BRYAN

A Political Biography of William Jennings Bryan

ERROR ON P. 365

OTHER BOOKS BY LOUIS W. KOENIG

THE INVISIBLE PRESIDENCY

THE CHIEF EXECUTIVE

BRYAN

A Political Biography

of William Jennings Bryan

BY LOUIS W. KOENIG

G. P. Putnam's Sons

New York

To Betty and Norb

Contents

➤➤✕◀◀

BRYAN

A Political Biography of William Jennings Bryan

1. A Rare Politician

IN the summer of 1897, almost a year after the Presidential election of 1896, William Jennings Bryan, the loser, spoke for the local Democratic ticket at a crossroads in the silver mining country of northwestern Utah. There he renewed his campaign pledge to lift from the masses of men the oppressions laid by privilege and power and to open the gates of the good life for all.

His figure dominated the balcony of the smoke-streaked wooden hotel from which he spoke. Thick among the crowd were men in their work caps topped with lamps, men with dust in their lungs and lines on their faces, all early candidates for silicosis and the nearby churchyard. His eyes flashing, his raven hair tossed with an actor's skill to underscore his argument, the speaker conveyed absolute earnestness in pledging himself to fight the battles of the common people, and to their cause he consecrated his life "through all the years to come."

When Bryan finished, there was silence, deep reverential silence, with no stir of conventional applause. One miner after another took off his cap until all stood with bared and bowed heads. Then a roar of cheers filled the valley, and their echoes rolled back from the hills. When Bryan came down from the balcony to enter his carriage, the miners crowded forward to shake his hand. So profound were their feelings that they could scarcely articulate their affection and gratitude. Many who could not shake his hand reached out to touch him.[1]

For twenty-eight years after that day, William Jennings Bryan toiled in fulfillment of his pledge. Forsaking the comforts of home and the pleasures of family, he walked and spoke in the midst of common men, and they in their number, whose devotion to him was unswerving and well nigh fanatical, were legion. If Bryan fondly regarded them as the "common people," there was nothing patronizing in the designation. To him, they were sovereigns whose judgment was supreme and who could not err. That they rejected him three times when he offered himself as their President never shook his trust in their worth and wisdom. He took his text from Psalm 138: "For though the Lord is high, he regards the lowly; but the haughty he knows from afar." He believed that it was the common people to whom the Bible "pays the highest compliment it ever pays to any class when it says that the common people heard Christ gladly." By establishing rapport with them, Bryan obtained more than simply rapport with God's anointed. ". . . it is from such as these that one can learn the drift of the public sentiment and best predict with certainty the things to be." [2]

Bryan's attachment to the workingman provided the base of a towering political achievement for which he has yet to secure even a modicum of recognition. More than anyone else, William Jennings Bryan is the founder of the modern Democratic Party. Well before the days of Woodrow Wilson and Franklin Roosevelt, Bryan brought it to champion the masses against the exactions of the classes, broadening the party's base to embrace the farmer, the city laborer, the immigrant, the small businessman, and to win the Negro.

As the apostle of the politically deprived, he brought into the political system those who were left out. He gave a sense of belonging to people who were unaccustomed to being heard and power to those who were powerless. He aimed to erase the distinction between the rulers and the ruled, to stamp out injustices, banish violence, and establish a supranational kingdom of moral and economic well-being in which all humanity would partake. Bryan toiled to transform the American dream into reality, to convert the old ideals of the Declaration of Independence into present fact, to instill in American life the democracy whose denial was blatant on so many sides. Toward such ends Bryan championed the breaking up of trusts, the regulation of railroads and banks, the popular election of United States Senators, the income tax to lift from the backs of the poor their disproportionate burden of public costs and to shift to the well-to-do a proper share, and suffrage for women, whose long exclusion violated democratic principle and elementary fairness. Bryan was justly coupled with his great political hero when he was called "the Jefferson of the new dispensation."

To be sure, he did not invent the proposals he championed. Like other great politicians, he excelled at borrowing, if not stealing, ideas from others. His favorite poaching ground was the tenets of the Populist Party, a source rich in ideas for political and economic reform. His own invaluable contribution lay in lifting these issues from the limiting and unpromising context of minor parties and state contests into the arena of national party politics.

Those who abided in the citadels of power and privilege did not hear Bryan gladly. Few American politicians have been subjected to so much criticism and vilification. To some men, Bryan's doctrines portended nothing less than the overthrow of established society, and they spent money and intimidated and coerced unmercifully to assure that he would not become President. He was widely labeled and feared as an "anarchist," a "Socialist," and a "Communist," and the New York *Times* carried letters from a reader who contended at length that Bryan was insane. Even in death,

Bryan was denounced. When Claude Bowers was assigned to write an editorial for the New York *World* on Bryan's passing, the paper's publisher was determined that no complimentary word should infiltrate what was written.[3]

Not the least of the punishments Bryan has suffered is the fate customarily allotted to the political pioneer. Others picked up the ideas he promoted and, as they gained in popularity, applied them to building their own monuments in history. Theodore Roosevelt was so impressed with the relevance of Bryan's proposals that he made many of them the warp and woof of his administration's major policies. And Woodrow Wilson, a late adherent to the progressive cause, took up policies that Bryan had long advocated at the price of ridicule, calumny, and electoral defeat. Even Franklin Roosevelt and his Presidential successors espoused measures of social reform and economic regulation whose spirit and substance are traceable to Bryan. Bryan, the pioneer, cut down the trees of the political forest, pulled up the stumps, plowed the soil, and planted the seed. Others reaped the harvest. Like General Nathanael Greene of the American Revolution, Bryan seldom won a battle, but every defeat turned eventually into a triumph. Bryan himself lost, but his causes prevailed.

Franklin D. Roosevelt saw the Great Commoner, as Bryan came to be known, as the prototype of one who would rather be right than President. To Bryan, Roosevelt noted, "political courage was not a virtue to be sought or attained, for it was an inherent part of the man. He chose his path not to win acclaim, but rather because that path appeared clear to him from his inmost beliefs. He did not have to dare to do what to him seemed right; he could not do otherwise." [4]

Bryan is a rarity among American politicians. Most treat politics largely as an enterprise in which competing interests and pressures are balanced and reconciled by adjustments and compromises. Manipulative skills are a large factor in their success. They view politics largely as a dialogue of reason and of fact, in which perception is unhampered by tightly held beliefs. In a country as diverse as the United States in regional makeup, in economic pursuits, in the nationality and racial origins of its people, such politicians have played a heroic role in displacing conflict with consensus, in extracting the strands of unity from the tangle of diversity. With the towering exception of the Civil War, they have managed to accommodate serious differences, but pragmatic politics has an underside. The continual trimming and adjusting may confine the possibilities of the political process to half steps and semisolutions. So nimble are some politicians that they can be at the forefront of political life for a decade or more and what they stand for remains a mystery, their future actions denying prediction. Politics can thus forfeit serious social change for a minimal disturbance of the status quo and permit urgent public problems to grow and drift.

Bryan was different. He was an ideologist devoted to a body of serious political beliefs that were germane to society's central problems, and he was willing to place them above victory. In the fashion of ideologists, he prized the formulation of lofty goals and saw the world about him within the blinders of tenaciously held dogma.

Ideological politics is given to moral emphasis, and Bryan perceived and discussed the social and economic issues of politics largely in religious terms, following the prescriptions of the Bible in his temporal as well as in his spiritual life. In his eyes, the Bible illuminated the choice between right and wrong that lay at the heart of every political issue. Bryan's religious background was evangelistic, and his discourse relied heavily on moralistic generalities. It emphasized purpose and mission while providing guidelines of such clarity that he could quickly take sides on a question once it emerged. Yet Bryan's convictions on some matters made him absolutely closed-minded. When he became Secretary of State, 1913–15, he stuck to his long-standing pacifist principles and resisted American involvement in World War I at enormous cost to his political well-being. As a liberal ideologist championing social programs for the deprived at home and peace abroad, Bryan had no counterpart on the American scene until Robert F. Kennedy's quest for the Presidential nomination in 1968.

Bryan, this is also to say, is an intensely contemporary man in old-fashioned dress. His clothes must not deceive us. To the youth of our day who despair over the moral sluggishness of public affairs and who look for nobler ends and more honorable means, he is a highly relevant figure. For all groups who today are politically deprived and suffer social injustices, whether Negroes, youth, consumers, the aged, or others, Bryan remains an articulate champion who viewed public problems through humane and moral lenses. To those who wish to eradicate the scourge of war, Bryan still speaks as one who was deeply involved in their purpose. Most of all, Bryan is relevant to those who feel that time is running out on our traditional pragmatic politics of half steps and semisolutions, who believe that bolder programs and more resolute action are required to free domestic society from injustices and suffering and all humanity from the cataclysm of war. Bryan, above all, is relevant because he pursued these highest of ideals by working and struggling in the mainstream of politics. He entered and played the political game for keeps, excelling at transposing moral principles into concrete action. He presents the paradox of a man with relatively fixed political beliefs who, except in the final years of his life, remained relevant in a nation which during his career of more than three decades, emerged from isolationism to internationalism and passed through two wars, which moved from an agrarian to an urban culture, whose industry, population, and learning grew miraculously in size and sophistication.

Just as human beings move through life cycles from birth to death, politicians too are subject to the physiology of change. Bryan fought continuously for his causes while passing through each major phase a career politician may encounter: ascent up the ladder of political influence; a crest or period of maximum effectiveness and status; a decline, with marked loss of impact and influence; and humiliation, when politics, a cruel and thankless master, exposes inadequacy and showers ridicule.

Not just a shooting star that flashed brilliantly in the political firmament and then vanished, Bryan was a flame that burned brightly and compelled the attention of millions for three decades. Not a single national convention of the Democratic Party transpired from 1896 to 1924 in which he was not a major, more often the dominant, figure.

His enduring influence has all the proportions of a political miracle, particularly since he had meager resources to work with. His campaigns were run on a shoestring, while his opponents spent lavishly to defeat him. Unlike other leaders who can cement the loyalty of followers by distributing rewards and favors, Bryan was conspicuous, from the beginning to the end of his long career, for lacking the most potent wherewithal of political leaders. He had no patronage to allot, no offices to give, no contracts to let, no honors to confer. He offered only ideals and purpose, the nobility of his causes. These he never blemished in his occasional desperation for political capital. He accepted no money to which strings were attached; he succumbed to no offers of high and lucrative position in the giant corporations and law firms. "No temptation ever induced Bryan," said Josephus Daniels, who observed him closely throughout his long career, "to sell the truth to serve the hour." [5]

The readiest explanation of Bryan's achievement leads inevitably to his superb gift of oratory, to the power of what Daniels called his "lute-toned voice . . . as melodious as possessed by any queen of song." With Webster, Calhoun, Lincoln, and Franklin Roosevelt, Bryan stands in the front rank of the nation's superlative orators.

But he achieved and maintained his place in politics by more than oratory. Bryan possessed a profound and practical knowledge of political organization and high skill at political maneuver. He understood the nature of public opinion and how to arouse and mold it. He was alert to the potentialities of pressure groups in the formulation and promotion of government policy, and he was concerned more with the machinery of government and its realities than with its façades. Taken altogether, his political talents moved Abram S. Hewitt, a veteran Democratic leader, to observe in 1900, "The Democratic party, as we knew it, is dead." [6]

PART ONE

✦

Ascent

2. Illinois Beginnings

WILLIAM JENNINGS BRYAN was born on March 19, 1860, the fourth child of Silas and Mariah Bryan. His birthplace was Salem, Illinois, on the great prairie of south-central Illinois, a modest town of frame and brick structures that rose out of an infinite vista of flatland and sky.

Silas Bryan as a young lawyer had helped hew the timbers to build his house, which was near the town's center, and William's coming brought cheer and hope into a family numb from the then-commonplace tragedy of the death of its children. Two years before, the first two children, Virginia and John, had died of whooping cough, a disaster that drove Silas to write from an anguished heart a disbelief "that I can ever be reconciled to their loss or that the Lord will ever bless me hereafter with children that will give me so much satisfaction. . . . Thank God that I feel that I am their father still and that I will be with them soon." [1] The birth of another child, Frances, in 1858 helped redress the loss, and William's arrival in 1860 was equally welcome.

The year 1860 was a time of tension and excitement in the Bryan household. Farmers in muddy boots were constantly arriving and departing after snatches of excited conversation with Silas in which they discussed the prospects of the "Little Giant," Democratic Senator Stephen A. Douglas of Illinois, in the forthcoming Presidential election. Silas, a leading Democrat of Salem, had made speeches for Douglas in his victorious race for the Senate in 1858 against his Republican opponent, Abraham Lincoln, but whatever joy Silas may have found in Douglas' Senatorial victory was demolished by the Presidential campaign of 1860. Douglas found his chances ruined when Southern delegates to the Democratic convention withdrew and named their own candidate, John C. Breckinridge. This division in the Democratic ranks made Lincoln's election a foregone conclusion.

Silas Bryan was the first member of his family in several generations who took up politics and made it at times the basis of his livelihood. Genealogists traced the family back to an Irish king of the eleventh century and discovered the first form of the name was O'Brien, with the O meaning "son of." The surname "Bryan" was understood to mean "having a thundering voice." With passing centuries, the family acquired a Scottish blend, and accounts of the lives of its members show the characteristics so often associated with the Scotch-Irish: thrift and industry, vigor and pugnacity, and an impregnable self-righteousness fed by the springs of a hardy conviction that this earthly life is ordered by divine guidance.

The first ancestor known to reach America, William Smith Bryan, arrived in one of the several waves of Scotch-Irish immigrations. He settled in 1650 in Gloucester County, Virginia, a frontier land in the foothills of the Blue Ridge Mountains. Some of his eleven sons and several daughters, upon maturity, scattered through Massachusetts, Pennsylvania, and New York; others remained in Virginia, and still others moved to what later became West Virginia, North Carolina, and Kentucky. A grandson settled near Winchester, Virginia, in 1710, and one of his children, William, William Jennings Bryan's great-grandfather, mustered troops to fight in the Revolution. William's son, John, married Nancy Lillard, of English descent, and built a double log cabin to accommodate his large family. After the seventh child, Silas Lillard, William Jennings Bryan's father, was born in 1822, the family crossed Virginia to settle at Point Pleasant, in what later became West Virginia, on the Kanawha River near its junction with the Ohio. After eight years, Nancy died, and two years later, when Silas was twelve, his father, John, also died. Uncles and aunts looked to the upbringing of Silas and his brothers and sisters. Among the more solid recollections of his childhood was Andrew Jackson's capture of the Presidency in 1828. Silas' kinsmen rejoiced in the victory of one of their own: a Westerner, a champion of the small farmer and a foe of Eastern money power. Silas continued the family tradition of moving westward by walking to Troy, Missouri, to live with his brother William, a farmer, and to work as a farmhand, woodchopper, and country schoolteacher. Valuing education as the gateway to a better life, he enrolled at McKendree College, a Baptist institution at Lebanon, Illinois. He was a good student who valued the classical curriculum, which he later extolled to his own children, and excelled in the literary or debating societies. A tall, gaunt youth with an aquiline nose and thin lips, he was a devout Christian; religion oozed from his pores. During a bout with pneumonia, in a fervor of supplication for divine help, he promised God that if he recovered, he would pray three times a day for as long as he lived. He kept this promise, abiding by a careful schedule of daily prayer at morning, noon, and night, and years later when the noon whistle blew, he would halt any proceeding and bow his head.[2]

After college, Silas read law and moved to Salem, Illinois, where two of his sisters had already settled. At twenty-nine, he was admitted to the bar and wet his toes in politics by being elected superintendent of schools of Marion County, of which Salem is the county seat. A year later, 1852, he married Mariah Elizabeth Jennings, a daughter of Charles Waters Jennings and Mariah Woods Davidson. Residing near Centralia, Illinois, the Jennings, like the Bryans, were a peregrinating family and had moved to Illinois from Kentucky in the second decade of the century. Mariah, at eighteen years, was a former pupil in Silas' classes and was nearly twelve years younger than he. Tall and straight-standing, embodying the freshness of youth and the strength of the mountain woman, Mariah possessed exquisitely balanced features. Luminous gray eyes looked steadily out beneath gracefully arched brows; her high cheekbones, long aquiline nose, brown hair tightly parted in the center, and full lips, presented a vision of arresting attractiveness. She loved the piano and singing, and her upbringing in the Methodist Church had opened to her broader horizons than the fundamental training of her Baptist husband allowed. Mariah was a good mother and wife, devoted to her older and more reserved husband, who she was convinced possessed the seeds of greatness.

Soon after his marriage, Silas was elected to the State Senate. There he grappled with the issues that steadily magnified into the Civil War. He witnessed the splitting of the Democratic Party, the death of the Whigs, and the birth of the Republicans. In the surge of strife and change, Silas discovered that the work he loved most was politics. But in 1860, the year William was born, he lost reelection. This rebuff simply diverted Silas to another political channel. That same year he was elected judge of the state circuit court, which embraced a half dozen surrounding counties. Until William was twelve, Silas was for much of the time away from home, out on circuit, and the burden of running the household and rearing the children fell upon Mariah.

The bench did not deter Silas from making political speeches exhorting his fellowmen to apply the eternal principles of Christian morality to the urgent and complex issues of the day. Nonetheless, when slavery had been an issue, Silas, his conscience doubtless muted by his Southern background, voiced no protest. In perspective, the chief effect of Silas' judicial career was that it delayed the coming of the full measure of his influence on William.

By 1866, when the nation began wrestling with the problems of Reconstruction, two other children had come into the Bryan family: Hiram (Harry) and Russell. (Harry died in infancy, and Russell survived only until his seventeenth year.) Since Frances, William, and Russell overtaxed the space of their little two-bedroom house, Silas now bought a holding of farmland on which he built a country home. Compared with his modest Salem house, his new abode was manorial in scale, inspired by the admiration Silas retained for the vast, gracious estates of the Virginia country squires of his childhood. His effort was substantial. A porch graced the front and rear of the main living room, and a hall ran through the center, in the style of Southern mansions, thus permitting the breezes of the hot prairie summer to flow through the house. Rising on a slight elevation, the house dominated a yard, 300 feet long and 200 wide. The main walk was shaded by a row of cedars on either side, in *allée* style, and behind them stood rows of maples. Around the house extended 520 acres, nearly all prairie. A small woodlot and pasture lay nearby, and 80 acres of timberland some 3 miles away. Silas even indulged his boyhood fancy for a deer park.

Although he stocked his farm with horses, cattle, hogs, sheep, and a full selection of poultry, Silas was not a farmer like his neighbors. Most of his land he rented out, cultivating only a few acres for himself. With their father busy in court, the chores fell chiefly on his sons, especially on William, the strongest. By pitching hay, digging postholes, hauling timber, and doing other standard feats of farmyard strength, he developed a solid physique that enabled him to command in his political career almost superhuman endurance against the rigors of incessant campaigning.

Farm life had its joys, as well as its chores: buckwheat cakes, sausages and slabs of pork, trips to the swimming hole, hay jumping in summer, sledding in winter; hunting for squirrels and rabbits the year around. Silas, who was something of a marksman, early trained his son in the art. Before he was old enough to use a gun, William hunted rabbits with a stick, tracking them in the snow and cornering and killing them in their lair. He passed first to a single barrel and then a double-barrel shotgun, molding his own bullets the night before.[3]

As nineteenth-century homes tended to be, the Bryans' was a place of parental dominance, in which Silas, with Mariah's support, asserted authority and discipline. As much as, if not more than, his brothers, William complied with his parents' demands and was rewarded with their approval and affection.

William did not go to school until he was ten because the nearest academy lay so far away that attendance was impracticable. Besides, his parents were convinced that the influence of their home life was more constructive. Mariah gladly and diligently served as schoolmistress. William learned to read early, and after committing lessons to memory, he would stand on a little table to recite them, with Mariah elaborately encouraging him in the art of declamation. Silas himself excelled at it and was in demand as an orator in the surrounding community. Both parents felt that oratory was valuable for securing recognition, approval, and dominion over one's fellowmen. Thus, perched on a table, the little boy would recite:

> You'd scarce expect one of my age,
> To speak in public on the stage.
> If I should chance to fall below
> Demosthenes or Cicero
> Don't view me with a critic's eye.
> But pass my imperfections by.[4]

In the Bryan home there was no distinction between religion and parental authority, for parental edicts were largely founded on religious prescription. The family, from father to youngest child, took their cues from a close,
literal reading of the Bible. Silas and Mariah aspired to live the good Christian life in dealings with one's fellows, in choosing one's work and purpose,
in close study of the Word, and in the observance of worship and ritual at
the hearth. The family prayed together at the beginning and close of each
day and at midday. If his circuit duties permitted, the judge rode home for
luncheon, and the entire family would share in a noonday religious observance, during which Silas would read to his family a chapter of the Book of
Proverbs and follow it with a discussion of its import. At the children's bed-
time there was further Bible reading and discussion, with William participating and urging his parents to read on.

Stories and poetry that William read, or were read to him, tended to
confirm the ethical ideals of the Bible. Silas' favorite poem was William
Cullen Bryant's "To a Waterfowl," which he often had William recite to the
family. Its last stanza was then and forever after William's own favorite
verse, what he deemed to be mortal man's most apt expression of divine
power outside the Holy Writ:

> He who, from zone to zone,
> Guides through the boundless sky thy certain flight,
> In the long way that I must tread alone,
> Will lead my steps aright.

The family's chief diversion was singing. Evenings and Sundays they
clustered around the piano, the most prized possession in the parlor. Mariah would play, while the judge, a competent and enthusiastic tenor, led his
children, each giving forth with spirit and vigor. On Sundays the repertoire
was confined to hymns and church school songs, while the freedom of the
weekdays permitted such popular melodies as "When You and I Were
Young, Maggie" and "Farewell, Mother, You May Never Press Me to Your
Heart Again." But nothing of this parlor culture budged by one jot the impact of parent and Bible.

The first serious challenge to the self-sufficiency of the Bryan homestead
and its monopoly of influence in shaping the mind and character of young
William was his advent to public school in 1870 at the age of ten. He was
hauled into Salem to a worn, cheerless structure known as the Old College,
a building once used as a girl's seminary. There to greet him was a teacher
whose manner utterly contradicted her name, Mrs. Lamb. Roaring out the
daily lessons with unabashed enthusiasm and holding her class in ramrod
discipline, she seems to have contributed no new important element to the

boy's firmament. At school he encountered the books that had furnished the staple of his education at Mariah's knee: McGuffey's *Reader,* Webster's spellers, and a standard geography. The emphasis was on learning by rote rather than on the nurture of intellectual inquiry. William would memorize his lessons until he could repeat the questions and answers without the book. At home, he still declaimed his lessons to Mariah.

According to Bryan's testimony and that of others, his performance as a student was undistinguished. He never recalled failing an examination, but neither was he ever at the head of his class. His strongest point, on which he clearly excelled all others, was deportment. Obedient, respectful, dutiful, he did what was required and had no truck with pranksters among his class-mates or with the roughnecks who loved nothing better than a bloody fight in the schoolyard with a throng of their more savage classmates urging them on. Big and strong enough to thrash much older boys, Bryan did not fight, not because he was afraid, but because to do so would violate the Christian precept, learned so well at home, that one loves his fellows as brothers.

A second potential intruder on Billy's home rearing was the church. His initial excursion into the formal household of God created a prickly di-lemma. Should he attend the church of his father, a Baptist, or his mother, a Methodist? The solution was a perfect compromise. He attended both: the Baptist on Sunday morning and the Methodist in the afternoon. At fourteen, he entered into still another denomination, the Presbyterian, to which he became converted at a revival, apparently with his parents' full approval. Actually, at this juncture at least, little difference existed among the three denominations. The Baptists, Methodists, and Presbyterians were the most conservative of the Protestant faiths. Each clasped the Bible in its most literal sense, prized form and observance, and was charged with a strong evangelistic current. Billy's "conversion" to Presbyterianism was not an explosive personal experience. "Having been brought up in a Christian home," he later wrote of it, "conversion did not mean a change in my habits of life or habits of thought. I do not know of a virtue that came into my life as a result of my joining the Church because all the virtues had been taught me by my parents." [5]

These parents practiced what they preached. Silas communicated an ar-resting sense of character and absolute integrity. Yet he also had moments of humor, and he participated unhesitatingly in everyday human affairs. He was an expert legislator, a respected judge, and a forceful political speaker and campaigner. His hallowed Biblical precepts often intruded mercifully on his deliberations as judge and tempered the severity of the temporal jus-tice he dispensed. By invoking divine guidance as a prelude to decision, he deemed his judicial holdings to be inspired and blessed by the Almighty, and he could never understand how anyone could feel that he erred. Once when told that the Illinois Supreme Court had reversed six of his decisions, he instantly replied, without a flicker of doubt, "The Supreme Court is wrong." [6]

Mariah reinforced Silas' way of life, accepted his temporal and spiritual leadership, and administered its principles faithfully in his absences. Having a sprightlier sense of humor than Silas and a more musical bent, she lightened and brightened the family's days.

In short, William's childhood provided the ideals, the precepts, a choice of vocation, indeed a master plan that inspirited and directed his life right up to the moment of his death. To a degree exceptional among children, he took his parents' view of life as his own and kept it intact in his later years. His subsequent career is a replica, done on a larger scale, of his father's. William seems never to have rejected, doubted, or even questioned any judgment entertained by his parents. What was right for his father was right for William unto eternity. No matter how the waves of crisis and change beat upon him through the years, no matter how unceasing the struggle with intricate problems and intelligent, sophisticated personalities, the parental heritage remained paramount and impregnable. Whatever William Jennings Bryan said or did in more than three decades of an intensely dynamic era of American public affairs sprang from principles learned in boyhood.[7]

Not a single wayward episode can be unearthed about his childhood. "He never argued or refused to do what was required of him," observed Mary Webster of Salem, who often helped take care of the Bryan children. "He was always truthful and obedient. Sometimes a look of sadness came into his face when he was refused things or pleasures. There was never a word of unkindness or impudence." [8]

Silas and Mariah severely tested their son's capacity for obedience. "My parents were quite strict with me," Bryan observed years later in retrospect, "and I sometimes considered the boys more fortunate who were given more liberty. . . ." Judge Silas was by his own testimony enormously pleased with William's conduct. "He is a fine boy, of sterling integrity of character . . ." he said in a rare burst of praise to an old family friend.[9]

Throughout his life Bryan never faltered in his imitations of his father. Although Silas smoked in college, he had given it up before William was born. Silas did not resume the habit, and his son never adopted it. Neither ever used liquor. William was an early and ardent supporter of temperance. By his twelfth year he had signed a fistful of pledges, and, according to report, when he and a friend were hired by a nearby farmer to bring refreshments to the threshing hands, Bryan, then in his thirteenth year, gladly carried water but refused to carry whiskey. Silas hated gambling and inculcated in his son an utter aversion to it. Neither could the Bryans abide swearing. William's parents so impressed their dislike of it upon him that when he entered school and came upon a crowd of boys who began to swear, he would withdraw at once.[10]

But the most significant contribution of the elder Bryans to William was their conviction of the desirability and the feasibility of applying Christian principles, through politics, to public affairs. Silas' own career was a living testimonial to this conviction. By unswerving party affiliation a Democrat, he deemed the underlying principles of republican institutions and those of the Christian faith identical. He regarded the conduct of government as second in importance only to religion. Republican government he understood as essentially popular government. At the Illinois Constitutional Convention of 1870, to which he was a delegate, he introduced a resolution that all offices, legislative, executive, and judicial, provided for in the new Constitution should be filled by popular election. Silas neglected no opportunity to combine the religious and the political. When someone dared to propose at the constitutional convention that the printing of the daily prayer be omitted from the convention journal, he took to his feet and made an impassioned protest. The most frequent guests in Silas' home were the emissaries of what in his eyes were man's two loftiest callings, the ministry and politics. "My father was as much at home with ministers as he was with politicians," Bryan wrote years later. "He saw no necessary conflict—and I have never been able to see any—between the principles of our government and the principles of Christian faith." It was also in token of the vocational partnership that Judge Silas at each harvest season sent a load of hay to every preacher and priest residing in Salem.[11]

The fires of William's enduring interest in politics were first strongly kindled when Silas ran on the Democratic ticket in 1872 for the United States House of Representatives. He was also the nominee of the Greenback Party, which proposed to fight falling farm prices and foreclosed mortgages by issuing large amounts of paper money, or greenbacks, as they had been called in the Civil War. Silas' nomination by two political parties was a lesson that was not lost upon his son, who in his day would build ties with the successor party to the Greenbacks, the Populists. For several years before Silas' campaign, William's political awareness had been pricked by the political news carried in the several newspapers that came into the homestead, especially the *Missouri Republican*, which provided the best coverage. But Silas' Congressional campaign charged the family with the excitement of immediate participation. At the dinner table he discussed ideas for his speeches, the attitude of the crowds, the skulduggery of his opponents, and the prospects of victory.

Bryan accompanied his father on the hustings, standing in the rear of many a courthouse yard, beholding the oratorical performance through the rose-colored glasses of a young son's pride, delighting in audience approval, and bearing criticisms of his father like arrow wounds. There is a story, doubtless apocryphal, that at the tender age of twelve years he actually made a campaign speech for his father.

Ultimately the election was won by a margin of 240 votes, not by Silas, but by his opponent. Report had it that Silas lost chiefly because he refused to contribute $500 to the party coffers, an omission that cooled the efforts of party workers. It was another lesson that William noted. In all his campaigns, he offered not only superb oratory but financial gifts as well. Silas' defeat did not, however, cast his household into gloom. The people, in all their wisdom, had spoken. No man, Silas reasoned, could question their judgment. William too showed no remorse; indeed his father's defeat provided him with a new ambition. Now when grown-ups asked, as they inevitably did, what he would do some day for a living, he would answer, "I am going to be a lawyer and go to Congress. . . ." [12] His father's defeat had left him work to do. He must win the office his father had lost.

3. *Education of an Idealist*

Early in his parental career, Silas Bryan had vowed that each of his children would receive a college education. From his own experience Silas was impressed that education gave sinew to character, was the gateway to the professions, and, above all, provided, better than any other source, the substance of leadership in public affairs. The leadership of men was Silas' ruling ambition in his own career, and he hoped with all his might that at least one of his progeny might surpass his own attainments as a public leader.

As William moved from grade school into high school and as college loomed a few years distant, Silas believed he should enter the much respected Illinois College at Jacksonville, a town close by and west of the capital, at Springfield. The college had begun as a kind of frontier outpost of Yale. Its first teacher was a Yale graduate, and other men from there were recruited to the college faculty. It had connected with it a preparatory school, the Whipple Academy, into which Silas placed William in 1875 as a middle student, or one who, on the basis of his previous high schooling, qualified for entry into the junior year.

The boy did not live at the rooms the academy provided its students, but at the spacious Victorian residence of Dr. Hiram K. Jones, a distant relative of Silas and a warm friend. A prominent physician, a leading local citizen, and a trustee of Illinois College, Dr. Jones very quickly took on the role of

William's father-away-from-home. The familiar high-minded atmosphere provided by Dr. Jones was moderated by his warm, openhearted wife, Cousin Lizzie, as Bryan and his family affectionately called her. A devotee of literature and music, owner of a serene temper and infinite compassion, she watched over Bryan's comforts with scrupulous attention. The Joneses were well practiced in caring for students. Having no children of their own, they provided, over the years, a warm, comfortable home for many a schoolboy.

Bryan passed all six years of prep school and college with the Joneses. In later life and prominence, he recorded his gratitude to the fine old couple. "As I view in retrospect my own life in the Jones family," he wrote, "I find it difficult to calculate the influence which association with them had upon my ideas and ideals."

Dr. Jones possessed considerably broader intellectual horizons than Silas. For some years he had lectured at the Concord School of Philosophy in Massachusetts, taught courses on medicine and philosophy at Illinois College, and numbered Ralph Waldo Emerson and Bronson Alcott among his friends. Talk abounded in the Jones household of Plato, Hegel and Kant, even of evolution. Although Bryan did not come to mirror Jones, as he did his father, he enlarged the realm of his reading and inquiry under the doctor's influence.[1]

At the academy, Bryan's studies involved no sharp breaks with his education in Salem. Only now his former subjects were pursued with greater rigor and more scrutiny. He took up first Greek and then Latin, and he marched ahead in the remorseless curriculum through the other subjects begun in high school. He promptly seized the opportunity, open to students at Whipple, to join the literary societies of the college. Much to his taste, they stressed speaking and debating, rather than literature. Sigma Pi, into which he was initiated, was a literary society, rather than a fraternity, and undeterred by his young years, he pushed quickly into prominence in its meetings, declamations, and debates. This, needless to say, was a world more exacting and competitive, more definite in its conception of oratorical skill, than anything he had known at home. His first speaking venture before his literary brothers, chiefly college men, whose eyebrows were raised in supercilious disbelief, was so unnerving that his quivering knees, Bryan acknowledged later, gave out more applause than his audience.

Every opportunity to speak that Sigma Pi presented Bryan grasped. His assurance grew by giant steps, and in the spring semester he dared to enter a declamation contest. He chose a theme taken from Patrick Henry, "Give me liberty or give me death," and cloaked a series of commonplace thoughts in orotund sentences and a spirited delivery. The judges were unimpressed. The next year, his senior year at Whipple, he tried again, on the subject "The Palmetto and the Pine." He managed to place third, a hurtful disappointment to a lad whose ambition focused so intensely upon success in public speaking. His delivery seemed to lack something, and he puzzled over what it was. Dr. Jones, who attended the contest, thought that Billy's trouble lay in his failure to articulate distinctly. The eager youth was not so certain that this indeed was the root of the trouble, but Jones' suggestion drove him to practice, for hours in his room and in the solitude of the nearby woods, long passages specially selected for their difficult diction. In his zeal to improve, he even resorted to Demosthenes' expedient of talking with pebbles in his mouth.[2]

In the fall semester of 1877, Bryan, no longer an awkward boy, but a strapping youth of confident bearing and solemn dignity, entered the freshman class of Illinois College. Here was a college tailor-made for a youth bent upon a career in public affairs, who proposed to make oratory the vehicle of the sturdiest and finest ideals. Even the environment of the college crackled with inspiration.

Situated in the very center of the Lincoln country, Illinois College was rich in Lincoln associations and traditions. Its president for many years, Edward Beecher, son of the eminent divine Lyman Beecher, was a close friend of Elijah P. Lovejoy, a martyr in the cause against slavery, who was mobbed and murdered in 1837 at his printing presses in Alton, where he published the *Observer*. Beecher witnessed the tragedy and returned to the college fired with zeal to liberate the slaves and to preserve the freedoms of press and speech against every assault. The faculty of Yale men he imported eagerly took up his causes, and the college quickly became the center of ferment in lower Illinois.

Lincoln's law partner, William Herndon, had been a student at Illinois College, until his father insisted on his withdrawal, fearful that his son was well along to becoming a "red hot abolitionist." A brother of Ann Rutledge, Lincoln's sweetheart, studied at the college, and Lincoln himself for a time intended to go there because Ann planned to attend school in Jacksonville.[3]

College offered Bryan the opportunity to fill out the general ideologies and moral principles learned in the Salem homestead with historic facts, economic analysis, and sophisticated studies of the political system. It afforded whatever intellectual foundation he would have for building his own life as an instrument for his ideals and for anticipating the kind of world in which they might function.[4]

As a freshman, he entered upon a curriculum representative of the good colleges of the day. His courses centered on the classics, with Latin studied for his first three years and Greek for all four. His favorite course was rhetoric, built around a reading of compositions and a reciting of declamations. A year of German constituted the modern language offering, and mathematics extended through trigonometry and college algebra, with calculus as an elective which Bryan did not take. Sandwiched in with the classics in the sophomore and junior years were scientific studies of physics, astronomy, chemistry, and geology. In the senior year the social sciences came to the forefront—economics, political science, American history, and elements of Christianity. The elective system had not yet appeared on the college scene, even in the East. At Harvard, President Charles W. Eliot was only beginning to introduce his concept of the free curriculum.

The subjects studied tended not to go beyond introductory courses. Class meetings were devoted largely to recitations and discussions of the textbooks. Except for the classics, there was no training in research methods and no particular cultivation of the spirit of scholarly inquiry and investigation. The college library was not accessible to the students but functioned as a repository of old and rare books, of costly reference works and scientific treatises, a treasure to be closely guarded, and was open for only an hour a day. Its administrators counseled the students that their reading needs could be well supplied by the collections of the several literary societies. According to Sigma Pi's records, Bryan was an average book borrower, taking out three or four volumes a year, chiefly fiction. Mostly he dipped into the novels of Charles Dickens which provided vivid insights into the abuses and miseries of urban industrial society. His borrowings from his literary society's library may be only a partial clue to his reading, for he also had access to Dr. Jones' well-stocked shelves.[5]

Yet for all the limitations of his adventure in higher learning, Bryan studied under great teachers with substantial reputations as scholars. Of these, the most important was Julian Monson Sturtevant, in the twilight of his career in Bryan's student days. A president of Illinois College for thirty-two years, Sturtevant had returned to teaching after superintending the college through its critical formative years. Author of a widely used text on economics, Sturtevant still possessed a fresh and penetrating mind in the classroom. On the economic issues of the day, Sturtevant was an independent and liberal thinker. With deft analysis, he expounded the cases for free trade and bimetallism. The merit of these doctrines immediately became a part of Bryan, like plasma injected into the bloodstream, for they provided nothing less than the substance of the policies with which his early political career was most deeply identified. Sturtevant was also a lay leader in the Congregational Church and thus reinforced the idea of the nexus between religion and public policy. Bryan's most inspiring teacher was probably Edward Allan Tanner, professor of Latin who later was president of the college. Gifted at inspiring an entire class, he produced over the years a remarkable crop of classicists of national reputation.[6]

In this new world of higher learning, Bryan developed skills and improved on talents decidedly relevant to the oratorical and ideological emphasis of his awaiting political career. He pursued the classical course, a not unguided decision, for his father and mother had, before he left home, made the selection for him. Just before Bryan departed for Jacksonville, Silas pulled down from the shelves of his library the two largest tomes in his possession, one a Greek and the other a Latin lexicon. Solemnly presenting these to his son, Silas instructed that one was to be used for six years of Greek study and the other for five years of Latin. At Illinois, William fulfilled this trust to the very letter, and in his later political life he valued his classical studies for their illumination of the meaning of words and their solicitude for form and cadence, which enabled him to impart a polish and precision to his oratory. His favorite subject was mathematics, and the disciplined reasoning it exacted sharpened in Bryan the capacity to employ a kind of steely logic in his later public speeches.

The English curriculum was ideal for the future orator with its courses in composition, logic, and declamation. His studies of American history and politics introduced him to two works that profoundly influenced him. George Bancroft's *History of the United States* glorified the Presidency of Andrew Jackson and defined democracy as "the voice of God 'as it breathes through the people,'" thus reaffirming the lesson Bryan had learned at his father's knee of the union of religion and politics. To Bancroft, "democracy is practical Christianity." From Alexis de Tocqueville's *Democracy in America*, Bryan soaked up concepts of equality, liberty, and privilege which provided the core of his later political opinions. Political liberty, according to De Tocqueville, could exist only under conditions of relative economic equality, and the most ominous peril to democracy, therefore, was privilege.

As a student Bryan impressed his professors with his industry, perseverance, and unfailing decorum, rather than with any brilliance. ". . . he never shirked a task and never seemed to think that if he could 'get by' that was enough," said his professor of natural sciences, Dr. Henry E. Storrs. "I always found him respectful and responsive to what I tried to do for him. . . . He was certainly a most exemplary student. . . ." [7] This was not a time when social and moral causes excited the campuses, and Bryan left behind no evidence that he was particularly concerned with finding crusades in which to march. At home, he conformed to a parental society; at Jacksonville, he conformed to the campus social order without reservation or remorse.

By the standard criteria of academia, Bryan was indeed a successful student. He became valedictorian of his class, but the glow of this distinction was dimmed by the smallness of the class of 1881, with seven members in the classical course and four in the scientific. Bryan laid claim to this highest honor with a respectable, but something less than overpowering, average of 8.93.

As at Whipple, Bryan was, from the beginning to the end of his college years, a diligent aspiring orator. Although he was blessed with a rare clarity, range, and resonance of speech, he achieved no immediate success. In his freshman year he entered the college's declamation contest and won second place with a melodramatic ballad, "Bernardo del Carpio." In declamations before his literary society, his chief recitations were "The Burning of Chicago," "True Eloquence," and Henry Clay's "Ambition of a Statesman." Bryan applied himself equally to trying to excel as an original speaker in debate.

Despite nature's generous gifts, Bryan did not achieve the recognition it seemed he should against his less endowed competitors. His era of lean success persisted until Professor S. S. Hamill, who taught elocution, took him in hand. Hamill smoothed off rough edges and stressed modulation of voice, gesticulation, and the rhythmical possibilities of language. By his junior year Bryan had surged to the top of the college's orators. "Next followed the treat of the evening," the campus paper reported, "in the shape of an oration by W. J. Bryan. In both composition and delivery it equalled anything that has been heard in Sigma Pi for years." The address was entitled "Master Motives," and it was clearly of the genre of speeches Bryan delivered so well in his adult political career. It celebrated an idealized way of life and summoned mankind to take it up. In his youthful oration, Bryan allowed that ambition and the desire for wealth and knowledge are laudable motives for promoting good ends, if controlled, but "a sense of right," he contended, was "the greatest and most powerful motive of all." [8]

"Master Motives" was a popular oratorical essay in college circles of the day. Bryan developed a number of these essays, which are clues to the young man's thoughts and budding convictions. In one he recorded in orotund style his belief in the importance of the individual in history. "History," he declaimed, "is but a grand biography. Time's hoary scribe writes indelibly upon the eternal page the actions of individuals." Here was the stuff of a profound sense of destiny that sustained Bryan in his own long, rough political journey. As an orator, Bryan was deeply impressed with the overriding importance of conviction in giving effect to oratory. "Virgil," he noted approvingly, "well says, 'If you would bid the tears of others flow, yourself the signs of grief must show.' "

An essay on "Perfection" recorded Bryan's view of the power of great oratory. The supreme Roman orator Cicero was both hero and example. "What a power has eloquence," Bryan declaimed. "What more enviable attainment is there than the ability to control by a stream of passionate words the thoughts of a multitude, to guide by a look the wills of your hearers or to excite action by a wave of the hand.' " But the road to oratorical triumph was gained by something more than glittering talent. Cicero's genius would have gone for little, Bryan noted, had it not been linked to the noblest causes—the causes of the unfortunate at the bar of justice. Perfection,

Bryan concluded, was "what is possible to man" through "pure purpose and persevering diligence." [9]

Bryan's own declamatory strivings were spurred on by a galaxy of contests and prizes. He displayed early a tendency to respond best to specific incentives. As a freshman, by capturing second prize, he gained the honor of representing his college in an intercollegiate contest at Galesburg, where he again was runner-up. The biggest competition of his college career occurred in his senior year, a gala oratorical tournament at Monmouth, which was won by James S. E. Erskine of Monmouth, with Bryan placing second. By general opinion, Bryan deserved top place but fell to second after a low rating by one of the judges. Two judges rated him the highest, but the third judge ranked him fifth, sufficient to drop him to second place. The Galesburg *Plain Dealer* offered a more sensitive and flattering appreciation than the wayward judge. Bryan, its reporter said, was "magnetic," his voice "full," articulation "clear," his modulation "not affected," his gesturing "natural." From the "first" he was "a favorite with the audience." [10]

For all of his prowess as a speaker, Bryan compiled no impressive record as a debater. In twelve contests, in which he represented Sigma Pi, he won six and lost six. The debates' topics dealt with matters on which he concentrated in his subsequent political life. "Resolved," read one topic, "that intemperance is more detrimental to mankind than war." Quite possibly his preparations influenced his later positions on prohibition, world peace, and international arbitration. Other debates on the tariff and the resumption of specie payments, too, may have shaped his later views. Whenever he was not a speaker in debate, Bryan was in the thick of the discussion that followed. On every occasion that provided an opportunity for an analysis of questions, Bryan was an eager participant, particularly if the matter at hand was moral or political, as it tended to be.

Bryan had little truck with another major extracurricular activity for which nature had amply endowed him. His 6-foot frame and solid, muscular 180 pounds seemed to burst with athletic potentiality, but his record in sport at Illinois was almost barren. Whatever exercise he got was in walking from the Joneses' to class and in running errands for his parents-away-from-home. The truth is that he had little facility except for jumping. He took his turn at the most popular of sports, baseball, but was regularly consigned to right field, where his general inefficiency least harmed the team. His batting average, which was never robust, utterly collapsed when the game, in a sudden change of rules, substituted the round for the flat bat. In jumping, Bryan did best at the running broad jump and won a prize with a leap of 12 feet 4 inches. He also jumped backward and once made a record of 9 feet. An avid competitor, he would begin jumping after the frost was out of the ground. Practicing until the muscles of his legs cried out in soreness, he would ease up briefly and then jump away the remaining aches. [11]

At college, Bryan maintained at high flame the two consuming interests he had brought from home—politics and religion. He followed national politics, particularly those of his father's Democratic Party, with minute attention. The summer before he entered college, he journeyed to St. Louis to attend the national Democratic convention and witness the nomination of undersized, spare, asthmatic Samuel J. Tilden for the Presidency. The impecunious youth bunked in East St. Louis in a room with thirty other people.

In the summer of 1880, Bryan decided to make his first political speech and devoted it to the cause of the Democratic Presidential and Vice Presidential nominees, Winfield Scott Hancock and William H. English. The occasion was a farmers' picnic near Salem, and the handbills announced in thick black print that there would be three speeches, with Bryan's last. Upon reaching the picnic grove on the appointed day, he found only his two fellow speakers and an audience of four, consisting of the grove's owner, the operator of the wheel of fortune, and the two operators of the lemonade stand. After waiting a full hour for an audience that never materialized, the meeting adjourned, and the frustrated Bryan hiked back home.

Despite indefatigable diligence, Bryan made no strong mark as a campus politician. His chief goal was the presidency of his society, an honor conferred less for popularity than for political and executive ability. If the number of offices Bryan held in his society is a guide, he was indeed a busy aspiring politician. At various times, he was sergeant at arms, chaplain, critic, and chairman of the finance committee. A political overturn in the society carried him into the vice-presidency in his junior year; this meant, according to custom, that he would become president in his senior year. But factional strife intervened, and Bryan lost. According to one report, he was done in by a maneuver launched by a personal enemy. Bryan, however, had the last word by managing the election of a close friend as president, and the friend happily displayed his gratitude by appointing Bryan to a second term as chaplain.[12]

Generally Bryan got along well with his fellow students. His science professor, Dr. Henry E. Storrs, noted that Bryan's friends were not the crude, roustabout types, but those of studious tastes and refinement. But Bryan was in no respect snobbish or exclusive. He had many non-college friends in town, whom he met as a result of his part-time employment in a Jacksonville haberdashery, where he worked to supplement his meager allowance. Bryan did not attract friends by spending, for that was not his style, and in any case he had no largess to flaunt. Father Silas encouraged and enforced the strictest economy. Once, as the Christmas holidays neared, Bryan discovered that his trousers had become too short, and he wrote to Silas for money for a new pair. In recommending postponement of the purchase until his son's homecoming, Silas directed his attention to other greater values. "My son," he admonished, "you may as well learn now, that people will measure you by the length of your head, rather than by the length of your breeches."

Students who were attracted to Bryan were struck by his generosity and kindliness and the depth of his Christian morality. "He was very good," a classmate noted, "but for some reason Bryan's goodness was not the kind that rubbed against you and turned the fur the wrong way." Probably Bryan's most intimate friend was Julian Wadsworth. When Wadsworth disclosed that he heard an unmistakable call to enter the Christian ministry, Bryan rejoiced and encouraged him in it. He too, Bryan said, had long felt that God was calling him, not to the ministry, but to another high endeavor: to the life of the Christian politician.[13]

Bryan's religious commitment underwent a brief but profound crisis of faith during his college years. Illinois College, like many another campus, was caught up in the controversy over the validity of Charles Darwin's findings and the implications of evolution upon traditional Christian beliefs. Speakers on both sides of the question visited the campus, and in his sophomore year, Bryan alluded to evolution in a prize essay. That this scientific doctrine deeply troubled him seems quite clear. He postponed joining a church in Jacksonville and seemed for a time uncertain whether to join at all. He wrestled with the grave intellectual task of reconciling what Dr. Storrs said in his science lectures with what the Bible said about the Creation, the Flood, and other epochal occurrences. Bryan was particularly vexed by the several theories of the Creation and, above all, by the nebular hypothesis, which assumed that matter and force existed and that when the latter acted upon the former, the universe was created. The hypothesis cast doubt upon the faith young Bryan had been reared on: that there was "a Designer back of the design—a Creator behind the creation . . . ," an assumption enjoined by Genesis, "In the beginning God created the heaven and the earth."

In the depths of his painful struggle, Bryan wrote to Robert Ingersoll, a prominent agnostic, requesting a statement of his views on God and immortality. Ingersoll's secretary answered with a perfunctory form letter and enclosed a copy of one of his addresses. Some time after this meager response, Bryan resolved his struggle. Years later, he attributed his doubts to the brashness of youth, to the circumstance that a young collegian is "just coming into possession of his powers, and feels stronger than he ever feels afterwards—and he thinks he knows more than he ever does know." The ultimate triumph of his faith, Bryan explained, was helped by his experience in church membership in Salem before his college years. With his belief in God restored, Bryan now put those trying days behind him. He joined the Presbyterian Church of Jacksonville, regularly attended Sunday school, and, according to a classmate, "was not ashamed to carry his Bible under his arm." [14]

4. Mary

On a brilliant fall day in 1879, an event took place whose significance would extend for the full duration of Bryan's life. As is common with such events, it afforded no clue to its ultimate importance. As a routine social occasion Illinois College boys were invited to attend open house at the nearby Jacksonville Female Academy, otherwise called the Jail for Angels. Bryan had no particular compulsion to attend; he was enjoying occasional dates with what the Joneses deemed the "nicest" girls in town.

The nineteen-year-old Bryan came that day with a cadre of classmates dressed in their best. For a few stiff moments, the social room was absolutely segregated with the girls on one side in their crinolines and pert upswept hairdos, and the boys on the other. After a great urn of tea had been trundled in along with plates of cookies, a general movement toward the serving table took place. The relaxing effect of the refreshments, the courage of some boys who introduced themselves to likely girls, and the enterprise of several academy faculty brought a general intermingling. Bryan moved toward one girl, whose attractiveness had instantly gained his attention. Her large gray-brown eyes; the perfect oval face they dominated; her lips full and curved to bowlike perfection; her soft brown hair, whose curls and ringlets occasionally strayed from their upswept discipline—all delighted him. They had barely exchanged a few sentences when he discovered to his complete delight that the personality infusing this lovely exterior—the quick humor, easy laughter, and graceful movement—was utterly attractive. In his instant rapture he may not have perceived the large intelligence lurking behind the penetrating gaze and the look of calculation that occasionally glimmered.

Eighteen-year-old Mary Baird was not equally impressed. Bryan's manner seemed a trifle didactic, and after the reception, when the girls exchanged experiences of the day, Mary learned from several classmates who knew him, that Bryan was really "too good"; he oozed rectitude, they said, and wore a halo, untouched as he was by such earthly habits as smoking, drinking, cursing or even dancing. But as she thought about Bryan's massive virtues, Mary realized that neither did she indulge in any of these minor vices. Finding the handsome, broad-shouldered Bryan otherwise attractive, she concluded with characteristic sensibility that it was better to have a man who was "too good" than "not good enough."

No temporizer, the thoroughly smitten Bryan now attempted to see Mary at every opportunity the Victorian niceties of Midwestern society allowed. This required some ingenuity, for the regulations of the academy did not permit callers. He found a sympathetic ally in Mrs. Edward Allan Tanner, wife of his Latin professor. They entered into a pact by which he called on her one evening a week and secured the use of that good lady's parlor to see Mary. Mary, in turn, received her academy's permission to visit Mrs. Tanner. According to the tradition at the academy, which is probably more legend than fact, the young suitor used to scramble up an elm and move out on a wide branch that carried him almost to Mary's dormitory window. From the branch, Bryan is supposed to have carried on much of his wooing.

If Bryan could see Mary through the good offices of Mrs. Tanner, surely there were other ladies who would provide the same cooperation, and indeed they did. A turn of events also increased their meetings. When Mary's mother fell ill that winter and was brought to a Jacksonville sanatorium, Bryan seized the opportunity to call on Mrs. Baird whenever Mary did. After Mrs. Baird's recovery, he also took Mary riding several times in a rented buggy in absolute violation of the academy's rules. By late spring, 1880, Bryan's diligent courtship had become so widely known that word of his machinations trickled down to the principal, the austere E. F. Bullard. He immediately summoned the young suitor and sternly informed him that he had violated both the academy's privileges and his honor as a gentleman. The distressed Bryan tried to assume the full blame, but Bullard waved him off, saying that since he could not punish him, Mary must be penalized.

The crisis brought Mary to understand the depth of her love for Bryan. Occasionally in these weeks in Bryan's company, she had grown weary of his relentless solemnity and probing inquiries concerning her ambitions, her religious life, and her parents' attitudes. But now she found that her love for him overwhelmed any exaction Bullard might levy. The principal was stern but not severe. He did not expel but suspended her for the remainder of the current spring term and required that she return home at once. In the fall she could resume her studies. The mountainous problem facing Mary was how to disclose and explain this sudden disruption of her education to her parents. When her anxious ponderings were intensified by the approaching hour of her departure, she wrote to Bryan: "Am going on the seven o'clock train, but it would not be safe for you to go down would it."

Bullard personally escorted Mary to the train, saw her seated, and watched from the station platform until the train moved from sight lest Bryan join her. As the train pushed beyond the city, Mary resigned herself to believing that Bryan had rightly deemed it best not to come, when suddenly he was beside her. The undaunted young man, exultant in her burst of surprise and delight, explained that he had hidden in the baggage car. In the joyous exhilaration of the moment, they exchanged rings that each was wearing. Bryan insisted on riding home with her to ask her parents' consent to their engagement. But Mary, believing that upheaval should not be compounded, induced him to get off at the next stop and return to Jacksonville.

Bryan resumed his romance when he and Mary returned to Jacksonville in the fall. Bullard restricted them to a single exchange of letters a week. When Bryan won $50 in a speaking contest, he bought a ring, a garnet set in gold. Then, with Mary's permission, he had a dedication cut inside the band, "Will to Mamie, June 4, 1880," the day they exchanged rings on the train. As the Thanksgiving recess neared, they planned for Bryan to approach Mary's father and, in the Victorian manner, ask his approval of their eventual marriage. "Hope you will not be frightened," Mary wrote, "though I imagine it would be a rather disagreeable task. Being a girl has a few advantages after all." If her father presented the least difficulty, she consoled, "there is a party concerned who *can* and will manage him." [1]

Bryan dutifully faced Mr. Baird, a man known for his reserve. Bryan cloaked his presentation in Holy Scripture. "Mr. Baird," he said, "I have been reading Proverbs a good deal lately, and find that Solomon says, 'Who-so findeth a wife, findeth a good thing, and obtaineth the favor of the Lord.'" Baird, a successful merchant and postmaster, was well read in the Bible and replied in kind. "Yes, I believe Solomon did say that," he acknowledged, "but Paul suggests that, while he that marrieth doeth well, he that marrieth not doeth better." This unexpected apostolic roadblock sent Bryan's mind racing through Proverbs, whose infinite wisdom had never before failed him in any situation. But it was his own ready wit as a debater rather than the sacred texts that now saved him. "Solomon would be the best authority upon the point," he replied, "because Paul was never married, while Solomon had a number of wives." Baird quickly warmed to the agile young man and approved the engagement.

Bryan also had to cope with his own father. This he did gradually, a strategy that was facilitated by a series of visits Silas paid to Jacksonville early in 1880. He was suffering from diabetes at the time and came to Dr. Jones for treatment. In March he decided it was high time to "look over" the young lady of whom he kept hearing such wondrous things. Mrs. Jones negotiated with Mary's principal, Mr. Bullard, to arrange the meeting. He agreed that Mary might come to tea at the Joneses on the second afternoon, March 30, following Silas' arrival. Silas retired early on the initial night to be at his best. Mary devoted that evening to searching through her entire wardrobe for her most appropriate dress. With several classmates standing by, in whose sartorial judgment she had the utmost confidence, she tried on dress after dress until one finally suited.

On the appointed day, as Mary looked from her window, there was a knock at her door. It was a message for her from the Jones household. Judge Silas Bryan, it said with stark directness, had just died. A tearful young girl put away the dress selected so carefully for the afternoon meeting.

Silas had died the victim of a paralytic stroke in his fifty-eighth year. On the morning of March 29, Dr. Jones had found Silas in bed unconscious. William stayed at the bedside, sent a message to Mary, optimistically anticipating that she could still meet his father, at least briefly, according to plan, the following afternoon. But Silas never rallied, and the next day he died. Mariah arrived in time from Salem to be with her husband at the end. On the thirty-first, mother and son accompanied Silas' body to Salem. His importance throughout southern Illinois was made evident by his sudden death. Mourning touched innumerable men and places. Local newspapers praised Silas' strength of public leadership and deep worth to his community and state. A crowd followed his body from the depot to the Bryan homestead, and when he lay in state in the county courthouse, thousands filed by in tribute. After the church service six of the leading lawyers and judges of Illinois bore his casket to the awaiting grave.[2]

We know nothing of Bryan's thoughts under the hammerblows of this sudden disaster that tore from him his preceptor and guide. The silence is perhaps itself indicative that his stoicism, his pride in new responsibilities as the family's eldest male, his religious faith revitalized after its own crisis, all drove him into a disciplined, undemonstrative response. In a very real sense, Silas was not gone. His moral leadership stood towering and firm as the cedars at his manor; his conception of the union between religion and public affairs was branded upon William's being; and his unfinished political career leavened his son's ambition.

Silas was fully prepared for his sudden departure from this life. He had arranged even for his funeral service, stipulating the psalms, text, and hymns. In the summer before his death, he had composed his will in his library, with Mariah present and William recording his words. Silas left no doubt about the purpose that his bequest was to serve. "It is my will," he declared, "that all my sons and daughters shall receive the highest physical, intellectual and moral education to be had in our generation. . . ." For William's education, Silas had formulated a specific plan in expressions and actions taken well before drawing up his will.

Silas wanted William, after finishing at Illinois College, to go to England for postgraduate study at Oxford. There he could acquire polish and sophistication from the world's most prestigious university. Oxford would furnish the gilt-edged credentials of the Virginia gentlemen Silas admired in his youth and aspired to imitate. One day William would inherit the manor. English-educated, he would become its squire in the old image. Like the

Virginian plantation aristocracy, he would be at the forefront of public affairs. But according to Silas' dream, William would be governed by a vital difference from the usual Virginia gentry: the wielding of his public powers would be tempered by Christian precepts. He would toil, not for the gain of a privileged class, but for the advantage of all men. His model would be Thomas Jefferson, apostle of equality and liberty, rather than an aristocratic, class-oriented Edmund Pendleton.

Some years prior to his death, Silas had taken steps to advance his plan for William's education at Oxford. He had purchased thirty steer and was fattening them for sale, expecting that the profit would underwrite a year at the English university. Even with Silas' sudden death, his plan would still have been practicable but for one unfortunate fact. In his openhearted way, Silas had signed security notes for a friend for almost $15,000. The friend had defaulted, and conceivably the Bryans could by legal action avoid paying. Since Silas, however, deemed the notes binding on the estate and since, furthermore, he ordered his "just debts" to be paid, the family chose to follow the mandate and honor the notes. William's program for study abroad evaporated, and he was fated to go through life without the intellectual and social breadth that Oxford might possibly have provided.[3]

After honoring the security notes, Silas' heirs were left with the manor, which was valuable and which they did not wish to sell, and a mere $1,500 in cash. In discussing their unexpected shortage of ready funds and the outlays required for the education of William and Russell, who was nearing college age, the family agreed on a common strategy. William would return to Jacksonville and complete his college course. If sufficient money could be scraped together, he would go on to law school. If, however, Russell should enter college, William would forgo law school and remain at home and run the farm. Uncertainty hung only briefly over William's plans. In August, 1880, Russell also died, and William proceeded to law school.

Bryan finished at Illinois College in a blaze of glory. As class valedictorian, he delivered an address on "Character" which delineated his view of life and its fundamental choices. "Character" he likened to "grooves in which are to flow the purposes of our lives." The grooves, in reality, were principles by which one guides and measures his actions. Bryan exhorted his audience to choose principles that are eternal, that conform one's life most nearly to the "Perfect Model." The result could not fail to be a background "on which to paint the noblest deeds and the grandest intellectual and moral achievements." To Bryan, the question of character, as with most other questions, was a choice between good and evil. There was no middle ground. "Character" was "the individuality of the person shining from every window of the soul, either as a beam of purity, or as a clouded ray that betrays the impurity within." The struggle between "light and darkness, right and wrong," continued interminably to the grave, and from moment to moment men faced and answered the question, "Shall those characters be good or bad?" [4]

The speech reveals a young man governed by a simplistic view of society and its complex problems and forces, innocent of awareness that one "good" may clash with another "good," that "good" is not always readily identifiable, and that something less than "good" may benefit society more than "pure goodness." Betraying no sense of history, no understanding of the confusing pressures facing men in authority, and the common unavailability of clear choices, Bryan's oration was more suitable for an eighth-grade exercise than a college commencement. One can imagine his professors writhing as they listened. It seemed to accept the old schoolbook maxims at face value without the least flicker of a question or a shred of doubt. But the most important aspect of the address was its revelation of a way of thinking and judging that would rule Bryan throughout his political career. Both men and issues he was prone to relegate to the absolute categories of "good" and "bad," and that which in his perceptions was "bad" suffered utter rejection. "Bad" men and causes carried no traces of good that he was willing to acknowledge and weigh in his estimations.

With his reduced educational budget, Bryan chose to attend the Union College of Law in Chicago. To study law would be to follow his father's professional path, and old yearnings nudged him toward it. A cousin had attended the Union College of Law and enthusiastically recommended it. The school was among the most distinguished in the state. Since 1873 it had been under the joint management of Northwestern University and the old University of Chicago, which closed in 1886 for financial reasons, with degrees granted in the names of both. In Bryan's day the school, which had been something of a peregrinating institution, was located on Dearborn Street, in a single building, and consisted of a solitary lecture room, an office shared by the dean and his faculty, a slightly larger room occupied by the secretary of the school and his assistants, and a combination coat, locker, and lounge room. A roof garden had been transformed into a library, and it was reached by students agile enough to climb two steep iron ladders. Despite the impossibility of bringing all its students, who attended classes by day and by evening, into the single lecture room simultaneously, classes were small, with the graduating body averaging only eleven in Bryan's years there. [5]

The two-year course carried Bryan through a curriculum that was standard for the day—torts, criminal law, pleadings, equity, jurisprudence, contracts, patents. Bryan's habits of faithful study, so well honed in college, grew even sharper in law school, and he steadily won high grades. His law studies fell in an era of transition in legal education. Like many another law school, Union had adopted the case method, by which the student read judicial opinions directly. Previously he had read treatises or commentaries

on the law and absorbed them in memory by drill and rote. In turning to
actual cases, he saw the principles of law applied to concrete problems. In
addition, as the great Harvard law teacher Christopher Columbus Langdell
demonstrated as early as 1871, original court cases could be exploited in the
classroom by a kind of dialectic or Socratic method. It drove the student to
search for implications, to be alert to gaps and lapses in judicial reasoning,
and to think for himself.

Bryan was enchanted by the classroom give-and-take and the endless
argument and discussion of students outside class. Law school was for
Bryan a debater's paradise, where he could sharpen the skills of dialectic,
think with finer precision and, what pleased him most, with greater rapidity.
In college debating, there was ample time for preparation, but in law school
the pace of the assignments, the acumen of his professors, and the unpredictability of their probing questions spurred Bryan to improve the tempo
and precision of his thought. He progressed smoothly through his courses
and stood well in his class. Law did not excite in him any marked interest in
its philosophy or foundations. He valued it as a tool or craft, indispensable
in a democratic society. His favorite course was constitutional law, which
related most closely to his future life in public affairs.

With the family fortune gone, Bryan lived in pinched circumstances.
Budgeting himself for room and board at a mere $4 a week, he had to locate
some distance from the school to find a room that was just barely tolerable.
In a drab cubicle with tattered furnishings and a total absence of sunlight,
he maintained his existence. He walked the four miles to school, rain or
shine, to save a five-cent transit fare. His forced parsimony developed habits that were never to leave him. The meager outlay Bryan made for his
room was further pinched by the somewhat disproportionate requirements
of his expenditure for food. Bryan's appetite seemed unbounded in its lack
of discipline. His large-boned frame had long required a lot of food, but his
mother and Mrs. Jones had both satisfied him and sensibly regulated the
amount. Bryan, now on his own, cast discretion aside and indulged in gas-
tronomic orgies. He would consume pigs' feet for breakfast, corned beef
and potatoes for lunch, pastry in midafternoon, and veal cutlets and buckwheat cakes for dinner.

Bryan ventured into law school politics with rather more success than he
had achieved at Illinois College. He was elected president of the junior class
and class orator. As in college, he attended church and joined the literary
societies and other organizations devoted to political discussion. He became
a member of the school's student senate, whose sessions were held at the
YMCA. Because of the pressures of study, the societies did not function
during the week, but on weekends in an age without movies, their programs
provided major entertainment. At each meeting a member delivered an address on some aspect of the school's work, on a public question or govern-

mental function. Afterward there were refreshments and conviviality. Of Bryan's several presentations, the one exciting the highest regard was his speech on "Eternal Vigilance Is the Price of Liberty," hailed for its magnetic eloquence.

The address is notable as a demonstration of Bryan's fast maturing political thought and as a testimonial of his faith in popular rule as the foundation of democratic society. "History teaches us," he declared, "that as a general rule, truth is found among the masses, emanates from them; a fact so patent that it has given rise to the old saying, 'vox populi vox Dei.' " But popular rule was not automatic, a political harvest that could be reaped without effort from the citizen. Indeed, the earnest young law student saw in the people the power either to preserve or destroy their liberties, and the key lay in the willingness of the people to exert themselves. If they did not, their liberties would be lost, as the political scene attested. Voter indifference in the cities had handed over their government to bosses and machines, to corruption and tyranny. Bryan's argument was doubtless spurred by the ugliness he beheld in Chicago's politics. The Cook County Democratic machine, managed by Mayor Carter Harrison, had desecrated the basic institutions on which popular rule rests: the suffrage and the administration of justice.

For "our best citizens" to stand aloof from politics, Bryan warned, served to surrender to "the worst classes" the control of elections. Good government could rise only from a clear and responsible conception of civic duty. ". . . every man who wished a pure administration, who is interested in having honest and upright men make and execute the laws, has a duty to perform at every caucus and every election; to shirk that duty is treason." [6]

It was during his law school days that Bryan developed another view of "the people," a view that vastly influenced his entire subsequent political career. The people in his address were seen optimistically, even euphorically, as the great body of "good citizens," while a far lesser minority comprised the "worst classes." Moral men plainly outnumbered, if they did not always prevail over, the corrupt. But there was another side of the question which presented itself to Bryan one wintry day as he strode by the city courthouse. Eager to reach the comfort of his room, he noticed a handful of unkempt little poor boys, in tattered clothes and broken shoes, who were gambling their pennies in a warm corner of the building. Bryan halted briefly to watch and then pressed on. As he walked against the cutting wind, a question leaped into his mind: Why were these poor little fellows born and reared with no higher ideals than to pass their hours gambling in the streets, while so many men were born into a far more favorable environment, nurturing ideals and opportunities that shaped their entire lives? Men, Bryan had learned, were not born equal, the Declaration of Independence notwithstanding. The discovery vexed him deeply.

The topics Bryan debated in his law school societies bear an extraordinary resemblance to the agenda of his future political career. He tackled the
intricacies of prohibition, woman's suffrage, and the tariff. On the last he
took the position of Democratic reformers in Congress and urged the abandonment of duties on all domestic manufactures except liquor and tobacco.
In letters to Mary, he articulated his convictions on another subject that
would loom large in his subsequent political career. He could not, he made
plain, abide imperialism. Even England, the most successful imperial
power, did not have enough saving qualities to justify her actions. "However much we admire England's power in war," he wrote, "or her eminence
in peace I can not but feel that her foreign policy is mercenary, tyrannical
and iniquitous in the extreme and a disgrace to her boasted civilization." [7]

Another enduring influence on Bryan of the law school years was provided by an arrangement of the law school schedule which enabled students
who needed more income or who wished to supplement their classroom
knowledge to take part-time jobs in Chicago law offices. It was Bryan's
great good fortune to find employment with former United States Senator
Lyman Trumbull. A good political friend of Bryan's father, Trumbull had
admitted Silas to the bar, and when the son of his old protégé appeared one
day to ask for a job, Trumbull quickly agreed. For $5 a week, Bryan swept
floors, copied pleadings, and managed the supplies of papers and ink. He
became a warm friend of Trumbull's son, Henry, a law school classmate. In
Chicago, the Trumbulls provided for Bryan what the Joneses had in Jacksonville, a kind of foster home and a center of culture.

Lyman Trumbull, when Bryan knew him, was in the twilight of a career
of the rarest distinction in its devotion to principle and to the causes of the
oppressed. Prior to the Civil War, he had broken with his own Democratic
Party on slavery and supported Lincoln, whose position on the issue
squared with his convictions. As a United States Senator, he drafted the
Thirteenth Amendment, which gave permanence to the Emancipation
Proclamation, and led the debate for its passage. Because of his lifelong
habit of obeying his conscience, he refused to vote for the impeachment of
Andrew Johnson, a decision that eventually cost him his Senate seat and
banished him to political retirement. But private affairs and advancing
years did not dim Trumbull's awareness of current injustices or his zest for
speaking out on them. In 1882, when Bryan went to work for him, he was
denouncing the evils springing from the growing concentration of wealth
and pleading that the tax power be employed to contain it.

Fighting his new crusade, Trumbull found a special joy in the youthful
Bryan. He loved to discuss ideas with him, was delighted by his receptivity
to the nostrums he proposed, and was stimulated by the thrust of his questions. But it was not merely the presence of a congenial spirit that brought
Trumbull to pass much time with his young assistant. Rather, he perceived

in Bryan the promise of an extraordinary political career. If he meant to shape its attitudes and beliefs, he succeeded remarkably. A. R. Talbot, Bryan's classmate and future law partner, noted the effects that association with Trumbull had on his young friend. "Will," he said, "was eagerly impressed with the idea that the people were being unjustly burdened by monopolies. He maintained even then that the menace of the country was the encroachment of wealth on the rights of the commonwealth, and he thought there was serious trouble ahead for the country."

Bryan's letters to Mary demonstrate the remarkable extent to which the thinking of his awaiting career years was already formulated. Or, less flatteringly, they show that he stopped growing while young. Interspersed with his avowals of love for Mary was an outpouring of his observations on politics and economics, spurred by Trumbull and his own reactions to the realities of Chicago. He was distressed that everywhere small business was vanishing as big business relentlessly achieved ever greater dominion. Huge corporations already ruled steel, railroads, and oil. The age of the trust had moved well beyond its dawn. Through the great corporations a few people were lavishly enriching themselves at the expense of the masses. The men who toiled from sunup to sundown in the factories, who worked in the stench of the packinghouses and in the grime of the railroad yards, were creating mountainous wealth, of which they were dealt only a meager portion. Bryan's impressions of the wretchedness of industrial labor were not gained at second hand. In those formative days he visited one of the most distressing industrial scenes in the nation, the shops of George Pullman. He rightly predicted that within a few years the laborers would revolt against wretched working conditions and low pay. Nor did it escape his notice that the worst exploiters of labor and the consumer tended to be affiliated with the Republican Party.[8]

During his two years in Chicago, Bryan and Mary faced the problem of separation. The adage that absence makes the heart grow fonder was proved by their experience; their ties grew firmer. Bryan, in his life of study and self-denial, put aside the large interest he displayed in girls in his college days. He solemnly abjured "flirtation," which he defined as "intentionally gaining the affections of another and then throwing them away." Flirtation, he said in his renunciation, is "the one unpunished sin." For these two years of law school, he saw little of Mary except for brief visits during school vacations. After graduating first in her class at the academy, she lived at home and pursued a kind of training course in housekeeping to ready herself for her impending marriage.

Their correspondence was prolific, affectionate, and solemn. Mary's letters bubbled with admonitions for Bryan to pursue a less rigorous schedule of activities, to adopt a sane diet, to avoid the occasional failures of health his letters recounted. But Bryan was not to be budged by counsel that he should not work so hard, not even from a charming, concerned fiancée. "Don't lessen my ambition," he protested, "it is my great spur to action. Excite and encourage me to work hard so that I may develop powers which exert a great influence for good." Neither success nor wealth did Bryan value in themselves, for he stressed in one report to Mary that "Success is the great perverter of virtue." Small wonder, on the basis of the evidence, that Mary sometimes wearied of Bryan's letters, finding them "a little didactic." [9]

Even as Bryan completed his legal studies, he was not yet ready to take the marriage vows, adopting the view that they ought not to marry until he was capable of supporting a wife. Given the customary uncertainties of a fledgling lawyer, his attainment of economic adequacy could not be precisely anticipated. After receiving his law diploma, Bryan set out at once to found a practice whose income would enable him to fulfill his aging promises to Mary. Fired by love and resolve, he had first to answer the question of where he should hang out his shingle.

5. The Young Lawyer

In point of fact, Bryan had been searching for some time for a suitable place to launch his practice. The summer before graduating he journeyed to Troy, Missouri, where his father had once lived, but felt the town too small. Then he pushed on to Kansas City, but it seemed too big, and its roaring, swashbuckling style and wide-open saloons repelled him. The city's high living costs also made him fear that the money left from his law studies would run out before he could become self-supporting.

Ultimately, Bryan did what most young lawyers do. He chose to settle in a community where he was already known, and by this criterion a return to Jacksonville was altogether logical. Mariah suggested Salem and a partnership there with two cousins, but Bryan chose Jacksonville, after exploring the matter with Dr. Jones. Mariah, always the good mother, observed stoically, "It is best you should go where you can do best," and since she had lately come into some cash through the sale of her farm's assets, she promised him $1,000 as a wedding present. Once he could earn $500 a year, Bryan said in acknowledging this deferred gift, he would immediately make Mary his bride.

Dr. Jones both encouraged his young ward and applied his considerable influence in his behalf. His word provided Bryan entrée and a place in one of Jacksonville's leading law firms, Brown, Kirby and Russell. Its partners ideally combined the skills necessary to a small-town firm. William Brown, a stellar cross-examiner, excelled as a trial lawyer. Judge Edward Kirby was the firm's "office lawyer," whose forte, with his outstanding knowledge of pleadings and precedents, was drafting briefs and settling estates. Younger than his partners, Robert D. Russell was a fast-rising star in the county's legal community. All the partners, having close ties with Illinois College, valued Bryan for his sterling record there.

On July 4, 1883, Bryan proudly nailed a fresh-painted sign, W. J. BRYAN, LAWYER, to the doorpost and prayerfully hoped that his deliberate selection of Independence Day for the commencement of his professional career would prove lucky. In his office on the first floor, Bryan stationed himself where he could see and be seen by potential clients, most of them intent upon proceeding to the second floor, where the firm's inner offices were located. He positioned his battered rolltop desk just inside the doorway, and whenever a visitor approached, Bryan would rush out to greet him with a cavernous smile, a warm handshake, and cheerful words. Though most clients still moved to the upper floor, Bryan managed to siphon off just enough trade to keep body and soul together.

Like any young adult entering a profession, Bryan had to humanize his values and adapt the absolute standards of his younger years to adult life. Ironically, almost cruelly, his very first case posed a conflict between one of his most basic youthful beliefs and his adult need to eke out a living. Bryan's energetic socializing corralled as his first client, John Sheehan, a saloonkeeper whose bills required collecting. For the utterly moral, high-minded, teetotaling Bryan to accept such an assignment seems an outrageous incongruity, but he batted not a whisker of the full beard which now, and only briefly, adorned his face. "I told him," Bryan wrote later of the terms by which he was retained, "that I did not drink myself nor advise drinking, but that I thought those who bought liquor ought to pay for it." His bill collecting proved to be a huge success, and he executed his mission in such gentle fashion that to Sheehan's great delight, the former debtors returned to his saloon and amiably compiled more debt.

The importance of not making debtors angry was not lost upon Bryan. Though his style was gentle, it was also firm and persistent. If the debtor could not pay when Bryan called, he asked him to suggest a day to call again. If the second call was unavailing, Bryan showed no annoyance and set another date. He pursued this procedure until the bill was paid, although his effort for weeks and months might yield only driblets. Bryan's impregnable goodwill even converted debtors into clients. A liveryman, after the young lawyer had called on him to no avail many times, finally declared he would gladly pay his debt if Bryan would make it possible by collecting debts owed him and long past due. Bryan gladly and successfully complied with the request.

Having gained a reputation as a bill collector, Bryan ranged far and wide in the affairs he handled. One lagger had failed to pay on an organ, another defaulted on the interest of a loan, and still another fell behind on his groceries. Bryan collected for Illinois College, which carried him to many communities throughout the state. His concentration in this area was further spurred by a change of circumstance in his firm. Soon after Bryan joined its ranks, Robert Russell resigned to move to Minneapolis, and much of the large collecting effort Russell had handled was transferred to Bryan. Fortunately, his practice afforded other opportunities. In November, Bryan teamed with another attorney, Ed McDonald, who had summoned his help with an assault case. The case dragged on all day, and just before dinner Bryan knew the thrill of making his first jury speech. When he got up on the floor, he afterward wrote to Mary, "my fright all left me and I never spoke with more fluency and earnestness than I did that day." After court, the judge and several attorneys, well impressed with their young colleague, complimented him on his performance.[1]

But the days of glory were far exceeded by empty days, utterly bare of clients, income, or even a flicker of activity. Even where there was business, more often than not its yield was small. In his first month of work, Bryan earned $9.60. When receipts fell one month to $2.50, he wrote despairingly of his circumstances to his classmate Henry Trumbull, who, because of his health, had opened practice in Albuquerque, New Mexico. But Henry provided no report of a land of litigious milk and honey, and Bryan dropped any notion he might have had of migrating to New Mexico. He also shared his despair with Mary, who waited patiently in Perry. As she would be in all his dark hours, Mary was the voice of patience and hope. "Don't be discouraged in your work, dearie," she wrote, "Father and I were talking about you last night and he said you were going 'through the narrows' now and would have it pretty hard for a while." As Christmas neared in that bleak year of 1883, Bryan wrote Mary of his intention to buy her a gold thimble as a gift, if he had the money.

As the new year dawned, the clouds began to break. The collections turned over to Bryan by Brown and Kirby became juicier. Dr. Jones sent him a few good clients, and John Sheehan, the saloonkeeper, brought in a client out of whose business, a grocery store, Bryan as assignee soon earned $200. Meanwhile, he was branching out into activities not directly related to the law. By giving an oration on "The American Citizen," he satisfied the then-simple requirements for a master's degree at Illinois College. Thanks to a railroad pass and an honorarium for an Independence Day address, he was able to attend the national Democratic convention in Chicago.

But the act that exulted him most was his start at building a house for his

long-waiting bride-to-be. Arranging to borrow against his share of his father's manor, he bought a site and contracted for the erection of a modest
dwelling. In this he was assisted by a mortgage taken by Dr. Jones. Bryan
and Mary set their wedding date for October 1, exactly five years after they
first met and four years after their engagement. These epochal intertwinings
of their lives were commemorated in the inscription Bryan placed on
Mary's wedding band, "Won, 1880. One, 1884." In a last letter to Mary just
before the ceremony, Bryan told how he was practicing diligently on that
portion of the wedding service requiring him to intone "and with all my
worldly goods I thee endow." He wanted, he wrote, to make that pledge
duly impressive, and "If you dare laugh when I say that I won't kiss you
when he tells me to salute my bride."

On October 1 the wedding took place at Mary's spacious Victorian home
in Perry. A little group of local friends witnessed the simple religious observance. Dr. Tanner, Bryan's former Latin professor and now president of
Illinois College, officiated, and Bryan's younger brother, Charles, was best
man. It was a day of contrasting moods, of Mrs. Baird's tearful reluctance
to part with Mary, which was more than offset by Mr. Baird's light charm.
The new Mr. and Mrs. Bryan passed their wedding night at a Jacksonville
hotel and next day journeyed to Salem, where Mariah honored them with a
reception for which seemingly half the town turned out. Ultimately they
reached St. Louis for their honeymoon and lots of shopping to stock their
new house. Because the house was not yet completed, Bryan returned alone
to Jacksonville, and Mary rejoined her parents at Perry. But separation
soon proved unbearable, and Mary came on to Jacksonville. Friends put up
the Bryans until their home was finally ready in late November.[2]

With his new responsibilities of a wife and a home on College Hill, Bryan
stepped up the tempo—if that was possible—of his efforts to succeed at the
law. His quickened enterprise was nicely, though not sensationally, rewarded. In 1884 his income reached $700; the next year it rose to $1,000,
and the following year to nearly $1,500. He compiled a part of his alto-
gether respectable earnings from the assorted sidelines in which a small-
town lawyer can exert himself. He sold real estate, was also an insurance
agent, peddled books on commission, and collected rents. His law practice
encompassed liens and bankruptcies and the settlement of estates. Like
many small-town lawyers, Bryan occasionally came upon opportunities to
turn a fast gain. George G. Waite, for example, was the bearer of fetching
economic tidings from far-off Lincoln, Nebraska. To "Friend Will," he
wrote of a national bank being organized there, with stock available at an
entrancingly low price. Lincoln was "a live city," and the investment would
most likely pay 10 percent interest.[3]

But Bryan's modest income left no residue for investment. Mary's parents, who were not well and required her care, occupied a suite in the new Bryan home. Comfortably fixed, they contributed to the household expenses, yet their presence added to his task. Bryan also had to reckon with another kind of increase of familial duty. Just one day short of their first wedding anniversary, he and Mary had their first child. On September 30, 1885, a daughter, Ruth, was born. This healthy, saucy girl was immediately the center of the lavish attention of four adoring adults. A loving, generous father, Bryan delighted in watching his new daughter grow and learn.

Despite his engrossment in the struggle to make an adequate living, Bryan found time to preserve his interest in politics and public affairs. He had every encouragement from Mary, who believed as an article of faith that they both should use their early adult years in ways that added to their knowledge and future usefulness. In one of those candid, stock-taking conversations that they were so often to have and that bespoke so well the fact that marriage had brought them into the fullest partnership, they canvassed what they should do with their leisure hours. Many of their young friends had urged them to join the several social clubs available in Jacksonville, and the step was altogether logical for a lawyer like Bryan with a new practice and the need to widen his acquaintanceship. This alternative the Bryans rejected in favor of activities contributing to community service and self-improvement.

Bryan invested a good many of his free hours in reading books on political economy and public affairs. He studied numerous volumes on the most controversial questions of the day: the railroads, the tariff, and money. Whenever the family chose a gift for him, it was apt to be a book on political economy. Mary, who did not take eagerly to housework, threw herself into several projects—a course in early English at Illinois College, membership in a German conversation club—and, most formidable of all, she embarked upon the study of law, pursuing the same course that Bryan had completed at the Union College of Law. She read his textbooks and supplemented them by borrowings from the remarkably good library at Brown and Kirby and from the collection of the county bar association.

Mary thus shared easily and without hesitation her husband's ways of thinking and his view of life, in a sense replacing the departed Silas as a monitor of his ambitions and performance. Her outlook, her optimistic assessment of Bryan's potential, her ready acceptance of his religious and moral concepts enabled her to make her relationships with Bryan of a piece with the older parental influence.[4]

Bryan, for his part, served as president of the YMCA, an organization to which he was devoted all his life, and early in 1887 he became chancellor commander of the Knights of Pythias. Eager always to help in the training and development of youth, he taught in Sunday school and continued to toil for his college literary society, Sigma Pi, as a coach and speaker. He attended Dr. Jones' sprightly monthly seminars on philosophical topics. He devoted himself to civic enterprises such as the organization of the local Fourth of July celebration in 1887. As the principal speaker for the event, he invited Senator Benjamin Harrison of Indiana, whose brilliant oratory made his Republicanism tolerable to the young Democrat. But the future President already had an engagement in the East, and Bryan had to settle for less glamorous talent.

Bryan's first and irresistible love was politics, and he continued the apprenticeship begun in his college days as a worker in the local Democratic Party. There he gladly performed unglamorous bread-and-butter tasks. Politics provided relief from the tensions of struggle and frustration encountered on the hard road of his legal career, offering a more exciting, broader, and more constructive arena in which to apply his skills than a law practice so far devoted largely to bill collecting. It was also an outlet for Bryan's gregariousness. Sociable, glad-handing, and extroverted, he could indulge in political endeavor while simultaneously advancing causes and purposes of public policy to which he was committed. Besides, the Democratic Party in Jacksonville attracted college faculty members and other young lawyers with whom he enjoyed associating.[5]

Bryan quickly learned such elementary practical politics as the rudiments of organization and campaigning. He grew versed in the mechanics of electoral administration and served his party at one election after another as a poll watcher. But his forte, for which his party brothers came to value him quickly and highly, was his work on the stump. Any election, local, state, or national, found him ranging the county, speaking for the ticket at picnic groves, in courthouse yards, and in schoolhouses. He became thoroughly adept in the homespun, coarse-grained ways of rural democracy.

Typical of his assignments was a speech he had to deliver at the village of Buckhorn, six miles southwest of Jacksonville. With a Democratic coworker at his side, Bryan set out in a buggy. Neither knew the way, and as they neared their destination, they asked a passerby for directions. He first told them to turn back half a mile but after a moment withdrew this advice and said they were proceeding correctly. His first response, he explained, was based on the impression that his interrogators were set upon disrupting the meeting.

In Buckhorn a scraggly throng of bearded farmers in dungarees and boots well splattered with the marks of barnyard life, their ladies in homespun toggery, awaited the day's speaker. A holiday spirit reigned, and menfolk bandied sentiments to one another rich in local meaning and productive of much hilarity. One burly type advanced upon Bryan with a hip-pocket-size bottle and pressed, not once but several times, an invitation for the speaker to partake of its contents. Bryan declined politely and repeatedly. Baffled by this rejection of his generosity, the local citizen shuffled off, muttering that he hoped the speaker would do as well as he could any-how. His stress of "anyhow" left Bryan believing uncomfortably that his would-be benefactor felt that he could not expect very much under the cir-cumstances. Just before the meeting began, another man shuffled up to Bryan and with earnest solicitude cautioned him not to speak too long. Only a few nights ago, he growled, a speaker had worn everybody out.

As Bryan made his way to his seat on the platform, a voice cried out in encouragement, "Hit 'em hard, there ain't a Republican here." The chair-man took pains to work out the proper form of the introduction. Never averse to using a political meeting to advertise his law practice, Bryan sug-gested that it might perhaps be best to say, "Mr. W. J. Bryan, an attorney-at-law of Jacksonville, will now address you." The chairman, who evidently was new to his task, advanced to the podium and was so overwhelmed that he was able to blurt out only that "Mr. O'Brien will now spake."

Elections apart, Bryan's favorite topic was prohibition, which nicely satisfied his desire to promote through politics causes for human uplift. Time and again to Jacksonville and county audiences, the earnest, hand-some young man, a radiant model of clean and frugal living, conveyed in his rich tone and with the emphasis of his flashing dark eyes the message of temperance. Jacksonville, like many another Midwestern community of the day, was visited by professional temperance speakers who crisscrossed the state, urging their listeners to swear abstinence by signing pledge cards and supporting local laws banning the evil drink. In his own contribution, Bryan spoke with evangelical style and fervor. The virtues of temperance, he contended, must be proclaimed "daily and hourly," for the "saloon is open all the time . . . wickedness never tires; vice never sleeps." He who drinks, Bryan thundered, is unwise and sinful. He sins "against himself, those dependent upon him, against society and against God," for strong drink "weakens the body," "poisons the blood," and "destroys the power of the mind."

With prohibition as his vessel, Bryan was entering the well-defined world of the young adult ideologue. Prohibition lent itself easily to his way of thinking, of seeing life and politics as a constant war between good and evil. It was a question on which Bryan could expend freely his moralist's right-eousness. He acknowledged no middle ground; he perceived in the regula-tions and restraints of prohibition no endangering of human liberty, no counterevil of a coercive government trampling on individual rights and freedoms.[6]

For all the good life that he and Mary enjoyed at Jacksonville, Bryan was restless. True, his law practice was building; he was at least an obvious peb-ble on the beach of local Democratic politics; both he and Mary were hap-pily enmeshed in the life of the college and in constructive activity in the community. But Jacksonville, as Bryan plainly perceived, was also a world of formidable constraints. After four years of faithful service in Jacksonville's Democratic politics, he had not been nominated for any local office, and even if he had, the overwhelming Republicanism of the people would have barred his election. The law practice was not growing fast enough, and several new efforts Bryan made to increase his professional income proved unavailing. He explored the possibility of leaving Brown and Kirby and setting up his own law office in partnership with Richard Yates, a college classmate and city attorney. Negotiations with Yates stumbled fatally upon Bryan's insistence on a larger proportion of the fees since he was earning more than Yates at the time. With a Democrat, Grover Cleveland, in the White House, Bryan pulled all the political strings within his grasp to win appointment as assistant district attorney for the Southern District of Illinois, even journeying to Springfield to press his claim, but he met only rebuff.

Disappointment sharpened Bryan's disenchantment with Jacksonville. The city, indeed the entire state of Illinois, had lost the dynamism of the frontier. A settled society, confining and stratified, had taken over. The well-circumscribed legal business of Jacksonville was divided among a few major law firms and the ever-augmented ranks of young lawyers. Bryan was admitting to friends that he had unfortunately overestimated the impression his college career made on the local people.

Bryan then tried to pull more strings. He made known his desire to hold a responsible and well-paying administrative post in Washington, but the Cleveland men gave not a blink of recognition. He wrote Robert Russell to disclose his willingness to join him in Minneapolis, but Russell gave no encouragement. Bryan always contended that one's life is largely molded by small occurrences that come to develop large consequences. Ample inspiration for that theory was provided by what appeared to be a minor journey in the summer of 1887. Seemingly simple and unpretentious, it would redirect and reorder his life.

The journey had modest, almost unpromising beginnings. Judge Kirby, who, in addition to presiding over his law firm, was treasurer of Illinois College, proposed that Bryan go to Kansas to collect interest overdue on notes held by the college as part of its endowment fund. In return for Bryan's calls on the notes' makers, the college could do no more than pay Bryan's travel expenses and a small commission on collections actually made. He undertook the journey not because of its economic possibilities but because he had never been West and his curiosity was pricked about that vast, newly settled region. Bryan's journey had another mission. Mary's father asked that Bryan, after completing his business in Kansas, go on to Creston, Iowa, to look at a tract the Bairds had held there for many years. In plotting his journey from Kansas to Creston, Bryan noted he could go by way of either St. Joseph or Lincoln. The fact that a law school classmate, Adolphus Talbot, lived in Lincoln, prompted Bryan to choose that alternative. He passed a weekend with the ebullient Talbot and inquired thoroughly into professional opportunities in Lincoln. On the way to the train, Talbot urged his friend to come to Lincoln, stressing that opportunities in this youthful city were far better than in Illinois. Bryan, with his superior speaking ability, would surely go far as a trial lawyer. Talbot made his invitation specific. He proposed that they form a partnership.[7]

There were other inducements for the move. On his busy July weekend there, Bryan met the owner of a weekly paper who offered to provide him a column in which to answer legal questions submitted by readers. The column, Bryan expected, would be invaluable in making him quickly known to the people of the county. Bryan always took pains to contend that no thought of politics spurred his move to Lincoln. That city, like all Nebraska, was as resolutely Republican as Jacksonville. But Bryan could have hoped, although he never confessed it, that Nebraska, as a frontier state with a fast-rising population, might one day shift its allegiance. He explored the possibilities and implications of a move with Mary. "You know Jacksonville," she said with quiet finality. "You have seen Lincoln. If you think that a change is for the best, I am willing to go." [8]

Bryan and Mary agreed that he should move to Lincoln first and that his family would come later after he had perfected living arrangements for them. On October 1, 1887, his wedding anniversary and a day he preferred throughout his life for commencing major undertakings, he reached Lincoln. The partnership of Talbot and Bryan began at once, with offices on an upper floor of the First National Bank Building. The sparse and battered furnishings proclaimed the humbleness of the new enterprise. Its business was at first decidedly small. Talbot had no ready practice apart from his employment as local attorney for the Union Pacific Railroad. The partnership functioned by several simple principles. At the end of each month the partner with the greater earnings gave the other half of the excess. Bryan, who on principle would not accept compensation from a railroad, insisted that Talbot's income from the nefarious Union Pacific must not be included in the partnership. He would neither be nor appear to be a minion of a railroad that held a stranglehold on so much of Missouri's and Nebraska's politics. It had state legislators on its payroll, helped finance their campaigns, and generously doled out railroad passes to influential politicians to assure both their free travel and their ready sympathy. When Nebraska passed from territorial status to statehood, it passed into the domination of the railroads. The two most powerful lines, the Union Pacific and the Burlington, were granted millions of acres of land, with twenty and more miles on each side of the right-of-way. The land was neither desolate nor remote but constituted the best acreage in the state. Needless to say, laws to regulate or control the railroads enjoyed small possibility of success in the legislature.

From the beginning, the partnership of "Will" and "Dolph" proceeded with idyllic harmony. To Bryan, Talbot was "a rare man—one of God's noblemen." Nearly the same age, height, and build as Bryan, Talbot too exuded a genial warmth that no adversity could wither, and as a staunch Methodist, he had the springs of Fundamentalism running deep within him. As an active Republican, he complemented Bryan's Democracy to give the partnership the bipartisan cast so often contrived and valued by law firms. Bryan and Talbot worked easily as a team. As a standard practice in preparing litigation, Talbot would develop their case, while Bryan put himself in the place of the opposing attorneys and conjured up likely arguments.

Bryan again had to pass through the ordeal of starting a law practice. As before, business came in driblets. Its principal source, in the beginning, was the German National Bank, in which he deposited $300 brought from Illinois. So impressed was the bank with its new depositor that it made him its attorney. The bank's affairs enabled Bryan to gain other clients. But the initial yields, despite his diligent gregariousness, were slim—from October to December he earned only $82.55, and to stretch his funds, he lived with the strictest economy. By sleeping on a folding lounge in his office, he saved room rent and he even skimped on his meals. For a time his diet was mainly apples and gingersnaps, and he remembered "with great distinctness" when the office receipts reached a sufficient total to justify three normal meals a day.

Despite his penury, Bryan's optimism about a Nebraskan future never faltered, and he proceeded with plans to build a house. In a Christmas visit to Jacksonville, he arranged for the sale of his house there and concluded an arrangement with his father-in-law by which the latter provided the money to build the house in Lincoln. Bryan subsequently paid back the entire loan with interest. In Lincoln, he entered into a contract with J. F. Harrison to build and complete a two-story frame house and barn for $3,290. These were to be ready for occupancy by June 10, 1888, "unless weather delays" and "all work is to be well done." The weather fortunately cooperated, and Bryan exultantly brought his family from Jacksonville on schedule. He, Mary and Ruth, and the Bairds clasped the new life with the eager anticipation of better opportunities and a faster-rising career, the very sentiments that brought thousands upon thousands to leave their settled communities for the frontierlands of the West.[9]

6. O Pioneers!

The Bryans moved into their new-built home on D Street in Lincoln in June, 1888. The house's glistening white exterior, the generous sweep of its veranda which crossed the front and curled around to the side, the breadth of its several clapboarded sections, its rise for two stories, beneath the crown of an observation tower and cupola, all made it the typical Westernized Victorian edifice of its day.

Even Mrs. Baird, who was not given to enthusiasm, expressed pleasure with her new surroundings. Mary, delighted with the house, happily rearranged the furnishings from Jacksonville, which had already been moved in. The possessions of their former and smaller home now seemed sparse. In the next weeks, Mary purchased chairs, pictures, and bookcases. Bryan, looking ahead to winter, bought an additional stove, an ax, a hatchet, and a good supply of firewood.

The city of Lincoln, to which they now committed their allegiance and their hopes, symbolized the swift success that Bryan aspired to. In a mere twenty years the city had changed from a wild prairie hamlet of fewer than 50 people to a city of more than 40,000. Lincoln's remarkable growth was owed in part to its being Nebraska's capital and in part to its being the principal radial railroad center west of the Missouri River. Into its yards cascaded the produce of the sprawling surrounding agricultural empire. Wheat, corn, all manner of fruits, grains, and vegetables, as well as ore from Western mines and cattle from the great ranches of Montana and the Dakotas, flowed toward the East. From the other direction, thousands of settlers passed through the city en route to the prairielands where a million acres lay open to claim under the Homestead Law. The human tide rolled in so fast that in the seven years prior to the Bryans' coming, twenty-two of Nebraska's counties were created.

Although the atmosphere of the frontier lay heavily over Lincoln, its streets, with their rows of trim frame houses, suggested the settled respectability of Jacksonville. Lincoln, too, was the scene of a considerable cultural life. The state university was situated there, and the abundance of Lincoln's churches prompted it to be called the Brooklyn of the West. Funke's Opera House, at the corner of O and Twelfth Streets, was a first-class theater, to which came traveling opera, plays, and lectures. The city was studded with moral, fraternal, and charitable organizations, including no fewer than thirteen temperance societies. Newspapers and periodicals in English and foreign languages thrived, from the Lincoln *Freie Presse,* the most successful of the newspapers serving the state's large German population, to the *Daily Stock Dealer.*

The banks, stockyards, two great packinghouses, numerous woolen and paper mills, woodworking factories, tanneries and stonecutting works of the city fed the hopes of the youthful Bryan.[1]

In February, 1888, the firm of Talbot and Bryan settled in new offices at Burr Block, near Funke's Opera House. There, from a reception room and two private offices, the partners carried on a practice which, according to their advertisements, was available for all the courts of the state. The services rendered included the preparation of briefs, the argument of cases in the State Supreme Court on behalf of nonresident counsel, and use of the firm's office and library by visiting attorneys. Bryan also wrote to attorneys roundabout, inviting them to engage him as their agent for business they might have in Lincoln, which, since Lincoln was the state capital, might be substantial. Despite his efforts to build a dignified practice, collections and tax foreclosures still constituted the greater part of his new work.

Occasionally he argued before the State Supreme Court. He appeared in a struggle between two communities to become the seat of Greeley County. He took on a case testing the constitutionality of a bond issue to support a bounty to the several beet sugar factories of Nebraska, and he defended an editor who had been arrested because cards advertising his paper had been thrown in the street in violation of a city ordinance. Bryan showed to best advantage in jury trials, where his quick mind excelled in the sudden turns of argument and where he became the master of the stirring plea. But, as in Jacksonville, legal business was short, and an abundance of able young lawyers scrambled for it. Bryan's first year, 1888, was disappointing, for it yielded only $800, substantially less than he had last earned in Jacksonville. The following year, however, his income climbed to $1,400.[2]

The offices of Talbot and Bryan seemed always to have visitors, although few of them were clients. Most belonged to an ever-growing circle of acquaintances and friends that the open, gregarious Bryan quickly built after his arrival in Lincoln. He welcomed them all, and it is not difficult to understand why they came in steady numbers. To see Bryan was, as many testified, like taking an elixir that magically lifted one's spirits and restored one's confidence. In conversation, he had the ready faculty of imparting a sentiment that lightened his visitor's burden or providing a joke or illustration that gave courage and broadened vision.[3]

As they had in Jacksonville, Bryan and Mary flourished in a variety of community clubs and activities. In quick time, he joined organizations at a rate that must have established something of a record: the Chamber of Commerce, the Rotary Club, the Lincoln Bar Association, the Elks, Odd Fellows, Masons, the Moose, the Knights of Pythias, the Royal Highlanders, and the Modern Woodman. Typically, these organizations manifested a philosophy congenial to Bryan's own and served to reinforce it. They stressed ideals of brotherhood and solidarity, disdained unjust privilege and legalized wrong, and at least several opposed any man's taking from the common store more than he contributed to the common good. In all these organizations, Bryan was an active and valued member.

His exuberance and high-mindedness, his handshaking heartiness, his soaring spirit enveloped every gathering. In the local Presbyterian church, he was a mainstay of the Sunday school, and he was on constant call to preach in churches around the city. He persisted as an industrious member of the YMCA and regaled its young men with lectures on moral themes steeped in Biblical texts.

In addition, the Bryans formed discussion clubs. Bryan started the Round Table by inviting ten close friends to his home, all Democrats except his Republican law partner, Talbot. The club quickly took on a more solid bipartisan cast when its ranks were joined by Charles G. Dawes, who one day would be a Republican Vice President; Dr. J. H. Canfield, chancellor of the University of Nebraska; S. H. Burnham, a Republican lawyer; and C. H. Gere, editor of the *Nebraska State Journal.* At Round Table meetings a paper was read by a member on a political, philosophical, religious, literary or scientific subject, and the reading was followed by discussion. After several meetings, the organization began to falter, but Dawes rescued it by supplementing the solemn presentations with doughnuts and cider and light talk. Mary's contribution was the Sorosis, a discussion club for women that she and Mrs. Albert Sawyer, wife of Lincoln's mayor, created. Of the several branches of knowledge covered by Sorosis, Mary deemed that dealing with political economy the most important.[4]

Despite the moral fervor of the Bryans' endeavor, their ceaseless devotion to community uplift, and their entrée into the elite circles of Lincoln, economic rewards did not follow. There was no upsurge in Bryan's law business, and he seemed condemned to the identical fate he had known in Jacksonville: the life of a moderately successful lawyer with an average practice from which not more than a genteelly respectable income could be extracted. But Bryan had another string to his bow, a string that to be sure had not carried his arrow very far in Jacksonville, but he would try again—politics.

The politics of Lincoln and of Nebraska were distressingly similar to those of Jacksonville and Illinois. Bryan's adopted city and state were satrapies of the Republican Party. Except for a lone forgotten Congressman, the Republican Party had won every state and national election since Nebraska gained statehood in 1867. Lincoln boasted a flawless record of victorious Republicanism.

Despite these cheerless auguries, Bryan lost no time in getting in touch with Nebraska's Democrats. He sent out a flurry of letters to Democratic politicans and editors, inviting their counsel to a newcomer such as himself who wished to enter Democratic politics. The responses were numerous and satisfying. In general, they depicted a deep split in the state party and predicted that the dominant issue in the approaching Presidential campaign of 1888 would be the tariff. From Illinois Bryan brought a letter of introduction to Jefferson H. Broady, a Lincoln attorney and leader of the city's Democratic organization. Another such letter was addressed to J. Sterling Morton, once the publisher of the Nebraska City *News* and at that moment the state's leading Democrat, a wealthy agriculturalist and arboriculturalist of international renown, and the founder of Arbor Day.

Bryan dispatched his letter to Morton, and the reply, dated May 23, 1888, a landmark in Bryan's budding political career, graciously invited the young aspirant to come to Arbor Lodge "for the day and also for the night if you care to stay over." In Nebraska City, an exquisitely appointed carriage drawn by sleek horses met Bryan at the railroad station and quickly transported him to a palatial estate. It stood on the crest of a hill to the west of the town; its winding avenues, lined with specimen trees, led to immaculate formal gardens and an enormous villa. Morton, who exuded culture despite his years in a frontier territory, had the air of authority of the enormously successful executive that he was. He discussed with his young visitor the Democratic situation in the state, the approaching campaign, its issues, and the part in it that Bryan might play. The encounter was evidently successful. In his diary entry for the day, Morton stated frankly that he liked Bryan.[5]

Anyone on the brink of joining Nebraska's Democratic politics faced the unpleasant choice of aligning himself with either the Morton wing of the party, otherwise known as the slaughterhouse Democrats, or with the anti-Morton faction, the packinghouse Democrats. The nature of each faction derived largely from its leader, his political beliefs and attachments. The leader of the packinghouse Democrats was Dr. George L. Miller, until 1887 the owner and editor of the Omaha *Herald,* a powerful organ in Nebraska's chief metropolis, whose population, wealth, and influence dwarfed all other communities of the state. In the 1870's Miller was the leading Western representative of Samuel J. Tilden's Democratic organization. With the incumbent Cleveland administration, his connections were imposing, and he possessed the most commanding voice in the disposal of Nebraska's share of the federal patronage.

If Miller was the state's leading Democrat in national politics, it was

Morton who dominated the politics of the state itself, as his nomination for the governorship in 1880, 1882, and 1884 attested. That Morton could and would freely demand party and public office in the future was the general sentiment of informed Democrats.

The political views of the two rivals did not even approximate Bryan's. Both were staunch conservatives. Miller was a neo-Republican who belonged to the high-tariff wing of his party. Morton, on the other hand, shared Bryan's aversion to subsidies of any kind, but the tariff was the limit of Morton's interest in reform. A "Bourbon Democrat," he cared not a whit about measures designed to lighten the burdens of his fellow farmers who were less fortunate and was, in fact, a lobbyist for the farmers' worst oppressors, the railroads, at handsome pay.

Buoyed by his visit to Arbor Lodge, Bryan cast his lot with Morton. His tariff views were acceptable; Miller's were not. Miller's usefulness to Bryan, eager to commence a political career, was limited to federal patronage, and at this juncture Bryan did not want an appointive post. Nor was there any sign that the Miller faction would push beyond its minority status in state politics. Morton was Nebraskan Democracy's dominant personality, and blessed with his sponsorship, Bryan could have access to office and preferment in the state.

Bryan really needed no letters of introduction to enter the ranks of Democratic politics in Lincoln. The city was so overwhelmingly Republican that any new Democratic talent that offered itself was eagerly welcomed. Good local orators were in short supply, and Bryan, whose skill was praised in the letters he presented, was given immediate encouragement to take to the stump. A political speaker needs issues, and for Bryan they were not hard to find. They were written large on the face of Nebraskan society.

Nebraska, like other states of the West, was a farmer's world. Only two cities of any size existed—Omaha and Lincoln—and their economies and culture derived from agriculture. At this juncture, the cities produced no indigenous problems—and therefore no potential political issues—of their own.

When Bryan appeared on the scene, Nebraskan agriculture was rife with problems and discontent finding ready political expression. The farmers were divided into two distinct groups. The southeastern half of the state contained the loess, a fine light-yellow loam of exceptional fertility, and was therefore the site of Nebraska's best productivity. But in the greater part of the state, west of Seward County, the glacial drift petered out, leaving a soil of clay, gravel, and sand, granite boulders, and green stone. Because of improvements in plant and animal varieties, expanding irrigation and hard work, the vast reaches of western Nebraska, once labeled on the maps as the "great American Desert," now produced millions of bushels of corn, wheat, oats, and potatoes and hundreds of thousands of farm animals. Waves of settlers poured in from the late sixties through the eighties to take advantage of the Homestead Act.

But free land also meant a life of hard work and limited rewards passed in isolation. Standing on a short-grassed hillock, one could gaze across endless miles of prairie unhampered by fences. The farmhouse, an inconspicuous object in the immense grain fields, was often a half-dug-out, half-sod house, its back part hollowed out of the side of a low hill, and its front consisting of squares of sod placed together and held up by a slight frame of wood. Life was hazardous. Snakes might wind down from the rafters or crawl past the door to reach any milk pans lying about. Coyotes and gray wolves might skulk in the poultry yard or howl by the window. Indian raids were not unknown. Disease could decimate the livestock; drought could set in, and a brilliant sun and a cloudless sky became a curse when accompanied by strong winds that curled the leaves of young corn and turned the buffalo grass brown. These hazards made the farmer prey to the hazards of economics. The heavy mortgage he carried could, with but a little push from nature, cast him over the cliff of foreclosure. Those not fortunate enough to occupy lands near the railroads had to haul their livestock and produce great distances to the nearest carrier.[6]

Any visitor who brought civilization to the farmer in his isolation was welcome. The approach of the peddler was the signal for excitement. Religion, too, was wagon-borne; ministers traversed the short-grass country bearing Bibles and pamphlets. Basket socials and literary and home talent plays in the distant towns relieved the rural monotony, and July 4 was a true holiday with horse races, foot races, sack races, broncobusting, a baseball game, climbing a greased pole, and catching a greased pig.[7]

The Nebraskan farmer, Bryan discovered, suffered from burdens and problems astonishingly like those that harassed Illinois farmers of the seventies and early eighties. From an era of rising income, expanding acreage, mortgage indebtedness, and hardy optimism, the Nebraskan farmer had passed into an era of declining prices and rising costs, the sure foundations of economic disgruntlement. The Panic of 1873 laid its blighting touch on Nebraska as it did on other agricultural states. The prices of corn and wheat, to which Nebraska's rural economy was heavily committed, plummeted, while the prices of commodities the farmer had to buy held their levels or increased. Railroad rates and interest charges failed to come down. His general economic misery brought many a farmer to see the grisly outlines of conspiracy by which merchants, banks, and the railroads were joined in nefarious common cause to strangle him economically and fatten themselves upon his carcass. Even after the panic passed, hard times persisted for Nebraska's farmers. The year of Bryan's coming to the state,

1887, was the first of a succession of years when rainfall dropped seriously below normal. For the farmer who required an annual crop to meet payments on his land, machinery, or stock, the situation was desperate. Helplessly, he watched as "Week after week, the hot burning sun glared down from the cloudless steel-blue sky. The dread hot winds blew in from the south. Day after day they continued. All fodder, small grain and corn were cut short. . . . The careful expert got some return for his work, though small."

For all the severity of the farmer's circumstances, for all his standing as the largest block of Nebraska's population, he was unrepresented in the mainstream of the state's political life. Neither the Republican nor the Democratic Party took up his causes. Another economic interest, far mightier in power and influence, dominated Nebraskan politics—the railroads. The Platte River, crossing the state from east to west, created two political satrapies reigned over by the state's principal railroads. To the north of the Platte's languid flow, the Burlington and Northwestern railroads ruled, and to the south, the Union Pacific. Nebraska's politics were securely in the railroads' pockets. The state legislature and the principal officials were minions of the lines; the Republican Party was an ever-dependable adjunct. Even though the Republicans won elections with monotonous regularity, the railroads were fully prepared for the eventuality of defeat. The leaders of the two principal Democratic factions, Morton and Miller, were securely under their thumb. Small wonder that the farmer and his ills won scant attention. But their growing numbers and deepening plight made the future less certain.[8]

As he had in Jacksonville, Bryan began his political career by speaking at local meetings, choosing the tariff as the theme of his first speech in Lincoln. The subject was a natural and potent issue in Nebraska, for the tariff conferred privilege and profit on the industrialist and gave little to the farmer except the scourge of higher prices. Spurred by an audience that was wildly receptive to his arguments, Bryan soared to a fiery climax, likening the tariff to a cow fed by Western farmers and milked by Eastern manufacturers. In the joyous tumult, Bryan learned the value of the telling metaphor in political oratory.

Bryan's brilliant successes and the dearth of talent in the Lincoln Democratic organization quickly enabled him to become city chairman, an office well beyond his reach in Jacksonville. Like any ambitious politician, he was watchful for opportunities to enlarge the territory in which he was known. His first speech outside Lincoln took him twenty-five miles west to Seward. There he spoke in behalf of Morton, who was running for the United States House of Representatives in the First Congressional District, which was where Bryan resided. In the audience was a group of veteran Democratic politicos, who had come to look over the meteoric twenty-seven-year-old campaigner and decide whether he should campaign throughout the state rather than be confined to a merely local schedule. The connoisseurs found him to their liking, and Bryan always rated their reaction that day as "one of the earliest assurances I received to exert more than an average influence thru the power of speech."

In April, 1888, as a delegate to his own Lancaster County convention, Bryan helped the Morton faction prevail. Morton was elected a delegate at large to the national convention that would soon renominate Grover Cleveland for President, and Bryan was chosen as a delegate to the Democratic state convention.[9]

If there was a hero in the state convention which gathered at Omaha in May, it was "the youngest member . . . a bright young Democrat from Lancaster county . . . who was rocked in a cradle made of hickory." In a dynamic address, Bryan, who never lacked audacity, offered a recipe for national Democratic victory. Let the campaign be based, he urged, on Cleveland's tariff message of December, 1887. Let the Democracy go to the farmers of Nebraska, as Democrats should do in every state, and lay bare the inequities of the tariff system. The boldness of Bryan's proposal in suggesting the abandonment of traditional state Democratic strategies and concentration on the farmer, coupled with the intoxicating effect of his oratory, made an enormous impression. In one jump, he leaped from being merely a Lincoln and Lancaster County politician to statewide prominence. Prodded by Morton, the convention managers offered "Bryan the Invincible," as the press was calling him, the nomination for lieutenant governor. When he declined, they asked solicitously if the post of attorney general would be more acceptable. He again refused.

To the puzzled managers, Bryan explained that he could not afford a campaign, which was true, and he would surely be defeated, a prophecy which the Democratic record, so utterly bare of victories for state office, undeniably supported. Bryan's declinations reflected an attitude which he held for his political lifetime. Never would he show interest in state office. Convinced that in Nebraska such an office led nowhere, he chose to wait for more propitious political opportunities. However, he did agree to campaign for the Democratic ticket in a heavy schedule of speeches that would carry him throughout the state.

With other top Democrats of Nebraska, Bryan attended the national convention at St. Louis. Although not a delegate, Bryan had access to the floor, thanks to Morton's courtesies as leader of the Nebraska delegation, and he bustled about collecting introductions to national leaders. The man who impressed him most, he cultivated most, United States Senator John Daniel of Virginia. This dark, forbidding figure with burning eyes and a hawk nose, supporting on crutches a body that had absorbed four wounds in the Battle of the Wilderness, made what Bryan deemed the best of the nominating speeches. From Daniel and from other speakers, Bryan absorbed ideas and arguments that were to highlight his speeches on tariff reform in the approaching campaign.

Bryan more than kept his word to the state committee and embarked on a stumping schedule that ultimately led him to thirty-four counties throughout the state. Each speech was a triumph, and its glories were trumpeted in the news articles of the Omaha *Daily World-Herald.* One Bryan speech in Columbus, it said, was "clear and forcible," "dispensing with the usual stump oratory," and adorned with "apt stories and bright quotations." That his speeches received these accolades in the *World-Herald* was ensured by Bryan's writing the news articles about them himself, even though a speech delivered, say, on July 20, might not be reported until August 15.[10]

But not even Bryan appreciated the full power of his oratory until one fall day when he spoke in Chadron, in the northwestern corner of Nebraska. Journeying by train to that far country, he passed from the well-populated eastern portions of the state into the great open country of the west. Often on the broad horizon he saw nothing but a solitary farmhouse or a trail of smoke hanging in curled suspense over an Indian tepee. At some "stations" where his train stopped, there were only weeds, and at others a mere sign or box. This was grazing country, dotted with herds, whose owners' cause he was carrying, and packs of buffalo restlessly seeking better grass. Each mile his train advanced, the vegetation grow perceptibly sparer until any glimpse of the low sumach, the yellow pine, the dwarf wild cherry, the buffalo berry, the golden currant was rare and welcome.

Chadron was situated on land as flat as a table, with hardly a tree or a blade of grass to be seen. Bryan's business there was not political but legal and concerned the construction of the new Dawes County Courthouse. Whenever he visited a strange town, Bryan diligently extended the circle of his acquaintances by seeking out local politicians and leaders. Thus he met C. W. Allen, editor of the Chadron newspaper, and the accommodating Allen took him to the old courthouse to introduce him to the sheriff, James C. Dahlman, an event of large consequence for Bryan's career and Nebraska's politics for the next twenty-five years.

Bryan and Dahlman, a spare, wiry, exuberant former cowboy, took an instant liking to each other. Dahlman was an enterprising type whose peppery dynamism appealed to Bryan. Once, for a Fourth of July celebration at Chadron, Dahlman arranged to have 200 Indians brought in to do a war dance. To his amazement, not 200 but 1,500 Oglala led by Chief Red Cloud filed into town, two days in advance. The Oglala had to be fed and entertained, and the sheriff delighted Bryan by recounting the ingenious, often hilarious expedients he resorted to to meet the challenge.

During their conversation, Dahlman induced his new friend to accompany him to Gordon in the next county, Sheridan, to attend a political rally. When the advertised speaker did not appear, Bryan volunteered to fill the gap, and Dahlman, who knew nothing of his prowess, was overjoyed by the results. "We had never heard such oratory before in northwestern Nebraska," gasped Dahlman afterward. "For two hours, Mr. Bryan held that crowd enthralled. When he closed, because he had to catch a train, the crowd yelled for him to continue. I believe they would have listened all night." [11]

Throughout the tedious journey homeward Bryan reflected upon his oratorical success. His mind was filled with thoughts of his new power. The shadows of doubt left by his partial success in college speaking contests now vanished. At Gordon he had demonstrated a skill and commanded effects far beyond Silas' and his own dreams, and he constructed and reconstructed the outline of a glorious political future.

At daybreak, Bryan tiptoed to his bedroom. Mary was asleep, but in his wonderment he could not resist waking her. Sitting on the edge of the bed, he said, "Mary, I have had a strange experience. Last night I found that I had power over the audience. I could move them as I chose. I have more than usual power as a speaker. I know it. God grant I may use it wisely." He settled upon his knees in prayer at the bedside.[12]

Most of Bryan's speechmaking was devoted to aiding Morton's candidacy for the House of Representatives. At some rallies Morton appeared in a double billing. At one Saturday night rally, after Morton, a mediocre orator, had spoken an hour and a half, cries rose around the hall for "entertainment." Bryan responded with a speech that so "captivated his hearers that they hung upon his words for over an hour and when [he] wished to stop they would not have it so." Morton, who by now treated Bryan like a favorite son, as well as a priceless campaign asset, took pains to introduce him to the most important state Democrats. When his protégé was flooded with invitations to speak, he told him which were the best engagements to accept.[13]

But despite Bryan's efforts, 1888 proved to be a disastrous year for the Democracy. Morton lost his race for Congress, and Grover Cleveland, although exceeding his Republican opponent, Benjamin Harrison, in popular votes, was defeated in the electoral college. Bryan wrote consolingly to Cleveland that "we would rather fall with you fighting on and for a principal [sic] than to succeed with the party representing nothing but an organized appetite." [14] Intrepidly the young politician even went so far as to offer a suggestion for the retiring President's future. Cleveland should move to Nebraska and run again in 1892, wrote Bryan. "As a Western man with friends you have in the East, we can elect you. Why not come to Omaha or Lincoln?" Whether Cleveland replied or not is not known.

Whatever else the campaign may or may not have proved, it confirmed Morton's estimate that "Bryan . . . is a remarkably promising man. He has gifts. He will be, with good habits and right directions, a benefactor to good government." [15]

In the two-year interlude until the next elections in 1890, Bryan returned to his law practice, a neglected orphan in the late campaign. His new fame imparted assurance and a better income, and now his work became a genuinely shared experience with Mary. After more than two years of study, she had passed the bar examination in Lincoln, firmly believing that a wife should always help her husband. In this interlude of political calm, Bryan and Mary's only son, William, was born on June 24, 1889.

The Bryans continued their dedication to community and church endeavor. Their discussion clubs were flourishing to the point where they now had an annual banquet. They became even closer friends with the Charles G. Daweses. Bryan and Dawes both had law offices in the Burr Block, and whenever business slowed, they would while away the hours in friendly argument, usually on the tariff. The Bryans delighted to take the Daweses riding in their one-horse surrey, a recent acquisition of which they were justly proud, and the Daweses were among the little group of close friends who helped them observe their fifth wedding anniversary. The high point of the festivities, which were complete with cider and cakes in the celebrating couple's home, occurred when Bryan donned a dark suit, Mary her wedding gown, and with a Presbyterian minister officiating, they renewed their marriage vows. In this interval, Dawes brought off what no one else ever succeeded in doing: He defeated Bryan in a jury trial. Another member of the Bryan circle was John J. "Black Jack" Pershing, commander of the cadet corps at the university.

But Bryan, for all his retreat to private pursuits, by no means let go of his budding political career. Convinced that the tariff would again be the dominant issue in 1890, he continued to study that intractably technical subject. His expertise reached a point where he thought he might well establish a national reputation by writing a book on tariff reform. He approached the New York publisher G. P. Putnam and Sons, which regretfully reported its estimate that "there would not be enough sales to warrant us undertaking it."

In 1889, Bryan's sparkling statewide reputation and Morton's sponsorship assured him a prominent place in the Democratic state convention. The most important business was the drafting of the state platform, and days before the delegates met, Morton put Bryan to work on a major plank attacking the state's bounty for beet sugar. With Morton, Bryan also wrote a plank condemning the protective tariff and the curse it laid upon agricultural states. There was a brief flurry of disagreement between Bryan and Morton and between them and other delegates over prohibition. Bryan opposed too strong a plank for fear of alienating too many voters. A compromise was contrived, and Bryan went on to make what the Democratic press reported as a "glowing speech" for his handiwork. But the convention was both the beginning and the end of his triumph. In the election for State Supreme Court justice, the chief prize of the campaign, the Republicans, as usual, swept the state. But there was an exception, as striking to the political eye as an oasis is to the nomad in the desert. The Democrats carried Douglas County, which included Omaha and which constituted the most populous part of Bryan's own First Congressional District. It was enough to set a man thinking.[16]

7. A Contrived Victory

Some two years prior to the elections of 1890, Bryan told Mary in absolute confidence that at the next opportunity he could both capture the Democratic nomination for Congress in the First District and win the election. She scoffed at this brash prediction; surely so important a place would be reserved for the party fathers and not allowed to slip away to a young, impecunious newcomer. And victory—for a Democrat? The string of Republican successes exposed the absurdity of the thought. Mary strongly urged Bryan to concentrate on his law practice and to ignore politics until he could afford to retire from the law.

But the siren call was irresistibly sweet. In February, 1890, several Democratic state leaders told Bryan the Congressional nomination was his if he wanted it. Letters to Bryan and callers in the capital who took pains to visit his office in the Burr Block all urged his nomination. Nebraska's leading Democratic newspaper, the Omaha *World-Herald*, related the opinions of a "rock rooted, mountain buttressed democrat" of Cass County that Bryan was the leading candidate and "one of the most promising Democrats in the state. He has a large following in both parties and would be able to poll a big vote, even if he was not elected."

Nonetheless, Bryan did not have a clear road to the nomination. Older leaders, as Mary had suggested, were available. Morton could run again if he chose to. In Omaha a movement started in behalf of Charles W. Brown, who could poll a big city vote and perhaps attract more Republicans than Bryan. In June, a few weeks before the nominating convention, Bryan's informant in Pawnee City, R. W. Story, reported that the local feeling was that either Brown or Bryan could prevail, and that many politicians in the county "will want to be for the candidate who will win the nomination." [1]

With the convention approaching and eager to avoid any struggle with the established leaders, Bryan wrote to Brown, seeking an understanding of who would be the nominee. It was a lengthy, candid letter, in which Bryan offered to subordinate personal ambition to party peace. "If either you or Morton ask for the nomination, you will get it," he assured Brown. True enough, "written offers of assistance" had come to Bryan from nearly every county, "but no one," he added, "is pledged to me. I have told them that the interest of the party is above the interest of anyone." Bryan explained he was considering the nomination because he was assured of a large Republican vote in Lincoln and was told that "the farmers and laboring men were friendly."

He took pains to disclaim having any part in what newspapers said about the nomination. "I have not inspired editorials against any one and will not, and if I suffer by the acts of indiscreet friends I will only suffer the lot of mankind in general." Among the news articles that prompted this remark was a Lincoln *Daily Call* story that Brown wanted the nomination "and doubtless has the money to buy it." The *Call* claimed that Bryan could capture more Republican votes than any other Democrat in the field, that he was not excessively identified with the older warring factions, and that even in Omaha he could attract "larger support than Brown." [2]

Bryan's bold letter yielded a rich dividend. Brown replied that he did not want the nomination and would help Bryan win it. Brown, of course, was not charmed into surrender. According to his own soundings of party opinion, he concluded that the progressive sentiment that backed Bryan had carried him securely into the lead. Morton, meanwhile, had made no move for the nomination. Older leaders wanted no part of what to them appeared to be certain defeat at the hands of the Republican incumbent, the popular William J. Connell. A month before the Democratic convention assembled, they gladly left the field to Bryan.[3]

But Bryan had cleared only the first jump toward realizing his bold prediction of nomination and election to the House of Representatives. There was a further, more difficult hurdle. A new party was forming—the People's Independent Party—and it meant to hold the balance of power in the coming elections. Ordinarily, a new party entertains more modest anticipations, but the People's Party drew commanding strength from sudden circumstances. It expected to be the one party to respond constructively to a long-building political tornado that was soon to strike Nebraska with full fury.

In Nebraska and in other corn and wheat states of the West, the farmer was deep in the trials of Job. A lingering economic depression had darkened the seventies. After a brief taste of prosperity in the early eighties, the farmer staggered through a succession of disasters. Each year, from 1887 onward, drought was the enemy. Rainfall had been abysmally below normal. Instead of moisture so precious to the vast arid lands of Nebraska, there were only a fiery sun and hot winds. Crops withered, and the terror and grief of failure were intensified by the mortgages affixed to most farmers' land, stock, and machinery. Requiring a good annual cash crop to keep their heads above the financial waters, countless farmers needed to feel that rough hand of nature but once to know disaster. Not only did nature lash the farmer in the summer, but for several winters he was also plagued with cattle-killing snow.

Even worse than the cruel weather were the ravages of the general economic deflation that befell the Western farmer in the eighties. The prices the farmer got for his staples took a long, deep tumble. Wheat, which was sold for $1.19 a bushel in 1881, brought only 40 cents in 1890. Corn, selling for 63 cents in 1881, fell to 26 cents in 1890. The deteriorating prices were naturally accompanied by a general collapse in farmland values. Land worth $8 an acre in 1870 and $30 in the boom following the closing of the frontier now sold for only $5 or less. The early eighties were boom years of wild speculation in farmlands, and the farmer, caught up in the feverish optimism of the moment, enlarged his holdings, his stock, and his debt far beyond any standard of prudence. In 1890, estimates of indebtedness in Nebraska suggested that there was one mortgage for every three persons, or more than one to a family. Even to the casual observer, the ravages of economic dislocation were everywhere patent. Thousands of foreclosures covered the land like blight. With corn so cheap, some farmers concluded that it was better to burn their crop for winter fuel than to buy coal. In Gosper County, Nebraska, farmers shot their hogs because they could neither sell nor give them away. Many a wheat and corn farmer found that the costs of raising these staples often exceeded, sometimes considerably, the prices they commanded.

Meanwhile, the busy migration from east to west was suddenly reversed. Young people in particular abandoned the despair of the farms for the promise of the cities. Nor did their elders lag. Long processions of covered wagons returned from the prairies and moved east under the banner:

> In God we trusted,
> In Nebraska we busted.

"In one season," observed an editor, "eighteen thousand prairie schooners passed east over the Missouri River bridge at Omaha—never to return." [4]

Several explanations for the farmer's economic torment have been advanced. In one view, he was caught by the Industrial Revolution, which had brought him to use machinery instead of hand labor and converted him from a manager of a farm that was intended to be largely self-sufficing into a commercial enterprise which sold most of what was produced. Although he competed with his fellow farmers, they all stood or fell together as the law of supply and demand, over which they had no control, decreed. No longer were household goods manufactured on the farms. Increasingly the farmer bought them from stores and factories. The railroads, as handmaidens of industrialization, increased his market, but they also made him acutely dependent on their services and charges.

Not a few economists and politicians contended that the root of the farmer's trouble was overproduction. The vast increases in productive acreages brought by mechanization, by the cultivation of free lands provided by the Homestead Act, and by the railroads chained the farmer to a cruel paradox: The harder he worked, the less income he got. Overproduction was not simply a domestic problem. The railroads and shipping were hauling wheat from Canada, the Argentine, Russia, India, and Australia into a world market to compete with American harvests. United States surpluses, added to those of the other countries, could only depress prices at home and abroad.

But farmers and their spokesmen declined to accord much weight to any theory of overproduction, maintaining that underconsumption, not overproduction, was the problem. The urban masses and no small part of the farm population lived in undernourishment, even semistarvation. "The makers of clothes were underfed," the saying went, "the makers of food were underclad." "Artificial barriers" were preventing the farmer from making his bounties available to the masses who eagerly awaited them. Influences were at work, cried one rural politician, "like thieves in the night," to rob the farmer of the just rewards of his toil.

The farmer saw many culprits. One of the more monstrous was the railroads. Western farmers complained that half the value of their wheat was eaten by freight charges, and Nebraskan farmers discovered they paid an average of 50 percent more for equivalent service than their competitors across the Missouri River in Iowa. In addition, there were the heavy tax burdens the farm communities assumed earlier in more prosperous times to lure the roads westward, the excesses of stock watering that increased freight rates, and the political ruthlessness of the lines. The railroads' influence ran across the entire gamut of politics, from nominating convention to the processes of legislation and administration. Railroad passes were conferred freely upon governors, judges, state railroad commissioners, and every variety of opinion maker, not excepting editors and ministers.[5]

The farmers saw malefactors other than the railroads. The trusts were visible everywhere on the economic landscape. Besides the beef, plow, fertilizer, and jute-bag trusts, the machinery the farmer used, the clothes he wore, the materials that went into his house, barns, and fences were bought from the trusts, and their exactions sent prices ever upward. The trusts made brutally clear to the farmer that while he sold his produce in a "free" market, or one responsive to the vicissitudes of supply and demand, he bought the goods he needed in a "controlled" market, or one so closely managed that almost nothing could halt the rise of prices.

The tariff was a villain in many a farmer's eyes, protecting one class to the detriment of another, the manufacturer at the expense of the farmer, the rich at the expense of the poor. The tariff fenced off the domestic market, enabling the American manufacturer, especially the trusts, to enjoy exclusive exploitation. But there was no tariff to help the farmer.

A less visible enemy lurked in the convoluted fabric of money and credit. The farmer seemed forever to be borrowing and mortgaging in circumstances prejudicial to the debtor and favorable to the creditor. Whenever the farmer needed money, it was scarce. Hostile fluctuations of currency tended to coincide with the harvesting of crops. When the farmer sold his produce, the dollar was dear and prices were depressed. After the crop was marketed and with the produce now in other hands, the dollar fell in value and prices climbed. Speculators reaped handsome profits, while the farmers broke their backs under the burden of debt. One angry farmer-editor wrote that Nebraska produced three great crops: corn, freight rates, and interest. The first was produced by the sweat of farmers who tilled the land; the others by men who sat in offices and behind bank counters and farmed the farmers.

The Western farmer saw a greedy, scheming money power concentrated in the East or, more specifically, in iniquitous Wall Street. The lines of conspiracy did not stop there, but ran on to Lombard Street in London and to the other financial capitals of the world. To foil the speculators and the money masters, rural spokesmen took hope in a simple expedient: Increase the quantity of money and, as a consequence, prices, including farm prices, would rise. To bring economic salvation to the farmer, diverse schemes were advanced, of which one was "the free coinage of silver." [6]

The farmer's awareness of his plight and his determination to escape it were sharpened by the contrast between the harsh realities of his circumstances and his ancient and lofty place in the national myth. More than anyone else, Thomas Jefferson had laid the foundation of that myth. To Jefferson, the farmer's industry, independence, and ability to produce a simple abundance made him the ideal man and citizen. The farmer, Jefferson said, was "the most precious part of the state." In the eighties, the farmer's spokesmen summoned the vision of a glorious past whose restoration would free him from present economic servitude and make him once again a sturdy yeoman, prosperous, democratic, and egalitarian.

Throughout the first half of the nineteenth century, the Jeffersonian myth remained powerful, Richard Hofstadter has noted, because the nation's politics revolved chiefly around the literate enfranchised farmer. It was trumpeted by the exponents of popular causes in the era of Andrew Jackson, who provided the momentum that carried it into the unsettled regions of the West, including Nebraska. Thus, the vast new Western expanse became charged with confidence in the farmer, his innate virtue and democracy.[7]

When economic reality endangered the myth, the farmer suddenly demonstrated a ready capacity to organize, for all his presumed commitment to self-reliance. In the deluge of woe in the seventies, the Patrons of Husbandry developed as a leading farm order and launched broadsides against the railroad abuses. Out of the swirl of agitation sprang the Granger movement, which fought to establish the right of the states to regulate the railroads and their appendages, the grain elevators, but it was thwarted by the courts and balky, even "bought," legislatures. A National Greenback Party, an instrument through which the debt-burdened farmers might speak, stressed the necessity of currency reform. In the late seventies and the eighties a corps of new farm' organizations appeared, the chief of these in the West being the National Farmers' Alliance, more commonly known as the Northwestern Alliance.

In Nebraska, galloping advances in freight rates gave extra impetus to the Alliance. In 1881, delegates from nearly twenty-five counties met in Lincoln, formed a statewide organization, and adopted a constitution more elaborate than that of the national organization. After faltering in the mideighties, the Alliance revived toward the end of the decade. Throughout the Northwest, membership soared and leaders called for ever more aggressive measures, including government control of railroads and free coinage of silver.

By 1890, with membership snowballing from defecting Democrats and Republicans in Nebraska's great farm population and from conviction that the major parties were impervious to rural suffering, leaders of the state Alliance decided to commit their resources to the approaching elections. They had sufficient strength, they believed, to hold the balance of power between the two major parties. To do so, however, it was plain that they had to become a full-fledged political party. Plans were quickly roughed out for a convention to gather in Lincoln to establish a new political party—the People's Independent Party—and the date chosen for that occasion, July 29, 1890, seemed deliberately timed to coincide with the Democratic convention. A new and most likely a powerful party that would nominate candidates and adopt a platform gave Bryan an arresting situation to ponder.[8]

Bryan's perception of the realities was identical with the Independents'. If a three-cornered race developed, the Republicans would surely win. If he became the nominee of both the Democrats and the Independents, quite possibly he would win. This judgment was supported by friendly observers in the counties of his district. J. W. Barnhart, editor of the *Nemaha County*

Herald in Auburn, urged Bryan first to secure the Democratic nomination and then to "cast an anchor" and try for the Independents' nomination. Bryan launched negotiations with an Independent state leader, Joseph A. Edgerton, through Constantine J. Smyth, Democrat, as intermediary. Edgerton questioned Smyth closely about Bryan's position on the tariff, silver, transportation, and the ballot system. He also imposed a condition that Bryan must pledge to the Independents that, if elected, he would not be bound by the Democratic caucus. What Bryan's response was to this politically embarrassing, if not impossible, condition is not known. Evidently Edgerton was sufficiently satisfied to take up with other Independent leaders the question of nominating Bryan.

Smyth was also Bryan's observer in the First Congressional District's largest county, Douglas, and its largest city, Omaha. A year older than Bryan, Irish-born and New York-educated, Smyth was a lover of books and a state legislator with a solid reputation as a foe of graft and privilege. Kindly and intellectual, he admired Bryan, for whom he predicted a brilliant political future in the cause of their common principles. Smyth's optimism was based more on long-term expectations than on immediate realities. He reported some doubt that Bryan could capture the Douglas delegation. True, the younger men were for Bryan, but many Democrats believed that a man "is to be considered a mere stripling until he reached fifty or sixty years of age and is entitled to no consideration at the hands of the party. . . ." Both in Omaha and in Lincoln the opposition to Bryan was grounded in two counts: that he had been in the state but a short time and that he was too young. But all doubts about Bryan's ability to capture the Democratic nomination vanished when Brown, who preferred to concentrate on his private career, declined to run. "Some men think a political honor or an office makes them great," Brown explained his decision to Morton. "What a derisive idea." [9]

If Bryan's fortunes were glowing in the Democratic Party, they fell suddenly under a cloud in the Independents. Edgerton's conclave with his fellow leaders failed to produce the support necessary for the nomination. The Independents chose as their candidate Charles H. Van Wyck, a former state and national Senator, a sterling vote getter, and a proved reformer. Bryan might profess his devotion to reform, but he would be running against an established reformer, the candidate of the reform party.

On July 30, the day after the Independents made their decision, the Democratic Congressional convention gathered in Lincoln. For all the lathery oratory and the cheering, stomping delegates, the proceedings that really counted were a kind of political chess game. Bryan was ahead in the game, but other candidates were still on the board, and their combined vote was not far behind his. With his superior strength Bryan resorted to the strategy of reversing the usual sequence of convention procedure by inducing the delegates to adopt the platform first, with the Congressional nomination to follow. Bryan was the platform's chief author, and its planks were shaped to accomplish two vital purposes. Their sharp progressive hue served to eliminate the candidacies of Democratic conservatives. They could not possibly stand on such a platform, and the field, in effect, was left exclusively to progressive contenders.

Bryan's maneuvers must have been unwelcome to his political godfather, the conservative J. Sterling Morton, but the young politician had anticipated this clouded state of affairs well before the convention. He had moved to neutralize Morton. "I would like to talk over the coming campaign with you," Bryan had written, and accompanied his properly solicitous request with flattery and attentions. He congratulated Morton for his recent letters on taxation and the necessity for reform. Bryan hailed the letters "for bringing the truth so well to the people" and added that he had quoted from them liberally in a letter to the New York *Post* attacking the sugar bounty. Morton was apparently mollified; he spoke no public word and made no overt move to stop Bryan's nomination. But neither did he speak or act in its favor.

In its further purpose, the Democratic platform was an adroit appeal to both Democrats and Independents. Bryan's was a fusion platform. It denounced the McKinley Tariff, which protected both established and infant industries and agriculture, but whose duties on farm products were proving ineffective in the depression. The platform called for deep reductions in duties on necessities and for wool, coal, lumber, sugar, salt, and iron ore to be placed on the free list. The platform demanded with unbridled optimism that trusts be abolished, that Congress prohibit landownership by nonresidents (in effect, absentee landlords), that government be the instrument of the people through popular election of Senators, the Australian, or secret, ballot, and the repeal of rules in the U.S. House of Representatives enabling the Republican Speaker, "Czar" Thomas B. Reed, to oppress the Democratic minority.

All these were causes dear to Independents and many Democrats. Bryan's platform, however, did not take up the loudly trumpeted Independent causes of public ownership of railroads and telegraphs. These presumably would be unacceptable to the general body of his party and even more so to Republicans he hoped to attract. On a subject that was to be the sun and moon of his future, Bryan wrote, "We demand the free coinage of silver on equal terms with gold, and denounce the efforts of Wall Street as against the rights of the people." Bryan stressed the tariff on a scale traditional with Democrats and exceeded the Independents on the subject. Silver was an Independent plank in mild, vaguer form. Bryan called for "equality" between gold and silver chiefly because, not having studied the complexities of money, he was not certain how "free" silver should be. It was enough that his constituents wanted "free silver." After the election and with a year of research behind him, he substituted for "equality" between the metals a precise demand for a ratio of 16 to 1. Free coinage of silver at a ratio of 16 to 1 called for abandonment of what in reality was the monometallic gold standard of 1890 and a return to the bimetallic gold and silver standard of the Coinage Act of 1837. Coinage in 1890 was governed chiefly by the Act of February 12, 1873, which ended the system of bimetallism established by the Coinage Act of 1837. Under the 1873 law, the silver dollar was dropped from the list of coins that could be freely struck at the mint. With no free coinage of silver, a single gold standard was legally established. Bryan was demanding the restoration of the Act of 1837, which authorized silver and gold to be coined in unlimited amounts as they were brought to mints of the United States government. The Act of 1837 fixed the coinage ratio between the two metals at the market prices then prevailing, or 15.9884 units of silver to 1 of gold—approximately—or 16 to 1. The dollar of the 1837 act contained 371.25 grains of silver or 23.22 grains of gold. Neither the money plank nor other planks were much discussed at the Lincoln convention.

After a quick brisk struggle between the progressives and conservatives, the platform was adopted. Bryan's nomination followed as a matter of course. His 86 votes on a call of the counties on an informal ballot provided him a majority against 73 votes divided among four opponents. On the formal ballot that quickly followed, Bryan moved up to 137 votes. A burly leader rose to announce in a foghorn voice that Omaha's First Ward was changing its vote to Bryan. After several minutes of shouted switches, the nomination was unanimous.

A committee was appointed to wait upon Bryan, and he came quickly to the hall. His entrance brought the delegates to their feet, wildly cheering. With excitement and solemnity illumining his handsome face, his large trim figure erect and heroic, Bryan consecrated himself in ringing moral phrases to the awaiting struggle of good against evil. "I shall go forth to the conflict as David went to meet the giant of the Philistines, not relying upon my own strength, but trusting to the righteousness of my cause." He would campaign in every county of the district, and before the convention adjourned, he wanted to meet every delegate. "I will visit you in your homes. I will call on you upon your farms," he cried in a final surge of eloquent dedication, "and help you make hay while the sun shines, and I shall expect you to help me make votes all the time."

Even after the convention adjourned, the mood of confident jubilation persisted. Bryan, exulted the Omaha *World-Herald,* is "the very best standard bearer who could have been chosen to lead the recently aroused masses against the fortification behind which the favored classes are entrenched." Seasoned politician William A. Paxton predicted that Bryan would do well in Douglas County because he had never become involved in a factional fight. And many a Nebraska Republican whose badly deteriorated personal economics had disenchanted him with the high protective tariff would choose Bryan, drawn by his advocacy of tariff reform. On the touchy issue of prohibition, Bryan struck a perfect political posture. As an abstainer, he was attractive to the growing body of drys. To the far larger number of wets he made himself wholly acceptable by putting aside his advocacy of prohibition and the crusading zeal of his Jacksonville days. Opportunistically he even now went so far as to speak against prohibition.

Bryan left behind no record of mental anguish caused by this reversal. Most likely, his appetite for victory and his granitic self-esteem enabled him to discard prohibition with no more remorse than if he were throwing away an old shoe. Decades later, late in his career, he would reembrace the cause, but in 1890 Bryan seemed to reduce issues to mere political tools to be used or discarded as the necessities of his campaign dictated. He was not attracted to prohibition by a conviction intense enough to bring him to sacrifice an opportunity for victory. Instead, he condemned prohibition as a misguided venture bringing government to regulate a private moral choice.[10]

In prohibition, Bryan faced, as he often would in his career, a conflict between his ambitions and his ideologies. When the two were intrinsically hostile, as they were in this case, the politician Bryan decided not to live by faith or ideology alone. Ideology is selfless; the politician is ambitious and self-seeking. Since public office is rarely conferred as a gift or honor, the politician must seek it with drive and calculation. If he had been a man with political beliefs but no political ambitions, Bryan could have subsisted on his law practice and found sufficient outlet for his convictions in his civic clubs. But his own preferences and the personal career his father had charted required the holding of elective office, and the circumstances of Nebraska's First Congressional District provided the several ingredients necessary for the furtherance of this ambition. Elections provide politicians with a standard of immediately defined success or failure. Bryan, like any politician, wanted to win, and his only choice was to deal cruelly with any belief that he thought might prevent victory.

Following his nomination, messages both flattering and derogatory flowed into Bryan's D Street home, ranging from one that hailed him as a "Moses" who would lead the Democratic faithful out of their bondage to "trusts, tariff abuses, and irrational taxation" to another that exhorted him to "Speak everywhere—kiss all the babies—you can do it—you have mouth enough for both." Conspicuous among the messages was one from J. Sterling Morton, which Bryan acknowledged by writing, "Of the numerous congratulatory letters received none has been more highly appreciated than the one from you." The single note of uncertainty sounded in the postconvention optimism came from the busy railroad lobbyist Dr. George L. Miller when Morton invited his rival factional leader to close ranks behind the sparkling new nominee. Miller growled, "Who the hell is Bryan?" [11]

Bryan quickly settled upon a campaign strategy. It was simply a logical extension of his preconvention planning. He followed to the letter the plea of his good friend John Sherman of Wahoo, to "be very careful you do not get after the Independent ticket as that is the people we have to get our votes from." At the state Democratic convention in Omaha, which nominated James E. Boyd for governor and inevitably called on Bryan for a speech, his crowning sentence was worthy of the most fiery Independent. "Let us hope," he cried, "that we are on the eve of a brighter day when equal laws will lighten the burden of the toiling masses." [12]

Bryan also aimed to detach many Republicans disgruntled by the hard times and by Connell's unflinching devotion to the high protective tariff. On tariff reform, Bryan being a moderate and not a radical, was palatable to Republicans who felt tempted in this election to abandon their party for the Democracy. In more than eighty speeches on his leading campaign subject, Bryan steadily advocated tariff "reform" rather than free trade. (At a later day he would take a position much closer to free trade.) His explanations and his oratory, nevertheless, were illuminated with all the fiery hues of the most fervent Independent. The tariff centralized wealth, created monstrous trusts, oppressed the farmer by robbing him of the fruit of his toil, and corrupted legislators. But Bryan's prescriptions against the tariff evil were modest. The lightning was a small measure of the great thunder. If the rhetoric was Independent, the solutions were those of a Democratic moderate. Bryan's double purpose seemed to work. His Republican listeners were pleased, and the Independent press, which, like its party leaders, had hitherto treated the tariff as of minor consequence, began to elevate its importance.

As a campaigner the kinetic, youthful Bryan performed in a whirlwind manner. Speaking almost every day and sometimes three times daily, he missed hardly a village or a crossroads in his sprawling multicounty district. His preferred format featured one subject—the tariff, trusts, or money— and these, for all their convoluted technicalities, he presented in simple direct terms that even the least educated could grasp—"a child can understand the points and follow the argument," a reporter claimed.

The audiences that overflowed the halls and parks were drawn as much by generous servings of hoopla as by Bryan's magnetism. In Lincoln, Boyd and Bryan Clubs launched gay noisy parades whenever the candidates appeared, and in Omaha, their speeches were preceded by extravaganzas in the city streets with brass bands, booming drums, and long lines of shuffling marchers bearing torches and flambeaux.

Bryan and Boyd did much of their campaigning together, joined less by comradeship than by the political good one could do the other. Bryan's electrifying oratory complemented Boyd's humdrum addresses, while Boyd, who was rated a wet, provided reassurance to those voters who were uneasy about the young candidate's wide reputation as a teetotaler. In his speeches, Bryan steadfastly courted the wet vote, repeating on numerous occasions that "it is unjust for any one man to say that another must 'live like I.' " In the themes and issues he stressed, Bryan tried to reach the various groups in his district who were short-changed in the dispensations of society. His most concentrated appeal was to the farmer, whose fortunes continued to deteriorate, but he endeavored to demonstrate that the evils that hobbled the farmer—the tariff, the trusts, the money power—also oppressed the laborers in the cities. "When you buy $1 worth of starch," he related to both farmers and city laborers and their wives, "you pay sixty cents for the starch and forty cents for the trust and the tariff. . . ."

Bryan also undertook the unpromising struggle to dislodge the substantial Negro population of Omaha from its thoroughly cemented loyalty to the Republican Party. "It seems to me strange," he declared in one speech, "that this party, which claims to love the colored man so well, fails to show its affection in any material degree. In the northern states there are 621,000 colored men. In many instances they hold the balance of power, but nobody ever heard of a colored man going to Congress from the north."

The climax of the campaign was a series of debates between Bryan and Connell. The press followed these closely, huge audiences turned out, and old-timers, recalling the days of '58, deemed them worthy of comparison as "intellectual treats" with the encounters of Lincoln and Douglas. The debates began in Lincoln before an audience of 3,000, who filled every available inch of Bohanan's Hall. For days before the encounter, Bryan was immersed in thought and planning, ordering and sharpening his arguments. In the manner of preparing for his law cases, he put himself in his opponent's position to anticipate his contentions and to construct his own answers. At the outset, the audience seemed evenly divided between the candidates. Each spoke twice, and when he came forward the first time to answer his opponent, Bryan, staggered by the importance of the event, for a moment lost his usual aplomb, and nausea stole over him. He quickly recovered and reached a climax of overwhelming effectiveness. He bombarded Connell's arguments with short crisp sentences, each with its vivid point or illustration. The vigor and boldness of Bryan's attack surprised and delighted his hearers, and applause swept the hall like a violent sea. To these people lately touched by the rough hand of economic depression, Bryan brought a message, not of revolution or of class vengeance but of equality and moderation. His audience found irresistible the sentiments that "When the poor and weak cry out for relief, they too often hear no answer but 'the echo of their cry,' while the rich, the strong, the powerful are given an attentive ear. For this reason is class legislation dangerous and deadly. It takes from those least able to lose and gives to those who are least in need. The safety of our farmers and our laborers is not in special legislation, but in equal and just laws that bear alike on every man. The great masses of our people are interested, not in getting their hands into other people's pockets, but in keeping the hands of other people out of their pockets." [13]

Bryan and Connell debated eleven times in cities and towns of the First Congressional District, and the younger man glaringly outshone his opponent. For all the pressure to succeed, the exchanges were always gentlemanly and good-humored. In the last debate, at Syracuse, Bryan, after his customary rousing closing, surprised and delighted his audience by presenting to his opponent a copy of Gray's *Elegy*. Connell responded graciously and, with an eye to his rural audience of simple faith, affirmed the Biblical truth "that it is more blessed to give than to receive." Merriment dancing in his eyes, Bryan stepped forward to invite his audience to join him in three cheers for "so able and gallant a defender of a lost cause." In a day when audiences threw flowers at orators they admired, Bryan won a rare tribute when he was presented with an elaborate floral wreath. On a large shield faced with pure white roses and a band of white carnations was inscribed "Truth," while beneath was a sword with a blade also of white carnations, and upon it appeared the word "Eloquence" in purple, extending from the hilt to the point.[14]

It was a sign of the rising tide of Bryan's campaign that his Republican detractors resorted to cheap ridicule and wild rumor. "Mr. Bryan," reported one paper, "went to church, leaving his mouth in the backyard practising on a new tariff speech." Other times, he was variously described as "effervescent as a bottle of soda pop," a "calamity howler," and one paper referred to him condescendingly as "the young Mr. Bryan." Worse than the ridicule were the rumors of a deal between Republicans and Democrats, by no means an unknown procedure in Nebraska politics for settling elections. Late in the campaign, Bryan received from a seasoned political observer in Omaha, W. E. Johnson, an ominous warning that "a scheme was brewing for a great political trade." Its object was to assure the election of candidates who could be counted on to fight against prohibition, the issue Bryan was treating so tenderly. But achievement of that purpose would cost certain candidates dearly in votes. The plot called for the transfer of many Republican votes to Boyd, an undoubted wet, and a corresponding number of Democratic votes to Connell, equally wet. Bryan's professed wetness was obviously not trusted. The trading would be done in the Omaha area, which boasted a concentration of breweries and a long, reeking record of irregularities in balloting. The plot did not come off, however, and Bryan was spared a fate that had destroyed many another candidate.[15]

Not all the proceedings of the political back rooms were directed against Bryan. Indeed one such episode had important, if not decisive, consequences favorable to his candidacy. In mid-September, his Independent opponent, Charles H. Van Wyck, who had been hesitating since July, chose to decline his party's nomination. A far weaker candidate was named to succeed him. A veil remains tightly drawn around the motives and movers of these events. Did they occur, one wonders, because Van Wyck and his fellow Independents had become confident that the unknown and untried Bryan could win and that such a victory would be preferable to Connell's?

At last, election day arrived, and at day's end the outcome was clear. It was glorious news for the Nebraskan Democrats. Bryan was elected to Congress and Boyd to the governorship. Never before had the Democrats fashioned this double triumph. Only once before in Nebraska's history had a Democrat been elected in the First Congressional District. Where Connell had defeated Morton in 1888 by 3,400 votes, Bryan topped Connell by 6,713. The rejoicing at Bryan's fireside and in the Democratic precinct rooms of the First District was not at all diminished by the likelihood that half of Bryan's victory margin was represented by fraudulent results in Douglas County. The ballot boxes had been systematically stuffed to shore up Boyd's gubernatorial candidacy, and while proceeding with their unsavory task, the stuffers could not resist helping Bryan. Evidence is lacking that he chose to subordinate his image as the good party man to moral principle. Certainly he made no public protest against the deep-sinning Omaha Democratic machine.

Why did Bryan win when in the general opinion of experienced politicians he would surely fail? Although specific causes are by no means always clear-cut in elections, Bryan's success appears explicable in terms of his campaign formula. He won by a combined rural and city vote, each an indispensable ingredient of success. The farmers, in their misery of drought and debt, looked for a savior and welcomed what Bryan said. In the cities, the liquor question absorbed attention, and the abstemious Bryan diligently—and successfully—cultivated an image of opposition to prohibition while riding the wet coattails of Boyd. A minor occurrence of the unexpected kind on whose outcome elections so often depend also worked in Bryan's favor. The Omaha Bankers' and Business Men's Association, as it was wont to do with Republican candidates, assessed Connell $1,200, which he refused to pay. The wealthy Boyd, sniffing instant political opportunity, leaped forward to pay the assessment in exchange for the association's support.

Bryan was also careful to keep J. Sterling Morton out of his campaign. This was something of an embarrassment, for Morton had graciously offered his services to Bryan's nomination, but the unpleasant truth was that Morton loomed as a liability. His free-tariff views were offensive to Republicans whom Bryan hoped to attract by his own moderate tariff position, while his conservatism on other issues would surely have troubled the Independents. After the victory, Morton in a congratulatory letter expressed pointed regret at having had no part in his protégé's campaign. Bryan squirmed his way through by explaining his campaign committee had little money, "and we did not feel like calling on people to make speeches when we were not prepared to pay expenses." The debates with Connell had occupied all of Bryan's time, and "except for a few speeches by Watkins, Allen and Cunliff [his chief local Democratic and Populist allies] hardly anything was done in the way of outside speakers." Bryan's note ended cordially. While he did not yet know what opportunities he would have in Congress to help his friends, "I want you to feel free to call upon me when I can be of service to you. . . ."

Even after the campaign was well under way, George L. Miller observed, "I do not suppose he has the least chance of election." Yet Bryan constructed a victory coalition on a scale and of a diversity previously unmatched in Nebraska politics. He united wets and drys, farmers and city workers, a new party with old parties. He succeeded in attracting both discontented Republicans and agitated Independents. He brilliantly capitalized upon the politics of instability, annexing to his own cause those no longer satisfied with their old organizations and their traditional loyalties. On the issues, he offered something for practically everybody: a mild tariff posture for Republicans, silver and other reform planks for the Independents, a renunciation of prohibition for the wets, and a solid reputation as a teetotaler for the drys. Bryan demonstrated convincingly an amazing possession of the politician's skill of creating a sense of common interest.

On the stump Bryan emerged as an enormously attractive candidate. His thrilling resonance, translucent sincerity, the freshness of his youth, his ability to sustain a campaign pace that would kill an ox, his articulation of what people felt, what they despaired over and yearned for—all were weighty. For at least the hour of his campaign, strife-ridden Democrats put their quarrels to rest, and like many Congressional candidates before and since his day, he profited from the vital fact that he ran in a midterm election as a member of the party not in the White House.

With this, their second Congressional victory in all of Nebraska's history, Democrats across the state exuded joy and hope. "The fruit was ripe," wired J. Sterling Morton. "You have wisely gathered it. . . . I rejoice and congratulate." The jubilant Bryan was a fountain of generous sentiment. Douglas County, that fertile land of votes, proper and improper, he promised, "will receive a full share of my attention, and your people will have a warm place in my heart." Mary, who had once doubted her husband's powers of political divination, now perceived him as an acute scrutinizer of trends. Nestled in the pile of congratulatory letters and telegrams was another prophecy, even bolder than her husband's. It was from Eli H. Doud, lately removed from Lincoln to Illinois. "It appears to me," Doud wrote to

Bryan, "that the dawn is approaching and that you are the morning star of the reformation which is moving fast upon your state." [16]

8. Congressman

The political calendar required that Bryan pass a full year in the status of Congressman-elect. Until 1933, when the Twentieth Amendment was added to the Constitution under sponsorship of another Nebraskan, George W. Norris, Bryan and every other Congressman passed through an inordinate period of waiting between election and assumption of office. Bryan, however, did not waste this time in political idleness. Instead, he capitalized upon his victory by propelling himself from the leadership of his Congressional district to the forefront of Nebraska's state politics.

It was in these free months that Bryan first discovered the value of an issue—silver—to advance his political purposes. It is doubtful that silver at this point had burrowed very far into the skin of his convictions. It was merely a fast-growing issue that increasing numbers of politicians were eyeing, politicians who might become his competitors. Although silver had been muted in his electoral campaign, because he and Connell agreed on it and because Bryan was little initiated in its bog of technicalities, he now steeped himself in the subject and cultivated his public identification with it. He devoured a diet of heavy reading that began with a pamphlet of the Bimetallic League, *Silver in the Fifty-First Congress,* and moved on to the distinguished University of Chicago economist J. Laurence Laughlin and his standard book on bimetallism, *The History of Bimetallism in the United States,* the report of the Royal Commission of England on the subject, and the works of various leading economists, William Stanley Jevons, Bonamy Price, Enrico Cernuschi, Emile De Laveleye, and Michel Chevalier. He also pored over the information in the *Congressional Record* and a long popular work on money, Edward Kellogg's *Currency: The Evil and the Remedy.* (Kellogg was widely believed to be Horace Greeley.)

All through Bryan's young life, money had periodically been the subject of furious public discussion. In his college days, his debate topics embraced greenbacks and the resumption of specie payments. Recollections of the grim Panic of 1873, whose causes were traced to monetary problems, burned deep in his memory. In his adult life, he had witnessed the unhappy economic life of farmers in Illinois and Nebraska, and he was impressed with the weight given in political discussions to the bearing of a faulty monetary policy on rural problems. He had noted that repeatedly debate over monetary policy was a contest between West and East, between debtors of the West whose holdings were mortgaged and creditors of the East, the bankers and countinghouses, that held the indebtedness. Manipulation of the monetary system also afforded a choice between inflation and deflation. To the extent that the system contributed to falling prices, it favored the creditor, while only rising prices helped the debtor.

The nation's experience with monetary policy had largely been dominated by efforts to establish and maintain a relation between the two precious metals, gold and silver, on which the monetary system was primarily based. The ideal relation between the metals, in the eyes of many, especially in the West, was the Coinage Act of 1837, which established a coinage ratio between them at the market price then prevailing.

Shortly after passage of the 1837 Act, new discoveries and increased production of gold caused its market value to decline in relation to silver. Under the fixed coinage ratio of 16 to 1, silver became undervalued, its flow was diverted to other, more profitable uses, and little silver was brought to government mints for coinage. The undervaluing of silver persisted through the Civil War and into the postwar era. In 1873 Congress passed a new monetary law, with little debate or publicity, which, after recognizing that silver was not being minted, omitted any provision for the metal's coinage. Subsequently silver underwent increased production, and its price fell. It was once again advantageous for producers of silver to have the metal coined under the 16 to 1 ratio of the Act of 1837. When, however, they approached the mints, they were turned away with the explanation that the new law of 1873 made no provision for silver's coinage.[1]

The distraught miners and other friends of silver perceived in the circumstances under which the little noticed act of 1873 was passed the raw elements of conspiracy. The web of seamy circumstances was soon spoken of as the Crime of 1873. According to the legislative record, the act slid through Congress unnoticed in the perfunctory fashion of routine legislation. James A. Garfield, chairman of the Committee on Appropriations, confessed that "having my hands over full . . . [I] never read the bill. I took it upon the faith of a prominent Democrat and a prominent Republican, and I do not know that I voted at all . . . nobody opposed the bill that I know of. It was put through as dozens of bills are . . . on the faith of the report of the chairman of the committee." The bill had been before Congress for several sessions; no legislator had promoted it or evidenced any more interest than Garfield.

In 1890, few silver men accepted this chronicle of unwary innocence. The Act of 1873, they felt, was the result of a plot, engineered not in Washington but in New York's Wall Street and London's Lombard Street. There, in their fiscal palaces, bankers perceived the unwelcome possibility that increased production of silver would prompt an inflationary rise in prices. Putting their heads together and coordinating their moves, they conspired to reduce the United States and the rest of the world to a single gold standard. The most commonly heard story in the circles of silver's true believers was that the evil genius who slithered the 1873 law through to passage was a mysterious international financial figure named Ernest Seyd. According to report, Seyd came to the United States with $500,000 in gold in his pockets, put there by the Bank of England, to salve the enactment of the American demonetization law. A great push was given the conspiratorial theory when Moreton Frewen, the important English economist, declared in a speech in 1889: "Still, it is only when we pass on to the deed done at Washington that the silver question fairly emerges as the biggest and best planned financial coup of the century. The whole affair was a vast 'job' and I believe that any jury would find a true bill on the evidence that comes to us from America." [2]

The year 1873 was also a year of economic panic, signaled by the failure of the great banking house of Jay Cooke and Company. Other business houses quickly collapsed like falling cards. Within a year 6,000 commercial failures transpired, long breadlines appeared in the larger cities, and tramps wandered through the countryside. As economic depression continued, politicians, particularly in the West, were suggesting that it was the savage consequence of a money shortage prompted by the Coinage Act of 1873, with its exclusion of silver. The persistence of the depression and the agitation of Western Congressmen led to passage of the Bland-Allison Act of 1878, which authorized the Secretary of the Treasury to purchase not less than $2,000,000 and not more than $4,000,000 worth of silver each month. The Secretary had the option of either coining the silver or issuing silver certificates based on it. The same pressures brought passage of the Sherman Silver Purchase Act of 1890, which instructed the Secretary of the Treasury to purchase 4,500,000 ounces of silver each month and to issue treasury notes to cover the cost of the purchase. The acquired silver was to be stored. Silver advocates, though they rejoiced in these laws, deemed them temporary expedients, to be superseded as quickly as possible with the free coinage of silver under the terms of the Act of 1837.

The argument for silver was founded on the quantity theory of money. Silver's champions contended that the amount of money in circulation determined the general level of prices and the level of economic activity. In 1890, the year of Bryan's electoral victory, both prices and economic activity were again falling to low levels, free silver men argued, because the amount of money in circulation was insufficient to sustain normal price levels and general prosperity, let alone the nation's growth in population and economic transactions. When money fell into short supply, it gravitated to the financial centers of the East and away from the Western hinterland. The quantity theory found support in the harsh realities of price behavior as farm prices underwent devastating declines. Corn in 1890 was selling at less than half its price in 1881, and wheat, by the same comparison, was even worse. Almost parallel to the decline in farm prices was the decline in the amount of money in circulation. From a high of $31.18 per capita in 1865, the amount had fallen to a low of $18.97 in 1875. In the interval to 1890, the supply remained relatively constant with only the slightest increase to about $20 per person. A bimetallic system, silver advocates argued, would pump more money into circulation than the prevailing monometallic system, or gold standard. When foes of silver recalled that the metal had been unable to maintain its position in the ratio of the 1837 Act, its advocates pointed to recent discoveries of silver in the great Western mining states of Utah, Nevada, and Colorado which assured that the white metal could easily be maintained in relation to gold at a coinage ratio of 16 to 1. With silver restored to its former place in the monetary system, more money would circulate, farm prices would rise, and the rural gloom of 1890 would be replaced by the prosperity of 1837.

The imputations of conspiracy and the desperation of the Western farmer quickened interest in the silver debate. The farmer perceived all too clearly the painful need of his economic circumstances. He had borrowed when wheat and corn were high in price and money was cheap. In the dawning nineties he had to repay when his staples had sagged in price and money was dear. As he in his shabby coveralls and dusty boots and his wife in her bonnet and calico, their faces creased with lines of worry and hard work in the merciless sun, gathered in spare country schoolhouses to discuss their plight with others who shared their fate, their words were angry, and their thoughts turned to violence and even to revolution.

In 1890 the mounting discontent, for all its force and fury, had concentrated on no particular panacea. The most articulate spokesmen trumpeted a variety of nostrums. Some called for government ownership of the railroads; others for a subtreasury system for the storage of perishable and nonperishable products. Prohibitionists who moved into the ranks of Independents pushed their chosen cause; and Western suffragists declaimed for votes for women. In May, 1891, a kind of political miracle occurred when spokesmen of these motley causes gathered in Cincinnati for a National Union Conference, which resulted in the birth of a national Populist Party. The Grangers, Farmers' Alliance men, Prohibitionists, Suffragists, Antimonopolists, Greenbackers, Single Taxers, the Knights of Labor—seemingly every grievance-bearing son of humanity—entered the new party. The platform that emerged was a mirror and catchall of the several inspirations of its motley authors. It called for national ownership of the means of transportation and communications, a graduated income tax, free coinage of silver at 16 to 1, abolition of the national banking system, the issuance of fiat money sufficient to transact the country's business in cash, creation of a postal savings system, economy in government, and the like.

Silver, then, to Independents and Populists was just one cause among many, and because it was viewed as a latecomer to the lists of remedies, even an interloper, it was therefore suspect. In Nebraska, Kansas, the Dakotas, and Minnesota, it was the fashion to distinguish "genuine Populists" from "free silver Populists." The genuine breed suspected that silver was a tool by which one faction in their polyglot party hoped to wrest control. Populism had more than its share of dynamic, flamboyant personalities, but none was committed to silver. The silver cause had its able technicians who understood its economic mysteries, but it lacked a major public leader. It dangled, a rich, fast-ripening political apple, waiting to be plucked.

Bryan's season of diligent reading in the convoluted mysteries of silver and the money question brought him to conclude that the case for silver was absolutely correct and meritorious. He lost no time in broadcasting his commitment. At the First Western States Commercial Congress, held in Kansas City in April, 1891, business and farm spokesmen of twenty-four Western, Southern, and North Central states gathered to discuss the persistence of economic depression. The congress was sufficiently important to attract a message from President Harrison. Bryan, who was a delegate, pushed himself into the limelight by introducing a resolution, adopted to the accompaniment of wild cheers and waving hats of whiskered silver men, that "all legal money of the United States should be made full legal tender for all debts, public and private, any condition in the contract notwithstanding, provided that this should not affect contracts already in existence." Bryan, in effect, called upon Congress to authorize anyone with an ounce of silver, then worth about 75 cents, to offer it as $1, or the equivalent of an ounce of gold, in payment of his debt. He was demanding for silver treatment even better than what was possible under 16 to 1. He accompanied his resolution with a captivating supporting speech. Fittingly for a Western audience, he made no bones about appealing to its seething debtors' prejudices against the creditor East. "We simply say to the East," he cried, "take your hands out of our pockets and keep them out." [3]

Bryan's resolution won national attention. A. J. Warner, then America's best-known silver editor, wrote to Bryan hailing his "good stroke." But the wise old hands of Nebraska's Democratic Party urged caution. J. Sterling Morton, his sensitive conservative antenna already humming with the silver heresy, warned Bryan against its perils. Even the tolerant, progressive Gilbert M. Hitchcock, editor of the Omaha *World-Herald* who was giving Bryan great play in his paper, declared with candor that he was delighted to see "Bryan fight for free silver coinage against the Eastern gold bug," but he hoped too that his good friend would resist "the demands of the wealthy mine owners who seek to get a bonus of 25% out of the American people."

As a combined silver orator and a Democratic Congressman-elect in a Republican state, Bryan was fast building a regional and national reputation. He raced into Iowa to campaign for Horace Boies, seeking reelection as governor on a free silver platform. He pulled wires which initiated an appeal that his talented services be brought to the aid of the embattled Ohio Democracy in its struggle with the rising Republican giant, William McKinley. By challenging the popular McKinley, Bryan drew even more national attention to himself. To arrange this useful event, so helpful to his own advancement, he wrote his Illinois friend Congressman William Springer that he wanted to combat McKinleyism "on its native hearth." He needed his expenses paid, as he was confident they would be, and, he added, "Perhaps a word from you to the committee in charge of the campaign would be of advantage." An invitation was soon forthcoming from Governor James A. Campbell for Bryan to stump in Ohio.[4]

By summer's end, 1891, with his extensive travels and soundings behind him, Bryan was convinced that silver was the great issue of the future. "If the Democratic party," he wrote to a political friend, "allows itself to be frightened away from the support of free coinage, I have little hope for our immediate success." That his party and its masters were thoroughly frightened, Bryan discovered at Nebraska's Democratic state convention in September. Even before the convention Bryan laid a strategy that proved he was far more than a brilliant young orator. It demonstrated again his ability to draw together disparate parts of the political landscape to produce an arresting, consequential effect. Coincidentally, he applied a full measure of audacity and shrewdness to reap maximum benefits from his political resources. At the convention Bryan, armed with his shining new lance—silver—and a bold strategy, proceeded to do nothing less than challenge the long-reigning potentates of the Nebraska Democracy for the leadership of the party.

Bryan, representing his own county of Lancaster on the Resolutions Committee, succeeded in having himself elected chairman. He was not in a position to lead the fight for a free silver plank. His committee colleagues, as he expected, responded like good puppets to those old conservatives Miller and Morton. Overnight the two factional leaders became united against the ominous peril of Lincoln's flaming young orator. The committee, which Miller and Morton dominated, rejected Bryan's silver plank, a step that he had well anticipated. The defeat enabled him to go to the convention floor with a minority report and present his plank in a speech of explosive eloquence. This was the first time the state's assembled political professionals had heard the fabled Bryan in action. So moved were they by the bombardment in behalf of a cause of fast-growing popularity that they came within a whisker of adopting his plank. The hard-pressed leaders, Miller and Morton, were driven to what for them was a rare public display of sharp vocabulary, itself indicative of the severity of the challenge to their power. They warned against the allure of a "cheap and nasty" dollar and proposed the adoption of "a bold and broad declaration for honest money." Eventually, because of the astounding silver strength, the issue was compromised, with the lion's share of the concessions favoring Bryan's forces.

Despite the convention's patched-up peace, the Bryan-Morton rupture deepened. Morton opposed silver not merely out of conviction; it was useful to him, as it was to Bryan, as a political issue. Morton's sagging political fortunes desperately needed a new cause, and his unfolding image as a defender of fiscal soundness was a promising restorative. But it was conviction, not mere calculation, that led him to warn his promising young friend soon after the convention, "Free coinage beckons Democracy to disaster in 1892." Bryan, by now well resolved to break with Nebraska's old Democratic leadership, retorted to his erstwhile benefactor in words as bold as his schoolboy scrawl, that he no longer needed J. Sterling Morton's counsel or support. ". . . I do not think we can afford to take a backward step on the money question, and if the Democratic party deserts its position as the champion of the mass of the people, it will have no place to go, for the Republican party is nearer to the classes and the corporations than we could possibly get if we wished." [5]

Bryan was fighting for more than control of the state Democratic organization. He was putting forth a novel and specific plan for the future management of his party that would build upon its recent successes and improve the possibilities of steady victory. The next round in Bryan's new struggle transpired a few days after the convention in a meeting of the Democratic state central committee at Omaha. The state leaders were hastily summoned when the nominee for State Supreme Court judge, Jefferson H. Broady, a Bryan man, declined to run. That Bryan may have encouraged him in the step is possible, for the young orator in his confrontation with the party potentates urged that the nomination be kept vacant and that the Democrats endorse the Independent candidate. While old political leaders shook their heads in disapproval of Bryan's unheard of proposal of Democratic-Independent fusion, he argued that a Democratic nomination would ensure a Republican victory. Bryan did not stop there in his program of fusion. He urged that Democratic candidates for the state board of regents should also withdraw. He was arguing openly for full fusion of Democrats and Independents as the recipe for electoral victory. It was, to be sure, a rather one-sided fusion, with the Democrats simply handing all their nominations over to the Independents. Morton and Miller men cried out against this seeming political insanity. "The Independent party," Bryan answered soothingly, "is Democratic on many questions. . . ." [6]

November did not bring victory to Bryan's fusion ticket, but it was the month in which, in the great chamber by the Capitol dome, Bryan took the oath of office as a member of the House of Representatives. He had come to the place that had been denied his father.

To his regret, Bryan had to savor the triumph alone. He had left his family in Lincoln, planning to bring them to Washington after he had found suitable living quarters, a difficult task for a young Congressman entirely dependent on his salary. In February the Bryans had had their third child, Grace Dexter, a beautiful infant who would come to bear a striking resemblance to her father. For all the thrill of the new life, Bryan deeply missed his family. He was delighted to find little William's mittens in his pocket, and he dispatched them back home by registered mail. To Mary, he professed in his letters his love and his loneliness and the assurance that "I have not seen many ladies yet and none I would trade you for." [7]

With the coming of the new year of 1892, Bryan finally found an apartment for his family. The search was difficult, for almost everywhere he tried landlords displayed a stony aversion to children. In February he returned to Lincoln to fetch his family. En route at last, they stopped for several days in Jacksonville to visit old friends.

The Bryans lived in a double house on B Street, facing the Library of Congress, then under construction. Bryan rented a suite on the second floor and there in neat and spacious comfort made his home for the next four years. Several other legislators lived on the premises, including Congressmen Samuel Busey of Illinois, Clinton Babbit of Wisconsin, William Sulzer of New York, and Edward Carmack of Tennessee, the last two of which were destined to become Bryan's staunch allies in the cause of free silver.

The owner of the B Street property, Cotter Timothy Bride, quickly succumbed to the charm of his warm, outgoing new arrivals. Living with Mr. Bride was a nephew, Daniel, lately arrived from County Cork, Ireland, whose health had buckled under the clammy rigor of the Washington climate. His despair scattered after the Bryans' arrival. Attentive to his cares, ready with comforting words and uplifting thoughts, they took him on as a member of the family. They had their meals together at the house, and he joined in the little religious observance the Bryans held each day after an early breakfast. Gathered in the living room would be the Bryans, their three children, Mary's father, who was now blind (her mother had died recently in Lincoln), and young Bride, a Roman Catholic, participating with the Presbyterian Bryans.[8]

When Bryan took his place in the House, he was quickly aware of the overwhelming predominance of his party. It enjoyed an almost 3 to 1 majority, what with 235 Democrats, 86 Republicans, and 14 who were either Populists or members of the older Farmers' Alliance, with which the Populists were now merging. Even more remarkable was the number of new Democrats—105, at least one from every state. The Democratic Party, anchored for decades in the morass of minority status, with Cleveland's term of office the only respite, seemed on the threshold of a new era. The colorless incumbent of the White House, Benjamin Harrison, almost guaranteed their future political prosperity. This House of Representatives enjoyed several distinctions. Its membership included eighteen generals of the Civil War and three men who one day would become serious candidates for the Presidency: Thomas Brackett Reed, Richard Parks Bland, and William Jennings Bryan.

The driving, ebullient Bryan could never be quiet and obscure in any organization, not even in the United States Congress, where freshmen legislators were expected to be seen and not heard. On Capitol Hill, Bryan employed a technique of self-advancement that had served him well in Nebraska. He widened the circle of his acquaintances, immediately giving high priority to meeting every one of his fellow Congressmen and as many Senators as possible. Success at this task came easily. Only the most gloom-encrusted human could resist his proffered friendship. Shining with good-will and exuberant optimism, Bryan was a companion who always wore well. He had a vein of quick bright humor and an infinite fund of stories with a twist of just the right appeal for most House members.

Bryan was delighted to discover that nearly thirty members of the House were under forty years of age, and what was even better, they seemed the brightest Congressmen. A favorite was Tom Johnson of Cleveland, thirty-seven, "and a big good natured fellow he is." Bryan was also impressed by the erudite, razor-sharp intelligence of Senator George F. Hoar of Massachusetts—"real pleasant, but a little eastern"—built upon his earlier acquaintance with Senator John Daniel of Virginia, and, as a native Illinoisan, quickly found ties with the delegation of his former state. Others whom he admired hailed from North and South, Henry St. George Tucker of Virginia, William L. Terry of Arkansas, and James N. Castle of Minnesota. "You will have a chance to display your social genius here," Bryan promised Mary even before she had left Lincoln. And Bryan kept his word by steadily bringing home those colleagues whom he liked most.[9]

While Bryan was still in Nebraska, his old friend Congressman William Springer, aspiring to become Speaker of the House of Representatives, wrote him asking that he corral the support of two new Nebraska colleagues—both Independents who had been elected with him. The Speakership was fought for with all the intensity of a Civil War battle. There were three major aspirants—Charles F. Crisp of Georgia, Roger Q. Mills of Texas, and Springer—and two minor contenders, Benton McMillin of Tennessee and William S. Holman of Indiana. The choice was far more than one of personalities. The foremost issue of the day—the tariff—and the most rapidly emerging issue—silver—gave momentum to the struggle. Mills and Crisp demanded tariff reform, but Mills was a gold man while Crisp embraced silver. Mills was the candidate of the Easterners promoting Grover Cleveland for President in 1892. Crisp was the candidate of the Western and Southern wing of the party and a band of Easterners who preferred Senator David Bennett Hill of New York, a bimetallist, to Cleveland, who was for gold. Silver Democrats and Alliance men rallied around Crisp. The strategy of Springer, who had modest support, was to preserve his own position until a deadlock between Crisp and Mills required a compromise candidate, a role for which he was ideally suited. A parliamentarian more interested in procedure and maneuver than in policy, Springer was identified with minor revision of the tariff, and on the emerging silver issue he had as yet taken no open position. Crusty "Uncle Joe" Cannon once complained that Springer had "a weakness for breaking into the limelight regardless of the inconvenience he caused other members."

Almost immediately upon his arrival in Washington, Bryan jumped into the fray, becoming "perhaps his [Springer's] most active supporter" with great relish. "The Speakership fight," he reported to Mary, "has given me a chance to 'fight' and you know that is my strong forte." There were several battlegrounds. The hotels where candidates stayed—Crisp and McMillin at the Metropolitan and Springer at the National—were scenes of incessant comings and goings. The Democratic caucus met at noon and worked through quantities of ballots until midnight. It could come to no consensus. Between ballots, there was fervish buttonholing to build votes. The corridors outside the caucus room were jammed with the press and throngs of visitors drawn by the excitement and the heavy stakes.

In the late balloting, Springer's strength slipped so alarmingly that Bryan was driven to ask for nine men "who would stand with me and promise to hold the fort." Sixteen men rallied to his side, and once again the strategy of the Springer camp was to maintain the balance of power and eventually to secure the election of their candidate after his stronger opponents had exhausted one another. If the strategy worked, Bryan reported to Mary, "Your husband will be on top. . . . It is a bold move and has dismayed the friends of both leading candidates. . . ."

The struggle took on new intensity with the arrival in the House lobby of Cleveland's former Postmaster General, Don Dickinson, presumably to represent the interest of that former and future President in Mills' election. But the presence of the astute, hard-driving Dickinson had little effect. Eventually the impasse was broken by a "deal" by which Springer withdrew from the race on condition that "my friends must be well treated," and most of his supporters cast their votes for Crisp. The specifics of the "deal" were clarified when Crisp as Speaker appointed Springer chairman of the Ways and Means Committee and Bryan a member. (At that time, the Speaker appointed the chairmen and members of the committees, a function that was the fountainhead of his power.)

For a freshman Congressman like Bryan, to be named to Ways and Means, the House's most powerful committee, was almost unheard of. In addition, as one of two leaders of the Springer faction, as its ingratiating, indefatigable negotiator, Bryan had immediately emerged from the sea of unknown freshman faces to the forefront of the House. "On the floor of the House today," the Washington correspondent of the Omaha *World-Herald* noted after the fight, "he was given unusual attention by both Republicans and Democrats. Bryan is everywhere and is pointed out more often than many old members of Congress."

Upon entering the Speakership fight, Bryan was resolved to maintain the goodwill of both Mills and Crisp. After the fight ended, he took pains to patch up any cracks in the wall of amiability he was patiently building to embrace every House member. In a statement to the press soon after the conflict, he declared that despite his championship of Springer and his dispensation from Crisp, he remained "a warm friend and admirer of Colonel Mills." [10]

According to the dictates of a tradition as old as Congress itself, a member of the House of Representatives is the emissary in the national capital of his district and his constituents, duty-bound to nurture their interests and concerns. This branch of Bryan's responsibilities posed a problem. If he were a whole-cloth ideologue, a legislator unreservedly devoted to policy and to mankind's improvement, he would look askance at this lesser task of satisfying the self-centered needs of individual constituents. The other extreme would be to ignore high-minded ideals for the pedestrian, sometimes amoral needs of his voters. Bryan easily found a middle course.

He responded to his constituents' concerns with initiative and dedication that soared far beyond the norm. Aided by an expanded pension law, he gathered up more pensions for the First District than had all his predecessors combined. He pushed his way through thickets of bureaucratic red tape to flush out action for the most intricate problems his constituents conjured up, and he was tireless at introducing special legislation to care for worthy citizens when all else failed. One of his better triumphs was inspired by Sarah Beck, widow of a Civil War veteran who, when Bryan came to know of her, was existing on forty cents a week. Dropped from the pension rolls after she remarried, she had passed into a life of penury after her second husband died until Bryan rescued her and a special act of Congress restored her public stipend.

Bryan took up all manner of causes for aggrieved Nebraskans. He secured payment for a grower who still awaited a balance due from the Quartermaster General's Office for corn supplied during the Civil War, and he gained permission from the Interior Department for the nation's most distinguished cowboy, William F. Cody, better known as Buffalo Bill, to engage 100 Indians from the Sioux reservation for his Wild West Show. Bryan did not wait for constituents to come to him with their troubles but sprang into action whenever his watchful eye discovered need or trouble. Spotting a news item that Solomon Gerber of Omaha had been arrested by Russian authorities, he promptly requested from James G. Blaine, Secretary of State, full information on the incident. The aggressive Bryan even dared propose to Benjamin Harrison's Republican administration that he be allowed to designate postmasters in his district, but the administration predictably and coolly rebuffed him. When a river and harbor appropriations bill underwriting the study of rivers in many states omitted any reference to Nebraska, Bryan moved to include his state, lest those, he said, who learn their geography through such bills in future years absorb the misconception that there are "no running streams in the State of Nebraska." [11] He worked to put a new bridge across the Missouri River near the city of Omaha. He introduced bills calling for appropriations for new public buildings in Lincoln, South Omaha, and Plattsmouth and for the establishment of a branch mint near Lincoln. Though these efforts went unrewarded, Bryan did succeed in pushing through laws that divided Nebraska into two judicial districts, obtained an extra fall term for the federal court in Lincoln, and got the Crop and Weather Bureau moved from Omaha to Lincoln, where it could work rewardingly with the agricultural experiment station at the university. Probably the most important bill Bryan sponsored was the last act of Congress signed by President Harrison. The legislation helped the debt-ridden farmers of his constituency by regulating the procedures by which federal court judgments could be imposed as liens upon real estate. Previously, an out-of-state creditor could foreclose on his Nebraska debtor with a minimum of public notice in that state. Henceforth, under the Bryan law, nonresident lenders who used federal courts to foreclose on land mortgages had to publish foreclosure notices in the county where the land was located. In effect, the law served to give farmers notice of loan sharks who were skulking in their territory.

In the bills he sponsored or voted on, Bryan was a latter-day Jeffersonian, jealous of liberty, confident of local government, suspicious of distant Washington, and respectful of the virtues of the small farmer. He supported an investigation of the use of Pinkerton detectives in the Homestead strike, holding that the preservation of order was a function appropriate only for government and that its transfer to private hands exposed lives and safety to the dangers of an irresponsible soldiery. Bryan struck at another form of tyranny when he joined the fight to repeal the Reed Rules, adopted under the previous Republican Speaker, Thomas B. Reed, which gave any incumbent Speaker autocratic power over the House proceedings. In one instance of House affairs, bringing into clear conflict loyalty to party versus individual justice, Bryan chose the latter. In a contested election, he voted against seating the Democrat because he deemed the Republican to have been fairly elected.

When expenditure did not flow to his constituents, Bryan would insist on economy in government. He attacked a proposed federal underwriting of an encampment of the Grand Army of the Republic in the national capital on the grounds that if the federal government helped the GAR, it would be called on to finance the "entertainment of any other civic body in our midst." He also saw the project as a kind of conspiracy of hotels and railroads greedy for federal money. Bryan also opposed expenditure benefiting any special group or class. When members of Nebraska's sugar beat industry petitioned for a bounty, he sent them running by tartly proclaiming his revulsion to bounties and special legislation and advised his visitors that if they could not make a profit in their present enterprise, they should transfer their investments elsewhere. The Lincoln *Daily Call,* upon hearing of the encounter, cried, "Give us that new post office and we'll forgive you your eccentricities."

On questions concerning the economy and government, Bryan took stances that gladdened his fellow progressive Democrats and the most resolute Independents back home. He backed amendments strengthening the powers of the Interstate Commerce Commission and added his voice to cries for stricter enforcement of laws regulating the trusts. In 1891 Bryan was years ahead of his time in demanding the physical valuation of railroad property as a basis of determining rates—a measure adopted some twenty-two years later in 1913—and regulation of speculation on the stock exchanges—a law passed forty-two years later in 1933.

To chronicle Bryan's initiatives and their actual implementation is to reveal the lumbering pace of the American political process. As a good Jeffersonian, he aimed to make government more responsive to the people. Distressed that an incoming President had to deal with a short-session (lame duck) Congress possibly dominated by the opposition party, he proposed to harmonize the timetables by which a new President and a new Congress took office. His efforts bore fruit some forty-two years later when the Twentieth Amendment was added to the Constitution. Another favorite Bryan project was the popular election of Senators, the subject of the first bill he introduced.

For the trust problem he put forth an ingenious solution that caught the attention of the lawmaking community. Bryan would place on the free list, by Presidential order, any article of commerce on which a duty is levied, whenever a United States circuit court found that a trust or monopoly had been found to control trade in that article. In effect, Bryan aimed to break up trusts by admitting competitive imports free of duty. Critics angrily assailed the proposal as "radical" and "experimental," as it was, and it suffered the fate that befalls such measures by dying in committee.[12]

The issue that first brought Bryan into the national spotlight and his oratorical gifts to the notice of the whole body of Congress was the tariff. The tariff was the province of the Ways and Means Committee, where the reform forces, led by Springer, outnumbered the protectionists. Springer and his band followed a strategy based on the fact of Democratic control of the House and Republican control of the Senate and Presidency. They concentrated on reducing duties on specific articles. Benton McMillin of Tennessee, a tariff reformer, commenced the play by reporting the wool and woolens bill, with Bryan responsible for binding twine, barbed wire, iron fence posts, lumber, and salt.

It was on McMillin's wool bill that Bryan made his first major speech on March 16, 1892. Momentarily smitten with stage fright, he launched a shrewd, well-planned attack on the protective tariff. To the young Congressman, the protective tariff was a simple but monstrous device by which "one man is authorized to collect money from his fellow men." It enabled industrial interests to profit at the expense of farmer, worker, and consumer. It transferred money "from one man's pocket to another man's pocket." The plight of the consumer under the protective tariff he likened to slavery. "It has been said," he cried at his full oratorical momentum, "that the slave was a slave simply because 100 per cent of the proceeds of his toil was appropriated by somebody else without our consent, we are simply to that extent slaves. . . ."

Traditionally, a speech on the tariff was like an expedition to a dull gray bog, utterly without excitement. The tariff put members to sleep or pushed them into animated conversation in brave efforts to stay awake, and, above all, it made members write letters. As Bryan's rich-timbred voice and its spirited message carried to the far corners of the House, however, the galleries quickly filled, and Senators came over in numbers to hear the extraordinary young orator. Most came as reports of his unbelievable skill spread like swamp fire. Others anticipated a kind of entertainment. "Let's go see our boys have fun with him," one Massachusetts Congressman was heard to tell another.

Bryan worked to rip aside the veil that covered the arguments for the protective tariff. Did it raise revenues as its defenders said? Hardly, he answered, since 80 percent of the customs were absorbed by the protected industries and only 20 percent dribbled into the Treasury. Did not the protected manufacturer or employer act as a trustee for his employees, who also benefit? No, said Bryan; the employer keeps the tariff bonus for himself. Let the employee dare ask for a higher wage and Pinkerton detectives are summoned to drive him away and foreign labor is imported to take his place. But manufacturers cry they cannot live without help of the tariff. They live, noted Bryan, not as ordinary men, but in stately palaces and give banquets that rival in magnificence the banquets of ancient times. "These are the men who can gather around a banquet board as they did, I think it was in New York, to celebrate 'home industries' at $10 per plate, when within a stone's throw of their banquet hall were people to whom a 10 cent meal would be a luxury." Moreover, the appetite of these tariff eaters was insatiable. Infant industries that once managed with 10 percent, then 20, then 30, were now accorded 40 to 47 percent by the McKinley Tariff.

Bryan also took up his own binding twine bill and proceeded to demonstrate that the McKinley Tariff rate of seven-tenths of 1 percent, which Republicans called "trifling," in actuality added $700,000 to the price of imported twine. None of this accrued to the government as revenue, but all flowed into the pockets of manufacturers. Bryan invited his listeners to indulge in a little arithmetic. There were thirty-five twine factories in the country, all controlled by the cordage trust, which meant that each, thanks to the tariff, received $20,000 a year.

When Bryan's allotted hour was up, an archprotectionist, Julius Burrows, asked unanimous consent for the brilliant young orator to proceed. The motion carried, and Bryan put in another two hours of running debate with the McKinley Tariff's best sharpshooters. In the swift exchanges, Bryan gave his own prescription for the tariff—collect part of the present revenue from customs, put raw materials on the free list, and levy the highest duties on luxuries and the lowest on necessities. When one high-tariff advocate asked how "in morality" he could justify the bill he was reporting, which called for a 39 percent tax on woolen clothing, Bryan replied: "If I found a robber in my house who had taken all I had, and I was going to lose it all or else get one-half back, I would take the half." When his opposition, sniffing eagerly to entrap him, queried whether the tariff did not protect the high wages of the American worker, he retorted that the American worker received higher wages than foreign workers because his output was one and a half times as high.

As the debate waxed on, Bryan's argument was increasingly infused with emotional oratory. More and more, the fight was between good and evil, between oppressors and oppressed, between the many and the few, between an equitable future and an unjust present. The tariff posed the kind of issue to which Bryan was dedicating his political life. Government, he contended, should be by and for the people, and, he predicted, it soon would be: "A marvelous change has taken place, and rising from the political mourners' benches throughout the Northwest, their faces radiant with a new-found joy, multitudes are ready to declare their allegiance to the cause of tariff reform. . . . Why are we right? Because, Mr. Chairman, we are demanding for the people equal and exact justice to every man, woman and child. We desire that the laws of the country shall not be made, as they have been, to enable some men to get rich while many get poor." [13]

Not for decades had Congress heard such oratory. Democrats and even Republicans rushed over to congratulate the Nebraskan. Crusty Congressman Constantine Kilgore of Texas snapped, "This is the first time I ever left my seat to congratulate a member, but it is the first time I ever had such great cause to break the record." The Democratic press was jubilant, hailing the effort as "an oratorical firecracker," "dramatic," and "wonderfully brilliant." Even Bryan's rugged opponent, Julius Burrows, next to Reed in his eminence among House Republicans, declared, "I am free to say that Bryan made the best tariff reform speech I have ever heard." [14] At one swoop, the speech had lifted Bryan from an obscure place on the crowded political canvas into national prominence.

Bryan's most attentive listener was Mary, perched in the gallery within an easy glance from the floor. Her presence inspired Bryan, and her nods and frowns and other little signs were useful guides as he spoke. Mary by now was more than a wife; she was a full-fledged political partner. She was a constant visitor at the Library of Congress, pursuing books and monographs, corralling facts and arguments on the tariff, silver, and other complex subjects with which Bryan grappled. Seated by her husband in his study, she worked with him in answering the mail, and in thoughtful, searching discussion they worked out the framework of his speeches, the themes, the memorable phrases, the telling rebuttal. No matter how intricate or colorless the subject, they could garb it in a simple attractive dress intelligible to the common man. To devote as much time as possible to her husband's fast-blooming career, Mary hired girls to help with the housework and with the care of the children and shunned organizations, like the Congressional Women's Club, whose social fritter might encroach on her precious time.

Because of Mary's availability and skill, Bryan, unlike other Congressmen, did not depend on a clerk, engaged for his term, as his chief assistant. He did hire clerks, but only for four or six weeks at a time. To these stints, he brought promising young Nebraska Democrats, simultaneously getting his Congressional work done and building personal strength in the youthful wing of the party. Since no Congressional office building had been built as yet, Bryan used a room at home for his office.

By their own choice, the Bryans did not participate in the ample social and literary circle of the capital which boasted such luminaries as Henry Adams, William C. Whitney, Whitelaw Reid, and Civil Service Commissioner Theodore Roosevelt. Almost nothing could lift the Western couple from their immersion in a Congressman's work. Not Mrs. John Wana-maker, wife of the Postmaster General and merchant prince, and her enter-tainment of Mrs. Ballington Booth, daughter-in-law of General William Booth of the Salvation Army, who spoke on "Rescue Work." Not the woman suffragists who capped a half week of meetings with an address by Julia Ward Howe at the opera house. If these causes that were so dear to the hardworking Bryans failed, there was no chance at all for Sarah Bern-hardt appearing in *La Tosca* at Albaugh's, for James Henry Moser's pleas-ing exhibit of watercolors, and for the Countess Esterhazy, who gave a large luncheon at the old Carroll Mansion in honor of the President's lady, Mrs. Harrison, with the wives of Washington's mighty present.

In their sparsely budgeted free time, the Bryans lived for themselves and a small circle of close friends who worked hard and lived as economically as they did. Their only true rest occurred on Sunday, which they observed as God's day, with churchgoing in the morning, followed by quiet, contempla-tive activity. In the afternoon, Dan Bride often took the Bryans out for a buggy ride. Their usual route was down the Good Hope Road, leading through neat little villages and rolling countryside. En route, the horse, upon coming to a particular saloon, would, as if from habit, turn into the yard. The teetotaling Bryan observed jokingly to his embarrassed host, "Dan, the horse must know this place."

In a day of Sunday calling, the Bryans exchanged visits with a wide circle of Capitol Hill folk. With more intimate legislative friends, there might be a singing of hymns and popular songs and light refreshments. On occasion, the gatherings were larger and merrier. Bryan's birthday was the cause for a special celebration as it would be all through his life. On the eve of his thirty-second birthday, his first in the capital, the young orator, returning from a speaking engagement in Virginia in the late afternoon, found, when he entered his apartment, a score of Senators, Representatives and their wives. The songs and laughter lasted until 2 A.M.

Among their legislative peers, the Bryans, despite their teetotaling ways, were unusually popular. Their ready song, Bryan's jocularity and wit, Mary's easy laughter and sprightly conversation made their home a kind of oasis in the capital's life. Legislators were delighted to come there, although a few at first held back, committing the easy mistake of misjudging Bryan. His Western boots, slouch hat, striped rumpled trousers, and clerical tie tempted them to conclude that the young man was simply "one more of those hayseed Congressmen." But Bryan's superb oratory, his rush to the forefront of the House of Representatives, his handsome features seemingly imprinted with commitment to all that was good and pure in public life quickly demolished such judgments. Men of Washington whose own ca-reers depended no little on their skill at detecting able men among the legis-lative newcomers perceived in the young man an extraordinary promise.

Bryan found no opportunity to launch an oration on the subject in which he was becoming steeped—free silver. Early in the session, there was a flickering sign that silver would make large gains. Speaker Crisp appointed Richard P. "Silver Dick" Bland of Missouri, dean of the silver men in the House, as Chairman of the Committee on Coinage. But despite a friendly Speaker and staunch silver men, Springer and Bland, at the leaderships of strategic committees, the cause foundered. It was slowed partly by the acumen of President Harrison, who faithfully applied the Sherman Silver Purchase Act and purchased "the entire product of our mines" while contending that full use of silver could not be made in the monetary system without international agreement. Silver was also caught up in a snarl of House procedure. Bryan managed to induce the Rules Committee to reserve time in House debate for consideration of a strong silver bill, prepared under Bland's aegis. The debate faltered on a motion to table the bill, but in the tie vote that resulted, Crisp saved the day by voting against the motion. However, another motion postponing action on the bill indefinitely was passed later. March 24, when this hot debate transpired, Bryan always referred to as "the night free silver was killed." Bryan and his silver cohorts labored valiantly at one last tactic—to force a vote by cloture. They pursued, buttonholed, and pleaded with their colleagues, gathering signatures on the necessary petition, which, under House rules, had to be subscribed to by a majority of House members. The effort fell short by ten signatures.[15]

From his lair in the East, Grover Cleveland, having announced his receptivity to a third nomination for the Presidency, put starch into the spines of gold Democrats by objecting to silver in a strong public statement and by declaring that tariff reform would be the chief issue of the coming national campaign. Bryan lost no time in challenging the former President and the party's undoubted nominee for 1892. In a nationally publicized statement, Bryan dared to characterize the silver-minded Governor Horace Boies of Iowa as "the most available Presidential candidate yet mentioned." The West, Bryan added, was unwilling to accept the two chief contenders from the East—Cleveland and Senator David B. Hill of New York.

Bryan was plainly moving to change the geographic power base of the Democratic Party. Silver was the issue which gave leverage to his purpose; its natural stronghold was the debtor west; in the creditor East it was anathema, a monster of inflation. In beating the drums for the Presidential nomination of Boies, Bryan was taking a first step toward educating the West, the East, and indeed the national Democratic Party to the possibility and the desirability of a Westerner as the Presidential nominee. Though the lesson was too large to digest in 1892, it might well be mastered in 1896.

In June, 1892, Bryan solidified his position as principal Congressional spokesman for silver when he led the attack upon a bill before the House calling for repeal of the 10 percent federal tax on state bank notes. The repeal, he contended, would restore the wildcat banking that cursed the country before the Civil War. Repeal would help the states authorize private banking institutions to put out substitutes for money among the people. Bryan made clear his opposition to the issuance of money by any source but the national government, contending that this "function should not be surrendered to any corporation or any private concern whatever." If the federal tax were repealed and the state banks were empowered to issue money, "we would have all over the country a flood of currency, not a legal tender, which would be redeemable, if at all, only on individual responsibility." Legal tender would vanish from circulation "and debtors would be at the mercy of creditors." Bryan offered his own prescription for the money system: "free coinage of gold and silver at the present ratio," with paper money "issued by the federal government alone and convertible into coin on demand. . . . I do not want a currency which will make it necessary whenever a man travels from one state to another to have telegraphic communication with all parts of the United States in order to know whether his money is good." The House cheered, and a majority, with differing motivations and convictions, was patched together to defeat the bill.[16]

9. An Uncertain Election

However much the new star of Bryan scintillated on the national scene, its continued presence depended on his retaining his Congressional seat. Since, as a member of the national House of Representatives, Bryan had to face reelection every two years, he, like any Congressman, was continuously watchful of local political trends.

In the spring of 1892 after the close of the Congressional session, he returned to Lincoln for a series of political tests that would be spaced over almost the remainder of the year. Good political friends, eager for his success, converted his homecoming into a gala celebration. To be reelected, Bryan again had to commandeer Republican votes, and lines were thrown out to corral Republicans and Democrats alike to indulge their pride in the young Congressman.

A reception committee was organized of citizens of "all shades of political opinion." Invitations were extended to state, local, and county officials, and to the public in general "without regard to sex or political affiliation," and to the Young Men's Republican Club to share in the festivities. The burden of hoopla and demonstrations was put upon Democratic agencies of absolute loyalty. The grand marshal of the procession, scheduled to move through Lincoln's main streets from the railroad depot to the Lincoln Hotel, was a steady Democratic subaltern, Colonel Victor Vifquain, and the great body of his dependable marchers was provided by the Jeffersonian Club of Lincoln; the music, dash, and color by the Irish-American Pikemen, all good Democrats.

On April 12, when the Bryans reached Lincoln, the weather, as though an omen of rough days ahead, laid a heavy hand on the proceedings. A great downpour gave Lincoln's busier streets a corrugated coating of mud. The crowd crushed into the station to hail the Bryans' arrival to the accompaniment of "Yankee Doodle" and then sloughed to the hotel lobby to hear the young Congressman, who was so overwhelmed by surprise at this demonstration that he dropped his strong clear voice to softened tones and declared, "This is one time when my mouth won't work well." [1]

The next day Bryan went to Omaha to attend the state Democratic convention, a battleground in this Presidential election year of 1892 for control of the Nebraska Democracy. The Bourbons—Morton and Miller and their allies—had been immensely strengthened by the pronouncements of Grover Cleveland in behalf of gold, by the top priority he accorded to tariff reform, and by his commanding lead for the Presidential nomination. The Nebraska convention would be a Cleveland convention and therefore an opportunity for the Bourbons to cut Bryan down to size. Putting their heads together, they agreed to box in Bryan, muffle his rhetoric, and rough him up a bit, but nothing more. His oratorical ability, his rare capacity for victory, his compelling appeal to youth made his continuation in the party imperative. He could be punished for fraternizing with the Independents and for taking up the heresy of silver, but he must not be alienated to the point of bolting. As the one Nebraska Democrat who could win an election, he was too valuable. The Bourbons soon discovered that they had made two miscalculations: They underestimated Bryan's audacity, and their reading differed from his reading of the political situation. They believed that Bryan was in an impossible position that could lead only to straddle and compromise, which was exactly what they wanted to happen. If Bryan insisted on a silver platform, they reasoned, he would alienate much of the state organization, which could be fatal in what loomed as a close election in the First District. Yet the Bourbons also had to concede that if Bryan failed to stand by silver, he would lose the votes of silver Democrats and Independents.

This first of the two state conventions to be held that year faced the tasks of selecting the delegates to the approaching national convention and of adopting a platform for state and national issues. Bryan was not long in showing his hand. What he did was hardly in the shape of the compromise the Bourbons expected. He announced in the most defiant language that he would not become a delegate at large to a national convention obeisant to the gold-loving Grover Cleveland and as a member of the convention's platform committee, although he found his silver views in a minority, he carried his fight to the floor by moving the addition of a single sentence to the platform: "We declare ourselves in favor of the free coinage of silver."

Politicians eager to dodge the money question cried that the convention should not have to pronounce on the issue since it had been shelved in Congress. Bryan, with his big voice, shouted over the din, "I do not believe it is noble to dodge any issue. Vote this down if you do not approve it, but do not dodge it, for that is not democracy." With the money question now before the convention, the Bourbons, evidently in absolute control, clamped on a gag rule that limited Bryan's oratory, with its dangerously intoxicating effects, to ten minutes. Midway in the angry, shouted debate leading to cloture, a delegate asked Bryan if he was for Cleveland for President. "I am first for Horace Boies," Bryan snapped.

His speech, confined strictly to its allotted time, urged that since the present and only Democratic governor of Nebraska, James Boyd, had been elected on a free silver platform, there must be no abandonment of that commitment. In vivid Biblical metaphor, he presented the silver question as a struggle between good and evil. On one side—silver—were the people; on the other, "the money power." Let the delegates choose. "If the Lord be God, follow Him. If Baal be God, follow him." The delegates were transformed into a cheering, whistling, stomping mob. Then the roll was called, the hall charged with tension. Upon the outcome turned the question of who would lead Nebraska's Democracy: the Bourbons, who always had, or the upstart progressives and their hero, Bryan.

The roll call moved through the counties until Douglas, the largest and perhaps decisive one, was reached. Douglas chose to vote as a unit and, under the unit rule, applied all its votes against Bryan's silver resolution. Before the results were announced, however, Bryan rose and raising his voice above the wild din, shouted that although Douglas would cast its 103 votes as a unit, many men in that delegation were for silver. Soon all the counties had been called, Douglas voting as a unit against silver, and the results were announced: 267 votes for the silver resolution and 237 against. The Bourbon faction, so confident of the outcome, was stupefied. Its leather-lunged spokesmen began to shout, "It isn't right," "You lie," and strings of profane expletives. "It was like a hot chamber in hell," the Omaha *World-Herald* reported. The object of this frenzied attention was the convention secretary, who, after anxiously rechecking his tallies, shuffled to the edge of the stage and said to a hushed and thoroughly confused audience, "I have kept this tally and I will swear by my last drop of blood that the count I have is correct, and I tell you it is 257 for and 247 against." The 10-vote variation from the first announced result and a comparison of many private tallies unleashed waves of demands for a recount. Bryan tried to soothe the convention into holding to the first result, but a recount was taken. Certain that they would be cheated, the silver men, in their turn, now became the angry mob. The recount reversed the original result. It showed 229 yeses and 247 noes. Bryan was defeated; yet for all this sudden trying disaster, he remained to his followers a heroic model of resolution. "Bryan's livid face, compressed lips and defiant eyes," one admirer said, "were a vivid reminder of Edwin Booth in his most dramatic moments."

In the hubbub a delegate introduced a resolution: "that we heartily endorse the actions of Hon. W. J. Bryan as Representative, and extend to him words of good cheer and encouragement in his public work." Most of the Bryan men had stomped off by this time. The resolution was the work of the Morton-Miller regulars, an anxiously proffered peace offering. It was enthusiastically adopted.

Despite Bryan's defeat, the April convention demonstrated that his faction was no longer a mere transitory minority. It had the strength and the will to seize control of the state Democracy.[2]

As for Bryan, he was left with an unobstructed path to renomination for his Congressional seat. Nebraska City, site of the First District's convention, outdid itself in providing symbols of enthusiasm and support. Its business streets and even its residential avenues were filled with bunting, their unsoiled splendor flapping in the prairie wind. The stage of the Opera House, where the convention took place, was laden with ferns and flowers. The only note of disharmony was a huge portrait of former President Cleveland who with stern eye and drooping mustache seemed to view the proceedings with implacable disdain. But even Cleveland was soon forgotten in the single-minded enthusiasm blanketing the convention. The paeans in behalf of Bryan soared to the farthest rafter. That it was strictly his convention became clear at once when Henry M. Boyeston read the poem "Bryan the Brave." Each verse of this unalloyed admiration in iambic pentameter was punctuated by cheers. John D. Calhoun, editor of the Lincoln *Herald,* was accorded the honor of nominating the hero of the day, and Calhoun wisely painted his candidate in the sharpest moral hues, with the final stroke: "He would rather be a doorkeeper in the house of his Lord than to dwell in the tents of wickedness."

When the convention chairman dared inquire facetiously, "I suppose if I asked if there were other nominations, I would be put out," the crowd yelled back good-naturedly, "That's right." Bryan was renominated by acclamation on a platform calling for free coinage of gold and silver "at a just ratio," language somewhat weaker than the plank of 1890, and the undoing of the deed "so clandestinely accomplished by Congress in 1873." Two days after these blows for silver, Grover Cleveland was nominated for the Presidency in a national Democratic convention thoroughly under the thumb of gold men.[3]

For Bryan, the 1892 election loomed as a grim struggle in which his political life was at stake with a host of unfriendly forces poised to make certain his demise. Since his first election, the First District had been recast, presumably in response to the 1890 census, with results that pointed like a dagger to the heart of his fortunes. The most powerful base of his strength, the city of Omaha, was cut off from his district, leaving him no choice but to reflect the decidedly rural character of his redefined constituency in the forthcoming campaign. Bryan was the victim of a blatant gerrymander contrived by Nebraska's Republican legislature.

If reapportionment pushed Bryan toward an agrarian campaign, the nature of his Republican opponent, Allen W. Field, made it imperative. A district judge slightly under forty years of age, Field was prominent in Lincoln, now the largest city of Bryan's district, from which he had been elected to two terms in the state legislature, the second as speaker of the House. The likelihood that Field would garner most of the Lincoln vote was increased by the fact that the two most influential newspapers circulating in the district—the *Nebraska State Journal* and the Omaha *Bee*—supported him. The *Bee*'s publisher, Edward Rosewater, as a national committeeman and director of the Republican Party's Western headquarters, had direct access to his party's ample resources to make good his observation that "any good man ought to beat Bryan, and Judge Field should have no trouble." [4]

Immediately after his renomination, Bryan journeyed to the national convention at Chicago. There he bravely, but vainly, resisted the Cleveland juggernaut by extolling the virtues of the silver-hued Horace Boies as the best available nominee. Even more important, he engaged in a struggle to control the Nebraska delegation. According to the gossip of Nebraska politicos, Governor James E. Boyd was to be elected chairman of the delegation to Chicago and Judge Joseph Ong, a Bryan man, the new member of the national committee. These well-laid plans were kicked asunder by Cleveland's overwhelming strength. The Nebraska Democracy, understandably unwilling to deal itself out of favor by boosting a Bryan silverite for the national committee, chose instead a Bourbon whose acceptability to Cleveland was undoubted—Tobias Castor, otherwise known as "Toburlington" Castor because of his devotion to the railroad. It threw a sop to Bryan by accepting his friend and fellow silverite William H. Thompson as its chairman, but Cleveland's certain nomination reduced Thompson's election to mere symbol.

After Chicago, Bryan rushed on to Washington for the current legislative session, where he and his fellow silverites worked mightily to push through a silver bill, hopeful that their forces might now rally and prevail. But Cleveland's capture of the Presidential nomination and his adamant stand on gold drove House Democrats to his side like cattle seeking cover in a hailstorm. Even though the bill passed the Senate, it was pushed aside in the House to languish for the remainder of the session, prompting Bryan's Nebraska Populist colleague Congressman William McKeighan to rise and declare: "Mr. Speaker, if Wall Street has no more business for this body to do, I move that this house now adjourn." 5

Simple political mathematics showed how desperate Bryan's fight for reelection was. The gerrymandering left him with a district whose voter distribution was estimated to be 13,000 Republicans, 10,000 Democrats, and 8,000 Populists. To win, Bryan had to arrange a fusion or some understanding with the Populists, in addition to mounting a campaign of strong agrarian appeal. The issue which above all others agitated his rural constituents was—everyone knew—silver. If any medicine could save Bryan's endangered political life, it was the white metal.

Bryan engaged in a series of secret conferences with his many personal contacts among the Populists. According to the evidence that seeped through, he persuaded them to postpone their party's convention, which normally met in June or July in the First Congressional District, to the extraordinarily late date of August 11. The step led to accusations that the postponement allowed inadequate time for the Populist nominee, should there be one, to wage an effective campaign and that it also gave Bryan more time for the lengthy politicking necessary to arrange fusion. Sensational reports circulated in the district's political circles. One said that Bryan had concluded an understanding with Charles H. Van Wyck, the likely Populist nominee for governor, whereby Democratic and Populist votes in the First District would be traded on behalf of their respective candidacies. Another foretold that Bryan would become the Populist nominee and in effect that party's director in his district. Many Populists resented these rumored bargains, and others feared that their outrageous character might send many Democratic and Populist voters into the Republican fold.

The Populists' eagerness to maintain their identity was evident when they finally nominated Jerome Shamp for the First Congressional District on August 11 with 60 votes; another aspirant received 22 votes and Bryan a mere 12. But it was one thing for Shamp to win the nomination and another for him to run a serious campaign. Shamp was a former Republican who now said that although he was carrying the Populist banner, he would always abide by "Republican principles." Charles H. Gere of the *Nebraska State Journal*, whose distaste for Bryan was more acrid than in 1890, claimed that the Congressman's campaign manager, T. S. Allen, immediately intimidated Shamp by informing him roughly that he would be in

Bryan's way and would only bring trouble. Gere's accusations did not stop there. He went on to contend that Bryan and McKeighan had made a spectacular deal calling for the interchange of Populist and Democratic votes on a statewide basis.

Other rumors followed. The sheer number and variety of them lent credence to their existence. In the extremity of an election, in which he faced political life and death, the ultramoralistic Bryan had to decide whether his political righteousness allowed him to make deals and employ intimidation and other acts of questionable ethics in order to safeguard the noble ends to which his career was dedicated. If he yielded to this temptation, he could follow a not uncommon tendency among highly moralistic people to do unethical things to advance noble purposes. Doubtless there were deals in Bryan's behalf, but his connection with them, if any, remains obscure. In no reported deal was Bryan mentioned as a negotiating agent. The "dirty work" seems always to have been delegated to trusted subordinates, chiefly to brother-in-law Tom Allen.[6]

A young Lincoln attorney and professional Democrat, Thomas Stinson Allen was credited with "discovering" Bryan even before he ran for office. Allen's achievement was assisted by his presence as a reader of law in 1888 in the firm of Talbot and Bryan, of which he subsequently became a partner. Thoroughly versed in the ways and byways of state and local politics, he managed Bryan's two Congressional races and was bound to him by familial as well as political ties, having married Bryan's sister Nancy, who had followed her brother, whom she idolized, to Lincoln. Tall, like Bryan, she towered over her shorter husband. In the fluid state of Nebraska politics, marked by much movement between the traditional major parties and the new Populist Party, no little of it sparked by sheerest opportunism, Bryan was hard put to find lieutenants who could be trusted. He was fortunate indeed to have political talent of high order in his own family.

Bryan's failure to effect official fusion by winning the Populist nomination drove him to rely heavily on his magnetism as a campaigner and to elevate silver as the dominant issue. But his slide toward silver was toughly resisted by conservative Nebraska Democrats.

The second Democratic state convention of 1892, which met on August 30, outdid itself in demonstrating fealty to Cleveland. Honor fell like manna upon the gold men. J. Sterling Morton was nominated for governor, and Euclid Martin, an Omaha paint manufacturer with large interests in the city and an absolute gold man, was named the new state chairman. The trio of Morton, Martin, and Castor, the national committeeman, solemnly pledged their talents and toil toward bringing about the election of Grover Cleveland. Let the heretic Bryan be elected, they reasoned, and let them win the patronage prizes.[7]

This trio of conservative Democratic leaders realized they must box

Bryan in at the Lincoln convention lest he disrupt it with a heady plea for silver or for fusion or by challenging Morton for the gubernatorial nomination. They resolved to divert him from silver to his old specialty, the tariff.

The stage of Funke's Opera House in Lincoln, where the convention was held, was arranged to give the most flattering homage to Bryan. In its center was a huge picture of him, his handsome countenance contrasting with the stern visages of the national candidates Grover Cleveland and Adlai Stevenson, whose portraits were placed in careful subordination on either side of him. Beneath the three portraits was a streamer, with words whose sentiments obviously referred to Bryan and to Bryan alone. They acknowledged his prowess, not for the cause of silver, but for the cause of tariff reform. "The people of Nebraska," the bold words proclaimed, "find their champion here, not in Ohio."

"In Ohio" was a reference to William McKinley, the most popular personality of the Republican Party and author of the tariff law bearing his name. Earlier that year, McKinley, retaliating for Bryan's previous invasion of Ohio, had come to Nebraska at Edward Rosewater's invitation and declaimed to audiences in Omaha, Lincoln, and Beatrice that Bryan erred on the tariff. Bryan, not overlooking the publicity involved in attacking a politician of major national reputation, rose to the bait. He accepted the triumvirate's invitation to deliver the principal address of the convention and their stipulation that it must deal with the tariff.

Everything went swimmingly. Bryan made a brilliant speech, spurred by the attention he knew his attack on McKinley would command. He probably went along with the tariff theme from a realization that it was a Cleveland year, and, therefore, a gold year. In the dangerous race he was running, he could well use any help from the state Democratic organization. In his desire to keep his Congressional seat, he would again soft-pedal his beliefs and blur his ideology. To win, he must satisfy both his electorate in the revised first district and the Democratic and Populist organizations whose willingness to back him held the key to his future.

The convention, having dutifully nominated Morton for governor and adopted Cleveland's Chicago platform, left silver an unmentioned subject but wisely gave its leading progressive his innings. With a mighty shout, it adopted a resolution "that we endorse the course of Hon. W. J. Bryan in Congress and point with pride to him as a resolute and brilliant champion of the masses against the classes." The likelihood is that a bargain was struck between Bryan and the conservative triumvirate. By its terms, they may have promised to help Bryan in return for his pledge to help Morton. But what titillated the triumvirate most was that they had been spared a Bryan oration on silver.

For the tight race he faced, Bryan needed all possible help. Without funds of his own for a costly campaign, he turned for financial aid to untoward places, sending a campaign aide, Jefferson H. Broady, to the silver-producing states to collect donations from the mineowners. Broady's "passing of the corn popper," as it was called, yielded some $4,000. Although he would one day criticize his Republican opponents for collecting from industries that profited from a high protective tariff, Bryan always contended that the collections were innocent of ulterior motive, such as influencing legislation. However, it was a hostile newspaper, not he, that disclosed the gifts a year after the election.

More respectable succor was provided by Gilbert M. Hitchcock, publisher of the Omaha *World-Herald,* the paper with the widest circulation in the First Congressional District. Hitchcock summoned his ace political reporter, Richard L. Metcalfe, from his post in Washington to cover the campaign and aid Bryan. The columns of the *World-Herald* sounded the tocsin for Democratic-Populist fusion and beseeched readers to contribute funds to the Bryan campaign. Good friends like Jim Dahlman journeyed from the western end of the state at their own expense to help in the struggle, and devoted supporters everywhere contributed their pennies and dollars.

Midway in the campaign, the Bryan-Morton concordat of peace dissolved into recriminations. In speeches, Bryan declared that he would not be diverted from espousing the silver cause by other men of his party—meaning Morton. The gubernatorial candidate declared from the stump, in mildest candor, that regretfully he must disagree with Bryan, convinced as he was that the young Congressman was wrong on the money question. Bryan men seized these temperate remarks and contended, with fierce exaggeration, that Morton was really hostile to Bryan and that anyone with an ounce of love for silver in his veins had no choice but to vote for the Populist Van Wyck for governor.

Bryan himself insisted that he and Morton were friendly and that he was in no way party to the stirrings against the gubernatorial candidate. But rumors kept recurring until Morton was convinced that silver Democrats as a body were conspiring against him. "They are thickest among Bryan's friends," Morton wrote to his sister Emma, "and seek to trade me off for Van Wyck to get in exchange votes for Bryan." Morton held to this opinion even though veteran political friends assured him that the rumors of a deal were "absolutely without foundation," and added that "the people who get wild over 'rumors' must be very young in politics." [8]

Morton, too, was playing a game. Although professing his desire for Bryan's reelection, he spoke against Bryan's key issue, silver, while resolutely advocating tariff reform. Morton's main interest was in helping Cleveland and laying the foundation for the reward this devotion eventually earned him—a place in the new President's Cabinet. The confusion of Bryan extolling silver and Morton praising gold amused Edward Rosewater, who predicted, "There are going to be some very cross-eyed Democrats in the First district who are endeavoring to believe Morton and vote for Bryan." [9]

Bryan committed his seemingly infinite strength and endurance to a speaking schedule that would kill a truck horse. As in 1890, every town, hamlet, and crossroads saw his presence. Weeping Water, Syracuse, Elmwood, Union, South Omaha—communities of all shapes and sizes—heard his voice and arguments. County fairs, which nicely coincided with the electoral schedule and afforded large, made-to-order audiences, were a favorite port of call.

At the Elmwood fair, he spoke to a crowd of more than 3,000. They were drawn less by his superb oratory than by the presence of twenty speed horses and by farm exhibits and a trade display that connoisseurs of such matters spoke of as comparable in quality with the state fair. At the Washington County fair at Blair, an even larger audience was augmented by 1,500 schoolchildren on holiday, admitted free. After speaking at the kite-shaped track, Bryan took a walking tour through the grounds and exhibit halls at a snail's pace, greeting and talking with hundreds of beaming constituents.

The campaign's high point was a series of eleven debates between Bryan and Field, running from September 12 to October 15. The contests began in the New Lansing Theatre in Lincoln, before a standing-room-only audience. Field started strong, delighting his supporters by coupling "calamity-howling" Democrats with drought and grasshoppers as Nebraska's foremost scourges, but he quickly demonstrated his ineptitude as an orator by reading, in uninspired tones, a lengthy statement on the tariff filled with figures and windy quotations from official reports. Bryan's presentation, with its ringing tones and simple, vivid argument, was in effective contrast.

In their forensic journeys through Nebraska, Bryan and Field carried gripsacks laden with pieces of dry goods, red flannel, and samples of cutlery, which were valued props in their tariff debates. Field would hold them up to his audiences as examples of good Nebraska produce at fair prices, manufactured in the era of the McKinley Tariff. Bryan, in his turn, proclaimed his pride in Nebraska's output but added that whenever he saw a fat steer, he reflected that the animal owed not a single ounce of its flesh to the protective tariff.

Bryan then would lay out his own valise on a table, saying, "I am something of a travelling man myself." Holding up his collection of butcher knives and dress goods, he would launch his attack against the high protective tariff, relating how on a recent trip to Mexico, he discovered that American-made cutlery sold for 50 percent less there than back home. The manufacturer, he said, thanks to the tariff wall, could charge the United States customer any price he chose, after which he could dump the surplus on the foreign market and still profit on a 25 to 50 percent reduction in price. Bryan next moved to the contrasting wretched prices received by the farmer. "What did you get for your wheat last year?" Bryan called out, and a chorus of rural voices answered, "Eighty-five cents." And Bryan, "What did you get this year?" "Fifty cents." "Great is protection," proclaimed Bryan, his hands raised. "And yet my opponent insists that you should buy his goods in order to keep some of his eastern friends warm and make them comfortable."

Toward his opponent, Bryan was a model of courtesy, generosity, and forbearance, listening smilingly to attacks on himself. As the debates wore on, and Bryan's forensic skill kept rolling up advantages, Field's thrusts became bolder and sharper, until they touched Bryan's rawest political nerves. How could Bryan, asked Field, support both silver and his party's Presidential candidate, Grover Cleveland, a staunch gold man? "Whatever may be the view of other Democrats," Bryan answered, "I propose to give my every endeavor and my earnest effort to the passage of a free coinage law. Though I should be left alone . . . I would not be turned from my course by the attitude of any other man in my party." Suppose, Field persisted, the Presidential election were thrown into the House of Representatives? Would Bryan vote for the Populist Presidential candidate, General James B. Weaver, or Cleveland? Bryan answered candidly that he preferred Weaver, but that as an elected Democrat he would vote for Cleveland. Likewise, he added, he would vote for Cleveland at the polls in November.[10]

Field's friends circulated a letter contending that Bryan was at heart a prohibitionist, a charge that clanged like a death bell in the hard-drinking, saloon-ridden Nebraska frontier land. Bryan worked overtime declaring his hostility to prohibition, and the Omaha *World-Herald* rushed to his defense by informing its readers that the prohibition charge was a canard based on a letter being circulated from a man in Illinois who was an old enemy of Bryan's father. Field stirred other broths of local prejudice. Bryan, he said, was Irish, and therefore he was also Catholic. Furthermore, the local Ancient Order of Hibernians was helping him. When this blatant appeal to Know-Nothingism had no evident effect, in almost a complete turnaround, Field denounced Bryan as a nativist connected with the American Protective Association, and anti-Catholic secret society, a potentially mortal charge in view of the heavy numbers of European émigrés in Bryan's constituency. The powerful Edward Rosewater charged that money raised in the Second District, whose fiscal strength was due to its inclusion of Omaha, would be used by the Bryan men in the First District to sway the saloon crowd and other votes that could be bought. But the evidence is clear that the Field men were casting their own sins upon Bryan. In Lincoln, they exploited the powerful whiskey interests by ordering the city's saloonkeepers to work against Bryan or face a likely rejection of their license renewals.[11]

Bryan fought not only Field but the national Republican Party, which seemed to regard him as a towering menace who had best be stamped out now and for all time. Stellar Republicans led by no less than William McKinley and Joseph B. Foraker, a former governor of Ohio and a flamboyant orator, rushed into the state. The Omaha *World-Herald* reported that a huge fund donated by Republican magnates around the nation was pouring in to underwrite Bryan's destruction. The *Herald's* correspondent learned from a Republican leader in Stella, Nebraska, that $20,000 had already been brought from the East to beat Bryan and that four times that sum would be supplied instantly upon word that it was needed. The reason for this money was Bryan's poisonous propaganda for free silver. "If he hadn't talked so much of free silver he might have stood half a show, but now he is up the shoot." [12]

Bryan's most delicate relationships were with his political cousins the Populists or Independents. His Populist opponent, Jerome Shamp, had but one function in the campaign—to draw away votes from Bryan to make Field's victory a certainty. For the good Populists who helped nominate him, Shamp turned out to be a colossal mistake. They did not know their man. Hardly had the campaign begun when, to their consternation, Shamp was exposed as one who was anything but a Populist. The astute Richard Metcalfe, the Omaha *World-Herald* reporter, uncovered evidence that Field's law partner, in behalf of the Republican state central committee, had delivered to Shamp's brother a 1,000-mile railroad ticket for the Populist candidate's personal use. Soon the mails were loaded with flaming posters depicting Shamp as one who "was owned body, soul, and breeches by the bloody corporations." The Lincoln Independent Committee for the First District investigated the charges and found that Shamp had indeed received the ticket but had returned it upon the advice of friends.

Independent leaders of statewide and national reputation regarded Shamp as an alien to their cause and worked eagerly for Bryan's victory. Mrs. Mary E. Lease, "the People's Joan of Arc," who won national fame with her fiery counsel to farmers—"Let 'em raise less corn and more hell"— spoke in Omaha and Lincoln on Bryan's behalf, and the Populist candidate for President, General James B. Weaver, orated for Bryan in Lincoln. Bryan reciprocated by speaking for Weaver's Presidential candidacy while refusing to take to the stump for Cleveland. The Independent Congressman, William A. McKeighan of the Third District, praised Bryan to the voters of the First District as one who "worked and labored for the passage of the silver bill with as much earnestness as it was possible for any man to give to any measure."

McKeighan spoke bluntly to voters of the First District: "While I am an Independent and desire the success of the Independent party, I cannot see how the Independents of your district could in any way assist in the defeat of Mr. Bryan, when all that they could derive from his defeat would be to place a man in Congress from your district that would vote against all the measures that the people's party is supporting, while Mr. Bryan supported all of them." Bryan for his part, reciprocated with expressions of assurance of his harmony with genuine Populists. Between himself and a Populist like McKeighan, he said, "There was no essential difference . . . except in name." [13] McKeighan's pronouncements sparked further rumors of a deal by which Independents would vote for Bryan while progressive Democrats of the First District voted for Van Wyck rather than Morton. Fuel was added to Morton's uneasiness when an informant in Lincoln wrote that ". . . here Bryan's 'fool friends' talk a good deal about voting for Van Wyck. They say there is no chance to elect you. . . ."

Bryan became a master at structuring his sentences so that simultaneously the silverites were pleased and the tariff reformers were not offended. "I don't know anything about free silver," he confessed to one rural audience. "The People of Nebraska are for free silver and I am for free silver. I will look up the arguments later." Low-tariff Democrats responded favorably when they learned that Bryan, queried by Independents anxious over his attitude on silver, replied that he had been so busy with the tariff in Congress that he had had no time to study the money question. Such modesty was feigned, for Bryan was by now thoroughly versed in its intricacies. J. Sterling Morton, witnessing these political acrobatics, observed sourly, "Bryan is so self-adjusting that—in his fine flexibility—he can agree with a greater number of persons who hold different views on the same question than any pinfeathered economist I have ever met." [14] In effect, the disdainful Morton was acknowledging the triumph of ambition over belief and ideology in Bryan's candidacy. With his political survival at stake, Bryan was freely trimming and adjusting his positions on the tariff and silver.

Further proof of Bryan's political agility could be found in Lincoln on election eve. Two great jubilant hordes marched, whistled, sang, and shouted his name through the capital's streets. One was Populist, the other Democratic. The spokesmen for these separate tides of humanity had a common message. J. Sterling Morton muted his discontent and declared: "No friend of mine, no Democrat, can vote against Bryan." The Populist spokesman was equally emphatic: "I have been travelling over the silver states and I am commissioned by the people's independent party of nine states to come here and say to you, of the first district of Nebraska, for God's sake, do not help the gold bugs of Wall Street by permitting them to defeat W. J. Bryan for Congress."

One veteran Republican leader declared that in the face of this miraculous unity of Populists and Democrats, his own GOP was "hanging on by its eyebrows." [15]

The people spoke, and a tally of their votes made their pronouncement clear, except for one office. Grover Cleveland was elected President; Nebraska's electoral votes, to no one's surprise, went Republican. The governor and other state officers and three of six Congressmen were Republican. Two of the remaining Congressmen, Populists Omer Kern and McKeighan, were reelected. The single unsettled question was—who was elected in the First Congressional District?

The known results revealed that the Populist Shamp had run a poor third, but Field and Bryan were so close that neither dared claim victory. On the morning after election day, the outlying counties were yet to be heard from, and their word would settle the question. For all the suspense and strain, for all the waiting for a decision that could perhaps in one breath snuff out his political career in its mere infancy, Bryan was a model of benign calm. The day after the election, he visited his Democratic headquarters, which, like that of the nearby Republicans, was jammed with anxious party workers. When an authoritative telegram arrived from one far county giving Field a margin of 116 votes, jubilant Republicans streamed out into the street to march with horns and hurrahs, while Democrats watched in gloom.

Midway in the triumphal procession, the returns from another county arrived, with news of a Bryan victory by 54 votes. Out marched the Democrats in jubilant redemption; back slunk the Republicans. For two days more the reports trickled in, seesaw style, and by the fourth day both parties were united in hoarseness and exhaustion. They were also wary. Watchers took their turn guarding the ballot boxes in every county, day and night.

At last, on the afternoon of the fourth day, the results became clear; the official totals were announced. By a razor-thin margin of 140 votes Bryan was the winner.

By any analysis the victory was extraordinary. Bryan led Morton, the Democratic gubernatorial nominee, in every county of the First Congressional District, from a low of 500 votes in Otoe County to a high of 1,600 in Richardson. He garnered more votes in his district than Cleveland and Weaver combined. While Bryan squeaked through to victory in the district, Morton was overwhelmed, losing it by 5,500 votes. In the state at large, Morton ran a poor third, trailing Van Wyck by nearly 25,000 votes, who ran nearly 10,000 behind the victorious Republican Lorenzo Crounse.[16]

Bryan withstood a massive assault of all means, fair and foul, against him: the decoy of Shamp, a Republican disguised as a Populist to beguile votes from him; the flood of Eastern money; the premier Republican national personalities who invaded the campaign; the merciless railroad influence; the ferocity of the Republican press and of Field's attack. Yet he somehow prevailed. As in 1890, he continued to enjoy distinction as Nebraska's only Democratic Congressman. Well could he say, in what for him was rare understatement, that "under the circumstances" he was satisfied.

Bryan won because he had developed a political personality which fitted the demands of an electoral campaign. On the stump he was an extrovert, confident, glad-handing, mingling easily with the crowds. He succeeded at politics because he loved politics, the oratory, the fight, the contacts with the people—whom he revered. He had overcome an earlier tendency as an idealist to shun the drab, mechanical, workaday aspects of politics, the local clubs and caucuses. He had learned to work easily in these humdrum appurtenances of political management and to comprehend their indispensable contribution to electoral success.

Bryan was made for Western audiences. His supreme gifts of oratory brought excitement and hope into their lives of plodding toil and economic distress. His flamboyance, sincerity, volubility, his impregnable self-confidence harmonized with the life-style and values of the frontier-land culture. Like his Western followers, he was unaffected, often the mark of the crusader. Bryan's power was his native force. His only mannerism was his taste for low collars and clerical ties, which gave him the appearance of a Kentucky judge, an air which pleased his audiences as a reminder that they were not merely new settlers but hailed from backlands of culture and worthy tradition.

Bryan's ease in politics was facilitated by a ready humor. Willa Cather, as a college student, was struck by this gift in her first encounter with Bryan, which transpired on a streetcar in his first Congressional campaign. Returning from an address in a nearby town, Bryan carried a huge, ungainly floral offering, doubtless a reward from his admirers, that was partially concealed by a wrapping of tissue paper. On the crowded streetcar, he had some difficulty keeping his floral piece out of the way of his fellow passengers. A talkative old lady sitting next to him asked sympathetically, "Is it for a funeral?" Bryan looked quizzically at his treasure and replied politely, "Well, I hope not, madam."

Although Bryan exuded moral purpose on the stump and lived in rectitude, his bearing did not seem oppressive to those around him. No fellow political worker complained that Bryan's morality was grating. Newspapermen who followed him on his campaigns and who probably are more sensitive than most to moral pretensions did not cavil at Bryan's manner. In private, Bryan wore his morality lightly. He did not seek to make converts. He was quick with humor, often employed in self-deprecation. Newspapermen first discovered that Bryan was a teetotaler not from any private highminded pronouncement on the subject—this he seldom did—but from a quiet episode they almost overlooked. After a campaign rally, Bryan and several reporters were riding back to their hotel when one suggested a stop for beer at the next saloon. Bryan quietly declined, saying simply, "I never touch the stuff." The reporters' thoughts quickly flew back over their association with him and found that what he said was indeed true, a fact that had utterly eluded them.

Bryan's high moral purpose was accompanied by incessant physical activity. At his home there was no rest. To anyone who knew them, it was utterly inconceivable that either Bryan or Mary should ever dawdle or loaf or engage in frivolous talk. The minds and tastes of husband and wife were always in step. They read the same books, discussed political issues and Bryan's stands. Mary knew every word of his first major Congressional address, on the tariff, and when Bryan delivered it, her lips moved, repeating the familiar phrases under her breath. Mary did much of the research for apt quotations and historical references for her husband's speeches. Some days before his tariff presentation was scheduled, Bryan delivered a eulogy for a dead colleague. Mary was in the gallery, noting the tones and gestures best suited to the House chamber. Then she and Bryan reconsidered the tariff speech as thoughtfully as an actor and director delineating an interpretation of a role.

With Bryan so absorbed in politics, many duties of his law office fell upon Mary, but like Bryan, her first love was politics. A woman of intellect, she handled easily the current topics of political debate, knew the political personalities Bryan dealt with, and was shrewder than he in assessing them. She had time only for serious endeavor and was seldom seen in public except for political meetings and university lectures. Her chief indulgence was a Wednesday morning swim with ladies of the university, her principal friends. She gave little attention to dress, for which the Eastern press one day criticized her. Her world centered on her husband, and she was confident that his beliefs and talents would be the salvation of the West.

Bryan was sustained by religious principles and moral generalities to such a degree that he never pondered and debated what to men of lesser faith would seem the painful dilemmas of political life, with their barbed intertwining complexities for which the canons of right and wrong were unclear. In making the moral decisions presented by his two Congressional campaigns, Bryan left behind no trail of doubts of searching thought and inquiry. For the thorny questions of political life, the general directives of the Bible and his moral upbringing were adequate. Where political necessity required that he modulate his views or even engage in conduct utterly hostile to them—as in his rejection of prohibition in 1890—Bryan automatically spread a blanket of self-justification over anything he did. He was a pragmatic ideologist and one who did not quail at occasionally permitting pragmatism to prevail over ideology. He valued immediate results. He preferred a half step forward to no step at all and was not loath to take several steps backward to a position from which many future strides forward might be executed.

Once when asked why he kept no carbon copies of his letters, he said the precaution was entirely unnecessary. All he need do was to see the original letter which prompted his own, and he would immediately recall the principle that governed his answer. Whatever letters there were were always brief and controlled. No associate—Mary, Charley, Tom Allen, or any one among his host of political friends or foes—made the slightest suggestion that he ever found any conflict between what he did and a possible framework of larger philosophical beliefs. Bryan's life was either all on the surface or seldom far below it.

That Bryan had little inner life is suggested by his library, that spacious, cluttered workroom in his D Street home. The walls were hung with mediocre old-fashioned engravings of early statesmen that were there because Bryan liked them. His books on political economy were not the works of the field's best talent, but favored one-sided tracts and treatises. The poetry was didactic or declamatory. The fiction tended strongly to the classics; the most recent was Thackeray. There were many of the old classics and French and Latin books, well worn, because Bryan apparently referred to them constantly, doubtless for his speeches. There was a good supply of the writings of early American statesmen, whom he was prone to emulate, with pages well marked in the manner of a student's annotations. Few books in evidence were valuable for their art or style.

If Bryan did not lose himself in books, neither did he lose himself in intimate friendships. In Jacksonville and Lincoln he was a man without close friends. There was nothing of familiarity in his manner. "You never came any closer to him than just within range of his voice," wrote one who observed him well. He loved and served the "people" collectively, but he kept them at arm's length individually. Only to his family, or, more precisely, only to Mary, his brother Charles, and to his brother-in-law Tom Allen did he accord his confidence and trust. Although he was favored with a band of devoted political workers, whose toil was indispensable to his electoral victories, their ranks remain largely faceless to history. No one became his intimate, no one his protégé. Under Bryan's generalship, no great captains developed.

To Willa Cather, Bryan embodied a perfect synthesis of the West, "all its newness and vigor, its magnitude and monotony, its richness and lack of variety, its inflammability and volubility, its strength and its crudeness, its high seriousness and self-confidence, its egotism and its nobility." [17]

10. The Silver Craze

Almost immediately after his hairline victory, the Nebraska political calendar hurtled Bryan into still another electoral crisis. Nebraska had to choose a United States Senator. Since the popular election of Senators was still many years away, the office was filled in Nebraska, as in most states, by joint vote of the two houses of the state legislature.

For Bryan to aspire to the Senate was altogether in accord with political logic. Since he was one of several leading Democrats of the state and the only national elective officeholder of his party, his ambition was predictable. Victory would bring him superior rewards: an office statewide in dimension. He would be Senator "below the Platte," a region more wealthy, populous, and influential than the domain of the Senator "above the Platte." Indeed, as the Kansas City *Times* perceived, Bryan, if elected, would represent the entire Northwest Democracy in the Senate, for not a single Democrat from the upper Mississippi Valley was in that body. A Senatorship would improve Bryan's claim to the nuggets of federal patronage, and he would enjoy the luxury of a six-year term in contrast with the harrowing biennial crisis of the House. It was far from a surprise, therefore, when on November 19, 1892, Edward Rosewater disclosed in the Omaha *Bee* that Bryan had let it be known that he wanted the Senatorship.

If the Senate seat was valuable to Bryan, it was also valuable to other leading politicians, and several special circumstances of the election whetted their interest. The national Senate was evenly divided between Republicans and Democrats plus five Populists and one vacancy. The tendencies of the next Senate might be shaped no little by the results in Nebraska. Furthermore, the distribution of party strength in the state legislature was indecisive, fostering a climate that encouraged candidacies to blossom. The Republicans and the Populists each had 53 votes, and the Democrats a mere 17. Clearly the path to victory was fusion between one of the older parties with the Populists.

With the situation so unclear, candidates flocked to the battleground, and the fast-growing list of the Democratic, Republican, and Populist entrants read like a Nebraskan political *Who's Who*. The crowded field encouraged alliances and bargaining and put a premium on money. Having, as usual, no money to set up campaign headquarters in a Lincoln hotel, as his competitors did, and pressed by urgent Congressional business requiring his presence in Washington, Bryan was given little hope. Arrayed against him was the Morton-Miller alliance, the Republican Party, and certain Populists. Bryan's chief trouble, reported his friend John D. Calhoun, editor of the Lincoln *Herald,* was that "Back of the candidacy of sundry democrats lies a jealousy of you, and it has been decreed that you are not to be elected. I am told that you would lack six Democrats at a pinch—but that you will not be allowed to have the 'pinch.' . . . The main trouble is that the Big Chiefs are against you, and the multitude that is for you has neither time nor money to spend in the lobby."

From Washington, Bryan set the ground rules of his candidacy in a letter to an emissary in Lincoln, C. D. Casper. "While I would prize an election myself," Bryan wrote, "you must not allow my interests to prevent election of an anti-Republican. Our national alliance is with the Independents. Let my friends so act that I cannot be blamed if a Republican is elected. I agree with Democratic Senators that any Independent is better than a Republican Senator. Show this to Democratic members. Rush." [1]

In the next uncertain weeks, fears burned like fever that enough Populist votes might be bought to elect a Republican or that Morton was so obsessed with stopping Bryan that he too might back a Republican. The reverse strategy also loomed, by which Republicans might unite and elect one of Bryan's Democratic foes, Morton or Boyd. Fusion became difficult to swallow when some Populists insisted that in any fusion their candidate, rather than any Democrat, must be elected. Out of the welter of rising and falling candidates a winner, William V. Allen, a Populist, finally emerged. An old friend and brother-in-faith of Bryan, Allen was a political hybrid, not unusual in the shifting party loyalties of the day. A former Republican who voted for Samuel J. Tilden in 1876, an unsuccessful Independent Republican candidate for Congress in the eighties, Allen had risen fast in the new Populist Party. In 1892, he was president of the party's state convention. A rival deemed him "a very sly as well as a very shrewd politician." By throwing the Democratic votes he commanded over to Allen, Bryan provided the margin of victory. C. D. Casper wrote the young Congressman from Lincoln that the word "all over the state" was that "eleven Bryan men elected Judge Allen." As *quid pro quo* for this vital support, Allen agreed to stand by Bryan on patronage and free coinage. "We told him," Casper wrote of a conference with Allen, "we wanted a Senator who would go among the silver Senators and organize opposition to Cleveland appointees in executive session" if the President attempted to punish Bryan because of his silver views.[2]

Although Bryan did not become Senator, he was able to elect a man thoroughly acceptable to himself. Nonetheless, the harrowing uncertainties of the shadowed bargainings and sly maneuverings of legislative politics redoubled Bryan's belief in the urgency of popular election of United States Senators. In this, his first application to state politics of the principle of fusion which led to his Congressional victory, he gained further insight into fusion as the key to his own future dominance of Nebraska politics. His thank you note to his friends was a model of generosity. "I have received good even beyond my deserts, and I accept defeat without complaint. I ask my friends not to cherish resentment against anyone who may have contributed to the result." [3]

Bryan's most powerful antagonist in the Nebraska Senate struggle was the disapproving, if removed, figure of his national party leader, President-elect Grover Cleveland. He openly expressed his hostility by naming Bryan's chief foe, J. Sterling Morton, as his Secretary of Agriculture. As if to italicize his feelings, Cleveland appointed Morton promptly upon conclusion of the Nebraska struggle.

Contemplating the prospects of his approaching administration, Cleveland was haunted by the specter of the silver Democrats of the House and Senate. "I don't like to think that there are alleged Democrats in Congress who do not desire the success of our Administration," he wrote to his future Secretary of the Treasury, John G. Carlisle, "but it is hard to keep such thoughts out of my head." For Democrats "who are heedless of the . . . duty our party owes to the people," Cleveland had already determined upon both treatment and punishment. "They must not expect me to 'turn the other cheek,' " he wrote, "by rewarding their conduct with patronage."

The President-elect made other moves to contain the gathering storm. Speaker Crisp was informed that Cleveland would not object to his reelection, provided he would reconstitute the membership and in some cases not reappoint the chairmen of the House committees most involved with monetary policy. Among the victims specifically designated for his purge was Bryan because of his "violent free silver tendencies." In his candid interdictions, Cleveland also let it be known that unless Congress repealed the Sherman Silver Purchase Act by his inaugural, he might summon it into special session to do so.[4]

Cleveland's ominous gestures did not for a moment deter Bryan from reaffirming his place at the forefront of the legions fighting for free silver. In the lame-duck Congress that met in cantankerous debate until the day of the inaugural, he was a key participant in the House's review of several measures that would abet Cleveland in throttling free silver. The Andrews-Cate bill called simultaneously for repeal of the Sherman Act and for empowering the national banks to increase the circulation of their notes. Other legislation would repeal the existing law and tax on state banknote issues. In his best oratorical style, in simple pungent arguments, Bryan opposed repeal of the Sherman Act on grounds that it would contract the currency and topple the price of both silver and farm products, thus placing a millstone on the back of the debtor. Repeal of what Bryan called "that cowardly makeshift," the Sherman Act, would make even more unlikely the restoration of genuine bimetallism. Helped by the aging, prestigious "Silver Dick" Bland, Bryan's impassioned leadership repulsed the attempt to repeal the Sherman Act. But the narrow margin of the victory, 153 to 142, augured ill for a future that would bring into the Presidency the resolute Cleveland, who already was set upon employing the enormous powers of the office to eradicate the silver heresy.

Bryan was also occupied in the lame-duck Congress with defeating a gold bond bill that in effect would cancel some $346,000,000 of greenbacks as fast as they were redeemed. Here, too, Bryan detected a diabolical plot to contract the currency and "to secure a solemn declaration from Congress that gold is the only coin and that silver is no longer legal tender money." Bryan's Herculean oratory was handsomely rewarded; the bond proposal was easily defeated.

In the emerging contest between the David and Goliath of Democratic politics, the youthful orator, this mere member of the House of Representatives, had drawn first blood against the future incumbent of the nation's mightiest political office. These two gladiators preparing themselves for inevitable conflict possessed striking similarities and differences as political personalities. Both were prone to view political issues such as the money question through moralistic lenses. In his devotion to "sound money" Cleveland was as much an ideologist as the silver-minded Bryan. Both had confidence in the people's judgment. Neither was given to compromise. In fact, if an inch were to be given here or there, Bryan would be the more likely of the two to do it. ". . . I have never seen the day," Cleveland wrote in the winter before his inaugural, "since I consented to drift with events that I have not cursed myself for yielding; and in these particular days I think I curse a little more heartily than ever." Both Bryan and Cleveland saw in stark outline the rich prize that would fall to the winner of their struggle. They were fighting for nothing less than control of the future course of the Democratic Party.[5]

Bryan continued to steep himself in the intricate lore of silver. From his Washington bookseller, Robert Beall, he obtained an assortment of monographs and treatises whose sober scholarship probably found few readers among professional politicians of the day. From the Treasury Department, he obtained the *Statistical Abstract* for 1892 and pored over the information on American cotton, wheat, and corn crops since 1870, with special interest in their farm value and market and export prices. From Cleveland's Secretary of the Treasury, John G. Carlisle, he asked for and got information on the quantities of United States government bonds outstanding, on bonds deposited with the U.S. Treasury by national banks to secure their circulating notes, and on the quantity of bonds held by the Treasurer of the United States to secure federal moneys in national banks designated as public depositories. All this was largely gloss upon the two years of hard study Bryan had already devoted to silver. He read through stacks of books on the subject, with Mary helping in their review. At the Library of Congress, she took notes from weighty tomes and selected from their numbers those of special value to take home and to pore over in the evening at Bryan's side.[6]

In the spring of 1893, as the silver movement gained momentum, Bryan was an indefatigable participant and leader in silver conferences and conventions, where new organizations were formed, structures rearranged, and fresh resolves taken. Bryan's zealous presence kept him at the forefront of the crowded field of emerging silver leaders and provided him an indispensable opportunity to build and mend the fences of personal relationships vital in fusion politics.

Accordingly, in that lively spring and summer of 1893, he seems always to be arriving or departing for meetings on the silver question. He made a speaking tour of the West and South with the vigor of a candidate and the zeal of a crusader. He thrilled the Trans-Mississippi Congress, meeting at Ogden, Utah, with an overwhelming denunciation of Cleveland's view of the currency issue and a plea for a fusion of silver Democrats, Republicans, and Populists, a combination, he was confident, that could overcome the *de facto* alliance of conservative Democrats and Republicans. The congress' invitation to Bryan was couched in the simple, true observation that "your reputation as an orator in defense of Western country interests has permeated the Western country. . . ." Everywhere that Bryan went became a scene of glittering triumph. He passed with flying colors the test of a cold-eyed intellectual audience in a banquet address to the University of Michigan Democratic Club at Ann Arbor. The warmth of his reception at Atlanta, where he spoke to the Young Men's Democratic League, gave heart to Populists and progressive Democrats. One correspondent who witnessed this triumphal climax of a Southern tour exclaimed in his dispatch, "Bryan of Nebraska has captivated the people of the South as he captivated the people of his own state." [7]

No gathering was too modest in importance to command Bryan's appearance. He would come when other emerging silver leaders would not. At the Bimetallic State Convention at Topeka, Kansas, he was the only one of a half dozen out-of-state guests who appeared, and a great crowd showered him with enthusiasm.

Bryan's untiring crusading was spurred when the Panic of 1893 seized the country. Only two months after Cleveland's inauguration, waves of business distress from Europe and Australia reached American shores. Major railroads, such as the Union Pacific and the Santa Fe, passed into the hands of receivers; the Reading failed. Bank failures spread like contagion, worst of all in rural areas and in the West and South. Within a year, 4,000,000 jobless were walking the streets in factory towns. The Pillsbury flour mills were forced to buy wheat with scrip; Southern farmers could not sell their cotton because purchasers could not find money to buy it. In nearly every large city committees were set up to provide food for the unemployed, and in many communities public agencies took over the burdening task.

Why did the panic strike? All sorts of explanations emerged. The trusts with their commonly attendant overspeculation; labor unrest, particularly the Homestead strike, which reduced purchasing power; the collapse of markets abroad; the long-persisting agricultural depression; the silver agitation—all were blamed.

Bryan, like other silver orators, had his own single, simple explanation of the complex economic disaster, which he articulated in his home city of Lincoln at an open-air meeting of the Bimetallic League in which a crowd of 3,000 stood jammed like baled wheat. The present crisis, he cried, was caused, not by the Sherman Silver Purchase Act, as certain comfortable Easterners claimed, but "by the monied sharks of Wall Street trying to frighten Congress into issuing bonds." [8]

Bryan's speeches told of an evil world that framed dark plots and launched secret maneuvers against the white metal. The chicanery extended beyond Wall Street and the East to arrogant English financiers, who pressured India into suspending the coinage of silver without the least consultation with the United States. The lesson for America was plain. "It is time," cried Bryan, that "we act for ourselves and not be consulting England." [9]

Grover Cleveland too entertained definite ideas concerning the cause and cure of the panic. It was, he believed, a business problem that the business community must work out. Government, of course, must not aggravate the depression, a maxim that in Cleveland's eyes was violated by the Sherman Silver Purchase Act of 1890. The act, the President was distressed to find, sent men rushing in panic to exchange the silver certificates, issued under its provisions, for gold, fearful that the Treasury's gold reserves would soon be depleted. The endless parade of men clamoring to divest themselves of certificates spurred a swift outflow of the Treasury's gold reserves. Cleveland subscribed to the widely prevailing view that the Treasury must maintain a gold reserve of at least $100,000,000 if the gold standard was to be preserved. As a key response to the depression, therefore, he summoned Congress into special session and requested that the Sherman Act be repealed.

Such a situation promised an enormous boost for Bryan's political career. The importance Cleveland attached to the silver issue, the dogmatic uncompromising tenor of his message, focused national attention on it. To a rising young politician like Bryan, the gathering struggle was also an opportunity to recast the hierarchy of the silver forces. It would create a new fluidity, permitting fresh leaders to emerge and would bring into the open the question of whether Richard P. Bland, whose name was stamped on the best silver legislation but who was an aging, indifferent orator, would give way to a younger champion, more daring, impassioned, and moving—in other words, Bryan. Here was his chance to be no longer merely an officeholder; he could push to the forefront of a political movement that was swiftly changing from regional to national dimensions. Happily, Bryan's ideology and his ambition coincided. He could, in good faith, commit his talent and energy to promoting silver and himself.

Bryan lost not a moment in the rushing to the front lines of the struggle. In a caucus of House Democrats held promptly after Cleveland's message, he demanded that the President's proposal for the Sherman Act's repeal be rejected. In another caucus, several days later, while others in his party searched for compromises and alternatives, Bryan was again a hard-liner. Ultimately he was appointed to a committee of seven silver men to negotiate, with a corresponding committee of gold men, the arrangements for floor debate. The committees agreed on a sequence of debates and votes by which attention would first be given to several silver bills sponsored by Bland, each calling for free coinage of silver at a different ratio—at 16 to 1, 17 to 1, and 20 to 1. The concluding step in the sequence would be consideration of the administration's bill calling for the Sherman Act's unconditional repeal.

In the early debate, Bland made the most impressive speech for silver, and as his own turn approached in the prearranged schedule, Bryan was consumed with tension and pangs of responsibility. "I never felt more deeply the gravity of a question," he confided to Mary, who was in Lincoln. "I believe our prosperity depends upon its right solution and I pray that I may be the instrument in the hands of Providence of doing some good for my country. . . ."

On August 16, the appointed day of Bryan's address, Congress crackled with expectation and the Capitol's corridors assumed an extra bustle. Virtually every member was present; outsiders with privileged access gladly stood along the walls; the galleries were crammed. On Bryan's desk lay proofs of the speech and by them a glass of malted extract of beef to sustain his strength. As he looked about the tense scene, he suddenly decided that his prepared text was not just right. He turned it facedown and began to speak extemporaneously.[10]

He stood tall and strong, handsome as a matinee idol, dressed with the simplicity of the people's delegate and yet with a consciousness of the honor of his politician's calling. As Bryan began, his colleagues were all attention. Big Tom Reed, the Republican leader and distinguished former Speaker, stood surrounded by lieutenants, some gnarled and rough, others benign and suave, all excelling in the game of parliamentary politics. Two future Speakers of the House were in the cluster about Reed—David B. Henderson of Iowa and Joe Cannon of Illinois—supplemented by such luminaries as Sereno Payne of New York, Julius Burrows of Michigan, and Jonathan Dolliver of Iowa. On the Democratic side, gold and silver men alike turned their chairs toward Bryan to await his word. The most attentive of all was Richard P. Bland, gray and aging, no sudden friend of silver but its steady champion for decades in fair weather and foul.

With a tremor of stage fright in his voice, Bryan acknowledged that he possessed no words to describe the weal or woe of all mankind that was poised in the balance, pending the House's action. He paid quick tribute to his President and party leader, to his honesty, courage, and sincerity, but mothers in India possessed those virtues too in superabundance, he noted, his voice rising, when they threw their children into the Ganges. President Cleveland was the victim of gross misconception if he thought repeal of the Sherman Silver Act was demanded by the people. Not from them or their representatives came the demand, but from "middlemen [and] the business interests." Cleveland could no more accurately make soundings of popular feeling by consulting such sources than "measure the ocean's silent depths by the foam upon its waves."

In sentences remarkable for simplicity and clarity, he expounded his principles for dealing with the complex subject. The world did not possess enough gold for all nations to go on the gold standard. America, England, France, and Germany owned about five-sevenths of the world's supply of gold coin, while containing only a fraction of the world's population. When the nations of the Orient too reached out for gold, its price would soar beyond comprehension. If Congress should destroy the demand for silver and increase the demand for gold by making it the only standard, the dangers would be even more exaggerated. "If the exchangeable value of the dollar is increased by legislation the debt of the debtor is increased, to his injury and to the advantage of the creditor." It was like lending a Nebraska neighbor a hog in winter weighing 100 pounds and the next spring demanding in return a hog weighing 200 pounds. A gold standard would create a drastic contraction of the currency in an era of burgeoning population. The step would bring idleness to labor, further distort the distribution of wealth, and force debtor farmers into tenancy to the point that "you must tremble for civil liberty itself." [11]

Bryan contended that the use of gold and silver in combination would bring more stable money than one metal alone. Even if, in a bimetallic standard, silver should drive American gold to Europe, he argued, we should still gain, for Europe would have gold with which to buy our goods. If the United States established gold as its standard, Europe's ability to buy from us would be diminished, for we would have to obtain gold from Europe. If, however, silver were made a standard with gold, the United States would become the trading center of nations using silver, constituting more than half the world's population. American mines would readily produce the silver needed. Thus the wiser step was bimetallism, which would enable our trade to flourish with both gold and silver countries. Admittedly, the stumbling block to international bimetallism was Britain, but the time had come for the United States to declare its financial independence. We were no longer a British colony, and the people living between the Alleghenies and the Golden Gate "are not afraid to cast their all upon the Republic and rise or fall with it."

There was, he acknowledged, "an honest difference of opinion as to the particular ratio at which the unlimited coinage of gold and silver should be undertaken." Thus, 16 to 1, 30 to 1, and other combinations were under discussion. Bryan, for his part, preferred the ratio that "will secure the greatest advantage to the public and cause the least injustice," criteria, he believed, that "the present ratio" best filled. Opening the mints to free and unlimited coinage of gold and silver at 16 to 1 would immediately raise silver, he was confident, to the coinage value of $1.29 per ounce. The coinage of silver would again be profitable "not only here, but everywhere. . . ." Thanks to the balanced supply of gold and silver, the gold dollar would not again go to premium because it could not find a better coinage ratio elsewhere and because it could be put to no purpose for which the silver dollar would not be as good.

Bryan did not propose to cope with the panic and corrosive social injustices merely by restoring silver and the bimetallic standard. The panic was strewing the landscape with wrecked and failing banks and ripping open to exposure a shocking array of malpractices. Bryan urged upon the Cleveland administration several immediate steps to restore confidence in banking institutions: Let bank deposits be guaranteed; let bank stockholders provide security for double rather than simple liability; increase the penalty for officers and stockholders who pillage banks at depositors' expense; stiffen the punishment of embezzlers.

Bryan visualized the Democratic Party as standing between two competing aggregates, each beckoning for its support. "On the one hand stand the imperious and compassionless corporate interests and moneyed institutions . . . which demand that the Democratic party become their agent and execute their merciless decrees; on the other stand the masses for whom the party would speak, work-worn and dust-begrimed, suffering from the inequitable distribution of wealth, unable to purchase necessities, beating in vain for relief against the outer walls of legislatures." The Democratic Party must decide which it will serve. "Will the party turn its face to the rising or the setting sun, choose blessings or curses, life or death—which, which?"

Applause and praise billowed upon Bryan. By general agreement, his address was the best on the silver side, and it catapulted him to an almost equal place with Bland in the leadership of the House's silver forces. A proud Congressman, William Springer, predicted that Bryan's silver speech "will rank with the best efforts of Clay and Webster or Wendell Phillips." The *Rocky Mountain News* was certain that Bryan had immortalized himself and deserved nothing less than the next Presidential nomination on a "people's platform." Bryan's mail shot up to 100 letters a day; invitations poured in for him to speak in twenty states. Senator William M. Stewart of Nevada ordered 5,000 copies of the speech for distribution, and it was expected that requests for its reprint would exceed 150,000.[12]

President Cleveland, a seasoned, foreseeing politician, had no intention of risking the struggle's outcome on the chance fortunes of legislative debate. With a forcefulness rarely seen, Cleveland employed the formidable political weapons provided by his office. He engineered his long-deliberated reshuffling of the several House committees concerned with the silver question. In the most drastic of these assaults, William Springer, now well identified with silver, was derricked as chairman of the most important of committees, Ways and Means, and replaced by William L. Wilson, whom the President could count on. Springer's good friend William S. Holman, also a silver man, was dropped from Appropriations and, according to the pattern, was relegated to an unimportant committee. Not a single House chairmanship was awarded to any Congressman from west of the Missouri River, the favorite habitat of silver politicians.

The maker of this rare rearrangement of committee assignments was Speaker Charles F. Crisp, who in his critics' eyes was a mere puppet of the President. Seeking reelection to the Speakership and mindful of his earlier narrow victory in gaining the post, he prized the President's support in his new quest. "By putting Wilson in as chairman," the distraught Springer wrote of Crisp's action, "he placated Cleveland." Bryan, too, was scheduled to be lifted from Ways and Means, but Crisp managed to fend off Cleveland by observing that the young orator would be useful when the administration moved later for tariff reform.[13]

Cleveland had become fully confident that he could win the fight to repeal the Sherman Act. He had stellar orators in the House to countervail Bryan—William L. Wilson of West Virginia, who presented a closely reasoned address against the act, and Bourke Cockran of New York, whose dynamic oratory rivaled Bryan's. The Cleveland men were highly organized. A recording committee kept a ledger of the votes and opinions of individual Congressmen and a proselytizing committee gained support. Although silver men enjoyed a fiery enthusiasm, they were handicapped by rival personalities jockeying for advantage and an abysmal lack of organization.

Cleveland's shrewdly plotted fight was rewarded with sweet victory. The Wilson repeal bill passed the House by 239 to 108. The voting pattern reflected Bryan's notions of the geography of the silver sentiment. Western and Southern states opposed repeal; Northeastern, Middle Atlantic, and Middle Western states favored it. The vote was both a reassurance from sections friendly to Bryan's cause and an emphatic revelation of those sections that must be wooed and won if the silver cause were ever to prevail. The Senate gave the President an even harder struggle. For a time, it appeared that he would be driven to compromise, but he was adamant, and on October 30, repeal was passed. "The iron firmness of Mr. Cleveland," as the New York *Times* put it, had at last prevailed.

If the fight against the President had the advantage of riveting public attention, it also invited penalties. Bryan had to be chastised, and the administering of this chastisement was gladly taken up by Nebraska Democrats eager to please the Chief Executive, a mighty source of preferment and favor. Licking their chops, Nebraska politicians planned to humiliate the young upstart at the state Democratic convention that would assemble in the final weeks of the Congressional silver debate. The humiliation, elaborately conceived and arranged, contributed invaluably to Bryan's education in the darker arts of party conventions.

Tobias Castor and Euclid Martin, shrewd emissaries of Cleveland and Morton, worked overtime to rig the convention against Bryan and in favor of the national administration. Every man endorsed by the state central committee for a post office appointment was summoned to Omaha for "a very thorough understanding" of the course to be followed in the coming convention. Those approved for other offices were sent letters setting forth the propriety of their coming as delegates to the convention and the necessity of having none but Democrats (*i.e.*, gold men) in the delegation. Tickets of admission to the convention hall were denied to known Bryan men.

Confident of his handiwork, Euclid Martin said that he had never attended a convention "in which the influence of organization was so apparent," and James E. North, the newly appointed Collector of Internal Revenue, observed that the convention would be "attended by the class of men who could not be run off from a principle through the eloquent appeals of a young Moses, much less Mr. Bryan." [14]

The machinery of humiliation began turning almost immediately upon Bryan's arrival at the convention in Omaha. When the state committee proposed that T. J. Mahoney be elected temporary chairman, Bryan quickly challenged the organization by moving that Judge Joseph E. Ong of Geneva be substituted for Mahoney. Acknowledging great regard for Mahoney, Bryan declared that he represented "an element" antagonistic to the "principles" of those supporting Ong. The vote was taken. Mahoney over-whelmed Ong, and Bryan, unaware of what was in store, did the standard courtesy of moving that Mahoney be elected unanimously.

A good silver Democrat proposed that Bryan as a kind of personal compliment—he was, after all, the party's only elected federal officeholder—be made a member of the Resolutions Committee. But the steamroller moved again when the huge Douglas County delegation, under the unit rule, voted against Bryan. His good friend C. J. Smyth jumped up to challenge the Douglas vote. The convention became an uproar. Bryan men yelled themselves hoarse with curses and epithets and menacingly waved hats, newspapers, and umbrellas at the jeering opposition. Bryan alone sat serenely through it all, an icy smile frozen upon his face. The demonstration was unavailing, and Bryan was soundly defeated. With six gold Democrats on the Resolutions Committee, one silver man was added. But this, as it turned out, was less a political courtesy than an entrapment. The silver man would doubtless make a minority report, and the convention, by overwhelmingly rejecting it, could again embarrass Bryan.

When the Resolutions Committee brought in a platform endorsing Cleveland and the Sherman Act's repeal, Bryan attacked it in a furious speech and urged the passage of the minority report extolling free silver. It did not matter a snap of his fingers, he cried, if the minority report was accepted or rejected. He was right—that is what mattered—and whatever the outcome might be today was immaterial. With fiery defiance leaping from his eyes, he made a ringing threat: "If you represent the Democratic party in saying you are for the gold standard of Wall Street, I want to tell you if the Democratic party ratifies your action, I will go out and serve my party and my God under some other name than as a Democrat." Bryan's followers roared with delight when he cried that he would not support in the next Presidential election of 1896 any candidate who advocated the gold standard. The convention, a crescendo of boos and jeers, conceded nothing to this threat. It rejected the minority report by 403 to 114 and nominated for the principal office at stake in an impending election a true gold man, Frank Irvine, for State Supreme Court judge.

The spectacle of Bryan, whipped and bloodied, aroused delight in many circles. President Cleveland privately expressed his pleasure. Upon the several convention leaders who had performed so faithfully and well, Morton bestowed federal offices and, for good measure, counseled, so that all might hear, that Bryan "ought to take a tumble to himself." Populists, who had long wanted to bring Bryan into their fold, were also delighted, because the day seemed not far when he would join their party. Populists of the federal House of Representatives even honored Bryan with a telegram joyfully welcoming him into their ranks, and Thomas E. Watson, the eminent Southern

Populist leader, proclaimed that Bryan must abandon either his principles or the Democratic Party.[15]

The Omaha convention left Bryan in an unpleasantly ambiguous position. Though he had threatened to leave his party, it became apparent soon after the convention that he had not the least intention of doing so. He quickly squirmed back into a position of Democratic respectability. In campaign speeches, he declared that the convention's resolutions did not reflect the great body of Nebraska's Democrats and that at Omaha he had been the victim of "the federal pie counter brigade"—those Cleveland men in Washington and Nebraska who administered the political prizes of the federal government against his interests. Bryan contended that his position on silver in Congress was in absolute accord with the last national party platform of 1892, that the Omaha convention, in voting down silver, had repudiated the national platform.

Would Bryan endorse and campaign for the gold-minded Irvine? Bryan was confronting an unpleasant conflict between his political beliefs and friendship and loyalty. Irvine had had "very much to do" with Bryan's first nomination to Congress. Among the most prestigious lawyers in the state, Irvine was considered "far better qualified for judge than all other candidates." Bryan lost no time in announcing his preference for belief over party and personal sentimentality. He acknowledged that Irvine was among his first friends in Nebraska and was "an excellent fellow, personally and professionally." But Irvine could not run, Bryan pointed out, without endorsing the state platform adopted at Omaha, "and I cannot write a letter appealing for votes for anyone who runs on that kind of platform." Bryan in the end supported the Populist nominee and preached the necessity of future Populist-Democratic fusion.

Seeking to belittle Bryan's influence in his party, the gold Democrats labored mightily to roll up a solid vote for Irvine. Morton exhorted every Democratic county chairman to work against fusion and for Irvine "for the sake of the Bench, sound money, and the national influence it would help the Democrats of Nebraska to gain." But it was all in vain. Irvine ran a poor third, and following the old pattern of Nebraskan elections, the Republican candidate was elected, with his Populist rival running a strong second. On the basis of the returns, a Populist-Democratic fusion candidate would have won easily. If anything, the election demonstrated that the conservatives who dominated the Omaha convention did not represent the general body of actual or potential Democratic voters. The farmers of Nebraska, bleeding from economic depression, viewed Morton and his ties to the railroads as a bleak symbol of the Cleveland administration's indifference to agricultural distress.[16]

President Cleveland, too, had his disappointments. He had fought tooth and nail for the Sherman Act's repeal, expecting that removal of this canker on sound financial policy would spur the restoration of prosperity. But the economy scarcely flickered. If anything, the Treasury Department, vehicle of Cleveland's sound money policy, passed into worse days. As holders of silver certificates acquired under the Sherman Act rushed to the Treasury and presented them for gold, Cleveland and his Secretary of the Treasury, John G. Carlisle, watched with horror as government gold reserves melted away to the point of threatening to disappear altogether. To stave off disaster, Cleveland ordered the Treasury to sell $50,000,000 of government bonds for gold. He was again distressed when few bids were made for the bonds, which cast a further shadow on government credit. A desperate Cleveland turned to a New York banking syndicate, headed by J. P. Morgan and Company, which accepted the issue and exposed Cleveland to the charge that he had sold out to Wall Street. For his anxiously taken steps, the President received small recompense. Purchasers of the bonds lost little time in presenting them and withdrawing gold from the Treasury. Cleveland and Carlisle had a new spectacle to agonize over; as fast as gold moved into the Treasury at one end, it moved out at the other.

Silver politicians on Capitol Hill had provided the President an alternative to the bond issue. While Cleveland was weighing his bond decision, Congressman Richard P. Bland introduced a seigniorage bill. Seigniorage is the gain government enjoys when it purchases bullion at a price lower than the value stamped on the metal. Bland proposed that the Treasury issue money based on reserves of silver accumulated from seigniorage charges. The step would realize nearly $55,000,000, approximately the sum Cleveland expected to gain from the sale of bonds. When Bland introduced his seigniorage bill, Bryan, alert to other alternatives to Cleveland's bond venture, sponsored a measure vesting in the Secretary of the Treasury, rather than in the holder of a government obligation, the option of redeeming it in gold or silver. The bill was approved in a subcommittee of Ways and Means but was never reported by the full committee.

Bland's seigniorage bill, however, passed both houses. Many Democrats who had voted for the Sherman Act's repeal voted for the seigniorage bill, eager to put themselves in a better light with constituents suffering in the depression who found little hope in the administration's devotion to sound money doctrines. A wide political consensus believed that Cleveland, with little disturbance to his conscience, could sign the Bland bill. The step would do much to reconcile free silver Democrats with their party. Democratic Congressmen urged the President to take a conciliatory course. Bryan, who deplored Cleveland's earlier assault on the Sherman Act as a lamentable unnecessary division of the Democratic Party into two massive hostile factions, saw in Bland's bill a sparkling opportunity to reunite them. Bryan even visited Cleveland to beseech him to sign the bill, but Eastern governors and financiers countered by telling him to veto. Cleveland never wavered; he vetoed. To accede to the bill, he believed, would reopen the entire question of silver policy that bankers and commercial men had thought settled by the Sherman Act's repeal. Uncertainty and distrust in the financial community could only exacerbate the depression. The House silver forces rallied to throttle the President's veto of Bland's seigniorage bill. That they fell a mere thirteen votes short of the necessary two-thirds demonstrated that great numbers of Congressmen were now marching under the silver flag. Bryan boldly predicted that the veto would do Cleveland enormous harm by exposing the moneyed interests' power over lawmaking.

Bryan's own philosophy of monetary policy was rapidly evolving. This philosophy was by no means limited to silver and carried him away from old positions, in which as a good Jeffersonian he once called for a minimum of government. In the crisis of depression, he took new positions which accorded government an ever-larger place in monetary management. His changed thinking is evident in his moves against a bill to repeal the 10 percent tax on state banknotes. He launched a counterproposal that the federal government alone issue paper money. He objected to the existing system of banks of issue—state and national banks—and its effect of placing in the hands of interested private parties the power to regulate the volume of currency and through it the market value of all other property. Also, he contended, banks of issue become interested in preventing the circulation of any money that might operate to the disadvantage of their currency and resisted any public regulation of their control over finances. He recalled Jefferson's remark to John Taylor, "I sincerely believe with you that banking establishments are more dangerous than standing enemies." [17]

What would Bryan substitute for private banks as sources of currency? He urged that government adopt a "managed currency," as many other nations had. In rhetoric that would become familiar four decades later in Franklin Roosevelt's New Deal, Bryan proposed that government put paper money into circulation to pay for public works. This pump priming, as the later New Dealers would call it, would jog the economy from the doldrums of the depression. Government as currency manager could render "complete justice" by inflating the currency sufficiently to restore the balance between prices that were in wild disarray since the "Crime of 1873." All government money, according to Bryan, should become legal tender, and contracts calling for payment only in gold should be banned. Again he anticipated the New Deal. Bryan's prophetic gifts also enabled him to give a kind of preview of elements of the future Federal Reserve System. Among other things, he proposed that banking reserves no longer be kept predominately in Eastern banks but be distributed among leading banks in every state.

Bryan's other great project for coping with the depression and enhancing social justice was the income tax. His friend C. H. Jones, now the editor of the St. Louis *Republic,* in which he published a widely circulated article on the silver question, suggested that "the most effective weapon against Plutocratic policy is the graded income tax." "Eastern Plutocrats" with soaring fortunes and inflated pensions "dreaded nothing more," Jones suggested. Contemporary publications, which Jones urged Bryan to study, revealed the extraordinary degree to which wealth was concentrated in the United States, a condition aggravated by inequities of the tax system, which lay heavily upon the poor and gently upon the rich. According to one study that impressed Bryan, the prevailing federal system of indirect taxes claimed 70 to 90 percent of the yearly savings of the poor, and only 3 to 10 percent of those of the rich. The nation's wealth was concentrated to the point where at one extreme 91 percent of its families owned only 2 percent of it, and at the other extreme 3 percent of the millionaires owned 20 percent. Advocacy of the income tax, Jones counseled Bryan, offered another attraction to a young Congressman. "I do not believe there is any way in which a member of the House could impress himself on legislation and on the country more effectively than by fighting such a measure through." [18]

As he did with silver, Bryan steeped himself in the technical lore of the income tax by wading through books and monographs and by soliciting the State Department's help in collecting information abroad on the tax systems of other governments. He accurately anticipated that an income tax bill would arouse bitter opposition in the East, among Democratic and Republican legislators alike.

In a shrewd tactical move, Bryan sought to link the income tax to tariff reform. On the latter subject, he saw more or less eye to eye with Cleveland and William L. Wilson, chairman of the Ways and Means Committee. This quondam triumvirate united on a tariff reform bill that dropped the duty on wool and the bounty on sugar, while increasing the free list. For the American manufacturer, the Wilson bill, as it became known, provided less protection than formerly; to the American consumer, it promised a substantial lightening of tax burdens. With a bright future apparently in store for the tariff bill, Bryan proposed to hitch his more controversial income tax bill to its progress.

At first the scholarly Wilson seemed to go along with Bryan's plan. He commissioned the Nebraskan to draft provisions for an income tax and appointed Benton McMillin of Tennessee, Bryan's like-minded friend, chairman of a subcommittee on internal revenue. However, as Bryan developed his tax proposal, Wilson became convinced that the cloudburst of controversy it would engender would jeopardize his own cherished tariff reform. The Cleveland administration reached the same conclusion. Although the President took no overt position on an income tax, he bridled at antagonizing Eastern and other Democrats and Republicans who had backed his fight to repeal the Sherman Silver Purchase Act and his gold bond sales policy.

Secretary of the Treasury Carlisle was soon sending word to House leaders that the administration wanted the income tax and the tariff to be separate measures. Bryan, mounting a counterattack with an appeal to House leaders, met only rebuff. Never one to be deterred by defeat, he set out on a hazardous course. He collected a sufficient number of petitions to call a caucus of Democratic Congressmen, and there, in an impassioned speech, and thanks to a careful marshaling of his Western and Southern colleagues beforehand, he secured the passage of a resolution calling for the merger of the tariff and the income tax into a single bill.

As a member of McMillin's subcommittee, Bryan drafted a proposal establishing a graduated income tax, beginning on incomes of $2,500. The tax was expected to reach from 50,000 to 80,000 incomes. Bryan's measure reflected a feature of Prussian law by which the citizen himself computed the tax and made his return. Guiding his plan through committee and floor debate, Bryan withstood several moves to separate it from the tariff, a step that would have been fatal, jousting again with his chief rival among Democratic rhetoricians, Bourke Cockran. Speaking probably at the instigation of Cleveland, in his far-ranging, flawlessly modulated voice, garnished with a charming, slight Irish twang, Cockran contended that an income tax was unnecessary as a revenue measure and predicted doom and ruination if those who enjoyed democracy were not required to support it equally. The tax, Cockran lamented, was a cheap bone thrown to the discontented and was an evil sign of an oncoming tidal wave of socialism.[19]

Cockran, Bryan cried, spoke for monopolists and millionaires, while he bore the cause of 60,000,000 common people. The country had had ten years of experience with an income tax adopted in the Civil War, and evidence was unknown of any weakening of the poor's participation in government. "If taxation is a badge of free men," Bryan exclaimed, "the poor people of this country are covered all over with the insignia of free men." Bryan argued that the income tax was the most just of all taxes since it was based on the ability to pay. He objected to condemnation of the tax as "socialistic," a view encouraged by the circumstance that the great body of the poor would escape its imposition. The tax must be seen in conjunction with customs and sundry federal domestic taxes that demand more from the poor than from the rich. Above all, Bryan objected to the tendency to tarbrush advocates of the income tax as "demagogues." "They call that man a statesman," he cried, "whose ear is attuned to the slightest pulsation of the pocket book, and they describe as a demagogue any one who dares listen to the heartbeat of humanity."

Bryan applied his oratorical hammer and tongs to a wealthy New Yorker who contended that adoption of the income tax would "compel many of the best people of New York" to move abroad where living would be cheaper. "Where would they flee to?" asked Bryan "—to England where the tax exceeded 2%; to Prussia, with 4%, or Switzerland at 8%, Italy 12%, and Austria, 20%? May God pity those whose patriotism was only 2% deep. We would be well rid of those who would flee abroad and live under a monarchy without an income tax rather than support a republic." Connoisseurs of Congressional oratory rated this the best speech Bryan ever made in the House. Members rushed to congratulate him, and the next day, Chairman Wilson, seeing how the tide was running, entered into negotiations with Bryan and other champions of the income tax. Wilson, acting for a Cleveland administration suddenly uneasy over the diminished revenues promised by tariff reform, now welcomed an income tax as a source of governmental prosperity but not as an instrument of social justice. Wilson hailed the income tax and incorporated it into his tariff bill after insisting on the abandonment of its graded features—the scaffolding of the bill's provisions for social equity. In its revised form, the tax called for an across-the-board 2 percent levy on personal and net incomes of over $4,000. With writhing reluctance Bryan accepted Wilson's harsh terms since Wilson's version had weaned away enough of his supporters to leave his own tax plan in a minority position. Nonetheless, Bryan still deemed the struggle worthwhile, if only to establish the principle of an income tax. The House adopted the tax in passing the Wilson tariff bill. A joyous Bryan and his colleagues, Henry St. George Tucker of Virginia and John Sharp Williams of Mississippi, lifted Wilson onto their shoulders and paraded in merry triumph around the House floor.[20]

But the bright sunlight of success was soon clouded over. Many a Senate Democrat, smarting under Cleveland's roughshod tactics with the Sherman Act repeal, did violence to the administration's cherished tariff reforms. By making no less than 634 amendments, the Senate undid much of the House bill, chiefly by raising rates. Bryan's income tax embedded in the Wilson bill remained untouched with help from a moving speech by his Populist ally, Senator William V. Allen. To House colleagues, angered by the Senate's depredations, Bryan offered a kind of counsel that he many times repeated in his political career. Although moralistic and ideological, he was not rigid to the point of impracticality. Where political forces were antagonistic and of roughly equal strength, he was prone to be pragmatic. The new tariff and income tax law, with all its imperfections, he contended, was much to be preferred to no law at all. Always the optimist, Bryan was confident that a bad law could be made a better law later. His House colleagues heeded his advice, and the House-Senate conference version of the Wilson-Gorman bill, as it was known, became law. Its tariff reform provisions riddled and mangled, it was a monument to the defeat of agrarian interests. Cleveland, to show his displeasure, permitted it to become law without signing it, but Bryan had his income tax law, the most substantial achievement of his legislative career. Even that triumph was not unflawed. Hardly had the law passed when its opponents commenced litigation to have it declared unconstitutional.

Bryan struck another blow for reform by introducing an "Antioption" bill, as he called it, to bar "gambling" in certain farm products. Directed at speculators in agricultural commodities, his bill was a precursor of the regulation of grain and cotton exchanges enacted as law more than two decades hence in the administration of Woodrow Wilson. "I deny," said Bryan in explaining his bill, "that it is just to the farmers of my district that gamblers should be permitted to bet on the price of their products to their injury after they have prepared their crops for the market." Commodity speculators— or gamblers, as Bryan called them—increase the price of the commodity speculated in to the purchaser, largely the city dwellers in his constituency, and decrease it to the farmer who sells. The legislation got nowhere. As on so many things, Bryan was decades ahead of his time.[21]

Humiliation in open convention was by no means Bryan's last punishment for defiance of Grover Cleveland. Perhaps the worst punishment he suffered was Cleveland's withholding of the juicy patronage, to which his position as Nebraska's only Democrat in either house of Congress entitled him. The appointment tied most intimately to his prestige was the postmastership of his own city of Lincoln. For the postmastership, he proposed J. D. Calhoun of the Lincoln *Herald,* but his guns were spiked when a Morton man forwarded to Cleveland clippings from Calhoun's paper critical of administration policies. The President turned down Calhoun immediately and absolutely, and a visit by Bryan to the White House to plead his case could not budge him.

This was only the beginning of Bryan's humiliating exclusion. The President, always less prone to compromise than Bryan, made not even the most infinitesimal effort to court or placate the young Nebraskan but turned the screws to the farthest notch. Cleveland handed over the Nebraska patronage to no one less than Bryan's archenemy Morton. In turn Morton committed to his like-minded ally, the Nebraska national committeeman Tobias Castor, the painstaking work of selecting from among the candidates. In an extended sojourn in Washington late in 1893, Castor transacted the bulk of patronage business. He visited the Post Office Department with a list of nominees—good Morton men, of course—for all twenty of the Presidential postmasterships to be filled in Nebraska. He made further calls at the Justice, Treasury, and Interior departments.

At Interior, Bryan was nurturing a friendship with the department's chief clerk, the shrewd, humanistic Josephus Daniels of North Carolina. This was the beginning of an affectionate lifetime alliance. Bryan advanced upon

Daniels with a clump of recommendations for receivers and registers of the land office in Nebraska. These the chief clerk dutifully toted to the Secretary of the Interior, Hoke Smith, but to his consternation, Smith announced that "The President will appoint nobody to office in Nebraska unless he is recommended by Secretary Morton. Go over and ask Mr. Morton for his recommendations for the vacant offices and make out the papers, to go to the White House, of the men Mr. Morton recommends." Daniels, warmly sympathetic to his young friend Bryan, could only chat vaguely about the patronage and, of course, could not convey the instructions of Secretary Smith. As days passed without result, Bryan, his patience fading, exclaimed to Daniels that if his recommendations "are to be turned down because I am to be denied rights granted to other Congressmen, let me know of it. I am at least entitled to that consideration." Daniels still was the soul of discretion in conversations with the despairing Bryan. As the names he proposed continued to be turned down, he said resignedly to Daniels, "Tell the Secretary I will trouble him with no more recommendations since the administration is using offices to get votes for repeal [of the Sherman Silver Purchase Act]."

Ultimately, a spare bone with precious few appointments was tossed to Bryan, but these never exceeded 1 percent of Nebraska's offices. The remaining 99 percent were filled with the henchmen of Nebraska's Bourbon Democrats. Probably the bitterest patronage pill Bryan had to swallow was the appointment of his remorseless enemy Dr. George Miller as surveyor of customs at Omaha. Miller could well repeat his earlier query, "Who the hell is Bryan?" with intoned defiance.[22]

Unmovable by failure or doubt, Cleveland increased his commitment to a sound money policy by arranging a second issue of bonds in November, 1894, again through a syndicate led by J. P. Morgan. Meanwhile, the silver movement was picking up momentum. The American Federation of Labor in its 1894 convention declared for free silver at 16 to 1. At the Fifth Trans-Mississippi Congress at Omaha, Bryan, supported by many Western governors, pushed through a resolution demanding "16 to 1 without waiting for the consent of any other nation." A convention of the American Bimetallic League expressed an identical sentiment, and at the Populist convention in Chicago, Lyman Trumbull brought delegates to their feet by charging that the money power, long dominant in most of the great governments of the world, was seizing control in the United States. With defiant cheers the convention adopted a resolution framed by Trumbull, paralleling Bryan's in Omaha. The state Democratic conventions of Nebraska and ten other Western and Southern states also echoed Bryan.

Cleveland, sticking to the guns of his conservative monetary policy, recommended to Congress an overhaul of the banking and currency structure.

In essence, he proposed to separate the federal government from banking and permit the banks to provide whatever currency they deemed necessary. This was exactly the opposite of Bryan's conception of a government which alone would provide the nation's money and regulate banking. From the conservative camp cries were rising for American legislation in support of an international gold standard.

In a free-swing oration in the House on December 22, 1894, Bryan flayed Cleveland and his policies. "Oh, if in the White House we had an Andrew Jackson," he cried. By adamantly opposing bimetallism and a graduated income tax as a device of social justice, Cleveland stood shamefully against the people's interests and with the East against the West and South. Cleveland alone was responsible for the Democratic Party's deepening division between conservatives and progressives. With his oratorical fists flying, the young Congressman went after "the money centers" that "present this insolent demand for further legislation in favor of a universal gold standard. I, for one, will not yield to that demand. I will not help to crucify mankind upon a cross of gold. I will not aid them to press down upon the bleeding brow of labor this crown of thorns." These telling metaphorical sentences, he would use again and again, most notably in the national Democratic convention of 1896.

Cleveland's bond issue of November, 1894, sustained the Treasury for only ten weeks. As winter came on, the depression still held the land in its deadening grip; unemployment, starvation, and bank failures rolled on mercilessly. Prices and wages continued to tumble, tattered and hungry bands of unemployed roamed the countryside, and fires from their camps flickered ominously and frightened more fortunate city residents. The nation was facing its worst days since the Civil War. With gold reserves and financial confidence plummeting, Cleveland was driven to a third bond issue which he prepared again to sell to Morgan and his associates, including the House of Rothschild. But the House of Representatives, carried by the momentum of the grave depression, had passed securely into the grip of the silver men. It defeated legislation implementing Cleveland's bond plan and brought Bryan to exult that the "voice of the people . . . therefore the voice of God" had vanquished gold and the greedy bankers.

An undaunted Cleveland nevertheless drove ahead with his contract with Morgan and in a terse note informed Congress of the *fait accompli*. He added that if Congress would substitute gold bonds for coin bonds within ten days, as provided in the Morgan contract, the government could save $16,000,000 in interest charges. Bryan in counterargument contended that the bonds would be unnecessary if the government used its option to pay in silver. Let Cleveland stop discriminating against silver and he would be rid of what good silver men spoke of as "the endless bucket." Sniffing a conspiracy in the making, Bryan said that Morgan was the hireling of Britain's sly attempt to "purchase a change in the financial policy of the United States for a given sum of gold."

The administration pressed William L. Wilson into introducing legislation to save the $16,000,000 in interest charges. In an unrestrained speech against the Wilson bill, Bryan said he would willingly lay down his life to defeat the President's policies. "Never before," he exclaimed, "has such a bribe been offered to our people by a foreign syndicate, and we ought to so act that such a bribe will never be offered again." Far more than $16,000,000 was at stake; nothing less than the welfare of all mankind depended on the vote. If Eastern Democrats and Republicans persisted in their joint aggressions, the rest of the country must unite to protect their homes and well-being. Thanks to an appreciating currency, Eastern creditors were enjoying an unearned increment at the expense of the debtors of the West and South: "They are seeking to reap what they did not sow."

When a Democratic Representative of the Bourbon persuasion suggested that good Democrats ought not criticize their President, Bryan answered tartly that in taking the oath of office, he had made no mental reservation not to speak out against outrages perpetrated against his constitutents "even when committed by the President of the United States." The Democratic Party, he added, should feel the same gratitude to the President "which a passenger feels toward the trainman who has opened a switch and precipitated a wreck." The party's duty, he said, "if it still loves its President," is "chastening him whom it loveth." Moments later, Bryan was demanding a political union of the West and South and the election of a Western President.[23]

The silver forces, thoroughly in control of the House, vanquished the Wilson bill and Bryan scored his first victory over President Cleveland at a cost to the nation, administration men pointed out, of $16,000,000. The Morgan contract moved ahead, bringing the syndicate a round profit of $5,000,000. This tidy, easily earned sum moved Bryan to new protests.

Congress was more than a forum for the great debate over monetary policy. It provided the spectacle of the Democratic Party locked in an ideological crisis in which Bryan and his allies endeavored to rip their party from its moorings of sound money and conservative social policy and move it into a new ideological channel more responsive to popular needs and standards of social justice. In setting his own conduct, Bryan accorded top priority to his silver beliefs. His commitment was unreserved. At this hour he preferred ideology to party and pressed his silver beliefs to the point of dangerously dividing his party. Few legislators have exceeded Bryan's headstrong audacity in pursuing their beliefs at the expense of party unity. Yet Bryan's conduct was not simply an exercise in blind belief. He became bolder and more accusatory in his attacks on the President as the tendency of his party on the money question became clearer. Democratic legislators were increasingly moving away from traditional monetary policies toward silver and progressivism. So far as the dominant tendency of his party was concerned, Bryan was on the right side and Cleveland on the wrong side.

By sheer oratorical power, Bryan had risen to the forefront of the silver movement. He responded in the most fundamental way to the needs of the beleaguered farmer and the unemployed. Both groups were grievously deprived of income and therefore of their ability to satisfy the basic biological needs of shelter, clothing, and food. These deprivations were now critical, and the environment that produced their misery made them eager for explanations and solutions. The message of silver provided both an explanation of why the world was as dark and oppressive as it was and the way to salvation. Bryan voiced the suffering and resentment of those whose own articulations were blocked by lack of education and by the ceaselessness of the struggle to keep body and soul together. Bryan more than anyone else lifted silver out of the technicalities of economics and made it comprehensible, imparting to the cause a sense of humanitarian concern and social justice. In contrast, Cleveland, wedded to the old financial system, seemed in partnership with the men of Wall Street, who were horrified by the thought of government aiding the people and whose pockets were lined thick with profits gained from the debt Cleveland ran up to preserve the gold standard.

In addition to fighting the President, Bryan was preparing the Democratic Party for 1896. Just as fusion was the key to his own victory in the First Congressional District, he looked to fusion in national politics for the eventual triumph of silver. Several pieces in the political puzzle had to be fitted together to bring into common effort those Democrats, Republicans, and Populists imbued with the silver sentiment.

The Populists were deeply divided on the question of fusion. Given the disparate elements of their membership, it was almost inevitable that they should be. The Populist Party was rooted in a succession of dissident parties of the earlier nineteenth century—the Farmers' Alliance, the Greenbackers, the Knights of Labor, followers of Henry George and Edward Bellamy, and the free silverites. Populism was flourishing because of the major parties' sterile attitudes toward current social problems. Despite the prolongation of the depression, neither the Democrats nor the Republicans had responded with remedies or even with energy. The Populists, as Richard Hofstadter has suggested, were the first important modern political movement in the United States to insist that the federal government has responsibilities for the common good and the first to attack seriously the social problems of industrialism.

The utopia conjured up in the Populist imagination was oriented to the past rather than to the future. Populism was a movement bent upon restoring the harassed farmer to a former, happier estate largely superseded by an industrial order in which a predatory minority enriched itself from the labor of the masses. Populists perceived a common interest among farmers, city workers, and small businessmen; all were victims of the parasitical few in the high places of the financial and industrial order.

The political Bible of Populism was the Omaha platform, developed in the national convention of the new party in 1892. Its planks called for public ownership and operation of railroads, telegraphs, and telephones; the reclaiming of railroad lands illegally held; establishment of postal savings banks; an eight-hour day for labor; barring of labor spies; curtailment of immigration; prohibition of alien landownership; the direct election of Senators; the Australian ballot; the initiative and referendum; a graduated income tax; a subtreasury system; free and unlimited coinage of silver; a flexible currency system controlled by government rather than banks, with an increase in the circulating medium to $50 per capita. In the East, especially, these planks were reviled as Communistic and as the pap of anarchism.

In the Presidential race of 1892 the Populist candidate, General James B. Weaver, had made a good showing, polling more than 1,000,000 popular votes and capturing 22 electoral votes. Eight Populists were elected to the federal House of Representatives, and even more Congressmen owed their elections to deals of various kinds with the Populists. In Kansas, North Dakota, and Colorado, predominately Populist governments were elected, and as many as 50 state officials and 1,500 county officials and members of the state legislatures were estimated to have won office under the banner of the new party. Well could Weaver hail Populism's "enviable record and surprising success at the polls." The 1892 elections nevertheless also produced several unpleasant political facts. The Populists failed to carry a single state of the Solid South. The entrenched Democratic Party, the white man's party, was largely controlled by Bourbons whose outlook on most issues opposed the Populists'. In the Far West, the silver-producing states approved the Populist ticket and supplied Weaver with half his electoral votes. But this success was not unblemished since the silver states supported Populism only because it advocated free silver. The silver states were uninterested in Populism's general program.

Populism was a political terrain of contrasting lights and shadows. One had to distinguish between "genuine" or "old-fashioned" Populists, devoted to the varied planks of the Omaha platform, many inherited from the older Farmers' Alliance, and a newer breed, the free silver Populists, who arrived in extraordinary numbers in the nineties from both major parties. "Genuine" Populists viewed silver as a distinctly minor issue. Populist platforms stressed not so much the cause of silver as the validity and necessity of the quantity theory of money. "We believe it possible," William V. Allen declared, "so to regulate the issue of money as to make it of approximately the same value at all times." The value of money, Allen believed, ought to bear as nearly as possible a fixed relation to the value of commodities. "If a man should borrow a thousand dollars on five years' time today, when it would take two bushels of wheat to pay each dollar, it is clear that it ought not to take any more wheat to pay that debt at the time of its maturity, except for the accrued interest." Silver and gold would be used as money, but, according to a leading Populist, Ignatius Donnelly, "if gold and silver cannot be issued in sufficient volume, by all means let us have paper money."

Older Populists scoffed at silver, deeming the potentialities claimed for it to be grossly exaggerated. Free silver, these critics agreed, would prompt far too small an increase in the currency to restore prosperity. In fact, so pessimistic were some older Populists about silver that they felt embarrassed and apologetic for the prominence their party was giving it. To Populist leaders eager to see their party grow, silver, whatever its deficiencies as an economic instrument, had enormous political value. In effect it was a bridge that brought many disillusioned Democrats and Republicans into the land of Populism. As the movement from the old parties to Populism increased, concerned Democratic and Republican politicians, anxious to halt the flight from their ranks, became more attentive to the money question by advocating free coinage or some variant of bimetallism as a substitute for it, including international bimetallism, which required adoption by most or all nations, but which, in light of experience, was altogether unpromising.

Populism not only was fragmented by doctrine, but was a party of many leaders, with none clearly towering over all the others. Colorful, idiosyncratic figures thrived on the Populist movement. In Kansas alone, where Populism ran strong, several stellar personalities held the Populist stage. One, Mrs. Mary Elizabeth Lease, Irish-born, sad-faced, a mother of four, had studied law, was admitted to the bar, and promptly turned to politics. Mrs. Lease knew the Western farmer's suffering at first hand, and her prescriptions for his salvation were rendered in fiery style. What farmers needed to do, she is reported to have cried, was to "raise less corn and more hell." The United States was no longer a government of the people, "but a government of Wall Street, by Wall Street and for Wall Street. The great common people of this country are slaves, and monopoly is the master. The West and South are bound and prostrate before the manufacturing East. Money rules. . . . Our laws are the output of a system which clothes rascals in robes and honesty in rags. . . ." Kansas' equivalent male Populist orator was "Sockless" Jerry Simpson, a Canadian by birth, a former sailor and captain on the Great Lakes, a slender, powerful man in his sixties, given to double-breasted short sack coats. His eyes gleamed with ready humor through old-fashioned glasses; his voice was crisp, deep, and pleasant. "He speaks with a Western accent mainly," wrote an intrigued Hamlin Garland, "and when he is making a humorous point or telling a story, he drops into dialect, and speaks in a peculiar slow fashion that makes every word tell. He is full of odd turns of thought and quaint expressions that make men think of Whitcomb Riley." As a Greenbacker and single taxer, Simpson was long familiar with third-party causes. His favorite mission was exposing the iniquities of the railroads. Simpson acquired his nickname Sockless when a natty opponent taunted him about his rural aspect and Simpson, flaying back, accused his detractor of wearing silk stockings. A reporter retorted that Simpson wore no socks at all, and thus the name was coined that Simpson was known by.

The most conspicuous Populist in the north-central states was Ignatius Donnelly of Minnesota, probably the party's foremost orator. A devotee of causes that included antislavery, Liberal Republicanism, and the Granger movement, first hard money and then Greenbackism, Donnelly had served three terms in Congress. It was once said that a reform convention without Donnelly would be "like a catfish without waffles in Philadelphia." Donnelly was of many talents: a lecturer on humorous subjects, a stout defender of the Baconian theory of the authorship of Shakespeare, author of the prophetic novel *Caesar's Column,* and an orator who excelled at denunciation. Clever rather than profound, Donnelly was chief draftsman of the Omaha platform.

The Far West boasted Governor Davis H. Waite of Colorado, defender of farmers and miners and all species of the downtrodden. Admirers spoke of him as "the Abraham Lincoln of the West," and his detractors as "Bloody Bridles," a name inspired by Waite's pronouncement that it is better "that blood should flow to the horses' bridles rather than our national liberties should be destroyed."

The other great sectional stronghold of Populism, the South, too had its vivid personalities. Chief among them was Tom Watson of Georgia, the red-haired, cadaverous, inspiring champion of tenant farmers and mill hands and of free trade, whose hates included the Democratic Party, which he considered a mere instrument of hypocrisy. Watson emerged from a planter background to become a distinguished criminal lawyer in his native Georgia. Rebellious and a fighter by nature, he revered the old agrarian order and rejected the New South. As a youth, he passed under the influence of Robert Toombs and Alexander H. Stephens, who imparted to his views many of the beliefs of the Confederate agrarians. As a political stripling, he fought the state Democratic machine dominated by capitalist-industrialists, and in 1890 he was elected to Congress on a Farmers' Alliance platform. Confronted with a choice between his reform planks and identification with an unsympathetic Democratic Party, he became a Populist. He was the new party's candidate for Speaker in the House of Representatives and introduced many of its measures. Marked for extinction by the state Democratic Party, he was defeated for reelection in 1892 in a violent, fraudulent campaign. Fearless and intense, Watson was made for the part of defender and avenger of the vanishing agrarian order. He was also a man of many sides, something of a poet and a humorist and the deft proprietor and editor of the *People's Party Paper*.

If Bryan had a counterpart in Southern politics—a Democrat with Populist principles—it was "Pitchfork Ben" Tillman of South Carolina. Of rural background, for seventeen years Tillman scratched out a living from his 400 acres of red lands in his native Edgefield County in South Carolina. Dark and savage-featured, his uncomely appearance exaggerated by the loss of an eye, Tillman owned a rasping voice, an irascible disposition, and careless manners. His neighbors were unanimous in the sentiment that to know Tillman was to dislike him. In the eighties, his declining farm income drove him into politics. Endowed with high demagogic talent, he rallied the farmers by declaiming that their interests were betrayed by lawyers and merchants and by demanding that the state cope with rural problems by undertaking a program of agricultural education. Proclaiming that he was the only man "who had the brains, the nerve and the ability to organize the common people against the aristocracy," Tillman captured the governorship in 1890 and was reelected until 1894, when he moved to the U.S. Senate. In South Carolina, he reigned for many years in high-handed style. He filled executive offices with his partisans, and when the legislature resisted him in 1890, he condemned it as "dead, rotten driftwood." In 1895, against bitter opposition, he induced a convention to rewrite the constitution. Despite his brassy style, Tillman's rule was constructive, resulting in the establishment of new colleges, a state normal and industrial school for women, and a state railroad commission with rate-making powers. A favorite object of his demagogery was the Negro, against whom he freely manipulated the political system. He easily won his Senate race by declaiming to excited rural audiences, "Send me to Washington and I'll stick my pitchfork into his [Cleveland's] old ribs!"

Insofar as Populism had a national leader, it was the party's standard-bearer in the Presidential elections of 1892, General James B. Weaver, whose quiet and poise contrasted with the dynamism of types abounding in his party. A lawyer and Union Army general in the Civil War, Weaver had migrated from his native Ohio to Iowa. After holding minor offices as a Republican, he became a Greenbacker and was elected to Congress. An experienced campaigner, with strong appeal to the soldier vote, Weaver inspired confidence among many who otherwise would dismiss Populism as a mere gathering ground of radicals.

Populist attitudes toward fusion and silver were profoundly affected by the elections of 1894. Carried by their heady electoral success in 1892, most Populists, West and South, adopted a "go it alone" plan for the Congressional and state elections two years later. Weaver was an exception in ac-

cepting nomination from both the Populists and Democrats in his unsuccessful race for Congress. The electoral results in 1894 were disastrous for
Populism. Most of the Western states the party had won in 1892 reverted to
one or other of the major parties. Every state that had voted for Weaver two
years before was lost. In the South, which was more receptive to fusion in
1894, the results were almost as bad.

The severity of electoral defeat made the Populists highly susceptible to
pressures from the free silver champions who intensified their efforts after
1894. Never modest, they boldly proclaimed their vision of the Presidency
as an attainable goal in 1896. The American Bimetallic League and the National Bimetallic Union and other nonpartisan silver organizations unloosed a flood of pamphlets and news releases to fill city dailies and county
weeklies with expositions of the money question. Reprints of speeches by
silver Senators and Congressmen were given similar distribution. To alert
party leaders, both Populist and Democratic, silver, with its burgeoning
popularity, posed new opportunities. Silver politicians and propagandists
meant to capture the Democratic Party for their doctrine and to entice Populists away from their traditional principles and commit them to a program
featuring silver. Populist politicians proposed to use silver as a lure to bring
disaffected Democrats and Republicans into their party. In effect, silver was
a conveyor belt in a time of political upheaval, by which the traffic of political human beings bent upon changing their party membership could flow
from the major parties to the Populists or from the Populists to the Democratic Party.

Many Populist leaders envisaged other kinds of growth and influence for
their party. One of the most cherished hopes of Populism was that city laborers, oppressed by the hardships of the depression, might unite with the
protesting farmers. Ample bonds seemed to join them. Both suffered from
oppressions of the industrial order, and both could be saved by similar remedies. The very logic of the title "The People's Party" required the amalgamation of these two great bodies under a single banner. From the Omaha
platform onward, the Populists were diligent in adopting the major labor reforms in courting support from labor organizations. But labor remained
aloof and uninterested. Its leaders looked askance at Populist advocacy of
silver. Silver could mean higher prices, as well as higher wages, and increasing the quantity of money might leave the city worker relatively worse off
than he was before. Not a few labor spokesmen were impressed that the
farmers' interests as producers might clash with the city workers' interests
as consumers. Samuel Gompers and other labor leaders suspected Populism
of domination by "employing farmers," many of them well-to-do, who were
using the party to defend interests inimical to labor. Labor, dissatisfied by
the old parties, was resorting more to Socialism than to Populism.

The strategies of both Populism and silver were directed toward an alliance of the South and West against the East and the Bourbon Democracy, the common enemy. Powerful similarities in their environment and circumstance drove the West and South toward combination. In both sections, agriculture predominated and other elements of the economy were subordinated to serve it. In contrast with the East, large cities were not numerous, and the problems inherent in them did not rival agriculture in their claims on public policy. Agrarian demands in both the West and the South were similar. Farmers wanted action on currency and credit, railroad practices, the tariff, public land disposal, and excessive landholdings by railroads and aliens. Political leaders and spokesmen in both sections perceived men of wealth, domiciled largely in the East, as the source of the farmers' misery. The political reality of a common West-South interest was reflected in Congressional voting patterns, and by the nineties many political leaders confidently expected a West-South agrarian alliance to replace the Democratic East-South Bourbon alliance. It was but a short step for fusion-minded Populist and Democratic silver leaders to conceive a West-South combination to capture the Presidency. With 224 electoral votes necessary to elect the President, the section west of the Mississippi River contained 83 electoral votes, and the South, defined to include Delaware, 159, or a total of 242. Even if Delaware, Maryland, and West Virginia, with a total of 17 electoral votes, should leave the Democratic column, a majority still remained. Or if the South remained solid, Iowa and any one of ten other Western states could be lost without destroying the majority. Conceivably a silver Democratic, or Democratic-Populist, Presidential candidate could win without carrying a single Northern state east of the Mississippi if he could hold his lines fairly intact in the South and could win nearly all the electoral vote between the Mississippi and the Pacific Ocean. If he could capture Illinois or Indiana, to say nothing of Ohio, Michigan, or Wisconsin, he would more than make up for possible defections in the Far West or South.

Optimistic assessments of the potentialities of a West-South alliance were predicated upon an assumption that Populists and Democrats would fuse their national tickets for 1896 and that the cement of union would be silver, to which both parties presumably would adhere. In the interval between 1894 and 1896, no general consensus prevailed among Populists concerning strategy. Western Populists widely favored silver and fusion, taking their cue from their Presidential nominee for 1892, General Weaver. The coming Presidential election of 1896, Weaver was proclaiming, should be fought on the money question alone, and he advised a Colorado audience that party lines had better be swept aside, and all Populists, Democrats, and Republicans who believed in currency reform must ready themselves to join hands. A sturdy minority of antifusionists among Western Populists warned that silver spokesmen within their ranks meant to wreck the party by subordinating it to the Democrats.

In contrast with the West, Populism's Southern branch opposed fusion. Southern Populist leaders distrusted and were repelled by the Democratic Party of their region, stronghold of the Bourbons they were seeking to escape. The Bourbons promoted policies favoring the well-to-do classes and therefore utterly opposed the program of the party of the people. Southern Populists distrusted the Democratic Party. If the Southern Democracy accepted Populist tenets now, they feared, it would do so with the motive of swallowing the People's Party later. Tom Watson put the matter less delicately. For the Populists to go back to the Democratic Party he said, would be to "return as the hog did to its wallow."

Many leaders of Southern Populism disdained the silver issue. They deemed silver a mild medicine for reform and a distraction from other more serious Populist planks against the trusts and transportation abuses. To them silver was a Trojan horse, which, according to one Southern Populist editor, would inject into Populist ranks outsiders who planned "to ruin our party and destroy the reform movement." Silver would also bring Republicans, as well as Democrats and Populists, under a fusion banner and in turn might revive the race issue, thus diverting attention even further from social reform.

For all their uneasiness and suspicion, Southern Populists leaders viewed Bryan agreeably and charitably. A reliable barometer of his standing was a jubilant reception accorded him in a visit to Atlanta in 1893. Tom Watson was intrigued by "our handsome and brilliant friend from Nebraska," by his sturdy ties with Nebraskan Populism, and his espousal of key Populist planks. But Watson was convinced that the Democratic Party could never become an adequate vehicle for Bryan's political beliefs. In fact, he had already told Bryan "that he would have to abandon his principles or leave the Democratic party." He hoped that Bryan would "choose principle—even though he loses office by it. There is such a thing in life as paying too much for office."

Leading Democrats of the West and South were more confident of the feasibility of sectional alliance and party fusion than their Populist cousins. "Silver Dick" Bland, Bryan, and another rising young Democrat and stellar orator, Congressman Joseph Bailey of Texas, were driven by the dream of an alliance of Western and Southern Democrats capable of defeating the Eastern wing. They toiled imaginatively to work out a compromise of Western and Southern differences. The fruit of their labor was "The Call to Silver Men," issued in March, 1895, a proffered compact of political fellowship between Democrats of the South and West, aiming to minimize their differences and to wrest control of their party from the gold men of the East. Since gold, "The Call" declared, had reduced the majority of people to financial bondage, no party could win the coming national elections by advocating the gold standard, least of all the Democrats who drew their strength from the "common people." The money question, "The Call" predicted, "will be the issue in 1896 and will so remain until it is settled by the intelligence and patriotism of the American voters." If the national convention did not endorse free silver at 16 to 1 or nominate a free silver candidate for President, free silver Democrats would bolt. Silver Republicans and Populists were exhorted to enlist under the Democratic banner. Silver Democrats were summoned to impress their views on party leaders, and the leaders were bidden to take up their pens for the cause. The text of "The Call" was followed by an array of signatures set down in the manner of those accompanying the Declaration of Independence. In the juxtaposition of the leading Democratic personalities of the silver movement, the name of the august Bland led the list. But at the head of the second column of names, in a bold John Hancock-like scrawl, was "W. J. Bryan." [24]

The sands were racing through the hourglass as Bryan's Congressional term pushed into its final months. One May evening in 1894, as a western breeze gently stirred the maples and cottonwoods along Omaha's treelined avenues, a group of staunch Bryan men gathered in the Paxton Hotel from communities across the state. They had hitched the wagons of their own political careers to his brilliant star. He championed silver; they did likewise: Judge Joseph E. Ong of Geneva, C. J. Smyth, and J. B. Kitchen of Omaha, Judge J. H. Broady of Lincoln, William H. Thompson of Grand Island, James C. Dahlman of Chadron, John Thomsen of Fremont, and half a dozen others.

The annual state Democratic convention was looming, and with some of these "congenial spirits," as Bryan called them, he had discussed the necessity of making a fight for control of the Democratic party organization in the state. On that May evening, the Bryanite band roughed out plans for a conference of silver Democrats to be held in Omaha on June 21. Bryan was the principal speaker, and his choice of topic—the free coinage of silver—made clear that the conference would trigger a general mobilization of silver Democrats preparatory to a take-over of the state Democratic Party.

Not only silver Democrats, but like-minded Populists and Republicans, attended the conference, whose vast audience jammed every inch of standing room in the giant Exposition Hall. It was from beginning to end a Bryan affair.

That this gathering was devoted to more than simply the future of the silver creed was apparent from the briefest glimpse at the meeting hall. Its decor suggested a wider concern than a discourse on monetary economics. Bunting in jaunty colors was wound around the galeries; big, luxurious palms provided an imposing background on the stage. The visitor's eye went not to the conventional table with its pitcher of ice water, not to two immense flags above it, flanking a sad-eyed portrait of Andrew Jackson and a barely more cheerful likeness of Thomas Jefferson, but above it, where there hung in a central position of honor a big, handsomely framed portrait, not of the President of the United States and leader of the Democratic Party, Grover Cleveland, not of Richard P. Bland, the patriarch of the silver movement. It was instead a huge, smiling picture of that fast-rising young Nebraskan William Jennings Bryan.[25]

Bryan's address did not disappoint his eager, clamoring audience. It was Bryan at his best. He refused to accept these great demonstrations as a personal tribute. The cause was greater than any man. "There is no way to secure public favor," he declared, "except to ally yourself to a great truth." Silver, which this mighty host was ready to fight for, was but a part of a greater cause. "The restoration of silver," he said, "is only one of the reforms, but if the Democratic party cannot accomplish it, it cannot accomplish the others, for the same power opposes all the reform demanded by the people today." The following speaker, Judge Ong, heaped praise upon Bryan and declared in the same breath that the next candidate of the Democratic Party for President of the United States would be "a western man." The crowd roared back its approval.[26]

The most important consequence of the Omaha conference was neither the personal triumph it brought Bryan nor its zealous affirmation of the silver doctrine. In the tête-à-têtes and committee meetings it permitted, the conference set up a statewide organization of silver Democrats, or the Nebraska Democratic Free Coinage League, as it became known. From a state executive committee on down to committees in each county and in each city precinct, silver Democrats were available to recruit new supporters, develop cohesion, and to lay strategies to take over the corresponding local official Democratic organization. With strong county and city organizations, the silver Democrats could wage a serious fight to control the impending state Democratic convention.

Bryan in 1894 was increasing the tempo of his speechmaking around the nation. Thanks to his fast-growing prominence, he was invited to more prestigious places to make addresses, and his fellow speakers now tended to be top-drawer Democrats. He was appearing more before college audiences and was delighted to woo intelligent young folk to the silver cause. National holidays, which then, more than now, were devoted to speechmaking, found Bryan sharing the rostrum with leading public figures. In a Chicago celebration of George Washington's birthday, it was Congressman William McKinley who offered the toast, but it was Bryan who delivered the principal address. His subject was "Patriotism," which he defined as rendering one's duty to his country "by conscientious performance of everyday tasks."

But Bryan's proudest triumph was his top billing in the Memorial Day orations in Washington's Arlington Cemetery. For this prize every denizen of Capitol Hill was in competition. The significance of the day was heightened when President Cleveland, putting aside at least for a moment his fuming disdain for the upstart Congressman, journeyed to Arlington with his Secretary of State, Walter Q. Gresham, to join the circle of Washington's top officialdom that provided a dignified background to one of Bryan's more superb efforts. It did not comfort Cleveland, when on the return to Washington with Gresham in his carriage, the Secretary was moved to say of Bryan, "We can be sure of one thing; while he lives he must be reckoned with as a force in American politics." [27]

11. The Almost Senator

The young prince of orators had to make a vital personal decision. Should he run for reelection to the House in 1894, or should he run for governor or U.S. Senator, as followers were urging? By May Bryan's ruminations had reached the point of choice. Having won reelection to the House in 1892 by the hairsbreadth margin of 140 votes and having, furthermore, aroused the hostility of the Cleveland administration in the meantime, another race, it was uncomfortably clear, would be risky. If, on the other hand, he were to run for the United States Senate, the statewide candidacy which the office represented would make him a symbol and inspiration for rallying his followers to overthrow the Bourbon state Democratic machine. Furthermore, the pattern of fusion, which he, more than anyone had masterminded in 1892–93, had led to William V. Allen's election to the Senate. Why then could it not do the same for Bryan in 1894–95?

On May 17 the die was cast when Bryan wrote to Judge Jefferson H. Broady, the Lincoln leader, declining to become a candidate for renomination in the First Congressional District. Bryan rationalized his step like an old-hand politician. Such a candidacy, he wrote, would be unwise, for it would confine him to the First District in the coming campaign. He disavowed that he was a candidate "for any office" and closed with the gratifying assurance that "I . . . shall return to private life with far more interest in public affairs than I had when I entered Congress." The letter, which was lengthy and was published, simultaneously presented a platform on which Bryan conceivably could run for another public office. Among other things, he urged free coinage, free trade, the income tax, and pleaded for Democratic-Populist fusion throughout the state. In a private, more candid letter, he wrote to Gilbert Hitchcock, "If I am footloose I can help make combinations . . . and I might stand a good chance for the Senate. . . ."

Giving up his House seat had for Bryan a bitter taste of remorse. It was from there, after all, that he had rocketed to national fame, with a rapidity and brilliance that compared with the rises of Clay, Webster, and Calhoun. As the time neared to leave the House, Bryan grew nostalgic. One sultry summer day, while sitting in the Senate gallery with the journalist Willis J. Abbot, listening to a dreary debate, Bryan whispered, "This place has no attractions for me. The other house is closer to the people, more thoroughly permeated by popular ideas. There the great battles for popular rights must be fought." However, the Senate, he continued, offered one not unimportant advantage. It would spare "a man of such slender means as I, the need for going back to his district every two years to seek reelection. . . ." [1]

In the eyes of the Morton-Miller camp, Bryan had for some time been running for the Senate. They interpreted his blatant warfare on Cleveland and love affair with silver as motivated by his desire to court favor with the Populists, without whose support he could not gain the Senate. From May onward, Bryan and his lieutenants began the hard, unglamorous work of winning over county delegations to the future state convention to his candidacy for the Senate. On August 4, in a public letter, he formally announced his candidacy and promulgated a platform, highlighting his favorite planks of free coinage, tariff reform, the income tax, and popular election of U.S. Senators. It was also an outright pilferage of all the major planks of Populism. Some indeed were planks that Bryan had never before advocated, or if he had, they were so far down his list of priorities that he seldom mentioned them. The most startling of Bryan's newer propositions was his advocacy of government ownership of the telegraph lines. With its membership growing by thousands upon thousands in the unrelieved misery of the depression, the Populist Party's favor was, more than ever, vital to Bryan's success. The way to overcome those Populists who opposed fusion, Bryan apparently believed, was to steal their best thunder—public ownership and strict regulation of the railroads "and other public corporations."

In his other planks Bryan reached out to the city laborer. As yet, free silver was proving to be no adequate issue to command the votes of the city workingman. "The sentiment outside the towns and cities is very strong for free coinage," Tobias Castor, always a shrewd political watcher, noticed at midyear in 1894. In his heavy-handedness toward the Pullman strike, Grover Cleveland provided Bryan the necessary issue for the cities. In May, 1894, workers of the Pullman Palace Car Company struck when the company arbitrarily refused to discuss grievances. Eugene V. Debs' powerful American Railway Union took up the workers' cause. Railroads throughout the North were quickly paralyzed, violence erupted, the situation grew critical. The Cleveland administration responded with strength. It secured a sweeping injunction from a federal circuit court barring obstruction of railways and the mails. When obstruction persisted, Cleveland dispatched a regiment of federal troops to restrain the strikers. The effect in the Western laboring community was like the dispatch of British troops against Boston colonials just before the Revolution. Bryan picked up the opportunity the situation afforded. He attacked the labor injunction and championed unionism in a patent appeal for support from the industrial population of Omaha.

In the eyes of Tobias Castor, Bryan was implementing a well-conceived strategy. He aimed to control the coming state Democratic convention so overwhelmingly that after nominating him for Senator, it would adjourn without making any nominations for state officers. Bryan would then be free, Castor believed, to work for the Populists' state ticket, while they in turn helped elect him Senator. Castor was confident that "the plan won't work with either the Populists or Democrats." The Populists would never "recognize Mr. Bryan unless he unconditionally joins their ranks and is one of them."

Bryan and his lieutenants rolled up their sleeves and applied themselves to the grinding toil of lining up the support of Democratic county delegations for the awaiting trial of strength with the Martin-Castor-Morton machine at the state convention. Tom Allen and his aides, Castor reported to Morton, "are very active in fixing up deals that will give Bryan a big send off from his own country and sit down on the administration at the same time." Trends quickly developed heartening to Bryan. The silver leagues were moving efficiently about their appointed task to control the county conventions or to prevail in the primaries that chose delegates. "Dodge County solid for you," John Thomsen wired from Fremont in a rendering of typical good news. "We will not lay down [sic] until you are elected U.S. Senator." The primaries in Lincoln were a personal triumph for Bryan. They swept his slate of delegates into victory by a wide margin. Press reports of "heavily organized voting" and "a big turnout" attested to the good work of the silver leagues. Soon Lancaster County was instructing for Bryan, then Platte County, Dodge, and Pierce. Others quickly joined the parade, including J. Sterling Morton's own county of Otoe. The defeat of Cleveland's Secretary of Agriculture and his principal political representative in Nebraska seemed the ultimate political mortification.

Equally devastating was Bryan's glittering triumph in Euclid Martin's stronghold, the city of Omaha. At the campaign's outset, Bryan's men were not expected to win there, but occasionally there were flickers of encouragement. The Nebraska State Federation of Labor, meeting in Omaha, adopted a platform, several of whose key planks Bryan had already taken up, and soundings among the delegates, who came chiefly from Omaha, revealed a "strong feeling" for the young orator of Lincoln. Bryan won in

Omaha because he was watchful to the degree that he seemed to have eyes in the back as well as in the front of his head. Over the years he had absorbed enough hard knocks from Omaha's ruthless machine politics to be wary of the grossest shenanigans. On primary day, he posted his best watchers at the polls, with a firm exhortation for unceasing vigilance, and he personally made the rounds of the polls several times. His diligence was not wasted. His men discovered quantities of bogus tickets at various polling places, designed to confuse and mislead the voter. Victory in Omaha meant that Bryan's silverites would outnumber the machine or gold Democrats by 3 to 1. He now stood, ready, willing, and able to snatch the Nebraska Democracy from the grasp of President Cleveland and his Bourbon plenipotentiaries.[2]

Bryan's chief contribution in the fight for delegates was his customary massive oratorical attack. In the three weeks prior to the primaries he toured the state, averaging several speeches a day. The fierce campaign also saw Bryan take on a new role and a different kind of political weaponry. On September 1, he became editor in chief of the weekly issue of the Omaha *World-Herald*, the largest and most influential Democratic newspaper in Nebraska. Circulating widely in rural areas, the paper enabled Bryan, whose campaign funds were minimal, to reach great bodies of voters. Gilbert Hitchcock, publisher of the *World-Herald*, announced that editorial policy would be "mapped out by Mr. Bryan from time to time along the line of his well known political convictions." The arrangement was also valuable to Hitchcock. Needing money badly, he had allotted the editorship to Bryan on condition that he invest $25,000 in the paper. Bryan provided only $9,000, of which $2,000 was his own, the balance being supplied by his father-in-law and friends. For years, stories circulated that silver mineowners contributed heavily, but these appear groundless.[3]

Not many editions of the *World-Herald* were required to prove that journalism was not Bryan's forte. His prose on paper was clear, but flat and devoid of sparkle. Although he was helped by his knack for apt Biblical quotation and homely illustration, he succeeded little in the unenviable task of making the dry-as-dust technicalities of free coinage, the tariff, and the income tax vivid and interesting to his readers. Bryan not only wrote editorials but often provided news accounts of his speeches. His descriptions of vast audiences that turned out and their passionate acclaim for his doctrines and candidacy infused his campaign with an air of invincibility. For the voter among his readers who preferred to cast his vote for the winning side—and studies suggest that his type is legion—Bryan's journalism cultivated the right psychological atmosphere.

Simultaneously, Bryan was conducting a subtler but intense fight within the Populist Party to advance his plans for fusion. Here, too, the struggle was for control of county delegations that would constitute a future state convention. The more radical Populists, the middle-of-the-roaders, suspicious of Bryan as a threat to their party's growth and survival, fiercely resisted his siren song. Reports trickling to him revealed that he could not hope to achieve among the Populists the same degree of sentiment for fusion as he had for his own candidacy in the Democratic county delegations. J. C. Ecker of Dixon observed, "Fusion here hopeless owing to the Middle of the Road Populists controlling their party and passing insulting resolutions." In contrast, S. B. Thompson of Broken Bow: "Bryan has the respect and esteem of *all* the populists here." From Fullerton, E. B. Spackman reported that the district Populist convention had instructed its delegates to the future state convention to vote for Bryan for Senator "in case the Populists were not able to elect one of their own men." With several Populist aspirants for state offices, Bryan made pacts of mutual aid, by which he would help their interests if they helped his.

The Populist state convention gathered at Grand Island in late August, and for Bryan it was the harvesttime of his efforts for fusion. Silas A. Holcomb, an attorney from Broken Bow, an honest, amiable man, was nominated for governor, a choice eminently satisfactory to Bryan. When Populist leaders sought from Bryan assurances of support for Holcomb's candidacy, he readily and enthusiastically gave them. But the Populists, egged on by the middle-of-the-roaders, turned stern-faced and offered Bryan precious little in return. Worst of all, they failed to nominate him as Senator. But fortunately for his candidacy, they did the next best thing: They made no nomination of their own. The door was left open for honorable cooperation between Bryan Democrats and his many Populist supporters.

It was the Democratic convention, meeting a month later, that lifted Bryan to a new crest of political fortune. But he had to survive a dark hour first. As the delegates gathered at Omaha, the Cleveland Democrats quickly showed their hand in all its roughness. They filled the galleries with leather-lunged supporters, withheld tickets of admission to Bryan men, and provided free railroad transportation exclusively to gold Democrats. The gold machine moved adamantly onward by nominating no one less than its chieftain, the Democratic state chairman, Euclid Martin, for the post of temporary chairman. With the chairman's opportunity to make rulings favorable to his faction and to further its strategy, his selection might well be the key to much of the convention's future course. The gold men launched another crafty maneuver. They made several further nominations for temporary chairman, each with a potential of siphoning off portions of Bryan's strength.

His face taut and grim, Bryan rose to meet the growing threat. "We might as well commence the fight right now," he cried. "We have had conventions in which the chairman refused to recognize the majority. I want to say that any delegate who comes here instructed for 16 to 1 cannot disregard it. I ask those who are with me to vote for Ed P. Smith." Heeding their leader, silver men eluded the gold machine's snares and elected Smith. Minutes later, Bryan's control was conveyed in flaming italics when the convention chose between two delegations claiming to represent Otoe County, one for Bryan and the other for Morton. The convention voted overwhelmingly to seat the Bryan group.

When the convention moved on to the business of choosing candidates, Bryan pressed his advantage mercilessly. At his signal, the delegates passed to the task of nominating their candidate for governor. They chose not a Democrat, but the Populist gubernatorial nominee, Silas A. Holcomb. The step, which a flabbergasted Euclid Martin could protest as "a most unusual proceeding," revealed that Bryan had overthrown the machine. He was also handing over his party's richest prize, the nomination of the head of its ticket, to the Populists.

Bryan was assisted in this audacious act by his revelation to the convention, in ringing accusatory tones, of a plan by which the Cleveland Democrats would support, not the Democratic nominee the convention might produce, but the Republican nominee, Tom Majors. In effect Bryan was charging his opponents with doing what he wanted to do, only it was wrong for them and right for him. No one could serve Bryan's shock treatment better than Majors, who, as a matter of common knowledge, was in the pocket of the Burlington Railroad. After Bryan's horrendous revelation, the delegations could with better conscience nominate Holcomb. Bryan's own nomination for Senator was unanimous.

Unanimity was possible because by this time the gold Democrats had stalked out of the convention in indignation. For them the nomination of Holcomb was a betrayal so gross that it constituted Bryan as a political Benedict Arnold. After emerging from the convention hall, jabbering threats and curses, the gold men assembled in the café of the Paxton Hotel and quickly organized a rump convention. In short order, they adopted a platform endorsing the Cleveland administration and reaffirming the gold standard, nominating a full slate of candidates, headed by a gubernatorial nominee, Phelps D. Sturtevant. A decade earlier, Sturtevant had gained distinction as the first Democrat ever to be elected to state office in Nebraska. He had won the state treasurership on a fusion ticket of Democrats and the Anti-Monopoly Party headed by no one less than J. Sterling Morton. In the ensuing campaign, Bryan and his friends did not permit Sturtevant and his fellow gold Democrats to forget that they too had once succumbed to the urge to fuse. Thanks to a quirk in the election laws, the gold Democrats could style themselves on the ballot as the "straight Democrats." [4]

The Nebraska elections of 1894 were fought with the same ferocity and thunder as the national elections of 1896. It was a struggle not of three major parties, Republicans, Democrats, and Populists, but of progressives and conservatives, between those who believed the depression could be overcome only by curbing economic abuse and bringing relief for hard-pressed debtors and those who saw the country's salvation in conservative financial policy and reliance on the business world to set the economy aright. Bryan's principal opponent for the Senate, John M. Thurston, the Republican nominee and general counsel for the Union Pacific Railroad, epitomized the conservative viewpoint.

Bryan, as usual, relied on unstinting oratorical effort. He made more than eighty speeches in a campaign run in faithful accord with the fusion ideal. From the stump he praised Populists, as well as Democrats. He crossed into Iowa to campaign for the most eminent of Populists, General James B. Weaver, and Weaver reciprocated with an excursion to Nebraska for Bryan. The American Protective Association again opened its coffers to achieve Bryan's defeat; the railroads gave their money taps a full turn. Banks and loan companies, whose clients in Nebraska were legion, unloosed a barrage of threats by which loans would be collected immediately unless their debtors had the good sense to vote Republican. Against this moneyed juggernaut, Bryan fought with piggybank resources. As early as mid-October the sparse funds of the Free Coinage League ran out, and the most desperate SOS's to comrades in faith in neighboring states failed to bring replenishments.

William McKinley felt behooved again to journey to Nebraska, as he had in 1892, to put down the Bryan menace. In a published letter, C. J. Smyth, the new Democratic state chairman, challenged McKinley to debate with Bryan the issues of the campaign. McKinley declined the invitation. The poverty of Bryan's campaign treasury put staggering burdens on his oratorical prowess. He resorted to the device that had served him well in his two previous races—a debate with his chief opponent.

Thurston at first wisely declined to enter this entrapment, but Bryan's insistence became embarrassing, and his opponent reluctantly agreed to two encounters. An able, logical but uninspiring orator, Thurston was no match for Bryan, a judgment his own aides concurred in. Bryan ended his campaign in Lincoln with a rally at the packed Funke's Opera House. The occasion was something of an ordeal for Bryan's already depleted vocal chords. The Republican managers employed 200 marchers, equipped them with tin horns, cannon crackers, and an assortment of other noisemakers to march and create a terrific din for a full half hour in front of the opera house. The *pièce de résistance* of this head-splitting demonstration was a traction steam engine, with a calibrated steam whistle, calculated, according to an oppressed bystander, "to set the teeth of a cross-cut saw on edge." The whistle was pulled wide open, and the general din continued until it was throttled by angry citizens, whose frayed nerves, regardless of party, could bear no more.[5]

Although United States Senators in Nebraska, as in other states, were elected by the state legislature, Bryan succeeded in bringing into use a state law, unapplied in eight years, permitting the popular vote to express its choice among the candidates. The outcome was a spectacular triumph for Bryan. He captured 75 percent of the popular votes and Thurston only 2 percent. Bryan, accordingly, would have been overwhelmingly elected if Senators were chosen, as they are today, by direct popular vote. The makeup of the new Nebraska legislature, however, bore no resemblance to Bryan's success with the voters. The legislature went Republican by a wide margin, and Thurston's election was assured.

Bryan's brilliance at the polls stood as a towering monument over the general shambles of his party. The election results proved Tom Reed's prophecy as the campaign began, that "The Democratic mortality will be so great next fall that their dead will be buried in trenches and marked 'unknown.' " And later he added, "till the supply of trenches gives out." The national House of Representatives, which before the election had 219 Democrats and 127 Republicans, was replaced with a new House with 104 Democrats and 244 Republicans. Both houses of Congress were solidly arrayed against the Cleveland administration. In Nebraska, Republicans won in every Congressional district except one, captured by a Populist. Bryan's own First Congressional District reverted to Republican control. For the Democracy, the election was what the young Missouri Congressman Champ Clark called the greatest slaughter of the innocents since Herod.

The election's fullest rewards fell upon the Populists who polled nearly a million and a half votes, almost half as many more as in 1892. They elected six U.S. Senators, although only four of these openly called themselves Populists. In addition they installed seven Representatives and twenty-one state executive officials.

In Nebraska, Bryan had demonstrated how the traditional major parties might adjust to the rising Populist tide. He had developed fusion into a fine art. Its fruits were evident not merely in his own spectacular showing. They were further revealed in the election of Holcomb as governor over the Republican Majors by 3,000 votes. Holcomb's victory was the victory of fusion. It was fashioned by indispensable help from Bryan and the Free Coinage League. Fusion's triumph in the Nebraska state election inevitably thrust forward the question whether fusion could work its magic on a national scale in the coming Presidential elections of 1896. Hardly had the returns come in on that crisp election night of 1894 when Bryan's thoughts were channeled to 1896 by a remark of James C. Dahlman, ". . . I have begun to talk you for president, —and I mean it. . . . No gift in the hands of the people is too high for you." [6]

12. Laying a Foundation

Come March 4, 1895, and Bryan would be out of a job. His House term would end, and the election of a Republican legislature in Nebraska doomed his chances for the Senate. On election night of the preceding November, as the inflowing election returns proclaimed the termination of his holding of public office, he was seated with Mary in the living room of their Lincoln home, taking stock of the past and weighing the future. Suddenly, with a kind of climactic air, Mary exclaimed, "Will, I want you to grant me one request."

Bryan, who excelled at sniffing trouble, answered in the semiformal, guarded manner that he donned as a kind of protective armor. "Mary," he said, "you know that anything in life that I can do for you, I will gladly do, unless you ask me the impossible."

Mary said she was not going to ask the impossible. "Now that you have been defeated for the Senate," she went on, "and know that political life takes you away from home a good deal, please remember that it is anything but pleasant for me to be left alone and try to raise a family." She came to the point. She hoped that Bryan would give up politics and return to the practice of law.

Bryan, his face wreathed in solemnity, replied, "Mary, I admit that all you say is true, but you have asked me the impossible. It would seem to me as if I was born for this life and I must continue to fight the battles of the people for what I think is right and just if I have to do so single-handed and alone. I care nought whether I am elected to office or not." [1]

Lacking his Congressman's salary and having to fend for his family, Bryan did return to the practice of law but steadily subordinated it to his political endeavors. He also eked out more income from his editorials in the *World-Herald.* His chief earnings were extracted from a wholly new career. Bryan now became a lecturer, enrolling in several bureaus and commencing at fees of $50, which soon rose to $100 and beyond. When the venerable Richard P. Bland, because of advancing years and faltering health, withdrew from a series of lectures on silver, his agent, the Brockway Lecture Bureau of Pittsburgh, recruited Bryan as a substitute. His oratorical skill and knowledgeability in what was fast becoming the country's favorite topic made Brockway and other bureaus eager for Bryan's services. He had scarcely begun his new career when Brockway dangled a tantalizing offer of four or five engagements a week at $200 per appearance. But Bryan's chief interest in relentlessly pursuing a demanding lecture schedule was not simply the amassing of a substantial income. He was also spreading the good word of silver. Often he spoke for a small fee, or for no fee at all, and in a small town in Delaware, where the sponsors were short of funds, he paid for the rental of the meeting hall out of his own pocket. He spoke all over the map. One week, he charted a tour with stops at Helena, Montana, Salem, Oregon, and Boise City, Idaho, and the next week he raced through the territory of Oklahoma with major addresses at Enid, Guthrie, Oklahoma City, and Purcell.[2]

Bryan's coming to these places was anything but a tepid, routine affair. His visit had the proportions of a Roman holiday. In Oklahoma City, where he appeared on a torrid June day to speak on the virtues of free silver, Smith's Grove, on the edge of the city, had all the trappings of a Fourth of July celebration. The speakers' platform was bedecked with bright spangled bunting, placards with simple resolute sentiments, and flags of the territory and the nation. At the edge of the gathering was a clutter of refreshment stands. Hawkers of "16 to 1" hats and other silver-oriented adornments moved through the crowd. Advance sales of July Fourth fireworks entertained children, and adults everywhere were engrossed in catchpenny games. A brass band noisily entertained the gathering of 2,000 sweltering human beings until the speaker arrived. The crushing heat did nothing to crumple his ardor or his listeners'. For a full 150 minutes, Bryan declaimed on silver, and his audience in his later moments displayed the same interested, exuberant responsiveness as at the beginning.

Bryan's practice in a city of any size was to make an outdoor speech in the afternoon and an evening address in the local opera house or meeting hall. In Oklahoma City the audience filled every nook and cranny of the Opera House and included dignitaries of all three major parties. Following Bryan's speech, the crowd adopted resolutions organizing a silver league for the territory and elected a full roster of officers. In an early hour of the morning, the gathering concluded its final business—passing a resolution thanking Bryan for his magnificent address.[3]

Bryan's lecturing, speechmaking, and editorial writing for the *World-Herald* provided far more than a comfortable living. They were part of a grand design the young ex-Congressman was unfolding to capture the Democratic Presidential nomination in 1896. Bryan built the foundation of his nomination in the sixteen-month interlude between the close of his Congressional term on March 4, 1895, and the Democratic national convention at Chicago in July, 1896. In those months, Bryan showed himself to be more than a brilliant orator; he was a masterful political strategist and tactician, who exploited the trend of events, the purposes of organizations, and the ambitions of men to the advantage of his political goals.

It is impossible to determine when Bryan resolved to set out after the nomination, but his activity throughout this sixteen-month period contributes consistently to the posture of a seeker of the nomination. In addition to any sentiments and desires that flamed inside him, Bryan was buffeted with suggestions and reminders of his Presidential availability. Even as early as his famous silver speech of 1893, the press, especially in the West, took to mentioning his suitability for the Presidency. In the months before the 1896 convention, letters came to him occasionally from party figures in various states suggesting his candidacy. John W. Tomlinson, a future Alabama delegate to the national convention of 1896, early articulated this sentiment. M. A. Miller, an Oregon delegate, and Governor John E. Osborne of Wyoming also took up the refrain.[4]

Bryan was indispensably assisted by the tides and currents of events. The economic depression continued on its oppressive course. Prices and wages persisted in their fall. The fate of Coxey's army, that little band of unemployed who marched upon Congress as a "living petition" only to be clubbed and trampled and arrested for trespass on Capitol grounds, was fresh in memory. So too was the Pullman strike.

The lengthening image of the national government as a ready ally of oppressive economic interests was fortified by three decisions of the U.S. Supreme Court. In *United States v. E. C. Knight,* the court dismissed a suit against the sugar trust, which controlled 98 percent of the country's sugar-refining capacity. This stark economic fact was insufficient to dissuade the court that the sugar trust was not a conspiracy in restraint of trade. In *Pollock v. Farmers' Loan and Trust Company,* the Court crushed Bryan's fondest legislative project for advancing the people's cause. It held unconstitutional the income tax provision of the Wilson-Gorman Tariff. The court's crowning blow fell when it remanded Eugene V. Debs to jail for contempt of court in the Pullman strike. Each of these judicial edicts provided Bryan new texts of protest and new planks for his platform of inequities. The cases lent substance to his contentions that the Court was excessively composed of justices whose sympathies lay with wealth, that an amendment embodying the income tax must be added to the Constitution, and that the labor injunction must be curbed.

The highest note on Bryan's political harp, the silver question, was gaining ever-widening popularity thanks to a sudden new phenomenon. A stupendous venture in mass education was afoot, launched by William H. Harvey of Chicago, author of an enormously popular pamphlet, *Coin's Financial School.* In dialogue and apt illustration, in discussion that was rigorously elementary, Harvey presented the essentials of the money question and highlighted the virtues of silver and bimetallism. Harvey first wrote on money in 1893, when he published an illustrated paper called *Coin,* and subsequently produced *Coin's Hand Book,* but *Coin's Financial School* surpassed the earlier publications, and by 1895 it was a national best seller. Silver organizations distributed it throughout the country, and train butchers cherished it as their hottest item. By midyear sales were in the hundreds of thousands. Harvey's pamphlets, soiled and dog-eared, were passed around eagerly among friends; discussion groups sprang up; speeches, lectures, and debates multiplied. Seldom, if ever, has a publication educated so vast a public on a serious political issue.[5]

As 1895 advanced, signs abounded throughout the West and South that silver had assumed the proportions of an enormously popular movement. Thousands sent quarters and dimes to silver organizations for lapel buttons, tiepins, and cuff links, insignia of their allegiance to the silver cause. Western lads, courting their sweethearts, took to boasting of the wonders they would work once the "bloated money holders" were chased from power. Muddied farmers spoke to one another knowingly of "furrin conspirators," and rural ladies interwove the silver question into their gossip.

Bryan in these sixteen formative months kept himself in the public eye at the forefront of the silver movement. Let any meeting or conference be summoned in the West or South, to lift the movement to some new crest of success, and Bryan was certain to be the star most brightly seen in the constellation of performers. Sometimes Bryan was pushed into prominence by his opponents, even by his foe in the White House, Grover Cleveland.

As the spring primaries approached in 1895, Cleveland moved to bolster his fellow sound money Democrats in the South who hitherto had posed a staunch barrier against Populist inroads. The kickoff for this important enterprise was made by Secretary of the Treasury Carlisle in an address to a sound money convention at Memphis, Tennessee. Carlisle delivered an eloquent, closely reasoned plea for a "safe and sound" money system. When the silver Democrats of Tennessee invited Bryan to answer Carlisle, he went after the Secretary with his favorite combat weapon, the Biblical analogy. Carlisle, once ranked with the friends of silver and now a staunch sound money man, presented, by his defection, an easy target. "How are the mighty fallen," cried Bryan, as David did for Saul. Not Carlisle's change of mind, but his "change of heart" was distressing. Once, as Congressman, Carlisle had voted for free coinage and had never acted against that noble conception until he enlisted in the cause of Cleveland's Presidential ambitions. Formerly the Moses of the common people, Carlisle, lamented Bryan, was now "the commander-in-chief of Pharaoh's army." [6]

An enormous opportunity opened up for Bryan when the governor of Illinois, John Peter Altgeld, summoned a silver conference in his state for June 5, a month prior to the convening of the Illinois Democratic convention. By happy coincidence, Altgeld's secretary of state and chief political lieutenant, William H. "Buck" Hinrichsen, had been Bryan's classmate at Illinois College. An invitation for Bryan to address the silver conference was soon forthcoming. Although 1895 was not a general election year, in Illinois and elsewhere, the silver Democrats sought to make the state conventions and the primaries which chose their delegates referenda on the silver question.

The invitation from Illinois would bring Bryan into association with a leader who at this moment was probably the most important Democrat in the nation. As the party broke away from Cleveland, Altgeld, more than anyone else, seemed to edge into the President's place of leadership. Once a collaborator with Cleveland, Altgeld became his enemy when the President, without consultation, sent federal troops to Chicago to quell the Pullman strike. Just before the 1894 elections, Altgeld read Cleveland out of the Democratic Party in Illinois. As a prelude to his 1895 silver Conference, Altgeld observed, "To laud Clevelandism on Jefferson's birthday is to sing a Te Deum in honor of Judas Iscariot on a Christmas morning!"

In the emerging struggle between plutocracy and the people, there was no doubt where Altgeld stood. He was already lastingly tainted in propertied circles for freeing the surviving prisoners accused of bomb throwing at the Haymarket riots. Forever after, Altgeld was known in those circles as Altgeld the Anarchist. Not a little of his tarnish would one day rub off on Bryan. In an address for ceremonies at the battlefield of Chickamauga, Altgeld did not, like his fellow speakers, Vice President Adlai Stevenson and William McKinley, praise the hero dead, but made a bitter arraignment of the social evils of the day. "Born of vast concentration of capital in unscrupulous hands," he cried, "corruption is washing the foundations from under us, and is tainting everything it touches with a moral leprosy. To be an eligible candidate now often means to stand for nothing in particular and to represent no definite principle, but to be all things to all men and, in the end, be contemptible."

To Grover Cleveland, the call for an Illinois silver conference was the beginning of the fight to control the next national convention. Firing a salvo in counterattack, the President addressed an open letter to an organization of Chicago businessmen who had invited him to address them. Among other things, Cleveland endeavored to demonstrate that urban workers, as well as business, would be harmed by a cheap money policy like free coinage. To silver strategists, Illinois glistened as a pivotal state. If, as they fondly hoped, their candidate in 1896 could collect the votes of all states south of the Ohio River and west of the Mississippi, plus one or two of the Middlewestern states east of the Mississippi, free silver could win both the Presidential nomination and the election.

So preeminent was Altgeld in reputation and influence that many believed he could have won the Presidential nomination had not his birth in Germany precluded it. He could use his enormous influence only to promote another man's candidacy. Altgeld was also exceedingly adroit. The thousand and more delegates assembled at Springfield were thoroughly under his thumb and swept through a string of silver resolutions. Hinrichsen, eager to promote Bryan's Presidential candidacy, darted hither and yon, introducing his protégé to the right people. Bryan's address was one of his best, a rafter shaker that brought the delegates to their feet when he declared, "We are confronted with a conspiracy greater than that attacked by Jackson, one international in extent and destined in its consummation to produce more misery than war, pestilence and famine." In a spirited peroration, Bryan hailed the convention as "the Sumter of the great contest for the restoration of the coinage of the Constitution." Even callous veteran politicians were stirred by the Nebraskan's oratory, and as delegates conversed in little groups afterward, "Bryan for President" was on many lips.

The Springfield meeting endorsed free silver at 16 to 1 and lamented the failure of the Democratic national committee to call a national convention on silver. Soon afterward, similar silver conventions met in Texas, Mississippi, Missouri, and several other states.[7]

From Springfield, Bryan moved on to Memphis, where some 2,000 delegates, mainly from the Southern and Western states, gathered on June 12 and 13 under the auspices of the American Bimetallic League. Although the convention was technically nonpartisan, Democrats were predominant. Senators already well identified with the silver cause attended—Isham G. Harris of Tennessee, James H. Berry, and James K. Jones of Arkansas, David Turpie of Indiana, Benjamin "Pitchfork Ben" Tillman of South Carolina, and William M. Stewart of Nevada. With his election as a vice-president of the league, Bryan came quickly to the forefront, and as was his custom, he secured appointment to the Committee on Resolutions.

The most dramatic moment came during a confrontation between Bryan and an emerging rival for the Presidential nomination, Joseph C. Sibley. Like Bryan, Sibley was a dark horse with impressive qualifications. Elected to the Fifty-third Congress from a Pennsylvania district by a fusion of Democrats, Populists, and Prohibitionists, he immediately moved to the front rank of silver orators with a single explosive speech on Washington's Birthday in 1895 in the national capital. Copies of the address were widely circulated, and he was immediately talked about as the Presidential possibility best able to unite the disparate forces of free silver. His largest asset was that as a Pennsylvanian he represented silver in a populous Eastern state, a region where Presidential elections traditionally were won.[8]

At Memphis Sibley urged that there be an independent silver ticket in 1896 to whose support all parties might contribute. This gambit threatened to destroy Bryan's strategy of pursuing the silver cause within the confines of the Democratic Party. Outraged Democratic leaders protested that their party was strong enough to champion free silver alone. Siding with them,

Bryan, first a Democrat and second a silverite, made the most effective speech against Sibley's position and pushed through a resolution calling merely for free coinage at 16 to 1. "We say to all parties," he cried, "go on with silver at your front and we shall not envy you one laurel on your brow."

Sibley surged back when the convention established a nonpartisan National Silver Committee to circulate literature throughout the union. Democratic Senators of the committee—David Turpie, Isham Harris, and James Jones—who looked askance at nonpartisan action, circulated their own letter to leading Democrats stressing the necessity for free silver men to control their party's coming national convention. Toward that end, they called a conference of kindred Democratic spirits in Washington on August 14. The Senators' language was conciliatory rather than militant, tactics utterly the reverse of Bryan's. As pragmatic politicians used to adjustment and compromise, they proposed simultaneously to promote a silver policy while avoiding the catastrophe of breaking up the Democratic Party. Firebrands like Bryan, they feared, made that disaster inevitable. The Senators' letter calling the conference contemplated an organization of silver Democrats separate from the Democratic Party in order "to avoid friction and complaint of such Democrats as oppose the free coinage of silver." The party's regular machinery had the duty ". . . to act for the whole party, without regard to differences of opinion upon a single question." [9]

The conference gathered in the sweltering parlors of Washington's Metropolitan Hotel, with thirty-seven states and the territories represented. A Bimetallic Democratic National Committee was formed, with Senator Harris as chairman. The conference settled for a bimetallic, or a gold and silver, monetary standard to placate party factions that were not willing to swallow free silver. So impressed was the conference with the need for conciliation that it listened courteously to a speech holding that Grover Cleveland "had a right" to entertain views different from those of free silver men and that not a single drop of prejudice was lodged in his Presidential veins. Bryan, to his regret, could not come to Washington. He was occupied in Nebraska with a crisis of the first magnitude.[10]

Bryan's dominance of the Nebraska Democracy, built up with such assurance in 1894, was suddenly in peril. The Populist administration of Governor Holcomb, in dispensing jobs and favors, had almost totally ignored hungry, deserving Democrats. C. J. Smyth and other embittered lieutenants were counseling Bryan that fusion was impossible and that significant reforms were attainable only through the Democratic party under his leadership. On a hot August day in Omaha, as delegates to the state Democratic convention seethed behind badges of native silver, aluminum, silk, and satin proclaiming devotion to free coinage, Bryan managed to forestall the adoption of hostile resolutions. As ironclad insurance against that catastrophe, he established himself as chairman of the Resolutions Committee. In an address heavy with nostalgia and optimism, he recounted the astounding growth of the silver sentiment and warmly hailed the little band of Democrats who had met at the Paxton Hotel to call the silver conference of 1894 from which sprang a movement that swept across the state and was now covering the land. Bryan's struggle to hold his ranks in line was eased when a cadre of gold Democrats moved to push through a plank reaffirming Cleveland's 1892 platform. With battle lust surging in their limbs, the Bryanites promoted the state convention's 1894 plan calling for free coinage of silver at 16 to 1. That the Bryan forces prevailed by vote of 500 to 5 attests to his success in preserving their solidarity.[11]

Bryan had surmounted the least of his hurdles. Most gold men, led by Morton and organized as the Nebraska Sound Money League, staged their own Democratic convention at Lincoln. After reaffirming the national platform of 1892 and adopting other conservative planks, they nominated T. J. Mahoney for judge of the State Supreme Court, the chief office at stake in the 1895 election, to oppose the Bryanite nominee, C. J. Phelps. Bryan pleaded desperately with the Populists to unite in fusion on a candidate, but the "Pops," whose soaring strength inflated their independence, were deaf to all pleas and nominated Samuel Maxwell.[12]

Organizing a rival convention was only the first step in the new war plan of Morton against his alienated protégé. Morton instructed his lieutenant Tobias Castor to petition the courts to have the "goldbugs" declared the "Simon-pure, unadulterated, original, and everlasting organization of the Democracy." Bryan's forces countered by protesting to the Nebraska secretary of state against the filing of the bolters' certificate of nominations. When the dust lifted, the candidates of the gold Democrats were certified to appear on the ballot, and both the gold and silver factions were permitted to use the name "Democrat." Since candidates were listed on the ballot alphabetically, Mahoney, the gold "Democrat," preceded Phelps, the silver "Democrat."

A thoroughly goaded Bryan waged a furious campaign for Phelps. But the Populist candidate Maxwell won; this did not displease Bryan. Disaster enveloped the further results, however, since Mahoney garnered 18,636 votes to 10,079 for Phelps. The humiliating showing is not to be explained by any sudden collapse of Bryan's popularity, for many of his followers voted the Populist ticket, as they were wont to do. Others, confused by the two Democratic tickets on the ballot, voted for the first candidate—Mahoney—and therefore unwittingly went against their leader and their convictions.

Morton and the gold Democrats rejoiced. "It places the Democracy on a respectable footing with Eastern people," exulted the squire of Arbor

Lodge, "and it raises the credit of the citizens individually and of the state collectively to see such an expression in behalf of sound finance where money fallacies have been preached so persistently, vehemently, and sonorously. . . ."

But the richest prize of their triumph was altogether visible to Morton and his friends. "The election," said Morton, "determined who shall represent the Democracy at the National Convention next year. . . ." When Bryan struck to puncture the goldbugs' chirping jubilation by proposing that the silver issue be put before the people in a state primary, they brushed him off with laughter and ridicule.[13]

As the silver movement caught hold, politicians flocked to its banner. Despite the ever more crowded political scene, Bryan remained prominent at the movement's forefront. His most strenuous and rewarding work occurred in hotel lobbies and meeting rooms where his hearty bear-hug greeting and bright humor multiplied acquaintances and his handsome, sincere presence inspired devotion.

His gift of audacity also stood him well. Presumptuously he wrote to Democratic leaders throughout the nation requesting reports on the progress of silver organization and sentiment in the state and local Democracy. Functioning as a kind of self-appointed clearinghouse, he became the conscience of the movement, exhorting to better effort, illuminating goals, and bestowing praise. He dealt with silver Democrats of all rankings, from top contenders for the next Presidential nomination to those far down the line, and he possessed sufficient importance that no one dared ignore him.[14]

Just as Bryan had plotted his career in Nebraska on a foundation of Democratic-Populist fusion, he proposed an identical silver strategy for national politics. How could this be arranged between the two proud and spirited parties? Bryan proposed first steps. Above all, silver must become the paramount issue of both parties, against which all other issues were to be subordinated or eliminated. Discussions between Populists and silver leaders in the major parties were increasingly preoccupied with the selection of a Presidential candidate whose personal record might prove reassuring to both Southern and Western Populists. Two names emerged. One was the Republican Senator of Colorado, Henry Teller, whose devotion to silver was unquestioned. Conceivably, he might become the Presidential nominee of the Populists and of a Democratic convention dominated by silver Democrats. Teller would be more acceptable than any Democrat to Southern Populists, who had long been allied with Republicans in local politics. His nomination would best assure the support of Silver Republicans, a precious commodity in a possibly close Presidential race. With Teller as their common candidate, both the Democrats and the Populists would have chosen an outsider, and neither party would suffer the dread feeling of having been taken over by the other. But Teller, under the scrutiny of some Populists, showed serious blemishes. He was, they said, nothing more than a political front for the silver corporations, who owned him "soul, body and breeches." He had never been a Populist and probably never would be. His record disclosed limited interest in the general body of Populist reforms.[15]

The other name to emerge was the most preeminent of silver Democrats, Richard P. Bland, although in Populist eyes he was too strict a party man and was deemed unreliable on such vital questions as the national banks and government issuance of all paper money. The Populists themselves had no indigenous leader of Presidential caliber. Their last nominee, James B. Weaver, lacked magnetism and was too old for the rigors of national campaigning, and their other possible candidates were either too local in reputation or too wildly idiosyncratic to count seriously in a national election. Bryan, accordingly, was pleasingly situated on the Populist terrain, for he could well satisfy the criteria of eligibility it was insisting upon.[16]

The smallest of the major party units committed to silver was the Silver Republicans, whose strength was concentrated in a few Western states. Elsewhere gold men dominated the Republican organization, most intensely in the East. Bryan aimed to detach the modest minority of Silver Republicans from their party and move them into an alliance with Democratic silver ranks. His hopes soared when the Republican State League of Colorado resolved that it would not cooperate in 1896 "with any national party which does not unequivocally declare in its platform for . . . free . . . coinage. . . ."[17]

The final party Bryan had to reckon with was the National Silver Party, which hovered like a scrawny vulture over the proceedings. Its future could be fattened only if it could feed upon the failures of the other parties to deal positively with the silver question, in which case the disgruntled might rush to join its ranks. This somewhat tentative party stemmed from the American Bimetallic League, an organization flourishing since the repeal of the Sherman Act. Strongly backed by Western silver miners, the league was committed to a nonpartisan course in boosting silver legislation in Congress. The floundering of the three great parties in the sudden storm over silver prompted A. J. Warner, chief executive of the league, to launch the National Silver Party in hopes of absorbing the Silver Republicans and providing a haven for silver Democrats if their party should not adopt free silver. Populists watched with alarm. If the silver sentiment continued its scorching progress, the Silver Party might push them off the political map.

The only prominent politician associated with the National Silver Party was Senator William M. Stewart of Nevada. No one in the party counted seriously in the Presidential race. At Memphis, Bryan had been elected a vice-president of the Bimetallic League, and leading Populists were among its officers. From their command posts, they could watch over the league's activities and the doings of Warner, who, in the fluid political situation, was not above suspicion of self-aggrandizement.[18]

A rival and even younger organization, the National Bimetallic Union, was broader in outlook, representing the strain of social betterment coupled with the silver movement. The union's membership also had greater geographical breadth. Its ranks included a swath of Western governors and mayors and wealthy Easterners such as Wharton Barker of Philadelphia and William P. St. John of New York, who were attracted by its potential for social uplift. With headquarters in Chicago and a weekly paper, the *Bimetallist*, edited by H. F. Bartine, a former Nevada Congressman, the union was a sturdy educational force for silver. Its editorials were widely quoted by the daily and weekly press. Union chapters were established in states and cities, with Bryan the prime organizer in Nebraska. But as 1896 approached, the league and the union subdued their differences. With the launching of the Silver Party, a formal consolidation took place, with Warner as president of the new organization known as the American Bimetallic Union.[19]

In season and out in 1895 and 1896 Bryan moved through a mountainous speaking schedule in the South and West. He lavished attention upon the South in the belief that since no Southerner could be nominated, Southern Democrats would prefer a Western to an Eastern nominee. His oratorical success knew no bounds. So ecstatic were his huge audiences that Sidney Brooks, the British journalist, wrote of him as "almost a second Messiah." Head and shoulders above everyone else as silver's premier orator, Bryan attracted crowds the size and enthusiasm of which exceeded the scale of any previous Presidential campaigner.[20]

One of his most important appearances was at the Texas State Fair and Dallas Exposition in November, 1895. After an address in his best form, Bryan met with leading Texas Democrats—former Governor James S. Hogg, Governor Charles Culberson, Senators Joseph Bailey and Horace Chilton, T. M. Campbell, Cone Johnson, and probably Colonel E. M. House. Bryan apparently made a powerfully favorable impression on these friends of silver, despite their partiality to Bland. Quite possibly, if these Texas potentates should subsequently drop Bland, whether at the convention or before, they might pick up Bryan. The young silver prince began concentrating upon making himself a second or third choice among likely delegates committed to Bland or other contenders.

During his Texas visit, Bryan was queried about his political future in view of his abdication of his House seat, his Senate defeat, and residency in a state normally and overwhelmingly Republican. Bryan answered wholly in terms of the approaching national convention. "Bland," he said, "is the most deserving and will have the most followers; Boies will have the backing of his state and possibly the delegates from other states," but, Bryan added, in his calm, assured manner, "neither will be able to make the kind of campaign necessary to win." The earnest young man left the implication that he possessed the necessary qualifications for the nomination. "It did not occur to me," mused a Texan who heard these words, "to imagine that one so young in years and so modest in demeanor could expect so soon to be elevated to the chief place in party leadership and become head of the nation." [21]

Bryan was also immersed in a correspondence, national in scale and devoted to several shrewdly conceived strategies to advance his own candidacy. He bombarded such leading Populists as James Weaver, Marion Butler, Ignatius Donnelly, and Clarence Darrow with letters enlisting their commitment to two principles: the right to bolt and the necessity of fusion. If he secured the Democratic nomination, Bryan reckoned, he could not hope to win without Populist support. He was fishing now for signs that Populists, South and West, would choose fusion with Democrats for the sake of the silver cause. By stressing the likelihood that free silver Democrats might be thwarted at their party's national convention, and therefore would be driven to bolt, he could more conveniently put to his Populist and Silver Republican friends the naked question: Who from their parties would fuse with the silver Democrats? To his delight, such Populist potentates as Marion Butler affirmed the fusion of all silver adherents regardless of party, and Ignatius Donnelly said that all parties would support a Democratic nominee who was a genuine silver man. A fusion strategy also pointed to the logic of Bryan's candidacy. Of the leading silver Democrats, he boasted the most solid experience with fusion. His two successful Congressional campaigns were based on fusion, and his entire Nebraska career was a working alliance with Populist leaders.

Bryan also undertook a kind of general superintendency of the vital job of establishing silver delegations for the future national convention. To Democratic state chairmen across the nation, he underscored the urgency of silver victories in primaries and conventions, out of which silver delegations might come. To ease the task, he enclosed copies of Nebraska's silver plank and practical suggestions on conducting silver campaigns. One after another, states of the West and, to a lesser degree, the South responded with uninstructed free silver delegations.

The uninstructed delegation was another indispensable part of Bryan's personal strategy for winning the nomination. As a dark horse, he could prevail only if the convention began with no candidate commanding a majority of instructed delegates. With a preponderance of uninstructed delegates, Bryan could hope to win them over eventually to himself. How could Bryan induce silver leaders to strive for uninstructed delegations? He acted on the basis of that most delectable of political rationalizations—highest principle. "Principles first" was his slogan. First and foremost, the silver cause—rather than any man—must triumph. Let every energy be bent to that end. Nebraska's position, he said, was "first for an unequivocal declaration for silver at 16 to 1 and after that for the most available man who fits the platform." This apparently selfless, high-minded counsel coincided absolutely with the necessities of Bryan's dark-horse candidacy.

Bryan's dedication to "Principles first" by no means shut the door to discreet promotion of his own candidacy. Often it appeared that Bryan applied the principles doctrine only to rivals and visualized himself as the Great Exception. As a standard procedure, Bryan, when corresponding with state chairmen, asked for the name and address of every probable delegate to the national convention. He kept up-to-date listings of delegates elected, and to these decision-makers of the future Presidential nomination he sent copies of his silver plank and interlarded his comments about the future campaign with unobtrusive suggestions of his Presidential availability.[22]

Sometimes Bryan tiptoed to his objective. Aiming to win the invaluable support of James Hogg of Texas, he wrote to the former governor, "I believe that you have all the qualifications necessary for President, and there is no man whom I would rather support than yourself. . . . I know that your interest in democratic principles is greater than your ambition to be President, and therefore you would not stand in the way of the success of any more available candidate if at the convention you found that you could not be nominated." Bryan's transparent bid for Hogg's support of his own candidacy did not offend the governor, who became an early supporter. Senator Charles S. Thomas of Colorado too was the recipient of a Bryan silver plank and the usual exhortation to work for its adoption. Thomas responded politely, the plank prevailed, and he became head of the delegation. Thereupon Bryan wrote Thomas a carefully contrived letter: "I don't suppose your delegation is committed to any candidate. If we succeed in getting a 16 to 1 plank in Chicago, our own delegation may present my name. Whether it goes further than a compliment will depend upon the feeling in other states. I am not saying this in public, but write you this in confidence. The state [Nebraska] would instruct for me, but I prefer to be a delegate, so that I can help to secure the right kind of platform."

Thomas was dumbfounded by the brazen aplomb. "Here was a young man," he mused, "barely thirty-six, living in a comparatively unimportant Republican state west of the Mississippi River, audaciously announcing his probable candidacy for the presidential nomination. The very seriousness of the suggestion emphasized its absurdity." [23]

It was in his own "unimportant Republican state" that Bryan faced hurdles. The first hurdle, Bryan's own Lancaster County convention, was easy.

The delegates who assembled in Lincoln's Germania Hall were thoroughly under Bryan's thumb and did their paces with the brisk exactitude of a vaudeville dog act. As a sign of his sure grip, Bryan rose, touching off a holocaust of applause, to move that the customary Resolutions Committee be dispensed with and the convention declare simply for the "free and unlimited coinage of silver without waiting for any nation on earth." With joyous shouts and yips, the convention followed where its hero led. His noble sentiment was suddenly, but only momentarily, flawed when a wayward delegate shouted, "Are you a Democrat or a Pop?" No answer was wasted upon him.[24] Bryan orated on his current theme of "Principles first."

The state convention of silver Democrats, meeting several days later at Lincoln's Funke's Opera House, was also entirely a Bryan affair. The confident, jubilant gathering declared itself the only true Democracy and chose sixteen delegates to the national convention, with Bryan at their head as delegate at large. Their platform resolved that 16 to 1 be the featured issue of the coming national campaign and renewed endorsements of such traditional planks as a tariff for revenue only, the income tax, direct election of Senators, the initiative, and the referendum. When an overpowering movement exploded among the delegates to endorse Bryan for President, he rose and earnestly asked that they forgo that step.

Circumstances suggest that this was a piece of premeditated dramaturgy designed to bring attention to Bryan. His lieutenant, Dahlman, presented a motion they must have discussed beforehand, that "The Democracy of Nebraska presents to the Democracy of the nation as its unanimous choice for President the Hon. W. J. Bryan and the delegates from the convention are truly instructed to present the name of our favorite to the national convention and to employ every honorable means to secure his nomination." The convention leaped to its feet with roars of ecstatic approval. Hats and hankies were waved; the howling persisted, converting a legion of white faces into red faces. In all the tumult, Bryan stood in the aisle, self-possessed and demanding permission to speak. Even when the din subsided and Bryan, his face filled with his illimitable smile, insisted on being heard, the chairman at first ignored him and seemed bent upon putting the motion to a vote. But he soon checked his incipient folly and recognized the handsome young man of Presidential timber. "I do not believe in contending for honors," Bryan began, commanding every ear, "until the contention for principles is settled. When we have framed our principles, there is time to put up candidates. Until then, the announcement of candidates only arouses jealousy and detracts from the main question of principles. I ask the withdrawal of the resolution. We can do better work for our country and for ourselves that way than by selecting our President before we know what platform he is standing on." Dahlman withdrew his resolution.

The sound money Democrats also convened, selected a delegation to the national convention, and airily dismissed "the claims of a small faction," the free coinage Democrats, who betrayed their party by accepting offices from a Populist governor and by adhering to "peculiar Populist notions." [25]

To Bryan's good fortune as a dark horse, the national convention was scheduled not for June, but for the relatively late date of the first week of July. He was allowed more time to court support among leaders and delegates. Like every other serious candidate, Bryan concentrated much attention upon the governor of Illinois, John Peter Altgeld. The most powerful politician of national reputation in the silver movement, Altgeld could sway the 48 votes of the Illinois delegation which could be decisive in clinching the nomination. When the Illinois convention assembled in Peoria late in June, the chief contenders for the silver leadership—Bland, Boies, and Teller—all were present and courting Altgeld. The uninvited Bryan dispatched a college classmate, Millard F. Dunlap of Jacksonville and a power in the downstate Democracy, to press his cause. Altgeld brusquely made known his preference for Bland, and Dunlap sat frustrated through proceedings that flamed with vituperation. The keynote address spoke of Cleveland as "traitorous" and of the need of a Moses for the common people. The observation brought shouts of "Bland" and "Boies." From afar, Theodore Roosevelt, warming up for the lusty role he was to play in the future campaign, characterized the delegates at Peoria as "murderers, horsethieves, burglars, libertines, crooks of all kinds—men who have been convicted of crimes ranging from pick-pocketing to arson." [26]

Altgeld, choosing to retain his freedom and to carry it into the convention to be applied as he saw fit, refrained from coming out openly for Bland. Bryan continued to court his favor. He sent the governor several of his speeches with a covering letter inviting comment that could move easily from approval of their substance to endorsement of his candidacy. Altgeld responded politely, but in terms of a gentle and unmistakable letdown. "These speeches," he wrote, "will give you a much more enduring and brilliant fame than has been made by most Presidents."

Bryan, whose audacity could never be tamed by mere rebuff, no matter how impressive the source, still pressed his cause. But Altgeld, who was also an immovable force, declared bluntly that Bryan definitely was not ready for the Presidency at this time, although perhaps he could capture the Vice Presidential nomination. Altgeld once explained his objections to Bryan to Clarence Darrow—that he deemed the Nebraskan a superficial thinker who did not really understand the implications and subtleties of the money question. Altgeld's criticism of Bryan was not known to be shared by other silver leaders.

Bryan, still pressing his case, even journeyed to Chicago. After what we can surmise was a spirited confrontation, a young barrister of Altgeld's firm saw from an outer office the governor patting Bryan on the shoulder and saying, "You are young yet. Let Bland have the nomination this time. Your time will come."

The initiatives in this tense relationship between the political potentate and the political stripling were not all Bryan's. As the convention neared, as Altgeld noted Bryan's rising favor in many quarters, he felt constrained to telegraph the Nebraskan: "Since seeing you I have canvassed presidential situation. Find everywhere great admiration for you but an almost unanimous sentiment that you are not available for President this time. All feel you should be in new cabinet if we succeed. Now situation looks dangerous because of possible divisions among silver men. . . . We must practically nominate before convention meets or we may yet be defeated. The enemy will try to divide and conquer." Altgeld proposed to Bryan that they have another "consultation" and offered to pay the expenses of the journey to Chicago. But no words from Altgeld could budge Bryan one jot from his ambition.[27]

By any consideration, Bryan's hardy, indestructible ambition was altogether reasonable. The signal fact written large across the political skies was that no aspirant for the nomination was anywhere near to grasping it. The leading candidates bore flaws from which there seemed no cure or escape. None of the lesser candidates, whose numbers were becoming legion, showed a potential for breaking through to the front of the pack.

Beyond any doubt, the front-runner was Richard Parks Bland of Missouri, a political careerist, with twenty-two years in the United States Senate and House of Representatives. Bland's entire adult life was in one way or another entwined with silver. As a youth he worked in Nevada's silver mines, a direct encounter with the white metal that none of its other political champions could boast. The dean of the silver advocates in Congress, Bland sponsored the Bland-Allison Act of 1878, which restored silver temporarily as legal tender after the "Crime of 1873," and he enjoyed the backing of the most influential silver politicians, Altgeld, Senator James K. Jones of Arkansas, Senator William J. Stone of Missouri, the great bulk of Senators and Congressmen of the silver persuasion, and most of the membership of the Bimetallic Democratic National Committee. Forecasts of Bland's strength on the convention's first ballot anticipated his receiving only one-third of the votes, with substantial additional strength expected on subsequent ballots. Yet his ultimate nomination was not confidently predicted by silver's friends or foes. A week before the Chicago convention, Republican Senator Shelby Cullom of Illinois, asked who the Democratic nominee was likely to be, snapped, "It will be Bland or some other crank." [28]

Cullom's ungracious proviso tacitly recognized weaknesses in Bland's candidacy. At the advanced age of sixty-one, his health uncertain, Bland was not equal to waging the combative campaign that a successful pressing of the silver cause would require. He was lacking in magnetism. Although his dignity and calm reason were a welcome relief to the strident personalities of the silver movement, Bland could never supply the verve, the rhetoric, and the vibrant idealism that the movement in its high gear needed. He suffered the further disadvantages of having lost his last election and of being unacceptable to leading Populists. General Weaver and Henry E. Taubeneck stated openly that their party would not support him. As if these defects were not enough, Bland had even two greater strikes against him. He hailed from the South, and the embers of ill feeling left by the Civil War were still hot. Mrs. Bland was a Catholic, and in an age when divisions between the faiths were intense, Bland as a candidate would lose Protestant votes by droves because of this.

The other major candidate, former Governor Horace E. Boies of Iowa, had started late and come on fast, a sign of Bland's weakness. Described as having "a Mona Lisa smile on his affidavit face," Boies had brought off the difficult feat of being elected to the governorship of a rock-ribbed Republican state. Boies' strength, as well as his weakness, was his middle-ground position on silver. While he favored the monetization of silver, he supported no particular ratio. The omission made him suspect among the more ardent silver devotees. After 1896 dawned, Boies spoke out for 16 to 1, but his earlier silence still vexed the true believers. He labored under other handicaps. Until 1884 he had been a Republican. He became a Democrat not because of any national issue like silver but because of the local issue of prohibition. Probably his worst offense was his condemnation of Altgeld's policy in the Pullman strike of 1894. Bland men decried this lapse without surcease, and Altgeld in a letter to Boies stated coldly that he would be unacceptable as a nominee. The closer the convention came, the more the Presidential bee buzzed in growing numbers of Democratic bonnets.[29]

Whether the nominee would be a moderate—a Governor Claude Matthews of Nebraska or an Adlai Stevenson of Illinois, the current Vice President of the United States—or an uncompromising silverite—a Bland, a Teller, or that dark horse in the far backstretch, Bryan—depended fundamentally on the force and vitality of the silver movement. The stronger the movement, the more likely the nomination of a silver ideologue. Weakness necessitated moderation. The proving grounds for the contending gold and silver forces were the Democratic state primaries and conventions of April, May, and June, 1896. By June 1 thirteen states had declared for silver and seven for gold. Since silver's strength lay in the West and South and the citadel of gold was the more populous East, the total count of delegates was rather evenly divided despite the preponderance of silver states. On June 5,

Kentucky declared for silver and assured that silver delegates would number a majority at the national convention. The Bluegrass Democracy, meeting under the disapproving eye of the Louisville *Courier-Journal,* which dismissed free coinage as "a fad rejected by every civilized nation on the globe," was a harbinger of the coming national convention. The silver men were thoroughly in charge and made short shrift of all opposition.

By the end of June silver delegates numbered almost two-thirds of the convention, the total which, under traditional rules, was required to nominate the President. The delegates, however, had made little progress in uniting on a candidate. Bland, the front-runner, was still some distance even from a majority. Seldom was an incumbent President so thoroughly repudiated as Grover Cleveland in the state proceedings of 1896. Those who had fought him tooth and nail were now poised to take over his party.

The Bimetallic Democratic National Committee, organized in the Washington conference of August, 1895, as silver's central command post, settled upon two immediate objectives. It girded for battle at the approaching national convention over several contested delegations. Bryan was vitally interested in the undertaking since gold and silver delegations were claiming to represent Nebraska. The outcome of that contest would determine whether he would attend the convention as a delegate, a capacity essential to his nomination. The outcome of other contests could well roll up for the silver forces the necessary two-thirds majority of the delegates to clinch the Presidential nomination. With the secretary of the Bimetallic Democratic National Committee, T. O. Towles, Bryan explored the procedures for deciding contests over delegations. Towles assured Bryan that precedents of previous national conventions had been searched and briefed and that all was in readiness for winning the fight in the national convention's Credentials Committee, where contests were adjudicated.[30]

The bimetallic committee also had the delicate task of making certain that the convention's machinery fell into silver hands. To mobilize an army to march over the treacherous terrain, Senator James K. Jones requested each silver delegation to send a representative to Chicago on June 30 to join him in visiting the regular Democratic national committee on which the gold forces were dominant. In the meeting, Jones hoped to induce the national committee to take no steps hostile to silver. Bryan agreed to represent Nebraska in this vital endeavor.[31]

No little part of silver's momentum derived from the political ineptitude of the goldbugs and sound money men of both the Democratic and the Republican parties. Sound money Democrats were handicapped by the ponderous, rigid opposition of Cleveland, who moved not a muscle to head off the silverites by accommodation and compromise. Even when silver reached tornado proportions, Cleveland clung absolutely to his monometallist position. Less than a month before the Chicago convention, the President, in a press statement, expressed confidence that the Democracy, which is "neither unpatriotic nor foolish" would eschew the free coinage doctrine which promised only defeat in the November elections. The President sounded a war cry. "A cause worth fighting for," he said, "is worth fighting for to the end." [32]

Cleveland's tenacity boxed in any possible compromises. Formulations of possible compromises were not lacking. Assistant Secretary of the Treasury Charles S. Hamlin, contemplating the hard realities, urged the political desirability of bringing before the Chicago convention "a plank providing for free banking . . . under uniform National regulation." The banks could issue notes, and "As against the cry of 'Free Silver,' " he went on, "we can offer 'free banking' with hope of influencing some delegates without sacrificing principle." In effect, Hamlin was proposing to increase the amount of money in circulation by increasing the use of currency issued by banks or, more specifically, the issuance of national bank notes. But Cleveland never warmed to the proposal and it withered.

The silverites conceivably might be undercut by international bimetallism, but Cleveland, clinging fiercely to the monetary status quo, largely ignored it. International bimetallism, although battered, was still very much alive politically. Just a few years before, after having attracted support from respectable public figures at home and abroad and from reputable economists, international bimetallism had been ground to a halt by the adamant opposition of Lord Arthur Balfour and a coterie of powerful British financiers. True, international bimetallism's poor past augured a weak future and its abundant technicalities barred interesting, even intelligible, political discussion of its merits; but international bimetallism did afford to American politicians the opportunity to lay their country's economic plight at the British doorstep. Although inveighing against British wickedness made for effective courting of the American voter, the utterly honest Cleveland was not given to fabricating issues.[33]

The defense of the embattled economic status quo and the prevailing power structure of the Democratic Party was entrusted to the thoroughly capable hands of William C. Whitney. A forty-three-year-old financier and lawyer of an old New England family, Whitney made an ideal gladiator for the established order. Shrewd, urbane, and an enormously efficient political manager, Whitney had demonstrated outstanding ability as corporation counsel of New York and as Secretary of the Navy. His role in the consolidation of the New York street railway system had swollen his already substantial wealth and brought him into the circle of such tycoons as Thomas Fortune Ryan and the Wideners of Philadelphia.

To take up his formidable task at Chicago, Whitney canceled a vacation trip to Europe and, on June 17, issued a battle cry, "I think I perceive . . .

that those Democrats who believe in the existing standard of money have a chance yet to control the convention." He conferred with Cleveland and with leading sound money politicians of the East. His wealthy Democratic confreres, including Perry Belmont and Charles S. Fairchild, also abandoned European sojourns to face the fray at Chicago.

Whitney had a strategy. Unlike the obdurate Cleveland, he proposed to venture down the avenues of retreat and compromise. He aimed to pull the sound money forces back from their place far out on the currency limb to more moderate positions, a move designed to enlarge the body of delegates attracted to his camp and to force the silver hosts to compromise on the platform and the candidate. By dint of this strategy, Whitney hoped to secure the nomination of an international bimetallist, preferably the able governor of Massachusetts, William E. Russell. Nonetheless, in public statements, Whitney continued to talk with a hard line, declaring that there could be no compromise at Chicago by the Eastern sound money Democrats and that if a free silver candidate were nominated on a free coinage platform, the party would be disrupted. The crisis, he said, was "the most serious one that has threatened the country since 1860."

Whitney and his followers put their hopes on the two-thirds rule. With the silver delegates possessing a majority, but not a clear-cut two-thirds majority, they hoped to use the two-thirds rule as a lever to force the convention into accepting a compromise candidate satisfactory to the gold Democrats. The goldbugs were not united on a candidate of their own. Cleveland himself favored his attractive, extremely able Secretary of the Treasury, John G. Carlisle, but gold Democrats outside Washington, after soundings of voter opinion, preferred a candidate free of associations with the Cleveland administration.[34]

Critical to Bryan's and silver's future were the deliberations of the Republican national convention which opened in St. Louis in mid-June. The Democrats, meeting some weeks later, would inevitably posit their course on the earlier Republican actions. The far-reaching consequences of the Republican conclave were foreseen by the perspicacious Charles A. Towne, a Silver Republican Congressman of Minnesota, who wrote, "Astounding things are possible. Should the determination of the eastern ultra-gold standard men . . . prevail in the framing of the coinage portion of the . . . platform, a new party will instantly take the field, full-panoplied like Minerva, with more than an even chance to win. And even a tame and ambiguous deliverance by that convention may lead to the same result."

Bryan attended the Republican convention as special correspondent for the Omaha *World-Herald.* All eyes were on the only serious contender for the nomination, William McKinley of Ohio, and Bryan interlarded his dispatches with accounts of McKinley's varying positions on silver in the course of his career. McKinley, Bryan demonstrated, championed silver from 1877 to 1891, after which he wavered. McKinley's proclivities for silver were most candidly revealed in a letter he allegedly wrote in 1890 to the Stark County (Ohio) Farmers' Alliance: "I am in favor of the use of all the silver product of the United States for money as circulating medium. I would have silver and gold alike." Queried at his Canton home if he knew anything about the letter, McKinley replied, "Why, no! This is the first I have ever heard of it." When reporters posed more questions, he declined further discussion. Not a few papers considered the letter genuine.

As Republican delegates deliberated, McKinley writhed in a quandary. With only ten state delegations committed to silver, the convention was solidly under gold control. Eager not to alienate the fast-rising silver sentiment of the West, which might tip the scales in a close race, McKinley prepared a plank on the currency that was a masterpiece of evasion. It promised "to maintain our present standard," with silver used to the fullest extent consistent with holding its parity with gold. But the convention's overwhelming gold strength forced a modification of McKinley's draft; more pointed language, that "the existing gold standard should be preserved," was substituted. Mindful of Western Republican sentiment for silver, McKinley insisted that a pledge be included to promote international agreement on free coinage. Of all the oceans of words spilled upon the 1896 election, nothing wielded more effect on the outcome than McKinley's astute, seemingly minor negotiation.

Despite McKinley's concessions, Silver Republicans, led by Senator Henry M. Teller, made bolder demands and were brusquely rebuffed. Bryan encouraged his friends to bolt, a step that was widely expected. In a speech notable for its mildness of phrase and weakness of voice and with tears rolling down his face, Teller bade farewell to the party he helped found and walked down the aisle. Senator Frank J. Cannon of Utah, also in tears, followed, and eventually silver delegates of Nevada, Colorado, and Idaho joined the exodus. In all, twenty-one delegates bolted. To offset the painful moment, the band struck up "Columbia," and delegates, springing to their feet, began to sing, and the galleries joined in.[35]

As the silver men marched out, Bryan, from his place in the press stand, watched them with a gleam in his eye and a slight, satisfied smile. The smile broke into a grin as voices cried, "Go to Chicago!" "Take the Democratic train!" In reporting the event, the gold press expressed little remorse. The tearful scene wrought by Teller and his colleagues brought *The Nation* to comment, "Silver is, we think, the first raw material that has ever been wept over." In Denver and other Western cities, a twenty-one-gun salute was fired in honor of the bolt.

Highly relevant to Bryan's fortunes was the question of Teller's future. His name was on the lips of more silver Democrats than ever for their party's nomination. The newer, or silver, Populists were impressed with his bravery for the white metal, and while acknowledging his silence on many traditional Populist measures, they hailed his stand on the income tax and the railroads. Professional silver leaders seemed enchanted. "I am hoping," wrote A. J. Warner, "that the South and West will unite on Teller. . . ." If anything, Teller was helpful to Bryan. His intrinsic modesty and sincerity remained intact against the sudden storm of adulation that his brave course raised. He refused to discuss his possible Presidential nomination publicly and insisted that all energy must be concentrated on the silver cause. Teller lived and breathed the doctrine of "Principles first" that Bryan never tired of proclaiming. It was essential to his strategy that this doctrine be carried right into the convention. He was grateful to Teller for helping to assure that it would be.[36]

Bryan was struggling not merely for primacy in a political party; he was contending for leadership of a social movement. The silver cause was a political and social response to a crisis situation. The elusive, long-running economic depression had not waned. Nothing the Cleveland administration had done in holding fast to conservative financial policies had significantly relieved the severity of the crisis. Silver as a social movement was the offspring of unrelieved economic disaster.

The economic misery of silver audiences made them willing to accept simple explanations of causality and receptive to almost childlike conceptions of the environment in which evil (the remote bankers) conspired against and chased away good (the white metal, silver), whose return to its former place would restore a once-known day of prosperity. Orators did not hesitate to exploit this "will to believe" in magnifying the evildoings of monstrous banking system, the trusts, and the capabilities of their heroic metal.

Like other social movements, the silver cause was one of shared values. It provided its members a general frame of reference that directed their specific opinions on such subjects as gold, prices, bankers, the East, England, and the like. These shared standards of judgment created a common subjective world of social values to which millions of Americans subscribed, while millions of others did not. In one perspective, the nation was divided into two vast social camps, one silver and the other gold.

The silver cause had other trappings of social movements generally. It had symbols, stamped on badges and embodied in songs. It had a plan—overcome the depression by increasing the supply of money—which orators could reduce to simple terms comprehensible to audiences of even little education. It enhanced its members' self-regard by attempting to restore the Jeffersonian image of the farmer as "the elect." A fast-expanding industrial society had trampled down this image and substituted one which beheld rural folk as coarse, ill-educated, poverty-prone. In the silver doxology, no man was nobler than the farmer, and his worst enemies—bankers, railroad executives, trust magnates—inhabited the cities.[37] Thus, the most important function of the coming Democratic national convention would be not the selection of a silver-minded Presidential nominee but the selection of a leader to head the entire social movement of silver.

Just as he stood at the gate of his awaiting test, Bryan lost two of the most influential persons in his young life. On June 27, he attended the funeral in Chicago of the sponsor and preceptor of his social idealism Lyman Trumbull. Three days later he journeyed to Salem to bury his mother.

In late years, Mariah had no longer lived on the manorial farm of Bryan's youth. After her children had grown and settled, Bryan had bought her a modest home in Salem, near her eldest sister. In visits and correspondence, Mariah and Bryan shared in the delights of his flowering career and the growth of his family. In the fall of 1895, illness that proved fatal fell upon Mariah. With a premonition that this would be his mother's last Christmas, Bryan and his family journeyed to Salem for the season's festivities. With four of her five children present with her and five grandchildren besides, Mariah sat up in bed, her spirits unflagging, and with traces of lustrous beauty still glowing in her face, she distributed the gifts, a not undemanding task for so large a gathering. To Bryan, Mariah never seemed happier, and her radiance lighted the reunion.[38]

From his mother's grave, Bryan journeyed to Chicago for the long-anticipated confrontation between the Bimetallic Democratic National Committee—the silver body—and the regular national committee, controlled by the gold Democrats, which was empowered to organize the convention and to prepare a slate of officers. Wary that this power should not be used against the silver interests, Bryan pressed the point that his colleagues had the right to know the mind of the regular national committee. The discussions yielded no agreement, concession or information, and confirmed the silver men's suspicions that the gold-dominated national committee would move against them. Confident that it could grab control of the convention, the bimetallic committee drew up a slate of officers who could be voted upon and installed quickly. Bryan was listed as permanent chairman.

When Bryan returned to Chicago, he was, in the fullest sense, a dark horse. On July 5, just two days before the convention began, several newspaper polls placed him last in a field of seven likely candidates. Only two papers, the Chicago *Times-Herald* and his own Omaha *World-Herald,* contended that he would become a serious candidate if the silver forces took over the convention. The Raleigh *News and Observer* engaged in a solitary act of courage when it carried Bryan's picture with the caption "May Be the Next Democratic Nominee for President." No leading politicians had as yet declared in Bryan's favor, even though their careers depended no little on a capacity for accurate forecasting.

Even Bryan himself, as Armageddon neared, was caught up in a rare mood of pessimism. He was impressed with the strength of the front-runners, Bland, Boies, and Matthews, and "as I looked over the situation," he wrote later, "I did not think that the outlook for my candidacy was encouraging." He advised John W. Tomlinson, an Alabama delegate who was pledged to him, "that I did not want him to feel bound by his pledge to me if he found it to his advantage to support some one else." [39] When, just before the Chicago convention, Bryan's old Republican friend of Lincoln, Charles G. Dawes, told McKinley and his manager, Mark Hanna, that for the first time both parties would nominate men with the same first names, the benign McKinley and the ruddy, avaricious Hanna heaved with laughter. McKinley emitted a string of polite jests, and Hanna crude jeers. They were confident that Richard Parks Bland would be nominated.[40]

13. Cross of Gold

The old myth that William Jennings Bryan captured the Democratic nomination in 1896 simply by sweeping the delegates into their decision by irresistible oratory dies hard. The superb "Cross of Gold" speech, one of the great political addresses of all time, had its indispensable place in an enterprise of many parts. Without it Bryan could not have won the nomination. But the address was more than a piece of soaring oratory. It was a part, a great part, to be sure, of an intricate strategy that young Bryan, scarcely old enough to be President, conceived and played out to win the nomination. As important as the brilliance of the oration was its timing. In the rush and confusion, in the unpredictability of convention developments, Bryan maintained a plan that looked toward his rendering of the address at just the right moment when he might maximize its magical effect in the interests of his nomination. Bryan was also the beneficiary of luck. Luck is a precious, essential commodity in politics. In his career luck would mostly elude him, but in Chicago, at several critical moments, when other men's actions were beyond reach of his influence, luck fairly cascaded upon him. In short, Bryan won the nomination by a perfect blend of oratorical brilliance, political finesse, and sheer luck.

All roads in those first days of July led to Chicago, that citadel of raw American strength, where every European state was represented by a colony, where wheat, corn, and cattle of the Western prairie were gathered up, processed, and speeded to markets in the East and across the sea. Chicago in July was overlaid with merciless heat, the smoke of its factories, and the saccharine stench of its stockyards. In return for these assaults on their sensibilities, delegates and spectators who poured into the city had the privilege of assembling in the Coliseum, of which Chicago was boastfully proud. It was the largest permanent exhibition hall in the world, with a floor area of five and a half acres, and the portion used for the convention could seat in excess of 20,000 persons.

William C. Whitney's New York Central special chugged into the city loaded with stalwart champions of the beleaguered order: the city street-railway millionaire Thomas Fortune Ryan; the handsome, astute Senator of Delaware, George Gray; the learned Charles Warren, Attorney General of the United States; the literate, influential publisher Colonel George Harvey. The men of wealth were accompanied by their faithful adjuncts from the political world—James Smith, boss of New Jersey; James S. Hinckley, the genial New York state chairman, and William F. Sheehan, astute leader of Erie County. En route, the train picked up more troops—David Bennett Hill, the suave and crafty Senator, clambered aboard at Albany, and at Detroit, Don Dickinson, Cleveland's Postmaster General and political manager. Silver men called this ever-enlarging company of the wealthy and influential "the millionaire contingent." Its chieftain, Whitney, tall, erect, attired in expensive, impeccable dress, his eyes dark and commanding, his hat tilted rakishly, was the epitome of authority and competence. Looking to the comfort of his little band, Whitney stocked his train with choice viands and beverages.

Major aspirants for the Presidential nomination and a cluster of dark horses were present in the city. The most impressive candidate in evidence was Horace E. Boies, whose rising stature was reflected by the efforts of the Bland boomers to belittle him. His lieutenants, worried by the unceasing cannonade of the Bland men, brought Boies rushing to the convention. According to a story that dirt farmers who were filling the city delighted to tell, Boies came flying to Chicago without time to blacken his shoes or clean his nails. Boies' managers kept his hotel suite filled with visitors, hoping his quiet magnetic charm would cause delegates to forget his past sinfulness in siding with Cleveland rather than Altgeld during the Pullman strike.

Altgeld, too, was in Chicago. He more than anyone excited the curiosity of the teeming, sweltering convention; he more than anyone sent chilling fear down the spines of men of property and conservative principle. Altgeld, by wide reputation, was an anarchist. The basis of this scariest of political images, which inspired endless cartoons of the governor with a lighted fuse in his hand and a mad gleam in his eye, was his action in freeing three accused bomb throwers of the Haymarket riots.

Altgeld was expected to become the kingmaker. That he nourished something of this ambition was evident in his comment to the Illinois delegation just before the convention: "We are so situated that Illinois will wield a great influence in the convention. The individual delegates from Illinois will wield a great influence on delegates from the West and South. Ours is a pivotal State." [1]

The front-runner, Richard P. Bland, was represented by the most elaborate organization. Bland men descended upon Chicago with twelve large packing trunks bearing a ton of literature on the life and speeches of their hero. The lobbies and corridors of major hotels were plastered with huge canvas crayon portraits of Bland, enclosed in festoons and bearing a confident emblem of success, a colored paper horseshoe in the lower left-hand corner. On the lapels of Bland men rushing hither and yon was a blue badge with a portrait of "Silver Dick" on a celluloid medallion suspended from a bar, one-half of which was silver-plated and the rest gold-plated, with the figures "16" on the silver side and "1" beneath the gold.

Bland himself remained at his farm in Lebanon, Missouri. There, according to the press, he was engaged in the altogether seemly occupation for a politician of taking in his hay, although he was in instant communication with the convention by means of a Western Union line that had been installed to connect his home with the Chicago auditorium. For all its vitality, the Bland movement was marred by its amateurishness and sparse imagination. The latter failing is suggested by its favorite marching song, chanted through many a Chicago street,

> Ha! Ha! He!
> Who are we?
> We are the Bland Club
> Of K.C.
> We're hot stuff;
> That's no bluff.
> Vote for silver
> And we'll all have stuff.

Bland men were also afflicted by an undercurrent of fear that their candidate might not win. Their clammy foreboding was reinforced when Senator James K. Jones, acknowledging that he was instructed for and would work for Bland, added, "If, however, the delegates from the Central and Western states believe that somebody else would be stronger than Mr. Bland, we will accept their judgment."

The prospect that the silver forces would control the convention had moved growing numbers of moderate Democratic politicians of national reputation to aspire for the nomination. Claude Matthews of Indiana was the leading governor in the race, and the United States Senate was a hotbed of moderate Presidential aspirants stirring under the silver sun. Joseph Blackburn of Kentucky, John Daniel of Virginia, Stephen White of California, and Vice President Adlai Stevenson were prominent dark horses. The wildest of this species was Senator Ben "Pitchfork" Tillman of South Carolina, that master of invective, who was strutting about the hotel lobbies with a silver pitchfork on his coat. Impaled on the prongs of the fork were three goldbugs. Already Tillman, according to the New York *Times,* was living up to his reputation "for swearing longer and louder than any other man in the city."

Yet for all the outcropping of candidacies, the appraisal by Bryan's good Kansas friend John Atwood made a month before the convention still rang with validity: "Boies is too new a convert; Bland is too old and not brilliant enough. Blackburn is too far south; you alone have every quality that goes to make up my ideal of the candidate; you are young, clean and brilliant. . . ."

The "young Lochinvar of the West" journeyed to his rendezvous with destiny in a special train of fourteen cars, bearing the Nebraska silver delegation and scores of clamoring enthusiasts. Each car was festooned with gay bunting and a sign variously inscribed in bold letters: "Keep Your Eye on Nebraska"; "The William Jennings Bryan Club"; "Nebraska Democracy 16 to 1"; "To the Chicago Convention—Without the Aid or Consent of Any Other Nation"; "Nebraska First to Declare for 16 to 1." [2]

If the silver men were not united on a candidate, they were of one mind on several vital elements of strategy. On July 4 they met in grand caucus at the Sherman House and, in an undersized sweltering conference room, constituted Senators Jones of Arkansas, Turpie of Indiana, and Daniel of Virginia, plus Governors Stone of Missouri and Altgeld of Illinois, as the permanent steering committee of the convention. No one of this committee was for Bryan; most favored Bland; and the Senators, all moderates, outnumbered the more radical governors. The caucus also established, to serve under the steering committee, a general silver committee composed of one member of each state with a silver delegation. Bryan represented Nebraska. The two committees were expected to permit general communication among silver men, to formulate action swiftly, to keep the ranks solid.

Since the silver men counted a majority of the delegates, they could control the convention's organization. The choice of officers, the writing of the platform, the adoption of convention rules, lay within their grasp. The most vital decision of the convention, however—the nomination of the President —could not be settled by a mere majority. Silver delegates were still less than a two-thirds majority, and under the rule that harked back to Andrew Jackson's day, a two-thirds majority of the delegates was required to nominate the President.

Conceivably, the silver men, with their convention majority, could repeal the two-thirds rule and then move on to choose the Presidential nominee by simple majority, but it was unlikely that the moderates who had moved into the silver camp would tolerate this blow against a hallowed rule of a great party hero. (Not until forty years later did the Democrats finally repeal the rule in the convention of 1936.)

The two-thirds rule was both a boon and a peril to Bryan's ambition. It made more elusive a victory for a front-runner like Bland and other leading candidates and enlarged the possibility that the delegates, tiring of the big candidates after a spate of futile balloting, might rush to a dark horse. But the two-thirds rule was latent with pressure for a possible compromise candidate, a moderate—a Matthews, for example—who might unite sufficient numbers of "silver" and "gold" delegates to fashion a nomination. An even more obsessive fear among silver's true believers was that in an impasse wrought by the two-thirds rule, their weaker brethren might be bought by gold men, whose pockets and trunks were thought to be crammed with money. So haunted were some silver men by this bugaboo that they dared not accept even a cigar from anyone even suspected of harboring sound money sentiments.

One of the most important elements shaping Bryan's future welfare was the nature of the convention hall. Ideally suited for the extraordinary carrying power of his voice, it was far less friendly to politicians of ordinary vocal endowment. The delegates, who numbered 906, were to be spread out in fan-shape style, in a space approximately 125 feet wide and 80 feet deep, divided into five sections. In conditions of normal quiet, anyone with a good carrying voice could be heard by the farthest delegates. But a mere glance at the hall showed that it would never know anything like normal quiet. Behind the delegates, on their floor level in the Coliseum, lay rows upon rows of seats for spectators and above stretched the vast reaches of the galleries.

That the convention was expected to be a rousing affair was indicated by the simple precaution of a minor convention official charged with responsibility for ordering the delegates' chairs. The ordinary frail folding variety, this official made clear, would not be acceptable. He chose to anticipate the possibility that stout delegates, as well as lean, might wax enthusiastic. "What I want," he specified, "are solid, oak-bottomed chairs, that three hundred pound men can jump on all day without weakening them." [3]

The first crisis in Bryan's strategy sprang from the necessity to choose a temporary chairman. The gold-dominated national committee proposed

David Bennett Hill for the post. There was a touch of subtlety in the move, for Hill was not a total gold man blindly devoted to the existing gold standard, but a bimetallist who would utilize both gold and silver in the monetary system at a carefully maintained parity. In addition, Hill's sturdy record of opposition to Cleveland might make him acceptable to the silver hosts. Since the temporary chairman makes the keynote address, which may set the theme and mood of the convention, the silver men were unwilling to surrender this privilege to one like Hill, a wriggly politician who mingled easily with gold men. "It would be absurd," announced Senator James K. Jones, "to allow a gold man to make the initial speech to a convention that has been ascertained to be for silver, and that will declare for it. For this reason we will not approve of Mr. Hill's nomination."

The silver men searched for one of their own to oppose Hill. Bryan with his oratorical prowess was immediately mentioned. To dark horses with Presidential ambitions, the temporary chairmanship normally has a value akin to the Holy Grail. The keynote speech it permits can bring the candidate into immediate prominence and provide the convention with a full view of his prowess at a moment when the delegates are hungry for inspiration. For Bryan, however, the temporary chairmanship was bad timing. The speech he would have to deliver would bring him into full prominence too soon, long before it was time for the Presidential nomination.

This first crisis in Bryan's strategy was resolved in the convention's opening moments on July 7 before 15,000 witnesses. From early morning, the great crowds moved upon the Coliseum as they had during the World's Fair three years before. The day was warm and sunny, not oppressive, but hot enough for the fan vendors to do limitless business. So dense were the multitudes around the Coliseum that marching clubs had to abandon their plans to parade into the hall. Viewed from on high, the vicinity of the Coliseum was a vast surging mass of assorted hats—soft hats with wide brims and narrow brims, straw hats, hard hats, conventional stiff hats, and sprinkled everywhere were women's hats, gay, drab, clutched, and askew.

Because of a lamentable architectural lapse, the entrances to the Coliseum were not arranged for quickly handling a great crowd. A railing with only three openings separated the crowd from the hall, and a meager number of doorkeepers were posted to take care of the ever-enlarging shoving humanity. Delegates had to run the same gauntlet as the crowd. Although there was a series of doors through which earlier arriving delegations had passed in comfort, these were now locked. Spectators were bemused by the spectacle of Governor John Altgeld and the full Illinois delegation beating vainly on the locked doors to gain admission. Sympathetic guards stationed outside joined in the beating. But the guards inside, who alone had the keys, did not respond.

Bland badges predominated in the crowd, from raised portraits to small buttons. Insignia for Boies and Governor Robert E. Pattison of Pennsylvania were next most prominent. Hawkers and dispensary stands offered refreshments limited to soft drinks—iced tea, lemonade, sweet milk, and buttermilk—for the Coliseum was situated in a district of the city where prohibition reigned.

The thousands who crushed their way in by 12:48 P.M. saw William F. Harrity of Pennsylvania, national committee chairman, call the convention to order by bringing down his gavel, whose effect was aided when an electric gong clanged simultaneously. Nestled in a gallery that reached close to the eaves, Mary Bryan witnessed the beginning of these proceedings, which eventually would grant their richest gift to her husband. From trusses of iron, which supported the arched roof, and from the fronts of the gallery, which extended around three sides of the hall, hung the national colors and other flags and banners. Just above the chairman's desk was stretched a bad picture of Thomas Jefferson framed in evergreen; to its left was a giant picture of Andrew Jackson; and to its right was what one reporter called "a counterfeit presentment" of James Buchanan done in crayon. Along the walls, at intervals, were pictures of other Presidents, the shields of the states, and various patriotic emblems. The speakers' stand and platform were on the east side, with seats for members of the national committee and special guests. Directly in front of the speaker's stand sat the sergeant at arms, and flanking him on both sides were chairs for several hundred reporters, rising in tiers. Immediately behind the platform was a telegraph room crammed with tables and operators.

The Reverend E. M. Stires, rector of the Grace Episcopal Church, a handsome, clean-cut young man, offered prayer. Promptly after the divine blessing, the gold and silver men fell upon each other in strife. The national committee reported its recommendation that David Bennett Hill be temporary chairman. Henry D. Clayton of Alabama rose to foil this plan by moving to substitute the name of Senator John W. Daniel of Virginia. Daniel's selection as the silver candidate reflected the ascendancy of the Senatorial moderates among the silver forces. The most finished speaker of the Senate, Daniel so electrified many audiences that the silver cohorts expected him, as temporary chairman, to make the great oration of the convention. The mention of Daniel's name transported the silver forces to ecstatic delirium. They cheered and shouted and stomped their feet like cattle racing across a gymnasium floor.

After a turbulent three-hour debate, Daniel was elected by a comfortable majority, but, to the dismay of silver leaders, by less than the two-thirds majority necessary for the Presidential nomination. Daniel soon launched into his keynote address. Measured by the standard of a great speech, his performance was disappointing. Since there were no amplifiers, a speaker could hope to make himself heard only if he commanded a strong carrying voice. Unfortunately, Daniel was suffering from hoarseness, and his words were lost in the perpetual buzzing of the restless audience. Luck thus smiled again upon Bryan. Daniel, who was being talked about as a dark horse Presidential candidate, had fumbled his opportunity. His victory in the balloting also served to tarnish the fortunes of Hill, a formidable possible compromise nominee.[4]

The failure of the silver men to muster a two-thirds vote underscored the importance of the Credentials Committee, which the silver forces controlled by 27 to 16. In adjudicating between contesting gold and silver delegations, the committee could become the stepping-stone to silver's two-thirds majority. For Bryan, much was at stake. Nebraska's gold delegation had taken its places on the floor, after he had challenged its right in vain before the National Committee. In reply, some of the more outraged silver men spoke of throwing the entire national committee into Lake Michigan. Fortunately the chairman of the Credentials Committee was Bryan's friend John H. Atwood.

The hearings of the Credentials Committee were scenes of vitriolic clashes. Certain that a committee majority sided with his position, Bryan was a model of composure and reasoned argument. When the debate finished, Atwood and his committee consulted, after which it was announced that Bryan's silver delegation should be seated rather than the Nebraska gold delegation, headed by Thomas J. Maloney. Atwood reported this decision to the convention and was immediately challenged by former Governor William E. Russell of Massachusetts, who demanded a roll call of the committee. Choosing to ignore the dissenters of his committee, Atwood declared coolly that it was unanimous, and Russell declined to press the issue. In further actions, the Credentials Committee increased the votes of the territories to silver's advantage and unseated four Michigan gold men, for whom silver men were substituted. Since Michigan was under unit rule —by which a majority of the delegation can determine how all its votes shall be allotted—its total vote, when added to Nebraska's 16 and the vote of the territories, assured silver a two-thirds majority of the convention. Bryan, accordingly, was indebted to Atwood's committee on at least two counts. It arranged for his seating at the convention, and it structured the two-thirds majority necessary for the nomination.

The committee also set the stage for the dramatic entrance of the Nebraska silver delegation into the convention. Atwood supplemented his report with a request that the delegation be supplied at once with tickets and places. The convention roared its approval, and while cheering and whistling rolled across the hall, a fat, ruddy-cheeked young man, wearing a bicycle cap, marched into the hall, with the blue flag of the "William J. Bryan Club of Nebraska" trailing from his shoulder and the victorious silver delegates marching in his wake. A country band in the southern gallery broke into a quickstep, and the fat youth waved his cap as a signal for silver men to yell. As their shouts came in rhythmical waves, the fat man waved the blue banner aloft. Cries for Bryan to speak leaped from everywhere in the hall, but the young Lochinvar of the West was nowhere to be seen. He was wisely saving his inevitable speech for that precise time when it would count most.

For Bryan and his Nebraska silverites it was a delicious victory. Their seating was as dramatic as Teller's withdrawal from the Republican convention. While thousands of witnesses roared approval punctuated with laughter and hisses, the Nebraska silver men chased their state's gold delegation from the floor into the galleries. Or, as Bryan himself put it with sweet contentment, "To be seated with the other silver delegations would have been one thing, but to walk down the aisle and put the gold standard delegation on the tip of my toe as they are being kicked out of the Convention is another." [5]

Bryan's plan to keep himself sequestered from speechmaking until just the right moment was threatened from still another quarter, the Committee on Permanent Organization, which was charged with recommending a permanent chairman to the convention. Committee representatives conferred with various silver leaders and the Bimetallic League for guidance. Three candidates quickly emerged—Bryan and Senators Isham G. Harris of Tennessee and Stephen White of California. Harris was soon dropped since the temporary chairman, Daniel of Virginia, was a Southerner, and it would be impolitic to have two Southern chairmen.

Bryan and his friends, distraught that his name had come forward, worked frantically for his defeat. Bryan was closeted for some time with the committee, and his friends moved about, talking down his candidacy. When the committee finally voted, its members did as he beseeched and voted against him. White, long a champion of bimetallism, was elected chairman. Bryan was spared a fate made all too vivid by Senator Daniel, now limp from duty as temporary chairman. Presiding over this great body of "representatives of the oppressed" was a savage assault on the vocal chords. The delegates were given to constant shouting and interrupting with no particle of regard for the presiding officer. Time and again, Daniel in a hoarse voice would call for order, restore it for a moment or two, and then disorder again would flare.

While Bryan was busy fending off moves that might launch his candidacy too soon, he and his friends also engaged in guarded positive actions for its promotion. He made his first appearance on the convention floor on July 8, in the afternoon following the seating of his delegation in the morning.

After most delegates and spectators had taken their seats, and just before the afternoon session began, the Nebraska delegation marched down the aisle with Bryan at its head, smiling and bowing to wild cheers and to many friends encountered along the way. Each smile or handshake ignited a chorus of "yaw-hoops." As Bryan approached Nebraska's place, an awaiting silverite let out a whoop, and Bryan moved to his seat with more applause. He was a picture of courtly rural grace, with his black alpaca coat, white lawn tie, and trousers that bagged at the knees. He prolonged the applause by moving about and shaking hands after depositing his hat upon his seat.

Bryan had no organization working in his behalf other than a few friends in the various delegations who, in an amateurish sort of way, kept his name in the consciousness of their colleagues. The hub of this modulated effort was the headquarters of the Nebraska delegation in rooms 5 and 6 of the Clifton House, a tattered, economy hotel. Its front porch was lined with placards announcing the delegation's presence, and a broad banner in the hall proclaimed that the headquarters of Nebraska's "regular" representatives were one flight up. The rooms were bedecked with flags and streamers, with a large portrait of Bryan and the national colors on either side.

To old friends at Chicago, Bryan freely acknowledged his confident expectation of the nomination. To Willis J. Abbot, a Hearst reporter and an ally from his Congressional days, he made the startling announcement: "I am going to be nominated by the convention." Stupefied, Abbot looked at Bryan "with doubt of his mental capacity." With Bland forces swarming everywhere and Bryan innocent of even a single delegation pledged to him, the young Nebraskan's pretensions seemed ridiculous.

Still in pursuit of his elusive purpose to move Governor Altgeld behind his candidacy, Bryan induced Abbot to approach the governor on his behalf. Conceding pleasantly that Altgeld was for Bland, Bryan wanted the governor to "come over to me when he sees that Bland's nomination is impossible." Altgeld, standing like a mighty oak against Abbot's considerable charm, would promise nothing.[6]

Nebraska's silver delegation elected Bryan to a committee on which his future acutely depended, the Resolutions Committee. In point of fact, Bryan aspired to be chairman of the Resolutions Committee but, upon discovering that Senator James K. Jones wanted the place, yielded it to him. The chairmanship would have automatically brought Bryan into prominence before the convention at just the right time—immediately before the nomination. Jones was much Bryan's senior and a kind of *éminence grise* of the silver movement.

If he could not be chairman, Bryan had at least the satisfaction of drafting several planks, including the most important one, on money. Just before the convention, Bryan, in an act of foresight, had called upon Charles H.

Jones, now the editor of the St. Louis *Post-Dispatch*. Finding him preparing the platform, Bryan induced Jones to permit him to draft the money plank, which was quickly adopted by the committee. Bryan had borrowed much of his phrasing from the Nebraska Democratic platform of 1894, whose sentiments and language had been taken up and endorsed by many other states.

In words that were becoming as familiar as the oath of allegiance, the money plank demanded "the free and unlimited coinage of silver at the present legal ratio of 16 to 1, without waiting for the aid or consent of any other nation. We demand that the standard silver dollar shall be a full legal tender, equally with gold, for all debts, public and private, and we favor such legislation as will prevent for the future the demonetization of any kind of legal-tender money by private contract." The money plank went on to retain for government the option of redeeming in gold or silver, condemned the resort to interest-bearing bonds in peacetime, opposed the issuance of notes by banks, and demanded that all paper money be provided by government and that it be redeemable in coin.

Tariff reform was subordinated to the money question. "Until the money question is settled," the platform read, "we are opposed to any agitation for further changes in our tariff laws, except such as are necessary to meet the deficit in revenue caused by the adverse decision of the Supreme Court on the income tax."

The platform denounced arbitrary federal interference in local affairs (a slap at Cleveland's handling of the Pullman strike), and it called for arbitrating labor disputes and strengthening the Interstate Commerce Commission against railroad trusts, pools, and consolidations. In addition, life tenure in the civil service had to be abolished, American labor protected against the influx of foreign labor, economy practiced in government, and internal waterways improved. Other planks opposed a Presidential third term (another slap at Cleveland); supported the Monroe Doctrine (a yank on the British lion's tail); and urged the early admission into the Union of the territories of Oklahoma, Arizona, and New Mexico (all likely silver states).

For all the furor the platform raised, both in its immediate announcement and in the later campaign, its substance was not radical. It was, instead, liberal, a kind of New Deal for its day. Most important, it was a silver platform, not a Populist platform. It provided nowhere for public ownership, and its demands for public regulation were mild compared with Populistic prescription. Tom L. Johnson, delegate and friend from Bryan's Congressional days, captured the significance of the document when he observed, "Not free silver in the platform, but its demand for free men, made it hated and feared."

The platform was an absolute and unequivocal renunciation of Grover Cleveland. The name of the only successful standard-bearer the Democratic party had produced since the Civil War was pointedly omitted, and his policies of sound money, the labor injunction, and his sundry expedients of public finance were unsparingly condemned. His only important policy to escape censure was his support of the Monroe Doctrine. The platform, in truth, attacked Cleveland and his administration at more points and with greater vehemence than it did the Republican foe.

With issues so great and consequences so enormous, the deliberations of the Resolutions or Platform Committee were inevitably a Donnybrook between the established possessors of power and the new claimants. "From the first assembling of the Platform Committee," Bryan noted, "it became evident that there could be no agreement. The differences between the delegates upon the money question were so radical and the convictions so deep that compromise was impossible." The sound money men incorporated their views in a minority report, and warning that the doctrines of the majority would serve to "diminish the purchasing power of the wages of labor and inflict irreparable evil upon our nation's commerce and industry," they took their fight to the floor of the convention.[7]

Just after the Resolutions Committee completed its task, a page, a small lad, his forelock glistening with sweat from running and pushing his way through the crowd, reached Bryan to gasp that Senator Jones wished to see him at once. The tall, courtly Senator, speaking in his mellow Arkansas drawl, had a request to make. Would Bryan take charge of the debate on the platform? As the Senator's words tumbled out, they utterly surprised Bryan. A wave of elation and confident expectancy swept over him. The presentation of the platform had long been a favorite procedure of Bryan, invaluable for accentuating policies he championed, for bringing his oratorical skills into play, and for thrusting his leadership upon a convention. Now, thanks to Jones, he found himself "in the very position for which I had at first longed." Commanding his emotions, as he always did, he managed to protest politely that it was the Senator, not he, who should lead the debate. But Jones was insistent. He suffered from a sore throat, he explained, and could never be heard in the din on the floor. Though he supported Bland, he deemed it a matter of elementary fairness that Bryan, the only prominent silver orator unscheduled to speak at the convention, should have an opportunity to do so. Bryan's prominence and long devotion to the silver cause, Jones felt, entitled him to the honor.

As manager of debate, Bryan negotiated the arrangements with Senator Hill, leader of the minority of the Resolutions Committee. In joint decision, they allotted an hour and fifteen minutes of debate for each side. The sound money advocates divided their time among three spokesmen—Hill, Senator William F. Vilas of Wisconsin, and former Governor Russell of Massachusetts. When the chips were down, Hill had confirmed the silver men's suspicions by aligning himself solidly with the sound money forces. From Jones, Bryan learned that only Senator "Pitchfork Ben" Tillman had expressed a desire to speak for silver. Bryan now proceeded to arrange the several ingredients of the situation for his own advancement. He did not solicit any further speakers for the silver cause. In the reality of the situation any of his partners in the debate were not simply allies; they were also his rivals for the attention and approval of the convention. It was also to his good fortune that his partner was the wild, bizarre Tillman. If Tillman looked bad, Bryan, looking better, would profit by the contrast.

Vital questions required decision—how the time would be divided and the order in which the speakers would appear. Tillman, who had never succumbed to a moment's modesty, did not now. He asked for nothing less than to close debate in a speech of fifty minutes. Of these two interlocking preferences, the first was to Bryan the more significant. He knew the inestimable strategic value of the last speech, with its rich opportunity to make the final impression upon the delegates. The first address would require a more or less technical presentation of the silver question; the last would permit a rough-and-tumble reply and an emotional peroration. The kind of speech Bryan needed to deliver was patently unsuitable for the opening, and the psychological effect he hoped to generate would be far more potent if he were positioned at the close of debate.

It would be better, Bryan counseled, for Tillman to use the substantial time he wanted to open the debate. To reinforce this suggestion, Bryan urged each silver member of the Resolutions Committee to induce Senator Jones to permit the young Nebraskan, rather than Tillman, to close the debate. Hill, who disliked Tillman and knew that if he were to precede the Carolinian, he would risk bringing down upon his own head a cloudburst of humiliating abuse, insisted that Bryan do the closing. With Jones also intervening, the schedule was arranged accordingly.

The platform debate was scheduled for the following day, and the news that Bryan would speak stirred his admirers with rapturous expectation. The Nebraska delegation, led by Gilbert Hitchcock and C. J. Smyth, now nursed his candidacy with redoubled effort. In their rooms at the Clifton, they readied a colossal portrait of Bryan, which they had been eagerly waiting to unfurl at a high moment of their hero's acclamation.[8]

A push of support was building for Bryan, although he still remained a dark horse. A most auspicious sign was the action of the North Carolina delegation which met that night and voted to support Bryan for President. North Carolina's entire vote was pledged to Bryan since it followed the unit rule. A majority of the Kansas delegation resolved to support Bryan if Bland could not be nominated. That night, too, word arrived that a part of the Iowa delegation supported him, and that the delegations of Georgia, Louisiana, and several other Southern states were discussing him as a possibility. When George B. McClellan, Jr., the gentlemanly New York politician and scion of the illustrious general, reached Chicago late and encountered Congressman Benton McMillin of Tennessee in the Auditorium Hotel, he asked the irrepressible question : Who was the nominee to be? It was to be Bryan, McMillin replied quickly. "There is something going on here that I can't get the hang of. There are a lot of men here who are going to try to slip him over, but how they are going to do it I can't find out."

But there were other bands of men working zealously to slip other candidates over. On the night before his address, Bryan was visited at his genteelly shabby rooms by the most distinguished political contingent that had yet found its way there. They were a trio of legislators, Congressman Charles A. Towne of Minnesota, Congressman Charles S. Hartman of Montana, and Thomas M. Patterson, editor of the *Rocky Mountain News.* At once they came to the point. They wanted Bryan to support for the Democratic nomination the hero of the Silver Republicans, Senator Henry Teller. They developed their arguments at length, and Bryan courteously heard them through. He then declared in his solemn, confident manner that he did not regard Teller's nomination as a possibility, although he was perfectly willing to vote for him because of his eminence in the silver cause. Silver Democrats, he elaborated, had won the fight in their party, while Silver Republicans had lost the fight in theirs. It was easier, he added with an air of finality, to lure disappointed Republicans over to the Democratic Party than to carry victorious Democrats over to the Republicans. The young Nebraskan's absolute aplomb swayed Patterson into asking, out of curiosity, who could be nominated. Bryan replied evenly and without blinking an eyelash that he himself had as good a chance as anyone. The incredulous visitors, after leaving this model of youthful certitude, all looked at one another, broadly smiling at the display of gross presumption.

Late that evening, when he finally managed to escape the ever-growing press of visitors, Bryan, Mary, and a Texas friend, Dr. Charles M. Rosser, had supper at the Saratoga Restaurant on Dearborn Street. As the trio ate an indifferent meal, they viewed from their table by the window the convention crowd outside pushing through the street, an endless river of human energy and excitement. Loud throbbing bands fueled the tempo, and the signs on their bass drums and on the banners of marchers who followed were overwhelmingly devoted to advertising Richard P. Bland. As Bryan and his companions gazed with irrepressible curiosity at the campaign buttons worn by passersby, they noted, too, the predominance of Bland. Boies periodically gained the spotlight when squads of shouters pushed by in great wedges, proclaiming his name. Bryan, looking out upon the waves of enthusiasm, broke into his confident smile and said, "These people don't know it, but they will be cheering for me just this way by this time tomorrow night. I will make the greatest speech of my life tomorrow in reply to

Senator Hill. . . . I will be at my best. Hill is the brains of the opposition, and when I have answered him, it will dawn on the convention that I am a pretty good man to lead the fight."

Mary, who knew of Bryan's optimistic assessment but as a dogged realist remained a trifle skeptical, turned to Dr. Rosser and asked, "Don't you think that Mr. Bryan has a good chance to be nominated?" Before Rosser could answer, Bryan, his confident smile unbroken, said evenly, "So that you both may sleep well tonight, I am going to tell you something. I am the only man who can be nominated. I am what they call 'the logic of the situation.' " [9]

The logic required illumination, for on the night before the great address, the press was predicting Bland's nomination at no later than the third ballot. Bryan's candidacy was conspicuously absent from listings of possible nominees. He earned his best notice that night from a cartoonist in a Chicago paper, depicting him as a very small and very dark horse, hitched to a sapling at the far outskirts of the political racetrack.

July 9, the day of the most memorable political address in American history, found the auditorium crackling with excitement. Delegates and spectators pushed their way into the hall for the opening, scheduled to begin promptly at 10 A.M. The reports of the several committees were to be made vehicles by which the silver forces were to solidify their hold on the convention. Whispers ran through the crowds like licking flames that Bryan at last would speak. "Wait until you hear Bryan," the silver men were saying.

A rush of breeze from Lake Michigan made fans unnecessary. The aisles and floor were swept free of debris. Fresh roses graced the platform desk. The monotony of whiskered faces was relieved by dashes of colors in the galleries of gay dresses and boutonnieres of roses. Pages and convention officers rushed about. The bands ground out the favorite tunes while thousands hummed, and when they broke out occasionally into "Dixie" and "My Maryland," the crowd let go. Soon after the session opened, a booming sound of music rose from the far northern end of the building. A marching club appeared and paraded uncertainly through the crowded galleries. A big blue silk banner unfurled to proclaim its identity—"The W. J. Bryan Club, 16 to 1." A strong wave of applause swept over the sea of hats and heads.

There were the usual delays of committees in readying their reports and the summoning of speakers to fill in time. The themes of the silver speakers grew bolder and more vituperative. Senator Blackburn proclaimed that "Christ drove from the temple a better set of men than those who for twenty years have shaped the financial legislation of this country." David Overmeyer, staunch silverite of Kansas, hailed the transfer of "the seat of empire" from "the Atlantic to the great Mississippi Valley."

At last the permanent chairman, Senator White, recognized Senator Jones for the reading of the platform. Jones, whose strong commanding presence contrasted strangely with a lackadaisical eloquence, commenced a droning reading. When he came to the silver passages, even he could not suffocate the enthusiasm of the vast audience. It broke into a delirium of joy. "It was," observed a dismayed reporter, "like bringing a new mess of playthings into the violent wards of an insane asylum."

His reading finished, Jones explained the order of debate to be followed. Bryan was seated with the Nebraska delegation, and his every move touched off applause—when he rose to shake a hand, wave across the hall, or whisper to a fellow Nebraskan. A. B. Macdonald, a journalist, sniffing for convention trends, approached Bryan. They shook hands, which transported the convention into an uproar. Leaning down to Bryan, who resumed his seat, Macdonald whispered, "Who will be nominated?" With a half-eaten sandwich in one hand, Bryan cupped the hollow of his other hand to the side of his mouth, and with a twinkle dancing across his eyes, he said, "Strictly confidential, not to be quoted for publication, I will be." Macdonald laughed, out of politeness, at what surely was a joke. In appropriate spirit, he bantered back, "I believe I'll take it myself."

The debate on the platform began. Tillman came forward to speak, his dark face flushed, his hair awry, his one eye gleaming, his collar and necktie askew, his coat rumpled. The solitary sign of ordered neatness was his inevitable pitchfork emblem on a lapel. His appearance of cultivated dishevelment was an omen of his oratorical style. Tillman perceived in the convention's brassy excitement a magnified replica of his rural South Carolina audiences. He resorted to the full bag of his demagogic tricks to exploit an opportunity at which he was a proved master. Defiant against the prejudice he could feel from non-Southerners against him, Tillman launched into the grating task of demonstrating that silver was a sectional issue. Introducing himself as one who came "from a state which is the home of secession," he contended that the financial system put the South and West, "the hewers of wood and drawers of water . . . in bondage to the East."

Northerners in the restless crowd who bridled at a righteous lashing from a Southerner cried "Time" and "Boil it down," driving Tillman deeper into vituperation. Each time he used the words "secession" and "sectional" in his angry sentences, the audience hissed. Only three things hiss, he cried, "serpents, geese, and men." It was the wrong speech to the wrong audience. When Tillman sat down, he and his friends knew that he had missed his opportunity.

An embarrassed Senator Jones took pains to repudiate Tillman's sectionalism, and Senator David B. Hill, the urbane, master manipulator, moved forward to speak. Many who distrusted Hill feared he might pluck the fruit of temptation by moving over to the silver side and capturing the nomina-

tion. But he was true to the colors of sound money and international bimetallism, and attacked the platform, Tillman, and free silver in an expert, aggressive performance.

As Hill began, Bryan was writing a reply to a note a page had brought
from Clark Howell of the Atlanta *Constitution.* "You have now the opportunity of your life," Howell had written. "Make a big, broad, patriotic speech
that will leave no taste of sectionalism in the mouth and which will give a
sentiment that will touch a responsive chord in the heart of the whole country." Bryan's reply was stronger than the weakness he always felt in the
depths of his stomach before making an important speech. He wanted to lie
down, but he bravely wrote to Howell, "You will not be disappointed. . . .
I will speak the sentiment of my heart and I think you will be satisfied."

Hill's speech, as it continued, was a reasoned exposition of the case for
sound money and a brisk attack upon the silver forces. He decried the presence in the platform of planks endorsing greenbacks as legal tender, supporting the income tax, and condemning the Supreme Court. He defended
the Cleveland administration and lamented the predominance at the convention of Populists "who never voted the Democratic ticket in their lives"
and who now "have organized this party." It was, in Bryan's words, a "very
strong speech," but, just as Tillman's was overheated, Hill's erred in lack of
feeling. Reasoned and logical, it failed to stir the emotions.

Senator William F. Vilas, the next sound money orator, "pounded," as
Bryan put it, "the advocates of free coinage without mercy," but his style
was bland, and when his voice faltered, the great crowd, mocking and insulting, made his continuation difficult. Vilas bravely held on, and strayed
into the time allotted the next speaker, Governor William E. Russell of
Massachusetts. Fearful of losing his turn to speak, Russell protested to Hill.
Bryan, who overheard the exchange, stepped up to suggest that the time on
both sides be extended ten minutes. Russell was delighted, Hill agreed, and
Bryan, by gaining for himself another ten minutes of precious speaking
time, enjoyed another "unexpected bit of good fortune."

Russell, a brilliant young man, a new political star in the East, contrasted
pleasingly with the older politicians who had preceded him. Suffering from
a serious physical weakness that would soon bring death in his fortieth year,
Russell concentrated his attack on the financial plank. His frailty made impossible the projection of his voice beyond a few rows. Fascinated by the
strength of this brave spirit, the crowd permitted him to finish. The silver
enthusiasts felt cheated; their cause had been pummeled by the sound
money gladiators. Their only spokesman, Tillman, had been ineffective.[10]

As soon as Russell finished, Bryan sprang from his seat, strode rapidly
down the aisle, and bounded up the steps two at a time to the platform.
Strong cheering began in the front and rolled back across the floor and up

through the galleries. He reached the speaker's stand, and the applause grew like a forest fire in fury and swept beyond the galleries into the lobby and out into the street. The galleries stood up, almost in unison; delegates rose; and even the distinguished guests stood. Crowds pressed around the entrance ways to the floor surged forward.

Tall, slender, "every inch an Apollo," his eyes flashing beneath a crest of raven hair, his great jaw set, sincerity and inspiration leaping from his face, Bryan assumed for a moment a statuesque pose. Head thrown back, foot thrust forward, his left hand on the lectern, his right hand extended over his head toward delegates and galleries, he appealed for silence. But the heroic stance only lured the great crowd on. Iowa raised her flags and touched off a display of waving handkerchiefs which rolled, like the whitecaps of the sea, up to the roof of the Coliseum. To cheer better, delegates climbed up on their chairs, and the Nebraskans tied red bandannas to their canes. The wild cheering was soon supplemented by a dull rumble. The vast crowd, their throats giving out, took to beating the floor with their feet, their umbrellas, and their canes. It seemed as though suddenly herds of buffalo were pounding through the entranceways. But within minutes, above the dull din, shrill cries grew quickly in intensity: "Bryan, Bryan, Bryan. What's the matter with Bryan?"

Bryan, still motioning for silence, maintained his pose, head thrown back and one hand on the podium. Everything in his manner suggested the accomplished actor standing as a central and heroic figure at an historic scene. His every motion renewed the cheering, until finally the energies of the great crowd were sufficiently spent for him to begin.

He immediately commanded his audience. Speaking clearly, distinctly and effortlessly, he projected his voice to the farthest seats. Other speakers had strained and lost their voices, but Bryan was the first to achieve this range. "He did not seem to raise his voice at all," Josephus Daniels noted. Bryan quickly produced a theme for the overwrought crowd to sink its emotional teeth into. "The humblest citizen in all the land," he proclaimed, "when clad in the armor of a righteous cause, is stronger than all the hosts of error. I come to speak to you in defense of a cause as holy as the cause of liberty—the cause of humanity."

The present issue involved in that cause was money, free silver, and never before had so great an issue been fought. He recounted the successive triumphs of the free silver movement, beginning with the Democratic Congressional Manifesto, or "The Call" of 1895 which aimed to place a silver plank in the national platform. The silver men, with "the zeal of Peter the Hermit," had gone forth to victory after victory and were assembled now not to condemn or protest, but "to enter the judgment of the people."

With every sentence, Bryan increased his dominion over his audience. As he uttered each contention, the crowd would rise and shout its approval and then sit down and with the stillness of a church congregation await his next contention. "The audience," Bryan said of this disciplined scene, "acted like a trained choir—in fact, I thought of a choir as I noted how simultaneously and in unison, they responded to each point made." As Bryan gazed down upon the delegates, his attention was drawn repeatedly to two great figures who stood like sentinels on either side of his vision. Both were well over six feet and beardless. By the aisle on one side former Governer James Hogg of Texas, and on the other, Congressman Ollie James of Kentucky. Delight and agreement illumined their faces. As Bryan, in his controlled speaking manner, turned from one side of the hall to the other, they were like two beacons guiding and encouraging his course.

As he continued, Bryan took pains to stress that the silver cause was impersonal. It was directed at no man or section, certainly not at Senator Hill or Governor Russell, who properly represented the interests of their states as they saw them. But, he contended, when the gold men "tell us" that the silver forces "are about to disturb your business interests, we reply that you have disturbed our business interests by your course." Easterners, he suggested, had too narrow a definition of the businessman.

He offered his own definition, to which he would advert for years to come. "The man who is employed for wages," he cried, "is as much a business man as his employer; the attorney in a country town is as much a business man as the corporation counsel in the great metropolis." And so he continued. "The merchant at the crossroads store. . . . The farmer who goes forth in the morning and toils all day . . . who by the application of brain and muscle to the natural resources of the country creates wealth, is as much a business man as the man who goes upon the board of trade and bets upon the price of grain. . . ."

As Bryan advanced to each step of his definition, the crowd went berserk with approval and delight. Farmers, when they heard themselves classed as businessmen, sailed their hats through the air. One enraptured farmer thrashed a vacant seat with his coat, exclaiming, "My God! My God!" When Bryan added to his definition "The miners who go down a thousand feet," he touched off a new uproar.

Unlike his colleague Tillman, Bryan declined to castigate the East. But he had a special word for the West (to which he pointed). Its pioneers, who had braved and tamed the wilderness and planted the institutions of civilization upon the plains, deserved as much consideration from the Democratic Party as any other people of the nation. "We have petitioned, and our petitions have been scorned; we have entreated, and our entreaties have been disregarded; we have begged, and they have mocked when our calamity came. We beg no longer; we entreat no more; we petition no more. We defy them!"

Bryan pushed the attack. "What we need is an Andrew Jackson to stand

. . . against the encroachments of organized wealth." He rejected the charge that the platform was made "to catch votes." Rather, he said, changed conditions make new issues, and Democratic principles, "as everlasting as the hills," must be applied to them. One such issue was the income tax, and it would be paid gladly by those worthy to enjoy good government. Another was that the right to coin and issue money belonged to government, a sovereign power, and "can no more, with safety, be delegated to private corporations than the power to enact penal statutes or to levy taxation. . . ."

Reflecting the priorities of the platform, Bryan declared that silver was the paramount issue. True, the platform was attentive to that most traditional of Democratic causes, the tariff, but silver now took precedence. For if the protective tariff "has slain its thousands, the gold standard has slain its tens of thousands. If they ask us why we do not embody in our platform all the things that we believe in we reply that when we have restored the money of the Constitution all other necessary reforms will be possible but that until this is done there is no other reform that can be accomplished."

Bryan viewed the nation and the world as scenes of struggles and choices involving the forces of virtue and evil. At home, it was the cities against the countryside. "You tell us the great cities are in favor of the gold standard. Burn down your cities and leave your farms, and your cities will grow up again. But destroy your farms and the grass will grow in every city of the Union." Men, Bryan found, must choose between two theories of government. One held that "if you will only legislate to make the well-to-do prosperous, their prosperity will leak through on those below." An opposing theory, or "Democratic idea," suggested that "if you legislate to make the masses prosperous, their prosperity will find its way up through every class which rests upon them." (Franklin Roosevelt's New Deal and the social programs of succeeding Presidents concurred in Bryan's choice.)

International affairs, too, could be presented in polarities. Let the United States legislate on any subject "without waiting for the aid or consent of any other nation. . . . It is the issue of 1776 over again . . . instead of having a gold standard because England has, we will restore bimetallism and then let England have bimetallism because the United States has it. If they dare to come out in the open field and defend the gold standard as a good thing, we will fight them to the uttermost."

Bryan moved into the immortal sentences: "Having behind us the producing masses of this nation . . . we will answer their demands for a gold standard by saying to them: You shall not press down upon the brow of labor this crown of thorns, you shall not crucify mankind on a cross of gold."

As he uttered the words "crown of thorns," Bryan raised his hands to the sides of his head; his fingers, spread inward, moved slowly down close to his temples, transfixing his audience into imagining the thorns piercing his brow and the trickling blood. Upon proclaiming the "cross of gold," he held out his arms in crosslike fashion. For almost five seconds, he assumed the posture of one crucified in the flesh. Then he lowered his arms to his side and took one step backwards. Delegates and galleries sat silent, as if mesmerized. He started toward his seat in a silence he found "really painful." He had almost reached the floor when the mighty volcano of human emotions, so long checked, erupted.[11]

Waves of tumultuous, almost frightening sounds pounded the auditorium, accompanied by furious motion. From end to end the vast interior was carpeted with fluttering objects, anything that could be waved—handkerchiefs, canes, umbrellas, hats, and newspapers. For the first time since the convention began, silver delegates could join in an act of unanimity. They went collectively crazy. No one escaped the madness. In the North Carolina delegation, a distinguished judge, with a bearing of seemingly impregnable dignity, grabbed up the North Carolina banner and, followed by the entire state delegation, joined a fast-growing parade around the hall.

Delegates of other states lifted their banners, fought their way through the aisles, and clustered around the Nebraska delegation. Silver men fell over one another in the effort to reach Bryan. Within seconds after he resumed his seat, Bryan was the center of a shouting, shoving mob, eager to grab his hand. Tennessee and Texas reached him first, and others quickly pressed in. Amid the wild noise the solid sitting Bryan was the hub of a growing circle of flags and banners. Several sturdy admirers lifted him to their shoulders and ventured several steps but were defeated by the surging crowd and the weight of their burden. They deposited him feetfirst upon a chair. Flushed and agitated, he mopped his brow with a great kerchief. A Nebraskan, standing by, fanned him vigorously. Every moment he reached out for some eager, congratulatory hand. Whenever the din waned a trifle, the Bryan men stirred up a fresh outburst. A full twenty-five minutes of turmoil passed.

A fat man carrying the Kentucky banner marched up the main aisle, and after him came the banners of Alabama, Nebraska, Louisiana, and a lengthening string of other states, Western and Southern. To the accompaniment of earsplitting yells, the growing procession, first of hundreds and then of thousands, began moving around the confines of the delegates' reservation.

Bryan's speech was a triumph of style over substance. It was significant, not for what it said, but for what it did not say. It was, despite the sectional overtones of the convention, remarkable for its modulation of the sectional spirit. It pointed to no villains; rather, it expressed understanding for the positions of the sound money spokesmen. Like the platform, the speech was not a Populist refrain. It was a silver speech, but just barely, for even on that subject it trod lightly. Bryan was ingeniously unspecific; although he broadly implied evil and abuse, he cited no details and exposed no realities. His words were a fabric of catchy but vacuous expressions, rich in cadenced appeals to an audience in which emotion, rather than reason, reigned. Midway in the uproar, Altgeld turned to Clarence Darrow and asked, with justification, "I have been thinking over Bryan's speech. What did he say, anyhow?"

Altgeld touched on the heart of the intent and design of the speech. To win the Presidential nomination under the two-thirds rule, Bryan had to appeal to a huge mass of delegates, not merely to those blindly committed to the silver cause. His cause could not be won by the West and the South alone but needed help from the border states, the Middle West, and, even better, the East. The speech was not a new speech inspired by or tailored for the convention. It was an old speech, tried and tested in many forums. Bryan had used parts of it in Congress and most of it in a debate at Crete, Nebraska, just a week before Chicago. Although he made minor adjustments to his text for the convention and added only one new argument, the definition of the businessman, its most notable feature was its almost universal inclusiveness. The "crown of thorns, cross of gold" metaphors, as has been noted, were also thoroughly pretested in Congressional speeches.

The metaphors were ideally suited to Bryan's purpose. They could evoke identity and approval from anyone with any kind of dissatisfaction with the world. They lent themselves to sonorous delivery, their Biblical source conveying absolute authority and unimpeachable prophecy. Delivered with Bryan's eloquence, they and their vague social message were irresistible. Josephus Daniels described the spell that enveloped the convention. "The fountains in the hearts of men were stirred," he wrote. "They believed that Bryan was a young David with his sling, who had come to slay the giants that oppressed the people and they felt that a new day had come and, with it, a new leader. Clean of limb, clean of heart, and clean of mind, he was a vital figure . . . like the others, I had been swept away on a tide of hero worship." [12]

While Bryan remained an island of composure in a sea of adulation, one jubilant politician after another approached to say that members of their delegations would vote for him. Others rushed to report that their entire states had just pledged to him. Some were eager to discuss a doubt or rumor that caused their commitment to dangle in suspense. Did Bryan drink to excess? one delegate asked anxiously, and he received the firm, reassuring reply that the Nebraskan was, and always had been, a teetotaler. Another delegate related how a colleague accused Bryan of saying that he would not support a gold candidate if one were nominated. Bryan answered that he would no more support a gold candidate than he would an army marching on his house. The delegate vigorously agreed and raced off with the gratifying intelligence.

Arthur Sewall, a delegate of Maine, bustled up to declare that Bryan could be nominated that very night if his friends would prevent adjournment. To Sewall, he gave the same answer that he did to the note a page had just deposited in his lap from Senator James K. Jones. "You can be nominated on the first ballot," it read. "Shall we begin voting?" With a smile and a shake of his head, Bryan wrote, "If my boom won't last over night, it won't last until November." Within moments, the convention adjourned, and the jubilant delegates and spectators trooped out into the streets.

Actually, several factors contributed to Bryan's decision to delay. His forces needed time to organize their new strength. His oratory had indeed moved the delegates, but those circumspect souls could not be expected to disregard commitments to Bland and Boies for a new attachment to Bryan. That night was a frenzy of agitated low-voiced discussions in hotel corridors and rooms between representatives of the rival candidates and delegates who were to be wooed and won. The eager, confident enterprise of the Bryan men contrasted with the nervous bustle of the Bland camp. The latter, led by Governor William J. Stone, Senator Francis M. Cockrell of Missouri, and Senator George G. Vest of Kentucky, rushed among the leaders inquiring anxiously if their delegations would hold for Bland. In addition, the Bland leaders were feverishly concocting a floor strategy to counterweigh the impact of the Bryan speech. They reposed their jarred hopes in the considerable oratorical powers of Senator Vest, who was to place Bland in nomination.

As for Bryan, he passed the evening serenely in his modest, dully lit rooms at the Clifton House. Through his door, which was never closed because of the incessant coming and going of visitors, trooped ecstatic friends and noisy supporters. Upon Bryan and Mary poured waves of congratulations and confident well-wishing. Willis Abbot, who stopped by late in the evening, was amused to find in the throng which pressed upon the young orator, many faces who, just hours before, had scoffed at his hopes and mocked his capabilities. He would have been even more amused had he known that Murat Halstead, a leading reporter, had telephoned William McKinley, tightly secluded in Canton. When Halstead ventured to predict that Bryan would be nominated, McKinley was incredulous. "That is rot," he said and hung up the phone.[13]

The wooing of delegates consumed all the next day, and not until 8:30 P.M. were nominations called for. A crowd of 25,000 filled every seat of the steaming, brightly lighted hall. Senator Vest nominated Bland in a speech that was lackluster until he hit upon a rhyme, "Silver Dick would make McKinley sick." This ignited a bedlam, but as one observer sensed, "Fear of Bryan and his sudden leap into favor stimulated the cheering."

An obscure Georgia delegate, Judge Henry T. Lewis, moved forward, presumably for a seconding speech. His first words enraptured the delegates. He wished to present, he said, a "sterling Democrat . . . a soul come to lead the Israelites to battle." The name that flew from his lips was not Bland, but "William Jennings Bryan." The judge was out of order, but the convention again convulsed with approval. The Bryan men, caught unawares, worked mightily to launch another stampede of state banners to Nebraska. Six states quickly took up the procession, but the banners of other states seemed glued to the floor. A picture of Bryan lifted in the air failed to attract a single additional banner. But the lusty fifteen-minute din belied Altgeld's prediction of the night before that the Bryan boom would be by now as "dead as a door nail."

One after another the major candidates and favorite sons were nominated: Boies, Matthews, Blackburn, McLean, Governor Sylvester Pennoyer of Oregon, and Pattison. The first real indication of the sound money men's intentions flashed when the Massachusetts delegation announced that the platform adopted made it impossible for Massachusetts to offer the name of Governor Russell or any other candidate.

At 12:55 A.M., July 10, an adjournment was forced until 10 A.M. by those who feared that to begin the balloting would prompt a stampede to Bryan. By no means was so flattering an assessment generally entertained. The discerning Altgeld, conceding the loss of several Southern states to Bryan, deemed the West intact and predicted inevitable victory for Bland. Not a few reporters were impressed that Bryan's strength lay far more in the galleries than among the delegates.

Through the night and into the morning, the delegations again were wooed and caucused. Rumors and reports sweeping through the hotel corridors had it that one Southern state after another was abandoning Bland for Bryan and that even Altgeld's Illinois delegation was teetering on that brink. A group of Bryan enthusiasts, unknown to their hero, began negotiations to swing Ohio over on the second or third ballot. That pivotal state, with Illinois according to the plan, might unloose a stampede. In exchange, John R. McLean, a wealthy newspaper owner of Cincinnati, was to be awarded the Vice Presidency. Dr. Rosser, who was party to this secret negotiation, rushed to Bryan to report the joyous news that victory was in sight.

The deal, Bryan acknowledged pleasantly, stood the test of "practical politics." Then a change swept over his face, "a look of decision I learned to recognize," Rosser said, and the young orator declared in measured words that the deal must be declined. McLean, despite his support of silver, was not politically "straight," he said, and in any event he could not afford to be nominated by any kind of trade. Furthermore, he said evenly, it was not necessary. "There are not enough politicians in the world to defeat me." The first ballot began. It quickly disclosed several pieces of vital political intelligence. Bland was toppled from his pedestal as the expected winner. The South began a strong movement away from the Missourian to Bryan. Florida divided between them, but Georgia, Louisiana, Mississippi, and North Carolina voted for Bryan. The other major disclosure was the alienation of the sound money men to the point where New York and New Jersey refused to vote, and in ten other states a part of the delegations abstained. In the totals, Bland led with an unimpressive 233, followed by Bryan with 103, Pattison 95, Boies 86, and the remainder scattered among a number of lesser candidates. The Bland strategy to sweep away Bryan by a great lead at the start had failed.

The second ballot saw both Bland and Bryan improve, Bryan gaining 92 votes and Bland 48. Pattison reached 100. The abstentions stood at 162. The size of this withheld vote and the wide scattering of votes cast among the candidates prompted a delegate from Louisiana to cry out against the specter haunting silver men—a deadlocked convention. The withheld vote and the two-thirds rule together could produce it.

The third ballot produced a further, although undramatic gain for Bryan, as he picked up 22 votes to only 10 for Bland. Of the dramas of arguing men that sprouted like brush fires across the hall, the most intense occurred when Illinois was reached on the balloting. Bryan's good friend "Buck" Hinrichsen, secretary of state of Illinois, anger leaping from his face, rushed down the center aisle and asked permission for his delegation to withdraw for consultation. As the delegates trooped out to an anteroom, they were besieged en route by Bryan and Bland men. As Altgeld, his face "as white as death," passed the Arkansas delegation, a member pushed into the aisle, clutched the governor's arm and cried, "For God's sake, stand by Mr. Bland." From the transom of the Illinois conference room, angry voices could be heard above the roar and stomping feet of the convention.

The fourth ballot showed the makings of a rush to Bryan. Alabama, voting first, switched to him. Colorado dropped its support of Teller and voted for Bryan, and Kansas switched from Bland. The Bryan men now launched a massive demonstration almost equaling the one following the "Cross of Gold" speech. Fracases broke out across the floor as they grappled to clutch the standards of states not yet committed to their cause. In the Virginia delegation, Carter Glass, a Bryan man, struggled to wrest his standard from a fellow delegate, who although Glass did not know it, was also committed to Bryan. The bulky figure of former Governor Hogg of Texas, moving with the unswerving determination of a stampeding elephant, tried to wrest the New York standard, but George B. McClellan, Jr., knocked him down. Rising quickly, Hogg moved away, shouting, "Bryan, Bryan, Bryan, Bryan."

The turmoil was accompanied by bands playing loud airs, delegations departing for or returning from caucuses, and resolute efforts by Chairman White to restore order. Somehow the roll call was finally completed, and for the first time, Bryan moved into the lead with 280 votes to 241 for Bland, with Pattison next with 96, McLean 46, Matthews 36, Boies 33, Blackburn 27, Stevenson 8, and Hill 1. The abstentions remained at 162. After announcing the results, Chairman White declared that proceedings were now at a point where the chair must state its construction of the two-thirds rule. The question to be settled was whether the two-thirds should be based on the total number of delegates or on only the number of delegates voting. The rule itself simply read: "Two-thirds of the whole number of votes given shall be necessary to a nomination for President and Vice President." Both a literal interpretation of this language and the fact that the convention was operating under the rules of the House of Representatives brought White to the judgment that only two-thirds of those voting would be necessary. His ruling made Bryan's nomination possible on the next and fifth ballot.

The growing body of Bryan states converged with their banners upon Nebraska. Pictures of Bryan were flourished and held high. A huge Bryan procession began to march around the hall. Delegates and visitors climbed onto their chairs, shouted themselves hoarse, and then screeched. Applause leaped in a new crescendo when an Illinois delegate dragged his state's banner into the procession, a sweet harbinger of victory, prompting Bryan men to hug one another with joy. Then other states, not previously voting for Bryan, joined the march. A fresh sensation exploded when the Ohio banner was seen to rock to and fro, as if tossed in a great gust. For a moment, it disappeared, and then it was seen again, held aloft by a Bryan man in the Ohio delegation. The handle had been broken in a struggle with the McLean forces for its possession.

The fifth ballot began at last. When the convention clerk reached Illinois, Altgeld stood up, all eyes upon the visage so familiar in the nation's cartoons, the close-cut beard, the penetrating eyes, and the patch of hair on top of his head, to announce a long-awaited result. "Illinois," he said, "casts its forty-eight votes for William Jennings Bryan of Nebraska." Altgeld had stuck with Bland until the Illinois delegates informed him they would no longer follow his lead. Under this pressure, he voted for Bryan. John R. McLean quickly mounted his chair to announce that "Ohio withdraws the name of John R. McLean and casts forty-eight votes for William J. Bryan." Again, pandemonium. The ultimate action occurred when William J. Stone of Missouri moved to the platform and read a letter from Richard P. Bland, authorizing the withdrawal of his candidacy whenever another silver delegate reached a majority. Stone now withdrew Bland's name and, on behalf of Missouri, raised the banner of his state and cast 34 votes for "the gifted and glorious son of Nebraska." After a rush of other states to the bandwagon, the nomination was declared unanimous.[14]

Mary, but not Bryan, was present to witness the glorious moment. From her seat in the gallery, she had watched each step in her husband's march to the grail. Admiring friends clustered to offer congratulations. She thanked each one pleasantly and brought the hypercritical New York *Times* to acknowledge that Mary's "quiet demeanor," even in the moment of glory, "impressed those about her."

Bryan was ensconced in his hotel rooms or what in reality was the command post of his convention campaign. There he had received reports of developments and moves, and in the occasional quiet moments he thought out the next steps of his strategy. Bryan had been, and always would be, the manager of his own fortunes at conventions. When a bulletin reached him announcing his nomination, he rushed downstairs to the barber for a shave. He had been so completely preoccupied in the morning that he had found no time. So excited was the barber that he could hardly control his quivering razor. When Bryan returned to his rooms, an avalanche of well-wishers awaited him, with a cadre of police, who futilely sought to guard the entrance and stairway against overcrowding.

A body of newspapermen were the first to congratulate him. As they gathered around, Bryan grabbed a piece of paper and, standing at a marble-topped bureau, wrote a telegram addressed, he said, "to the American people." "In order that I may have no ambition," he wrote, "but to discharge faithfully the duties of the office, I desire to announce that, if elected, I shall, in no circumstances, be a candidate for reelection." He explained that the President's power is so great that "no temptation" should be "thrown in his way to cause him to use it for his personal advancement."

Among the first reporters to reach Bryan was Willis J. Abbot, his friend of the Hearst staff. Bryan, painfully aware that the press would be arrayed overwhelmingly against him, grasped at this straw of potential support. He granted Abbot a private interview. They repaired to Bryan's favorite place for tête-à-têtes at crowded political gatherings—the bathroom. Behind its closed door they discussed the fact that while Abbot's employer, Hearst, had up to this point opposed free silver, he was aspiring to build up a great newspaper in New York City, the *Morning Journal*. Willis was seized with the inspiration that since most, if not all, important New York and Eastern papers would oppose silver, the *Journal*, if it supported the cause, might in one jump become the leading Democratic paper of the East, with the joyous prospect of a swift rise in circulation. Bryan was titillated by the plan, and with the din outside crashing upon their ears, he helped Willis prepare a comprehensive telegram to Hearst. Hearst soon threw in with the silver cause.

Having finished with Abbot, Bryan rejoined the mob that packed the hotel and surged to grasp the hand of the new leader. Bryan stood midway on the stairs and reached as many hands as he could. Here and there, instead of a hand, there was extended a gift. "Here is a bit of wood from the old Breckinridge home in 'Kaintucky,' " called Jack Chinn, handing Bryan a walking stick. "It may bring you good luck and has a sentimental significance." Bryan, accepting it with a benign smile, said, "My friends, I feel this is going to be a campaign of sentiment." In the next hours, he shook hands with thousands. Finally exhaustion compelled him to catch a twenty-minute nap, but his doors remained open to afford the passing crowds a glimpse of their slumbering hero.

When he managed to escape for dinner, Bryan, whose thinking had jumped to the coming campaign, composed a telegram to the New York *World*, largest Democratic newspaper of the East, objecting to its references to the cause of silver as a "craze." The *World*, he recalled, had, to its great credit, promoted the income tax. Let it now take up the even greater cause of restoring silver to its ancient place and permit the return of prosperity.

Bryan was not merely writing telegrams; they poured in upon him bearing congratulations in every form imaginable. His rivals for the nomination —Bland, Boies, Matthews, Blackburn, and Pennoyer—sent warm messages with pledges of support. His old Nebraska foe John M. Thurston and the labor leader Eugene Debs were generous with praise. "The young giant of the West," wired Governor Pennoyer of Oregon, "will lead the reform forces of the nation to victory. The story of David and Goliath will be repeated." Other wires soared far and high. "The day breaketh and the shadows flee away," or again, "Glamis thou art and Cawdor thou shall be." From Bryan's old friend W. F. "Buffalo Bill" Cody came congratulations, joined in by "Every member of Nebraska's wild west exhibition including Indians." J. H. Broady telegraphed exultantly from Lincoln: "All Lincoln rejoicing, whistles blowing; bells ringing, and bonfires burning, in pride of your genius which rises with a mantle of Jefferson in a blaze of oratory unsurpassed in all the ages and moves toward the chair once occupied by him, for whom this city was named."

But if there was praise for Bryan, derogation also abounded. Wrote *The Nation*, "only a small fraction of the people . . . have ever heard of him. All of our Presidents heretofore have been men of experience, sufficiently tested in public life to form some idea of their capacity and moral fibre. This is not the case with Mr. Bryan." Beneath the disdain lay a pervasive fear. Henry Cabot Lodge wrote to his English friend Moreton Frewen of the Chicago convention: "They have set up an unknown stump orator as their candidate and they have filled their platform with all kinds of revolutionary and anarchistic doctrines. It is a very serious fight . . . and involves a great deal more than a money standard." [15]

The convention's remaining duty was to nominate a Vice President, a traditionally anticlimactic act. Late in the evening of July 10, Senator Jones, the acknowledged manager of the silver forces, summoned a caucus at Sherman House and to it invited one representative from each state delegation committed to silver. Arriving a trifle late, Bryan settled his solid frame on a gilded Louis XIV chair in the front circle, and through the cigar smoke, his handsome face quickly settled into an expression of intense, concentrated interest in the brisk discussion.

Suggestions about a suitable Vice Presidential nominee sprouted like weeds after a spring rain. Let the nominee, some urged, be one of the principal candidates defeated in the Presidential race. Bland was immediately mentioned, but he sent word that he would not accept. Then Boies' name was put forward, but his friends, who were present, were certain he would decline. Matthews, Daniel, and several other Presidential contenders were thrown into the hopper, but stirred no enthusiasm. The disposal of these names illuminated several basic conditions of Bryan's candidacy. No top-ranking silver politician would become his partner in the race and commit his reputation to the second place on the ticket. None of the lesser silver figures had sufficient resources to arouse any general enthusiasm.

Anyone in that caucus gazing at the heroic figure of Bryan could readily perceive the essential function of the Vice Presidential nomination. Bryan was impecunious, and he was totally lacking in access to wealth. Even worse, his reputation and the platform he was running on would alienate the traditional sources of the party's financial aid. A serious national campaign could not be run without major expenditure.

Several Senators, led by Blackburn and Hernando Money of Mississippi, stressed the absolute necessity that the Vice Presidential nominee be a man of wealth. Their specific candidate was John R. McLean, the multimillionaire publisher of the Cincinnati *Enquirer,* whose pages staunchly promoted the silver cause. In addition to being able to pay campaign bills, McLean had been a Presidential favorite son, and as a candidate for office he was a proved vote getter in a state whose electoral vote would be precious.

The talk of money and electoral votes prompted several New England delegates to advance the name of Arthur Sewall of Maine, a multimillionaire shipbuilder of Bath, who operated a merchant fleet and was a director of many enterprises, including the Maine Central Railroad. Sixty-one years old, long a member of the national committee, Sewall was one of the few important businessmen in the nation who were convinced of the wisdom and justice of the silver movement. He believed fervently that an inflation of the currency would stir business from its slumber.

Throughout the discussion, Bryan had kept silent and those who watched his face saw it harden when McLean's virtues were recounted. Now, as the talk petered out inconclusively, Senator Jones turned to Bryan and said, "You are the nominee of the party and you are the chosen leader. We would like to have a suggestion from you if you have any to make."

Bryan rose. The infectious smile that everyone was accustomed to had vanished. His massive jaw was set, his muscles taut, and fire gleamed in his eye. But that extraordinary, omnipresent self-discipline asserted itself, and he began very pleasantly by observing that having just been chosen as the standard-bearer, he had given little consideration to the Vice Presidential question. He hoped that the delegates might bring a larger wisdom and knowledge than he could summon to the selection of a nominee. It was of supreme importance, he added, with a touch of emphasis, that the ticket be harmonious. It would be fatal if the Presidential and Vice Presidential nominees disagreed on principles.

He turned to the names suggested and said, with an air of impressive finality, "If the convention should nominate John R. McLean, I would decline the nomination for the Presidency. I would not run on a ticket with that man. He is an immoral man. He preaches free silver but all his connections and all his interests are with those who give a lie to our professions. We would be selling the party's birthright for his campaign money. We cannot win the election by appealing to men who stand for privilege. There are too many clean and honest men who believe in the new doctrine we shall preach in this campaign for the party to tie to a man of McLean's standards."

This full and solemn pronouncement was received in flabbergasted silence. Veteran politicians, who had developed to the finest art the ability to mask their feelings behind an expressionless gaze, now visibly gasped. Senator Blackburn leaned over to whisper to Josephus Daniels, "Josephus, this is magnificent, but it is not war. You cannot win victory by driving off everybody who isn't 100 per cent virtuous." But any reservations about Bryan's position remained strictly private. Other names were mentioned for the Vice Presidency, and as the discussion again dwindled, Bryan offered the opinion that it might be wise to award the nomination to the East. Just as in his "Cross of Gold" speech, he had sought to delineate the silver movement as national rather than sectional in character, so now he urged the nomination of an Easterner such as Sewall to help offset the impression of silver as a sectional union of West and South against the East.

When the convention assembled next day, July 11, to make its decision, it quickly demonstrated that Bryan was by no means freely accepted by the polyglot factions that marched under the silver banner. No fewer than sixteen nominations, including Bland, McLean, Sibley, and Sewall, were put forward. As the balloting proceeded, Sewall became the beneficiary of a political trend strikingly similar to the one that had brought victory to Bryan. The hard-core silver strength of Bland now moved to him, and by the fourth ballot he had pulled within forty votes of the leader, McLean. For Sewall, the fifth ballot was the victory ballot, as it had been for Bryan. Both, then, were nominated on a relatively late ballot, Sewall triumphing when McLean withdrew. The belatedness of the victory and McLean's prolonged strength exposed the tenuousness of Bryan's leadership. But Sewall could possibly be a healing and binding agent. His advanced age balanced Bryan's youth and provided reassurance to those troubled by it. As a successful businessman, he was an impressive testimonial that men of wealth and practical experience could identify with a cause whose damning caricature was that it was a haven only for the wooly-headed.

Perhaps the worst omen of the balloting was its disclosure that the number of gold delegates absent or not voting had risen to 250. Well toward one-third of the delegates had in effect seceded. Not all gold men were pleased with the chosen road of decorous dissent. Frederic R. Coudert, New York delegate at large, observed, "Have we not condemned ourselves to silence? There is a parable in this: 'Silence is golden; speech is silver!' "

Bryan had gained the victory, but his prize was the headship of a broken party. What did the gold men propose to do? The answer was not yet clear. This great and vanquished faction looked to New York, and James S. Hinckley of Poughkeepsie, chairman of that state's Democratic committee, said simply, "It is our policy to wait until we reach New York before we come to conclusions. When we reach home and have a little time for consideration, we will act." [16]

PART TWO

Crest

14. The Popocrat Candidate

T HE convention was over, and like any other delegate, the party's new leader, for all his sudden glory, was caught up in such humdrum duties as checking out of his hotel and arranging his journey home. It tickled his parsimonious fancy to discover that the entire expenses for Mary and him during the convention week were less than $100, "a sum," he later noted, "probably as small as anyone spent in securing a Presidential nomination." His reputation as a foe of privilege did not deter a major railroad from offering a private Pullman car for his return to Lincoln. Willis Abbot, Bryan's journalist friend, who was present when the invitation arrived, cried, "Mr. Bryan, you should not accept this offer. You are the great Commoner, the people's candidate, and it would not do to accept favors from the great railroad corporations." Bryan instantly agreed, and the unconsciously minted title, Great Commoner, stuck.[1]

The Bryans took a long way home. The next day, Sunday, they spent in Chicago with the family of Lyman Trumbull, who, despite their mourning, rejoiced in Bryan's sudden political fortune. Bryan paid homage in this sublime moment to another place of his youth. He and Mary made a sentimental journey to Salem. Leaving their train at Odin, they set forth with a few reporters in a stage drawn by mules. It was a gay journey of Bryanesque banter and reporters' hilarity, a mood heightened by several threatened upsets at bad places in the roads. Salem was bedecked for a hero's welcome. Nearly every house put out a flag, and the porch posts of homes fronting the main streets were entwined with red, white, and blue bunting.

Even a drenching rain could not cool the ardor of the townfolk. The courthouse yard where Bryan spoke was a mire, but 3,000 citizens crowded into it to hear his message. He recalled, in strains of affection, his parents, "who took me to the farm" where he built the "physical strength which will be needed in the campaign." Over yonder at the fairgrounds, he had delivered his first political speech. He remembered, too, "the silent city of the dead," where reposed his father "whose upright life has been an inspiration . . . and whose counsels lingered in my ears," and his mother, "patient . . . gentle . . . and . . . kind. . . ."

The long train ride from Salem to Lincoln was busy with politicking and speechmaking. En route, Bryan met "Silver Dick" Bland, their first encounter since the convention. Bryan was delighted by Bland's cordiality and by his declaration to the crowd that "if I had been the one to select the leader in this great contest, I would have selected my friend, the Honorable William J. Bryan." Since Bland had announced himself as a candidate for Congress, Bryan, for his part, reciprocated with a hearty endorsement.[2]

The train pushed into Nebraska at Rulo, a little village tucked into the southeastern corner of the state. As the train rolled off the bridge, the Rulo Gun Club, assembled in full strength, fired several volleys in salute. An Eastern newsman could not resist asking Bryan, in archly sectional overtones, whether it was a reception or a holdup. Each town along the way outdid itself in demonstrating pride in Nebraska's hero son. The arrival of the train in Lincoln touched off an explosion of firecrackers, steam calliopes, cannon, shotguns, horns, and drums. The first person to reach Bryan was not the mayor, who aimed to, but a plain citizen in high boots into which his trousers were tucked, who wore rings in his ears, and whose beard was long and tawny. He came right to the point. He wanted to be the White House coachman, a position, he noted, that paid $600 a year and had living quarters attached to the stables. Benign merriment lighted Bryan's eyes, as he replied, "There is one thing I can say to you, and that is that I have not promised the position to anybody else." In a sprightly address, which he endeavored to hold within the nonpartisan confines appropriate for a general turnout of the citizenry, he noted that all could "join in celebrating the fact that at last the nomination for President has crossed the Missouri river," the first time that this was so.[3]

Bryan did not tarry long in celebration but immediately set to work capturing the Presidential nomination of two other substantial parties, the Populists and the National Silver Party. The Populists, preparing for their party's national convention at St. Louis, wrestled with an horrendous dilemma. If they nominated Bryan, they feared they would destroy the independence of their party. If they withheld support, they would jeopardize, if not destroy, the chances of a major political leader who, regardless of his Democratic affiliation, was running on a platform with many Populist planks.

The Populist leaders, responding to pressure from the silver Democrats, the American Bimetallic Union, and Bryan himself, had scheduled the Populist convention after the Democratic. Radical Populists bemoaned the decision. Henry Demarest Lloyd concluded, to his enormous distress, that the Populist leaders had been "flimflammed." Once Bryan was nominated by the Democrats, Lloyd was certain that the Populists would be left with "the Hobson's choice" between accepting Bryan and fusing with the Democrats or of naming their own ticket and developing an issue other than silver. Taubeneck and Weaver took pains to assure that the St. Louis convention would approve their stewardship by altering the basis of state representation to increase the numbers of free silver delegates.[4]

As there had been in past years, there were several shadings of Populist opinion divided along sectional lines. Most Western Populist leaders urged their party to nominate Bryan, whom they deemed a Populist at heart, and to accept silver as the central issue of the platform and campaign. The more traditional Populist planks of public ownership and intensive public regulation, they were willing to put aside. The more radical, oddly named middle-of-the-roaders, who were a minority in the West but a major force in the South, abhorred any political alliance with the Democrats. Tom Watson urged them to "avoid fusion as they would the devil." The ties of Southern Populists were with Republicans who had helped build the young party, and fusion would destroy its independence.

Marion Butler, the middle-of-the-road leader, hoped and prayed, when the Democratic convention approached, that the silver forces would not prevail. "If the silver Democrats should succeed in controlling the Chicago Convention, and they should insist on nominating a candidate . . . without consulting the other silver forces, it would be a worse blow to the cause of financial reform than it would be for the gold men to control the convention, for the result would be that the Republicans would carry the country on account of the free silver men being divided." Free silver Democrats would never move into the Republican Party, nor would the Silver Republicans move into the Democratic ranks. Butler had nourished the impossible hope that the silver Democrats, should they control the Chicago proceedings, would adjourn the convention without making a Presidential nomination and then move on to St. Louis. There they might join with Populists and Silver Republicans to put up a joint candidate.[5]

But this was not to be. The Populist convention that met at St. Louis was beset with tensions. The 1,400 delegates who poured into the city were a motley legion of the discontented—old-time third-party politicians of the Granger and Greenback days, rustic Southern Alliance men, reformers with diverse causes, freshly converted silverites. It was predominantly a convention of poor men. Some, lacking funds, had walked all the way. Others had gone without places to sleep to save nickels for scanty meals. Some were faint from lack of food. All were sustained in deprivation by fierce devotion to their cause. One reporter, surveying the gathered delegates, was convinced that there existed "some mysterious connection between Populism and hair." The vast hall was a sea of whiskers—long, short, red, black, forked, and pointed. The great hairy sea undulated in unison when the delegates sang their favorite song, "We'll Shoot the Gold Bugs, Every One."

The common expression on the faces beneath the whiskers was anxiety. Southern delegates feared they would be sold out to fusion with the Bryan-Sewall ticket. Anxiety, too, seared the faces of the fusionist managers as they feverishly caucused. With fusion and national victory within their grasp, they feared that the pertinacious folly of the middle-of-the-roaders might smother their opportunity.

Bryan's fortunes at the convention lay in the capable and experienced hands of Senator James K. Jones; his longtime ally of Nebraskan fusion, the former U.S. Senator William V. Allen; and Governor William J. Stone of Missouri. Jones and Stone were emissaries of the Democratic national committee, and Allen was chief agent of the Bryan interests in the Populist Party. The trio enjoyed staunch support from James B. Weaver and other leading Western Populists. J. H. Turner, secretary of the Populists' national committee, openly predicted that the convention would adopt the Chicago platform and ticket. Clarence Darrow, his eyes sparkling at the prospect of national victory, announced his support of Bryan and Sewall in "a year in which we are to fight the greatest battle of modern times between the plutocrats and the producers." And that legendary leader of Western Populism, "Sockless" Jerry Simpson, uttered the general sentiment of his section: "I care not for party names. It is the substance we are after, and we have it in William J. Bryan." [6]

Several powerful leaders were arrayed against Bryan's nomination, however. The national chairman, Henry E. Taubeneck, wanted the Populists to nominate their indigenous candidates and then combine with the Democrats upon a single set of electors. Dissenting middle-of-the-roaders were led by Texas, the largest and most militant of the delegations. Its most evident figure was James H. "Cyclone" Davis, a string-bean type with a booming voice. For all their rugged individuality, the middle-of-the-roaders finally agreed on a ticket to oppose Bryan and Sewall. Without much enthusiasm, their representatives from twenty-one states combined to support S. F. Norton of Illinois for President and Frank Burkett of Mississippi for Vice President.

Norton was a second choice of the radicals. Their hopes centered originally on the dynamic Socialist and labor leader Eugene Debs. Fully a third of the delegates were pledged to his support, but he forbade any promotion of his candidacy. Convinced that Bryan and the silver movement represented a "grand opportunity to strike at economic privilege and oppression," he did not choose to undermine that opportunity by fighting for the nomination. He instructed his supporters to vote for Bryan.

The first night of the convention the middle-of-the-roaders made their strength felt after the temporary chairman, Marion Butler of North Carolina, flayed both major parties as malefactors charting their country's ruin. They planned a massive demonstration to sweep the convention into adopting their position. As the raucous marching began, the convention hall was suddenly plunged into darkness. With grumbling and oaths, the demonstrators stumbled and pushed their way onward. The lights could not be restored, and their absence produced a weird scene: the string-bean figure of "Cyclone" Davis holding aloft a flickering candle; the peppery heroine of Populism, Mrs. Mary E. Lease, yelling from the platform; hundreds of frustrated delegates hurling from the darkness accusations of "ugly work." The villain of the piece was suspected to be a Bryan emissary, Governor Stone.[7]

Distressed by the show of radical strength, the Bryan forces worked through the night to entice delegates into their ranks. That they did their work well was revealed the next day in the election of the permanent chairman. The Bryanite Populist leader, William V. Allen, won handily by 758 to 564. Asked to comment on this victory, which foretold his own nomination, Bryan discreetly declined.

With Bryan's nomination apparently assured, the middle-of-the-roaders turned their attention to the most vulnerable spot in the fusion armor, the Democratic Vice Presidential nominee, Arthur Sewall. Man of wealth, railroad director, Easterner, Sewall was anathema to many men of Populist principles. Bryan's managers, Jones and Stone, confident of their strength, demanded that Sewall be accepted, too. Resentment flowed like wine, even beyond the middle-of-the-road ranks. "Texas is here to hold a Populist convention," cried a delegate, "and we're going to do it before we go home." [8]

The machinery of compromise began to turn. Marion Butler and others urged the Democrats to drop Sewall and to substitute a radical Southerner as Bryan's running mate. Butler specifically had in mind Thomas Watson of Georgia, that hero of the intransigent Southern Populists and a figure widely admired in Western circles. As he always had been, Watson was still a resolute opponent of fusion in any form. Even during the St. Louis convention, he declared to the press that "I am opposed to the nomination of Bryan and Sewall or either of them separately. The Populist party has good material within its own ranks." His fiery devotion to radical Populist principles made him an ogre to men of orderly instincts like Theodore Roosevelt, who was to say of him: "Mr. Watson belongs to that school of southern Populism who honestly believe that the respectable and commonplace people who own banks, railroads, dry goods stores, factories, and the like, are persons of mental and social attributes that unpleasantly distinguish Heliogabalus, Nero, Caligula, and other worthies of later Rome. . . ." [9]

To lure Watson into a Vice Presidential nomination required a measure of finesse. Messages dispatched to him in far-off Georgia led him to understand that the Democratic emissaries had agreed to withdraw Sewall from their ticket and that he, Watson, would also become the Democratic nominee. He was not told that middle-of-the-roaders had already settled upon their own ticket—Norton and Burkett—and, in fact, did not learn of this until after the convention. "Reluctantly," he wired, "yes, if it will harmonize all factions." Later, he declared that had he known of the middle-of-the-roaders' ticket, it "would have received my hearty support. . . ."

There was a companion and even more bizarre step in the maneuvers of the Bryanite Populists. They proposed for the convention a procedure of almost outrageous irregularity. It was, simply, that the Vice Presidential nominee be chosen first, before the Presidential nominee. Several compelling reasons prompted this inspiration. Although many Populists would support Bryan's nomination, few could swallow Sewall. General agreement prevailed among fusionists and middle-of-the-roaders alike that the Populists should nominate one of their own. Equally compelling, the fusionists feared that the middle-of-the-roaders would bolt the convention if they were not appeased. To nominate a middle-of-the-roader for Vice President would commit that faction to the convention and its ticket and lend the party an aura of independence.

But these brisk maneuvers had another problem to cope with. As the fires of sentiment against Sewall began to rage, Senator J. K. Jones, in distress, wired Bryan: "If it is not Sewall, what shall we do? I favor declination in that event. Answer quick." Bryan replied with an ultimatum: "I agree with you fully. If Sewall is not nominated, have my name withdrawn." He wired a similar message to Allen, requesting him not to make it public until Jones approved the step. Jones, who apparently changed his mind, now agreed with Allen that Bryan must win the Populist nomination, despite awkwardness over the Vice Presidency. Hereupon, Jones and Allen, in a conspiratorial consensus, kept their messages tucked away while the convention nominated Watson. (For the rest of his life, Allen denied receiving any message from Bryan.)

After Watson was securely nominated for Vice President, Allen wired Bryan asking that his telegram of declination be withdrawn. He evidently received no answer. Bryan was now nominated for the Presidency by the illustrious Weaver. According to plan, the name of S. F. Norton, choice of the middle-of-the-roaders, was also advanced. As the balloting proceeded, word raced through the convention that Allen had just received a telegram from Bryan stating that he would not run if nominated. One delegate, aflame with curiosity, asked Allen point-blank if the report was true. The big Nebraskan boomed that it was not. When Governor Stone, who seemed agitated by this reply, flagged Allen's attention and requested permission to read the convention the message received from Bryan, Allen refused to give him the floor. The baffled Stone continued to signal, but in vain. Later Allen explained with perfect aplomb that a Populist convention was hardly a proper place for hearing and considering a purely Democratic negotiation. Under Allen's sheltering hand, Bryan was elected on the first ballot, with 1,042 votes to 321 for Norton.[10]

The platform reported by General James B. Weaver highlighted free coinage of silver at 16 to 1, demanded national money issued solely by the national government and the emancipation of the financial and economic

system from European control. Reflecting the venerated Omaha platform of
1892, the new platform called for a national income tax; postal savings
banks; public ownership of railroads and telegraphs; direct election of the
President, Vice President, and Senators; public works projects for the unemployed; acquisition of Cuba, and prompt statehood for it and other territories; curbing the labor injunction; and a "full, free, and fair ballot and an
honest count." But the platform, after citing these traditional Populist
issues, opened the gates for fusion. It declared that ". . . the great and
pressing issue of the impending campaign . . . is the financial question, and
upon this great and specific issue between the parties we cordially invite the
aid and cooperation of all organizations and citizens agreeing with us upon
this vital question."

To a Populist ideologue such as Henry Demarest Lloyd, the platform of
1896 was the ultimate in political sacrilege. It was an act of the slickest legerdemain. The new platform seemed to mirror the old faith, but in reality it
was different. By elevating silver as the paramount issue, the platform
shoved the traditional planks far into the background. To Lloyd silver was
only the "tenth dilution" of an issue; it was a "fake," claiming or implying
that it could effect marvelous economic and social changes when in fact it
could command merely a fraction of them. To Lloyd, "Free silver is the
cow-bird of the Reform movement. It waited until the nest had been built
by the sacrifices and labor of others, and then it laid its eggs in it, pushing
out the others which lie smashed on the ground. It is now flying around
while we are expected to do the incubating."

To Lloyd the platform was proof that the convention was "gagged,
clique-ridden, and machine ruled." As he and other disgruntled Populists
were painfully aware, brutal precautions were taken to assure that a platform would come forth compatible with the overriding purposes of fusion
and Bryan's nomination. The Committee on Resolutions was shamelessly
packed, and in its proceedings any effort to introduce new and radical positions into the platform were summarily squelched. When protesting Populists threatened to carry their fight to the convention, Chairman Allen informed them with private and cynical candor that he would never permit
them to catch his eye and obtain the floor. When the platform was reported,
the machinery of domination began promptly to turn. The previous question was moved at once, and with a shout, it was declared carried.[11]

What emerged from the Populist convention was a political product battered into monstrous shapes. Bryan was nominated, but Sewall was not.
Watson was the Vice Presidential nominee, but under the misapprehension
that he would also become the Democratic Vice Presidential nominee,
when Sewall, impressed that he must now resign, vacated that place. The
Populist convention had done its work, but would it stick? Would Bryan
and Watson, once they knew all the facts, accept their nominations?

The convention adjourned without any definite commitment from Bryan. In a press interview in Lincoln, after the grotesqueries in St. Louis, Bryan said that his acceptance "will depend entirely upon the conditions attached to the nomination. I shall do nothing which will endanger the success of bi-metallism, nor shall I do anything unfair to Mr. Sewall." Senator Jones, after the Populists finished, journeyed to Lincoln to render an account of his strange stewardship. When he emerged from the meeting, Jones gave out a statement to the press that could only have had Bryan's approval. Bryan, Jones said, "will act with deliberation and . . . nothing will be done which can justly be criticized by those who are interested in the success of bimetallism. He begs all friends of the cause in all parties to refrain from harsh criticism of those who, however much they may differ, agree in desir-ing the immediate restoration of free coinage. He feels sure that the solution of all difficulties will be found in due time . . ." [12]

Bryan's awkward silences and prayerful pronouncements and outcrop-pings of intrigue and machine tactics at the St. Louis convention were symptoms of the difficult and uneasy coalition that had somehow to be hammered out between the Populist and Democratic parties. For Bryan, the coalition was both necessary and costly. As a *sine qua non,* he required the Populist nomination and the support of the substantial Populist elector-ate to win the November election. From Bryan's standpoint, the ideal ar-rangement would have been simply a Populist adoption of the Democratic nominees and platform. But the strength and divisiveness of Populist fac-tions dictated otherwise. Bryan had no choice but to acquiesce to running with a twin-tailed ticket, with Sewall and Watson as the Vice Presidential nominees.

Although Bryan's forces corralled the Populist platform within a frame-work that did not allow fresh radical departures, he paid the price of assum-ing the liabilities of the Populist caricature in the moderate political com-munity. The Populist nomination gave Bryan a reputation for radicalism well beyond anything he deserved, and it especially imperiled his support in the East. After St. Louis, the New York *Sun* predicted "repudiation, revolu-tion, and national dishonor" if Bryan won. The New York *Times* deemed it altogether logical that the "freaky Coxeyites" (Populists) had chosen "an ir-responsible, unregulated, ignorant, prejudiced, pathetically honest and en-thusiastic crank" for President.

If Bryan was willing to accept a twin-tailed ticket, the eccentric, strong-willed Watson was not. One of the Georgian's constant preoccupations in the campaign was the elimination of Sewall as a Vice Presidential nominee. Promptly after St. Louis, Watson proposed to Marion Butler that they jour-ney west to attend Democratic state conventions to press the cause against Sewall. "The Democrats do not ask much odds in the South," Watson noted, "but in the West we have them at a disadvantage. If we can get Kansas, & other Western states to endorse the St. Louis ticket, Sewall will have to come down." [13]

Bryan was also the nominee of the National Silver Party, the adjunct of the new American Bimetallic Union. The chief strategist of both organizations remained General A. J. Warner. Still in infancy, the party was committed to establishing organizations and distributing literature in every state and to maintaining headquarters in Washington. The party offered means by which Republicans, Populists, and Democrats might join together in the West, and it was a haven for Republicans of the silver persuasion who did not want to pass through the portals of the Democratic and Populist parties. The new party also aimed to promote interparty cooperation on behalf of the free silver movement. Originally it had pushed Henry Teller for the Democratic nomination, with Bryan reputedly its second choice.

The convention of the National Silver Party met in St. Louis simultaneously with the Populist convention. There all resemblance between them ended. If the Populists were factional and garrulous, their brothers in faith discharged their business with expedition and serenity. The National Silver Party's unanimity rendered it colorless. It nominated Bryan and Sewall by acclamation after a surging speech by Edward C. Little of Kansas, who hailed the Nebraskan as "a gifted young Joshua who shall bid the golden sun and the silver moon stand still while he fights the battle of human freedom."

But in another of its purposes, the National Silver convention was less successful. A conference committee it dispatched to the nearby Populist convention to secure endorsement of the Bryan-Sewall ticket failed. Yet even that rebuff stirred not a ripple of apprehension in the National Silver leadership for the ultimate triumph of their cause. "The nomination of Bryan by the silver convention in St. Louis," Warner wrote, "secures to him every state west of the Mississippi, which, with the Southern states he will surely get, will elect him." [14]

Bryan was also the nominee of such minor parties as Henry George's Single Taxers, Edward Bellamy's Nationalists, the Reverend W. D. P. Bliss' Christian Socialists, and the "broad-gauge" Prohibitionists—those interested in various social issues harmonious with prohibition—who endorsed silver and Bryan and broke off from their "narrow-gauge" brethren, who concentrated on prohibition exclusively.

Warner's anticipation of the pattern of victory implied that William McKinley, if he were to win, had to carry every Northern state east of the Mississippi, including New Jersey, Connecticut, and Delaware. After such a sweep, he would fall one vote short in the electoral college of the required number. Of these states, New Jersey had gone Republican but once since

1856 (in 1872). Delaware had never gone Republican in Presidential years, and Connecticut had cast its votes for Democratic candidates at every election since 1872 but one, when it voted for Garfield by a small plurality.

It was clear then that the attitude of the Eastern Democracy would have much to do with Bryan's electoral fate. Presumably, such Democrats might be influenced by expressions from their national party leader, President Cleveland. At this hour of repudiation by his own party, Cleveland was off on a fishing trip at Buzzards Bay, and his secretary announced that concerning Bryan's nomination "the President will have nothing to say. . . ." Cleveland's lieutenants were less reticent. William C. Whitney, political manager of the sound money forces, announced ominously that he would not vote for or assist the Chicago ticket. *The Nation,* the leading intellectual journal with a Democratic outlook, after damning the Chicago convention as a "collection of inflammatory and reckless men," predicted that the Eastern branch of the Democratic Party would refuse, virtually in a body, to support the national ticket. Indeed, on the Eastern scene, the chief party resource from which Bryan conceivably might draw support was Tammany Hall. Nestled among its hard-boiled chieftains and ruthless hatchet men was one of the Wigwam's strongest vote getters, Congressman William Sulzer, who was openly and vigorously committed to free silver and the Chicago ticket.

Hostility to Bryan was not confined to the East, but seethed in men of property wherever they might be in the Middle West, Far West, and, to a lesser degree, the South. The Western Bourbon Democrats were at the forefront of the opposition. From his comfortable lair in Nebraska City, J. Sterling Morton viewed with alarm the massing of Populists and free silver Democrats and Republicans under one flag. Together they constituted "a dangerous party in a country like ours where the elective franchise is the privilege of the ignorant and vicious as well as the enlightened and good." To the many Democrats who sought his counsel, he said, "I think it the duty of every patriotic citizen to do all in his power to bring about the defeat of Mr. Bryan and those who support him and the platform upon which he stands." [15]

The great body of sound money Democrats who were repelled by the Chicago proceedings possessed several options in the approaching campaign. They could ignore the national ticket and concentrate their political efforts on state and local tickets representing the sound money sentiment. They could openly or covertly support the safe and sane Republican candidacy of William McKinley. Or, as a demonstration of their commitment to the monetary doctrine they were so resolutely defending, they could form a new party, in effect the Sound Money Democracy.

From the moment the shape of things at the Chicago convention became clear, cries were heard from propertied men across the political map for the launching of such a party. Promptly upon Bryan's nomination, former Governor Thomas M. Waller of Connecticut declared that if the Democratic Party were to hold together in the East, a convention must be called to produce a gold nominee and a gold platform. The Louisville *Courier-Journal* deemed these steps necessary both to repudiate the "foolhardy and bastard leadership" of Chicago and to help elect Sound Money Democrats to Congress. Sound Money Leagues and Honest Money Democracy clubs spread like pox over the East and Middle West.

On August 7, 900 delegates of the gold Democrats gathered in Indianapolis and issued a call for a convention to meet September 2 to adopt a platform and nominate national candidates. The convention duly assembled; its ranks, *The Nation* found, were composed chiefly of "the intelligence and character of the Democratic party." The convention enthusiastically and smoothly performed its allotted tasks and nominated Senator John M. Palmer of Illinois for President and an erstwhile Confederate general, Simon B. Buckner of Kentucky, for Vice President. The age and staidness of the ticket contrasted absolutely with the youth and vitality of Bryan or, as the keynoter expressed it, with the "populism and anarchy" of the Chicago ticket.

For its emblem the National Democratic Party, as it was formally known, chose the hickory tree. Borrowed from Andrew Jackson, the symbol was in Bryan's eyes grotesquely inappropriate, because the party in reality represented the very forces that were arrayed against that late, heroic President. Once his own campaign began, Bryan discovered that the new party was prepared to undertake a fight against him "more bitter, if possible, than that waged by the Republicans." Much of the fight was underground, with money, false rumors, and intimidation. After being exposed to this harassment, the embattled Bryan concluded that a more appropriate emblem for the new party was the owl— "It looks wise and does its work in the dark," or the mole—"a smooth animal and works underground all the time." [16]

15. The First Battle

His ascent to the pinnacle of American politics, the Presidential nomination, was so swift and unpredicted that Bryan had no time to waste in basking in his success. The trim bastard-Victorian house on D Street was transformed into a political beehive. Leaders and personalities, Democrats,

Populists, and Silver Republicans, all species of the doers and thinkers, flocked to Bryan's home. Telegrams and letters deluged him, offering congratulations and counsel and imploring him to journey here or there for a major address.

A common theme of advice was caution. The older men, the veteran politicians who were his managers and promoters, urged that until the formal opening of the campaign, marked by his speech accepting the nomination, he should keep silent or speak only guardedly. For Bryan to be silent, they were asking, of course, for the impossible. Senator Jones warned of "Telegrams, asking all sorts of questions all intended to injure you. . . ." For the Sewall-Watson dilemma, James G. Hogg wired, "Take time. Do not let anyone rush you." And Governor Stone cautioned against "an unscrupulous enemy will seek to distort every utterance you make and turn it to your disadvantage if possible." [1]

If Bryan sought a model of discreet behavior, he need turn only to his Republican opponent, William McKinley. Popular and beloved, McKinley was a surefooted politician who could traverse the most treacherous political quicksands. His magic weapons were silence and the noncommittal statement. In the maneuvering prior to the Republican convention at St. Louis, he and his astute manager, Mark Hanna, had beaten down the chief challenger to his nomination, Thomas B. Reed of Maine, largely by his popularity, which he did not imperil by taking any clear position on issues. Instead he stood on his record.

He infuriated opponents by remaining silent on the money question. Eager not to impair his popularity in the Western mining states, he aimed to capture the nomination by stressing the tariff issue. Gold-minded Easterners demanded that he express his intentions toward money, and when their pressures became undeniable, he advocated a bimetallic standard, based on a ratio between gold and silver to be established by international agreement. He hoped the appearance of solicitude for silver would placate Western Republicans. Surely, the long-proved futility of international negotiation would reassure Eastern Republicans that the nation's *de facto* gold standard would remain undisturbed in a McKinley Presidency. A strong surge of gold sentiment in the Republican national convention at St. Louis induced McKinley to alter a draft money plank he had supplied the delegates. His original words pledged the party "to maintain our present standard." Gold-loving Republicans forced the substitution of "the existing gold standard should be preserved." Although Henry Teller and others saw no significant difference between the phrases, gold-minded Republicans were impressed that the introduction of the single word "gold" signified crisis and commitment.

At his home in Canton, Ohio, McKinley listened by telephone to his nomination in St. Louis. The sound, a reporter with McKinley said, was "like a storm at sea with wild, fitful shrieks of wind." The voting began, "Alabama, 18 for McKinley." The candidate kept score at his desk. Other states rushed swiftly to him, and Ohio's 46 votes clinched the nomination. McKinley went to the parlor, kissed his wife and mother, and told them that Ohio had given him the nomination. Garret A. Hobart of New Jersey, a wealthy, little-known corporation lawyer and businessman, handpicked by Hanna, was named for Vice President.

Within minutes after McKinley's nomination, Canton was transformed into a maelstrom of jubilation. Bells, cannon, and firecrackers expressed communal joy. A huge crowd raced to the nominee's home. A friend who had sat with McKinley by the telephone to listen to his nomination, upon hearing the approaching mob, fled out the back door, exclaiming to his host, "You have my sympathy." McKinley mounted a chair on his front porch and pleased the crowd with generalities. He then moved through his kitchen to address another deputation at his back door. By midnight an estimated 50,000 people had called at McKinley's home. Most shook his hand. The grass was trampled, the fence was broken, and the shrubbery, rosebushes and geranium beds were crushed.

Bryan's campaign was scheduled to begin on August 12, when he would deliver his acceptance speech at Madison Square Garden. The choice of New York City revealed a fundamental strategic decision. Bryan was unwilling to write off the East as hopelessly lost to McKinley. He proposed to wage a national campaign, and he would begin it in New York, lair of the richest treasury of electoral votes and of the most intense hostility to the silver cause.

Actually, the campaign began with the long, slow journey eastward. Thousands of exuberant fellow townsmen crushed into the Rock Island depot at Lincoln to see the Bryans off. In brief, off-the-cuff remarks to the crowd, Bryan committed a slip that his opponents would mercilessly exploit throughout the campaign. Explaining pleasantly how he really preferred to make his acceptance speech in Lincoln, he added that he had chosen New York "in order that our cause might be presented first in the heart of what now seems to be the enemy's country, but which we hope to be our country before the campaign is over." The phrase "enemy's country" was ripped out of context and pointed to incessantly as proof of his hate and fiendish intent toward the propertied classes.

Otherwise, the tour was a gala of acclaiming crowds, of Bryan's stirring speeches, of reunions and intense discussions of plans and problems with silver leaders met en route. At Canton, Ohio, McKinley's hometown, Bryan indulging an impulse, paid a surprise call on his astounded Republican rival. As he crossed into Pennsylvania, Bryan's voice was weakening badly under the ceaseless punishment. At Harrisburg, when cries for a speech rolled forth, he pointed to his throat and shook his head. He was anxiously consulting doctors and taking medication, and his white hat had been displaced by a black skullcap that gave the man, whom many feared as a firebrand anarchist, a reassuringly pious look. At last the Bryan special rolled into New York. When reporters moved to shake Bryan's hand, his host, William P. St. John, pushed them back, explaining that it was badly swollen and could not bear even to be touched.[2]

On the night of Bryan's acceptance speech, Madison Square Garden had the atmosphere of a mammoth county fair. In stifling 88-degree heat, 12,000 were jammed inside while 15,000 more outside hoped by some miracle to get in. Hucksters quickly sold out their "Bryan silver fans." Bryan walked rapidly into the hall with Jones, Stone, Bland, and Elliott Danforth, national committeeman of New York. Danforth had been induced to preside after the far more prestigious David Bennett Hill had adamantly refused. The hall was embarrassingly barren of major New York Democratic leaders except for a sprinkling of Tammany chieftains. As Bryan stood on the platform, a huge American flag was lowered behind him, touching off an eight-minute ovation distinguished by a stomping of feet, a new style of applause that the silver men had discovered at Chicago and that seemed similar, to those who knew the West, to the clatter of hooves.

The crowd obviously expected Bryan to demolish the goldbugs with his most pulverizing oratory. He had spoken for only a few minutes when his audience knew it was to be disappointed. Putting aside his accustomed oratorical style of the seemingly extemporaneous speech, Bryan read from a prepared text. Bryan also abandoned his usual gestures and inflections that heightened emphasis and captured attention. His reading was formal and hurried. Within minutes after he began, spectators started filing out, their curiosity slaked. They had seen this much-heralded political phenomenon of the West, and not a few wondered what the excitement was all about. Some who departed were Republicans, big of limb and heavy of foot, posted in the audience to make a noisy getaway, but most who left were unwilling to sit through the wilting heat. When the hour-and-forty-minute address was over, half the audience had vanished.[3]

Bryan deliberately sacrificed his audience to a higher interest. This, his first speech of the campaign, would be attacked by the opposition press, and a precise written statement would be less vulnerable. Besides, the press would provide better coverage if supplied with the text in advance.

In its substance, the speech strove to reassure the East and other opposition that Bryan was no fuming Jacobin who coveted other people's property. He would reconstruct society not by leveling it but by uplifting it to the point that all would stand equal before the law. He did not challenge the Supreme Court's authority but believed the Court had erred in striking down a measure for social justice like the income tax. Someday, he hoped, the Court might reverse its unfortunate opinion. He presented a lengthy reasoned exegesis of the money question in both its domestic and its international aspects. He closed with a plea that the East join with West and South in a regeneration of America conducive to its prosperity and independence.

The scattering of loyal Bryan press hailed the speech. "Distinctly creditable and dignified," proclaimed the Chicago *Record.* Hearst's New York *Journal* deemed it "unanswerable." But if it was a good lecture, its constrained delivery made it a poor speech. The style of Bryan's performance touched off a rush of lampooning in the opposition press. A typical caricature represented Bryan as a boy, reading a lengthy roll of manuscript, while Father Knickerbocker returned to his house, a complacent look on his face and a fire extinguisher under his arm. The caption read: "A false alarm."

But more important than its style was the speech's reflection of a fundamental strategy Bryan had adopted in his approach to the campaign. It was, essentially, a decision that elevated the silver question to paramountcy among the issues. The many other planks of the Chicago platform—tariff, labor, income tax, and the like—were conspicuously subordinated. The wisdom of this choice was dubious against the background of big-city politics. Silver was not an issue that aroused the labor leaders at Madison Square Garden and their union memberships, or the immigrant colonies, or the general body of urban voters. As an issue silver was handicapped by technical obscurities, and outside rural America it lacked bread-and-butter appeal. In fact, labor and city people were apprehensive that a silver policy would prove inflationary and drastically reduce the buying power of existing wage scales. In elevating silver, Bryan grossly underplayed two planks of wide appeal to Eastern workers and union members—government by injunction and the income tax. In the eyes of his foes, Bryan was committing an enormous blunder. Mark Hanna, McKinley's campaign manager, rejoiced in the discovery that Bryan's "talking silver all the time and that's where we've got him." And Joseph B. Foraker, another Republican potentate of Ohio, declared triumphantly, "Mr. Bryan made himself by one speech and now he has unmade himself by one speech." [4]

Bryan's early effort to woo and win the East moved into a second and, as it turned out, a final phase the next day. According to plan, he and Mary held three receptions at the Windsor Hotel, for which invitations had been broadcast to everybody who was anybody in the political community of the New York region. While a steady procession of humanity trooped in to greet the candidate, one conspicuous fact emerged. Extraordinarily few of the callers were politicians of note. Even the Tammany chieftains whose soiled presence had been welcomed to fill the chairs of honor at the Garden now stayed away. Beneath the talk and laughter, the Bryan men were seized with clammy despair. Bryan was not a victim of this mood. He was master of an impervious optimism that did not falter even in his most candid moments with Mary. As always, in such gatherings, he was all cheeriness, free with smiles and pleasantries. When some ladies were introduced, Bryan said he expected each of them to secure sixteen votes for free silver. " '16 to 1', you know," he explained.[5]

After the reception, Bryan and Mary met with Chairman Jones and other national committeemen over the ashes of disaster at the Garden and the reception. The atmosphere was somber, almost funereal. Key decisions had to be made. Jones and the committeemen quickly vetoed Bryan's plan for an extended tour of the East, requesting that he concentrate on the West and South and write off the East as lost. The pullback was spurred by a desperate shortage of funds. While money was cascading into Mark Hanna's coffers, the flow to the Democracy had been reduced to barely discernible rivulets.

A lengthy animated discussion centered on selecting the location of the national campaign headquarters. Jones and other Senators urged that Washington be chosen, contending that, for one thing, the franking privilege would be available for mailings, a not unimportant consideration in an impecunious campaign. An unarticulated consideration was that the choice of Washington would enhance the influence of the Senatorial clique over Bryan and the campaign. Bryan, forcefully supported by Mary, pressed for Chicago, the place of his triumph and well removed from the Senators who advocated a campaign of mild discourse and a benign slurring of the issues. Chicago, besides being in the heartland of a potentially more radical approach to the campaign, was the state of the fiery Altgeld, who excoriated "Wall Street," "plutocrats," and "British domination." Bryan prevailed, and headquarters quickly sprang up in Chicago.

The abandonment of an Eastern tour necessitated a quick rearrangement of Bryan's plans. He was scheduled for a Labor Day address in Chicago, with speeches en route as he journeyed from the East. He was now in an awkward position. He had nearly two weeks of time to kill. The utter simplicity of Bryan's solution astounded Eastern politicians accustomed to devious motives and slick actions. He and Mary journeyed to Upper Red Hook, a hamlet in northern Dutchess County, New York, for an extended visit with Edward C. Perrine. Mrs. Perrine had been Mary's teacher in Jacksonville; she had wanted to visit her for years, and what better time could there be than now?

Bryan's departure from New York City was silent and unattended. No Democratic politician, no Tammany chieftain, no emissary of the city's government, was on hand to see him off. A cluster of reporters was present, and Bryan, after giving each a campaign button with his picture on it, thanked them with smiling warmth. "The press of your city is against me, of course," he said, "but you boys have treated me very nicely."

Bryan, Mary, their host William St. John, a Nebraskan, John W. Cutright, who was acting as secretary, and John Brisben Walker, a publisher and prominent Democrat, boarded the "Croton local" of the New York Central Railroad. Their destination was Irvington, where the Bryans would stay for two days at Walker's manorial residence overlooking the Hudson before moving on to Upper Red Hook. Bryan and his party trooped into a musty day coach. A special car had been offered, but he declined, saying that he was too poor to afford it and he would not accept anything he could not pay for.[6]

As publisher of *Cosmopolitan* magazine, Walker arranged interviews for Bryan at Irvington with two leading figures of the New York publishing world, Dr. Albert Shaw of the *American Review of Reviews*, a journal of political reporting and analysis that circulated widely among an informed and influential readership, and William Randolph Hearst. What transpired between the hulking, shy Hearst, now deep in his sensational newspaper career, and the youthful Presidential candidate is unrevealed. Bryan had every reason to lavish thanks upon Hearst for a lonely, vigorous championship of his cause. And Hearst, in his muted but determined way, must have spoken in accents of renewed commitment. It was surely a portentous meeting, the first of many times the paths of these sharply different men would cross, Bryan devout and puritanical; Hearst amoral and nonreligious, and both joined in common cause.[7]

The journey to Upper Red Hook was completed by Hudson River steamer, train, and carriage. The little village, with its solitary clapboard hotel, a post office, a store, two churches, its few residences and shaded drives was a perfect bucolic haven for a Bryan wounded in his first encounter with the great metropolis. The Perrine home was a pretty frame structure in the village's center, next to the general store kept by Bryan's host, who, it turned out, was a leading Republican and was once the local postmaster in the Harrison era.

Midway in Bryan's rural sojourn there occurred in New York City and again at Madison Square Garden an event indicative of the severity of the Democratic cleavage. Bourke Cockran, who was the champion Democratic orator of the East, as Bryan was of the West, answered the Presidential nominee in an address that rallied the sound money cause. It was interesting that gold's rhetorician strikingly resembled silver's. Cockran, too, was Irish in his antecedents, flashed an oratorical style similar to the Westerner's, and leaned to black clothes, although he did not indulge in Bryan's clerical tie. Again the Garden was filled with clamorous humanity; prominent Democrats who had shunned Bryan were now present and blatantly on display. Unlike Bryan, Cockran spoke without notes, in a pugnacious speech of unbridled accusation and insinuation. The country, he said, would not "consent to substitute for the Republic of Washington, Jefferson, and Jackson the Republic of Altgeld, Tillman, and Bryan." The country would not accept "the fantastic dream of Populist agitators." Cockran, who made Bryan's performance seem a model of the innocuous, defined "Bryanism" as "a conspiracy between professional farmers who want to pay low wages and unreconciled slaveholders who would like to pay no wages." In a climactic passage, Cockran challenged Bryan to debate.[8]

Bryan saw in Cockran's challenge an opportunity for publicity and thrust. He announced that he would answer Cockran but not debate him. He would debate with only one man—William McKinley. The Republican campaign manager, Mark Hanna, paused in his collection taking among wealthy businessmen, from whom he was amassing a record fund, to disclose that McKinley valued too highly the dignity of the Presidency he was seeking to indulge in "catch-penny schemes" to win publicity. Bryan retorted that he preferred to have it said that he lacked dignity rather than backbone to meet the public's enemies.

McKinley persisted in a decorous campaign. Instead of going to the people, as Bryan planned to do, the people came to him. Delegations visited him from all parts of the country, taking advantage of the low excursion rates of cooperating railroads which prompted one paper to remark that visiting McKinley was "cheaper than staying at home." Sporting campaign badges, caps, and neckties, the delegations poured off the trains and into the arms of greeters who led them to McKinley's home. Soon the candidate appeared on his front porch, bade the crowd welcome, and treated the campaign issues briefly.

In answering Cockran, Bryan cast aside the reserve of Madison Square Garden and resumed the bravura of Chicago. He pleaded the cause of the common man. Just as businessmen used politics to their advantage, he urged the "toiling masses" to make politics their business "this once" and demand equal rights to protect their homes and families. The people, he contended, have sufficient intelligence to "sit in judgment upon every question." The great political issues are in their final analysis "great moral questions, and it requires no extended experience in the handling of money to enable a man to tell right from wrong."

Bryan used the remainder of his sojourn in attempting to build support out of the morass of antipathy against him among New York Democrats. With Mary he visited the state Democratic chairman, James S. Hinckley, but no tangible gain emerged. However, Tammany chief Richard Croker did endorse his candidacy. Clearly, to have the least chance to win New York and its rich electoral votes, he needed the campaign support of local Democratic organizations. Croker's pledge of support emboldened Bryan to push on the Albany to court David Bennett Hill, leader of upstate Democrats.

In a reception of rare enthusiasm in New York's capital, 10,000 squeezed into City Hall Square to hear Bryan declare—doubtless with Hill in mind—that he expected the support of many Democrats who could not agree to all that the party platform endorsed. Afterward, Bryan went to Hill's luxurious suburban home, Wolfert's Roost, where other politicians were gathered with their wives for dinner. Everything about the meal was perfect in the Hill manner, the viands, the wines, the service. The talk was light and gay, but little of it was political. At no time was Bryan closeted with Hill, and after his guests had departed, Hill had nothing to say to the press. His silence made his absence from the speech at City Hall Square all the more painfully conspicuous.[9]

If Hill and other New York leaders chose to remain cold to his candidacy, Bryan had available a further course. He could rally the people, and they, in turn, could prod the party chieftains. Having failed to arouse Hill, he now labored to awaken his constituency, the people of upper New York State. The same tactics could be used against other lagging leaders in Pennsylvania, Ohio, and elsewhere.

From Albany, Bryan embarked on a man-killing schedule of daily campaigning which brought him into every major city and most towns and hamlets astride his long slow route to Chicago. In a single day, August 26, he addressed fully 40,000 in lots from 100 to 10,000. By the day's end, his used-up voice could hardly be heard a hundred feet. He uttered his themes of social justice with new fervor and candor. His opponents feared him "because they know that the Chicago platform aims its blows at the real enemies of this country—those who think they are greater than the Government and can make the Government their instruments for private gain."

Labor Day in Chicago was a gala occasion for Bryan and his host, the Building Trades Council, a grouping of labor unions. After a parade of 40,000 in the morning, Bryan spoke in the afternoon at Sharpshooter's Park, located at an inconvenient distance from the city and poorly accessible. But the workingmen and their families were undeterred from coming, both to hear Bryan and to enjoy the unions' annual picnic. Thousands filled the grounds, and men and boys climbed trees overlooking the speakers' stand. Inevitably as in all Bryan's outdoor meetings, the crowd crushed toward him, and the jam became so severe that several women fainted and were trod on before they could be rescued. Bryan pleaded with the crowd to stay back and several times paused in his speech to pour a glass of water to be passed to a fainting woman.

Apart from an invitation to labor to share in everybody's better future, Bryan made no promise to support labor's immediate bread-and-butter aims. He was silent on the most relevant planks of the Chicago platform, including labor's uppermost political demand: the end of the court injunction in labor-management disputes. For the disputes he advocated "arbitration," which was "an impartial tribunal, before which a man may come to settle his differences, instead of resorting to violence to settle them." But arbitration has never appealed to labor leaders, both before and since Bryan's time, and there is no evidence that it did on Labor Day of 1896. But the crowd had come to hail Bryan, not to dispute him, and when he stopped, they turned to enjoy their picnics under the oaks.[10]

In formulating his attitude toward the East, Bryan knew that in the two Presidential victories scored by the Democrats since the Civil War (and in a third the party would have won in 1876 but for extraordinary irregularities) lay a common pattern. In all three elections, the Democrats carried New York, New Jersey, and Connecticut.

According to most advice pressed upon Bryan, the East was lost, and he should fight, therefore, only for the West. But there were dissenting voices. One of Hearst's star reporters, Alfred Henry Lewis, contended that Bryan should not be fooled by the hostility of Democratic leaders in New York State, adding that William Whitney and Congressman George B. McClellan, Jr., acknowledged privately that the silver ticket "will carry the state." From Pennsylvania, Joseph Sibley rendered a similar estimate. True, the Pennsylvania state organization was "not so friendly . . . as it should be," but the local Democratic clubs were "enthusiastic in the belief that Pennsylvania can be carried for you." [11]

The amount of attention Bryan could allot to the East depended on the demands of the West and South. In the West, it was clear, Bryan would pursue the policy of fusion that had been so successful in Congressional campaigns. In addition, he had to break Western Republicans into two main segments, gold and silver, and lead the latter into the new coalition. But to bring about these realignments, he would have to enter into lengthy, painstaking negotiations with organizations and leaders.

Interlocked with the strategy of sections was the strategy of issues, which, in actuality, was the strategy of groups. The Chicago platform, with its many planks, attracted a wide gamut of possible supporters, all with grievances against the social order. Bryan could try to appeal to each separate group or, as he finally decided to do, try to rally them under a single broad banner. His broad definition of the "businessman" at the Chicago convention, his identification of labor with "the great middle class," and above all the primary status he accorded silver indicated the latter course. Silver, as Bryan envisioned it, not only offered surcease for all who suffered injustice, whether farmer or city dweller, but imparted a powerful evangelical flavor to the campaign. It enabled Bryan to paint the struggle as a clash of good and evil.[12]

Silver was more than a monetary issue. It was a symbol of the deeply felt needs, hopes, and anxieties of millions of men who could not hope to participate in the detailed formation of policy, but who could find in silver an outlet for their frustrations even though they could not understand some of its technicalities. Silver came to represent such other planks of the Chicago platform as the income tax, tariff reduction, the trusts, and curbing the labor injunction. Silver was also a shorthand reference to the enduring depression and its hardships and to Wall Street's alleged conspiracies. It identified the Republicans with gold, despite McKinley's efforts to associate himself with international bimetallism, and polarized the campaign into a contest between two clearly defined adversaries. By fostering a dual value conflict, Bryan intensified enthusiasm, fears, and voter interest.

The Republican strategy was largely woven by McKinley's campaign manager, Marcus "Mark" Alonzo Hanna. Rolling in wealth and avid for power, Hanna was the nearest approximation to a national political boss the United States has ever known. A longtime sponsor of the gentle McKinley, Hanna believed that business interests should govern the country and that the Republican Party should promote business concerns. The resulting prosperity would filter down to farmers and city workers. Hanna was a formidable opponent in 1896. Highly intelligent, although contemptuous of learning; personally honest, although tolerant of corruption; hard and cynical in dealings with his fellowmen, Hanna had managed McKinley's political fortunes step by step in a swift, sure march to the White House.

The fear of Bryan among the well-to-do enabled Hanna to launch a mighty attack, which, at least in the campaign's early stages, was largely underground. Hanna resorted to his most proved weapon in confrontation and struggle—money. He subjected the giants of the business community to a grand shakedown. From railroads, insurance companies, big-city banks, and other likely givers he demanded generous contributions, and so efficient were his exactions that the Republican National committee ultimately reported expenditures of $3,500,000. The amount actually spent by local and national committees approached $16,000,000.

In addition, Republican orators pulled out all the stops in picturing, should Bryan win, the country's immediate and utter ruination. Although Bryan was often depicted as an "anarchist," Theodore Roosevelt and other Republican orators were given to speaking of him as "a mere boy, without intelligence or power." The real danger, they maintained, was that Bryan as President would constitute a Cabinet of Altgeld, Tillman, and Debs, apostles of radicalism whom Roosevelt expected to meet someday "on the field of battle, sword in hand. They are dangerous men, a menace to the nation." [13]

The stridency of Republican oratory was accompanied by the fear of big business that the prevailing depression would deteriorate into a complete economic collapse in the event of a Bryan victory. Businesses advised their employees that their work would cease if Bryan triumphed. Bryan had scarcely begun his campaign when the Indiana Bicycle Works, the largest of its kind in the world, with 1,500 employees, shut down. There was too much uncertainty in the world, its president explained: "We cannot risk in further manufacturing until our monetary contest is settled."

To an audience, Bryan displayed a membership card of a "Railway Men's Sound Money Club," distributed by railroads to their employees. The card pledged its signer "to use my vote and influence for the defeat of free coinage at the forthcoming election." The authoritative voice of Andrew Carnegie was raised in gloomy prophecy: ". . . a paralysis strikes the business world, mines close, factories shut down, millions of spindles stop, railroads retrench, wages fall, labor is dismissed, confusion reigns in finance and commerce, failures increase and confidence is gone."

The courtly, temperate McKinley did not propose to meet Bryan on his own ground. The Republican nominee had no intention of resorting to the campaign trail. But as the momentum of the Democratic campaign climbed, Hanna in alarm urged McKinley to reconsider his judgment. "Things are going against us, William," he said. "You've got to stump or we'll be defeated." McKinley drew himself up and said with his quiet air of finality, "You know I have the greatest respect for your wishes, Mark, but I cannot take the stump against that man." McKinley's reasoning was quite explicit. "If I took a whole train, Bryan would take a sleeper; if I took a chair car, he would ride a freight train. I can't outdo him, and I am not going to try." McKinley continued to prefer his "front porch" campaign.[14]

September. Blooming with hope and confident effort, the Bryan campaign, after Chicago, turned to the border states and the upper South. A high-priority subject in Bryan's speeches was McKinley's late pronouncement demanding that the "mills" be opened before the "mints." "That reminds me," rebutted Bryan, "of the man who said that his horse would go well enough if he could only get the wagon started. It is, so to speak, putting the cart before the horse. Of what use are mills unless the people can buy what the mills produce? . . . There is no more effective way to destroy the market for the products of the mills than to lower the price of the farmer's crops."

In St. Louis, Bryan was provided his theme when, a day before his arrival, many banks of the city joined in a public letter announcing that they could not supply gold to their customers, but promised to renew that service once "a correct settlement" of the money question was secured. In a huge meeting at Sportsman's Park, Bryan ridiculed the flighty undependability of gold. Laughingly referring to St. Louis, he noted how the metal disappeared whenever anyone dared to discuss the financial question.

In Louisville, the great crowds were so brimming with enthusiasm that they cheered at anything. Matt O'Doherty, a Silver Republican and chairman of a Louisville meeting, made a speech in which, among other things, he held that Bryan was "the greatest anarchist that ever lived." This contention thoroughly agitated the anti-Bryan press, which featured it, with flamboyant satisfaction, while omitting O'Doherty's citation of Bryan's social concern and patriotism as the basis of his "anarchy." Folly was twice compounded when Senator Joseph C. S. Blackburn, acting as a cheerleader for the exuberant crowd, asked for the identification of some American with one or another superlative capacity or achievement, each time evoking the hearty cry, "Bryan." Mindful of O'Doherty's speech, Blackburn went on to demand from the happy crowd, "Who is the recognized leader of anarchists in this country?" "Bryan! Bryan!" they roared back in jubilation.

"The recognized leader of anarchists" pushed through Kentucky, missing scarcely a hamlet and giving no surcease to his hoarse voice, and then moved into Tennessee. Knoxville was a gala celebration. Excursion trains from surrounding districts brought in carloads of farmers to swell the local crowds. In his speech, from a stand erected in front of the courthouse, Bryan explained why 16 to 1 would not entail grave inflation, as opponents were predicting. While leading the crowd through the mysteries of how money is put into circulation, Bryan was interrupted when someone yelled, "Mark Hanna is going to put it into circulation." The candidate rose to the opportunity: "That is increasing the circulation just before election in order to contract it after election." [15]

Each place outdid the other with demonstrations of support. At Asheville, North Carolina, Bryan was met by a great cavalcade of men and women mounted on all kinds of horses from spirited thoroughbreds to used-up donkeys. His route to Raleigh was lighted by burning tar barrels. At this moment the New York State Democratic convention was deliberating at Buffalo. Apprehension raged like plague in the Bryan camp that the New Yorkers would not endorse the Chicago ticket and platform. In his Raleigh speech, Bryan hurled a thunderbolt of warning. "The man who leaves the Democratic party today, when the party is taking up the fight for the common people, must understand that if he comes back he must come back in sack cloth and ashes." Gesturing like a preacher, countrified in dress, and heavy-jawed, Bryan was a vision of moral strength. But a closer look revealed the imprint of fatigue. His complexion was sallow; his eyes were dull. He was no longer an apple-cheeked "Boy Orator of the Platte."

The next day, at Goldsboro, brought joyful news. The state Democratic convention at Buffalo had endorsed the national ticket and platform. Bryan felt his leaden fatigue suddenly lighten. "There within the shadow of Wall Street," he rejoiced, "there, against the combined opposition of those who were once the leading Democrats of New York, the delegates had rallied to the national party standard." From North Carolina, where he gathered thirty rabbits' feet from well-wishers, Bryan entered Virginia. Upon reaching the Rappahannock River, he inevitably recalled the feat of young George Washington in throwing a silver dollar to the other side. He went on to lament that nowadays American financiers could throw gold dollars across the Atlantic and then bring them back "by an issue of bonds." [16]

In Delaware, the taut thread of Bryan's endurance snapped. On a dreadfully hot night in Wilmington, Bryan suddenly collapsed at the home of a friend. The spectacle of his huge, limp figure made his associates fear for his life. Nurses rubbed him through the night with alcohol, and a doctor attended him. The next morning the patient seemed miraculously transformed. He was, as Josephus Daniels, an anxious onlooker, put it, "as fresh as a daisy." Daniels attributed the collapse to fatigue combined with a sudden crisis. In the New York State Democratic convention at Buffalo, Bryan was assaulted with a grave, untoward development. The convention nominated for governor John Boyd Thacher, a thoroughgoing gold man, whose first statement as a candidate was a prompt and complete repudiation of the Chicago platform.

Bryan, angry and desperate with the rising stream of defections of leading Eastern Democrats, telephoned the New York State chairman, Elliott F. Danforth, and declared that, unless Thacher were removed from the ticket and a candidate nominated who would support the Chicago platform, he, as national candidate, would denounce the action of the New York Democrats and decline to fill any speaking engagement in the state. "He was very much excited, deeply outraged, and highly indignant," observed Josephus Daniels. To Bryan's immense relief, Thacher soon withdrew, and another candidate who did not repudiate the Chicago platform was nominated. Bryan, with restored equanimity, kept his schedule of New York appearances.[17]

Bryan's campaign route now led him once again into the "enemy country." Pennsylvania, New Jersey, New York, and New England turned out in lavish numbers. This time Bryan abandoned the pallid style of his Madison Square Garden speech and in his New York appearances subordinated silver to stress two issues of more immediate concern to the city workingman —the labor injunction and the income tax. This time in New York candor was the watchword. Senator Blackburn of Bryan's entourage cried to a Brooklyn audience that "From President to dog catcher, your leaders are skulking in the rear."

In New Haven, Bryan experienced a new kind of confrontation. In an outdoor meeting, his sympathetic audience was suddenly joined by a large, noisy contingent of Yale boys. When a student threw an egg at Bryan, pandemonium loomed, but he expertly dominated the situation by forceful sentences that recaptured the attention of his supporters. "I have been so used to talking to young men who earn their own living," he said through the Yale men's catcalls and cheers for McKinley, "that I hardly know what language to use to address myself to those who desire to be known, not as the creators of wealth, but as the distributors of wealth which somebody else created." The Yale boys shouted back "Ho-ax, Ho-ax" and brought in a brass band that blared as Bryan struggled to speak. To those of his listeners who could hear, he said, "Do not blame the boys. You could not expect much more of some of them. Their fathers, some of whom have gotten rich by the oppression of the poor, have threatened their employees with discharge if they vote their convictions. . . ."

New England was rife with aggressive opposition to Bryan. In Worcester, Massachusetts, he spoke beside a huge underwear manufacturing plant, on whose wall was spread a great portrait of McKinley with the American flag as background, while alongside was the red standard of anarchy with a bristling picture of Bryan. In another industrial town, giant placards covered most of a factory front, reading, "This factory will be closed on the morning after the November election if Bryan is elected. If McKinley is elected, employment will go on as usual." As Bryan preached the cause of silver, the employees listened quietly, refraining from applause lest they be reported by spotters posted in the crowd by their employer. After the New England journey, Josephus Daniels concluded, "It was a reign of terror in industrial communities, the like of which never was seen before in this country." [18]

Foreign observers were mystified by the ferocity of the American campaign. To Sydney Brooks, the distinguished British journalist, the real issue of 1896 was a narrow one: the Democrats' demand that bimetallism be adopted by the United States at once independently of other nations versus McKinley's ambivalent loyalties to gold and to bimetallism promoted by international agreement. Had Bryan campaigned on his platform in England, Brooks believed, it would have aroused only mild reaction. It was not "half so revolutionary" as the English Liberal Party's Newcastle program calling for extensive political and economic reforms for the working classes. The English could calmly debate the liberation of trade unions from age-old restrictions, national abolition of child labor, and free trade, and the British industrialist not only paid an income tax, but was accepting greater governmental intrusion into his affairs on behalf of social justice. The American industrialist, in contrast, was little trammeled by national regulation, and the laws applying to railroads and trusts were generally hobbled by lax enforcement and crippling judicial interpretation. The alert industrialist or financier could extract huge profits, unburdened by income or inheritance taxes. Inevitably American society became an order of sharp differences between a small group of the fabulously wealthy titans and the squalid poor whose numbers were enlarged by the heavy immigration.

Meanwhile the men at the top wielded their wealth and power freely. No one better symbolized private strength than J. P. Morgan to whose financial citadel on Wall Street the President of the United States had to venture twice, seeking help to save the gold reserve. If Bryan was, as Sydney Brooks called him, "the first American Radical," his radicalism derived less from his program than from the background against which it was expressed. If in America he was a radical, in Europe he would barely have been considered a moderate.

For Bryan, the Eastern political skies, under which private wealth and power were so lavishly concentrated, were not always leaden. Everywhere in New England and New York he was received by vast, warmly demonstrative crowds. For all the hostility of the press, the pressures of factory owners, and the manipulations of sound money Democrats and alarmed Republicans, "the people" seemed to be overwhelmingly for Bryan. When Daniels remarked upon the lavish outpourings of approval, Bryan replied, "If you think you have seen enthusiastic people you ought to go with me to Ohio, Indiana, and Kansas. These people have given us a great welcome in the East, but the West is on fire." A jubilant Daniels wired to his newspaper, the *News and Observer* of Raleigh, North Carolina, the prediction that Bryan would be elected by an overwhelming majority of the popular vote and a large majority of the electoral vote. His expectations were reinforced by the contagious optimism of Bryan. With the trend in the West running strongly in his favor and the Eastern trip exploding with popular interest wholly unforeseen, Bryan exuded confidence from every pore.[19]

While Mark Hanna threw money around like confetti, Bryan's chief resource was his own granitic endurance and ardor. His ability to deliver several speeches each hour for most of the day and night, his survival on a few hours' sleep were the marvel—and worry—of friends. One predicted with alarm that Bryan's managers "will kill him the way they are working him" and urged that they "lighten up."

Even crusty newspapermen were solicitous. Despite the hostility of journalism's owners and editors to Bryan, reporters developed a warm regard toward the Commoner, as many called him. Some counseled him to retire for the night at a civilized hour and resist every demand that he rise from his sleep for an appearance or speech. Bryan was amused to detect in this concern a large kernel of self-interest, for the newsmen could prepare and send in their dispatches only after Bryan went to bed.

His chief aide and counselor in the campaign was not some seasoned politico or facile expert in public relations. It was Mary who usually traveled with him, coached and advised him on his speeches, and oversaw the endless tons of correspondence. Mary helped conserve Bryan's strength by meeting the reception committees at the succession of railroad stops, thus permitting her husband more rest between speeches. And Mary was shrewd in her estimates of political people who came into Bryan's presence.

Bryan's efforts were supplemented by a band of silver orators who fanned through the country. Chief among them were Charles A. Towne, whom many deemed superior even to Bryan. A farm boy, Towne had been graduated from the University of Michigan with high honors and then read law. Restless and struggling to establish a practice, Towne began at Lansing before moving on to Marquette and Chicago and, in 1890, to Duluth. An indefatigable orator, adept with the telling phrase and impassioned plea, he became a busy Republican campaigner and in 1894 was elected to the U.S. House of Representatives. A convert to silver, he refused to accept renomination from his gold-minded party and ran independently as a Silver Republican. So consumed was Towne by zeal for a Bryan victory that he neglected his own Congressional race and was defeated by 719 votes.

In the East, Bryan's best gladiator was George Fred Williams, a powerful speaker who had mastered the complexities of the money issue. Born in Dedham, Massachusetts, in 1852, the son of a sea captain who died rescuing his passengers, Williams seemed destined for high office, with a distinguished presence, ease in making friends, and wealth to the point of his boasting of the finest wine cellar in Massachusetts. He was also well educated at the universities of Heidelberg and Berlin and at Dartmouth. In his student days, when France and Prussia were at war, Williams went to the battlefields near Metz to aid the wounded of both sides.

As a man of conscience, Williams was not always predictable. Originally a Republican, he joined independents of his party in rebelling against James G. Blaine's Presidential nomination in 1884. Eventually Williams became a Democrat and in 1890 was elected to the House of Representatives. He immediately dismayed his party leaders by refusing to vote for their candidate for Speaker. After an unsuccessful race for the governorship, Williams journeyed to the Chicago convention, sporting a long record of devotion to sound money. But at the convention he experienced a shattering conversion to silver and Bryanism. To the dismay of fellow Massachusetts Democrats, Williams returned home to campaign for 16 to 1. Vilification awaited him at every turn, and when Bryan came to speak in Boston, Williams sighed that he was "gratified to meet a man who had been as bitterly assailed as myself."

A young orator who breathed Western radicalism with fiery verve and could transport an audience of farmers was Congressman Charles A. Hartman of Montana. Born in Indiana, he migrated to Bozeman, Montana, and became a bookkeeper in a banking house while simultaneously reading law.

Admitted to the bar in 1884, he turned to politics and later that year became probate judge of Gallatin County. In 1892 he was elected to the first of his many terms in the U.S. House of Representatives. A gifted, fiery speaker, he was much in demand throughout the West. An early recruit to the silver cause, he took on heavy burdens for the 1896 campaign.

In addition, such amply tried and proved Populist orators as Mary Lease, "Sockless" Jerry Simpson, and Ignatius Donnelly were tireless on behalf of Bryan.

In contrast with the zealous, unsparing effort of Bryan and the silver orators, the top structure of the Democratic Party was a picture of lassitude. The national chairman, Senator James K. Jones, had little taste for the duties of party management. He was so slow in naming key committees that much of the influence of the Chicago headquarters slipped away to auxiliary organizations in Washington and New York. Jones, in point of fact, had not been appointed because of any presumed political skills. His primary function was to reassure old-line Democrats who might bolt their party and to lure the votes of Silver Republicans who might be more responsive if the respectable Jones held the Democratic reins. But if Jones was valued in the community of respectables, he was distrusted by the reformers. Senator Marion Butler's paper conveyed a wide feeling when it said of Jones, "He is a strong representative of the worst type of Bourbon Democracy, and would rather vote for Cleveland today, and be thick with Whitney, Hill, . . . than support Bryan or any genuine reform Democrat."[20]

The commodity in shortest supply for the Democrats was money, a numbing frustration since a campaign based on the complex theme of silver required gigantic expenditures for literature and speakers. While the community of financiers and industrialists provided Mark Hanna with princely sums, the substantial men in Bryan's ranks were as scarce as hen's teeth. A handful of well-to-do Eastern and Middlewestern Democrats like Sewall, McLean, and Henry Gassaway Davis made sizable contributions, but neither individually nor collectively were they in the same league with Hanna's men of wealth. Although stories circulated that Western silver mineowners, who stood to profit handsomely from a Bryan victory, were doling out contributions, the actual sums they offered were niggardly.

To meet payrolls, campaign leaders borrowed money, sought volunteers, and launched appeals through the press for the general public to make small contributions which cumulatively might offset the bulging Republican coffers. But the press campaign yielded little. Only William Randolph Hearst in New York gathered a sum of any size. Promising to match by half every dollar contributed, Hearst eventually handed over $40,000 to the campaign fund, of which he provided $20,000 himself.

Perhaps the most vibrant part of the campaign organization was what amounted to its Eastern headquarters in Hearst's fledgling enterprise, the

New York *Journal,* the only paper in New York City and the most important of the several Eastern papers that supported Bryan. To its offices flocked party leaders with stories and arguments on the silver issue they wanted published. For his political temerity, Hearst took heavy losses in advertising revenues, but he was building for the future a fast-expanding readership.

The most potent literature of the campaign was provided by the issue and reissue of the writings of William H. "Coin" Harvey. Thousands of readers still poured over his *Coin's Financial School.* Coin was a thoroughly composed little man, blessed with invincible intelligence and attired in dreamworld pedagogical finery: evening tails and dress shirt, or bow tie, knickerbockers, and silk stockings. To Coin's school came eminent figures and their sons, bank presidents, journalists, and economists. Humbly they asked questions and were not long in acknowledging their conversion to the silver gospel. Those who like Lyman Gage, president of the First National Bank of Chicago and a former Secretary of the Treasury, sought to entrap Coin were foiled. Gage emerged from Coin's classroom "in a thoughtful manner" and was "compelled to give assent" to the boyish instructor and his "plain and unanswerable views." As important as Harvey's texts were the accompanying drawings by H. L. Godall, which distinguished vividly between the forces of monetary good and evil. An American cow, for instance, was depicted as fed by the West and milked by New York bankers while New England financiers carted off the milk. Other times, a farmer paid for a restaurant meal with four bushels of wheat and four of corn; England strangled the fair maiden "Prosperity," as heroic Silver, in chains, looked on helplessly.

Bryan one day visited his great benefactor in his Chicago home. The orator could hardly make his way through the hallways because of the stacks of the *School* piled for mailing to thousands of readers. It was a warm meeting between two battered warriors, and there began a friendship that was to carry through years of common struggle.

The election of 1896 was a war of cartoons. Bryan and his cause suffered under the ridicule doled out by the skilled cartoonists of Republican journalism. The Democratic response was lacking in verve and incisiveness at least in part because of the low visibility of William McKinley. Exuding kindness and integrity, a devoted husband, and free of scandal, he was a poor target. Easily the most effective of the pro-Bryan cartoonists was Homer Davenport, a Hearst hireling, whose renderings included a drawing of Mark Hanna dressed in dollar signs. Copies were distributed throughout the country and made a memorable impression. A circus hand in his youth, Davenport drew with a free line and with telling force but was handicapped by the utter barrenness of his imagination. Left to himself, he was apt to produce some variation of the American eagle and depended on resourceful editors to keep him supplied with ideas. Silver's campaign songs, which were sung lustily, used melodies that were tried and true, but the lyrics rarely verged beyond the pedestrian. The favorites were "Sixteen to One," sung to the tune of the "Old Oaken Bucket"; "Cross versus Thorns," sung to the "Old Hundred"; and "Down with Plutocracy," sung to "Auld Lang Syne." [21]

Academicians, professional economists, and the more serious journals almost unanimously opposed Bryan's free silver position. The greater part of the silver argument was devoted to rejecting their claims that free coinage would bring horrendous disasters upon the economy. There was first the suggestion that upon the adoption of free silver American mints would be inundated with silver from Europe and the East. But Europe, the silver advocates answered, has no silver except her silver money, and the foremost silver nation of the East—India—is a "perpetual sink of silver," absorbing all she can attract.

Under free silver, opponents contended, a kind of Gresham's law would operate; "bad" money would drive out the "good," and gold would vanish from circulation. Free silver men replied, with amusement, that gold was already in retirement, reposing, with little exception, in the U.S. Treasury and in banks, where it was held as a reserve against liabilities. Free silver will hurt the city workingman, cried its critics. Prices will rise sooner than wages, and the workingman will be less well off than he is now. This, at most, will be a short-term condition, retorted free silver advocates. Rising prices will quickly encourage commerce, increase employment, and eventually raise wages, with labor, as well as merchants and manufacturers, benefiting.

"It is the people against the dollar," wrote Professor Frank Parsons, "men against money, the public good against the privilege of accumulating wealth that others create. The vital question is whether we shall fill the offices with men who will continue the policy of legislating in favor of moneylenders, banks, trusts, combinations, corporations, and syndicates, or whether we will fill the offices with men who are opposed to special privileges and will inaugurate a policy of legislating in favor of the people, a policy favoring the creation and fair distribution of wealth among the whole people rather than the gathering of millions in the hands of the privileged few."

Those who could not bear the policy of free coinage saw it as a device of confiscation. Creditors would be fleeced for the sake of debtors. Those with property would see its value shrink. Free coinage was a bull in the china shop of business confidence. By its threatened uncertainties, it would induce a panic. No one, not even the farmer, would gain from its establishment. If what the farmer produces rises in price, what he buys will also rise. The savings of the thrifty would be corroded by inflation, and those on pensions and salaries would suffer. Only three classes would gain—those who own silver mines and exchange their yield for "50-cent dollars"; speculators who, as in wartime, would profit by fluctuations in premiums on gold, foreign exchanges, and commodities; and exporters of manufactured goods who could pay their labor in depreciated money and sell the goods in foreign countries for gold.

Such a meticulous economist as J. Laurence Laughlin of the University of Chicago was troubled by an inconsistency in Bryan's argument. On the one hand, the candidate contended that free coinage would bring higher prices; on the other, he claimed that free coinage would cause such a demand for silver that it would be kept at par with gold. Prices would then remain on the level of gold, exclaimed Laughlin triumphantly, "up to which silver would be lifted. The irreconcilable inconsistency in these two grounds for urging free coinage of silver is fatal to the claims of the silver party."

Even social reformers were critical of free coinage, claiming that its high priority in public discussion blocked consideration of more serious issues. At best, its impact upon social and economic ills would be limited. Free silver would not cure the evils of monopoly. The monopolist could fix his prices whether the currency was gold or silver or both. Free coinage would not check the spread of city slums, curtail the liquor traffic, make government honest, or free the nation of the abuses of wealth. These social critics hoped that silver could be got out of the way, once and for all, in 1896, and the country could move on to issues of larger significance for its life and future.[22]

As the crowds turning out to see him grew, as expectations that he might win rose, Bryan escaped the constraints of the conservative Senators led by Jones and became the master of his own campaign, sketching out his routes, choosing the stops at which he spoke, and performing or overseeing scores of crucial little details. Marion Butler, who accompanied him over a part of the terrain, was appalled at Bryan's absorption in such trifles as looking up train schedules, buying tickets, and taking care of baggage and mail. Bryan would rise in the middle of the night to make train changes and connections rather than engage a special car in which he might have enjoyed unbroken rest. Newsmen beheld with wonderment Bryan carrying his heavy grips from the train to his hotel. Whenever local committees forgot to arrange for a carriage to be on hand for his arrival, Bryan, jovial, kindly, imperturbable, never lamented these lapses.

A common scourge of the campaign was the pickpocket, who found the close-packed crowds ideal for his nefarious purposes. Reporters noticed that as many as fifty pickpockets might clamber aboard Bryan's train as the day began, take seats in the smoker, and pile out at each stop for their work. They were aided by Bryan's frequent rhetorical device of asking those in the crowd who had gold in their pockets to raise their hands and then those who had silver to raise theirs. As Bryan proved his point that both metals were commonly accepted, the pickpockets moved upon their self-revealed victims. The problem became so serious that Bryan employed a Pinkerton detective and would sometimes stop midway in a flight of eloquence to point out an offender and demand his arrest.

At Marion Butler's recommendation, the national committee eventually provided Bryan with a special railroad car, known inappropriately as the Idler. The car afforded enough room for the press and local committees to travel comfortably in it and for meals to be prepared. It also contained a cot, which Bryan sometimes preferred to a hotel. The car usually carried stacks of campaign literature. "At every town, village, railroad crossing and farmhouse," according to one worker aboard, "we threw off copies of the New York *Journal* & other documents." Those who accompanied Bryan fast wilted under the pace, while the candidate seemed to thrive. According to one worker, "He can make twenty speeches a day & travel 300 miles without its having the slightest effect apparently upon him. Every morning he seems to be the freshest man in the car." [23]

In addition to campaigning, Bryan was preoccupied with forestalling further defections to Palmer Democrats and with combating those Eastern Democrats engaged in subversion and sabotage. Although the principal figures of the Cleveland administration ostensibly were for Palmer, their support was nominal; in actuality they worked for the Republican ticket. Even many Democrats affiliated with Bryan backed him only to the extent that it served their local political interests. Mrs. Mary E. Lease, the flamboyant, eloquent Populist, had only scorn for those who took an ambiguous stance toward the Bryan campaign. "When the future historian," she cried, "shall write the story of this campaign he will give as the two principal causes for the defeat of William Jennings Bryan the support given him by David B. Hill and the support given him by Hoke Smith." Smith, Secretary of the Interior in the Cleveland administration, "supported" the Bryan ticket but, as a sound money man, rejected the Chicago platform. In the campaign, he limited himself to two addresses for Bryan and refused to speak outside his state. Intermixed with his presumed backing were elaborate tributes to Grover Cleveland, endorsements of sound money, and emphasis of issues Bryan was ignoring.

If Hoke Smith's course was marked by vexing contradictions, David Bennett Hill's attitude was a mystery thrice compounded. Mary Lease screamed to the heavens that an unholy alliance had been entered into by Bryan and Hill, by which the latter, in the event of the former's election, would control the federal patronage of New York State. Undoubtedly, the Bryan camp through the agency of Chairman Jones endeavored to bind

Hill to the national campaign and through him work to keep New York in the Democratic fold.[24]

From every side, the Eastern voter was bombarded with messages hostile to Bryan. With rare exception the Eastern press was massed against Bryan, and its discourse was choleric. The Philadelphia *Press* cried that "the Altgelds and Tillmans," who had seized the reins of control, "incarnate a spirit of Communism and Anarchy." The New York *Post* saw a "mob of repudiators," and the Richmond *Times* dismissed Bryan as a "mere youth," given to "sophomorical rhodomontade." The Louisville *Courier-Journal* scorned Bryan as "a boy orator . . . a dishonest dodger . . . a daring adventurer . . . a political fakir . . . not of the material of which the people of the United States have ever made a President, nor is he even of the material of which any party has ever before made a candidate." [25]

Torrents of abuse poured forth from the clergy who beheld Bryan and the Chicago platform as equivalents in evil to the Devil and the Great Temptation. "That platform," cried the Reverend Cortland Myers in Brooklyn, "was made in hell," and he promised to denounce it each Sunday until election. The Reverend Thomas Dixon, Jr., spoke of Bryan at the Academy of Music in New York, as "a mouthing, slobbering demagogue, whose patriotism was all in his jawbone." His listeners howled their agreement. Other clergy likened the silver movement to theft. Free coinage, cried one, "will wipe out about one-half of every existing promise to pay." Another saw a Bryan victory as inaugurating a "revolution, the destructive consequences of which no man can picture," and the congregation applauded. Distinguished clergymen everywhere—Dr. Charles H. Parkhurst in New York, T. de Witt Talmage of Washington, and Dr. Robert S. McArthur of New York joined the attack, although with a trifle more forbearance.[26]

From church and press, hostility to Bryan fanned out to other institutions. University presidents, college deans, and eminent professors of economics joined in the chorus. Willis J. Abbot, Bryan's journalist friend, noticed that he and like-minded friends were cold-shouldered in their clubs and were denied admission to others they hoped to join.

In the East, Bryan was referred to as "the Boy Orator of the Platte" and identified with William F. Cody, then in his heyday as "Buffalo Bill." Cody's shows of a legendary Wild West, complete with broncobusters, scenarios of Indians attacking stagecoaches, and crack shooting exhibitions by cowboys and cowgirls, roused visions of gracious Washington society adopting the uncouth ways of frontier life should Bryan be elected.[27]

Through most of the campaign, the presence of two Vice Presidential nominees plagued Bryan. There was an almost continuous agitation for one or the other nominee to step down. As the campaign wore on, leading Populists continued to seek new schemes for dumping Sewall. The Maine state election, coming on September 14, was expected to go badly for the Democracy and would prove that even in his home state Sewall brought no strength to the ticket. The somber auguries materialized; the Democrats did not even carry Sewall's precinct. A Maine Populist promptly leaked to the press that he had assurances from the Democratic national committee that Sewall would be withdrawn. But Sewall moved not a flicker.

Possibly Tom Watson might be edged off the Populist ticket. A plan was hatched in a New York meeting, whose participants included Bryan, "Pitchfork Ben" Tillman, and sundry national committeemen but not Sewall, to send an emissary, Captain Evan P. Howell, armed with telegrams from Chairman Jones, to visit Watson. Howell, a skillful diplomat, worked up to offering a cabinet post to Watson if he would retire, but he indignantly refused.[28]

Two Vice Presidential candidates made it necessary for the Democratic-Populist fusion to reach accommodation on the arrangement of the electoral college ticket in each state. Under the workings of the Presidential and Vice Presidential election system, the citizen voting in November chooses electors, who in turn choose, in separate votes, the President and Vice President. Quite conceivably if the popular vote in a given state was closely divided between a Sewall slate and a Watson slate, the Republican Vice Presidential nominee, Theodore Roosevelt, could capture a plurality or a majority of the electoral votes of that state. An horrendous possibility loomed that Bryan, as President, might have Theodore Roosevelt as his Vice President.

Democratic-Populist negotiations over the composition of electoral college slates were conducted with wariness, a thirst for self-advantage, and a sense of mission. Various formulas were invented to reduce the friction. The easiest solution, which was adopted in some states, was for Democrats and Populists to vote for a common slate of electors. If the aggregate Democratic popular vote in a state was greater than the aggregate Populist vote, then all the electoral votes should go to Sewall, and vice versa. But such a formula was rejected elsewhere. In Indiana, Populist officials were offered bribes to prevent agreement on a joint electoral ticket. From Kansas, the state Populist chairman wrote, "I have absolute evidence that Mark Hanna's money is at work in Kansas and I know that some of the men who are clamoring for another electoral ticket in this state have received a portion of this fund." [29]

In campaigning, Bryan was careful never to refer to himself as the Populist candidate or to extol the Populist platform. He ran as though he were exclusively a Democratic nominee, a fastidiousness that was not lost upon Populist leaders. "It irritates me," wrote the Populist Colorado state chairman, "to hear Bryan constantly talking of Democracy and the Chicago platform. It makes me mad to hear him deny that he & his kind of Demo-crats are Populists as if there was a stigma attached to the name." [30]

Bryan ignored his Populist running mate, Tom Watson, even when Wat-son ventured West to help in the campaigning. The political explanation of Bryan's aloofness is not hard to find. To win the Presidency, he had to at-tract the great body of voters, whose convictions would hardly respond to Watson's radicalism. In addition, Watson was a free political spirit with a large gift for malapropism. Watson, observed Josephus Daniels, "was to be a thorn in the side of all the silver men . . . until the election. Nobody could quiet or silence him. He was obsessed by his ego. . . ." In a Dallas speech, Watson seemed to say that Bryan must be defeated and McKinley elected if Sewall was not dropped. Horrified Populist managers urged him to soft-pedal his opinions. In a Western speech, he proclaimed: "This is a movement of the masses. Let Bryan speak for the masses and let Watson speak for the masses and let Sewall talk for the banks and railroads."

Yet although Bryan kept his distance from the Populists, they were a bal-ance wheel against the intrinsic conservatism of Jones and other Demo-cratic leaders. Tom Watson perceived the value and necessity of this func-tion. "Unless the Populist Party can be held together as the champion of reform principles," he wrote, "the Democratic leaders will tie Bryan's hands, and the Silver movement will not materialize." Bryan, in point of fact, was in the strange position of having his like-minded friends in the Populist Party and his managers, who were neither friends nor fellow think-ers, in the Democratic party. "If Mr. Bryan were the same kind of man that the leaders and managers of his party are," wrote Marion Butler, "there would not be a Populist in America who would think of voting for him. The fact is, a large number of the managers of the party would secretly be glad if he was defeated." [31]

Yet if Populism received scant recognition from Bryan, he never disa-vowed it. Wrote Ignatius Donnelly after the campaign, "We put him to school and he wound up by stealing the schoolbooks." Populism permeated Bryan's oratory; its doctrines went well beyond the beliefs of his Demo-cratic heroes Jefferson and Jackson. It was the Populist rather than the Democratic Party that agreed with Bryan that the federal government has responsibility for the commonweal and must protect its citizens against the injury and wrongdoing of industrialism. It was the Populist rather than the Democratic party that provided Bryan with the main planks of his cam-paign.

Bryan's view of the world was Populistic rather than Democratic. He saw America as a bountiful land whose riches eloquently contradicted the farm-er's poverty and the worker's unemployment. Monetary policy, or free sil-ver at 16 to 1, was the magic key to unlock the door through which the peo-ple might escape from a barren present to an elysian future. This utopia would essentially be a restoration of the past, from which the nation had strayed and fallen into evil ways.

Bryan, with his intense moralism, found instantaneous agreement with the Populistic interpretation of politics as a struggle between good and evil, between the people and the plutocrats, between the toiling masses and the money power. His readings of American monetary history brought him to conclude, with the Populists, that evil worked in conspiratorial ways. Lombard Street and Wall Street incubated dark plots against the masses. British and Continental bankers, particularly the House of Rothschild, masterminded and manipulated against the people's interests. Populists, employing the Rothschilds as their point of departure, moved quickly down the road of anti-Semitism. Indeed so vehement became their expressions that Bryan, midway in the campaign, issued a statement of disavowal. "Our opponents," he declared, "have sometimes tried to make it appear that we were attacking a race when we denounced the financial policy advocated by the Rothschilds. But we are not; we are as much opposed to the financial policy of J. Pierpont Morgan as we are to the financial policy of the Rothschilds. We are not attacking a race; we are attacking greed and avarice, which know neither race nor religion. I do not know of any class of our people who, by reason of their history, can better sympathize with the struggling masses in this campaign than can the Hebrew race." [32]

While the Bryan campaign had a dual appeal for labor and the farmer, the perspective of each was different. For the farmer, Bryanism was the last fight against the encroaching industrial order; for labor it could be the beginning of a glorious march toward political power and social revolution.[33]

Since the disposition of labor leaders was crucial, Bryan was exhilarated when, promptly after the Populists nominated him, Eugene V. Debs, president of the American Railway Union, wrote exultantly that "in the great uprising of the masses against the classes, you are at this hour the hope of the Republic—the central figure of the civilized world. . . . The people love and trust you—they believe in you as you believe in them, and under your administration the rule of the money power will be broken and the gold barons of Europe will no longer run the American government." James R. Sovereign, head of the Knights of Labor, supported Bryan and joined the executive committee of the Populist Party. But both men had flaws as sources of support. After the Pullman strike in 1894, Debs' union fell into rapid decline, and Debs' personal influence in union affairs and politics dwindled with it. Sovereign's Knights of Labor were in their twilight and as a fading organization could provide little real aid.[34]

The object of Bryan's most assiduous courtship was Samuel Gompers, head of the American Federation of Labor. Although each AFL convention since 1893 had endorsed free silver, Gompers refused to support Bryan. As a new, fast-rising organization, the AFL was stressing bread-and-butter economics and political restraint. Gompers' European background made him unaccustomed to working with farmers in political alliance. To Gompers, agrarians were "employing farmers," who could hardly share labor's perspectives and interests. In actuality, Gompers seemed to oppose the agrarians for being too radical. Generally, the member unions of the AFL and their leaders were prepared to move further into political action than was Gompers. Bryan was indefatigable in seeking to coax Gompers away from his position of political neutralism. At a Chicago banquet, with Gompers present, the candidate declared that, if elected, he would appoint the labor leader to his Cabinet. Gompers, true to his beliefs, at once declined, but Bryan said he would persist in the hope that Gompers would change his mind. For the remainder of the campaign, Gompers spoke out in support of free silver, but not for any candidate or party. His reticence earned him the distinction of being the only major labor leader who did not endorse Bryan.[35]

October. The campaign in high gear. The "enemy" in alarm. A projection of the New York *Herald* gave Bryan 237 electoral votes, 13 in excess of victory. Mark Hanna was doleful. Shaken by anticipations of defeat, he commanded his lieutenants to "Quit blowing and saw wood." Senator Jones fanned Republican alarm by predicting that Bryan would carry thirty-six of forty-five states.

Bryan turned away from the East, to the relief of colleagues who lamented his devotion to what they deemed a poor gamble, and carried his fight into the American heartland, the Great West. His train puffed across the stolid peaks of the Alleghenies. A fierce fall rain pounded at his car window, and as the train pulled over its winding route at night, Bryan's sleep was broken by shouts from throngs gathered at the lonely mountain rail crossings, who, even with no hope of seeing him, cheered as he passed.

Harpers Ferry, Cumberland, Keyser, Grafton, West Virginia—all heard Bryan's voice. At Keyser, he was introduced by ex-Senator Henry Gassaway Davis, a wealthy man who said he feared no harm from Bryan's election. The young candidate exulted in the open support of a rich man who "is not afraid to trust the government in the hands of the people." In Wheeling, Bryan reported that a prominent corporation executive had boasted that the Republicans had $300,000 to spend in West Virginia to prevent its electoral vote from passing to the Bryan ticket. But the zealous young candidate was confident that "in times like these, when the people are in earnest money cannot change the result." [36]

Stirrings in the national and international economy were ominously suggestive. On October 3, three steamships puffed into New York Harbor, bearing $1,200,000 in gold for deposit in the Subtreasury, $1,500,000 for Lazard Freres, and lesser sums for the National City Bank, the New York Produce Exchange Bank, and other New York financial institutions. A week earlier, the Treasury reserve had gained almost triple this amount from European shipments. Indeed in the weeks just prior to the election, the importations of gold rose to $47,939,500, with Lazard Freres making the largest gains, $16,350,000. The financiers were stealing Bryan's thunder by making money plentiful.[37] In mid-October, more than $5,000,000 in gold arrived from Europe. The masters of finance were preparing to counter Bryan's call for inflation by making an inflation on their own terms. Silver fell to its cheapest price in three years, a result that Bryan hoped to achieve, but only through his election. On October 13, wheat, whose price Bryan aimed to increase, rose 1⅛ cents a bushel. Four days later, it soared to a record high of 81¾ cents. The accumulation of price rises since August amounted to 22 cents. The sudden improvement in the principal staple of America's rural voter was accompanied by inevitably heavy trading on the Chicago grain market. The prices of another great staple, corn, also advanced. This sudden increase came from a large expansion in foreign demand, which in turn prompted heavy domestic buying for storage, for the big operators were eagerly anticipating further price jumps within the next several weeks. Their optimism spread like swamp fire through the Western agricultural community. How could Bryan sound his notes of woe and reform when his rural audiences could see in the distance the outline of the very prosperity his campaign was promising?

Meanwhile, Bryan was pushing into Tennessee to address vast crowds in major cities and to boom the Congressional candidacy of Edward W. Carmack, the brilliant, doughty former editor of the *Commercial Appeal,* an early champion of the silver cause. Bryan personally intervened to quell a Populist-Democratic electoral college ticket wrangle. Each party had insisted on a separate ticket, putting Bryan in the unhappy position of running against himself until he managed to induce the Populists to withdraw. For Bryan, Tennessee was a land of adulatory welcomes. At Humboldt, his pathway from the train to the speaking stand led between rows of young girls, each wearing a Bryan and Sewall uniform, consisting of a cap, blue blouse and white skirt. The "16" of "16 to 1" was constantly used as a symbol. In a Nashville banquet, sixteen young ladies of Belmont College waited on table, and each presented a red American Beauty rose to Bryan.

His trail led through Kentucky, Ohio, and Indiana, where he stepped up the number of one-minute appearances from the platform of his car. He fired scorn at the National Democratic Party in Indiana, the state of its birth. That "so-called party," he declaimed, "calls itself the National Democratic Party when it does not expect to carry a single county in the whole Nation. It calls itself a Democratic Party when it was organized for the express purpose of electing a Republican candidate for President."

To the great crowds, Bryan spoke candidly of employers in Indiana cities
·ho notified their employees that they would shut down their businesses if
ryan was elected. After observing dryly that no corporate charter authorized the business it created to run the politics of the state, Bryan went on to
contend that "the restoration of bimetallism will not hurt any legitimate
business. The election of the Chicago ticket will help legitimate business. It
only interferes with the man who wants to eat the bread that someone else
has earned." [38]

For the last three weeks of his campaign, Bryan concentrated on the
upper Mississippi Valley. He crossed first into Iowa, and, at Burlington,
when a man cried out, "Three cheers for McKinley," Bryan retorted,
"Which McKinley are you for? The McKinley of 1890 or the McKinley of
1896?" From McKinley's earlier speeches, he read passages sympathetic to
silver and bimetallism, and added, with a flourish: "We can support every
contention we make by quoting Republican authorities. . . ." In South
Dakota, the men and women of Sioux Falls pulled Bryan's carriage through
the muddy streets. At Aberdeen, thousands waited his delayed appearance
by listening to six hours of oratory until he arrived at 2:30 A.M. The crowds
were equally faithful in North Dakota, and Bryan's journey through Minnesota was an unbroken triumph. In St. Paul, organized labor gave him a gold
pen and silver holder which he promised to use, if elected, to sign a free
coinage bill "at the earliest possible moment."

In Minneapolis, Bryan pressed the priority of the claim of "the producers
of wealth" upon the fruit of their toil. "I believe," he said, "that all the
classes which rest upon the producers of wealth can only prosper permanently when the producers of wealth are prosperous, and, therefore, I am
not unselfish when I desire such legislation as will enable the people to have
more than enough to eat and drink and wear. I want them to have enough
to be comfortable, because until they produce there is nothing to distribute,
and if they simply produce without enjoying, the production of wealth will
be so discouraged that production will finally cease." [39]

In Michigan, he dared address the workingmen of Mark Hanna's Iron
Mountain Mine, although he made no direct reference to his archfoe. Then
he darted back for heavy rounds of speeches in Ohio, Indiana, and Illinois.[40] In Jackson, Michigan, where the crowd was so dense he could not
reach the speaker's stand, Bryan took delight in introducing a local political
veteran, the eighty-year-old Albert Williams, as "a typical anarchist." "He
must be an Anarchist," said Bryan, broadly applying his opponents' reasoning, "because he is with us this year." Two years before, Bryan added,
Williams had been hailed by McKinley as the only survivor of sixteen men
who had founded the Republican Party.[41]

Increasingly, Mark Hanna was employing the tactic of sending out
squads of speakers who would move just ahead of Bryan and tell the wait-

ing audiences what he would say. By studying his addresses, memorizing his favorite phrases, and mastering his standard arguments, they aimed to rob his presentations of their effectiveness. With gleeful thoroughness, they told his little stories, sprang his jokes, and burlesqued his arguments. Bryan was soon finding that in some towns his serious, climactic presentation evoked merely roars of laughter.

The excoriation of the press increased. Among other things, Bryan was accused of being insane, of being a thwarted actor rebuffed in a quest for a stage career, of being in the employ of silver mineowners, and of being consumed with religious prejudice. There were even more ominous rumblings. In New York City, a group of wealthy men stated openly that if Bryan won, "We will not abide by that decision." A similar group in Chicago resolved that if intimidation and bribery did not work, they would resort to force of arms. As the campaign moved into its final days, feelings soared. Despite his repeated requests that silverites not abuse the gold men, Bryan learned that former Secretary of the Treasury John G. Carlisle was pelted with eggs in a Kentucky speech. The occurrence was viewed by gold men as part of Bryan's anarchistic plan. "Most of my friends think Bryan will be elected," John Hay reported to Henry Adams, "and we shall be hanged to the lampions of Euclid Avenue." [42]

In the final days of the campaign Bryan was hobbled by a cold which his hectic pace prevented him from throwing off. Yet somehow he held on, and after moving through Iowa, he reached Lincoln on Sunday morning, November 1, ending his longest trip of the campaign, totaling 12,837 miles. Early Monday morning, he left with Mary and Grace for a 344-mile journey through Nebraska, chiefly to aid the Congressional tickets. Republicans and gold men wearing big yellow ribbons freely infiltrated his crowds. Bryan rose to the challenge. He counseled any gold-minded farmers who might be among them that a more fitting emblem was a bunch of straw since it not only would provide the golden color they wanted, but would attest to their devotion to a financial system that turned over wheat to the Wall Street financiers and left only straw for the farmers.

Bryan put in eighteen-hour days of campaigning, which included seven speeches in Omaha before overflow crowds. He finished his speaking in the early minutes of election morning at Creighton Hall in Omaha, side by side with his old Populist ally Silas Holcomb, seeking reelection as governor. Bryan thus concluded a Presidential campaign which, although it omitted the Far West, in sheer application well exceeded all others before his day. Its raw statistics made Bryan seem a hybrid of Atlas and Demosthenes, with a total effort of almost 3,000 speeches and journeys of 18,009 miles. In a public letter to Chairman Jones, Bryan urged that all Democrats and other good friends of silver devote all election day "to our cause." In states where the bolting Democrats employed the party name, workers of the

Bryan clubs must warn voters "of the deception," and at polling places they must cope with misrepresentations circulated too late to be handled by Democratic speakers. "The gold syndicate and the trusts," Bryan warned, "are fighting for existence, and we must be prepared to meet them at every point." Mark Hanna too sounded an urgent call to "unfurl your flags, show your colors, and vote for the protection of your family." [43]

In the late morning of election day, November 3, Bryan and Mary voted in Precinct F of the Fifth Ward of Lincoln in a fire engine house. They were escorted to and from the polls by a marching group of local Democrats known as the Bryan Home Guards. All through this day of decision, the candidate was a model of serenity. At breakfast in the dining room of the Paxton Hotel in Omaha, where he had begun his day before returning to Lincoln, "he did not look like a man with an anxious mind." But by late afternoon his sudden emancipation from the demanding campaign had overwhelmed him with fatigue almost to the point of collapse. At 6:30 P.M. he went to bed. But fatigue and the suspense of the awaited results did not ruffle his aplomb. "Dan," he said to his aide, Dan Bride, "I have presented the issues to the American people. I have done my part. It is up to the people to decide if they should choose me. If they elect McKinley, I will feel a great burden lifted off my shoulders."

Mary and Dan faced the election night on the lower floor of the D Street house. Both the Western Union and the Postal Telegraph companies had wires run to the house to bring in special bulletins. Three telegraph operators were on hand, and twenty-eight newspaper reporters. The nerve center was the library, where the returns were received. Mary brought the more important bulletins to Bryan. From her expression he could immediately divine their import. By 11 P.M. Bryan was convinced from the reports that defeat was to be his lot. There is no evidence that faced with this prospect as the final reward of his months of commitment and travail, he uttered a single word of despair or lamentation, even to Mary. There simply vanished from his mind "the vision of the President in the White House perplexed by the cares of state, and, in the contemplation of the picture of a citizen by his fireside, free from official responsibility, I fell asleep." [44]

Although Bryan lost, the defeat was far from inglorious. True, he was overwhelmed in electoral votes, 271 to 176, but the popular vote was impressively close, McKinley receiving 7,107,822 to Bryan's 6,511,073, or 50.88 percent for McKinley and 46.77 percent for Bryan. He could extract various kinds of statistical small comforts. He won in 26 states and in the territories, while McKinley won in 21 states. Bryan polled 1,000,000 votes more than Cleveland in his victory of 1892 and only 84,212 fewer votes than the combined Democratic and Populist vote of that year. (There were about 2,000,000 more popular votes in 1896 than in 1892.)

A closer scrutiny of the results affords a clearer profile of Bryan's strengths and weaknesses. He failed to carry a single industrial state. The key to McKinley's victory was his sweep of eight states—New York, New Jersey, Pennsylvania, Ohio, Indiana, Illinois, Michigan, and Wisconsin— which polled one-half of the nation's total vote. In only one area was the Republican lead overwhelming—New England—where McKinley's vote was more than twice Bryan's.

In the nation as a whole, Bryan received a much smaller percentage of the votes of the cities than of the rural sections, yet he did better in the cities in the more urbanized and industrialized sections of the nation than in the cities of the less populous and more agricultural states. In the East he won strong support in many urban centers, while heavy majorities often opposed him in the rural areas. In the South the cities tended to be more conservative than rural areas, and only in Virginia did Bryan do better in the cities than in the countryside.

Bryan's best showing was in the Mountain States, where all six states (Utah, Colorado, Montana, Idaho, Wyoming, and Nevada) opted for him, some by enormous majorities. He also scored victories in the East-South-Central section (Tennessee, Alabama, and Mississippi) and in the West-South-Central section (Arkansas, Louisiana, and Texas). Bryan carried the remainder of the traditional Solid South: Virginia, North and South Carolina, Georgia, and Florida. His showing was utterly barren in New England and the Middle Atlantic States, and his victories sparse in the North-Central States and the Middle West (South Dakota, Nebraska, Kansas, and Missouri). Of the Pacific States, he won only Washington.

The 1896 election was a watershed election, which commenced a regrouping of supporters of the two major parties along lines that extended well into future elections. In his campaign appeal, Bryan worked for a realignment that would move farmers, city workers, and small businessmen into Democratic ranks. Instead, a different realignment resulted, with the Republicans drawing new support in nearly equal degree from all kinds of economic and social classes so that for the first time the aggregate vote of the Republicans in urban areas nearly matched that in the rural sectors.

So strong was Bryan's race that a shift of 19,436 votes in California, Oregon, Kentucky, North Dakota, West Virginia, and Indiana would have brought him victory. His total popular vote was larger than that of any previously elected President.[45]

Postelection analysis cast a pall of suspicion over the McKinley victory. Leading figures in the Democratic and Populist camps were agreed that Bryan had been victimized by the grossest electoral irregularities. "I have no doubt," George Fred Williams wrote to Moreton Frewen, "that there were tremendous frauds in the recent election, and no doubt much colonizing by which the doubtful states were carried for McKinley." A. J. Warner

THE FIRST BATTLE 253

contended: "It is impossible to believe that the vote in such states as Ohio and Indiana was an honest vote. . . ." Altgeld believed that fully 100,000 fraudulent votes were counted in Illinois alone and that the fraud in other states was so great that Bryan was actually the winner. Josephus Daniels was convinced that Bryan was the victim of frauds as outrageous as those that had kept Samuel J. Tilden out of the White House in 1876. "The difference between 1876 and 1896," he added, "was that the Mark Hannas got in their dirty work before the election, and twenty years before, it was perpetrated after the polls were closed." Various Washington correspondents following the election, some of them Republicans, told Daniels that if the votes had been counted as cast in California, Kentucky, Indiana, Ohio, Maryland, and Virginia, Bryan would have won. James B. Weaver called the vote in Iowa "absurd and dishonest." Bryan himself was quick to offer his own explanation: "I have borne the sins of Grover Cleveland." Thousands upon thousands of voters, unemployed or hard pressed by the collapsed economy, eagerly heard McKinley's sirenlike promises of prosperity. To some, like Ignatius Donnelly, the defeat was incomprehensible. "We had a splendid candidate," he lamented, "and he made a gigantic campaign; the elements of reform were fairly united, and the depression of business universal, and yet in spite of all, the bankrupt millions voted to keep the yoke on their own necks! I tremble for the future." [46]

One political analyst was convinced that the sensational rise in wheat prices cost Bryan Minnesota, North Dakota, Iowa, California, and Oregon. It overwhelmed the silver issue and seemed automatically to vitiate the contention that gold had depreciated every other commodity. The wheat price rise was the consequence of crop failure in India and a sudden increase in the production of gold resulting from the discovery of new deposits in the Klondike, South Africa, and Australia, made operational by the cyanide process. The validity of Bryan's quantitative theory of money was demonstrated—unfortunately for his own political welfare—before his election, rather than after, and to his opponent's profit.

It is clear, too, that Democratic bolters cost Bryan the election. Although the National Democratic ticket, headed by Palmer, garnered only 133,146 votes, it tipped the scales in several rural states. In Kentucky the Palmer vote ensured McKinley's victory. In Minnesota more than 15,000 ballots were voided because the voters in the confusion of facing a ballot bearing two Democratic tickets, marked everything "Democratic." According to one analysis, merely 14,000 Palmer votes, properly distributed, could have elected Bryan.

As well, Bryan suffered from the presence of John Peter Altgeld, a kind of political albatross that the young candidate could not cast off. Ironically, Altgeld played a minor part in the campaign, yet the most agitated attacks on Bryan were conducted by depicting Altgeld in monstrous terms as the campaign's central figure. Louis F. Post, editor of *The Public,* perceived a larger purpose in the attacks upon Altgeld: ". . . it was necessary to discredit him in order to keep open the channels for respectable and legal plunder; and the hint was taken from the method of housebreakers who poison the watchdog in the yard before venturing to climb into the dwelling at the window." [47] And there was too little money. The Democratic expenditure was a miserly trickle compared with Hanna's lavish outlays.

Elections are measured not only in terms of victory, however mountainous in importance that result may be. Elections are productive of lesser results, and these were of enormous importance to Bryan's political future. His strong race left him the dominant leader of his party, but it also fastened on him an issue that would stick like cough plaster. The great body of political supporters who in the wake of his defeat pledged their fealty in 1900 did so on the assumption that silver would again be the major issue.[48] "The sentiment here," wrote Henry T. Rainey, young attorney of Carrollton, Illinois, and future Congressman, "is universal that you must continue at the head of the free silver movement until we are finally successful." But some saw the issue both in 1896 and in the future in a larger and nobler context. "Too bad, too bad," cried Henry George, when the results were known on election day. "The people lost again." [49]

For all the clamor, outrage, and wild accusation of the campaign, Bryan had displayed gifts of leadership that won respect even beyond his own vast body of followers. Bourke Cockran, who fought him in the hustings, deemed Bryan's leadership magnificent. His unflagging spirit, his fervor, courage, and candor excited admiration, and even to his opponents, he was a breath of fresh air from the general run of shilly-shallying politician so perfectly typified by McKinley. Something of their hidden admiration is conveyed in a letter from Mrs. Henry Cabot Lodge, patrician and Republican, to Sir Cecil Spring-Rice, the British ambassador. "The great fight is won and a fight conducted by trained and experienced and organized forces, with both hands full of money, with the full power of the press—and of prestige—on the one side; on the other, a disorganized mob at first, out of which there burst into sight, hearing, and force—one man, but such a man! Alone, penniless, without backing, without money, with scarce a paper, without speakers, that man fought such a fight that even those in the East can call him a Crusader, an inspired fanatic—a prophet!" [50]

16. The Legacy

Through the mists of defeat and in the waves of messages rushing upon him in his somber study, Bryan perceived the awaiting task. An army of millions devoted to the cause and ready to fight on needed to be led. One correspondent stated his vanquished idol's obligation in homely verse:

> A just cause can never be gained or lost in one battle.
> We are buffeted to fight better, fall to rise again.

The general expectation in these initial postelection weeks, of his friends and foes alike, was that Bryan would again be the Presidential nominee four years hence in 1900. Letter after letter from admirers sounded that refrain. "Kansas will be for the young Gladstone of America again in 1900," wired a delegate to the Chicago convention, "and we will triumph." "We organize here today with Bryan Silver Club, five hundred strong for nineteen hundred," wrote a member from Sherman, Texas. A Presidential elector who had cast his ballot for Bryan looked forward to repeating this act in 1900. Even a competitor for the 1896 nomination, Governor Claude Matthews of Indiana, wrote to Mary expressing hope that the rigors of the late campaign would not deter Bryan in 1900 from leading "in the march to certain victory." And from the U.S. House of Representatives came the booming, authoritative voice of the Democratic leader, Congressman Joseph W. Bailey of Texas, who announced his well-considered judgment in June, 1897: "Mr. Bryan is identified with the Chicago platform and the issues of 1896 indissolubly. No man can so fully represent that platform in 1900 as the candidate of the Chicago convention of last July. Mr. Bryan is a better Democrat now than when he was nominated. . . ." [1]

For all these heady paeans, Bryan could hardly expect a smooth path to the 1900 nomination. But as the months slipped by, no serious competitor loomed on the horizon. None of his rivals for the 1896 nomination appeared to acquire new strength. Joseph Sibley, the young Pennsylvania firebrand who briefly lighted the skies in 1895–96, declared in a letter that somehow fell into Bryan's hands that he had no interest himself in becoming President and he looked forward to supporting the commoner in 1900. Bryan's old friend and political emissary M. F. Dunlap, of Jacksonville, Illinois, reported on the latest cerebrations of the man whose support Bryan most coveted. John Peter Altgeld, according to Dunlap, informed him in a tête-à-tête in Chicago, that "he had no further political ambition and his whole object now is to make you President." [2]

If the known and older leaders gave no sign of bestirring themselves to serious challenge, the possibility of the sudden emergence of a bright new star in the political firmament was also to be reckoned with. In the spring of 1897 such a star appeared in the adjacent state of Kansas, where Bryan could easily view it. For weeks the fusion forces of silver in the Sunflower State gossiped avidly over the prospect that U.S. Senator William A. Harris would capture the next Presidential nomination. The Topeka *Daily Capital* acknowledged the presence of this new element. "A little political cloud no bigger than Senator Harris has arisen over Mr. Bryan's chances for the leadership of the Populistic forces of 1900. The former is being urged by his friends to make the race." [3]

The danger of a rival candidacy would be twice compounded if it had the endorsement of what was remembered from the Chicago convention as the Senatorial ring. This was a group of party leaders, chiefly Senators, who supported the silver cause but whose devotion ranged from considerable ideological commitment to rank expediency. The Senatorial ring, above all, were "safe men," a temper they displayed in cutting out Bland from the nomination in 1896 and in sharpening their knives for Bryan, only to be thwarted by his oratory. According to reports, they did not mean to be thwarted again. "They now are formulating plans," an informant disclosed to Bryan, "to defeat the will of the people in the next national convention, and get the place for some one of their body." [4]

On November 16, 1896, just days after the election, Bryan opened his campaign for 1900 in a speech at Denver. It was a clarion call to action: "Those who fought in the battle will continue in the ranks until bimetallism is restored," he cried and his audience of thousands shouted back their fealty.

In speeches that followed, silver was the central theme, expounded to vast audiences still throbbing with the excitement of the late campaign. A few days later, again in an address at Denver, he reinforced the paramountcy of silver. "This issue," he declared, "goes down deeper and towers up higher than all others that have confronted us in years. It is a grapple between the producers of wealth and the monopolists, and the monopolists were the victors, but the masses were with us." Bryan's preachments contained concrete suggestions for enlarging the ranks of the cause. "We failed in our campaign to reach the business men," he acknowledged, "and I believe in the next four years that we ought to give especial attention to bring our arguments before them." He pictured the businessman as a forlorn victim of the money system, unable to secure needed capital in his local bank "because the banks have insisted upon a policy that ties money up in the Treasury at Washington that ought to be in the banks to be loaned out." [5]

If fusion was the staff and reed in 1896, let there be more fusion in 1900. Bryan hailed a new Bimetallic League forming in Nebraska as a model for other states to emulate. Let all friends of silver, regardless of party, enroll in such leagues under one banner. Let state election laws be amended to protect voters better from intimidation, and let corporations be curbed in employing funds to sway elections. To his Lincoln audience, before whom he made these proposals, Bryan noted, with beaming satisfaction, that bimetallism, though defeated at the polls, had made many Republicans hope that it would become law before the next Presidential election. Some silver men, he acknowledged, feared that the Republicans would steal their bimetallic thunder. Since the triumph of the cause was more important than candidate or party, he would gladly place his thunder on his front porch, where it would be in easy reach of the thieves.

Throughout 1897, Bryan crisscrossed the country on the scale of an electoral campaign. The sacred Democratic holidays commemorating the birthdays of Jefferson and Jackson were devoted to the silver theme. Invitations flowed from state legislatures for Bryan to address them. He highlighted silver but sometimes moved on to ancillary themes which stressed the need for better regulation of railroads and trusts, matters on which the state legislatures could act.

His comings and goings were attended with all the fanfare of the campaign: torchlight parades; foregathered local notables who basked in his popularity; vast audiences supercharged with the excitement of his oratory. Inevitably, as during the campaign, an occasional snarl or embarrassment bedeviled Bryan or his sponsors. The Arkansas legislature, for example, invited Bryan to address it, and local Democrats made elaborate preparations. One legislator in his exuberance dared to offer a resolution calling for the temporary removal of a picture of Jefferson Davis from the chamber's wall. In its place would be hung, for the brief duration of his visit, a portrait of Bryan painted by a local artist. The reading of the resolution erupted fierce excitement and vigorous protest. "Never." "Not on your life," members yelled. "Jeff Davis will not come down." The motion was tabled, and honor was done Bryan in other ways.[6]

When he was not out on the campaign trail, Bryan maintained his presence before the country via the lecture tour. The tour responded admirably to his two indispensable needs. It provided him a living and simultaneously brought him into the presence of great audiences where he could perpetuate attention to himself and his cause.

Bryan launched into lecturing on a major scale through the offices of W. E. McBee of Portsmouth, Virginia, and Alexander Comstock of Atlanta, recommended by the former as "a smart, a smooth advertising man." Com-

stock mapped out a tour of large Southern cities, in each of which he arranged for excursion trains within a radius of 150 miles. Pledging not to
make "any theatric or bombastic display," Comstock cleared all advertising
matter with Bryan. When word of the prospective tour was bruited about,
Bryan's political colleagues, particularly the Senators and banker William
P. St. John, were seized with despair. "I trust the rumor is untrue," wrote St.
John. "I feel deep interest in the next campaign. I dread the effect upon the
voter who can command an hour of your utterance for a dollar or two."

Never one to retract decisions in the face of objections from colleagues
and counselors, Bryan proceeded with the lecture projects. The moment
that word of Bryan's plans slipped out, his managers found themselves "almost overwhelmed with applications and invitations from all parts of the
country to name dates and amounts required to guarantee your coming."
According to the New York *Times,* Bryan was to receive $50,000 for fifty
lectures. He commenced these labors in Atlanta, on the subject "The Ancient Landmarks." By general consensus, Bryan in treating this apolitical
subject was far from his oratorical best. His managers, at least, were decidedly of this judgment. "We had a frost in Atlanta," said one, and another
offered, "Bryan, I am convinced, is a better speaker on the money question
than he is on other topics when there is no campaign." [7]

Bryan, too, was displeased and disengaged himself from the tour and its
managers. Quickly recruiting new managers, he embarked on another tour,
this time concentrating on the money question. He moved triumphantly
through the South and dwelled long in the East, where education on his
subject was badly needed. His drawing power assured packed houses. Although the charges varied somewhat, Bryan was prone to stipulate in his
contracts with the lyceum bureaus that the general admission should not
exceed the popular price of fifty cents. When critics sometimes lamented
that the common man had to pay to see his hero and presumed benefactor,
Bryan explained that his lectures were not free "because the free silver people are too poor to hire halls. Our adversaries at first accused me of being in
the pay of the mine owners. Now they censure me for charging the people
to hear me lecture. It is hard to satisfy the gold bug."

He lectured in locales as widely different as Carnegie Hall in New York
City and a tent in Beatrice, Nebraska, where he earned $163.66, or one-
third of the gate receipts. The draft for that amount was accompanied by a
note from the local manager, bearing the apology "Too bad weather
knocked us out." Although the precise total of Bryan's earnings from lecturing in 1897 is not known, it was well beyond the salary he would have commanded had he been elected President of the United States.[8]

Bryan resorted also to the written word to communicate his hopes to
even greater audiences, and the newspaper and magazine articles added to
his income. In the East, he still had Hearst's New York *Journal* as an outlet,

with Willis Abbot as his intermediary, but the *Journal* was not available for all that he wished to place. Hearst, who during the campaign had driven up the paper's circulation at a dizzy pace by advocating silver, had, after the election, noticeably chilled toward the cause. Abbot, explaining one rejection by the Great Chief of a proffered Bryan article on silver, pointed out that while the gains in circulation were gratifying, it was now necessary to coax back the advertisers that had been driven away. "Personally," Abbot added soothingly, "I think other qualities of the paper repel advertisers, but Hearst is inclined to charge all to the silver issue in which he never was a believer." But Bryan had another outlet in New York, the paper of Hearst's archrival, Joseph Pulitzer. In the *World*, Bryan placed occasional articles on issues and political developments of the day. Aside from the $1,000 he received for each article, the Sunday edition of the *World*, to which he was partial, offered the advantage of a vast audience. Its proofs were used by major papers across the country, some in the Pulitzer chains, and afforded a readership of from 3,000,000 to 5,000,000.[9]

Bryan's most ambitious literary enterprise was the preparation of his book *The First Battle*, published early in 1897. From silver leaders far and wide, he collected speeches, documents, and photographs and strung them together with an absolute minimum of connecting narrative. The result, in the most positive view one may take of this hasty scissors-and-paste compilation, constituted a kind of history of the silver movement from 1889 through the election of 1896. The political journalist and historian Mark Sullivan termed it "a weird hodge-podge of autobiography, Bryanesque philosophy, and propaganda—but nevertheless with attractions for those who can see reality in unconventional forms."

The First Battle instantly became an outstanding commercial success. In its first two months it sold 1,000 copies a day, and total sales eventually reached almost 200,000. His first royalty check exceeded $35,000. However, no sooner had he signed his contract for publication with the W. B. Conkey Company of Chicago than friends cried out in horror that Conkey had a history of seamy labor relations and that Bryan, presumably the friend of the workingman, had put himself into a position of gross embarrassment. As it turned out, the company, although blemished in its labor relations in the past, had in the meantime made contracts with the gamut of publishing unions. As a kind of ultimate insurance, the union label, as it appears on articles of clothing, was printed, at Bryan's request, on the frontispiece of the book.

The First Battle was intended to sustain continued interest in the silver movement, to underscore its dependence upon fusion politics, to provide a memory album of its milestones, and to express appreciation for assistance in the campaign. For years to come, in the parlors of silver families, *The First Battle* was customarily found in an honored place next to the Bible.

Bryan turned over the income from his book to the silver cause. To distribute the proceeds, he proposed to create a commission with representatives from each of the silver parties, but the Populist leaders, William V. Allen and Marion Butler, declined to participate, probably from fear of criticism from the middle-of-the-roaders, whose hostility to fusion was unabated. Bryan eventually distributed the earnings himself to the several parties in proportion to the votes they contributed in the late election.[10]

In these early months following the election, Bryan moved to counteract the image of youthful inexperience that his foes had delighted in exploiting. In April, 1897, with C. J. Smyth, now attorney general of Nebraska, Bryan appeared in the United States Supreme Court to argue what became a landmark case in governmental regulation of railroad rates. In his presentation, Bryan demonstrated that his talents were not confined to campaign stumping. On the day of the hearings the Court was jammed with spectators, many of them women, eager for a view of Bryan. When he appeared at noon, they broke into applause. Bryan spoke with decorously modulated force, on behalf of the Nebraska Board of Transportation and against several railroads, with his old foe, the Union Pacific, at their head. For two hours, he argued that Nebraska could set maximum freight rates based on a formula reflecting the value of railroad properties in terms of the cost of reproducing them, less depreciation. The railroads contended that original investment costs, less depreciation, and the value of stocks and bonds should be weighed in rate making. Bryan scoffed that original investments were made in eras of inflation and that railroad stocks and bonds were mostly watered. The conservative Court rejected both arguments but concluded that in evaluating railroad property, many factors must be weighed.

In his Washington sojourn, Bryan, with Smyth and Congressman Benton McMillin, paid a courtesy call upon the newly inaugurated President McKinley. The visitors were immediately ushered into the President's private office, where McKinley was conferring with a delegation. The President quickly broke away to greet his late rival. Cordiality reigned. After an exchange of small talk, McKinley acknowledged that a copy of *The First Battle* had recently arrived, but as yet he had no opportunity to read it. "There is no law which compels you to read it," said Bryan, smiling. Upon emerging from the interview, Bryan was besieged by newsmen, clamoring for his views on the Michigan and Ohio elections, in which the silver forces had scored impressive triumphs. Bryan was delighted to oblige. Mindful of the charge in his own campaign that silver politicians shook business confidence and aggravated the former economic depression, Bryan noted the present happy coincidence of silver's victory with business prosperity.[11]

Bryan applied another stroke to developing a firmer image of maturity and sophistication by making a triumphal visit to Mexico in December, 1897. In this neighboring nation which had committed its economic destinies to silver, Bryan, as the metal's outstanding champion, was given a hero's welcome. The high point of the visit was Bryan's address to the Chamber of Deputies. Doubtless inspired by events a few miles distant, where Cubans were locked in savage struggle with their Spanish masters, Bryan proceeded to interpret the Monroe Doctrine as an instrument for the promotion of liberty in the Americas. He noted that Mexico shared with the United States an interest in the doctrine, which was promulgated to bar the extension of monarchical institutions in the Western Hemisphere. Mexico and the United States will "hold up the torches of freedom before the nations of the world and prove that the governments derive their just powers from the consent of the governed and not from the rights of hereditary power." [12]

As a defeated Presidential candidate with strong prospects for a second nomination and as the leader of a powerful social movement, Bryan was engaged in a vital kind of politics, the politics of maintenance. To keep the silver movement at the forefront of the Democratic and allied parties, to assure its dominance in the national Democratic convention of 1900 and his Presidential nomination as the cause's champion, Bryan had to hold intact the elaborate array of party and silver organizations distributed throughout the nation. In addition, he had legions of personal contacts in parties and private organizations, ranging from governors and senators to precinct workers, to keep alive and to strengthen. The faith of these troops and leaders in the cause, their availability, their resistance to deviation toward rival causes had to be sedulously watched over and assisted. Together these men and women and their committees and clubs had fired the silver cause in 1896 with zeal and energy, and they provided an indispensable resource for the future. Urey Woodson of *The Messenger* of Owensboro, Kentucky, grasped their worth, when he wrote of Bryan's renomination in 1900: "Never before did a man have such a compact army behind him in our history."

Bryan had to inspire and instruct hundreds of silver organizations and Democratic clubs in the fine art of keeping their ranks intact, of increasing their memberships, and of spreading the good news of silver in their local communities. A general plan for carrying off these responsibilities was brewed during a hunting trip in the Missouri interior in December, 1896, with Bryan, Senator Jones, Governor Stone, and other illustrious Democrats participating. They drew blueprints for a national bureau of volunteer speakers with headquarters in Washington. The speakers would be assigned to every county in the nation and would be equipped with arguments and statistics. In the most optimistic projections, they might even be called on to pass an examination demonstrating their mastery of the complex subject of silver. Bryan and his friends dared to hope that 5,000 speakers might be sent out within three months. An honor roll would recognize those who brought off notable exploits in recruiting new members, collecting funds, or holding to an ambitious speaking schedule. Bryan became the official overseer of the honor roll.

In succeeding weeks, many a silver club repeated the course of the Bryan Free Silver Club of Manhattan, Kansas. This club changed its name to the 1900 Free Silver Club, in deference to Bryan, who now frowned on the inclusion of his name in club titles. But the Manhattan Club, after observing his wishes, went on to resolve itself as "emphatically in favor of his [Bryan's] renomination for the Presidency in 1900." As one silver club leader explained, "We realize these organizations cannot do their best possible work unless we have a head—a central head—for the movement."

The movement's faith and principles, its plans and rationale had to be communicated to the multitudinous following. Shortages of literature and the paucity of newspapers friendly to the silver cause were severe handicaps in the campaign of 1896. John P. Altgeld proposed that a plan he was developing in Illinois be extended throughout the nation. Altgeld aimed to establish in each precinct of his state a small circulating library, to be known as the Economic Circulating Library, which would contain the latest and best standard works on financial and other economic questions affecting popular welfare. Altgeld, with the aid of Professor J. W. Coultas, developed a book list, negotiated with authors and publishers for price reductions in the interest of education, and worked out mechanics of money raising and administration. Bryan took up Altgeld's idea, and libraries devoted to silver economics began sprouting around the country.[13]

Bryan, pursuing the politics of maintenance, had to hold Nebraska in a favorable posture toward silver, of providing through her example an inspiration to other states. Since Nebraska was Bryan's home base, it would be a dreadful humiliation if that state were to falter in her devotion to the cause. In Nebraska's elections of 1897, Bryan and his friends demonstrated how good silver forces ought to function throughout the nation.

In September, 1897, Nebraska's three silver parties—Democrat, Populist, and Silver Republican—held simultaneous conventions in Lincoln. Nearly 1,000 delegates gathered. Despite the minor character of the offices at stake —a Supreme Court judge and a regent—heroic national figures of the silver movement were present: Weaver, Towne, Davis, and Simpson, among others. Delegates and national figures alike happily took up the task of demonstrating how efficient, harmonious fusion could help the common cause.

Early in the proceedings, delegates of all the conventions met in Bohanan's Hall, and a glance at the interior disclosed the theme of the evening. On the stage, behind rows of palms, hung a huge and solitary picture of Bryan. The principal speaker, Jerry Simpson, after delighting the audience with a description of the present government in Washington as divided into "departments—these being the legislature, the judiciary, the executive, and Mark Hanna," moved on to prophecy. The fight for silver, he cried, would be maintained until March 4, 1901, when "we could all go to Washington" and see Bryan inaugurated as President.

Each of the three conventions met and made its resolutions separately, but with marvelous unison. Yet for all the watchfulness and close management by Bryan and his deputies, not every variety of untoward event could be avoided. The temporary chairman of the Democratic convention, A. C. Shallenberger of Alma, did everything in his keynote address that the most dedicated silverite might want. If anything, the address was too effective. It roused the convention to a shouting pitch. But it also prompted connoisseurs of Nebraskan oratory to whisper to one another in awe that this newcomer, this handsome thirty-five-year-old son of the frontier, was superior even to Bryan. A new star—and a local rival for Bryan—had been born.

Any gathering of livewire young men, whose meaningful acts are closely regulated, requires some outlet, and at this convention, they found it in a spirited debate over an issue of minor consequence. The fused forces of silver required an emblem, they agreed, and various delegates sallied forth with their pet suggestions, often with impassioned speeches. Eventually the choices narrowed down to two: the rooster and the Liberty Bell. Pat Gering of Cass shouted that he could tolerate no picture of a bird that fed on dunghills. Friends of the rooster blazed back in indignation. A bitter forensic brawl might have ensued had not Bryan then entered the hall. The delegates, upon seeing him, rose to their feet as one and, waving their hats and coats, gave out with deafening cheers. After the noise faded, the emblem was voted upon, and the rooster prevailed. Bryan's appearances at the Populist and Silver Republican conventions were also noisily appreciated. All three parties united upon a common ticket and on the principle that bimetallism "is the paramount issue" of the campaign.

In a windup celebration at the statehouse grounds, Bryan declared that "the money question must be settled before other questions can be seriously considered. To fight each other in the face of a united and unscrupulous enemy would not only postpone the restoration of bimetallism but endanger the success of every other necessary reform." He had soothing words for Populist middle-of-the-roaders who despaired that the price of cooperation with Bryan for their party was its thorough subordination to the Democrats. Not at all, contended Bryan. Cooperation did not mean "that any one of the parties will swallow the other two. It simply means that they will travel together while they can and separate only when they must." [14]

Bryan was even more preoccupied with the establishment of newspapers favorable to the silver cause in major cities. Of highest priority was the founding of a silver paper in Chicago. The enormous original investment still loomed as an insuperable obstacle, but it did not deter journalistic ideas of some originality. "Coin" Harvey spoke eagerly of a tabloid-size daily devoted to a condensation of the news and to highlighting silver, which would sell for five cents a week. But the project foundered, as so many others did, on securing original capitalization.

Bryan seemed always under siege to contribute articles, make personal appearances, and arrange meetings of financial backers on behalf of journalistic entrepreneurs who promised unflagging devotion to silver. J. Q. Thompson, editor of the Washington, D.C., *Chronicle,* impressed that no daily paper in the capital supported Bryan in the latest campaign, aspired to found "a clean family literary political paper . . . advocating bimetallism and aimed at a national clientele." Would Bryan please agree to furnish signed articles on occasion, and could both he and Mary be listed as "contributing editors"? One founder of a paper proposed to kick off his popular subscription campaign with a rousing public meeting at which Bryan would be the star attraction. Bryan was implored from many sides to dispense approval to the editor of *Der Deutsch-Amerikaner,* a German weekly paper of Chicago, whose growing tolerance of silver views promised to be invaluable in moving German-Americans away from their sound money proclivities and into the silver ranks in 1900.

Bryan also had to provide succor to keep good and faithful friends in office, as well as encouragement for new silver candidates in the elections of 1897. This often required him to choose, on occasion, between candidates competing to bear the silver banner and clamoring for his approval. The most insistent demands for Bryan's help centered on the several Senate races. Since this was a day when state legislatures elected United States Senators, Bryan, in effect, was petitioned to participate in statewide fights to elect legislatures that in turn would choose friendly Senators.

The most savage of these fights in 1897 transpired in Ohio, and it pitted Bryan against Mark Hanna. By an adroit bit of political legerdemain, Hanna was serving an interim term as Senator, filling the vacancy left when McKinley moved the incumbent and aged John Sherman into his Cabinet as Secretary of State. In 1898, Hanna would face the test of election, but the preliminary and actually the decisive stage of that test transpired in 1897, when the Ohio legislature was elected. "You ought to be willing to do anything to help beat this man," observed A. G. Thurman, a leading Ohio Democrat, in urging Bryan to bring his oratorical thunder into the state. Bryan came and took off his gloves for the fight. Barnstorming the state, he termed the first six months of the McKinley administration "the most disastrous in the history of the country." He pointed to Hanna as the enemy of labor's interests and the master conspirator of the late Presidential campaign, who achieved his results by fraud and coercion traceable to "the money powers" of this and other countries. Bryan even warned of frauds in the coming elections.[15]

Bryan was also importuned to support specific Democratic candidacies for U.S. Senatorships. To extricate himself from these thorny predicaments, he took refuge in a rule he had long applied in Nebraska politics "not to get involved in any political contests . . . among rival silver candidates." By and large, he managed to hold to his rule, but sometimes an ambitious candidate strove to budge him from it. "I presume"—one aspirant warmed to the subject—"there are some here to whom you could speak without attracting the notice of the general public. . . ."

Then there were the scrambles of aspirants of the several parties that were uniting in fusion behind a common ticket, as in the quest of U.S. Senator Fred Dubois of Idaho for reelection. Dubois was a Silver Republican and probably, next to Henry Teller, was that party's leading advocate of the silver cause. Trouble erupted for Dubois—and, as it developed, also for Bryan—when Populists and Democrats of Idaho agreed to unite behind a Populist candidate. Leading silver Democratic Senators such as John W. Daniel and James K. Jones besought Bryan's help for Dubois the veteran. Dubois himself was driven to write to Bryan, in mixed desperation and understanding, ". . . I can win with your help but I must not ask you to aid me to the disadvantage of the cause. . . ." The knowledge that Mark Hanna was working for Dubois' defeat did not make Bryan's task any easier. Within private and rigorously circumscribed confines, Bryan did give a measure of aid to Dubois, but to no avail. A combination of Democrats and Populists dominated the Idaho legislature and moved invincibly on to the selection of a Populist, Henry Heitfelt, to succeed Dubois.[16]

As 1897 waned, the silver issue was becoming more and more for Bryan the Great Temptation. Should he in the future accord it the paramount status it enjoyed in the 1896 campaign? Or should he, sobered by electoral defeat, henceforth take up other issues that might broaden his political base and enhance the prospects for victory in 1900? Or, further, should he abandon silver altogether as a used-up issue? Silver was, on the one hand, the foundation of his brief, sensational national political career. He was committed to it by the most solemn, unqualified, and repeated pledges. Yet, on the other hand, silver had dwindled as a political issue in the late election's final weeks. New discoveries of the metal and rising farm prices had pulled much of the rug out from under Bryan's argument. But silver, for all these changes, had not been "restored" to its former place in a bimetallic monetary system. The erasure of the "Crime of 1873," silver's recovery of its status in the eras of Jefferson and Jackson, was still denied.

Bryan was buffeted by counsel and entreaty from every side. Arthur Sewall was impressed that "there are more silver men in our country today than there were on election day." The sudden economic upswing that lifted McKinley into office, he regarded as "accidental," thanks to crop failures in

India and Argentina. Foreseeing "bad times" for the next four years, Sewall was convinced that "this battle beyond a question must be fought over again in 1900 and my present judgment is that it ought to be fought on the single issue of free coinage of silver." The chairman of the Democratic national committee, Senator James K. Jones, was impressed that "the cause of bimetallism is stronger today than it has ever been in this country." Elwood S. Corser, a Silver Republican leader and shrewd campaign manager, pleaded that Bryan hold to silver and the Chicago platform and press state Democratic organizations to follow his course. The 1896 campaign, he contended, was "too short to educate the Democratic voter," but that task could now be completed, making victory attainable in 1900.

However, there were also voices of dissent. The prestigious John Peter Altgeld warned that while silver stirred the agricultural states, in Chicago and other great cities and in the rural East, silver sparked little response. In those political communities were substantial bodies of men "who desire to act with us solely because they believe that through the Democratic party they can achieve reforms regarding municipal corruption, etc., they cannot do through Republicans." Altgeld recalled that in the late campaign many audiences, although attentive to discussions of silver, were far more demonstrative toward other issues. The case against silver was put on other grounds. The perspicacious Louis R. Ehrich, author of a standard work, *The Question of Silver,* observed that silver had gained its high momentum in 1896, not by any intrinsic merit as a political issue, but by the coincidence of "hard times" with Bryan's candidacy. "Such a condition will not exist in 1900," Ehrich warned, "and the first continued period of prosperity . . . will expel the last echoes of this troublesome issue." [17]

Bryan was not long in making his position known. At the Jackson Day banquet in Chicago on January 7, 1897, he declared, "The contest for the restoration of the money of the Constitution will go on with renewed vigor. The people who advocated free silver before the election advocate it now. The election has . . . not overthrown the convictions of those who believe that the gold standard is a conspiracy against the welfare of the producing masses, nor has it changed the convictions made to obey the law." Altgeld and others of his opinions could take heart that Bryan, although declaring again for the paramountcy of silver, was at least linking it to the growing issue of the trusts.

Steadily, in decision and act, Bryan in 1897 reaffirmed the primacy of silver. In Nebraska he made it the paramount issue of the campaign. In lecture tours and political addresses, it was his constant topic. If anything, McKinley's policies spurred his attentions to silver. His harsh indictment of evil liaison among the money changers, the trusts, and a compliant President was given credence by two major actions of the Republican administration. One, the Dingley Tariff, raised duties to new protective highs, to the anguish of the consuming masses on the farms and in the cities. The second, the currency "reform" plan of Secretary of the Treasury Lyman J. Gage, was exposed by Bryan, Bland, Teller and other silver spokesmen, as a transparent maneuver to retire greenbacks and Treasury notes by the issue of national bank notes, a procedure long and bitterly opposed by silver spokesmen. Organized labor, distressed by the contraction of the currency which the Gage program augured, took new interest in Bryan's monetary preachings. Gold Democrats who had voted for McKinley felt betrayed by his raising of tariff duties.

McKinley sought to paper over these cracks by carrying out his campaign pledge to appoint United States members to an International Bimetallic Commission, charged with exploring the possibilities of an international bimetallic monetary standard. The President's special emissary was Senator Edward O. Wolcott of Colorado, long an apostle of international bimetallism. The endeavor of Wolcott and his fellow delegates raised not the least concern in the silver camp. As the Wolcott mission commenced, Henry Teller confidently predicted that Britain would never budge from its adamant rejection of silver. Altgeld suspected that Wolcott's colleagues "derive too much pleasure from *waiting* for bimetallism to desire any change in the conditions at present." Wolcott toiled diligently; the commissioners met in earnest plenary sessions, but few tangible results emerged. Asked of the implications of the Wolcott commission's apparent failure, Bryan answered: "It proves what the Democrats have always claimed—that international bimetallism is impossible, except through independent action. The Republican party must now keep itself before the public as the champion of the single gold standard. That tub must stand on its own bottom, if it can." [18]

The proving grounds of Bryan's principles and personal strength were the state conventions of 1897, which were strongholds of the professional politicians. As Davis H. Waite, the Populist former Governor of Colorado well observed, these professionals, although they rushed to clasp the silver faith in 1896, were anything but ideologues. All too often, Waite noted, " 'Silver' Democrat . . . is only another name for 'professional politicians' out of a job. . . ." Their interest in 1900 was victory and their view of what issues might best produce it might well differ from Bryan's.[19]

When at last the dust cleared, convention after convention had declared for silver and the Chicago platform had proclaimed pride and confidence in Bryan or subscribed to his nomination in 1900. The territory in which he was weakest was, as it had been in 1896, the East. It was the scene of several formidable struggles in 1897.

The chief of these centered in New York State and New York City. In the state the state committee was charged with writing a platform and making the party's nomination for the principal elective office to be filled in November, the chief judge of the Court of Appeals. Bryan men, working through three organizations they dominated—the Loyal Democratic League, the Democratic Alliance, and the United Democracy—pressed for reaffirmation of free silver and the Chicago platform. After a harsh confrontation, the state committee declined to act on any platform. From Washington, Chairman Jones shrugged off this seeming rebuff by declaring that in his opinion the committee utterly lacked authority to frame a new platform or to endorse the Chicago convention. For chief judge, the committee nominated Alton B. Parker of Ulster County, who, though he had voted for Bryan in 1896, was infected, good Bryan men believed, with the virus of loyalty to Cleveland and the gold standard. Outraged Bryan men spoke of rejecting the Parker nomination but were dissuaded.[20]

New York City was electing a mayor, and the struggle within the Democratic Party between Tammany and forces tied with Bryan was bitter. At best, Tammany's deportment toward their hero in the 1896 campaign had been ambivalent, if not downright disloyal. A new boss had risen in Tammany, a churlish, tyrannical son of the old sod, Richard Croker, who experienced his first brush with Bryan when he invited the Nebraskan to speak before Tammany, provided he did not discuss the silver question. Bryan replied tartly that he would not appear at any function where the Chicago platform was taboo, and he added, for Croker's further edification, that "Tammany needs the Democracy of the nation as much as the national party needs Tammany, and Tammany should recognize that fact."

Breathing fiery defiance to Tammany's nomination of a mayoralty candidate uncommitted to the Chicago platform, New York City's free silver Democrats entered into an alliance with labor unions and progressives and nominated Henry George, the single taxer. Bryan himself behaved guardedly in the New York City struggle, declining to rush to the aid of his forces. Croker even dared to say publicly, "Mr. Bryan doesn't wish the national issue introduced into the municipal campaign." In a telegram Bryan even went so far as to declare: "I have not expressed any opinion in regard to the New York mayoralty campaign, and do not care to express any opinion in regard to it." Tragedy was piled upon confusion several days later when Henry George died. His son, Henry George, Jr., took his place in the race.[21]

Judge Robert Van Wyck, the Tammany candidate, carried every borough of Greater New York and was swept into victory by a comfortable margin. In a field of four, Henry George, Jr., ran last, with pitifully few votes. Had Bryan entered decisively into the New York campaign, its consequence for him would have been disastrous. He would have put his prestige on the line, seen it mangled by defeat, and suffered an open break with Tammany. He could be pragmatic when it paid to be.

One of the knottier questions facing Bryan was the future of the gold Democrats who had bolted the party and who, according to the electoral data, caused his defeat in 1896. Days after the defeat of 1896, Bryan had made it clear that their repentance must occur on his own absolute terms. In a press interview, he said, "The gold Democrats, if they come back to the Democratic party, must come as silver men. There is no room for two Republican parties in this country." Months later, he prophesied a lasting alienation between gold and silver men. "Monometallists and bimetallists," he proclaimed, "will not associate in the future any more than they have done in the past. Any man who will come into our ranks and go with us in the fight, will have his sins forgiven; but he cannot bring his sins with him."

Bryan's stern demeanor only stiffened the will of the gold Democrats. Grover Cleveland wrote, ". . . Democracy is not disorder . . . the care of only a portion of our people . . . its aggressiveness does not mean class hatred and sectional vituperations, and . . . mere partisan triumph at the sacrifice of principle and patriotism." William D. Bynum, chairman of the National Democratic Party, after noting Bryan's belligerency, pledged that "the National Democratic party will last as long as there is any danger to the country from agitation along the lines of the Chicago platform." [22]

To Bryan of higher importance than a most rigorous screening of the returning gold prodigals was a thorough purging by the Democratic Party of all gold men who remained within it. Of the two types of gold Democrats, those who bolted and those who stayed, Bryan was decidedly more interested in the latter: ". . . while the fight is on," he said, "the man who is with us and not of us is more dangerous than he would be on the outside." A model for Democratic self-purification was provided by the Jacksonian Club of Omaha. Soon after the 1896 election, the club dropped from its rolls all its members who had refused to support Bryan in the campaign. Heading the list was Bryan's long-standing foe Euclid Martin. The victims cried out in mingled surprise and wrath and wrote scathing letters to the entrenched leadership, but all in vain. The banishment was final and without appeal.

The most sensational act of purification was levied against William F. Harrity of Pennsylvania, recent chairman of the Democratic national committee, who had sinned by withholding his support from Bryan in the 1896 campaign. With Bryan's full knowledge and approval, the Pennsylvania Democratic state committee passed a resolution declaring Harrity's seat vacant and replacing him with James M. Guffey of Pittsburgh, "who so loyally supported William J. Bryan. . . ." The proceedings that produced this result were attended by flashing tempers and angry confrontations between rival factions. At one stage a policeman was called in to help the presiding chairman keep a semblance of order.[23]

Worn by strain from the election, the ties of fusion were further tattered by new stresses and frictions. Populists, restive over the return of Eastern conservatives to the Democratic Party, doubtless spurred Bryan's severity toward gold Democrats. The Populist Party's identity, obscured by its support of Bryan in 1896, needed restoration. Populist leaders, looking for fresh causes that might enhance their party's distinction and vitality, were encouraged to do so by Bryan's insistence on silver as the issue of the future. Marion Butler urged both Bryan and his party to spotlight transportation. Given the vast distances of the nation, the general dependence on the railroads and their potential as a natural monopoly, Butler was sure that a scrutiny of the railroad industry must soon come to the forefront of national politics. George F. Washburn of the Populist national executive committee contended that focusing on public ownership and widening public regulation of the economy would best shore up Populist identity. But Bryan, who meant to give the same exclusivity to silver as he had in the late campaign, was unimpressed and noted that Washburn "no doubt is sincere, but I question wisdom of the position . . . taken." [24]

More than ever leaders like Butler and Washburn were pressed by the middle-of-the-roaders to sever ties with the silver Democracy. "Our party will have to be reorganized," wrote Tom Watson, "and the fusion heresy stamped out." Middle-of-the-roaders enjoyed a brief inning of glory when Bryan, in distributing his earnings from *The First Battle,* bestowed $1,500 upon the Populists. Professor L. C. Bateman of Auburn, Maine, a middle-of-the-roader and previously a Populist candidate for governor, cried out that the evil of bribery lurked in Bryan's gift. Despite the modesty of the sum involved, Bryan took pains to declare publicly that in distributing his book's royalties it would have been "an inexcusable slight" to omit the Populists. Tom Watson had the last word. "We could wish," he snorted in his *People's Party Paper,* "that Mr. Bryan had kept his money in his pocket." [25]

With his other major partner in fusion, the Silver Republicans, Bryan's relations were serene. Many Silver Republicans looked to the day when all silver forces might be united under a single party banner. Silver Republican leaders—Towne, Dubois, Richard F. Pettigrew, and Hartman—were hammering out plans to extend their party's organization from its Western base to every section of the country. One of the party's heavier handicaps was the shrinkage of its membership in Congress because of the ravages of the late election. But Towne, an inveterate optimist, could report to Bryan in the spring of 1897: "Work is going favorably and increases in ranks are happening daily from the ranks of disillusioned gold standard Republicans." Most likely, Towne's finding was based more on hope than on fact.[26]

The success of Bryan's politics of maintenance was subject to visible test in the elections of 1897, but the results were necessarily fragmentary. Statewide contests occurred in only twelve states. In the general picture, Bryan held his strength in the West and South, but in the East his weakness deepened.

The contest in which Bryan was most interested, the Massachusetts governorship, saw his staunch friend and ally George Fred Williams go down to defeat. Eastern Democrats swarmed back into power, but they were of the sound money rather than the silver variety. McKinley's striking pluralities of 1896 in the major Eastern and Middlewestern states all but vanished. "Never before," editorialized the New York *Times,* "has any Presidential leader of a party seen so magnificent a following dwindle so far and in such degree." Critics tended to lay the decline to McKinley's clasping of the Dingley high protective tariff rather than to any general awakening to the merits of Bryan and his cause.

Not unexpectedly, Bryan viewed the results through silver-tinted glasses. "The sentiment in favor of the Chicago platform," he told the press, "shows a healthy growth throughout the country . . . Free and unlimited coinage at 16 to 1 is nearer now than it was a year ago." [27]

17. *Colonel Bryan*

Bryan's political engrossments were rudely jarred on the night of February 15, 1898, by an explosion about 1,200 miles from his home. In the harbor Havana, Cuba, the United States battleship *Maine* blew up and quickly sank with the loss of 250 men. The disaster was the capstone of years of turmoil and strife in unhappy Cuba. Economic depression, the corrupt and dictatorial government of the Spanish overlords, oppressive taxation, riot, and revolution plagued the island. The heavy-handed rule of the Spanish governor-general, General Valeriano Weyler, poured fuel onto the flames.

President McKinley, instinctively a man of peace, found approval for dealing with the Cuban question by diplomacy among the business community, on whose support his political career depended. But while McKinley worked for peace, powerful pressures pushed for war with Spain. The "yellow" journals of Hearst and Pulitzer stirred their readers with lurid, often invented accounts of Spanish atrocities. An expansionist clique, avid for the enlargement of American territory, raised loud and influential voices for intervention: Senator Henry Cabot Lodge, Assistant Secretary of the Navy Theodore Roosevelt, and other Eastern patricians; Admiral Alfred T. Mahan, the distinguished naval theoretician and apostle of imperialism;

Whitelaw Reid of the New York *Tribune* and Albert Shaw of the *Review of Reviews,* among others. Clergymen and the religious press provided spiritual gloss to their urgings.

Hearst in the New York *Journal* laid the foul deed to Spain. Theodore Roosevelt stated that "the Maine was sunk by an act of dirty treachery on the part of the Spaniards. . . ." In the face of these words, McKinley redoubled his efforts to resolve the situation by diplomacy while peering nervously over his shoulder at the racing political clock that made the elections of 1900 seem just around the corner. Bryan, as the McKinley camp nervously appreciated, had in Cuba a political issue superior to that of silver, which, after all, was an amorphous movement and a complicated subject.

By placing himself at the head of a movement for war, by fanning patriotic passions and jingo spirits, and by promoting a cause attractive to influential citizens, he could place himself in an overpowering position to unseat McKinley in 1900. Mark Hanna, whose doubts were growing daily over the political wisdom of McKinley's pacific course, warned a gathering of Republican Senators in the Marble Room, "Look out for Mr. Bryan. Everything that goes wrong'll be in the Democratic platform in 1900. You can be damn sure of that!"[1]

Bryan's past public record provided little basis for predicting his course in the Cuban crisis. As a Congressman, while Cleveland was involved in foreign policy decisions over Hawaii and Venezuela, Bryan was engrossed in the domestic questions of the tariff and the currency. His silence then did not diminish the fears of McKinley men, but to their surprise Bryan refused to discuss Cuba until a report was made on the *Maine.*

As McKinley worked fervently to avoid war, Bryan, a month after the *Maine* disaster, asked an aroused people to support the President. A few days later, he veered slightly, but his discourse was still that of national unity. On March 9 he publicly advocated a defense appropriation, holding that it would "show the world that Congress and the American people, without regard to political differences, are ready to support the administration in any action necessary for the protection of the honor and welfare of the nation."

In the fast-moving politics of the Cuba situation, Bryan faced risks equal to McKinley's. In essence, his danger was that his followers might move in one direction—war—and leave him abandoned, marching behind rather than ahead of his army, his voice unheard. The war spirit was indeed rolling over his legions. The West, his stronghold, its ready humanitarian instincts aroused by reports from Cuba, viewed the conflict as a struggle between autocracy and self-rule. In Washington, silver leaders, Democratic, Populist, and Republican alike, demanded action. Henry Teller cried that events in Cuba constituted war "at our borders," and considerations of humanity required the United States to tell Spain that it must desist "let the consequences come what may." The silver Democratic Congressman William Sulzer of New York announced that he would go as far as anyone to bring freedom to Cuba. Senator Richard Pettigrew agreed, but for different reasons. ". . . I want a war with Spain," he said, "because I believe it will put us on a silver basis."

Bryan was not long in moving with the tide. His assessment of events, he announced, brought him to regard war as inevitable. From his lecture platforms, he raised audiences to frenzy by waving a small American flag in his right hand and a Cuban flag in his left. William V. Allen introduced in the Senate a resolution recognizing "the independence of the Cuban Republic," the outgrowth of a conference of Populist and Silver Republican Congressmen to find common ground on Cuban policy.

Hours after the Allen resolution was introduced, Bryan enunciated his position: "Yes, the time for intervention has arrived. Humanity demands that we shall act. Cuba lies within sight of our shores, and the sufferings of her people cannot be ignored unless we, as a nation, have become so engrossed in money making as to be indifferent to distress. . . . War is a terrible thing, and cannot be defended except as a means to an end. . . ." Now it was McKinley who was overcome with sensations of political alarm.

Elihu Root wrote to Theodore Roosevelt, "I sympathize with McKinley . . . but . . . if the administration does not turn its face towards the front and lead instead of being pushed, its seems to me it will be rolled over and crushed and the Republican party with it." So insistent was the push for war in Congressional and popular opinion that McKinley suppressed a message from the American minister at Madrid reporting Spanish capitulation to the administration's terms: an armistice for Cuban insurgents and dissolution of the reconcentration camps, as they were known, into which people of the countryside were crammed to die by the hundreds. Congress quickly passed the equivalent of a declaration of war. Word of the momentous step reached Bryan during an address in Boston to an audience of 20,000. The great crowd, upon learning of the news, rose to its feet and cheered wildly. Bryan led the demonstration by waving a Cuban flag.

Events were rushing to a climax. On April 21, after McKinley conveyed to Spain the demand of the Congressional resolution to "relinquish its authority and government of the island," she broke off diplomatic relations with the United States. On April 25, Congress declared that a state of war existed, and the United States began to fight for ends that Spain had already conceded. America was seeking to win by war what it had already won by diplomacy.[2]

Even before Congress declared war, McKinley issued a call for 125,000 volunteers, of whom Nebraska's quota was 2,114. Arguments, put chiefly by older counselors, flowed upon Bryan, admonishing prayerfully against his offering himself as a volunteer, lest he jeopardize his safety and his political future along with it. His leadership was irreplaceable; his highest duty was to steer the silver cause which he alone could bring into victory's sweet harbor in 1900. If he volunteered, the administration would then enjoy the option of sending him to the fighting fronts or to tropic swamplands where he could contract yellow fever and succumb to an inglorious death. James K. Jones, fearful that the war would churn up new issues and new leaders, felt that Bryan could better guard against these hazards by retaining civilian status.

All this counsel was unsolicited, for Bryan possessed a tough self-sufficiency in making decisions, and he was not one to anguish over them or to seek out the opinions of others. Nor did he overlook the political fine points of his new position. On the day that Congress declared war, Bryan wrote to the President, making a clear, astute offer, "I hereby place my services at your command during the war with Spain and assure you of my willingness to perform to the best of my ability any duty to which you, as the commander-in-chief of the Army and Navy may see fit to assign me." Of Bryan's silver compatriots, some found satisfaction in his step. Joseph Sibley wrote, "I am very much gratified that you have made the tender, because you have removed the weapon of reproach from those who would have been delighted to have forged and used it." [3]

For McKinley, Bryan's letter was a thorny dilemma. If he failed to commission Bryan or employ his services, he would appear petty and mean, while if he sent Bryan to the battlefield, he would be accused of cruel manipulation to rid himself of his once and future rival. He waited twelve days to reply and then asked merely for what branch of service Bryan considered himself best qualified. Totally lacking military training and experience, Bryan had absolutely no basis for choosing between the services. The hot potato was burning his hands.

One of Bryan's preferences for resolving the knotty situation was to become a staff aid to General Joseph Wheeler, an old family friend, an ex-Confederate general, and a senior member of Congress, who at the moment was posted in Florida. James K. Jones made discreet inquiry of Wheeler if the appointment would be possible. Wheeler expressed warm delight to have "our eminent friend" on his staff, and noted a ruling of the Judge Advocate General that aides must be detailed from those having commissions in the army. The problem, therefore, was for Bryan to secure a commission by means that unfriendly politicians could not exploit. The quest was complicated by the quota of commissioned officers assigned to each state and by the speed of the mobilization. On May 12 the established First and Second Regiments of Nebraska were mustered into service. Four days later the First embarked from Lincoln to Manila. On May 19 the Second departed for training camp. With seemingly all of Nebraska's soldiery on the point of vanishing, Bryan immediately enlisted as a private in the Nebraska National Guard for a three-year term. The day before Bryan committed himself to the military life, Governor Silas Holcomb issued a public statement empowering Bryan to recruit a third regiment of Nebraska volunteers. The understanding prevailed that Bryan was to be elected colonel, its being the practice for volunteer regiments to elect their officer.[4]

These well-laid plans were suddenly imperiled when the War Department ordered companies already mustered to expand their enlistment in lieu of organizing new companies. Both Governor Holcomb and General Wheeler telegraphed the War Department their strenuous objections to the order. In the darkest moment of this new impasse, salvation suddenly burst upon Bryan when the governor of Missouri, Lon V. Stephens, telegraphed: "Knowing of your patriotism and anxiety to go to the front in the service of our country, I tender to you, if under the second call I am empowered by the Secretary of War to make an appointment, the Colonel of a Missouri Volunteer regiment." On the heel of the Stephens offer, Secretary of War Russell Alger suddenly overlooked his own order and permitted the organization of a new third regiment for Nebraska to proceed. Bryan expressed gratitude to Stephens but declined his offer, saying he was duty-bound to Nebraska.

Since the Third Regiment was clearly marked as Bryan's regiment, there was an eager scramble by young silver enthusiasts to sign up. Lieutenant Colonel Victor Vifquain, a professional soldier and Bryan's longtime political friend, assigned by the governor to recruit Company A of the new regiment, set up quarters in the Lincoln Hotel and in less than a day had recruited more than enough men. Bryan was among the first to enlist, to the accompaniment of rousing cheers. Evidently only the cream of local manhood volunteered, or the physical examination to which Bryan and his compatriots were subjected was extraordinarily flexible, for only two candidates were rejected. Recruitment proceeded throughout Nebraska under a plan by which all parts of the state were to be represented in the Third, much in the manner of a party convention. Bryan took pains to recognize each Congressional district and, except for Lincoln and Omaha, avoided recruitment from communities that already had companies in Nebraska's other regiments. The several officerships were eagerly sought for. One "old veteran" of Ewing, Nebraska, petitioning to be appointed quartermaster, offered to raise an entire company "if necessary." On June 11, Bryan and his aides moved to Fort Omaha on the northern limits of the city. A month later, nearly 2,000 men were assembled under his command, and on July 13, Governor Holcomb, honoring their election of officers, appointed Bryan colonel of the Third Regiment.[5]

Bryan's entry into the military life by no means closed the door to politics. Indeed it is doubtful that any military system, even one in the iron-disciplined Prussian style, could have separated Bryan from politics. To Fort Omaha came a steady trek of visitors with state and national political business. As a scintillating national figure, Bryan was a favorite "tourist attraction" of vacationers and convention-goers in Omaha and the nearby states. To "shake hands with Colonel Bryan" was a standard divertissement of any conference. For the Republican press, Bryan's new career provided ready grist for ridicule. "The military life," one paper observed, "is having an excellent effect upon Mr. Bryan in assisting him to thoroughly command his will. He made an address to his troops the other evening and not a word did he say about the output of silver or the relation of coinage to seigniorage."

Bryan was in military service less than a month when he made a major speech on the emerging issues prompted by the war and its likely consequences at the Trans-Mississippi Exposition at Omaha. Bryan and C. J. Smyth were among the scheduled orators. What Bryan said was patently a precursor of the 1900 campaign.

Bryan accepted the war within distinctly more narrow and reasoned limits than other public leaders, whose statements pulsated with blood-and-thunder patriotism. He revealed himself as a near pacifist, motivated by a religious conception of brotherhood. War with Spain was justified because the United States had exhausted diplomacy in seeking a peaceable solution and taken up arms only when it was compelled to choose between war and "servile acquiescence in cruelties which would have been a disgrace to barbarism."

Bryan dwelt on the hardships and suffering of war and prayed for the time "promised in the Holy Writ when the swords shall be beaten into plowshares." But this time could never be "until justice is enthroned throughout the world." This war must not be a war of conquest and, therefore, of injustice. The nation must take a higher road. These views committed Bryan to the arduous task of bringing a war-obsessed nation to renounce the temptation of imperialistic territorial aggrandizement.

Bryan's announced commitment to anti-imperialism was produced by no significant political pressures and with no expectations of political profit. He was simply articulating moral principles that he had long embraced, derived from the holy commandment "Thou shalt not kill." Man, in his eyes, had a higher mission than to murder his brothers, than to commit them to the whip and misery of arbitrary, exploitative rule.

Bryan's views brought rejoicing in the camp of his opponents. Henry Cabot Lodge, ardent apostle of war and of imperialism, wrote to Theodore Roosevelt noting Bryan's opposition to colonization and the country's apparent taste for it. "We shall sweep the country. . . . Republican conventions are all declaring that where the flag once goes up it must never come down." [6]

Nebraska's new Third Regiment was a motley collection of amateurs, and Bryan's military innocence, coupled with the contradictions between his religious convictions and the demands of the military art, created a blissful harmony of ignorance between the rank and file and their leader. For military professionalism, the Nebraska Third depended on its second-in-command, Lieutenant Colonel Vifquain, who had been educated in the military academy of his native Belgium. Migrating to Nebraska, he settled in Saline County before the Civil War. Enlisting as a private, he won rapid promotion, and in 1865 President Lincoln made him a brevet brigadier general. For bravery in capturing the Rebel flag at Fort Blakely, Alabama, he became the only Nebraskan to earn the Congressional Medal of Honor. After the war, he tasted politics as a delegate to the Nebraska Constitutional Convention of 1871 and served in subordinate diplomatic posts in Panama.

Vifquain was instrumental in overcoming Bryan's reluctance to abandon his early plan to enlist as a private in lieu of taking a colonelcy. "But I know nothing of military matters," Bryan had protested. "I then told him that I would help him," Vifquain wrote later of their interview, "that if he who had received 6,500,000 votes for commander-in-chief of the army and navy of the United States could afford to become a colonel, I could afford to come down a peg or two and become a lieutenant colonel." Bryan's other bulwark was his quartermaster, William F. Schwind. Schwind functioned as a majordomo who simultaneously cared for Bryan's multifarious political affairs and for the accustomed duties of a quartermaster. A private secretary to Bryan in the 1896 campaign and one deeply conversant with the lore and personalities of Nebraska's politics, Schwind offered impressive credentials for his major task. Not the least part of his value was his affability.[7]

On July 13, Bryan was inducted into the Army as a colonel. Military ceremonies marking his assumption of the Third's command took place on the evening of the following day with both Mary and the children present. Bryan, whose horsemanship was excellent, rode into the hollow square formed by his awaiting regiment and gave his first order in his clear, sonorous voice. His uplifted sword flashed in the sun, and the motionless lines of men began to move.

The raw troops went through their paces far more smoothly than anyone dared hope, and each new evolution of their drill was cheered. When the drill ended, Bryan gave a brief fatherly talk to the men, stressing his hope that no one would in any way discredit the regiment and promising his loyal support of every worthy endeavor. The ceremonies ended with a homely affectionate touch. Private W. R. Simpson of Company L presented Bryan with a magnificent bridle made entirely of horsehair, except for four tassels which were of ladies' hair.

Bryan immediately telegraphed the Adjutant General in Washington of his mustering into service and estimated that his command "will be uniformed, equipped, and ready to move within a few days."

For his part, Bryan took pains to preclude any behind-the-scenes interventions on his behalf. To Senator William V. Allen, he wrote, "Please do not make any requests or suggestions as to destination of 3d regiment. I have no preference. If the War Department asks my wish, I expect to leave matters entirely with my superior officers and go wherever they see fit to send me." News soon arrived that the Third would join the Seventh Corps of Major General Fitzhugh Lee on the Florida east coast.

On July 18, five days after the mustering in, the Third was to depart. It is doubtful that any regiment of the war was accorded a more elaborate send-off. A day was set aside at Omaha's exposition to commemorate the event, and no fewer than 15,000 gathered to attest their homage. The high point was a display of fireworks, put together with obvious affection and solicitude for the untried Third. The most elaborate fireworks ever seen in Omaha filled the skies—rockets, bombs, serpents, spreads, and countless set pieces. Of the latter, the most spectacular was an explosion that filled the darkness with a multicolored "Welcome Third Regiment," followed by a huge portrait in fire of Colonel Bryan. The approval of the crowd was not diminished by reports that Spain had sued for peace.[8]

Bryan on his last day at Fort Omaha was immersed in an avalanche of private business. Mary was at his side, assisting with deftness and grace. Vifquain and his aides oversaw the issue of "travel rations" and countless other details of the impending journey. The long route by rail to Florida was attended by crowds whose enthusiasm and curiosity were reminiscent of the campaign. At stops along the way, local communities outdid one another in attentions to the troops' comfort. At Nashville, a major stop, the entire city seemed to turn out, and a local organization brought off the prodigious task of distributing to Bryan's troops, or "Willie's Wonders," as critics dubbed them, 350 gallons of coffee and 1,800 box lunches. In Atlanta several old friends met Bryan at the depot and escorted him to the Hotel Kimball in a kind of Pied Piper's march. When the hotel was reached, the crowd was so dense that Bryan and his hosts could not pass through the doors. Inevitably there were cries for a speech and Bryan responded graciously, expressing his pleasure that his regiment "will have an opportunity of seeing the Confederate veterans and know that in our present struggle they will have an opportunity to fight with some of these old soldiers and their sons."

The next day, July 22, six trains of the Plant System railway brought the Third into Jacksonville, Florida, and to their ultimate destination, Camp Cuba Libre, located five miles north of the city. General Fitzhugh Lee immediately made a welcoming call. To an inquiring correspondent of the New York *Journal,* Bryan declared that he would be "out of politics" for the duration of his tenure as an Army officer. Four days after the Third was fully encamped, Spain sued for peace.[9]

Camp Cuba Libre was situated in a huge grove thick with pine, along the St. Johns River, seven miles from the seacoast. The camp was deemed one of the healthier places in Florida, whose clawing heat and oozing swamplands bred both malaria and typhoid. Disease and the McKinley administration's resolute ineptitude in coping with it combined to kill more troops than the enemy.

If Camp Cuba Libre was one of the choicer Florida locations, its temperature nonetheless hovered frequently at 110 degrees; all manner of harmful, biting insects and reptiles abounded; and the water, warm and heavily sulfurous, was unpalatable unless cooled, for which fifty pounds of ice a day were allotted to each company.

Bryan and his troops adjusted. Morale soared when wood flooring was provided for the tents. Bryan had two tents. One was his living quarters, shared with Dan Bride, who had come along as a general factotum. The second tent, called the White House, was his office where he worked on a rough-hewn desk, built by a soldier who was a carpenter. "If we go to Cuba," Bryan wrote to William, Jr., "I will send it home and you can claim it as yours."

As a military commander, Bryan was far removed from the method and decorum of West Point. His easy attitudes, his tendency in late years to sloping shoulders and shambling walk utterly contradicted any military stereotypes. He made short shrift of military protocol, blithely ignoring procedures and regulations in his partiality for shortcuts to swift action. His religious and political credo, which esteemed every man, brought him to see no distinction between officers and enlisted men. No soldier of his command was treated with aloofness and reserve, and no commander in the Seventh Army Corps more diligently championed his men's privileges. He even failed to learn the commands in the manual but instead read them from slips of paper. If the commands were not all they might be, the Third derived solidarity from the uniqueness of their leader. Inevitably, it was known as the Silver Third and special dispensations permitted its officers to wear the name "3d Regiment" upon their coat collars in gilt lettering. The "3," however, was not in gilt, but had a silver hue.

As a military administrator Bryan was scrupulously attentive to the countless details that maintained the health of his men. While other camps were ravaged by illness and death, Bryan's escaped the scourge of disease. He could well write to Mary in triumph, "We have been here two weeks and not a case of serious illness yet. If no one out of 1,300 is seriously ill you need not fear for me—the most robust of them all."

Bryan was also a model in guiding the social and religious life of his troops. Swimming, boating, and fishing were promoted and became the favorite sports. Competitive athletics were encouraged. Social life centered on a YMCA tent well supplied with games, books, and magazines. Songfests and musical instruments abounded. Church services were held regularly, and the soldiers were constantly encouraged to attend. Bryan, by natural preference, became very much a part of the lives of his men. He remained in camp more than they did, declined to share in the privileged social life of officers, and shunned, if he could, functions where liquor was served. Although Bryan freely warned his troops of the evils awaiting them in the city, his charges generally ignored his counsel, gambling away their money and paying the high prices greedy merchants charged them.

Bryan invested enormous quantities of time in getting to know his men personally. His critics deprecated this intimacy as a chumminess injurious to proper Army discipline. Sometimes Bryan's well-intended efforts seemed misdirected. Once, for instance, when some of the boys were feeling "low," he had the chaplain lead in a singing of "Home, Sweet Home." [10]

Bryan, too, deeply missed his home and family and was solicitous for the children. Had Ruth recovered from her bruise? To Grace, he sent candy via Governor Holcomb, who visited the camp. To young William he wrote an account of camp details that would enthrall a lad of nine and closed with the admonition, "Write to me every Sunday and remember that you are to be a little papa while I am gone." Above all, he wanted Mary with him. "It is only two weeks today since I left home," he wrote, "and yet I would give the best raddish [sic] on the farm to see you." But Mary was engrossed in the care of her badly ailing father and could not respond to Bryan's summons. He, as always, was a model of generous understanding; someday he and Mary would suffer the frailties of age, he acknowledged, and it was better that they be forbearing now if they expected others to be in their own twilight years. Mary buoyed his spirits by sending him a little collection of poems, selected for their constructive sentiment and copied in her own hand.

However much geography separated Bryan from his family, geography was powerless to sequester him from politics. Despite his solemn forswearing of political activity, Bryan at camp was in politics up to his ears. Scarcely had Bryan settled down in camp, when the scheduled Democratic state convention for early August brought the Nebraska political pot to a boil. A statewide ticket, headed by the governorship, was to be nominated. Lured by the glistening prizes of patronage that would be theirs if one of their number were elected, Democrats were eager to name one of their own on a fusion ticket to replace the outgoing Governor Holcomb, constitutionally barred from succeeding himself.

What better way to capture the governorship than to offer the nomination to Bryan? On behalf of these eager Democrats, O. N. Humphrey telegraphed Camp Cuba Libre: "We are anxious to nominate you for Governor." Bryan's reply was swift and sure. He wired Humphrey: "Am not candidate. Do not allow my name to be mentioned for nomination." [11]

Back in Nebraska, things were set aright, but not without a fight. Bryan's lieutenants, Dahlman and James Manahan, supported the Populist gubernatorial nominee, W. A. Poynter, state senator and farmer of Boone County, for the Democratic nomination. Other Democrats bucked and wrangled, even after Judge William Neville warned that such tactics would both destroy fusion and imperil Bryan's chances for 1900. That the struggle was considerable was evidenced by the circumstance that Poynter did not gain the Democratic nomination until 5:55 A.M. With a mighty sigh of relief, Bryan telegraphed his workers in Lincoln: "While I have not yet seen an extended report of the convention I am gratified to know that harmonious cooperation was secured among the reform forces." In November, Poynter and the fusion ticket swept into victory. Bryan's political image continued to cast a warm glow, and good Nebraska Democrats continued on a starvation diet of state patronage.[12]

For all of Bryan's solicitous observance of health and sanitation standards, the Silver Third was eventually struck by illness and disease. After three weeks at Camp Cuba Libre, there was an outbreak of typhoid. In August, there were fifty cases and several of malaria. In early September, Bryan reported ninety-five in the camp hospital, and eighty were sent home. Deaths quickly began to mount. For his men, Bryan was the soul of solicitude. He visited them religiously in the sick bays, looked to their comforts, and redoubled his efforts to elude the invisible enemy. Morning after morning, he and Dan Bride would bring together the personal belongings of the deceased—the watches, rings, and sundry effects—and forward them to next of kin with a careful personal letter of sympathy.[13]

The McKinley administration's incompetence in dealing with disease infuriated Bryan, but faithful to the soldier's duty and discipline, he was angry only in private. He did agitate within channels for a relocation of the Third. Another possibility was for the regiment to be mustered out.

The war was over. On August 12, Spain agreed to and signed a peace protocol, and on August 17, McKinley announced his decision to release from 75,000 to 100,000 volunteers. With the war ended and with the autumn election campaigns impending, Bryan was feeling and acting like a caged lion.

When he would be discharged was a question to be decided by his commander in chief, McKinley. Technically, Bryan could resign at any time, even if his troops were not released, but such a step had the obvious drawback of making him a leader who forsakes his men. Bryan decided to work quietly and with reasonable dignity behind the scenes for the Third's release. The faithful Governor Holcomb, now nearing the final days of his

term, journeyed to Florida to confer, preparatory to serving as his intermediary in negotiations with the administration. Bryan urged Mary to come,
too, to have the benefit of her counsel, but she was still confined by the care
of her ailing father and the children.

Out of the Holcomb-Bryan discussions emerged a plan. The governor enlisted the good offices of Congressman William L. Stark of Nebraska's
Fourth Congressional District, who approached the War Department to ask
how many of the Nebraska volunteers it would need to retain in service as
an army of occupation in the conquered territories. Bryan and Holcomb
coached Stark to point out that a Nebraska regiment was already posted in
the Philippines, and if the department required still more Nebraskans, a
fourth regiment could be organized specifically for occupation. This new
regiment could be constituted in equitable proportions from men of the
Second and Third Regiments who wanted to go to Cuba. Men who did not
volunteer would be released, and presumably, Bryan would join them in the
exodus. But the plan was foiled when the War Department immediately ordered the Second Nebraska Regiment to return home for release.[14]

As September dawned and political campaigns around the country
picked up tempo, illness and death ravaged the Third. In early September
sixty of its men lay in the camp hospital, and ninety-seven were sick in
quarters. Holcomb spread the figures before the War Department on September 5, with a request that the Third be mustered out. When the governor
failed to spark even a flicker of encouragement, Senator Allen addressed a
confidential telegram to Secretary of War Russell Alger: "It is being suggested that the retention of the Third is for the purpose of keeping Colonel
Bryan from participating in [the current electoral] campaign or forcing him
to resign that administration press may criticize him." Alger replied that he
had "never heard the motive you suggest spoken of at headquarters" and
relayed the telegram to the President. McKinley maintained absolute silence.

Meanwhile, Bryan men were nervous lest their leader make a misstep.
With the fires of patriotism burning high, any act or word that suggested a
wavering of desire on Bryan's part to serve or sacrifice for his country could
blight his political future. Warnings sped from the political capitals to
Bryan becalmed in Florida. Congressman William L. Stark reported that
"the politicians in and around Washington are very anxious that you should
quit the service, and knowing you are tenacious in your purpose, they desire
to force you to resign, particularly if your regiment is likely to go into active
service; they could then furnish such motives for your action as would best
help their schemes." Members of the Democratic Congressional campaign
committee told Bryan that "we think it more important to you and cause
that you remain with regiment and patiently await turn of events." [15]

The single concession the administration yielded to Bryan was permission to move the Silver Third to a new site, Pablo Beach, in the hope of escaping the mounting disease and illness. For two days after the move on September 8, Bryan's troops worked diligently at cutting away the underbrush and palmetto roots and at applying the standard sanitary measures. To Bryan's despair, the new campsite was no better than the old, and he continued deep in the grim duty of visiting sick wards, disposing of corpses, dispatching personal effects, and conveying sympathy to the grieving.

Bryan's spirits were not lifted by the report of his Washington emissary, Congressman Stark, on a conference with McKinley. The President was charming and gracious as always, but the result was inconclusive. It was his practice, McKinley explained, to leave any technical matter, such as the release of troops, to professional military decision. "He told me," Stark reported, "he desired to extend every courtesy to you and that if at any time I felt there was something demanding his personal attention to present the matter in person to the White House."

Driven by the enormous stakes involved, Bryan on September 22 journeyed to the capital to oversee personally the efforts on his behalf. At this point wobbly in health, Bryan, with Holcomb and Stark, called on the Adjutant General, Henry C. Corbin, to set forth a new plan for the discharge of those Nebraskans who wanted to go home. Corbin responded only that the proposal must "go through channels." Bryan and his friends moved on quickly to the White House. McKinley, attended by Secretary of the Treasury Lyman J. Gage, met with them in the Cabinet Room. Bryan outlined the essentials of his plan, and an elaborate verbal sparring match began. "Colonel Bryan," McKinley observed quietly, "has expressed no wish in the premise whatever." Bryan gently suggested that he had expressed no wish out of consideration for his commander in chief, the President. McKinley, squinting as he often did when aroused, said that he did not understand. Bryan attempted a clarification. "If I expressed a wish in the matter," he said, "and you did not think it right to grant it, you might, in view of all the circumstances, find yourself much embarrassed in refusing, even if you felt it your duty to do so." McKinley said evenly and pleasantly that he did not agree. If Bryan made a request that should be granted, he would grant it, and if he made one that should not be granted, he would not be embarrassed in declining it. Driven to greater candor, Bryan declared that his men felt they had a "right" to be mustered out because the war's character had changed. Originally, they "volunteered to attempt to break the yoke of Spain in Cuba, and for nothing else. They did not volunteer to attempt to subjugate other peoples, or establish United States sovereignty elsewhere." McKinley asked for no further elaboration and said only that he would consider the matter.

The next day Bryan succumbed to fever and was at once put under a physician's care. Mary rushed in anxiety to Washington. After several days in bed, Bryan improved and journeyed with Mary to Culpeper, Virginia, to visit relatives, and then they moved on to Hot Springs, Arkansas, for further rest. Scarcely had Bryan unpacked his bags in the exquisite resort, when the War Department ordered him to rejoin his regiment at once. Bryan and Mary proceeded to Jacksonville, while Governor Holcomb, now in Lincoln, persisted in trying to pry his friend loose from the Army. He scored a telling blow upon McKinley by pointing out publicly that Nebraska was being required to provide more than its quota of troops for garrison duty. McKinley wriggled free by leaving it to the governor to decide which and how many Nebraskans were to remain in service.

Holcomb, who had his own political reputation and future to consider, declined to make a choice that would surely offend more Nebraskans than it would please, leaving it up to Bryan to develop a formula for his military emancipation that could withstand the rigorous scrutiny of his political opponents. "The right thing to do," it seemed to Bryan, was to give priority to the First Regiment, which had distinguished itself in combat in the Philippines. In anticipation of the possibility that the First might not wish to be mustered out or if, in addition to the First, other troops could be demobilized, Bryan would consult his own regiment to determine its attitudes. He polled his men and found that he and his officers "had no preference," but that 87 percent of the men wished to be discharged. With this data, Holcomb informed McKinley that the retirement of simply one regiment would obviously work hardship on a heavy percentage of men in the other. If, therefore, McKinley desired to retain an entire regiment, he as the Commander in Chief must decide which one it was to be. The President, faced with what he perceived as a trap with potential political embarrassment, took refuge in inaction.[16]

The weeks melted away, and when, at last, the administration responded, it was with another salvo aimed at Bryan's discomfiture. The Third was alerted for occupation duty in Cuba. It was immediately and painfully conceivable that Bryan might languish there for much of the next year of 1899, when political forces would be shifting and settling, with enormous consequences for the Presidential nomination, platform, and possibly even the election in 1900. In the mounting torment of his imprisonment in military service, Bryan continued to wrestle with his future. "The one question which I am considering," he wrote to Mary on October 26, "is whether I can be more useful in the army or out of it." Perhaps, he added, he should let the question drift. With the new year, pressures upon Congress to muster out all volunteers might become unbearable.

There was another reason for Bryan's anguish. "Added to this," he wrote, "is the uncertainty in regard to the President's policy in the Philippines."

The nation was poised on the springboard and must soon choose whether to plunge into the adventure of imperialism or hold to traditions and values basic in American life. In his frustration, Bryan again bade Mary, "Come *at once.*"

But Mary, for the usual reasons, could not come, and Bryan was eaten with guilt that he had to make demands upon her. The confluence of his several dark moods drove him, in his letter, to pour out his view of the life it was their lot to share and of his duty in the turmoil that beat upon them: "If I consulted my own comfort or happiness, I would come home and forsake public as well as military life forever but I am not free to please myself. I have consecrated whatever talents I may have to the service of my fellow men. To aid in making the government better and existence more tolerable to the producers of wealth is my only ambition. . . . Unhappy woman to be yoked to such a companion! . . . As I tell people, you have a remarkably well balanced mind and your judgment has often been helpful to me in deciding knotty questions." [17]

The Third, meanwhile, moved on to Savannah, to ready itself for transshipment to Cuba. Scarcely had Bryan arrived in the city when he succumbed to a mild case of typhoid, which cost him twenty-five pounds and left him pale and weak. His good recovery and a grant of sick leave by the War Department in a sudden burst of mercy enabled him to return to Lincoln in time to vote in the November elections. His military status had shielded him from committing his reputation to the outcome, and he did not give in to the temptation to speak out on public questions.

Although Bryan kept his prestige intact in Nebraska, thanks to fusion's victory, the national picture made his future look dim. Democrats lost seats in Congress, and the Republicans retained control in both houses, with small but sturdy margins. Even though McKinley's strength declined in the East, he had been saved in the West, Bryan's stronghold in 1896, by the efforts of Mark Hanna. "I milked the country," Hanna confessed, and he wisely invested his booty in the West. McKinley and Hanna glossed over the scandals of war—the grim record of illnesses and deaths in Army camps within the United States, the gross corruption of war contracts, the abuses of the War Department—by clasping to themselves the issue of imperialism. In his hesitant, reluctant way McKinley built up a solid imperialist stance in the late weeks of war. He supported the annexation of Hawaii, resolved to maintain a foothold in the Philippines, and eventually chose to take the entire archipelago, Guam, and Puerto Rico.

William McKinley was demonstrating again his ability to hold his ear to the ground, hear what the people said, and render what they wanted. As early as May 21, *The Baptist Standard* in Chicago noted a developing "popular craze" for annexations. Chauncey M. Depew confided to the Republican Club of New York that "in my daily business I have clipped out for me reports in the papers from all over this country. . . . I can't help seeing what a strong feeling is spreading over the whole land in favor of colonial expansion." Two of the earliest papers to take up the annexationist chant were silver papers whose hero was and remained W. J. Bryan, the Washington *Silver Knight* and the Denver *Rocky Mountain News.* Countless congregations heard some variation of the note sounded by one clergyman: "The Philippine Islands . . . should be made the garden of the universe." With unerring political sense, Henry Cabot Lodge remarked to Henry White, "I have never seen such a universal feeling as there is against handing the islands back to Spain." [18]

Bryan felt moved to comment publicly on the outcome of the election, both to provide his own hopeful analysis of it and to lay guidelines for the future. In a statement to the press, he noted that military service had kept him out of the campaign, but with the election past he would exercise his citizen's duty to comment on the results. Any assessment of Republican successes, he stressed, must acknowledge the administration's advantage in conducting a victorious war and its cry that a Republican defeat would handicap McKinley in negotiating the peace.

The election, he contended, was not in even the least way a trial of the money, banking, and trust questions. The war had pushed them into the background. With peace restored, they must again be faced. The Chicago platform, he declared, "will be reaffirmed in 1900, because it gives expression to the hopes and aspirations of a large majority of the party." The election could not be viewed as the endorsement of "any definite foreign policy." The peace negotiators were now busy, and until they revealed the terms of the treaty, the people could not pass judgment. "Whether the war will raise any question of sufficient importance to turn public attention away from domestic problems remains to be seen."

Hardly had Bryan spoken when that supreme domestic issue—silver— surged briefly to the fore again. In the tumultuous uncertainty of the late Congressional campaign, the President had pledged that if both houses of Congress went Republican, by dint of the voters' decision, he would bring Congress into special session to enact a gold standard law. Good silver men were outraged that McKinley had originally made the pledge in private and did not reveal it until after the election. George Fred Williams, eager to make the Democratic race for governor in Massachusetts, perceived the resulting McCleary bill for "currency reform" as a battle between "the bankers who are fighting within the lines through Gage and the Republicans who think more of Republican success than of bankers' profits." He rightly predicted that the latter Republicans and Democrats in the House would combine to defeat the administration bill.

The disciples of silver were beset by another emerging crisis. Market conditions affecting the precious metals had changed so radically since 1896 that the prevailing market ratio between gold and silver was 22 to 1. The cry of 16 to 1 of 1896 was now badly outdated, and that economic fact created political risks. Rumors cropped up that India and France would adopt the 22 to 1 ratio. Senator Edward Wolcott, avidly on the hunt for an international bimetallic agreement, might conceivably secure it at 22 to 1. Charles A. Towne was fearful that Wolcott, encouraged by India and France, might commit the United States to 22 to 1, "backed by our New York financiers acting on tips from Lombard Street." [19]

Lest their thunder be stolen by their Republican opponents, many silver leaders felt that party doctrine needed updating to square with the new realities of the marketplace. James K. Jones proposed bringing a dozen silver leaders into conference to join in pledging themselves to the new ratio. With few exceptions, silver leaders, Democrats and Populists alike, announced their willingness to subscribe to 22 to 1. The British economist Moreton Frewen bespoke his blessings. But the fast-building momentum suddenly screeched to a halt. Bryan, with absolute and immovable finality, announced that any ratio but 16 to 1 would violate the Chicago platform and distress the great body of followers. International bimetallism, he said emphatically, was a canard, for Britain and the European nations never would commit themselves to it, and the Republicans, it was long plain from their record, would never press the cause. As a silver doctrine 16 to 1 stood undisturbed and a little hoary waiting for 1900. [20]

Bryan finished out his extended sick leave and, still pale and debilitated, returned to his troops in Savannah, December 4. An honor guard met him at the train and escorted him to camp.

In the world outside Savannah, new and powerful currents were stirring. The treaty of peace was being drafted in Paris. McKinley communicated to Congress a lengthy message on the emerging issues. Cuba was to be independent, but on the Philippines, the President was the soul of ambiguity. Bryan, although driven into private rage by the contention that the late elections endorsed expansion, made no public statement, holding, as before, that his Army service barred political discussion.

In the cloakrooms and lobbies of Washington and other major political habitats, rumors were stirring that Bryan, rebuffed by the administration's unwillingness to discharge his regiment, would resign from the service. On December 10 the peace treaty was signed, and Bryan chose to regard this event as a wholly new context for the question of his remaining in or withdrawing from military service. Coming quickly to a decision, he wrote to the Adjutant General in Washington, "Believing that under present conditions, I can be more useful to my country as a civilian than as a soldier, I hereby tender my resignation, to take effect immediately upon its acceptance."

Two days later, December 12, the Adjutant General granted what he had so long and so anxiously wanted, an honorable discharge.[21]

Bryan plunged at once into the turbulent political sea. He conducted a press interview in Savannah, with reporters cramming his hotel room, and set forth the views on imperialism that with the utmost strain he had kept bottled inside him in deference to his military status. He came quickly and emphatically to the point. The nation "is in greater danger just now than Cuba. Our people defended Cuba against foreign arms; now they must defend themselves and their country against a foreign idea—the colonial idea of European nations." Colonialism violated the sacred doctrine of the American fathers—of Jefferson and the Declaration of Independence—that governments derive their just powers from the consent of the governed and that "this nation cannot endure half republic and half colony, half free and half vassal."

To be sure, Jefferson, as architect of the Louisiana Purchase, the largest territorial aggrandizement the nation had known, was the source of a little awkwardness for Bryan and other anti-imperialists. Bryan invited those who raised this question to distinguish between imperialism and expansion. Furthermore, one must distinguish between expansion that secures contiguous territory for future settlement and expansion that acquires "alien races for future subjugation."

Despite his beliefs, Bryan thought it "easier" to end the war at once "by ratifying the treaty and then deal with the subject in our own way." The issue of imperialism could be promptly faced by a resolution of Congress proclaiming the nation's policy. He noted that the President in his message declared that our only purpose in taking possession of Cuba was to establish a stable government and then to turn that government over to the Cuban people. Let Congress reaffirm this intention and "assert the same purpose in regard to the Philippines and Puerto Rico." The resolution would mark out a clear distinction between "the doctrine of self-government and the doctrine of imperialism." [22]

Despite his strictures on imperialism, Bryan did not advocate a renunciation of all rights and interests in the Philippines and Puerto Rico. In both countries we should reserve a harbor and a coaling station "in return for services rendered and I think we would be justified in asking the same concession from Cuba." Should the people of Puerto Rico desire annexation, the step would be proper, "but the Philippines are too far away and their people too different from ours."

Bryan left Savannah for Washington to work for his convictions. With both truth and prophecy, he observed, "I had five months of peace in the army and resigned to take part in a fight." [23]

In Washington, Bryan was a busy lobbyist. He passed several days buttonholing legislators and speaking to groups in the cloakrooms on his conception of Congress' duty. His message was a simple one: Treat the Philippines as Cuba was treated, and therefore hold them no longer than necessary for the United States to establish a stable and independent government. Midway in his toil on Capitol Hill, Bryan journeyed to New York to confer with Andrew Carnegie. The mighty public-minded industrialist had emerged as a spirited foe of imperialism and of Philippine annexation.

Their meeting was warm, constructive, and of abundant goodwill. In fact, so impressed was Carnegie with Bryan and his opinions that he prepared an article for the New York *World* recounting the interview and endorsing Bryan for the Presidential nomination in 1900. Bryan's New York friends reacted with high alarm. It simply would not do, they cried, for Bryan or his party to be publicly endorsed "by the promoter of the Homestead riots." Bryan immediately wired Carnegie that he wanted nothing said of their interview and his future candidacy. "I am not a candidate for an office at this time. Whether I ever shall be again, depends upon circumstances." [24]

Meanwhile, the treaty negotiators had just completed their labors in Paris, and Senate debate on their handiwork was scheduled for some weeks hence in January, 1899. In the hiatus, Bryan journeyed home to celebrate Christmas. Arriving the day before, he was greeted with a lavish demonstration arranged by the Bimetallic League and student followers from the university. Governor Holcomb and Governor-elect Poynter led the hundred dignitaries who sat on the stage. Reminiscence and sentimentality hung heavily over the proceedings.

Bryan, in an address delivered with his old fire, laid out the political work of the future. "The American people have not accepted the gold standard as final. It has wrought more injustice in our country during the last twenty-five years than Spain has wrought in all her colonies. . . ." The trusts flourished more than ever, and other questions pressed for immediate attention. One was the President's request to increase the permanent Regular Army to 100,000 men to meet the new tasks of occupation. As a preferable approach, Bryan urged that the Army of Occupation be separated from the Regular Army and that it be recruited at once so that the volunteers could be mustered out.

The most immediate issue, though, was imperialism. The President, Bryan contended, had badly misinterpreted popular sentiment. In his newly revealed exuberance to keep the Philippines, he had asked, "Who will haul down the flag?" The flag, cried Bryan, was a national emblem, whose use must obey the popular will. "When the American people want the flag raised, they raise it; when they want it hauled down, they haul it down." For McKinley's edification, he cited chapter and verse of two occasions when the flag was hauled down: on Canadian soil in the War of 1812 and at Chapultepec in the war with Mexico. Both times it was lowered when peace was restored.

Although initially Bryan was the solitary major political figure to take a stand against imperialism, other leaders in all parties quickly rallied to the cause. As an ideological issue, imperialism, like silver, attracted a polyglot of supporters. Old allies in the silver cause now joined him in the fight against imperialism. Senator Ben Tillman saw the sugar trust working its nefarious influence to bring about the annexation of Pacific territories. Old comrades-in-arms like James K. Jones and George Fred Williams gave zealous support. In the Populist camp, Senator William V. Allen developed arguments and theses similar to Bryan's. The Silver Republican leader Senator Richard F. Pettigrew roared that the United States was already big enough and that he would resist the acquisition of any territory.

Grover Cleveland emerged from political retirement to oppose expansionism. The New York City Central Labor Union, composed of unions representing callings from cigar makers to actors, declared against expansion, imperialism, and alliance with England. Other union leaders, fearful of the competition of poorly paid Philippine labor, rushed to the banner. Bryan, for the first time, saw eye to eye on an issue with many influential Easterners, who established an Anti-Imperialist League, with an executive committee and headquarters in Chicago, and the New England Anti-Imperialist League in Boston. A list of the vice-presidents of the leagues attests to the organizations' impeccable respectability: Grover Cleveland, Andrew Carnegie, Charles Francis Adams, Bishop Henry C. Potter, Governor Hazen S. Pingree of Michigan, and Samuel Gompers, president of the AFL. Administratively and politically, the two most important men of the Anti-Imperialist League were Edwin Burritt Smith, chairman of the executive committee, and Carl Schurz. A leader of the Chicago bar, a founder of the Municipal Voters' League of Chicago, and a booster of many other reform efforts, Smith excelled as an organizer and had keen political sense. With his lofty prestige among German-Americans, Schurz brought great numbers of his admirers with him into the cause. Irish-Americans joined in, too, for they were prone to think of imperialism as essentially English.

The Anti-Imperialists, like any polyglot political movement, had difficulty in agreeing on a common strategy, and least of all could they acquiesce to Bryan's idea of accepting an expansionist treaty now and pruning its imperialist branches later. From January, 1899, onward all eyes were focused on the United States Senate, before which the treaty with Spain was placed. Bryan, by working for its ratification, immediately separated himself from most of his anti-imperialist allies.[25]

From the outset of the treaty debate, which began on January 4 and ran until February 6, Bryan was arrayed with a strange lot of political bedfellows. His support of the treaty put him shoulder to shoulder with President McKinley, the majority of Republicans, and the majority of Democrats, especially those from the South. The minority opposition included conservative Democrats such as Arthur Pue Gorman of Maryland and Donelson Caffery of Louisiana, silver Democrats Vest of Missouri and Jones of Nevada, and Silver Republicans Teller of Colorado and Pettigrew of South Dakota. Joining forces in the opposition were such unlikely figures as George F. Hoar, the genteel intellectual Senator of Massachusetts, and William E. Mason, a countrified demagogue of Illinois. When debate began, the precise strength of the anti-imperialist minority was unknown. This information was vital because the constitutional requirement that two-thirds of the Senators present and voting must approve would enable a minority of sufficient strength to defeat the treaty.

While the Senate wrestled with the problem, Bryan moved about the country making major speeches on the entrapments of imperialism. He dwelled little upon his complex plan for approving the treaty and dealing with the Philippines later. Instead, he toiled to expose imperialism as an alien and false god. In Denver to an audience that overflowed the Coliseum, he warned that imperialism was wrong in principle, expensive, and harmful to both the American and Philippine peoples. "It is not a step forward toward a broader destiny, it is a step backward toward the narrow views of Kings and Emperors." Bryan reminded his audience of the lesson provided by Ahab, the king who wanted the vineyard of Naboth. In his plottings and manipulations, sacred commandments were broken—Thou shalt not covet; thou shalt not bear false witness; thou shalt not kill; thou shalt not steal. Imperialism and the wars of conquest that support it "have their origin in covetousness, and the history of the human race has been written in characters of blood because rulers have looked with longing eyes upon the lands of others. Covetousness is prone to seek the aid of false pretense to carry out its plans. . . ." [26]

As Bryan was preaching on imperialism's evils, McKinley provided skillful leadership for the treaty forces, while Henry Cabot Lodge annexed Republican votes in intensive behind-the-scenes consultations. Republican Speaker Thomas B. Reed, who opposed the taking of Hawaii and the Philippines, felt that the outcome would turn upon Senators who could be influenced by labor leaders. But he despaired over the indifference of the labor men, who, after an initial burst of interest, had absorbed themselves in their traditional concerns on the American mainland.

Bryan now chose to assume a more forceful and he hoped a more decisive part in the struggle. Aid and comfort for his plan to approve the treaty simultaneously with a resolution for Philippine independence were provided by Senator Augustus Bacon of Georgia, who, on January 24, 1899, introduced a resolution declaring that when the Filipinos organized a stable, independent government, the United States would hand over to it the sovereignty of the islands. As the struggle neared its critical stage, Bryan came to Washington against the warnings of loyal friends and old allies, who believed that grave risks for his political future lurked in the slippery situation. Teller informed Bryan with naked candor that he could not influence the outcome. James K. Jones painted a canvas of awaiting rejection and humiliation. Republicans, he warned, would gladly accept his help to win the treaty's ratification but would laugh in his face when he pressed for Philippine independence.

With his usual tenacity, Bryan could not be budged. On Capitol Hill, he took up his battle station in the Marble Room in the rear of the Senate chamber. He summoned Democratic Senators and in his agreeable but firm and confident way urged them to vote for the treaty. He thoroughly rehearsed his plan for the treaty and quick passage of a resolution committing Congress to Philippine independence. His bearing, his surroundings, and the circumstances left no doubt that Bryan deemed himself to be acting as the leader of the Democratic Party.[27]

Bryan's efforts were suddenly pushed into rude disarray by an occurrence in the Philippines. In one of those cruel ironies, while Bryan was working for Filipino independence in his national capital, sentries of the First Nebraska Regiment in the Philippines exchanged fire with a Filipino patrol. The firing spread, and American and Filipino lives were lost. The Filipino revolt, led by Emilio Aguinaldo, an artist in guerrilla warfare, had begun its lengthy, costly course.

To Bryan these new events proved the warning he had sounded that "If we enter upon a career of conquest we must expect bloodshed." The object now was to prevent further trouble, and this could be best assured if the resolution promising independence were passed before the treaty's ratification. If this were not possible, ratification would not prevent the passage of the resolution later and would throw responsibility on the imperialists for any further trouble. Until the nation's policies were determined, Bryan publicly and fully supported the nation's soldiers in their mission "to defend American interests at any cost." [28]

Two days after the exchange of fire, on February 6, the Senate voted on the treaty. Senator Gorman, leader of the antitreaty forces, privately and confidently predicted that the treaty would be defeated by a single vote. Other political soothsayers saw only defeat, but the outcome made their reputations suspect. The treaty passed the Senate, 57 to 27, or by a single vote in excess of the required two-thirds.

Precisely what converted likely defeat into narrow victory is not easy to define. Doubtless the sudden Filipino revolt fetched some Senators who were on the fence. Leading conservatives of the Senate—Nelson W. Aldrich, William B. Allison, Stephen B. Elkins, Charles W. Fairbanks, John C. Spooner, and Mark Hanna (elected in his own right from Ohio in 1897)— who had opposed the war, the annexation of Hawaii, and initially the takeover of the Philippines, abandoned their position in the later stages of debate. Aldrich and Hanna, according to well-substantiated report, swayed votes by promises of federal judgeships, lesser patronage, and money. Spooner delivered a compelling oration on the constitutionality of annexation. Hanna, in a postmortem analysis rendered to McKinley, felt that Elkins was the key factor in the victory.

The precise measure of Bryan's influence on the result is difficult to calculate. Senator George F. Hoar, who was dedicated to the treaty's defeat, wrote to Bryan afterward, "Next to McKinley, you are the person in the country most responsible for [its] adoption. . . ." Estimates of the number of Democratic Senators Bryan influenced have ranged up to ten, although of these, eight were known to support the treaty before he began his effort, and the two others who were uncommitted seem to have been won over by Republican promises of patronage.[29]

Bryan's conduct provides no scintillating lessons in astute politics. He was faithful to his convictions, and his devotion to popular rule and to Jeffersonian principles required his rejection of Philippine annexation. By opposing imperialism, he harmonized his foreign policy with his domestic positions. Government had to be the instrument of free men, both at home and abroad.

But while Bryan's purpose was praiseworthy, his strategy and tactics served him ill. By supporting a treaty inspired and managed by his opponent, William McKinley, he badly circumscribed his ability to face down the President on the issue of imperialism. Regardless of his sincere and apt explanations, he appeared oppportunistic. In climbing far out on the limb of the treaty, he also exposed himself to wide repudiation by Democratic Senators who rejected it.

A by-product of Bryan's conduct was the emergence of Senator Gorman, a shrewd conservative Democrat, as a leader of the treaty's opposition. So aggressive was Gorman in resisting Bryan's work in Washington that the press widely interpreted his conduct as carving out a sizable area in which to seek the nomination in 1900. Senator Allen, often Bryan's spokesman, felt driven to play down the late events and their implications for the Presidential candidacy of Gorman. "I have at no time promised to enlighten the country concerning what Senator Gorman is doing or proposes to do," he declared to the press. "I do not know, nor am I concerned in knowing what Mr. Gorman's intentions may be."

Yet it is also inappropriate to apply to Bryan the criteria of failure or success that fit the purely pragmatic politician. Bryan was a practical ideologue, nurturing ideals rigorously separating right from wrong in public policies and contriving political strategies to give effect to his high purposes. As in his support for the treaty, he lived by the conviction that half a minor retreat now might lead to a major gain later. And however roundly his course in the treaty was condemned, it came within a whisker of succeeding.

After the treaty was passed, the Senate was confronted with rival resolutions defining future Philippine policy. McKinley and his Senate lieutenants supported the McEnery resolution, which said simply that permanent annexation of the Philippines was not contemplated but did not contain a positive pledge of future Philippine independence. The Senate's anti-imperialists fought to have the Bacon resolution, which promised ultimate independence to the Philippines and reflected Bryan's views, added as an amendment. After rumors and reports of "trades" and "deals," the vote was taken on the Bacon resolution, and the result was a tie. The Constitution empowered Vice President Garret A. Hobart, always a perfect mirror of McKinley's attitudes, to break the tie. Hobart administered the *coup de grâce* by voting in the negative.

For Bryan, Hobart's vote was the opening round of a new and vital political struggle. Bryan defined its nature in an address on Washington's Birthday. Choosing as his title "America's Mission," he derided talk of "Manifest Destiny," a phrase that was falling from many an official's lips, "the last resort of imperialists who cannot reconcile colonial policy with our principles of government. . . ." He denounced imperialism as an ancient doctrine, "banished from our land more than a century ago," that has recrossed the Atlantic "and challenged democracy to mortal combat upon American soil." The supreme irony of America's inauguration of an imperialist policy was that its own people had had no voice in the decision. "The people have not voted for imperialism; no National Convention has declared for it; no Congress has passed upon it. . . . We have reached another crisis." His listeners had no doubt that imperialism would become a major issue in the awaiting 1900 campaign, unless by some miracle it was resolved before then.[30]

18. New Issues

The year 1899 was a time of mocking paradoxes. Bryan preached social doctrines predicated on the distress and maltreatment of the great majority of the people by an avaricious minority of economic overlords. Yet the country was enjoying a period of luxuriant prosperity. Even for the once-impoverished Western farmers, the grim days of the eighties and foreclosed mortgages, depressed prices, and oppressive railroad rates faded into memory in the wartime boom. In the cities, high employment rates and climbing wages brought workingmen to share in the contentment and optimism. To proclaim silver as some magical key to a better life would appear almost ludicrous.

Likewise, any further preachings on the wickedness of imperialism seemed futile. The war had at least brought America onto the world stage and provided it a glittering, heady entrance. With an ease implying enormous reserves of might, it had whipped a major colonial power and extended its dominion to new lands and peoples. A future of burgeoning trade in the Pacific, of access to rich resources of the new tropical territories instilled in the people a sense of achievement, strength, and optimism. How, then, could Bryan expect to march into the Presidency with a message depicting imperialism as immoral and contradictory to the nation's traditions?

Louis R. Ehrich, a wise, intellectual friend in Colorado, urged Bryan to put the silver fight behind him and undertake a searching reassessment of his position in light of the country's and the world's changes since 1896. "I know the allurements of so-called 'consistency,'" Ehrich wrote in candor, "and also the paucity of men who have the courage and the noble self-control to be willing to say: 'I was wrong; I have changed my mind.'"[1]

The question of the immediate future of the Democratic Party was, of course, no monopoly of Bryan. Its leaders and subalterns throughout the country had at stake their own political futures. But Bryan was, in addition, leader of a fusion of parties and reform forces joined by the common thread of their devotion to silver.

Something of the quickened concern of this alliance was revealed in conferences at Hot Springs, Arkansas, in the closing days of March. Bryan was to lecture in the opera house, and to this resort town, silver leaders gathered like birds assembling for flight. Governor William J. Stone led a body of Democrats. Populists and Silver Republicans were represented by Senator Lee Mantle, Senator Richard F. Pettigrew; former Senators Fred T. Dubois of Idaho and John H. Reagan of Texas. John C. Sheehan, a Tammany leader, vacationing at Hot Springs, postponed his return to New York to join in the discussions.

The deliberations of the fusion leaders were cloaked in tightest secrecy. No clue of the outcome leaked out of the elegant, shuttered Eastman Hotel where they transpired. Bryan would reveal his attitudes and formulations in speeches and scheduled lectures. The positions of other leaders might not lend themselves so easily to discovery. They might be revealed in speeches, but they might be more fully disclosed in scores of seemingly minor acts or deliberately camouflaged from the public eye.[2]

In 1899, Bryan covered the country with speechmaking on the scale of a Presidential campaign. That Louis Ehrich's counsel of reconsideration and revision fell upon deaf ears was revealed in Bryan's message to the Jefferson Club of Milwaukee. ". . . I am taking no risk," he declared, "when I say that those who in 1896 gave their allegiance to the Chicago platform are as united today in the determination that no step taken in 1896 shall be retraced." The recent great discoveries of gold in Alaska provided not the least basis of a cause to abandon bimetallism. If anything, the discoveries proved the validity of the quantity theory of money. The establishment of bimetallism was the only possible way to assure that in the future the money supply would remain adequate for the needs of a growing economy. In New York City, Bryan, in the strongest language he had yet employed, consigned all who questioned or doubted the wisdom of highlighting silver in 1900 to the ranks of the enemy. The Chicago platform of 1896, he reminded his listeners, "was a menace to those who rob others," and it was "disliked by those who have their hands in the pockets of their neighbors." [3]

In Des Moines he took pains to deny a press report that he had said that silver "must go to the rear." The report was nothing but a "false rumor" laid by "the gold press." In another interview, Bryan dealt with the same question with a homely analogy that reinforced the primacy of silver. His remarks were inspired by the comments of reporters that other issues such as imperialism, militarism, and the trusts were superseding silver. With genial patience, Bryan lectured that "when a new baby is born in a household the parents do not expel the other children. We should gather all these children into our arms and fight for them."

The most that Bryan would allow was for other issues to take their place beside silver. He continued to battle imperialism and was the staunch champion of the Philippine cause. Let assurances be given to the islands for their independence, he demanded, and of our intention of "establishing a stable government, which, when established, will be their Government, not ours." For the Philippines, the United States should stand by "like an elder brother, and say to other nations 'Hands off! Let this republic work out its destiny.' " [4]

The issue on which Bryan commented most, right up to the 1900 convention, was the trusts, which had long been a target of political orators. Populists had featured the trusts in their first platform, and Henry D. Lloyd, their scholar-writer, had depicted the trust as a menace to liberty in his impassioned *Wealth Against Commonwealth.* In popular usage, "trust" came to apply to any combination of intensive or substantial control.

The first of the giant trusts was the Standard Oil Company, founded in 1872. John D. Rockefeller, its head, cast ethics to the winds and destroyed competitors or forced them into his organization. At its peak, Standard Oil controlled upward of 95 percent of the petroleum industry. Such devices, as price fixing agreements among many concerns, holding companies and interlocking directorates quickly spread to whiskey, sugar, glass, copper, coal, reaping machinery, and a host of other commodities. Industrial giants such as the American Sugar Refining Company and International Harvester shut down competitors, paid lower prices for raw materials, and exacted higher prices for finished products. In the eighties imperiled individual businessmen and small corporations brought suits against the trusts; state legislatures launched investigations and passed antitrust statutes. The Republican national platform of 1888 declared its opposition to trusts, and in 1890 Congress passed the Sherman Act designed to end all trusts. Its sponsor, John Sherman, warned that unless the depredations of trusts were halted, his legislative brothers must "be ready for the socialist, the communist, and the nihilist."

In the nineties, the trust octopus continued to flourish despite several potent court decisions. Trust makers, with their richly paid legal staffs, found ways to evade the rulings, and Republican Presidents grew lackadaisical in enforcement. The entry for Charles R. Flint in *Who's Who* proudly averred that he was "widely known as the 'father of trusts.' " A leading promoter of trusts, John B. Dill, began a lecture at the Harvard Law School: "I am the lawyer for a billion dollars of invested capital." William Nelson Cromwell, head of one of the trusts' favorite law firms, acknowledged that he was an "officer or counsel of more than twenty of the largest corporations of the United States." The great Eastern banking houses of J. P. Morgan and Company; Kuhn, Loeb and Company; Kidder, Peabody and Company; and Lee, Higginson and Company, closely associated with the largest New York commerical banks, were instrumental in fashioning the industrial combines. Together this community of industry and capital virtually controlled the credit resources of the nation. The trend was blessed by leading academic economists who saw these developments as an inevitable stage in the economy's maturation, affording gains of efficiency in production and marketing in which all society might share.

Bryan was one of the more articulate politicians who rejected these arguments. All trusts, without exception, he contended, merited condemnation. He could not accept the view that one had to distinguish between "good" and "bad" trusts. "There can be no good monopoly in private hands," he said, "until the Almighty sends us angels to preside over the monopoly." The evil of monopoly was mirrored in the nature of its antithesis, competition. Competition required the employer to strive and excel, "to get a good man," to exceed the efficiency of rival enterprises. In the absence of competition, however, "anybody can sit in the office and receive letters and answer them because everybody has to write to the same house for anything he wants." Bryan freely granted that a trust might sometimes lessen the costs of distribution, but society, he added, "has no assurance that it will get any of the benefits from that reduction of cost."

The trust and the monopoly it tended to produce perpetrated other evils.

It dictates terms to those who buy its products and to those who sell the raw material and provide the labor. When competition is eliminated, price is controlled, "not by reason, but by . . . greed. . . ." To cope with the fast-spreading evil, Bryan posed a specific plan of attack. He urged that the states and the nation apply concurrent remedies. Let Congress require that no corporation organized in any state do business outside that state until it receives, from a federal regulatory agency designated by Congress, a license authorizing it to do so. The license should be granted under carefully prescribed conditions designed to prevent the watering of stock and the spread of dominion over other enterprises and to provide public airing of the corporation's affairs and transactions.[5]

As he was wont to do, Bryan illuminated the trust question by a Biblical analogy. God made man, Bryan recalled, as the climax of the Creation. The corporation, upon which the trust rests, "is a man-made man." God made men relatively equal, each not much stronger or taller than his fellows, and imposed limitations upon their existence, not the least of which was death. The man-made corporation can be "a million times" stronger than God-made man and can be endowed with the gift of perpetual life. God "in the next world" holds man accountable for deeds done in the flesh. The corporation, or "man-made man," has no hereafter to worry about, a lacking that made all the more urgent the imposition of government control. "Man-made man," too, must be admonished: " 'Remember now thy Creator in the days of thy youth and throughout thy entire life.' "

A National Anti-Trust Conference gathered in Chicago in February, 1900. Bryan did not attend but was represented by loyal and articulate spokesmen. The results of their handiwork were reflected in the conference's platform, which carried two principles highlighted in Bryan's speeches: All trust-made goods should be placed on the free list, and patents, as hotbeds for propagating trusts, should be closely supervised.

Bryan's spokesmen struggled to keep the trust issue within moderate confines. The middle-of-the-road Populists, who were strongly represented, pushed a resolution pledging the delegates not to vote for any party that did not incorporate into its platform planks for government ownership of railroads and the initiative and referendum. Another group moved to create an antitrust party. But Bryan's representatives expertly blocked both moves, which were obvious thrusts at the Democratic Party. The antitrust issue was, consequently, kept under the wing of the Democracy, and the antitrust leagues were behooved to divide their loyalties between the Democratic and Populist parties.

On the campaign trail, especially as the national convention neared, Bryan was less rigid than in the conference rooms. In speechmaking, he seemed to distribute his emphasis over the triad of silver, trusts, and imperialism on the basis of geography and talked most about the issues that local people liked most to hear.[6]

In the period preceding the national Democratic convention, Bryan was pulled and pushed by old supporters, by new groups that perceived him to be useful for their purposes, and by old enemies in his party who sought reconciliation by bringing him to modify his positions. Meanwhile, forces opposed to Bryan were manipulating issues to stop what seemed his inevitable march to the 1900 nomination.

The most intense of the several struggles centered on the status of the silver issue in the coming election. Bryan's continued insistence that it have the same importance it enjoyed in 1896 was regarded by elements of the Democratic Party as a certain prescription for defeat. They derived what comfort they could from the fact that Bryan, despite his avowals for silver, was giving it less attention than he bestowed on trusts and imperialism.

Eastern Democrats were as opposed to Bryan as they were to silver. A Bryan race, they were convinced, would bring certain defeat. His tenacity on silver provided Tammany leader Richard Croker with a convenient pretext for opposing him while enlarging his political role from that of a city machine boss into a national political influence. Croker proclaimed publicly: "The time has gone by when the Democrats can accept the doctrine of 16 to 1. I feel sure that the Democratic party will nominate some one else as their candidate in the next Presidential campaign."

In Richard Croker, Bryan was pitted against an archetype of the party boss. A former bartender, prizefighter, and alleged murderer, Croker, once having attained exalted station in Tammany, put aside certain of his rough-hewn ways for exterior gentility. The principal symbols of this change were a veneer of tolerably good manners and meticulous attention to clothes. The well-proportioned Croker wore expensively tailored morning dress, complete with silk hat, and after dark, he blossomed out in formal evening attire. Tammany braves quickly imitated his tastes, and this rough city machine suddenly transacted its hard business with sartorial elegance. Croker was also given to a sardonic mien and shunned laughter. His substantial entourage of sycophants managed never to smile in his presence, no matter how great the provocation.

Croker's style in transacting business was unremittingly regal. Once, to help a friend who owned a huge hotel in New Jersey that was doing poorly, Croker came to the sumptuous structure for a month's stay. Inevitably, there followed in his wake a flood of politicians, businessmen, and courtiers seeking his favors and thus buoying up the hotel's revenues by their patronage. In the Croker manner, everyone dressed for dinner, a procedure reinforced by his preference to transact business in the evening. When Croker appeared in the huge hotel lobby, every Tammany man present would

spring to his feet. With several selected companions Croker began his prolonged ambulatory conferences up and down the lobby's carpeted prome-
nade. At intervals those consulting with him would fall away, and by a
barely discernible nod or glance he would summon another awaiting peti-
tioner.

Emissaries running between Bryan and Croker accommodated themselves to this imperial style. One of the busiest of these was Willis Abbot,
whom Croker pressed into service to take soundings of any latent willingness on Bryan's part to soft-pedal silver. Not only did Bryan refuse to
budge; he made his sentiments known in a manner that left Abbot writhing
with embarrassment. Bryan composed a long letter for Abbot to read to
Croker. With the letter in hand, Abbot proceeded one night to a club where
Croker was holding court and took his place among the petitioners who
hovered around the boss. Finally, there came the slight nod and a gruff inquiry, "Heard anything from Bryant?" (Croker always said "Bryant" instead of "Bryan.") Abbot took up the unpleasant task of reading Bryan's
letter. "Please say to Mr. Croker," it said, "that I say to the Chicago platform, to every plank in it, including the silver plank, as Ruth said to Naomi.
'And Ruth said, Intreat me not to leave thee, or to return from following
after thee, for whither thou goest, I will go; and where thou lodgest, I will
lodge; thy people shall be my people, and thy God my God!' " After hearing several more sentences of emphatic consecration to silver, Croker
stopped Abbot in his reading and said with gruff finality, "I didn't think
that Bryant was that kind of a feller. You can tell him from me that I'm
through." Bryan promptly escalated the conflict by instructing Abbot to release the letter to the press.

In Washington there were also flutterings of unrest over Bryan's adamancy on silver. Democratic Senators, of the South and West, as well as of
the East, were searching for formulas that might both satisfy the stubborn
Bryan and breathe reality into the Democracy's position. A coterie of Senators, led by John Morgan of Alabama, Francis Cockrell of Missouri, and
Arthur Pue Gorman of Maryland, pressed Senator James K. Jones to apply
his influence as national committee chairman to have the Chicago platform
reaffirmed merely in general terms without any specific reference to silver.
But neither pressures nor blandishments could budge Jones. "The Democratic party will, in my opinion," he declared, "stand on all national issues
in 1900 precisely where it stood in 1896. None of the issues for which it held
out at that time will be abandoned in 1900." [7]

From every quarter, counsel poured in upon Bryan urging abandonment,
or at least substantial toning down, of his silver position. "I have become
convinced," wrote William Randolph Hearst, "that the people do not want
free silver and that if we try we will lose the opportunity to do great good in
other directions." Several of Hearst's stellar hirelings, who knew Bryan well,

put this argument with even greater insistence. James Creelman, a reporter of international reputation, wrote with utter candor: "I have seen most of the leaders in every part of the country and they all oppose any specific mention of free silver in the platform and want simply to reaffirm the platform of 1896 in general terms and devote the new platform to new issues. If they say anything else to you they lie; and if you require 16 to 1 in the platform you will be simply forcing the delegates against their will." [8]

The anti-imperialists, that body of respectable citizens—lawyers, businessmen, clergy, and educators—who hoped to find in Bryan a viable political champion, were distressed by his adamancy on silver. Dr. David Starr Jordan, president of Stanford University, argued that silver was killed as an issue by the nation's tinsel prosperity. To continue the agitation for silver "is to work for imperialism." Jordan further maintained that the McKinley administration was working for Bryan's renomination so that the campaign could be fought on the issue of silver, one which it was certain to win. Jordan's arguments, which abounded with kernels of truth, might have had more force if there had been a Presidential candidate whose chances for victory were better than Bryan's.

In reply to Jordan, Bryan wrote, "I receive a great many letters, all from honest and well-meaning men, some advising me to drop everything else and make the fight against imperialism, some advise me to drop everything else and make the fight against trusts, some advise me to drop everything else and make the fight against the gold standard. As I cannot follow all the advice and as no adviser is able to prove that his advice and his only is good, I am compelled to follow my own judgment." [9]

In addition to attracting the intellectuals and respectable citizens identified with the Anti-Imperialist League, Bryan, in his anti-imperialist stance, conceivably could corral other support. The Philippine insurrection increased daily Eastern dislike of this new adventure in the Pacific. Bryan's staunch friend Philo S. Bennett of New Haven predicted in February, 1899, that if Bryan, in a projected speaking tour of the Eastern states, stressed imperialism and the trusts and soft-pedaled silver, he "could carry New York, New Jersey, and Connecticut on those issues in 1900."

For all his severity with David Starr Jordan, Bryan continued to emphasize imperialism, often at the expense of silver. Less than a month before the convention he declared that it was the question that most interested the general body of the people. He even managed to link insurrection in the Philippines to the trusts, proclaiming that the nation's blood was being poured out in the Philippines "to satisfy the greed of the trusts and the monopolies seeking to gain commercial advantage." [10]

The trust question was very much alive. Other political enterprisers besides Bryan were according it a lofty place in their attentions. Hazen Pingree, the reform-minded governor of Michigan, told a Cooper Union audience that "there is no more important problem before the people today than the trust and what to do with it." The trusts, like imperialism, could serve to restore the Cleveland gold Democrats to the party. Ohio in 1899 provided a heartening illustration. Gold and silver Democrats in that state moved to unite in the gubernatorial race behind the one-word slogan of "Beef!" By shouting "Beef!" up and down the state, they hoped to remind the voters of the incompetence of McKinley's Secretary of War Alger in the late war and the beef trust's ruthless exploitation of his weakness. Included in the troops' ration were quantities of odorous, hideous canned meat, or "embalmed beef," as it was known. Supplied by leading American meat processors, the beef contributed to the illness rampant among the troops, who were well called "an army of convalescents."

Bourke Cockran, who relied on publicity to curb trusts, presented another example of a distinguished Cleveland Democrat making highly flattering references to Bryan. Bryan, said Cockran, in a nice turn of phrase, had "a monopoly of excellence" and "a monopoly on the Democratic hearts of the country."

The most extensive statement of his position that Bryan made was set out in a letter to Bradford Merrill, editor of the New York *World.* However much his supporters might differ over the relative importance of silver, the trusts, and imperialism he, for his part, preferred to regard all of them as important. The Democratic Party could not hope to win in November without the cooperation of all forces opposed to Republican policies, "and that cooperation can only be secured by making the fight *all along the line.*" Bryan had no doubt that his position mirrored the sentiment of the vast majority of his supporters. "The people who oppose the gold standard also oppose the trusts and imperialism and there are *nine* who oppose all three to *one* who favors the gold standard and yet opposes the trusts or imperialism. Why alienate nine in order to please one?"

To reject or downgrade silver would be an act of heinous disloyalty to his supporters of 1896. To elevate imperialism would gratify those who "left the party and did what they could to defeat the ticket." Their clamor to elevate the issue of imperialism and downgrade silver concealed a malicious motive. "Now they want to drive away the populists and silver republicans who came to us when the gold democrats deserted." His formula for 1900 was simple and tolerably clear. "Whatever influence I may have will be exerted toward holding what we have and gaining enough from the outside to defeat the republicans. . . ." [11]

Bryan's major task in the pre-election months was to mobilize the state and city organizations of the Democratic Party behind his self-chosen platform. Of the many battlegrounds upon which he ventured, none was more important, or more treacherous, than New York State. Without New York's support he could not hope to win in 1900. But New York was the citadel of the unbelievers. Gold Democrats inhabited the canyons of Wall Street and the city's political clubhouses, and it was the home of Tammany Hall, whose corruption and perfidy toward national tickets were seldom excelled in an era of booming city machines.

Nonetheless, Bryan did not yield when Perry Belmont, the transit system millionaire and solid gold Democrat, joined with Richard Croker in arranging a local Jefferson Birthday dinner that was presumably to be a feast of reconciliation. Leaders of the several party factions, from Grover Cleveland to Bryan, were invited to speak, and all speeches were limited to twenty minutes. The prospective hosts took pains to build an atmosphere of harmony, dropping a plan to invite a representative from each of the states formed out of the Louisiana Purchase, as a symbolic recognition of America's capacity for expansion, lest it offend the anti-imperialists among the guests.

Bryan's response to Belmont's letter of invitation was confined to posing a question: ". . . Remembering that you openly repudiated the democratic platform in the last campaign, I desire to know, before answering your invitation, whether you have since the election publicly announced your conversion to the principles set forth in that platform." Belmont's reply was politely evasive. Bryan bore down. "The antagonism between our opinions is so great that we cannot with propriety join in a political banquet given in honor of Democracy's patron saint," going on to make it clear that he, rather than Belmont, espoused Jefferson's principles. "I believe in harmonizing personal differences," Bryan wrote, "but differences in principle cannot be harmonized, and, in my judgment, no party advantage is to be derived from political communion between Jeffersonian Democrats who stand upon the Chicago platform and the Republican allies who masquerade as democrats between campaigns in order to give more potency to their betrayal of democratic principles on election day." [12]

Bryan's declaration did not leave him without a Jefferson Day dinner to attend in New York. In lieu of Belmont's posh celebration, he was invited to a "dollar dinner" organized by other local factional leaders who openly embraced the Chicago platform. Eventually these factions brawled over the dinner plans and broke apart so that each might organize its own occasion. Bryan found himself attending two dollar dinners on separate nights. The more important, given by the Chicago Platform Democrats took place in Grand Central Palace and was heavy with the embellishments of a political campaign. Festoons of bunting and flags filled the hall, and Bryan's entrance at the head of a long line of speakers touched off a thunderous ovation. It was far more a Bryan rally than a Jefferson celebration. On the stage was a huge floral horseshoe bearing the inscription "16 to 1" and "Bryan." When he was introduced, the chairman flourished a bouquet of American roses at least four feet long bearing the motto "You, like these roses, are the Nation's choice." Bryan's speech, although attentive to all the major issues, set forth his recipe for the purification of the party. "All that we contend for is that those who deserted us in 1896 shall divorce themselves either from our party name or from the political principles of opposing parties."

What was lacking in this triumphal evening was the presence of New York Democratic leaders. To avoid the embarrassment of being a solitary political eminence at his own celebration, Bryan took the precaution of bringing along his own luminaries—George Fred Williams, Charles Towne, and O. H. P. Belmont. However there was some speculation that the New York Democracy was represented by the band that played from the gallery. When the soup was served, the band broke into "You're Not So Warm," and intermittently throughout the evening, it regaled the dollar diners with blaring renderings of "Get Your Money's Worth."

Those who broke bread with Bryan comprised a sizable body of reformers, silver doctrinaires, dissident Tammany figures and conceivably could become an important weapon for Bryan in dealing with New York. With growing strength and wise leadership, they might, in the view of C. H. Jones, editor of the St. Louis *Post-Dispatch* and political counselor, "bring Tammany into line." The Chicago Platform Democrats could also fight to secure representation in the national convention of 1900 at Tammany's expense. But professional politicians looked askance at these dreamings. In faraway Kansas, Jerry Simpson regretted the entire course of events that pitted Bryan against the Belmont-Croker alliance. "Tammany," he suggested, "runs the Eastern Democracy, and controls thousands of votes. By antagonizing Tammany, Bryan may lose these votes, and he will need them later. . . ." Simpson perceived still another threat in the unfortunate situation. "They may," he warned, "put up another man against him." [13]

Bryan, who apparently saw wisdom in Simpson's words, took up the task of gaining Croker's support. His prospects were improved by the fact that Croker, as Willis Abbot noted, "For some reason . . . took great fancy to Bryan." Perhaps the cause was personal chemistry; perhaps Croker, who admired strength, perceived in Bryan a Christ-like tenacity. Bryan began the courtship by dispatching O. H. P. Belmont, a reformer and Chicago platform advocate, albeit a brother of the gold-minded Perry, as his personal representative. The ensuing discussions were wrapped in absolute secrecy, but something of their tenor can be deduced from articles on the initiative and referendum and other "better government" concerns. Soon after the discussions, however, Belmont began running rhapsodic essays in his magazine, *The Verdict*, on the value of party harmony, on Tammany as a "pure well-spring of absolute Democracy," and on Croker as "a Democrat of Democrats." The climax of these flattering attentions was a brave forecast that Croker would support the Democratic ticket of 1900 no matter who the candidates were or what the platform.[14]

To woo Croker further, Bryan also employed the good offices of Norman E. Mack of Buffalo, a national committeeman and newspaper publisher who had supported Bryan and silver in 1896. Chairman of the State Committee of Western New York and the dominant personality of the Erie County Democracy, Mack was a self-made man of great social grace. Broad-shouldered, with balanced features and attractive coloring, a fine brown mustache, and a glint of steel in his eye, Mack was close to Bryan both socially and politically.

Croker was passing the summer at his Irish estate where he kept a choice string of racing horses, and Governor William J. Stone is credited with conceiving the inspiration of having Mack, who was also in Europe, see Croker. Mack approached bearing letters from Bryan and O. H. P. Belmont attesting friendship and goodwill.

Although no communiqué disclosed the outcome, the political world was soon apprized of its far-reaching consequences. Croker shortly returned to the United States and in a dockside interview unveiled his new political positions. Once noncommittal upon Bryan's future, Croker now lavished praise upon the Nebraskan. Once smitten with the fever of expansionism, Croker now called for war upon imperialism. Once outspoken against the silver issue, he now chose to straddle it.[15] In private discussions, Croker boasted of bringing the gold Democrats back into the party, declaring, with his air of imperial confidence, "I will have Perry Belmont making speeches for Bryan before the campaign is over."

Although the diplomatic talents of Mack and O. H. P. Belmont were considerable, their velvet glove of diplomacy concealed a mailed fist. Croker's headship of Tammany was being challenged by John C. Sheehan, a staunch Bryan supporter. The Bryan men of New York could mount a considerable force to fight Croker in the state convention and an overwhelming force in the approaching 1900 national convention. Like other Tammany leaders before him, Croker's political needs dictated that he support the national ticket in exchange for a free hand in New York City. "Croker," George Fred Williams put the situation succinctly, ". . . cannot afford even to have an outside organization attack him. . . ."

Croker's local insecurity was emphasized by Sheehan's success in retaining his position as leader of the Ninth District. As 1900 dawned, sweet goodwill radiated between the Bryan and Tammany camps. O. H. P. Belmont gave an elaborate dinner for Bryan at his New York home. The banquet table stretched the entire length of the ground floor of his sumptuous town house, from the entrance hall to a study far in the rear. The menu was elaborate, the service perfect, and the American beauty roses conveyed an appropriate suggestion of affection; but the most gladdening sight for Belmont, a dedicated peacemaker, was the Tammany men's effusive goodwill toward Bryan.[16] Sheehan, who had a hardy capacity for forgiveness, seems never to have resented the fact that he gave more to Bryan than he received and that in his hour of peril Bryan did not come to his aid.

Norman Mack, with his successful London mission behind him, was deputed by Bryan to court the remaining major power center in New York, the upstate organization of David Bennett Hill. Mack emerged from his encounter with the wily Hill wreathed in enough optimism to declare in a press interview that Hill would support any nominee and platform of the next Democratic convention. James Creelman, a leading Hearst correspondent, made a similar assessment, telling Bryan that Hill "will make a hard fight for you." But Creelman deemed it wise to add a caveat: ". . . he is not your friend: Keep your eyes wide open."[17]

In his quest for renomination, Bryan, the seeming idealist and purist, his future soldered to the Chicago platform, had to break political bread with men whose hands were morally unclean. Of the various states posing problems for Bryan, none surpassed Kentucky, which had followed the general pattern throughout the West and South of endorsing Bryan for President in 1900 and free coinage at 16 to 1.

For all this evident unity, a deep, ugly factional split developed, resulting in two self-styled Democratic conventions and two nominees for governor, the incumbent William Goebel and John Young Brown. Both endorsed Bryan and the Chicago platform, condemned imperialism, and beseeched him to campaign on their behalf. As Bryan hesitated, John P. Altgeld provided urgent counsel. Goebel, Altgeld argued, in addition to being connected with influences embracing "trimming, trading, trickery, fraud and thugism, breach of faith, and when necessary, crime," was close to the corporations, and his record was bare of any stand on behalf of popular rights. Eastern gold influences supported him and were pouring $100,000 into the Kentucky primaries. These same gold influences, "bent on overthrowing us," controlled the mayors of Milwaukee and Detroit, had "friendly relations" with the mayor of Indianapolis, and once enjoyed "a perfect understanding" with the mayor of Chicago.

Exercising his customary self-sufficiency, Bryan chose to ignore Altgeld. Instead, he applied a simple test. He would support whoever was the legitimate Democratic nominee. That it was Goebel, Bryan had no doubt, and he journeyed to Kentucky to campaign on his behalf, reminding the huge audiences that turned out for him that Kentucky was a testing ground for 1900. Several factors weighed heavily in Bryan's decision. He was impressed with the high worth of an election law Goebel had guided through the legislature. "There is no doubt," Bryan wrote to Altgeld, "that the Republicans stole the electoral vote of Kentucky in 1896 and the Goebel law was passed to prevent the recurrence of this." Bryan too was eager for Joseph C. S. Blackburn to continue as U.S. Senator, a wish that could be gratified only through Goebel's election, since Brown, his rival, had Senatorial ambitions of his own. Bryan toured Kentucky in a mighty campaign and was rewarded by Goebel's victory.

Bryan faced another crisis in the Ohio gubernatorial candidacy of John R. McLean, the wealthy politician and press lord whom he had stigmatized as politically immoral in 1896. McLean had opportunistically offered, in exchange for the Vice Presidential nomination, to underwrite much of the campaign and to launch a free silver paper in Chicago. In the postelection interlude McLean's enthusiasm for silver, like that of countless other politicians, had declined sharply, but he remained, at least outwardly, identified with the Bryan forces. Now, as governor of Ohio, he would immediately become a formidable rival in 1900. "If he wins," warned one Bryan supporter, "all of the East from Maine to Virginia, and maybe some of the Southern states will rally around him. They will control one-third of the votes of the convention, and if they cannot nominate him they will never permit you to be the nominee."

Bryan again shunted aside the counsel of respected friends partly because he was confident of his ability to subdue any pretension McLean might have for the Presidency but mostly because he believed the gold Democrats were a greater danger. They meant to reclaim their party and would succeed if their candidate won the primary. Bryan rushed to Ohio and by frantic speechmaking and private prodding of local leaders was credited with defeating them.[18]

Election results in 1899 provided heartening affirmations of Bryan and strengthened his primacy in the national party. His succor to Goebel in his Kentucky victory and to Maryland Democrats, who wrested their state from Republican control, put a high gloss on his prestige in the border states. In New York, where his representatives and their organizations put out a big effort, Republican pluralities were scaled down impressively. In Ohio, Bryan had the best of all possible worlds. McLean was defeated and therefore eliminated as a potential Presidential rival in 1900, but Bryan and Ohio Democrats could rejoice in their party's showing. The combined vote of McLean and the reform mayor, "Golden Rule" Jones, of Toledo, who ran as an independent, comfortably exceeded the total of the Republican candidate.

"Taken as a whole," Bryan said, "the election returns from all the states give encouragement to those who hope for the overthrow of the Republican Party in 1900. . . . It is evident that those who believed in the Chicago platform in 1896 still believe in it." Theodore Roosevelt, after scanning the results, concluded to his distaste that Bryan was stronger now than in 1896.

In one respect Bryan's exultant words were a long, lonely whistle in the dark. A striking feature of the state campaigns of 1899 was their utter deemphasis of silver. Although Democratic state conventions politely included silver planks in their platforms, their candidates tended to ignore the issue. Any brightening of the national Democratic picture owed far more to Bryan's personal popularity and to the quality of the party's Congressional membership than to zeal for silver. If anything, the tempo of the silver cause seemed to falter. But Bryan declined to give even the barest nod of acknowledgment to the change. "I stand just where I stood three years ago," he proclaimed, moving the Republican editor of the New York *Press* to write, with emphasis on the last word, "Sit down, Mr. Bryan. You must be awfully tired, too." [19]

Bryan's most sparkling—and indispensable—electoral victory occurred in Nebraska. Although the highest state offices were not at stake, elections of a supreme judge and two regents of the state university presented statewide contests in which Bryan's security in his home base could be tested. Faced with the opportunity of humiliating and hobbling Bryan, his foes responded with zest and enterprise.

Bryan, as usual, mounted a fusion campaign. The Populist, Silver Republican and Democratic conventions that gathered in Omaha nominated a ticket headed by the ever-reliable Silas A. Holcomb for State Supreme Court judge. The two major conventions, Populist and Democratic, met simultaneously and were Bryan extravaganzas. While Bryan busied himself at the Populist gathering, Mary watched the Democratic proceedings from a proscenium box. James Creelman sat with her, and delegates came in steady numbers to pay their respects. With joyous shouts they reaffirmed the Chicago platform and free coinage at 16 to 1, with texts drafted by Bryan personally as chairman of the Resolutions Committee.

Bryan campaigned for the fusion ticket with an effort that was unprecedented even for him. Moving through Nebraska's towns, he mastered a speaking schedule that often began at 5 A.M. and continued far into the night. At Oakland, where hundreds could not get into the meeting hall, Bryan after his address indoors, came out to repeat it, perched on a lumber wagon. Everywhere he appealed for Holcomb's election by a big majority as a rebuke to the McKinley administration and sounded the trumpets for silver, for curbing the trusts, and for bringing peace and independence to the Philippines.

The scene at North Bend was a page out of the 1896 campaign. The *pièce de résistance* of an elaborate parade was a float of sixteen lovely girls dressed in silver and waving American flags, and a girl in a yellow gown wearing a golden crown. Republican agents circulating through the crowd with yards of yellow ribbon urged Bryan's listeners to affix a piece to their lapel to attest their commitment to the gold standard and sound money.

Enthusiastic Bryan newspapers, such as the Omaha *World-Herald,* reported the miraculous effects of their hero's oratory. A blond young Swede, according to the *Herald,* who came wearing a yellow ribbon tore it off and trampled it after hearing Bryan's address, exclaiming, "If God will forgive me I will never vote another Republican ticket. I'm for a free country and a free people after this."

Each town vied with the others in Democratic testimonials to Bryan. At Papillion, a pole eighty feet high, known officially as the Bryan Pole, was erected in his honor. Its shiny newness contrasted sharply with an old, weather-beaten Republican pole that stood nearby, and leaned, as Bryan quickly pointed out, toward "Wall Street and England." A longtime female resident was said to be in tears at the close of a powerful Bryan address. "I am a Christian woman," she exclaimed, "and I am not afraid to say as a Christian that I honestly believe William J. Bryan is inspired of God."

Bryan thrived upon the hecklers who dotted his crowds. "Why didn't you go to Cuba?" a voice would call. "When the treaty of peace was signed," Bryan replied, "I resigned because I believed this country was more in danger than Cuba and I came home to fight Republicans. I had five months of peace in the army, and have had constant fighting since I came out." Sometimes, as Bryan launched into a telling argument, a voice would cry, "Hurrah for McKinley." Bryan came to delight in this interruption. "Well, friends," he would say, "you know I've frequently felt like hurrahing for McKinley myself when I've thought of what he used to say, but has since denied. When I hear a Republican in my audience hurrahing for McKinley I think he is hurrahing for the old McKinley, who denounced Grover Cleveland for trying to make money the master, all things else the servant. I think he is hurrahing for the McKinley who denounced forcible annexation as criminal aggression."

It was not difficult to understand why Bryan, in the words of McKinley's Assistant Secretary of War George Meiklejohn, was making "the fight of his life." Early in the campaign, word rushed into Nebraska from McKinley's political representatives in Ohio and New York that Nebraskan Republicans must "whoop it up" against Bryan, and administer the severest possible blow to his awaiting 1900 candidacy. As the campaign moved into its critical weeks, talk was rampant of a lavish Hanna slush fund flowing into Nebraska to buy local votes. National Republicans were unstinting in their efforts to defeat Bryan. Theodore Roosevelt agreed to lead a band of orators through the state to counteract Bryan's oratorical successes. J. Sterling Morton openly allied himself with the Republicans, and his paper *The Conservative* published letters Bryan had written to his mentor a decade before. One of these requested Morton's intercession for a clerkship in the Board of Transportation, cherished for the salary rather than for the honor. The letter was reproduced in quantity and circulated by the Republican state committee. Rumors multiplied that Morton had received a letter from Cleveland holding that a fusionist defeat in Nebraska would destroy Bryan's claim to the Presidential nomination in 1900.[20]

By every appearance, Bryan welcomed the Republican strategy of making himself and his policies the central issue. He and other fusion orators trumpeted the theme that the campaign was a prelude to the next year's major battle. Holcomb made absolutely clear to his audiences that turning down the ticket would constitute a body blow to Bryan's nomination. Almost uniformly, fusionist orators avoided state issues and concentrated on national questions. Bryan too brought in a troupe of all-star orators—John P. Altgeld, "Cyclone" Davis, Congressman Towne, and W. H. Harvey, among others.

The Bryan camp passed through a moment of dark despair after the first day of registration under a new law that required the voter to declare his party affiliation. The results showed a sharp upsurge in Republicans, but the succeeding days restored Bryan's hopes. As the elections neared, he left nothing to chance and went about the state, bidding the voters to "do your duty and don't husk corn."

The voters heeded his counsel and gave Holcomb—and therefore Bryan—a smashing victory. The gross personal attacks on Bryan boomeranged in the face of Nebraskans' resentment of the invasion of Republican outsiders to destroy their local hero. Most political professionals agreed with Assistant Secretary of War Meiklejohn's assessment of the role of the silver issue in the struggle. "Prosperity," said Meiklejohn, "has killed the silver question as dead as a door nail." [21]

In the sweet high grass of fusion victory lurked a serpent of future trouble. Weeks after the election, Nebraska's junior U. S. Senator, M. L. Hayward, a Republican, died, and the new Populist governor, William A. Poynter, faced the task of appointing a successor. Bryan, whose guidance Poynter expected, faced the unpleasant task of choosing from three Nebraskans seeking the appointment, each his close and loyal partner: ex-Senator William V. Allen, Gilbert Hitchcock, and William H. Thompson. Allen was Bryan's chief tie with both Nebraskan and national Populism. Hitchcock had made available the Omaha *World-Herald,* Democratic Nebraska's foremost organ of publicity, to assist Bryan's early political rise and to maintain his primacy in the state. What's more, Hitchcock's favors had persisted in even the thinnest years of his own and Bryan's fortunes. Creator of the Omaha *Evening World* in 1885, Hitchcock had purchased the *Morning Herald* in 1889, consolidating the papers into the *World-Herald.* The searing depression of the nineties had driven him to the point of insolvency. Fortunately bank loans on his papers and on real estate tied in with their purchase were extended and expanded when his creditors perceived that they would gain little by foreclosing. After years of aiding and promoting Bryan's political career, Hitchcock was eager to commence his own.

The third aspirant, William H. Thompson, "The Little Giant" of Grand Island, Nebraska, for years had done yeoman work for Bryan's causes. The short, slight, mustached, bow-tied Thompson, whose hair bunched behind his head, matched the stereotype of a Western politician. After practicing law at Brush Creek, Iowa, he moved to Grand Island and rose quickly in that fast-growing community as an organizer and director of the state bank of Grand Island, city attorney, and county attorney for Hall County. In the fierce floor struggles of Democratic state conventions and in the state committee, the shrewd, keen-eyed Thompson was invariably on Bryan's side and unfailingly represented his interests. Bryan gave him precious little in return—no prominent place on the state ticket, since under Bryan's fusion formula, the leading state nominations were yielded to the Populists.

Faced with the necessity of disposing of the Senatorship to one of the three claimants, Bryan fell back upon his formula and suggested that it be given to the solitary Populist among the three. "Good faith," he felt, required the appointment of Allen, "the most prominent Populist in the United States." Hitchcock, whose ambition burned fiercely for the appointment, confronted Bryan with an ultimatum: "If you insist on sacrificing me, we part company forever." But Bryan held to his choice and thereby began a break with his long-standing ally that soon divided Nebraska's silver Democrats into two main factions, each identified with one of the alienated leaders.

Near midyear of 1899, the national Democratic committee gathered at the Planters' Hotel in St. Louis to discuss the approaching Presidential campaign. Predictions were rife that free coinage would be well subordinated to the fast-rising new issues. These expectations soared when one committeeman said in an interview that " 'Anti-trust' and 'anti-imperialism' will be the salt and pepper with which we will flavor 16 to 1." Bryan took no notice of any latent dissent over the issues and urged the members to put their state organizations into good repair for next year. Afterward he told the press that although it was too early to discuss the next national platform, "I am sure of one thing, and that is that silver will not be relegated out of sight. It cannot be. It is an issue that has come to stay, and the people will not allow it to be put in the background."

If Bryan was troubled by those of little faith, he was buffeted even more by silver's true believers and hard-liners. Through their chief spokesman, Senator William J. Stone of Missouri, they pressed for a "loyalty test," by which admission to the next national convention would be denied to any delegate who declined to reaffirm the Chicago platform. Staunch silver men of the West and South were titillated by the idea, but cooler heads saw the step as widening and hardening the alienation already rife in the party. Bryan preferred a looser, almost ambiguous stance. Although stressing devotion to principles, he would leave the door open wide for Democrats who had forsaken the party in 1896 to return in 1900. "We desire," he wrote to Urey Woodson of Kentucky, "that all Gold Democrats shall return, provided they will accept the Democratic Platform and support candidates pledged to that Platform." Stone also promoted fourteen new rules on the national committee's organization which promised to shear the national chairman, Senator James K. Jones, of much of his power and to subordinate the national committee to the National Bimetallic Union, now the chief organization pressing the silver cause, as a kind of double insurance that Jones would have little part in the coming campaign.

Bryan now repulsed the ardent silverites. Always faithful to Jones, he rushed to his defense and turned a receptive ear to the entreaties of O. H. P. Belmont to reject the loyalty tests. With the aid of George Fred Williams and Ben Tillman, Bryan rebuffed Stone's thrust. The national committee's primacy was kept intact, and a formal loyalty test was rejected. Stone was given the consolation prize of election as vice-chairman of the committee, but with a mandate of closely circumscribed subordination to Jones.[22]

Having saved Jones, Bryan engineered several changes in the national committee's structure to enable the coming campaign to avoid the delays of 1896, when precious time had been lost in readying the committee for battle duty and collecting funds. Among other things, an executive committee was established with Jones as ex officio chairman, along with a ways and means committee and a press committee. Bryan put great store in a financing plan developed by "Coin" Harvey, predicated upon the party's inability to "appeal to classes that enjoy special privileges for money because it is opposed to the granting of special privileges." Harvey's plan called for every Democratic voter to send one dollar to the Ways and Means Committee of the national committee. Foreseeing massive responses, Bryan was confident that a full national campaign could be mounted with squads of speakers, ample literature, and a vigorous effort in every precinct.[23]

Bryan rightfully anticipated that he would again enjoy the support given in 1896 by the Populists and Silver Republicans. Unfortunately, fusion had declined sharply in value as a political commodity. The Populists and Silver Republicans were weaker versions of their former selves. As yet no magic formula was evident for avoiding the snarls and embarrassments of the earlier fusion effort—the bizarre spectacle of two Vice Presidential nominees and the wrangles over the distribution of electoral votes.

The Populists were suffering a crisis of identity. The party's strength was so reduced that it lacked ascendancy in any state and it was without hope of victory in the nation. The political principles of the party's dominant forces more or less coincided with Bryan's program. Even the more radical Populists, who beheld Bryan with acute reservation in 1896, viewed him fondly in 1900. Bryan, wrote Henry Demarest Lloyd, his onetime critic, was "in truth more progressive" than his public statements and on "government ownership," the referendum, and other issues was "as advanced . . . as we need him to be." Furthermore, Bryan was "much more of a radical than Lincoln was," and if sentiment warranted "any aggressive step in economic, political or social legislation he would encourage it."

To satisfy their appetite for identity, the fusion Populists held their national convention in 1900 prior to the Democratic gathering, a decision that brought no rejoicing in the Bryan camp. True, a Populist nomination for Bryan was a foregone conclusion, but the timing of the convention raised the specter of a possible Vice Presidential nomination that would not be acceptable to the Democrats, and the repetition of the Sewall-Watson tragicomedy of 1896. To forestall the looming disaster, the fusion leaders hastily arranged a conference in Chicago several days before the Populist convention.

Senator Marion Butler of North Carolina, General James B. Weaver and Senator Benjamin Shively of Indiana represented the Populists; Senator Richard Pettigrew of South Dakota and former Senator Frederick T. Dubois, the Silver Republicans; and J. G. Johnson of the Democratic national committee organization and Daniel J. Campau, a national committeeman of Michigan who was close to Bryan, appeared for the Democracy. Bryan was absent, presumably to avoid the appearance of dictation, although he acknowledged that he "had seen the men of the three parties present. . . ." From the conference emerged a plan for the imminent Populist convention, calling only for Bryan's nomination as President and the creation of a committee to negotiate with the subsequent Democratic and Silver Republican conventions on the selection of a Vice Presidential nominee satisfactory to all three parties. If the negotiations proved abortive, the committee could then choose a Populist Vice Presidential nominee.

But, alas for Bryan, the plan adopted at Chicago could not weather the realities of the Populist national convention at Sioux Falls. The Populists, eager for self-assertion, chose to make a Vice Presidential nomination. Marion Butler, who apparently dissented from the prevailing opinion of the interparty meeting, viewed the nomination as a matter of life or death for Populism. "If the party is sacrificed and dies," he said, "then reform dies with it. When you destroy the party you will find you have destroyed Mr. Bryan." Senator William V. Allen, who again served as Bryan's emissary, urged his fellow Populists to abstain from any nomination and "wait to see what the Democrats do." Since, by general expectation Charles A. Towne, a Silver Republican, would become the Populist nominee, Allen warned: "The way to defeat Mr. Towne in the election is to nominate him here today. Let us take counsel by our mistakes of the past and not make a mistake here today."

But Dr. Howard S. Taylor of Illinois shouted that any objections to Towne were grounded in the fact that he is "too fully the embodiment of the Chicago platform. They," he added, referring to the East, or "the Tory end of the country, want a moderate man—a veneered man." The delegates nominated Towne overwhelmingly.

Bryan was again faced with the prospects of not one, but two, running mates. With his own National Democratic Convention looming at Kansas City, he maintained a tight public silence. "Towne must be nominated at Kansas City if you want to win," wrote Senator Richard F. Pettigrew, "and it is your duty to say so." To win, in Pettigrew's analysis, Bryan must carry Illinois, Ohio, and Michigan, and "Towne's nomination will help do it more than any one's." Pettigrew importuned Bryan not to sacrifice the Vice Presidency "again" for illusory Eastern support.

Bryan also had the counsel of the good and faithful Towne. "I regret the embarrassment to you," he wrote, "but it cannot be serious. Your nomination is certain, and you have assumed no responsibility for me and need not do so." [24]

As a defeated Presidential nominee, as the champion of doctrines profoundly hated and feared in quarters of entrenched power, and as a political phenomenon viewed with curiosity and distaste by machine politicians, Bryan witnessed an eager search for candidates who might snatch the 1900 nomination from his grasp. The months before the national convention quivered with booms and boomlets for old and shopworn politicians whose images were desperately refurbished and for newcomers, utterly innocent of political experience, who were suddenly brought or pushed before the voters.

The star of Arthur Pue Gorman, veteran Maryland machine politician, was briefly infused with new light. For a time he stirred interest among anti-imperialists, Tammany Hall, and Southern conservatives. But his chances collapsed when Eastern Democrats who found inspiration in Cleveland saw only the machine and expediency in Gorman. Anti-imperialists came to deem him too evasive, and others discovered that their fear of Bryan was not balanced by confidence in Gorman. [25]

Attention then shifted to Augustus Van Wyck of New York City, a former gubernatorial candidate and a brother of the mayor of New York City. His backers included William F. Harrity, the deposed national committeeman of Pennsylvania, and a wide assortment of Eastern gold Democrats and conservative Southerners. But under scrutiny Van Wyck, with his ties to Tammany, seemed little more than a machine politician, and old Cleveland men again recoiled in distaste.

If machine politics failed to conjure up a suitable competitor, there was another avenue to be explored. This was the availability of a war or military hero, an invaluable type in Presidential competition. The Spanish-American War conveniently provided a modest number of possibilities. The chief of these was the war hero whose exploits, next to those of the Republican Rough Rider, Theodore Roosevelt, had most jogged the public imagination: Admiral George Dewey, victor in the Battle of Manila Bay, who crushed the Spanish fleet without loss of a ship or a man.

His candidacy was launched at a gala reception in Washington at the John R. McLean mansion—the admiral was McLean's brother-in-law. (Besides being a Democratic power in Ohio, McLean published the Washington *Post,* and his regal suburban estate, Friendship, built on old cemetery grounds bought at a bargain price, was a center of capital society.) Ambassadors, Cabinet Secretaries, and legislators crammed the handsome ballroom and were regaled by the Baltimore Symphony Orchestra, by Madame Schumann-Heink, the contralto, and by an equally distinguished tenor and baritone. Prestigious political voices rose in acclaim of Dewey. Perry Belmont exclaimed in New York, "Admiral Dewey's nomination would be a glorious ending of the dead issues of 1896." In Louisville, Kentucky, the influential editor Henry Watterson fondly foresaw a Democratic ticket comprised of Admiral Dewey for President and General Fitzhugh Lee for Vice President—"the great admiral and the gallant General" with the issue of free silver "relegated to the limbo of busted shades."

Dewey's sudden injection into national politics was not without embarrassment. The researches of an enterprising journalist disclosed that the admiral had never voted. Major Van Wyck of New York, presumably at Tammany's behest, undertook a secret visit with Dewey that was leaked to the press. The Wigwam's solons quailed at their exposure of shopping around for yet another viable candidate.

But Dewey's prospects too quickly languished. The admiral, who photographed well on the bridge of his flagship, proved to be a cardboard figure in the sprightly, variegated arena of politics. His failure to identify with either party, but to imply his availability to both, served only to blur his image. Governor C. S. Thomas of Colorado voiced the sentiment of astute silver politicians when he wrote to Bryan, "It is clear that if your nomination is to be prevented, Dewey's is not a name to conjure with."

With Dewey's collapse, other war heroes were trotted out, General Nelson Miles and Admiral W. S. Schley, among them, but they too fell flat. Politicians of lesser national standing were desperately thrust to the fore, not only by the unbelievers, but even by those who had supported Bryan and silver in 1896. The Kansas City *Times,* after an unblemished record of toil on Bryan's behalf, urged the Presidential nomination of U.S. Senator Francis Marion Cockrell. Now in his fifth Senate term, Cockrell was hailed as "an old-fashioned Democrat, who stood for what the Chicago platform contains long before that platform was promulgated. . . ." The silver-minded former governor of Oregon, Sylvester Pennoyer, wrote candidly to Bryan, "My opposition to your renomination is not prompted by a difference of opinion or dislike of you, but simply because I wish for the success of the Democratic party." [26]

For all of the opposition to Bryan, no substitute could be found. Bryan's own decorum in the face of candid doubts and open rejection was constructive and correct. In private correspondence and in public discussion, he would declare, "I have never assumed that it would be necessary for the Democratic party to renominate me, but I do believe that the party should nominate some one who believes in the Chicago platform." [27]

The Bryan steamroller moved on with inexorable momentum. By early June twenty-two of twenty-four Democratic state conventions that had met had endorsed Bryan, and several weeks later his delegate strength exceeded the two-thirds required for nomination. It was also a reliable harbinger of Bryan's nomination that from the spring months of 1900 forward an ever-growing trek of politicians moved upon his Lincoln home. Conspicuous in the unending parade were the New Yorkers: Mayor James K. McGuire of Syracuse, Eugene Hughes of the New York Democratic state central committee, Congressman William Sulzer and Fred Feigel of Tammany, and David Bennett Hill. Hill, who came several days before the convention began, was closeted with Bryan in a three-hour conference. Although its substance was tightly sealed, it was commonly speculated that Hill made an eleventh-hour appeal to omit any specific declaration for 16 to 1 from the platform.

By every indication, Hill ran into a stone wall. Bryan, for all the hospitality he lavished upon the New York leader, declined to budge the least fraction. In the leading article of the *North American Review* of June, Bryan provided what could well serve as the Democratic platform for 1900. The fight for bimetallism at 16 to 1 must be preserved. The current monetary system created a "paper-money trust," one of a host of trusts waxing in society. The article's dominant theme was that wealth was becoming a dangerous factor in national life and monopolies must be controlled and curtailed. The Filipino insurrection made all the more urgent both a forthright promise of independence to that unhappy land and American guarantees against interference by outside powers.

Despite the dour cast of an occasional visitor, Bryan, in his public pronouncements, was unremittingly optimistic. "The Democratic party is sure to win," he said in a typical rallying cry. "The people are with us this year and they are in sympathy with the principles which shall be embodied in the

Kansas City platform, which represent the feeling of the great mass of American people." [28]

Not the least of Bryan's assets was that he was a charismatic leader, richly endowed with the several common qualities of that political breed. His extraordinary gifts of oratory, translucent sincerity, magical talent at arousing belief and passion in his followers, and contagious optimism even in defeat inspired his legions. His boundless energy and endurance sent him continually rushing on rounds of campaign and lecture tours. "Living near him," observed Willa Cather, "is like living near Niagara. The almighty, ever-renewed force of the man drives one to distraction. . . ." Without the audiences that sprawling continental America never failed to provide, it is difficult to see how Bryan could have survived. Their willingness to assemble, listen, and vote was the bread and butter of his career and the provender of his self-regard. To impose his hold on these audiences, he tended to stress goals and ends and to underplay means, which are more apt to be technical and therefore baffling.

Bryan also excelled as a selector and simplifier of issues. His penchant for moral issues and moralistic rhetoric satisfied a pronounced taste among his following. He truly was the spokesman for the common man. His devotees were farmers and laborers, the less well educated rather than intellectuals and academics; the less well-to-do and the poor, rather than the wealthy and business leaders.

For all his political enterprise, Bryan never invented his own issues. He clasped them after others had developed them and after they achieved substantial popularity. Carrie Chapman Catt, champion of the emerging woman suffrage movement, was distressed by Bryan's slowness in taking up her cause, but as a selector of causes he worked under limitations. Since his constituency was nationwide, he could choose only issues that promised to appeal to a vast mass audience.

There is no denying Bryan was in many ways an opportunist. He embraced ideas when they suited the necessities of his political position of the moment. Yet, unlike the general run of politicians, he was pragmatic within well-defined ideological confines. He espoused only issues which in his eyes were conducive to economic and social justice, whether by improving the lot of his own people or sparing the Filipinos from imperialism's oppressions. Bryan did not fear rejection at the polls because he was confident of the righteousness of his causes and the ability of the common people eventually to see them in their true light.[29]

19. The Second Battle

Kansas City, home of the 1900 Democratic national convention, was in spirit and atmosphere utterly at odds with the mood of the arriving delegates. They were ruled by uncertainty and reservation toward the decisions awaiting them. But Kansas City was a gaudy extravaganza of Western braggadocio, a wide-open town, day and night. Roulette, keno, and card games thrived. Barrooms did a gold-rush business, and minstrels and vaudevilles played to sellout crowds. Huge pink silk badges were seen everywhere, flaunting the information, in bold lettering "Delegate from Samoa." To "What does it mean?" a wearer said. "Why Samoa beer, Samoa whisky, or Samoa anything else." The pride of the busy sight-seeing guides was Jesse James' cigar store, operated by the outlaw's son, who was suspected of following his father in holding up railroads. In a barbershop on Walnut Street, the barbers danced ragtime while shaving their customers to the syncopated music of a young Negro at a piano.

The mood of the convention, however, was more in tune with the wilting July climate. Day after day, the sun beat down mercilessly. The great majority of the delegates, unaccustomed to the driving heat, felt drained, and a general dispiritedness pervaded their attack on the party's problems. That there had been no significant reconciliation of gold and silver Democrats was attested by the absence in many state delegations of the gold leaders of four years ago. Not a few delegates hoped that by some eleventh-hour miracle a candidate might appear who would bring the convention to abandon Bryan. Far more delegates, many of them Bryan's close friends and allies, were eager for a pullback from silver in the new platform. Even Josephus Daniels endeavored to induce Bryan not to insist on a restatement of the money plank of the Chicago platform, but he met with stony rejection. There was far-ranging unrest over the possibility that the Vice Presidential nomination might go to the Silver Republican Towne in preference to a "regular Democrat," possibly one from New York State who would strengthen the ticket in the East.[1]

Unlike 1896, Bryan did not attend the convention. Many friends urged him to, but he deemed it in bad taste to present himself in the attitude of a seeker of the nomination. His spokesman and representative was Richard L. Metcalfe, or Met, as he was called, an associate editor of the Omaha

World-Herald and a friend and confidant of the Commoner. In his mid-thirties, Metcalfe had little of the appearance and air of men of organization politics. Emaciated, if not asthmatic in appearance, he was given to the positive, earnest manner of speaking and argumentation so characteristic of staunch Bryan men.

Metcalfe was a delegate at large from Nebraska and was in immediate touch with Bryan's Lincoln home by a special long-distance telephone. To gain maximum effect for his role as emissary, Metcalfe was Nebraska's member of the Committee on Resolutions. Promptly upon arriving at Kansas City, he revealed the substance of his mission in terms that were absolute and admissible of not the slightest deviation. "Mr. Bryan," he announced, "is firm in the demand for the reiteration of the free silver plank of the Chicago platform. There can be no evasion, no compromise. We must stand firm for 16 to 1."

Bryan also took pains to provide the draft of a platform for C. H. Jones, who had prepared the one at Chicago. He doubtless found inspiration and substance for his assignment in Bryan's preconvention speeches, but most of all he found them in his own handiwork of 1896.[2]

Meanwhile, Bryan in his modest Lincoln home entertained Western delegations en route to Kansas City, and once the convention began, telephone calls and telegrams poured in upon him. Reporters were always at hand, and Bryan entertained them with readings from the *Old Curiosity Shop* and its tale of a convention, terming it a fair example of how reports should be written by newspapermen, and from the proceedings of the *Convention of the Mudfog Association for the Advancement of Everything*. At an impromptu social, he delivered, at their request, the Declaration of Independence. The inspiration for this derived from the convention, where the historic document had been recited by Charles S. Hampton of Petoskey, Michigan, otherwise known as the foghorn of the Skillajalee. Hampton had come into his special name, according to story, when a foghorn on the Skillajalee was broken and a gray mist set in endangering a group of mariners, Hampton among them. His mighty voice, summoned in the emergency, proved equal to the unfortunate foghorn and quickly reassured the crew. At the convention, the portion of his reading of the Declaration of Independence that was most appreciated were the passages denouncing George III. A delegate struck a favorite chord when he cried, "Is it Hanna you're talking about?" The convention gleefully interpreted the remainder of the passages as an excoriation of the Ohio boss.

Along with high officialdom and famous reporters a steady parade of local friends and neighbors passed in and out of the Lincoln home. At one point, when the convention moved into a crucial stage and Bryan was poring over telegrams and facing clamoring reporters, a neighbor, in his shirt sleeves, called from the sidewalk, "What's the news?" and Mary quickly invited him to come on the porch and take a seat on the divan beside her. Reporters were impressed with Mary's growing public role, her quiet strength and dignity, and utter lack of affectation.[3]

Although Bryan was not present, the convention at Kansas City settled for the next best thing, a sculptured bust that was unveiled as the proceedings began. As the party's hero was revealed, 2,000 delegates and 20,000 spectators rose with a mighty shout. An observer wrote that the attendant who turned the bust around, so that all could see, was the only man who ever "moved" Bryan.

The convention's most intense and controversial deliberations took place in the Resolutions Committee and concerned the fate of silver. If this plank had vexed and divided party leaders before the convention, it now redoubled their agitation. Bryan's position had grown more adamant. When the Colorado delegation stopped at Lincoln, he had spoken in the most absolute terms: "But I want to say to you that when Colorado forsakes the principle of 16 to 1, and when the people have ceased in their support of the principle, I will be found still fighting, even though alone."

Bryan's stubbornness persisted even when so old and true a friend as Millard Dunlap of the Illinois delegation ominously informed him that while he could be a candidate if he chose, "the platform should be made in Kansas City." The Illinois delegation, Dunlap stated emphatically, "did not wish to make the fight on the lines of 1896 entirely." In reply, Bryan pointed to the free coinage plank of 1896 and said evenly that he would insist on it, "no more, no less."

At Bryan's invitation, David Bennett Hill journeyed to Lincoln to discuss the silver issue. By the several extant accounts, the meeting of these titans of East and West took place beside a huge oak desk heaped with letters and telegrams. To the Bryan household, Hill seemed the epitome of Eastern elegance and insensitivity. "The way he handed his hat to the maid and walked"—Grace was impressed—"showed he was used to being both demanding and commanding," and his manner of greeting Bryan revealed a man with "a very exalted opinion of his own importance and ability." Hill, for his part, was no better pleased with Bryan's conduct. "I have a reputation for being somewhat cold at times myself," he acknowledged, "but I am not an iceberg." [4]

In the steaming, littered, overcrowded Club Room in the convention hall, the stage for battle was set when three draft platforms were introduced, one by Metcalfe representing Bryan's views and others by a delegate of Georgia and Augustus Van Wyck of New York, a member of the state Democratic committee and the man who had run unsuccessfully against Roosevelt for

governor in 1898. The two latter drafts simply reaffirmed the Chicago platform, without reference to the ratio of gold and silver. Otherwise the three
were remarkably similar.

Earnestly, Van Wyck explained that his draft was predicated upon four
issues—imperialism, militarism, the trusts, and finance. Of these, he believed that only the first three possessed present significance, the money
question having been crowded well into the background. Senator John
Daniel, to everyone's surprise, announced his support of Van Wyck's position. It was well known where he stood in 1896, Daniel declared, and his
sentiments on silver were the same now as they were then. But he was anxious to bring back into the party those who had left four years ago, and if
that could be achieved by simply reaffirming the Chicago platform without
any reference to the ratio, he proposed to do it.

George Fred Williams plunged into a fiery rebuttal. The Democrats, he
cried, had become a new party since incorporating the financial question
into their declaration of principles. They had become alive and virile, and
the hero of this transformation was Bryan. It would be an act of basest cowardice and ingratitude to demand that Bryan recant the text of his preachings up and down the country the past four years. It would, in effect, repudiate him while becoming a disaster for Populist fusionists in their struggle
with the middle-of-the roaders. "Are we going to drive the Populists into the
middle of the road in order to get back these traitors?" cried Williams. "Are
we going to sell our principles to the Tories of the Democratic party and
desert our real friends? By such a course, the trusts will take complete command of the Democratic party as they have of the Republican, and then no
ark of refuge will be left for the plain people." Waves of speakers joined the
debate, which roared into the early morning hours. Clearly, the vote would
be close.

By telephone and telegraph Bryan made it explicit that unless a specific
16 to 1 plank were adopted, he would not accept the nomination. If the
committee, in the face of this threat, rejected 16 to 1, he would not let the
matter drop but would go to Kansas City and take the fight to the floor. He
was spared these drastic steps, when the subcommittee on the platform
adopted by a single vote a specific plank of 16 to 1. His victory was something less than total, and there remained the possibility that a minority report might bring the silver issues squarely before the convention. A delegate
vote could possibly have gone against Bryan, but Norman Mack's heroic
and skillful negotiations, reinforced by Croker, checked any such movement.

By every sign, the avoidance of a minority report was part of a bargain by
which the Resolutions Committee made imperialism rather than silver the
dominant issue. By telephone, Bryan agreed to this move "because I be-

lieved that with changed conditions the question of imperialism was at that time more important than the money question." [5]

Even so, the convention still had to pass upon the platform, and the outcome was by no means a foregone conclusion. Waiting by their telephone for word of the delegates' decision, the Bryans passed the night in grim suspense. Even worse was the awareness that Daniel, an old ally, Dunlap, an old friend, and others like them either doubted or rejected Bryan's silver position. Never had Mary seen her husband more distressed. When the good news of the platform's adoption arrived at 4 A.M. Bryan still could not stop pondering the defections from his silver views. He put his arm around Mary and said, "Well, I have my wife left anyway." And Mary added, "Yes, and 16 to 1." Their laughter chased away the cobwebs of Bryan's gloom.

Bryan's tenacity on the silver plank was based on more than whim or ideological blindness. During the four years of national campaigning since 1896, he had become convinced that a watered-down silver plank would cost perhaps 1,000,000 Populist and Silver Republican votes, a number far in excess of the Democrats who voted for Palmer and Buckner in 1896 and who presumably might be brought back by a deflated silver plank. In addition, Bryan reasoned that the Republican foes of imperialism—Carl Schurz, former Governor George S. Boutwell of Massachusetts, and others—were so engrossed in anti-imperialism that they would support him regardless of his silver position. The platform's plank establishing imperialism as the "paramount" issue was a double insurance of their commitment.

But Bryan's adamancy on silver carried evident costs. It endangered whatever possibilities he had of carrying the gold-minded East. It provided a cover for the Republicans to throw over the gross inadequacies of their administration of the war and the fallacies of imperialism laid bare in the Philippine insurrection. Not for nothing could Thomas B. Reed observe of Kansas City that Bryan "had rather be wrong than President."

Yet it is difficult to deny that Bryan was not more right than his critics and his well-meaning friends. Even if he had retreated on silver, the gold Democrats and the East were hardly likely to cast off their vision of him as a monstrous radical and come rushing to his support. Their more probable response would have been overwhelming ridicule that would have laughed him off as a charlatan. The Resolutions Committee compromise fitted the necessities of the situation. It preserved Bryan's integrity on silver, while granting top priority to imperialism, the most urgent of the newly emerging issues.[6]

The handiwork of the Resolutions Committee was read to the convention by Ben Tillman, fiery, one-eyed, and leather-lunged. Eager to minimize the silver plank, he cried in expectant climax: "We recognize imperialism as the paramount issue of the campaign," shouting the word "paramount," and stirring a burst of cheering that endured only a minute and a half. Dismayed at the slight response, Tillman turned to colleagues on the stage for succor in this trying moment. "Read it again," someone called. Tillman read it again, shouting and pausing between each word. When he screamed "paramount," he threw his hands in the air and shook his manuscript; the delegates understood, responded as they would to a cheerleader, and rose for a raucous demonstration. Around and around the floor they circled, carrying flags that were hastily handed out, some bearing the inscriptions "The Constitution and the flag are one and inseparable now and forever. The flag of the Republic forever, of an empire never," "A republic should have no colonies." A wild, shouting parade of thousands followed, spurred by several bands and fully justifying Tillman's observation: "If Mark Hanna had been here for the last twenty minutes, he would have thought that hell had broken loose."

Eventually, Tillman resumed his reading and reached the silver plank. It drew cheers that lasted only four and a half minutes and brought only one-third of the delegates to their feet. The radical silver men labored mightily to throw the convention into an uproar, but failed. Colorado, Missouri, and the Indian Territory carried their standards to the front of the hall and beckoned other states to join the rally, but none did. Bryan, that moment made painfully clear, had forced his silver plank down the throats of the delegates.[7]

William B. Oldham, a delegate at large of Nebraska, made the nominating speech for Bryan, who had personally chosen him for the task. A huge thirty-five-minute demonstration, well fit for the hero of 1896, followed, and each seconding speech touched off additional demonstrations. Bryan's managers suffered an anxious moment when Texas, reached in the call for nominations, had one of its delegates stand on a chair and shout, "Texas wants to hear David Bennett Hill. He is a Democrat from the top of his head to the soles of his feet. Texas is Democratic and honors Hill." The New Yorker was almost carried to the platform. He quickly snuffed out any incipient revolt by seconding Bryan's nomination—"His integrity has never been questioned"—by commending the platform, and pledging the support of "a united Democracy."

When word of Bryan's nomination reached Lincoln, Grace was playing croquet with press correspondents on the front lawn, and William, Jr., was entertaining visitors on the porch with his pet kitten. The good news was received by Dolph Talbot, who ran into the parlor, shouting, "You're nominated, old man! You're nominated!" But Bryan showed no elation. "I fear this is too sudden," he said. "If congratulations were based on sound judgment, November would be a good time to extend them." [8]

If Bryan was chosen without opposition, the Vice Presidential nomination became tense. Daniel J. Campau, who was a possibility for the office, said at the outset of the proceedings that in view of the Republican nomination of "Rough Rider" Theodore Roosevelt, the Democracy would do well to nominate "Buffalo Bill," William F. Cody. Bryan abstained from showing any preference, although according to his convention manager, Metcalfe, certain ground rules were to be observed: "that he shall be a man who has been a consistent and active supporter of Mr. Bryan and the platform of 1896."

Privately, Bryan favored Towne, but his party could not swallow a non-Democrat, and when the eleventh hour of the nomination approached, Bryan's managers, eager to widen the ticket's appeal, turned to Adlai Stevenson of Illinois, Vice President in Grover Cleveland's second administration. Stevenson was that rarity, a major politician who straddled both the Bryan and the Cleveland camps. In 1896 he had supported the Chicago platform and Bryan's candidacy. Poised and dignified, Stevenson was twenty-five years older than Bryan and could therefore balance his youth. His selection might also achieve an objective Bryan deemed unattainable—the reconciliation of gold Democrats to the new national ticket. The ultimate choice of Stevenson deeply disappointed Bryan, and it dejected the Populists, who had counted on Towne's strength to help their state and local tickets.

As for the Silver Republicans, their national convention was proceeding simultaneously in Kansas City to promote what supposedly would be a harmonious, joint party enterprise. After they nominated Bryan unanimously for President, the trouble began. When a delegate moved that Silver Republicans endorse Stevenson for Vice President, angry shouts swept the hall, "We want Towne! Nominate Charley Towne!" At last Towne got the floor and engaged in an act of heroic self-denial by declaring, "The Silver Republicans have made a good fight. They have been defeated, but it is your duty to support the ticket nominated by the national Democratic convention." But the anger raged on, and the convention adjourned without nominating a Vice President, pushing the thorny problem into the hands of the national committee and granting it full authority to act.[9]

For all the impasses and stress, Bryan emerged from the several conventions with impressive political profit. He had dominated the proceedings as they affected the two most significant criteria of his personal success—his nomination and the adoption of a full restatement of the silver plank of 1896. The remainder of the platform was framed in a fashion affording him flexibility to adjust the themes of his campaign as circumstances might change in the months ahead. In Kansas City a new rapport had been built with the foremost machine of the East, Tammany Hall, Richard Croker's support of Bryan's cause at every crucial turn raising hopes that New York might also be carried, without which victory seemed scarcely possible.

Having been defeated once for the Presidency after conducting a campaign unprecedented in the number of its speeches, of people reached and communities visited, Bryan was not lacking in counsel urging revision of his conception of Presidential electioneering. Although Bryan did not choose to imitate McKinley's front-porch style, he acquiesced to the view pressed by James K. Jones and most of the Democratic executive committee that his coming campaign should be a well-reduced scale of his effort of 1896. Following a meeting of the committee on August 10, Bryan disclosed that "No regular program of speeches by me will be mapped out, and no especial itinerary arranged. I shall make a few speeches during the campaign: the times and dates will be announced from time to time. . . . Every speech will be independent of all others." [10]

Bryan's principal appearances in the campaign's first weeks coincided with major party occasions and ceremonies. The chief national party rite preceding the opening of the campaign was the notification, when Bryan and Stevenson were officially apprized of their nomination. Bryan did not again repair to New York's Madison Square Garden for his acceptance speech but chose the friendlier and more central locale of Indianapolis. The journey from Lincoln was the usual triumphal procession—the abundant stops for speeches, the huge enthusiastic crowds that gathered from around the countryside to view and hear the charismatic hero, the state and local dignitaries who clambered aboard for portions of the journey. The "Bryan special" that eventually pulled into Indianapolis was a gay aggregation, with ten of its twelve cars filled with jolly, carousing members of the Cook County Democracy of Illinois, an eleventh by the press. The final car, whose atmosphere was more solemn, carried Bryan, Mary, and young William and an assortment of Democratic dignitaries—Governor and Mrs. Charles S. Thomas of Colorado, Sergeant at Arms John I. Martin, various members of the national committee, Mayor Carter Harrison of Chicago, Samuel Alschuler, Democratic candidate for governor of Illinois, and Webster Davis, a former Assistant Secretary of the Interior in the McKinley administration who was repelled by its expansionist policies.

The notification ceremony had an afternoon session for country audiences who could attend and return home the same day and an evening program for the citizenry of Indianapolis whose work barred their presence during the day. Estimates of a total crowd of 40,000 were not exaggerated. Bryan's afternoon presentation was rendered in Military Park, a shaded, thirty-acre tract in the center of the city. So dense was the crowd that a hand once raised could not be lowered. Old people and children were endangered, and a few persons fainted.

When Bryan began to speak, those in the rear pressed forward, stirring screams and groans. But with his first sentences, a light breeze mercifully sprang up, and the crowd settled down and greeted his oratorical sallies with strong hurrahs. Bryan, on the platform, against the background of his own and Stevenson's families and party dignitaries, was a striking figure. Handsome, erect, his hairline receding, he masterfully coordinated his words, cadences and gestures. His attire, as usual, was that of the Western lawyer-statesman—a black sack coat, loosely buttoned about his waist, a white shirt front, and a white necktie. Onlookers marveled at the range of his voice as they saw listeners on the far edge of the crowd in deep attention.

Bryan's acceptance speech was a cogent analysis of imperialism and made no allusion to silver. Imperialism, Bryan contended, was a new chapter in the struggle between plutocracy and democracy. The two major parties were instruments of the struggle. The Republican Party was dominated by those "influences which constantly tend to elevate pecuniary considerations and ignore human rights." The Democratic Party, in contrast, was friendly to "the honest acquisition of wealth; it has no desire to discourage industry, economy, and thrift." It sought indeed to give "every citizen the greatest possible stimulus to honest toil" and to protect him in "the enjoyment of the proceeds of his labor." Property rights, he argued, are most secure when human rights are respected. Democracy strives "for a civilization in which every member of society will share according to his merits."

The roadblock to this utopia was thrown up by "a comparatively small, but politically and financially powerful, number who really profit by Republican policies. . . ." Imperialism offered new possibilities of profit "to the army contractors, . . . to the shipowners who would carry live soldiers to the Philippines and bring dead soldiers back," to franchise holders, and colonial officialdom. But to the farmer and the laboring man, Bryan argued, imperialism would bring "expenditure without return and risk without reward." Imperialism's most insidious aspect was its erosion of the nation's loftiest political values. "We cannot repudiate the principle of self-government in the Philippines without weakening that principle here."

Bryan also viewed the Filipino insurrection and Filipino rights in the framework of the most elementary perceptions of the nature of humanity. "God Himself . . . never made a race of people so low in the scales of civilization or intelligence that it welcomes a foreign master." Bryan's attitude led him to assume an explicit position of pacifism, unknown, before or since his day, for the Presidential nominee of a major party. "It is our duty to avoid killing a human being, no matter where the human being lives or to what race or class he belongs."

To solve the Philippine problem, Bryan unrolled his earlier proposals, all of them incorporated in the new Democratic platform. If elected President, he would call Congress into special session and urge the immediate adoption of a declaration of purpose to establish stable government in the Philippines and to accord independence to the islands just as it had been promised to Cuba. The United States would protect the Philippines as they worked out their destiny.

For all the solemnity of his preachings on imperialism, Bryan's address contained both humor and optimism. The gold Democrats, according to the press, had deserted the party by tens of thousands in 1896; "now it requires an expert mathematician to stand at the door and count them as they come back." The nation's cities—New York, Chicago, Baltimore, Indianapolis, Buffalo, San Francisco, Denver, Kansas City, and Jersey City—glowed with a promise utterly lacking in 1896, for their mayors were now Democratic, and this could be the key to the coming election.

This emphasis of the bright municipal picture augured a substantial city-oriented campaign, and Bryan's fighting, optimistic address, his highlighting of imperialism and subordination of silver evoked only praise from his party, even from so severe a critic as Senator George F. Hoar of Massachusetts, who said that Bryan had put his case "With great power and with great dexterity." Mark Hanna, too, was forced to forgo criticism. "I think," he observed, not without prophecy, "that that speech was put forth as a feeler and was devoted to the line it took in order chiefly that Mr. Bryan might see whether the country took the bait." [11]

From triumph in Indianapolis, Bryan returned to struggle in Nebraska. He was again faced with a determined assault by national as well as local Republicans upon his base of power. The full state ticket and two U.S. Senatorships were at stake. This year Bryan carried new liabilities in the struggle. The incumbent Governor Poynter was unpopular with the fusionists, and his renomination required the application of pressures that threatened to split the parties of fusion asunder. Henry Edmiston, the Populist state chairman, was also disliked and had driven many workers from the field.

The magic cement required to restore the broken pieces was Bryan. In a generous response, considering his obligations to the Presidential race, he invested days and weeks in August and September in the bitter Nebraska struggle. A mighty spur was the equally busy presence in Nebraska of the Republican Vice Presidential candidate, Theodore Roosevelt, whose swashbuckling charm was supplemented by generous infusions of national Republican money.

Bryan became an omnipresent figure at Nebraska's fairs and picnics. In a vast picnic in Omaha's Syndicate Park of the Jacksonians of Nebraska, speeches by Bryan, Stevenson, and state candidates were sandwiched in with a series of games and prize awards, a fat man's race, a married woman's race, a boy's race, a girl's race, a sack race, and an egg race for the ladies. One day, while aiding the Congressional candidacy of George Berge, Bryan, nearly two hours behind in his appointments, drove his team at a fast gait in a twenty-two-mile trip from Tecumseh to Pawnee City. En route he noticed a horse was badly entangled in the rope by which it was tied to a fence. Its desperate attempts to free itself only worsened its plight. Bryan, faced with a choice between helping a struggling dumb creature and the political favor of the awaiting crowds, halted his carriage to aid the horse. When he was unable to complete the rescue alone, he called others to help. After the horse was freed, Bryan stood for some moments patting its muzzle and then hurried back to his carriage.

Whenever he could in his Nebraska campaigning, Bryan linked state affairs with national issues. In Nebraska City he pointed to the Argo Company, a nearby factory, which was part of the starch trust controlled by the National Starch Company in New York City, to demonstrate that a substantial evil of the trust was that it wrenched enterprise from local control and placed it in remote, absentee hands. Thus, the economy of Nebraska City lay with men in New York, who probably never had and never would see the Western city.

For all the ferocity of the struggle, Bryan was scrupulous in honoring the several rules of political sportsmanship, notable for the infrequency with which they were observed in a hard, corrupt age. When Theodore Roosevelt was about to barnstorm through Lincoln, Bryan wrote a letter to the press requesting his political friends to remove pictures of himself from their windows. Needless to say, Mark Hanna and his subalterns did not reciprocate.[12]

At the dawn of the 1900 campaign, Bryan's gifts of leadership had come into full bloom. To the great mass of his followers and even to the most hardened politicians among them, he possessed a glittering allure. His youth, his handsome mien, his unparalleled ability to move men, his consecration to the purest and most noble of American public purposes, his invulnerability to temptation—all were part of the garment of the Great Hero that others placed upon his shoulders.

Bryan's performance in holding fast to 16 to 1 against overwhelming pressure moved the crusty, hardheaded John Peter Altgeld to a rare outburst of encomium. "Your heroic stand . . ." he wrote to Bryan, "not only saved our cause, but made you the grandest figure in the civilized world." Edgar Howard, Nebraska journalist, politician, and staunch Bryanite, declared: "It is time for us to quit saying we are not hero worshippers. Truthfully I confess . . . that I am. No man has ever confronted me in public or private life who has exercised such an influence over me. . . . He brightens and betters all those who come into contact with him. Then why not go before the world and preach this man—the personification of purity—as well as his principles."

Upon any politics he touched, Bryan left a personal, inspirational imprint. "Once remove hero worship from the politics [of Nebraska]," wrote Charles H. Gere, conservative editor of the *Nebraska State Journal*, "and Republican control will be permanent." Senator Henry M. Teller of Colorado made a similar assessment of Bryan's place in national affairs: "If there is a man in the United States today who comes near to Abraham Lincoln, that man is William Jennings Bryan. . . . I say Bryanism is Americanism, and if we could have less Hannaism and more Bryanism we should be better off." [13]

Yet there were dangers lurking in Bryan's personal magnetism. His vast following might only hear, but not listen; see, but not understand. The huge, enthusiastic crowds that turned out might be exhilarated by his sentiments and enthralled by his rhetoric, but their final disposition might be lamentably like that toward their Sunday preacher. Willingly they harkened to the evils of the temporal kingdom on the Sabbath, but they devoted the other six days to tilling the imperfect soil and gathering the blemished fruits.

The gap between the brilliantly proclaimed vision of Bryan's rhetoric and its ability to command results is garishly demonstrated by the fate of the anti-imperialism issue in the 1900 campaign. For Bryan's political necessities, anti-imperialism was an issue rich with promise. It could impart to the young candidate an aura of respectability among cultivated and concerned men. It was an opportunity for Bryanism to shed its stereotype as the gospel only of the poor, the indebted, the disinherited. Two main groups constituted the anti-imperialist community. One consisted of Republican Mugwumps like the Boston Brahmin lawyer Moorfield Storey, who saw a war waged for liberty betrayed for conquest and domination. The second was the gold or sound money Democrat who was sufficiently offended by imperialism to rally to Bryan's standard.

The most sensational conversion of a gold Democrat to Bryan's cause was Bourke Cockran. To the dismay of the McKinley administration and diehard gold Democrats, the supreme orator for sound money in 1896 joined hands with Bryan in the fight on imperialism. When sound money Democrats begged to know how Cockran could abandon their high cause, he replied that he was as much opposed to free silver in 1900 as he was in 1896 but he was convinced that the election would leave monetary policy unaffected. The Senate, Cockran reasoned, "will remain Republican for two years certainly, and probably for four. Even if the people raise Mr. Bryan to the Presidency, the Democratic party cannot possibly achieve any power of legislation during the existence of the next Congress, and without legislative sanction no change in the standard of value . . . could be accomplished." [14]

The anti-imperialists provided the sinews of campaigning. They could gather money, and although they produced only a modest war chest, it was substantial in the eyes of the impecunious Bryanites. A superlative orator like Cockran took on a sizable burden of speechmaking through the East and Middle West. With logic and eloquence, he toiled to convince audiences of gold Democrats that the attitudes of 1896 must not govern 1900 issues: "We cannot hope to deal intelligently with the issues of this campaign until we liberate ourselves from the domination of the questions, discussions, and passions of the last campaign. Within four years political conditions have changed decisively and as conditions change, issues change with them." [15]

Bryan's campaigning harmonized with Cockran's reading of the political scene. He continued to emphasize imperialism in his speeches. In his homecoming from Indianapolis, he declared from his front porch to the vast crowd that escorted him from the railroad station that "those who today say that the dollar of trade is superior to the rights of the Filipinos will be saying in a few years that money is more important than man. . . ." At Topeka, Kansas, where he accepted the Populist nomination, he devoted fully half of his forty-minute address to a discussion of imperialism as the most important issue.[16]

With insurrection raging in the Philippines, the Boer War in South Africa, and the Boxer Rebellion in China, Bryan could apply to his moral texts vivid illustrations from the day's events. For the Boxer Rebellion, he urged the nation to repose its trust, not in the troops McKinley had dispatched, but in the principles of justice and fair dealing. Though other nations might choose to "slice the Chinese melon," the United States must provide for other nations an example of ethical conduct. These moral precepts he also commended to two archagents of imperialism—the merchant and the missionary. He counseled merchants that trade is profitable only when mutually advantageous. He admonished missionaries that their duty was to teach the gospel of love and not to act as advance agents for fleets and armies.

Yet for all the commitment of Bryan and prestigious public men to the cause of anti-imperialism, the movement fell flat on its face. Bryan is blameless for the sad result. The causes of failure lay outside him. His effectiveness with the issue was limited partly by the vagaries of anti-imperialist politics. On the one hand, a week after Bryan's acceptance speech, the Democratic Liberty Congress of the American League of Anti-Imperialists emphatically endorsed his Presidential nomination. Every mention of his name at its convention triggered enthusiastic applause. But on the other hand, a rival anti-imperialist league, which looked askance at Bryan, pursued an independent course and supported no Presidential nominee. Many other anti-imperialist organizations regarded him with highly diluted approval. Moorfield Storey declared that he would support Bryan until some better champion of anti-imperialism came along. Carl Schurz accepted

Bryan only because it was the means of defeating McKinley, whose foreign policy he could not abide. E. L. Godkin, editor of *The Nation,* turned to Bryan, less from admiration than from repugnance for the aggressive nationalism of Roosevelt and Henry Cabot Lodge.

The anti-imperialist campaign is a classic example of lofty ethical resolve articulated with masterly eloquence going for naught. It was a kind of appeal Bryan did best, aimed to rouse people to justice and generosity. But in 1900 the American people lay deep in moral slumber. The country was never as stirred about the Philippines as it was about silver. In reasoning and phrasing, Bryan's speeches on imperialism outclassed his earlier presentations on silver. But the people, confident after a victorious war, proud of their new place among nations, comfortable in domestic prosperity, were deaf to a prophet proclaiming the error of their ways and their transgression of the faith of the fathers. Josephus Daniels and others who followed Bryan on his campaign tours made the distressing discovery "that the American people could not be aroused by any wrongs done to people across the sea." Even Bryan's anti-imperialist political manager, Elwood S. Corser, for all his devotion to the cause, felt compelled to acknowledge that "we have failed to awaken the lethargic American conscience." [17]

For William McKinley, the paramount issue of the campaign was not imperialism but free coinage of silver at 16 to 1. He wanted it that way. The money question had provided his ride to victory in 1896, and he looked for a like route in 1900. The Democrats' explicit reaffirmation of the Chicago platform greased his tracks. In 1900 the electorate witnessed the spectacle of Bryan seeking to minimize the money question and McKinley working adroitly to maximize it.

McKinley and his fellow Republican leaders lost no time in pushing the money question forward as the campaign's big issue. Henry Cabot Lodge, who took aristocratic glee in the trend of political events, chose to highlight, in his letter of notification to McKinley, the theme that his reelection guaranteed the maintenance of the gold standard. McKinley's reply devoted twice as much space to silver as it did to imperialism, and a subsequent letter on September 8 explicitly endorsed a single gold standard. McKinley was less a bimetallist in 1900 than he was in 1896.

Always careful to preserve the dignity of his person and office, McKinley left the rougher play to his subordinates. They, inspired by the victory pattern of 1896, again resorted to a scare campaign. Secretary of the Treasury Lyman J. Gage suggested in an interview that Bryan as President could order his Secretary of the Treasury to pay out silver in the settlement of all interest on the public debt not specifically payable in gold and to make daily disbursements to the government's creditors in silver. Having painted a nightmarish spectacle of creditors suffering hardship and loss from a debased currency, Gage went on to suggest the absolute essentiality of the election of a Republican President. Carl Schurz, although he had no truck with Bryan's money doctrines, was moved to protest that for Gage to claim that a silver policy could be installed by executive fiat was to confess the inadequacy of the McKinley administration's monetary laws. Congress, Schurz pointed out, could easily and immediately amend these laws to keep monetary policy securely in its own hands. The real purpose of Gage's interview was "to alarm the business community." [18]

To foil these Republican maneuvers, Bryan responded with ridicule and stepped up efforts to keep the newer issues before the voters. After omitting silver from his acceptance speech, he referred to it infrequently during the campaign and discussed it only in those sections where it still possessed voter appeal.[19]

The third major issue—the trusts—offered enormous potentiality. Unlike imperialism, it touched the lives of the masses visibly and directly and, therefore, could conceivably become the means by which Bryan might attract the city people and rally them behind his banner. In 1896 he hoped that silver might awaken them; in 1900 it was the trust.[20]

It was in a speech in St. Louis to the National Democratic Committee of Commercial Travelers that Bryan most fully developed his portrayal of the trust evil. The trust, he argued, by the logic of its nature, becomes a monopoly. In its fullest development, the monopoly exposes each branch of industry to control by one or a few men. The fruits of monopoly, "like the divine right of rule," will remain in the possession of a few "from generation to generation, while the real producers of wealth will be condemned to perpetual clerkship or servitude." Bryan warned his listeners of a future day when "your son will buy a finished product at the price which the monopoly fixes; and, if he works for wages, he will work for such compensation and upon such conditions as monopoly may determine."

The sanction of publicity, which some Republicans proposed, was not enough to stop the grasping tentacles of the trust octopus. Trust practices must not simply be exposed; they must be prevented. Bryan put great store in the Democratic plank demanding that trust articles be placed on the free list, a step, he was confident, that would "protect the people from much of the extortion going on under high tariffs." Where a trust operated entirely within a state, he would leave its regulation to the state legislature. Congress must "cooperate" with the states in preventing interstate monopoly by providing that corporations organized in any state shall not do business outside the state until "certain necessary conditions are complied with." Such measures would prohibit a corporation from controlling more than a specific percentage of the production of a given commodity. In a word, a corporation would be barred from becoming a trust.

In a letter of September 18, Bryan pledged himself to vigorous measures to curb the trusts. He would choose an Attorney General dedicated to enforcing existing laws. He would propose new legislation to dissolve every private monopoly doing business outside the state of its origin. If, contrary to his opinion, a constitutional amendment should be necessary, he would propose one "without impairing any of the existing rights of the states." [21]

In 1900, as in 1896, Bryan devoted his campaign to mass themes and a mass format. Yet there were several substantial interest groups that Bryan wooed, and it is clear that he envisioned their coalition as the foundation of victory.

For Bryan, the most important and the most elusive grouping was city labor. James K. Jones voiced Bryan's and the prevailing Democratic sentiment when he remarked that the laboring forces "are the ones who are to decide this election." But labor bore certain tantalizing limitations. Its political consciousness was dim and weak. Samuel Gompers and several other key leaders of craft unions eschewed politics as the avenue to their goals and were prone to rely upon private economic strength. For all of Bryan's dire lamentation about the trusts, workingmen believed in an American dream suffused with an Horatio Alger ethic, holding that all may rise in a society of opportunity by hard work, thrift, and other kindred virtues.

The Democratic platform of 1900 carried planks designed to constitute, as Charles Daniel, chairman of the Order of Railroad Telegraphers, put it, "the only hope for the workingmen. . . ." The platform condemned two practices inimical to labor's well-being, the injunction and the blacklist; pandered to its fears by opposing Asian immigration; underscored the contradiction between militarism and labor's self-interest; called for a federal "labor bureau"; and carried Bryan's own pet proposal for avoiding strikes and lockouts, a plan of voluntary arbitration. He abhorred labor-management strife just as he did conflict between the nations.

In his courtship of labor, Bryan depended on a heavy outflow of campaign literature from the national party headquarters to labor organizations and on his sturdy personal relationships with a corps of labor leaders who envisioned the Democratic Party and his candidacy as their best available political vehicles. Frequently in his speeches he tended to mute and thus avoid the "anarchist" image of 1896. Yet Bryan never regarded himself as labor's special pleader rather than as champion of all the people.

In his Labor Day speech in Chicago, he declared, "Our desire should be not to separate the people into warring factions, but to bring them into better acquaintance and greater sympathy with each other." Bryan called for love, compassion, and justice among classes, but in the social scheme, he accorded highest priority to "producers," of whom labor was the major but by no means exclusive constituent. "Why should the man who eats at a well-supplied table forget the man whose toil furnished the food? Why should the man who warms himself by the fire forget the man whose labor in the forest or in the mine brings forth the fuel?" Bryan stopped with his questions. He offered no prescription or program. Eugene V. Debs had ample cause to sniff: "There is nothing in the platform, program or attitude of the Democratic party that points toward socialism." [22]

Bryan's chances for political gain seemed to soar when a strike called by John Mitchell of the United Mine Workers quickly spread to become one of the worst labor disputes the nation had yet known, eventually involving 134,000 miners. But this advantage sank like mercury on a winter day when Mark Hanna moved easily to a position not much different from his in demanding arbitration and better pay for the miners.

A further substantial group that Bryan hoped to bring into his coalition was the great body of German-American voters. The heavy migrations of Germans to the United States in the eighties, added to the several waves earlier in the nineteenth century, made the German-Americans one of the largest nationality groups. Hardworking and thrifty, they tended overwhelmingly to affiliate with the Republican Party. Bryan's inflationary monetary position in 1896 had repelled them, but in 1900, Bryan counted upon imperialism to lure them to his fold, for imperialism meant militarism, and many of these people had fled their homeland to avoid conscription.

In certain states, particularly in the Midwest, Bryan considered the German-American vote critical. ". . . I regard our chances in Illinois as almost even," he wrote to Mayor Carter Harrison of Chicago. "If the German vote comes to our ticket there will be no doubt of success." Bryan was enormously aided by the support of Carl Schurz, and through Norman E. Mack, Bryan wooed the backing of the New York *Staats Zeitung,* the most influential and widely circulated German-American newspaper. While the paper rejoiced in Bryan's stand on imperialism, it, like most of its readers, was appalled by his insistence on an explicit 16 to 1 plank. The campaign was not long under way when it became clear that Bryan's silver views, rather than his excoriations of imperialism, counted most with German-American voters.[23]

Bryan also worked to bring the Negro voter to put aside his traditional Republican allegiance on the promise that the Democratic Party would be more attentive to his plight in American society. The Republicans, he charged, were attentive to the Negro only during an electoral campaign and afterward settled into numbing indifference: "The Republican party has taken the Negro for thirty years to an office door and then tied him on the outside. The Negro has bestowed Presidents on the Republican party—and the Republican party has given to the Negro janitorships in return." [24]

Bryan, to be sure, had towering handicaps to overcome. The white Southern base of the Democratic Party frightened off Northern and Western Negroes. Their disenchantment deepened when "Pitchfork Ben" Tillman, ostensibly campaigning for Bryan, chose to include offensive remarks in a Michigan speech, thereby leaving to Bryan the well-nigh impossible task of recomposing the wounded feelings.

Bryan sought out the Negro community through the Negro press, most of whose owners and editors were friendly to his cause. He and Democratic aides were in close touch with diverse Negro organizations, each politically alert and skillful. He was enormously aided by the United Colored Democracy of Greater New York and its efficient local proselytizing campaign. The 1900 convention of the Negro National Democratic League, with twenty-eight states and the territories represented, was the largest of its kind ever assembled. A delegation of its leaders worked out with Bryan the details of ambitious plans to increase the numbers of Negroes voting Democratic. Other groups of Negroes journeyed to Lincoln to pledge their support. One of Bryan's happier campaign days was a meeting with a delegation headed by Bishop J. Milton Turner, minister to Liberia in the Grant administration. Turner and his followers stressed their dissatisfaction with McKinley's policies and predicted an upsurge of Negro votes for Bryan, as did W. P. McAllister, president of the Afro-American Protective League, who confidently predicted the support of "free thinking Negroes."

The organization on which Bryan was most dependent—the national Democratic Party—succumbed again to the major defects that had plagued it in 1896. Once more Bryan had to wage a campaign desperately short of funds. Chairman James K. Jones daily and accurately portrayed the national committee's acute poverty. "You are aware," he wrote to a donor, "that our committee is very seriously handicapped by the want of money with which to defray the current expenses of the campaign. We are very grateful for your liberality in sending us a check." So bare was the party cupboard that speakers who took off substantial time from their normal employment could not be compensated, for there was no speakers' fund worthy of the name. Expenses usually were reimbursed, but one of the busiest of the Democratic speakers, Bourke Cockran, was so appalled by "the meagre treasury" that he declined even this proffer.[25]

As in 1896, Bryan again stressed the distribution of great quantities of literature expounding his views. Imperialism and trusts, unfortunately, produced no master chronicler with the skill and popularity of "Coin" Harvey, but Bryan did enjoy the aid of the fully matured journalistic talents of William Randolph Hearst. The flamboyant Hearst established the Chicago *American* and at last gave Bryan what he had craved so long, a friendly newspaper in the city that Bryanites regarded as the country's political center. The campaign was not long under way when Hearst decided to prepare and publish a campaign book, to be illustrated by his master cartoonist,

Homer Davenport, who knew his finest artistic moments when he took out after Mark Hanna with pen and ink.

Special pamphlets prepared by the national committee and runoffs of Bryan's speeches were funneled to the Democratic clubs whose central function was to nurture citizen interest in the campaign. Bryan, who banked heavily on the clubs, called for a "great civic army" in which "every citizen should be a politician." Let Democratic clubs be organized "in every city, town, village, and precinct in the United States." The omnipresent Hearst was the aggressive, enterprising president of the national association of the clubs, and his factotum, Max F. Ihmsen, was its secretary.[26]

The diffusion of Bryan literature and Bryan sentiment was aided by a variety of magazines and specialized journals that were invaluable as counteragents to the predominant hostility of the national press. The Commercial Travelers' and Hotelmen's Anti-Trust League, for example, provided to its vast membership 100,000 copies of *Talkative Facts* with "up-to-date arguments from a travelman's point of view" on the trust evil. From such readings, the league's president expected his members to become "travelling evangelists" for Bryan's cause as they trudged around the nation with their sample cases, bringing both merchandise and a political message.

To spur the growth of Democratic clubs, James K. Jones employed the *National Watchman,* originally a silver paper but now devoted to all issues and published by the Democratic National Publishing Company. Jones developed a plan by which 100,000 names were collected from Democratic national and Congressional committees, and these were grouped to include a leading Democrat, Populist, and Silver Republican in each precinct. This trio was responsible for organizing a Democratic club and bringing together local people to discuss, under its auspices, articles and editorials of the *National Watchman.* Local folk would pay a subscription fee for the paper, which already circulated in every state. Jones confidently looked forward to the development of a body of informed and committed workers. In operation, Jones' plan achieved at best only a shadow of the success hoped for it. It produced nothing like the rash of silver clubs that had imparted so much vitality to the campaign of 1896. The handicaps of the Jones plan were not flaws in conception or management, but rather the absence of an inflammatory issue in 1900 comparable to silver in 1896.[27]

Bryan himself took a new step in campaigning by reciting portions of his Indianapolis acceptance speech for phonograph records which good Democrats, who might never see him perform personally, could hear and enjoy in the comfort of their homes. The phonograph industry was still in a technological state which required a megaphone attachment for Bryan to be heard, but proud Democratic professionals hoped that the record might become an effective weapon against McKinley.[28]

By every rational political calculation, Bryan could not hope to triumph unless he carried New York State. His road there was straight uphill. In 1896, McKinley won the state by 268,000 votes. Even worse was the presence, in New York State and local Democratic politics, of rival personalities and fiefdoms, productive of political strife waged with the ferocity of Kilkenny cats and the diabolical skill of Mephistopheles.

In 1900 the flames of political war in New York leaped high between Tammany boss Croker and upstate leader Hill, who were contending for the dominance of the state Democracy. In a Labor Day speech, Hill unloaded heavy salvos upon Croker and the Tammany machine. Although Hill's discourse was indirect, everyone—and, above all, Croker—knew the identity of the object on which it concentrated. After citing "the cohesive power of public plunder," Hill spoke at length of wealth amassed by "political plunderers," who first control a ward, then a city, and reach out to control a state. In a public interview, an outraged Croker denounced Hill as an "untruthful sneak," "liar," "coward," "trickster," and "peanut politician." [29]

Faced with the prospect that his campaign might be forgotten in New York while its local organizations were embraced in a colossal brawl, Bryan looked to a succession of peace emissaries. He counted heavily upon James K. McGuire, mayor of Syracuse, a suave diplomat and the new state chairman. Steadfast in loyalty to Bryan and his cause, McGuire labored heroically to restore order and plied Bryan with reassuring reports that newspaper accounts of the local strife were exaggerated and that eventual victory was certain. The national committee's top command, James K. Jones and William J. Stone, repaired on separate occasions to New York, and Norman Mack, the Buffalo leader, was also drafted to make peace.

The Hill-Croker struggle raged most intensely over selecting a Democratic nominee for governor. Bryan had more than a modest stake in the decision, for an attractive candidate might brighten his chances while a lackluster nominee could be the seal of his defeat.

Bryan's preference was Bird S. Coler, a youthful Wall Street broker, now comptroller of New York City, where he performed capably. Reformminded and an advocate of good government, Coler was resolutely antiTammany. When the Kansas City convention searched for a Vice Presidential nominee, Bryan had dispatched William Stone to sound out Coler on his availability, but the New Yorker at thirty-three proved too young. Now Stone came on his second mission to Coler and, during a stay in New York of some weeks, freely gave out to influential local politicians the opinion that Coler ought to be nominated for governor. Croker was not long in informing Stone, in his pugnacious way, that such talk was personally distasteful. Stone desisted but did not retract his statements.

The struggle passed to the New York State Democratic convention at

Saratoga. The Bryan camp momentarily rejoiced when David B. Hill threw his support to Coler. Croker countered by bringing forward the name of John B. Stanchfield, an examplar of the colorless machine hack. By an interesting coincidence, Stanchfield, who hailed from Elmira, was also Hill's former law partner. As the struggle rolled on, the influence of the Bryan camp shrank dramatically since its members could not afford to break with Croker, whose Tammany machine possessed incomparable facilities for getting out the vote in New York City. Eventually, Hill accepted Stanchfield as the nominee, and the opportunity to buoy up Bryan's New York campaign with an attractive gubernatorial nominee went up in smoke.[30]

In other states, Bryan's fortunes were also traversing a brambly path. From North Carolina, Josephus Daniels wrote in high alarm of incipient betrayal by Marion Butler, state fusionist leader in 1896, now seeking reelection to the U.S. Senate. "I know that Butler stood with us in 1896," wrote Daniels, "but he thought it was to his interest to do so. This year he intends to 'run with the hare and hold with the hound.' He would betray us to Hanna and Hanna to us if he could make it pay." Indeed, Butler did eventually abandon the Democrats and ally with the Republicans as the surest path to reelection.[31]

For all his experience on the rough seas of fusion politics, Bryan was put to new tests of rigor in 1900. Unlike 1896, when he had dealt with the single issue of silver, on which the Populists, Democrats, and Silver Republicans were tolerably united, Bryan now juggled three major issues upon which these parties were sharply divided. In 1896 all three parties had luxuriated in rising strength, productive of confidence in fusion and hope of victory. In 1900 the Silver Republicans and Populists suffered sharp declines and growing defections, and their mood at the fusion conference table was one of despair and sharpened concern for self-interest, making cooperation difficult.

Silver Republican leaders who hailed Bryan on silver were distressed by his anti-imperialism, for they and their followers were staunch nationalists and expansionists. Former Senator Lee Mantle of Montana abandoned the Silver Republican Party and returned to the regular Republican fold, proclaiming that silver was "a dead issue" compared to "maintaining the honor and dignity of the Nation, and the supremacy of its flag wherever it is rightfully floating." Senator William M. Stewart of Nevada found that while silver took him out of the Republican Party in 1896, anti-imperialism put him back in in 1900. He made his newest transition, grumbling about the "political ghosts and hobgoblins created by the feverish imagination of Mr. Bryan. . . . He raves about imaginary imperialism, which does not exist." To stem the Silver Republican desertions, Bryan stepped up his attention to the silver question in addresses to Western audiences.

If any path was easier for Bryan in 1900, it was that the Populists had nominated for the Vice Presidency Charles A. Towne, whose personality and political views were wholly different from their 1896 nominee's, Tom Watson. The combative Watson's social stands were considerably more radical than Bryan's. Towne, in contrast, was a close friend of Bryan and they were resolutely like-minded. The ever-accommodating Towne not only withdrew as the Populist Vice Presidential nominee but declared in a published letter that Stevenson was quite as good a Populist as he. The Populist national committee soon replaced Towne with Stevenson. The transition, which took place in a Chicago meeting, was not altogether smooth, for Marion Butler sought first to nominate a Populist in place of Towne and, that failing, to make no nomination at all. But Bryan was also on hand in Chicago, and it required little effort in the face of his robust strength to vanquish Butler.[32]

For Towne, this was not the end, but merely the beginning of an engrossing campaign. A brilliantly rousing speaker, he became the second busiest of the Democratic campaigners. His special mission was to serve as an oratorical antidote to Theodore Roosevelt, "that predestined and incorrigible eccentric," as Towne called him. Preceding or following the voluble Rough Rider and ladling out hearty, vivid oratory, Towne continued to act as though he were the nominee and executed a speaking schedule whose pace and competence would have been beyond the elderly Stevenson.

October. Bryan was midway in a campaign tour on the scale of 1896. Convinced that his strategy of shunning the stump was producing only a pallid response among the voters, he launched a tour of seventeen critical states. In this enterprise of five and a half weeks, Bryan journeyed some 16,000 miles and made approximately 600 speeches. His geographical strategy was to concentrate on an area bounded by the Mason-Dixon Line, the Mississippi River, and New York State. To New England and the South he gave scant attention, and in the West, he made only several speeches in Kansas and Nebraska, where his efforts were invested in the state contests.

Bryan again put in thirteen- and sixteen-hour days, speaking from dawn until well into the night to vast city audiences and to crowds who gathered with numbers and enthusiasm at hamlet crossroads. Most of the trip was done in day coaches. Bryan's chief departure from the common man's way of life occurred in West Virginia, where the Democratic national committeeman, John R. McGraw, provided a private car. But this aberration was suddenly halted at the Ohio border, where railroad authorities refused to attach the car to the regular train. The suspected perpetrator of this shabby discourtesy was H. H. Rogers, who headed both the railroad involved and one of the most notorious of the trusts against which Bryan was thundering, Standard Oil.[33]

A high point of the journey was Bryan's address at Madison Square Garden where friend and foe alike waited with interest to see whether he would repeat the fiasco of 1896. This time, to the delight of the thousands who filled every nook and cranny of the Garden and in the approving presence of the potentates of all the major New York factions, Bryan resorted to his usual speaking style—what appeared to be an extemporaneous speech but what in reality was worked out painstakingly beforehand in structure and key sentences.

Bryan talked of the trusts, imperialism, and labor's rights and needs. He dared to employ a favorite speaking device, the rhetorical question, put in a fashion that invites responses first from the audience and then the speaker. The result is a kind of spontaneity, not without risk. Bryan took his first gamble by ridiculing the Republican campaign slogan of the "full dinner pail" and noting that the Republican image of the workingman was "all stomach, without heart and head . . . and . . . like a hog. . . ." As a bridge to the broader Democratic conception, Bryan asked, "What does the working man want besides a full dinner pail?" Voices in the crowd cried, "A full coal bucket," "A full ice box." Shunning these untoward answers, Bryan launched into the Democratic program for the workingman, as it ranged from curbing the injunction to reducing the workday.[34]

By general consensus, the speech was a huge success. Bryan made no reference to silver, that most tender of Eastern sensitivities. His themes and language were temperate and bare of suggestion of class strife. In deft strokes, he portrayed Democratic-Republican contrasts. One party supported honest wealth, and the other predatory wealth. Republican leaders were "trust lovers," nurturing that evil institution under shelter of the tariff and by the distracting thesis of "the full dinner pail." Republicans were infatuated with marching armies, returning war heroes, and the splendors of empire. But Democrats "want the light of liberty to shine so brightly here that it will be seen around the world and everywhere inspire people." Eastern Brahmins, the most devoted of anti-imperialists, could not but be delighted by Bryan's performance.

The next day he spoke at Cooper Union, and on the crest of his heady triumph the night before and in the ebullience of the moment produced by a wildly enthusiastic crowd, Bryan uttered a single sentence, instantly productive of one of the worst blunders of his career. Its damaging effect was inflated by his sturdy, almost beatific image as a foe of evil, a lighter of the way to an earthly kingdom of moral and political cleanliness. In acknowledging the contribution of Tammany Hall to the success of his New York visit, Bryan moved to where its leader was seated on the stage, and holding his hand over the head of that square-faced man, he declared, "Great is Tammany, and Croker is its prophet!"

A volcano of political ill effects immediately erupted. Jacob Gould

Schurman, president of Cornell University and chairman of the first commission on the Philippines, declared that the homage to Croker made it impossible for the large class of independent citizens of New York to support Bryan, for it revealed "alliance with Tammany Hall, and . . . worship of its despotic leader. . . ." Theodore Roosevelt accused Bryan of seeking to vest Croker with control of New York State and to "bring it down to the level of infamy to which he has reduced the government of New York City." Carl Schurz, outraged as was many a fastidious anti-imperialist, exclaimed, "Bah! Wasn't it awful?" [35]

After this lapse, Bryan speedily reverted to carefully deliberated and moderately phrased speeches. He dwelled increasingly on the trust issue and treated imperialism largely in terms of the Philippines. His restraint contrasted with much of what the Republicans were doing. McKinley was again devoting himself to a front-porch campaign, leaving the orating to his slashing Vice Presidential candidate, Theodore Roosevelt. In speeches whose drastic opinions and cutting phrases sometimes made Bryan's orations seem like somber Emersonian lectures, Roosevelt attracted crowds and enthusiasm on a grand scale. Other Republican speakers spread roseate puff clouds, telling of prosperity at home—"the full dinner pail"—and victory in foreign war. "There is only one issue in this campaign, my friends," cried Mark Hanna, almost at Bryan's doorstep in Omaha, "and that is, 'let well enough alone.' " Republicans labored mightily in portraying Bryan as a many-splendored ogre. Secretary of War Elihu Root, in an uncharacteristic display of interest in the workingman, prophesied that Bryan, if elected, would follow his 1896 doctrines and put labor on a fifty-cent dollar. A Bryan running amuck in the Presidency would deprive the judiciary of its power and destroy the protective tariff. As corroborating evidence, Root pointed to Aguinaldo fomenting revolution in the Philippines, inflamed by the Kansas City platform and Bryan's campaign speeches.

"Wake up," Hanna cried to his lieutenants as Bryan's strong attack on the trusts made Hanna's invitations to the corporations for campaign contributions hard to resist. This almost-legendary titan of political money raising amassed a war chest of $5,000,000, compared to a fund of less than $500,000 for the national Democratic managers.[36]

As in 1896, the 1900 campaign was heavy with economic intimidation and coercion. To vote for Bryan, workers were flatly warned again, was to invite a mad bull into the china shop of prosperity. Manufacturing firms once more gave employees notice that operations would be suspended the morning after Bryan's election. Contracts were made conditional on Bryan's defeat. "I believe the time has come," declared Bryan after exposing one of the more blatant instances of intimidation, "when the corporation should be compelled to keep its hand out of politics, and tend to the business for which it was organized. I am not willing that the independence of the citizens should be destroyed."

In addition, Bryan was continuously denigrated and lamented by a variety of opinion makers of commanding stature in society, as when Archbishop John Ireland of St. Paul announced that he would vote for McKinley and Roosevelt to assure "the maintenance of the country's material prosperity, and of peace and good will between the several classes of its population. . . ." [37]

Bryan finished out the last week of the campaign in Nebraska in desperate frenzy, as though his political life depended on it. In fact, it did. The national Republican organization was intent not only upon Bryan's immediate defeat, but also upon his absolute political extinction. Should Bryan fail to carry Nebraska, and should the Democratic ticket of the state be defeated, he would be knocked out of the contention for another office as well—the United States Senate—which, Republican leaders were convinced, Bryan coveted, and elected to the Senate, he conceivably could run again for the Presidency.

Even while Bryan was campaigning in the East, there moved through Nebraska a parade of Republican luminaries, including Hanna, Theodore Roosevelt, Postmaster General Charles Emory Smith, several distinguished Senators, and Mary Ellen Lease, who had forsaken Populism for Republicanism. Their attacks on Bryan were unsparing. Hanna announced that Bryan was not fit to be elected constable, moving the latter to retort, "I am not running for that office. Constables are to punish little thieves and presidents to punish big ones." In the hot struggle, provocations abounded. A mighty trust magnate, Charles R. Flint, distributed a circular among Nebraska Democrats advising them to vote for McKinley. "I am glad that Mr. Flint has taken that position," Bryan told a crowd at York, Nebraska, "for I don't want him or any other trust magnate coming to the White House, if I am elected, and telling me what to do." [38]

The effectiveness of Bryan's Nebraska campaign was imperiled by rumors that if defeated for the Presidency, Bryan might have the state legislature elect him to the United States Senate. Utter consternation seized several Nebraskan quarters. Conceivably Bryan might depose his Populist friend William V. Allen and deprive that party of one of its last important offices. Conceivably, too, Bryan might push aside such deserving Senatorial aspirants as Gilbert M. Hitchcock and William H. Thompson. Hitchcock demanded that Bryan clarify the situation by announcing publicly that he would not accept a U.S. Senatorship "under any circumstances." Bryan promptly issued such a statement enabling his supporters to return to their strenuous campaigning for his election with renewed peace in mind.

Bryan interrupted his Nebraska efforts to journey to Chicago for three days of furious speechmaking. He finished out the campaign in Omaha, delivering, on the day before the election, nine speeches in the city, in various forums that included a park, a small and large hall, a tent, several theaters, and the Good Shepherd Fair atop the Schlitz roof garden.

For all the heroic inspiration of his effort, the atmosphere on the eve of the election dripped with pessimism. Betting stood at $4\frac{1}{2}$ to 1 in favor of McKinley. The discourse of insiders was disspiriting. Elwood S. Corser, secretary and treasurer of the Silver Republican national committee, wrote to his counterpart in the American Anti-Imperialist League, "The campaign is closed except the final payment of cash down by the Hannaites and in my judgment, we have failed to awaken the lethargic American conscience. . . . I pray that my fears are groundless." A reporter at Lincoln, making the rounds of the county headquarters of the several fusion parties, was struck by the prevalence of the darkest pessimism in what little conversation there was. The rooms in which these utterances were heard were dimly lighted, and the lack of illumination mercifully befitted the gloom.

But Bryan, at least in public view, was untouched by the inky mood. The battle for the Presidency, he announced on his final return to Nebraska, has been fought and won. Money and intimidation may have deprived him of victory in 1896, but they could not control the outcome "this time." In 1900 voters were "angry rather than fearful." [39]

The most precise similarity of 1900 to 1896 was the scene at Bryan's home on election night: the extra telephones and telegraphs jangling and tapping, the omnipresent reporters, the solicitous presence of old friends, and Mary presiding over the hubbub with grace and quiet humor. Bryan's brother Charles, his former law partner Dolph Talbot, his secretary and aide-de-camp of the Spanish War William F. Schwind, his staunch old political ally cowboy Jim Dahlman were on hand, and Mary was attended by Mrs. Charles Bryan and Mrs. Dahlman. Conversation and laughter were easy. The tension of the election was as alien to this gathering as the devil himself.

The first returns from Poughkeepsie, New York, a heavily Republican community, gave McKinley a majority of 1,722. This small number, said Bryan, was encouraging. Bryan and his friends were further heartened when Norman Mack telegraphed to report that McKinley's majority in upstate New York was one-fourth of what it was in 1896. The good tidings suddenly stopped, like the turning off of a faucet. Thereafter the dispatches became increasingly discouraging, and by late evening and well before midnight it was clear that Bryan had been defeated.

In confronting this second rejection by the people, whom he loved and whose judgment he revered, Bryan was composed, confident, and cheerful. One by one the reporters who had followed him through the campaign approached to say farewell. For them, Bryan had a slight joke, a kind word, or an apt epigram. Despite the apparently irreversible result, Bryan declined to make any public comment on the election. The next day he conceded in a public statement and sent a telegram to McKinley: "At the close of another Presidential campaign it is my lot to congratulate you upon a second victory." [40]

Republican propagandists and the anti-Bryan press inflated McKinley's new success into a "popular landslide." It was in fact anything but that; McKinley's victory in 1900 was not substantially larger than in 1896. In 1900, McKinley received 292 electoral votes, and Bryan 155, compared to McKinley's 271 electoral votes in 1896 and Bryan's 176. McKinley gained about 5 percent of the total electoral vote. The increase of McKinley's popular vote was merely 1 percent, rising from 51 percent in 1896 to 52 percent in 1900 with a plurality of 886,000. In net result McKinley gained a little more than 100,000 votes, and Bryan lost approximately 150,000. Bryan carried the Southern states (Alabama, Arkansas, Florida, Georgia, Louisiana, Mississippi, North Carolina, South Carolina, Texas, and Virginia), border states (Kentucky, Missouri, and Tennessee), and most silver states (Montana, Idaho, Nevada, and Colorado). Nebraska forsook him, and the Republicans captured both state senatorships, casting a grave shadow over his future power. McKinley carried all the states he had won in 1896, except Kentucky, and six that had gone to Bryan (Washington, Utah, Kansas, Nebraska, South Dakota, and Wyoming. Bryan also lost the one electoral vote he had won in California in 1896). Though Bryan carried New York City by 30,000, he lost the state by 145,000, a significantly better showing than in 1896. In New York, Bryan ran behind the state ticket, but in Nebraska he exceeded it. Compared with 1896, Bryan made large gains in the East, most impressively in Massachusetts, where the anti-imperialists enjoyed their foremost strength. Much of Bryan's Eastern gain is attributable to the return of gold Democrats to the party. McKinley's greatest gains were in the Far West, where imperialism, focused as it was in the Pacific, enjoyed high favor.

In his own postelectoral analysis, Bryan attributed his defeat to three major causes: the war, "better times," and Republican money. The nation was luxuriating in victory and newly won empire. It was prosperous, and the grim days of the Cleveland depression were all but forgotten. In the contest between the heart and the stomach, the latter won. Champ Clark, a young Missouri Congressman and ardent campaigner for Bryan, gained a preview of the outcome while pleading with a rural audience to reject the ways of immoral imperialism. As he rose to a fine oratorical pitch, a farmer called out: "Well, I guess we can stand it, so long as hogs are 20 cents a hundred."

But Dr. H. K. Jones of Jacksonville, Illinois, guardian of Bryan's college days, saw a deeper cause. Bryan and his campaign, Jones was impressed, were ahead of the times. The American people suffered an immaturity, a lack of moral resource fit for their obligations at home and abroad. ". . . as a people," wrote Dr. Jones, "we are in our teens yet, and are but entering the experience, nationally, that 'the love of money is the root of all evil' . . . the love and worship of the God Moloch—the love and worship of the power and dominion of wealth. We have thus been enticed and led astray from the worship of the God of Our Fathers, but—not yet reached God's time for the sense and the smart and the retribution of transgression—the bitter dregs of the cup we have taken. . . ."[41]

Bryan again suffered badly from a merciless smear campaign. Republican orators, prestigious citizens, and the press—all poured out abuse. With the exception of Hearst, the press lords were almost unanimous in their hostility. Gross cartoons, envenomed editorials, unabashedly slanted news articles moved like an endless avalanche upon Bryan. In the various portrayals of him and his movement, he was represented as a demagogue, an officer in Aguinaldo's army, a fakir, a Janus-faced politician, a blatherskite, a quack doctor, the chief of anarchists. To be a Bryan follower was to be demented, a ne'er-do-well, and a sure sign of financial indebtedness.

Much was made of Bryan's "wealth." He was widely represented as a politician who inveighed against plutocracy, but who used politics to become a plutocrat himself. Bryan was forced to deny these glowing accounts of his economic well-being. Acknowledging that since 1896, he had made money from his book *The First Battle* and the Chautauquas and other lecturing, he added, in a partisan counterthrust: "What I have made has been made from people who came because they thought they got what they were paying for, but if I had been the attorney of the Standard Oil trust, like a Republican Senator from Nebraska, no Republican paper would have condemned me for making money." Bryan's actual worth at this time was probably about $20,000, chiefly in real estate. Although his book was profitable, he gave away $17,000 from its royalties, and his contributions to churches and charities were large, as they always were in his good earning years.[42]

In defeat, Bryan paid a price customary for a loser. He had to face a heavy tide of letters and telegrams variously bearing despair, commiseration, and resurgent hope. "I write from the battlefield," reported Elwood S. Corser, "sore and defeated. It seems to me that the American people have passed under the yoke, and are now committed to a plutocratic imperialism. . . . We had magnificent leadership in our presidential candidate." William A. Croffut, secretary of the Anti-Imperialist League, observed, "It seems now as if the country was given over the carnage and plunder—to blood and ashes . . . has not our 'laboring man' joyfully fitted their necks to the yoke? And will they not be made to bear it yet? 'Ephraim is wedded to his idols.' " [43]

Though political storms burst upon his head, though opponents sprang fierce maneuvers and hurled cruel epithets, though electoral defeat crashed upon him, Bryan endured a vision of cheerful serenity and unfaltering optimism. Despair and anxiety were utterly alien to his character. He seemed to put them behind him when he abandoned his legal career and its uncertainties for the greener pastures of politics. He loved politics as he could never love any other vocation, and in it he found fulfillment for his rare oratorical skills and gifts of leadership. To the demands of politics—the arduous campaigning, the danger of defeat, the explosion of new issues—Bryan responded brilliantly. His extraordinary physical strength and endurance outmatched the most rigorous campaign, and his genial extroverted presence charmed the crowds and party workers. The Christian principles absorbed at his father's knee and reinforced by his education and youthful experiences gave him ample anchorage to cope with every variety of new political experience.

Bryan possessed a sense of identity as distinct and resolute as the rock of Gibraltar. Spurred by the conviction that he was doing God's work, he dealt creatively with the world of politics and applied his talents with volcanic gusto. But there was a danger for the confident young politician who was fast becoming an older politician. Satisfied as he was with himself and favored with an absolute minimum of anxiety, would he change sufficiently in his attitudes and perceptions with advancing years as the world around him changed?

20. A Divided Party

American politics, in their customary workings, relegate one, such as Bryan, who has been twice defeated for the Presidency to a place of honorable neglect. With his proved capacity for defeat, his further candidacy for the top office is unwanted. His voice will be heard with respect, but not heeded. It is difficult for him to run for lesser office, and if he does and is defeated, he is affixing another, more final seal of doom to his political future. The more worn and the immensely more comfortable course for the twice-defeated Presidential candidate finds him moving into a well-cushioned place in private life, preferably in a respected law firm or business corporation. He rounds out his working years in well-paid anonymity.

As a consequence of his second defeat, Bryan became subject to something of these temptations. He was offered the post of editor in chief of a major magazine with such alluring trimmings as a $25,000 annual salary, 100,000 shares of stock, and a house in New York City valued at not less than $50,000. A group of well-intentioned friends, including O. H. P. Belmont and Dr. Rosser, put before Bryan a plan to organize a syndicate to establish or purchase an outstanding life insurance company, with Bryan as its president. The lucrative dignified position would enable him to face the future with his now substantial family without a shred of concern for money.

To these good friends, Bryan expressed a fitting gratitude, but he had to take his cue, he explained, from the psalmist David: "My heart is fixed, oh God! [*sic*] My heart is fixed." "Our party," Bryan said, "is in much more need of defenders now than if it had been successful at the polls, and I am deeply devoted to the principles and in the work I am trying to do, as long as I am able to see progress and maintain my family in decency and comfort." There were other good reasons for Bryan to heed the counsels of David. At forty years of age, he was moving into the prime of life. The crowded years of demanding political work had made no dent in his enormous resources of strength and endurance. Above all, he commanded a greater cohesive following and was a stronger influence for social progress at this moment than any other American political leader. There was no apparent figure prepared to succeed him at the head of his legions for social justice. To abandon his followers now would be a cruel act of callous self-interest. "We have lost two battles," wrote Altgeld, "but the war is still going on and you are still the idol of our people."

If Bryan chose to remain in political life, both his friends and his enemies nourished a sprightly interest in the framework and terms within which he would participate. In a speech to the Jefferson Club of Lincoln, gathered for its annual banquet on December 26, he presented a more positive statement of his plans, in developing his topic, "Principles Live." Officeholding, he said, "should not be an end, but the means for the accomplishment of a purpose." Whether he would be a candidate for office again he could not foretell, but he would be "content if it is my lot to aid in the triumph of the principles while others enjoy the honors and bear the responsibility of office." The principles for which he had fought still lived. An election—a mere event—does not change principles: "It only determines what principles shall be for the time being applied." [1]

Bryan's Lincoln speech presaged the gigantic effort he mounted over the next four years to maintain both his principles and his person in public view. Principles must be carried by a human vessel, and in the Bryan political order there was but one oracle—himself.

Day in and day out, he kept himself in the national press, accumulating a footage that rivaled the space accorded McKinley and his successor, Theodore Roosevelt, who was also a glutton for publicity. The clamorous Roosevelt had been thrust into the Presidency after the beloved McKinley was assassinated at the Pan-American Exposition at Buffalo on September 6, 1901. At the Temple of Music, among the hundreds who passed to greet him was the anarchist, Leon F. Czolgosz. As McKinley extended his hand, Czolgosz fired two bullets into the President's body from a revolver concealed beneath a handkerchief in his right hand. The President slumped forward, gasping, "Am I shot?" When the crowd seized his assailant, McKinley implored, "Let no one hurt him." On September 14 the President died.

The assassination of McKinley deeply grieved Bryan, and immediately upon learning of the dreadful deed, he declared in a public statement that "the grief of personal friends and close political associates may be more poignant but their sympathy is not more sincere than that extended by political opponents. . . ." Since the assassin was a professed anarchist, a breed that Bryan's detractors were given to identify him with, a leading Midwestern newspaper was not long in laying at his doorstep a share of the responsibility for the murder. ". . . if Colonel Bryan and others of his stripe had not made so many speeches stirring up class hatred and misrepresenting the government, the tragedy might not have occurred." Well before this attack, Bryan condemned the anarchism of the assassin in noting: "Free governments may be overthrown, but they cannot be reformed by those who violate the commandment, 'Thou shalt not kill.' Under a government like ours, every wrong can be remedied by laws. . . . Anarchy can be neither excused nor tolerated here." [2]

Bryan commanded the attention he wanted for himself by several trusty expedients. He was an inveterate giver of speeches on major party occasions and against backgrounds that maximized the public attention accorded them. The birthdays of the party heroes, Jefferson and Jackson, found Bryan invariably occupied in devoted commemoration in a large city with a headline-making address, delivered at a dinner with hundreds, if not thousands, of fellow celebrants present.

Sometimes what he said on these occasions was heightened by an accommodating backdrop of local affairs. Bryan, who never missed rendering up a Labor Day speech, enjoyed the advantage of a tailor-made locale at Kansas City in 1901. Preceding his address was a parade of 8,000 union members, with the marchers of each union wearing a distinguishing uniform made by girls of the Garment Makers' Union locked out by their employer in a current labor-management dispute. In the wake of a long strike, the girls had founded their own cooperative factory, and the uniforms were a handsome token of their craftsmanship. A striking feature of the parade was the Hod Carriers' Union represented by 225 Negroes wearing white shirts and black caps and led by a Negro band whose syncopated tunes delighted the street-lining crowds. Bryan's carriage was at the head of the line, followed by a tallyho coach filled with girls dressed in white who had founded the cooperative factory.

In this atmosphere of confident solidarity and jubilation, Bryan could develop bold themes from his chosen Biblical text: "Muzzle not the mouth of the ox that treadeth out the corn." Though every decade revealed a greater production of wealth, he argued, the men who produce it "have less to show for it." For redress, he said, labor must seek legislation assuring equal justice before the law. Labor's best weapon, the strike, was "weak and insufficient," but, "If the laboring men are half as active on election day as they are in the enforcement of their strikes they would wield a force that would right the evils which beset them. . . ." Bryan warned labor not to heed the suggestion of some who counseled it that it divide profits with the trusts. This, he said, would be like "permitting a man to rifle your pockets and then offer to divide the proceeds with you. . . ." Labor must ally itself with another natural resister of the trusts, the farmer, and Bryan mixed into this advice the spice of self-interest by observing that "when the farmers can no longer pay trust prices, then there will be no more demand for the products of your toil and you can make no wages." [3]

Kept well posted by emissaries and watchers across the jumbled political land, Bryan revealed a knack of showing up in the right political place at the right political time. When the Cuban relief bill suddenly foundered in Congress because of a burst of indifference by the House Democratic leadership, Bryan ignited support among his good House friends, and the measure was quickly saved. He was adept at converting a newsworthy observation another notable made to his own attention-catching advantage. When president Arthur T. Hadley of Yale warned that "We shall have an Emperor in Washington within twenty-five years" unless public sentiment was stirred against the trusts, Bryan offered that the evil which Hadley feared was already existent, that he long had deemed and called McKinley "an Emperor," thanks to the administration's devotion to imperialism.

Theodore Roosevelt, both as Vice President and President, with his glorification of the strenuous and the soldierly life, provided the occasion of many a Bryanesque moral lecture. When Roosevelt advised the cadets at West Point that "A good soldier must not only be willing to fight, he must be anxious to fight," Bryan accused Roosevelt of preaching "a bloody and brutal gospel of imperialism. . . . The Ten Commandments and the Sermon on the Mount will be discarded and the yellow back novel substituted. . . ." A prominent gold Democrat, after noting for some time the high and imposing crest of attention Bryan enjoyed in the nation's newspapers, observed: "If the press of the country would not mention the name of William J. Bryan, the Nebraskan would be as dead as a doornail, politically, in less than three months." [4]

Bryan's chief occupation after his 1900 defeat was public lecturing, a pursuit that continued to bear both political and economic fruit. His tours in one summer took him to such varied locales as Watertown, New York; Philadelphia; Norfolk, Virginia; Monteagle and Union City, Tennessee; Bowling Green, Kentucky; and Madison, Indiana. He was a favorite with college audiences and made appearances at Harvard, Princeton, the universities of Wisconsin and Michigan, and a host of smaller colleges. In academic quarters, he was received with courtesy, as well as curiosity. Sometimes the lecture most in demand was a critical moral essay on contemporary public affairs. A favorite soon after Theodore Roosevelt took over the Presidency was "A Conquering Nation," which reflected Bryan's growing concern over the rampant militarism manifested by Roosevelt's popularity and his lusty trumpeting of the military virtues. [5]

No other political leader, not even Roosevelt, was on such continuous and intimate terms with a vast national following. In fact, no other American political figure, before or since Bryan's time, has enjoyed such a relationship. His repeated crisscrossing of the country enabled him to keep in touch with the latest efflorescences of public opinion and to gauge its receptivity to new issues. The tours that wound through the cities, towns, and countryside were in effect a continuous political visitation, enabling him to fortify his myriad political friendships and acquaintances while receiving an honorable income.

Since Bryan interlarded interviews with local political leaders with his lecture appearances, his life on circuit was given to long workdays and to bizarre hours dictated by railroad schedules. Not without cause, Willa Cather was impressed that Bryan "takes no care of himself," yet "his vitality comes up with the sun and outburns the street arc lights."

Lecturing for Bryan meant countless meals at railroad lunch counters, where he must have set something of an all-time record for the consumption of hamburgers. It also meant countless adjustments of personal ways to a life spent for weeks on end in railroad travel. In the summer, he shunned a linen coat because it soiled so easily and adopted the more practical alpaca which became his trademark. He was given to white clerical ties since they laundered and could be carried easily. He wore square-toed shoes in a day of pointed toes, because in boarding trains on the run, as he often did, he was less apt to stub his toe. Bryan coped with the laundry problem by carrying in his gripsack two or three dozen soft shirts. Handkerchiefs posed a special difficulty. Bryan, while declaiming, would usually have a block of ice before him, on which lay an oversized handkerchief. Occasionally, he would stop and apply it to his face and forehead. Between applications, on hot days, he comforted himself with a large palm-leaf fan. When his handkerchief stock ran low, he replenished it with the cheap cotton squares hemmed on a sewing machine. Although generous to many charities and to the comfort of his family, Bryan treated himself with parsimony and self-denial. He did not indulge in the expensive dress his rising income permitted. He had no rings or scarf pins; he was no frequenter of expensive hostelries and restaurants. His tastes were plain and his needs few. His single luxury was his shoes, made to order, of the best leather, but their style was simple and always the same.[6]

Bryan's lecturing was supplemented by a companion endeavor equally suited to keeping himself and his doctrines before the public. He was editor in chief of a newspaper, not as the hireling of a press lord but as proprietor. Published weekly and titled *The Commoner*, the paper was an immediate success. Selling for one dollar a year, *The Commoner* had 17,000 subscriptions before the presses began to turn, and additional subscriptions and newsstand sales pushed the first issue beyond 50,000. In *The Commoner's* first editorial, Bryan avowed that the purpose of this new journalistic venture was "to aid the common people in the protection of their rights, the advancement of their interests, and the realization of their aspirations." As he had in his political campaigning, Bryan accorded a wide inclusiveness to his concept of the common man. The range of humanity in this heaven-blessed classification included "the rich man who has honestly acquired his wealth and is not afraid to entrust its care to laws made by his fellows," and excluded was the poor man "if he fawns before a plutocrat and has no higher ambition than to be a courtier or a sycophant."

The Commoner, which began as an eight-page paper and was soon enlarged first to twelve pages and then to sixteen, was published in a commodious but cluttered building on South Twelfth Street in Lincoln. *The Commoner* was blazoned across the upper half of the street-side window, while the lower half, to afford privacy, was covered with a modified fleur-de-lis. *The Commoner* was, from its very first copy, which was sent to Senator James K. Jones in an affectionate gesture, in the fullest sense a family paper. Its best space was given to expositions of Bryan's political views, editorials set forth his opinions, and his speeches were fully reported. Over the years, the issues of *The Commoner* constitute an encyclopedia of Bryan's positions on every issue of significance that emerged, either by its own force or with his help. A favorite department was "Current Topics," little moral and political essays whose viewpoints were not attributed to Bryan but were hardly ever inconsistent with his preferences. A home department covered a gamut of activities from sewing to cooking. Useful articles and helpful hints abounded not only for mother and daughter, but for father, husband,

and son. There was a busy "Query Box," as well as an endless procession of delectable recipes for items such as strawberry Bavarian cream and gooseberry jam. Like other journals of its type, *The Commoner* carried a "News of the Week," a brief summary of the world's important news, and a "Weekly Press Forum," which corralled editorial opinion from other papers.[7]

After *The Commoner*'s initial issues, Bryan played a removed role in the paper's daily operation. His forte was writing editorials, and these he supplied to the extent that his lecturing and travel permitted. *The Commoner*'s regular staff had to be prepared for the frequent eventuality that an editorial promised by Bryan might not arrive. The chief managerial responsibility for *The Commoner* was carried by Bryan's younger brother, Charles. "Brother Charley," as he was known, had always been close to "Will," his elder by seven years, whom he revered. In the 1896 campaign, Charles had given up his job as a traveling man for an Omaha wholesale house to help rescue his brother from an avalanche of correspondence. For a time Bryan received some 3,000 letters a day, and Charles passed the year of 1897 answering them. Thereafter, he, with brother-in-law Tom Allen, devoted himself to Bryan's political needs. Possessed of an extraordinary capacity for self-subordination, practical and scrupulous in detail, Charles took easily to politics, where he was invaluable with his encyclopedic memory of names and faces and his skill in overseeing political machinery. A big man with the bald Bryan dome and piercing eyes, restless and quick in speech and movement—his hands were never still—Charles was credited with being more practical in politics than Bryan. Like his brother, Charles had a solid reputation for combativeness. A reporter of the Albion, Nebraska, *Argus,* a Democratic paper, said of him, ". . . people will find no dove of peace nestling about him. . . . He knows politics like an open book and believes that all is fair in politics as in love."

Charles oversaw the myriad administrative details of subscription lists, printing schedules, layouts, and a score of other tasks. Both he and Mary contributed editorials on a wide range of political questions. Richard L. Metcalfe, an editor of the Omaha *World-Herald,* was a busy contributing editor and later joined *The Commoner* as associate editor. The Home Department was handled by Helen Watts McVey, a journalist of national reputation specializing in home subjects.

One of the favorite departments was "Whether Common or Not," a blend of jokes, verse, and wise saws, by the elfin-spirited Will Maupin. Born in Missouri in 1863 and educated in its public schools, Maupin served his journalistic apprenticeship with the *Holt County Sentinel* of Oregon, Missouri, and moved on to the editorship of several county journals. His path soon led to the editorial staff of the Omaha *World-Herald,* and like his close friend Metcalfe, he eventually moved to *The Commoner.*

Maupin's homely, uncomplicated verse is in no danger of slipping into the poetry anthologies. But it often carried a social message, luminously reflective of Bryan's own views, and found its best expression when it dealt with children, to whom Maupin was sensitive and devoted, having lost a daughter and son in their young years in an age of high child mortality. One of Maupin's most popular poems was "Whip Behind," pointedly Bryanesque in sensitivity and viewpoint:

> . . . [the] meanest man on earth is the one who, when a little lad
> hitches his sled to a waggon "always whips behind.": God bless
> the man who's kind enough
> To smile and look ahead; Who never growls because a boy
> Hooks on a little sled.
> May health be his, and length of years,
> And may he fortune find.
> For nothing is too good for him
> Who never whips behind.

Maupin's verse was often openly directed at the social evils Bryan inveighed against in his speeches. Typical of Maupin's poetical lancer's charge is "Protected":

> Mary had a little lamb
> Its fleece was thin and sickly!
> She vainly tried a tariff pill
> To make it come in thickly.
> The wool she from her pet lamb
> By Dingley law protected
> She sold the trust, but at a price
> Much lower'n she expected.

Maupin's column abounded in imaginary conversations and "modern definitions." One installment of "Modern Definitions," for example, offered the following: "Syndicate—$ and H-2-o; Trust—Legalized grand larceny; Assimilation—synonym of grab; Aggression—Refusing to be benevolently assimilated; Moral Code—Product of an elastic conscience; Infant Industry—a key to the public treasury." The invented conversations also cast a disapproving glance at selected arenas of turpitude in the nation's political life. "Hello, Boomerleigh!" one conversation went. "I thought you were holding down a seat in the Senate at Washington!" "Nope. Had a streak of bad luck." "How's that?" "Just as I got my legislators rounded up for a final vote my bank failed." [8]

The Commoner carried advertising unexceptionably observant of a principle that Bryan laid down from the beginning: that trust-made goods would be given no space in its pages. Although the growth of trusts made the maintenance of this prohibition difficult, Bryan never wavered. Advertising of liquor or tobacco and anything else "unfit for a family newspaper" was also strictly taboo. Bryan's devotion to principle probably cost him $200,000 a year in revenues. In the fashion of the day, advertisements of patent medicines were numerous in *The Commoner*—the kind where a little girl, applying a hair tonic, is able to grow luxuriant hair that reaches to her feet. *The Commoner,* which always exuded the air of crusading zeal, was given to promoting postcard campaigns. One of the earliest of these urged readers to send postcards to members of Congress demanding passage of a constitutional amendment calling for popular election of Senators.

Several expedients were employed to maximize the attention given in the country generally to *The Commoner*'s pages. The paper was not copyrighted, and newspapers were therefore free to reproduce anything appearing in it. Advance copies of important *Commoner* articles were furnished to the Associated Press and any interested journals. The arrangements, needless to say, harmonized with Bryan's own necessities for political publicity. Through *The Commoner* facilities, advance copies of his important pronouncements were distributed to the press sufficiently early for treatment in the news columns. New subscribers were wooed and won much in the style of political parties courting votes. Soon after his paper was launched, Bryan, actually brother Charley, working from his ample political files, moved to set up in each county of the nation "some good Democrat" to act as agent for *The Commoner*. From among the county agents, a state agent was chosen for each state. Within a year, the Bryan brothers' energetic salesmanship and low subscription rates built up a subscription list of 140,000, chiefly in rural areas.[9]

As editor and proprietor, Bryan was a model employer. His pay scales were 50 percent over prevailing wage rates, and he was a pioneer in observing the eight-hour day. Each year *The Commoner*'s birthday was celebrated with a party of all the employees at Bryan's home. There were short speeches, recitations, and singing, and Bryan in his remarks said that what pleased him most was that most of those present had been employed at the paper's first issue and that to the best of his knowledge no one had a grievance and everyone was happy and contented.[10]

The Commoner reflected Bryan's style of dignified homiletics, with strong moral themes applied to issues and the day's events. William Randolph Hearst, who belonged to a wholly different school of journalism, tendered some fatherly professional advice by urging the application of several expedients to enliven *The Commoner*'s pages, but Bryan always eschewed muckraking and sensationalism.

In the interlude between the dawn of 1901 and the Democratic national convention of 1904, Bryan advocated a variety of reforms in *The Commoner*

to advance popular government and social justice at home and peaceful
relations between nations. As he preached, the nation was moving into the
twentieth century, prosperous and confident. Even the farmer fared tolerably well. In the first decade of the new century, the prices of farm products
would increase by nearly 50 percent. The city worker continued to enjoy the
boom sparked by the Spanish-American War. Unemployment withered;
job security bloomed. Pittsburgh was underselling British steel in world
markets, and the nation exported more manufactured goods than it imported. Senator Albert J. Beveridge of Indiana dared proclaim, "The trade
of the world must and shall be ours." New York, it was predicted, would
soon become the world's financial center. Foreign visitors were impressed
with the hardy optimism and rushing pace of Americans, and the prevalence of material artifacts. "Life in the States," wrote a friendly English
visitor, Frederic Harrison, in 1900, "is one perpetual whirl of telephones,
telegrams, phonographs, electric bills, motors, lifts, and automatic instruments."

But America's mammoth production machine was attended with problems. The nation's fabulous wealth was sliding into relatively few hands.
Men who organized and administered the trusts, which continued to grow
at a rampant pace, were fantastically rewarded. Those who created the
United States Steel Corporation, according to a conservative magazine, received fees never equaled "from the beginning of the world. . . ." Politics
was an annex of business. United States Senators were servants of such
masters of capital as J. P. Morgan and Jay Gould and such captains of industry as Andrew Carnegie and John D. Rockefeller. Municipal corruption
was a contagion. The ethics of brutal, calculating business were the ethics of
politics. And the ethical code of an individualistic, agrarian society proved
ill suited to a highly industrialized and interlocking economic order. At the
base of society lived millions of Negroes and immigrants in wretched poverty.

The reform spirit, which in the nineties found its chief expression through
Bryan, now took on new shape and a broadened base. The wretched conditions of the urban poor pricked feelings of guilt in sensitive individuals
unaffected in the nineties. Innocence and indifference were superseded by
quickened concern for the underprivileged, for women and children, for the
immigrant, the Negro, and the Indian. The reform spirit, or progressivism,
as it became known, called for new standards of honesty in business and
politics, and overhaul of political machinery to make it more responsive to
the people. Progressivism rejected unbridled laissez-faire, demanded public
regulation, and valued strong government. Like Bryan's silver doctrine, progressivism had roots in religion and faith in man's capacity for improvement. Religion, especially Protestantism, was a major contributor to progressivism's humanitarian impulse. The older, pessimistic, otherworldly

Calvinism gave ground to doctrines stressing human improvement in this life and the incompatibility of social squalor and unscrupulous business tactics with Christian love. In many respects, progressivism was Bryanism adapted to industrial, urban America.

Just as Bryan was aided in the nineties by such authors as Henry George, Edward Bellamy, W. H. Harvey, and Henry Demarest Lloyd, so, in the new century, zeal for reform was being fired by powerful writers. Thorstein Veblen published *The Theory of the Leisure Class,* a brilliant attack upon "predatory wealth," the absentee landlord, and the idle rich. In *The Octopus,* the young novelist-reformer Frank Norris revealed the paralyzing pressure of the California railroads upon wheat farmers, and in *The Pit,* the malefactions of Chicago wheat speculators. By 1902–3, a group of journalistic muckrackers, as Roosevelt came to call them, were laying bare with inspired pens the muck of social evils. Lincoln Steffens launched his series of articles, "The Shame of the Cities"; Ida Tarbell wrote a piercing exposé of the Standard Oil Company. Other journalists joined the muckrakers' list.

In these first years of the new century the momentum for social reform was a tidal wave of many elements. It embraced a remarkable array of reform mayors, governors, and national leaders, Democrats and Republicans alike. Bryan was the principal national Democratic figure of the progressive faith, but beside him stood eminent Republicans, including President Roosevelt, who overcame an initial hesitancy, and the fast-rising Wisconsonian Robert M. La Follette. Gubernatorial zeal was supplied by Joseph W. Folk of Missouri, Charles Evans Hughes of New York, La Follette, and Hiram Johnson of California. In the cities, progressivism's shining stars were "Golden Rule" Jones of Toledo, Ohio, and Tom Johnson of Cleveland.

Who were the progressives? William Allen White said that Populism simply had "shaved its whiskers, washed its shirt, put on a derby, and moved up into the middle class. . . ." But while Populism was born of depression and was rural in its roots, progressivism was the offspring of prosperity and the city. Its leadership was recruited largely from the professional and business classes. Patrician and wealthy names appeared in its ranks: Du Pont, Spreckels, Morgenthau, Pinchot, McCormick, and Patterson.

Predominantly, the progressives of the early 1900's were the conservatives of the 1890's. Republican progressives had supported McKinley, and many Democratic progressives had backed the gold Democrats or ignored the 1896 election. In the new century they still disdained Bryan's monetary views, although they now accepted many planks of his old program. Except for his paramount issue of silver, Bryan, despite his electoral defeats, was enjoying an hour of vindication. His efforts to quicken social conscience, to awaken the people to wrongdoing and injustice, were yielding a sudden harvest. Men in the East, men in the cities, men in high places who were deaf to his importunings in 1896 and 1900 were at last alert and concerned. He had lost men's votes, but not their consciences.

Between Bryanism and progressivism, there remained significant differences. Segments of progressive thought venerated the strong public executive applying his talent and will for social improvement. "The world wants *men,* great, strong, harsh, brutal, men," wrote Frank Norris, "men with purpose who let nothing, nothing, nothing stand in their way." Men like Roosevelt and La Follette approximated Norris' ideal, but Bryan rejected it. Like his fellow Populists, he remained suspicious of the strong executive, advocated the single term to check his powers, and venerated the people and the popular assembly as the paramount sources of decision. Progressive leaders like Roosevelt and La Follette and, at a later day, Woodrow Wilson deemed themselves apart from the people and reflected the progressive credo that social advance occurs through the ministrations of a few great and good men. Bryan identified himself with the people; he was their servant, and they might accept or reject his work.

In the initial years of the new century Bryan advocated yet unrealized Populist planks calling for popular government. The reforms he championed largely coincided with pleas of a great wing of progressivism committed to pure democracy and belief in the efficacy of popular rule. For the sake of better, more popular government, Bryan urged a single term for the President, the popular election of Senators, and an end to lame-duck sessions of Congress. He hailed the growing movement to curtail the arbitrary powers of the Speaker of the House of Representatives and continued his fight to bar corporations from contributing to campaign funds. The initiative and referendum, the direct primary, the recall of judges he eagerly added to his list of causes. He proposed to banish stock speculation, establish guarantees of savings deposits to protect against bank failures, and to institute a postal savings bank. He would have the people rule through municipal ownership of utilities and afford them a better life through tighter railroad regulation and the building of good roads. He decried the exploitation of child labor, and he unreservedly supported those spokesmen of American labor who perceived in Asian immigration a threat to domestic labor standards.

In *The Commoner* in these years, Bryan faced the emerging questions centering on the place of the Negro in American life. Spurred by his moral principles and deep humanity, Bryan unshackled himself from many, although by no means all, of the constraints of his Southern roots. In *The Commoner,* he never failed to condemn the Negro lynchings that beset the nation as "atrocities that were inexcusable." When Virginia weighed a constitutional amendment stipulating that appropriations for Negro schools should be in proportion to the taxes paid by Negro people, Bryan wrote forcefully against the plan, which, he contended, violated the tradition of the states that education is paid for by general taxation, not on a basis of class.

Bryan sometimes decried the Northern tendency to lecture the South on race relations, holding that the problems of the two sections were wholly different. Bryan also entered a candid reservation to Theodore Roosevelt's attention-catching act in entertaining the distinguished Negro leader Booker T. Washington at dinner at the White House. "It is a grievous mistake," Bryan wrote, "to turn the Negro's thoughts from the substantial advantages of industrial, intellectual and moral progress to the unsubstantial promises of social recognition. The amalgamation of the races is not the solution of the race question, and that would be the logical result of social equality." Bryan saw the races as equal in rights "to life, liberty, and the pursuit of happiness," which for each should be protected "with jealous care." Educational advantages should be open to both races, and both should be encouraged to secure "all the mental discipline possible." [11]

Causes that Bryan later fought for in the national political arena were sometimes heralded years earlier in the pages of The Commoner. Well nigh two decades prior to his advocacy of the woman's suffrage amendment in his public speeches, Bryan in his editorials championed the cause of the "new woman." This woman, he contended, should not be limited to her ancient familial duties but should have her talents developed by education and the opportunity to apply her business and professional capacities. "The world," he wrote, "needs the brain of woman as well as the brain of man, and even more does it need the conscience of woman. . . ."

In these years, Bryan was articulating more fully and more precisely the random strands of pacifistic thought that outcropped in the tumultuous aftermath of the Spanish-American War. His utterances, in this new interval, would shape, if not control, his demeanor toward future war. The Commoner gave great play to two addresses on themes of war and peace. In one, a Thanksgiving address in 1903, Bryan argued that the world had reached a point in its progress, by which "today you cannot justify bloodshed except in defense of a right already ascertained, and then only when all peaceable means have been exhausted." Bryan summoned mankind to move from its admiration of the man who dies defending his rights to a higher, more noble moral ground. "There is yet to come," he predicted, "a greater man still— the man who will die rather than trespass upon the rights of another. Hail to the nation . . . that leads the world towards the realization of this higher ideal." [12]

In a widely noticed address to the Holland Society in New York City, Bryan outlined a new social order for people everywhere and the foundation of international peace upon which it must rest. This new order, he said, could not emerge from a conception of civilization "as measured by the mastery of the human mind over the force of nature." Rather, he contended, it must be defined "as a harmonious development of the human race, physically, mentally and morally." Of this trio of resources, Bryan deemed one more important and more elusive than the others. Physical perfection and intellectual training, alone or together, would be insufficient unless "the spiritual man will be considered and his welfare guarded." Not "the plutocracy of wealth" or "the aristocracy of learning," but "the democracy of the heart" was the key to world peace. Once let mankind achieve the glorious moment of universal love, and "We shall then arraign every evil at the bar of public conscience."

Both in his lectures and in his writings for *The Commoner,* Bryan increasingly applied to public problems his concepts of Christian ethics. Those who in his eyes committed the wickedest transgressions upon the people were the titans of the trusts and monopolistic wealth. Bryan rejected the rationalizings of an Andrew Carnegie or a Daniel Drew, who, while conceding that moneymaking suffered ignoble lapses, maintained it was justifiable and even holy when the wealth accumulated was spent for good causes. To Bryan it mattered not that the chief villain of his strictures, John D. Rockefeller, indulged in good works after acquiring his wealth by dark and evil acts. If only a few of the facts set out in Henry D. Lloyd's *Wealth Against Commonwealth* were correct, Bryan observed, "no criminal now incarcerated . . . for larceny has shown more indifference to human rights and property rights than this same Rockefeller. Does it lessen his sins that he has given liberally to churches and colleges? Nay, it exaggerates them, for he attempts to make others share with him the odium that his conduct merits." The worst effect that gifts from a source such as Rockefeller had, Bryan claimed, was that the recipients would fall under a "silencing influence." Time and again, Bryan averred that he had no quarrel with an honest accumulation of wealth or with its inheritance, but he condemned the process of building a personal fortune through a trust or private monopoly as "a menace to government and civilization." [13]

Bryan rejected, too, what he deemed a precondition to monopoly: the acquisition of privilege in public affairs by special interests. These interests, he contended, took money indirectly from the pockets of the taxpayers with government's sanction and even direct help. The trusts, the financial system, imperialism—all were the masks of this legitimized larceny. It was no cause for surprise that corporations spent money wildly to win elections. It was a small investment for potentially huge returns. Bryan offered the fullest exposition of his views in an address in Madison Square Garden in January, 1904, when he declared, "When I tell you that the first and most important object of government is not money-making or the extension of commerce or even the care of property, but rather the protection of human rights, I am not asserting an original proposition. . . . I am simply giving expression to a fundamental truth. . . ." [14]

With two Presidential campaigns behind him and their accompanying enrichment of his understanding of governmental processes, Bryan had come to definite conclusions concerning the priority and strength of the forces involved in the affairs of men. The most powerful of these forces were "principles." He interpreted his own experience and the possibilities of the future in the observation of his doctrinal hero, the popular historian and Navy Secretary of the Polk administration George Bancroft, that "It is alone by infusing great principles into the common mind that revolutions in human society are brought about. They never have been, they never can be effected by superior individual excellence." Bryan, holding Bancroft's mirror to himself, perceived that he had been twice nominated by the national Democratic Party not simply because of his own merit or talent, "but because of my advocacy of democratic principles." These principles, borne in the Chicago and Kansas City platforms, he expected to advocate "during the remainder of my life." New issues surely would arise, but established principles would settle them.

As his experience so amply revealed, there were also advocates in politics of bad principles. These, he contended, must never be surrendered to. "Yielding to a bad principle," Bryan wrote in a *Commoner* editorial, "because it seems triumphant is simply an easy method of avoiding labor and sacrifice. It is a complacent but unsound philosophy which teaches compromise with wrong merely because the enemy is strongly entrenched. No one has a right to assume that error will be permanently victorious." [15]

The test of good principles was whether they were "democratic" or conducive to the good of the people, in contrast with "bad principles" that contrived to feed privilege and profit only to a few. "Democratic principles" are established by open means, by reason, discussion, and truth. "Truth," wrote Bryan, "grows in the open field; the sunshine nourishes and strengthens it." The foremost sources of resistance to democratic principle, in contrast, are secrecy and deception. "The people have nothing to fear from open enemies," for their erroneous principles can then be easily exposed. "It is secret influence which is constantly corrupting government and securing special privileges for the few at the expense of the many. The man who advocates a thing which he believes to be good for the people as a whole has no reason to conceal his purpose, but the man who tries to secure an advantage which he knows to be beneficial to some class or a combination but hurtful to the public naturally and necessarily employs stealth." [16]

These were years when Bryan moved from the modest home in Lincoln to a handsome farm four miles from the city. In March, 1902, he celebrated his forty-second birthday by settling his family into a commodious barn on his extensive rural property for a few months until the spacious house was completed.

Fairview, as the new country estate of Bryan was called, fulfilled a boyhood dream. "A home of brick and stone had been in my mind from youth," Bryan explained to *The Commoner*'s readers, "I having inherited it, as it were, from my father." Just as Silas had provided Bryan with a rural manor in the Virginia style, where he could pass his boyhood, Bryan now provided a comparable princely setting for his family. William, Jr., already past twelve, was at an ideal age to luxuriate in farm life, and it was, as Bryan wrote, "pleasant for the rest of us."

Fairview was long abuilding. The ground on which the commodious house was situated was purchased in 1893. The then young Congressman Bryan, home in intervals between sessions, found relaxation, after poring over treatises on the intricacies of the money and tariff questions, by horseback riding in the verdant countryside outside Lincoln. Soon he was returning, repeatedly and unconsciously, to a little knoll which afforded a panoramic view of Antelope Valley. Bryan was intrigued with the frequently changing coloration of the scene, wrought by the successive plantings of several kinds of crops, and by the checkered patterns of corn and wheat fields and groves and pasturelands.

Sometimes, in good weather, Bryan repaired with his books and papers to this place to prepare his speeches for the coming Congressional session, and at lunchtime Mary pulled up in a buggy with their meal. Together they dreamed of a house there, and Bryan soon sought out the owner, purchased his five acres in 1893, and by purchases in succeeding years accumulated a holding of forty acres. Over the years, he set out orchards and shade trees. On October 1, 1901, Bryan, a sentimentalist who embarked on family ventures on the dates of significant family anniversaries, broke ground for his house on the day that was the seventeenth anniversary of his marriage and the fourteenth of his emigration to Lincoln.

But Bryan and Mary were not immune to the fate that befalls all parents, the growth and departure of their children. They had scarcely settled in their new home when their eldest child, the vivacious, articulate Ruth, left home for the world of study and action. After two years at the University of Nebraska, Ruth, now nineteen years old, set out for Chicago to work in Jane Addams' Hull House. Mary had long been interested in Miss Addams' pioneering social enterprise, and the eminent sociologist was a fervent supporter of Bryan. He and Mary rejoiced that the freethinking Ruth subscribed to their social views and was resolved to advance them.[17]

Bryan's entry into the role of country squire, although on a modest scale, brought the inevitable outcries from his even more comfortable sound money critics. Hostile newspapers carried accounts of Bryan luxuriating in sensationally growing wealth. One newspaper, allowing itself a generous margin for error, estimated that Bryan was worth anywhere from $150,000 to $500,000. It was but a short step to depicting Bryan as a demagogue and a sharpie, quick at turning evangelism for social justice into rich personal profit. In retorting to his detractors, Bryan estimated his worth in 1903 to be about $20,000. This was doubtlessly well on the conservative side, although it is unlikely that his worth was anywhere near the extreme figure of his critics.

The Commoner, because of its puritanical advertising policies and the paper's need for capital, rendered Bryan an annual income of only $5,000. In discussions of his worth, Bryan never acknowledged a specific sum from lecturing, his major source of income. But this, too, was shaped by ideological considerations that reduced its yield. As always, Bryan devoted a substantial portion of his earnings to educational, religious, and charitable purposes. The effect of his Presidential campaigns and his lecturing, he said, was an ever-rising number of outstretched hands beseeching his support for worthy causes.

A clue to Bryan's domestic well-being is found in his correspondence with his close personal friend, admirer, and political ally Philo S. Bennett of New Haven. A retired wholesale grocer experienced in personal financial planning, Bennett in the months following the 1900 campaign guided Bryan in investments of his savings. After extended painstaking correspondence, Bennett sank a little more than $5,000 for Bryan in government bonds. This, of course, was but a part of his savings, but it constituted an amount suggestive of an income and worth far short of the waist-high riches in which Bryan's detractors had him wallowing.[18]

Bryan's relationship with Bennett was a special one. To the comfortably situated Bennett, young Bryan was the hero of a righteous cause, whose welfare was worthy of his benefactions. After the 1896 campaign, Bennett gave Bryan $3,000 for his personal use, and after the venture of 1900 a smaller sum. Each gift was intended to reduce the personal financial loss Bryan suffered in the campaigns. Whenever Bryan journeyed to New York, Bennett visited him, and occasionally the Bryans were his guests in New Haven.

Late in May, 1900, during a sojourn in Lincoln, the amiable, hero-worshiping Bennett dictated his will to Bryan and appointed him its executor. From his total estate of nearly $300,000 he left $100,000 to Mrs. Bennett, $20,000 to Bryan to be administered to help educate poor children, and a special bequest that soon became the subject of a lawsuit and bad publicity. According to his bequest, Mrs. Bennett was to hold in trust for Bryan $50,000 to be used for purposes set forth in a sealed letter. The letter, addressed to "My Dear Wife," explained that the $50,000 was placed in a safety-deposit box in New York City and was to be given to Bryan "so that he may be more free to devote himself to his chosen field of labor," inasmuch as political work barred him from making money. Should Bryan not choose to use the money, the letter stipulated, he was to distribute it to educational and charitable institutions.

Nearly three years later, in 1903, Bennett died in an accident. He apparently had never apprized his wife and daughter of the will. Largely because Bennett left $20,000 to his mistress, Mrs. Bennett refused to apply the will's provisions in behalf of the two benefactors who were not members of the family, Bryan and the mistress. Deeming himself clean and blameless, Bryan entered suit in New Haven's Superior Court. Eventually, the case rose to the Connecticut Supreme Court. In the difficult situation, Bryan acquitted himself well by candidly describing his relationship with Bennett and rendering convincing testimony in a voluntary cross-examination.

The case was eventually settled against Bryan on the technicality that the letter concerning his $50,000 was inadequately identified in the will to justify its being incorporated by reference. Respected lawyers who subsequently studied the case agree that the courts erred. Meanwhile, the indomitable Bryan launched a countersuit to have the will and letter executed. He informed the court of his intention to use none of the $50,000 himself, but to distribute the entire sum to educational and charitable institutions. He sought not gain for himself, but the faithful performance of his good friend's plan and purpose.

Again the courts ruled against Bryan. On a vital point in the controversy he was nevertheless successful, for the courts found that in the will-drafting meeting at Lincoln he had not exercised any undue influence over Bennett. The worst light cast upon Bryan by the case was that as a lawyer he had acted with unlawyerlike indelicacy. He had served in the double capacity of counsel and legatee, a tandem arrangement barred, at the time, in some states, and at least professionally frowned upon in others. The heaviest losers in the case were Bryan's undying political enemies who approached the trial with lecherous expectations of seeing the anarchist from the Western prairie boiled in acid disgrace. The caldron was never lighted; the hostile press found precious little fuel for its headlines. Before many years, Mrs. Bennett came to regret the entire struggle and was thoroughly reconciled with Bryan.[19]

With the Bennett case behind him, Bryan looked with favor upon a proposal Mary had long been pressing: that this was an opportune moment in his career to journey to Europe, to observe its governments and policies, and in the leisure of sea travel to reflect upon the wild jumble of his full political experiences and consider his future course. Mary could not travel because she thought—erroneously—that she was pregnant. Nonetheless, she urged Bryan to undertake the journey with young William, who was now fifteen, in a rare opportunity for a major father-son venture.

In mid-November, 1903, Bryan and William left New York on the White

Star liner *Majestic.* He had decided so suddenly to take the journey that his name was not even on the passenger list. As he glided out of the great harbor, he wrote to Mary from his stateroom, "How I miss you, sweetheart. There is no one else in all the world to whom I can unbosom myself and tell all my plans and ambitions—no one who can be as you are a part of myself." Bryan and William landed at Liverpool and journeyed through England, Ireland, and Scotland and the countries of western Europe and Russia. As the twice-chosen candidate for President of the United States, Bryan was everywhere accorded the highest honors. Ambassador Joseph Choate, who had called him a Communist in 1896, gave a dinner in his honor, replete with England's top officialdom. He had a private interview with Prime Minister Arthur J. Balfour. He listened in Parliament to debates on the tariff, then an issue at high flame, and schooled himself in the young Labour Party's politics in discussions with John Burns and the party's imposing intelligentsia, Sidney and Beatrice Webb. Irish patriots regaled him, and throwing discretion to the winds, he proclaimed his support of home rule. In Scotland, Germany, and other western countries, Bryan was impressed with public ownership of utilities as a counterweapon to private corporate abuse.

Bryan, who left warm good feeling in his trail, proved highly popular with Europeans. His address in London on peace received high acclaim, and in a much-publicized meeting with the Russian czar, he impressed Nicholas II with his democratic ideas and ideals. For Bryan, the climax of his journey was a visit with Leo Tolstoy at his estate near the village of Yasnaya Polyana, about 130 miles south of Moscow. To the Henry Whites of the American embassy in London, Bryan had confided his eagerness to meet the Russian literary giant. Which of Tolstoy's books had impressed him most? Mrs. White asked. "Oh, I have not read Tolstoy's works," he replied, "but I have read a great many articles in the magazines and the Sunday newspapers about him." The Whites, who had dreaded their approaching luncheon with Bryan as a passage of utter boredom, were delighted by his solid goodness. Practiced in judging the denizens of their rarefied diplomatic world, they found that Bryan excelled as a talker more than as a listener and was better schooled in public affairs than in the arts and letters and history.[20]

The visit with Tolstoy was a success far beyond Bryan's most avid expectations. A sojourn originally scheduled for several hours stretched to several days. These men of literature and politics took long horseback rides and walks together through the rough countryside and against the cutting wind, all the while deeply engaged in conversation, thanks to Tolstoy's competence in English. Bryan eagerly probed his host's beliefs on passive resistance and found that in substance they remarkably paralleled his own conceptions of Christianity proscribing violence. The encounter with Tolstoy doubtless lifted Bryan a giant step toward the sturdy pacifism he was later to display in World War I. Bryan, at this juncture, had reservations about its practicality; the persuasive Tolstoy broke through the doubts.

For Bryan, Tolstoy provided a reaffirmation of basic tenets. Tolstoy, too, believed that "there is more genuine joy in living for others than in living upon others—more happiness in serving than in being served." In Bryan's and Tolstoy's eyes, love was the dominant power in the world, superior to force and selfishness or any other behavioral competitor. The sojourn at Yasnaya Polyana began a friendship that endured until Tolstoy's death in 1907. The Russian watched closely Bryan's ensuing struggles in the political arena, all the while exhorting him to "help the working people to enjoy the whole fruits of their toil." [21]

Bryan, being Bryan, tenacious of ideals and principles, possessed of infinite energy and superb oratorical skill, stirred no predictions that he would fade into the political background. The nice question confronting him was the form and substance of his future role in his party's affairs. The European visitation injected fresh elements into his national image. His dialogues with European rulers, his study of European governments and policies softened the stark lines of youth and immaturity, of Western parochialism so elaborately dwelled on by his detractors. By going to Europe, Bryan, like other politicians since his time, could appear to talk more authoritatively about the problems of America.

The contours of Bryan's new role were filled out sometimes by himself and sometimes by the press of political forces and events. Not surprisingly, he sounded the bugle of no retreat from the Chicago and Kansas City platforms. In 1901, in the railroad station of Roanoke, Virginia, on a July day heavy with heat, Bryan told a vast body of local citizens that the Democratic Party excelled at addition rather than subtraction. The party's duty was to advocate its adopted principles. "I am fighting on," he exclaimed, "not so much to win, for I would rather die fighting for right than win fighting for something else."

Bryan had to dispose of maneuvers and rumors linking him to candidacy for major office. When a leading newspaper suggested the possibility of his future national candidacy as early as 1901, he felt driven to declare: "I am not planning for another Presidential nomination—if I were I would not be editing a paper." But he did not shut the door tight. "If I ever become a candidate again," he added, "it will be because it seems necessary for the advancement of the principles to which I adhere, and that does not now seem probable." If not a candidate for President, then what of other prestigious offices—a U.S. Senatorship or the governorship? As the Nebraska's Democracy's best vote getter, Bryan was importuned to run for these offices by career politicians eager to ride his coattails. But since either race would risk defeat and banishment to the political netherworld, he declined.[22]

Bryan's chief preoccupation was his retention of control of the national Democratic Party. This filled the interlude from 1900 to 1904 with fierce and raucous combat between Bryan and his followers and the sound money Democrats. The struggle was not wholly of Bryan's choosing. Given the existing realities of power, his foes took the initiative. He controlled the national party structure; they were behooved to drive him out.

Their project brought together a band of forceful men of impressive political power. Grover Cleveland emerged from retirement at Princeton to give his blessings and encouragement to the venture. The most astute and practiced political lieutenants of his administration, William C. Whitney, Don Dickinson, Abram S. Hewitt, and Charles S. Hamlin rushed to the colors. Leading Democrats at the party's several major strongholds came, too: David Bennett Hill and Alton B. Parker in New York; Arthur Pue Gorman in Maryland; Carter Harrison and John P. Hopkins in Illinois; John G. Carlisle and Henry Watterson in Kentucky; J. Sterling Morton and Albert Watkins in Nebraska; Rolla Wells and David R. Francis in Missouri, among others. These hardheaded, practical men proposed to "reorganize" the party—that is, wrest its control from the deathly clutch of Bryanism.

But Bryan had formidable legions, too. His lectures and political speeches made vividly clear that his popularity had not diminished. He was still the hero of the "plain people" and the rank and file of his party. Major politicians supported him—doughty old warriors from the silver wars like Altgeld, Richard Pettigrew, J. C. S. Blackburn, and his Silver Republican friend, who had just become a Democrat, Charles A. Towne; rising new politicians like Blair Lee and Champ Clark; and those prestigious apostles of "good government" Mayor Tom Johnson of Cleveland and "Golden Rule" Jones of Toledo.

Bryan, too, resorted to pugnacious discourse as the struggle hardened. When the reorganizers spoke of running Grover Cleveland as their candidate in 1904, Bryan scoffed that the ex-President could not carry a single state and acidly described his sorry place in the party. Cleveland, Bryan said, was "a leader in the Hessian forces which had attacked the Democrats in the rear while the Republicans were attacking them in the front." Cleveland's Democracy, he added, was of the variety "which would make the waterlogged enterprises of the trust promoters seem bona fide and honorable." [23]

Bryan's verbal cannonading moved the reorganizers to employ in retaliation the sweet political talk of "harmony." For too many years, they contended, Bryan had sounded strident notes, fomented cleavage and dissent, and driven decent Democrats from the party. Let harmony now prevail and restore unity to a divided party. Bryan was quick to warn his followers of the dangers of the "harmony" theme: ". . . there is no condition more delightful to contemplate or to enjoy than 'harmony,' and there is no phrase more shamefully abused than 'harmony.' " Those now sounding the high note for Democratic unity provided a case in point. "Their promises and guarantees read like the advertisement of a sorceress, 'Estranged friends reconciled, lost property found and a happy and prosperous life ensured.'. . . No one should be deceived by this pretended desire for harmony. No process has ever been discovered for welding together into one harmonious party men who differ in conviction and desire the triumph of opposite principles." [24]

To Bryan, political issues were always moral issues, and politics was a battleground of moral struggles. He perceived the jumbled landscape of contentious politics not as a sprawling, confused canvas where meaning was difficult to untangle, but a scene that was stark and precise and readily interpreted. In the fashion of moral thinking, everything admitted classification. The behavior of men and institutions was either right or wrong, good or bad. These absolute categorizations followed the older religious patterns of thought and their absolute dichotomies between God and the Devil and demons and saints. In the religious style, too, Bryan perceived the outcomes of political struggles as largely foreordained. Just and righteous causes always triumphed. They might be temporarily rebuffed, as were the proposals he offered in his unsuccessful Presidential races, but eventually they prevailed. The time and energy expended in achieving the ultimate triumph were of no consequence against the noble worth of the cause.

Bryan accordingly rejected the nonmoral, nonreligious styles of thought which view politics as a conflict of causes and antagonists, none of whom may enjoy a monopoly of truth and right, which value compromise and consensus and acknowledge the uncertainty of the outcome and the merit of the result. Bryan did not see politics as an arena crowded with minor issues and causes, as well as occasional major ones, where small gains are made and futility often reigns. Instead, he entertained a heroic conception of politics. Whatever was done in politics was always important. Politics dealt with the foremost issues facing man, and it was a place where one such as Bryan could achieve greatness by mobilizing men to march in the armies of Good against Evil.

Bryan's moral emphasis was strongly imprinted upon his political style. His evangelical manner flamed with sincerity and was preoccupied with principles and goals rather than with plans and operating details. It was devoted more to promise than to action and often to broad, if not hollow, generalization. As is common with moral crusaders, Bryan's political endeavors sometimes appeared unsophisticated. Moral certitude left him poorly read in the growing literature of the social sciences and his arguments unfettered by its findings. It tied him to dogmas formulated early in his career whose abandonment was justifiable and would have been politically helpful. It made him reserved in his courtship of labor and it inhibited conciliation and compromise with the great body of gold Democrats whom he was prone to assign collectively to Evil.

Yet Bryan was not a moralist, pure and simple. He was, within limits, also a pragmatist. Although he spoke in moral terms, he could respond to the demands of the situation. He could persist in championing the hallowed cause of silver and simultaneously seek out and enter into alliance with Tammany Hall. He could damn imperialism but support the Spanish peace treaty, itself a vessel of imperialism, which he planned to reconstruct later. Bryan, this is to say, worked within the arena of national majoritarian politics. He succeeded in keeping the essences of his moral principles intact, while engaging in trading and in alliances with unclean partners. His extraordinary achievement was his steady success in keeping his moral causes high and dry above the lapping, impure waters into which he had to wade.

The presiding genius of the war against Bryan was that wily political field commander David Bennett Hill of New York. Hill's multipart strategy called for the crushing of Bryan's influence in New York, toward which a giant step might be made with the overthrow of Richard Croker. Hill drew into his purpose Grover Cleveland, who imparted the prestige of his open approval, Gorman of Maryland, Richard Olney of Massachusetts, and machine leaders of New Jersey. The ready success of his local probings encouraged Hill to fan out his efforts for support in the South and the border states. Rumors flamed that Hill had already promised the Vice Presidency to the South, on the assumption that the next Presidential nominee would be a New Yorker. The Brooklyn *Eagle,* a trusty journal of the reorganizers, reported that Hill would fight in Illinois and in Ohio for the elimination of Tom Johnson, whose ideological camaraderie with Bryan made reorganizers blanch with anger. Even in Nebraska, the *Eagle* said, Bryan would be overthrown, and the state would send a delegation to the next national convention committed against the Kansas City platform and from whose ranks Bryan would be conspicuously absent. With Bryan eliminated, sound money Democrats would come into a new day.

From 1901 to 1904 the combat reached its savage worst in those states that constituted the absolute foundation of Bryan's strength in the national party. State and local conventions and elections assumed a national significance.

The year 1901 produced as one of its hotter battles the mayoralty election of St. Louis. After anxious entreaty by William J. Stone and other loyal silver Democrats, Bryan in the pages of *The Commoner* declared himself opposed to the nomination of Rolla Wells for mayor. The gold Democrats, Stone wrote, "have come back to power after opposing you and voting for McKinley," and Wells was their tool. After a bitter convention struggle,

Wells was nominated. The Bryan men of St. Louis faced a difficult question that his followers elsewhere were to confront. Having been defeated in the local party, should they bolt and nominate their own candidate? The St. Louis Bryanites opted for that choice, formed "a Kansas City—public ownership platform" and nominated Lee Meriwether, who distributed 100,000 copies of Bryan's *Commoner* article opposing Wells. Wells swept on to victory, aided, as Norman Mack wrote in candor, by Bryan's interference, "not only getting Republicans to vote for their candidate, but, no doubt, raising large sums of money from both Republicans and gold Democrats to apply rather to your defeat than to that of the Republican organization." Mack, needless to say, had counseled against Bryan's intervention.[25]

The political warfare abounded with boobytraps. With Carter Harrison seeking election as mayor of Chicago, Bryan was invited to address the Harrison League at the height of the campaign. Ordinarily, he would have accepted such an invitation, but a loyal local follower frantically waved him off. Characterizing the Harrison crowd as "a set of tricksters working only for their personal gain," the informant related how in the 1900 Presidential campaign they "did no work," raising only $14,000, compared with $300,000 for the city campaign the following year, devoted to electing an "independent" ticket, consisting of Harrison and a quantity of Republicans. The informant offered proof that Harrison conspired with the Republicans to give Illinois to McKinley in 1900 while he took the city in 1901. Bryan was enough impressed by this testimony to maintain silence in 1901 while Harrison campaigned and won the mayoralty of the nation's second largest city. Harrison retaliated and showed his colors by fighting and trouncing John Altgeld and his silver forces in the election of a gold man as chairman of the Illinois Democratic state central committee.

Adversity flowed like wine. In Ohio an alliance of John R. McLean and Judson Harmon rejected a reaffirmation of the Kansas City platform. In Pennsylvania, Bryan men refrained from pushing a plank endorsing the Kansas City platform for fear that it would bring rejection and humiliation. Indiana elected a goldbug chairman of the state committee. The Michigan Democracy was reported by a Bryan observer to be "hopelessly divided." Bryan's chief comfort emerged from the Nebraska Democratic convention and its endorsement of the Kansas City platform and the nomination of Edward M. Shepard, a progressive and a supporter of the Nebraskan, to be mayor of New York. But joy over Shepard soon turned to remorse when the Republican Seth Low defeated him in the November elections. The elections indeed were a Republican sweep. Republicans won five governorships, while the Democrats captured one, prevailed in the principal city elections, and in Nebraska won the chief office at stake, Supreme Court judge. Prosperity, the McKinley-Roosevelt popularity, the emergence of local issues, and Democratic factional strife combined to bring electoral defeat and to push Bryan several rungs down the ladder of his national prestige.[26]

In the 1902 Congressional elections, Bryan's fortunes were no better. Democratic state conventions moved en masse away from the Kansas City platform, and in many states reorganizers returned to party power. Probably Bryan's worst defeat was the entrenchment of John P. Hopkins as Illinois state chairman. "With Hopkins in control of the party machinery," Bryan remarked, "the platform is immaterial because he cannot be trusted with the carrying out of a platform embodying the Sermon on the Mount." Not only the Kansas City platform, but even the display of Bryan's picture was a matter of contention at some state conventions. Good New York Democrats, convening at Saratoga Springs, fell into grievous dispute over the display of pictures of past party heroes in the convention hall. As a huge Bryan portrait was readied for hanging, there was objection that it might offend gold Democrats. When Samuel J. Tilden, former Presidential nominee and expert legal counselor of great corporations was proposed, Bryan men expressed distaste. An eventual compromise brought in a huge portrait, not of any Democrat, but of the unimpeachable George Washington.

As Bryan faced the mounting tide of rebuff, he had also to restrain diehard supporters who in the face of defeat proposed to break away from the Democratic Party and launch new state parties devoted to their principles. It took his strong letter of disapproval, for instance, to check his followers from supporting the proposed Liberal Democratic Party of New York. All fighting, Bryan in effect said, should be done within the Democratic Party. However low his stock was falling, Bryan was the good soldier on the campaign trail. The exuberance of his discourse was undimmed. "There are more righteous men in Sodom and Gomorrah," he told a Missouri audience, "than there are tariff reformers in the Republican party." [27]

The outcomes of the 1902 elections continued Bryan's downward slide. Normally, at the President's midterm, the Congressional elections show an upsurge for the out party, but the Democrats in 1902 did not enjoy that beneficence. Instead, with bumper crops, prosperity in the cities, and the passivity of the voters on national issues, the Republicans gained nationally. Even more important for Bryan's future was the election's failure to show that the Democratic Party fared better at the polls if it followed Bryan's recipe for success or heeded the opposing cries of the reorganizers. Where Democratic victories occurred, they materialized under either formula. Bryan's strength in his home base was further diminished when Republicans carried Nebraska. Populists and independents all but vanished from the victory columns, and the general decline of Bryanite strength in Congress and the states now clearly precluded the Democratic nomination of 1904 for any apostle of the Commoner's teachings. More and more Democratic ears were prepared to hearken to the cry of Congressman Jacob

Bromwell of Ohio midway in the campaign: "The Democratic party can never make any headway until it gets rid of Bryan. He is a millstone around its neck."

There was also the matter of the new President Roosevelt's booming popularity. The incomparable, cyclonic TR was dominating the national scene. His bared teeth, flung hands, thickset neck, puffy cheeks, and voice which at oratorical heights cracked in a weird falsetto, captivated the nation. ". . . a very likeable, a big figure," Justice Oliver Wendell Holmes described him, "a rather ordinary intellect, with extraordinary gifts, a shrewd and I think pretty unscrupulous politician. . . ." Roosevelt was a caldron of contradictions. The policies of his early Presidency were conservative, compared with its closing, more liberal years. At moments he took pains to describe himself as a conservative and confessed to "an almost Greek horror of extremes." An ardent conservationist, he embarked upon a hunting trip, eager to kill a grizzly bear with a knife, because it "would be great sport." Roosevelt was possessed of deep social consciousness, yet in his eyes, men, races, and nations were divided into the superior and inferior. Toward the "banana republics" of Latin America and the "inferior races" of south and central Europe, as he termed them, he was disdainful. Yet he was also moved by a strong sense of right, faith in man's capacity for progress, and the aristocrat's *noblesse oblige*. About the great immigrant groups dwelling in the slums of Eastern cities, many deriving from his "inferior races," he was genuinely concerned.

Conservative Republicans were deeply alarmed when "that damn cowboy," as Mark Hanna called him, moved into the White House. Reassuringly, Roosevelt said that he would "continue absolutely unbroken" the policies of McKinley. The new President's conservative posture was fortified by his first message to Congress in December, 1901. It endorsed existing tariff schedules, termed great corporations "natural," urged a subsidized merchant marine and educational and economic screening for future immigrants. But interspersed in the message's 30,000 words were flickers of reform sentiment—references to the "real and grave evils" of large industry, the need for conservation and reclamation and reciprocal tariff treaties. Each suggestion was embedded in cautious qualification.

The year 1903, a time of political prelude to the coming national convention, carried Bryan even farther in his descent. Democratic state conventions abandoned the Kansas City platform in greater numbers. Nebraska and a few states which endorsed Bryanism and Ohio, which nominated Tom Johnson for governor, were blotches of hope upon the country's darkened political map. New York persevered as an anti-Bryan stronghold; at the Jefferson Day banquet in New York City, diners hissed Bryan's name when the state committee chairman accused him of failing to aid the state tickets in 1902. Tammany, under new leadership, hailed the septuagenarian Grover Cleveland as the best available candidate for President.

Again the elections went badly for the Democrats. But Bryan was undeterred. In statements to the press and in his *Commoner* editorials, he moved to refute the suggestion that the Kansas City platform was the operative cause of the Democracy's defeats. Let the reorganizers, said Bryan, explain defeats in Massachusetts, Pennsylvania, and Iowa where the Kansas City platform was not endorsed. The lesson of the election, Bryan contended, is that "The party can make no progress while it spends more time trying to reconcile irreconcilable elements than it does in trying to make converts." The electoral results of 1903 disclosed a marked progressive trend that looked to strong government as an instrument of social justice and whose agenda embraced the ills of farm and city.[28]

By now President Roosevelt was skillfully riding the progressive trend. He had dropped his initial conservatism, and his liberal Square Deal, as it was known, was fast growing, thanks to his skill in gaining new laws. He won passage of the Expedition Act, adding two Assistant Attorney Generals to speed antitrust suits. The new Department of Commerce, established at his recommendation, contained a Bureau of Corporations, to collect information on interstate industrial activities. When conservative legislators faltered in supporting the measure, the President released copies of telegrams sent by the Standard Oil Company to stop the legislation. In the outcry, Congress rushed to pass the bill. In addition, Roosevelt helped push through a reclamation law and the Elkins Act, barring railroad rebates to large industrial enterprises, long their bludgeon against smaller competitors. Roosevelt trod cautiously on the tariff but won reduction of duties on Cuban and Philippine goods. He settled the coal strike of 1902, with distinct advantage for the miners, and startled Morgan, Rockefeller, and other titans by launching an antitrust prosecution of the Northern Securities Company, a giant holding company of three large Northwestern railroads. James J. Hill, the railroad magnate who had an interest in the company, remarked bitterly, "It really seems hard that we should be compelled to fight for our lives against the political adventurers who have never done anything but pose and draw a salary."

While the ideological Bryan was warring with conservative Democrats, the pragmatic Roosevelt was coping with conservative Congressional Republicans with expediency and audacity. Roosevelt was succeeding in the politics of give-and-take with such lights as Senator Nelson W. Aldrich of Rhode Island, Republican Senate leader and a multimillionaire thanks to street railways and franchise politics. His belief came easily that wealth should rule the country. In the House reigned Joseph G. "Uncle Joe" Cannon, the Speaker, a rough, shrewd politician. Cannon's reputation for conservatism was so strong that it was said that had he participated in the Creation, he would have voted against God for chaos. Yet by astute bargaining and pressure, Roosevelt extracted laws from his unwilling partners. "We cooperated," the President once said, "I pulling forward, and they holding back."

The elections of 1902 and 1903, in addition to deciding the immediate contests, distributed power and influence in state and local organizations that would determine the crucial decisions of the approaching national convention of 1904—nominating a President and drafting a platform. Bryan, despite his fading strength, articulated his views concerning the proper substance of these decisions. Not surprisingly, he wavered not one iota in this interval of personal political dearth from the expressions of his earlier political prosperity.

The Presidential nomination, he wrote in the New York *Independent*, depends on what the party wants to do—"if to bid for the plutocratic element, it will nominate a gold Democrat; if it wants to bid for support of the masses, it will nominate a silver Democrat." He allowed for a further possibility: "If it does not want any support at all and does not care to take part in the contest between man and Mammon, it will find a man who lacks neither the brains or the heart to take a position." [29]

One bright element in Bryan's generally desolate situation was the failure of any Democratic personality to emerge as the clear challenger of his national party leadership. As for the gold Democrats and those who tended toward their faith, none rose head and shoulders above the rest. Indeed, the figures who popped to the surface were decidedly shopworn. It was perhaps indicative of the parlous state of Bryan's opposition that the Democrat most spoken of in 1903 for the next Presidential nomination was Grover Cleveland, already three times the standard-bearer.

In the summer of 1903, New York politicians returning from the St. Louis World's Fair, where they had viewed the exhibits and closeted themselves with other politicians converging from everywhere in the country, concluded that Cleveland was the chief prospect for the nomination. Theodore Roosevelt, anxious for reelection and fearful that Wall Street in distaste for his progressivism might turn to Cleveland despite his sixty-six years of age, marked him as a very formidable candidate. Bryan was so impressed with the prospects of Cleveland that he attacked him at every opportunity and with a vehemence that he dealt out to no one else. Cleveland, he warned, "represents as no one else does the plutocratic element of the party, and is the logical candidate if the party returns to its wallow in the mire."

Like a procession of patriarchs, old party figures emerged to claim the mantle of Bryan's political slayer. Arthur Pue Gorman, in the words of his first political lieutenant, was the logical Presidential nominee for 1904, for "the great business interests of the country must have absolute confidence in the nominee of any party." A mention of Gorman drove Bryan, writing in *The Commoner,* to words of utter condemnation. "There is not a single reform for which Mr. Gorman stands nor is there a single remedial measure which can be said to have his earnest and hearty support." And there was that perennial aspirant for the Presidential nomination David Bennett Hill.

Powerful Democrats beat the drums for Hill. "Governor Hill," declared Hugh McLaughlin, the Brooklyn Democratic leader, "is the biggest man in the Democratic party. . . ." Cleveland, he added, had already served his party "long enough," and Bryan "has done damage enough for one man." Hill himself behaved like a serious candidate. At major party functions, he declared that the tariff would be the campaign's next chief issue. He scarcely alluded to the currency question.[30]

But the most consternating aspect of Hill's conduct to the Bryan camp was his brash venture to detach several of their key men—Nebraskans among them—and annex their support at the next national convention. There, concealed as members of the Nebraska and other delegations, they could work in Hill's behalf and help engineer Bryan's dethronement. Edgar Howard, angry and writing in his Columbus, Nebraska, *Telegram,* condemned these "shameless traitors" who stood "close to Bryan." While they might deceive Bryan, "who is faithful to his friends," they are not deceiving other Bryan men. "The traitors are marked and their every move in behalf of Hill will be met and checked. . . . The man who imagines that Dave Hill can induce the democracy of Nebraska to spit in Bryan's face belongs to the order of imbeciles."

There was another star, which as the national convention neared shot more and more into prominence. Judge Alton B. Parker, after years as a lower court judge, had been elected in 1899 to New York's highest court, the Court of Appeals. His triumph in a statewide election, in the state of the Union richest in electoral votes, gave Parker an arresting political glamor. Furthermore, his long career on the bench had barred his participation in political controversy; his views on issues were unspoken and unknown. He was, accordingly, remarkably free of those liabilities that encrust politicians in the active arena. Easterners, whose tendencies were conservative and who would have no more of Bryan, looked to the judge as an ideal prospect, but good Bryanites cast a cold eye. They openly proclaimed their distress at the general ignorance of the judge's position on current issues. As insistence grew that he speak out, the judge's friends made known the Parker strategy. He would not speak on political subjects until after the convention at St. Louis. As a loyal Democrat, he would willingly let the party make the platform. His modest deportment seemed almost to suggest that there had been altogether too much personal pretension in the Democratic Party in late years. Parker's reticence increased the attacks by Bryan men. John Brisben Walker of New York, Bryan's friend, in an address entitled "The Democratic Party," characterized Parker as a creature of Hill, August Belmont, and the Brooklyn boss Patrick H. McCarren. Though Parker was aware of corruption all about him, Walker contended, including the bribing of legislators by "the great interests," he was "too safe and sane" to protest. "What do you think about Judge Parker of New York?" Bryan was asked. "I am not thinking about Judge Parker at all," he snapped.[31]

Much of Parker's strength lay in his function as a counterweight to the rising candidacy of another New Yorker of opposite political persuasion, William Randolph Hearst. The brazen, enterprising journalist was not without credentials. He had supported the Nebraskan with his papers and his wealth in 1896 and 1900. Doubtless his support was not unalloyed, and now he stood on the brink of turning his past deeds to the profit of his current candidacy. For ample reason, Bryan in public pronouncement had always employed the vocabulary of gratitude and approval in speaking of Hearst. In 1903, at a Jefferson-Jackson-Lincoln dinner in Columbus, Ohio, with Hearst present, Bryan extolled the great journalist for his "immense service to the party" and for demonstrating that "wealth need not lead a man away from the people. . . ."

Bryan presumably made himself free to endorse an aspirant for the nomination, when, in a press interview early in 1904, he was asked, "Would you become a candidate if conditions should indicate the necessity of your making the race?" Bryan replied, "I can imagine no circumstances under which it would be either wise or necessary for me to become a candidate." An enterprising reporter pressed on: What did Bryan think of Hearst? "I appreciate the work Mr. Hearst has done for the Democratic party," Bryan replied, "and count him among my personal friends, but I am not advocating his nomination or that of any person. I am avoiding any expression of preference for anybody."

Hearst's candidacy, to be sure, suffered flaws that presumably served to encourage Bryan's reticence. He was very weak in the South, and his foremost strength was among the more radical sectors of the party and less among the moderates. To Democratic conservatives, he was anathema. Henry Watterson, editor of the Louisville *Courier-Journal,* uttered the common prognosis when he said, "Hearst has no more chance of being nominated than he has of being carried to heaven in a wicker basket handmade by Bryan."[32]

By the same rationale, Bryan withheld endorsement from another who loyally supported him, Tom Johnson, Cleveland's mayor, disciple of Henry George, and a national political figure whose views on social issues were even more positive than Bryan's. Bryan not only did not endorse Johnson, but in a speech in Cleveland, Johnson's home ground, actually discouraged his Presidential candidacy. "Mr. Johnson," noted Bryan, "says he has no higher ambition than to be mayor again. Well, God speed him in the realization of that ambition."[33]

Toward the nomination, Bryan pursued another tactic that confounded his friends and titillated his enemies. He devoted himself to the thesis that the Democratic Party abounded with Presidential talent, and he employed the pages of *The Commoner* from time to time, to direct attention to the eligibles. A pattern quickly emerged. Those whom Bryan favored either were unknowns or, if they possessed national reputations, suffered serious political blemish. "Why not Francis Marion Cockrell of Missouri for President?" began one of Bryan's presentations. The U.S. Senator's "Christian character" and "long experience" commended him to Bryan. Cockrell, he acknowledged, suffered the liability of service in the Confederate Army, "but the war is over," he added, "and his record commends him to blue as well as gray." Or, again, according to a Bryan editorial, "The Honorable John W. Bookwalter of Ohio ought to make an ideal candidate. . . ." Bookwalter's last candidacy for public office had transpired twenty-three years earlier in 1881. But he was also a silver publicist who had supported Bryan in 1896 and, as a self-made millionaire, was "one of the foremost business men of the country." As Bryan continued to draw little known names from his political hat, his detractors laughed and teased about "The Little Unknowns from Nowhere." [34]

Bryan's behavior was motivated by several purposes. His tactic of supporting almost everybody and of endorsing nobody left him totally free for maneuver and decision at the awaiting convention. He preserved intact his full veto over any emerging candidate. His veto was a real one thanks to the two-thirds rule, by which he, supported by one-third of the delegates, could stop any nomination. He also left himself free to seek the nomination, and in doing so, he would not suffer the opprobrium of violating a pledge of support to others, for he had given none. Bryan, it was clear, meant to cut a big figure at the convention. He did not envisage playing the part of a passive spectator, acquiescing to the dismantlement of his influence, his causes, and the legions of his followers.

21. From the Ashes of Weakness

Bryan journeyed to the St. Louis convention as a delegate at large and as chairman of the Nebraska delegation. He came into these honors by the exertions of capable lieutenants and by applying his own practiced political hand. Before the Nebraska state convention, the clouds of crisis gathered when several of Bryan's oldest and most devoted supporters, eager to remove the albatross of silver from their necks, issued a brief statement opposing a reaffirmation of a free coinage plank. "Our fight is not against Mr. Bryan," the statement read, and its signers pledged themselves to support as delegates only those who backed "the regular Democratic nominees in 1896 and 1900."

But the revolt was quickly squelched, and the state convention that gathered at Omaha was from beginning to end a Bryan affair. Bryan served as chairman of the Resolutions Committee, and since his fellow members were his most trusted and devoted followers, he was able to write his own platform. The convention joyously adopted his handiwork, which reaffirmed the Kansas City platform. A clue to Bryan's absolute hold was a resolution offered by Edgar Howard and adopted unanimously, with shouts and cheers. "The Democracy of Nebraska heralds to the Democracy of the Nation its steadfast respect for, confidence in, and loyalty to Nebraska's great champion of pure Democratic principles, and bids him God speed in his splendid efforts to prevent the National organization from falling under the baneful control of the enemies of the real Democracy." [1]

Bryan arrived in a torrid St. Louis on July 3, several days before the convention began. His modest room at the Hotel Jefferson was besieged by friends and admirers, although the hostile eastern press was impressed that few major figures trekked to his door. Bryan exuded confidence in his ability to dominate the convention's decisions, and by evening he had issued a prepared statement that was equivalent to a declaration of war upon the reorganizers.

The statement announced Bryan's "unalterable opposition" to the nomination of Parker and denounced Hill and August Belmont, whom he designated as Parker's sponsors, as "tools of Wall Street and the corporations." Bryan told reporters that more than one-third of the delegates were behind him, and his statement acknowledged that "There has been no concentration upon any anti-Parker candidate." The Parker camp immediately launched a counterblast. Elliott Danforth, Hill's trusted lieutenant, declared to reporters: "The trouble with Mr. Bryan is that he does not know when he is licked, or if he does, he does not know how to take his medicine with good grace." If anything, the major preoccupation of the reorganizers at this moment was not the Presidential nomination, of which they were confident, but the burial, once and for all, of Bryan. "I am in favor of making a slaughterhouse job of it," growled John P. Hopkins. "The first duty of this convention is to kill Bryanism, root and branch." Enterprising reporters, sniffing a mighty battle, rushed to Bryan. He did not disappoint them. "I shall," he said, casting aside all diplomacy, "stand here until the last dog is dead." [2]

Nonetheless, Democratic conservatives were worried lest Bryan, defeated at the convention, bolt the party. They recalled, not altogether comfortably, that gold Democrats had deserted Bryan by the thousands in 1896 and cost him the election. Much of the apparatus of party workers and organizers throughout the West consisted of staunch Bryanites, and without them the Presidential race would be lost from the start. One night a group of delegates huddled in the Jefferson lobby were puzzling over the fateful question of Bryan's likely course, when one of them, R. L. Holt, a major cotton manufacturer and reputedly one of the wealthiest men in North Carolina, cried, "Let's go upstairs and ask him." They shuffled into Bryan's presence, and Holt, with glacial aplomb, related how he had voted for him in 1896 and 1900 before marching on bravely to the anxious question: Would Bryan bolt in 1904? Bryan listened to this presentation with fixed and unchanging expression. As the delegates looked at him expectantly, he placed his hand upon his heart and said with absolute solemnity, "I do not ask any person or party how I shall vote. This [meaning his heart] is responsible only." Taken aback by Bryan's dramatic response, the group did not miss its essential vagueness. They restated their question. Bryan, now more direct, said that he could not answer until the convention adjourned and he had studied the platform. Throughout the convention, Bryan was to use the fear that he would bolt as a personal tactical weapon.[3]

The first major battle of the convention was begun by Bryan himself. He challenged nothing less than the seating of the Illinois delegation, comprised chiefly of henchmen of the Hopkins machine. Bryan contended that an awaiting body of Hearst men should be recognized instead. In his bill of particulars, he said that the Illinois convention had been intimidated by the Hopkins crowd to the point of frustrating the will of the majority, which was for Hearst. Bryan related how the Hopkins machine posted a gang of its most menacing characters at the speakers' stand in Springfield before a temporary chairman gaveled through a series of rulings that resulted in a delegation opposed to Hearst. Although Hearst himself showed no heart for making a fight, Bryan, with his old friend M. F. Dunlap of Jacksonville, laboriously toured Illinois following the Springfield proceedings and collected signatures from the state convention members petitioning that delegates friendly to Hearst be seated at the national convention. Bryan launched a second credentials fight by pressing the case of a contesting delegation from the District of Columbia, headed by another old friend, Cotter T. Bride.

In the sweltering conference room of the Credentials Committee, filled to overflowing with ancient enemies, grinning and licking their lips in happy anticipation of his humiliation and defeat, Bryan opened and closed the argument for the contesting delegations. The Hill-Parker men, firmly in control of the committee, ruled uniformly and jubilantly against him.

The first moved to the convention floor where Bryan presented a minority report. By careful prearrangement, he was to perform his task against a background of wild and noisy approval. The Hearst camp, friendly leaders of Tammany Hall who could not stomach Hill, the retiring sergeant at arms, John I. Martin, and others pooled their respective resources and influences and, by issuing special tickets of admission, packed the galleries with hundreds of Hearst supporters and posted leather-lunged shouters at strategic places around the floor. Hitherto Bryan in several appearances on the floor had stirred hardly a ripple of attention. But thanks to these special measures, his entry into the hall was now hailed with a sudden sharp cry, "Bryan, Bryan, Bryan," which quickly rolled into a roar. As he smilingly made his way to his seat, thousands of palm leaf fans—his famous symbol —waved and hats soared. C. D. Casper jumped for the Nebraska standard, only to find it bolted to the floor—a precaution the Hill men had taken against a Bryan demonstration. Giving the standard a mighty wrench, the brawny Casper brought out all the screws. Holding the banner aloft, he commenced a parade. Everywhere men, sweating and shouting, began tugging at their standards, some succeeding, as Casper did, others improvising a banner from shirts and materials at hand. Soon almost every state had joined the march.

At first the Hill-Parker men watched the unexpected rampage with passive disdain, but within minutes, exhorted by their managers, they rushed to retrieve their standards from the Bryan-Hearst demonstrators. Struggling and fighting spread around the floor. Although the Bryan forces were far outnumbered, the shouting galleries created an illusion of enormous strength.

Somehow order was restored, and Bryan presented his minority report. He recited his facts without effort at oratorical effect, although the convention was triggered to a new outburst by his vivid concluding judgment of events in Illinois: "No band of train robbers ever planned a robbery upon a train more deliberately or with less conscience than they did."

Frank P. Quinn, chairman of the Illinois state convention, whom Bryan referred to as "a gavel ruler," delivered an angry rebuttal, attesting to his belief in majority rule, his revulsion to bolters, and his support of Bryan in 1896 and 1900. When Quinn finished, Bryan jumped to his feet, his face gripped in anger. In his sudden movement, he bumped against Quinn, prompting the crowd to think there was a fight and triggering a new uproar. From the edge of the platform, Bryan made a fiery rejoinder, the crowd punctuating his argument with yells and cheers.

When the vote was put on Bryan's report, the scattered ayes were dwarfed by an overwhelming roar of noes. Bryan rose at once and demanded a roll call. In effect, he was forcing a test of strength of the Parker and anti-Parker forces. The tedious call of the states found Bryan voted down 647 to 299.

Although defeated, Bryan had chiefly been intent upon inspiriting and mobilizing his forces, which, for all his articles in *The Commoner* and speeches around the country, had been distressingly moribund. His respectable vote in the floor struggle and the mountainous enthusiasm of the galleries served notice on the Hill organization that their steamroller tactics would meet noisy and dogged resistance. It was hoped the convention majority might henceforth be more prone to compromise and moderation.[4]

Bryan, who said he attended the convention out of obligation to the millions who supported him in two campaigns, meant to extract the best platform possible for them and "make the convention partly Democratic." The Nebraska delegation chose him as its representative on the Resolutions Committee, and Senator John Daniel of Virginia, the committee chairman, put Bryan on the subcommittee to draft the platform, doubtless with a shudder of foreboding. But Daniel also aimed to isolate Bryan by naming no other anti-Parker delegate to the subcommittee, although shortly after its sessions began, Francis G. Newlands, a staunch Nevada silverite, was added.

Drafts of platforms were introduced by John Sharp Williams of Mississippi, Charles S. Hamlin of Massachusetts, and John Poe of Maryland, and "a written interpretation," as it was called, was prepared by Bryan. Bryan's interpretation, according to Hamlin, consisted of "planks on national banknotes, against melting silver dollars, favoring greenbacks, against Aldrich Committee bills, etc., etc. Richard F. Pettigrew of South Dakota offered [of course, with Bryan's connivance] planks for public ownership of railroads and telegraphs and others. . . . Bryan also advocated an internal revenue tax on all corporations selling products cheaper abroad than in the United States."

While Bryan was away fighting the Illinois case, the resolutions subcommittee, despite Newlands' heroic resistance, adopted a platform with a gold plank by a vote of 7 to 3. Bryan attended the meeting of the full Committee on Resolutions which began at eight o'clock in the evening and raged on until noon of the next day, July 8. Each time the Hill-Parker forces moved a conservative plank, Bryan moved to substitute a progressive plank of his own.

The bitterest fight centered on money. Bryan threw down the gauntlet by moving the reaffirmation of the Chicago and Kansas City platforms. He was overwhelmingly voted down. The gold plank, fathered by Hill after consultations with August Belmont and other Eastern financiers, contained a tiny sop for Bryan by affirming the quantity theory of money. Recent discoveries of gold, according to the plank, have "contributed to the maintenance of a money standard of value no longer open to question, removing that issue from the field of political contention."

Sniffing that Hill was building a gold platform to fit the real but carefully undisclosed views of his candidate, Parker, Bryan asked the wily New Yorker precisely when he had decided that a gold plank was necessary. Hill answered evenly that his decision had been made just a few days before the convention gathered. Fire leaping from his eyes, his jaw set like a taut trap, Bryan moved his 200-pound frame toward the dapper Hill and shook his finger dangerously near the New Yorker's nose. "You ought to have a gold platform to go with the gold candidate you are forcing upon the country," he shouted. Hill, with unruffled aplomb, replied that he knew nothing of Parker's monetary views.

"Do you mean to say that you do not know Judge Parker's financial views?" cried Bryan, his gaze sweeping the committee members with incredulity.

"I mean just that," said Hill.

"You have no knowledge of the subject?"

"None."

"Have you never asked him?"

"I have not. I have never sought to secure an expression of his views and he has never sought to convey them to me. I only know that he is a Democrat and a high-minded and patriotic man, and I believe that he can be trusted implicitly on this, as upon other matters of public policy." [5]

When Chairman Daniel asked whether committee members believed that a gold plank such as that which Hill proposed would weaken the party in their states, more than half of them stood up. Eager to avoid serious division over what he deemed a secondary issue, Hill offered to compromise. Bryan, sensing that the best he could do, both in the committee and in the convention, was to prevent any mention of the money question in the platform at all, held out for that position in the bargaining and prevailed. When diehard conservatives proposed to submit a gold minority report, Hill talked them out of it by eloquently stating that such a report, if defeated in the convention, would be interpreted as a further rejection of the gold standard by the Democratic Party. It might also open the gates for the nomination of a radical candidate.

The income tax plank also sparked a bitter wrangle. John Sharp Williams of Mississippi called for a constitutional amendment to establish an income tax. Hill declared adamantly that New York could not be carried with such a plank. But Bryan, unwilling to see the income tax, in his eyes a profound social measure, discarded, picked it up, offered it as an amendment to the platform, and launched into a fervent speech. While votes, he said, might be lost among the very rich, the party must consider the mass of the people who bear the burdens of taxation and the expenses of government.

Senator Daniel, although chairman, dropped any pretense to acting as moderator and attacked Bryan savagely. He wanted to win, the Senator declared; he was tired of being in the minority; and it was absurd for the Democratic Party, facing the prospect of victory, to take any action that threatened defeat. To lose New York meant defeat. He wanted a platform that would bring into the party voters who had left when Bryan led. Looking the Nebraskan in the eye, the fiery Daniel declared, "Conditions have changed in the last few years, and heroic changes demand heroic remedies. We must consider New England, New York, and that section of the country. . . . [Bryan] has reviled every man whom any state has recommended for the Presidency, and, so far as I have been able to learn, has as yet presented no candidate of his own." There were cries of "Order! Order!" Bryan shouted that Daniel should be allowed to proceed. Ben Tillman, master of vituperation, quickly quieted Daniel.

But the outburst did not in the least deter Bryan, who moved like a juggernaut toward his purpose. He proposed a bold bargain. He would withdraw his income tax plank, he said, if the committee accepted the anti-trust plank of the Kansas City platform, whose language was substantially more muscular than the present draft plank. A committee member observed with candor that such a plank would "frighten capital and scare away campaign contributions." The effect of these words was like waving a red cloth at a mad bull. Bryan cried that a bargain had been entered into with the trusts for campaign money. Soon Bryan and Hill were redrafting the anti-trust plank, strengthening the language to the point where the Nebraskan, with his acute political antenna, felt that a committee majority would still sustain it.

The tariff touched off another battle in which allies came more readily to Bryan. The original plank, overseen by the confident Hill, carried a bias for protection. When Bryan thundered against it, Charles S. Hamlin, Cleveland's deputy, several Hearst men, and a sprinkling of Parker supporters joined in the protest. Southerners threatened to make a minority report unless all vestiges of protection were removed. Bryan and his fellow protesters easily prevailed.

For all the strife, Bryan and Hill emerged from the committee room when their work was done exuding smiles and cheer. "Now, boys," Bryan called to the waiting reporters, "be sure and get Hill's platform right."

With a laugh, Hill retorted, "I think we will have to share honors on that."

"We are all satisfied," added Bryan. "We all wanted some things put in that the committee has rejected, but on the whole the document is perfectly satisfactory."

Hill, too, was pleased. "Will Mr. Parker stand on the platform?" a reporter asked.

"I do not see why not," replied Hill, his tired face fleetingly lighted by a confident smile.

In retrospect, Bryan felt he exerted more influence upon the platform's substance in 1904 than even in his glorious year of 1896. His success in 1904 sprang from a complex of factors. Though holding a minority position in the convention, he championed issues appealing to men like Tillman, Carmack, and others who now supported Parker, but were loyal to the old causes. Bryan's best support emerged from a broad spectrum of Western states. The South, thirsting for victory, moved strongly into partnership with the East.[6]

Indispensable to Bryan's successes were his tenacity, zest for combat, and total disconcern for the consequences of his insistence on what he thought was right. With the vote looming close, Bryan, time and again, resorted to massive personal attacks that were long resented by their victims. "All the leading members . . ." Hamlin wrote afterward, "begged Bryan almost with tears in their eyes to be reasonable for the sake of the party, but he was obdurate. He insulted almost everyone and seemed more like an insane man. He insulted Judge Parker—called him a tool of trusts—and even attacked Senator Daniel. He insulted me. . . ." In 1920, as late as sixteen years after the convention, Parker wrote: "I have been told more than once by men who sat in that committee, that they doubted whether any man living could have kept his head absolutely level with the insulting speeches of Bryan which he had to meet." But other onlookers discerned in Bryan's struggle personal qualities of heroic proportions. In the judgment of the staunch Republican journal the St. Louis *Globe-Democrat*, "Rarely have eloquence, courage, sincerity, and persistence won over brute numbers in any great assemblage as the Nebraskan has just achieved."

While Bryan deemed platforms the vessels of his ideology and set far higher value upon them than upon mere candidacy, David Bennett Hill, a craftsman of pragmatic politics, lived by processes of adjustment and compromise. It was at the St. Louis convention, soon after his set-to with Bryan, that he remarked, "Platforms are like sausages; the more you know about how they are made, the less respect you have for them."

Bryan's behavior in the brawling Resolutions Committee illuminates his tendencies toward ideological politics. The ideological politician is prone to display a "closed mind" toward political issues. The pragmatic politician, in contrast, veers toward the "open mind," eager to build agreement and ready to compromise. The stereotype of the ideological politician represents him as dogmatic, self-imprisoned in closed ways of thinking, and authoritarian in outlook, with a low tolerance of those opposing his beliefs and free sufferance of those who agree. The closed mind manifests itself on a network of issues and is particularly prevalent in politics and religion in debates over what is right and what is wrong.

The test of the closed mind can be applied in terms of Bryan's acceptance or rejection of several more or less distinct elements: ideas and beliefs, people, and authority. Conceivably, the state of Bryan's open- or closed-mindedness might be identical for all these elements, or it might vary significantly for each.

Bryan's beliefs lend themselves to charting like a map. They include a hard core held with closest tenacity; an intermediate region, important, vigorously asserted, and to a degree open to compromise; and a peripheral region deemed of minor importance and readily available for compromise. However, the latter was virtually nonexistent, for few beliefs were peripheral with Bryan.

If a label were applied to the hard core of Bryan's beliefs, it would be "1896." For the Bryan of a decade later, the platform of that year was a Bible of ideas and issues. His impassioned confrontations in the committee room were sparked by the ideas incorporated in the Chicago platform and reaffirmed at Kansas City. He asserted these ideas against the heavy majority that opposed him, including old allies and friends who now rejected his counsel as hopelessly impractical and a sure recipe of defeat. He held rigidly to his views despite vitriolic rejection from the hero of his younger political days, Senator John Daniel of Virginia. Ridicule, jeers, personal abuse, the smashing of old friendships—nothing deterred Bryan. Goaded by ideas that symbolized the struggle between "the people" and "plutocracy," he bombarded his detractors with ever greater ferocity. Bryan sweepingly rejected the relevance of his two Presidential defeats and the hunger of long-denied Democratic politicians for victory. A mind less closed would have acknowledged these stark realities and tolerated discussion of other planks of widest possible appeal to Democrats, conservative and progressive alike.

For Bryan, the ultimate authority, the basis on which he attacked problems or judged his fellow politicians, was the Chicago platform. Men were "good" or "bad" according to their fealty to its provisions. As Bryan applied the platform judgmentally, there were several categories of sinners. The worst offenders were those who bolted the regular Democratic Party and worked for the National Democratic Party, whose presence had cost Bryan the 1896 election. These were absolutely and forever banished from his dispensations; their sins were unforgivable. Slightly less reprehensible were those of the gold persuasion who had remained in the Democratic Party in 1896 but who had actively opposed him after the nomination or sat out the campaign. No matter how faithfully they supported his further candidacy, they could never atone for their initial lapse. David R. Francis of Missouri is a case in point. In 1896 Francis had abstained from aiding

Bryan. In later years he lent vigorous, effective support. Though his social relations with the delightful Francis were easy, Bryan never lifted a finger in reciprocity to help his friend in the fiercely competitive politics of Missouri. Bryan applied his beliefs more severely in judging others than in judging himself. That is, he was more open-minded toward himself, a not uncommon human condition. Although he defended the Chicago platform with ferocity in the Resolutions Committee, he was open to and did indulge in compromise. Even the most sacred of planks—silver—was susceptible to the one compromise he found tolerable. In the face of the gold men's adamancy, he agreed that the money question should not be mentioned, the least damaging of all conceivable compromises to silver. Bryan exhibited no readiness for further retreat on the question. Not all the planks of the Chicago and Kansas City platforms weighed the same in Bryan's estimation. He valued the antitrust plank more than the income tax plank, and within the cruel limits of the Resolutions Committee, he chose to bargain away the latter as the price for the former.[7]

Bryan continued to decline to endorse any major candidate. The Nebraska delegation, under his tight control, planned to scatter its vote, allotting more to the front-runner, Alton Parker. As the nomination neared, Bryan declared in a press statement: "While the opposition is not centralized upon any particular candidate, it is an aggressive opposition, and likely to be recruited by accessions from the instructed states when it is seen that Parker cannot be nominated."

Toward Parker, Bryan's opposition was open and unrelenting. There was the deep suspicion that Parker's candidacy shrouded the purposes of Eastern wealth. Shortly before the St. Louis convention, *The Commoner* published a speech by Bryan's old ally John Brisben Walker, highlighting the following passage: "I have it on good authority that seven months ago, in London, the friends of Mr. Pierpont Morgan were announcing confidently that a man had been found who could beat Theodore Roosevelt—a man by the name of Parker, a protégé and friend of David B. Hill—and that sufficient money would be spent to corrupt the democratic politicians and control the democratic convention . . . this gentleman is absolutely the creature of four men—Mr. David B. Hill, Mr. August Belmont, Mr. Patrick McCarren, and Mr. Francis Lynde Stetson, a well-known lawyer of Mr. Pierpont Morgan who was the intermediary between Mr. Cleveland and Mr. Morgan in those same bond deals."

At St. Louis, Bryan repeatedly gave out statements to the press that Parker's strength was faltering and opposition was rising. In his most aggressive move, Bryan promoted a petition committing its signers to remain firm against Parker's nomination for three ballots. Asked repeatedly how many signatures he had collected, Bryan declined to disclose any precise count, but continued to predict confidently that more than one-third of the convention "will stand out against the nomination of Judge Parker." [8]

Bryan was under intense pressure to cast his prestige behind a serious rival candidate. John G. Johnson, a key national Democratic manager in Bryan's own Presidential campaign, in a lengthy, prayerful letter urged his endorsement of William Randolph Hearst in order to bring "our kind of people to concentrate on some candidate and make a straight fight . . . for him." But Bryan moved not a muscle. At the convention, his only effort relevant to Hearst's progress was his fight to seat Hearst delegates in the Illinois contest, but Bryan fought less for Hearst than to further his feud with the Hopkins machine. When the convention got under way, a reporter asked Hearst's manager, Max Ihmsen, if Bryan would make "a Hearst speech." Ihmsen's reply was a smile wreathed in acid.

Behind Ihmsen's unspoken rancor lay a sharp drama between the giants, Bryan and Hearst. At a late hour in the convention, at the peak of the effort to nominate Hearst, the mighty press lord dispatched an intermediary to Bryan, asking that he place Hearst's name in nomination. In effect, Hearst, who had lavished support upon Bryan in 1896 and 1900, was requesting a return of favors. Bryan promptly turned down the request, with the explanation that he had just promised to nominate Senator Francis M. Cockrell. Because Cockrell had absolutely no chance, Hearst dismissed the excuse as flimsy and unreal.

In withholding support from Hearst and any other major candidate, Bryan was committing a patently selfish act. Discredited by two defeats for the Presidency, he was at a stage in his political career when he was acutely vulnerable to fresh rivals who might displace him. In St. Louis he faced the task of preserving his monopoly of leadership of the party's progressive wing. Any endorsement of Hearst would have thrust the press lord into a posture of influence and power where his voice would, in the future, rival Bryan's.[9]

As it was, Bryan spoke glowingly of Senator Cockrell, who "stood for everything that I had been fighting for" and who, as an ex-Confederate soldier, might erode Parker's vital base of Southern support. Simultaneously, Bryan engaged in behind-the-scenes probing actions in behalf of several other men. He made gestures to promote former Governor Robert E. Pattison of Pennsylvania, a gold man—but "I will trust his honesty on all questions!"—and Joseph W. Folk, a thirty-five-year-old circuit attorney for St. Louis, who had been catapulted into national prominence by his brilliant prosecutions of Missouri corruption. But all these candidates were so minor that they carried not even the faintest marks of dark-horse contours.

Bryan's bizarre attitude toward the candidates invited the suspicion that he was playing a subtle game to grab the nomination for himself. In far-off New York, Parker was impressed that Bryan was looking for some opportu-

nity for a moving speech by which "he might . . . fascinate the Convention,
. . . in the belief that there would not be mustered for my nomination two-
thirds of the Convention, that Hearst would be able to control little more
than a third, and that ultimately the Convention would take him, although
he was not openly a candidate." [10] Bryan's neglect of Hearst and his support of hopeless candidacies had given credence to Parker's perceptions. So,
too, does the carefully contrived speech that Bryan was about to deliver.

Martin W. Littleton, the distinguished New York attorney, placed Parker
in nomination with a masterful address. Bryan, who had caught a cold
which passed quickly into fever, had risen from his bed, covered his chest
with plasters, escaped his doctor, who warned of pneumonia, and taken his
place in the Nebraska delegation. As the convention moved relentlessly
through its schedule of nominating speeches, Littleton approached Bryan,
perspiring and pale and seated with his fellow Nebraskans, to ask politely if
he planned to speak before the day's adjournment. "Yes, Martin," Bryan
answered pleasantly. "After a little while I think I shall submit a few remarks."

In a seconding speech for Parker, Bryan's staunch ally of the silver wars
Edward Carmack betrayed the depths of their present break. "I have yet to
learn," cried Carmack, "that laryngeal activity is the supreme test of statesmanship . . . that the width of a man's mouth is commensurate with the
breadth of his understanding or that the length of his tongue measures the
depth of his wisdom." But when Clarence Darrow, seconding the nomination of Hearst, mentioned Bryan by name, a great cheer ran through the
hall.

At 4:30 A.M. Bryan's turn to speak came. The delegates were surfeited
with oratory and weary from the heavy heat and lack of sleep. Many ate
sandwiches imported from nearby saloons; others slept determinedly in
their chairs against the roar of thousands of voices; and most had their
coats off and collars unbuttoned. Doorkeepers were letting anyone in, and
discipline had long since vanished. Despite the late hour, some 20,000 filled
the auditorium.

The gray dawn was pushing through the convention windows, which resembled the portholes of a ship, when Bryan rose to speak. Attired in his
characteristic black alpaca jacket, he made his way to the platform. The
crowd was more respectful than demonstrative toward this giant who faced
incipient defeat after eight years of firm rule of the national party. His face
was flushed with fever, but the cheers which suddenly rose stirred a smile,
and exultation leaped into his dark eyes. The bored, undisciplined convention was suddenly galvanized by his presence, and an ever-increasing roar
continued for ten minutes until Bryan lifted his arms for silence, frowned

darkly at shouters who disobeyed, and imperiously motioned for order. The thousands fell quiet for his word.

He apologized for his voice, rasping and cracking from his cold and "two nights without sleep." He moved immediately into his theme, which he couched in Biblical phrases, adapting to his need Paul's letter to Timothy. "Eight years ago at Chicago," he began, his voice suddenly clearing and its sonorous tones carrying to the far corners of the hall, "the Democratic National Convention placed in my hand the standard of the party and commissioned me as its candidate. Four years ago at Kansas City that commission was renewed. Tonight I come back to this Democratic National Convention to return that commission and to say to you that you may dispute over whether I have fought the good fight, you may dispute whether I have finished my course, but you cannot deny that I have kept the faith."

Asserted in perfect intonation and gesture, these heroic sentences, rising to their climax, "I have kept the faith," brought the convention into its most tumultuous demonstration. Although Parker men sat immobile, the vast filled galleries and one-third of the delegates voiced thundering approval. Bryan told of his love for his party, excoriated Roosevelt's gross militarism, and implored the delegates to choose a nominee who would lead the party "away from the Scylla of Militarism without wrecking her upon the Charybdis of Commercialism." With trembling voice, he avowed that he asked nothing for himself. He had never been a dictator, he said, pointing a finger at Hill. His work in the Resolutions Committee had helped unite the party and was not undertaken to advance the cause of any candidacy. "I led you twice," he continued, "and you once followed me and believed in me. Now you have overruled me and cast me out. I accept because I am a loyal Democrat. But be merciful to your former leader."

There were many good men, he said, from whom the convention might choose its nominee. He named some—Hearst, Wall, Pattison. Let the convention take one—"Any one—whether he is a free silver man or not." But he implored the delegates not to make him take anyone who worshiped "the god of gold, not this candidate of yours, for he represents the money interests, and to take him would be too bitter a dish of crow." The candidate thus rejected was, as every rapt listener in the great hall knew, Alton Parker. Bryan's own choice? At the crest of his measured eloquence and the crowd's wild approval, he declared that he seconded the nomination of Marion Cockrell. The announcement of this little-known name hit the convention like a wet pancake. Bryan had reached the end, almost toppling from exhaustion, and the crowd let forth another vast ovation.

Men who had never voted for Bryan and gleefully awaited his defeat looked at one another and nodded in agreement that "This is a great speech, the greatest he ever made." Bryan himself felt that this was his best speech "because," according to Josephus Daniels, "he converted a convention hostile to him into one that gave him a larger measure of applause than he ever received, before or afterwards." August Belmont, ancient enemy and symbol of all that Bryan opposed, was heard to exclaim as Bryan closed, "My God! I can now understand the power of the man." Belmont maintained this generous appreciation even though Bryan, as he spoke his bitterest sentences about gold, stared directly at him. From afar, Republican Senator Albert J. Beveridge, who had taken a poor view of Bryan, hailed him as "the hero of conscience." [11]

A politician invariably on the side of his party's majorities was now cast with the minority, a status Bryan's address accepted with dignity and asserted with reason. His magical eloquence, proved once again, restored his wavering leadership of the Western branch of the Democratic Party and won new strength in the South. But for all its grandeur, the speech did not, in the manner of the "Cross of Gold" oration, sway delegate votes. When the first ballot count finished at 5:45 A.M., Parker had nine votes less than a two-thirds majority; Hearst placed second with 181 votes; and Cockrell had only 42. The rush for the bandwagon began, and Parker was quickly nominated.

Bryan was not present at the moment of Parker's nomination and therefore at the moment of his own fall and ejection from the headship of his party. After concluding his speech, he fell into his seat, and friends half carried him to a cab and drove him to his hotel. At the instant that Parker succeeded him in the party leadership, his fevered frame was fast asleep, and his doctors worried anew that he would succumb to pneumonia.[12]

All five of those placed in nomination for the Vice Presidency had supported Bryan in his Presidential campaigns, although the eventual nominee, Henry Gassaway Davis, an eighty-year-old multimillionaire and former West Virginia Senator had rejected free silver in 1900. Journalists were inevitably intrigued by his middle name. Bryan was amused to read in the press that "looking over the candidates we can't find any trace of Bryan, unless he might be related to Henry *Gassaway* Davis by his middle name."

When Texas was reached on the roll call for the Vice Presidential balloting, Senator Charles A. Culberson rose and said, "We want to know, before a candidate for vice president is nominated, who will be the nominee of this convention for President." For some minutes before Culberson spoke, the convention had suddenly assumed a distracted air. Delegates were running about, talking and gesticulating excitedly in little groups. Though the galleries were not aware of it, a crisis of magnitude was boiling up, and Culberson's statement served to articulate it.

As increasing numbers of delegates learned, to their consternation, William F. Sheehan had just received from Parker from his home in Esopus, New York, a telegram that, to say the least, was jarring. It read: "I regard the gold standard as firmly and irrevocably established, and shall act accordingly if the action of the Convention shall be ratified by the people. As the platform is silent on the subject, my view should be made known to the Convention, and, if it is proved to be unsatisfactory to the majority, I request you to decline the nomination for me at once, so that another may be nominated before adjournment." Culberson, in his version of the telegram, contended that Edward Carmack had known all along of Parker's insistence on a gold plank as a condition to his nomination and that Hill had ordered the telegram withheld from the convention, reasoning that if Parker wanted to reveal his thoughts to the delegates, he would have sent the telegram directly to the convention.

Culberson's bombshell unloosed a new frenzy of activity on the floor. Sheehan and Hill talked excitedly. "Pitchfork Ben" Tillman rushed over to Hill and shook his clenched fist in the New Yorker's face, shouting, "Why did you not tell us? You knew what Parker's views were. Why did you let us get into this hole? The message is an opprobrious and malicious insult." Western and Southern delegates, wild with rage, tore their badges from their coats, threw them on the floor, and stamped on them. The angry, hulking Tillman came upon Senator Daniel, who had done much to swing him over to Parker. Tillman shouted at the bewildered Daniel that he had been "deceived, seduced, maltreated, and horsewoggled." Hearst supporters began calling his name again, and a boom was started to nominate Bryan for President, who, at this moment, stood as the convention's towering hero. Charles A. Towne, now a Democrat, and Willis J. Abbott rushed to the Commoner's bedside to convey the sudden, shattering development. Other factional leaders withdrew to confer on the spiraling crisis; the convention was adjourned for several hours, and the delegates spilled out into the streets in vigorous conversation, attacking or defending Parker.[13]

When the convention reassembled, John Sharp Williams, Tillman, and Carmack were skillfully handling the situation when Bryan, his face chalk white and attended by his brother, Charles, and Willis Abbot, entered the hall. There was an instant uproar; calls of "Bryan, Bryan" rolled across the floor. Tillman, who was speaking, was reading a reply, prepared by the reorganizers, to Parker's telegram, "The platform adopted by this convention is silent on the question of a monetary standard because it is not regarded as a possible issue in this campaign. . . . Therefore there is nothing in the views expressed in the telegram just received which would preclude a man entertaining them from accepting a nomination on said platform." As Tillman read, Bryan walked rapidly up the side aisle, his lips compressed in a thin line and his brows drawn straight. He fanned himself nervously and ignored the hands stretched out as he moved by.

When Tillman finished, Bryan, in a voice weak and hoarse, told of the struggle in the Resolutions Committee over the gold plank and of his long unavailing efforts to divine Parker's views. The telegram drafted by the reorganizers was unacceptable, he cried; ". . . if you are going to declare for the gold standard, you should be honest and manly and say so in the platform." But if the convention chose to omit the gold standard from the platform, then Bryan insisted that Parker be queried whether he favored "the melting up of the silver dollars, the asset currency, a branch bank, and the national bank currency or not." His voice now resonant and clear, Bryan added, "I want you gentlemen to know that if there is discord in the convention, you cannot lay it at my door. I have been the harmonizer." [14]

The reorganizers, fearful and at bay, fought Bryan with insults. John Sharp Williams accused him of hypocritically pleading for harmony when his was the only voice of discord. For minutes, as the personal attack continued, Bryan sat fanning himself, his face immobile. Finally, he sprang to his feet and declared that his delegation would support the candidate for Vice President that New York wanted and that for the sake of harmony, he would withdraw his amendment to the reply to Parker. "We are not going to do one thing to mar the harmony of the convention," he said, to great applause. The delegates quickly adopted the telegram to Parker, completed Davis' nomination, and adjourned.

If there was a hero in the 1904 convention, it was Bryan. Burdened with the stigma of two Presidential defeats, forsaken by droves of former lieutenants and followers, he seemed foredoomed to political humiliation and burial. Instead, he had risen from the ashes of weakness, and skillfully exposed the vulnerabilities of his foes. He retained his eminence as the most authentic voice of Democratic progressivism and towered, alone and unrivaled, as the rallying point for those of his party who conceived of government as the agency of commonwealth rather than the preserve of wealth.

From Fairview, Bryan issued a statement that dispelled the suspenseful uncertainty in the political world of his attitude toward the Democratic ticket. "I shall vote for Parker and Davis," he said, and gave his reasons: Roosevelt "stands for the spirit of war"; the Democratic ticket "stands for peace, for reason, and for arbitration rather than for force, conquest, and bluster." But Bryan also entered a reservation to his support. He would not, he said, "misrepresent the situation or appeal for votes for the ticket upon false grounds." He had much to be candid about. A Democratic victory, he said, will mean "little if any progress on economic questions. . . . Nothing good" could be expected of Parker on the money question, and although the Democratic antitrust plank was better than the Republican, Parker "nullifies" both the advantage and the plank.

How, with such ample reservations, could he bring himself to vote for the party's nominees? Because, Bryan confessed, he was a Democrat first and an idealogue second. ". . . the Democrat . . . who loves his country has to make his decisions upon conditions as he finds them, not upon conditions as he would like to have them." But party regularity afforded a compensation that he proposed to capitalize on. "As soon as the election is over," he said, "I shall, with the help of those who believe as I do, undertake to organize for the campaign of 1908, the object being to marshal the friends of popular government within the Democratic party to the support of a radical and progressive policy to make the Democratic party an efficient means in the hands of the people for securing relief from the plutocratic element that controls the Republican party and for the time being is in control of the Democratic party. This plan of organization will be elaborated soon." [15]

Bryan's task of rationalizing and reconciling the hostile forces of progressivism and gold conservatism was only half done. His handiwork had yet to pass under the critical eye of his Nebraskan supporters, from whom there were ominous rumblings. His long-standing Populist comrade-in-arms William V. Allen let it be known that Bryan had "made a mistake" in announcing that he would vote for Parker, thereby forsaking the Populist national ticket of Tom Watson and Thomas H. Tibbles. Bryan, observed Allen, had committed himself to remaining in the Democratic Party "whether it accomplishes reform or not."

The prospect of Republican victories in the state brought trouble to a high boil in Bryan's caldron, as he labored to piece together a fusion state ticket. As usual, the Populist and Democratic conventions met simultaneously. But the shrunken fusion framework within which Bryan could toil quickly became obvious. His old political partner Silas Holcomb, whose nomination for governor was long expected, was suddenly scorned by the Populists. Holcomb was suspect of a grave offense—of swallowing "Parkerism." A Populist of the younger generation, George W. Berge, was advanced for the headship of the state ticket. Bryan induced the Democratic convention to accept Berge.

Bryan had difficulty fleshing out the Democratic ticket. The backslide of his own political fortunes encouraged long-building resentments against his tight rule of state party affairs to break through to the surface. In this most difficult of years, Bryan and the party urgently needed to put into the field A. C. Shallenberger, one of the Democracy's best vote getters. But Shallenberger scornfully declined a proffered nomination for Congress in the Fifth District. He explained his decision to the press. At an earlier time, he said, when he wanted the gubernatorial nomination, with solid chances of being elected, "Bryan refused to let me run." Now, with ill winds blowing for the Democracy in 1904, Shallenberger did not choose to run. "Now I hold the whiphand," he elaborated, "and I do not intend to help him and his ambition to run things. I am tired of the dictation of Bryan, and I am glad to let him get the party out of the hole in which he has placed it." [16]

In toiling for fusion, Bryan was handicapped by the small advance of progressivism among Nebraska's Republicans. He was therefore deprived of an external pressure to force Populist-Democratic fusion to preserve their progressive identity. He was also handicapped by the heavy return of conservative gold Democrats to the party fold. By adroit back-room negotiations, Bryan eventually got his fusion ticket, after much trimming and adjusting to the new realities. When a goodly number of Democrats, chiefly gold Democrats, emboldened by Parker's triumph, showed disinclination to accept Berge, the Populist gubernatorial nominee, Bryan, in a brisk floor debate, applied the tarbrush to the malcontents. He welcomed back to the party, he said, "Those who went to the Republicans in the past," but he did not want them to override the Populists now. He moved into an eloquent plea for fusion and endorsement of Berge for governor. "I for one," he cried, "am not willing to say that a Democrat brand shall be upon a certain office than that relief shall be brought to the people of the state."

Fusion was also forged by deals. In exchange for Democratic support of Berge, M. F. Harrington, the Populist intermediary, pledged his influence to achieving Bryan's election as United States Senator, should the fusionists, by grace of the election, control the state legislature. Fusion, however, stopped at Nebraska's borders. The Populists, for understandable doctrinal reasons, refused to accept Parker and fielded their own slate of electors rather than share a common slate with the Democrats.

Bryan also patched together a working rapport with his chief rival faction in the Nebraskan Democracy, headed by Gilbert Hitchcock, who was battling for reelection to Congress. In a mutual aid pact, Bryan helped Hitchcock's campaign, while he supported fusion and the election of a state legislature capable of boosting Bryan into the U.S. Senate.[17]

One of Alton B. Parker's gravest problems was the necessity of luring Bryan into active support of his candidacy. With his millions of followers and his proved capacity as a mighty vote getter in his two national races, Bryan was indispensable if Parker was to garner electoral votes in the Mid and Far West. Since county and local Democratic organizations in those regions were loyal to Bryan, the effort they put out, whether small or large, depended on Bryan's disposition toward the Parker campaign.

Parker and his associates courted Bryan's favor. As an early step toward writing his acceptance speech, Parker secured from Bryan a copy of his 1900 acceptance and searched its paragraphs for cues on colonial policy. In composing his letter of acceptance, Parker gave his "careful consideration" to suggestions that Bryan freely offered. And when Bryan poured praise upon the vehement anti-imperialism of Parker's acceptance, the nominee reciprocated with warm gratitude and the hope that "the outcome in your state will be your election to the Senate. You could render very great service

. . . to the people. . . ." David Bennett Hill also applied his magical ministrations to lure Bryan into the campaign.[18]

But Bryan, too, had interests to be weighed in choosing his attitude. His
loyalty to his party and his standing as a "good Democrat" must not be
doubted. He could not, therefore, assume a do-nothing posture. He must
support the ticket, but how he would do so was subject to almost infinite
choices in degree and kind. These choices would be based on strategic formulations reflecting both present politics and Bryan's future course in the
party. In conversation with Bryan, shortly after the Democratic convention,
Louis F. Post, editor of *The Public*, a progressive journal, absorbed something of the Commoner's perspective. ". . . I am *sure* Bryan really hopes
for Parker's election," Post reported to Tom Johnson. "He thinks it would
take the race question and the Philippine question out of politics and leave
the way clear for economic questions. . . . Bryan would regard Parker's
election by small majorities in pivotal states, yet by a smaller popular vote
in the whole country than he himself got in 1896 and 1900, as ideal from the
point of view of the future radical Democracy."

But waves of developments drowned whatever intentions Bryan entertained of helping Parker. Those archetypes of financial conservatism
Thomas Fortune Ryan and August Belmont opened their purses wide for
Parker. Wall Street titans like James J. Hill and Jacob H. Schiff cried his
praise, and press barons Joseph Pulitzer, Adolph Ochs, and Henry Watterson, who numbered among Bryan's most resolute enemies, sang paeans for
Parker. David Bennett Hill and Grover Cleveland's most capable subalterns, Dan Lamont and Charles S. Hamlin, were his leading counselors.
Viewed from Lincoln, it seemed as though every evil spirit in the East was
dancing favors upon Parker. Worst of all, most Democratic leaders with
whom Bryan was comfortable preferred the triumph of Theodore Roosevelt, who was far more one of their kind.

Faced with this complex of pulls and pressures, Bryan released a press
statement in which he offered "a plan for party reform." Since he was neither an officeholder nor an office seeker, he was at last "free to undertake a
work which until now I have avoided, namely, the work of organizing the
radical and progressive element in the Democratic party." Acknowledging
that Parker's election was "a good beginning," Bryan delineated a platform
that was the very antithesis of anything Parker could stand on. In gathering
planks, Bryan resorted to one of his oldest tactics. He appropriated from
the Populists their best present thinking and exploited it for tomorrow's
Democratic needs. Bryan's recipe for a reformed or reorganized Democratic Party called for state ownership of railroads, government control of
telegraphs, abolition of private monopoly, the income tax, and popular election of judges. His plan marked a turning point on the money questions,
which he acknowledged is "for the present in abeyance." Rising production

of gold and silver "lessened the strain upon the dollar," he conceded, "and while bimetallism is as sound in theory as it ever was the necessity for it is not so apparent." A full decade after the "Cross of Gold" speech, Bryan at last agreed that the silver question was buried beyond resurrection. His platform for the future, Bryan insisted, must be fought for "whether the party wins in November or not."

Bryan continued to dawdle over lending succor to Parker. When at last Bryan took to the hustings, he helped, not Parker, but the Missouri gubernatorial campaign of the brilliant young prosecutor and progressive Joseph W. Folk. After rendering his blows for Folk, Bryan unexpectedly announced that he would now remove himself to Arizona for all September to assure his full recuperation from his illness at St. Louis. Withdrawal and solicitude for health were uncharacteristic of Bryan. Most likely his instinct not to campaign was confirmed by the opinion of radical counselors who bade him to "sit out time." After Arizona, Bryan passed more days on the Chautauqua trail. His favorite lecture, "A Conquering Nation," was a convenient vehicle for lambasting the militant Roosevelt. Although in lectures and in *The Commoner,* Bryan dealt sternly with Roosevelt, he said little of his party leader, Parker.

Bryan's reticence encouraged reports that his behavior in national politics was dictated by a "deal" helpful to his fortunes in Nebraska politics, most particularly his election to the U.S. Senate. Rumors raged of an agreement between Tibbles, the Populist Vice Presidential nominee, and T. S. Allen, Bryan's brother-in-law and political representative, to the effect that Tibbles would support the fusion state ticket if Bryan refrained from booming Parker. Another kind of deal was suggested by Chancellor E. Benjamin Andrews of the University of Nebraska. According to Andrews, votes of the Bryan Democracy in Nebraska were to be cast for Republican electors in exchange for Republican votes for the fusion candidates for the state legislature. Presumably the exchange would produce a legislature disposed to elect Bryan as Senator. Under reporters' questioning, Andrews admitted: "I am not prepared to offer proof that there is an out and out deal . . . but that is the talk throughout the state, and I am convinced that all of Mr. Bryan's personal following and another following which he is able to control will not support Judge Parker." [19]

But these sins were morsels compared with the misfeasance springing from the Roosevelt camp. Disclosures made years after the election revealed that Roosevelt, alarmed at the heavy flow of industrial money into Parker's campaign chest, entreated the magnates for financial support. "He got down on his knees to us," Henry Clay Frick in later years told Oswald Villard. "We bought the son of a bitch and then he did not stay bought."

Frick was referring to contradictions between Roosevelt's behavior before the election and after. Months before the Republican national convention, the President feared that a Wall Street-Mark Hanna coalition might deny him the nomination. In 1903 a brief but sharp financial panic seized the country, with a steep decline in the stock market and an alarming rise in commercial failures. Business leaders, looking for the cause of the malady, cited Roosevelt's harassment. They also spoke of the desirability of the conservative Mark Hanna for President. To reverse the economic trend and to safeguard his imperiled nomination, Roosevelt, prior to the election of 1904, shut down his program of progressive legislation. No unsettling proposals emanated from the White House. Cordial letters were dispatched to J. P. Morgan, E. H. Harriman, H. L. Higginson, and others of their ilk, soliciting their advice on future laws, and pro-administration journalists spewed forth articles proving Roosevelt's concern. Illness and death removed Hanna as a Presidential threat, but Roosevelt, to win contributions for his campaign, continued to be solicitous. His quest for funds was not limited to entreaty. His campaign manager, George B. Cortelyou, employed methods approaching blackmail. Parker attacked Roosevelt and his campaign financing, and the President uttered indignant and unconvincing denials. Promptly after winning the election, Roosevelt resumed his progressive program, to the distress of Frick and other business leaders.

Parker's plain talk of financial malpractice by the moralistic Roosevelt spurred Bryan to bring his voice into the national campaign. As October dawned, Bryan moved into Indiana, Missouri, West Virginia, Illinois, Ohio, and Kentucky. His Indiana schedule was on the scale of his own peak Presidential campaigns. Bryan's speeches were more notable for their zestful attacks on Roosevelt for campaign financing, his militarism, and other lapses than for their attention to Parker. When he did get around to Parker, Bryan was hardly a spectacle of quivering enthusiasm.

In discourse on Parker, Bryan was given to speaking of the nominee and himself as a kind of Moses-Aaron tandem. Moses, Bryan explained, was slow of speech, and Aaron fluent. The crowds quickly learned that Parker was Moses and Bryan, Aaron. ". . . the Lord selected Aaron as his speech maker," Bryan explained and added, in a pointed reference to Parker, "I am willing to be the Aaron of the party if our Moses, who has been slow of speech, will but lead the people out of the wilderness." [20]

"I found it difficult to arouse enthusiasm," Bryan wrote of his efforts for Parker, and the results squared with his assessment. Parker, judicial rather than political in temperament, yielded to Roosevelt the grandest Republican victory since 1872. By every conceivable standard, Parker's race compared badly with Bryan's. He received 1,400,000 fewer votes than Bryan had in 1896 and 1,300,000 fewer than in 1900. Parker carried no Western state, and he lost New York, where his strength was instrumental in gaining him the nomination, by a greater margin than Bryan had to McKinley in 1900.

The chief dent made upon Bryan's scutcheon was Roosevelt's sweep of Nebraska, a disaster for the fusion ticket. Berge fell in defeat, and Hitchcock lost his quest for reelection. With a solid Republican legislature, Bryan's Senatorship went up in smoke. Fortunately for Bryan, his reversals in Nebraska were obscured by the disaster of Parker's national race, and like many another Democratic disaster in the state contests, a goodly share of the blame could be pushed onto the judge's shoulders.[21]

The Parker debacle, in one of its most significant consequences, meant the political redemption of William Jennings Bryan. He lost no time in analyzing the nature of this event in an extended statement to the press. The cause of Parker's defeat was not the candidate, but "mistaken party policy." The defeat was not local, but general, as serious in the East as in the West and South. In essence the American voter repudiated the reorganizers, who had been in "complete control of the party" and had "planned the campaign and carried it on according to their own views." Silver was blameless, "for the campaign was run on a gold basis." The root of the trouble was that the Democratic Party "attempted to be conservative in the presence of conditions which demanded radical remedies. It sounded a partial retreat when it should have ordered a charge all along the line."

In 1904, Bryan contended, the Democratic Party strove to bring back into its ranks "the plutocracy" who had been driven out in 1896. The Republican Party occupies the conservative position—"That is, defends those who, having secured unfair advantage through class legislation, insist that they shall not be disturbed, no matter how oppressive their actions may become." It is sheer political folly for the Democracy to court the plutocracy, for "it cannot do this without losing several times as many votes as that course would win." [22]

What of the future? ". . . hundreds of thousands of honest and well-meaning Democrats who a few months ago favored the 'reorganization' of the party now must choose between turning to the Republican party or join with the Democrats of the West and South in making positive, aggressive, and progressive reform organization. There is no middle ground." The party need not wrestle with the elusive business of choosing the next candidate—that could come later. The need now was to form the line of battle, to take positions on issues featured in Bryan's speeches and lectures: opposition to imperialism and militarism, independence for the Philippines, tariff reform, the income tax, bimetallism, the trusts, improving the position of the wage earner, popular election of the Senate, and the initiative and referendum.

Bryan's recipe for the future had other ingredients unarticulated in his public statement. To Louis Post, he confided his further plan to encourage local Democrats to organize municipal ownership clubs to bring public ownership into their communities. Successful municipal ownership would be the stepping-stone to state ownership of the railroads. To Post, too, he sketched the first steps to implement his call of all good Democrats to the colors. He envisioned a series of huge dollar dinners in Chicago, St. Louis, and Indianapolis to celebrate Jackson's Birthday, arranged over a series of days so that Bryan could attend each. The movement could be continued through the Mississippi Valley and carried into the East. To minimize factionalism, as many elements as possible should be included in the dinners, although participants must be committed to "positive reforms." The goal of the dinners should be the adoption of resolutions "that would put the party right before the country." [23]

Bryan's prescriptions were planted in several fragile assumptions. Not the least of these was his projection of an enduring conservative image for the Republican Party. Roosevelt's Presidency already overset that image, so much so that not a few of Bryan's admirers were clamoring that the Republican President was shamelessly stealing their hero's thunder. With the resources of the Presidency at his command, Roosevelt could give Bryan a mighty struggle for possession of the progressive banner.

Bryan was not alone in feeling the need for immediate action. The "safe and sane" Democrats of the East were like-minded. Now in control of the national party, they meant to shore up their position and hold it on their own terms. Soon after Bryan's public statement, leading Eastern Democrats gathered in New York City at the Manhattan Club for dinner. Parker reportedly sat at the head of the table, and the withholding of the guest list from the press suggested a larger purpose well beyond the announced intention to honor W. S. Rodie, manager of the late upstate campaign.

Tom Watson, speaking from the ruins of the Populist Party, saw only woe for Bryan's political future. Bryan, Watson predicted, would remain the prisoner of his concordat of 1904, venturing that ". . . even if Mr. Bryan should win the nomination on his populist platform in 1908, the plutocratic element in his own party will bar his progress and compass his defeat just as they did before." [24]

22. The Road Back

The November election results had thrust into Bryan's hands the possibility of a political comeback. He might become that rarity, a thrice-nominated candidate for President, a feat that in American annals was the rare distinction of Henry Clay and Grover Cleveland who was rewarded by two victories in his three attempts. The fact that few enjoy the distinction suggests the obstacles to winning it, and Bryan faced the substantial problem of displacing the image of an aging, defeat-prone politician with one of vitality and hope.

In the first weeks after the November debacle, in accord with time-honored politicians' behavior, he gave off a casual air of absorption in diverse private pursuits, all conducive to an appearance of lively, positive, broadening interests. Yet by pronouncement and act, Bryan moved to establish and entrench himself as the premier national spokesman of the Democratic Party. In a January address in Memphis he hailed Roosevelt for pressing for larger powers for the Interstate Commerce Commission and ventured to prescribe the course for all good Democrats in Congress to follow. "The President's attitude," he said, "will cause a split in the Republican party, but Democrats will be found siding with the President."

Bryan's pointed words were quickly followed by his movement onto the Washington scene. His appearance on Capitol Hill was a bold act and a barometer of his new position in the party. For two hours he stood in the lobby of the House, shaking hands and giving opinions to the throngs of Congressmen who crowded about him. He conferred with Democratic Congressional leaders, whose friendly cooperative spirit was marked. In conversation, Bryan did not assume a righteous "I told you so" pose by dwelling on the fiasco of the past campaign. What he said was oriented to the future and to progressivism as the party's salvation.[1]

Bryan's triumphal visit extended to the other end of Pennsylvania Avenue, where he had an audience with President Roosevelt. He found the President deep in work on his Square Deal program of economic and social reforms. Following his impressive electoral victory, Roosevelt cast aside the reserve of his first term and launched a vigorous attack upon abuses. His proposals for new laws included power for the Interstate Commerce Commission to establish reasonable railroad rates, federal licensing for interstate business, safety and maximum working hour regulations for railroad labor, and model social welfare practices for the District of Columbia. After his White House visit, in comments to reporters, Bryan again endorsed Roosevelt's efforts for stronger railroad legislation and federal licensing. Both reposed in Bryan's armory of reforms long before Roosevelt ever dreamed of them. When reporters sniffed incipient fusion between his own and Roosevelt's progressivism, Bryan allowed that "I believe in speaking well of any policy that is good, regardless of which party is supporting it." He anticipated a hazard of his new venture in cooperative politics. "I have often been accused of being a Populist," he said, "merely because I have given my support to some things advocated by that party. I suppose I shall now be accused of being a Republican because I agree with President Roosevelt's views on some things." [2]

Bryan embarked upon a heavy schedule of speechmaking to fortify his place in his party. Notable Democratic political events in the West and South tended to have Bryan as the featured speaker. He got top billing at the inauguration of Joseph W. Folk as governor of Missouri. The most sacred of Democratic holidays—Jefferson's Birthday—saw Bryan in Chicago, sharing the podium with such congenial spirits as Tom Johnson, George Fred Williams, and Mayor Edward F. Dunne.

Bryan moved in further directions in his quest for serviceable issues for 1908. He declaimed upon the virtues of arbitration for disputes between nations. His support of Roosevelt's efforts to secure railroad regulation, he explained, was but a step that "will lead ultimately to public ownership." Bryan, these days, was acting responsively to Mayor Dunne's prescription for a happy Democratic future: "Aggressive Democracy is in the saddle, and if it remains aggressive it will carry the country. If the Democratic platform contains one plank in favor of the Government ownership of railways, telegraphs, and express companies . . . I have no doubt that it will win." [3]

For the restoration of the progressive Democracy, there was much organizational work to do. *Commoner* editorials urged each Democrat to pledge himself to participate in all primaries until the next national convention and to "use his influence to get clear, honest, straightforward definitions of the party position on every question on which the voters of the party desire to speak." *The Commoner* helped provide information and prepared a pledge for each voter to subscribe to, committing himself to the ideals of political participation.

In Western states, new local Democratic clubs were forming, spurred by the accelerating currents of progressivism. In their ebullience, many took on the name of their hero, as they had in 1896. In *The Commoner,* Bryan moved to deter this development and its attendant embarrassments. Better to use the word "Democratic," *The Commoner* suggested, or some old venerated name like Jackson or Jefferson. "Whether Mr. Bryan is ever a candidate for any office again," *The Commoner* explained, "will depend upon circumstances; the question can not be decided now." [4]

A measure of Bryan's comeback was the political importance of the voices raised to laud or condemn his course. Norman Mack, now national committeeman of New York, was typical of party leaders who after twice supporting Bryan crossed over to Parker in 1904. Now they were beating their wings in return flight to Bryan. Bryan, Mack was proclaiming, was "the national leader of the Democratic Party." He had polled more votes than any other living Democrat, and "Until some other Democrat receives a larger number of votes Mr. Bryan will continue to be the national leader of his party."

William Howard Taft, Secretary of War, who was already emerging as Roosevelt's likely successor, seemed to calculate that Bryan would be his opponent and was acting accordingly. In a speech in Akron, Ohio, he let fly a salvo. "It is perfectly apparent," Taft observed, "that Mr. Bryan is gradually resuming control over the Democratic party and proposes to assume the aggressive in a controversy in which he hopes to array the poor against the rich, to shake the present system of private property and freedom of contract." Bryan did not reply directly to the Taftian barrage but quoted with approval in his paper the comment of the Fulton, Missouri, *Gazette*: "Mr. Taft decries the arrayal of the poor against the rich, yet he seems to think it legitimate to arouse popular feeling against Bryan. Is it any worse to array the poor against the rich than to array the rich against the poor?" [5]

The most vital relationship for Bryan in his comeback was with the President. As 1905 proceeded, Bryan assumed a variety of postures toward the Roosevelt administration, each true to his principles and faith. When Roosevelt faltered or erred, Bryan rebuked him. The President's tepid inaugural address prompted Bryan to write, "With the people marshalling for a hand-to-hand struggle with plutocracy there is no bugle call—no inspiring or encouraging word." Repeatedly, Bryan protested the President's taste for violence—his admiring of military ways and his zest for hunting wildlife. A report that a Presidential party on one hunting trip killed six bears and two cats stirred *The Commoner* to plead for stricter game laws. Bryan was free with praise when Roosevelt did what he urged, which was frequent. And nestled in Bryan's praise might be exhortation to Roosevelt to lift his solid achievements to yet higher planes, as when Roosevelt brought off the glittering diplomatic feat of a negotiated peace to end the Russo-Japanese War. His public letter, after hailing Roosevelt as "a peacemaker," swiftly moved on to the observation that the President must realize "how the peaceful victory thus achieved by you outshines your military exploits." He then exhorted Roosevelt to take up an even greater cause—one that Bryan long had advocated—winning the agreement of nations to arbitrate their disputes in lieu of going to war.[6]

Meanwhile, Roosevelt's domestic program was assuming new boldness. The President was pushed by governors pleading for action and muckrakers who laid bare railroad rebate scandals and gross profiteering. Roosevelt's message to Congress in December, 1905, forcefully reiterated his call for legislation requiring railroad services on an equal basis to all at "reasonable and just rates." He demanded that railroads be barred from granting free tickets, passes, and other favors to anyone. In bolder moves, Roosevelt proposed that the railroads' books be open to the ICC's inspection, that overcapitalization of corporations be stopped, interstate insurance transactions supervised, corporate campaign contributions barred, and the misbranding and adulterating of food regulated. Recalling the great coal strike of 1902, Roosevelt proposed that future strikes involving interstate commerce be investigated and "the facts officially reported to the public." Lamenting the courts' role in labor disputes, he proposed to "regulate the procedure" for granting labor injunctions. These were bold steps for a Republican President, but several strides short of Bryan's long-standing positions. Unlike Bryan who sought to lure reluctant labor unions into the political arena, Roosevelt was merely reacting to their presence. Labor's top leaders at last were actively participating in political campaigns, conducting themselves on the principle of rewarding their friends and punishing their enemies.

Roosevelt's tendency to take up ideas that Bryan had long advocated and to incorporate them into the policies of his administration sometimes excited comment by the press and political leaders. He had settled the coal strike by arbitration, which the Democratic platform provided for in 1896 and 1900, and he had recommended railroad legislation, which the Democrats had demanded but on which the Republicans had been silent. Equally popular was his enforcement of the criminal law against the trusts. *The Commoner* illuminated for its readers the obvious lesson: "If the President can achieve popularity by being spasmodically democratic, what would be the popularity of a President consistently and persistently democratic?"

The press delighted to query Bryan concerning Roosevelt's appropriation of his ideas, expecting and perhaps hoping to expose a vein of resentment and frustration. In an interview a reporter asked, "Is it true that President Roosevelt caught you in swimming and stole your clothes?"

"He didn't get all my clothes," Bryan replied, laughing. "I doubt whether what he did get fit him very well. It is hard, uphill work for Mr. Roosevelt to make his administration respond to the country's evident demand for reforms, for the country gave him no mandate." His platform, Bryan pointed out, did not declare that "Our laws and our government should aim at the welfare of the whole people nor that the unjust treatment of the many for the benefit of the few must cease. Mr. Roosevelt's party is not committed to that sort of doctrine, nor is it likely to be." Bryan did not refrain from suggesting that "if a Democratic President is chosen in 1908 he will undoubtedly represent a party committed to this reform idea and will be in quite a different situation from Mr. Roosevelt." [7]

Roosevelt's road indeed was not easy. His railroad proposals advanced at a snail's pace in Congress, encountering strident industry hostility and the opposition of Republican Senate conservatives. Yet he ultimately managed to extract a law—the Hepburn Act—by brilliant use of publicity through sensational revelations in antitrust suits of railroad malfeasance. The muckrakers, whose contributions he did not always welcome, unloosed more exposures. A milestone in federal regulation of industry, the Hepburn Act empowered the ICC to set aside railroad rates upon complaint and prescribe reasonable rates subject to court review. The ICC could examine the railroads' books and regulate other aspects of their conduct. The act was a compromise, and in the legislative struggle, Roosevelt rejected Senator Robert La Follette's demand for physical valuation of the roads as the only sound basis for rate making. Roosevelt pushed through a pure food law, including meat inspection, aided by Dr. Harvey Wiley, chief chemist of the Agriculture Department, and Upton Sinclair's novel *The Jungle,* exposing unsanitary conditions in the Chicago packinghouses. Roosevelt's other successes included an Employers' Liability Act, applicable to common carriers and the District of Columbia, and statehood legislation for Arizona, New Mexico, and Oklahoma.

Roosevelt was sustained by the swelling tides of progressivism, which attained new heights in 1905 and 1906. The statehouses of Missouri, Minnesota, and Iowa were occupied by progressive governors. In New York, another progressive, Republican Governor Charles Evans Hughes, was exposing a web of wrongdoing by the officialdom of major insurance companies, encompassing heavy contributions to Roosevelt's late Presidential campaign. "Fighting Bob" La Follette was a tireless gadfly in the rich man's U.S. Senate, and a former proud conservative, Republican Senator Albert J. Beveridge of Indiana, had been transformed into a reformer, dedicated to winning income and inheritance taxes, a national child labor law, and direct primaries for all elective offices. To David Graham Phillips, author of a brilliant muckraker's exposé of the Senate, Beveridge wrote, "You have no idea how profound, intense, and permanent the feeling among the American people is that this great reform movement shall go on. . . ." As progressivism grew stronger, the shrewd adjusting Roosevelt shifted leftward.

So too did Bryan, and always farther than Roosevelt. His function was to prod and outpace the President, applauding his achievement, scolding if he stumbled, and ever urging him on by example. In those years of political change, Bryan was developing and adjusting his philosophy. He was becoming less a Populist and more a progressive, more urban and less agrarian; less reverential of Jeffersonian decentralization and more receptive to federal action. He placed less reliance on substantive policy such as free coinage at 16 to 1 in the fashion of progressivism and accorded higher value to improving political institutions and processes—to establishing primaries and eradicating political corruption.

Bryan was also engaging in conversations with Professor Edward A. Ross, a sociologist of fast-rising reputation of the University of Nebraska faculty. He was intrigued by Ross' concept of "social sin," founded on the observation that men may harm others not simply by direct violence or threat, but by means not involving close or proximate contact. Thus, stock swindling, adulterated foods and drugs, the employment of children, the failure to use safety appliances in dangerous occupations were social sins. "Too often," Bryan concluded, "educated and cultured men are found increasing their dividends by methods that must be called criminal when measured by any moral law."

Even worse, respectable men's sinfulness worked distortions of society that in their accumulation touched everyone. Fast-spreading trusts closed the doors of opportunity to the wage-earning class. All too commonly, ostentatious displays of wealth were seen "without rendition of equivalent service." Farm tenantry rather than ownership was growing, and "gambling upon the market is being substituted for productive industry." Fabulous fortunes and destitution existed in the cities in the same square mile. The politics of privilege produced a federal tax system falling relatively lightly upon those best able to pay and heavily upon the masses. Great corporations contributed liberally to campaign funds, reaped huge benefactions from government, and polluted the suffrage and bribed officials. "Predatory wealth" blanketed all levels of government with corruption.[8]

Bryan had little confidence that legislatures would provide relief and reform, for they were dominated by lawyers with ties to corporate power. The nation's salvation was possible, he was convinced, only if the citizenry became morally aroused and committed to participation in public affairs and the enforcement of corrective principles. To combat social sin, each individual "owes it to his Creator" and to society to fit himself for the largest possible service and to attain a maximum efficiency in his work. Compensation should be commensurate with service, with each person drawing from society in proportion as he contributes to its welfare. Let every man strive to give reality to the doctrine that "government is made by the people for themselves, deriving its just powers from the consent of the governed, and to be used for the protection of each citizen in the enjoyment of his natural rights and for doing jointly of those things which the community can do for itself better than individuals or corporations can do for it." Every individual must help advance these principles by working to place his party on "the right side" of questions and to nominate for office only those "in sympathy with the common people."

Despite the spread of social sin, Bryan was optimistic of society's capacity for redemption. Just as an individual can be transformed by moral sensitivity "from a fiend incarnate into a ministering angel," so, he asserted, can the conscience of a nation exert a "dynamic force sufficient to destroy any threatened evil and to propagate any needed truth."[9]

Bryan acted by both word and deed. He drove the Nebraska state Democratic convention through the paces of adopting planks demanding that legislators and judges surrender their railroad passes. He engaged in headline-making altercations over the growing ties between the academic community and corporate wealth. He condemned a large financial gift by John D. Rockefeller to the University of Nebraska toward the cost of a new building, rejecting Rockefeller as an "odious eminence" who, having manipulated the railroads' rebate system to bankrupt competitors, would use gifts to bribe a college into silencing its criticisms. At Illinois College, where Bryan and his fellow trustees faced a growing deficit, the college's president, Charles H. Rammelkamp, insisted on seeking funds from Carnegie, Rockefeller and other trust magnates. The trustees passed a resolution sanctioning the step, and Bryan, after fierce resistance, resigned by public letter. By accepting gifts from such sources, he wrote, colleges were selling out to "the plutocrats of the land who are seeking to strangle economic truth. . . . Our college cannot serve God and Mammon. It cannot be a college for the people and at the same time commend itself to the commercial highwaymen. . . ." Bryan's revised philosophy, like his earlier silver philosophy, thus continued to see the political struggle in absolute terms, between good men and bad men. And bad men, while mired in evil, were incapable of good.[10]

Bryan added still another dimension to his political attractiveness when, on September 21, 1905, he and all his family, except Ruth, left San Francisco for a trip around the world. He devoted a year to this enterprise, affording visits to most countries, meetings with statesmen and private personalities, and abundant sight-seeing. Despite his earlier trip to Europe, Bryan had long been pained by his bucolic image, a politician from a small Western state, with farm dust on his boots, and experience that seldom reached beyond his country's shores.

It was an ideal time for this family adventure. Bryan was riding a high-arching curve of popularity; political men believed, with assurance or resignation, that he would win the nomination of 1908. A world journey would impart a knowledge of conditions and acquaintance with foreign leaders at a moment when America's sudden thrust upon the international stage made familiarity with affairs abroad a desirable, if not necessary, qualification of any serious aspirant to the Presidency.

Ample family reasons justified the trip. Grandfather Baird, that blithe spirit Mary had lovingly cared for for twenty years, had died in May, and travel would ease her grief without thrusting a burden upon Bryan's ample income. In fact, the journey would cost him nothing since it was underwritten by articles about the trip that Bryan contracted to supply for the Hearst and other newspapers.

Before departing, Bryan dispatched a farewell letter, bearing counsel and encouragement, to President Roosevelt: "You have the contest of your life before you and I desire to render you all the assistance in my power." Acknowledging the formidable opposition facing the President, of pugnacious industrial titans and crusty railroad magnates, Bryan exhorted, "Stand by your guns! You have developed a reform element in the Republican party; you must lead it or suffer the humiliation of seeing the leadership pass to some one else. . . . Go forward! You owe it to yourself, you owe it to your party, and more than all, you owe it to your country." The mind boggles at the thought of Roosevelt, who deemed Bryan an American Marat, reading this letter.[11]

The Bryans embarked from San Francisco on the *Manchuria,* a giant steamship owned, alas, by E. H. Harriman, a king of the trust makers, whose empire embraced the Union Pacific and Southern Pacific railroads. The *Manchuria* thoroughly conveyed to its passengers the atmosphere of the Orient. The crew, mostly Chinese, wore queues and their national dress. There was a joss house in the steerage and an opium den. After six days of calm seas, the *Manchuria* reached Honolulu, where the Bryans were exuberantly received by a welcoming committee of Democrats, Republicans, native leaders, transplanted Americans, and a coterie of Bryan's fellow Elks. Garlands of flowers, a huge reception at the Royal Hawaiian Hotel, surf riding in native canoes, and the standard tourist routines of watching sugar being processed and seeing the tropical fish in the aquarium took up the brief stay in Hawaii.

In Japan, as in most countries he visited, Bryan was honored at high official functions, but his periodic insistence that he traveled as a private citizen and journalist enabled him to escape from the *haut monde* and resort to gatherings of the common man. Everywhere the Bryans labored gamely to adjust to the idiosyncrasies of Oriental style. They practiced the Japanese custom of removing one's shoes at the front door and donning slippers. This was something of a problem for Bryan, who, being considerably larger than the Japanese, could not find slippers long enough.

The highlight of his sojourn in Japan was a banquet for Admiral Heihachiro Togo, fresh from his glorious triumphs over the Russian Navy. Bryan maintained toward the many toasts that were offered the attitude of an immovable teetotaler. Promptly upon taking his seat at the table of honor, he turned down all the liquor glasses set at his place, and when toasts were offered to the admiral, Bryan drank his with water. Togo, who was startled at noticing this preference, indignantly demanded from the interpreter an explanation of why the distinguished American was not drinking his health in champagne. Tension rolled over the assemblage. Smiling and unruffled, Bryan explained that he was a teetotaler and added, "Admiral Togo won his great victory on water, so I drink to him in water. When he wins a great victory on champagne, then I will drink to him in champagne." Togo was mollified and even delighted by the quick humor. Japanese generally were impressed by Bryan's remark: "Steam has narrowed the Pacific and made us neighbors. Let justice make us friends." [12]

In Korea, Bryan was distressed by the huge numbers of Japanese soldiers in evidence and by the royal family's mood of resignation to incipient abdication. Although the Bryans were the last visitors received at court before the Japanese seizure of the kingdom, the royal interview was an interlude of dignity and grace. Even in this moment of utter peril, the emperor prepared a tray of gifts bearing a large incense burner, a silver box, fans of brocade and ivory, and rolls of exquisite linen and silk of delicate hues and image.

China Bryan characterized as an empire "awakening from a sleep of twenty centuries." Japanese, American, and European influences were permeating the old order, and the emerging China was "a democracy of opportunity for intelligence and ability and perseverance." But there was much in China that repelled him—the congestion, the dirt, the stench. The visit gave him new perspectives on the knotty political question of Chinese immigration to the United States and its implication for the American worker. ". . . no one," he later wrote, "can become acquainted with the Chinese coolie without recognizing the impossibility of opening the doors of our country to him without injustice to our own laboring men, demoralization to our social ideas, injury to China's reputation among us, and danger to our diplomatic relations with that country."

Bryan's advent to the Philippines was awaited by the hostile American and conservative island press as an incipient orgy of indiscretions. Long the outspoken champion of Philippine independence, Bryan was expected in his Manila appearance to thunder away at his old themes and to take the local administration and American policy roundly to task. Setting his teeth to thwart these unflattering premonitions, Bryan was a soul of restraint. He was attentive to the local American community and officialdom, and took Christmas dinner with the secretary of the American Philippine Commission. Then he called upon the revolutionary leader Aguinaldo with a local judge as a kind of chaperon. "Am keeping the interests *balanced up,*" Bryan wrote to brother Charles. One paper, the Manila *American,* impatient with the discreet silence, suggested that Bryan's earlier interest in Philippine freedom was, in truth, stirred by its potential "as a vote-getter." "Hot air," the *American* counseled its readership, "will never build a Filipino nation."

In private conversations with American officials, however, Bryan was utterly forthright. To the governor of Moro Province, General Leonard Wood, he made known his careful opinion that most Philippine problems originated in the circumstance that "the country is governed by laws made for it, but not binding upon the country which makes the laws." Governor Wood found considerably more palatable Mary's opinion that whatever her husband might say about the rest of the Philippines, "the people of the Moro province were not yet ready for self-government." Doubtless the unexpected congeniality of this view assisted Wood's judgment that "Mrs.

Bryan is a sensible level-headed appearing woman and I have no doubt has a restraining influence on her husband." [13]

Moving through Borneo, Java, Ceylon, and Burma, Bryan reached India, which, like the Philippines, was caught in the tentacles of imperialism. Despite Bryan's known hostility, the resident British rulers permitted him to interview subordinates, as well as high officials, and to mingle freely with Indians of his own choosing, including those having ties with agitation led by Mohandas Gandhi. Indians and British alike put before Bryan an abundance of statistics, reports, and petitions unavailable in the United States. "British rule in India," he concluded, "is far worse, far more burdensome to the people, and far more unjust . . . than I had supposed." India, he was impressed, was used for England's benefit, not India's; officials who owed their appointments to England and expected to return there committed their sympathies to the motherland rather than to the natives. The tax system was "nearly twice as heavy in India as in England," and the tax on salt, a vital commodity, was "especially burdensome on the poor." [14]

Spring, 1906, found the Bryans in the Holy Land, marveling at the sensation of discovering the places they knew from the Bible and comparing their reverent imaginings of them with the reality. At the Sea of Galilee they gathered shells and pebbles as mementos for church friends. Cairo, Athens, Constantinople, Vienna, Berlin, the Bryans passed through the capitals of the Mediterranean and northern Europe savoring of their distinctions and delights. From Berlin, they journeyed to Hannover, Germany, to a comfortable pension where Mary and Grace had stayed the summer before and where Bryan proposed to regain thirty pounds he had lost in the Orient. His healthful sojourn was interrupted by reports of the likely dissolution of the first Russian Duma, or legislative body. He rushed to St. Petersburg, and the United States ambassador, George von L. Meyer, arranged for his admission to the diplomatic gallery, whence he could view the assembly, which he admired as unique in the variety of classes and shadings of opinion represented.[15]

The Bryans had a taste of monarchical splendor in Norway when they attended the coronation of King Haakon VII and were accorded the privilege of seats near the throne. For all their democratic proclivities, the Bryans were entranced by the regal spectacle, by the robes of crimson and ermine, the clergy with their miters and scepters, the soft light of the old cathedral restored for the occasion at Trondheim, the chanting of coronation hymns by the people.

In the even greater monarchic splendor of London, the patrician United States ambassador, Whitelaw Reid, took them under wing and heralded their presence with a gigantic July 4 reception at midday, where they shared the limelight with Mrs. Alice Longworth, President Roosevelt's daughter.

For the occasion, there was a general turnout of the English *haut monde* that included the Prime Minister, Sir Henry Campbell-Bannerman, and Winston Churchill. In the evening, Bryan addressed a banquet of the American Society of London. Reid, who had predicted to Roosevelt that Bryan would use the occasion to make a flagrant political address illuminating his claim to the next Presidential nomination, was surprised—and the audience, expecting an impassioned discourse on social evils, disappointed—when the honored guest read an address on "The White Man's Burden in the East." Under this topic, Bryan condemned imperialism and predicted, with an unrestrained optimism, that Christian nations, by their example, "were gradually reforming the world."

Driven by curiosity to view more closely this quaint American cousin from the Western prairie and by a providential instinct that he might become the next President and therefore it was well to cement relations with him, Englishmen in high places pressed forward to make his acquaintance. Even Sir Edward Grey, Secretary of State for Foreign Affairs, withdrawn and grieving from the loss of his wife, emerged to ask Reid to arrange a private meeting with Bryan. The ambassador had not requested that Bryan be presented to the king, believing that it could not be arranged. But King Edward himself asked to see Bryan.

These imperious folk, ensconced in their high places and privileges, unanimously looked down their long noses at this bucolic American cousin. King Edward concluded that Bryan was "agreeable and intelligent but a little gaseous, you know," and Lord Grey found that Bryan "does talk interminably." Bryan's own judgments of these supremely confident men were more charitable. He found the king genial and was delighted by his interest in the promotion of world peace, and he perceived in the cold remote Grey a fine presence of strength. He admired most the Prime Minister, Sir Henry Campbell-Bannerman, both his easy humor, persuasive gifts, and expressed interest in a cause close to Bryan's heart, the promotion of arbitration to settle international disputes.

The chief figures of the American embassy, who tended to think like the British on many topics, entered disparaging and patronizing judgments of Bryan. Ambassador Reid was impressed that Bryan "like all half-educated people . . . dogmatized dangerously on a multitude of topics." [16]

As Bryan crossed the continents, the American political scene was stirring with anticipations of the next national nominating conventions due to gather two years hence. A firm momentum was building for Bryan's nomination. State legislatures, West and South, hailed his talents and commended him for the Presidential office. Prestigious Democrats, conservative and progressive, were speaking of Bryan's nomination in terms of inevitability. David R. Francis of Missouri, once Cleveland's Secretary of the Inte-

rior, hailed Bryan as "Our next President." The conservative Francis acknowledged that he "had differed with this man on a question of principle,"
but asserted that "never have I doubted his integrity, his singleness of purpose, and his loyalty to what he believes to be right." John Sharp Williams,
a reorganizer who had fiercely opposed Bryan in 1904, announced, after
careful soundings of far-flung sources, tht Bryan would be nominated on
the first ballot.[17]

Reporters bearing this good news from the American political mainstream occasionally intercepted Bryan on his journey. To the glad tidings,
he responded in the time-honored manner of Presidential aspirants. He
acted with resolute coyness. "This is so sudden," he said, laughing, to reporters in Berlin. "I have been off the caravan route for some time and have
been absorbed in what I have been seeing and doing." As the momentum
rolled on, Bryan dispatched a letter for release to the press: ". . . who will
be most available in 1908 is a question that cannot be answered now. I shall
not do anything to secure another nomination, and do not want it unless
circumstances seem to demand it—time alone can determine that." For
good measure, Bryan put forward, for responsible citizens to consider, the
names of other qualified Democrats—Congressman Hearst, Senator Bailey,
Governor Folk.[18]

American politics did not stop at the Atlantic shores but leaped across
the waters to Bryan's presence in London. During those summer weeks of
his lengthened stay in the British capital, a succession of American political
figures directed their vacation travel straight to Bryan's presence. Because
of the substantial investment an overseas journey involved, the visitors, although Democrats, tended to be of comfortable economic circumstances
and of conservative persuasion.

Several visitors subjected Bryan to a kind of trial that was the equivalent
of the Great Temptation. Distressed by Roosevelt's increasing tendency to
progressive utterance and impressed by Bryan's controlled and cautious deportment abroad, they now fondly hoped that what many were calling the
new Bryan might take on a conservative image for 1908 in contrast with the
radical Roosevelt. Wealthy Democrats whose purses could underwrite a
campaign on a scale spectacularly beyond anything he had known discreetly scattered their economic blandishments before his presence.

One tempter, George Harvey, president of Harper and Brothers and a
man with strong ties to the financial and political worlds, was at the moment supporting Woodrow Wilson for the Presidency. Nonetheless, he
urged upon Bryan the desirability of a meeting with Thomas Fortune Ryan,
the insurance and mining millionaire who had long been a favorite figure of
the Nebraskan's condemnation. Bryan allowed that he would meet privately with Ryan but voiced fears that knowledge of the event would leak to
the press and kindle suspicion that he was falling under Ryan's moneyed

sway. Bryan outlined the ground rules for any Bryan-Ryan cooperation. So severe was their substance that their likely effect was to dissuade Ryan even from a private meeting. Let Ryan realize, Bryan said, pacing the length of his commodious room at the Hotel Cecil in London, that anyone so rich as he could not join the fight for popular rule "unless he was not only absolutely free from entanglements, but in a position to convince the public that he was free." Bryan pointed the way to this emancipation. Ryan, he said, "should rid himself of all personal pecuniary interests, at least, all corporations having to do with public utilities, railroad stocks and bonds, and all such properties, and invest his money in Government bonds. Then he could stand before the people as having but one interest in the world, that of his country. There his money would be and there his heart would be." [19]

John Sharp Williams, minority leader of the House of Representatives, addressed his charming, persuasive presence to inducing Bryan to renounce his talk of government ownership, heard before this world journey began, and to adopt a conservative stance in contrast with Roosevelt's radicalism. Let Bryan do that, Williams stressed, and he would become the strongest Presidential contender. Bryan's old Tammany friend, Richard Croker, emerged from retirement at his Irish baronial estate, to present similar tidings from Nathan Straus, a public spirited dry-goods merchant. To all these advices and emissaries, Bryan was stone deaf.

To this heroic adamancy there was one exception. George B. McClellan, mayor of New York, came to London to report on a mission undertaken at Bryan's request. Before leaving the United States for his around-the-world trip, Bryan, through William Randolph Hearst, asked McClellan to sound out Grover Cleveland's attitude toward his nomination. "Well," Cleveland had said, "I don't feel as bitterly about Bryan as I once did." A delighted Bryan pressed McClellan for a further disclosure: "Do you think he will back me for the nomination?" he asked anxiously. McClellan replied that this was highly doubtful. Bryan pressed McClellan to continue his courting of Cleveland and launched into a background briefing of his current political position. For almost an hour, Bryan talked at an eager tempo. The tenor of his discourse, McClellan found to his surprise and amusement, was overlaid with a restraint and a conservatism extraordinarily similar to Cleveland's own views. McClellan, who knew Bryan well, viewed the incident only as a demonstration of the high value he had come to place on the attitude of Cleveland. [20]

In London, Bryan attended the Peace Congress of the Interparliamentary Union, and on July 24, 1906, he was the featured speaker of this convocation of delegates from many nations devoted to the quest for peace. Bryan did not disappoint the crowd that jammed the Royal Gallery of the House of Lords. He was at the top of his oratorical form. The London *Standard* reported that his voice rang out like "a silver clarion," and the *Daily Mail* that his audience listened "with rapt and appreciative attention." Bryan's efforts that day reflected his fast mellowing ideas concerning world peace. He supported a resolution deploring the "intolerable expenditures on armaments," and when a model arbitration treaty excluded questions of national sovereignty and honor, he proposed an amendment committing even these subjects to arbitration. His amendment also required that nations in dispute "shall not resort to any act of hostility before separately or jointly inviting . . . the formation of an international commission of inquiry or mediation on the part of one or more friendly powers." Bryan's amendment was unanimously adopted, a miracle that was speeded by his fervid oratory. Even the most hard-bitten old diplomat was moved when, in a dramatic volley, Bryan pointed his long finger to a painting of the death of Admiral Nelson and exclaimed, "There is as much inspiration in a noble life as in a noble death."

In this final phase of his European sojourn, Bryan crossed to the continent for a lightning tour of Holland, a trip up the Rhine, and a sweep through Switzerland, Italy, France, and Spain. With Mary he had resolved that they must be home in time for the children to start the school year.

Bryan was eager to return. Except for the London period, with its passage of lively politics, he had been protractedly wrenched from his trade for the first time since taking it up and forced to be an observer rather than a participant. For much of the trip, his indomitable spirit had to fight off gnawings of ennui. From Damascus, he had written Charles, "It will only be about 4 months until I reach home and I am counting the days." Several months later: "While we are enjoying ourselves I shall be glad to be home again." As a traveler, Bryan had strongly specialized tastes. For political institutions and religious practices he had a keen eye. But Henry White, who journeyed with him through Italy, was struck by his slight interest in historic places and things.[21]

On August 20, the Bryans departed from Gibraltar on the *Princess Irene* for their voyage home. It was a happy crossing, enlivened by Edgar Lee Masters and Millard Dunlap and their families. In the ten-day journey Bryan kept to his cabin, drafting and refining a major address to mark his homecoming.

For weeks, the American mainland had seethed with plans to make his return a gala monumental event. Madison Square Garden had been hired as the forum for his address. Legions of friends from everywhere in the country migrated to New York. Western trains put into force excursion rates for passengers heading for the Bryan reception. From Omaha a special train left with a delegation of Nebraskans, led by Mayors Frank W. Brown of Lincoln and James C. Dahlman of Omaha. Important Democrats across the country contributed to the reception's expenses, and when Bryan's steamer was sighted off Fire Island, New York resembled a political convention with its concentration of major Democrats. Mayors, governors, Senators, and Congressmen stood shoulder to shoulder awaiting Bryan's imminent arrival.

When his steamer moved into New York Harbor, the whistles of ships and factories blew, and some 300 Nebraskans jammed themselves into two tugs. Moving alongside his liner, they greeted him with wild, affectionate acclaim. "Cowboy Jim" Dahlman expertly slipped a lasso around Bryan, who cried in his huge voice, "The sight of you is good for sore eyes." Soon Bryan was hugging Dahlman and a succession of Nebraskans. Mary, too, was greeted and hugged, while reassuring a new family pet acquired in their travels, a dachshund fondly named Richard Croker.[22]

The following day provided the climax of the homecoming, Bryan's address at Madison Square Garden. Circumstances now constituted it one of the most important utterances of his career. For more than a year he had made no public address, and except for a random editorial in *The Commoner* and several slender interviews with the press, he had withdrawn from political discussion. His fortunes at this moment had risen to a new plateau of opportunity. Despite his two defeats for the Presidency, the rare privilege of a third nomination seemed well within his grasp. Even more important was the circumstance that never before in his quest for the office had his chances for winning it been more impressive than at this moment. For the first time, stirrings of acceptance and even of cooperation were evident in quarters of his party that always had rejected and resented him.

His awaited speech, therefore, could both reaffirm and speed up the processes of healing the party divisions that were the remnants of his previous candidacies and solidify even more his claim to a third nomination. He was not lacking for advice as he drafted and redrafted his address. Democratic politicians, hungry for victory in the approaching elections, perceived on the roseate horizon a cloud, larger than a man's fist and more ominous than a bomb with a lighted fuse. They were troubled by reports drifting across the waters that Bryan in his European visit was hunting for new issues and that he had joyfully settled upon the national ownership of railroads. Alarmed that advocacy of this position would blow the new-forming party unity to smithereens, Democratic leaders—Senators Joseph Bailey and Charles A. Culberson of Texas and the Democratic leader of the House, John Sharp Williams—pleaded with Bryan, virtually on their knees, to avoid all reference to the railroad question in his coming speech. From Mary, too, there was counsel, of a different sort. Mindful of earlier experience, she begged him not to read his speech. Ever self-willed, Bryan rejected both proffers of advice. To Mary he explained that he would be misrepresented unless he read from a prepared text. She retorted that he would be misrepresented anyhow, but he was not to be budged.

Madison Square Garden on that August night was a sweltering pit overflowing with about 12,000 human beings. Bryan's appearance on the stage touched off a vast crescendo of cheers, a tribute so affectionate and so moving that, although his lips were set in a firm line, he could not hold back his tears.

He began his hour-long address by reporting his finding in the Old World of "a growing sentiment against war, and in favor of the substitution of arbitration for force." Henceforth he would seek to bring his own nation "to enter into a treaty with every other nation, submitting every question for investigation before commencing war." He confessed that as he grew older, he found his aversion to the killing of men increasing, and in moving tones he recounted how "I stood but a few weeks ago at the birthplace of Shakespeare and asked myself what would the world have lost if he, in the enthusiasm of the youth, had entered the army and had been killed upon the battlefield." To a hushed, respectful audience, he cried, "Oh, my friends, we have reached a point where I deny that our Creator ever made the progress of the human race dependent upon an occasional blood-letting." For the cause of peace, he urged that the United States withdraw from colonialism, free the Philippines, and renounce the use of the Navy as a collection agency for private debts.

His journey, he said, had brought the unpleasant discovery that some European governments were more responsive to the popular will than his own. To improve the American posture, he urged the popular election of Senators, a national income tax, an eight-hour workday, and arbitration of labor disputes. These, he said, were "nonpartisan" questions.

As for future issues, most likely the antitrust question would dominate the political struggle of 1908. Bryan demanded laws coping with the holding companies that trusts were weaving together to avoid regulation. He again called for federal licensing of interstate corporations and regulation of corporate campaign contributions.

He then moved into the railroad question, the subject of intense apprehension to his victory-hungry Democratic counselors. He began reassuringly by hailing the President for his strivings at railroad regulation but quickly warned that an appointed regulatory commission, which Roosevelt contemplated, might prompt railroad leaders to choose a President friendly to their interests. In that event, Bryan said, "The sentiment in favor of government ownership is likely to increase as rapidly throughout the country as the sentiment in favor of municipal ownership has increased in the cities." Acknowledging that he did not know "that a majority of my own party favor" government ownership, he nevertheless ventured to offer his own plan. He opposed federal ownership of all the railroads because it "would so centralize the government as to almost obliterate state lines." He preferred to see the interstate lines operated by the federal government and the local lines within a state by the states. Public ownership, he noted, was common in Europe, and the plan he proposed was operative in Germany. Bryan concluded with a fierce volley against plutocracy, its incompatibility with a republic, its drain upon national strength, its vulgarization of society, its mockery of morals. "The time is ripe for the overthrow of this giant wrong. . . ."

The railroad passages of the speech required less than four minutes of the hour-long address to read. But the newspapers, particularly the hostile Eastern press, blazoned in their headlines Bryan's proclaimed commitment to government ownership. The brevity demanded by headlines and the lead paragraph of the news story tended to strip the press accounts of the several qualifications Bryan attached to his proposal. Those who had fondly hoped that a year of foreign travel and removal from domestic politics had produced a new Bryan now drank the dregs of disappointment. The Bryan of Madison Square Garden in espousing government ownership, the hallmark of outright Socialism, seemed enormously more menacing than the young impassioned silver orator of 1896.[23]

Throughout the political community, Bryan's position produced no wheat, but only the chaff of concern, fear, and disparagement. Conservative Democrats, taking up a heavyhearted search for another candidate, were disposed to take a second look at the young governor of New Jersey and a newcomer to the national political scene, Woodrow Wilson. Southern Democrats such as Joseph Bailey, John Sharp Williams, and Thomas S. Martin simply writhed in anguish. Some of these men and "others of their kind," in the opinion of George Fred Williams, drew spirit for their opposition from the fact that they were "under the direct influence of the railroads." Grover Cleveland's recent slight mellowing toward Bryan evaporated, and he openly doubted that "the recent symptoms of Bryan insanity" would again overtake the party. Among Republican leaders, rejoicing and new confidence in the future reigned. "I drew a sigh of relief after reading Bryan's speech," Roosevelt wrote to Henry Cabot Lodge. "I think he has helped us immensely. Down at bottom Bryan is a cheap soul. He felt that he had to take an attitude that would show that he was really a great deal more radical than I was." [24]

The furor over his railroad remarks distressed Bryan, and Mary regretfully found vindication in her forecast that even a read address, couched in the most careful qualifications, would be artfully distorted by a malevolent press. In a speech at Louisville, Kentucky, a stop on a tour of the border states and the upper South to help local tickets, Bryan took pains to clarify his position on railroad ownership. His effort consisted largely of repeating the qualifications couching his pronouncements in New York that he did not know if the country was ready for such legislation, that a majority of his own party might not favor it, and that indeed, "If you ask me whether the question of government ownership will be an issue in the campaign of 1908, I answer I do not know." At Raleigh, North Carolina, he went on to recall that Roosevelt had declared in two messages that if railroad regulation should prove ineffective, government ownership might follow. Why, Bryan wondered aloud to his audience, should his remarks cause such a stir when the President's did not?

Bryan's campaign for Congressional and state tickets of 1906 led through Indiana, Illinois, Ohio, and Iowa and to Nebraska itself, for his customary big effort for the fusion slate. "The vote this year," Bryan told his Nebraska audiences, "will be taken as an indication of the trend of public sentiment. We are entering upon a great fight for the extermination of the trusts and the protection of the public from injustices at the hands of the railroads." The trend the elections revealed, as Bryan implied they would, was toward progressivism. The South demonstrated that preference in electing its governors. The new state of Oklahoma, with Bryan's help, approved a progressive constitution and a Democratic ticket. But Republican progressivism had its innings, too. Hughes triumphed in New York, and in Nebraska, where Bryan's fusion ticket lost, Republicans elected a reform governor and a progressive legislature. Of the Democratic Congressional tickets, only Gilbert Hitchcock squeaked through. Although Bryan made upwards of thirty speeches in George Norris' district, the young Republican, a new meteor in Nebraska's firmament, prevailed.

The 1906 elections swung Roosevelt, as sensitive to shifts in public opinion as the finest seismograph, to positions more left than ever. For the remainder of his term, in word and act, he was the exemplar of progressivism. Where once he had distinguished between good and bad fortunes, now he dismissed all great fortunes as "needless and useless." His newly acknowledged mission was to forestall "the least attractive and most sordid of all aristocracies," a plutocracy. He inveighed against the "ruling clique" of the houses of Congress and the Republican national committee "who seemed to regard every concession to decency as merely a matter of bargain and sale." Once La Follette was "a shifty self-seeker"; now Roosevelt expressed approval of the Senator. Even Bryan, whom the President earlier called an American Marat, became tolerable, a "kindly, well-meaning, emotional man." To intimates, Roosevelt confided his purpose to transform his inherited "ultra-conservative" party into one of "progressive conservatism or conservative radicalism."

Roosevelt's mood was accompanied with enlarged requests for new legislation and bold executive action. When ranchers, mineowners, power com-

THE ROAD BACK **417**

panies, and lumbermen pressed Congress into passing a law forbidding, in effect, the creation of new forest reserves in Western states without legislative assent, Roosevelt foiled their underlying purpose to open up public lands for private exploitation. He delayed signing the law while moving millions of acres into the national reserve. Legislators and their thwarted Western friends cried of executive "impudence" and "dictatorship." The President hammered away at his earlier tax, labor, and railroad proposals and espoused La Follette's plan for railroad rates based on physical valuation. He urged federal regulation of stock-market gambling and struck at "predatory wealth," or the dishonesty of men of great wealth who injected "rottenness" into business and fought every public regulation and reform. Roosevelt was specific. Executives of Standard Oil and the Santa Fe Railroad, he said, had opposed "Every measure for honesty in business that has been passed during the last six years . . . with every resource that bitter and unscrupulous craft could suggest and the command of almost unlimited money secure."

If imitation is the highest form of flattery, Bryan must have been overwhelmed with gratification. Roosevelt's boldest words and acts were pages out of his own past. The President was demanding and sometimes accomplishing what Bryan for years had been preaching, but Roosevelt's conversion to the true gospel posed a special problem for its originator. Since 1896 Bryan had been the most advanced spokesman in national politics of popular causes. The leftward-galloping Roosevelt threatened to overtake him in that proud role.

Bryan's advocacy, accordingly, of government ownership of railroads was a response to the dilemma posed by Republican progressivism. The pronouncement, however qualified, moved Bryan into a new, advanced position, distinguishable from the competition. But as the consequent outcry demonstrated, it worsened the other element of his dilemma. It outraged conservative Democrats, especially in the East and South, just as they were faintly stirring toward a kind of acceptance. And if the elections of 1896 and 1900 had taught anything, it was the simple lesson that Bryan could not win, unless somehow he rallied behind himself both wings of the Democratic Party.[25]

In *Commoner* editorials, in lectures and speeches, in a torrent of activity whose quantity and tempo were doubled by his year's absence from the political scene, Bryan set forth a platform of beliefs and positions responsive to the fast-maturing progressive age. The age, he believed, was dominated by a moral awakening which rejected the old view that life's success is measured in material accumulation. For a generation plutocracy had been running riot, compiling new records of extravagance. Now people increasingly realized that money must be no longer the master, but only the means to just ends. Legislation was a supplementary force to conscience in protecting the citizen from the injustices of other citizens. But legislation could not perform that function when government was subservient to plutocracy and exploited for its enrichment. The time had come when democracy in its literal Greek meaning—the people rule—must be genuinely applied. Bryan joined in the advocacy of two measures widely discussed in progressive circles: the direct primary and public regulation of campaign contributions.[26]

He also singled out several areas where governmental action was necessary to offset lapses in private conscience with consequent injustices and hardships. High on his list was vigorous prosecution of the trusts under the Sherman Law and the prohibition of specific activities such as interlocking directorates that advanced the trusts. For the most controversial issue, the railroads, Bryan demurred from Roosevelt's recommendation to Congress to provide either for their national incorporation or for licensing by which they might engage in interstate commerce upon satisfying certain federal conditions. To equate these as alternatives was unacceptable. National incorporation, Bryan stressed, was clamored for by the railroads to escape the control of states with stringent regulations, but a licensing system, properly devised, would not infringe on the states. Bryan soft-pedaled government ownership. Although he referred to it as "the ultimate solution," he cheerfully acknowledged that "a large majority of the people still hope for effective regulation, and while they so hope, they will not consider ownership." Regulation, he said, "must be tried under the most favorable circumstances" before the masses would be ready "to try a more radical remedy." Since regulation could not be sufficiently tested within a year, "there is no desire anywhere to make government ownership an issue in 1908." There was, needless to say, a wide rejoicing in the community of Democratic politicians at Bryan's statement.

Bryan could put the quietus on the government ownership issue with a modicum of grace, thanks to the emergence of William Howard Taft in 1907 as Roosevelt's chosen successor. On the night of his electoral victory in 1904, Roosevelt, impressed with the wisdom of the two-term tradition, had declared, "Under no circumstances will I be a candidate for or accept another nomination." Having abjured the race, Roosevelt did the next best thing and handpicked his own candidate, Secretary of War William Howard Taft. Of a venerable, moderately wealthy family of Cincinnati, Ohio, Taft had never run for public office. His career had been passed in the judiciary and in appointive administrative posts. From a judgeship in Ohio's Superior Court, Taft became U.S. Solicitor General, a federal circuit court judge, president of the Philippine Commission, governor-general of the Philippines, and Secretary of War. An elephantine man of some 300 pounds, amiable, and placid, Taft was unambitious, of high character, and

amply endowed with the lawyer's trained mind. Devoted to order and repelled by strife, Taft while on the bench delighted business with his antilabor decisions. Cautious, literal, and legalistic, Taft, compared with the
progressive Roosevelt, seemed obdurately conservative. Because Bryan was
now running against Taft, rather than Roosevelt, the pressures to assume a
more advanced progressive stance were reduced.[27]

Bryan, ready to lead the people farther into the Elysian fields of the progressive age, went among them as Chautauqua lecturer and political campaigner to bring the tidings. His two speaking roles, one private and the
other public, were not readily separable. "Bryan," noted Dr. George L. Miller, his old foe in Nebraska politics, "is lecturing on everything on the face
of the earth. . . . He is a thrifty fellow. All this talking all over the country
brings him in money, and keeps up his political machine at the same time."
His lecture on "The Moral Awakening" fitted equally well the Chautauqua
circuit and political audiences. In Richmond, Virginia, an audience of
about 4,000 assembled for proceedings of a religious nature, with Bryan's
address the awaited climax. But politics, too, was in the air, as evidenced by
the presence of Governor Claude Swanson and other Democratic officials
of the state on the platform. Bryan's remarks were devoted in part to religious themes, and to them were added some fiery strictures on Rockefeller,
Roosevelt, the trusts, and "tainted money."

That Bryan roamed far and wide and into the tiniest of byways is evident
from his adventures and misadventures on the oratorical trail. Because he
missed a train, he had to keep a Chautauqua date by riding by auto from
Goldfield to Iowa Falls, Iowa, through forty miles of hub-deep mud, no
small evidence of his unflagging persistence. At St. Johnsbury, Vermont,
following a lecture, a harness snapped, and the horses of Bryan's carriage
broke at a run down a hill. He jumped out of the vehicle and landed safely
just as the horses began their mad gallop. At another removed place, Storm
Lake, Iowa, Bryan, driven by auto following a lecture, was crashed into by
another auto, driven by a matron and carrying a second matron in the back
seat, who was thrown to the ground and slightly injured. Bryan sprang out,
lifted the lady back into her car, cranked it for her, and off she started.

Bryan's major speeches stressed the fact and the necessity of unity in the
Democratic Party. In a key midyear speech in New York, he declared with
satisfaction that the party was "never more united," and he went on to
plead for a closer union of East and West and better understanding between the farmer and the trader. A favorite Bryan tactic was a dwelling on
the failings of his chief Republican rivals—Roosevelt, when it appeared he
might run again, and then Taft, when he emerged as the President's successor. Bryan delighted to demonstrate how Roosevelt's Square Deal program
of social reforms stole Democratic thunder but left much to be desired by

Democratic standards. "If you ask me if he is Democratic," he told one audience, "I answer after the manner of Peter Cartwright, the pioneer preacher of Illinois, who when asked if he was sanctified, replied, 'Yes, in spots.' The President is Democratic in spots, and while the spots are not as large as they ought to be, or as numerous as I might wish them, a Democratic spot looks beautiful to me, no matter upon whom I see it." [28]

With William Howard Taft, Bryan seized upon several evident political traits of the Secretary of War for jest and ridicule. Taft was the "great postponer." Taft had advised Oklahomans, engrossed in the transformation of their territorial government into statehood, to reject a proposed progressive constitution until a better—and less progressive one—could be devised. (In reality, Bryan explained, Taft sought to keep Oklahoma's potential seven electoral votes from the Democrats.) Bryan belabored Taft for other procrastinations: He favored tariff reform, but not until after the next national election; he favored an inheritance tax, but would postpone it; and the income tax, he would "postpone indefinitely."

Bryan's hostility to Taft extended to the point of openly bestowing his blessings upon the national Republican figure whose sentiments most closely matched his own on national issues, Robert M. La Follette. In *Commoner* editorials and articles, Bryan viewed with disdain the ascendance of Taft and the ignoring of La Follette. "What has Secretary Taft done to indicate that he is a reformer," asked Bryan, ". . . who will give bond that, if elected, he will stand up bravely against the demands of Wall Street?" And he added, "If the Roosevelt policies are all they are represented to be it would seem that Senator La Follette would be Mr. Roosevelt's first choice." [29]

Bryan was carefully cultivating old political friends and new potential supporters around the country. As the year wore on, these influential figures spoke out for his candidacy. Mayor Tom Johnson of Cleveland was early in proclaiming he would work to get an Ohio delegation for Bryan. Senator R. F. Pettigrew proclaimed from Washington that Bryan deserved to be President to carry out the policies he long had advocated and which Roosevelt achieved with only mixed results. Both an old personality like Ben Tillman and a new one like Tennessee Senator Robert L. Taylor told the world that Bryan was to be the next nominee. These welcome endorsements were by no means left to chance. At midyear, Bryan's good friend, the "cowboy mayor" of Omaha, Jim Dahlman, embarked upon an extensive expedition as Bryan's political emissary. In his first stop, Wyoming, Dahlman made ten speeches and consulted with local leaders throughout the state. He moved on through the central states and into the East. Everywhere, he furthered a well-defined objective: "We want solid delegation support for Mr. Bryan," he said, "and we want him nominated unanimously on the first ballot." Had Bryan authorized his tour, Dahlman was asked. "He doesn't exactly consent," the cowboy mayor replied, "but he knows just what I am doing, and what I intend to do."

The opposition to Bryan was scarcely visible, being largely city bosses who tended to hug the shadows. Alarmed by the Bryan momentum, they gathered in New York City to lay plans to halt it. The assembled bosses included Tom Taggart of Indianapolis, national committee chairman; Roger Sullivan of Illinois; Colonel James Guffey of Pennsylvania; James Smith, Jr., of New Jersey; and William J. "Fingy" Connors, the New York State chairman. Hailed irreverently as Standard Oil Democrats, all were connected with Standard Oil and other corporations. For a dire problem, they hoped to construct a simple solution. If they could but control their state delegations, they could defeat Bryan's nomination. The New York meeting was the first of several conclaves of the bosses. Fingy Connors emerged from the deliberations to laugh, for the enlightenment of gathered reporters, at the idea of Bryan's nomination. Bryan, he stressed, was "worse than Roosevelt." The country wanted a conservative administration.[30]

As in his two previous quests for the nomination, Bryan was aided and his opponents were handicapped by the failure of any serious rival to emerge. Old and new personalities flickered only dimly on the horizon. William Randolph Hearst, one of the few strong national Democratic figures, had suffered the damage of crushing defeat in his late gubernatorial race in New York against Charles Evans Hughes. Nevertheless, Hearst men were stirring for the Presidential prize of 1908. In late summer, leaders of his Independent League from many states gathered in New York. New York Democrats were eyeing with fond hope their lieutenant governor, Lewis Stuyvesant Chanler, who by some electoral miracle had squeaked through to victory while Hearst collapsed in utter defeat. "He is the only man I know who can carry New York State," former Congressman Jacob Ruppert said.

Otherwise, the scene of Democratic Presidential hopefuls was thinly peopled. To those eager to block Bryan, the young progressive Governor John A. Johnson of Minnesota was a shining knight, but he spread withering discouragement over efforts on his behalf by declaring of Bryan's candidacy that "To attempt to wrest the honor from him would only result in suicide." Conservative Democrats looked hopefully to Woodrow Wilson. George Harvey, a leading promoter of Wilson, viewed Bryan with distaste and referred to him publicly as a "leader who hobbles like a cripple in the wake of his successful rival, gathering as he goes the few scraps that are left of his own fallacies." Wilson, too, thought ill of Bryan and declared to the press: "There are specific objections that I could point out in Bryan, political propositions in his platform that I consider absurd. . . ." But Wilson continued to resist all entreaties that he become an active candidate. Privately, however, he possessed an ambition nurtured in many Democratic breasts, which he conveyed in a letter to the industrialist Adrian Joline: "Would that we could do something, at once dignified and effective to knock Mr. Bryan once and for all into a cocked hat." [31]

23. Let the People Rule

The Mr. Bryan upon whom Woodrow Wilson proposed to wreak such devastation already bore the marks worked by time and his own hard pace of nearly two decades in national politics. The luxuriant crown of raven hair was replaced by a bald pate, whose hairy fringe was flecked with gray. New lines crossed his face, and old ones were deeper. The solid athletic stance had given way to a bulgy waistline and puffy cheeks. The gargantuan appetite was now a trifle regulated. The years of eating hard and rushing about had made his table manners aggressive and unkempt. In a new dietary policy, Bryan was consuming large quantities of water between meals, but at mealtime no glass or cup was set for him. The water diet required him to absent himself frequently for trips to the lavatory. His habit of leaving the door open was not appreciated by fastidious reporters.

Bryan was no longer a national bogeyman. Theodore Roosevelt had helped rescue him from that infamy by adopting many of his ideas. No more did Bryan inspire clergymen to thunder reproach at him as the bearer of anarchistic ideas and the conjurer of class hatred. Here and there a man of property still might tremble, but as *The Nation* observed, "People really can't work themselves up into a fright . . . any more. . . . How can they be expected to despise in Bryan what they have applauded in Roosevelt?"

If anything, the strongest element in Bryan's image was that of an evangelical missionary whose parish was the United States of America, its churches, YMCA's, schools, colleges, lyceums, and Chautauquas. This man, who seemed utterly without blemish, fervently championed all the virtues and pitilessly denounced all the vices. His most popular lecture, "The Prince of Peace," was a masterpiece of pure translucent goodness. Some who witnessed these evangelical sallies were impressed that Bryan's nearly two decades of concentrated platform experience, of easy success in captivating audiences, had slowed his mental growth and lent unctuousness to his manner. Had his career been passed differently—say, in a legislative body—where his views could have been challenged in dialogue and his thinking processes sharpened, his intellectual development might have acquired a profundity precluded by years passed before approving, adulating audiences that never talked back.

Undoubtedly Bryan acquired acceptance by the mere process of growing older. Some correspondents who had trailed at his busy heels through the years perceived that the aggressive flamboyant youth had been superseded by a middle-aged man, endowed with a more patient comprehension of life's realities. "Mr. Bryan," wrote James Creelman, "is mellower and sweeter. He is graver." As most other humanity would be, Bryan was impressed with the importance of age. "When you first knew me," he reminded a reporter, "they called me, in derision, 'The Boy Orator of the Platte.' I have outlived that title and my grandchildren are now growing up about me." [1]

The grandchildren in question were the tiny son and daughter of Ruth, who at eighteen had married William Homer Leavitt. The attractive, brilliant, self-willed Ruth decided at seventeen that she wanted more than anything else in the world to marry Leavitt, who had come into her Lincoln home to paint a portrait of her father. The handsome, worldly artist intrigued her, but Bryan and Mary, perceiving in the situation the ingredients of disaster, warned Ruth against the marriage and worked strenuously to prevent it. The havoc Ruth's adamancy cast upon Bryan's loving, close-knit family was evidenced by Mary's absence from the eventual marriage ceremony. Bryan, the dutiful father, attended, grief creasing his face, and his solitary act at the close of the service was to press a formal kiss upon his daughter's brow. After the children were born, the marriage unfortunately fulfilled Bryan's prediction and collapsed. Leavitt fled to Paris, and Ruth sued for divorce in Colorado. With the elections approaching, Bryan was watchfully supervising Ruth's journey through the distasteful legal processes.

Bryan's younger daughter, Grace, posed the problem of frail health. Of all his children, Grace resembled him most. Dark-eyed and raven-haired, tall, and magnificent-looking, Grace was now seventeen and a student at Hollins Institute near Roanoke, Virginia. In Bryan's second Congressional term, the girl had fallen critically ill with pneumonia and was weakened for years to the point of requiring special care and sojourns in warm climates. Whereas Ruth was daring and flamboyant, the author of a play produced in New York, president of the Women's Democratic Club of Denver, and a lecturer in the extension service of the University of Nebraska, Grace was quiet and studious, fond of music, fiction, and horses, as all Bryans were.[2]

William, Jr., at nineteen was, in Mary's estimate "one hundred percent boy," with a mischievous streak and a facile mind that enabled him to do good work in school with little effort. He long thwarted Bryan's and Mary's earnest hope that, like his father, he would excel in public speaking. But

William, despite urgent parental encouragement, developed only an aversion to it until at Culver Military School he somewhat relented.

Although the children had grown to maturity, Bryan and Mary were never lonely at Fairview. Ruth, in this unsettled interval, passed half her time there, and Grace, for whom there was no more cherished place in the world, returned at every opportunity. From school in nearby Indiana, William could come easily. Fairview, which overlooked the little settlement of Normal, was easily accessible to visitors. In Lincoln one could board a trolley which, after brushing tall sunflowers overhanging the roadbed, halted at Bryan's mansion.

From the moment they arrived in their new home the Bryans started building friendships with their neighbors. To the farmer across the way, Bryan was "the squarest Christian I ever knew. When my pasture gave out last September, he said to me, 'Why I've plenty, Jim; just turn your cows in with mine.' " Down the road, Bryan trudged up to the porch of another farmer to deposit a bushel of potatoes. "They're my best Carmens Number 1," he explained. "I thought maybe you could use them."

In the little Methodist church at Normal, which the Bryans attended because it was closer than the Presbyterian Church in Lincoln, where they were members, Mary and Bryan taught Sunday school whenever they were at home. They belonged not to the Country Club, which had a bar, much to their distaste, but to the Farmers' Club, which embraced most of the farm families round about. The focus of local social life, the Farmers' Club in slack winter months would arrange meetings at members' homes, where as many as fifty people would gather from morning until dark. Each family brought chicken, roasted, broiled, or fricasseed; pies, mince, custard, and pumpkin; and all the cakes in the cookbook. At the Bryans' the high point of these gatherings transpired when their host sat down at the grand piano and turned on the pianola attachment. "Now let's have some music," he said. "What'll it be?" "Let's have Pentecostal Hymn Number Three," someone would reply, " 'I'll Go Where You Want Me to Go.' " This, as everyone knew, was Bryan's favorite hymn, and his clear baritone led the motley voices.

Like everything else in their lives, Fairview was for Mary and Bryan a shared experience. Local folk were accustomed to seeing Bryan helping in the field in an old straw hat and hitching suspenders and Mary in a blue sunbonnet, with a tin pail on her arm, throwing corn to the White Wyandotte chickens.[3]

One after another the states were choosing delegates for the national convention and instructing for Bryan. In the South and the Far and Middle West, support for him rolled on like an invincible juggernaut. In the winter and spring of 1908, Bryan toured the country, fulfilling one of his heaviest schedules ever of lectures and speeches. His appearances sometimes took place just before a state convention gathered to choose its delegates. If plans to oppose him began to flutter, his sudden appearance would bring recalcitrants to their senses. With a popularity among Democratic masses that equaled Roosevelt's among Republicans, and with friends, supporters, and politicians in his debt scattered throughout the country, the heritage of his continual campaigning, Bryan had the elements of a national personal machine. In the West or South, he could ignite a revolt against any politician who dared oppose him. "If a Southern Representative or Senator," *The Nation* noted, "were to come out publicly for a candidate other than Bryan, there would instantly be talk of sending another man in his place." "To be suspected of disloyalty to Bryan," noted the experienced reporter Arthur W. Dunn, "was like buying a ticket to private life."

As the election year of 1908 dawned, rumors multiplied that a delegation of distinguished Democrats would visit Bryan and urge him not to accept the nomination. So that all might hear, he snorted to the press that "Men who come to speak for the Democratic party must show their credentials." When rumors persisted that many Democratic Congressmen opposed his nomination, he rushed to Washington, presumably to receive a reported delegation bent upon telling him that he ought to be the Warwick and not the candidate in the coming campaign. For two days Bryan posted himself in the Capitol, waiting for the delegation and meeting quantities of Congressmen and Senators. His greeting seems to have been extended to every legislator who ever dreamed of urging him to drop his candidacy. He subdued this wayward humanity by very much the same sort of cheerful glare that John L. Sullivan employed against opponents in the ring. Before many hours of Bryan's presence, those most anxious to arrange his withdrawal were following at his heels and shouting his acclaim.

As a kind of double insurance against possible trouble, Bryan's good friend Senator Francis Griffith Newlands organized a dinner party in his honor and arranged a guest list in which were adroitly mixed Bryan's most diehard Congressional adherents and those suspected of incipient defection. After dinner, the guests retired to the smoking room, and Bryan at once took charge of the conversation. He fairly invited the legislators opposing his nomination to speak by telling the story of a cowpuncher in Texas who went uninvited to a ranch dance. The floor manager took him by the arm and rather abruptly led him outside. Soon the cowpuncher returned again. The manager now tackled him violently and threw him out. As he picked himself up, the cowpuncher turned to some loungers and said, "Those fellows can't fool me. I know what they mean. They don't want me." After some laughter, there was a solemn hush. No one accepted the story's invitation to tell Bryan that he was unwanted. After a decent "I dare you" pause, he proceeded to tell them that "Bryan policies" would become the chief issue in the coming campaign and that because these policies were also "Roosevelt policies," they would be the most popular in the campaign. With appropriate delicacy of phrase, he confided to his dutiful listeners his belief that as between Republicans represented by Taft and Democrats represented by Bryan, the country would surely choose the Democrats.

When a Southern party leader objected to his advocacy of the initiative and referendum, Bryan replied imperiously, "That ought to be an issue. I will drive every man out of the Democratic party who does not support it." Former Senator James H. Berry of Arkansas dared to suggest that Bryan ought to promote only issues that would win. "Win! Win!" cried Bryan in high indignation. "That's it! You want to win! You would sacrifice principle for success. I would not. I would not desire to be elected if the principles I stood for were not incorporated in the platform. I am not sure that defeat is not better than victory, if victory comes with the sacrifice of principles."

"But," said Senator John Daniel, joining the conversation, "some of the things you have stood for in the past have proved wrong, and you may prove wrong again."

"I have always been right," Bryan retorted.

Many states that in the past harbored trouble for Bryan were now compliant. Ohio instructed for him even though it rejected his old ally and kindred spirit Tom Johnson and his gubernatorial candidate, Atlee Pomerene of Canton. Illinois, in these late years a scene of invariable trouble and woe for Bryan, behaved like a lamb. The sudden calm had its origins in the counsel of Norman Mack. Eager that Bryan be nominated and elected in 1908, Mack urged Charles Bryan that the old fight against Roger Sullivan, the Chicago boss, be dropped. Charles reported Mack's views to Bryan, that in the convention and campaign Sullivan could "shape things up for you." Charles recited to Mack that Bryan could not tolerate having in his campaign organization anyone such as Sullivan who had ties to the corporations. However, said Charles, if Sullivan should choose not to seek reelection to the national committee, "the fight would be over so far as we are concerned." Mack eagerly pressed his opinion that Sullivan "could be trusted to be for you if you would repudiate Dunlap and Thompson," loyal Bryan men, and others fighting Sullivan in Illinois.

Bryan made no repudiation, but the warfare against Sullivan suddenly abated. The boss' minions sat politely through the state convention as Raymond P. Robins uttered the pointed and hostile sentiment that "the great struggle [is] between the group of plunderers on the one hand and the group who toil on the other. The real issue is between the people who work and do not get a living and the people who get a living and do not work." The convention swept through the business of choosing delegates to the national convention instructed, in language utterly charming for a boss-run convention, to "use all honorable means" to secure Bryan's nomination. The negotiated Bryan-Sullivan peace did not pass unnoticed. "In order to pick up the Illinois delegates to the Democratic convention," observed the Columbus, Ohio, *Evening Dispatch*, "Mr. Bryan has dropped his quarrel with Roger Sullivan. The delegates will better serve his purpose." [4]

But New York, presenting its customary spectacle of quarreling factions, lay beyond reach of Bryan's magic. Norman Mack toiled valiantly for an instructed delegation for Bryan, but the divisions between upstate and New York City and the struggles for influence between factional leaders produced a national delegation uninstructed and presumed to comprise a majority opposed to his nomination. After the convention at Carnegie Hall in New York City was over, Bryan rushed to New York to recompose the situation. He journeyed from Rochester to New York City, with stops at several of the major political byways in between. Midway in these consultations, the state chairman, William J. Connors, felt driven to deny that he had promised that New York's delegates would ultimately vote for Bryan, in return for which the state's Lieutenant Governor Chanler would be nominated for the Vice Presidency and the wealthy Tammanyite Lewis Nixon would be appointed to the Cabinet.[5]

Bryan did not have a clear field. There were other candidates, aided and abetted by pessimism in many quarters toward his ability to defeat the Republican nominee. Joseph Pulitzer sardonically attributed Bryan's vitality "to the pusillanimity or cowardice of Democratic leaders and thinkers who privately admitting that Bryan has no earthly chance still publicly either remain silent or like Tillman, Watterson, Tom Johnson still pretend to favor Bryan's nomination. It is the 'What's the use' cry accepting the apparently inevitable."

Of the candidates thrust forward to halt Bryan's march, the most formidable was Governor John A. Johnson of Minnesota. Of Swedish descent, Johnson and another Swede, John Lind, had been the only Democrats to capture the governorship in forty years of Minnesota politics. In office, he pursued an aggressive tax policy against big business, increasing the assessed valuation of steel properties in the state, recommending successfully a tax on sleeping-car companies doing business in the state and unsuccessfully a royalty tax on the output of iron mines. He vested union labor with control of the Free Employment Bureau and provided leadership in arranging for ownership of public utilities by Minnesota cities and towns. Articulate and zestful, Johnson seemed to many victory-hungry Democrats immensely preferable to the twice-rejected Bryan. Headquarters for Johnson's Presidential candidacy were opened in New York and Chicago, and the governor took on a busy schedule of speeches and appearances. Simultaneously, pamphlets circulated, charging Bryan with full responsibility for years of Democratic defeats and lauding Johnson's capabilities for carrying every state that Bryan could and ten more besides.

The response of the Bryan forces to the Johnson movement was swift and muscular. They mercilessly crushed the Johnsonites in several state conventions, a catastrophe from which the rebel candidacy became permanently stunted.[6]

As the Johnson boom faltered, Judge George Gray of Delaware was pushed forward. Hailing from the Democracy's conservative Eastern wing, Gray at sixty-seven was a U.S. circuit court judge, a Cleveland type of Democrat, a former U.S. Senator, and an ardent foe of imperialism and the protective tariff. The Bryan forces did not move against Gray as they did Johnson, partly because his candidacy developed even less potency and partly because Bryan eyed the conservative judge as an ideal Vice Presidential nominee.

Bryan's candidacy had to surmount all manner of adversity. As his grip upon the nomination grew more secure, an article in the New York *World* contended that Thomas Fortune Ryan, whom Bryan time and again denounced as a monster of Wall Street, had contributed $20,000 to the expenses of the 1904 Nebraska campaign. This generous gift had been made in a manner calculated to disguise its embarrassing source. Ryan, according to the *World*, had given his check to his attorney, who in turn gave his own check for the amount to Bryan's brother-in-law, Thomas S. Allen, chairman of the Nebraska state committee. Allen denied the story and said that the only outside money had come from the Democratic national committee. Bryan replied, too, in language that was a trifle qualified: "If Mr. Ryan contributed to the Nebraska campaign, it was not with my knowledge or consent. While I had but a remote personal interest in the Nebraska campaign that year, I am always interested . . . and I am not willing to be, in even the slightest degree, obligated to any favor-seeking corporation." [7]

If Bryan seemed well along the road to mastery of his own party, it was clear from all the signs that for the first time in his career, a fusion campaign was beyond his grasp. The Populist national convention gathered in St. Louis in April, and, with the middle-of-the-roaders in control, declined to follow its custom of nominating Bryan. Instead, it chose Thomas E. Watson, to whom Bryan was now a political abomination. Bryan's Populist forces resisted the result in a dogged fight. Nebraska and other delegations challenged the legality of the convention and then withdrew. "We do not hesitate to say," cried the Nebraska chairman in a parting shot, "that if Mr. Bryan is nominated at Denver by the Democrats, the Populists of Nebraska will support him to a man."

Another staunch ally of bygone campaigns would surely be absent from the fold in 1908. William Randolph Hearst had supported Bryan in 1896 and 1900 and in the spirit of reciprocity had expected Bryan to assist his quest for nomination in 1904. Now Hearst was still smarting from what he considered Bryan's perfidy. The question inevitably arose of the great journalist's demeanor toward the awaiting election. In a context that clearly indicated he was discussing Bryan, Hearst declared with grand disdain: "I do not think the path of patriotism lies in supporting a discredited and decadent old party, which has neither conscientious conviction nor honest intention, nor endorsing chameleon candidates who change the color of their political opinion with every varying hue of opportunism."

One of Bryan's problems was to determine his stance toward his ideological ally and partisan foe Theodore Roosevelt. As his Presidential term moved into its final stage, Roosevelt sounded an increasingly progressive note. As he had in the past, Bryan continued to praise Roosevelt whenever he acted upon some principle or policy which the Democratic leader had for years been advocating. No longer, he told his audiences, were Democrats regarded as dangerous . . ."it is not I who has moved forward toward radical innovations. . . . I have remained with the principles I announced twelve years ago. I may congratulate the others who treat my views with this, the highest form of flattery." Repeatedly in his praise, Bryan employed his favorite metaphor of Roosevelt stealing his clothes.

Joseph Pulitzer, in his lair at the New York *World,* boiled in indignation at Bryan's tactic. Pulitzer felt that Bryan was "spiking" the Democratic guns: "Bryan the greatest Roosevelt man in the U.S., most effective. The more he talks about Roosevelt having stolen his clothes and what not, the more he makes Democratic votes for Roosevelt." Furthermore, Pulitzer mused, "Bryan himself stole the clothes. They were never made for him originally. He stole them from the Greenbackers, Farmers' Alliance, etc., etc." When the economy suffered a drastic downswing in the Panic of 1907, Pulitzer was even more distressed that Bryan did not attribute the disaster to Roosevelt but instead praised Roosevelt's subsequent message to Congress for championing progressive principles. "Sham opposition if any," growled Pulitzer. "There seems to be one Republican party with another one led by Bryan."

The Panic of 1907 was a substantial political fact. In January of that year, John D. Rockefeller publicly prophesied the coming of hard times from Roosevelt's increasing attacks on big business. Stock prices soon fell, production sagged, and by October business distress was acute. Several large industrial corporations went bankrupt; small banks in the South and West closed. In New York the Knickerbocker Trust Company collapsed, the entire New York financial community seemed in jeopardy, and international financial institutions trembled. To hold back the crisis, Roosevelt entered into cooperative understandings with J. P. Morgan. In the inevitable discussions of the causes and blame for the panic, critics flayed Roosevelt and his war on business and its erosion of confidence. Roosevelt roared back, attributing the panic to "certain malefactors of great wealth" who conspired the debacle "in order to discredit the policy of the government." Cooler analyses stressed the inelasticity of the currency and the overextension of credit as major factors. Bryan's old doctrines of the quantity theory of money and free silver suddenly were again relevant, but in his mood of restraint he did not choose to reassert them.[8]

In his busy speechmaking around the country, Bryan portrayed the economy and politics as the domains of evil masters. Politics, national and state, were dominated by "favor-seeking corporations," and in a winter address at Carnegie Hall, he contended that "larceny" included both that which was in violation of the law and that which occurred through operation of the law. The largess of the tariff for business corporations was a ready illustration of the latter, and "inequality in taxation is merely a form of larceny . . . As a rule, a man who steals a million dollars has a better chance of escape than a man who steals a thousand." So prevalent had the distinction become in current society that the ancient commandment should have been amended to read: "Thou shalt not steal upon a small scale."

With the Panic of 1907 cutting a broad swath of devastation, Bryan stressed the necessity of adopting more careful regulations for the conduct of bank officers and of establishing a system to insure or guarantee bank deposits. Arguing that "the depositor is the best friend the banker has," Bryan proposed the general adoption of a bank guarantee system which he had had a hand in fashioning for the new state of Oklahoma. Under the Oklahoma system, every bank in a defined district stood behind every other bank, so that all the banks guaranteed one another. The heart of the arrangement was a tax of one-fourth of 1 percent on the amount of each bank's deposits. This common financial pool could be applied to the economic fires which threatened any individual bank with disaster.

Bryan's other prescriptions for the Panic of 1907, which raged through the months of 1908, were remarkable precursors of Franklin Roosevelt's planks for his New Deal program in the Great Depression of the thirties. As unemployment mounted, Bryan advanced what in his day was a daring radical doctrine: that government should act to relieve the suffering of unemployment. "We must meet an immediate need immediately," he said at Cooper Union, "furnishing labor if labor can be furnished, giving work if the government can supply it, and giving aid if work cannot be supplied."

Unlike his earlier campaigns, which dealt almost wholly with economic subjects, Bryan in the months before the national convention of 1908 was also stressing political issues. These were devoted to the common theme of the necessity of popular rule. To advance this cause, Bryan in late May invited William Howard Taft to join with him "as leading candidates in our respective parties" in asking Congress to pass a bill requiring the publication of campaign contributions prior to the elections of 1908. Taft answered that he had already written privately to Senator Julius C. Burrows, chairman of the Committee on Privileges and Elections, approving legislation calling for publicity. Taft, however, did not endorse the timing of Bryan's proposal.[9]

Bryan was accumulating delegate strength with the assurance of a moving glacier. By April the New York *Times* had conceded that he was "a sure nominee," and by mid-June estimates of his delegate support were running to 707 votes, with 672 necessary for nomination under the two-thirds rule.

In this atmosphere of certainty, Bryan, aided by his remorselessly efficient brother, Charles, and the enterprising, ubiquitous Norman Mack, began drawing the blueprints of a smoothly functioning convention. Responding to his explicit wishes, the national committee chose Theodore Bell of California as temporary chairman and Congressman Henry Clayton of Alabama as permanent chairman. For chairman of the Resolutions Committee, Bryan turned to a new political ally, with whom he was getting on famously, Governor Charles N. Haskell of Oklahoma. "It would be a compliment to the newest democratic state," he wrote to Haskell, "and then Oklahoma has been giving Bryanism a trial."

As the Denver convention neared and delegations stopped over at Lincoln in a carefully scheduled part of their journey, the mood was amiable and even jocular. When the Illinois delegation en route to Denver by automobile, reached Lincoln after a desperate struggle through rain and mud, Bryan called out, as they made their weary approach, "Will you support the good roads plank at the Denver Convention?" To this question, put with a serious air, a delegate replied, "We are unanimously for it." [10]

In his specific attentions to the East and Middle West, Bryan concentrated on keeping in his fold supporters of his past campaigns and on building friendships with old enemies. He dispatched Richard F. Pettigrew as a special emissary to court the new boss of Tammany Hall, the enigmatic Charles F. Murphy, and to woo an old enemy against whom he had once thundered with hair-curling epithets, boss Roger Sullivan of Illinois. For these bosses who presided over the caldrons of corruption in the nation's two largest cities, Pettigrew brought a simple message. Bryan, in victory, would accord them patronage and political recognition in return for their support in the coming election. Sullivan, viewing Bryan's nomination as inevitable, pledged his support. Murphy remained noncommittal. Pettigrew even dared visit Arthur Brisbane, Hearst's editorial writer, in an effort to rally Hearst's strength in New York behind the Bryan candidacy. But Hearst, still quavering with indignation, incited Brisbane to declare that Bryan was now as conservative as the Republicans. "Bryan," Brisbane added, in vengeful tones, "is an ignorant man. You need in the White House a good brain, and you don't need a mouth. Bryan is a mouth."

In his attentions to the East, Bryan evidenced no resolve for further concessions, least of all on issues. His conduct reflected a strategy stated by his brother, Charles: "I believe we will have to win the election in the West and Middle Western states, and if the corporation element in the East come to our support, we could not come as near carrying the eastern states as if they fought us there, and their support in the East would destroy our chances in the West, where the people want to get rid of the domination of the East in finance, tariff and other questions." [11]

In his swift travels about the country, Bryan's preconvention manager, Mayor James C. Dahlman, fostered the organization of Bryan Volunteers in every precinct. It was hoped they would become collection agencies for massive numbers of small contributions to offset the Republican war chest.

Bryan was also preoccupied with combating another heavy Republican advantage, the power of the press. Democratic papers were as scarce as pearls on an Eastern seashore. Bryan launched two main attacks. For a journal like Joseph Pulitzer's New York *World* that fired fusillades of disparagement against him without letup, he asked, through the pages of the Omaha *World-Herald,* "Who is paying for it?" When the *World* in an editorial, "We Confess," acknowledged that the *World* was paying for it, Bryan's counterattack became more focused. "What is the extent," he asked, "of the financial interest held by Joseph Pulitzer, owner of the New York *World,* in railroad companies and in great corporations commonly known as trusts?" This time, the *World*'s answer was less successful.

In an extended article in *The Commoner* early in 1908, Bryan urged that a Democratic weekly newspaper be immediately established in every county of the nation. The investment involved is small, he wrote reassuringly, and one person could both own and edit it with but a slight overhead. "It has far more influence," he wrote, "in proportion to its circulation than the city daily—because it has behind it a person known to its readers and whose character adds force to its words. . . ." *The Commoner* offered to supply editorials, cartoons, and columns.[12]

Above all, Bryan's disposition toward the 1908 campaign was shaped by the deliberations of the Republican national convention. There Theodore Roosevelt imposed upon the delegates the nomination of the man he loved like a brother, his Secretary of War, William Howard Taft. Good Bryan men promptly proclaimed that the nomination was "dictated." In public statement and *Commoner* editorial, Bryan depicted the Republican convention as a triumph of conservatism. The platform was a "silent repudiation" of Roosevelt's principles. It carried no plank for the popular election of U.S. Senators; it glossed over the issue of publicity for campaign contributions. It was utterly silent on the income tax and the inheritance tax, two potent instruments by which popular rule might advance through taxation. The trust plank made no demand for serious enforcement or the use of available criminal penalties. The promise of tariff revision was "vague," and Senator La Follette's proposal to enlarge the powers of the ICC was voted down. Samuel Gompers, seeking adoption of his anti-injunction plank, was rejected and humiliated by shouts of "Go to Denver." But worst of all was the nominee, Taft, a conservative who too easily commanded Wall Street support and who too plainly caused the trusts to rejoice in his nomination. Even Pulitzer had to acknowledge that Bryan now best represented the "Roosevelt type of candidate." [13]

If the Republican convention seemed the product of "dictation," the Democratic gathering at Denver, at least at its outset, bore marks of being "managed." When the convention opened, 618 delegates were instructed for Bryan, and from 50 to 200 more were pledged to him in a more or less binding manner. He was well beyond the necessary two-thirds vote, and he would surely win on the first ballot.

In addition, Denver was in the heart of the silver country, and the local citizenry in the gallery were unabashed Bryan enthusiasts. This Western city and the convention itself exhibited much of the ebullience of its political hero. Every delegation was met at the station and escorted to its hotel by a band. Twenty thousand people functioned as a kind of walking information bureau, by wearing buttons inscribed "I live in Denver. Ask me." Trainloads of snow were hauled down from the mountains and dumped in shady streets, allowing Southern politicians who had never seen snow before to pelt one another with snowballs with the zest of schoolboys.

The tallying of votes promised to assume a new efficiency, thanks to the unheard of presence of a battery of four automatic adding machines. In another innovation, each chair had on its back a small placard, with the name of the state in large black capitals and the word "delegate" beneath it. It was hoped that this new arrangement would overcome traditional confusion by showing where the territory of each state began and ended and would avoid the usual good-natured scrapping over boundary lines. Beaming down upon the convention was a huge oil portrait of the party's founding father, Thomas Jefferson, and of the party's last President, Grover Cleveland, who had just died.

Bryan was not long in acquiring pictorial representation. After all the delegations, except Nebraska and California, were seated, the representatives of Bryan's state made a spectacular entrance by marching in a solemn column down the center of the aisle, holding a huge banner of red, white, and blue silk on which was painted an effulgent portrait of Bryan. Hard on the Nebraskans' heels, the California delegation marched in with a banner of white, blue, and gold, bearing a likeness of Bryan. Each Californian bore their hero's trademark, a palm-leaf fan, and a small American flag. Not

until after some minutes of wild cheering by delegates and spectators standing on chairs, waving hats and handkerchiefs, could proceedings begin.

Through it all, Bryan remained at Fairview, where the trek of visitors
continued. Although he passed much time in the field bringing in alfalfa,
Bryan was in close touch with the convention thanks to a direct telegraph
wire running between Denver and an office in the basement of his home. A
telegraph operator was imported for Bryan's needs.

At Denver, Bryan's fortunes were entrusted to the most devoted and
tested of his lieutenants, brother Charles, who was in general command of a
steering committee consisting of his brother-in-law, T. S. Allen; the preconvention manager, Jim Dahlman; old Bryan stalwarts George F. Williams of
Massachusetts, Ollie James of Kentucky, and Norman Mack of New York;
and more recent associates John E. Lamb of Indiana and Charles N. Haskell of Oklahoma. All would play leading parts in the awaiting campaign.[14]

Scarcely had the managers taken up their posts, when an ominous threat
suddenly materialized from a seemingly innocuous situation. Grover Cleveland's recent death required that the last Democratic President be memori-
alized. Etiquette suggested that the late President's state, New York, discharge this reverential act, and to commit it there appropriately stepped
forward that state's and the party's last Presidential nominee, Judge Alton
B. Parker. Consternation exploded when word circulated among the delegates that Bryan's enemies proposed to employ the tribute to discredit him
and to ignite a factional struggle. Parker, after a suitable speech, offered a
resolution which hailed Cleveland as one who had "maintained the public
credit and honor, stood firm as a rock in defense of sound principles of
finance. . . ." Bryan's managers sprang to bottle up the hostile words, and
a late recruit to his cause, Colonel Henry Watterson, the editor of the
Louisville *Courier-Journal,* erstwhile foe of Bryan and now an ardent supporter, struck Parker's move with his journalistic birch rod: "The attempt to
drag the dead body of Grover Cleveland from its newly made grave is the
art of shameless hypocrites. Nor was ever a professional ghoul inspired by a
more mercenary spirit." The Bryan men pushed the resolution aside and
watched over the writing of a new draft, doing Cleveland honor and
scrubbed clean of all hostile and oblique references to Bryan.[15]

The Bryan forces also had an altercation with the Pennsylvania boss,
James M. Guffey. This was long building. In April, Bryan ran up an impressive triumph in the Pennsylvania primaries. Guffey, openly opposed to the
Bryan candidacy, clamped machine controls on the state convention which
chose delegates at large to the pending national convention. These delegates
were uninstructed and violated Bryan's dictum at the time that delegates
should mirror the expressed will of the people of each state. "I have known

of his underground work," Bryan wrote of Guffey, "and am very glad to have him now where he has to make his fight in the open."

When a delegation of the Bryan Democratic League of Pennsylvania stopped off at Fairview, Bryan hailed the members for symbolizing "the overshadowing issue in this campaign . . . 'Let the people rule.' " At the convention, Bryan Pennsylvanians moved to unseat Guffey Pennsylvanians. As expected, the national committee upheld Guffey, and the fight moved to the Credentials Committee, where the Bryanites, under Charley's watchful eye, held sway. From Fairview, Bryan, despite earlier accusatory words about Guffey, now became fearful of disrupting convention harmony. He wired Charles to confine the attack on Guffey to revelations of corrupt tampering with elections in Philadelphia and to drop the project to unseat him. "Tell them," he added, "that they can trust me to take care of Guffey."

But this new strategy evaporated when Haskell, perceiving in the situation an opportunity to boost his own reputation, made a fiery speech on the convention floor, moving to a climactic shout of "Go back to Standard Oil." Quaking with rage, frantically motioning for support from his friends, Guffey suffered the humiliation of being voted out of the convention. Defiantly waving good-bye from his place in the Pennsylvania delegation, his small spare figure puffed with rage, he left the hall, and with him went the precious harmony Bryan had hoped to preserve.[16]

As the Credentials Committee dawdled over its contests, the convention officers were hard put to use up time on the floor. Thomas P. Gore, the blind Senator of Oklahoma and a highly gifted orator, was drafted to fill out an hour with an address. In the course of a stirring recital of the Democracy's blessings, Gore, with nominating speeches yet to come, innocently let fall the name of William Jennings Bryan. Gore used Bryan's name only casually and with no intention of commencing an explosive demonstration. But in an instant the convention turned into a cyclone. At first there swelled a long loud shout that seemed to have no beginning or end. Parades formed; state standards were pulled from their places. Young men grabbed for the banners of the Bryan Volunteers and pushed toward the platform. The Kentucky banner could not be disconnected from a chair, and both the banner and chair were carried around the hall. Seated in a box, Ruth and her companion, the President's daughter, Alice Roosevelt Longworth, waved their scarves and cheered.

The spontaneous outbursts soon developed a purpose. Men quickly saw in the strength of the demonstration the possibilities of a record, the forty-seven-minute uproar that followed the "Cross of Gold" speech. A new record must be set that would long endure. A thousand men suddenly assumed responsibility for it. The band played; men tramped through the aisles with collars open, ties torn to shreds and faces streaming with perspiration. Jim Dahlman, holding a red and white umbrella, jumped up and down, shouting encouragement. Ruth was led to the platform, a Colorado standard was thrust into her hands, and she waved it gaily. "Have we gone over the time yet?" sweating delegates inquired. Here and there among the 15,000 spectators and delegates who joined the fandango was a nonparticipant. Tammany leader Charles F. Murphy, lounging disdainfully in his chair, sniffed to a companion, "It must be pretty nice down at Rockaway, just about now." At last, after an hour and seventeen minutes, the exhausted marchers stopped. No one was more pleased than the man who had touched off the demonstration, the blind Senator Gore.[17]

The next day, July 10, with the Resolutions Committee locked in difficult deliberations, the convention took up the Presidential nominations, with speeches to be made, but no vote taken, pending the committee's report. I. J. Dunn, Omaha lawyer and Bryan's longtime friend, placed his name in candidacy. Dunn's skillful, persuasive half-hour address, was followed by a carefully arranged extravaganza. When he mentioned Bryan's name in a moving peroration, a white dove was released, and in a moment scores of others followed, circling around and around the high open space of the auditorium. An immense painting of Bryan was suddenly lowered from the ceiling, obscuring a picture of George Washington and substantial enough for a pigeon to perch comfortably upon its top.

At midnight, after the candidates were nominated, Governor Haskell brought in the platform, which was adopted without dissent. The balloting for the Presidential nomination began, and all possibility of stopping the inevitable vanished when Charles Murphy, Tammany's chief, rose to cast all of New York's votes for Bryan. In the final tally on the first ballot, Bryan emerged with 892½ votes, Gray 59½, and Johnson 46. Bryan's nomination was quickly made unanimous to the accompaniment of exultant yells, catcalls, war whoops, shrieking horns, roaring megaphones, and the strains of a band's anthems. Upon receiving word at Fairview of his nomination, Bryan told the gathered reporters that if he were defeated, he would not run again.[18]

The most managed aspect of the convention was the platform, with Bryan holding tight the strings. As it finally emerged, it combined elements of the Oklahoma constitution, the Nebraska state platform, and positions taken by the American Federation of Labor.

The superintendency of the platform was entrusted to Haskell and an old personal favorite, Mayor F. W. Brown of Lincoln. As the convention gathered, Brown, after a final full day with Bryan at Fairview, departed for Denver with a bulky package under his arm, consisting at least partly, presumably, of the platform. At the convention, the mayor was seen to carry around a long mysterious envelope, which reporters, who managed a glimpse of its contents, found to contain clippings from *The Commoner* and several type-written sheets of suggestions from editor Bryan.

All ultimate decisions were kept in Bryan's own hands. Charley, Brown, and Haskell, operatives at the convention scene, each had a limited function. Charles was the intermediary between the convention and Bryan, the interpreter of developments at Denver to the leader at Fairview. Brown, Nebraska's member of the Resolutions Committee and recently arrived from Fairview, was the chief expositor of his leader's wishes. Haskell, as Resolutions Committee chairman, was Bryan's field general, who, after shedding his coat, letting down his "galluses and rolling up his sleeves," appointed a subcommittee on the platform, to which he read the suggestions brought by Mayor Brown.

Haskell also appointed ten specialized subcommittees, assigning each an involved or controversial subject such as the labor injunction, the tariff, the railroads, and the guarantee of bank deposits. The subcommittees posed certain advantages for Bryan. Because they were numerous, they tended to assure that only their members—two or three men—would speak on a subject, and by meeting simultaneously in the big committee room they permitted several speeches to be made at once. Since observers noted a good deal of old-fashioned Populistic garrulity at the convention, the arrangement proved to be a wise economizing of time. As each subcommittee developed its plank, it was submitted through Charley for Bryan's approval at Fairview. Ultimately, the platform would bear Bryan's comprehensive blessing.

Although Charles and Haskell scrutinized every word beforehand, Bryan subjected the planks to meticulous review and frequent revision. In all, he invested forty hours at the telegraph table and a platform of almost record length evolved. At the subcommittee stage, the platform was estimated at from 20,000 to 25,000 words long, or sufficient, as one committeeman put it, "to reach from Pike's Peak to Fairview." Many committee members were aghast at its length, particularly those who had taken seriously a prediction that it would be brief enough to print on a postcard.[19] Occasionally, an air of insane confusion assailed the committee when Bryan changed his mind. He would order alterations and then retract or revise them. Sometimes, before his orders could be carried out in subcommittee, Bryan would be struck with the inspiration of a better word or phrase while committeemen still struggled with the earlier change.

The platform making followed certain ground rules. "Be careful," Bryan instructed Charles, "that no economic issue is declared to be paramount. We have already said that the overshadowing issue is 'Shall the People Rule?' and that this manifests itself in all the questions at issue." But while Bryan was sounding the high note for popular rule, he indulged in the scuttling of one of its most potent instruments, the initiative and the referendum. This was an act of the crudest expediency. Although Bryan eloquently championed forms of popular rule in his 1900 platform, they were omitted in 1908. The moving force of this about-face was an alliance with Tammany. "The omission of any such declaration in 1908," Arthur Mullen wrote years later, "alienated many of his liberal supporters, among them Tom Johnson of Cleveland, who angrily said Bryan would live to rue that elision." A further ground rule set by Bryan was that the platform must be silent on government ownership of the railroads.

One of the severest tests of Bryan's craftsmanship was the fashioning of the labor planks. After Gompers' rebuff by the Republican convention, Bryan was eager to accommodate labor, particularly on the injunction. Yet he also wished not to offend the Parker school of New York conservatives. Parker, as a jurist, entertained quite definite ideas on the question of limiting court injunctions, and not unexpectedly he drafted a plank. To Charles, who anxiously looked for guidance in a threatened devastating conflict, Bryan telegraphed a serene, buck-passing solution: "As New York is the center of wealth and business, it is well enough to have that state take the responsibility for the injunction plank, if the plan is satisfactory to the laboring men."

Gompers, Parker, Charles, and Haskell entered into intensive negotiations. What emerged was a modified version of the Nebraska platform's treatment of the labor injunction. "We deem that the parties to all judicial proceedings should be treated with rigid impartiality, and that injunctions should not be issued in any cases in which injunctions would not issue if no industrial dispute were involved." The plank was cushioned in language, doubtless inspired by Parker, deferential to the courts. Bryan, borrowing freely from the AFL's program, included in the labor planks a call for an eight-hour day in all government work, a general employers' liability act, and the creation of a Department of Labor with Cabinet rank. When the labor provisions were at last settled, Bryan telephoned Gompers to inquire if he was satisfied and to invite him to stop off at Fairview upon his return from Denver.[20]

Eastern conservatives made such a determined assault on the trust plank that Bryan was moved to remind Charles that "a failure to put in a strong trust plank will lose me a million votes." Arrayed against Bryan were Parker, ex-Senator James Smith, Jr., of New Jersey, and conservative forces that opposed any expression on the subject at all. So powerful was the opposition that Bryan at one juncture proposed to incorporate his own views in a minority report calling for the substitution of the Nebraska antitrust plank for the Easterners'. But Charles composed the situation.

Bryan moved with less travail through quantities of other planks on the tariff, guarantee of bank deposits, Republican extravagance, conservation, swollen fortunes, a postal savings system, the railroads and cooling-off treaties to preserve world peace. As the heavy toil of drafting and redrafting moved past twenty-four hours, Bryan wired to Charles, "How much longer had I better stay up? We are cutting our alfalfa and I will not be in shape to work in the field unless I get some sleep." Charles replied confidently: ". . . Corporation bunch trying to make changes in important planks. We have the situation in hand and can put lid on any time."

Bryan's homemade platform was the most conservative of his three Presidential races. At most, it constituted the unfinished business of Roosevelt progressivism. It carried nothing comparable to the silver issue as a potential spark of social revolution. Controversial economic questions were subordinate to political planks. "Let the people rule" was a sloganized restatement of the Declaration of Independence. The lack of novel or specific prescriptions by which they would rule took the edge off any boldness the proposal might have had. Bryan's moderation was encouraged by the nomination of Taft and the lessons of 1896 and 1900, that victory was unobtainable without the combined effort of Democratic progressives and conservatives. Had the Republicans nominated Roosevelt, La Follette, or another progressive, Bryan would have been pressed toward more radical positions. The platforms of 1896 and 1900 were the work of chronological and political youth, that of 1908 of chronological and political middle age.[21]

Bryan's quest for a running mate was a long, uncertain process. Weeks before the convention, Bryan and his deputies made soundings on prospective candidates, and the East was combed for a likely name to strengthen the ticket. A criterion of eligibility implicit in Bryan's developing confraternity with Samuel Gompers was that the nominee must not be offensive to labor. But simultaneously, he must be acceptable to the general body of the Eastern Democracy.

Judge George Gray, who was palatable to labor and Eastern Democrats and to Bryan, declined to run. For a time, the name of John Mitchell, president of the United Mine Workers and hero of the coal strike of 1902, sparkled in the skies, but Eastern Democrats caviled, and Bryan backed away. New York State, with its rich electoral votes, was scoured from head to toe. Chanler evinced no interest, and no eligible was discovered. Easterners and Middle Westerners were inventoried and found wanting. Eventually Bryan and the convention chose John W. Kern, a twice-defeated candidate for governor of Indiana. Popular and widely known in the Middle West, Kern was quick in debate and a spellbinder. His gubernatorial race in 1900, which he lost narrowly, outstripped Bryan's own performance in Indiana.[22]

Fairview was a mecca for the delegations returning from Denver. The Minnesota delegation came, formed a wide circle on the lawn with Bryan seated in the middle, and vows were exchanged. This delegation, which had stuck to the candidacy of its governor, John Johnson, until the end, now assured Bryan that Minnesota Democrats would give their best to elect him. "I remember no fights after they are over," Bryan replied. "Minnesota had a good man and stood by him. Mr. Johnson has telegraphed me offering his support, and I have no doubt he will do much good for the ticket. . . ." The Minnesotans celebrated the happy exchange by lining up at a hydrant and imbibing the clear fresh water supplied by Fairview's merrily whirling windmill. It was a day of reconciliation. From Denver, Alton Parker proclaimed, "I am going to support the ticket of Bryan and Kern, and I want my friends to do the same thing."

Samuel Gompers came too, with the first vice-president and the secretary of the AFL. Bryan, with Kern by his side, spent most of the day conferring with them in his library. When they emerged, Gompers announced that he had assured Bryan that labor would vote heavily for him. Reporters, conscious of dissent in AFL locals to Gompers' new Democratic proclivities, asked if labor would act as a political unit in the campaign. Gompers said merely that he and his fellow officers had been instructed to work for "political declarations" by both parties, but "the Republicans turned us down at Chicago, while the Democrats at Denver met us fairly and squarely."

One after another the state delegations came, Tammany chieftains, the national committee, a committee of Negroes resident in Lincoln with suggestions for increasing the vote of their race for the Democratic ticket. While coping with streams of visitors, Bryan managed to sandwich in formulations of campaign policy. No money would be accepted from any corporation, no more than $10,000 from any individual, and not more than $100 from any person within three days of the election. From October 15 onward all contributions exceeding $100 would be published each day. Bryan's strides forced his rival, Taft, to take a step in the same direction. The Republican candidate announced that he would not accept corporate funds.

Bryan's most drastic adjustment to the campaign was his resignation as managing editor of *The Commoner*. The efficient Charley took over the controls, with the articulate Richard L. Metcalfe moving up as editor. Bryan planned to contribute an occasional signed article, and he pledged that any profits *The Commoner* might yield until election time would be turned over to the national committee for use in the campaign. In dealings with the press, Bryan displaced his traditionally free and buoyant style and now had a stenographer by his side to take down everything he said.

Of the myriad changes demanded by the oncoming campaign, there was at least one to which Bryan would not surrender. He would not permit temporal affairs to displace a simple spiritual commitment, honored whenever he was at home in Fairview. On the Sunday following his triumph in Denver, he appeared at the little nearby country church. For an hour a benchful of adult Bible students were engrossed in a discussion of the story of Saul and David, led by the Democratic nominee for President of the United States.[23]

As chairman of the national committee and, therefore, as general manager of the campaign, Bryan chose Norman Mack. Mack's selection was more than a recognition of an old friend and invaluable soldier in the earlier campaigns. It revealed Bryan's strategy for 1908: He would fight for votes in the East and to carry New York. Publisher of the Buffalo *Sunday and Evening Times,* Mack was a self-made man, born of Scottish-Canadian parents and reared in Williams, Ontario. Having migrated to the United States, he passed through a series of small jobs until he founded a newspaper in Jamestown, New York. Soon he sold out, took the proceeds to Buffalo, and with a credit of $2,500 established the *Times* in 1883 and soon converted it into an enterprise worth several million dollars.

Bryan and Mack were close politically and personally. Bryan admired Mack's simplicity and generosity and the presence he conveyed as a Christian gentleman. Their families also got on famously, exchanging visits and delighting in one another's company. Mack brought to politics the same verve and enterprise he gave to journalism. If Mack symbolized the East in Bryan's strategy, the two other major appointments recognized the West and South. For vice chairman of the national committee, Bryan chose L. P. Hall of Nebraska, a veteran of state politics, and head, as Bryan noted, "of one of our largest banks." For Democratic treasurer, Bryan designated Governor Haskell, who also had a substantial business background. As the nature of the appointees suggested, Bryan looked to the national committee to flush out funds.[24]

Bryan's speech of August 12, accepting the nomination, officially opened the campaign, and it fitted into a kind of master plan for the entire body of subsequent speeches. Bryan explained the plan beforehand to Henry Watterson. The acceptance speech would be wholly devoted to the issue considered overriding in the platform: "Shall the People Rule?" Planks devoted to economic questions—the tariff, trusts, railroads, and the like—would each be taken up in separate speeches as the campaign evolved. Above all else, Bryan wished to avoid issues that divided Democrats in previous campaigns. There is no use discussing the silver question, wrote Bryan, "because it is not in the campaign. . . . I shall confine the fight to the platform, so far as I am concerned."

The acceptance speech, a model of brevity, one-third the length of Taft's, was delivered on Lincoln's statehouse grounds, before a solid mass of jubilant humanity. Its rendering was heralded by the William McKinley memorial chimes of the nearby Methodist church, which played "America" and

"The Star-Spangled Banner," after which a band played "Dixie." Building upon his theme of popular government, Bryan argued that the nation faced a choice between a government devoted to the protection of the people's rights and the promotion of their welfare or a government ruled by privilege. To bar the latter alternative, Bryan urged the popular election of Senators and publicity for campaign contributions. Not otherwise could there be genuine tariff reform or adequate regulations of the railroads. The Democratic Party pledged both changes in its platform; the Republicans were committed to neither. As a third thrust for popular rule, Bryan demanded reform of the rules of the House of Representatives, which were so despotic that they placed this presumably popular legislature "under the absolute domination of the Speaker, who has entire control of its deliberations and powers of legislation."

Bryan depicted the Democratic Party as the party, not of revolution, but of reformation, not the enemy of any "legitimate industry or honest accumulations," but the friend of industry "and the steadfast protector of that wealth which represents a service to society." The Democratic Party favors "such an administration of the government as will insure, so far as human wisdom can, that each citizen shall draw from society a reward commensurate with his contribution to the welfare of society."

Bryan's opening salvo earned a generally favorable press reaction, an almost unheard of experience. *The Nation,* long hostile, was free with compliments, and *Outlook,* which adored Roosevelt, allowed that Bryan had shown himself to great advantage. Crusty Joseph Pulitzer deemed the speech "a wonderful improvement on the old Bryan of '96 and 1900. If these words could stand alone without regard to the past or fear of the future, it is difficult to see how anybody could be afraid of Bryan. . . ." [25]

As he had been in 1900, Bryan was again torn between a heavy schedule of speeches and the front-porch type of campaign, perfected by William McKinley and others who had *won* the Presidency. Among Bryan's counselors the view persisted that he would do better if he said less and raised less apprehension that he was a monster of revolution; if he followed more traditional Presidential electioneering by staying home and projecting an image of dignity and serenity and rendering well-deliberated discourses on the issues.

As in 1900, Bryan initially subscribed to this viewpoint. To Henry Watterson, who doubtless was delighted to hear of the decision, he wrote that he expected to spend nearly all October at home writing articles or giving out interviews, answering Republican arguments, and concentrating the fight on the immediate questions. "I believe," he added, "I can do more good in this way than I can by travelling and making brief speeches." On July 29, Bryan announced this plan in a public statement.

In August and September, in accordance with his plan, Bryan did present a series of speeches devoted to the major issues. At Topeka, Kansas, his address was wholly concerned with the guarantee of bank deposits. The unrelieved Panic of 1907, with its spectacle of failing banks, pulled him at once to this theme, and he chose Kansas because the governor had just proposed a guarantee law for the state. As was his custom, Bryan coupled the guarantee principle with tighter regulations on the conduct of bank directors and officials. The chief causes of bank failures, he contended, were the excess loans made to banks' own officials. The wobbly banking structure sent millions of American dollars in flight to European savings banks offering greater security. In the current panic, much money was in hiding or, in effect, withdrawn from circulation at a time when it was most needed.[26]

At Indianapolis, in ceremonies honoring John Kern, Bryan presented a second major issue, the trusts. To a wildly cheering crowd, Bryan underscored his differences with Taft and Roosevelt, who accepted, as they variously put it, "good," "lawful," "reasonable" trusts. Bryan's position was simply that all trusts should be exterminated, and he taunted the Republicans for excessive forbearance that left most trusts undisturbed. In diagnosing this failure, Bryan concluded that Republicans could never enforce the law against the trusts because so many of the party were connected with them. A trust was, he said, a corporation which controls "so large a proportion of the total quantity of any article . . . as to be able to regulate the price and terms of sale. . . ." Since the proportion controlled determined the power of the trust for harm, some conception of proportionate control, in turn, must be applied to forestall the rise of trusts. Bryan employed what he acknowledged was an arbitrary figure of 25 percent; when a corporation achieved that degree of control over an industry, it became a trust.[27]

Labor Day, 1908, was awaited with anticipations that Bryan would celebrate it on a scale worthy of a campaign that might bring organized labor and the Democratic Party into a new relationship and even, possibly, an alliance. Bryan spent the day in Chicago. Standing on the balcony of the Auditorium Hotel, he won the applause of thousands of workers marching by in a huge Labor Day review. Many labor personalities addressed him familiarly as Bill or William.

In his address, Bryan dwelt upon the rejection Gompers had suffered from Republicans and the open hospitality rendered by Democrats. Both labor and the Democratic Party were agreed upon goals: the establishment of a Cabinet-level Department of Labor; restriction of the antilabor injunction; an eight-hour workday; and an employer liability law. The labor question at this time, he suggested, was chiefly a question of distribution, and the measures advocated in the Democratic platform were directed to securing to each man what his services entitled him to. Bryan likened prevailing employment practices to the military system. Some issue commands, and others carry them out. The commanders largely determine the wage "and appropriate the better part to themselves." Bryan took pains not to appear as a blind friend of labor but acknowledged that labor, in its present plight, needed governmental succor, for the labor organizations "have been yoked by the trusts." [28]

Having expounded his positions on the major issues, Bryan abandoned his plan of restricted campaigning and in the remaining half of September moved through a heavy schedule of speeches in Midwestern, border, Eastern, and north-central states. What he said was less expository, and his vocabulary took on more the cutting edge of partisanship. The crowds compared in size and enthusiasm with the best turnouts of the earlier campaigns. With his secretary Robert Rose and former Governor William Jennings of Florida accompanying him and helping with the arrangements, Bryan managed the hard-driving journey tolerably well. An awkward moment materialized at Deer Park, Maryland, where on a brilliant Sunday afternoon a local committee on arrangements and a crowd of several thousand awaited a Bryan address. The program had been planned without his knowledge, and when he arrived at Deer Park, he at once made known to the committee his policy never to make political speeches on Sunday. The committee argued and pleaded, but Bryan was adamant. In a rare concession, he finally agreed to shake hands with those in the assemblage.

In Eastern addresses, Bryan bathed his audiences in lotions of reassurance. He stressed that he was not a champion of government ownership and that his attitude on the subject had been misrepresented. The silver question, he said, was "dead." Bryan attended the New York State Democratic convention at Rochester and conferred with party leaders. The happy scene unloosed an air of confidence. Never before had Bryan evoked such receptivity and harmony in the state. At the convention, Chairman Alton Parker again declared his devotion to Bryan's success, and as four thousand onlookers roared their approval, Parker and Bryan clasped hands and faced the delegates. Thanks to Norman Mack's excellent groundwork, Bryan moved serenely through conferences with Parker, former U.S. Senator Edward Murphy, Hill, and other leaders. Afterward, Hill said Bryan's visit was "very pleasant" and that the campaign was off "to a strong start." [29]

In Delaware, Bryan's discourse took on a tougher weave when he charged that officials of the U.S. Steel Corporation were supporting the Republican campaign in exchange for immunity from prosecution. The next day he adopted milder discourse by taking pains to explain that the "Democracy is the friend, not the enemy, of every honest business." Buoyed by confidence, Bryan, in another presentation, conducted an imaginary cross-examination of Taft in which he placed his competitor in the position of admitting, after much pressure, that the Republican platform was errant and unsatisfactory and the Democratic platform was wholly right. The novelty of this sprightly inquisition delighted the crowd.

The great turnouts, the New York successes, the unprecedented friendliness of Eastern newspapers gave the campaign a sturdy surge of hope as it neared the two-month mark. According to the prevailing opinion among political professionals, he was running ahead of Taft. The Republican nominee was now pressed from all sides to drop his passivity and to take up the fight.[30]

Some 1,500 newspapers publicized Bryan's mass campaign for funds and engaged in eager solicitation. Contributors were rewarded with a button bearing a picture of Bryan and the caption above his head, "I gave my dollar," and beneath, "Did you?" Some newspapers carried banners or boxes: "Every dollar sent is a soldier to be used in the battle against plutocracy" or "A dollar voluntarily contributed to the democratic campaign fund may result in making it impossible for the trusts to make you unwillingly cough up ten or fifteen times that amount to the Republican fund in future campaigns." In some counties, Democratic clubs and Bryan Volunteers canvassed farmers and laboring men for thirty-cent donations. This modest sum was set to permit every Democrat to contribute, without burden. "Won't somebody give thirty cents to the Bryan campaign?" cackled the Republican New York *Tribune*.[31]

A consequence of the "popular subscription" campaign was an enormous swelling of Bryan's mail. Already ponderous, it developed an enormous tonnage, which soared from the tendency of thousands of contributors to send their gifts in coin. Each day groaning wagons would wend their way to Fairview. Several stenographers were kept busy handling the mail, acknowledging the receipt of the money, and dispatching drafts, checks, money orders, and cash to the bank twice a day. By mid-October contributions of less than $100 totaled $115,355.22, while contributions of more than $100 totaled $90,712.23. The year 1908 was no exception to the general pattern of Bryan campaigns: There were few large contributors. The Bryan effort was again bedeviled by lack of funds, and the Democratic resources were like a parched spring compared to the Republican financial ocean. "The work here is great," Josephus Daniels wrote to his wife from national headquarters, "and the *money is scarce*. We see so many things needed to be done & so little money with which to do it that it is a strain." [32]

In this, a people's campaign, Bryan was alert and inventive in arranging ways to spur the mass of voters. He made a movie of his several activities on Labor Day in Chicago. In part the movie was a talking picture, long before the industry itself made the transition. While Bryan was shown declaiming his Labor Day address, his voice was heard simultaneously from a phonograph record. In the movie's making, Bryan was put through all the paces of a Hollywood star. Riding from the railroad station to the auditorium, he was photographed from an automobile ahead of the one in which he rode. While the director shouted instructions, Bryan amiably gestured and moved about and even retained his tolerance when a shot of his car drawing up to his hotel in a sweeping curve had to be made three times. He was sustained in this drudgery by the spectacle of Norman Mack and other party leaders standing at the curb for these long minutes, gamely smiling and waving at his approach.

Bryan, who believed in a great deal of literature, had a Democratic campaign textbook prepared by the press committee, chaired by Henry Watterson, with Josephus Daniels providing the principal authorship. In the textbook, the voter could find data on the beef trust, the prices it fixed for the beef-growing farmer, and the prices it charged the public. The voter could also absorb an extensive exposition of Taft's labor record as a federal judge and a quantity of grim data on the Panic of 1907. As the campaign moved into high gear, Bryan also founded the practice of writing a letter each week to every Democratic precinct club in the nation, outlining plans for bringing issues more clearly before the people.[33]

In 1908, Bryan continued to work the vineyards of mass politics. The issues he highlighted—popular rule, the trusts, bank guarantees, the tariff— possessed mass appeal, for they represented concerns of every voter, regardless of who he was, where he lived, or what he did. But 1908 also marked a fundamental change in Bryan's campaign strategy. For the first time, he distinguished substantially among the groups constituting the mass of voters and courted them with attentions, insights, and pledges.

He gave specialized attention to economic, racial, and nationality differentiations in city groups, while simultaneously stressing issues upon which rural and urban groups could unite in large combinations. In the annals of the national Democratic Party, Bryan's innovations in 1908 constituted major pioneering. Woodrow Wilson, to a degree, and Franklin Roosevelt, far more, were to build on Bryan's efforts. The coalition of groups that Roosevelt contrived and that sustained his party for decades after his death had its beginnings in 1908.

The political object Bryan wooed most ardently in 1908 was the AFL. The Bryan-Gompers alliance became personal and close. They and their lieutenants conferred constantly, and Gompers boldly employed his position for the advance of Bryan's candidacy. He pressed workingmen to vote for Bryan, a matter that had to be handled with some delicacy since he was a leader and not a boss, and the AFL was not a monolith but a structure that left local unions with much power and discretion.[34] When Gompers called, most unions answered, but a few did not. Among the notable exceptions was the Western Federation of Miners. Gompers also solicited campaign funds from AFL unions. AFL organizers roamed through critical states on political missions, and labor orators sang the praises of the Democratic ticket. *The Federationist* carried articles admiring of Democratic doctrine, and the raw material of these efforts was provided by the press bureau of the Democratic national committee. Josephus Daniels, who ran the bureau, even dared feed words into Gompers' mouth. When Taft unloosed a salvo at the AFL's course in the campaign, Daniels urged Gompers to make a pithy reply, "and say that when labor asks for bread, Taft offered them a stone." [35]

Bryan acted to spur labor on. Midway in the campaign, his men organized the National Anti-Asiatic Immigration League. In denouncing Oriental immigration to the United States, the league struck a responsive chord among legions of American workingmen who feared the competition of Asian labor. When the campaign moved into its more critical weeks, Bryan pledged that if elected, he would include a wage earner in his Cabinet, "to represent the toiler of this country."

To the other major economic groups, Bryan was alert with attentions. The farmer, he said at a Western state fair, had not received his share of prosperity and was robbed of his earnings. Bryan again painted himself as the friend of the businessman, a species to which he gave the same sweeping definition he had accorded in 1896. When the National Association of Manufacturers called on its members "to bury Bryan," if only because of his comprehensive support of labor's demands, he pointed to what he perceived as the underlying fallacy of the recommendation. "Has the manufacturer," he asked, "an interest so distinct from those whom he employs, and through whose labor he produces that he has a 'vital concern' in opposing legislation beneficial to his employees?" Bryan's rather novel claim to represent the interests of both labor and capital drove Eugene V. Debs, Socialist candidate for President, to exclaim between laughter and tears that Bryan's position was just as impossible as "to ride two horses at the same time, going in opposite directions." [36]

As Norman Mack busied himself with setting up the national campaign apparatus, Bryan prodded him to pay full heed to the several bodies of nationalities constituting the American voting community. Bryan avidly courted the German-American vote, and his effort to detach this grouping from its traditional Republican moorings was enormously aided by the New York *Staats-Zeitung,* widest circulating newspaper of its kind, whose publisher, Herman Ridder, served as Democratic treasurer in the crucial second half of the campaign. Lest the Irish stray from their Democratic dispositions, Bryan, in an address to the Ancient Order of the Hibernians, proudly alluded to the Irish blood in his veins and hailed Irish-Americans for playing "the most important role in every part of the nation's work."

And in an address to the Young Men's Hebrew Association in New York, he hailed the Jewish people in a parallel encomium.[37]

It was the Roman Catholic voter who gave Bryan his gravest concern. "The Republicans," he acknowledged to Henry Watterson, "are making an effort to reach our Catholic Democrats, but we are planning to meet this. . . ." Many Catholics looked favorably upon Taft, who, as governor of the Philippines, had negotiated with the Vatican over the Friar Lands in the islands and agreed to terms pleasing to Rome. The Friar Lands, choice farm holdings of the Spanish Dominicans, had been seized by Aguinaldo in the Philippine revolution, and Filipinos were tilling them as their own. In negotiations with the Vatican, Taft had agreed to pay nearly 50 percent more than the appraised value of the lands and to abandon a demand that the Vatican withdraw the Spanish friars from the islands. Bryan, in contrast with Taft, had passed under a shadow in Catholic estimation because in writing of his journey to the Orient, he had heaped praise upon Protestant missions there but omitted any reference to Catholic endeavor. Throughout the campaign, Bryan was diligent in seeking to restore himself to Catholic graces. In an open letter, he referred to reports that he was unfriendly to Catholics and categorically denied them. He cited the large number of Catholics among his friends and in responsible positions in the party organization. Omitted was the name of Norman Mack, who, when he was appointed national chairman, was believed to be a Catholic. But to Bryan's deep chagrin, it was subsequently discovered that Mack, although of a Roman Catholic family, was not himself a Catholic.

There was another string to Bryan's religious bow. "There is considerable opposition to him," Bryan wrote privately of Taft, ". . . on account of his religious views." This, Bryan felt, might chase away his own dark clouds. Many a cleric criticized Taft for being not a Christian but a Unitarian. Indignantly they stressed that no man who denied the divinity of Christ was fit to be President of the United States. Even the minister of the other Tafts in Cincinnati astounded the family by declaring emphatically and publicly that Taft was not a Christian and that his father in a court ruling had "put the Bible out of the public schools." Therefore, the Tafts' minister concluded, he would vote for Bryan.[38]

In Bryan's two earlier Presidential campaigns, there were stirrings that gave him hope that Negroes might in some numbers move away from the Republicans to support him. For years Republicans seemed to have taken the Negro for granted. Negro dissatisfaction was spurred by an episode in Brownsville, Texas, in 1906, when members of the Negro Twenty-fifth Infantry were charged with shooting up the town, killing one man and wounding two others. The actual wrongdoers were never identified, the infantrymen were reticent about testifying, and President Roosevelt approved a report of the Inspector General that all three companies of the twenty-fifth be discharged without honor. Many Negro leaders and spokesmen cried out against the injustices of Brownsville, citing them as indicative of underlying Republican hostility, and urged their race to support the Democratic ticket.

W. E. B. Du Bois, the distinguished Negro intellectual, declared, "It is high noon, brethren—you are free, sane and twenty-one. If between two parties who stand on identically the same platform you can prefer the party who perpetrated Brownsville, well and good! But I shall vote for Bryan!" Other Negro leaders sounded this call as well.

Early in the campaign, reports spread that Bryan was eager for Negro support. Bishop Alexander Walters of the AME Zion Church and president of the Afro-American Council, was reported to have said that Bryan had told a delegation of Negroes that he deemed Roosevelt's handling of the Brownsville affair "unjust," and that in the event of his own election he would appoint Negroes to office. Subsequently, when questioned by a reporter, Bryan said he had not discussed the Brownsville question for publication and did not recall "ever having stated any positive attitude upon either of the questions propounded." [39]

Bryan faced the political task of reassuring his Southern supporters, while subtly encouraging a Negro breakaway from the Republicans. To a query at Cooper Union, "Is the policy of disenfranchising the Negro, advocated by the Democrats of the South, in accord with the spirit of brotherhood?" he endeavored to show, with the political debater's ingenuity, that Republicans were guilty of racial sins exceeding the Democrats'. The Negro in the South, he argued, who was disenfranchised by an educational qualification, "has a chance to bring himself within the qualifications. Many Southern Negroes do vote." The Northern Republican, he continued, who objects to this system, has fastened upon the Filipino a colonial system under which no man, however intelligent, "has a chance to bring himself within the qualifications. Many Southern Negroes can hope to share in the destiny of this nation." Bryan's other tactic at Cooper Union was to argue that just as the Southern white man resorted to voting qualifications for self-protection, "There is not a Republican community in the North that would not put it on when necessary."

In grappling with the Negro question, Bryan seemed always to be slithering about in ungainly postures. His Southern roots surfaced, and Negro leaders must have quailed when he said at Cooper Union that Southern disenfranchisement of the black man was "a matter of self-protection. . . ." The logic of his religious conceptions required him to embrace all races into the brotherhood of man. Both he and Mary indeed contributed to Negro charities and causes, and in his contests for Congress he openly solicited Negro votes. But in running for the Presidency, ever mindful of the Southern Democracy as the foremost bastion of his strength, he was affected by a hardheaded calculation of what Negroes could do for him. For Bryan, working in the realities of Presidential politics, the potential of Negro voters to assist his own needs materially was unimpressive. The deep state of Negro passivity was revealed when several prestigious leaders, Bishop Walters, Monroe Trotter, and William H. Scott of the Boston Suffrage League, sent out a call for a national Negro convention to determine a course of action for the Presidential campaign. The call declared that the Brownsville episode required a reassessment of the Negro position. The convention, which met in Philadelphia, was instantly overwhelmed with gloom when only forty delegates appeared. They achieved a ready unity, however, in pledging themselves to support Bryan and to oppose Taft, but generally there was no sign of any substantial movement of Negroes from their Republican base to the Democratic fold.

One of the most widely circulated pieces of literature of the campaign was an issue of a leading Negro newspaper, the *Broad Ax,* of October 24, 1908. It recounted how Democratic leaders were friendly and politically partial to the Negro, how the Bryans contributed to Negro schools, how Kern appointed a Negro as his chief clerk, and former national chairman Thomas Taggart made many Negro appointments. So widely did the Democratic headquarters circulate this issue that C. H. Williams, Democratic committeeman, indignantly protested, and added, "I sincerely hope Mr. Bryan, to whom we of the South have been so true, is not a party to the distribution of this paper."

As the campaign wore on, attendance and enthusiasm of Negro voters at rallies climbed. Brownsville remained the spark. Bryan, meantime, persisted on his narrow cautious path of encouraging a Negro breakaway from the Republican fold. His pioneer endeavor of striving to bring the Negro voter into the Democratic coalition remained a young unnoticed fruit on the vine until a far day when Franklin Roosevelt nurtured it and plucked it in its ripeness.[40]

As the contest proceeded, Bryan anxiously eyed the powerful Hill faction in New York. In the campaign's climactic weeks he trekked to Albany to consult with Hill, and the latter, for the first time in Bryan's twelve years in national politics, allowed himself to be seen publicly with the nominee. This concession it was hoped would rally many gold Democrats to the Presidential ticket. Hill's protégé, Alton Parker, continued to be generous with warm endorsements. Yet for all of Bryan's avid visits and consultations and the healing ointments and lotions applied by Norman Mack, New York remained a buzzing, faction-ridden hornet's nest. New York City was hobbled by strife between Tammany and the McCarren machine of Brooklyn, and in Buffalo a local faction battled with supporters of state chairman Wil-

LET THE PEOPLE RULE **451**

liam J. Connors. Repeatedly Brian was showered with warnings and lamentations that Tammany was making no serious effort on his behalf.

One of the more enheartening factors was the unprecedented friendliness of the Cleveland wing. The Bryan camp could view the beautiful spectacle of every living member of Cleveland's Cabinet expressing approval or working actively for their hero. But the atmosphere of reconciliation was suddenly punctured by anti-Bryan diehards of Cleveland's subcabinet. The late President's remorseless hostility to Bryan was recalled when Colonel Felix A. Reeve, former Assistant Solicitor of the Treasury, released a letter written by Cleveland shortly before his death saying, "I am dumbfounded when I see [the Democratic party's] apparent willingness to turn again to Bryanism—sugar coated, but otherwise unchanged. . . ."

More disruptive for Bryan was the disaffected William Randolph Hearst's igniting of the *cause célèbre* of the campaign, the case of Charles N. Haskell, governor of Oklahoma and Democratic treasurer. Hearst papers began spilling out details of Haskell's earlier years of sharp railroad transactions in Chicago and connections with Standard Oil. Haskell had stopped an antitrust suit against the company in Oklahoma. In a New York speech, Hearst charged Haskell with receiving $50,000 for services rendered in organizing the Federal Steel Company. "So you see," cried Hearst triumphantly, "this Haskell's not only a Standard Oil tool and the promoter of crooked railroads but also an organizer of trusts."

The revelations about Haskell were not a total surprise to Bryan. Nearly a year before, E. T. Russell, editor of the Ardmore, Oklahoma, *Morning Democrat,* had laid before him Haskell's connections with Standard Oil. Bryan had expressed disbelief and had thrown away Russell's letter relating the charges. The steady drumbeat of Hearst's accusations evoked only silence from Bryan. He was suddenly jogged from this posture when Roosevelt found in the Haskell case raw material for many Presidential sermons.[41]

Up until the Haskell affair, the Republican campaign had been mild, almost placid. When the party fared poorly in the Maine elections, Roosevelt and other leaders nervously urged Taft to do something. Taft abandoned his front-porch campaign and launched a speaking tour that soon drew crowds rivaling Bryan's.

Hearst's accusations also implicated an Ohio Republican Senator, Joseph B. Foraker, whom Taft quickly renounced, but concerning Haskell, Bryan still held his silence. In a public telegram, he demanded that the President produce proof of Haskell's connections with Standard Oil. Bryan recalled how he had himself aided Roosevelt's Presidency by offering measures for the nation's welfare and rallying Democratic support. He would not permit the Democratic Party to be misrepresented by Republicans.

Roosevelt, who had urged Taft to "smash and cut Bryan," brandishing the Haskell affair as the knife, now demonstrated to his protégé the workings of this political art. Bryan, cried the President, must have known when he appointed Haskell to his party posts of his permission as governor to a Standard Oil subsidiary to build a pipeline in Oklahoma "without the color of law." After contrasting Bryan's silent indulgence of Haskell with Taft's prompt and utter disavowal of Foraker, Roosevelt marched on to a large conclusion. No law-defying corporation, he declared, need fear anything from Bryan "save what it would suffer from the general paralysis of business which would follow Democratic success."

Daniels, Mack, and other Democratic leaders agreed that continued concentration on Haskell could scuttle the campaign. Daniels laid their joint opinion before Bryan, and regretfully he agreed that Haskell must leave, seeing embarrassment in Haskell's withdrawal and even greater embarrassment if he remained. Acting for Bryan, Daniels secured Haskell's resignation. Meanwhile, Taft dropped his gentlemanly passivity and, in the Roosevelt manner, attacked Bryan for his love of "financial theories that are full of sophistries and are impractical . . . his election would mean a paralysis of business. . . ." Bryan, for his part, now moved upon Roosevelt and dared him to match the publication of Democratic campaign funds of 1896 and to disclose, before the current elections, the contributors to Taft's campaign. Roosevelt, he pointed out, had paid more heed to the mote in the Democratic eye than to the beam in the Republican. Roosevelt, at this juncture, chose to abandon the debate.

Taft's and Roosevelt's allusions to possible setbacks in the economy from a Bryan victory were supplemented by business pressures on employees to vote Republican, a tactic that haunted Bryan's other campaigns. In Philadelphia, a separator works, with 1,000 employees, announced it would move away if Bryan won. The Atchison, Topeka, and Santa Fe railroad disclosed that in the same contingency it would abandon a $3,000,000 program of extensions and improvements, and the New York Central Railroad threatened its employees with reductions in wages.

For all of Roosevelt's hard talk and Taft's own enlivened effort, the camp of the Republican nominee, as the campaign moved into its most crucial weeks, was jittery. Ohio, termed by Taft's private secretary, Charles D. Hilles, as "The battlefield where the fiercest fighting is being done," found Republican chances weakened by the defection of the Foraker forces, "a deep-seated labor union prejudice, the disgruntled Negro vote. . . ." Even Vermont, as solid as its granite in Republican devotion, was reportedly stirring with doubts. "The discussion of the bank guarantee planks," an observer reported, ". . . made a profound impression on Vermont, especially among those persons who have been incredulous about Mr. Bryan's sanity on financial matters." [42]

As the campaign moved into the homestretch of October, Bryan concentrated his speechmaking in the middle Atlantic, north-central, and northern Great Plains areas. He ignored New England and the West Coast, which were predominantly Republican, and the Deep South, which was safely Democratic. In his hurrying and scurrying, an electoral vote strategy is evident. With 242 votes necessary for victory, Bryan was certain of 120 from the Deep South, and most likely would capture 13 more from Kentucky and 7 from Oklahoma, or a total of 140. The remaining 102 votes Bryan hoped to garner from the sections in which he labored. He could win by a combination of New York (39), Illinois (27), Indiana (15), Missouri (18), and Nebraska (8), constituting 107 electoral votes.

On the Eastern seaboard Bryan gave almost equal attention to labor issues and to the bank deposits guarantee plan. As Taft continued to oppose the plan by stressing that it would help bring "bad men" into banking, Bryan retorted that far too many bad men got into banking under the existing system. He would be delighted to support this contention, he said, by furnishing a list "of former bankers who are in Canada, another list who are in the penitentiary, and still another list who have committed suicide." As his train pulled out from Eastern industrial communities, Bryan was given to shouting that his listeners must not be coerced into voting as their employers dictated.[43]

In October's last week, Bryan and Taft arrived simultaneously in New York City for their last stands, both appearing exhausted from the grueling pace. As Bryan emerged from his train, Nathan Straus greeted him with a cablegram from Oxford, England, announcing that "American Rhodes scholars, after debate, emphatically support you for Presidency." In New York City and its vicinity, Bryan made a furious final effort that included a two-hour address to an overflow crowd at Madison Square Garden. With a close schedule of speeches in the city and suburbs, Bryan was forced at times to discourage applause. At a Brooklyn speech, he and his local hosts were taken aback by a storm of cheering, which after a full five minutes, showed no sign of subsiding. After more minutes and no letup, Bryan, mindful of his awaiting schedule, showed impatience. The controller of New York City, who presided, came to his rescue by shouting, "Give three cheers and shut up!" Bryan moved on to Albany, where David B. Hill, in an unprecedented act, cried that the candidate Bryan was "absolutely right upon every contested question in this campaign." In Cleveland, Ohio, Bryan declared that the endorsement just given by John D. Rockefeller and Andrew Carnegie to Taft's candidacy proved his contention that the Republican Party was allied with the trusts. Samuel Gompers, in an extra edition of *The American Federationist*, exhorted labor once more to vote for Bryan and warned that union members must expect "misrepresentation, coercion, and threats of discharge."

Bryan finished out the campaign in a hectic round of speechmaking in Illinois and Indiana. Everywhere the crowds were mammoth, the political decorations profuse, and each community seemed to vie with the other in the hospitality proffered. Mary was deluged with flowers and lunch baskets. At nearly all his stops now, Bryan was proclaiming that "Mr. Taft today is heading an army that has in it every financial pirate, every trust magnate, and I have not one single man who has his hand in another man's pocket. I appeal to the people who have been the victims of these men." [44]

Election night presented its familiar scenes at Bryan's Fairview home. Neighbors and friends dropped in. He passed much of his time in the enclosed porch that still served as a telegraph and newspaper office. The evening began happily when the Bryans entertained at a dinner in honor of the correspondents who had traveled with the candidate on his campaign.

When an occasional report arrived from a state chairman or the national committee, he read it aloud. His interest seemed most piqued by results from New York State. As the evening moved on, he read to reporters and guests letters from cranks advising him what to do if he became President. The atmosphere brightened when it appeared that he had carried his home precinct of Normal and the city of Lincoln. He quickly issued a statement of appreciation. But before long the returns took a definite trend against Bryan. As the hours passed, they did not improve, and at 9:30 P.M. Bryan announced that he would have no statement to make that night. The spirited Ruth would not concede that her father had lost and stayed up until the late hours, confident the trend would turn.

But, alas for Bryan, it was firmly set, and Taft emerged with 321 electoral votes, to Bryan's 162, and a popular majority of more than 1,000,000. Bryan prevailed in the Solid South and in Kentucky, Tennessee, Oklahoma, Nebraska, Colorado, and Nevada, none a major electoral vote state. It was a crushing defeat, the worst in his three Presidential races. When his family expressed their heartfelt regret, Bryan was, as always, a model of stoicism. "My only personal regret," he told Grace, "is that your mother will never be the First Lady of the Land to the nation, as she has always been to me, and that you, dear girl, will not make your debut in the White House." For himself, he was not sorry to be spared from an office that would have claimed "ten years" from his life.[45]

Yet Bryan was bewildered by the election's outcome. He could "not understand," he wrote to Louis Post, "how we were so badly beaten." And to Josephus Daniels, he added, "As far as I can see, no mistake was made." From all sides came explanations of the political disaster. Louis Post had no doubt that "a great deal of corruption entered in." No Democratic organization was more widely suspected of treachery than Tammany Hall. "Let Tammany explain," thundered an incensed *Commoner* editorial. Although

Tammany leader Charles Murphy made indignant denials, Raymond Robins, a social worker and friend of Bryan, related how the day before the election, Tammany men circulated throughout the state thousands of sample ballots—Robins had one—marked for Taft and the state Democratic ticket. New York City newspapers reported a deal between Murphy and Herbert Parsons, president of the Republican New York County committee, by which in a trade of votes each knifed the reformer on his party's ticket—the Democratic Bryan for President and the Republican Hughes, who was reelected governor. Murphy dismissed the report airily: "The days of deals of that kind are past."

The workingman, the results made clear, had again let Bryan down. Although he committed his campaign heavily to labor's cause, labor responded poorly. Louis Post was satisfied that "organized labor was pretty solid for you," but the union worker was no more than a minority of the labor force. *The Commoner,* presumably speaking for Bryan, exuded appreciation and understanding for organized labor's stance in the campaign. It heaped praise on Gompers and his fellow leaders. While labor faltered, the corporations and trusts, according to reports flowing in to Bryan, applied pressure and coercion mercilessly. General James B. Weaver, the Populist eminence, wrote that "the trust and monopoly magnates, having made their peace with Roosevelt and Taft, united to intimidate the so-called business men, from peanut vendor to country bankers." More damaging than coercion was the widespread expectation of the business community that prosperity would thrive better under Taft than Bryan, an impression that rubbed off on the work force and moved their votes toward the Republican candidate.[46]

The letters coming to Bryan to explain the defeat stressed the loss of the Catholic vote, traditionally Democratic, more than any other factor. Many cited the exceptionally heavy vote for Taft in large Eastern cities and contended that instructions to vote for Taft were read widely in Catholic churches the Sunday before the election. Various of Bryan's Roman Catholic friends discredited these reports, and Bryan himself seems to have given no credence to the thesis.

The most evident cause of Bryan's failure was his inability to stir the nation as he did in 1896. Friends and foes alike had become accustomed to his presence. It no longer created the stark excitement of old because he had altogether outworn his novelty. No issue that he advanced could rescue him from the painful penalty of voter indifference. Radicals were displeased by his apparent wooing of the East through trimming his issues and dropping free silver, government ownership of the railroads, and direct legislation. "Evidently he had determined to ignore dangerous problems," declared Clarence Darrow, who declined to stump for him.

With Republicans spending three times as much, the Democrats again ran poor. Negro voters were disenchanted by a sudden burst of Jim Crow laws in Democratic-controlled Southern states. The minor parties—Populists, Socialists, and others—no longer admired Bryan, and defections of their voters from his ranks doubtless cost him Missouri. That residue of resistance, the hard-core gold Democrats, persisted in opposition. Others less demonstrative in their rejection sat on their hands in joyful anticipation that awaiting defeat would put Bryan out of the way once and for all. The New York *Times,* promptly after the results were known, administered its own *coup de grâce* to Bryan's political future. "For Mr. Bryan this is annihilation," read an editorial, "and in his case the crushing defeat of ambition evokes not one spark of pity. In the criminal law the third offense is visited with an exemplary penalty, and no jury makes the recommendation to mercy." [47]

Any estimations of Bryan's future would have to reckon with the circumstance that he was an ideologist. Incorporated in his being was a set of ideas, about which he was passionate and articulate, which infused his calls for action, and whose validity he perceived as absolute and unqualified. In the fashion of ideologies, his ideology dealt with issues that are centuries old and are never settled. He dwelt on fundamental questions of politics, of relations between the rulers and the ruled, of how the rulers are to be selected, of the working principles and structure of the economic and international orders. As an ideologist he was deeply concerned with basic social change as an opportunity to reform and convert institutions into more morally responsible organs and therefore to make them more responsive to the people. Bryan, also in the tradition of ideologists, discerned the need for political reform in terms of causality. Reform was necessary because some men, highly placed in economic, political, and social institutions, were avaricious and immoral and employed them for outlandish personal gain at the expense and pain of the masses. The worst sources of oppression were the big institutions of an advancing industrial society—the corporation and the trust—whose masters freely and selfishly manipulated political organs and decisions.

Implicit in Bryan's ideological preachings is a theory of the nature of man. Man intrinsically is good, but man is corrupted when he is embraced by man-made institutions, above all, the business corporations. These institutions, powerful, immoral, and brutally manipulative, spread deprivation and misery. But the vast body of men—"the common people"—are good. Their essential characteristic is captivity in or subordination to big economic institutions. The farmer, the city worker, the small businessman, and the professional man of town and village constituted their main body. In Bryan's perceptions, the common man was suffering, meritorious, and heroic. He could do no wrong, and no word of criticism or reproach ever fell upon him from Bryan's lips.

Bryan's ideology also possessed a geographical dimension. It conveyed a sense of place. Its homeland was the West and the South, the latter being the section from which his ancestors had come and the former the land to which he had migrated. His ideology appealed for political union of these two regions, which he pictured as deprived and oppressed by an arrogant, exploitative East. Bryan perceived the nation's affairs to be manipulated by a conspiracy. The farmer oppressed by his mortgage and the low prices commanded by his produce; the city worker bedeviled by poor wages and transformed into a soldier and posted in the Philippines to keep the islands' peoples in subjugation; the consumer paying the exactions of the tariff-protected trusts—all were victims of a common conspiracy. Greedy men, moving behind the scenes and lacking any vested legitimacy, manipulated society and public policy to their own immense profit and brought misery to the general citizenry. These malefactors were concentrated in the East and, above all, at that gathering ground of evildoers, Wall Street.

In the manner of ideologists, Bryan, in his discourses, revered a body of sacred political texts. The chief of these was the Declaration of Independence, whose canons of freedom and equality, so long denied in practice, he strove to apply as the foundation of a better future. There were the venerated older figures, Jefferson and Jackson, perceived as political father-heroes, whose principles, pronouncements, and eras portrayed that which was noblest and best for the society of Bryan's day. From these saintly figures, Bryan derived his solutions for the problems plaguing contemporary society.

Like those of other ideologists who address their endeavors to the mainstream of politics, Bryan's proposals were directed to swaying a national popular majority. Since through a free electoral process they were designed to move a majority of the nation, Bryan's proposals, whether pertaining to silver, imperialism, the trusts, or otherwise, were never radical, for all the fright and screams of his opponents. In the time-honored style of reform leaders appealing to a vast following, Bryan, in constituting his package of proposals, combined the best of old institutions and practices with the best of the new. His proposals were weighted toward the restoration of a simpler, more idyllic past. If the ponderous trusts of today were oppressive, restore the smaller economic units of yesterday. If money was scarce because of the gold standard, revive the nation's historic commitment to bimetallism from which it had strayed. When Bryan espoused innovation in institutions and practices, his demeanor characteristically was cautious. His most extreme thrust was national ownership of railroads, from which he retreated several steps in the face of a substantial critical outcry. At most, Bryan offered a modest program of reform, whose planks already enjoyed wide acceptance when he took them up.[48]

PART THREE

≫≪

Decline

24. Keeping the Progressive Faith

BRYAN faced a crisis of role. In this, his third defeat for the Presidency, he confronted the adamant historical fact that no unsuccessful candidate for a major party had ever been accorded a fourth try for the Great Prize. Statistically, his chances for the office were at an end, and admirers and well-wishers, in affection and commiseration, provided fitting words of comfort. "The greatest men of this nation—Webster and Clay," he was reminded, had never become President, and he could now join their exalted company. "You will have a larger place in the history of the country than most of our Presidents," wrote Mayor William J. Gaynor of New York, "larger than any of them except a few."

But these appraisals, however well intentioned, relegated Bryan to a function akin to that of a political museum piece. They did not acknowledge that any new dimension could be added to his political career. Surely, the kinetic, morally haunted Bryan, in the full vigor of his forty-eighth year, would mean to act. But in what capacity, in what role? The question disturbed his admirers and enemies alike. Gaynor visualized Bryan as leader of the opposition and reminded him that "the opposition in a constitutional government often does more good . . . than those in actual control of government."

But "opposition," with its implicit negativism, was too narrow a function. Bryan's whole political career had been affirmative, given to positive proposals and generous in according approval to competing parties and leaders when, in his eyes, they deserved it. In speeches, correspondence, and press interviews, Bryan outlined his own perceptions of his future. An address near Christmas, 1908, entitled "A Battle Over, a War Begun," professed his resolve to continue the fight for reform and his regrets that he could not gratify those clamoring for his retirement. When Norman Mack and less friendly party figures expressed disbelief that Bryan would ever again be a Presidential candidate, he took pains to assure the press that "I hope it will never become necessary to run for office again, but I will not attempt to decide that question, until the time comes to act."

Yet if Bryan were not to engage in idle talk, he had to face a real threat. Since 1896, almost as if by some miracle, no one had emerged in the Democratic Party to challenge his place as the most conspicuous and effective leader of progressivism. But a new generation of Democratic personalities who might become formidable rivals was arising. Bryan had given the party inspiration and ideals, but never victory. Democrats were hungry for a new hero who could master the arts of victory and open the gates to its fruits.[1]

This was a transitional interlude for Bryan both in the political arena and in the ever-moving cycle of life and family. Within a year, Bryan yielded his two older children to marriage. William, Jr., was wed to Helen Berger, daughter of a prominent Milwaukee businessman. Accounts of the wedding noted young William's resemblance to his father at his age and his devotion to his ideals. The couple settled in Tucson, Arizona, where William began the study of law at the university. Ruth remarried. In a simple ceremony against a background of palms, Easter lilies, and lilies of the valley, she wed Lieutenant Reginald Owen of the Royal Engineer Corps of the British Army, stationed in Jamaica. Officiating at both ceremonies was the Bryans' old family friend the Reverend Harry F. Huntington of Crete, Nebraska.

As another evidence of their solid advance into middle age, Bryan and Mary celebrated their silver wedding anniversary. Festivities rolled through the day and into the night, with some 600 guests, chiefly from Normal and Lincoln, passing through Fairview. It was a day of pure, decorous joy. The younger Bryans and their spouses enlivened the receiving line. Dolph Talbot announced the guests with a gay flourish, and after greeting the honored couple, they trooped on to a curio room to inspect the clutter of objects accumulated on the Bryans' world travels and during three Presidential campaigns. Gifts had been prohibited, but floral offerings, which escaped the general injunction, crammed tables and hallways. The dining room, decorated in green and white, featured a quaint suggestion of older days—cakes with frosting inlaid with candied peppermint hearts.

Bryan also pursued the obligations incident to responsible Christian living. In 1910 he was ordained and installed as an elder in the Westminster Presbyterian Church, and in remarks to his admiring fellow members, he dwelled on the principles of forgiveness and of returning good for evil. Only these principles, he declared, could lead eventually to peace on earth. Bryan, on occasion, was summoned to perform duties as First Citizen of Lincoln. When William Howard Taft inaugurated the custom of throwing out the first ball to open the baseball season in the national capital, Bryan performed the same service for Lincoln's professional baseball club.[2]

But the major part of Bryan's life was concentrated on the lecture circuit. After sixteen years of his political speaking and moralistic lecturing, his appearances were still clamored for. He was more in demand than any other speaker in America. By train, auto, and wagon, he crossed and recrossed the United States, bringing his word to cities and hamlets. A reporter who followed him about on a midwinter tour of lyceums and banquets was impressed with how Bryan was constantly stopped for handshakes. "I was on the committee when you spoke in Keokuk in 1896," a man would say. "Yes," Bryan would reply, "I have been there twice since."

Even Bryan's journeys abroad were a kind of political busman's holiday. With Mary and Ruth, who met her second husband on the trip, Bryan early in 1910 toured Central and South America. Only spasmodically was the journey a vacation; its regimen was speeches before legislative bodies and rounds of official receptions. At midyear, Bryan and Mary journeyed to Edinburgh, Scotland, for a church-sponsored international peace meeting. In a soaring optimistic address, Bryan recounted the forces working for world peace. There existed, he contended, a stronger sense of brotherhood than was ever known before on earth. From the conference emerged resolutions, subscribed to by the delegates of the participating nations, that called for treaties to be entered into that would bind the contracting nations not to declare war or commence hostilities until the question in dispute had been submitted to an "impartial international tribunal" for arbitration and report. Afterward Bryan wrote of the conference to President Taft, who also hopefully looked to arbitration treaties to spare the world the scourge of war: "The plan gives time for peace influences to work, besides giving a chance to separate questions of fact from questions of honor." Though the plan left the nations free to act independently after the report, "the chances are greatly against war if time can be secured for reflection and investigation." [3]

Bryan's most solemn responsibility, to which he committed his might and main, was the keeping of the progressive faith. The economic reforms highlighted in the struggle of 1908 he continued to extol and plead for with voice and pen. He urged Democratic Congressmen to put their shoulders behind a bill to guarantee bank deposits. To President Taft he wrote an open letter urging his support of a constitutional amendment establishing the income tax. The amendment, he assured Taft, "would make your administration memorable—and I pledge you whatever assistance I can render in securing . . . ratification. . . ." Bryan manned the old bastions of tariff reform. The tariff plank of 1908 was his battle flag, calling for free wool, lumber, oil, twine, and a host of other commodities. When seventeen Democratic Senators voted for duties on lumber, and only eleven supported free lumber, Bryan cried, "Which element represents the Democratic party? If we are going to do anything in the next Congress, . . . we must elect congressmen who can agree as to what ought to be done."

When Congress at last bestirred itself to face problems for which Bryan for years had been urging action, he watched the proceedings in Washington with an Argus eye. Bryan was an articulate conscience, who did not mean to allow conservative legislators to hoodwink the public into believing that half measures of reform were really full measures. He sounded the alarms against the proposal of Nelson Aldrich, dean of Senate conservatives, calling for a central bank, privately controlled, as the heart of a far-reaching financial "reform" plan. Such a bank, Bryan warned, would be " a gigantic money trust. It is hard enough to control the financiers when there is some little competition between them—it will be a hopeless task when the finances of the government are turned over to them." Bryan was driven to pointing out that another Aldrich proposal calling for federal incorporation of big business was simply a dodge to escape state regulation. The great corporations, to be sure, required further control, and the best way to provide it appeared in the Democratic platform of 1908. This was the device of federal licensing (in contrast with federal incorporation) "which does not surrender any of the rights of the state but adds a federal remedy to existing state remedies." The licensed corporations would be supervised by federal authority, and indulgence in trustlike conduct would be prohibited and punished.

In his open letter to President Taft, Bryan also solicited support for the constitutional amendment calling for direct election of Senators. He reminded *Commoner* readers that "One of the important tasks of the American citizen is to reform the U.S. Senate. The Senate will be reformed when it has been brought closer to the people." The House, too, fell under his critical eye. "We denounce the despotism of Cannonism," he cried, and called for amendments to the House rules to "insure majority rule on every question." Bryan's reforming gaze turned also to the courts. He endorsed a plan, already used in several states, providing for the recall of judges. When critics argued that recall made judges subservient to the popular will, Bryan argued that this was as it should be.

Bryan's interest in the judiciary extended even to the United States Supreme Court. When the Court spewed forth a quantity of decisions hobbling the Sherman Antitrust Law and the regulatory acts governing the railroads, Bryan was indignant that Taft should appoint one of its most conservative members, Edward D. White, as Chief Justice. He invited Taft to make public the written and oral recommendations on which he relied in making appointments to the Court. The New York *World* mirthfully observed that Bryan, in reality, was attacking Taft because of his failure to appoint Bryan's own kind of court. Who would constitute such a court? Bryan himself, the *World* answered, most surely would be the Chief Justice, and the Associate Justices must include Jeff Davis of Arkansas, Theodore Roosevelt, Robert M. La Follette, Ollie James, James Martine, the New Jersey reformer, and others whose views of the world approximated Bryan's.[5]

Bryan, in his speeches and editorials, offered his listeners and readers a philosophy that illumined pathways to the good or better life. He commended to his followers the Bible, particularly the New Testament, and the moral code it posited, "which is destined to conquer the world." There was no greater endeavor than the life of Christian service. The saving of one boy, he contended, accomplished for the world greater things than money spent in any other way can buy. "Much as I am interested in government," he acknowledged, "I am more interested in religion. Anxious as I am too that man will vote right, I am more anxious that men shall live right."

Increasingly in lectures and writings, Bryan attested his devotion to pacifism as an attainable goal. "The day will come," he said in an address in Havana, Cuba, "when the world will see the folly of the doctrine that you can justly settle a difference of opinion by shooting the man who may differ from you." At a peace conference at Lake Mohonk, New York, in 1910, Bryan, as one of many distinguished speakers, discussed the teachings of Tolstoy on love and nonresistance. Bryan thrilled his peace-minded audience by urging that the United States "tell the world that it did not believe in war, that it did not believe that it was the right way to settle disputes, that it had no disputes that it was not willing to submit to the judgment of the world, and if this nation did it, it not only would not be attacked by any other nation on the earth, but that it would become the supreme power in this world." [6]

As the Democracy's vanquished Presidential candidate, Bryan was still the titular leader of his party. In the interests of a progressive legacy, he had to superintend the selection of the next Presidential nominee. The worst disaster would be the passing of the nomination into conservative hands.

In the interval between the election of 1908 and the national convention of 1912, Bryan devoted brain and sinew to keeping the Democratic Party in the progressive fold. His chief foes were the reorganizers, who had given the party Alton Parker in 1904 and who in 1912 would surely promote a similar standard-bearer. After this, his third defeat for the Presidency, with its drain of prestige, Bryan was undertaking a struggle against enormous odds. ". . . we will have a hard fight on hand," wrote Bryan to Henry Rainey, "and I think it is important that our people should know that those who criticize me personally are as a rule opposed to the things that we have been fighting for. . . ." [7]

The fragile character of Bryan's grip upon the party was exposed by early resistance to his continued leadership. Norman Mack, his longtime supporter and national committee chairman, who presumably would be the quintessence of loyalty to Bryan, showed signs of defecting. Promptly after the 1908 election, Mack took pains to declare that Bryan would never again seek the Presidential office. Months later, Mack took another long stride away from Bryan when he attended a highly guarded meeting in Texas with Chicago boss Roger Sullivan, who was also national committeeman of Illinois; R. M. Johnson, committeeman of Texas; and other important figures.

An ominous suggestion was allowed to slip out of the meeting that the conference was "emphatically antagonistic to the continued leadership of W. J.
Bryan. . . ." [8]

The first major testing of Bryan's progressive stewardship was the Congressional election of 1910. Distressed by Democratic support for the
Payne-Aldrich Tariff bill with high duties, Bryan urged vigilance in Democratic nominating processes across the country. "Put none but the faithful
on guard," he wrote in *The Commoner.* "The privileged classes never sleep;
their agents are always at work." He went about recruiting *The Commoner*'s
Million Army whose members pledged themselves to secure the nomination
of only "worthy and incorruptible men" as Democratic candidates. Bryan
betook himself to Texas for an extensive tour to speak against Senator Joseph Bailey, a defector to the high tariff ranks, and to keep Democrats from
endorsing the protective tariff in their 1910 platform. In actuality, Bryan
was working for a quiet purge of the Democratic Party. Only the progressive faithful should remain.[9]

On the face of the electoral results of 1910, Bryan contributed to an imposing Democratic triumph. The Democracy swept the country. The House
passed under solid Democratic mastery which the party controlled by 40
votes. In the Senate the party gained 10 seats and moved into possession of
major governorships. Woodrow Wilson triumphed in New Jersey, John A.
Dix in New York, and Judson Harmon in Ohio. In Massachusetts, Connecticut, Indiana, and Iowa, among other places, the Democracy had surged to
victory. Bryan, looking ahead to 1912, saw a glittering, beckoning vision of
success.[10]

When the new Congress gathered in 1911, Bryan rushed to the capital.
Congress was to be organized in an extra session, its leaders chosen, its
committees constituted. For two weeks, Bryan was seen hurrying and
scurrying on Capitol Hill and in hotel lobbies, buttonholing legislative
friends, and talking animatedly. Bryan's and the House's wills happily coincided in the choice of Champ Clark as Speaker. A generous, unswerving
supporter of Bryan in each of his three Presidential races, Clark offered impeccable credentials. "In the selection of Mr. Clark for Speaker," observed
the Washington *Star,* ". . . Bryanism had triumphed." Indeed when the
House formally opened its proceedings, with the galleries packed and the
benches on the floor filled with members awaiting the oath, Bryan walked
through a side door onto the floor to the accompaniment of electrifying
cheers. Clark followed a moment later, earning a good recognition from the
crowd, but "the peerless leader," an observer noted, "got the cream of their
ardor."

For Bryan, the Senate wore an altogether different face. The Republicans controlled it, but the election had increased both the Democratic progressives in the chamber and the combined total of Republican and Democratic progressives. Since progressive control of the Senate was mathematically ruled out, the monster Bryan chose to fight was the evident overrepresentation of Democratic conservatives in positions of leadership in the Senate party and on the important committees. The organization of the Senate, Bryan argued, posed the "issue of seniority vs. public interest . . . individual ambition versus the people's welfare."

Bryan directed his zeal for a more representative Senate to the selection of the Democratic minority leader. The leader would have much to say about the Senate's agenda and priorities and the assignment of legislators to committees. Senator Thomas Martin of Virginia, who was slated for the post, symbolized everything that Bryan wanted to avoid. Martin, *Commoner* readers learned, is a "master of manipulation. He is a machine politician . . . ," and, in Bryan's eyes, was one of the worst of the Senate Democracy's tariff renegades.

Progressive Democrats contested Martin's election as minority leader by rallying around Benjamin Shively of Indiana. Bryan electioneered for Shively and, in a step of exceptional audacity, declared in a public statement that if he were a Senator, he would not vote for Martin. In the final tally, Martin prevailed 21 to 16. The division seemed to follow the tariff voting lines, although several nonprotectionists threw in with Martin, professedly out of resentment against Bryan's impudence in interfering in the Senate's internal affairs. Yet Bryan was not wholly vanquished. He helped wring out concessions from the Martin camp for greater progressive representation in the Senate's Democratic organization. Shively was elected vice-chairman of the Democratic caucus, and Martin appointed a steering committee which contained two progressive Democrats: Bryan's recent running mate, John Kern of Indiana and Gilbert Hitchcock of Nebraska.[11]

While Bryan concentrated on the Washington scene, a corps of conservative Democrats who had voted the Republican ticket in each of Bryan's three Presidential races laid plans for a banquet and speeches in Baltimore, to result, they hoped, in the delineation of a party platform that would titillate the most adamant of the Cleveland Bourbons. Two young journalists, Judson Welliver and Louis Brownlow, who watched the unfolding of the project, labeled it "a tory scheme designed to commit the newly victorious party to conservative policies." Speakers were scheduled, dinner plans made, and Bryan was carefully not consulted. When driblets of news of the Baltimore developments reached him, he smote the machinators hard in a stern *Commoner* editorial denouncing the proposed conference and its organizers. The salvo was sufficient to wither interest to the point that the conference was called off, a Jackson Day ratification banquet was substituted, and Bryan was invited as one of the principal guests.

But the Jackson Day occasion was not all cleansed and purified. The speeches, while decorous, were given not to the trusts or banking reform or other items highest on the progressive agenda, but to the tariff, a subject of lower priority and one dear to the hearts of the Cleveland Bourbons. Even more than what was said, the menu and appointments revealed the sentiments of the occasion. Oysters, diamondback terrapin soup, Jersey capons of highest quality, canvasback ducks and Smithfield hams, 1,000 cocktails, 552 quarts of champagne, and 400 quarts of sauterne constituted an uncharacteristic Democratic extravagance. "This could not have happened in Bryan's day," observed the Cleveland *Leader*. "Then dollar dinners were the limit of Democratic indulgence . . . Then anything more costly was deemed improper in the party which laid claim to the special guardianship of the poor and humble." [12]

Cries for harmony were heard from many Democratic sides, and the voices raised most clearly belonged to Bryan's former foes. Warning his followers that "harmony" was a pleasing but deadly siren call, he cheerfully acknowledged that "We have not had harmony in the party for fifteen years, but we have seen the progressive element of the party dominate the political thought of the country and it is ready to sweep the country." He warned that under the cry of harmony, "the interests" would seek to nominate a Democratic Presidential candidate in 1912 unsympathetic to progressive principles and committed to halting their advance. Rather than harmony and the spirit of compromise that begets it, the Democrats, Bryan contended, required strength and unflinching moral purpose. "The cleaning out of the stable," he predicted, "will be a Herculean task." [13]

For well nigh a decade and a half, Bryan's dominion over Nebraska's Democracy was unchallenged. His monopoly was owed in no small way to his large gifts for political management which kept would-be rivals in their place. His employment of fusion politics fortified his preeminence in the Democratic hierarchy since the gubernatorial nomination was allotted to the Populists, a tactic that barred any Democrat from emerging to the top state post and therefore to leadership of the state party.

Changing political circumstances imperiled Bryan's local eminence. A fast-declining Populist Party drained fusion of its value; new Democratic faces were appearing; and one of them, A. C. Shallenberger, Democratic nominee for governor, was elected in 1908 with a larger popular vote than Bryan commanded in Nebraska for the Presidency. This was a shattering event, demonstrating that Bryan was no longer the Nebraskan Democracy's supreme vote getter. Two of Bryan's closest allies—Gilbert Hitchcock and James C. Dahlman—had also come into political maturity, and they could well collide with Bryan and his necessities in the interval prior to the national convention of 1912.

Hitchcock had been a key ally through every step of Bryan's career. Urbane and responsible, and a social crusader, Hitchcock, in editorials, struck at railroad abuses, commiserated with the suffering farmer, and lamented the ineffectiveness of the major parties. He championed the emerging Independent Party and became the journalistic patron of Bryan's budding career. When the young orator won his first Congressional victory in 1890, a rejoicing Hitchcock hailed it as an event that would launch Bryan, with his gifts, into becoming one of the most remarkable figures in the history of the nation. Over the years, Hitchcock was a close personal friend of the Bryan family.

In 1902, a drab political year for the Nebraska Democracy, Hitchcock was elected to Congress from the Second District. Defeated for reelection, he triumphed in 1906 and again in 1908. His combined Congressional tenure of six years was the longest of any Nebraska Democrat, including Bryan. A fiery orator despite his gentility off the stump and a proved vote getter, Hitchcock could hardly be denied political advancement.

James C. Dahlman, too, was deserving of preferment. From the day he chanced to discover Bryan's oratorical prowess in Chadron, Dahlman had been a worshipful, trusted promoter of Bryan's fortunes, who, to put it mildly, deserved better than he was to receive at his leader's hand. Dahlman was his skillful commander at the most crucial field posts—chairman of Nebraska's Democratic state committee in the Presidential races of 1896 and 1900 and a member of the Democratic national committee, 1900–1908, eventful years when Bryan was battling party conservatives and building toward his third Presidential nomination. Adroit in political negotiation and management, Dahlman was a main cog in Bryan's organization and career.

While serving Bryan, Dahlman had been building a career of his own in elective politics. After completing terms as mayor of Chadron and sheriff of Dawes County, he came east to Omaha and rose quickly in the city organization, where his vote-getting prowess was welcome and he was soon elected mayor. Omaha reelected him five times to its highest office. Dahlman headed the mighty Douglas County Democratic machine, whose support enormously eased Bryan's ascendancy in the state party. Like Hitchcock, Dahlman was a close and affectionate friend of Bryan and his family. He was also one of Nebraska's more colorful politicians. Proud of his background as a Texas cowboy, he was a star rider and roper at county fairs and rodeos until he was fifty. One of his first acts as mayor was to drive a nest of crooked gamblers out of town, and when more of their ilk threatened him, the wiry little man marched into their gambling rooms and coolly demonstrated his flawless marksmanship upon a chandelier high above the astonished crowd.

By 1910 the popular Dahlman, with his long string of electoral successes, was training his eye on the governorship. He announced his candidacy at a huge annual picnic of Omaha Democrats, who received the tidings while enjoying endless quantities of free beer and movies, one featuring a dancing skeleton and beneath it the label "Governor Shallenberger, the Dead One." The press reported that all kinds of gambling apparatus were in operation, free of intrusion from law officers.

The elements of change and incipient crisis in Nebraskan politics were also aggravated by Bryan's hesitation and blurred perception of his course. Gilbert Hitchcock announced that he would run for the Senate and commented on Bryan's intentions. He had first ascertained, he said, from "a personal interview with Mr. Bryan," that the latter was definitely not a candidate, that he was delighted Hitchcock was, and that "he would not take any part as between me [Hitchcock] and other Democratic candidates who had been equally loyal." But a pall of ambiguity was cast over Hitchcock's definition of the situation when Bryan men in Lincoln circulated petitions across the state demanding that Bryan run for the Senate. Some 2,000 signatures were collected, a shadow of the 15,000 hoped for by the managers. Bryan soon announced that he definitely would not be a Senatorial candidate.

Apparently concluding that it was the better part of wisdom not to lay his prestige on the line by personally entering the race against Hitchcock, Bryan did the next best thing. He endorsed the candidacy of a stand-in, *The Commoner*'s associate editor, Richard L. Metcalfe. While expressing gratification that Hitchcock and another rival, W. H. Thompson, were in the race, he hailed Metcalfe as "fearless and incorruptible . . . the most available man for the place." Metcalfe, Bryan added for good measure, would be a stronger candidate than he would himself.[14]

This was but the first rent in Democratic Nebraska's political fabric. A. C. Shallenberger, whose gubernatorial administration was popular and who had committed the cardinal sin of outpolling Bryan, had to be cut down. Because Shallenberger was popular and effective, he could not be vanquished on personal grounds. Bryan could reach him only through a policy issue, manipulated in a fashion to expose the governor as an unbeliever, an ingrate, and fit, therefore, only for the outer darkness. Bryan, his power challenged and influence slipping, pursued a course altogether at odds with his career image of a politician devoted to issues for their intrinsic worth. What he did was governed less by principle and conviction than by personal ambition and political necessity. Bryan now acted for the good of Bryan.

The issue he took up was temperance, a topic highly agitated and propagandized for by agents of the Anti-Saloon League, who were swarming across Nebraska spreading indignation at Demon Drink. Nervous and wary toward the budding issue, the Democratic Party in the 1909 elections maintained total silence. Bryan had also assumed a gingerly stance. In none of his Presidential campaigns did he raise the issue, and in 1908 he took special pains to prevent its intrusion into his campaigning in Nebraska. In his first Congressional campaign of 1890, his victory could not have been won without his open, articulate opposition to prohibition, a stand that pleased Omaha, the largest electoral enclave in his district and a city rich in breweries and saloons.

Statewide prohibition was politically out of the question, what with the heavy proportion of German-American and other European stock to whom the banning of alcoholic beverages would be an outrageous, unthinkable deprivation of a precious liberty. Temperance advocates resorted to the next best political thing, county option, by which each county, in a popular referendum, could decide what course to pursue within its borders. In 1909 prohibitionists invited Bryan to state his position on county option and, they hoped, to support it. But he graciously declined to enter into any discussion because county option "was not in the platform." The Reverend D. N. Tinder of Exeter, Nebraska, was one of many in the community of teetotalers distressed by Bryan's chosen silence. "Is not that something like the Pharisee?" the Reverend Tinder wondered. "But did you not hear a sound a few months ago ringing from ocean to ocean, from Canada to the Gulf, 'let the people rule'?"

Ironically, in 1909 Governor Shallenberger, whom Bryan was about to pillory on the temperance issue, pushed through a daylight saloon law, by which all saloons had to close at 8 P.M. Arthur Mullen, who introduced the law, was impressed that it made Nebraska nights "As dry as Death Valley." Omaha was omitted from the law—otherwise, it could not have passed— and a county option bill was defeated, thanks to brisk activity by the liquor lobby. Bryan and his chief lieutenants, brother Charles and brother-in-law Tom Allen, were conspicuously absent from these struggles.

In 1910, a year of state and Congressional elections, Bryan suddenly came out for county option, demanded that Governor Shallenberger call a special session of the legislature to pass it or refer the question to popular vote under the initiative and referendum. Only by such steps Bryan argued, in a letter sent to all Democratic legislators, could temperance, a local issue, be kept out of the impending Congressional elections, which ought to be devoted to national issues. Shallenberger declined to call a special session in the conviction that it would be abortive and indeed might unloose unwanted hazards to the Democracy's electoral fortunes. Many saw the issue Bryan was posing to be an exceedingly narrow one: He wanted a special legislative session now to act on the liquor question in lieu of waiting for the regular session a mere four months hence. The aroused Bryan began a busy campaign through the state for a special session, for a county option plank in the Democratic state platform, and a candid declaration by every gubernatorial aspirant of his position on county option. Since soundings found little statewide sentiment for county option, Shallenberger, preferring not to commit political suicide, kept silent.

Meanwhile, Nebraska was treated to a rousing temperance debate. Bryan thundered against drink and the nefarious liquor interests. Clarence Darrow, with his national reputation as a champion of political liberties after his court defenses of Eugene Debs and the striking coal miners of 1902, was imported to assert the doctrine that men have a right to do as they please. To an audience of 4,000 in Omaha's city auditorium he suggested teasingly that cardplaying, dancing, tea and coffee all were bad and ought to be voted out.

A further essential step toward Shallenberger's degradation transpired with the entry of Dahlman, a proud, vociferous wet, into the gubernatorial contest. In the ensuing Democratic primaries, which were open to all eligible voters, Bryan men, aided by wet Republicans, overpowered Shallenberger. Bryan, by now, had thrown principle to the winds; ambition dictated the crazy logic of his course. Having berated Shallenberger for displaying only limited commitment to prohibition, he made a crude about-face and joined hands with the wets of both parties. Whatever commitment Bryan had toward prohibition yielded to his higher purpose to cut down Shallenberger. Later at the Democratic state convention at Grand Island, Bryan paid the expected price. He was overwhelmingly defeated in his effort to implant his temperance views into the platform. Dahlman was nominated for governor on a platform expressly opposed to making county option "a question of party creed."

Although he had expertly blackened Shallenberger's eyes, Bryan put himself into a potentially embarrassing position. With the dry movement gathering momentum about the country, and particularly in his strongholds, the South and the West, he presented the appearance of supporting Dahlman, a wet, who was also openly and generously backed by liquor interests. At the peak of Nebraska's 1910 campaign, Bryan addressed himself to the problem. His speech, in Lincoln, one given many times in other states in support of Democratic Congressional tickets, contained no reference to the liquor question. At its close, however, he drew a paper from his coat pocket and said, "I have before me a very unpleasant duty, but I must perform it. Principle is important. Men are not important. What I have to say is so important that I want no misquotation. Therefore, I wish to read this statement." A pall of silence fell over the crowd. "My God, he's going to bolt Dahlman," Arthur Mullen groaned to his companion, Dr. P. L. Hall. In his statement, Bryan acknowledged that Dahlman had secured a majority in an open primary, which "gives him the legal right to the nomination," but "it does not give him the moral right to the Democratic vote of the state." The audience sat appalled. "Had it been anywhere but in Lincoln," wrote Mullen, "Bryan would have been mobbed; but there was enough of his spirit in the Lincoln crowd to save him." Thus was Dahlman rewarded when push came to shove.

In the remaining campaign, Bryan stumped for Democratic tickets, including the Senatorial candidacy of Gilbert Hitchcock. For his part, the cooperative Hitchcock reminded puzzled Nebraskans that Bryan had made the Democratic Party "stand for the best there is in government."

When the pieces of the wild Chinese puzzle that was the Nebraska election fell into place, it was evident that Bryan, after totaling up his political debits and credits, emerged with a clear profit. Of the three Democratic personalities rising to challenge his preeminence in Nebraska politics, two had sustained defeats, and it would be long before they could recover. Shallenberger went down in the primary, and Dahlman lost the governorship to the Republican Chester Aldrich. Only Hitchcock remained. Although he had foiled Bryan's effort to topple him in the primary through Metcalfe, he had, with Bryan's support, won the Senatorial election. Bryan thus eliminated two rivals while maintaining a working partnership with a third. His temperance plank had been rejected in the state convention, but his national prestige was immense enough to sustain that brief setback. A year later, in 1911, the state convention, with "Get together" its slogan, was a model of sweet harmony. Factionalism suddenly became invisible. The platform "pointed with pride" to the leadership of Nebraska's Democracy of the past quarter century. The measures listed as fought for and won were, all of them, Bryan's.[15]

The elections of 1910 were but the harbinger of those of 1912. In looking ahead, Bryan resorted to a familiar tactic. He began publishing in *The Commoner* extended lists of those who in his eyes were likely candidates.

To assure that the best available man be chosen, Bryan suggested, his record and views and character of his supporters must be thoroughly examined. By these tests, a major candidate, Governor Judson Harmon of Ohio, passed under an inky pall. There was pathos in Harmon's mischance. In 1908, Harmon had campaigned far and wide by Bryan's side, often to the sacrifice of his own gubernatorial campaign. So concerned was he about the dismal consequence of a fourth successive Democratic defeat, Harmon wrote to Congressman Henry T. Rainey of Illinois, "that I said everywhere in my speeches that I would gladly consent to be defeated if that course would insure the election of Mr. Bryan." Suddenly, in 1910, Harmon's standing in Bryan's estimation crumbled. Technically, the Ohio governor moved into ill grace by failing to support a pet Bryan project—a constitutional amendment calling for popular election of Senators. Bryan, in a public statement, suggested that Harmon by such lapses could not hope to remain long as a national leader. An indignant Ohio newspaper questioned by what dispensation Bryan could come to say that Harmon "shall surrender his right and class as a national figure" if the "Democrats of Ohio do not do as he [Bryan] wishes."

To those potential Presidential nominees who conducted themselves according to progressive lights, Bryan registered appreciation with generous praise. "Good for Governor Wilson," he exclaimed in *The Commoner*, when the governor of New Jersey and former university president took a progressive turn. Champ Clark, Democratic leader of the House of Representatives, also evoked Bryan's high praise. Clark played a central part in the successful revolt in 1910 against the tyrannous Republican Speaker, "Uncle Joe" Cannon. A rock of conservatism, with a well-oiled machine, Cannon for years blocked social legislation. Nebraska's young progressive Republican Congressman George Norris led the revolt by introducing a resolution depriving the Speaker of membership on the powerful Rules Committee and making the committee elective. Democrats, headed by minority leader Champ Clark, joined with the insurgent Republicans to pass the resolution. The Speaker was curtailed, and long-stalled progressive legislation began to move. An ecstatic Bryan hailed Clark in *The Commoner*. "Measured by courage, candor and fidelity, there is not a man in the democratic ranks who will deserve better things of a triumphant Democracy than the present minority leader of the House of Representatives." [16]

As the calendar raced through the months of 1911, Bryan's surveillance of the field of candidates took on a new urgency. "The interest shown in the nomination of the next Democratic candidate by the plutocratic press and corporation attorneys," Charles Bryan wrote to Louis Post, "shows their determination to nominate one or both of the candidates of the two dominant parties in 1912." Charles deemed it vital that the nation's progressive Democrats settle on their candidate "and let the work of organization be started throughout the country." By mid-August Bryan was announcing, "I intend to devote all my time between now and the nomination to finding out things about the candidates. . . ." He was delighted that the Democracy was blessed with "so many available men," and when the time for selection arrived, "I will not be silent. . . . I intend to devote my time to driving plutocracy from the throne and putting the rights of man in the seat. I haven't a friend in the United States whom I would reward at the expense of my party or my country."

Bryan now completed the erasure of Judson Harmon from his candidates' slate. At the Jefferson Club's barbecue in Columbus, Ohio, literally in Harmon's political backyard, Bryan performed this solemn punitive act. Taking as his topic "The Passing of Plutocracy," Bryan filled the air with bitter attacks on politicians with ties to Wall Street and indirectly, although unmistakably, included Harmon in this sorry classification. [17]

Champ Clark, in contrast, who became the House's new Speaker in 1911, continued by every appearance to balloon in Bryan's favor. "Champ Clark's real name," observed the New York *Sun,* "is W. J. Bryan." Clark was picking up most of Bryan's following in the Middle and Far West. The Hearst press backed him, and its influence was decisive in Illinois, California, Massachusetts, and other states. Most of the state organizations and regular party workers supported the Speaker. The chief discordant note was sounded by the New York *World,* which warned that Clark's provincial, narrow outlook, undistinguished intellectuality, and lack of identification in a long career with any important legislation would bring disaster to the Democratic Party and, with his election, to the United States. Suddenly a cloud the size of an elephant moved over the Bryan-Clark nexus. The political atmosphere did not produce the cloud; it was Bryan-made. The House of Representatives, at this moment, was wrestling with a new tariff bill. Speaker Clark, after soundings taken among House Democrats, discovered a predominant sentiment for a low tariff on wool, dealt with in Schedule K. Bryan proceeded to apply to Clark the same weapon he used to cut down Shallenberger. He manipulated an issue to advance his personal purposes. He chose this moment to demand free wool. Although since 1892 the tariff had occupied a lesser position in Bryan's political priorities, he seldom, if ever, displayed passion over the small difference involved between a low tariff and no tariff. In fact, in his own Congressional days, he had pooh-poohed the difference.

In an extraordinary letter to Clark, Bryan declared that "the fight over wool will prove a crisis in your life as well as in the party's prospects. . . . Don't inquire about how the fight is going to go—make it go the right way, if you can. If you fail you lay the foundation for a future victory. The right wins in the end—don't be afraid to wait." Clark, who was impressed that House Democrats "had gotten . . . together for the first time in twenty years," did not propose to help divide the Democracy again "and have another long spell of wandering in the wilderness." In actuality, Bryan was demanding that the Speaker imperil or even throw away his chances for the Presidential nomination at a moment when he was clearly leading the field.

The tariff also involved Bryan in a set-to with Oscar Underwood, chairman of the House Ways and Means Committee, who was emerging as the favorite Presidential candidate of conservative Democrats, following the apparent eclipse of Judson Harmon. Bryan, in a public statement and using information evidently fed him by a Congressional insider, charged that Underwood had sidetracked the efforts of Speaker Clark and others to revise the iron and steel tariff schedules. "The real Underwood," wrote Bryan in a *Commoner* editorial, was now "revealed." Flushed with indignation and speaking in a rising angry voice, Underwood explained to the House that he had engaged in no maneuver, deliberate or diabolical, to sidetrack the iron and steel tariffs. What he had done was to put them next in line after wool for committee consideration. The duties for wool, he explained, had not been revised for many years, while those for iron and steel had been reduced in all three of the last tariff laws. Underwood moved on to other explanations while Clark, from his Speaker's chair, beamed approval, and the House, rallying to one of its own, accorded the Alabama Representative a spirited five-minute ovation. From afar, Bryan retorted simply that what he had said was founded on a Washington dispatch published by an Omaha newspaper. The House Republican leader twitted the Democrats by noting that "When Oscar W. Underwood . . . in parliamentary language called Mr. Bryan a liar, not a man rose in the House to protest." [18]

Three major candidates had now passed under Bryan's microscope and had been found wanting. On two of these candidates, Harmon and Underwood, he had vented his judgments publicly. On the other, Clark, he was rankled by doubts, and by candid private warnings, he hoped to nudge the straying Clark back onto the progressive path. But Clark was doing little to gladden Bryan. The Speaker, to the delight of the liquor interests, was holding at a standstill a bill regulating the interstate shipment of liquor. Simultaneously Clark was running the best-financed campaign for the nomination, with the grateful liquor interests contributing generously. Another big donor was the railroad magnate James J. Hill. Clark persisted in his unblemished record of not identifying himself as the champion of important progressive legislation. "If we could only get him to work," an exasperated Bryan mused. "Why doesn't Clark do something aggressive? People will not follow unless he leads." A fourth major potential candidate remained, the governor of New Jersey, Woodrow Wilson.

On the record, Wilson seemed most unlikely to measure up to Bryan's stern expectations. He had voted against Bryan in 1896. He owned a substantial record of conservatism. "Government supervision," he said in 1907, ". . . will in the long run enslave us and demoralize us." While Bryan was thundering against the Aldrich plan for a central bank, Wilson embraced it with praise, and in a step that surely qualified him for the hottest depths of a Bryanesque hell, he recommended that no one less than J. Pierpont Morgan be chairman of a "common council," to guide the people's destinies.

By word and act, Wilson had on occasion been directly hostile to Bryan. In a 1907 press interview he said he could "point out in Bryan" an advocacy of political propositions he considered absurd and could never endorse. In 1908 Wilson refused to dine and speak with Bryan from the same platform in Philadelphia. After agreeing to speak at the Jefferson Day dinner of the National Democratic Club in New York, he withdrew upon learning that Bryan was also to speak. "I have even wished at times," Wilson told a reporter, "that every fool could be also a knave instead of being, as they often are, people who possess attractive manners and excellent intentions. Take

Mr. Bryan, for example. He is the most charming and lovable of men personally, but foolish and dangerous in his theoretical beliefs."

Just as St. Paul underwent conversion on the road to Damascus, so Woodrow Wilson experienced a political conversion from conservatism to progressivism. The time and place of this historic incident cannot be fixed for Wilson with the exactitude that it can for St. Paul. Apparently over a two-year period, from 1908 to 1910, Wilson made this sweeping metamorphosis. He broke with the original sponsors of his political career, James Smith, Jr., a powerful New Jersey boss, and Colonel George Harvey, whose Wall Street connections were massive and gold-lined. He dispatched a progressive program to the New Jersey legislature, and his addresses became devoted to progressive themes. After a Wilson speech of 1911, holding that "the great monopoly in this country is the money monopoly" and that "its power is used for personal ends," Joseph Pulitzer exclaimed from his editor's chair at the New York *World*, "Is Woodrow Wilson Bryanizing. . . . How like Mr. Bryan's language of sixteen years ago!"

From its very beginnings, Wilson's conversion was encouraged and applauded by Bryan in *Commoner* editorials. Bryan was exultant when Wilson backed the Democratic nomination for the U.S. Senate of James E. Martine, the leading Bryan Democrat of New Jersey and, in the Nebraskan's words, one of "America's stalwart democrats." Moved by Wilson's faith and courage in his trial by fire, Bryan seemed inclined to forgive and forget Wilson's multitudinous past sins. "If Governor Wilson," wrote Bryan, "had known in 1896 what he knows today he would have fought shoulder to shoulder with the Democrats of that year. . . ."

The growing Bryan-Wilson ties were cemented by personal visitation. Bryan delivered an address in New Jersey, which Wilson attended, and that evening the Reverend Charles T. Erdman of the Princeton Theological Seminary, with Mrs. Erdman, entertained at dinner Bryan, the Wilsons, and Thomas H. Birch, one of Bryan's warmest New Jersey supporters. In this first exposure to Bryan's oratory and presence, Wilson was most impressed. To Ray Stannard Baker, a former muckraking journalist and a confidant of the governor, he wrote of the meeting with Bryan, "I feel that I now can say that I know him and have a very different impression of him from that I had before seeing him thus close'at hand. He has extraordinary force of personality, and it seems the force of sincerity and conviction. He has himself well in hand at every turn of the thought, and talk too; and his voice is truly delightful. A truly captivating man, I must admit."

Bryan continued to watch with benign care over Wilson's emerging progressivism. When the governor averred that the Philippines were not yet ready for independence, Bryan gently suggested that he read the Democratic platforms of 1900, 1904, and 1908, and Bryan's own speech on "Imperialism" in the second volume of his addresses. Colonel Edward M.

House, now a major Wilson adviser and once the Bryans' neighbor during a winter sojourn in Texas to boost Grace's brittle health, began an industrious courtship to secure the Nebraskan's endorsement of Wilson. Just as House was taking heart in this difficult mission, there occurred an horrendous disaster that seemed to dash the Bryan-Wilson relationship into a thousand pieces. A Princeton trustee, Adrian H. Joline, released the letter from Wilson, clearly private and confidential, written four years earlier in 1907, with a prayerful wish that Bryan be knocked "into a cocked hat."

Intermediaries for Wilson and Bryan anxiously negotiated to resolve the incident without further embarrassment. Their toil had a frantic air, for close on the heels of the Joline letter, Bryan, Wilson, and other leading Democrats were scheduled to speak at the Jackson Day dinner in Washington. The imminent face-to-face meeting filled the Wilson camp with overflowing despair. But they soon swam with joy when Bryan, upon reaching Washington, said he had nothing to say about the Joline letter. At the dinner Bryan went out of his way to show cordiality for Wilson. He spoke warmly of the governor in his address and, while the two were standing on the rostrum, put his arm around his shoulder as photographers snapped the happy scene. Early in the evening, Wilson told an aide afterward, Bryan had said not to worry about the Joline letter, adding, "I, of course, knew that you were not with me in my position on the currency." Wilson answered, "All I can say, Mr. Bryan, is that you are a great big man." [19]

The year was 1912. State conventions and primaries now fell to the crucial task of choosing delegates to the national convention. In Bryan's eyes, the nominee would symbolize the outcome of the struggle between progressivism and conservatism.

The surest way to defeat progressivism was to eliminate Bryan as an influence in the national convention. This could be achieved through a simple process of political mathematics. His national political base consisted of the long-standing allegiance of two great sections, the West and the South. Let either or both of these be separated from his political legions, and he and progressivism surely would be defeated.

On the crowded canvas of struggle and maneuver in the states, Bryan perceived the outline of a plot calculated to achieve his political undoing. The "reactionaries," as he called them, advanced Oscar Underwood as a candidate in half a dozen Southern states, and his success would plainly cripple Bryan in his strongest bastion. Simultaneously, Harmon as a candidate was advanced in the West and East. In addition to whatever pledged delegates Harmon and Underwood might win, the plan included a further step, Bryan believed, to "work in as many reactionaries as possible in other delegations pledged to a progressive, with the expectations of having these delegates support a reactionary candidate, after the one for whom they may be instructed, is out of the race." To foil this subtle play, Bryan urged readers of *The Commoner* to be on guard that "No reactionary should be sent as a delegate to represent a progressive constituency." He warned progressive voters, faced with the task of choosing delegates to the national convention, to determine the delegates' second choice for the Presidential nomination "in the likelihood that no candidate will win a majority on the first ballot."

In further counterthrust, Bryan campaigned throughout Ohio against Harmon, pouring out a steady fire of criticism. Inevitably, admirers of Harmon, who had achieved something of a political miracle in winning in Taft's normally Republican state, demanded proof of Harmon's unacceptability. Exactly how was Harmon "a reactionary and a tool of Wall Street?" Bryan was asked. He answered that he had never charged that Harmon was "a tool of Wall Street." Rather, "he is a reactionary and the choice of Wall Street." As a reactionary, Bryan elaborated, Harmon refused to support the Democratic ticket in 1896. In 1904 "he helped the Belmont-Ryan crowd in putting Wall Street in control of the Democratic organization." In opposing adoption of the initiative and referendum at the Ohio Constitutional convention, he was "a repudiator of platform pledges. . . ." But what proof did Bryan have that Wall Street backed Harmon? ". . . Wall Street acts in secret," replied Bryan, "and . . . it is difficult to furnish written proof of the movements and endorsements of the men who control the financial affairs in our business centers." Harmon was attorney for Morgan and Hill interests, and "Wall Street controlled papers" favored his candidacy.

Toward Champ Clark, who presumably was his favorite candidate, Bryan maintained an ambiguous posture. His conviction did not soften that Clark was too conciliatory to "the special interests" in fashioning new tariff legislation. He encouraged the Presidential candidacy of Joseph W. Folk and journeyed to Missouri to seek a divided delegation between Folk and Clark, but the scheme was dashed when Folk withdrew. When Clark in the struggle with Folk accepted help from the Harmon men of Missouri, Bryan wrote darkly in *The Commoner* that Clark, before accepting this succor, "should inquire about the price" lest it "come too high." [20]

Woodrow Wilson's relationships with Bryan, meanwhile, progressed swimmingly. In breaking with George Harvey, Wilson had indulged in the most admirable of acts; he had given duty precedence over ambition. "It should matter little to him whether he reaches the White House, or not," wrote Bryan, ". . . the joy that comes from the faithful rendition of service surpasses any satisfaction that one can derive from gratification of political ambition—the joy that makes one strong enough to endure even the severest of strains, namely, the breaking of the bonds of friendship." Wilson also passed with flying colors the occasional probing questions that Bryan put to him concerning past political conduct and present attitudes. For whom did Wilson vote in 1900 and 1908? At both elections, Wilson "very cheerfully confessed," he voted for William Jennings Bryan. Did Wilson agree that publication of prenomination subscriptions should be made obligatory by law? He did, wholeheartedly. Originally expected to bring the Democracy back "to the old conservative camping ground," Wilson seemed to have gone over body and breeches to Bryan, and some thought him more radical than Bryan had ever been. "A more complete change," gasped the Washington *Star,* "was never made by a man seeking high political office in this country."

Whom was Bryan for? In Washington, Democrats in Congressional cloakrooms and at social gatherings played a kind of game: "Bryan, Bryan, who's got Bryan?" The Commoner, as yet, had declared outright for no one. Whom was Bryan for? "Bryan is for Bryan," a considerable chorus rang out. Many a Democrat viewed Bryan's attacks on Harmon and Underwood and his insistence on leading Clark and Wilson around by their political noses as a calculated plan to eliminate rivals and create deadlocks which eventually would drive the national convention to award him a fourth nomination. Repeatedly, Bryan declared that he was not a candidate. "I shall never be President," he told a crowd at Arapahoe, Nebraska, "but I would rather go to my grave with the consciousness that I have done right and that I have done all in my power to give to my country the best possible form of government than be President." And to the Jefferson Day dinner at New York in 1912, he declared, "I am not a candidate. . . . Give me a chance to fight in the ranks for a progressive candidate and I will show that I have fought not for myself but for a cause." [21] Not everyone believed these words, least of all the camps of the leading candidates.

The inexorable advance of the political calendar brought Bryan ever closer to the point where he had to indicate a specific preference. To participate most effectively in the impending convention, he had to attend as a Nebraska delegate. Given his preeminence in the state party, it was fit that he be not merely a delegate, but a delegate at large, a position which, since it reflected a statewide decision, would provide fresh ratification of his state leadership.

In Presidential nominating politics, Nebraska had become almost a model application of Bryan's campaign slogan of 1908, "Let the people rule." The state possessed a Presidential preference primary, by which the popular electorate expressed its will toward the several Presidential aspirants, each of whom was identified with would-be delegates. The primary's results, technically, were not binding on the state parties, which retained an ultimate power to choose each delegate, but the parties' choices were expected to reflect the voters' preferences.

Presidential nominating politics were thoroughly entwined with Nebraska politics in 1912. In the political civil war of 1910, Bryan had put down two competitors, Shallenberger and Dahlman. A third, Gilbert Hitchcock, had escaped the devastation, won election as U.S. Senator, and stood at this moment as the most formidable rival. He was a dominant force in the most populous city and county of Nebraska—Omaha and Douglas— and commanded the allegiance of its efficient Democratic machine. He owned the widest circulating and most influential newspaper in the state, the Omaha *World-Herald.* Above all, he was the first Democrat elected to the U.S. Senate in Bryan's political career. Bryan, on the other hand, held no office, and was tarnished by three Presidential defeats. Inevitably, the selection of Nebraska's delegates became a battleground between Hitchcock and Bryan for ascendance in Nebraska's Democracy.

Hitchcock carefully limited the ground he was defending to reduce the eventuality of defeat. He announced that his first choice for President was Harmon but added, by way of leaving a door open for honorable retreat, that he would support Wilson or Clark if Democratic voters so instructed at the primaries. Bryan, for his part, staked out a different ground. He was unwilling to be a delegate if Harmon won a plurality at the primaries. "As between Mr. Wilson and Mr. Clark," he did not care "to express a preference." He regarded both as "progressive" and he would be "glad to vote in the convention for either if instructed to do so by the Democrats at the primaries."

Hitchcock, Bryan declared, aimed "to misrepresent the Democracy of this state in the matter of the Presidential nomination" and "to prevent any cooperation" between the two progressive candidates, Clark and Wilson, "with a view to securing, not a majority, but a plurality for Mr. Harmon." Hitchcock could then proceed to the Baltimore convention "and ally himself with the plutocratic influences that are attempting to force Mr. Harmon upon the party." At the national convention Hitchcock and other Nebraska delegates who shared his attachments could help write a platform, "which will assassinate our party in advance and make it impossible for even a progressive to win." There was a further danger. However progressive the candidate Nebraska voters might instruct for, if that candidate could not be nominated at the national convention, Hitchcock would be released from further instructions and could then employ his influence "to foist upon the party any reactionary who may be nominated." [22] On his editorial page of the *World-Herald,* Hitchcock indicted William Jennings Bryan and his dark arts in recent Nebraska politics. In effect, Bryan was decreeing, wrote Hitchcock, "that no Democrat has a right to think for himself in determining his preference for the Presidential nomination. . . ."

Although Bryan had assumed a public position of neutrality between Clark and Wilson, in private talk and gesture, he became increasingly unneutral. A meeting of progressive Democrats in Lincoln adopted a resolution declaring that Clark's candidacy, "in view of the rival candidacies of

Wilson and Harmon," invited "the success of Mr. Harmon." The resolution urged Clark to withdraw in Nebraska. In the event that Wilson could not be nominated, the resolution proposed that Nebraska vote for Clark as its second choice. When speculation soared that Bryan was father and sponsor to these moves, he took pains to state publicly that he was "in no way responsible" for the progressives' actions. However, in a private letter to Clark, Bryan urged his withdrawal from the Nebraska primary to avoid the risk of Harmon's success. Clark rejected the advice and declared that he had no doubt that he would carry Nebraska. He was a good prophet. Clark swept Nebraska with 24,000 votes. Wilson ran a poor second with 14,000, and Harmon a bad third with 12,000. If progressivism was vindicated, it was the Clark and not the Wilson variety. Both Bryan and Hitchcock were elected delegates at large. Bryan quaffed a full cup of prestige when his popular vote was larger than Hitchcock's; he was still at the top of Nebraska's political mountain. Nebraska's people had spoken, and it remained for their delegates to demonstrate in the national convention that the people ruled.[23]

By mid-June the Republicans were gathering at Chicago for the first of the national conventions. As delegates streamed into the torrid city, there sauntered into their midst a most improbable figure. He was indeed W. J. Bryan, the most powerful of Democrats, present, he explained, as a reporter for the New York *World*. Once again, Bryan was demonstrating that in matters of personal advantage he could be extraordinarily open-minded. Working for the newspaper that ranked among his severest critics was profitable, and in this instance he did not permit political principle to impair his private economics.

When Bryan took his place in the press stand, Republican delegates, recovering from their disbelief, gave their old rival a heartfelt ovation. There were delicious moments when Bryan, pencil and notebook in hand, set out on the trail of an elusive news item. He would call at a delegation headquarters, and his expression wreathed with gravity, he would inquire into the situation and the prospects. For a moment the delegates would look startled, appreciating in a glimpse the paradox of the leader of the rival party now an inquiring reporter seeking out the secrets of their innermost proceedings. "Aren't you Colonel Bryan?" a puzzled delegate would ask. "That's right," he said, "but I'm only a reporter at present." He was greeted with effusive warmth and little information.

What Bryan witnessed at Chicago was a dreary affirmation of his suspicion that organized interests could easily subdue the progressive cause. Theodore Roosevelt, the overwhelming popular choice in thirteen Republican primaries, the obvious hero of the rank and file of delegates, was overwhelmed. The Taft juggernaut mercilessly cleared the way for the President's renomination, and the platform was boss-made, colorless, and

KEEPING THE PROGRESSIVE FAITH

unprogressive. "At Chicago," wrote Bryan, "I saw the Republican convention choose its candidate under the pressure and influence of Wall Street." If Wall Street could take over at Chicago, could it not also at Baltimore?

Bryan's uneasy ruminations were interrupted by a telephone call from Baltimore. It was Josephus Daniels, now a national committeeman. Daniels spoke the words of disaster. The national committee had just selected Alton Parker as the awaiting convention's temporary chairman. "What on earth does anybody want Parker for?" cried Bryan in angry stupefication. "He would start us off on a reactionary basis that would give the lie to all our progressive declarations." Daniels unrolled the details of the garish incident: The Clark men had supported Ollie James, Bryan's old friend, Kentucky Congressman, and Senatorial nominee, and the Wilson men Senator James A. O'Gorman of New York. Progressive forces, divided between the two candidates, became deadlocked, an eventuality Bryan long had feared. In a backsliding search for a compromise, the Clark men turned to Parker. Small wonder that Bryan was more concerned about second choices at Baltimore than first choices.

In face of this crashing disaster, Bryan resorted to an audacious move. He addressed identical telegrams to each candidate who appeared to fight under the banner of progressivism. He invited Clark, Wilson, and several favorite sons to join himself and his friends in opposing the selection of Parker as temporary chairman, either by the full national committee or the convention. Clark was again found wanting. ". . . the supreme consideration," he replied, "should be to prevent any discord in the convention. Friends of mine on the subcommittee of arrangements have already presented the name of Ollie James to the sub-committee. I believe that if all join the interest of harmony in an appeal to the entire national committee to avoid controversies in matters of organization that committee will so arrange as to leave the platform and nomination of candidates as the only real issues on which delegates need divide."

Woodrow Wilson, too, teetered momentarily on failure. Initially, he dismissed the Bryan letter in a cute straddling statement to the Baltimore *Evening Sun.* His political adviser Joseph Tumulty and Mrs. Wilson, however, successfully insisted that he give a straightforward answer to Bryan's appeal. "You are quite right," wrote Wilson. "The Baltimore convention is to be a convention of progressives—of men who are progressive in principle and by conviction," which must, moreover, "express its convictions in its organization and in its choice of the men who are to speak for it." Where Clark was noncommittal and harmony-minded, Wilson had assumed a heroic progressive pose of force and principle.[24]

Of all the Democratic personalities arriving at the humid convention city of Baltimore, Bryan was the most hailed and attended. "They all seem to be coming in to see me," Bryan said to a friend. "As soon as I have finished with one crowd another is on hand, so I have to begin it all over again, but I am pleased to see them—very pleased. This is a good Democratic year."

With the assistance of Mary and Charles and Mayor Frank Brown of Lincoln, his moon face beaming with joviality, Bryan received with warmth and banter waves of political friends from the old wars. One after another of Bryan's visitors suggested, in words naked of subtlety, that he ought to be the party's choice for President. "I will be for you for President," proclaimed a Minnesota delegate. Bryan, with a deep laugh, exclaimed, "I haven't thought of that at all. I have something more important on hand just now." The warm reunions were a kind of marshaling of the forces against a mighty host gathering elsewhere in the Belvedere and the Emerson, the two convention hotels. Arrayed against Bryan and progressivism were the city bosses and the community of financiers and lawyers, symbolized by that political epithet "Wall Street." Charles Murphy, Roger Sullivan, Tom Taggart, the most prestigious of the bosses, already were highly visible and extremely busy. The rooms of Murphy and August Belmont were in the same corridor at the Emerson, and visitors moved easily between them. Belmont and the nation's premier financier, J. P. Morgan, an old-style Bourbon Democrat, were members of the New York delegation. The delegation, largest and most influential in the convention, was securely under the thumb of Murphy, a posture that was doubly secured by the unit rule. Murphy and Morgan reputedly were joined in a well-cemented politico-economic nexus. The other towering financier to be reckoned with was Thomas Fortune Ryan, a Virginia delegate, owing to a home he maintained in the Old Dominion.

The president of the Erie Railroad arrived on his yacht with a bevy of politico-corporate attorneys, John B. Stanchfield, Morgan J. O'Brien, William F. Sheehan, and De Lancey Nicoll. "Big business," arrayed against progressivism, was represented, in the estimate of the New York *Times*, "by some of the ablest financiers and lawyers," supplemented by crowds of young men, the practiced press agents for the corporations. Well dressed, articulate, they moved smoothly through the hotel lobbies, warning with easy plausibility against the perils of progressive ideas.

Against the mighty forces of the assembled money changers, Bryan maintained an outward optimism and inner concern. There was weakness, he acknowledged, with progressive strength divided between Clark and Wilson, and neither could make his nomination certain, but together they commanded a majority, "possibly two-thirds of the convention. . . . The chances are largely in favor of the nomination of one or the other of them . . . unless some contingency, now unforeseen, arises. . . ."

The battlelines were drawn; the convention was ready to begin. James Cardinal Gibbons of Baltimore pronounced an impressive invocation.

Bryan, who had not taken his place with the Nebraska delegation, stood by his chair, alone, at the rear of the platform. He appeared tired and worn, lines of exhaustion deep upon his face. Seeking to conserve his dwindling strength, he had asked friends not to shake hands. As the cardinal's prayer began, Bryan stood with closed eyes, swaying noticeably, his lips moving as if he too were praying.[25]

Both sides had endeavored to avoid a fight over the temporary chairmanship. Bryan had personally appealed to Parker to withdraw, to no avail. "I made no impression on him than to arouse his ire," Bryan reported. Bryan then set about in quest of a suitable progressive, someone other than himself to run against Parker. He approached the behemothian, popular Ollie James, original candidate of the Clark men for the post. But Clark's managers objected, and James respected their wish. Bryan then approached Senator O'Gorman, the original Wilson candidate, but he, as a member of the New York delegation working under the unit rule, was pledged to Parker. Bryan moved upon Senator Kern, his 1908 running mate, but Kern, not wishing to jeopardize the Presidential candidacy of his fellow Indianan, Governor Thomas Marshall, too declined. Kern, however, agreed to participate in a complicated maneuver should a contest on the convention floor become necessary.

The Clark men, meanwhile, labored to avoid the fight. Soon after Bryan's arrival, a Clark emissary, Senator-elect James K. Vardaman of Mississippi, went to him. If Bryan would drop the fight against Parker for temporary chairman, Parker's friends would vote for him to be permanent chairman. Vardaman, Bryan's close friend of many years and a persuasive button-holer, was confidently expected to sway Bryan. No sooner had Vardaman set forth his proposal when the interview became a harrowing experience. Bryan stiffened, his manner suddenly caked with arctic frigidity. The Senator-elect nervously snatched up his hat and bolted toward the door. "I thought," he managed to gasp, "our personal and political relations were intimate enough to permit me to talk about the matter to you." Bryan quickly put his arm around Vardaman's shoulders, saying he did not mean to give offense. They talked about the matter further, and amiably, but Bryan budged not a speck.

Even more than the fight, the Clark men feared that Bryan, if he should become the temporary chairman, would exploit, with sensational effect, the perquisite of that office, the keynote address, and the convention would lose its head, in the manner of 1896. The Presidential nomination would again be his.

Promptly after the convention began its business, Bryan came forward to oppose the report of the Committee on Arrangements respecting the temporary chairman. He was pale, and his manner heavy; his black brows were contracted over penetrating eyes; his hawk nose had an extra downward twist. He held his head erect, the grizzled fringe of his dark hair ruffled and moist with perspiration. "He made a fine figure, standing up there," wrote a reporter of the New York *World,* "in an old dark sack suit, with a low collar and white string tie, holding his right hand up to quell the applause." Bryan employed his best arts to move the convention, citing his own record of service to the people and, climactically pointing to a motto lining the wall, cried that this quotation from Jefferson applied to himself. He read it, with arresting resonance: "He never sold the truth to serve the hour." By proved experience, this oratorical technique should have swept the assembly into a fit of clamorous admiration. But the crowd, heavily women and children, and the delegates, lost in a thousand distractions, responded only with sporadic cheers and clapping.

For temporary chairman, Bryan put into nomination John W. Kern of Indiana. When Bryan finished, Kern, according to prearranged plan, rose and appealed to Parker to join him in withdrawing from the contest in order that the convention might agree upon someone who would command its united support. In a carefully contrived moment, Kern paused for Parker to answer. There was only deathly silence. Kern, undaunted, appealed to Murphy. Surely the chairman of the New York delegation would apply his influence to move Parker to withdraw. Again cavernous silence. Since, apparently, there had to be a contest, Kern said, William Jennings Bryan was the only man to lead the people's side. He put the Commoner's name into nomination as temporary chairman.

Within minutes, the roll call proceeded, and the pattern of delegates' loyalties quickly emerged. Parker's support consisted of Harmon and Underwood delegates and many Clark delegates. The Wilson delegates moved massively behind Bryan. The final vote was close; Bryan lost 579 to 510, defeated by the tendency of large numbers of delegates to support the Arrangements Committee's report, and therefore Parker, as a matter of good, normal party behavior.

As soon as it was clear that he had lost, Bryan, Mary, and the children trudged back to the Belvedere. The press carried the day's happenings far and wide, and an avalanche of telegrams descended upon Bryan's suite: telegrams from old friends and supporters, telegrams to which many had subscribed, angry telegrams, and telegrams high with praise. Bryan now knew that he could use the convention not only to move the delegates but also to influence the country.

He also had uncovered the enemy. Bryan the reporter wrote in his "Baltimore Letter" that "There are many instructed for Clark who have no sympathy with progressive ideas, men who if they are ever released from Clark support may be expected to take up with a reactionary." The Wilson men had emerged from the fracas as shining Galahads. But Bryan did not declare for the governor even though it appeared easy and natural for him to do so. Perhaps Bryan was reserved because he had decided to be a candidate himself. The Wilson camp was deeply fearful of that eventuality.[26]

On the evening of Bryan's defeat for temporary chairman, a committee of Clark men called at his suite to offer him the permanent chairmanship of the convention. Exuding courtesy and solicitude that no ordinary mortal could resist, they sweetly pressed Bryan to accept the honor. Mary and old friends who were on hand encouraged Bryan, too. But he declined without hesitation. Those, he said, who owned the ship should furnish the crew. Whenever his friends controlled a convention, they never asked the minority to supply the officers.

The next morning there came another peace offering. A committee waited upon Bryan bearing this time the glittering gift of the chairmanship of the Resolutions Committee. But Bryan again declined. His visitors continued to press their favors. If Bryan would not serve as chairman, let him then name another in his place. Unhesitatingly, he recommended John Kern, who was quickly elected. Bryan agreed to serve on the subcommittee on the platform.

Since his potential enemies were exuding tolerance and concession, Bryan proposed that the Resolutions Committee depart from customary procedure, agree on a platform, and withhold it from the convention until after the Presidential nomination. The candidate, he said, could then be consulted before the platform was finally adopted. An Eastern delegate, quivering with incredulity, asked how the convention's nominee could ever object to the convention's platform. "Our candidate did in 1904," Bryan retorted. Amid laughter, his plan was quickly adopted.

The Clark men and the New Yorkers fell over themselves in permitting Bryan to have his own platform. "The subcommittee," he wrote afterward, "was a harmonious crowd." The eventual platform was an extended document, with, said Bryan, "many of the planks contained in previous platforms which I had helped to write. . . ." One of these planks pledged that the next President of the United States, should he be a Democrat, would serve only a single term.[27]

The balloting for the Presidential nomination began. The leading candidate was Champ Clark, who entered the convention with a lead so great that any time New York's 90 votes, controlled by Tammany boss Murphy, swung to him, the nomination was his. But Clark, who under ordinary circumstances could have waltzed into the nomination, bore a heavy cross of liabilities. In the Bryan-Parker fight for temporary chairman, Clark's managers had divided his vote, hoping to please both sides. The maneuver provided Bryan an opportunity to contend that Clark, despite his progressive raiment, was a candidate with deep Wall Street connections.

A chill air of uncertainty touched other flaws in Clark's posture. A heavy portion of his delegate strength consisted of old Bryan men, and some of these the aroused Nebraskan might detach. The Clark candidacy was largely financed by William Randolph Hearst, a far from revered name in Democratic circles, a circumstance that shed further unflattering light. His momentary political weakness served to underscore any seeming personal defects. It lent currency to a criticism Bryan was spreading among the delegates that Clark was too easygoing. "His managers show no judgment," Bryan would lament, "and he is letting them run things. If Clark cannot manage his managers, how can he manage the government?" And others were vexed by opinions akin to Woodrow Wilson's that Clark was "a sort of elephantine 'smart Aleck.' "

The second leading candidate, Wilson, emerged from the temporary chairman fight as the only major aspirant solidly identified with progressive sentiment. But the Wilson candidacy at this juncture was heavily dependent on Bryan, who even at this late hour had not endorsed the governor. Though delegates pressed to know his attitude, Bryan kept his counsel.

The men who lived atop great mountains of wealth and who were habituated to using the opportunities of government to increase their fortunes were almost brazenly conspicuous. Charles Bryan, who moved constantly through the convention in his black silk skullcap, with his easy smile and catlike tread, came upon evidence, which he laid before Bryan, that Clark's managers had concluded an agreement with Tammany by which New York's 90 votes would move to Clark early in the balloting. The agreement, Charles was impressed, would put Clark under obligations to Wall Street and would bar Clark from carrying out a progressive program as President. Charles also had a plan. With Bryan's approval, he called together several dedicated Bryan men now functioning as Wilson managers and proposed that one of them introduce a resolution calling for the expulsion from the convention of Thomas Fortune Ryan and August Belmont, both ringleaders in the plot to capture Clark. The assembled leaders quailed at the proposal as harsh and unwise. No one volunteered to introduce it. Though discouraged by this poor response, Charles suggested that Bryan write out a resolution naming Belmont, Ryan, and Morgan as Wall Street conspirators and lay it before the convention.

Bryan wrote out a resolution, but other opinion he and Charles consulted ran heavily against it. The Bryans nevertheless retouched the most criticized language, and on the morning of June 27, when Presidential nominations were to begin, Bryan tucked the draft in his pocket and started out to the convention hall, uncertain whether he would use it. Midway in his journey, he decided to go ahead, "more from conviction that it was my duty to act than from reasons with which I could justify the act." [28]

As Bryan moved down the aisle toward the platform, a friend pulled him aside to introduce him to Mrs. Taft. In deference to the First Lady, Bryan dropped a sentence from his resolution castigating Taft's renomination at Chicago as an event master-controlled by Wall Street. He strode to the platform, and his appearance, the first since the temporary chairman fight, was greeted by tumultuous applause. The band struck up "See the Conquering Hero Comes," as Bryan, pale and trembling, bowed and smiled.

He quickly read his resolution: "We hereby declare ourselves opposed to the nomination of any candidate for President who is the representative of or under obligation to, J. Pierpont Morgan, Thomas F. Ryan, August Belmont, or any other member of the privilege-hunting and favor-seeking class; be it further resolved, that we demand the withdrawal from this convention of any delegate or delegates constituting or representing the above named interests."

Utter bedlam erupted. Cheers, hoots, hisses raged over the convention. "My God," gasped Josephus Daniels, "what is the matter with Bryan?" Ollie James exclaimed, "Does he want to destroy the Democratic party?" "Go over to Roosevelt," came cries from all sides. Former Governor W. A. McCorkle of West Virginia shouted that the party could not afford to cut off all hope of victory by offending the big material interests of the country. "If thy right hand offend thee, cut it off," Bryan shouted back above the tumult, "and if it is necessary to cut off Morgan and Ryan and Belmont to save the Democratic body politic, then cut them off."

Delegates were on their feet shaking fists and screeching denunciation. A member of Congress rushed to the platform and, gesticulating violently, upbraided Bryan until he frothed at the mouth and, flailing the air hysterically, was carried away. Hal Flood, a Virginia delegate, a short, stocky man with bushy black hair and eyes blazing with indignation, ran to Bryan's side at the speaker's platform. The Commoner held out his hand. Vigorously shaking his head, Flood ignored the proffered hand and shouted that Virginia rejected "the insolent proposition" of the only man who wanted "to destroy the prospect of Democratic success." The statement ignited a tumultuous roar. Senator James K. Vardaman, in a frock coat and "his hair as long as a patent medicine man's," pleaded for silence. Bryan, braving hisses and boos, declared above the din that Virginia wanted the expulsion resolution withdrawn. Looking directly at Murphy, Bryan said, "If a delegate authorized to speak for New York will rise and ask that the last part of the resolution be withdrawn. . . ." Tumult again crashed upon the convention. Congressman John J. Fitzgerald of Brooklyn rushed across the platform to Bryan and shook his fist in his face. Bryan replied by shaking his fist in Fitzgerald's face.

Ex-Governor McCorkle also reached the platform. For a moment Bryan looked upon him with an expression of hope that perhaps he might speak in his support. But McCorkle quickly erased Bryan's yearning by declaring that the resolution was "senseless and foolish." Flood, again on the platform, shouted that Virginia asked nothing of Bryan. If he withdrew the second part of his resolution, it was not at Virginia's request. The crowd again lashed at Bryan, "Sit down! Sit down!"

Amid the din, Vardaman suggested that Bryan withdraw the second part of the resolution. The Commoner agreed to the deletion and demanded a roll call. In the angry babble of discussion, Bryan became impressed by the protest of some delegates, whom he respected, that the second part of his resolution violated the right of states to constitute their delegations. He also anticipated that some delegates might use this argument as an excuse to vote against the first part of the resolution. ". . . I thought it best," he explained afterward, "not to give them that excuse, and the purpose was served, anyhow, in a condemnation of the men and the system that they represent."

As for the roll call, Bryan calculated that whatever its outcome, he could not lose, for it would now be difficult to nominate a candidate supported by the New York delegation. Even if the resolution was voted down, Bryan was confident that the outcry of an aroused public opinion would bar New York from choosing the nominee. The roll call, as it moved from state to state, unleashed new fury. A state would be called, its chairman would announce its vote, and delegates would jump to their feet and demand a poll, shaking their fists and shouting in violent language. As the roll call proceeded, Vardaman rushed over to Murphy to urge that he vote for the resolution. "If you do, Murphy," Vardaman exclaimed, "[you] will make Bryan look like a fool." The vote was moving overwhelmingly behind the resolution. The New York leaders, Murphy and Mack, held a hurried animated conference. Deeply fearful that Bryan, like Roosevelt, would bolt, they agreed to support the resolution. As New York prepared to vote, Murphy turned to Belmont and said cheerfully, "Augie, listen to yourself vote yourself out of the convention."

Nearly all the Wilson and Clark delegates supported the resolution. At the final tally, it carried overwhelmingly, 883 to 201½. The Presidential nominating speeches began at once, and Bryan strode from the hall to the accompaniment of lusty cheers. To reporters who followed him, he observed, "It leaves the convention absolutely in the hands of the progressives." And to make that fact starkly clear was the purpose of his resolution.

Did the effect of the resolution, a reporter asked, now put Bryan against Champ Clark's candidacy? "No, sir," Bryan answered, "I regard Mr. Clark as a progressive. I am instructed to vote for him." But suppose, a reporter persisted, Nebraska, as balloting proceeded, abandoned the unit rule.

Would Bryan then be permitted to vote for Wilson? "Not at all," he answered quickly. "And I have refused from the beginning to express any preference as between Mr. Clark and Mr. Wilson." [29]

One by one the ballotings were taken, Clark leading, Wilson with a solid vote, both gaining, and the remainder of the field well behind. Nebraska, employing the unit rule, cast all its votes for Clark. Murphy electrified the convention by transferring New York's votes from Harmon to Clark, and with 556 votes, well over a majority of the convention, and with ample historical justification, the Speaker prepared, in his office on Capitol Hill, a telegram accepting the nomination. Not since 1844 had a Democratic candidate with a majority in the convention failed to win nomination by the required two-thirds.

Not a few of Bryan's Nebraskan compatriots were convinced that Murphy's move to Clark signified that a concordat existed between the Clark leaders and the New Yorkers. Bryan had given no aid and comfort to these brooding conjectures, and the Nebraska delegation continued solid for Clark. Bryan expected that New York would soon abandon Clark and throw its vote to Underwood. If Clark then secured the nomination, he would do so predominately by progressive votes.

By the thirteenth ballot Bryan had begun to revise his expectation of a New York abandonment of Clark, as did many other Nebraska delegates. Senator Hitchcock came to Bryan and declared that in light of the shift of sentiment about Clark he would have to demand a poll of the delegation. Bryan told his rival that if a poll were taken, he would have to take the platform and explain his vote. "I was willing to continue voting for Clark if the delegation was not polled," Bryan wrote later, "but expecting at any time that I might be compelled to change my vote, I was not willing to announce a vote for him that I might have to take back at any time. I decided, therefore, to make the change at that time if the poll was taken. . . . I believed . . . that if the nomination of our candidate was brought about in such a way that the country would regard it as a triumph for Wall Street, he would be defeated no matter who he was." Hitchcock said he would insist on a poll.

That Bryan was about to abandon Clark had been thoroughly bruited about the convention. When Nebraska was reached on the fourteenth ballot and asked to pass, the convention stirred with expectation; the storm was coming. Nebraska again was reached in the roll call; a wild uproar leaped from the floor and galleries. Chairman Ollie James, anticipating bedlam, had recruited William Sulzer of New York to preside with him.

Bryan rose and called, "I want to explain my vote." Sulzer, acting under orders from Murphy, at first refused to permit Bryan, his friend and hero of many years, to speak. As Bryan men exploded with rage, Sulzer, through an intermediary, pressed Murphy to rescind his order. But the Tammany boss was adamant. Bryan meanwhile stood on the floor, his arm around the Nebraska standard, insisting at every lull on his right to speak. The entire Texas delegation, forty strong, climbed up on their chairs and shouted, "Free speech! Free speech!" As the storm grew more thunderous, Bryan ascended the platform and stood beside Sulzer, facing the crowd. Murphy, at last impressed that the convention would not be bossed, rescinded his order.

In quick incisive sentences, Bryan stated his position. There were no oratorical devices, no gestures, no artful pauses. Nebraska, he assured the delegates, was a progressive state whose delegates were instructed to vote for Clark "with the distinct understanding that Mr. Clark stood for progressive democracy." The national convention, too, by the anti-Wall Street resolution, was pledged against any candidate subservient to the evil influence of Tammany and Wall Street. Nebraska was unwilling to be party to the nomination of any man who would not, when elected, "be absolutely free to carry out the anti-Morgan-Ryan-Belmont resolution and make his administration reflect the wishes and the hopes of those who believe in a government of the people, by the people, and for the people."

The party's nominee, Bryan continued, should "not be compelled to suffer the humiliation and act under the embarrassment that I have, in having men participate in the management of his campaign who had no sympathy with the party's aims and in whose Democracy the general public has no confidence." Bryan was unmincing in naming several New Yorkers who were well beyond the pale. Alton Parker was "a Democratic reactionary." Charles Murphy controlled the New York Democracy, which made it impossible for Bryan to participate in the nomination of a candidate supported by New York.

He was now prepared to administer the *coup de grâce,* by switching his vote and explaining his reasons. Suddenly former Governor McCorkle raced to the platform, planted himself in front of Bryan, and began waving his arms and jumping up and down, yelling, "Are you a Democrat? Are you a Democrat?" After a moment's hesitation, Bryan thrust his palm-leaf fan straight into the livid face of the locomoting McCorkle and in his thunderous voice replied, "My Democracy has been certified to by six million and a half Democratic voters. But I will ask the secretary to record one vote in the negative, if the gentleman will give me his name."

"Mr. Chairman," a delegate shouted, raising a point of order, "haven't we anything to do in this convention except to listen to Mr. Bryan's speech?" There was another outburst of yells and catcalls. At last Bryan mastered the crowd into silence. "Now I am prepared to announce my vote, unless otherwise interrupted," he said. "Speaking for myself and for any of the delegates who may decide to join me, I withhold my vote from Mr.

Clark as long as New York's vote is recorded for him. And the position that I take in regard to New York I will take in regard to any other candidate whose name is now or may be before the convention. . . . Now I am prepared to announce my vote, with the understanding that I stand ready to withdraw my vote from the candidate for whom I now cast it, if Mr. Murphy casts the ninety votes of New York for him. I cast my vote for Nebraska's second choice, Governor Wilson."

Wild cheering and prolonged applause. Clark's manager, Senator William J. Stone, red-faced and angry, took the platform and shouted, "So far as Speaker Clark is concerned, I have just this one sentence to utter. I pledge his great record as a Democrat and splendid service rendered his party for more than a quarter century, and no part of it was more conspicuous than that during the campaign of William J. Bryan."

In all the excitement, it was almost unnoticed that Bryan had not endorsed Wilson. He voted for Wilson only because a reactionary group was supporting Clark. In fact, Bryan had even threatened to withdraw his support from Wilson if New York ever voted for him.[30]

Thanks to Bryan, Baltimore had become a city of confused and desperate politicians, of shouted indignations, and ingenious conniving and maneuvers. Champ Clark, seeing the great prize that lay within his grasp slipping away, entrained from Washington to Baltimore to appear before the convention to contradict Bryan's insinuations. Clark embarked upon his desperate journey on Saturday night, June 29. Before he arrived in Baltimore, A. Mitchell Palmer, a Wilson manager, successfully moved that the convention adjourn until Monday. Clark always felt that a Bryan "henchman" spied him in Union Station in Washington and forewarned the anti-Clark forces in Baltimore, enabling Palmer to make his move.

Clark had to content himself with a public statement: "Today in the national convention," it read, "an outrageous aspersion was cast upon me and through me upon the Democratic party, by one who of all men ought to be the last to besmudge or betray his friends or his party." Clark denied absolutely having entered into the alliance Bryan accused him of. "If I have not entered into such an alliance," he added, "then the Democrat, however distinguished, who wantonly charges me with this act is a traitor to the Democratic party, and to his professed friendship to me."

The Speaker demanded immediate "proof or retraction" of Bryan's charges. Bryan endeavored to accommodate in a lengthy statement. Clark, he said, had not acted wrongfully, but he was culpable in failing to act. He had declared his neutrality in the fight over the temporary chairmanship, "a contest between progressive Democracy on the one side, and reactionary Democracy on the other." And he was guilty of another sin: ". . . the activity of Clark's managers is as objectionable as his own inactivity. They have been in constant cooperation with the reactionaries. If Mr. Clark did not authorize them to act, he has so far as I know failed to rebuke them for acting." [31]

The managers of the candidates, major and minor, huddled in anxious consultation to discover some formula to put together the political ingredients that would somehow produce a Presidential nomination. There began a quest for a compromise nominee. Simple political arithmetic showed that Clark could be nominated if his forces coalesced with Underwood's. Managers of the two camps engaged in eager negotiation, but no movement developed. Then the anti-Bryan constituency within the Clark following put might and main into moving strength to Underwood, and when this venture appeared unpromising, they turned to Wilson.

As for Charles F. Murphy, the Bryan-designated villain as emissary of Wall Street, the Murphy men shared the instinct of many convention sophisticates that Bryan's next move would be one at which he was a proved master; he would electrify the convention by some new maneuver or articulation and stampede the delegates into nominating himself. The injured Clark concurred in this view. Bryan, Clark wrote, "wanted to create a deadlock and grab off the nomination for himself. He had no more idea of nominating Governor Wilson for President than he did of nominating him as Ahkoond of Swat. His well-considered plan was to kill off both Governor Wilson and myself. As I was leading, I must be killed off first. . . ."

Repeatedly Wilson's managers expressed the suspicion that Bryan was really aiming to prevent the governor's nomination. These suspicions soared when Bryan on June 30, at a moment when Wilson's strength was rising, declared that the delegates ought to nominate a President and Vice President at least by the following day. Who should be the nominee? Bryan responded in characteristic fashion. There were many good candidates: John W. Kern, Ollie James, James A. O'Gorman, Charles A. Culberson, and Senator Isador Rayner of Maryland. All were minor figures, with not the least chance for nomination. Furious Wilson managers, reading between the lines, reckoned that Bryan meant to put his own name at the head of the list.

In addition, there was Mary's attitude and counsel. In this year of expected Democratic victory, Mary was eager for Bryan to capture the nomination. The Republican Party had been ripped asunder at the Chicago convention. At the head of the party's insurgent progressives stood Theodore Roosevelt, their candidate for the Presidential nomination. Roosevelt had swept through the primaries and carried even Taft's Ohio. But the President, leading what Roosevelt called the "reactionary" forces, gained renomination, thanks to smooth-running party machinery and the massive support of Southern delegates, a region where Republicans had not won for decades. The Roosevelt camp challenged the right of several hundred Taft delegates to be seated, but most of these contests were arbitrarily squashed by a well-run Taft steamroller. Crying "fraud" and "theft," Roosevelt men were expected to launch a third-party crusade with the fiery hero at its head. The 1896 spectacle of a broken party was about to be repeated; only this time the Republicans were divided.

At this moment of almost certain Democratic victory, Mary pressed Bryan to take the nomination. Bryan responded to her importunings by saying he did not want to run and that he would seek and accept the nomination only in the face of overwhelming demand. As the convention moved along its tortuous way, Mary saw the stark outline of awaiting opportunity. If the convention were deadlocked, her husband could be nominated. The formula for deadlock called for increasing Wilson's strength to the point where it balanced Clark's, and Mary encouraged this development. She passed out word to friends in her box that they were to cheer for Wilson at the slightest provocation, rightly calculating that the delegates, seeing Bryan's family allotting their plaudits to Wilson, would assume that this reflected her husband's sympathies. Here indeed was the signal to abandon Clark.[32]

Yet if Bryan's supreme purpose was to be the nominee, he would have accepted the post of temporary chairman, offered by the national committee, well before the convention began. In that capacity, he could have delivered a mighty address and set the magical mood that would have brought the delegates rushing to him after a Clark-Wilson deadlock. In attacking Murphy and the New Yorkers, Bryan was alienating the most powerful constituency of the convention, and as events proved, New York's support was vital to capturing the nomination under the two-thirds rule. Norman Mack believed that if Bryan had remained quiet and done nothing, he would have been nominated, "for the New Yorkers would have preferred him to Wilson. . . ."

Bryan's rough tactics exposed him to all manner of opprobrium and accusations from those he offended. For his newspaper coverage of the convention, he was reportedly receiving $1,000 a day. In effect, he was earning this princely stipend by writing about the fights that he himself perpetrated. As critics pointed out, while other delegates saw their expense money melt away as the convention dallied day after day in deadlock, the longer proceedings continued, the more money Bryan made. By fertile contrivance, he was, in the worst imaginings of the delegates, prolonging the convention deliberately to line his pockets.[33]

On the thirtieth ballot, Wilson moved past Clark and on the thirty-ninth pushed beyond 500 votes. At last on July 2, Wilson was nominated. Bosses Taggart and Sullivan threw their support to Wilson, and Murphy was expected to follow, but he did not. Instead, Senator John H. Bankhead of Alabama released the Underwood delegates, who provided the margin of victory and ended the deadlock. In the rush to make the nomination unanimous, Murphy rose to announce that "New York casts 90 votes for Woodrow Wilson." As he spoke, he cast a sidelong glance at the Nebraska delegation. Not a tremor was seen in that locale.

The convention marched quickly through its remaining business. Governor Thomas R. Marshall of Indiana was nominated for Vice President after two ballots. The platform, largely the fruit of Bryan's authorship, was cheered and adopted without debate. At last, the tumultuous convention was over.

Bryan had accomplished his supreme purpose in coming to Baltimore. His strenuous maneuvers had made the Democratic gathering progressive. He had escaped the most dreaded of disasters—a conservative Democratic nominee. A conservative Democratic ticket, side by side with the conservative Republican ticket produced at Chicago, would, in Bryan's words, give "to the third party the hope of defeating the reactionaries divided between two parties. . . ."

Although Bryan had painted the Baltimore convention in progressive colors, he was not a Warwick, not a kingmaker. At no point did he make Wilson his personal choice for President. Wilson's managers looked upon Bryan as "a mighty aid" in the triumph of their candidate, though they acknowledged that at times Bryan was "a hindrance rather than help." In the late balloting, William F. McCombs, Wilson's chief manager, telephoned the governor to report that he could not pick up necessary conservative votes without Wilson's assurance that if elected President, he would not appoint Bryan as Secretary of State. Wilson refused absolutely to make any such promise.

Wilson was put across the goal line of the nomination when political bosses Roger Sullivan, Thomas Taggart, and others swung their support to him. But this they did only after they tried by might and main and ruse to defeat Wilson and nominate some other candidate who was unprogressive or whose progressive ties were thin. No act of Bryan's moved a substantial body of votes to Wilson. Rather, Bryan imparted a progressive coloration to the convention; his audacious moves alerted public attention to a "reactionary plot" and illuminated Wilson as the chief Democratic exponent of progressive doctrine. Thousands of telegrams rained upon the delegates demanding that they stand by Wilson. "I believe," said McCombs, "that these expressions of public sentiment had more to do with the result than anything done here while the convention was in progress." [34]

"Will you take the stump?" Bryan was asked as he packed his bags at the Belvedere. "Take the stump," he replied, a giant smile sweeping his face. "I should say I will. Just watch me." Bryan journeyed home to Lincoln, but

Charles made a detour to Sea Girt, New Jersey, Wilson's summer residence, for closely guarded consultations.

Into his summertime lectures on the Chautauqua circuit, Bryan intermixed generous quantities of partisan comment. Wilson he hailed as the highest type of man ever presented to the people, and it was time, he added, for the nation to try the experiment of putting a broad-minded educator in the highest position in a country of education. Bryan was a pillar of the Wilson campaign. For seven weeks, he spoke every day, averaging ten speeches a day. His voice and stamina never faltered in the onslaught. As he had in his own campaigns, he portrayed the present contest as one between good and evil; only this time the political Galahad was Wilson, not Bryan. The Democratic nominee, in Bryan's words, had "intelligence, moral courage and sympathy with the people." The villain of the campaign, Roosevelt, suffered from "overpowering self-confidence. He thinks he cannot be mistaken." Bryan saw George W. Perkins, a financial backer of Roosevelt and a banking partner of J. P. Morgan, as a Wall Streeter who aimed to elect a President "who will look after the trust magnate's children." Taft, on the other hand, was a good man, but his failing was an inability to "trust the people." [35]

Bryan followed close behind Roosevelt as he spoke through the West and Far West. The paths of the Democracy's two foremost campaigners crossed when Wilson's campaign trail led to Nebraska in early October. Since the convention, he and Bryan had not seen each other; only letters united them. Bryan met Wilson as the candidate stepped from his private railroad car almost into Bryan's arms amid the din of thousands clamoring their approval. The slender governor was heard to exclaim, "Hello, Mr. Bryan; hello, Mr. Bryan," and Bryan, paunchy and loosely dressed, called back resonantly, "Welcome, welcome, Governor." The crowd committed every fiber to making this first meeting of the old party leader and the new warm and fraternal. As the two supreme politicians sat side by side in the last car of a motor cavalcade, crowds cheered, factories blew their whistles, autos tooted, and bands followed in their path.

The evening's program was bathed in a warm glow of political brotherhood. A huge dollar dinner at the Lindell Hotel, attended by Democratic state candidates, county committees, and officers of Nebraska's Democratic clubs was a political love feast. Wilson and Bryan outdid each other in strewing rose-petaled platitudes about the other. At the Auditorium afterward, where the crowd bulged into the street, Wilson received a crashing ovation as Bryan, shaking his handkerchief, egged the crowd on. Wilson was visibly touched by the enthusiasm. Bryan introduced the nominee as "a worthy leader of the great democratic forces of the nation," and Wilson launched into an hour's address, delivered in his best form. He paid tribute to Bryan: "Mr. Bryan is the man who set the party free at Baltimore. . . . I am proud to stand shoulder to shoulder with Mr. Bryan."

Bryan and his guest returned to Fairview at midnight, and they talked about the campaign easily and candidly into the night. Next day, Sunday, they attended services, unheralded, at Bryan's Westminster Presbyterian Church. Afterward the tiny congregation gathered around its distinguished worshipers for an informal reception. The repast at Fairview that day was what Bryan delighted to call an "Interstate Dinner." Its culinary treasures, supplied by devoted Bryan admirers, included melons from Los Angeles, olives from San Francisco, potatoes from South Dakota and Idaho, and a fresh catch of brook trout supplied by Governor John Osborne of Wyoming.

After dinner, Bryan and his guest met with the press, and what they said was given more to badinage than information. Reporters who knew Wilson well had rarely seen him so delighted. "I have had a splendid time," the nominee said, "especially with Mr. Bryan." That afternoon, the two new friends departed on separate ways to advance their common mission. Wilson headed west, and Bryan left for a heavily scheduled tour through the Dakotas.[36]

As he did in his own Presidential races, Bryan campaigned for the national, state, and local tickets wherever his trail led. His ability to bring out crowds, to stir voter appeal, especially in the West, was undimmed. For territory into which he did not venture, such as the East, he made helpful statements to the press for the candidacies of old allies and others whose platforms were right.

Bryan campaigned for Champ Clark, seeking reelection to the House of Representatives. Not even the most blistering condemnation of his demeanor toward Clark at Baltimore stopped Bryan from fulfilling what he saw as present duty. Both the Speaker and Mrs. Clark excoriated Bryan in public statement. "I have known for all these twelve years," she said, "that William Jennings Bryan was a false friend to my husband. I have warned him over and over again. Mr. Bryan is too selfish, too self-centered to be a friend to anyone. He has thus, under the cover of this false friendship, been Champ's foe." Would Bryan comment on the Clarks' animadversions, he was asked in a campaign swing through Missouri, as he paused for a breakfast of hamburger and onions in Kansas City's Union Station? Bryan refused to discuss the matter. "He is the Democratic candidate for Congress in his district," the Commoner elaborated, "and I am anxious to see him elected. . . . I am not a candidate for anything and I will wait until after the elections to answer any criticisms. . . ."

Above all, Bryan campaigned in Nebraska. The state Democratic convention met soon after the Baltimore convention. That the state gathering would, among other things, ratify Bryan's course in the East was presaged when his own Lancaster County convention hailed him as the "Hero of Baltimore." At Grand Island the state platform overflowed with praises for Bryan, who "transformed . . . what at one time seemed to be a reactionary gathering into a real Democratic convention. . . . We congratulate him upon a magnificent victory." Gilbert Hitchcock deemed it all in dreadfully bad taste. "This is a poor time," he wrote in the Omaha *World-Herald,* "to engage in the delectable enjoyment of kicking the body of the politically slain." [37]

According to his custom, Bryan passed the last week of the campaign touring the length and breadth of Nebraska for the national and state tickets. On his final full day of campaigning, he made no less than nineteen speeches, the last in Omaha's Auditorium. Bryan spoke nostalgically of Nebraska as a pioneer in political reforms that the nation subsequently adopted. "I am more interested in the election of a Democratic President this year than is Woodrow Wilson himself," he cried in an emotional peroration. "I have travelled more miles; I have spoken more times; I have spoken more hours, and I will rejoice more next Tuesday night over the election of Woodrow Wilson, than that gentleman himself." [38]

At midevening on election night, Bryan rode in from Fairview to the Lindell Hotel. The election returns, as they were read, clearly foretold a Wilson victory. Like a proud beaming king on the mountain, Bryan stood high on a stairway, wearing his most expansive smile. The joyous crowd below clamored for remarks from their leader, who, after sixteen years of fighting and denial, was tasting, at last, the honey of victory for their cause. "I am happier than Governor Wilson," said a smiling Bryan, beginning a rambling, jubilant discourse, "for his joy is repressed by a sense of responsibility, while I am happy and free. My confidence in Governor Wilson has grown with acquaintance and I feel sure that he will live up to the expectations which his campaign has excited. . . ." Bryan elaborated upon Wilson: "I have confidence in him because I believe he listens to his conscience. I have little faith in a man who does right only when he thinks he is being watched. . . . Mr. Wilson is free to be a people's President. . . ."

Mary was not with Bryan in this long-awaited hour of triumph. In late October she had journeyed to Washington to visit Ruth and her husband, Reggie, before they sailed for Britain. She saw them off in New York and then happily acquiesced to an invitation to come to the home of Mrs. E. M. House to meet Mrs. Wilson. "Found Mrs. Wilson a sweet, nice woman," she recorded the visit, "I liked her." Mrs. Wilson thoughtfully invited Mary to spend the next day with her in Trenton. But Mary, who was feeling ill, went to Washington and with young William, who was there, arranged to have a minor operation at Providence Hospital. On election day, as she lay in bed, she heard newsboys calling, "Extra! Wilson elected! Wilson elected!" The next day she read the returns she always hoped to read for her husband.

Bryan sent Wilson a generous, exultant telegram. The President-elect responded warmly. "I have thought of you very constantly throughout the campaign," he wrote, "and have felt every day strengthened and heartened by your active and generous support. . . . We have won a great victory, and it is now our privilege to show that we can live up to it. It is delightful to see the forces of the party united, and their union should now bring fruit of the richest sort."

Inevitably in the surge of Democratic joy, Wilson's vote was compared with Bryan's past races. A mere glance at the figures disclosed that Bryan was still the champion vote getter of his party. His popular vote in 1908 exceeded Wilson's in 1912 by nearly 100,000. In only two sections was the Wilson vote greater than the largest Bryan vote: in New England and in the Pacific states. Outside the former Confederate states and Kentucky, Wilson polled a majority of popular votes only in Arizona.[39]

"If I am elected, what in the world am I going to do with W. J. Bryan?" Wilson asked Albert S. Burleson of Texas during the campaign. "Make him Secretary of State," Burleson replied. It was a question the political community took up with zest. Democratic politicians and editors across the country wholeheartedly confirmed Burleson's recommendation. Conservatives, a species still heavily concentrated in the East, remonstrated that Bryan's appointment would "seriously alarm the entire business community," that Wilson could not appoint Bryan without becoming tainted with Bryanism, and that his presence in the administration would constitute "the worst example of demagogy assailing the National credit known to our history." Asked how his mail was running on the Bryan question, Wilson revealed that for every four letters supporting Bryan, only one opposed him. "Then Mr. Bryan still has friends?" a reporter asked with resignation. "He numbers them by the hundreds of thousands," Wilson answered.

Wilson was poised in indecision. For all the success of the convention and the campaign, he had poor regard for Bryan's judgment, and he dreaded the prospect of disagreement over policies. Mrs. Wilson shared these judgments. A rupture would be inevitable, she predicted, and bringing Bryan into the Cabinet was "unnecessarily inviting trouble." Henry Watterson, Bryan's late political ally, summarized the problem succinctly: "Two dogs and one bone—the saying hath it—two cats and one mouse, two women and one house can never agree. As to Mr. Wilson and Mr. Bryan that appears to be the size of it." At least four times in November and December, Wilson raised the Bryan question with his confidant, Colonel Edward M. House. Resourcefully, House searched for a solution and variously suggested Bryan's appointment as Secretary of State, ambassador to Britain, and ambassador to Russia. Watterson thought the British ambassadorship a fitting and honorable exile for Bryan. "Besides," he added, in an editorial, "we do so want to see Mr. Bryan in knee-breeches and silk stockings."

Feelers from the Wilson camp to ascertain Bryan's availability for an ambassadorship brought an utterly negative response. In this moment of his cause's triumph, Bryan meant to oversee the harvest. "I do not intend to get that far away from Washington," he said to a friend. "I intend to watch this administration and see what it is going to do." While Wilson puzzled, Bryan did nothing to advance his prospects of a Cabinet appointment. In a *Commoner* editorial, he even counseled Wilson to avoid appointments based upon "past service rendered." "The individual," he stressed, "counts for little; the cause counts for much." [40]

At last Wilson was ready to act. On December 21, Bryan journeyed to the statehouse at Trenton. For more than three hours they discussed Cabinet selections, the party platform, and party policies. Over luncheon, Wilson offered Bryan the post of Secretary of State. Although he preferred appointment as Secretary of the Treasury, Bryan quickly and graciously made a tentative acceptance depending on several matters that he needed to lay before the President-elect. Bryan recounted how he and Mary objected to the serving of intoxicating liquors at their table. Their position could conceivably prove embarrassing at state functions. Wilson promptly responded that it was a matter on which "we could feel perfectly free to follow our own wishes." There was another matter. Before he could accept the proffered office, Bryan said he must know whether he would be allowed to negotiate a series of peace treaties in accord with a draft that he produced, a typewritten version of a model treaty. Wilson read the draft and said that he had no objection. Bryan declared that this was not enough, that what he sought was an expression of Wilson's willingness to make the peace treaties an integral part of his foreign policy. Wilson agreed, and Bryan stated with finality his acceptance of the post of Secretary of State. [41]

The Wilson-Bryan bargain was interpreted in the political community as a bold stroke by the President-elect for party harmony. Bryan, according to the rationale, would, if he were left out of the administration, be a busy, articulate critic, a political thorn in the new administration's side. But by bringing him into the administration, Wilson might hope to mute Bryan's incipient criticism and promote his understanding and tolerance by involving him in its work. Wilson's step brought a mixed chorus of praises and lamentations. Arthur Mullen, speaking from solid experience in Nebraska's politics, warned Wilson "that when it came to a crisis someday Bryan would desert him and do it in the name of God."

Bryan was utterly delighted with the appointment. When Colonel House visited him at Miami in January, 1913, to discuss Cabinet and diplomatic appointments, he found Bryan in "a delightful humor," "as pleased with his new place as a child with a new toy," and eager to help without interfering. As newspapers filled the air with gloomy predictions of future relations between the two great Democrats, Wilson wrote Bryan a light note "merely by impulse from the heart." "How contemptible the efforts of the papers are, the last few days, to make trouble for us and between us—and how delightful it is—to me, as I hope it is to you—to know, all the while, how perfect an understanding exists between us!" [42] Woodrow Wilson would soon be doing less than honor to these words.

25. A Pacifist Secretary of State

March 4, 1913. Woodrow Wilson was inaugurated, the first Democratic President of the twentieth century. On that dank gray day, 100,000 massed before the Capitol to hear his inaugural address of acute, lean eloquence. "Men's hearts wait upon us; men's lives hang in the balance; men's hopes call upon us to say what we will do." As Wilson moved from one telling sentence to the next, approval filled Bryan's face. When the new President stopped, the Nebraskan was wrenched from his blissful mood by cadenced cries from the crowd: "Bryan, Bryan, Bryan, we want a speech from Bryan." Embarrassed, Bryan turned away to discourage further demonstration. Afterward, as the cavalcade of automobiles moved down Pennsylvania Avenue to the White House, the cheers followed a definite rhythm: first a volley for Wilson at the head of the procession and then an outburst for Bryan, whose car was not far behind. To Mary at his side, he exclaimed joyously, "It is worth sixteen years of hard work to have devotion like this, isn't it?"

The crowds that regaled Bryan with their plaudits that day doubtless concentrated their admiration on his political deeds of the past. But March 4 had a far larger significance, which surely escaped his admirers. In applauding Bryan they were manifesting approval of an event that all had seen, but none had perceived. It was an event unusual, almost bizarre, in its proportions. This newborn administration would have as its Secretary of State a pacifist committed, with remarkably few reservations, to nonviolence in dealings between the nations. Neither before nor since Bryan's day has a near pacifist such as he occupied high place in a Presidential administration. A leading world power, with a substantial record of war-making, was entrusting major responsibilities for its foreign policy to a proclaimed near pacifist.

Asked what the foreign policy of the new administration would be, Bryan answered that he was "in hearty accord" with Wilson in his desire "to promote world peace and good will." His own views, he said, remained exactly as he expressed them in his Indianapolis speech of 1900. He envisioned the ideal of the American Republic proclaiming and practicing in its relations with the world the principle that all men are created equal. He aspired to see "a republic standing erect while empires all around are bowed beneath the weight of their own armaments—a republic whose flag is loved while other flags are only feared." Let the United States hasten the coming of a "universal brotherhood"; let it be "the supreme moral factor in the world's progress." For Bryan the awaiting Secretaryship of State was a Promethean opportunity. In that office, as he conceived it, he could become a lasting benefactor of mankind. He could banish the scourge of war from the face of the earth.[1]

Bryan was deterred from making any immediate strides toward his noble purpose by the human swarm that besieged his office day in and day out, seeking appointment and preferment in the new administration. For sixteen years, the Democracy had been denied the fruits of office, and now its starved appetite knew no bounds. When Wilson, with an eye to his own salvation, announced that no place hunter could henceforth appeal to him in person, the diverted hosts of office seekers moved upon the departments.

Nowhere did they concentrate more than on the State Department. Bryan's office was the scene of a continual reception from early morning until long after the close of the business day. He conducted, in effect, a continuous open house for Democrats from everywhere. Friends, allies, collaborators of well nigh a quarter century of politics came to offer well wishes or their services. Entire state delegations from Congress arrived to pay their respects. Inevitably, in the steady influx of distinguished visitors, even those of lofty political ranking had to take their place in line. Senator John Kern, Democratic Vice Presidential nominee in 1908, labored mightily for a top priority to see his former running mate. But Eddie Savoy, the Negro messenger who had served every Secretary of State since the administration of U. S. Grant and who strove to impose a semblance of order upon the chaos, was driven to declare, "I'm sorry, Senator, but you can't come in; Mr. Bryan is busy." After an hour's wait, Kern crossed the threshold into the Secretary's happy presence.

Bryan took up gladly the burdens of dispensing patronage. In reality, he had a huge national army of good and faithful followers who awaited their deserved reward. In responding to them, he was unhampered by reverence for the merit system or bureaucratic expertise. It had long been a cardinal tenet of his Democratic-Populist faith that the specialist and the career employee, with their protected tenure and segmented knowledge, assured a privatism in policy making that was inimical to popular control. As well, the great body of departmental employees had been appointed in the long unbroken Republican sway. The appointees were heavily Eastern in their origins and educated at Ivy League colleges, places that long had convincingly demonstrated their inhospitability to the person and social doctrines of Bryan. A tremor passed through the department's employees when the new Secretary in his greeting declared, "I am not yet prepared to discuss tenure in office. . . . I have not had time to learn from the President the general policy that will be impressed on the various departments. . . ."

In the weeks and months that followed, Bryan covered the world in recommending ambassadors and ministers, consuls, and first secretaries. Senators and state chairmen, the President's intimate counselor Colonel Edward M. House, and, above all, Wilson offered names, expressed judgments, and pressed the search for competent and loyal appointees.

Initially Bryan was preoccupied with building a team around himself, an absolute requisite if he were to oversee foreign policy effectively. As his private secretary, he brought in Benjamin "Ben" T. Davis, his stenographer in his Congressional years. Soon after the administration commenced, Bryan rediscovered Davis, an obscure clerk in the office of the Adjutant General in the War Department. They had scarcely finished a heartfelt reunion when Davis was ensconced in his new job at State. Before many a month, the cool, efficient Davis was functioning as chief clerk, in effect the department's administrative manager. As his confidential secretary, Bryan then imported Manton Marble Wyvell, a middle-aged lawyer of New York City. Wyvell was an old friend, whom Bryan had first met at a political rally at Cornell University in the campaign of 1900. Owner of a massive head crowned with luxuriant hair and a voice that bellowed like a sideshow barker's, Wyvell had so unstintingly articulated his approval that Bryan sometimes had to stop his speech. Afterward he sought out the young man and invited him to come along on the remainder of his New York tour. Over the years, their friendship continued, and Wyvell was delighted to shed the anonymity of a placid law practice for the excitement of sharing in Bryan's long-awaited advent to a position of power and influence.

For his principal Assistant Secretary of State, Bryan brought in John E. Osborne, a former governor of Wyoming, an old and close friend and longtime political supporter. In contrast with his predecessor in the Taft administration, Huntington Wilson, a career official, Osborne brought to his new capacity absolute innocence of any background in foreign affairs. Originally a druggist, Osborne took up stock raising and by shrewd management became the largest individual sheeprancher in Wyoming. A Democratic national committeeman, he had contributed generously to Wilson's campaign.[2]

One crucial appointment that Wilson declined to yield to the wave of Bryan amateurs was the post of counselor. A prestigious office held by distinguished incumbents, it was the principal organ of legal advice to the Secretary, and to it had been entrusted delicate negotiations of key foreign policies. Wilson himself oversaw the disposal of this post and worked strenuously to bring into it, and keep there, John Bassett Moore. A Third Assistant Secretary of State from 1886 to 1891, Moore was a distinguished scholar and professor of international law at Columbia University who had served as a consultant to the department in the intervening years and knew its affairs intimately. Gifted with a delicate wit and obvious charm, Moore was an island of professional erudition among the personal and political appointees Bryan was amassing.

Moore was also punctilious, a trait that was aroused by the somewhat ambiguous status of the office of counselor vis-à-vis the assistant secretaryships. Furthermore, he anticipated that Bryan would be given to freewheeling administration with little regard to niceties. In an extended, meticulously drawn letter to Bryan, Moore noted that in the official Register of the State Department the post of counselor ranked below the several assistant secretaries. Yet the counselor's work was conducted directly with the Secretary, and "personally," wrote Moore, marching to the climax of argument, "I should be unwilling to be subject to the direction of the Assistant Secretaries and to be required to wait upon them." Bryan and Wilson quickly acquiesced to this and several other stipulations.

Wilson himself filled another key appointment, the Third Assistant Secretary of State, who was in charge of personnel. He named his friend Dudley Field Malone, and when Malone shortly moved on to become collector of the Port of New York, he assigned the post to Colonel House's young friend, the able career officer William Phillips. To Bryan, the President yielded the post of Solicitor, into which he brought his old ally and former governor of Missouri, Joseph W. Folk, and when Folk abandoned the post after a short tour of duty, Bryan turned to another old friend, Cone Johnson of Texas.

Bryan tried manfully to wreak changes in the department's formidable bureaucratic structure, but he was, with few exceptions, thwarted by the tenure system. The bureaucracy was jarred when the chief clerk was asked outright for his resignation. He refused, but by a permissible personnel procedure he was "reduced" to a position as chief of the Bureau of Accounts. "I know that others among the chiefs of division are to be asked to resign or to take places in the foreign service," wrote the talented young consular officer Wilbur J. Carr. After much prying and tugging, Bryan appointed Boaz W. Long, a protégé of Vice President Marshall, as chief of the Division of Latin American Affairs, and Albert H. Putney, dean of the Illinois College of Law, as head of the Division of Near Eastern Affairs. For Bryan these were important selections, for he was to undertake significant foreign policies in both these regions. For lesser posts not under civil service protection, he appointed outsiders with political backgrounds. Seizing upon a permissive civil service regulation, he later transferred them to the diplomatic or consular service. For all his sprightly ingenuity, Bryan, in net effect, made little impact upon the department's tenured personnel.[3]

Bryan, unawed by the steely decorum of the career system, meant to be an innovator. He moved toward a single goal: a more democratic and a more moral diplomatic administration. It was "undemocratic," he stated in a report to Wilson, "to have citizens otherwise competent, debarred from any department in the public service on ground of lack of means to meet the requirements of the position." He lamented that "no one without fortune" could afford to accept a diplomatic position in Europe. To reduce the increasing concentration on "a limited class" in the recruitment of ambassadors and ministers, Bryan urged "a new departure," calling for governmental purchase or building of homes for its principal diplomatic representatives. Let government also furnish these homes in a fashion avoiding misrepresentation of "our people" by "extravagances" or "parsimony." Bryan rejoiced to see his proposal win Presidential and Congressional approval, and he was soon deep in real estate transactions on behalf of American diplomacy.

As a responsible official, Bryan proved less devoted to a principle highlighted with flaming eloquence in his previous political endeavor. An articulate apostle of the doctrine "Let the people rule," Bryan presumably would usher in an age of maximum publicity in the conduct of foreign policy and was expected to transform the State Department from a treasure trove of sealed mysteries into something of a goldfish bowl. But Bryan, who began charitably with the press, was soon shocked by its tendencies toward sensationalism, distortion, and premature disclosure, with crippling effects upon diplomatic processes. With Wilson's approval, Bryan formulated a rule that henceforth the department would announce policies on international questions only "when the President thinks that public interests will be promoted thereby." Until such announcements were made, "questions concerning such policies will not be answered."

To the press' discomfort and regret, Bryan became the watchful guardian of this new rule and quickly built a reputation as the most absolute stickler for secrecy seen at the department in many a year. Whenever a reporter posed a query that he regarded as premature, Bryan would declare, "I shall say nothing about any matter pending in this Department until the conclusion has been reached." His large mouth would shut grimly, leaving across his face a long, thin line, a signal of impregnable firmness. Journalists were soon recalling with new appreciation the pleasant manners and customs of John Hay, Elihu Root, and Philander Knox, all of whom at one time or another were tagged in the Bryan rhetoric as the secretive agents of conspiratorial Wall Street.[4]

Bryan, not surprisingly, aimed to improve the moral foundations of diplomacy and struck an early blow at his first diplomatic luncheon, a farewell for the distinguished British Ambassador James Bryce and Mrs. Bryce. For the eighteen guests gathered in the Bryan suite at the Willard, a happy modulated affair was in prospect, suggested by bountiful decorations of white roses and maidenhair ferns, and little candlesticks with green and white shades. When the guests were seated, Bryan rose to ask their indulgence for a moment. To Mary, he seemed a trifle pale, but he marched bravely into his discourse. He quickly related how, before becoming Secretary of State, he informed the President that he and Mary and their fathers had been teetotalers, and therefore, they could not depart from familial custom at diplomatic functions "without contradicting all our past." Wilson had said that Bryan might use his judgment, and now, having exercised it, the Bryans hoped "we might show our hospitality in other ways." The guests applauded, the meal was served, with the libation consisting of grape juice and rock water. By every evident sign, the luncheon was successful. Jean Jules Jusserand, the French ambassador and dean of the diplomatic corps, and Bryce made charming speeches. "When we left the table," Mary wrote afterward, "I believe they were as gay under the stimulus of the speeches as they would have been had we served wine."

Diplomatic circles were quickly pulsating with comment on the strange wineless ways of the Bryans. Veterans of the capital scene were brought by Bryan's preferences to recall the far days of President Hayes and Mrs. Hayes, known familiarly as Lemonade Lucy, who barred wines and liquors from the White House table. The press, particularly the British press, made merry with ridicule. In London the *Pall Mall Gazette* lamented that official life in Washington held out "little prospect of gaiety" since Bryan had chosen to ignore the lesson that "the long accumulated experience of man demands wine to make glad the heart on festive occasions."

In all the furor, Bryan remained benign and composed. To inquiring reporters he allowed himself the temperate recollection that his remarks at the luncheon "were applauded and we never spent a more enjoyable evening." People with impressive credentials of one kind or another rushed to Bryan's defense. Mrs. Thomas R. Marshall, plain-speaking wife of the Vice President, declared: "What Mr. Bryan serves at his own dinners is Mr. Bryan's own business." Mrs. Marshall added that at none of her functions, including state dinners, would wines be served. Approving letters from clergy and temperance orders around the world poured in. In Britain, George Bernard

Shaw urged Bryan to advance one step more and convert all state affairs into vegetarian dinners.

Inevitably, capital hostesses vied with one another in inventing solutions to keeping both wine bibers and teetotalers among their guests happy simultaneously. Perhaps Madame Pezet, wife of the Peruvian minister, hit upon the most ingenious solution. At her diplomatic functions, while other guests drank champagne, according to their preference, she supplied Bryan not with grape juice—for it contrasted too obviously with champagne's color. Instead, she provided pineapple juice, which, with carbonated water added, presented an extraordinary resemblance to champagne.[5]

Bryan had another idiosyncrasy or two that Washington suffered some difficulty in accepting. In all his adult years, Bryan had always held two or more jobs simultaneously. As Congressman or Presidential candidate, he was also a journalist and a lecturer. Against such a background of multiple employment, it was too much to expect that simply because he had become Secretary of State, he would cast aside some or all of his various other occupations. Soon after taking office, Bryan arranged for *The Commoner* to be published henceforth on a monthly basis, rather than on its traditional weekly basis. Although Bryan wrote fewer editorials, he still was fertile with topics on which others should write. His continued light chores for *The Commoner* aroused no hostile comment.

A less placid reaction greeted another branch of employment to which he had long been devoted and which he meant to continue. Before accepting office, he secured Wilson's consent that he might continue his Chautauqua lectures. Although Bryan abandoned his usual summer-long schedule of Chautauquas, he devoted the month's vacation to which he was entitled to the lecture tours. Afterward he delivered occasional lectures at places near Washington. Often he would travel through the night to be at his desk at the normal opening hour the following day.

These oratorical peregrinations provided a field day for his legions of detractors in the press and in Congress. The Senate, for the better part of an afternoon, was the scene of a sprightly debate on the compatability of Chautauquas with official duty. Senator Joseph L. Bristow, Republican of Kansas, introduced a resolution calling on the President to inform the Senate of what an appropriate salary might be to enable the Secretary of State to live in comfort so that Congress might "take immediate steps to relieve the country from the great loss which it suffered by being deprived of the services of the present Secretary of State." Devoted Bryan men in the Senate defended their hero. Senator John Kern, after Bristow's resolution was read, exclaimed, so that all might hear, "Pooh!" Senator Henry Ashurst of Arizona, another of the Commoner's admirers, asked Bristow if he had always held such views of the sacredness of public service and went on to read an old letter in which Bristow had sought appointment to a board of the Panama Canal which imposed few duties and left him free to pursue a full schedule of other remunerative extracurricular activities. Senator Stone of Missouri read the names of a long list of Republican Senators who had spoken on Chautauquas during sessions of Congress.

In an article, "Making a Living," Bryan said the real question was not whether a Cabinet officer could live on a salary of $12,000 a year "if he had nothing to consider except the expenses attendant upon living in Washington." It was "whether he could add the expense of official life to his other expenses and meet them all out of his salary." His own obligations, he pointed out, included church, charity, and insurance contributions that could not be discontinued and "amounted to $6,800 a year." For more than twenty years, he had derived his income from lecturing and writing. Since these were "honorable professions," Bryan felt he was just as entitled to supplement his income from them as other officials might be to enjoy returns from business or investment.[6]

Bryan's loftiest hope as Secretary of State was so to contribute to international affairs that war might be banished as a curse of mankind. He aspired by the skillful use of the arts of government to overcome any dispute among nations without the employ of force. It did little good, Bryan realized, to create a bountiful and just domestic society if man, thanks to the chaos of international relations, had to devote himself to war, to killing and accepting the risk of being killed.

In his quest for international peace, Bryan was optimistic. Just as he was confident that a better domestic society would materialize, he was certain that man was progressing toward lasting peace. He conveyed this mood in a major address at the Hotel Astor in New York City to an international conference assembled to formulate plans to celebrate the centenary of the signing of the Treaty of Ghent and the hundredth anniversary of peace among English-speaking nations. Bryan's erstwhile political enemy Joseph Choate, a king of corporation lawyers and former ambassador to Great Britain, was toastmaster, and their old differences lay forgotten in their common concern for peace. Bowing gravely to Bryan, who sat behind a bottle of grape juice while the glasses of other diners sparkled with wine, Choate asked forgiveness as he portrayed the Secretary of State as one who for many years had "labored in the vineyard" of peace.

Bryan's speech that happy evening, innocent of the least awareness of an approaching world war, was suffused with eloquent optimism. People, he said, were learning the terrible cost of war. As men rise in intelligence, they more and more insist that their contests be "upon an intellectual plane and not upon the plane of the brute." There was an even greater force—"the moral progress of the world." More altruism, he contended, flourished on earth than ever before. And another great force was "the spread of that conception of government that puts increasing power in the hands of the people." Governments, therefore, ever more reflect "the real welfare" of the people, and that welfare is advanced "not by war, but by peace."

No nation, he said, should outstrip the United States in its work for peace. The United States enjoyed the advantages of "increasing intelligence," of "growing brotherhood," and popular government. More than any other country, the United States had a population to which all nations have contributed. The restraining influence of blood and kinship worked to keep us from engaging in war, and "our isolation keeps us from danger." [7]

To advance the cause of world peace, Bryan relied on peace treaties, which he had outlined to Wilson before accepting appointment as Secretary of State and which he now proposed to negotiate with other governments. With the President's encouragement, he introduced his peace plan into the Cabinet for discussion and consulted with the Senate Foreign Relations Committee. The committee approved his plan in principle, and he joyfully moved on to its presentation by memorandum and oral comment to a meeting of representatives of all the nations in the Washington diplomatic community. In essence, Bryan's peace treaties, known officially as Treaties for the Advancement of Peace, set up procedures for conciliation rather than for arbitration. They provided that all questions in dispute among the signatories must, after diplomacy has failed, be submitted for investigation and report to a standing commission of five members. The commission's makeup was to be agreed upon promptly after the treaty was subscribed to and therefore well before any dispute arose. When, subsequently, a dispute flared up, the signatory nations would refrain from declaring war or commencing hostilities until the investigation and report were completed. Neither disputant would use the period of investigation to alter its military or naval program. Bryan noted that his treaties would supplement the several arbitration treaties already in force. Eloquently, he stressed that the treaties assumed "that we have now reached a point in civilization's progress when nations cannot afford to wage war." He was confident, too, that public opinion, a rising force in the world, might form and express itself, while the commission studied a dispute.

The peace treaties were Secretary Bryan's proudest venture. To them he devoted his boundless energy and drive. He signed the first treaty on August 7, 1913, with El Salvador, and in the following year negotiated similar pacts with twenty-nine other nations, including France, Britain, and Italy. Eventually twenty treaties were ratified and promulgated. Each step taken was for Bryan an exultation. "I have a piece of news so good," he wrote to Wilson, "that I cannot postpone its communication until Monday." It was Britain's willingness, just revealed, to negotiate a treaty. Wilson, for his part, was generous with encouragement and praise. As Bryan progressed with the French treaty, the President, in a characteristic note pecked out on his little typewriter, wrote: ". . . congratulations on your progress. You are handling it in just the right way." And Bryan's pride in this work never dimmed. After many nations approved the treaty, he prepared souvenir paperweights, which he presented to each of the plenipotentiaries who had signed on behalf of their country. The weights were made of steel derived from melted army swords, justifying the inscription on the base: "They shall beat their swords into plowshares." Unfortunately, the general body of signers did not share Bryan's enthusiasm for the peace project. They gladly complied with its pleasant demands, but largely in the spirit of perfunctory approbation of something that could do no harm. Hardened, sophisticated diplomats were privately amused at Bryan's simple faith in man's moral progress as a force dominating all others in the life and future of the world.[8]

Bryan's first opportunity to apply his theories of nonviolence—his "peace-drag-out idea," as it was sometimes called—transpired in an American crisis with Japan over a discriminatory landownership law under consideration in the California legislature. Although both the Japanese population and Japanese landholdings in California were small, racial prejudice and unconscionable politicians fanned the situation into a holocaust. The California Assembly adopted an alien land bill barring persons "ineligible to citizenship" (i.e., Oriental aliens) from landownership. The Japanese government protested strenuously, spurred by the soaring excitement and war fever of extremist groups at home.

It was inconceivable to Bryan and Wilson, as devotees of states' rights, that they should employ the federal power to coerce a state, as Roosevelt had done in a similar crisis with California. The administration leaders were hopeful that personal diplomacy, goodwill, and constructive counsel to both Japan and California would dispel the crisis. The task of negotiating with California's aroused legislature and governor fell, by the President's choice, upon Bryan. The Secretary did not gladly undertake the venture, about which no one was optimistic. The mission's chief purpose, Secretary of Agriculture David Houston noted, was to convince the Japanese that the United States government was friendly and was doing "all it could." As his train sped westward, Bryan poured over information assembled by his departmental staff on the land question. In his researches, Bryan discovered that many states barred alien ownership of lands, and of the several laws, he considered an Illinois statute on the subject the best available. In Illinois, alien ownership was limited to six years, allowing five years for naturalization and a further year for disposing of the property if the alien failed to become a citizen. Wilson, by wire, agreed that the Illinois statute was a "valid and sensible solution."

Bryan was soon standing before an executive session of the Califronia legislature, the members rising and applauding warmly. He quickly presented four propositions for resolving the crisis, including the adoption of the Illinois law. As he spoke, his secretary Robert Rose was at his side, making a shorthand transcript for dispatch to the President.

In a question and answer period the discussion assumed a tough weave. Had the Japanese government, a Senator asked, done anything constructive in the crisis, such as deterring its citizens from acquiring land in California? Bryan declined to answer directly. When he conferred with Japan, he said, he tried to present the "California point of view." Now, in California, "I feel it my duty to present the point of view of Orientals." He was confident he could have Japan's cooperation "to limit the evil of which you complain."

Bryan's efforts bore uncertain fruit. The next day the California Senate approved a bill drafted by the state's attorney general, U. S. Webb. Under its terms, all aliens "eligible to citizenship" might own land in California just as citizens could. All other aliens might own land in keeping with any existing treaty between the United States and the country of which the alien was a citizen or subject. In a further appearance before the legislature, Bryan declared that the words "eligible to citizenship" were as offensive to the Japanese as the earlier "ineligible to citizenship." Certainly its legal effect would be the same. Under existing laws, Oriental aliens were ineligible to citizenship. The laws were spawned by American labor's fear that its jobs and wage standards would be imperiled by Oriental immigrants and the belief prevalent in Western states that they would quickly constitute a disproportionate share of the population. Bryan also feared that the Webb bill embraced a quagmire of litigation, since the United States–Japan treaty would require interpretation. He pleaded that California leave the problem to diplomacy.

But momentum for the discriminatory Webb bill mounted rapidly. Bryan made an eleventh-hour address to the legislature, indicating plainly that the President objected to the bill and suggesting that it be reviewed in a popular referendum before taking effect. Although the legislature continued to lavish warm courtesy upon Bryan, it passed the Webb bill, and progressive Governor Hiram Johnson lost no time in signing it.

In Washington the Japanese government protested California's action in language whose vehemence hovered at the far border of peaceful diplomacy. Secretary of War Lindley M. Garrison presented recommendations from the professional military for an immediate deploy of forces against the possibility of war with Japan. Garrison spoke forcefully to his fellow Secretaries, with Bryan, just returned from California, among them, and implied that on military questions such as these, the opinion of civilian Cabinet officials was not particularly valuable. "At this," noted Secretary of Agriculture Houston, "Bryan flared up for the first time. He got red in the face and was very emphatic. He thundered out that army and navy officers could not be trusted to say what we should or should not do, till we actually got into war; that we were discussing not how to wage war, but how not to get into war, and that, if ships were moved in the East, it would incite to war." The Cabinet was divided, and Wilson, after deliberation, decided not to move the ships.

The war clouds quickly vanished when Wilson declared that war with Japan would be preposterous. In official notes and in the representations of its ambassador in Japan, the United States avowed its friendship. But the Japanese government, goaded by hostile domestic opinion, continued to protest the California law. Bryan, with Wilson's approval, moved to develop a treaty affirming for Japanese subjects in the United States the privileges accorded to subjects "of the most favored nation" with which it dealt. But the Senate dawdled, and the Japanese government fell. A new government broke off negotiations of the treaty, holding that it was unacceptable to Japanese opinion. Bryan's drag-out kind of diplomacy, with its stress on negotiation and cultivation of an atmosphere of goodwill and friendship, had at least avoided war. But it did not resolve the conflict, whose lingering hostilities were to haunt future relations between the countries.[9]

The most available proving ground for Bryan's approach to foreign policy—with its stress on goodwill, moral uplift, and the advance of democratic processes—was Latin America. With no body of nations was the United States thrown into more continuous and involving relationships than with these neighboring countries. Under the late Republican administrations of McKinley, Roosevelt, and Taft, American policy was everything that Bryan did not want it to be, and he thundered against it in his Presidential campaigns, in the pages of The Commoner, and from the lecture platform.

The policy Bryan and Wilson inherited centered on preserving the security of the Panama Canal. This, in the estimations of previous administrations, required nothing less than the assertion of absolute supremacy of the United States in the Caribbean and the Central American region. A variety of strong-armed measures fostered the policy—military intervention, annexation of territory, protectorates, and dollar diplomacy.

In speeches and public statements, in letters and recommendations to the President, Bryan articulated the ideals and posture of a new policy for Latin America. The Latin American republics must be able "to work out their own destiny along lines consistent with popular government." Let the United States "protect the people of these republics in their right to attend to their own business free from external coercion, no matter what form that external coercion may take. . . ." When Wilson prepared his first State of the Union message, Bryan suggested as a theme that American trade might grow in Latin America "only by the maintenance of high standards of business integrity, Americans giving in service an equivalent for the money they drew out." In a speech at Mobile and in other pronouncements, Wilson gladdened Bryan with ringing demands that the United States and Latin America conduct their dealings with mutual confidence and trust, "for the lasting interests of the people of the two continents," and for no special group or interest. Bryan and Wilson were agreed on another particular. A progressive and humane foreign policy must fit in with the security needs of the United States. In the Bryan–Wilson prognosis, the United States must still maintain its supremacy in the Caribbean; the security of the Panama Canal must be paramount.

Bryan's first foray into Latin American diplomacy was a self-assumed effort to make amends to Panama and Colombia, both angry victims of Roosevelt's bludgeoning, piratical onslaughts upon their interests in building the Panama Canal. Bryan set out to dispel the lingering hostility in both countries toward American high-handedness and to displace earlier injustice with equity and goodwill. When Panama stirred with interest in building a railroad to advance the country's development, Bryan quickly formulated ideas to speed the project. For Panama's financing, he aimed to avoid the private bankers who had waxed rich on previous Latin American enterprises. Instead, Bryan proposed a direct loan by the United States government. But Wilson was apprehensive that this would strike the country "as a novel and radical proposal" and required instead a private loan, superintended by Bryan, to assure the best terms favorable to Panama.

As for Colombia, the country most aggrieved by Theodore Roosevelt's machinations, Bryan and Wilson presented a convincing spectacle of remorse and atonement. After some sprightly bargaining, guided by Bryan, the United States agreed to pay an indemnity of $25,000,000 to Colombia and, in a further step that was a model of honorable behavior, acknowledged its "sincere regret that anything should have occurred to interrupt or to mar the relations of cordial friendship that had so long subsisted between the two nations." Not the least of Bryan's duties was to guide through the Senate this agreement not easily swallowed by those of intense nationalistic feeling.[10]

Nicaraguan policy was another embarrassing heritage for Wilson and Bryan. The departing Taft administration had negotiated a treaty with Nicaragua, granting the United States a renewable ninety-nine-year lease of the Great and Little Corn Islands, the privilege of establishing a naval base on the Gulf of Fonseca, and a perpetual option on a canal route. In return, the United States was to pay $3,000,000, a sum the Nicaraguans would apply to obligations outstanding to American bankers. As the United States Senate pondered the treaty, the Wilson administration came to power. Nicaragua, on the verge of financial collapse, clamored for the treaty's approval. Although the blatant features of dollar diplomacy which studded the treaty offended Wilson and Bryan, they deeply valued the canal option and its foreclosure of a competing canal route under control of a major European power. Germany particularly showed interest in building a canal. Wilson sought to add to the treaty provisions making Nicaragua an American protectorate, but the Senate rebuffed him while accepting the treaty's other features. Critics noted that the new administration was making Taft's dollar diplomacy more nearly resemble ten-cent diplomacy.

Bryan negotiated the treaty with Nicaragua's counsel in Washington, Charles A. Douglas. In doing so, he turned his back on certain of the high-minded denunciations he had been making of Republican imperialist policies since 1898. The treaty was clearly within the heavy-handed, dollar-minded traditions of Roosevelt and Taft. He was unhappy that the $3,000,000 the United States agreed to pay would be applied to bankers' loans to meet Nicaragua's current expenses and the payment of claims from previous revolutions. "My own preference," Bryan wrote, "would be to have the money used for education or permanent public works."

Bryan's most heroic progressive stance in the Nicaraguan episode occurred as he delved into the agreement between Nicaragua and the American bankers in the Taft era. He was sickened by the exactions made upon the little country. Nicaragua, he found, owed the bankers approximately $711,000 but gave a security of outrageous magnitude: its customs, returns from its railroads, and, worst of all, an option of 51 percent of the railroads' stock. Altogether, Bryan estimated, the profit to the bankers amounted to something like $1,500,000. In its current fiscal crisis, Nicaragua was again beguiled by the same American bankers, who offered financial rescue at an even higher price.

The United States government, Bryan argued to Wilson, must become "a good Samaritan" and help those "who have fallen among thieves." He proposed a plan to extricate Nicaragua from its usurious bankers' loan and free its railroad. "I feel," Bryan wrote by way of preamble, "that we have an opportunity to help these nations in a disinterested way that will cement them to us and give us a standing among the Latin American countries which no outside influence can shake." Bryan proposed that Nicaragua issue bonds to be taken by the U.S. government at low interest. Bryan's plan represented an enormous saving over private alternatives, but Wilson, alas, rejected this proposal, and Bryan was forced to look for Nicaragua's financial salvation among profit-minded American bankers.[11]

In the Dominican Republic, Bryan's diplomacy ran afoul of another principle to which he was devoted, the appointment of "deserving Democrats." As minister to plundered, debt-ridden Santo Domingo, he endorsed James M. Sullivan of New York, whose background, in addition to party service, included prizefight promotion and a reputation as a somewhat dubious lawyer.

When revolution broke out soon after his arrival, Sullivan sided with his friend José Bordas Valdés, incumbent President of a widely unpopular government. In dispatches to Bryan, Sullivan misrepresented the revolutionaries as "malcontents" and "enemies of law and order." He was confident that "the right instruction from the Department to me, delivering to these outlaws our ultimatum, will end the matter summarily." Bryan complied by wiring that "we can have no sympathy with these who seek to seize the power of government to advance their own personal interests or ambition." Those who feel aggrieved, Bryan pointed out, should resort to agitation rather than insurrection. "Say to [them]," Bryan instructed Sullivan, "that the good offices of this Government can be counted upon at all times . . . in the remedying of abuses, and in the promotion of the welfare of the people." For nearly a year Sullivan kept Bordas in power by distorting his reports to Bryan and by threatening the rebels with punishment from United States forces.

Sullivan had great stakes in Bordas' continuation in power. Sullivan's appointment as minister had been pressed by William C. Beer, New York agent of Samuel M. Jarvis and his Banco Nacional of Santo Domingo. In return for Jarvis' support of his candidacy, Sullivan successfully applied his influence to move the deposits of the American receiver general of the Dominican customs from the National City Bank of New York to Jarvis' Banco Nacional. A cousin of the minister, Timothy Sullivan, who also went to Santo Domingo, was showered with government construction contracts, and the minister himself was suspected of profiting from government favors. None of this seamy background was known to Bryan.

The successes of the revolutionaries and plain-speaking, accusative reports from the American receiver of Dominican customs, Walker W. Vick, opened Bryan's eyes to Sullivan's flaws. With Santo Domingo rapidly sinking into chaos, Bryan dispatched an investigating commission, and Wilson intervened to end the civil war by threatening to occupy the country. The nefarious Sullivan was dismissed. An election, held under American supervision, elevated a revolutionary leader, Juan Y. Jiménez, as President. Elderly and enfeebled, Jiménez clung tenuously to power in a still-explosive situation.[12]

The Dominican Republic's neighbor Haiti, was another testing ground of Bryan's benevolent diplomacy. The shaky hold of its government upon power and the dominance of factionalism in its political life severely strained Bryan's principle of popular, reform government as the supreme goal of diplomacy. The new Haitian President, Michel Oreste, was overthrown in a revolutionary coup by the Zamor brothers, Charles and Oreste, and the latter, early in 1914, was elected President. Bryan wrestled with the slippery problem of determining whether the new government was sufficiently popular to warrant American recognition. He instructed the American minister to stress to the new Haitian leadership that the principles of constitutional government must be observed and "that there can be no freedom without order based upon law and public conscience and approval." On Bryan's desk lay plans for seizing control of Haitian customshouses and for establishing an American naval base at Môle-St.-Nicolas, as well as other measures to convert Haiti into an American protectorate. These plans, with their strong imperialist flavor, were fashioned by Boaz W. Long, chief of the Latin American Affairs Division, who had close ties with Wall Street, and Roger L. Farnham, agent of the National City Bank of New York in Haiti.

Soon the Zamor brothers were racing into exile. Convinced that "there will be no peace and progress in Haiti until we have some such arrangement as we have in Santo Domingo," Bryan was reluctant to intervene. Although there was "sufficient ground" to do so, "I do not like the idea," he wrote to Wilson, "of forcible interference on purely business grounds." The new government of Davilmar Théodore, which replaced the Zamor regime, was also buffeted by revolution and corruption to the point that Bryan concluded that the United States "cannot consent to stand by and permit revolutionary conditions constantly to exist there." As 1915 dawned, Bryan and Wilson dispatched former Governor John Franklin Fort of New Jersey and Charles C. Smith to Haiti to negotiate a convention as the foundation of future stability. When they arrived, Théodore had fled, and another new President, General Vilbrun G. Sam, refused to negotiate in the absence of recognition.

As he puzzled over the situation with Wilson, Bryan remained temperate and disinclined to force a drastic convention upon Haiti that would make it a United States protectorate. Wilson, in contrast, was consumed with exasperation and eager to bring the mercurial situation under control. The wonder is that Bryan was able to hold the President in check.[13]

As much as anyone, including Wilson, Bryan was the architect of American policy toward Mexico in the administration's early years. Bryan's disposition toward Mexico was shaped by his humanitarian ideals, his sympathy with the deprived Mexican masses, and his resolve to replace tyrannical, exploitative leadership with popular, progressive government. Shortly before the Wilson administration came to power, the humanistic Francisco I. Madero, whose regime sought to reconstruct Mexican society on a democratic foundation, was murdered. A chief perpetrator of the crime was General Victoriano Huerta, who occupied a trusted position under Madero and who was the master conniver of his destruction.

Huerta quickly seized power. Britain, France, Germany, and other countries recognized his new regime as a matter of course, and the American ambassador at Mexico City, Henry Lane Wilson, advised his government to do likewise. State Department experts urged recognition, for Huerta's government was in fact the only government in Mexico, and for the United States to withhold recognition, as Bryan was urging, would foment unrest and revolution. "We regard governments as existing or not existing," declared the scholarly counselor, John Bassett Moore. "We do not require them to be chosen by popular vote." The President's course of withholding recognition, taken after his ready concurrence with Bryan, Moore contended, was unsound in history and law and would lead to endless interference in other nations' affairs.[14]

The Wilson-Bryan policy was boosted by the quick emergence, after Huerta's seizure of power, of a rival, anti-Huerta faction, pro-Madero in outlook, which styled itself the Constitutionalists. They quickly fielded an army and dominated the northern Mexican states. Their leader, Venustiano Carranza, declared himself provisional President of Mexico and vowed to overthrow Huerta. In the first bloom of his new movement, Carranza, not surprisingly, praised Wilson and Bryan lavishly in a private interview.

Bryan recommended that Huerta be told that the United States will recognize "a constitutional President, if the [Mexican] Congress will call an election for an early date, and supervise the election so as to give a fair chance for an expression of the opinion of the people." Wilson accepted this counsel by announcing that a test of "constitutional legitimacy" would be applied to any Mexican government considered for recognition. The test, as Bryan proposed and Wilson adopted it, would examine whether the new government complied with its own constitution and with genuine electoral processes.[15]

A second major Mexican policy whose groundwork was laid by Bryan was expounded in a lengthy memorandum to the President on July 19, 1913. Bryan urged that the United States tender its "good offices" to restore order, facilitate popular elections, and establish "permanent peace" in Mexico. The step was justified, he argued, by our proximity to Mexico, by "our deep interest in conditions in North America, and by the "large number of Americans residing in Mexico." Equally, foreign investors had interests deserving protection.

The Wilson-Bryan pronouncements of high-minded policy produced no visible results. Civil war, devastation, and disruption raged and spread. The holdover American ambassador, Henry Lane Wilson, suspected of complicity in Madero's overthrow, was recalled, and Wilson and Bryan dispatched special emissaries for on-the-scene observation and negotiation. Of these several missions, the most important was undertaken by John Lind, a solid Bryan man of Wisconsin, whose appointment symbolized Bryan's large hand in Mexican policy. Although lacking diplomatic experience or relevant background, Lind was to go to Huerta and offer the United States' good offices of mediation between the several contending Mexican factions and forces. Huerta, upon learning of Lind's mission from the press, cried, "I will resist with arms any attempt by the United States to interfere in the affairs of Mexico."

Lind was instructed to seek an early and free election, the consent of Huerta not to be a candidate, and agreement by all parties to abide by the results. Lind managed to present his proposals, but the reaction of the Huerta regime was totally negative. The shrewd Lind was not long on the Mexican scene when he was warning Bryan that "we simply cannot expect elections to be held in the sense they are conducted in the United States. . . . Judged by our standards they are a farce, nothing but the homage of a people to the forms of democracy." Lind, meanwhile, in conversations with Huerta's representatives, toiled to wear down their utter negativism, chiefly by threats of more forceful American policy. Just as Lind reached the rock bottom of despair, Huerta, in a vital concession, eliminated himself as a candidate for the Presidency. Bryan was exultant when Huerta's appealing Foreign Minister, Federico Gamboa, was nominated. "I feel that we have nearly reached the end of our trouble," he wrote to Wilson.[16]

For Bryan, the Mexican problem also involved the large American oil, mining, and ranching interests there, who were urging that the administration employ all possible means to protect their holdings, including military intervention. Rumors of a likely pullback of American troops from the Texas-Mexican border to diminish the possibility of incidents distressed them. These wealthy, self-concerned citizens were angered by Bryan's attitude and deportment. They must think of the principles involved, Bryan lectured sternly, and not of "dollars and cents. You seem to be afraid that one of your steers will be killed and eaten by the Mexicans," Bryan said in disdainful accents. His visitors spoke of the necessity of protecting American lives in Mexico, but the Secretary accused them of pretending to seek the safety of American women and children when in reality they were thinking of their own selfish interests. The visitors retorted that American women and children were some miles from the border and from railroad stations and could not get out of Mexico safely. Bryan snapped, "Give me their names and addresses and I will get them out." When they persisted in lamenting the reduction of border forces, Bryan shot back: "You needn't think that all the red blood of this country is in Texas." [17]

Bryan's optimism about Mexico was suddenly wiped out. A new British minister, Sir Lionel Carden, came to Mexico City. The American chargé, Nelson O'Shaughnessy, reported to the Secretary of State that Carden, in previous Latin American service, "has done his utmost . . . to oppose the interests of the United States. . . ." In actuality, Carden was the agent of Lord Cowdray, who had enormous oil holdings in Mexico and wielded strong influence over the Huerta government. Coincidental with Carden's arrival, Huerta moved upon the Chamber of Deputies, a stronghold of Maderistas, and had 110 members arrested and imprisoned. Although O'Shaughnessy reported that the deputies were safe, a military dictatorship was at hand. Simultaneously, Carden put himself in prominent display at Huerta's Presidential Palace.

Wilson, angered by the blatant interference, in a speech at Mobile on October 27 envisioned the day when Latin America would be free from the dominance of foreign concessionaires. The next day, to help Wilson round out his thinking, Bryan suggested, in a lengthy, carefully drawn memorandum, that the Monroe Doctrine be extended to Mexico. "The right of American republics," Bryan wrote, "to work out their own destiny along lines consistent with popular government is just as much menaced today by foreign financial interests as a century ago by the political aspirations of foreign governments. We must protect the people of these republics in their right to attend to their own business, free from external coercion, no matter what form that external coercion may take." It is doubtful that Bryan included in his view of "coercion" his own pressures upon Mexico to follow democratic ways.

Wilson's manifest concern prompted the British to curb their hostile policies, and the United States, in turn, gave promises to safeguard foreign nationals and properties in Mexico. Meanwhile, the Constitutionalists, whose success the Wilson administration was openly encouraging, were making impressive progress on the battlefield. Led by the brilliant Francisco Villa, they swept through the northern provinces, and captured the key oil centers of Tuxpam and Tampico. The successes, however welcome to Bryan and Wilson, also tested the United States' ability to live up to its assurances that foreign persons and properties would be protected. United States warships rushed to the embattled scenes.[18]

As 1914 dawned, it became clear that Wilson must, if he was to achieve Huerta's overthrow, make American arms and munitions available to the Constitutionalists or send American forces into Mexico. The President chose the former alternative, and under Bryan's supervising eye, the State Department arranged for a supply of American arms in exchange for the Constitutionalists' pledge to respect "just and equitable" concessions. Villa, who got the news while riding his old pinto pony, waved his hat and exclaimed with joy, "The war will soon be over!" While Villa rejoiced, angry voices were heard in Congress. Representative Frederick H. Gillett of Massachusetts rose to declare that the administration was "floundering" in its policy, and the inevitable result of this sorry scene would be war. He laid "the entire responsibility" for the debacle to Bryan: "The Secretary's policy" was making the United States "the laughing stock of the world." What the Mexican problem needed, cried Gillett, was a man "of blood and iron," like Theodore Roosevelt, who, were he pressed into service, would quickly restore peace and calm.[19]

While Wilson and Bryan sloughed in the quandary of how to depose Huerta, an opportunity to intervene materialized when his soldiers at Tampico arrested the paymaster and crew of the USS *Dolphin* after they had landed their shore boat without permission. The Americans were promptly released, but Wilson quickly magnified the controversy, laid it before Congress, and requested authority, which was granted, to use the armed forces to obtain redress.

Although Bryan worked loyally within the framework of the President's emerging policy of intervention, he had a softening influence on certain of its prickly rigors. The Congressional resolution was originally drafted by Robert Lansing, an upstate New York lawyer who had succeeded John Bassett Moore as the State Department's counselor. Lansing, a hard nose, called for "an unequivocal apology." Bryan altered the draft to read "unequivocal amends," and the Cabinet, which reviewed the language, approved Bryan's change.

A new ingredient was added to the confusion when a German steamer, the *Ypiranga*, loaded with ammunition for Huerta, approached Veracruz. To prevent the landing of these supplies, which might possibly be used against American forces, Wilson ordered the Navy to seize the city. Mexican resistance produced casualties on both sides, but Veracruz quickly fell into American hands. Meanwhile, the President discussed with his Cabinet plans and preparations for war with Mexico. Secretary of War Garrison urged an immediate march on Mexico City, while Bryan argued vehemently against further preparations or provocations.[20]

For the pacifistic Secretary of State, the dark night of violence suddenly edged into a favorable dawn. The ABC Powers of South America—Argentina, Brazil, and Chile—offered to mediate the dispute, and Huerta and Bryan quickly accepted. Though Wilson visualized the mediation as a tactic for eliminating Huerta and bringing the Constitutionalists to power, Bryan saw the enterprise as an opportunity for the triumph of the instrumentalities of peace over violence. In a speech before the Brooklyn League, Bryan declared that the impending mediation augured that "the dignity and welfare of Mexico may be preserved with a new era in prospect of greater progress in civil affairs. Loving order as I do, I do not believe that it is necessary for man to shed blood to be great. If it is not greatness in the man, it is certainly not the way of greatness for a nation."

The mediation, unfortunately, did not live up to Bryan's expectations. From May 20 to July 2, 1914, the talks of American and Mexican delegates crept on at Niagara Falls, Canada, under the guidance of the ABC powers. The meetings' progress was dominated by Wilson's purpose to depose Huerta and to bring the Constitutionalists to abandon the fighting and accept American superintendency in establishing a provisional government. But Carranza foiled this plan by pressing the drive of his armies toward Mexico City and by refusing to accept a Wilsonian program for Mexican economic and social reform. The mediation, burdened with Wilson's constraining objectives, proceeded with Bryan's alert support. Simultaneously, he prompted other expedients to bring the Mexican fighting to a close. Through the American commissioners at Niagara Falls, he encouraged a plan by which Huerta might appoint a foreign minister who would be acceptable to the Constitutionalists. After that, other steps toward general harmony might be taken. Bryan oversaw an exhaustive search for a likely candidate, but the adamancy of the Constitutionalists spoiled the project.

Not mediation at Niagara Falls, but the battlefields of Mexico controlled events. On July 15 Huerta, faced with the unchecked drive of the Constitutionalists, resigned, and on August 20 Carranza swept into Mexico City. Just as the Wilson administration's policy seemed to enjoy the sweet fruits of success, a split developed between Carranza and Villa. Peon, outlaw, and bandit, cruel and volatile, Villa aspired to become leader of Mexico. To Wilson and Bryan, Villa was an opportunity to escape from the uncooperative, unpredictable Carranza. From conversations with George Carothers, the American diplomatic representative closest to Villa, Bryan was impressed that the general would be more dependable than Carranza in carrying forward agrarian and other reforms. A new civil war erupted, and Bryan, depending on informants, assumed that Villa and his ally Emiliano Zapata would quickly overcome the Carranza forces. But the underestimated Carranza, by shrewd political moves and by the exploits of his brilliant general Alvaro Obregón, rapidly restored his fortunes and put Villa's armies to rout. Bryan was soon pointing out to Wilson that "the situation in Mexico is, in some respects, worse than it has been before since Huerta left and I believe it is quite important that we do something at once." Concretely, Bryan proposed that all the American republics be invited to join in an appeal to the Mexican factions to adjust their differences and agree on means to establish a stable and orderly government. But Wilson dismissed the idea as something that "would be without effect and might bring irritation."

Ultimately, an exasperated Wilson warned that unless the factions stopped fighting, the United States would intervene. Although the weakened Villa offered to make peace with Carranza, the lofty First Chief, encouraged by the success of his arms, indignantly declined. Bryan, as a kind of last resort, proposed the launching of a program of organized relief to suffering Mexico. Wilson agreed and Bryan had reached the end of his string. His policy of peace through negotiation had failed the test of Mexico. After months of conference, negotiation, threat, and exhortation, there was no peace—only war, ruin, and starvation.[21]

On behalf of Wilson's ambitious program of legislation, Bryan was making frequent pilgrimages to Capitol Hill. No one in the administration, not even the President, was as well known personally in Congress as Bryan. No one had as many friends and old associates there, nor as many enemies.

For all his influence in Congress, Bryan conducted himself in strict subordination and loyalty to his chief. Although time and again opportunities flowered for Bryan to make recommendations of new laws he deemed desirable, the Secretary scrupulously followed the rule that he should make no recommendations on legislation since such activities were "not part of his official duties." Actually, Bryan suffered no hardship from this self-imposed restraint. Wilson's New Freedom program of legislation, itself a golden age in social reform, had been advocated for years and decades by Bryan. He was now experiencing the sheer joy of transposing old dreams into new realities. "President Wilson," wrote a delighted Bryan in *The Commoner*, "is in touch with the people and fully awake to the demands of the times."

The Secretary of State had even more reason to rejoice because two amendments he had fought for for decades had at last been adopted. Weeks before he joined the administration, the nation approved the income tax amendment. Bryan advocated the tax in his earliest days in Nebraska politics, pressed for it in Congress, insisted on its inclusion in the platform of 1896, and in each succeeding national convention persisted in the struggle for what he deemed the most just of taxes because it was based on the ability to pay.

Even after the amendment's adoption many dissented from Bryan's admiration of the income tax. Some feared that Congress, impressed with the overwhelming sentiment for the amendment, would impose a heavy tax, believing that it would be popular. Others feared that the states, inspired by the federal tax, would levy their own. Well-heeled Easterners feared the tax would fall most heavily on their section and lightly on other sections where wealth was not so luxuriant. "Nothing could be more fatal," warned the New York *Times*, "to the solidarity of patriotism."

Soon after Bryan became Secretary of State, a second old cause triumphed as a constitutional amendment. From his earliest political days Bryan had also championed the popular election of United States Senators and successfully fought for the inclusion of such a plank in four national Democratic platforms. For the Seventeenth Amendment, adopted on May 31, 1913, Bryan had the happy duty as Secretary of State to sign the proclamation of ratification. He made it a gala occasion. Around him were gathered the principal gladiators, old and new, of the long struggle—former Congressman Henry St. George Tucker of Virginia, floor manager of the first resolution ever to pass the House of Representatives calling for the popular election of Senators; Congressman William W. Rucker of Missouri, who managed the House resolution leading to the amendment; and Senator

William E. Borah of Idaho, a leonine progressive Republican, who directed
the Senate fight. Also on hand were Mary and Miss Mary Sharp, a sister-in-
law of Tucker, and many departmental officials.

A beaming Bryan used four silver pens to sign his proclamation, one each
for his first, middle, and last names, and the fourth for the date. One pen
was tied with a red ribbon, another with a white, another a blue, and the
fourth had two white ribbons. Tucker, Rucker, Mary, and Borah each received a pen, and the blotter was given to Eddie Savoy, the State Department's chief messenger. "That marks the end of a long fight," Bryan exulted
as he rose from his chair. It was, he added, the most important reform of the
century for the federal government.

Of the two Congressional houses in 1913, it was far easier for Bryan—and
Wilson—to work with the Senate than the House. Although the Senate had
been chosen prior to the Seventeenth Amendment's adoption, it mirrored
the country's progressive sentiment, and allies of the old Bryan wars constituted its leadership.

John W. Kern was chairman of the Democratic caucus and the party's
floor leader; Francis J. Newlands of Nevada was caucus vice-chairman;
and Willard Saulsbury of Delaware, an important 1908 campaigner, was
secretary. The House, in contrast with the Senate, tended to conservatism;
its leaders were two rejected aspirants for the Presidential nomination of
1912, victims of bruising battles with Bryan: the Speaker, Champ Clark,
and the floor leader, Oscar Underwood.

Soon after he was ensconced in his secretaryship, Bryan took steps to
effect a reconciliation with Clark. He had every inducement to do so, for
shortly after the Wilson administration began, Clark spoke ominously of
"self-styled Democrats, whose chief business is to stir up strife by foully
slandering any Democrat who has earned their enmity. . . ." A luncheon
meeting between the two longtime friends and shorttime enemies was arranged by Ira E. Bennett, editor of the Washington *Post.* To prevent the
stoking of new fires of animosity, Bennett and his co-planner of the occasion, former Congressman Theodore A. Bell of California, invited a quantity of distinguished guests and proven pacifiers, including Vice President
Marshall, Interior Secretary Franklin K. Lane, Senators Kern and O'Gorman, and Presidential secretary Tumulty.

At the luncheon table, Bryan and Clark were several seats removed from
each other but exchanged badinage, at which both were adept. Afterward
Bryan and Clark each issued statements to the press. Bryan said that their
"misunderstanding" was now cleared up and "that I have always regarded
and do now regard him as a good clean progressive Democrat. If my language at Baltimore created any impression that I was charging Mr. Clark
with being in sympathy with any of the reactionary forces, I am glad of the
opportunity to correct [it]." Clark, in his statement to the press, was a shade

less conciliatory. He earnestly wished cordial cooperation with the Secretary in the interests of administration politics. But neither "Colonel Bryan or anyone else" could "correct the injustice that was done to me at Baltimore." [22]

A degree, at least, of reconciliation with Clark was essential if Bryan was to perform a function Wilson very much depended on, promoting New Freedom legislation in Congress. In 1913 and 1914, the high season of his program, Wilson was still little known to the Washington political community. After long residence in academia and a stint in state politics, he was only briefly on the national stage. His limited acquaintance with Congressional figures was a handicap for the New Freedom program, which would require lots of buttonholing and a cashing in on old political debts on Capitol Hill. For such tasks, Bryan was ideal. He was a master at personal persuasion, and his years of campaigning for Democratic Congressmen gave him political credits to draw on.

The most important and the most controversial of the New Freedom legislation was the plan to establish what became known as the Federal Reserve System. The plan was prepared by Senator Robert Owen of Oklahoma, an old Bryan ally; Congressman Carter Glass of Virginia, a semicritical Bryan acquaintance; and sundry Treasury officials and consultants, all of whom were buffeted by conservative legislators, to whom obeisance had to be paid if their handiwork was to succeed in Congress. Conservatives demanded a huge private bank of fifteen branches, which presumably would work closely with the money trust, the elite corps of private financiers that Bryan for years had been fighting. Progressives, reflecting his doctrines, favored a decentralized banking system under government control. This latter version dominated the Federal Reserve Act, which passed late in 1913. It created a Federal Reserve System of twelve Federal Reserve Banks, each located in a region into which the country was divided. At the system's apex was a board of governors, appointed by the President with the Senate's approval. The twelve Federal Reserve Banks were led by a board of nine directors, three chosen by the Federal Reserve Board and six by member banks of the region. The regional banks were privately owned and controlled, except for supervision by the Federal Reserve Board. All national banks became members of the system, and state banks might join. The Federal Reserve Board was to determine the nation's general monetary and credit policies, which were to be carried out through the Reserve Banks and thousands of member banks. A new type of currency was authorized: Federal Reserve notes secured by short-term commercial paper and a 40 percent gold reserve. The new system aimed to introduce greater flexibility into the credit of the country, a sounder distribution of banking facilities, and safeguards against bankers' speculation with their depositors' money.

When a draft bill was completed, Wilson, not without apprehension, invited Bryan to the White House to discuss it. In this early version the bill provided for emergency notes to be issued by the regional reserve banks, and the Federal Reserve Board was to be composed partly of representatives appointed by the banks, while the government representatives were to be in the majority. He hoped, the President said, that Bryan would be able to support the bill. In the amiable conversation that followed, the issues dividing the President and the Secretary of State became sharply evident. "I called his attention to the fact," Bryan wrote afterward, "that our party had been committed by Jefferson and Jackson and by recent platforms to the doctrine that the issue of money is a function of government and should not be surrendered to banks"—the draft bill called for emergency notes to be issued by regional reserve banks, in effect a private banking decision. Bryan added in his candid statement to Wilson: "I could not consistently indorse the authorization of more bank notes and that to do so would forfeit the confidence of those who trusted me—this confidence being my only political asset, the loss of which would deprive me of any power to assist him." Bryan also objected to the feature of the draft which divided the membership of the top governing board between banks and government representatives. Bryan wanted the entire board to consist of representatives appointed by the President.

Despite these differences, the conversation remained cordial and even-tenored. Bryan, or W.J.B., as Wilson spoke of him to Tumulty, "conducted himself in the most generous way, and I was deeply touched by his personal attitude of friendliness toward me. He even went so far as to say that in order that I might not be embarrassed in the handling of the bill, he was willing to resign and leave the country and make no public criticism of the measure."

Wilson commenced a kind of friendly siege to bring Bryan around. He dispatched his overpoweringly persuasive Secretary of the Treasury, William Gibbs McAdoo, to work on Bryan's conversion. On another day he sent the adroit Tumulty to Bryan's home. The Secretary of State was the soul of graciousness. "We went at once to the library," Tumulty recounted, "and in his boyish way, he showed me a picture which the President autographed for him only a few days previous. As we stood before the picture, Bryan expressed admiration for the President." Eventually, after adjustments in the bill, although it was not by any means altogether to his liking, Bryan moved to support it.

On Capitol Hill, he lobbied for it unstintingly. When the bill seemed stalled in the House Currency Committee, Bryan got it moving again. "I have arranged," he reported to Wilson, "to meet a couple of Democrats on the Currency Committee tonight to urge immediate action. If you hear of any persons with whom I might have influence, let me know." When the bill lagged again in the House Rules Committee, Bryan, emerging from a tête-à-tête with his old friend Congressman Robert L. Henry of Texas, brought the exhilarating news that the committee "would report any rule you wanted." In addition, Bryan took to the stump to combat the avalanche of propaganda from banking circles against the bill. Hailing it as "the most remarkable currency measure we ever made," he argued: "It gives the bankers enough to make them happy and does not enable them to take enough to make the people miserable."

The Federal Reserve bill was eventually enacted and for other New Freedom laws, Bryan was a gadfly, both in the Cabinet and on Capitol Hill. Wilson, who was lukewarm toward a program of agricultural credit, found his instincts reinforced when his Secretary of Agriculture, David F. Houston, observed in a Cabinet meeting that a proposal to lend farmers $2 billion from the national treasury was "class legislation." An aroused Bryan made an unmincing rebuttal. "Why shouldn't Congress lend the farmers money out of the Treasury?" he cried with some heat. "You have created a national banking system in the interest of bankers and lend the bankers money at 2 percent. Why not lend the farmers more at 4 percent?" Ultimately, the President came around to Bryan's position. When Houston on another occasion urged that the administration go slowly on antitrust legislation lest business take alarm, Bryan confessed to long experience with that brand of argument. Trusts, he had often heard, should never be touched when business is good or when business is bad. He insisted that there was but one test: The party must keep the promise for new antitrust legislation made in its platform. The promise was fully kept.[23]

In the 1914 Congressional elections, the first testing of Wilson's stewardship, Bryan campaigned more than the President did, sweeping widely through the Middle and Far West, through Ohio, Illinois, and Indiana, north to Minnesota, south to Tennessee, and, in the Far West, ranging from Colorado to Washington. While campaigning for Democratic tickets and progressivism, Bryan was also renewing old associations and maintaining his vast devoted following. Mary, who accompanied him, wrote, "It warmed our hearts to see the loving good will extended to us in these states. People certainly love him. . . ."

Bryan's long journey was not wholly an excursion in political altruism. He championed most energetically his oldest and closest allies, such as Senator Stone of Missouri and Newlands of Nevada. Here and there on the political landscape were blossoms of uncertainty whether Wilson would run for reelection. The Democratic platform of 1912, thanks to a plank insisted upon by Bryan, called for limiting the President to a single term. If Wilson did not run in 1916, who would? Senator James E. Martine of the President's own state of New Jersey, progressive Democrat and a good Bryan friend, proposed an answer. "Bryan," he declared in a public statement, "will be the logical candidate. People have come to know and understand him better. People think that he has become more stable in his views, struck an equilibrium, as it were. The fact is that Mr. Bryan is just as radical today as he was twenty years ago, but the people have grown up to him." As talk of one term for the President persisted and as a constitutional amendment limiting the President to a single term gained in Congress, Wilson smothered the movement by letting it be known that he opposed both the amendment and the Baltimore plank.[24]

The 1914 elections brought the long-simmering unrest of Nebraska's Democratic factions to high flame. A major struggle loomed between Bryan and Hitchcock. In the spring, Charles, whose own eye was fixed on the gubernatorial nomination, laid before Bryan an optimistic assessment. Little was to be feared from the Hitchcock faction: "Their forces are badly organized" and "we have the strength to win."

But Charles' optimism melted in the warm political rains of May. John T. Maher a rising Democrat of Lincoln, in published statements, declared that the issue facing his party was whether "we are to have government of the people or of the Bryan family. If the rule of the people is to be supplanted by the rule of King William and Prince Charlie what is the use of keeping up the party?" Charles' ambitions for the gubernatorial nomination excited rumblings of discontent across the state. Their common theme was that one office-seeking Bryan was enough. The incumbent Democratic Governor John Morehead let it be known that he would run again, and there was a rush of county chairmen to his support. Charles' ambitions were sidetracked, and the convention at Columbus, Nebraska, burst with harmony as Richard "Met" Metcalfe in a speech recalled the days of struggle and progress when W. J. Bryan and Hitchcock were joined in fraternal Democratic union.[25]

But a factional contest that could not be subdued was the continuing struggle between Bryan and Senator Gilbert Hitchcock for the control of patronage. According to orthodox political etiquette, the dominant voice in the disposal of the Nebraska patronage should have been Hitchcock's, but Bryan, standing at the head of the Cabinet and as Wilson's chief political lieutenant, did not propose to yield. Since Hitchcock had supported Harmon rather than Wilson for the nomination, some of his candidates for federal appointment offered what at best were clouded credentials. When Hitchcock promoted F. L. Whedon for the Kearney postmastership, for example, Bryan remonstrated that Whedon was "unfit for a reward at the hands of a Progressive party. . . . I do not know of any Republican in the town whose appointment would be more harmful than his."

Months of deadlock passed as Nebraska's job-hungry Democrats waited in vain. Wilson, who suffered the unpleasantness of standing in the middle of the conflict, looked eagerly for a solution. Ultimately, the President proposed a meeting between Bryan and Hitchcock, which took place late one morning in the meeting room of the Senate Foreign Relations Committee. In the prickly atmosphere, Hitchcock suggested a division of major patronage by which he would name the United States marshal, Bryan the district attorney, while the collector of Internal Revenue would be chosen by agreement between them, with Hitchcock proposing three names and Bryan selecting one of them. Bryan responded that while he would not reject the proposal, neither would he assent to it, and on balance he preferred to have the whole matter held over until after the approaching elections. The elections came and went, but still no agreement emerged.

Finally, as 1915 dawned, Bryan reminded Wilson that "It is nearly two years since you took the oath of office, and the Democrats of Nebraska are still denied opportunity to assist you in your administration." The terms of many offices had expired, and "Republicans hold these which might be held by Democrats." To break the impasse, Bryan suggested that Wilson "feel free to follow your own opinion, after consulting with *anyone* whose judgment you may desire to have. If, in any case, you desire to have my opinion or ask me to make a recommendation, I shall be pleased to give you the name of a progressive democrat. . . . If you make the appointment relying upon the opinion of some one else, I ask that I may be permitted to inform the Democrats of Nebraska that my opinion was not asked. . . ." Bryan had stirred the becalmed waters just a trifle, but the patronage logjam remained largely unbroken.[26] In Nebraska, both the Bryan and the Hitchcock factions remained strong and warring, each maneuvering toward the approaching 1916 elections, which both viewed as momentous for their fortunes.

Washington's finest, most awesome miracle was the spectacle of Wilson and Bryan working in sturdy harmony. These two autonomous spirits, prideful and unyielding in conviction, constantly gave rise to rumors of clashes, but the Cassandras were always wrong.

As Wilson's subordinate, Bryan revealed a side of his character undisclosed in his earlier career. The three-time Presidential nominee who never in his life had worked for another man was demonstrating remarkable capacity for self-effacement. To Wilson, Bryan was a loyal subordinate. By both his own avowal and his acts, Bryan, who had labored so long to become President, was uncomplaining that another was in the place. ". . . if any one thinks that I was disappointed because the leadership fell to another," Bryan declared in a speech, "let him disabuse his mind of that thought. I rejoiced that there was one who could win where I lost. And I was so much more interested in the cause than in any title that could come with it that I am sure the President was not happier than I was."

Wilson, too, grew in admiration for his Secretary of State. After two years of their partnership had passed, Wilson wrote to Bryan that "I have learned not only to value you as a friend and counsellor, but, if you will let me say so, I have found a very strong affection for you growing in my heart. Your high motives and constant thought of the public interest have been an example and stimulation to me. . . ."

Bryan's affection for Wilson was of a strength sufficient to withstand the assaults of several of the President's more idiosyncratic work habits. A perfectionist in the use of language, Wilson was given to revising the documents and drafts prepared by his subordinates, including Bryan. "I felt," Wilson wrote to Bryan of a telegram the Secretary of State had just submitted, "that perhaps it was wise to make the telegram to Gerard [the United States ambassador to Germany] a little more explicit than the one you sent me yesterday, and I, therefore, suggest the enclosed." Occasionally, Wilson circumvented the Secretary of State and dealt directly with his subordinates, but Bryan harbored no resentment.[27]

On June 28, 1914, there began a train of events, far removed from Washington, that exploded into the ruination of Bryan's confident oft-expressed theory that a progress-making mankind was on the brink of eliminating war. That assumption fed the verve with which Bryan was negotiating his peace treaties and the great store he laid in their practicality. On that June day, in far-off Sarajevo, Bosnia, a place unknown to most Americans, Archduke Franz Ferdinand, heir to the Austro-Hungarian throne, was murdered by a Serbian nationalist. Over a succession of nightmarish days, one after another of the European nations went to war.

The war's sudden explosion found the State Department ill prepared to cope with the crises thrust upon it. In France, the holdover Republican ambassador, Myron T. Herrick, still waited for his Democratic successor to arrive. Assistant Secretaries John Osborne and William Phillips, who were away on vacation, were recalled at once to Washington. Bryan, who with Mary was preparing for a quiet sojourn in a favorite resort, Asheville, North Carolina, put aside his plans.

Thousands of American tourists, caught by the unexpected war, streamed from the Continent to England. Swift authorization was given American embassies in London and other capitals to enlarge their staffs. Volunteer workers helped to combat the crisis. In Washington, Bryan, working interminable hours in his shirt sleeves, was faced with a myriad of inquiries, resolves, and arrangements.[28]

For Bryan the most important objective in the bloody turbulence was the prompt restoration of peace. Although war had eluded the apparatus of courts and procedures so painstakingly established, Bryan, in this darkest hour, did not surrender to despair. As foreign minister of the world's most powerful neutral nation, as one obsessed by the essential turpitude of war, as one certain of the availability to man of a destiny nobler than killing his fellowman or of sacrificing himself and all his talent for good upon the altar of the war gods, Bryan felt driven to take every step to bring the war to its earliest possible close.

In these first weeks of battle Bryan was a conduit of peace-oriented ideas incubated in private minds and in governmental organizations, foreign and domestic. The New York Peace Society looked for Presidential encouragement of its plan to raise $1,000,000 to underwrite a study by neutral governments of the causes of the war and the elements necessary to a settlement, all as a prelude to mediation. But Wilson detected potential dangers, and the proposal languished. Another day, the Bolivian minister put before Bryan the suggestion that the Pan-American Union might pass a resolution commanding mediation to the warring nations. Wilson saw no "harm" in the step.

Bryan eagerly picked up the proposal of the Federal Council of Churches of Christ setting aside a day of prayer to be offered in the churches for peace. "[I] am sure a request from you would be generally complied with," he wrote to Wilson. When the Prayer Day eventually transpired, Bryan contributed an address on the theme that "Most of the errors which man commits in international affairs arise from a failure to understand the fundamental truth—that moral principles are as binding upon nations as upon individuals. . . . 'Thou shalt not kill' applies to nations as well as to individuals." [29]

Bryan's hopes were suddenly lifted by reports drifting to him of an intimate dinner given in New York by the banker James Speyer. His guests included Oscar Straus, United States member of The Hague Tribunal, and the German ambassador, Count Johann von Bernstorff. From the intensive conversation of that evening, there emerged the gleaning that Bernstorff believed that the Kaiser would accept mediation if the other nations also expressed their willingness. Straus asked if he could report the conversation to Bryan, and the ambassador agreed. Straus rushed to Bryan's home for a secret conference, and the Secretary swiftly and exultantly relayed its substance to the President. Meanwhile, Straus took into his confidence the French and British ambassadors, who instantly expressed the fear that Germany would not accept reasonable terms. Bryan, however, felt that even a failure of attempted mediation would be useful in forcing the belligerents "to explain to the world their attitude, the reasons for continuing the war, the end to be hoped for and the terms upon which peace is possible. This would locate the responsibility for the continuance of the war and help to mould public opinion."

To Bryan's deep delight, Wilson was willing to offer mediation "in the interest of European peace." Anxiously and hopefully, the Secretary awaited the belligerents' responses. They, unfortunately, were utterly negative. In London, the Foreign Minister, Sir Edward Grey, told the American ambassador, Walter Hines Page, that Britain and Russia were agreed not to make peace without common consent and not to accept a temporary truce in lieu of "permanent" peace. In Paris, Ambassador Herrick learned that although France longed for peace, it could not discuss its terms until the invader was driven from its territory and Belgium compensated. Germany laid the blame for the war on its enemies, averred that it was their duty to make peace, and concluded that for it to accept mediation would be interpreted as a sign of weakness.[30] Bryan, contemplating in the privacy of his office the dreary answers of the belligerents, was reminded of the passage in the Scriptures, "that they all with one accord begin to make excuses."

The drive for American mediation, although badly crippled, was not dead. Bernstorff remained confident that Germany would agree to evacuate and indemnify Belgium, while Grey acknowledged that the Allies could not decline a reasonable German offer. Bryan himself pressed Wilson to persist with the mediation proposal no matter how frail its prospects. With four months of war already past, the Secretary argued, chances were slight that either side would win and dictate terms. "Mediation," he wrote, "does not mean that any of the combatants shall accept terms that are unsatisfactory, but that they shall propose terms. . . ." Each belligerent, he acknowledged, disclaimed responsibility for the war. But this question was not at the moment important; mediation could fix responsibility for "a continuation of the war," a far graver question. It was "this nation's duty, as the leading exponent of Christianity and as the foremost advocate of world-wide peace, to approach the warring nations again. . . ."

Wilson eventually decided to renew his peace soundings. On January 13, 1915, he informed Bryan that Colonel Edward M. House would soon journey to belligerent capitals on a peace mission. House, a well-to-do Texan, who occupied no official position in the government, had promoted Wilson's Presidential candidacy and cultivated close personal relations, as the administration began, through visits to Washington and undertaking confidential assignments. Secretive and a subtle flatterer, House was bringing off the rare feat of working successfully with the prickly Wilson. Wilson perceived House as the "friend who so thoroughly understands me," "my second personality . . . my independent self. His thoughts and mine are one."

When Wilson disclosed that House would undertake the peace mission, Bryan was upset. House was an Anglophile, and his concern for peace would be subordinated to British self-interest. Bryan did not conceal his distress. He candidly told Wilson that he had planned to go to Europe himself. But the President was adamant, and Bryan declared loyally that House was the best choice if the mission was to be executed by a private person. Later Wilson told House that he was disturbed by Bryan's reaction but that he would permit the Secretary to resign before permitting him to undertake such a delicate assignment, for which he considered him unfit. Wilson's selection of House also revealed his partiality for House's narrower view of American policy for peace, in preference to Bryan's demand for bold action to halt the war.

Colonel House was soon absorbing and acquiescing to the hostility of the British Cabinet to any talk of peace. Bryan persisted at the State Department, besieged by organizations, delegations, and concerned citizens begging, demanding, and praying that more be done for peace. "Two ladies called here the other day," he reported to Wilson, "and asked me to present certain matters to you in connection with the peace question. . . ." Bryan kept his promise but assured Wilson that "I explained to them that I did not think it was possible at this time for this Government to do anything more than it has done." [31]

In the making of Far Eastern policy, Bryan's influence was major. His proudest achievement in that sector of the world was the withdrawal of the United States from a six-power consortium of banks formed in the Taft years to make a $125,000,000 loan to the Chinese government for construction of the Hu-kuang Railway. Bryan entered the situation on March 10, 1913, when representatives of J. P. Morgan and Company, the bankers involved on behalf of the United States, called at the State Department. As his conversation proceeded with these men of Wall Street, Bryan was appalled that the prospective loan was to be secured by Chinese revenues and that the bankers expected the United States government to furnish such support as might be necessary, including the use of force, to make China live up to its loan obligations. The lending powers acquired a monopoly of China's financial affairs. Horrified at the callous destruction of China's political independence that would be wreaked by the loan's terms, Bryan laid the matter before Wilson. Both shared a moral revulsion to the loan's terms, and both agreed that the United States should withdraw. Wilson's announcement of the step stressed that the loan's conditions impinged upon "very nearly the administrative independence of China itself." .

With the outbreak of the World War, Bryan labored strenuously, but vainly, to prevent its spread to the Far East. Japan declared war on Germany and moved to take over German territory and interests in China and otherwise to enlarge her dominion. Early in 1915, Japan made twenty-one demands on China, to the alarm of State Department officials. But Bryan and Wilson moved with caution and tolerance. Japan and China must remain "neighborly," Bryan wrote to Wilson, "and the neighborly spirit cannot be expected if Japan demands too much, or if China concedes too little." Bryan's perceptions of international relations were preserved in a singularly uncomplicated state by his simple moralism. He did not see these relations in terms of national interest; his thinking was unencumbered by the economic data his departmental experts could provide, by appreciation of historical and cultural influences, and by political pressures. He judged nations' actions by a simple moral scale: whether what they did was right or wrong.

For a time the Bryan-Wilson policy of restraint seemed to have a salutary effect on Japan. But in April, 1915, word leaked out that Japan was foisting secret and sweeping demands on China, running roughshod over its sovereignty, with warnings that it was futile to expect support from the United States. The Tientsin *Times* reported that a leading Japanese had said that "The Secretary of State is so much under the influence of Baron Chinda that he is not saying a word against the wishes of Japan." Sutemi Chinda was the Japanese ambassador to the United States, with whom Bryan's relations were very close. Following the *Times'* report, Wilson and Bryan stiffened. The Secretary of State informed Chinda that the United States could not decline to take a public position on Japan's move, since its silence was being understood as acquiescing to Japanese demands. Soon the State Department was announcing that the United States had never contemplated surrendering its treaty rights in China. When Japan sent an ultimatum to China, Bryan dispatched a lengthy memorandum to the Japanese government, specifying American objections to the demands contained in Article V of the treaty Japan sought to force upon China. Bryan somewhat balanced this emphatic official statement with a personal message to Count Shigenobu Okuma, the Prime Minister, urging understanding and peace. Under the combined force of these appeals, Japan yielded to American pressure and, at least for the time, dropped the demands incorporated in Article V. Japan's retreat was one of the proudest accomplishments of Bryan's style of personal diplomacy.[32]

The American people and their government were also striving to remain neutral. Promptly upon the outbreak of war, Wilson advised his countrymen to be calm and to keep a frame of mind enabling the country "to help the rest of the world." The President appealed for "absolute neutrality," and "impartiality and restraint." Bryan rejoiced in the President's preachings of neutrality as the best possible insurance for keeping the United States at peace and for holding in readiness its enormous potential influence for reconciling the belligerents.

Bryan not only believed in but practiced absolute neutrality. He devoted himself to neutrality as a way of life, with the assiduity he rendered to the dictates of temperance. As tiny Belgium was locked in resistance to the mighty German invader, countless Americans committed their sympathy and their dollars to the little nation. But Bryan maintained a posture of strict neutrality. Solicited to contribute to Belgian relief, he acknowledged his eagerness to relieve distress, but he felt behooved to distinguish between his public duty and its consequent restrictions, in contrast with the freedom of the man in the street. Neither he nor President Wilson, said Bryan, "could make any statement which might arouse the feeling that we were favoring any one nation of those now at war." As reports of atrocities in Belgium soared, demands sprouted across the United States for the Wilson administration to lodge a forceful protest. But the administration, reflecting Bryan's view, made not a sound. At Oyster Bay, Theodore Roosevelt, red-blooded winner of the Nobel Peace Prize after he helped end the Russo-Japanese War, writhed in disgust. "What can you expect," he cried, "when the Secretary of State lives in the clouds—no, not in the clouds, in a world of tenth-rate fiction."

As the wild dance of war swirled through its infinite convolutions, Wilson and Bryan were pressed to make their general, high-sounding principles of neutrality meaningful in the face of concrete problems and contingencies. A representative of J. P. Morgan and Company telephoned to learn from Bryan the government's attitude toward a loan that the Morgan Company was contemplating to the French government. In preparing his answer, Bryan first consulted Robert Lansing, who had succeeded John Bassett Moore as counselor. A native of Watertown, New York, Lansing was a fine legal craftsman and a distinguished international lawyer. He had served the United States in the complex Bering Sea arbitration in 1893 and since then had participated in other important international litigation. A former county chairman and candidate for mayor of Watertown, Lansing was well connected among New York Democrats, who urged his appointment to the State Department. From head to toe, Lansing was a legal technician. All else was subordinate—politics which he did not bear gladly and the world of social reform to which Bryan was devoted were utterly alien to him. In advising on the Morgan loan to France, Lansing's thought followed predictable lines. He reported that legal precedents deemed the loan compatible with neutrality. Bryan reminded Lansing that far more than legal considerations were at stake. The loan, the Secretary argued, would surely violate the spirit of neutrality, because money, since it could purchase other contraband materials, was itself the worst form of contraband. Lansing at once agreed with Bryan's position and suggested an analogy to support his argument: that just as a government discourages its citizens from enlisting in foreign armies and withdraws the protections of citizenship, so it should discourage the money of the country from taking part in foreign wars.

Thoroughly aroused by the specter of the Morgan loan as a looming strangler of American neutrality and peace, Bryan wrote an extended letter to Wilson, recounting his conversation with Lansing, emphasizing the reality of money as contraband, and warning that if the Morgan loan proceeded, the financial interests involved "would be tempted to use their influence through the press to support the interests of the Government to which they loaned. . . ." To Bryan's enormous delight, the President agreed with his position and composed on his portable typewriter a statement to the press that "In the judgment of this government, loans by American bankers to any foreign government which is at war is inconsistent with the true spirit of neutrality." For Bryan the President's decision was a landmark in the progress of peace. "It is the first time," he wrote in *The Commoner*, "that a great nation has taken this stand on the subject of war loans." He recalled how the subject had been canvassed at the Hague and at peace conferences without an inch of progress.[33]

Not all problems of neutrality left Bryan in such exultation. As the months of war passed, and Britain, with its superior navy, won increasing mastery of the sea's surface, Bryan and Wilson faced growing agitation in the country and on Capitol Hill to curb the sale of arms in the United States to the belligerents. At the war's beginning, the availability of American arms to all belligerents was deemed harmonious with neutrality. Now, however, with its increasing control of sea lanes, Britain and its allies became the predominant customers in the American munitions market. One day Bryan was pressed for his opinion by the House Foreign Affairs Committee on a proposal to limit American arms sales. Unhesitatingly, the Secretary replied that interference with belligerents' purchase of arms would be construed as an unneutral act because its effect would be to assist one party (Germany) at the expense of the other (Britain). Although Wilson wholeheartedly supported Bryan's response, an old political friend, Senator William J. Stone, did not. Doubtless mindful of his large German-American constituency in Missouri and of his place as chairman of the Senate Foreign Relations Commitee, Stone accused the administration of pursuing an arms policy partial to the Allies and unfriendly to the Central Powers. But Bryan budged not one jot.[34]

Keeping America neutral and at peace was complicated by the differences in status of the two warring sides in American society. A common language and culture and a long, close *de facto* alliance after two far-distant wars drew the United States toward Britain. Men of Anglo-Saxon ancestry dominated the power structure of the economy; they filled top professional positions in Bryan's State Department, in the influential Eastern universities, in the communications and cultural media. Furthermore, Britain and its allies were identified with democracy and freedom, and the Central Powers with imperial militaristic autocracy.

Yet for all these ties, the United States had rights, the most important of which attached to its shipping and trade. The nation's position as the largest trading neutral made these rights of enormous value. But Britain, with its dominant naval position and in the tradition of policy which had led to the War of 1812, issued a series of Orders in Council making sweeping definitions of contraband and intercepted American vessels to enforce her stringent regulations. Soon American direct trade with the Central Powers and indirect trade through neutrals were cut off. Britain's conduct sparked notes and protests from the United States, well couched in learned legal analysis, prepared by expert State Department attorneys. Bryan dutifully affixed his signature to these documents. Evidence is lacking that he was ever particularly exercised over these squabbles, chiefly because they never amounted to any real threat to Anglo-American peace, and the American trading community was not, for him, a favorite constituency.

If anything, Bryan was eager to forestall only serious trouble with Britain over trade. Once, when American tempers were boiling over some new British high-handedness, Bryan wrote to Wilson, "My own idea is that we cannot afford to make merchandise a cause for the use of force. If we have any disputes about merchandise which cannot be settled during the war, they can be settled afterwards, and if we have any disputes which cannot be settled by agreement between the parties, they can, in due time, be submitted to investigation and arbitration. . . ."

The aspect of British policy giving Bryan the deepest distress was its prohibition of food in the naval blockade it threw around Germany. It created for Bryan a nightmare of starving civilians, women and children, in Germany and the Central Powers. His humanity wounded and pained by this vision, he consulted with the German, Austrian, and British ambassadors and pressed inquiries in their capitals to contain the growing horror. One evening, in the quiet of his office, he wrote a lengthy soul-baring letter on the problem to Wilson. He did not know in what direction the President's mind was moving on this grim subject, he acknowledged, "but I feel myself more and more inclined in the opinion that the British position is without justification." From his inquiries he was impressed that the German government "is willing to give assurances that the food imported will not be taken by the Government." Even more, Germany was willing that American organizations distribute the food. "This, it seems to me," he concluded, "takes away the British excuse. . . ."[35]

Bryan's distress over the food blockade coincided with Germany's imposition of a war zone around Britain and proclamation of unrestricted submarine warfare. These ominous steps were laden with danger to American neutrality and peace. Bryan, in his letter to Wilson, proposed to deal simultaneously with the German and British problems at one fell swoop. He recommended setting "one of these propositions off against the other." He meant to see whether Britain would withdraw its objection to food entering

Germany, with distribution "through American instrumentalities," in return for Germany's cancellation of the war zone. Unless the dual problems were resolved, Bryan feared, "We are approaching the most serious crisis that we have had to meet."

With Wilson's warm approval, Bryan moved ahead with his twin diplomatic enterprise, working through the American ambassadors in London and Berlin. In both capitals, his hopes were quickly smothered. Germany, at least, seemed willing to retreat many giant steps from the war zone concept, but Britain budged not an inch. "The right to stop foodstuffs," Grey wrote to Ambassador Page, "destined for the civil population must . . . be admitted if an effective 'cordon' controlling intercourse with the enemy is drawn, announced, and maintained." Keeping food from the civilian population, the Foreign Minister asserted, was "a natural and legitimate method of bringing pressure to bear on an enemy country. . . ." [36]

Increasingly in the councils of the administration, Bryan was becoming a lonely voice for the policy of neutrality. Secretary of the Navy Josephus Daniels was his chief supporter, as he faced the overwhelming reality that those most concerned with foreign policy were ardent and unabashed partisans of the Allies, particularly the British cause. Wilson himself deeply admired England's culture and democracy, was steeped in its poetry and essays, and venerated its parliamentary system. His most trusted counselor, Colonel Edward M. House, whose influence in foreign policy well exceeded Bryan's, was ardently pro-Ally.

At London the American ambassador, Walter Hines Page, like Wilson, was an admirer of British society and culture, possibly even more so than the President. Thanking "Heaven I'm of their race and blood," Page was easily amenable to the thesis advanced by the captivating British Foreign Minister, Sir Edward Grey, that the Allies were fighting America's battle for democracy. Time and again, Page toned down his instructions and presented American protests in ways that left the British impressed that the United States was not serious. "I have now read the despatch," Page said one day in handing Grey a document signed by Bryan, "but I do not agree with it; let us consider how it should be answered!"

Most potent of all those with the Allied bias was Robert Lansing, counselor of the State Department. Presumably Bryan's subordinate, Lansing enjoyed an access and influence with Wilson that exceeded the Secretary's. On one important matter after another, Lansing wrapped neutrality in a blanket of legal technicalities and manipulated freely in favor of the Allies and against Germany. "I saw with apprehension," he wrote, "the tide of resentment against Britain rising higher and higher in this country. . . . I did all that I could to prolong the disputes . . . by preparing . . . long and detailed replies and introducing technical and controversial matters in the hope that before the extended interchange of arguments came to an end something would happen to change the current of American public opinion or to make the American people perceive that German absolutism was a menace to the liberties and to democratic institutions everywhere." [37]

Bryan at least is to be credited with clairvoyance. The German proclamation of February 4, 1915, erecting a war zone around the British Isles was a Pandora's box overflowing with grim trouble that an anguished Bryan amply foresaw. Every enemy ship found in the war zone, according to the proclamation, would be destroyed. Neutral ships would be "in danger" because of the "hazards" of naval warfare and the frequent practice of British vessels to fly neutral flags.

Wilson summoned his Cabinet to weigh the German proclamation. Bryan was in the West on a speaking tour and took no part. On February 10 the United States protested against the German step as an "indefensible violation of neutral rights" and pointedly declared that if American lives or vessels were lost, Germany would be held to "strict accountability." The note was well nigh the ultimate in severity of diplomatic language. The United States position contrasted sharply with its reaction to a comparable policy announced in November, 1914, when the British government proclaimed the North Sea a military area. This transgression of the ancient American doctrine of freedom of the seas was accepted without a murmur of official protest. Later, Bryan was to write, doubtless inspired by his country's contradictory behavior, ". . . I submit the thought that the administration was lacking in neutrality—not in commission, but in omission; not the notes which were written, but the notes which were not written, threw the delicate machinery out of balance. . . ." [38]

On March 28, 1915, the British passenger liner *Falaba* was sunk in St. George's Channel. Of the 111 passengers lost, one was Leon Chester Thrasher, a United States citizen. The *Falaba* was returning to the Gold Coast, where Thrasher was employed, when a German submarine struck. The thoughts of an anxious world turned to the language of the American note protesting the creation of the war zone: that the destruction of an American vessel or the loss of an American life would produce a "critical situation in respect to the relation between this country and Germany. . . ."

Within the State Department a profound division of opinion over the Thrasher question quickly emerged. Chandler P. Anderson, a top-ranking adviser and lawyer and until recently counselor to the American embassy in London, contended that the incident involved no offense to the United States because Thrasher's death was incidental to the destruction of the *Falaba*. At most, Anderson said, the United States was entitled to pecuniary damages. Robert Lansing, on the other hand, argued that the *Falaba* incident was so grave a violation of international law that the United States must demand that Germany disavow the act, punish the submarine commander, and pay damages. Lansing candidly acknowledged that these demands might lead to war. Wilson seemed to agree with Lansing, although he agonized about commencing a major confrontation with Germany and he wished to give House's peace mission, which was in progress, every chance for success.

Heartened by Anderson's argument, Bryan strove to dissuade the President from moving to a confrontation. He dispatched a series of letters and memoranda to Wilson, desperately reaching for any kind of serviceable argument and pressing the theme that the United States should grant the same freedom to violate international law to Germany that it had to Britain. Bryan argued vigorously that the doctrine of contributory negligence bore upon the case, that an American who took passage upon a British vessel, knowing of the German methods of warfare, "stands in a different position from that occupied by one who suffers without any fault of his own."

Days later, Bryan wrote Wilson concerning another angle of the Thrasher case. Should an American citizen, the Secretary asked, "by putting his business above his regard for his country, assume for his own advantage unnecessary risks and thus involve his country in international complications? Are the rights and obligations of citizenship so one-sided that the government which represents all the people must bring the whole population into difficulty because the citizen, instead of regarding his country's interests, thinks only of himself and of his interests?" Bryan also urged that this "most delicate question we have had to meet" be decided not simply on legal grounds, but on practical considerations as well. ". . . a large element of our population," the Secretary noted, was sympathetic with Germany and "has criticised us violently" for partiality to the Allies. The hostile domestic atmosphere aggravated Germany's unfriendliness. Whatever was done on the Thrasher affair, Bryan concluded, had to be "so obviously defensible as to appeal to the judgment of the entire country."

At last, on April 22, Wilson made his decision known to the circle of his administrators and advisers. He shunned legal technicalities and took a high ground. He protested the *Falaba* incident—"not on the loss of this single man's life, but on the interests of mankind which are involved . . . ; on the manifest impropriety of a single nation's essaying to alter the understandings of nations. . . ." An undaunted Bryan objected that a note incorporating this decision would "very much inflame the already hostile feeling against us in Germany . . . in part because of its contrast with our attitude toward the Allies." The Secretary urged that an appeal be made to the belligerents at once to consider the terms of peace and to accept American mediation.

Bryan's argument, Wilson acknowledged, "made a deep impression on me." The President was "not confident" that his proposed note was "on the right track." An offer of mediation, at this time, however, he considered "futile. . . . We would lose such influence as we have for peace." Wilson ended his candid letter in a conciliatory spirit. "I am afraid, Mr. Secretary," he wrote, "that there is much in this that will seem to you to be disputable; but I can only state my conviction in the matter, and God knows I have searched my mind and conscience both to get the best, the nearest approach to wisdom, there is in them."

Quite possibly Wilson, with more time and moved by doubts and Bryan's pleading, might have accepted the Secretary's approach to the decision, which, in essence, was "do nothing." As it happened, the Thrasher case was lost from view and all but forgotten by a new disaster whose magnitude utterly dwarfed it.[39]

The sinking of the *Falaba* and other vessels did not deter British liners from plowing to their destinations through the war zone. Time and again, Bryan urged the President to stop the practice of American citizens who laughed at danger and booked passage. "There is no more reason," he wrote in one appeal, "why an American citizen should take the risk involved in going in one of these vessels than there is for taking the risks that are involved in going near the fighting on land." But Wilson insisted upon upholding the clear legal right of Americans to travel on belligerent vessels. German representatives in the United States shared Bryan's concern to the point that they took the unusual step of publishing an advertisement on May 1, 1915, warning Americans that they sailed on Allied vessels at their own risk.

Six days later, on May 7, the appalling tragedy so long feared and forewarned struck when the British liner *Lusitania* was sunk off the Irish coast by a single torpedo launched by a German submarine. Some 1,200 noncombatants perished, including 128 Americans. Bryan was at luncheon at the Shoreham Hotel with several Cabinet colleagues and the Presidential secretary Tumulty when word of the horrendous deed first reached him. He rushed to the department, declining to comment, as newsmen calling out questions trailed him to his car.

To Mary that evening, in the midst of uttering his remorse and apprehension, Bryan remarked, "I wonder if that ship carried munitions of war? . . . If she did carry them, it puts a different phase on the whole matter! England has been using our citizens to protect her ammunition!" The *Lusitania,* as it turned out, was carrying munitions, and several odd circumstances surrounded the disaster. The liner had no convoy or protection, and the captain ignored the Admiralty's instructions to proceed at full speed with a zigzag course on an irregular route upon entering the war zone. Instead, the captain exposed the liner on the regular track of shipping and even slowed down. On the other hand, under long-standing international practice, the presence of munitions on the *Lusitania* did not absolve the German submarine commander from the procedure of visit and search. As for the newspaper warning, arranged by the German embassy, it had no legal effect. The embassy lacked any authority to communicate with American citizens through newspaper advertisements. Bryan, however, was unconcerned with legal niceties. His object was to avoid war.

A few militants led by the irrepressible Theodore Roosevelt demanded that the nation go to war. But the dominant voices of governors, Senators, Congressmen, and other leaders, called for peace. Two powerful Democrats, Senator Thomas S. Martin and Congressman Hal D. Flood, both of Virginia, declared that the country did not want war and that the President, should he seek it, would find it impossible to obtain a war resolution from Congress. A voice that was conspicuously silent was the President's. His secretary said only that Wilson was considering the problem "very earnestly, but very calmly." The President became extraordinarily inaccessible; for days he saw no member of his Cabinet and passed the time in motoring and golfing. Bryan, too, maintained silence, allowing only that "This is no time to rock the boat." At last the President broke his silence in a speech at Philadelphia on May 10. Bryan and the country applauded his restraint, when he declared: "There is such a thing as a man being too proud to fight."

Although Wilson's words to the American public were calm and reassuring, his advisers were locked in struggle over the tenor and substance of a note to Germany. As usual, Lansing was the hard-liner and Bryan was the soft voice of pacifism. The Secretary forwarded to Wilson an editorial of the Washington *Post,* observing that ammunition was carried by the *Lusitania* and that Germany could rightfully prevent this contraband from reaching the Allies. To rely on passengers to protect it from attack, the *Post* added, would be "like putting women and children in front of the army." [40]

Drafting the note to Germany protesting the *Lusitania* tragedy was the work of the usual triumvirate of Wilson, Lansing, and Bryan. At first, Wilson moved toward the high ground of the *Falaba* note and then abandoned it. Wilson's eventual draft reviewed the submarine actions climaxed by the torpedoing of the *Lusitania* and, in effect, demanded that Germany abandon submarine warfare against unarmed merchantmen. Bryan labored to diminish the severity of the note, while Lansing wanted the United States to demand that Germany disavow the attack on the *Lusitania,* apologize, pay an indemnity, and guarantee the future safety of United States citizens. If Germany declined, Lansing urged that diplomatic relations be severed. As the drafting proceeded, Wilson veered more and more toward Lansing's position. The President turned down Bryan's recommendation that the administration issue a statement warning Americans against taking passage on vessels like the *Lusitania* as "weak yielding to threat and danger." Wilson momentarily accepted Bryan's proposal to issue a statement proposing arbitration of the *Lusitania* incident, but under pressure from other Cabinet Secretaries, the President recalled the statement after it had been cabled to Berlin. To the end, Bryan urged that the United States should not relinquish its "role of peacemaker." But the note which Wilson finally approved at this juncture asserted the "indispensable" right of United States citizens to sail the high seas and demanded repudiation of the act and reparations for the damage done. It was issued under signature of the Secretary of State, but Bryan wrote to Wilson, "Mr. President, I join in this document with a heavy heart." [41]

Bryan's efforts to preserve at least the semblance of a balance in American dealings with the two warring camps brought him into important relationships with the ambassadors of Germany and Austria in Washington. The German ambassador, Count Johann von Bernstorff, was regarded by Colonel House as the ablest in Washington, and Lansing termed him "a master of the art of diplomacy." Broad-shouldered and slender, with a military bearing, immaculate in dress, and with a blonde mustache turned up at its ends like the Kaiser's, Bernstorff was "adroit and able," Lansing noted, "in time of difficult negotiations." The mustache did not hide the ambassador's mouth, and his lips writhed when he talked or smiled, Lansing noted, "in a very unpleasant way." The ambassador's supreme aim was to maintain peace between the United States and Germany. His career appeared to depend on it, and he was given to stretching his instructions to diminish conflict. Bernstorff was ill regarded by the Berlin hard-liners led by Grand Admiral Alfred von Tirpitz, who meant to unseat him. His devotion to peace made his relationship with Bryan comfortable and cooperative.

With the Austrian ambassador, Dr. Konstantin Theodor Dumba, Bryan's dealings were less easy. Sixty years old, stoop-shouldered, partially bald with thinning straight gray hair, Dumba, too, had a mustache, a heavy, drooping gray affair which failed to hide his thick lips. Dumba was an artist in handling subjects obliquely, and he excelled at luring others into committing themselves to certain facts or views to strengthen his position before taking up his real subject. After several bad experiences, Lansing warned Bryan on the perils of candor with Dumba. But "the genial, trustful . . . Bryan," as Lansing termed him, fell victim to Dumba's convolutions in the *Lusitania* crisis. The ambassador construed something Bryan said to mean that Wilson's earlier note to Germany declaring that it would be held to "strict accountability" was meant for home consumption in the United States and was not to be taken seriously by Germany. Dumba relayed this intelligence to the German Foreign Office. When Bryan learned of the play, he quickly had Berlin apprized of the absolute earnestness of the American position and demanded and got a correction from Dumba. Bernstorff, too, reacted by sending a special agent to Berlin to emphasize that Wilson meant everything he said.[42]

The German reply to the American note on the *Lusitania* was strong in tone. The *Lusitania,* because of the munitions it carried and other circumstances, was not "an ordinary unarmed merchant vessel." Though deploring the loss of lives, the note held that destruction of the *Lusitania* was an act of "just self-defense."

When the German note arrived, Wilson and Bryan were caught up in Memorial Day observances. In Arlington National Cemetery, where Wilson spoke, a preceding orator drew spirited applause when he declared, "The President of the United States is making a successful effort to keep us out of the broils of Europe," and when Bishop Earl Cranston of Washington prayed that the United States "might be led aright in the present crisis," Wilson uttered an audible "Amen." During the extended program of speeches, the President was seen writing on the printed program, stirring speculation that he was at work on another note to Germany. In his own Memorial Day address, Bryan observed how for long months the people had been surfeited with accounts of war. "We are depressed and distressed," he said, "by the reports of battles, of skies reddened by the glare of guns and the soil crimsoned by the blood of men, of homes made desolate, and of hospitals filled to overflowing of babies born fatherless, while sires are burned like worthless stubble in the fields over which the grim reaper has passed." [43]

The President, faced with the task of responding to the German reply, wrote to Bryan, "Please give, for the guidance of my thought on this anxious matter, an outline of the answer you think we should make. . . ." Wilson acknowledged that he was requesting a similar opinion from Lansing, and to gloss over the embarrassment of treating equally Bryan's opinion and that of his official subordinate, he added, "I feel that I very much need all the counsel I can get, and I shall, of course, chiefly value yours."

Otherwise, Wilson remained in solitude, totally removed from his Cabinet Secretaries and advisers. He kept to his study, dined with his daughter, Margaret, and cousin Helen Woodrow Bones, and took a short motor trip in the evening. Bryan, too, was much alone. His chief visitor was Bernstorff, eager, as usual, to do everything possible to prevent a break in American-German relations. In Bryan he found a kindred sentiment. His tenure as Secretary could well become a mockery if his country slid into a war and contributed its prodigious efficiency to multiplying the slaughter.

Wilson, Lansing, and Bryan labored intently on the reply to Germany. Simultaneously, Bryan urged the President not to make "an immediate answer." All the time necessary for drafting a careful reply should be taken,

Bryan contended, and in the intense atmosphere blanketing both Germany and the United States, "time itself is a factor of no mean importance." He recalled that in "our peace plan we have emphasized the advantage of time for investigation and deliberation." After beholding a preliminary draft by Lansing, Bryan lamented to Wilson the counselor's approach to the note of taking the points raised by Germany and "treating them like a case in court" and drawing distinctions between "material and immaterial propositions." A broader perspective than sheer legal forensics was imperative for an issue which in the past has "given excuse for armed conflict." The notes previously exchanged on the *Lusitania* were "couched in terms of friendly language." Better to avoid contentious legal debate for the sake of an amicable settlement.

Bryan was hardly gladdened by Wilson's responses, which plainly were rebuffs. The President rejected Bryan's counsels of delay, holding that "time [though not, of course, haste] is of the essence in this matter in order that the German Government should be made to feel that we regard it as pressing. . . ." Nor did it cheer Bryan when Wilson noted that the German Foreign Office "always misses the essential point involved, that England's violation of neutral rights is different from Germany's violation of the rights of humanity."

On June 1, Wilson laid before a meeting of the Cabinet the draft of the reply to the German note. "Bryan was a few minutes late," David Houston wrote of the meeting. "He seemed to be labouring under a great strain and sat back in his chair most of the time with his eyes closed." After the President concluded his reading, a spirited discussion sprang up over his draft, and after some minutes, proceedings suddenly veered in a different direction when a Cabinet Secretary asked what the administration proposed to do concerning British interferences with our trade. This Secretary proposed that a vigorous note be sent to Britain, protesting the holding up of American exports, especially cotton. Several Secretaries quickly and strenuously objected. One deemed it reprehensible that material interests should be advanced when the grave *Lusitania* incident, involving human lives, was at stake.

Bryan now opened his eyes and, his jaw set and his voice rising, exclaimed that all along he had insisted on a note to England, for it was illegally preventing our exports from going where we had a right to send them. The Cabinet, he said, with emphasis, his eyes hard and flashing, was pro-Ally. The overwhelming opinion of the Cabinet objected to sending a note to England. Amid the cacophony of objections, the President "sharply rebuked Bryan, saying that his remarks were unfair and unjust. He had no right to say that any one was pro-Ally or pro-German. Each one was merely trying to be a good American." Wilson recalled that a protest had been lodged with England and another might be again "at the proper time. . . ."

With a grave controversy with the Germans before the Cabinet, the President remarked, "it would be folly" to force an issue now with the British. After several Cabinet members spoke on the point, Bryan asked, again with heat, "if we thought we ought to ask the British authorities what we might do." [44]

In notes and letters, Bryan persisted in pressing his views on Wilson. The Secretary stressed that the *Lusitania* episode must be submitted to investigation and arbitration. The thirty peace treaties committed the United States to those procedures. Since a peace treaty had been offered to Germany and accepted by her in principle, "we cannot consistently refuse to apply the document to all questions arising between us." In addition, Bryan pointed out that the United States' expressed concern thus far in the *Lusitania* dispute was "for the protection of our people." The United States had not dealt with submarine warfare in general when other vessels not bearing Americans have been sunk. Bryan deduced that the United States was "compelled by duty to do what we can to prevent our citizens incurring unnecessary risks." Let the United States, Bryan urged, henceforth prohibit the carrying of American citizens on passenger ships that also bear ammunition, a regulation, he felt, that would have a beneficial effect on both the American people and the German government.

A further Cabinet meeting in the President's study on June 4, according to Houston, resulted in "tiresome discussion." Although the meeting was brief, "It tried the President's patience greatly and tired him." Evidently the Cabinet seemed more divided than at its previous meeting, for the next day, June 5, the President telephoned Houston to ask what the Secretary of Agriculture considered to be "the settled sentiment of the cabinet. . . ." Houston quickly replied that the general judgment was that his note was admirable and needed only slight modification. Meanwhile, at the State Department, Lansing and Bryan, in notes and conversation, were engaged in polite debate over Wilson's draft. Lansing's manner was confident and assertive from his obvious position of standing closer to the President, in influence and attitude, than Bryan, who was now only technically his superior.[45]

Bryan was passing through the agony of the damned. Each Cabinet meeting was a consuming ordeal. Mary was becoming accustomed to greeting him afterward as he trudged into the house with bloodshot eyes and weary steps. His voice tired and heavy, he would cry, "Mary, what does the President mean! Why can't he see that by keeping open the way for mediation and arbitration, he has an opportunity to do the greatest work man can do! I cannot understand his attitude." As defeat for his position grew more certain, Bryan suffered increasingly from insomnia. He would lie awake for three or four hours in the night, turning and rising to jot down a sudden idea that tumbled across his mind for his next memorandum to the President. Mary, anxious and comforting in his trial, would induce him to take hot baths, to eat something light, and to resort to that imperishable standby, counting sheep.

When, at last, the President's completed draft was sent to the State Department early on Friday, June 4, Bryan told Mary he could not sign it. After the Cabinet meeting in the President's study that day, Bryan drew Wilson to one side and wearily told him that he was determined to resign. The President was overwhelmed with surprise. As Bryan moved through the devouring experience of that day, Mary was attending a small luncheon for the wife of the Russian ambassador. In midafternoon, as both were homeward bound, their cars drew up alongside each other on Massachusetts Avenue. From her car, Mary hailed Bryan. He joined her, told her of his conversation with the President, and said that he had just called on Secretary McAdoo to tell him of his decision to resign. Bryan had consulted no other Cabinet colleague, wishing not to implicate anyone else. He had turned to McAdoo because he was the President's son-in-law.

Upon reaching his home, the magnificent Georgian-style mansion, Calumet Place, which he had leased, Bryan lay down for the rest of the afternoon. He told Mary that he fully previsioned the consequences. It would mean abuse and misrepresentation, but, he stressed, "If I wait until this note goes out and a curt rejoinder is returned, it will then be too late. The President evidently feels he is voicing the sentiment of the country. I feel sure there are comparatively few Americans who want our country to be involved in this cataclysm. If I resign now, I believe it will be possible to bring the real sentiments of the people to the surface. The President may then feel at liberty to take steps which he now feels are unwise to take."

Though Bryan worked at the department on Saturday morning, Mary was resolved to get him out of town for Sunday. They journeyed to the comfortable rambling old home of their good friend Senator Blair Lee in Silver Spring, which they had often visited to escape the fierce heat of the capital. That Sunday, as they so often did, they picnicked beneath a spreading magnolia tree, and Lee, who had no inkling the resignation was pending, took Bryan for a long walk. That night the agitated Secretary, facing another sleepless siege, read and drowsed over a tattered book, printed in 1892, titled *A Wreath of Appreciation of Andrew Jackson*.

While Bryan sojourned in Silver Spring, Wilson summoned McAdoo and Houston to the White House. The President immediately disclosed Bryan's intention to resign. McAdoo recounted that he had told Bryan that the step would not be fair to the nation, the President, or himself. Wilson expressed apprehension that if Bryan resigned now, it would create the impression among the American people and in Germany that the administration wanted trouble and was bent on forcing the issue. Houston discounted these apprehensions, and the trio agreed that there would be no use or wisdom in trying to change Bryan's mind. Wilson remarked that on personal grounds he was genuinely sorry and spoke of his affection and admiration for Bryan.

Wilson apparently reconsidered the desirability of urging Bryan not to resign. After Bryan returned from Silver Spring, he dispatched McAdoo to inform the Secretary that the President preferred that he remain in the Cabinet. McAdoo earnestly warned Bryan that if he resigned, he would be heading into political oblivion. "I believe you are right," Bryan replied, "I think this will destroy me; but whether it does or not, I must do my duty according to my conscience, and if I am destroyed, it is, after all, merely the sacrifice that one must not hesitate to make to serve his God and his country."

In the wake of Bryan's persistent talk of resigning, Wilson restudied his draft of the *Lusitania* note. It was further delayed by what the press termed the President's "severe headache." By Sunday, June 6, Wilson had finished the draft and dispatched it to Lansing for final touches in the interests of legality and diplomatic usage. Lansing completed his chore on Monday, June 7.

In final form, the second *Lusitania* note took the high ground that Wilson selected earlier for the *Falaba*. He urged Germany to renew its allegiance to "the rights of humanity, which every Government honors itself in respecting." Wilson asked for assurances that Germany "will adopt the measures necessary to put into practice in respect to the safeguarding of American lives and American ships" the principle that the lives of noncombatants must not be jeopardized in the destruction of unresisting merchantmen. In addition, Germany must honor "the obligation to take sufficient precaution to ascertain whether the suspected merchantman is in fact of belligerent nationality, or is in fact carrying contraband of war under a neutral flag." The tenor of the note was moderate.

Early on Monday morning, McAdoo again came to Bryan's home, where the two Secretaries engaged in spirited, but inconclusive, conversation. Once more Bryan prepared an extended memorandum laying his views before Wilson. He observed that if Wilson sent the note in its present form, the situation would be healthier if the President announced a policy of refusing port clearances to belligerent vessels carrying American passengers and to American vessels carrying ammunition. These steps, Bryan argued, would diminish tensions, deflate the jingoists, and win popular approbation.

With McAdoo, Bryan went to the White House. For an hour, he argued passionately with Wilson that the note would surely lead to war. Wilson yielded no point to Bryan but strove to keep him from resigning. As the discussion proceeded, the Secretary of State became increasingly distraught. He tried to drink a glass of water but upset some of it as he raised it to his lips. With quivering voice he cried that his decision to resign was final. "Colonel House has been Secretary of State, not I, and I have never had your full confidence."

After the interview, Bryan returned by car to Calumet Place. As he entered his home, Mary and Grace were anxiously waiting in the reception hall. A glance at his face, which had a feverlike flush, prompted the women to rush forward to support him. They led him to a sofa. "We have come to a parting of the ways," he gasped. "The President does not seem to realize that a great part of America lies on the other side of the Allegheny Mountains. These people have a right to be considered. I would not be true to the trust that thousands of Americans have imposed in me if I joined any action that might lead to the loss of life and property when they are so greatly opposed to it. By resigning I will be free to assist them in their struggle against entering this heart-breaking conflict on either side." Within an hour, a member of the household was en route to the White House with Bryan's letter of resignation, dated the following day. Dinner that evening was a hollow procedure. Little was said or eaten. After it was done, Mary, whose thoughts dwelled upon a coming storm of abuse for her husband's action, went to her room, locked herself in, and gave herself to loud hysterical sobbing for the first and only time in her adult life.

The letter of resignation, written in Bryan's own hand, was couched with warm praise for the President. Bryan's words were true to his conviction that he must leave the administration in a spirit of Christian love. The letter bore no trace of resentment that his policy had been rejected, that he had suffered humiliations from Lansing, his subordinate, whose counsel was preferred, that Colonel House, a minor political figure, had more influence than he, that the President avoided and rebuffed his Secretary of State time and again. The resignation, as Bryan phrased it, was "to take effect when the note is sent unless you prefer an earlier hour." Wilson promptly accepted the resignation.

On Tuesday morning, June 8, the Cabinet had its regular meeting. After some discussion of the revised note to Germany, a messenger entered the room, and Wilson said to his assembled Secretaries, "Gentlemen, Mr. Bryan has resigned as Secretary of State to take effect when the German note is sent. He is on the telephone and wants to know whether it would be desirable or agreeable for him to attend the cabinet meeting. Would it be embarrassing? What do you think?" From the murmured response it appeared there would be no embarrassment, and it was entirely agreeable for Bryan to attend. In a few minutes he entered. All the Secretaries rose; the President made a gracious greeting. Places were resumed, and discussion continued. To Houston, Bryan appeared "exhausted" and "under great emotional strain." For most of the meeting he leaned back in his chair with his eyes closed.

When the meeting adjourned, Bryan invited his colleagues to luncheon at the University Club, and six of the Secretaries accepted. The conversation was pleasant and general, though Bryan seemed preoccupied. As the company broke up, he observed with his mountainous solemnity that this was their last meeting, that he valued their association and friendship, and that he had to take his chosen course. As always, he spoke admiringly of the President. "You are the most real Christian I know," Interior Secretary Franklin K. Lane remarked to Bryan. The departing Secretary of State continued to speak in soliloquy, almost as though he had forgotten his friends. "I must act according to my conscience," he said. "I go out into the dark. The President has the prestige and the power on his side." He stopped, emotion seizing him, and his listeners feared he would break into tears. But after a pause, he added, "I have many friends who would die for me." [46]

Bryan and Wilson parted in an atmosphere of genuine good will. On the day of Bryan's leave-taking from the State Department, he declared feelingly that his affection for Wilson remained unchanged and he knew that the President felt as warmly toward him. Bryan shunned the press, and he kept his resignation locked in secrecy until the last possible moment. To his old friend Senator Henry Ashurst of Arizona, whom he saw minutes before the announcement, he gave no hint of what was in store. When finally the note to Germany was sent, Wilson wrote to Bryan, "I need not tell you again how sincerely I deplore what is to accompany its dispatch." On that final day, Bryan went to the White House for a warm farewell to the President, and reporters heard them say to each other as they broke away, "God bless you."

The news of Bryan's resignation brought an eruption of editorials and politicians' statements, but fortunately, they were lacking in the vituperation that Mary had anticipated. Those knowledgeable of Washington currents had for sometime expected the step but were curiously surprised when it was taken. Governor Richard I. Manning of South Carolina said that he regretted the resignation "for party reasons," and Governor E. F. Dunne of Illinois was certain that both Bryan and Wilson had been actuated "by the highest of motives."

In the White House and the State Department, in the aftermath, puzzlement reigned. To his friend Cleveland Dodge, Wilson wrote of the resignation, that "I must admit a certain degree of amazement at his present action, but I suppose it was inevitable that it should come." At the State Department, Chandler Anderson's puzzlement was based on his belief that the second *Lusitania* note, compared with the first, which Bryan signed, "goes no further and in some ways is less rigid." Anderson suspected that this circumstance would lead to accusations that Bryan's resignation was influenced by political motives. Yet, he discovered, from one closest to the

Bryan-Wilson scene, Robert Lansing, that "Lansing is convinced of his absolute sincerity and loyalty to the President and that he did not resign for political reasons." In Bryan's homeland of Nebraska, an editorial writer confidently described the key to understanding Bryan's action. "William J. Bryan never does things by halves. When he fights he fights like a berserker, and what commoner men consider as audacities become to him the very commonplaces of warfare. . . . When he wars for a principle he dares to put his fortune to the touch. . . ." [47]

As the Nebraska editor implied, Bryan's whole being was deeply involved in his political and moral causes. Upon them his attitudes and values were concentrated with utmost intensity. "Silver," "imperialism," "popular rule," "peace" evoked his unstinting commitment to demanding rounds or speechmaking, to suffering merciless counterattacks from his foes, to grinding tasks of political management, and to risk of rejection at the polls or to his countrymen's ridicule of his resignation. Over years and decades, Bryan was seldom distracted, even for a day, from his causes. From his father, his teachers, and his readings, Bryan derived a body of attitudes that were remarkably integrated and consistent, and these were absorbed into his being and held with relentless tenacity throughout his public life.

Bryan's most important attitudes were social. The way Bryan viewed particular persons, groups, and institutions shaped and directed the enormous energy and skill he devoted to politics. One can evoke whole chapters of his political life and struggles by the mere mention of "war," "railroads," "banks," "trusts," "city bosses," or institutions which oppressed and corrupted the common man, to whose well-being he was devoted. Bryan never lived a day when he did not detect situations and trends inimical to the common man. Even when the generality of his fellow citizens was lulled by prosperity and peace, Bryan was pointing to immorality and injustice and rallying his audiences to the banner of reform.

Bryan's deep commitment to his social values affected his perceptions, discrimination, and judgment. He saw the war only as sanctioned mass murder and not as a struggle between autocracy and democracy. He could discern in the trust only evil and not the possibility or actuality of merit: of economies in operation, of higher quality management, of superior resources for research, product improvement, and the like. Or, in a larger perspective, although he highlighted the deprivation and deceit rampant in the economy, he did not in his strictures acknowledge general rises in production and in the standard of living, conditions that weakened his cause.

Bryan was endowed with a combination of attitudes that spurred him to deal creatively with society. He cherished moral values and precepts to which men gave lip service in the church but which they and their institutions betrayed in the workaday world. Bryan toiled to alter what society would accept as "good," "right," or "desirable" and to substitute the higher moral standards preached from his platform. As a political evangelist Bryan was expressing himself in creative actions that simultaneously brought change in the political and social environment and contributed to the actualization of himself. He developed to fine precision the oratorical skills so fondly nurtured in home and college. He fulfilled the ideals absorbed from his father, and reinforced in his education and experience, to consecrate himself to the life of service, to improve through a career in politics the lot of his fellowmen.

With ample cause, Bryan was moving through his political career supremely satisfied with himself. He was never deterred by criticism, struck by doubt, or bowed—even a cubit—by defeat. He was favored with a self-regard that was strong, if not overpowering. Like any other human being, Bryan had continuously to engage in activity significant to himself to maintain his self-regard. But Bryan, to his good fortune, was never lacking in opportunities. The society he knew was never free of flaws and suffering, and Bryan, thanks to his formidable political skills, enjoyed ready access to his party, the electoral processes, and the public to promote his ideals and reforms.[48]

26. War and Peace

By his resignation, Bryan chose a complex path by which he hoped to promote his ideals without coming into opposition to the President. That Bryan could bring off this kind of feat was by no means confidently expected in the political community. "Bryan is mistaken," observed David Houston, "if he thinks he can promote his program on the outside and not be drawn into opposition to the President. . . . He is already in opposition." The Alabama editor and Princeton classmate of the President Frank P. Glass warned Wilson "to be on your guard. He [Bryan] is liable to give you trouble in the future. He is very emotional, and his vanity will lead him into courses he does not foresee." [1]

Bryan's chief activity in his first days as a private citizen was to lay his case before the people. Minutes after the controversial note was dispatched to Germany, he characterized it as conforming to the "old system" of firmness based on potential force. He styled himself a champion of a new system of "persuasion," instead of force, and "an humble follower of the Prince of Peace." The next day in another statement, addressed to "German-Americans," he urged those citizens to exert their influence to impress the German government that the President wanted peace. He feared that Germany might break off diplomatic relations with the United States, and he hoped that the German government, aware of the President's devotion to peace, would acquiesce to his note's demands. "The more generously she acts in the matter," he told the German-Americans, "the greater will be the glory which she will derive from it." Bryan continued to insist that the United States submit the *Lusitania* dispute to the processes of his peace treaty.

Bryan's behavior unsettled his friends, as well as his enemies. His longtime ally and ideological confrere Louis Post wrote that after studying the note to Germany and Bryan's statement, he feared that "the country will not understand why you resigned." The "average man," he felt, would see in Wilson's note only "a friendly request for assurances" which will not impress him as "inconsistent with your plea for persuasion instead of force." Bryan's critics passed severer judgment on his current deportment. The New York *World* lamented that he had "publicly betrayed" Wilson. The Atlanta *Constitution* termed Bryan "a public nuisance" and promised that "no more of his statements will be printed." In the Louisville *Courier-Journal* Henry Watterson abandoned his approval of Bryan rendered in the 1908 campaign and resumed his former role of critic. Watterson was distressed that Bryan's present conduct proved once again that he was "unfeeling and disloyal by nature, inordinately selfish, avaricious, egotistical, without any sense of the true relations of life and duty, or decent regard for the fitness of things. . . ."[2]

Undaunted, Bryan continued his struggle for peace. Wilson he gave a prod and a hint by declaring that "in all history no other peacemaker has ever been in a position to claim so rich a blessing as that which will be pronounced on our President when the time for mediation comes—as come it must." Bryan struck at the growing agitation for military preparedness by declaring that it provokes war, as the conflagration in Europe all too sadly demonstrated.

From statements to the press Bryan moved to gigantic public rallies. At New York's Carnegie Hall under the auspices of the Central Federated Union of New York, he drew a standing-room-only audience, generously sprinkled with labor leaders from across the country. To the wildly cheering crowd, Bryan delivered two speeches. Fearful of that old bugaboo—inaccurate, prejudicial reporting—Bryan donned glasses and read the first of them from a prepared text. Twice drafts of wind sweeping through the hall snatched from his hand the sheets he was reading, but he jumped nimbly forward and caught them each time. His second speech, done in his customary pseudo-extemporaneous style, rallied the crowd. Bryan argued: "It is necessary for those who love peace to advocate it, so that the jingoes will not seem to represent the sentiment of the country." For America's differences with Germany, he again urged the investigative processes of his peace treaties. "How about Mexico?" a heckler cried. "We have spent two years and three months investigating that, and we are still investigating it," Bryan replied. "And when we have spent over two years investigating the question with Mexico, why should we not spend at least one year investigating questions that arise between us and powers of Europe?" Bryan led another huge peace meeting at Madison Square Garden.[3]

With his case before the public, Bryan and Mary journeyed home to Nebraska. At Omaha their train paused twenty minutes for a changeover, for years an interval when politicians would crush about Bryan eager to hear his word. This time he did not leave his car, and no one came to see him.[4]

Lincoln was different. It rendered the vast tumultuous turnout that always marked the Bryans' major homecomings. Brother Charles, now the city's mayor, bade them official welcome. Governor John H. Morehead presided over ceremonies on the south balcony of the Lindell Hotel, witnessed by 5,000 below. Bryan, speaking on "The Farmer's Interest in Peace," cast barbs at his old scourge, the Eastern press, congratulated his listeners on living thirty-six hours from New York, and hailed the Alleghenies as a dike that saved the rest of the country from a flooding of New York's "prejudice, venom, insolence, and ignorance. . . ." In office, he had been "hand-tied and tongue-tied," but now he was free. "I have a larger work outside the cabinet," he cried, "than I ever had within it."

Eventually they reached Fairview, and the sight of their beloved home, wrote Mary, "made me sick at heart." Untenanted during their absence, Fairview bristled with signs of neglect—weeds and spent growth ruled the flower beds; vines reached far beyond their allotted place. During these first hours back, Mary and Bryan reached a decision toward which they had been building. Henceforth they would pass summers at their Asheville home and winter in Miami. Only politically would Fairview be their home, for, Bryan explained to the press, "I shall do my voting there." [5]

He tarried only briefly and then was off and away on a full schedule of speeches through the West on "The Causeless War." It was a grueling summer of suffocating railroad coaches, small hotels, vast shouting crowds, rain and wind, wild auto rides across roads either dusty or muddy, and the grinding work of two speeches a day. "Mama," Bryan said one night to Mary, who accompanied him, "maybe it is a good thing I make my living this way. I believe I do good and it needs the spur of necessity to keep me at it." [6]

If anything, Bryan was more sweeping than ever in condemning war. It was the evil derivative of the doctrine that "might makes right." It created the "mockery that men who worship God shall kill each other." It fed upon revenge and sacrifice. Driven by the death of a hundred Americans in ship sinkings, the nation was asked to avenge them by going to war and sacrificing "a million more killed before we get out of it. . . ." In his perspectives on the war, Bryan did not view the nation's interests to be at stake in the victory of one side over the other. Nor did he see the war as a contest between good and evil, between democracy and autocracy. "They are fighting over questions which do not affect our welfare or destiny. . . . An American must have more interest in one of the belligerents than he has in the United States if he desires to see us dragged into the contest as the ally or the opponent of either side."

To keep America at peace, Bryan offered specific prescriptions. Let Americans stay out of the war zone and off vessels carrying contraband. Bryan was by no means alone in his opinion. The distinguished Catholic prelate Cardinal Gibbons declared: "It seems like asking too much to expect the country to stand up and fight just because a few are over-daring." Further sinkings and loss of American lives lent urgency to these opinions. Bryan's preachings were soon reflected in the McLemore Resolution before the House of Representatives, barring American travel on belligerent ships through the war zone. In *Commoner* editorials and in correspondence with the influential Claude Kitchin of North Carolina and other friends in the House, Bryan backed the resolution's passage, arguing that since Congress, constitutionally, declares war, it has the right to determine what shall and shall not be the cause of war. At one point the House was on the brink of adopting the McLemore resolution by a two-to-one vote, but Wilson reacted strongly, holding that he could not consent to abridgment of American rights, and the resolution was sidetracked.[7]

Bryan and Wilson clashed head on over the issue of preparedness. Although the American Navy was strong, the Army, with some 100,000 regulars, was extraordinarily weak, ranking fifteenth among the armies of the world. As the European war raged, such military-minded leaders as Theodore Roosevelt and General Leonard Wood demanded rearming and founded numerous summer training camps like the one at Plattsburg, New York, where trainees, facing shortages of equipment, drilled with broomsticks. Isolationists, pacifists, and pro-Germans inveighed against these ventures, and the anti-preparedness mood inspired the popular song "I Didn't Raise My Boy to Be a Soldier." At the outset, Wilson, who also had strong pacifist leanings, bridled at preparedness and tended toward Bryan, who said: "To arm the nation to the teeth in preparation for wars that should never come, and expect such a course to preserve peace, is as absurd as it would be to give a dose of poison to a friend and expect it to preserve his life." To Bryan, "The real inspiration" for war was "the greed of the preparers of preparedness and the manufacturers of munitions." Preparedness in the hands of men like Roosevelt, Bryan argued, cultivated hatred against nations and contributed to the prevalence of "the duelist standard," which was that a man "had no right to think of his wife, his children or his country, but only that he must kill somebody or be killed to avenge what he regarded as an insult." [8]

But as the sinkings of passenger ships by the German U-boats continued, Wilson was converted. In December, 1915, the President bade Congress enact an elaborate program of national defense. In the East, monster parades, including one led down Pennsylvania Avenue by a flag-holding Wilson, backed the President's demands. In the West and South, Bryan's political heartland, the preparedness sentiment was only lukewarm. The President's turnabout left Bryan's Congressional friend Claude Kitchin of North Carolina "sorely disappointed," and it "has worried me more than anything in my political life." Bryan instantly resolved to place himself at the head of the opposition, while acknowledging that prospects for his success were bleak. "I have seen members of the House," he wrote to Kitchin, "throw away their convictions so often to please him that I can conjure up no reason to hope that his program can be defeated, though I shall try my best."

Against overwhelming odds, Bryan marched into battle. At his Washington home, which he still retained, he wielded his most powerful weapon— publicity. In a statement to the press, he deplored the President's preparedness plans as "a departure from our traditions," a "menace to the spirit of Christianity, which teaches us to influence others by example rather than by exciting fear." On Capitol Hill, Bryan toiled tirelessly, but Bryan versus Wilson was a grossly one-sided contest. By the summer of 1916 Congress had enacted the several parts of the President's preparedness program.[9]

Bryan's strategy was not entirely defensive. Early in December, 1915, Bryan called on the President to request from the belligerent powers a statement of the terms on which they were willing to make peace. Simultaneously, Bryan urged that Congress assure the President of its support should he undertake mediation. Bryan's new-sown seed fell on fertile ground. Inside the administration, Robert Lansing was impressed that Wilson aspired to the role of mediator and "to stand forth as the great neutral peacemaker." Restive toward Wilson's ambition, Lansing feared it might deflect the President from "the true policy which is 'Join the Allies as soon as possible and crush the German autocrats.'" The President's confidant, Colonel E. M. House, was persisting with exploratory talks at home and abroad to clear the way for Wilsonian mediation. But House, also intensely pro-Ally, laid plans to manipulate the mediation to the disadvantage of the Central Powers.

Both publicly and behind the scenes Bryan pressed the belligerents to state their war aims, which presumably could become the basis of a peace settlement. Employing contacts made while Secretary of State and asserting himself in his own right as a world figure, Bryan through 1916 lighted fires around Wilson to bring him to offer mediation. From Bernstorff, Bryan won assurances that the Central Powers' peace terms "will be reasonable." To the British Prime Minister, David Lloyd George, Bryan dispatched an appeal, urging British consent to negotiations and stressing that "Every guarantee that can possibly be secured by war can be stated as a condition precedent to peace."

Like a great winter thaw, the belligerents spoke under the sun of House's and Bryan's and other men's efforts. Both sides either expressed willingness to negotiate or outlined their aims. Wilson promptly offered to assist in developing statements of terms and to make soundings to learn "how near the haven of peace may be. . . ." An exultant Bryan hailed the President publicly for his "invaluable service" in opening the way to negotiations, "and when negotiations begin they are not likely to terminate until an agreement is reached. . . ." Unfortunately, nothing came of the negotiations, for neither side, at this moment, really wanted peace. Germany flourished on the battlefield, and the Allies were confident of ultimate success.[10]

As 1915, with its unrelieved bloodbath, drew to a close, many foreign newspapers of the United States urged Bryan to visit Europe in the interest of peace, as did former Congressman Richard Bartholdt of St. Louis and Shailer Mathews, president of the Federal Council of the Churches of Christ in America. Bryan, who was warming to the idea, made discreet soundings of Wilson's attitudes. Doubtless because they were not encouraging, he dropped the idea.

Late in 1915, Bryan was confronted with a concrete opportunity to journey abroad in the quest for peace. Henry Ford, seized with the inspiration of organizing a peace ship, busied himself with inviting a galaxy of peace-minded personalities to share in the venture. In addition to Bryan, former Congressman Bartholdt, John Wanamaker, the merchant of Philadelphia, State Senator Helen Robinson of Colorado, Judge Ben Lindsey of Denver, and Cardinal Gibbons of Baltimore were among those approached to sail on the *Oscar II*, chartered from the Scandinavian-American Line. Expressing hearty sympathy for Ford's plan and his confidence that it would "accomplish much good," Bryan decided he had better stay home, where he could render "A greater service" fighting the President's preparedness program.

When the Ford peace ship readied to set sail from New York, Bryan boarded the vessel with Ford. In the salon, two peace-minded passengers were married, and the two eminences affixed their signatures to the certificate of ceremony as witnesses. Bryan then left the ship and stood in the crowd to await the commencement of the pilgrimage he likened to the

voyage of Noah's Ark. Close by Bryan stood Ford's old friend Thomas
Alva Edison. As the *Oscar II* pulled away from the dock, the crowd
cheered, and Bryan did not leave the pier until the liner was lost from view.
It passed into an unhappy future. Dissension soon hobbled the pacifists,
and before many weeks, Ford himself returned home.[11]

War and peace were not Bryan's only preoccupations. Increasingly he
took up the cause of prohibition. The fast-building progress of drys in states
and local communities, the sturdy efficiency of the Anti-Saloon League, and
the passage of the federal Webb-Kenyon Act of 1913 barring shipment of
liquor from a wet to a dry state were transforming prohibition into a formidable national movement. Marching into states where prohibition was
weighed for adoption, Bryan joined the fight to win converts to the cause.
With the great evangelist Billy Sunday, he ranked as prohibition's foremost
orator. Sometimes Bryan and Sunday worked together, a contrast in evangelical styles. Sunday raced, jumped, and threw himself about the platform,
stamping until nails gave way and boards bulged up, wrestling with the
devil, whacking the pulpit until a water glass sitting on it bounced to the
floor. Bryan, in contrast, stood solid, almost immovable, on a single spot on
the platform, his right arm behind his back, half hidden in the folds of his
coattails. Only at intervals would he cut the atmosphere with a tightly
clenched fist, shake the forefinger of his right hand at the heads of his audience, or stretch out both arms and slowly raise them.

Bryan was the star attraction of the largest prohibition rally of 1915,
when thousands crushed into a Philadelphia tabernacle. As the crowd
moved to their seats, a choir sang "Brighten the Corner Where You Are."
When Bryan and Mary appeared with an honor escort, a cacophony of
songs, honking auto horns, shrill coronets, and drumbeats turned the hall
into bedlam. Cheerleaders of nearby colleges gave their college yells, and
high school boys sang a song, ending with "William, William Jennings
Bryan, we'll all drink grape juice yet," as Bryan smiled. Eventually he delivered a stirring attack upon drink and called his listeners to the colors raised
by the National Abstainers Union for "Health and Home and Humanity!"

Reaching his peroration, Bryan turned to a table beside him and from it
raised a glass of water high above his head. "Rise," he cried to his audience.
"Let us pledge our support to the cause in water." In organ tones, he rendered a laudation of water: "It ascends from the seas, obedient to the summons of the sun, and descending, showers blessings upon the earth. It gives
beauty to the fragrant flowers; its alchemy transmutes base clay into golden
grain; it is the canvas upon which the finger of the infinite traces the radiant
rainbow of promise. It is the drink that refreshes and adds no sorrow with
it. Jehovah looked upon it at creation's dawn and said: 'It is good.' "

Four thousand came down the aisles with pledge cards, while Bryan, kneeling on the platform, helped by assistants, accepted them. When Bryan announced he would autograph any cards, hundreds moved upon him, and for an hour he signed his name, while a choir intoned "If Your Heart Keeps Right." Hailing the mounting progress of prohibition in the South and West, Bryan refrained from making it a national issue, lest it divert attention from economic policies in the awaiting elections of 1916.[12]

Bryan was also espousing woman's suffrage. He fought for it when it was submitted to Nebraska voters in 1914, declaring, "I shall claim no privileges for myself that I do not ask for my wife." In 1915 he campaigned in New Jersey, New York, and Pennsylvania, advancing the simple, Bryanesque argument that since "man trusts woman everywhere else; why not at the polls?" If men learn most of what they know about government from women schoolteachers, "does it not create a presumption for woman suffrage?" Bryan welcomed women's stress on ethical questions, their social compassion, and, above all, their presence as the supreme force for peace.[13]

In other particulars the contours of Bryan's life were changing. In the new year of 1916 he and Mary gave up their Washington residence and moved to their palatial Spanish-style mansion, Villa Serena, in Miami, Florida.

It was a different world from the wheat- and corn-swept Nebraska prairies. The Bryans had been introduced to it in 1909, when, preparatory to their trip through Latin America, they stayed at the home of Bryan's cousin W. S. Jennings. Mary was so charmed by the warmth and beauty of the Miami region that she wanted to buy the acreage adjoining "Cousin Sherman's." Bryan fulfilled her wish and in the fall of 1912 began building Villa Serena. In its first years, it served as their winter home. Blooming bougainvillaea vines met in a full scarlet covered arch over an entrance reached by a gracefully curving drive through woodland. There were palms of every variety—traveler's palm, date palm, screw palm, fish-tail palm, and, towering majestically above all else, a royal palm. Strong-hued flowers vied for the eye's attention—flaming poinsettias reaching from windowsills of the second story; coleus in huge tubs on the edge of the wood; and scattered plantings of nasturtiums, roses, sweet alyssums, geraniums, foxgloves, and petunias.

In the winter of 1916, when he was not summoned to Washington by crisis or venturing onto the lecture trail, Bryan passed stretches of time at Villa Serena. There he and Mary, after the turmoil of decades, discovered a sudden tranquillity. Bryan indulged in one of his favorite activities, felling excessive trees, pruning and cutting off dead limbs, and splitting wood. During respites indoors, they read aloud from *The Life of John Bright,* which they had begun more than a year before at Asheville, and when that was finished, they began Ruskin's *Ethics of the Dust.* Each day they commenced by reading a few pages, followed by Bible verses and prayers. Then there was the mail, always heavy, and the telegrams, which, during some venture like the Ford peace party, were considerable. Telegrams for that project in the month of January, Mary was horrified to discover, totaled $103.97.

Although the manorial Villa Serena was well removed from the highways, the Bryans did not live in isolation. Their fame brought a heavy stream of acquaintances and curiosity seekers. Lest the constant influx rob them of all time for themselves, Bryan and Mary soon decided to hold open house on Fridays, with tea, cakes, sandwiches, and fruit punch in a huge bowl that once belonged to Thomas Jefferson. Four or five ladies helped Mary and her skillful butler, Jefferson. Bryan, attired in his customary alpaca coat, stationed himself on the lawn to greet the influx of anywhere from 300 to 500 visitors.

Each Sunday when he was at home, he conducted a Bible class in the local Presbyterian church. Originally, Bryan had taken on the class as a substitute teacher, but its snowballing popularity made him its prisoner. The first session began in a church classroom, but it quickly burgeoned to fill the church auditorium and then moved to a nearby ball park, where the grandstand filled to overflowing. As he did as a Sunday school teacher in Normal, Bryan selected several Bible verses, embroidered interpretations upon them, and wove in extended discourses on his current political preoccupations—peace and prohibition. Understandably, Bryan's class was sometimes called the Tourist Class, since it was a haven for visiting ministers, for traveling pillars of Northern churches, and mere visitors whose religion was less intense than their curiosity.[14]

Although Bryan's home was now in Florida, his political lifeline still lay in Nebraska. Despite his absence, his organization possessed such vigor that brother Charles had been elected mayor of Lincoln on a progressive platform. In state politics the Bryans were solidifying their positions by prominently and securely identifying themselves with the fastest-rising political issue of the moment, prohibition. While Bryan, in speeches and pronouncements, was building a national image as the leading public figure devoted to the cause of temperance, Charles was developing a similar role in Nebraska.

But the real test of Bryan's strength arose in the state election of 1916. In the spring primaries, Charles announced his candidacy for governor, a step that brought an affectionate endorsement from Bryan. I. J. Dunn, who had nominated Bryan for the Presidency, declared he would seek the Democratic nomination for the United States Senate. For lesser state offices, good Bryan men offered themselves. As for Bryan, he announced his candidacy for delegate at large for the awaiting Democratic national convention, heading a full slate of delegates known for their devotion to him.

Spring in Nebraska in 1916 saw a bitter, no-holds-barred struggle be-

tween Bryan and Hitchcock for primacy in the state party. By solidly identifying himself and his organization with prohibition, Bryan drew a sharp
line, for Hitchcock was equally identified with the wet way of life. While
Hitchcock portrayed Bryan as a foe of prohibition for most of his political
life and a late, opportunistic convert to the cause, Bryan depicted the Senator as a tool of the liquor interests. His split with Hitchcock, Bryan declaimed to the crowds, "came four years ago when I refused to bow to the
beer keg element." Despite their respective dubious records, Bryan and
Hitchcock jockeyed to show themselves as the loyal friend of the President.
Bryan reminded Nebraskans that Hitchcock had opposed Wilson in 1912,
and in the interval since then, his voting record in Congress demonstrated
that he was "a traitor to Nebraska," who had tried, and failed, to deliver the
state and the nation "into the hands of Wall Street." [15]

Bryan was concerned that Wilson might intervene in the race in
Hitchcock's favor. To Secretary of the Navy Josephus Daniels, who functioned as something of an intermediary for Bryan in Washington, he wrote
of his hope that "the President will not give Hitchcock any letter of endorsement." Wilson not only refrained from that step, but indulged in an
act partial to Bryan. It was an act little perceived by the general voter, but it
was highly intelligible to Nebraska's professional politicians and the army
of party workers. At the peak of the race, Wilson made an award of patronage, appointing Ross G. Moore, a devoted Bryan man, as head of the Broken Bow land office.

Bryan campaigned in forty-four counties, making two and three speeches
a day. The campaign against him was conducted with a venom unknown in
previous struggles. He was weakest in Omaha and Lincoln, where the liquor
interests were strongest, and his best prospects lay in the countryside, where
old-guard Bryanites still flourished. Lest his prohibition plank alienate
heavy numbers of beer- and schnaps-loving German voters, Bryan stressed
his hostility to the administration's preparedness program. To vote for
Bryan and his ticket provided the German-Americans of Nebraska their
best opportunity to register displeasure with Wilson and his policies.

On primary day the heavy city vote of Omaha and Lincoln overpowered
Bryan. With four delegates at large to be elected, he placed fifth, trailing
3,300 votes behind the fourth elected delegate. Brother Charley was even
more decisively defeated by Keith Neville, the wet candidate for the Democratic gubernatorial nomination. The defeat, needless to say, was a nasty
smirch on Bryan's prestige and place in Nebraska politics. It proclaimed to
the state's political world that Bryan was slipping, and veteran politicos
began to ponder how fast this trend might become.[16]

From political desolation in Nebraska, Bryan looked hopefully to the national party conventions in the Presidential election year of 1916. For Bryan

the mission that must not fail was the renewal of the Democratic tenancy of the White House. For all of Wilson's strength and seemingly inevitable renomination, there were flare-ups of speculation over a possible Bryan candidacy. Following his resignation, talk was so rife of his presumed ambitions for the Presidential office that Bryan issued a statement: "I have no political expectations whatever and no plans looking to the holding of any office in the future." In the springtime of 1916, when Presidential primaries stirred in many states, Bryan found it necessary to checkmate moves to put his name on the ballot. "No," he telegraphed to an ardent California disciple, "I will not consent to any delegates being instructed for me in California or anywhere else."

Defeated as a delegate, Bryan attended the national conventions in 1916 in his other accustomed capacity of working journalist. He covered the Republican and Progressive conventions in Chicago and the Democratic convention in St. Louis. He witnessed the Republican nomination of the cold, bewhiskered, intellectual Charles Evans Hughes, who simultaneously appealed to progressives and placated his party's conservatives. But to Bryan and Mary, who was at his side, the most interesting spectacle in a convention that was enveloped in rain from beginning to end was a parade of suffragettes viewed from their hotel window. Against merciless rain, women marched for the ballot, with the wind blowing so hard that three or four women clutched a single banner against the gusty torrent.

By every forecast, the Democratic convention would be tame. Woodrow Wilson would dominate it, and for the first time in two decades, Bryan, as many a paper noted with relief, could not "make trouble." Neither a delegate nor an alternate, he could get on the floor only by proxy and speak only by tolerance. Journalist Bryan came to St. Louis with modest ambitions. "I have no plan except to report this convention," he announced, in an impromptu reception in his hotel lobby, and pushed his way to his room through crowds of handshakers.

Yet it was Bryan who provided the convention's first excitement simply by taking his place among the press. The convention rose and cheered with evident enthusiasm and warm personal feeling. The ovation seemed to chase from Bryan's face the anxious, careworn look that had stolen over it in his labors for peace. "The convention," observed a hostile paper, "took Bryan from the scrapheap and raised him to the riding pole." [17]

There were other signs that Bryan was to be more than a mere reporter. His rooms were flooded with callers, whose visits were devoted to more than fraternity and reminiscence; they dealt with the delegates' business. As it happened, the convention's two most important officers were old Bryan friends. The temporary chairman and, therefore, the deliverer of the keynote address, Martin Glynn, talked over his pending speech with Bryan and wrote Mary afterward, "we thought it a most satisfactory speech." Ollie

James, the permanent chairman, came to "discuss matters," and delegates poured in to express assurances of loyalty. Yet for all this display, Bryan made no visible move or gesture to influence the convention. His restraint applied even to his favorite battleground, the Platform Committee. "I called on William J. Bryan today," reported a committee member, Samuel A. King of Utah, "and asked if he would submit any planks. He replied: 'I have no planks to offer but one, and that is the President's. Determine what he wants and his plank will be mine. I expect to go before the people in his behalf on your report.' "

It was, of course, Wilson's convention to manage, inspire and direct. Its most vital decisions were his decisions. His renomination was assured, and the platform was his to write. But a convention is more than decisions and resolutions. It creates and reflects moods which may balance or even overshadow its formal acts. In St. Louis there emerged a mood which Bryan, more than anyone else, helped fashion. In that enterprise, he enjoyed certain advantages over the President. Wilson possessed the power and resource of his office, but Bryan was present in St. Louis, and Wilson was not.

It began with the keynote address of Martin Glynn, a laudation of Wilson, although from the special perspective of his success in keeping the country out of war. Glynn's choice of theme evidently was wholly unexpected by Wilson's managers, and the delegates' response surprised even Glynn. The passages of his address evoking his audience's most intense reception were intrinsically dull, but he had retained them, planning to rush over them in his reading. These consisted of several paragraphs in which Glynn recalled provocative incidents from history to which the United States did not respond with war. Included in his enumeration were a British violation of American neutrality in the Pierce administration; a Canadian attack in the Van Buren administration killing several crewmen of an American vessel and sending her adrift over Niagara Falls; and the most memorable provocation, the British *Leopard* firing on the American *Chesapeake.* This last was cited in the schoolbook histories of the day as a supremely despicable example of weakness and cowardice, but in Glynn's hands each illustration gloriously depicted the nation's capacity for restraint and love of peace.

A deft and powerful orator, Glynn cast a spell over the crowd from which Bryan himself did not escape. Seated in the press stand, he was seen to weep with emotion as Glynn depicted the victories of peace. The mood was suddenly jostled when a Texas delegate, leaping onto his chair, yelled, "And don't forget that policy also is satisfactory to William Jennings Bryan." The crowd laughed, and Bryan with them.

Each instance that Glynn cited was received with rapturous cheers, and a pattern of response quickly developed. As Glynn finished his statement of a provocation, delegates from all over the hall yelled, "What did we do?" and the question was taken up in an exultant chant, "What did we do? What did we do?" Glynn answered: "We didn't go to war." A joyful roar greeted this response; men jumped upon their seats, danced about the aisles, waved flags, shouted, and screamed. With puzzlement creasing his face, Glynn read from his text, "American ambassadors who sought to adjust these wrongs were refused recognition and openly insulted at the French court." "What did we do?" came the yell again, and the chant swept around the hall, "What did we do? What did we do?" Glynn answered, "We did not go to war," and again American flags waved and the delegates shouted deliriously. "It was probably the first time in the history of conventions," an observer noted, "that one of them ever became frantic with joy over a mere recital of diplomatic precedents." When Glynn praised or mentioned Wilson, he got only perfunctory applause.[18]

In the ordinary etiquette of conventions, Bryan, as an historic, prestigious party figure, would be called on to speak. Spurred by the unexpected and unwanted peace emphasis of Glynn's address, the Wilson managers permitted no provision in the convention's order of business for a Bryan address. But the managers could not forestall the delegates from demanding it. Each time the former Secretary of State entered the press stand, cries swept the convention for "Bryan! Bryan!" Hard upon these demands one evening a resolution was offered from the floor and carried with a great shout to suspend the rules and hear Bryan. A committee headed by Senator John Kern of Indiana escorted the party's three-time nominee to the speaker's place as the floor and galleries roared approval.

Introduced as "one of the leading citizens of the world and America's greatest Democrat," Bryan, standing a solid figure of rectitude, satisfaction gleaming in his eye, raised hackles of fear in good Wilson men. But consternation evaporated when Bryan immediately proclaimed an unlimited admiration for the President and the absolute necessity of the Democracy's continuation in power. Bryan acknowledged he had differences with the President, but raising his voice, he uttered a sentence that triggered a mighty shout: "I join the people in thanking God that we have a President who does not want the nation to fight." As Bryan proceeded, murmurs ran through the delegates that this was surely Bryan's greatest speech, a magnificent selfless act, devoid of personal ambition. Not for a moment did Bryan suggest a distinction between foreign policy during his tenure as Secretary of State and that of his successor, Robert Lansing. In both intervals Wilson's foreign policy was equally valid; in both, Bryan stressed, Wilson had kept the country out of war. In another exhilarating speech, the permanent chairman, Ollie James, continued the peace theme: "I can see," he cried, "the accusing picture of Christ on the battlefield, with the dead and dying all around him, with the scream of the shrapnel and the roll of cannon, and I can hear the Master say to Woodrow Wilson, 'Blessed are the peacemakers, for they shall be called the children of God.' " The convention screamed approval.

Bryan made a second speech at the City Club of Chicago. This time, while extolling the glories of peace, he attacked the follies of preparedness. "If individual pistol toting is a menace to the peace of the comminuty," he cried, "pistol toting by nations in logic must be a menace to the peace of the world." He did not want to see "a single American mother's son shipped across an ocean 3,000 miles wide to bleed and die in the settlement of some King's dispute." Wilson was duly nominated, yet it was Wilson's convention less than it was Bryan's. He and his allied orators had created for the Presidential campaign of 1916 a theme and slogan that unquestionably were unwelcome to the party nominee: "He kept us out of war." [19]

Bryan campaigned for the Wilson ticket in nineteen states, chiefly in the West. He suggested to the national committee that he campaign where sentiment for prohibition was strong, and sentiment for it in the West was soaring. But, above all, the West was peace-minded, and Bryan, with other Democratic speakers in the region, treated the peace issue as paramount.

Bryan campaigned at least as hard as Wilson, and not a few observers felt the quality of his performances surpassed anything he did in his own races. Bryan told David Lawrence, the journalist, he had never seen such enthusiasm in his own campaign days. "Just why that is," wrote Lawrence, "may be hard to say, but I suspect he is also making more votes for Mr. Wilson than he ever made for himself." Bryan's theory was that in his campaigns, he could offer only promises; now he could build upon Wilson's performance "a record greater than any administration of our generation."

This was no empty boast. Wilson (with Bryan's help) had pushed through Congress an extraordinary array of social justice legislation that exceeded even Theodore Roosevelt's. Congress passed the Underwood Act, which scaled down the tariff to moderate levels and applied the first income tax under the Sixteenth Amendment; the Federal Reserve Act; an act creating the Federal Trade Commission; the Clayton Antitrust Act, barring various business practices that lessened competition, created monopoly, or imposed objectionable price discrimination; a Federal Farm Loan Act, which made credit available to farmers at low rates of interest, a reform long clamored for by Populists; a wage and working-conditions law for seamen; a workmen's compensation act; and an eight-hour workday law for railroad employees.

Although Wilson campaigned through the West, he and Bryan did not meet. Neither did Bryan devote his campaigning wholly to Wilson's cause. In states where prohibition was being weighed, Bryan, after striking his blows for Wilson, would take up the dry crusade. He also worked for the re-election of such politically congenial Congressmen and Senators as Henry

Myers of Montana, Key Pittman of Nevada, Henry Ashurst of Arizona, John Kendrick of Wyoming, and William H. King of Utah. Bryan refrained from endorsing his Nebraska rival Senator Gilbert Hitchcock in his race for reelection, but Wilson declared, "I sincerely hope that Senator Hitchcock will be reelected, and I am sure that the hope is shared by those who had the pleasure of being associated with him in the Senate." [20]

Election night Bryan and Mary observed at Fairview in the tradition of his own Presidential races. Family and friends, fourteen in all, sat down to a turkey dinner and a huge fruitcake, a gift for their wedding anniversary. The fruitcake was baked in the shape of a book, with an outside cover of glazed gingerbread which looked convincingly like brown leather. The edge of the leaves consisted of ivory-colored frosting. On the back in white sugar letters were the words, "Happy Days, Vol. 32"—this being the thirty-second anniversary.

In late evening, when the gathering broke up, the mood was anything but festive. Everything pointed to the election of Hughes. Bryan, Charley, and Tom Allen tried manfully to see hope in the late returns, but discouragement permeated Fairview. The final result lay in doubt for several days until California moved into the Wilson column. Hughes, who had swept the East, lost to Wilson's command of a solid South and a near-solid West.

A joyous Bryan wired to Wilson "earnest good wishes for the success of your second term. Am proud of the West—including Nebraska. The states beyond the Missouri have rallied to your support and saved the day. . . . They have been largely benefitted by the great reforms secured under your leadership, and they stand with you for peace, prosperity and progress."

Wilson responded promptly: "May I not say how much I have admired your part in the campaign and what a vast deal of effective work you seem to me to have done in the very part of the country which has now aligned itself with the forces of progress?" To the press, Bryan rendered an analysis of Wilson's victory. The "country is against war . . . against being drawn into the war in Europe." Prohibition, too, Bryan noted, as a dominant factor. Of the twenty-three dry states, seventeen voted for Wilson. Above all, the election spelled victory for a strategy Bryan aspired to in his own campaigns. Wilson won thanks to the West and South and "without the aid or consent of the East." [21]

Analyses of the victory put great store in the campaign slogan Democrats widely chanted, "He kept us out of war." Theodore Roosevelt was a factor, exploding and misfiring, avid for war and offending German-Americans, whose votes Hughes badly needed. Bryan, too, was accorded a major role in the result. The trail of victory seemed to lead to where Bryan campaigned. In fourteen of the nineteen states where Bryan spoke, Wilson won. Brother Charley noticed a persistent theme in letters and newspapers that Bryan was "responsible" for Wilson's "nomination and election four years ago and that you could be properly credited with his reelection at this time. . . . Quite a few of them mention the campaign of 1920, and expect you to lead it." [22]

Wilson took seriously the mandate implicit in the campaign slogan, "He kept us out of war." In December, 1916, on the theory that the best way to continue to keep the United States out of war was to bring it to a close as quickly as possible, the President called on all the warring nations to state the terms on which the war could be ended. Although his letter was couched in modest phrasing, Wilson made plain his willingness to serve as world mediator. Overjoyed at the President's step, Bryan from Miami praised it generously in a public statement. But the belligerents' responses again were disappointing. The Allies were both more candid and more resentful of Wilson's effort to draw them out, and his statement that "the objects . . . both sides have in this war are virtually the same . . ." infuriated the British. "Everybody is mad as hell," Lord Northcliffe informed Ambassador Page. Since both sides still expected victory, little hope for mediation gleamed through their replies.

An undaunted Wilson went before the Senate on January 22, 1917, and, in an address Ben Tillman termed the "noblest utterance since the Declaration of Independence," stated, to the consternation of the Allies, that a victor's peace would not bring victory. "It must be a peace without victory," he declared. "Only a peace between equals can last." The President called for a League of Nations to establish world accord. An exultant Bryan again acted to bolster Wilson by urging his friend Kitchin, the House leader, to bring Congress to pass a resolution endorsing the President's peace appeal.

But the response was even more distressing than before. Germany astounded Wilson by announcing that the submarine campaign would be reopened and henceforth all merchant ships found in the war zone would be sunk. German decision-makers were confident that U-boats could knock out Britain, before the United States, thanks to its lagging preparedness program, could throw its full weight onto the scales. Wilson, committed in a previous ultimatum to breaking off relations if ruthless submarine warfare was resumed, reluctantly did so on February 3.

Bryan, who had just completed a peace speech at Madison Square Garden, was overwhelmed by the news. He rushed to Washington, took a room at the Lafayette Hotel, and summoned friends to counsel on the alarming crisis. Senator Henry Ashurst, who came, found Bryan "excited" and apparently could do nothing to recompose him. "I studied this emotional man," Ashurst wrote later, "this man so eloquent in utterance—and let him talk peace and acquiescence; then asked him: Does Americanism mean peace at any price?" Senator Robert M. La Follette came, too, to hear Bryan declare morosely that the President's action was bearing out his worst fears upon resigning. The two peace-minded men discussed animatedly what should be done next. Bryan proposed a huge mass meeting, but La Follette dismissed it as ineffective, counseling that Bryan would do better by calling in as many Democrats as possible while La Follette courted progressive Republicans. Let both groups unite on "a well-considered resolution which would start a discussion that could run along for a few days in the hope of things cooling off."

Bryan fought like a man possessed against the Demon War. He issued "An Appeal for Peace to the American People," outlining specific steps for war's avoidance: Keep Americans off belligerent ships; postpone until after the war any question that cannot be settled now by peaceful means; refuse clearance to American and other neutral ships carrying passengers and contraband; withdraw protection from American citizens who travel as seamen with contraband on American or other neutral ships; keep all American vessels out of the danger zone "just as the mayor of a city keeps citizens in their homes when a mob is in possession of the street." Since Congress "has exclusive power to declare war," Bryan demanded that the declaration be submitted to a national popular referendum. He urged the people to wire immediately their sentiments to the President and their Senators and Congressmen. "A few cents now may save many dollars in taxation and possibly a son." The response was quick; telegrams advocating Bryan's measures poured in.

During several days of frantic effort, Bryan addressed a huge District of Columbia Anti-War League meeting, reaffirming his proposals, and told the press that he was "at the President's command," should Wilson wish to see him. Bryan also met with Bernstorff, with whom he was always friendly, to make the unusual suggestion that the retiring ambassador remain in the United States for the sake of promoting any possible amicable relations between the United States and Germany. Bryan's main endeavor was buttonholing legislators to stiffen their resolve for peace. The results were not rewarding. It is "distressing," he wrote to Mary, "to see so many men afraid to act." He returned to Miami, La Follette felt, "quite discouraged." [23]

The steps toward war were inexorable. The President, goaded by the economic paralysis of ships docked idly in port, asked Congress for authority to arm American merchantmen against German U-boat attack. When a filibuster of Western Senators ("a little group of wilful men," Wilson called them) blocked the proposal, he found authority in an obscure law, and American merchantmen soon went to sea armed. The fires of incipient war were further stoked by the Zimmerman note, which burst into headlines on March 1 with sensational effect. Its author, the German Foreign Secretary, Alfred F. M. Zimmerman, called for an alliance of Mexico and Japan against the United States. The anti-Mexican Southwest and anti-Japanese

Far West abandoned their indifference toward the war. Indeed the whole nation was aroused. An alarmed Bryan again rushed to Washington.

Patience with Bryan's agitations for peace was wearing thin. Wilson's inaugural address, commencing his second term, called for a "unified nation for the sake of a more active assertion of our rights." Theodore Roosevelt disdainfully cast aside a suggestion that he debate Bryan on preparedness. To do so, the former President said, would be "on a par with . . . the morality of abolishing patriotism . . . or the propriety of action such as that of Benedict Arnold." The Democratic standard-bearer of 1904, Judge Alton B. Parker, burst into notice by wiring Bryan, "If you and your friends, Senator La Follette and your joint followers and sympathizers, had gone to heaven three years ago Germany would not have attempted to drive the United States from the seas or to conspire to make war upon her. . . ."

While Bryan was excoriated, German U-boats sank three unarmed American merchant vessels with the loss of thirty-six lives. From Miami, Bryan, gasping with despair, addressed an appeal to the Senate and the House urging an exhaustive effort to obtain a suspension of Germany's unbridled submarine campaign. Specifically, he urged the application of his own peace plan, calling for an investigation of the dispute with Germany before a resort to war. Since Congress declared war, he urged it to consider that the step "may mean the signing of the death warrant of thousands, even millions of your countrymen. . . ." Let Congress remember, he pleaded, that "the wrongs you would punish, cruel and unjustifiable as they are, are not intended primarily against this country, but are acts of desperation, directed against other nations with which the offenders are at war." Bryan reminded Congress that "our land is not threatened with invasion, but that we are asked to go 3,000 miles for a chance to fight." Neither, he believed, did the United States have "the excuse for going to war that the European nations had." If Congress should prefer war, let it first consult by referendum those who must "defend the nation's honor with their lives."

Days later, on April 2, President Wilson asked Congress to recognize a state of war, holding that "the right is more precious than peace. . . ." Bryan remained in Miami, glassy-eyed with despair, after word from Senator James Vardaman: "Things look gloomy. God alone can save this Republic it seems to me from the horrors of the European slaughter." On April 6, Congress adopted a resolution of war.[24]

At this moment, Bryan ceased to be pacifist—for the war's duration. "Now . . . the discussion has ended," he explained to a crowd in Columbus, Ohio, "and the people of the entire country will stand undivided behind the President. In no other country should the people be so willing to make extreme sacrifices as in the United States."

On the day war was declared, Bryan dispatched a telegram to Wilson tendering his services: "Please enroll me as a private whenever I am needed, and assign me to any work that I can do." To Daniels, Bryan explained that he volunteered as a "private" because, having been a colonel, he thought the President and the Secretary of War might feel it necessary to offer an equal rank. He did not want a command, Bryan added, for he was "too old to learn the art of war." Wilson responded immediately and graciously: "I am sure that the whole country will believe that you are ready to serve in any way that may set its interests forward." Days later Bryan volunteered to Secretary of War Newton Baker to serve as a regimental "assistant chaplain" to satisfy the religious needs of the troops. Bryan cited the relevance of his "1898 war experience."

Although his proffer of services to the armed forces was not accepted, Bryan was the good soldier on the home front. Moved by the theory that a vigorous prosecution of the war was the fastest restorative of peace, Bryan vigorously supported administration measures of mobilization. He was a busy speaker promoting bond drives and Liberty Loans and a public example by his purchase of a $1,000 Liberty Bond. To audiences everywhere, he extolled the virtues of Garden Golf, played by the victory gardener wielding his hoe. The ice chest, he would declaim, was the nineteenth hole, and the game's success was measured by the number of potatoes driven home. Thousands of Nebraska soldier boys, en route to Camp Funston, would stop at Lincoln and march from the Burlington depot to a hotel for dinner, after which fifty pretty girls dressed as Red Cross workers would pin flowers on them and give them candy and cigars. The capstone of the day would be Bryan's speech in the Auditorium, a thrilling articulation of the theme that it was the highest privilege and honor to fight for democracy.

In the full bloom of his patriotism, Bryan was not oblivious to abuses in the civilian economy, to the opportunities for greed and fat profits by the kind of men and enterprises whose malfeasances he had fought throughout his career. In *Commoner* articles and in speeches, he supported the tax proposals of Claude Kitchin—to increase levies on wealth, to go lightest on those of slender means, and to apply generally the test of "ability to pay." "Why not draft money?" Bryan asked in *The Commoner*. "If the citizen must give his life to enable his country to carry on war, why should the property owner be dealt with more leniently? Is money more precious than blood?" In wartime, Bryan was still the country's conscience. But *The Commoner* carried that burden with moments of lighthearted relief. "An optimist," read a Maupin-like entry, "is a man who believes that the rich men of the country will give solid support to the proposition that all incomes in excess of $100,000 a year shall be commandeered for the war chest." [25]

Bryan by no means gave up politics for the duration. He stood at the head of the two most popular political movements: prohibition and woman suffrage. Both were adopted as amendments to the Constitution. On these and other questions, he took positions at odds with Woodrow Wilson's, a tactic that served to preserve Bryan's identity as a national leader, championing a distinctive body of emerging political issues.

Prior to America's involvement in the war, Bryan had refrained from elevating prohibition to status as a national issue. Now with the elections past and the country at war, the political hour for national prohibition had struck. Days after America's entry, Bryan was writing to Kitchin that although he did "not want to raise any issue with the administration," it was time, "if the President did not object," to bring forward a national prohibition amendment. Bryan readily ticked off reasons for the step: Because of war needs, grain must not be wasted in alcohol; victory garden patches would avail the nation little if 7,000,000 acres were wastefully devoted to grain for drink; and the supreme need of war was men "with clear brains and steady nerves. . . ."

Bryan moved with high-flaming zeal onto the campaign trail against the Demon Drink. A Bryan prohibition speech subjected the liquor interests to merciless oratorical bombardment. In a meeting at the Second Baptist Church in St. Louis, for example, he depicted brewers as "wielding the ox-whip" on bankers and businessmen, compelling them to sign wet endorsements for candidates in Missouri's state elections, where prohibition was an issue. "The brewers are the real anarchists," Bryan cried in one sally, "when they tell you in advance that prohibition will not prohibit because they will defy the government and will disobey the laws." [26]

In 1917 and 1918, Bryan systematically toured state capitals to pressure Democrats into pushing prohibition as a party issue. Fired by the war spirit, Bryan's new crusade had all the excitement of a Presidential campaign—his acclaimed arrival at the railroad station, this parade escorting him to the local auditorium, the audience of thousands with thousands more turned away, the captivating oratory, the rush into the late night to the next engagement. For prohibition, Bryan employed the kind of simple, telling argument that he had provided decades before for silver. "The fact that some who begin the use of intoxicating liquor," he told a Madison, Wisconsin, audience, "never become drunkards furnishes no justification for the saloon. A city would not license the establishment of a rifle range in a public park even if it could be assured that not more than one passerby in one thousand would be killed by a stray bullet—the percentage killed by drink is greater than that."

Like any other issue of his political career, prohibition cost Bryan a loss of friends, including his important ally Samuel Gompers. Gompers was indignant that the American workingman, on whom fell the main burden of war, should now be deprived of his pail of beer. To Gompers, Bryan rejoined that it was "a worse slander still to intimate that the great laboring classes of this country have got to measure their patriotism by the quart or schooner."

On a dank December day of 1917, Congress adopted the resolution for a prohibition amendment to send to the states. Bryan was on hand to quaff the sweet, nonalcoholic libation of victory. Seated in the press gallery, he observed the House debate and, after the vote, rushed onto the House floor to share in the jubilation. "The sentiment has now reached a point," Bryan observed afterward to the press, "where it carries with it those who might have opposed it had there been a prospect of successful opposition." [27]

In March, 1918, he was elected president of the National Dry Federation, consisting of twenty-eight different national groups, including the Federal Council of Churches, the Prohibition Party, and the Women's Prohibition League. Prohibition was prompting Bryan to veer toward a nonpartisan stance. As the elections of 1918 approached, Bryan, eager for the temperance forces to prevail in the state legislatures, appealed that "the voters should lay partisanship aside, and vote for the *Dry* legislative candidate against the *Wet* candidate regardless of party. A Republican legislator who will vote to ratify the national prohibition amendment is better than a Democratic legislator who will vote to defeat the amendment and retain the saloons." Even in the face of such exhortations, some saw in Bryan's endeavors for prohibition the fine hand of personal ambition. The New York *Sun,* never his admirer, perceived that Bryan was using prohibition to make himself "a political leader of the Democratic party, and has pushed his new moral issue to the front as a preliminary to the next campaign." [28]

The other major political issue of the war espoused by Bryan was woman's suffrage, for which he orated far and wide. "It is presumed," he explained to a New York audience, "that when a man has confidence enough in a woman to give himself to her, that he ought to have confidence enough in her to give her the ballot. The husband turns over the children to the wife for intellectual and moral training, and makes her his financial partner."

Bryan called on the Democratic Party to "take the lead in this great reform." President Wilson cast aside an original reluctance and espoused the amendment as "a vitally necessary war measure." In the House of Representatives, which passed a resolution for an amendment, many more Republicans supported the step than Democrats. Most Democratic Senators rejected the amendment, which showed Bryan to be at odds with the national wing of his party on the issue. In both the Senate and the House, old Bryan Progressives furnished the strongest support and old Bryan foes the most virulent opposition. [29]

Because of the war, Bryan also thought the political iron was hot for reintroducing his controversial plan for government ownership of railroads. He had ample cause to crow in self-congratulation that time was vindicating a proposal he had long ago made and for which he had suffered scorn. Pointing to the creditable record the United States government was compiling in operating railroads in the war, Bryan urged the cause of enduring government ownership. He proposed a "dual plan," with the federal government owning trunk or connecting interstate lines and the states owning local lines. Asking rhetorically why support for government ownership had grown, he stressed the economic advantages found in the elimination of watered stock and waste caused by the duplication of roads between competing lines. Other justifications, he felt, were the traditional resistance of railroad managers to regulation, the "corrupting influences" of railroads upon "legislators, other officials, and upon young men, who in the ambition to secure lucrative railroad positions, separate themselves from the mass of people and use their influence to shield the railroads from needed supervision." But Bryan's was a lonely voice. Wilson could never even dream of joining his demand for government ownership, and no other major Democratic politician supported him.[30]

In the war years, Bryan was speaking to more people than any other living man. His emphasis on prohibition was symptomatic of his growing preoccupation with moral issues and his movement away from his more traditional political and economic questions. His resignation as Secretary of State and, therefore, his abandonment of the Wilson administration alienated many power centers of his party and gravely damaged his ability to command results through party processes. Weakened as a party leader, he was still strong as a public leader, and moral questions provided far sprightlier fare for winning and holding his audiences than the politics of wartime in a unity-minded nation.

Bryan remained the champion of the American lecture circuit, now in its heyday. His lecture trails led most frequently to the smaller cities and towns of America. A scheduled visit from Bryan transformed the community into a holiday, with flags and bunting and special trains loaded with crowds from adjoining towns. When his train chugged into the depot, a band struck up, necks craned, and as Bryan emerged, cries rose, "There he is! There's Bryan." The familiar bald and portly figure would climb down, a reception committee would close in, and Bryan, with his massive smile, would say, "Glad to see you." Bryan would pass the interval before the lecture shaking hands and exchanging brief words with long lines of citizens. After the lecture, he would continue grabbing hands and telling everyone how glad he was to see them until his train pulled out. To all who approached, Bryan offered quick, cheerful hospitality, regardless of their station or dress. All were the people "who believe in me and stick by me."

On the Chautauqua platform, Bryan remained a vision of composure and ease. The savage heat of the summer day, the huge restless throngs that overflowed into adjoining groves, the children racing, crying, and chattering found Bryan on the platform serene, leisurely, and supremely good-humored. His palm fan and a pitcher of ice water were the props of this unruffled disposition.

Bryan spoke on simple moral themes, and if he depicted an imperfect present, it was, in his hands, always followed by a triumphant uplifting future. Listeners were wafted by Bryan's passionate treatment of lofty issues to high clouds of aspiration and moral nobility; their whole beings almost swelled with goodness. One observer of Bryan's platform magic, however, discovered a considerable flaw. "But when the audience," he noted, "got back to earth sufficiently to inquire what practical means they could employ to produce the millennium; lo: Mr. Bryan was on the train again hurrying off to his next lecture."

Mary was concerned about the dietary chaos of Bryan's journeys. She would write to him solicitously, ". . . 'eternal vigilance' is the price of good health. Do not begin a lot of starches and sugar. I realize that you can't be as careful when travelling as you are at home, but do your best." In return for hardship, there was always the reward of a faithful patient audience. To a Chautauqua scheduled for 8 P.M., Bryan arrived, because of misadventures, at 12:40 A.M. "But the Chautauqua audience was still there and shouting," he wrote to Mary. He spoke until 2:08 A.M.—"it almost equals my political meetings." [31]

In the politics of Nebraska the war years saw the decline of the Bryan organization and the ascendance of the rival Hitchcock-Mullen alliance. Bryan was faced with the horrendous problem of the erosion of his political base.

To forestall this approaching political crisis, Bryan and his organization endeavored to annex to themselves rising ideological movements in the state. Bryan men placed themselves securely at the head of the prohibition movement in Nebraska. The chairman of Nebraska's Dry Federation was W. T. Thompson, and Bryan continued to identify himself more with prohibition as a nonpartisan movement and less with the state Democratic Party. Telling evidence of Bryan's growing separation from the Democracy and his deepening attachment to prohibition derives from the Bryan birthday celebration of 1918, which instead of reaffirming progressive doctrine and bringing national Democratic personalities to Lincoln consisted of a mass meeting in the Lincoln Auditorium of prohibitionists of the Anti-Saloon League, the WCTU, and the State Dry Federation. Bryan's speech consisted chiefly of an attack on the wet Democratic governor, Keith Neville, for not pressing ratification of the national prohibition amendment in his recent special call to the state legislature. And concerning the Nebraska Senate, which had resisted prohibition, he cried, "The member of the Nebraska Senate who votes against this ratification must show whether he owes his seat to the German-American Alliance or to the people." The alliance was a pressure group, especially strong in Western states, devoted to causes close to the hearts of German-Americans: prior to 1917, keeping the United States out of war with Germany and thwarting prohibition. When Bryan spoke, war-minded Americans were suspicious of the patriotism of German-Americans. Bryan and other propagandists for prohibition identified their cause with winning the war; to be a wet was in their eyes to be unpatriotic. Among longtime Nebraskan politicians whose memories went back to the state's elections in the century's first decade when prohibition was a top issue and Bryan did not rally behind it, there were mutterings that "During all of the years that prohibition was making an uphill fight Mr. Bryan was very careful not to take sides; now that the battle is practically won, he cannot restrain his impatience for a complete clean-up."

The Bryan organization's other tactic, in its hour of weakness, was the building of ties with the Non-Partisan League and a studied take-over of the league's principles. From North Dakota, where it was founded and controlled the state government, the league's influence was spreading into neighboring states. The league aimed to bring government under farmers' control and to establish state-owned institutions for their benefit. Bryan, in a word, was behaving in the style of his youthful advent to Nebraskan politics. Just as a young politician he had borrowed—or stolen—freely from the Populists, now he acted similarly toward this other rising movement. His address to the state Democratic convention at Hastings, on July 30, was devoted not to Democratic principles, but to advocacy of the Non-Partisan League's program. It was indicative of his weakness in the party that the old custom of a laudatory resolution in his honor was abandoned and he was relegated to an inferior place in the order of speeches. Not until 11:30 P.M. did Bryan get the floor, after the audience and half the delegates had departed. He spoke again like the agrarian of old. He declaimed upon the necessity of grain and livestock commissions to protect the farmer, of municipally owned markets, slaughterhouses, and coalyards. He dwelled upon his own past attentions to the abuses of grain elevators and flour millers. The Hitchcock-Mullen machine, he declaimed, would give no support to this program. Not Bryan alone, but Charley too, espoused the league's platform when he entered the primary race for governor against the Democratic incumbent.

In 1918 the Bryan organization's alliance with the Non-Partisan League proved to be no blueprint for victory. Charley was badly beaten. But the November elections were even more disastrous for the Hitchcock-Mullen alliance. It was a Republican sweep for the entire state ticket, including the reelection of Senator George W. Norris. In the ashes of Democratic defeat, Bryanism took on a sudden allure of hope and salvation.[32]

In Europe, victory for Allied arms was in sight. The German armies reeled in full retreat; the Kaiser fled. Wilson promulgated his Fourteen Points as a basis of peace, which his European allies accepted with grumbling and formal reservations. In a message to Congress on January 8, 1918, delivered when the Allies were lagging and a staggering Russia seemed likely to drop out of the war, Wilson advanced his fourteen-point plan which established him as the moral leader of the Allied cause. He aimed to inspirit the Allies, entice enemy peoples into surrender, and attract discontented minority peoples. His first five points had wide appeal: abolish secret treaties; establish freedom of the seas; remove economic barriers between the nations; reduce armaments; and examine colonial claims in light of the interests both of the natives and the great powers. Among Wilson's other points were promises of independence to oppressed minority groups and the establishment of a League of Nations to provide collective security and guarantee political independence and territorial integrity to all nations. Allied leaders, whose dreams of annexation were recorded in secret treaties, feared that Wilson's idealistic Fourteen Points would thwart them. Colonel House, acting for Wilson, hinted at a separate German-American treaty if the Allies were uncooperative. Badly needing American help for postwar reconstruction, the Allies reluctantly agreed to negotiate a peace based more or less on the Fourteen Points. On November 11, 1918, the armistice was signed, and the war to end war had ended.

More than anything else in the world at this moment of his life, Bryan wanted to be a member of the United States commission which would negotiate the future peace. He was "heartily in accord" with the President's Fourteen Points, and he deemed himself "especially qualified" for the task. "Acting on the theory that I may be put on Peace Commission," he informed Josephus Daniels, "I am preparing myself in advance by reading up on principal treaties & European politics of last century." There is no doubt that Bryan had a specific prescription for future peace. It should follow the mold of his peace treaties. In the critical weeks before and after the war's end, Bryan besought the intercession of influential Washingtonians to bring the President to include him in the commission. But it was all in vain. Wilson himself headed the delegation to Paris, and the nature of its other members—Colonel House, Secretary of State Lansing, General Tasker Bliss, and Henry White, all tending to quiescence and subordination—made clear why Bryan was not appointed.

Bryan lost no time in self-pity, nor did he lapse into resignation. He had his own ideas on immediate questions, on longer-term peace, and on the issues debated in Paris that seeped through the tightly secretive conference rooms. In public statements he exuded support for Wilson, expressed abhorrence of "the balance of power" as a mechanism of peace, and endorsed the final appeal of Theodore Roosevelt, who had died unexpectedly of a blood clot in the heart on January 6, 1919, "to bring the boys back home." He lent his support to causes of the hour like independence for the Armenians and the Irish.[33]

Most of all, he watched with a close eye the unfolding of the League of Nations. The initial provisions that emerged contained extraordinary similarities to those of the Bryan peace treaties—the year's delay in a dispute before war might be declared and the employ of a special investigating commission. Toward Wilson's arduous and not unflawed labors in Paris, Bryan was tolerance itself. Something of the handicaps of the Paris diplomatic workshop was conveyed to Bryan by the reporter David Lawrence. To Charley, Bryan wrote after a lengthy discussion with Lawrence, "We have not overestimated the trouble they have had." By March, as the League assumed firmer outline, Bryan had begun to speak publicly about the handiwork in Paris. For some time he was resolved to be the approving constructive critic. "My position," he wrote to Charley, "is that we should take the League as the best thing we can get but that we must make it as good as possible." In a statement issued in Washington, he hailed it as "the greatest step toward peace in a thousand years." He was delighted with the stress on disarmament and secret treaties. He nevertheless offered suggestions: stronger representation of the United States in light of its size and power; easier admission of future members (no nation should be blackballed in a world organization); a clear exception for the Monroe Doctrine; freedom for a nation or people to accept or reject mandatory status; no interference by the League in a nation's internal affairs; freedom for each nation to decide whether to undertake actions determined by the League's Council.

The League, Bryan felt, needed additional powers. It had to be able to face the problem that certain nations, because of population, require expansion. The League had to be able to "deal with claims" made for "waste places" of the earth.[34]

For the League's chances in the Senate, Bryan maintained at least outwardly hearty optimism. As early opinion was expressed in the Senate, some of it bristling with hostility, Bryan resolutely predicted that the peace treaty and the League would be approved "by an overwhelming majority." The basis of this optimism? "I know they know they are elected by the people," Bryan explained, "and they are more than anxious to keep an ear to the ground all the time. I know that some of them mourn the fact they are not so constituted physically they can keep two ears to the ground."

But events conspired to undo these predictions. Once again Bryan, as he stood at the brink of seeing a dream transformed into at least a semblance of reality, was confronted with formidable obstacles. Once again the most forbidding hand raised against his hopes and dreams appeared in the East. The hand this time belonged to Senator Henry Cabot Lodge of Massachusetts. Patrician and Harvard-bred, Lodge, according to a critic, had a mind like the soil of his native New England, "naturally barren, but highly cultivated." Lodge and Wilson, both "scholars in politics," came to hate each other totally, and this with other raging political forces, quickly smothered the League's prospects in the Senate.[35]

As the political conflagration grew, Bryan took up his battle station in Washington. He marched daily to Capitol Hill to rally those Senators he could. "Expect to see Senator [William S.] Kenyon [of Iowa] this afternoon," he reported to Charley, "he is the best of the Progressive Republicans." Old Bryan stalwarts were leading defenders of the League. Senator Robert Owen of Oklahoma excoriated Lodge for "blind partisanship," and Senator Claude Swanson of Virginia delivered a three-hour speech warning against reservations to the League covenant. Bryan, too, made speeches in Washington, the most notable at a vast rally at the Mount Vernon Place Methodist Episcopal Church. Five thousand packed the church, streets, and nearby parks. Bryan and his speaking partner, Secretary of War Newton D. Baker, who probably constituted the most formidable oratorical team ever put together in American politics, each made three speeches in the several locales on behalf of adopting the League without amendments and without reservations. In the growing Senate impasse, Bryan advanced a formula to resolve the difficulty, lifted from his own experience in past peacemaking. He proposed that the example of 1898 be followed: Approve the treaty now and fight later for changes, and "If this nation cannot secure the changes it desires it can withdraw from the League if it chooses."

But opposition to the League was formidable. Legislative Republicans were restive under six years of Wilsonian rule and eager to assert themselves, particularly in the Senate, where they enjoyed a majority. Deep-rooted American isolationism was imperiled by America's awaiting obligations under the League. Senator Hiram Johnson of California thundered that through the League, "The British Empire can demand American blood to subdue Ireland." Above all, there was the image of Wilson, cultivated by his opponents, as a mere dupe at the hands of wily Europeans. Said the Republican Senator Frank B. Brandegee of Connecticut after discussing the treaty with the President, "I feel as if I had been wandering with Alice in Wonderland and had tea with the Mad Hatter." Meanwhile, Senator Lodge, operating as chairman of the Senate Foreign Relations Committee, was busy with machinations and manipulations against the treaty, which had come to his committee for study and report. In a strategy to delay and confuse, to Americanize and Republicanize the treaty, he formally read, in a deliberate tactic, the entire 204-page document aloud even though it was printed. He and others developed numbers of devastating reservations. Wilson, taking the fight to the people in an oppressive schedule of speeches, was felled by a paralytic stroke in Colorado. As the struggle wore on, Wilson, his fighting instincts flaring even in illness, refused to compromise. He wanted all of the treaty or nothing. When the Senate finally voted in November, 1919, the necessary two-thirds vote on behalf of the treaty failed to materialize. Republicans voted heavily against it, and substantial numbers of Democrats and a headstrong President would tolerate no compromises.[36]

Democratic leadership was in crisis. Woodrow Wilson, ill and headstrong, locked in a feud with a selfish, vindictive opponent, had allowed the banner of leadership to fall into the dust. The world waited, aghast at the strange American political spectacle; the enduring peace the war was fought for remained unstructured.

In the crisis of leadership, other men lay aside their feuds and united if only to extricate their country and party from political paralysis. Senator Gilbert Hitchcock, forgetting for the time his factional quarrel with Bryan, wrote to him, urging that he lay before Wilson an acceptable compromise. Bryan did not deal with either Wilson or Hitchcock but acted independently of them and in cooperation with trusted allies on Capitol Hill. In a word, since the standard of Democratic leadership had fallen, he was now abandoning his circumspect cooperation with the President, maintained through the war and the dawning hours of peace, and chose instead a course independent, self-assertive, and designed to solve the Senatorial impasse on the League of Nations. Not the least element encouraging Bryan to assume a new posture was the dawn of 1920, a Presidential election year. In such years, Bryan invariably nurtured more political strivings, and he was more combative.

Through such Senatorial faithfuls—John Kendrick of Wyoming, Kenneth McKellar of Tennessee, Claude Swanson of Virginia, and others—he presented a set of compromise treaty reservations, which he and they had drafted, to Senator Lodge. It was hoped that Senate Democrats in general would support the Bryan plan, and he aimed to win backing from Senator Charles L. McNary of Oregon, a mild reservationist and other like-minded Republicans.[37]

As he had in 1898, Bryan persisted in the supposition that some treaty, however imperfect, was far better than no treaty at all. The void of no treaty, he believed, demoralized world affairs, hurt the American economy, and placed the Democratic Party in a position of fighting for policies that popular opinion rejected. The Bryan-inspired compromises of the Lodge reservations were important but not impossible modifications of Wilson's position. Where Lodge would permit Congress to withdraw the United States from the League by concurrent resolution, Bryan would require a joint resolution, in which the President would have his word. Where Lodge would give the United States the sole right to interpret the Monroe Doctrine in the context of the League, Bryan would eliminate the provision entirely, while retaining the reservation that the League should not have power to impair the Doctrine. Bryan would do away entirely with those Lodge reservations concerning matters that required legislation in any event—appropriations for the American share of League expenses and limiting the power of a reparations commission to interfere with German-American commerce without Congressional assent. Other Bryan modifications proceeded in a similar vein.

Bryan's plan for compromise was cursed with a deadly flaw. It materialized not from any weakness of substance, but from its identification with Bryan. Many a Democratic Senator openly declared he would not accept the plan, regardless of its merits, because to do so would be to restore Bryan as leader of the Democratic Party. And even if Bryan's plan should be accepted in the Senate, the legislators argued, it would surely be doomed to rejection at the White House.

Bryan was not alone in urging Wilson to accommodate to his Senate opposition. Gilbert Hitchcock and other Senators also cried for compromise. Secretary of State Lansing appealed to Wilson to negotiate an accommodation as quickly as possible with Republican moderates. But the President angrily rejected the advice. In March 1920, the treaty again came up for vote in the Senate. Unless it were approved with the Lodge reservations, the entire document would be defeated. An ill and sequestered Wilson, his eyes shut to realities, again demanded that good Democrats reject the Lodge reservations. Twenty-one Democrats defied the President and voted with the Lodge Republicans. Although the treaty won a simple majority, it failed to gain the necessary two-thirds vote. Moving to the next step in his strategy, Wilson called on the Democratic Party to carry the fight for the treaty to the people in the coming Presidential election. Bryan, firmly implanted as the chief anti-Wilson spokesman, lamented that the isolated President had failed to receive information "essential to sound judgment and safe leadership." He urged the treaty's immediate approval, with any reservations necessary to command that result. The League issue must be taken "out of the campaign," and approval of the treaty would "speak peace to war-distracted Europe." A petition bearing fifty distinguished names, headed by Bryan, Herbert Hoover, the popular administrator of war relief, and A. Lawrence Lowell, president of Harvard, was presented to Wilson, urging compromise to secure Senatorial approval of the treaty. But Wilson would not budge. He was intent upon finding a mandate in the melee the 1920 campaign promised to become.[38]

If Bryan was frustrated in building the peace of the world, a fond project to which he had deeply committed himself to improve American man's moral and physical health had borne fruit. On January 16, 1919, the prohibition amendment was adopted when Nebraska, to Bryan's booming pride, became the thirty-sixth state to ratify. Under its terms, the amendment became effective one year later. The amendment's signing was observed with sturdy nonalcoholic gaiety. Prohibition's leading personalities, led by Bryan, gathered around Acting Secretary of State Frank L. Polk, to witness his signing of the official proclamation. The adoption of amendments is disclosed by proclamation signed by the Secretary of State. Bryan's successor as Secretary, Robert Lansing, was not present for the occasion, having recently resigned. Lansing was not long in his post before Wilson began meting out to him the same treatment he had dealt to Bryan. The President steadily rejected Lansing's counsel, accepted the advice of the Secretary's subordinates, and made other hostile gestures until Lansing in despair presented his resignation. Wilson accepted it "effective at once." Bryan never commented publicly on the similarity of Lansing's experience to his.

After the ceremony at the State Department, Bryan and his fellow witnesses enjoyed a decorous celebration at the Nebraskan's favorite lair, the teetotaling Hotel Lafayette. In an ebullient speech, Bryan generously conceded that "We ought to share our gain with other nations" and as a first step suggested that "Germany ought to know that she will not advance very far if she puts a brewer on the throne in the place of the Kaiser."

A trifling cloud passed over the noble aspect of Bryan's toil for prohibition when the critical press disclosed that, in exchange for his temperance speeches, he was generously paid for some months by the Anti-Saloon League. What was left unsaid was that Bryan made a score of free speeches for prohibition for every one for which he was paid. After the press furor, he declined any compensation for future addresses on the movement's behalf. Though reports snowballed of laxity in enforcement of state and local prohibition, Bryan maintained an inveterately optimistic stance. "If prohibition can be enforced in Omaha," he declaimed, "it can be enforced anywhere on earth." Of that city's five great breweries, one was idle and the other four were spewing out temperance beverages; the city's most famous saloon, Johnny Kern's, known across the country and a favorite watering place of actors and politicians, was as still as death; and the famous Rajan & Boysen's saloon had been replaced by a flower shop.

At last the year of waiting for national prohibition ended. Bryan and a group of fellow toilers for the movement again gathered at the Lafayette to celebrate the passing of America from the wet era to the dry. The distinguished gathering accorded Bryan the place of honor and the privilege of making the last speech before the nation became saloonless. Bryan spoke for half an hour, and then at midnight the audience rose and signaled the great change with the Doxology. For his text, Bryan chose "They are dead that sought the young child's life" and explained that since King Alcohol had slain a million times as many children as Herod did, no words could be more appropriate.[39]

Months later, in August, 1920, the woman suffrage amendment was added to the Constitution. In this final hour of triumph of Bryan's long project, opposition and doubt still simmered. Tennessee, the last state to ratify, did so not altogether graciously. Thirty-eight members of the legislature, which ratified for the state, absented themselves by journeying to Alabama. This left slightly less than a majority or a quorum of members who voted for the amendment, a lacking that cast doubt upon the legality of their action. Not without cause, the chaplain prayed for "God's richest blessing on our absent ones." The legality of Tennessee's action was challenged in the U.S. Supreme Court. The amendment's foes were repulsed when it was found that the Tennessee legislature had long followed the custom of accepting something less than a majority of its members as a quorum. On August 26, woman suffrage was proclaimed part of the United States Constitution. President Wilson, who had once opposed it, termed the amendment's adoption in his administration "one of the greatest honors of my life." Bryan rejoiced in a *Commoner* editorial. Notes of caution were also sounded. Cardinal Gibbons of Baltimore declared, "I regret very much that the women have taken the plunge into the deep. I would much prefer that things had remained as they were." It was difficult to say what the effect would be "upon the morals of the country." He was confident that very few women would vote "after the novelty wears off."

With the attainment of his two great wartime moral and political projects—prohibition and woman suffrage—Bryan began to reach out in the postwar era for a new agenda. As rapidly as possible he urged abandonment of all the trappings of war and swift return to the peacetime order. He exhorted the Attorney General and the Federal Trade Commission to stop the profiteers who waxed fat even in peace. He recalled some of his older prescriptions shelved in the exigencies of war—the guarantee of bank deposits; a national initiative and referendum; public ownership of railroads, telephones, and telegraphs; and publication of a national bulletin, an idea which evolved from his own experience that newspapers were overwhelmingly conservative and hostile to progressive political candidacies. Published by the federal government, "under the fair and equitable control of the two leading parties," the bulletin would supply information on campaign issues and editorial space in which the rival candidates might present their views. Bryan opposed universal military training, which was under discussion, and the Boston police strike—"the policeman cannot have a divided allegiance—his whole duty is to his government." In testimony before the Senate Labor Committee, he urged the creation of permanent tribunals for the investigation of labor-management disputes. Confined to investigation, the tribunals would have no enforcement power, and the parties to the controversy would retain full freedom of action. The several economic, social, and moral issues Bryan was seizing upon possessed at least a single common characteristic. Not one of them excited the nation's attention and interest. As 1920 dawned, Bryan was without a major issue.[40]

It was part of Bryan's burden in this cycle of political decline that his closest adviser and partner, Mary, was felled by crippling illness. Severe arthritic seizures overwhelmed her knees and legs so that she could not walk. There now began months of alternating improvement and decline in an illness that was agonizingly mercurial, of visits to doctors, hospitals, and curing places, of rising and declining hopes. At first Mary was taken to Baltimore to Johns Hopkins Hospital for treatment by Dr. J. Thomas Kelly, in whom the Bryans had great confidence and who combined medical excellence with genuine belief in the doctrines of his famous patients. Initially, Dr. Kelly was hopeful of quick improvement, but the illness deepened. In one interval Bryan despaired for her life, but when once again the symptoms lifted, he was writing joyously to Josephus Daniels, "It looks like the Lord is going to let her be my companion for the rest of my pilgrimage." For the Bryans, life entailed scores of adjustments involving pilgrimages to spas like Hot Springs, Arkansas, the sale of their Asheville home, and increasing stays in Florida at Villa Serena, owing to the benign climate. The faithful Dan Bride helped in the early stages of Mary's care, but as the illness wore on and she could get about less and less, a full-time valet was retained to carry her about.[41]

In 1920, Bryan attained his sixtieth year. As a man who all his life was lavished with birthday parties he was favored with a full commemoration of his advance into a new decade. At a big affectionate celebration at the Aldine Club in New York, he was presented with a birthday cake, three feet by two feet in size and bearing sixty candles. The toastmaster requested each guest to make a wish as Bryan blew out the candles, and someone called out, "All right to wish for the White House?"

Bryan looked older than his sixty years. The strain of ceaseless campaigning and speaking, the ill-regulated diet of travel gave him a used-up appearance. The flesh around his cheekbones was no longer firm; his forehead and crown were totally bald, only gray fringes of hair reached over his ears and at the top of his collar. The lines around his mouth were slack and tired except when caught up in the full stride of a speech or a smile. As always, Bryan remained addicted to the black alpaca suit, the "boiled" white shirt, low collar, and clerical tie.

If the flesh showed weakness, Bryan's spirit did not. Viewing the state of the nation and the world, he still surged with optimism for man's potential for progress, just as he had as a young green politician of 1896. ". . . my faith is even greater now," he said at his birthday celebration, "since I have seen reform after reform accomplished and great principles that were at first scoffed at, written into the unrepealable law of the land." And the years

ahead he viewed as a crowded unfinished agenda. ". . . they will be spent,"
he said, "in an earnest effort to aid in putting the American people in complete control of their government, and to promote peace among all the nations, to the end that the conscience of our country and the world may more
surely and more speedily overthrow injustice. . . ."

More and more, Bryan was dealing in real estate. For years in his oratorical peregrinations, he had kept an eye cocked for bargains in land. In California and Texas he had accumulated extensive holdings, but it was Florida, above all, that he beheld as a land of promise. He swiftly increased his
holdings and profits in Forida lands, spurred by a fast-evolving real estate
boom and his own vast confidence in the state's future. He saw Miami, still
a fledgling city, as a favorite convention site of tomorrow and a crossroads
of the United States and Latin America. When an aviation station south of
Miami was abandoned and put up for sale, Bryan agitated for its use as a
plot on which might be built a school of government whose students would
be "the young men of Central America." In time he envisioned Miami as
the educational center and "the natural northern metropolis of the entire
Latin American world." [42]

For Bryan, the Presidential election of 1920 was an opportunity for re-
gaining personal leadership of the Democratic Party. Woodrow Wilson was
debilitated by illness and caught in the quagmire of the peace treaty. Urgent
new problems of the postwar era were demanding strong new leadership.

The first of several battlegrounds for the future command was the Jackson Day dinner in Washington on January 8, 1920. A galaxy of party speakers, of whom Bryan was one, graced the meeting. Wilson, who did not attend, dispatched a letter that was read in which he came out squarely for
the treaty "without changes which alter its meaning." The Wilson letter,
with its forceful, telling phrases, evoked repeated bursts of wild enthusiasm.
Several times the diners rose en masse and cheered, most vociferously when
the President demanded a popular referendum. Throughout the reading
and demonstration, Bryan remained silent and motionless. After the letter
was read, the diners rose and waved flags, and at the guest table everyone
stood except Bryan and Senator Robert Owen.

When Bryan, who came late in the succession of speakers, was introduced after midnight as "a beloved Democrat . . . ready to render any honorable service to the cause of Democracy," the diners again cheered lustily,
but he impatiently motioned the demonstration to a halt. He startled the
crowd by saying, "You are not inspired by the thought that you are hearing
from a candidate. . . . Possibly because I have nothing to ask of you, I may
be more free to speak than those who have something to ask. . . . I am
going to state the situation as I see it whether you approve it or not. And in
stating it I yield to no man in this country or in my party in my devotion."

The message that followed this preamble directly controverted Wilson's letter.

Robert Lansing, who witnessed the occasion, was impressed that Bryan, in a masterful speech, had raised "a fine rumpus." Good Democrats were utterly bewildered, and old Bryan men were sorely distressed. Loyalty and their keen instinct for victory moved them to applaud Bryan, but loyalty made them equally anxious to support the President, still the chief provider of their political blessings. "They stand first on one foot," noted Lansing, "and then on the other, like turkeys on a hot stove."

Bryan's speech, reported widely in the press, fired speculation about his possible candidacy. "I am not a candidate," Bryan stated with exemplary directness. Did this mean he would not be a candidate? On this question, Bryan was noticeably less candid. "I am only trying to do my duty to my country," he said. "I do not care who approves or disapproves."

Bryan, as was his custom, spoke out freely as candidates for the Presidential nomination began to emerge. When, early in 1920, a boom was launched for Governor Edward Edwards of New Jersey in the hope that one New Jersey governor might succeed another in the White House, Bryan went after Edwards with talons flying. The governor, Bryan noted sourly, came from one of three states that had failed to ratify the prohibition amendment. Edwards was not merely wet, Bryan lamented, he was "a soaking wet," and had once boasted that he would make his state "as wet as the Atlantic ocean." Herbert Hoover, the celebrated relief administrator, was talked about. Hoover would not do, Bryan quickly counseled, and the reasons why were plain from his own public statements. He did not know yet, Hoover had said, which party he would support in the fall. He must first study the respective platforms, and then he would choose the party most in accord with his views. ". . . can a man big enough for the Presidency," cried Bryan in disgust, "be content to do nothing to influence party action in a crisis like this if he waits until parties act?" [43]

For other candidates of prominence, Bryan seemed always to have an ill word. Attorney General Mitchell Palmer had dealt "too lightly" with the profiteers, and he was performing badly in the primaries. McAdoo's voting appeal was largely untested, and since he had announced no platform, his position on issues was unfathomable. Worst of all, his presence in Wilson's family made him an easy target for the President's many enemies. Governor James Cox of Ohio, Bryan was certain, would eventually be "the residual legatee of all wet candidates, the final rallying point for those with financial interests in liquor or fondness for intoxicants." When critics suggested that Bryan was indeed tarbrushing each leading candidate in order to advance his own candidacy, he scoffed at the accusation.[44]

The greening wheat, the rising corn, the infinite azure skies flecked with white were infallible signs of a traditional gentle Nebraska spring. But in

1920 they did not betray the convulsive primary battle that was raging across the state. Nebraska voters were asked to make two decisions—to express their preference for a Presidential nominee and to elect delegates to the national convention.

Bryan, although he was living primarily in Florida, offered himself for election as delegate at large. He made explicit the terms under which he would serve in that capacity. Under no circumstances, he said, through a statement issued by Charley, would he vote for the Presidential nomination of Gilbert Hitchcock, who was running as a favorite son, even though Nebraska voters instructed that he do so. He would, if Nebraskans declared for Hitchcock and elected himself a delegate, "stand aside" and permit an alternate to vote in his place. Bryan in his statement explained why he could not tolerate Hitchcock. Hitchcock, he said, had opposed prohibition, woman suffrage, and the Federal Reserve bill; in a word, everything that "Wall Street opposed," Hitchcock opposed too.[45]

Nebraska's Democratic primary in 1920 was an earthshaking factional fight between Bryan and his organization and the Hitchcock-Mullen alliance for paramountcy in the state party. Bryan excoriated Hitchcock as one who "does not stand for the things that the Democratic party stands for." Hitchcock retorted that Bryan "almost invariably denounces those who oppose him or his hobbies as the tools of Wall Street" and that "If he goes to the convention it will be to run amuck." Hitchcock scoffed at Bryan's pretensions of friendliness to the administration by noting that he never mentioned Wilson in his speeches and was aiding and abetting the Republicans in their opposition to the peace treaty by taking a position "identical with Senator Lodge's." Lamenting over Bryan's recent conversion to prohibition, Hitchcock took pains to recall that two decades before Bryan had been adamant against allowing the least word about prohibition to seep into the platform and "once insisted on a great brewer, Fred Metz, Sr., of Omaha, carrying the electoral vote of Democratic Nebraska to Washington." [46] Bryan's turnabout on prohibition was symptomatic of his general political decline. His dwindling strength made him hungry for a viable issue.

Hitchcock demanded an instructed delegation consisting of his supporters, who would vote for a plank in the national platform calling for a modification of prohibition to legalize light wines and beer. Similar movements were transpiring elsewhere across the country, but Nebraska was a special battleground, upon which both state and national liquor forces concentrated. Bryan was the political figure most feared by the wets, who anticipated that if he eventually appeared at the national convention as a delegate, the plan to modify prohibition would probably be foiled.

According to sophisticated estimates, Bryan by espousing prohibition was fighting under a substantial handicap since the Nebraska Democratic

Party was wet by fully 10,000 votes. Bryan, however, had a recipe for victory. His possible salvation was woman suffrage. Thanks to the recently adopted Nineteenth Amendment to the Federal Constitution, women could now vote in Nebraska. Since the state's primaries were open, Bryan campaigned heartily to move women of both major parties to vote in the Democratic primary.

The organized women's groups, to Bryan's good fortune, were closely allied to the prohibition movement. His campaign was generously aided by the staff of the Women's Christian Temperance Union, the state suffrage association, the leaders of the federation of women's clubs, and others prominent in welfare and prohibition work. Bryan in his campaigning appealed repeatedly for feminine bipartisan support. The necessities of bipartisanship led him to sing tunes seldom heard from his normally partisan voice. Not all good, he was now contending, was found in one party and all bad in the other. Differences between the parties were "not fundamental, but merely superficial," and in crisis, people forget party differences and unite for the common good. Since women were voting for the first time, Bryan in his speeches bade them not to be intimidated or terrorized by "the rummies." [47]

His shrewd, industrious campaign paid off. Nebraska's women saved his cause. He was elected delegate at large, and the majority of the other delegates elected were Bryan men. Hitchcock won the Presidential preference vote, an issue that Bryan wisely did not dare take up. Bryan, Hitchcock's paper, the Omaha *World-Herald*, acknowledged, "won one of the most notable triumphs of his long public career." The primary election also meant, the *World-Herald* acknowledged with an obvious shudder, "that there will be 'hell-a-popping' at San Francisco with Mr. Bryan the chief fireman and troublemaker." [48]

By every sign, it was Woodrow Wilson's convention. Its principal posts were filled by men bearing the President's approval. Congressman Carter Glass of Virginia, who had guided the Federal Reserve bill through the House of Representatives, became chairman of the convention's most likely battleground, the Resolutions Committee. Bryan's early soundings among the delegates concerning the chances of a candidate he and other dissenters might promote drew responses that were stonily negative. Those who had given the President trouble in late years fared ill at San Francisco. The keynote address, delivered by Homer Cummings of Connecticut, a member of the national committee and until recently its chairman, was clothed in the thoughts of Wilson. The coming election, therefore, must be "a great and solemn referendum" on the League, with the Democratic plank on the subject diametrically opposed to the Republican. Bryan's counsel to keep the League out of the campaign seemed well on the way to rejection. Feelingly he wrote in his first dispatch as a reporter of San Francisco's proceedings: "The fog has not risen. . . ."

Bryan was elected to represent Nebraska on the Resolutions Committee. Upon its subcommittee, charged with drafting a platform, converged the various shadings of conviction on prohibition. But as the subcommittee moved into its work, dissenters from the Wilson administration's tendency to a wet position quickly faded away. When Bryan expressed determination to continue the fight for a dry plank, good friends shook their heads and bemoaned the prospect of a defeat that would further tatter his prestige and speed his decline as a party leader.

Even Bryan remarked on the ever-increasing loneliness of his position. He was feeling, he said, like Daniel in the lions' den. But when a delegate asked him privately if he thought he could win, Bryan replied icily that "a Christian ought not to ask that question. If you are on the side of a righteous cause you never know what you can do until you try. The Bible says that one with God shall chase a thousand, and there are about that many delegates in this convention." When the delegate looked incredulous, Bryan again turned to the Good Book. "The Bible says," he added, "that two shall put ten thousand to fight. I am looking for the other man."

Although defeated in the Resolutions Committee after a hard fight, Bryan carried the struggle to the floor by presenting a minority report. After praising the platform, he offered a prohibition plank pledging honest enforcement of the Volstead Act and other planks calling for a national bulletin, condemning profiteering, opposing compulsory military training in peacetime, praising the peace treaty, and proposing a constitutional amendment giving Congress the same power to end war as to begin it.

The floor debate was brisk, sparked by Bryanesque sallies that reminded old-timers of his soaring eloquence of 1896. Counseling that the League of Nations must not be made a partisan issue, he cried, "You cannot call me an enemy of Woodrow Wilson. It was my treaty plank that he took to Paris. If I could get the treaty without reservations and make Woodrow Wilson immortal I would walk up to the scaffold and die with a smile. But I cannot do it. Nobody can do it . . . there shall be no blood on my hands of people who were slaughtered while I talked politics." [49]

But it was prohibition that stirred the debate and brought the convention to high pitch. Prohibition was here to stay, Bryan proclaimed. And the liquor traffic was now a "corpse." "It's a pretty live corpse," a delegate shouted. To a wet delegate's argument that with Bryan's dry plank many men would abandon the party, he answered, "You can't do any good thing without some men leaving the party." From the gallery came a cry, "Why not leave it yourself?" When another wet called out, "I voted for you," Bryan replied, "Yes, friend. If you are sorry you did, if you go back on me because I stand for the home against the saloon, I'll get two in your place." [50]

As the tense discussion moved on, Bryan flung defiance at his enemies, his body shaking with emotion. With fire in his eyes, he stood on the edge of the platform, and as the wet barrage became almost overwhelming, he adroitly shifted the debate to woman suffrage and turned chaos into order by lifting up his hands and relating to the suddenly hushed crowd the Bible story of Elijah at the mountaintop and showing that how the veil that was rent then was being rent now. Women and children, he declared climactically, were coming into their own. Since few would wish to quarrel with this thesis, Bryan at last had reached safe ground. Good Bryan men, sensing that their hero was not altogether free of trouble, expertly moved to rescue him. A roaring whoop went up from Southern delegations. A lanky Texan seized his delegation's banner and started a parade. Oklahoma, Washington, and Idaho joined in, and other states followed. The roar increased, the galleries stood up, delegates climbed up on their chairs, and everyone seemed to join in the yells. Bryan stood erect on the edge of the platform, his eyes glistening and his anger dissolved into a broad smile. Eventually a vote was taken on his prohibition plank, and it was defeated overwhelmingly. [51]

The convention was deadlocked over the Presidential nomination. Wilson wisely maintained silence in a situation he could not control. But Bryan, for whom silence was rarely an acceptable course, offered a way out of the impasse. Let the three principal contenders, McAdoo, Cox, and Palmer be considered elminated, and let the convention instead choose a dark horse. Obligingly, Bryan offered a list that included Joseph W. Folk, former governor of Missouri, former Governor Thomas M. Campbell of Texas, Senator David I. Walsh of Massachusetts, Supreme Court Justice Louis D. Brandeis, former Governor Martin Glynn of New York, and former Senator John F. Shafroth of Colorado, almost all of whom were former officeholders who had seen their best political days.

But no dark horse of consequence emerged, and the convention again rejected Bryan's counsel. The contest for the nomination narrowed to a struggle between the two strongest contenders, McAdoo and Cox. Since the latter was decidedly a wet candidate, McAdoo's friends, at a decisive stage in the struggle, waited for Bryan to throw his influence to their man, whose leanings were dry, in order to beat Cox. Bryan declined the opportunity, recalling that in the platform fight "Mr. McAdoo's friends had joined with friends of Governor Cox to take away my weapons." Now, he noted, the McAdoo men wanted him to move against "the giant of the Philistines." Bryan acknowledged that "I had the pebbles—I do not know whether this Goliath had a forehead—but I had no sling. They took that away from me when they defeated the dry plank." A dry plank, Bryan contended, would have precluded a wet nominee. He added that he was "not in favor of McAdoo" because, as Wilson's son-in-law, he embodied the danger of establishing "a reigning family in the United States."

At last on a late ballot, Cox captured the nomination, with the youthful, photogenic Franklin D. Roosevelt as his running mate. Defeated and distressed, Bryan hurried back to his hotel to seek commiseration from Mary and others of his family. While pondering her ready words, he gazed out of his window high above the park below where delegates were laughing and talking animatedly in obvious relief at having discharged their somber responsibilities. Asked by a reporter who edged to his side what his disposition would be toward the Democratic ticket in the coming campaign, Bryan said, with a tinge of sadness, "My heart is in the grave with our cause. It must pause until it comes back to me." [52]

Fear flamed among Democratic professionals that Bryan in the despair of defeat might accept the Presidential nomination of the Prohibition Party, which was certain to carry strength in the election in the face of the avoidance of any clear stand on that unsettling subject by the major parties. The Prohibition Party, at its convention in Lincoln, quickly selected Bryan, a delegate exclaiming that "God Almighty would not let W. J. Bryan decline this nomination."

Temptation now stared Bryan full in the face. Rejected by his own party, should he accept prize and honor from another? His answer was swift. "My connection with other reforms," he said, "would make it impossible for me to focus upon the prohibition question alone. . . ." There were other considerations: He could not leave the Democratic Party that had brought the prohibition amendment into being, the party "which has signally honored me in years past."

In further proof of his steadfast Democracy, Bryan in a *Commoner* editorial announced that after comparing the acceptance speeches of Cox and his Republican rival, Warren G. Harding, he concluded that the Democrat's was better. But beyond tepid approval of Cox, Bryan would not go. When Pat Harrison, on behalf of the national committee, eagerly invited Bryan to bring his incomparable talents to the campaign trail, he "for the first time in forty years" felt driven to decline. He had no speeches, he said, "that fit into Governor Cox's campaign . . . such speeches as I have been in the habit of delivering would alienate the elements to which he is making his appeal." Cox too courted Bryan. Journeying to Nebraska, he hailed his influence, recalling that his own newspapers in Ohio and other states had supported Bryan in all three races for the Presidency and acknowledging that many of the progressive ideas he was advocating in the current campaign he had absorbed as a young man from Bryan. As the campaign wore on, Cox's speeches became less wet and more dry.[53]

Bryan's eventual role in the campaign was considerably more than that of a mere passive Democrat. Despite his protestations to the Prohibition Party, his supreme interest in the struggle was the protection and advance of prohibition. For it he worked along nonpartisan lines, and he concentrated his energies not on the Presidential but on the Congressional elections. In *The Commoner* and in speeches, he warned that the supreme danger was the election of a wet Congress. He authorized Wayne B. Wheeler of the Anti-Saloon League to sign telegrams bearing his name, supporting dry candidates for Congress regardless of party. If two drys ran against each other, he supported the Democrat.

Bryan made no speeches in the campaign, although on election day he let it be known that he had voted for Cox and Roosevelt and the Democratic state and Congressional tickets. Many a Democrat was not impressed by this simple act of duty but shared the sentiment of an old Bryan supporter who belabored his idol for "sulking in his tent." [54]

Election day revealed that Bryan was not the only Democrat missing from the ranks. Warren G. Harding, the glorious stuffed shirt, overwhelmed the ineffective Cox by more than 7,000,000 votes. It was the worst Democratic defeat in Bryan's political career. In a public statement cutting through the thick party gloom, Bryan observed that Wilson had "laid the foundation for the disaster" and that Cox "completed the structure." He excoriated Wilson for seeking to drive Democrats who did not agree with him—"even in minute details"—out of public life, for alienating Republican support, and for shunning workable compromise on the issue of the League. Bryan was some miles removed from his youthful role as a heroic unbending champion of free silver.

Bryan, who gave these opinions in a press interview conducted while shaving, did not quail in suggesting at least the first step toward a better future. He recommended that Wilson appoint Harding as Secretary of State, after which both the President and Vice President Marshall should resign to allow Harding to succeed to the Presidency at once and spare the country further months of Wilsonian ineffectuality. He was inspired to this suggestion, Bryan claimed, by the wisdom of one who had long antedated the Democratic Party. It was Job who said: "The Lord hath given, the Lord hath taken away."

Bryan's headline-making proposal drew inflamed responses. His Nebraska rival, Gilbert Hitchcock, declared that if the national administration were to be altered, it would not be done by those "outside the Democratic party." Bryan's good ally in the war years Claude Kitchin said, with Bryan evidently in mind, "Let us have less talk about leadership and more action toward harmony in our ranks." Congressman Hal D. Flood, chairman of the Democratic Congressional committee, dismissed Bryan as one who was "no longer a factor in the party organization" among men "at the forefront in party councils." But Bryan contemplated a reorganization made by the people rather than the leaders. The Congress to be elected two years hence, in 1922, he said, could become the foundation of a Presidential victory in 1924. The wisdom of the people made him confident of the party's future. "The Democratic party," he observed, "is normally a progressive party and will gather about it the progressive forces of the nation." [55]

27. Normalcy

Now in the seventh decade of his life, Bryan was well on the way toward the Bible's allotment of three score and ten to mortal man's earthly journey. He moved into these years with ready serenity. "The latter days of life like the autumn months, have joys of their own," he observed, "that make them welcome in spite of the silent warning that they bring. They are harvest days and are gladdened by the results of early labors." He saw his own life's successes symbolized by four amendments added to the United States Constitution through no little investment of his words and effort—the popular election of Senators, the income tax, prohibition, and woman suffrage. Like Pollyanna, he was still given to infinite optimism. "God is on His throne," he proclaimed, "and the teachings of the Prince of Peace exert an unceasing influence on the hearts of mankind." After such pronouncements, the Optimists Club of his native Illinois readily and unanimously elected him to membership. Composed largely of business and professional men, the club was a civic organization with state and local chapters. In mock solemnity, Bryan accepted the honor as "the most unanimous election that I ever had."

Age was but one of several basic changes in Bryan's life. In 1921 he moved his citizenship, as well as his home, to Florida. Mary's sagging health could not bear the rigors of Nebraska's climate, and he could no longer leave her for long intervals. The move was, he said, "a decision reluctantly reached. . . ." Watchers of politics gleefully predicted that his becoming a Floridian would speed his political decline since the South was not a hunting ground of political parties for national leaders. Yet there was no anticipation that Bryan would fade away altogether from the political scene. "As easily could a fish live out of water," lamented the Washington *Star,* "a born agitator cannot live in a clam."

Florida was a fertile locale for Bryan's increasing labors in religion. His Bible class, like the ongoing Florida real estate boom, was flourishing as never before. It remained Miami's foremost tourist attraction, superior even to the tantalizing real estate opportunities. With an attendance of between 4,000 and 5,000 each Sunday, the class met at the Royal Palm Park in Coral Gables, where standing room behind the seats and benches was at a premium. In simple language, expressed in faultless diction and a charming delivery, Bryan freed the thousands from their impression of the Scriptures as forbidding and unfathomable and led them to an understanding of the great Biblical truths and their relevance to every man's life and problems. Bryan's Bible lessons were syndicated in more than 100 newspapers, which drew into his class readers across the country, making, as he proudly noted, "the largest Bible class in the world." In addition to providing Biblical learning and uplift for countless thousands, Bryan drew an income of more than $20,000 a year from this new branch of journalistic enterprise.[1]

Bryan was holding as closely as ever to the lecture circuit, to the Chautauquas in summer and the lyceums in winter. Attendance and gate receipts never faltered, although his endurance sometimes did. He was known to deliver his messages on occasion sitting down, and midway in several presentations in 1922 he stopped to take medicine and rest. For years, Bryan's health had been of some concern, less to himself than to Mary. In 1914 he developed a diabetic condition and was immediately put on a special diet, which he observed better at home under Mary's eye than on his journeys. She constantly worried about his health, and her letters were studded with admonitions—"be careful," "don't catch cold." Neither age nor infirmity dented Bryan's oratorical effectiveness. His voice continued to command its phenomenal carrying power. Decades later, when the head of the RCA Laboratory in Hollywood heard recordings of Bryan's lectures, he exclaimed, "Look at that meter! Look at that voice! Why, it has absolutely no bass tones. We have recorded thousands of voices, but never a voice like this."

Sometimes Bryan traveled with a secretary, but more often he did not. Like the young silver orator he once was, he still made his own travel arrangements, toted his own gripsacks, and cared for his own laundry. Thus, when finishing lectures, say, at Indianapolis, he would send on his used clothes to his next stop, Paducah, Kentucky, with instructions to the young Congressman Alben Barkley (which Bryan spelled "Barkeley") to have everything laundered and ready. After Bryan's visit, Barkley's tutelage in the valet's art persisted when his guest left behind a pair of pants ". . . dark blue with a faint white stripe . . . not very valuable . . ." but let the young Congressman please mail them to the next lecture stop. In 1922 Bryan's audience partook a new dimension when he made his first radio address, reaching an estimated 60,000,000. For this magical new device of communication, Bryan was fired with enthusiasm. Painfully recalling that the press was heavily Republican, he hailed radio as "the gift of Providence" to the Democratic Party.

In a small way, Bryan returned to his original profession, the law. Midway in 1921, he associated himself with the Washington law firm of Charles A. Douglas, the announcement emphasizing that he would specialize in international law. Bryan at that moment was handling for the firm a case involving claims of an American citizen against a Latin American government. In this and other conceivable litigation, Bryan would deal with the State Department, with whose personnel and machinery he was well acquainted. As for Douglas, he had acted as Washington counsel for the Carranza government when Bryan was Secretary of State. But if the law called, Bryan heard it little. The lecture trail, politics, and the Bible were such demanding masters that they left little time for anything else.

Mary was ever Bryan's preoccupation, haunted as he was by the dread that her condition might grow worse. William, Jr., and Grace, whom the elder Bryans frequently visited in California, shared in the vigil. Ruth did, too, when she was not caught up in her multifarious enterprises. Blessed with talent and her father's grit and drive, Ruth infused almost anything she did with excitement and surprise. Mother of four children, a feminist, an ex-war worker and nurse, a student of Oriental customs and playwright, she had lately become a motion-picture director. Having completed a film, *Once Upon a Time,* based on the story of the *Arabian Nights,* she planned more films for children, which she deemed a promising, little-touched field. At a preview of her first film, reporters asked Ruth how her father held on to his vast and loyal public for so many years. Unhesitatingly, she answered, "I think it was because he practiced what he preached. He started out in life with high ideals and he has kept them." [2]

A new Republican age had dawned. Warren Gamaliel Harding was in the White House, broad-shouldered, silver-haired, warmly liked, the ideal image of what a President ought to look like. Easygoing and glad-handing, Harding was disposed to smooth and pat his way through trouble and acquiesce to whatever his subordinates proposed. In such a political household, the scandals of Teapot Dome were not far away.

Bryan, who tended to treat Presidents of the opposition party better than Presidents of his own, was, from the beginning, warmly disposed toward Harding. Soon after the 1920 election, he visited the President-elect at his home in Marion, Ohio. Although the substance of their discussions remained undisclosed, Bryan presumably aimed to spur the new leader's interest in that flagging institution for world peace the League of Nations. In

Harding's beaming presence, Bryan spoke at the Laymen's Convention of the Marion Presbytery, stressing that he and Harding stood for the same fundamentals in politics and religion and that "I would rather stand behind a man of that kind than one of my own party whose errors might hurt the country."

Subsequently, Harding visited Miami. Under benign March skies, he and Bryan passed a delightful day, with luncheon at the Flamingo Hotel, and late in the afternoon, the President-elect called on the Bryans at their home. In *The Commoner,* Bryan approved, almost lavishly, the simplicity of the inaugural and the good sense of the Presidential address. In visits to Washington, Bryan called on the new President and in letters offered counsel on the day's issues.

Although Bryan genuinely liked Harding, and their relations were cemented by the proximity of their ages and the fact that politically they "looked at some things in much the same light," his approval was not disinterested. More than once in his career, he had got the things he wanted in public policy not through his own party, but through the opposition. As well, Bryan's own fading fortunes as a Democrat could be charged with new vitality if he established a good rapport with the incumbent Republicans.

Bryan hoped through Harding to remove the League of Nations question from partisan politics and convert it into an enterprise fit for bipartisan support. He endorsed Harding's "association of nations," vaguely alluded to in the campaign, as a valid substitute. The name "League" or "Association" made no difference. While courting Harding, Bryan was attentive to another, even more significant personality for the League's future—Senator William E. Borah, its leading Republican opponent. Against Bryan's fervid argument and pleas, Borah proved intransigent. The Idahoan, an isolationist who took literally George Washington's warning against "entangling alliances," opposed American involvement in any degree in any international confederation. Before many a month, the League had sunk hopelessly beyond sight in American political waters.[3]

Bryan had another string to his bow of peace. Before the Harding administration began, he was pleading the cause of disarmament. With arms races widely regarded as a root cause of the late war, debates and discussions swept America on the necessity of arms limitations to prevent another holocaust. But how could nations be induced to set aside narrow self-interest in arming to the teeth for security? Bryan in his preachings, proposed that the Allied war debts be employed to purchase world disarmament. Let each debt be canceled on condition that the country which owed it agreed to disarm. Riddled with impracticality, this plan was short-lived.

Bryan was more successful in adding his own declining political weight to the considerable pressures beating upon Harding to do at least something for the cause of disarmament. At a session in Chicago of the Congress on the Reduction of Armaments, just after the administration began, Bryan was the featured speaker. He urged the United States to take the lead in arms reduction "by agreement if possible, by example if necessary." When Harding was soon declaring in an address over the soldier dead in Hoboken, New Jersey, that "It must not be again," Bryan lighted fires of encouragement around the bumbling, indecisive President. Let Harding, he cried, in an address to 12,000 Christian Endeavorers in New York City, summon a disarmament conference and take other steps to lead the nations "to the vale of perpetual peace," and the speech at Hoboken would be forever compared "to the Gettysburg address."

A conference was eventually arranged, destined to be known as the Washington Disarmament Conference of 1921–22, in which France, England, Japan, and the United States participated. Men's hopes soared, and Harding addressed himself to the hard business of selecting the American delegation. Bryan thirsted desperately for appointment to it. Wilson had ignored his ambition to participate in the Paris Peace Conference, but just as Wilson had been besieged with petitions and advice on behalf of Bryan, so Harding was pressed. So eager was Bryan for this to transpire that he escalated his pressures to the point where Mary wrote to Mrs. Harding urging his appointment.

Florence King Harding's reply to Mary was a gracious put-off. The President held Bryan "in very high esteem," believed him to be "great and good," and moved by "high ideals." The President did not yet know whom he would appoint, except that he must, in light of Wilson's experience, make appointments from the Senate and from both parties. Mrs. Harding, however, was glad to "second" the selection of Bryan. Eventually, Harding made his choices, and again Bryan was omitted from the delegation of peace planners.

The rebuff did not for a moment deter Bryan from applauding the positive works that emerged from the Washington Conference and from spurring the President on in plain-speaking letters. As the conference proceeded and European negotiators threatened to shackle it with impossible conditions, Bryan openly advocated an appeal by the United States government over the heads of the negotiators to the people of Europe. And when Secretary of State Charles Evans Hughes advanced his proposals for a ten-year naval holiday, Bryan told a packed house at Carnegie Hall that he "was never happier in my life." In its ultimate result, unfortunately, the Washington Conference afforded Bryan much less cause for jubilation. The conference took half steps rather than full steps. It dealt not at all with land forces, and the scaling down of navies was cautious and reserved. But enough was accomplished to deter Bryan from any public lamentations.[4]

When Bryan said that politics stopped at "the water's edge," implying that foreign policy must be forwarded with bipartisan cooperation, he was also acknowledging that Harding's domestic policies were fair game for partisan scrutiny. Bryan was encouraged, if not propelled, in this distinction by the tax policies of the quiet silver-haired Secretary of the Treasury, Andrew Mellon, an aluminum millionaire soon to be hailed as "the greatest Secretary of the Treasury since Alexander Hamilton." Mellon's tax program called for tax relief for millionaires and big business on the theory that high taxes both discouraged business and yielded less revenue than moderate taxes for the rich. Mellon's recommendations called for repealing the excess profits tax and the gift tax and lowering the income tax, estate taxes, the surtax, and excise taxes. The rich were spared, thanks to Mellon, and a heavy part of the tax burden was shifted to those of middle income.

Bryan, who for years had proudly championed the income tax as an equalizer that could right wrongs worked by the private economy, was outraged. "If anyone needs a little favoritism the farmer surely does," Bryan cried. As laws were passed mirroring Mellon's proposals, Bryan was roaring in public protest that America had now passed "under the rule of the rich" and that "Big Business is in control." The scaling down of taxes on big incomes—eventually the wealthy Mellon paid no income tax at all—provided ample fodder for Bryan's thesis "that Republican leaders are giving to those who have large fortunes and taking from the poorer members of society." In sum, the Republicans, with Mellon as their oracle, "are giving the Democrats the greatest issue they have ever had. The revenue bill . . . is the boldest, most unblushing effort to favor the rich at the expense of the poor ever presented to Congress." [5]

In the twilight of his political career, Bryan was championing the farmer as he had in its dawn. The farmer did not share in the prosperity that was cascading over American society. The tiller of the soil was cruelly shut out. The prices he won for his crops sagged miserably, and the harder he worked and the more bountiful his harvests, the deeper he dug his own misery. To Bryan and others, it was the nineties all over again. Farmers of the West and the South were wallowing in debt, falling prices, and foreclosed mortgages. The industrial East, fattening on soaring prosperity, freely employing government for its own ends, was coldly indifferent to rural hardship. As in the nineties, these were the sure ingredients of a leavening agrarian revolt. From his quickly assumed place at the forefront of the rural forces, Bryan urged the agricultural community to unite on a program and force it through Congress, which he characterized as showing "more fear of the farmer's power" than at any other time in his experience. [6]

Bryan was still the leader of the nation's chief moral crusade and its most troubled cause, prohibition, which he persisted in hailing as "the greatest moral reform ever brought about in the world's history." His devotion to prohibition was also buttressed by its general popularity in his own political territory, the West and the South. But in the East, particularly in the cities, prohibition became a mockery. City folk failed to cast off the drinking habit; foreign-born people were loath to drop their ancestral drinking ways; and Washington was unable to oversee leaky local enforcement.

Like other leaders of the prohibition movement, Bryan remained in the heady clouds of lofty moral principle, largely oblivious to the enforcement shambles below. He looked forward to the expansion of the prohibition movement, to the day "when there will be no saloons under the flag of any civilized country." He badgered the Harding administration to work harder at plugging the dikes through which King Alcohol still spilled. He called for diplomatic protest and sterner measures to halt the rum-runners, who got their stuff in the Bahamas and in other British possessions and whisked it to Florida and other Eastern points. In pulpits and assemblies he deplored the seemingly endless machinations to undermine enforcement, like the administrative ruling enabling physicians to prescribe beer as a medicine. Prohibition stood in danger of repeal by the simple medical act of changing the word "drink" to "dose." When pressed by questioners in his audiences to explain the ragged state of enforcement, Bryan answered, "The great trouble with enforcement is that the wets have been entrusted with enforcement. No drunkards should be appointed to enforce our prohibition laws." For the lapses of the great moral experiment of prohibition, Bryan offered a political remedy—elect drys to every office, local and national.[7]

At a decent interval after the disastrous elections of 1920, Bryan in statements and broadsides proclaimed the necessity of reorganizing the Democratic Party. Inevitably the common theme was that the party must get a new start. "The party," he said, so that all might understand, "cannot run with water that has passed over the dam." Bryan's reorganization plan called for a return to "progressive principles." Just as at the beginning of his career he had called for renewal of the Jeffersonian and Jacksonian faith, this time it was simply the abandoned Bryan faith that needed to be restored.

The party must "take the people's side of every question." It was therefore necessary to "purge the organization of the representatives of the special interests so that the people will believe in the party's sincerity." Marked for purge were the city bosses Bryan had traditionally fought with in earlier days. Bryan's further aim was to push Cox into oblivion, and his welcome mat was out to growing numbers of Democratic leaders who were abandoning the Ohioan in quest of a securer future.

In the manner of his early career, Bryan was proclaiming that policies rather than leaders were important, that it was more necessary to advance a program than to struggle over the selection of the party's next Presidential nominee. He frowned upon those who "have no higher purpose than to give some Presidential candidate the inside track. . . ." As between what by general consensus were the two ranking leaders of the party, Cox and McAdoo, Bryan maintained a careful neutrality. Presumably McAdoo's positions on public questions best approximated his own, but he gave no nod to the former Secretary of the Treasury. To his friend Louis Post, he explained that "I want to stay neutral between the Cox and McAdoo factions so that I may be in a better position to persuade them both to put policies above personalities."

In the nineties, Bryan had worked to remake the Democratic Party in the image of a creed accepted by some but not all of its members. Belief in silver had become in effect the admission card to party membership; nonbelievers had been given short shrift. The year 1921 also had its simple card of admission. "No one can be counted as progressive," proclaimed Bryan, "who is reactionary on the liquor question." Bryan was not simply indulging in idiosyncratic judgment; many progressives had long regarded prohibition as a key plank of their movement. Prohibition had become a significant cause midway in the nineteenth century. Its goals exceeded the narrow one of individual betterment. It anticipated that a society of liquor-free, better-functioning individuals would enhance democracy. As progressives grew concerned with the welfare of women and children, they realized that a husband, captive to drink, could be the chief source of their misery. Prohibition, too, fulfilled the Biblical edict that man is his brother's keeper. Platforms of the Prohibition Party during most of Bryan's career endorsed the breadth of social and economic reforms he championed. However, many at the forefront of the prohibition movement of the 1920's did not share the social doctrines of progressivism.

For Bryan silver had possessed far more symbolic power in 1896 than liquor possessed in 1921. Silver was a shorthand representation of a host of economic and social policies, as prohibition could never be. And prohibition was a declining issue, whereas silver, when Bryan had taken it up, had been beginning a spectacular rise. Bryan in 1921 required from reorganized Democrats a second proof of their commitment. Progressives, he said, "must also oppose Wall Street schemes for the exploitation of the masses."

His concrete program was a potpourri of proposals, some leftovers from his earlier campaigning and others specially contrived for the times and trends. His now-old, dog-eared proposals for a national bulletin, a referendum on war, membership in a League of Nations founded on the Bryan peace treaties, one term for the President, the absentee ballot, a ban on monopolies, a national primary, guarantees of bank deposits, and labor-management arbitration all were embraced. For pressing needs of the day, there were new proposals. In the continuous orgy of speculation on the stock market, by which butlers overnight might become richer than their masters, Bryan championed national legislation to curb market gambling. It was time, he said, for a national minimum living wage law. To leave it to unions to extract such a wage from bargaining with management he deemed impractical. It was also unjust that "any one group of laborers should be singled out and given this protection without regard to its effect upon others equally worthy." It was high time to establish a department of health and a department of education. (A little more than three decades hence his wish was granted when the Department of Health, Education, and Welfare was created.) Inspired by his real estate experiences in new, fast-developing Miami, he was enthusiastic about public parks. "The park is a Democratic institution; it is the people's playground." He preferred many small parks to the large park, and he labored strenuously to have cities include them in their plotting and subdivision of property.

Monopolies, which were growing apace despite years of his thunderings against them, were condemned as "indefensible, intolerable." The Federal Reserve Board, which he perceived as "largely responsible" for the sudden drop "by one-half" in farm prices, needed overhaul. "Why not have as one of the Directors . . ." he asked, "a farmer who actually farms and is, therefore, in sympathy with agriculture?" In the same vein, he suggested the addition of a laborer and a businessman who was not a banker and who presumably was in sympathy with the businessmen of the community. Let profits be limited as interest is limited; let the public know the difference between cost price and selling price; eliminate unnecessary middlemen; and prohibit gambling in foodstuffs.[8]

In the manner of the old free-silver cause, the Bryan-honed platform was to be carried forward through intensive educational and organizational work in every political constituency of the country, from precinct and county committee upward through the party hierarchy. The platform would be promoted in county and state conventions preparatory to its embodiment in the coming national convention of 1924. Like Bryan's political enterprises of old, the new venture depended on coalition with outside groups. In 1924, it was hoped, progressive Republicans, despairing of the Republican marriage to wealth, would seek new happiness in an understanding Democratic Party. Presumably, too, Bryan would project on a national scale his courtship of women political workers and voters, whose support had brought his recent victory in Nebraska.

"But what of the paramount issue?" cried a nonadmirer after scanning his score and more of planks. "A Bryan platform without a paramount issue were a Daneless Hamlet." The critic, after assessing Bryan's political history, concluded that the plank that might ultimately be so honored would best promise "the restoration of Mr. Bryan to imperial, absolute leadership," when as of yore he could cast unbelievers "into the outer darkness." Bryan, of course, at this late day, was well beyond any such restoration, which would remain only a figment of his critics' nightmares.[9]

In the twilight of his political life, Bryan embarked on a tentative venture of the utmost daring. He, a Westerner and long-standing national figure, dared to take up residence in the South and to consider offering himself for candidacy for one of its principal offices. Florida, despite the veneer of swift growth and change and the influx of monied outlanders with talent for economic exploitation, remained essentially a Southern state, a stalwart member of the vanquished Confederacy. Yet Bryan's audacity appears less prickly when one recalls his Virginia ancestry, his long popularity in the South, and his now substantial years of residence and economic entrepreneurship in Miami.

Midway in 1921, Bryan began emitting unmistakable signs of future candidacy. He wangled an invitation to address the Florida legislature and in far-ranging remarks offered a program for the state's improvement combining local issues and his established views on national questions, threaded together by his social ethic. He advocated reform of the state's prisons and the establishment of places where discharged prisoners could work voluntarily until they reestablished themselves in society. For the Everglades and other areas in the state, he urged the establishment of experimental stations to demonstrate how livestock, vegetables, and fruits could be produced at a profit. He proposed the establishment of state stockyards and slaughterhouses, junior colleges with normal courses, the teaching of Spanish, particularly at Miami and Tampa, and a state trade commission to protect consumers against profiteers. Once again, he urged the protection of bank deposits, the initiative and referendum, and conciliation of labor-management disputes.

The doors of Florida's Democratic establishments swung open easily to Bryan, thanks not only to his own gifts but to the circumstance that he had a cousin, William Sherman Jennings, who was a former governor of the state. Very quickly the concept of Bryan as United States Senator from Florida materialized. Mrs. Jennings, first vice-president of the General Federation of Women's Clubs, reported that "your stock for the Senate is going up all the time." John T. Crawford, the state's national committeeman, she added, was eager to sound out "the old political guard over the state" on the question of a Bryan candidacy. Charles E. Jones, editor of the Jacksonville *Observer*, reported that he had discussed Bryan's candidacy with about one hundred leaders around the state and "it was practically unanimous" in his favor. Many newspaper editors and businessmen realized that Bryan's identification as a Florida political symbol would be highly fruitful for the fast-growing state. The Miami *Herald* believed that most of the state's people "would consider it an honor for Florida to be represented in the Senate by a man of the international reputation of Mr. Bryan." And the Jacksonville *Observer* announced, "Bryan as a Senator from Florida would place

Florida on the map as no other state has ever enjoyed . . . he would directly be worth millions to it in advertising. . . ."

Despite these heady overtures, Bryan was racked with doubts about his course. Powerful factors operated against his running. He was now sixty-two, Mary was ailing without prospect of surcease and needed looking after, he himself was struggling with diabetes, and he was already well occupied with a wide range of activities. Above all, Bryan was haunted by the specter of possible defeat. To run, he would have to pit himself against the popular Democratic incumbent, Senator Park Trammell. A "cracker," widely known in the state, Trammell was a glad-hander with the politician's gift for remembering everyone by the first name. As signs of Bryan's candidacy grew, Trammell thrust at a weak spot by terming him a "rank outsider."

In mid-February, Bryan issued a carefully hedged statement mirroring the doubts that still gnawed at him. If the Democrats of Florida, he said, felt he "could render sufficient service" to the state, the party, and the nation, he would "consider the matter from the standpoint of duty and in connection with other claims upon me." He added that he had no thought of "entering into a contest for the office." All his past nominations, he stressed, "have been tendered me practically without opposition, and I have prized them as expressions of confidence." He looked forward to a continuing pleasant association with Florida Democrats, "my co-laborers for a quarter of a century," which could best be maintained so long as his plans did not conflict with their ambitions or preferences.

The passing weeks, despite insistent overtures from friends confident of his ability to win, brought Bryan to look on his candidacy with growing distaste. It was increasingly obvious that with Florida a luxuriant marketplace for rum-runners, prohibition would figure heavily as an issue. Bryan's strictures on law enforcement would be ill received as implicit criticism by an outsider of the local way of life. By mid-April he had made up his mind and announced that "I cannot at my age turn . . . to personal politics. . . . I shall not be a candidate." To a friend, he explained that to enter the race would invite "a purely personal contest." He added, "I dreaded the thought of it and am greatly relieved to be out of it." [10]

Bryan's removal of his legal residence from Nebraska by no means ended or even diminished the Bryan organization's ascendance there. Shrewd brother Charley now played a double role—his traditional one of political manager and strategy maker and Bryan's vacated role of candidate for office. In 1915, Charley had been elected mayor of Lincoln, and in 1921 he was again elected a member of the City Commission, which by law chose one of its members mayor. Having won the largest popular vote of the commissioners, Charley, by standing practice, should have received the office.

Because he had campaigned on a platform calling for a municipal coalyard and municipal sale of ice, big business moved against him, and instead of being elected mayor, Charley was relegated to the position of commissioner of streets. He easily transformed this skulduggery against the popular will into a political asset.

Charley's fortunes remained highly relevant to Bryan's. If the Bryan name and the Bryan organization could remain atop Nebraska's politics, then the brothers Bryan had a Western bastion from which they could operate to influence the coming national convention of 1924. If Bryan could also maintain acceptance and approval among the Florida Democrats, he would enjoy a Southern as well as a Western base in 1924. In 1922, Charley moved to nail down Nebraska. His task was eased by the rise of a solid third party, the Progressives, whose leadership Charley reported to Bryan was "composed of our close friends."

Within the Democratic Party, the chief threat to the Bryans remained Gilbert Hitchcock. Charley now proceeded to subdue this opposition by using the Progressive Party as his whip. Charley wanted nothing less than nomination for the governorship, and when "the Hitchcock fellows" began muttering that "any Bryan man" except Charley would be acceptable, he acted. In January, at a Hitchcock banquet in Omaha, a prelude to the Senator's renomination, Charley sent word via five Democratic guests from Lincoln that he intended to file for governor "and that if any of their crowd did too, I would assume that they were looking for a fight and that I would name a whole Progressive ticket, including a candidate for Senator." Charley concluded a report of these events to Bryan by observing—altogether accurately—that he had Hitchcock "over a barrel."

The old war between the Bryan and Hitchcock factions suddenly ceased. The terms of a quickly arranged peace became apparent when Charley won the gubernatorial nomination and Hitchcock the Senatorial. The latter's Democratic Harmony Club of Omaha endorsed the nominations, and Harmony Clubs sprouted like crocuses after a spring thaw across the state. Charley's platform and the remainder of the Democratic ticket delighted the new Progressive Party. Campaign oratory was not Charley's forte, and at the peak of the contest, Bryan came to Nebraska to take to the hustings for his brother, Hitchcock, and the Democratic ticket in general. Once more, Bryan made a big play for the female vote. Farmers' wives, because of the rural depression, were writhing under high taxes and high prices, and their city counterparts suffered a similar discontent. Bryan courted Democratic and Republican ladies alike and in speeches up and down the land deplored the unconscionable sums taken from the family income for taxes and coal bills. A standard feature of Bryan's speeches was an imagined colloquy between a Republican wife and her husband. The Republican husband said to his wife, Bryan reported, "My dear, I wish I could afford to give you and the children a little vacation at some inexpensive summer resort, but we can't really spare the money." The wife replied, "Why not let me have the amount that you are sending down East every year to help the tariff barons take their wives and children to Bar Harbor in the summer time, Palm Beach in the winter time, and to Europe between seasons?" On the stump and in editorials, Bryan beat the drums for Hitchcock's reelection. He painted the Senator as "a champion of the overburdened taxpayer," overlooked his earlier wet stand on prohibition, and stressed his current advocacy of its enforcement in state and nation. The embattled Hitchcock wrote thankfully to Bryan "that the old relations of political cooperation have been naturally and honorably restored between us."

Election day was a glorious vindication. Charley won the governorship by the largest majority ever accorded in the state's gubernatorial contests. Although Bryan was aging and ailing, his organization decidedly was not. With Charley at the pinnacle of Nebraska's politics, the brothers Bryan were sure to figure as a force in national politics in 1924. The Bryans' present ally and potential rival Gilbert Hitchcock was defeated in his race for another Senate term. It was proof of Nebraska's new Democratic solidarity that Bryan observed in tribute that "The defeat of Senator Hitchcock is a distinct loss to the Democratic party in the Senate." [11]

Bryan's campaigning in 1922 was by no means confined to the towns and crossroads of Nebraska. He carried off a full schedule of speeches for Democratic Congressional and Senatorial candidates throughout the West. Although campaigning, thanks to the automobile, was easier for Bryan than in his horse-and-buggy days, it had lost none of its perils. Near Rochester, Minnesota, his car plowed into the rear of the car of Mrs. Lillian K. Gault, Democratic candidate for the Third Congressional District. Everyone was badly shaken up, and Bryan was heard to exclaim, "If I am going to die, I want to expire campaigning, and not in a bed." At the campaign's end, letters of thanks from Congressional candidates poured in upon Bryan, and the national Democratic chairman tendered "unmeasured thanks for your invaluable service . . . you were in the thickest of the fight everywhere. . . ."

Nationally, the election results were a dazzling Democratic triumph, foretold almost to the point of inevitability by the scandals of Teapot Dome and the Harding administration's blooming image of ineptitude. The Republicans lost seventy-six seats in the House, leaving them with a scant five-vote majority, and in the Senate the Democrats achieved a net gain of six. The proportion of progressive Republicans also increased to the point where they held the balance of power in both houses. Bryan was not long in proclaiming that Democrats "by proposing progressive measures" might gain their passage with the aid of progressive Republicans. For Bryan, there was also disappointment. A surge of dry strength in Congress that he had confidently predicted did not materialize. Foreign-born citizens resented their forced abandonment of the drinking ways of the old country. Soldiers returned from the wars rejected prohibition as something that was "put over" on them while engaged on the battlefield. Workers resented the loss of cheap beer, while the rich could buy all the alcoholic beverage they wanted. Libertarians deplored the invasion prohibition represented upon private rights. Flaming youth and curious elders delighted in discovering and gulping bootleg liquor. Even now a strong minority, if not a majority, opposed prohibition. Bryan faced a mankind that did not want to be saved from the scourge of King Alcohol.[12]

Throughout his career, Bryan had accepted and applied his father's dogma that religion and politics were closely intertwined, and not a few observers of his career felt that the moralistic, evangelical fervor of his political messages lent them a distinctive vitality and attracted and held a massive devoted following. In the priorities he accorded to the two realms, religion and politics, Bryan was altogether clear. In his lecture "The Prince of Peace," which he gave scores of times, beginning in the first decade of the twentieth century, he said, "I am interested in the science of government . . . but I am more interested in religion than in government . . . and I shall be in the church even after I am out of politics. I feel sure of my ground when I make a political speech, but I feel even more certain of my ground when I make a religious speech." [13]

In the 1920's Bryan did at least as much work in religion as in politics. His famous Bible class, his syndicated "Bible Talks," his heavy schedule of speeches to church groups and meetings dominated his attention. He presented his handsome, spacious former home, Fairview, to the Presbyterian Church "for a home and sanitarium for sick or superannuated ministers and missionaries and their wives, widows, and orphans, or for any other religious use. . . ." Bryan also began moving into top-level deliberative bodies of the Presbyterian Church. In 1921 he was appointed a member of its General Assembly's Special Committee on Christian Life and Work, one of the most important of the church's committees, and subsequently he joined another key committee on Sabbath observance.

A growing focus of Bryan's religious preoccupations was the impact of evolution or, more precisely, Darwinism on faith. His concern was not sudden. As far back as his "The Prince of Peace" lecture, Bryan declared that he was not yet convinced that man is a lineal descendant of the lower animals. Further, he did not know of any argument that could be used to prove that man is an improved monkey that could not be used, just as well, to prove that the monkey is a degenerate man. Conceding that man in some characteristics resembles the beast, Bryan stressed that "man has a mind as well as a body, and a soul as well as a mind. The mind is greater than the body and the soul is greater than the mind, and I object to having man's pedigree traced on one-third of him only—and that the lowest third." Bryan, for his part, found it "just as easy" to believe "that God created man *as he is. . . .*" To the thousands who heard his lecture, Bryan objected that Darwinism caused man to "lose a consciousness of God's presence" because it pictured man as having reached his present state "by the operation of the law of hate—the merciless law by which the strong crowd out and kill off the weak." By Darwinian logic, "we shall turn backward towards the beast in proportion as we substitute the law of love." But if some men want to embrace Darwinism, "I do not mean to find fault with you if you want to accept the theory."

Darwinism was also objectionable on political grounds. It was the progenitor of Social Darwinism, which undertook to explain and justify the very political and economic conservatism which Bryan had spent his best years fighting. In the economic jungle, only "the fittest" survived. A Rockefeller, by ruthlessly eliminating competitors, came to control 95 percent of the country's oil refineries and extracted enormous profits. Rockefeller's ways of Social Darwinism were hardly the ways of democracy. Darwinism also had a politico-military dimension. Nations and peoples competed and fought with one another on the basis of might makes right.

During the war years, Bryan was enormously influenced by an American war relief worker's account of conversations with German officers which revealed Darwin's shaping influence on their thought and studies via an unbroken continuity from Darwin through Nietzsche to German materialism, nationalism, and militarism. In an address to the World Brotherhood Congress in 1920, Bryan condemned Darwinism as "the most paralyzing influence with which civilization has had to contend during the last century" and Nietzsche as a disciple who denied God's existence, subverted moral standards, idealized man as superman, praised hatred, "and endeavored to substitute the worship of the superman for the worship of Jehovah." [14]

In 1920, Bryan, in his concern with Darwinism and the seeming enfeeblement of religion, turned his attention increasingly to schools and colleges. In an address to Nebraska's constitutional convention in 1920, he declared, "The greatest menace to the public school system today is . . . its Godlessness. We have allowed the moral influences to be crowded out. . . . We do not ask public school teachers to teach religion in the schools, and teachers, paid by taxation, should not be permitted to attack our Bible in the schools. . . . We cannot afford to have the faith of our children undermined." Bryan carried his cause to the college campus when, in a lecture at the University of Michigan, he dealt with the evils of Darwinism and evolution. Afterward, there were clear rumblings of regret and friendly protest. Clergy at Ann Arbor urged Bryan to desist from pursuing this new cause. "You raised an issue that has been dead and buried for nineteen out of twenty students," wrote the Reverend Arthur W. Stalker of Ann Arbor's First Methodist Episcopal Church. "Be assured I would not offer the criticism, except in your own personal interest and that of the Christianity we both believe and love."

In 1921 Bryan persisted in developing and articulating his views in several lectures that were printed and widely circulated. The chief of these was "The Menace of Darwinism," which he began by observing that all morality and virtue depend on religion and belief in God. Anything which weakens belief in God weakens man and his capacity to do good. Evolutionary theory worked these deleterious effects by subtly "putting the creative act so far away that reverence for the Creator is likely to be lost." By destroying man's belief in immortality, evolution deprived him of a motive for righteous living and his principal source of hope. Evolution was as unscientific as it was dangerous. Darwin's pages were strewn with words like "probably," "apparently," and "we may well suppose." Darwin, Bryan concluded, "is guessing. . . . Darwinism . . . is a string of guesses strung together. . . ."

In a subsequent lecture, "Back to God," Bryan contended: "The supreme need of the day is to get back to God—to a love of God that fills the heart, the mind and the soul, and dominates every impulse and energy of the life." Evolutionists were leading their followers away from the Creator by teaching that "man . . . has in him, not the breath of the Almighty, but the blood of the brute." By rejecting the first chapters of Genesis and Matthew, the evolutionists denude "life of its spiritual elements and make man a brother to the beast." [15]

If there was any group that Bryan was concerned about in his view of Darwinism, it was youth. Mary observed that "helping one to make a good start in life was more important to him than anything else." Bryan was now most attentive to the college population because the expansion of science courses exposed them in great numbers to Darwinism. Bryan was also sensitive to college youth, because it was during his own college years that he succumbed for a time to the lures of Darwinism and underwent a crisis of faith. "I passed through a period of skepticism," he acknowledged in his lecture "The Prince of Peace," "when I was in college, and I have been glad ever since that I became a member of the church before I left home for college, for it helped me during those trying days." The college years, he was convinced, were a critical juncture in man's pilgrimage. They cover, he said, "the dangerous period in the young man's life; he is just coming into possession of his powers, and feels stronger than he ever feels afterwards—and he thinks he knows more than he ever does know."

Both from his frequent visits to colleges and from a book by James H. Leuba, professor of psychology at Bryn Mawr, *The Belief in God and Immortality,* Bryan was impressed with the adverse effects of college education on belief in God and immortality. Leuba's study concluded that while young people enter college with Christian faith, the probability is that "on leaving college, from 40 to 45 percent" denied or doubted basic Christian tenets. Leuba also found that among scientists and academicians, nonbelievers were preponderant. In 1921, word coming to Bryan from the campuses provided alarming affirmation. In lectures and magazine articles, he related how a girl educated at Wellesley informed him that no one believed in the Bible now; how a Columbia teacher began his lessons in geology by requesting his students to put aside "all that they had learned in Sunday School"; how the president of the University of Wisconsin heard with complacency that a professor there told his class the Bible was a collection of myths, "but was very angry when I presented to the students the other side of Darwinism." "Are you prepared," he cried to audiences, "to have your children trade a crowded intellect for a pure heart and come back with a swelled head and a shriveled heart?" [16]

Educators far and wide, particularly in prestigious Eastern establishments, took out with full cry after Bryan. Addressing a National Education Association annual convention, Professor Edwin R. A. Seligman of Columbia likened opposition to evolutionary theories to an expression of the ideas "of the childhood of society." If the nation must return to childhood, let it go all the way, he suggested, and teach that the earth is flat and the sun moves around it. Edwin G. Conklin, professor of biology at Princeton, noted that Bryan lacked training in that field and was misled by a widely prevalent view, particularly in politics, "that one man's opinion is as good as another's on any subject whatever."

The struggle escalated when Bryan was enlisted to support a bill in Kentucky barring the teaching of evolution in educational institutions supported by state funds. In an address to the state legislators, the first half of which was devoted to urging the establishment of a state trade commission, Bryan condemned the "teaching of irreligion in our public schools and universities." He proposed that if "agnostics or atheists or unbelievers of any sort" wish to teach their beliefs, they "should have the right to establish their own schools as Christians do" but should not be permitted to teach them in schools maintained by public taxation. In lending support to the Kentucky bill, Bryan was careful to advise against including "any penalties . . . on the ground that they were not dealing with a criminal class but with persons who would obey the law if it were merely stated."

"Christ went about doing good," Bryan said. "The young need Him as their guide throughout life." The service one rendered to his fellowmen depended on both capacity and disposition. Education could increase capacity, but "it goes for naught" unless religion, as only it could, provided disposition. "Nothing less than a sense of responsibility to God can give the coercive power necessary to insure the consecration of all our energy and time to that which is the highest and best." Darwin and evolution made man accept and adjust to the world as it is. Belief in Christ, a giving of oneself to the power of Christian love, made man a reformer. Only then could man obey Christ's commandment "Let him who would be chiefest among you be the servant of all." And only then could man perceive that "Love makes money-grabbing contemptible; love makes class prejudice impossible; love makes selfish ambition a thing to be despised. . . ." [17]

Bryan's increasing preoccupation with Darwinism and evolution did not in any way curtail his promotion of political questions and reforms. In the most absolute sense, his endeavors in religion and politics were interlocking. He could not do one to the exclusion of the other. "We need this belief in God in our dealings with nations as well as in the control of our own conduct; it is necessary to the establishment of justice," he said in his lecture "In His Image." "Belief in God is the basis of brotherhood; we are brothers because we are children of one God."

With such a faith, Bryan steadfastly pursued his efforts to establish an effective League of Nations supported by full United States membership and participation. He viewed the United States as possessing unique resources, and therefore singular responsibilities, for bringing enduring peace. In the late war, "We were the only great nation that sought no selfish advantage and had . . . no spirit of revenge to gratify. . . . Our nation being made up of the best blood of the nations of Europe, we learn to know the people at home through the representatives who come here. Because of our intimate connection with the foreign elements of our country our sympathy goes out to all lands; and because we have received from other nations as no other nation ever did, we are in duty bound to give as no other nation has given."

As the months of the Harding administration slipped by and the President took no real step to honor his campaign promise of an "association of nations" in which the United States would participate, Bryan was diligent in spotlighting the lapse. When France entered German territory, apparently to force payment of indemnity, Bryan, discerning the possible beginnings of another war, reminded his countrymen of their deep responsibility for that eventuality. The United States, "with the confidence of the world such as no other nation has, has failed to throw its influence into the balance . . . how shall we escape responsibility for the calamity that may befall the world?" Those steps that Harding took toward bolstering world peace Bryan generously applauded. The President's recommendation that the United States assume a seat in the World Court he quickly endorsed. And as new issues arose which jarred relations between nations, Bryan called for American leadership.

On the domestic political scene, Bryan persisted as the alert guardian and promoter of social justice. The Supreme Court's holding in 1923 that a minimum wage law was unconstitutional drew from Bryan as bitter a lamentation as it did from any union leader. The Court's handiwork, he said, was "another Dred Scott decision," and if any good might come from it, it should "awaken the country to the heartlessness of plutocracy." Bryan was wholly sympathetic to the demands of war veterans for a bonus to compensate, at least to a degree, for their niggardly pay in the Army, which contrasted so sharply with the fat profits of their brothers at home. Critics, including Harding, saw the drive for a bonus as a kind of political holdup and cried that the bonus would clean out the public treasury. Bryan quickly trundled out a plan to finance the bonus while avoiding the levy of any new tax on the general public. It was the simple recommendation that the government go after the full legions of tax dodgers whose artfully withheld contributions would more than pay the bonus. Bryan's chief villain was the wealthy, prestigious Secretary of the Treasury, Andrew Mellon. Intent upon rescuing the poor rich man from wartime taxes, the Secretary was making swift progress with his plans to repeal and lower taxes. Indignant at such brazen favoritism for high-income citizens, Bryan urged a reenactment of the excess profits tax which "would enable Congress to reduce taxes on the masses. . . ." [18]

Even more beleaguered than the tax system was the fast-sinking ship of prohibition, upon which pounded the waves of the speakeasy, the bootlegger, the gangster, and bathtub gin. Begun as a vast project for man's moral improvement, prohibition had become a grand accelerator of the moral decay of the 1920's. In these dark days for his cause, Bryan repeatedly called for holding the line of nonalcoholic rectitude. He endorsed a proposal by Congressman W. K. Upshaw of Georgia inviting the President and the Cabinet to sign a total abstinence pledge to provide an example to the nation. Indeed Bryan was so enthusiastic that he urged that ". . . Mr. Upshaw's proposal . . . be carried farther. Why would it not be well for each cabinet officer to have a pledgebook and ask all the employees of his department to join him in a total abstinence pledge?"

In Southern and Western states, when bills were weighed to repeal the enforcement law, Bryan would be asked to address the legislature. In less hospitable states, he lobbied in legislative corridors and offices, spoke at nearby churches, and wrote in the local press. His defense of prohibition brought him into a head-on clash with the leading wet Democrats and the principal contender for the next Presidential nomination, Governor Alfred E. Smith of New York.

In an age of lawlessness, gross corruption, and spreading moral breakdown, Bryan spoke no word against the chief governmental officer who presided over the chaos, the President of the United States, Warren Harding. Though the sticky defiling fingers of Teapot Dome reached one prominent figure after another around the President, Bryan's disposition toward the embattled Harding was one of absolute tolerance and restraint. In the midst of exposures and uproar, Harding was wafted away from the rising tides of political embarrassment by death. No eulogy for the late President was more tender or warm than Bryan's. Harding, he said in a public statement at Miami and in a voice showing deep emotion, was "a big-hearted, lovable fellow." But more important, in Bryan's estimation, Harding was, as no other President in Bryan's career had been, one of the common people, "a boy, born of humble parentage and reared upon a farm, without the prestige of a name, without the possession of wealth and without even the aids that come from scholastic training. . . ." His ascent was "proof of the wonderful advantages offered by our form of government. . . ." [19]

Bryan, now an elderly sixty-three, found that the process of aging brought no letup in the demands from the world about him. *The Commoner,* moving into its third decade, was a robust specimen of personal political journalism. Even in his political decline, Bryan kept in touch with his followers through its pages, which reached thousands of subscribers. In 1923 the year's first issue of the paper began with a solemn pledge: At the beginning of this, its twenty-third year, *The Commoner* rededicated itself "to the cause of the common people; for their interests against the interests of special classes." But a mere four months later, *The Commoner* carried "A Word of Farewell." With Charley well occupied in Nebraska's governor's chair and Bryan in far-off Florida, the paper's continuation had become impossible. "I am not retiring from politics," Bryan's final editorial assured his readers, "nor shall I lose interest in public measures." Various papers and magazines would carry his interviews and articles. His "Bible Talks" appeared in newspapers with a circulation of 4,000,000, and his traveling would continue, though with some decrease "with advancing years," and he hoped still to have the pleasure of meeting *The Commoner's* subscribers.

Charley oversaw the sad, sentimental task of dismantling the enterprise and its homely quarters. Subscribers had to be cared for, paper stocks disposed of, a box with a cast of Bryan's face had to be shipped to Florida, and two busts stored unless Grace or William could provide them sanctuary. Files had to be dug through for letters to save or burn. Worst of all was the breaking of old, firm human ties. "It is really distressing," Bryan wrote, "to have to part company with these faithful employees who have been with us so long, and I would not do it if it did not seem necessary." Bryan proposed that the magazine's surplus of $7,500 be divided among the small work force and Charley.[20]

If this was the period of Bryan's political decline, it coincided with the continued physiological decline of himself and his closest political partner, Mary. Illness was now a pervasive factor in Bryan's existence. Arthritis still clutched Mary mercilessly. Mary "is taking much more interest in affairs than she did last year," Bryan wrote in 1923. "It is wonderful how patient she is and how cheerful." Bryan struggled to resist the lures of speeches and lectures to be with her as much as possible. When the Reverend J. Frank Norris, the Fundamentalist divine, urged Bryan to undertake a lecture tour to fight "the evil doctrine" of evolution, Bryan remonstrated that he had already taken four trips north that winter, and he was now going to keep his resolve that "I owe it to her to give her such comfort as I could by my presence."

By 1923, after trying a sequence of doctors and water cures, the Bryans took to looking for a faith healer, and in 1924, deep in desperation, they consulted one. When Bryan was forced to leave Mary, she dominated his thoughts. Just before the 1924 national Democratic convention began, Bryan, sitting on the bed of his New York hotel room, poured out to a reporter the sorrow of his heart for Mary. With tears running down his cheeks, Bryan related at some length what she had been to him, blurted out his fear that she would not last long, and declared that he did not care to survive her.

Bryan too felt the scourge of poor health. His diabetes continued to force him to follow a prescribed diet, and he consulted regularly with doctors. A good friend, the Reverend Percival H. Barker of Pittsburgh, directed Bryan's attention to the glorious news that a doctor in Toronto was curing diabetic patients "with a serum called insulin." Solicitous friends such as Samuel Untermyer, the distinguished New York attorney, reading of Bryan's "unceasing activities—flying around the country" warned that "you are challenging fate, and that it is not given to mortal man to keep up the pace. Please do 'put on the brakes' while there is yet time." [21]

In lectures, press interviews, and correspondence, Bryan continued his fight against Darwinism and evolution. He developed a network of correspondence and consultation with Fundamentalist leaders—with Billy Sunday, who said that evolution is "bunk, junk, and poppycock"; with the Reverend J. Frank Norris, who had already secured the expulsion of several evolutionists from Baylor and Southern Methodist universities; and others. Bryan stepped up his visits to college campuses, and when biologists confronted him in the question period, he delighted to ask, "Why does a red cow, fed on green grass, give white milk?"

In aligning himself with Fundamentalists, Bryan, as Lawrence Levine has noted, was keeping strange bedfellows. His common cause with them stopped at anti-evolution and a shared belief in the infallability of the literal Bible. Bryan's politics and his program of social reform, which he continued to promote with unflagging gusto, were wholly unacceptable to the professional Fundamentalists. Billy Sunday flung fire and thunderbolts at advocates of the social gospel. Another evangelist taught that "Man has no inalienable right except the right to be damned." And the geologist Professor George M. Price, who enjoyed wide acceptance among Fundamentalist churchmen, observed, "When Christ himself was here, though surrounded by crying abuses, oppression, and tyranny, he attempted no civil reforms, nor has he left his Church any commission to purify the governments of the earth." With his left hand, Bryan was defending church forms; with his right, he was leading the earthly house of God away from its traditional noninvolvement in social issues. Ironically, Bryan's social gospel was more radical than that of the emerging body of his critics among the clergy—the Modernists, as they were called.[22]

Bryan's involvements in Fundamentalism assumed a new direction with his attendance as a delegate to the General Assembly of the Presbyterian Church in 1923. Before the assembly gathered at Indianapolis, rumors abounded of Bryan's possible election as the church's moderator. Days before the delegates gathered, his friends among the Fundamentalist clergy were making soundings of the feasibility of a departure from orthodox practice permitting the elevation of a layman, Bryan, rather than a cleric. Upon arriving at Indianapolis, Bryan declared that he did not know if he would be a candidate for moderator, and he cautioned reporters: "This is not like a political campaign where a man announces his candidacy and then goes out to secure the delegates."

But Bryan was not long in deciding to run. His opponents, the Modernists or liberals, united upon Dr. Charles F. Wishart, president of Wooster College, Ohio, where evolution was taught as fact. Bryan led on the first two ballots, but on the third, by preagreement, other candidates withdrew, and Wishart won with 451 votes to 427 for Bryan. To the astonishment of some delegates, Wishart abstained from the customary practice of appointing the runner-up as vice-moderator and from appointing Bryan to a key committee for which he had made his desires openly known. "When you win out on a question of policy," a pro-Wishart clergyman explained, "you don't put the execution of the policy in the hands of the opposition."

His defeated candidacy and pointed slights in no way diminished Bryan's purpose and activity at the assembly. He introduced several resolutions incorporating his views of the fit church and the proper churchman. In one, he moved to require ministers and church teachers in every Presbyterian school, seminary, or college to subscribe to a total abstinence pledge. After a hard fight, the assembly adopted the resolution. Bryan's second thrust provided that no part of the Educational Fund of the Presbyterian Church should support instruction that teaches as proved fact either Darwinism or any other evolutionary hypothesis that linked men in a blood relationship with any other form of life. This proposal touched off a fierce, cacophonous debate, spirited volleys of applause, and hasty motions and amendments to motions. At one juncture, the moderator was driven to remind the assembly that it constituted "a court of Jesus Christ."

In an unsparing summation Bryan exclaimed, "We have preachers in this audience who don't believe in the resurrection of Christ's body. We have preachers in this hall who don't believe in the miracles." These several failures of belief he blamed upon evolution. To a Modernist detractor he cried, ". . . Did you do more than I did to put across women's suffrage? Did you do more than I did to put across the election of Senators by direct vote of the people? Did you do more than I did to levy an income tax so that those who had wealth would have to pay for it? There has not been a reform for twenty-five years that I did not support and I am now engaged in the biggest reform of my life. I am trying to save the Christian Church from those who are trying to destroy her faith." Amid yells and screams, the moderator pounded his gavel and demanded "Christian decorum."

But the Modernists prevailed, and a mild substitute motion which fell well short of the wishes of Bryan was adopted. Bryan openly expressed displeasure with the result. "I have had experience enough in politics to know a machine when I see it, and the machinery in control of this Assembly works perfectly. The so-called liberals have everything their own way. I found that out as soon as I arrived. . . ." He also let fly a volley at the Eastern press, which according to its habit was magnifying his rebuffs and discomfiture. In these days at the assembly, he said he was becoming better acquainted with the editors of the New York press, "and I think the only Bible verse they know is 'The three wise men came from the East.' They think that if a reform does not start in New York it does not amount to anything. But no reform ever does start in New York." [23]

Bryan's efforts at the assembly to advance the purification of the church in light of Fundamentalist doctrines also centered on the question of the future status in organized Presbyterianism of Dr. Harry Emerson Fosdick of New York. One of the most influential of the Modernists, Fosdick was the author of numerous widely read books, a professor at Union Theological Seminary, and a consummate preacher. The assembly could not touch Fosdick since he was a Baptist, but it could direct the New York Presbytery to rescind its action of allowing Fosdick to preach regularly in the First Presbyterian Church. The Fosdick question again dispatched the assembly into an angry clamorous debate and a series of convoluted maneuvers. Eventually the assembly condemned the pulpit utterances of Fosdick and directed the New York Presbytery to require that preachings and teachings in New York's First Presbyterian Church "conform to the system of doctrines taught in the Confession of Faith." These included the Resurrection, the Virgin birth, and all the miracles—all Fundamentalist tenets.

The differences between Bryan and Dr. Fosdick continued to rage, as each authored widely circulated books in 1924. Bryan insisted on literal acceptance of the Bible's account of the Creation, the Virgin birth, the Resurrection, atonement, and other articles of faith. "To be a living vital force, a civilizing influence, and a spiritual power," he wrote, "the Christian Church must be true to the Christ of the Bible; apostasy means death to the Church and despair to civilization." Dr. Fosdick, in contrast, posed a view of Christianity as "not a finished article but a growing movement. . . . It is like a tree whose roots are deep in the spirit of Jesus. Sometimes it puts forth misshapen branches that must be pruned. . . . Because it is a growing, living, vital thing, it has never been quite the same thing in any two generations." Like many Modernists, Fosdick denied that true science and true religion could conflict. "The only clash can be between an unbelieving science and an unscientific belief." Fosdick visualized Bryan not as the Bible's defender, but its attacker. Bryan, he wrote, rejected the Bible as a record of God's progressive unfolding of his character and set it up for what it was never meant to be, "a procrustean bed to whose infallible measurements all human thought must be forever trimmed."

In addition to his struggle to purify the church, Bryan continued his struggle to purify the schools. In 1923 and 1924, he addressed a succession of state legislatures, most of them in the South, to promote the passage of bills prohibiting the teaching of evolution in tax-supported schools. "Evolutionists," he declaimed to the West Virginia legislature, "rob the Savior of the glory of virgin birth, the majesty of His deity and the triumph of His resurrection. They weaken faith in the Bible by discarding miracles and the supernatural and by eliminating from the Bible all that conflicts with their theories. They render that book a scrap of paper." [24]

Aging and ailing, freely acknowledging that "my power in politics has waned," Bryan still meant to be a directing influence on the approaching national Democratic convention of 1924. He had ample grounds for optimism in his purpose. The national Democratic Party was in a state of acute disarray. Woodrow Wilson lived in secluded retirement and would soon be claimed by death; the last standard-bearer was discredited with defeat and a residuary image of ineptitude. Bryan, for his part, still possessed powerful assets: unlimited audacity, large gifts for imaginative political enterprise, and an undimmed capacity for political generalship that enabled him to wrest the attention of national conventions and move them into directions he initiated.

As early as the winter of 1923-24, Bryan began devoting his surging activity to preparing for the 1924 campaign. In correspondence with key party personalities and in visits to Washington with Congressional leaders, he delineated the posture he deemed best fit for the party in the approaching contest. It must, above all, be a progressive party, in both its platform and its Presidential nominee. Progressivism encompassed the array of social and economic reforms Bryan had been preaching in late years, including prohibition. The rising public disenchantment with the Noble Experiment, the strong movement in the states to curb it, the rejoicing of wet Democrats in the antiprohibition trends, the last elections in the Eastern industrial states were spurring growing numbers of Democratic leaders to seek a platform calling for changes that would satisfy the South, which was incurably dry, and Northern urban centers, which were thoroughly wet. Conceivably the Volstead Act, on which enforcement was based, could be modified; its definition of intoxicating liquor, which included any beverage with more than one-half of 1 percent alcohol, might be amended to exclude beer and light wines. Since compromise was not for Bryan, the seeds of conflict were sown.

The issues of 1924, Bryan felt, would be largely shaped by the policies of the Harding-Coolidge administration. After Coolidge's State of the Union message of 1923, Bryan wrote to Charles, "I do not know of any large group that he has not offended." Farmers, he noted, "were not even treated with courtesy." By midsummer, 1923, Bryan had in hand the elements of a progressive platform. The farmer's condition was wretched; he was selling at prices of prewar levels and buying at levels 50 percent higher. "Something must be done to raise farmer's prices or to lower the prices of things he buys." The Federal Reserve banking system, which was "instituted to benefit the people has been captured by Wall Street," must be remade into an agency for protecting the public interest. Labor and capital were drifting apart, and a tribunal to investigate their disputes was essential. The profiteer was running riot; industry was entering into ever-larger combinations, "leaving the masses the victims. . . . The exploiters were never more fully in control of the country than now. . . ." Bryan's chief Republican target remained Andrew Mellon, Secretary of the Treasury in the Harding-Coolidge administrations, author of "the most reactionary revenue bill ever drafted."

Although Bryan had a platform, he did not have a candidate. Each of the leading candidates, he made glaringly clear, was unacceptable. The Oscar Underwood of 1924 was no different from, and therefore no better than, the Underwood of 1912. Underwood was dangerous to Bryan for other reasons besides his possible candidacy. As one of the few Southern Democrats of national stature, he rivaled Bryan for influence among the Southern delegations. As Democratic leader of the House of Representatives, he possessed strength in the Southern wing of the party far beyond anything the declining Bryan commanded. Among Bryan's Alabaman informants, fear was rife that Underwood, a wet, would sell out to Alfred E. Smith of New York, another wet, and be rewarded "by being made Secretary of State or some other rich plum." In the Alabama Presidential preference primary, Bryan marched through the state in a heavily scheduled speaking tour, blasting Underwood as "wet and reactionary." During a Bryan speech, circulars were distributed bearing a photographic copy of a letter in which Underwood requested that three double rooms and a parlor be reserved at the Waldorf-Astoria during the coming convention for Charles M. Lewis, described as the "chief lobbyist in the United States for the brewery interests." When Underwood men threw doubts upon the authenticity of the letter, Bryan retorted, "The liquor interests have such a keen sense of smell it is not necessary for Charles Lewis to engage rooms next to Underwood as they will find him anyhow."

Each of the leading Presidential candidates, in Bryan's eyes, carried some major blemish. Governor Smith was so thoroughly wet that he was well beyond the pale of acceptance. Toward William Gibbs McAdoo, Bryan in the earlier stages of the preconvention maneuvering was, at best, ambivalent, and he made several gestures that were decidedly unhelpful to his candidacy. In Texas, where McAdoo men hoped to win the state delegation, Bryan proclaimed that Governor Pat M. Neff, a dedicated dry, was ideal Presidential timber. Conceivably with this encouragement, Neff could become a candidate, and the canons of political etiquette dictated that McAdoo should not oppose him. In Nebraska, where McAdoo had entrusted the task of winning the state delegation to Arthur Mullen, he was again blocked by the favorite son gambit when Governor Charles Bryan announced his candidacy for the Presidency. Very quickly McAdoo withdrew his name from the Nebraska primary. To a sleek prancing dark horse who was emerging ever more distinctly, John W. Davis of West Virginia, Bryan applied the tarbrush in a public statement. It was not necessary, he declared, "to consider Davis further than to say that he is now attorney for J. Pierpont Morgan. That sufficiently describes his connections and political views." [25]

Once again, Bryan was indulging in his old ploy of trotting out candidates with regional but not national reputations and without any significant chance for the nomination. This year he was partial to Southerners, supporting at one time or another Governor Pat Neff of Texas and Josephus Daniels, whose chief function was to offset Underwood. The candidate Bryan eventually chose as his own had far fewer political credentials than Neff or Daniels. As the political year of 1924 dawned, Bryan announced that his choice for the Democratic nomination for President was Dr. A. A. Murphree, president of the University of Florida. "He is a rare combination of intellect and heart. He is a splendid executive, as shown by the success of the university under his management. . . . He is 'dry' and progressive and sound on economic questions. His popularity will grow as he becomes known."

Bryan's unveiling of the politically anonymous Murphree touched off waves of mirth and derision. In an editorial headed "The All Too Obvious Mr. Bryan," the Miami *Herald* proclaimed, "This gesture by Mr. Bryan can but lower public opinion as to his political sagacity. The assumption cannot be gainsaid that he is resorting to political legerdemain in order to regain a rapidly slipping foothold in the confidence of the public . . . and it is to be regretted that he has taken so good a man as Dr. Murphree as a doormat to obtain fairly clean footsteps in order to reenter the door of political opportunity."

At midyear, 1923, Charley was pointing out to his brother that "you have all the natural elements of strength that I had here, and I can prepare a national economic program that will bring you all support of the farmer, wage earner, middle classes, wet or dry." Charley's proposal was accompanied by counsel that Bryan must tour the country and present the issues. Old supporters besieged Bryan to allow them to enter his name in their states' primaries. But he resolutely discouraged these efforts. He would not, he wrote to John J. Lentz, a former Democratic Congressman of Ohio, "put myself in the attitude of seeking the nomination, but really dread the thought of being a candidate and would not consider it except as it came in the form of a duty—and that does not seem to me very probable."

Investigations of Teapot Dome in 1924 which revealed McAdoo's connections with the scandal brought new waves of demands for Bryan to make the race. Honesty in public affairs would now be the main issue, his friends cried, and "You are one of the few public men whose public and private lives are absolutely above reproach." Or again, "People look for a moral leader as well as a political one, and again you fill the bill." To all implorings that he enter the primaries, Bryan was adamantly negative, saying that he did not want to be President and that it was better for the office to go to a younger man. In a letter to Charley, carefully exploring the situation, Bryan foresaw that he might be available in the remote contingency "that after the Republican convention there might be an attempt to unite all the Democrats and progressive forces against a reactionary Republican candidate. If there is such a situation and no Democratic candidate before the convention is able to unite the forces, there might be a disposition to turn to me." [26]

Yet in the months preceding the national convention, Bryan maintained a schedule of speaking appearances that a serious Presidential candidate would follow. He moved through the Southern and border states, spoke in Chicago and Springfield, Illinois, at Des Moines and Topeka, and finally at Lincoln for a giant celebration of his birthday. As the convention neared, the New York *Times* reported from Lincoln that Mary was saying openly that Bryan had an excellent chance of winning the nomination and that after McAdoo and Smith were eliminated, the convention would turn to him. Mary, according to her Lincoln friends, reflected Bryan's thinking.

An old admirer and political sophisticate, John Temple Graves, a top Hearst editor, put before Bryan a recipe for action to make the dream attributed to Mary come true. "Make a great speech nominating or seconding McAdoo," Graves counseled. "Then 'sit steady in the boat.' Make no enemies on the floor of the Convention. After days of wrangle and bitterness . . . there will surely come to that great body, a receptive moment—which you of all men will know—Take the floor. Put the whole glory of your great moral convictions into a great plea for Democracy and the people. Make it the speech of your life. Build in it a sentence that will be as immortal as your 'cross of gold and crown of thorns.' The rest will be history."

Bryan meant to go to the convention as a delegate at large from Florida. Before announcing his candidacy for that designation in the primary, he was the soul of propriety in consulting the state's Senators and governor to ascertain whether they desired the honor, but they declined. In his quest for a primary victory, Bryan toured Florida by auto and spoke in the county seat of all of its sixty-six counties. Mary was delighted to see his wan appearance replaced by the tan of the winter sun, his eyes beaming with happiness in knowing once more the excitement of an electoral contest. Arthur Brisbane, who came into the state to help, discovered that only the railroads and "those to whom the dollar looks bigger than the Washington monument" were opposing him, while the people "will have sense enough to send you." Brisbane's forecast proved absolutely correct. Bryan won an overwhelming victory, running well ahead of the field.[27]

Bryan was the main attraction as more than 3,000 delegates, alternates and their families took dinner in the grand ballroom and adjoining lobbies, wings, and anterooms of the Hotel Commodore in the convention city of New York. Mayor John Hylan presided over what was described as the largest dinner ever held in the city, flanked by Governor Alfred E. Smith, Norman Mack, and Bryan. Throughout the repast, Bryan seemed the object of almost everyone's interest. Guests stood on chairs and fathers held up little children to see him. Old friends kept moving up to shake hands and exchange a word at such a pace that Bryan barely found time to put away a mouthful of food. When the dinner ended, waves of loud demands swept across the floor for a speech. Guests again climbed onto their chairs and shouted for him to rise, and cries of "Bryan! Bryan! Bryan!" filled the ballroom. But he merely smiled and kept his silence until the diners eventually filed out.

Bryan made at least two careful prearrangements for the convention. Weeks before the delegates gathered, he secured reservations at the Waldorf-Astoria Hotel which assured that both the Florida and the Nebraska delegations would be on the third floor, and he hired rooms for the joint occupancy of himself and Charley "so we can be in constant conference. . . ."

In addition, Bryan came with a series of planks for the party platform.

The convention's organizers, doubtless with an air of resignation, conferred upon him the chairmanship of the subcommittee of the Resolutions Committee charged with drafting the platform. As he trotted out his planks, Bryan seemed to meet with no resistance at all. His proposal for a war referendum was quickly accepted. When a delegate urged a plank calling for immediate independence for the Philippines, Bryan bespoke enthusiasm, and it was at once adopted.

The first sour note was sounded by Miss Helen L. Baughan of the National Liberal Alliance, who demanded a plank calling for modification of the Volstead Act. She recalled that Wayne Wheeler of the Anti-Saloon League had already said that "There will be no beer and wine plank in the Democratic platform," an assertion encouraged by Bryan's chairmanship of the platform subcommittee. "This is dictatorial gall personified," cried Miss Baughan, "and should be resented by every upstanding delegate." Miss Baughan enlarged her indictment to couple Bryan with Wheeler in the ambition to dictate to the convention. Wheeler added fuel to the fire when he declared that the liquor interests had brought vast quantities of their evil product to New York "to obtain a wet platform plank and a wet candidate through debauching the delegates." The resolutions subcommittee, after stirring debate, rebuffed the efforts of wets to win a liberal plank on prohibition. A League of Nations plank also raised a brisk struggle, but the most devastating encounter was over a plank denouncing the Ku Klux Klan, whose burning crosses and reign of terror were meant to keep the Southern black man in his place. The Klan was also anti-Catholic, anti-Jewish, anti-almost anything that did not fit into a Protestant, Anglo-Saxon, native American mold. Alternate resolutions were quickly introduced, including one by Bryan that did not name the Klan but reaffirmed the Democratic Party's devotion to the fundamental constitutional principles of freedom of religion, speech, press, and assembly. Bryan begged committee colleagues to shun any action that would divide the Democratic Party. He was confident that four years hence the Klan would have been forgotten, and he could not support any movement that would array Northern Democrats against their Southern brothers.

For two days, Bryan and his colleagues from both sides of the Mason-Dixon Line met seeking agreement. On the last night of their deliberations they gathered at nine o'clock and remained continuously in session for fifteen hours. From the outset the conference room crackled with tension. Committee members scattered around the room variously glared or had sullen looks cemented on their faces. Speakers tended to be crotchety and were easily offended. Several times violence seemed imminent.

Suddenly Bryan, who presided over these ominous proceedings, noticed a sharp change in atmosphere. For reasons that he could never altogether explain, a spirit of reconciliation seemed to displace the combativeness. Instead of remaining scattered around the room, committee members drew their chairs up to the long table at whose head Bryan sat. Several members made conciliatory remarks, and Judge John H. McCann of Pennsylvania delivered an eloquent appeal for harmony which further softened the delegates' attitudes.

When McCann finished, Bryan suggested that the long, exhausting meeting now end with prayer and that McCann, a Catholic, and he, a Protestant, lead the devotions. At about 6 A.M., as the first flicker of sun reached into the smoky tumultuous room, McCann led the committee, with all heads bowed, in reciting the Lord's Prayer. Thereupon, with the room still silent, Bryan prayed: ". . . We need Thy counsel, Lord. We are carrying great responsibilities and dealing with mighty problems that vex and trouble us. We are subject to prejudice and passion and unconscious bias. Cleanse our minds of all unworthy thoughts and purge our hearts of all evil desires. Show us Thy ways and help us to know what Thou wouldst have us say and do and be. . . . Help us to advance in our day and this day the brotherhood Thou didst establish; may it include all mankind. . . ."

The prayer's appeal to the Southerners for humanity and tolerance was not lost upon them. The committee voted, and the plank critical of the Klan but not naming it was reported to the convention. Bryan's prayer was, for the moment, the subject of talk and admiration among the delegates. Here and there derogatory comment was heard. Arthur Mullen observed sardonically: "It would have been more effective had not someone recalled the story of the Scottish sailor who was told after a shipwreck that the captain was in his cabin praying. 'That's all very well for him,' he said, 'but I'll start swimming.' "

On the convention floor, debate on the Klan issue was sharp and bitter. The climax was Bryan's speech, begun amid mingled applause, boos, and hisses, pleading against the adoption of an amendment specifically naming the Klan. He entreated the delegates to observe the supreme ethic of party unity and contended that "we have no moral right" to be diverted from the Democratic mission. ". . . it requires more courage to fight the Republican party than it does to fight the Ku Klux Klan. Here we have farmers driven into bankruptcy. . . . We find monopoly spreading. We find nearly every great line of industry in the control of gigantic combinations of capital . . . we have a war-worn world across the Atlantic that needs our help . . . Anybody can fight the Ku Klux Klan, but only the Democratic party can stand between the common people and their oppressors. . . ." The Klan could be exterminated "better by recognizing their honesty and teaching them that they are wrong." Bryan, his most resolute critics agreed, spoke with his old-time fire and enthusiasm. He had also demonstrated that prohibition occupied a higher place in his value scheme than the civil rights and civil liberties imperiled and destroyed by the Ku Klux Klan. On the Klan issue, he asserted the ethic of party unity. On prohibition, which also divided Democrats, he showed not the least concern for party unity.

At last, at 2 A.M., the count was taken, and the amendment naming and censuring the Klan was defeated by but a single vote. Bryan's purpose of preserving at least the outward unity of his party had been achieved. The next morning, when friends rushed to his room, exclaiming, "You did it," Bryan replied, "No, it must have been the Lord's work! I would not have been willing to risk so small a margin." [28]

At least one member of the Florida delegation regarded his colleague Bryan with bristly suspicion. Former Governor Albert W. Gilchrist told the press with unveiled disgust that Bryan was seeking the Presidential nomination. "In all his speeches," Gilchrist noted, "Bryan has accentuated that the convention must nominate a 'dry' and a progressive candidate on a dry platform. In my opinion that means Bryan." As the convention turned to select its Presidential nominee, Gilchrist could test his theory.

The early balloting was a three-way contest among McAdoo, Smith, and John W. Davis. A former member of the United States House of Representatives from West Virginia, Solicitor General, and ambassador to Great Britain in the Wilson administration, Davis, one of the most distinguished of constitutional lawyers, was shedding his status as a dark horse, although still running well behind Smith and McAdoo. Bryan bustled among the delegations working for McAdoo and remonstrating against Davis, whose strength increased steadily as the balloting progressed. Bitter at Bryan's opposition, Davis men recalled that their hero's father, John J. Davis, had zealously supported Bryan in his Presidential campaigns, and they flaunted an old picture of the three-time nominee and the elder Davis riding in an open carriage and radiant with confraternity in an evident campaign setting. Confronted by reporters, Bryan acknowledged that he recalled the elder Davis' support gratefully and added that he had nothing against the son except his Wall Street connections. He counseled reporters to read his own articles in Hearst's New York *American* on the convention, where he had praised Davis' personal qualifications but added, "Are the sympathies of Mr. Davis on the side of the common people? Would he take their side in matters of legislation and of administration? That question is largely determined by environment. . . . Mr. Davis is the attorney of J. Pierpont Morgan, the foremost representative of the big financial interests, and he has a law practice, both large and lucrative, derived from big business corporations." Bryan was patently less generous in moral judgment to Davis than to himself. Condemning him for the company he was keeping, Bryan was writing about him in a newspaper whose proprietor was William Randolph Hearst. But Hearst and Bryan willingly modified their old enmity for mutual commercial advantage. In Davis' case, however, Bryan was unwilling to allow the least professional or pecuniary considerations for those of the candidate's clients who were wealthy.

"And who is Mr. McAdoo a lawyer for?" a delegate asked, as others cited Davis' devotion to social causes, a record Bryan chose blithely to ignore. Davis, they recalled, in a great West Virginia coal strike was counsel for Eugene V. Debs and "Mother" Jones when they were indicted for sedition and inciting to riot. And in late years, Davis had served as counsel to the National Window Glass Workers. But Bryan only smiled and added that Robert La Follette, the Progressive Presidential nominee, would take more votes away from Davis as the Democratic nominee than he would from any conceivable Republican nominee.

As the drive for McAdoo reached its peak and then floundered desperately in a night drive to reach a majority, Bryan took the platform on the plea that he must explain his vote. The crowd was tired and inhospitable. Resentfully they recalled his bitter attacks upon their wet candidate, Alfred E. Smith. But Bryan's big voice, applied immediately to progressive themes to which Smith's followers were partial, quickly stilled them. However, when Bryan cited the need to nominate a progressive candidate and the fitness of McAdoo, the mention of this name unleashed a new uproar. "Oil, oil," came the cries across the hall. "Tell us about Doheny and McAdoo and oil," a delegate called. Edward L. Doheny, a California petroleum millionaire, was a central figure of the Teapot Dome scandal. Doheny and Harry F. Sinclair made a "loan" of $100,000 to Secretary of Interior Albert B. Fall, after which they leased oil-rich government lands. When Congressional investigating committees probed the murky scandal, Doheny disclosed that McAdoo and three other members of Wilson's Cabinet had been employed by his petroleum company. McAdoo had assisted Doheny in his Mexican interests and was in no way connected with the oil leases, but the mere injection of his name into the scandal tarnished his reputation, to which the clamors of the delegates testified. In truth, by these signs, McAdoo's candidacy was hopeless. As Bryan moved to defend McAdoo and his employ by Doheny, a voice called out, "Who is paying you?" amid a cacophony of catcalls, boos, and applause.

Bryan, thrashing desperately about in the noisy onslaught, named other suitable candidates for President—Thomas J. Walsh of Montana, Senator Samuel M. Ralston of Indiana, Senator Joseph Robinson, E. T. Meredith, former Secretary of Agriculture in the Wilson administration, Josephus Daniels, and Dr. Murphree. "A thousand dollars a speech," came a derisive cry. "Same old Dollar Bill," a delegate shouted. The cries spread like slick. "Oh, get out." "Tell us about oil." "Cut it short." "How about coal contracts?" When Bryan mentioned his brother, Charles, as a desirable nominee, new waves of ridicule broke out. In a box, a well-dressed man who looked like a president of a corporation sat perfectly erect through the uproar, waiting for a quiet moment, whereupon he would shout "Hypo-crite." A reporter counted his use of the word twenty times.

As Bryan fought the heckling, the piercing klieg lights of motion-picture cameramen played full upon him. Each of the many lines of his face stood out pitilessly in the white glare. The large mouth was drawn tight; the strong cheekbones glistened with sweat; it was the face of a man who looked far older than his years, who was fighting desperately and was being beaten. As he swung his arm out and pointed a trembling finger at a heckler and snarled that it appeared that oil was not the only thing his detractors were interested in, the image of benign suavity, known through the years, had vanished. Senator Henry Ashurst, who witnessed the painful scene, was struck with the melancholy thought that "Twenty-eight years ago . . . at Chicago, W. J. B. with raven locks and frame of oak, spoke eloquently and won a Presidential nomination. Tonight, emotionally sore, barren of hope, no longer handsome, eyes like occult jewels, he seemed to be a crotchety, crabbed, played-out man."

Soon after the savage onslaught was over, Bryan moved slowly down the aisle, looking utterly tired, and fanning himself with his big palm-leaf fan. He was at this bleak moment all but completely ignored. A devoted admirer noticed the forlorn apparition and wrote afterward: "It seemed a shame to me. I arose as he approached, shook his hand and congratulated him on a great fight. He actually seemed surprised and he was evidently pleased. As he passed on, I turned to look after him and he, too, had turned and was looking back." [29]

In the aftermath of Bryan's rough encounter, brooding speculation was rife over his purpose. Some viewed it as a sincere, desperate, last-minute effort to put McAdoo across in a dwindling cause. Others thought he was using McAdoo as a way to promote one of his own candidates. Still others were convinced that Bryan was bent upon stampeding the convention for himself. The old fire and eloquence still burned, but the convention, tired, overlong, the galleries filled with Smith partisans hostile to Bryan, was in no mood to be thrilled and swayed.

Bryan may have been bowed, but he was not broken. The next day he was on the floor, moving actively among the delegations to plead McAdoo's cause. At one point he stood in the aisle arguing for twenty minutes with three women who demanded that he vote for Davis. The galleries seemed utterly fascinated as Bryan continually toured about the floor, handshaking, buttonholing, and whispering. Eventually, McAdoo's vote in the balloting for the Presidential nomination shrank to a pitiful 12, and Thomas J. Walsh alone of Bryan's other candidates built a significant total. The galleries seemed to enjoy this further sign of Bryan's undoing.

The struggle for the Presidential nomination was the most protracted marathon in Democratic history. At last, the hundred and third ballot put Davis across. The tall, magnetic white-haired Davis possessed two ideological virtues that Bryan insisted on in the nominee—he was a dry and an advocate of the League of Nations. But he carried the worst of stigmas—he was a Wall Street man and lawyer for J. P. Morgan, and he was almost as conservative as his Republican opponent, Calvin Coolidge. No more bitter brew could have been concocted for Bryan to swallow.

The Vice Presidential nominee emerged from a late-hour conference at the Manhattan Club whose participants included Davis, Bryan's ancient enemy Joseph Guffey of Pennsylvania, and bosses such as George E. Brennan of Illinois and Mayor Frank Hague of Jersey City, whom the Commoner classed among the lowest order of political reptiles. Bryan's old friend Josephus Daniels was also present. Out of the deliberations came an astonishing decision. Charley Bryan was to be the Vice Presidential nominee. It was hoped that his progressivism would at least partially detract from the glaring taint of Davis' Wall Street connections.

Well before the decision that emerged from the moguls' conclave, Bryan had been working for this end. But this fraternal toil was not based upon the assumption that a Wall Streeter would head the ticket. When the choice eventually fell upon Charley, tied in tandem to Davis, Bryan gave forth no immediate utterance expressing delight or even approval. His daughter Grace, in her memoir, wrote that Charley's acceptance of the nomination was a bitter disappointment to her father.

After some delay, Bryan again gave witness that he was the good soldier of his party. "You can say that I shall support the ticket," he declared, explaining that his position would be the same as in 1904, when the conservative Alton Parker was nominated. He would support Davis as he had supported Parker. He added that he preferred "to make my fight within the Democratic party and to correct within the party any mistake the party might make, instead of attempting to correct them by securing defeat of my party and the triumph of another party." And of Charley, he said, "They wanted a Western man who was dry and a progressive, and Governor Bryan fitted into the requirements of the case in every way. . . . I do not think they could have found anyone who could bring more votes to the ticket in a section of the country where the fight will be hardest and hottest." [30]

The temptation to leave his party was spread before Bryan in vivid, dancing colors. With conservatives like Coolidge and Davis heading the Republican and Democratic parties, liberals rushed in droves to support the Presidential candidacy of "Fighting Bob" La Follette, heading a new Progressive grouping and running on a personal platform that included public ownership of waterpower, farm relief, a war referendum, and downward revision of the tariff and railroad rates.

Bryan declined to support La Follette and gave of himself generously to the Democratic campaign. He traversed the West and Far West with a heavy schedule of speeches. With Charley he fought hard to check the movement of Western "farmers, wage earners, and middle classes" to La Follette and to preserve in these groupings a faith in the Democratic Party. The Bryans in reality were fighting to hold on to their old constituencies against a threatened take-over by the invading La Follette. Davis and Bryan got on handsomely during the campaign. A deferential Davis sought the veteran candidate's advice on his acceptance speech and used it. He was attentive to unsolicited counsel that Bryan offered from time to time. And Bryan was generous with private praise to Davis for the quality of his campaign and in public statements declared that his original reservations about Davis had evaporated and he was convinced of his progressivism.[31]

But neither Bryan nor anyone else could prevent the Coolidge landslide that brought "Silent Cal" almost twice as many popular votes as Davis. The public was apparently far more impressed with Republican high-riding prosperity than with Republican oil-besmirched scandal. La Follette's capture of nearly 5,000,000 popular votes, nevertheless, signified the existence of a broad progressive base capable of enduring the assaults of high prosperity.

Yet there were silver linings for Bryan and Charley in the debacle. They rejoiced that the Democratic ticket outpolled La Follette in Nebraska and in states south and west of Nebraska. Although La Follette had seriously weakened the Democratic showing, the Bryans' earlier fears of a La Follette take-over of Western progressivism justifiably receded.

In the gray morning of defeat, Bryan, as usual, was undespairing and forward-looking. "It was a severe defeat," he acknowledged, "and we must begin at once on the campaign for 1928." [32]

PART FOUR

❧≫❂≪❧

Humiliation

28. Ordeal at Dayton

BRYAN was a watchdog of the Coolidge administration, and with its warm, almost unlimited sympathies for the business community, he often had occasion to bark. When Coolidge, in a typical move, nominated Commissioner Thomas F. Woodlock to the Interstate Commerce Commission, Bryan cried out that the appointee was a director of two railroads and "has been identified practically all his life with Wall Street. . . ." Supposedly the ICC's purpose is "to protect the rights of the patrons of the railroads," but "No matter how honest a man Mr. Woodlock might be, his business connections and his environment make it impossible for him to sympathize with railroad patrons." Yet Bryan, for all his periodic outrage, maintained personal relations with Coolidge that were always cordial. Regularly he sent the President quantities of coconuts and citrus fruits from Florida and, upon coming to Washington, customarily visited him. Together they viewed at the White House the eclipse of the sun in January, 1925. Afterward, Bryan said of the experience, "It's just like a Democratic defeat. The sun will shine again."

In seeking to bring the Democracy securely into the progressive fold, Bryan looked to Franklin Roosevelt, Josephus Daniels, and Senator Thomas J. Walsh of Montana as comrades-in-arms. Bryan's contribution to his party's betterment included his possible candidacy in 1926 for the Senatorial seat of Duncan U. Fletcher. A superb vote getter, with a solid progressive record, Fletcher would be a formidable adversary. Ideologically, a race against Fletcher could not be easily justified. Nevertheless, Bryan's Florida friends began to murmur his name whenever the next Senate race was mentioned. To these friends he acknowledged: "I dread the idea of taking on any additional load of care but I feel that this is my last opportunity to render a service to the party which has made me what I am and given me all I have." When Frank Harris, publisher of the Ocala *Banner,* bemoaned the likelihood of defeat in a race with the popular Fletcher, Bryan's attitude was well nigh beatific. Should he be defeated, he said, "I will feel that I have at least tried to pay back the debt I owe the party and can rejoice if there is someone considered more deserving than I." [1]

Bryan's willingness to undertake candidacy came in the face of his deteriorating health. Early in 1925, diabetes was laying a stern hold upon him.

His doctor was concerned from his tests that he was taking in too much carbohydrate and sugar. His daily consumption of rice and potatoes was closely regulated, and he was placed on a diet that banned honey and sugar. Nuts, olives, beans, peas, cucumbers, and pickles, among other things, were permissible if prepared according to prescribed directions. The inroads of disease and the strain of caring for Mary drove Bryan easily to fatigue.

Wobbly health did not prevent full observance of Bryan's sixty-fifth birthday. Friends and followers accorded it the status of a seminational holiday. There was a dinner at Bryan's old standby, the Lafayette, in Washington. More than 100 well-wishers assembled, including Senators and Congressmen and members of the General Council of the Presbyterian Church, whom he had specially invited. Bryan delighted to have his Congressional friends witness the church company he kept.

The message Bryan cherished most on that joyous day was from Mary: "Will not undertake to write you a flowery birthday letter, but simply remark that I love you better and better each year & have an increasing desire to do all I can for your comfort and happiness. I would not trade you. . . ." Bryan's reply was an earnest renewal of their partnership: "I am going to stay with you for a long while yet. Our work is not yet done." [2]

The work remained richly varied. Bryan began to write his memoirs, and in snatches between speaking engagements, he managed to compose chapters. At one point, in the exhilaration of his new task he announced that, to complete it, he would soon retire from the platform. With his old law partner, Dolph Talbot, he planned another new venture—to lead a party of good friends to the Holy Land early in 1926.

In church affairs, Bryan's fortunes had taken an upward turn. In the General Assembly of the Presbyterian Church of 1924, the Fundamentalists had prevailed over the Modernists. Dr. Clarence E. McCartney of Philadelphia, a leading Fundamentalist and a critic of Dr. Harry Emerson Fosdick, was elected moderator. Bryan, an elder and a commissioner from the Presbytery of Southeast Florida, made the nominating speech for McCartney. The victorious McCartney appointed Bryan vice-moderator and hoped that "in a year or two" Bryan might become moderator "without the intense conflict marking the last two elections." In the assembly of 1925, Bryan broke with the militant or extreme Fundamentalists when he supported the candidacy for moderator of Dr. W. O. Thompson, president of Ohio State University, who advocated the resolution, through peaceful methods, of the problems afflicting the church. Thompson humiliated Bryan by rejecting his support, and another theological conservative, Dr. Charles R. Erdman, was elected moderator. [3]

Bryan was still deeply preoccupied with the status of religion in education. In an address to the Men's Fellowship dinner at the General Assembly, Bryan, citing the Loeb-Leopold murder as an example, declared that educational institutions were building great intellectual ships and turning them loose upon the seas of life without a spiritual rudder to keep them off the shoals. He called for bringing this problem into national politics. He criticized both major political parties for the failure of their last platforms to say "a single word about the greatest need of the world—religion." His criticism was unsparing. "One candidate in particular," he added, "I should have expected to recognize this need, but he did not. That was my brother."

Bryan continued to carry his fight against Darwinism and evolution to the college campuses. At Brown University, he declaimed on his subject for two hours before a crowded house, but during the question period treated a persistent interrogator injudiciously by declaring, "I have come a long way to address you, but I shall certainly have to retire before this magnificent, bubbling fountain of wisdom." As the student audience booed and hissed, Bryan walked off the platform. At Harvard, he managed two speeches without serious verbal altercation. At church meetings and conventions, on the campuses, and in a growing body of correspondence, Bryan contended that "the taxpayers have a right to say what shall be taught . . ." and "to direct or dismiss those whom they employ as teachers and school authorities. . . . The hand that writes the paycheck rules the school, and a teacher has no right to teach that which his employers object to."

When correspondents or interrogators in his audiences protested that his line of reasoning was the very negation of free speech, Bryan denied that this was so. "We concede the right of any man," he wrote, "to be an atheist or agnostic. . . ." But he who was a teacher "represented" his school or the taxpayer or both, and he who was a church member "represented" his church. He who took membership or position in school or church had a different status. "The collective right is bound to protect itself from misrepresentation and is just as sacred as the individual's right to think for himself as an individual. These two rights do not conflict when a man is put out of a church because he does not agree with it, or put out of the ministry because he misrepresents it."

To teach or preach, one took his place in organizations, the school and the church. Just as the political party was conducted by majority rule, so, in Bryan's eyes, should the institutions of faith and scholarship be governed by majority. The exponents of Darwinism and evolution, therefore, were attacking an essential tenet of Bryan's handling of the human issues of daily living, the right of the majority to rule. In that rule all were equal, with the scientist or scholar having one vote, no more or less, and each taxpayer, be he schooled or unschooled, possessing an equal vote. Expertise, specialized knowledge, or scientific investigation were entitled to no privilege by dint of qualification or place. All men were equal before the throne of God and before the ballot box. Since a majority of the people were Christian, and Darwinism was anti-Christian, Darwinism should not be taught. "By what logic," Bryan asked, "can the minority demand privileges that are denied to the majority?" [4]

A not uncommon final phase of the politician's career is the experience of humiliation. After years of seeking and winning office or of championing causes with substantial success, he may be brutally and contemptuously rejected. He may be defeated or even overwhelmed at the polls and banished into forced political retirement. His party may deny him renomination. He may be the victim of investigation and scandal. Time may have passed him by; the views and opinions with which he is identified may have become outmoded and in voters' eyes rendered him fit only for a political relic heap. Bryan, in a long, controversial, seemingly unending career, was vulnerable to this cruelest of politicians' experiences. As 1925 dawned, he had thus far escaped personal political disaster. His losses of three Presidential contests were noble defeats, after which he retained influence and a place at the forefront of his party. His races for delegate at large in Nebraska and Florida courted a lacerating electoral rejection, but he generally escaped by winning the contests handily. As one who attached greater importance to issues and beliefs than to offices, Bryan was open to the political risk of being absolutely wrong on a very bad issue. That disaster, with a severe accompanying humiliation, materialized in 1925 in what history remembers as the Great Monkey Trial at Dayton, Tennessee.

Bryan was pushed into the disaster; it occurred from a minimum of choices and acts of his own volition. On January 21, 1925, John Washington Butler, a little-known member of the Tennessee House of Representatives, a strong, tanned farmer of Macon County and a former schoolteacher, introduced a bill making it unlawful for a teacher in any school deriving support from state funds "to teach any theory that denies the story of the divine creation of man as taught in the Bible, and to teach instead that man has descended from a lower order of animals." Earlier Butler had campaigned on a platform advocating the literal Bible and opposing the teaching of evolution in the schools.

In preparing his bill, Butler did not consult with Bryan; its drafting was entirely his own handiwork. After passage in the House by an overwhelming vote, the bill moved to the State Senate, where Senator John A. Shelton, a friend of Bryan, supported it. Shelton, who had himself unsuccessfully introduced an antievolution bill, turned to Bryan for suggestions. He wrote, "If necessary we can defer final action for a few days longer in order to have the benefit of your advice." Bryan objected to the feature of the Butler bill that imposed a penalty—a fine of not less than $100 and not more than $500 for each offense. Writing of his experience in promoting several state laws, Bryan warned that a penalty could be used by opponents to divert attention from the law. A similar bill in Kentucky, he felt, had been defeated by its penalty provisions, which imposed a fine of "not less than fifty nor more than five thousand dollars" or imprisonment for "not less than ten days nor more than twelve months" or both, at the jury's discretion. In addition, Bryan stressed to Shelton, "we are dealing with an educated class that is supposed to respect the law."

Bryan's counsel was rejected, and after several belittling attacks in the Senate, the bill passed with its penalty provision intact. While the bill was under legislative discussion, Tennessee's intellectual community remained strangely silent. The state's Education Department and the University of Tennessee uttered no word of objection. No leading citizen spoke against it. Inexorably the little considered bill moved to the desk of Governor Austin Peay. Although reported to have commented privately that the law was absurd, Peay, faced with the lack of any significant outcry against it and with a politician's instinct to avoid unnecessary trouble, signed the measure. Bryan, despite regrets over the retention of the penalties, congratulated the governor on his "great service. . . . The Christian parents of the state owe you a debt of gratitude for saving their children from the poisonous influence of an unproved hypothesis. . . . The South is now leading the nation in the defense of Bible Christianity. Other states north and south will follow the example of Tennessee." [5]

No real controversy over the new law began until the American Civil Liberties Union, apprehensive of Bryan's prediction that more and more states would pass similar laws, decided to support a test case. It sent word to Tennessee newspapers that it would provide legal and financial assistance to any local teacher who would cooperate in challenging the Butler Act.

An early reader of the Civil Liberties Union's message was a thirty-one-year-old slender, dark, bushy-haired, garrulous mining engineer of Dayton, Tennessee, and an émigré from New York City, George Rappelyea. A resolute evolutionist, Rappelyea was eager to begin a test case at once. One April afternoon, Rappelyea entered the local drugstore and crossed to a table where two young Fundamentalist lawyers were praising the Butler law and asserting that the Bible must be taken literally. Joining the discussion, Rappelyea ridiculed the new statute and contended that the Bible was "mere history." The debate reached the point where Rappelyea was proposing the desirability of a test case in Dayton. The drugstore proprietor, the balding F. E. Robinson, who had several substantial irons in the economic fires of the community, was enthusiastic about the idea. It would put Dayton on the map, he said, and it would be good for Dayton's business.

Discussion quickly got around to making as guinea pig a twenty-four-year-old science teacher in Dayton High School, John Thomas Scopes. Young, unmarried, popular, and modest, the tall, freckled, stoop-shouldered Scopes was by any measure ideal for the assignment. Like Bryan,

Scopes was born in Salem, Illinois. After a year's study at the University of Illinois, he had become the science teacher and athletic coach at Dayton for $150 a month. Local folk called him "Professor." On that April day, Scopes was summoned from a tennis court and brought into the discussion at the drugstore. Coming quickly to the point, Rappelyea asked Scopes if he could teach biology without teaching evolution. When he replied that he could not, several voices cried out, "Then you've been violating the law." The fast-talking Rappelyea then told Scopes of the Civil Liberties Union and stressed his duty as citizen and educator to overcome an iniquitous law. After some hesitation Scopes agreed to cooperate in the test case. An exultant Rappelyea quickly laid out a plan by which he would swear out a warrant for Scopes' arrest and invite the ACLU to honor its proposal and promise of support. The ACLU acquiesced, a spokesman declaring, "We shall take the . . . case to the U.S. Supreme Court if necessary to establish that a teacher may tell the truth without being thrown in jail." On May 7, Scopes was arrested, and the wheels had begun to turn on what Rappelyea was confident could become "a big sensation." As the sun set behind the ridges at the close of the discussion, he cried, "Why not bring a lot of doctors and lawyers here? Let's get H. G. Wells and a lot of big fellows! " [6]

A participant in the drugstore conversations, Sue K. Hicks, a young Dayton lawyer, a male named after his mother who had died in giving him birth, quickly singled out Bryan as a celebrity capable of attracting national and international attention. Hicks dispatched telegrams to Bryan, who was lecturing in Pittsburgh, inviting him to enter the case. Bryan wired back that he would gladly serve without compensation if "it is agreeable to the Law Department of the State." Bryan was assured that "great joy" reigned in the Fundamentalist camp over his acceptance. "We will consider it a great honor to have you with us in this prosecution," replied Hicks.

Bryan was immediately swamped with messages of approval and encouragement. Church congregations west and south adopted resolutions hailing him and reaffirming that religion should be taught and not assailed in the public schools. Chapters of the Women's Christian Temperance Union endorsed his "bold, determined, courageous and righteous defense of the Holy Bible . . ." His comrade-in-faith, the Reverend J. Frank Norris, offered to send an experienced stenographer to record the trial, whose main features could subsequently be put into book form. ". . . you are now in the great work of your life," wrote Norris, "and are rendering ten thousand times more service to the cause of righteousness than a dozen presidents." [7]

Phalanxes of extraordinary legal and political talent were quickly organizing for what ordinarily would be a simple misdemeanor trial requiring several hours. No sooner had Bryan declared his availability as counsel, when several of the nation's most skillful trial attorneys enlisted for the defense. The chief of these was Clarence Darrow, whose path had crossed Bryan's several times over the years. They had been comrades-in-arms in the 1890's for the silver cause and had spoken from the same platform. In 1904, Darrow had fought side by side with Bryan in resisting the restoration of Eastern conservatives to control of the national Democratic Party. In late years Darrow, who was thoroughly discomfited by Bryan's sorties against Darwinism and evolution and his absolute devotion to the literal Bible, had engaged in a newspaper debate with his former ally on the emerging issues that would come to dominate the trial at Dayton.

In 1925, Darrow, sixty-eight years old, was almost as well known throughout the land as Bryan. Tall, big-boned, and slouching, Darrow had a large head crowned by limp brown hair, cavernous blue eyes, a sallow complexion, a rutted face, and a rasping voice whose register was perfect for his lacerating cynicism and benign deference. His expensive clothes were maintained in almost studied disarray. As a trial lawyer he was crafty and ruthless, and he abided by no restraints in serving his clients' needs. His legal career was built on defending underdogs. He had an enviable record in murder trials, having lost only one client to the death penalty, and had enjoyed strong success in causes involving labor unions and leaders at a time when they were ill regarded in the courts.

In one view, Bryan and Darrow were gladiators contending for opposing approaches to life, in which they had been indoctrinated by their fathers. Each son had absorbed the beliefs, values, and loyalties of his parent. The sons, now sexagenarians, still beheld their fathers as models for imitation and deemed the paternal heritage imperiled by events building to the confrontation at Dayton. Whereas Bryan absorbed a home life of Biblical orthodoxy and piety, Darrow's upbringing was a journey in rational skepticism and individualism. "Neither of my parents held any orthodox religious views," wrote Darrow. "My father was the village infidel, and gradually came to glory in his reputation." In mental processes, the two prospective opponents were wholly opposite, Bryan beholding truth as something that is conferred and whose possession is guarded and prized, and Darrow regarding it as something discovered through reason. In religion, Darrow was an agnostic, or one who deemed available knowledge inadequate to determine the existence of God. In Bryan's eyes, Darrow was an inappropriate and unwanted opponent. Time and again, Bryan pointed out that his real concern was not the atheist or agnostic, who openly stated his position, but the Modernist, whose beliefs and expressions were concealed and subtle and therefore more insidious.

Bryan's path had also crossed with a second principal defense attorney, Dudley Field Malone, a stocky, ruddy, round-faced man of medium height, eloquent and big-voiced. Malone had served as Third Assistant Secretary of State under Bryan and in the late Democratic convention of 1924 had been

one of his more conspicuous tormentors. Although a Catholic by upbringing, Malone had divorced and remarried and was no longer a communi-
cant. A stellar international divorce lawyer, Malone, like Darrow, be-
friended underdogs. Among the other principal defense attorneys was
Arthur Garfield Hayes, swarthy, with a wrestler's build, and straight hair
combed back from a high forehead. Of all the trial's attorneys, he probably
possessed the keenest legal mind. Scopes' local attorney was John Randolph Neal, a law school dean, exponent of academic freedom, and an unsuccessful candidate for governor.[8]

Arrayed with Bryan were the Hicks brothers of Dayton. The elder, Herbert Hicks, was acting county attorney, handsome, wavy-haired, neatly attired; Sue Hicks was short, dynamic and articulate. The chief of the prosecution was the attorney general for the Eighteenth Judicial District, A. T.
Stewart, a slender, young-looking man in his mid-thirties, melancholy in expression, known as a shrewd courtroom lawyer and a rousing orator. Reports persisted that Stewart was receptive to evolutionary theory, but if he
was, this conviction never surfaced. Among other counsel for the prosecution were Ben G. McKenzie, dean of the local bar and a former assistant attorney general; his son, J. Gordon McKenzie, a stout, solemn local lawyer
and former judge; Wallace C. Haggard, a tall, good-looking young lawyer
and son of Dayton's first citizen; and William Jennings Bryan, Jr., now, at
thirty-six, a Los Angeles attorney who had long been eager to join his father
in the Fundamentalist crusade. William, Jr.—or Willie, as Bryan called
him—was a big, handsome, carefully dressed man, but unlike his father, he
was retiring and self-effacing, and his indifferent voice was utterly lacking
in resonance. Bryan proposed to these colleagues that distinguished Jewish
and Catholic lawyers be added to afford the advantage of a well-rounded
representation of faiths. He suggested Samuel Untermyer of New York and
Senator Thomas J. Walsh of Montana, both close friends and partners in
the political wars. But his colleagues thought their ranks were sufficient.
Walsh was never approached, and Untermyer, who was, was rendered unavailable by a trip to Europe.

Bryan had the arduous task of corralling witnesses willing to testify and
resorted to Fundamentalist clergy and any variety of scientific opinion opposed to Darwinism that he could find. At his approach, those who once expressed enthusiasm became fainthearted and made excuses, or whatever
traces of agreement they supposedly had with Bryan suddenly vanished.
One writer, whose book *The Dogma of Evolution* was opposed to Darwinism, objected to the use of law to enforce his views. The discovery of truth,
he reminded Bryan, should be by free discussion, and laws that regulate belief "are extremely unfortunate." Since reputable scientific opinion was as
scarce as hen's teeth for the prosecution, Bryan banked heavily on George
McReady Price, whose writings were critical of "organic evolution" and

who was not without criticism in the scientific community. Price contended that Darwin was vague concerning evolution's starting point, uncritical in his use of evidence, and given to loose assumptions in his belief in the powers of chance and finality as explanations of nature. Price, too, was abroad and unavailable. One minister could not attend because he needed to stay home to help dedicate a wing of his church. The extreme Fundamentalist Reverend J. Frank Norris contributed a stenographer but could not appear himself, and John Roach Straton, the apocalyptic Baptist of New York, took off for his summer home in the Adirondacks.

Friends and political allies of long years were utterly alienated by Bryan's current venture. C. S. Thomas of Colorado, who dispatched a letter to Scopes, with a copy to Bryan, regarded the awaiting proceedings as further ugly proof of his former friend's "monstrous egotism, his colossal assumptions" which threatened to launch "a new inquisition throughout the boundaries of the Republic." Bryan, in writing to Thomas of his regret over their separation, noted that having passed through a succession of controversies, he had become accustomed to realignments among his friends, to both losses and accretions. "In this controversy," he added, "I have a larger majority on my side than in any previous controversy, and I have more intolerant opponents than I ever had in politics." [9]

Each side was engrossed in working out a division of labor and a devising of strategy for the trial. Sue Hicks proposed that he, Stewart, McKenzie, and their other associates handle all legal phases of the case and that Stewart and Bryan do the cross-examination. Writing to Bryan from London, Samuel Untermeyer urged that the issue be strictly confined: "I would seek to exclude all discussions by experts or otherwise on the subject of Evolution (which to my mind has nothing whatever to do with the case . . .), and rest squarely on the proposition than the plain letter and spirit of the law have been violated, and that the burden rests upon the Defence to establish the unconstitutionality of that law not by introduction of evidence, but by discussion of the legal problem involved. I am fearful however that there is so much of 'grandstand play' involved in this prosecution and so great a desire on the part of local influences to convert it into a sensational controversy instead of adhering closely to the issues involved, that it will not be easy to keep the trial within the legal limits."

As he prepared to move on to this bizarre litigious battle, Bryan overflowed with characteristic optimism. "There is no reason why the Scopes trial should not be conducted on a high plane without the least personal feeling," he wrote. ". . . The trial will be a success in proportion as it enables the public to understand the two sides and the reasons on both sides. Every question has to be settled at last by the public and the sooner it is understood the sooner it can be settled." [10]

All roads led to Dayton, and they were heavily travelled. The town to which the people came consisted of fewer than 500 families, situated in the southeastern Tennessee hill country. Strung out along Market Street, Dayton was a long, narrow town, the seat of Rhea County which, paradoxically, was named after John Rhea, a pioneer in Tennessee education. H. L. Mencken was impressed with "The houses . . . surrounded by pretty gardens, with cool green lawns and stately trees. The two chief streets are paved from curb to curb. The stores carry good stocks and have a Metropolitan air. . . . Nor is there any evidence of that poisonous spirit which usually shows itself when Christian men gather to defend the great doctrine of their faith." To the surprise of its visitors, Dayton was no typical Southern town but could just as well be situated in Ohio or Pennsylvania. It embodied more a Northern tempo of ambition and efficiency than the expected Southern languor and charm.

Far more than its own folk, Dayton's visitors provided the eccentric examples of the human species. Religionists, curious spectators, and tourists; lawyers, freethinkers who insisted that the Bible was a superstition; animal trainers with chimpanzees represented as the fathers or the sons of man overran the town. The New York *Post* lamented that "Greenwich Village is on its way to Rhea County. . . . The Scopes case teachers, research workers, biologists and other men of science are being smothered in the rush of long-haired men, short-haired women, feminists, neurotics, freethinkers and free-lovers who are determined to shine in reflected glory. The vital issues of the trial in Tennessee are being lost in the stampede of professional martyrs and a swarm of practicing egotists."

Commercialism, too, moved in on the town. Banners strewn across the main streets gave Dayton a carnival atmosphere. Stores sold monkey dolls made of stuffed cotton, watch fobs shaped like monkeys, and umbrellas imported from Germany with handles shaped like monkey heads. Pressure on the monkey's throat made him roll his eyes and stick out his tongue. The monkey notion was exploited to the breaking point. Children played with lifelike monkeys with long tails. Motion-picture men got pretty girls, decorated as monkeys, to pose in front of the courthouse.[11]

Bryan left Miami on July 6, with Mary and his secretary, Walter Thomson, aboard the Royal Palm, which made a flag stop at Dayton to deposit him early the next afternoon. When Bryan appeared on the rear platform of the last car, clad in a dark jacket, a white shirt, a dark bow tie, and a large white tropical cork helmet purchased on a trip to Panama, a cheer went up from the crowd of 300 residents gathered to greet him. After an automobile procession down the main street, Bryan doffed his jacket and strolled through town to get acquainted. He enjoyed an ice-cream soda in the drugstore where the case began, conferred with fellow counsel, and was interviewed by the press.

The Bryans stayed at the home of F. Richard Rogers, another Dayton druggist, who moved out for the duration of the trial. But Bryan was destined to spend little time there. On the night of his arrival, he spoke before the Dayton Progressive Club and put the challenge to his formidable foes: "The contest between evolution and Christianity is a duel to the death. . . . If evolution wins in Dayton Christianity goes—not suddenly of course, but gradually—for the two cannot stand together. . . . The atheists, agnostics and all other opponents of Christianity understand the character of the struggle, hence this interest in this case. From this time forth the Christians will understand the character of the struggle also. In an open fight the truth will triumph."

The next evening, Bryan journeyed six miles into the hills to Morgan Springs, a resort on Walden Ridge. After dinner, he spoke from the worn porch of a plain wooden hotel. A great crowd of hill folk gathered around the veranda, and Bryan, as he spoke, was illumined in outline by a narrow shaft of lantern light stretching from an open door. A fading summer storm touched the distant hills with flickers of lightning, and a rumble of thunder rolled across the valley. Undistracted by nature's eruptions, the audience was quiet and reverential as Bryan spoke. A crippled old man in a wheelchair looked up at him with an air of rapturous inspiration. The only person close to Bryan was a tall mountaineer, who stood motionless throughout the address, holding a glass of water should the speaker falter.

Bryan's address, largely a repetition of his remarks to the Progressive Club, expressed his pride in the South and predicted the coming of a marvelous religious revival that would spring from the South and traverse the nation. When Bryan concluded, there was no applause, only the reverential silence earned by a moving church sermon. A New York *Times* reporter, who witnessed the occasion, wrote that Bryan "is more than a great politician, more than a lawyer in a trial, more even than one of our greatest orators, he is a symbol of their simple religious faith." [12]

The trial began on Friday, July 10. The eyes of the world turned to the Rhea County Courthouse, which dominated a two-acre park on the northwest side of Market Street, a large rectangular two-story structure of red brick and Romanesque arches. In one corner, the courthouse boasted a three-story tower, with clocks on its four faces and a gazebo on top. Someone described it as "a mixture of Moorish and Wesleyan Methodist," and the result "looked as though it had been designed by a Congressman." The courthouse was surrounded by grass and tall, spreading maples and water oaks.

The courtroom was filled long before the trial began. Men and women of Dayton, bronze-faced farmers from the hill country, clad in overalls, filled every seat and stood in the aisles and around the walls of the room. When the scene was crowded to the point of suffocation, Judge John Tate Raulston entered, beaming. Tall, broad-shouldered, his round face flushed, with a dimple deep in his chin and a permanent smile, he spoke slowly, in a singsong way, and his manner was busy and friendly. A lay preacher in the Methodist Episcopal Church and a leader of revival meetings, Raulston, defense counsel feared, was too much of a Fundamentalist to give Scopes a fair trial. There was a bustle at the room's big doors, and the defense, led by Clarence Darrow, trooped in. Trailing them was Scopes, looking almost apologetic for instigating the tremendous commotion. Scopes was a model of the room's standard attire; he wore no necktie, his collar was open, and his sleeves were rolled to the elbows. Darrow suddenly shared his style by pulling off his coat, revealing a pair of light-blue suspenders and a pongee shirt. Twisting his mouth and carrying a quizzical twinkle in his deep-set eyes, Darrow conveyed the unmistakable air of the professional skeptic.

Again there was a stir at the big doors and a rattle of handclapping. Bryan now entered with Attorney General Stewart and their corps of associates. Judge Raulston walked briskly over to greet Bryan, who wore an expression of absolute confidence. They shook hands, as did counsel on both sides. Darrow and Bryan stood for a moment chatting with their hands on each other's shoulders. Motion-picture cameras caught the scene, an achievement that required photographers to climb up onto chairs and tables. Efforts to photograph the spectators were defeated by the moving fans of the sweltering crowd, which produced nothing but blurs.

The selection of the jury chiefly occupied the trial's first day, a task that was completed with surprising rapidity in a few hours. Darrow handled the cross-questioning, and several prospective jurors were barred because of their too-concentrated devotion to the church. On the jury that emerged, ten members were farmers, and the remaining two were a schoolteacher and a shipping clerk. All were Bible readers except one who acknowledged that he could not read. Mary, who was carried up the courthouse stairs to her reserved seat, was intrigued by the teacher-juror who, with his long gray mustache and hair, white trousers, black coat and gold watch chain, looked like a Kentucky colonel.

Saturday and Sunday, July 11 and 12, the court was adjourned and of the luminaries with whom the town bulged, Bryan was most in demand as a speaker. On Sunday, talking from the pulpit of the Methodist Episcopal Church, with Judge Raulston in the front pew and Dr. Neal, chief defense counsel, on the church platform, Bryan in shirt sleeves and with his ever-present palm fan conducted a "Sunday school." From the pulpit, he ranged widely and candidly over his life's experiences and touched on themes relevant to the awaiting trial. "While God does not despise the learned," he said, "He does not give them a monopoly of His attention. The unlearned in this country are much more numerous than the learned. . . . Thank God

I am going to spend the latter years of my life in a locality where there is a belief in God, and in the Son of God, and in a civilization to be based on salvation through blood."

In the afternoon, Bryan spoke to a huge audience on the courthouse lawn on the topic "He Calleth Thee." Religion, he contended, was in the world before education, and Christ's doctrines are "so complete a moral code that no scholar has dared add a word to it." He denied the report of several major newspapers that he had said that he intended to "put God into the Constitution. Our purpose," he said, "our only purpose, is to vindicate the right of parents to guard the religion of their children against efforts made in the name of science to undermine faith in supernatural religion. There is no attack on free speech, or freedom of the press, or freedom of thought, or freedom of knowledge, but surely parents have a right to guard the religious welfare of their children." [13]

On Monday, July 13, the trial began in earnest. Bryan arrived coatless and collarless, in a shirt with a starched bosom. His Southern colleagues, who held to light coats, appeared to bear up better under the heat. Counsel were intrigued by the presence of microphones to broadcast the proceedings and to connect with loudspeaker systems carrying to several parts of town. Most of the day was passed in argumentation among counsel over motions and technicalities. Bryan sat silently fanning himself and abstained from joining the huddles among the attorneys for the prosecution.

The day's high point was the attempt to quash the indictment, offered for the defense by Clarence Darrow, whose bent, shuffling presence, seamed brown face, and blue suspenders had made him a figure of the greatest interest. Darrow's movements were followed by a craning of necks, and locally he was now known, even somewhat affectionately, as "the infidel." Darrow quickly demonstrated his mastery of courtroom histrionics. After according sweet and gentle acknowledgment to counsel on both sides, identifying them by name and place of origin, whether New York, Chicago, or California, he suddenly and startlingly passed from his mood of light banter to hard solemnity. In an instant he glared and pointed a gold pencil at Bryan, exclaiming, "And who is responsible for this foolish, mischievous, and wicked act who comes from Florida!"

With shoulders hunched and his thumb in his suspenders, Darrow declaimed: "This is as brazen and bold an attempt to destroy liberty as was ever seen in the Middle Ages." Prowling around the big arena of the courtroom, he let his voice sink into a whisper one moment and rise the next into a burst of rage. He held the crowded, uncomfortable audience in absolute silence. Save for his voice and the clicking telegraph keys, not a sound could be heard.

When the court reopened the next morning and Judge Raulston ordered the customary prayer, Darrow objected. The startled Raulston declared that in his responsibility for the conduct of the court he was accustomed to beginning with prayer. But Darrow objected that the daily prayer would influence the jury. Most of the attorneys were on their feet clamoring for attention. Bryan flung down his fan to glower at Darrow.

As the trial moved through its third and fourth days, Bryan remained a picture of oratorical passivity, sitting silently in the overpowering heat of the courtroom, waving his great palm fan. Only once was his voice heard in court, and then he uttered hardly more than a sentence. Some believed he was husbanding his strength for the final, more critical stages of the fight. Even after the defense's motion to quash was denied and the prosecution began presenting its case, Bryan did not join in. He left it to his fellow counsel, who were schooled in Tennessee court procedure, while he was not, to argue their case, which consisted simply of calling four witnesses. All testified that Scopes had in fact based his biology lectures on Darwin's work.

When Malone and Darrow began to present the case of the defense, Bryan's mien suddenly changed. He was more attentive, his posture more tense. Malone declared that the state must prove two things—that Scopes' teachings denied the theory of Divine Creation posed in the Bible and that he taught instead that man was descended from an order of lower animals. The defense, Malone added, would prove that millions of people believe in evolution and in the Biblical account of the Creation and find no conflict between them. Essentially the relation between the two was a matter of faith and interpretation which each individual must decide for himself. Malone lifted the proceedings to new intensity by quoting from an early writing by Bryan, commending Jefferson's contention that truth can and must stand by itself and has nothing to fear from error, provided free discussion is permitted.

A. T. Stewart objected to the use of Bryan's name. Judge Raulston quickly said, "Yes, Colonel Malone, I would like that you not make further reference to Colonel Bryan. Let that be excluded."

"Yes, your honor," replied Malone, "I do not think Mr. Bryan is the least sensitive about it."

Bryan was now on his feet, to speak officially for the first time in the trial. Necks craned toward him; silence reigned. What oratorical sensation would the Commoner unloosen? He said, "Not a bit." When Raulston and Malone moved into further argument, Bryan explained his position: "The Court can do as it pleases in carrying out its rules; but I ask no protection from the Court; and, when the proper time comes, I shall be able to show the gentlemen that I stand today just where I did, and that this has nothing to do with the case at bar." A thunder of applause demonstrated that the trial had not as yet accomplished anything to reduce the great body of Bryan's admirers who dominated the crowd.

The proceedings moved on to other things, and court soon adjourned. As the court disbanded, Bryan went up to Darrow near the bench and presented him with a carved image of a little monkey, saying with a smile, "A friend of mine sent me this and asked me to give it to you. It is carved from a peach pit, and it is so pretty I'd like you to keep it."

"I'm glad to have it," Darrow replied, smiling. "I have one almost like it, and I'll give it to you in exchange."

It was the last act of a friendship of nearly four decades.[14]

Thursday, July 16. The heat wave continued unmercifully. Additional electric table fans were brought in to supplement the scores of palm leaves rustling in the heavy air. The crowd had somewhat dwindled, bored by the long undramatic legal arguments, and farmers and laborers could no longer continue their absence from work.

The day was devoted to a most critical issue: Should the defense be permitted to introduce as witnesses men of science and learning who, as Darrow contended, might show that their interpretation of the Bible "is not in conflict with any story of creation; while the Bible, in many ways, is in conflict with every known science, and there isn't a human being on earth believes it literally"? The defense had fifteen scientists and clergymen available, and as Darrow began to examine Dr. Maynard M. Metcalf, a zoologist of Johns Hopkins University, Attorney General Stewart and former Attorney General McKenzie, for the prosecution, objected to introduction of the testimony. William, Jr., suffering from a cold, opened the state's argument in a weak voice. Bryan hitched his chair closer and leaned forward to listen. In essence, William, Jr., argued that experts should not be permitted to offer opinions on matters that were for the jury to determine. One attorney after another on both sides spoke, and when the court adjourned near noon, reports circulated that Bryan at last would speak when the court resumed in the afternoon. As the crowd filed out for the midday break, a chimpanzee was happily riding a tricycle along the sidewalk.

That afternoon the rumors that Bryan would speak brought a great human surge into the courtroom. With aisles and doorways jammed, lawyers and reporters had to struggle to reach their seats. Judge Raulston, anticipating that Bryan's entry into the struggle would touch off an outburst, warned the spectators against applause for fear of endangering safety in the old courthouse building.

Raulston recognized Bryan, who rose and took a long drink from a jug of ice water. As he set himself to begin, silence fell. His scores of admirers leaned forward, eagerly anticipating that, after a week of delay, wrangling and indifferent progress, he might sweep away the drab chaos with his magic voice and ringing phrases. Most of all, he might deliver a speech as stunning as his "Cross of Gold" masterpiece of 1896. Stern-faced, in a white shirt and starched collar, a black bow tie and dark trousers, a belt with a silver buckle, and a heavy watch chain looped from a watch pocket to a side trouser packet, Bryan held in one hand his inveterate fan and in the other a copy of *Civic Biology,* the text used in Scopes' biology class. Bryan's hands were markedly trembling, to the concern of Mary and William.

They were quickly reassured by the clear tone of his voice and ready humor. He had not so far taken part in the case, he explained, since Tennessee laws and court procedures had been under discussion, and this, he believed, was better left to fellow counsel whose knowledge of them was far closer than his. He referred good-humoredly to the defense's efforts to draw him into the case by labeling him as its archconspirator. He restated the prosecution's arguments that the law was clear and that those who did not like the law should take it up with the legislature and not the courts. "We do not need any expert to tell us what the law means," he said, "an expert cannot be permitted to come in here and try to defeat the enforcement of a law. . . . This is not the place to try to prove that the law ought never to have been passed. The place to prove that was at the legislature."

Sensing that his admirers were awaiting anxiously a surging attack from him that would put the infidels to rout, Bryan laid aside Untermyer's advice and charged ahead. Holding high a copy of Hunter's *Civic Biology,* used in Scopes' course, Bryan turned to page 194, which had a diagram classifying all the animal species. "We are told just how many animal species there are, 518,900," he began. He pointed to circles on the diagram, differing in size according to the number of species in them.

"Of course it [the diagram] is only a guess, and I don't suppose it is carried to one or even to ten. I see they are round numbers, and so I think it must be a generalization of them. (Laughter).

"8,000 protozoa, 35,000 sponges. I am satisfied from some I have seen there must be more than 35,000 sponges. (Laughter).

". . . Now, we are getting up near our kinfolks, thirteen thousand fish. Then there are the amphibia. I don't know whether they have not yet decided to come out, or have almost decided to go back. (Laughter).

". . . and then we have thirteen thousand birds. Strange that this should be exactly the same as the number of fishes, round numbers. And then we have mammals, 3,500, and there is a little circle, and man is in the circle. Find him; find man.

"There is that book! There is the book [from which] they were teaching your children, teaching that man was a mammal and so indistinguishable among the mammals that they leave him there with 3,499 other mammals— including elephants! (Laughter and applause).

"Talk about putting Daniel in the lions' den! How dared those scientists put man in a little ring like that with lions and tigers and everything that is bad?

"Tell me that the parents of this day have not any right to declare that children are not to be taught this doctrine—shall not be taken down from the high plane upon which God put man? Shall we be detached from the throne of God and be compelled to link our ancestors with the jungle—tell that to these children?"

Bryan picked up a copy of Darwin's *Descent of Man,* apologized for its long words, and regretted that Darwin had man descended "Not even from American monkeys but from Old World monkeys." He suddenly became serious and combative. Pointing to Metcalf, he cried, "I suppose this distinguished scholar who came here shamed them all by his number of degrees. He did not shame me, for I have more than he has. . . . Did he tell you where life began? Did he tell you that back of all there was a God? Not a word about it. Did he tell you how life began? Not a word and not one of them can tell you how life began. . . . They want to come in with their little padded-up evolution that commences with nothing and ends nowhere."

Evolution, he continued, was wrong both scientifically and morally because it destroyed moral standards. He held up Nietzsche (he pronounced it "Nitchy") and the Chicago murderers Leopold and Loeb as the offspring of evolutionary teachings and recalled that in defense of Loeb and Leopold, Darrow had argued that the professors who taught Nietzsche's doctrines to young Leopold were "just as responsible for the murder as Leopold himself." When Darrow sprang to his feet to deny this, Bryan read verbatim extracts from Darrow's argument to support his point. After further jousting with Darrow and Malone, Bryan concluded, his face flushed, his voice trembling, and his arms stretched out over the audience: "The facts are simple, the case is plain, and if those gentlemen want to enter upon a larger field of educational work on the subject of evolution, let us get through with this case and then convene a mock court, for it will deserve the title of mock court if its purpose is to banish from the hearts of the people the Word of God as revealed."

By any evaluation, Bryan's performance was well removed from his "Cross of Gold" sensation. The applause was strong but not overwhelming; the faithful were pleased but not ecstatic. Mary was impressed that the speech was "very well received." Defendant Scopes reported: "I did not pay much attention to the text of the speech, but it was well received. . . . I remember being lulled into a feeling that I cannot accurately describe. Since I was not listening to what he was saying, but to how he was saying it, I was letting his oratorical talents hypnotize me. Every gesture and intonation of his voice blended so perfectly that it was almost like a symphony. . . ."

After some minor wrangling between Bryan and Darrow, Dudley Field Malone commenced what by general agreement was the most eloquent speech of the trial. "Mr. Bryan," he cried, "is not the only one who has spoken for the Bible. . . . There are other people in this room who have given their whole lives to God." And in a stirring peroration, he declared, "The truth always wins. . . . The truth does not need the forces of Government. The truth does not need Mr. Bryan. . . . We feel we stand with progress. . . . We feel we stand with fundamental freedom in America. We are not afraid. Where is the fear? We defy it!"

When Malone finished, virtually everyone in the courtroom, Fundamentalist as well as Modernist, broke into what was easily the most resounding applause of the trial. In the din, a journalist heard Darrow mutter, "Tennessee needs only fifteen minutes of free speech to become civilized!"

After the court emptied out, Bryan, who had remained behind, said to Malone, "Dudley, that was the greatest speech I ever heard."

"Thank you, Mr. Bryan," Malone replied, gathering up his papers, "I am terribly sorry that I was the one who had to do it." [15]

When the court convened next morning, Friday, July 17, the air had cooled and a general expectation prevailed that after yesterday's speeches the trial was all but over. This opinion seemed confirmed when Judge Raulston read from a typescript his ruling on the critical question of the admissibility of scientific witnesses for the defense. After analyzing the issues of the case, Raulston concluded that "the evidence of experts would shed no light" on them and upheld Stewart's motion to exclude their testimony.

Defense counsel made angry objections, and Stewart took exception to them. In the strident exchanges, the defense and prosecution agreed on the next step, which was to permit the defense to put into the record the expert testimony that they would have obtained from their witnesses if the judge had allowed them. This testimony would not be submitted to the jury but would form a part of the record of the trial. Thus an appellate court could examine it, and if the higher court decided that the evidence was pertinent and Raulston in excluding it was in error, the court could admit and weigh the testimony. Friday's proceedings were devoted to determining how the evidence should be presented. In the verbal jousting, Malone fired a barb at Bryan when he remarked on "the campaign of propaganda which has been begun by a distinguished member of the prosecution." A nettled Bryan asked if the witnesses allowed to testify as experts for the information of the judge would be subject to cross-examination. Raulston ruled that they would be. Technically, the proper answer to this question was no, and when Raulston in effect said yes, the defense exploded with rage. A rash of gibes developed between Darrow and Raulston. Eventually, a modicum of good feelings was restored, and the court adjourned until Monday.

But Friday's battle was not yet finished. Darrow and Bryan fired salvos at each other through statements to the press. Darrow lamented that "Bryan has done everything in his power to prevent any discussion in court of the subject of evolution and the Bible. . . . Bryan made the issue and then, when he found that no reputable scientist and no preeminent theologian could be found to support his views in a court of justice, Bryan fled from the issue and sought the protection of technicalities. . . ."

Bryan quickly responded: "Personally, I am anxious to see the fullest discussion of the subject of evolution, but I cannot ignore the laws of the state of Tennessee relative to the introduction of evidence. The decision of the court could hardly have been otherwise under the law of this state. . . . I want it distinctly understood that the state has no fears of its ability to care for its own side of the question if the witnesses were on the stand, but with such evidence so unquestionably inadmissible, it could not go on without making a travesty of procedure in Tennessee."

On Saturday, Darrow and his fellow counsel worked on affidavits incorporating the experts' testimony, and from the Rogers home, where his temporary study was littered with books and papers, Bryan issued a laudatory statement on the trial—that it had "uncovered the conspiracy against the Bible Christianity." Afterward he and Mary drove to Chattanooga to see Lookout Mountain. William, Jr., after issuing a statement about the trial similar to his father's, departed for California. Darrow, not to be outdone, retaliated with a statement holding that "the scientist is as kind and humane and tolerant as the Fundamentalist. In fact, no one ever heard of a scientific man who ever sought to call the aid of the law to enforce belief in his theories. . . . I have no desire to have the Christian world give up its belief in God or its Bible, but at least a very large portion of the Christian world does not regard the Bible as a book of science. . . ." Then Darrow was off to Chattanooga, too, for a round of sight-seeing and dinners.

On Sunday, Darrow lectured on Tolstoy in Chattanooga under the auspices of the Young Men's Hebrew Association. Bryan also took to the platform that day. At Walden Ridge, he addressed an audience of 500 gathered at the farming community of Pikeville, in the Sequatchie Valley. He again spoke of the trial as "a gigantic conspiracy" of atheists and agnostics against the Christian religion. Other counsel on that quiet Sunday were less obtrusive. Attorney General Tom Stewart lolled in Robinson's drugstore, eating ice cream. And Scopes, who was all but forgotten, went swimming by day and dancing by night at Morgan Springs. Reporters were impressed that he fully expected to be found guilty as charged. He owned that he never did care much for teaching and hoped to return to college to study more science. Church services in Dayton were filled to overflowing, and most pulpits were occupied by visiting clergy and resounded with evangelical inveighings against evolution.

That evening at the "Monkey House," as the rambling structure where defense counsel lived was called, Darrow and Hays discussed with Dr. Kirtley F. Mather, a Harvard geologist, an inspiration that had struck Hays several days before. Why not call Bryan to the stand as a defense witness, notwithstanding that he was one of the opposing attorneys? As fodder for such an enterprise, Darrow had a list of fifty questions he had put to Bryan in 1923 in an open letter to the Chicago *Tribune* and a list of inconsistencies and errors in the Bible, prepared by a modernist clergyman. The trio, intrigued by the idea, moved on to a rehearsal, in which Mather answered questions, put by Darrow and Hays, in the manner in which he thought Bryan would reply.

After two intensive hours, Mather asked a question of his own. "How in blazes do you expect to get Bryan on the witness stand?"

"That's our job," came the smiling reply, "and we think we will succeed in doing it. Just leave that part of it to us." [16]

Monday, July 20. The courtroom was so packed that spectators sat on the clerk's desk. The assumption that the day would see the final arguments of the case had attracted an audience of record numbers. The morning was given over to technical matters, and then the court reconvened in the afternoon. Judge Raulston, at the urging of the fire commissioner, ordered the court to adjourn to the courthouse lawn. "The floor may give way," the judge explained, "the plaster is cracking downstairs. This floor was never intended to hold so many people. . . ."

On the lawn below, Raulston took his place on a platform built against the wall of the courthouse where, under the maple trees scarcely a week before, Bryan had delivered a sermon. Benches had been placed near the front, which quickly filled, while hundreds stood fanning themselves and squaring off into opposing Modernist and Fundamentalist cheering sections. On the platform, Raulston sat at a little table in the center, with prosecution attorneys to his left and defense at his right. Huddled around them were a few newspapermen and privileged persons who managed to squeeze past the guard. Small boys climbed onto the branches of a tree that overhung the platform. The courthouse's windows were crowded with people leaning out. In the rear of the courthouse yard, little children played on seesaws made from pine boards set on long sawhorses. Small boys moved through the crowd selling soda pop. Most of the men wore hats and smoked, and here and there was a Negro among the spectators. In all, some 2,000 human beings had gathered.

The affidavits of the experts were read. For a time the proceedings were devoted to technicalities and wrangling. Suddenly, after a blaze of argument, Hays was saying in controlled tones, "The defense desires to call Mr. Bryan as a witness. . . ." Spectators gasped, prosecution lawyers made startled movements, and, according to a reporter, "Judge Raulston's eyes goggled, and the Commoner's palm leaf froze in his hand." All of the prosecution's attorneys except Bryan leaped to their feet at once, shouting and waving for attention. But Bryan, convinced as always of the righteousness of his cause, consented to testify. Raulston remained vexed with doubts. It was virtually unheard of for a lawyer on one side of a case to call a lawyer on the other side as a witness. To reporters who watched him, Bryan appeared confident and even jaunty despite his familiarity with Darrow's deadly skill as an interrogator and the enormous risk, therefore, of public humiliation. Bryan, of course, was never lacking in confidence in his own forensic abilities. Thus far, the trial was lacking in any conspicuous triumph for the antievolution cause, and quite possibly he could seize this opportunity to fashion it. God, too, as he always believed, would protect him in a confrontation with the infidel. Above all, he could not turn away this challenge without dreadful loss of face.

Bryan sat down in a wooden office swivel chair, and Darrow in a blue shirt and blue suspenders began easily, "You have given considerable study to the Bible, haven't you, Mr. Bryan?"

Smiling and polite, he answered, "Yes, sir, I have tried to."

". . . Do you claim that everything in the Bible should be literally interpreted?"

"I believe everything in the Bible should be accepted as it is given there. Some of the Bible is given illustratively; for instance: 'Ye are the salt of the earth.' I would not insist that man was actually salt, or that he had flesh of salt, but it is used in the sense of salt as saving God's people."

With his thumbs in his suspenders, Darrow asked, "But when you read that Jonah swallowed the whale—or that the whale swallowed Jonah; excuse me, please—how do you literally interpret that?"

Bryan corrected Darrow to say that the Bible mentioned not a whale, but a big fish. "And I believe in a God," he added, "who can make a whale and can make a man and can make both do what he pleases." (Applause.)

Darrow returned to the attack. ". . . You don't know whether it was the ordinary mine-run of fish, or made for that purpose?"

"You may guess; you evolutionists guess," said Bryan, fanning himself vigorously.

"But when we do guess, we have the sense to guess right. . . . You are not prepared to say whether that fish was made specially to swallow a man or not?"

"The Bible doesn't say, so I am not prepared to say. . . ."

"But do you believe he made them—that he made such a fish and that it was big enough to swallow Jonah?"

"Yes, sir," said Bryan. "Let me add: One miracle is just as easy to believe as another."

"It is for me," said Darrow sarcastically.

"It is for me," Bryan retorted heatedly.

"Just as hard," smiled Darrow.

"It is hard to believe for you, but easy for me. A miracle is a thing performed beyond what man can do, you get within the realm of miracles; and it is just as easy to believe the miracle of Jonah as any other miracle of the Bible." Applause rippled through the Fundamentalist ranks and the state's attorneys beamed.

After some minor fencing and an objection by Stewart to the entire procedure, Darrow returned to the attack. "The Bible," he said, "says Joshua commanded the sun to stand still for the purpose of lengthening the day, doesn't it? And you believe it?"

"I do."

"Do you believe at that time the entire sun went around the earth?"

"No, I believe that the earth goes around the sun."

There was more bickering, and Stewart jumped up and cried, ". . . It has gone beyond the pale of any issue that could possibly be injected into this law suit, except by imagination. I do not think the defendant has a right to conduct the examination any further, and I ask your honor to exclude it!"

Bryan said he wished to speak, and Raulston acquiesced.

In a similar manner of questioning, Darrow extracted from Bryan statements attesting to his belief that the Great Flood actually took place, that the world's languages dated from the Tower of Babel, that Adam and Eve were the first human beings. Indicative of Darrow's questioning manner is the following:

"Mr. Bryan, do you believe that the first woman was Eve?"

"Yes."

"Do you believe she was literally made out of Adam's rib?"

"I do."

"Did you ever discover where Cain got his wife?"

"No, sir; I leave the agnostics to hunt for her."

". . . The Bible says he got one, doesn't it? Were there other people on the earth at that time?"

"I cannot say."

"You cannot say? Did that ever enter into your consideration?"

"Never bothered me."

Darrow's questions aimed to expose Bryan as an unthinking religionist who had failed to contemplate the elementary implications of his faith. Darrow also intended to reveal Bryan as impoverished in relevant knowledge, as one who knew little about the older civilizations and nothing about Zoroaster, Confucius, or Buddha. In angry questioning, Darrow wrung from Bryan an acknowledgment that he had never read a book on philology to test his views concerning the Tower of Babel, and that he had never thought about how long men had been inhabiting the earth.

Darrow was artful in extracting from Bryan a professed belief in the absurd implications of certain parts of the literal Bible. Referring to the serpent in the Garden of Eden, Darrow asked, "And you believe that is the reason that God made the serpent to go on his belly after he tempted Eve? . . . 'And the Lord God said unto the serpent, Because thou has done this, thou art cursed above all cattle, and above every beast of the field; upon thy belly shalt thou go, and dust shalt thou eat all the days of thy life.' Do you think that is why the serpent is compelled to crawl upon its belly?"

"I believe that."

Darrow grinned with the glee of the cat who had cornered his quarry. "Have you any idea how the snake went before that time?"

"No, sir."

"Do you know whether he walked on his tail or not?"

"No, sir. I have no way to know."

From the press table came a joyful whoop, which touched off great laughter among the spectators. The vision of the serpent bounding on his tail was utterly titillating.

Bryan rose to his feet, his shoulders dropping with exhaustion, the fan shaking violently in his hand, his face heavy with sweat, and in a trembling voice he said to Raulston:

"Your honor, I think I can shorten this testimony. The only purpose Mr. Darrow has is to slur at the Bible. But I will shorten his question. I will answer it all at once, and I have no objection in the world." Facing the crowd, his arms raised above his head, he cried, "I want the world to know that this man, who does not believe in God, is trying to use a court in Tennessee—"

"I object to that!" Darrow shouted.

"To slur it," Bryan continued, "and, while it will require time, I am willing to take it!"

"I object to your statement!" Darrow yelled, shaking his fist at Bryan. "I am examining you on your fool ideas that no intelligent Christian on earth believes!"

The spectators now rose as though a sudden wind had pushed them up and shouted and screamed, the din overwhelming the voices of the two elderly men, who stood glaring and shaking their fists in each other's faces.

A riot threatened, and Judge Raulston, thoroughly alive to the possibility, crashed down his gavel and shouted, "Court is adjourned until nine o'clock tomorrow morning!"

Bryan's ordeal, which he had endured for nearly an hour and a half, was over. He sank into his swivel chair, muttering, "Slurring the Bible . . . slurring the Bible. . . ." [17]

The excitement quickly evaporated. Many spectators pushed up to Darrow to shake his hand, but Bryan was largely ignored. Several ministers offered their congratulations, but scores of Fundamentalists who previously had regarded him as their champion seemed to feel let down and turned away. The cause of their disaffection was not any apparent defeat that

Bryan may have suffered from Darrow. Rather, Bryan had failed the Fundamentalists by taking a more enlightened position than the narrower views to which they clung. In the discussion of Joshua, for instance, Darrow brought Bryan to acknowledge, although reluctantly, that he believed the earth moved around the sun and that in telling that Joshua made the sun stand still, the Bible simply spoke in terms that people of the day could understand. Equally heretical, in Fundamentalist eyes, was Bryan's admission, in discussing the Creation, that the six days described in the Bible were probably not literal days but periods that might embrace millions of years. Darrow's interrogation made what for the Fundamentalists was the distressing disclosure that Bryan, the man who presumably was their champion, did not in actuality believe as they did, did not accept the literal Bible in all its parts. Some Fundamentalists spoke of sending a delegation to Bryan's house to protest the errors of his professed beliefs.

Bryan seemed to demand a literal reading of the Bible only when it served to combat theories he deemed inimical to the welfare of mankind. As Lawrence W. Levine has written, "His literal acceptance of the Bible did not lead to his rejection of evolution so much as his rejection of evolution led to his willingness to accept literally certain portions of the Bible in the face of the educated portion of the community." [18]

Yet he did his cause no good, and indeed much harm, by the grotesque argumentative positions that Darrow forced him to assume. Darrow's performance, too, was not unflawed. Although he posed as the defender of reason and light, as the protector of free scientific inquiry, the proceedings under the hot sun at Dayton did not altogether reflect these noble functions. Chiefly, they revealed that Darrow, the adroit lawyer, could score points in a mercilessly pulverizing way upon a less adroit opponent.

Whereas Darrow had carefully planned his attack in the preparatory scrimmage with Hays and Dr. Mather, anticipating replies and gauging his counterthrusts, it is clear that Bryan waded into his ordeal without a glimmer of preparation. He was overconfident, because of his faith either in his cause or in divine protection, and thus permitted himself to face a wily opponent without looking to his arms or armor. The forensic contest with Darrow was also one for which Bryan had little relevant experience save in those few distant years of his short-lived law practice. His public career had been largely a monologue conducted for more than three decades. From the platform, Bryan had expounded, preached, and declaimed in a one-way oratorical process. He was seldom questioned or debated in anything remotely approximating his experience at Dayton. In facing Darrow, in addition to the indefensibility of many of his positions, he carried the further leaden handicaps of being ill prepared and untrained.

On Tuesday, July 21, the day was dank and rainy. In light of Monday's cataclysm, the night was passed in anxious consultations. Sheriff R. B. Harris met secretly with Judge Raulston and warned that feelings were so roused by the Bryan-Darrow debate that rioting and violence threatened. "This thing must be stopped," Harris said emphatically. ". . . Someone is likely to get hurt." On Monday night, in a meeting of state's counsel, at Stewart's insistence Bryan's plan to grill Darrow the following day and expose him as an agnostic and infidel was quashed. Bryan undoubtedly accepted this decision in deep disappointment. Technically, he was still on the witness stand when the court convened, but neither side seemed to desire to act accordingly.

Bryan's position in the trial was further affected by a ruling Raulston delivered. He ordered Bryan's testimony of the previous day stricken from the record. Bryan rose and, looking tired and weary in voice, complained that he had not had an opportunity to ask a question, but added, "I fully agree with the court that the testimony taken yesterday was not legitimate or proper. I simply wanted the court to understand that I was not in position to raise an objection at that time myself, nor was I willing to have it raised for me without asserting my willingness to be cross-examined. . . . Now that the testimony has ended I assume that you expunge the questions as well as the answers." The court agreed.

Bryan presumably still had an opportunity to assert himself. Each side under usual procedure would make a summing up. This surely would be the vehicle best suited for Bryan's speaking style. It was widely reported that Bryan had composed a magical oration that would more than make up for yesterday's adversity. According to press accounts, he had been toiling over his presentation "for three months." [19]

Darrow and his colleagues again worked out a precise plan to cope with Bryan. With consummate craftiness, they would allow, in the summing up, the first speaker for the state—most likely Stewart—to make his presentation. The defense would then decline to argue the case further. The trial would end, and the hapless Bryan would have no opportunity to speak.

The plan did not go into operation, thanks to moves by Judge Raulston, which nonetheless served to achieve the same objective. Promptly after court began, the judge, in expounding on the case, declared that "the issue now is whether or not Mr. Scopes taught that man descended from a lower order of animals. It isn't a question of whether God created man as all complete at once, or it isn't a question as to whether God created man by the process of development and growth. . . ." Darrow, after some perfunctory wrangling, cooperated with the tendency of Raulston's observations. ". . . we have," declared Darrow, "no witnesses to offer, no proof to offer on the issues that the Court has laid down here, that Mr. Scopes did teach what the children said he taught, that man descended from a lower order of animals. We do not mean to contradict that, and I think to save time we will ask the Court to bring in the jury and instruct the jury to find the defendant guilty. We will make no objection to that, and it will save a lot of time, and I think that should be done."

Stewart jumped up quickly to say, "We are pleased to accept the suggestion of Mr. Darrow."

For Bryan, these swift maneuvers were a fatal blow. Now not only would he have no opportunity to examine Darrow, but he could not even deliver his carefully wrought speech. He protested: ". . . I had not reached the point where I could make a statement to answer the charges made by the counsel for the defense as to my ignorance and bigotry. . . . I shall have to trust to the justness of the press, not to the Court, the questions that I would have asked had I been permitted to call the attorneys on the other side."

After posing for photographers holding the paper bearing his charge to the jury and looking more sober than he was wont to, Judge Raulston read it to the assembled jurors. Darrow spoke briefly and after some minor disputings, in which Bryan shared, the jury filed out to deliberate. They were not long; in eight minutes they returned. The verdict, to no one's surprise, was "guilty." Nor was the verdict to anyone's disappointment; Darrow and his associates eagerly awaited it in order to move the case to a higher court.

Raulston passed sentence upon Scopes, fining him $100 and costs. Bond was fixed upon the young high school teacher at $500, which was supplied by the Baltimore *Evening Sun.* Counsel quickly worked out arrangements to appeal the case. As spectators rose and photographers took their last pictures, Raulston, who seemed reluctant to have his hour in the limelight fade, blurted, "Does anyone have anything to say?" Newspapermen, spectators, and attorneys joined in a round robin of comment. Bryan, who contributed somewhat rambling remarks, predicted: "The people will determine this issue . . . this case will stimulate investigation, and investigation will bring out information. . . ." After Raulston made an elongated statement of observations, the words ran out; there was nothing more to do. A locomotive whistled shrilly, as if to signal the end of the ordeal. Benediction was pronounced, and the court adjourned sine die.[20]

Despite his several disappointments, Bryan was the soul of optimism. If many onlookers at Dayton and in the world at large felt that Bryan had been humiliated and disgraced, there is no shred of evidence showing that he even for a moment shared in this impression. No word fell from his lips or his pen betraying remorse over his performance on the witness stand. If anything, Bryan's encounter reveals him as the possessor of a self-confidence that was impervious to Darrow's worst barbs. The world of Bryan's day and posterity may feel he was humiliated, but the experience failed to make the least dent on his self-image.

The night the trial ended he issued a statement to the press of extended observations on the proceedings and their significance. "The State has won its case. The Tennessee law has been vindicated . . . the followers of our Lord . . . are at last awakened to the insidious attacks which have been made, under cover of a scientific hypothesis. . . ." He was pleased that Darrow, "the most conspicuous of the opponents of religion in the nation," had participated. He posed again what he perceived as the central issues: ". . . a militant minority, made up of atheists, agnostics, and other dissenters from orthodox Christianity, is seeking to use the courts to compel the majority to pay teachers to undermine the religious faith of the children of the taxpayers who employ teachers." He advanced nine questions which he said he would have asked if he could have put Darrow on the witness stand. In a statement to the press, Darrow answered the questions cleverly, many with what amounted to an agnostic's "I don't know." Bryan issued another statement, his only concession that his performance was not altogether adequate, in effect contending that because he had devoted so much time to political, economic, and social problems it was unfair to expect him to be expert on the sciences about which Darrow had interrogated him.

Regardless of Bryan's own self-satisfied assessment of the trial, in the world's eyes Darrow had subjected him to humiliation on a scale rarely suffered by a major American politician. His stumbling under Darrow's questions ill served his cause. He brought upon himself a heap of ridicule and derision, and even to this day he remains buried under it. Yet the brawling, circus aspects of the trial which worked so much to Bryan's disadvantage have obscured its other effects. If Bryan failed to meet the challenge of science, Darrow failed equally, although not so obviously, to meet the challenge presented by traditional religion to modern philosophy. Darrow's performance served to put anti-Fundamentalism in a poor light. Modernism was unrepresented at Dayton, and Darrow, after hacking and scarring the faith of millions of Fundamentalists, offered only threadbare negativism and cynicism in its place. The American Civil Liberties Union received a flood of protests from liberal Christians among its supporters deploring the encounter at Dayton. Raymond B. Fosdick, a prominent liberal divine, declared that the trial was "not a very dignified proceeding." The accumulated complaints soon forced Darrow off the case.

But the worst failure at Dayton was Bryan's, and it was a failure, in his responses to Darrow's prickly, tricky, but entirely foreseeable questions, to demonstrate the connection between Fundamentalist religion and morality, or the relevance of Fundamentalism to modern-day problems. Ironically, on the basis of his own public record, of his years of struggle for social causes, there was no one better qualified than Bryan to explain these connections. His own life was an eloquent refutation of Darrow. Driven by faith in God's word and purpose, he had worked for decades, courageously and against crushing odds, to overcome America's social injustices and the murderous strife between the nations called war.

His worst lapse at Dayton was to permit the wily Darrow, posing as the champion of truth, to slide past that record without acknowledging it and to create a false image of himself that has endured in posterity. The portrayal of Bryan that is cemented in the stage drama and the motion picture is the gross distortion that Darrow contrived at Dayton. It is that of a bigoted, ill-informed, hopelessly outdated old man. Darrow and the dramatists who have taken their cues from him have cheated posterity of knowledge of the whole man, of the better man, the resolute champion of social justice who for decades prior to the Monkey Trial made religion and the Bible the foundation of an earthly kingdom of social justice and brotherhood among men and nations which today and as far into the future as the mind can see deserves the best efforts of men of goodwill.[21]

Although, with the trial over, visiting lawyers, journalists, entrepreneurs, and other assorted humanity fled Dayton, Bryan stayed on to dictate and revise the address he had planned to use on the summing up to the jury. He arranged with George Fort Milton, editor of the Chattanooga *News,* to have the speech printed. He visited a proposed site on a hill south of Dayton for a Fundamentalist school to be named in his honor. Before the trial began, a fundamentalist millionaire, George F. Washburn of Boston, and others announced that they would give $250,000 toward a $1,000,000 fund to build "the first fundamentalist university in America." The site delighted Bryan, but instead of a university, he favored a coeducational secondary school in which the students should wear blue and gray uniforms to symbolize the reconciliation of the North and South.

On Friday, July 24, Bryan journeyed to Chattanooga to confer with Milton about the publication of his speech, and that evening he was delighted to read the first proof sheets. Early Saturday morning Mary was driven down from Dayton to pick up Bryan. Together in the family limousine, with their chauffeur, William McCartney, at the wheel, they drove to Winchester, stopping briefly in the village of Jasper, where Bryan made a speech from a stand with a huge flag to an audience attired in shirts and overalls.

When they resumed their drive to Winchester, Mary and Bryan discussed the implications of his current cause. They dwelled on the "narrow margin," Mary wrote later, "between this perfectly legitimate work as touching the public servant, and an encroachment on individual religious belief which is a sacred domain. We agreed that care must be taken at this point that no religious zeal should invade this sacred domain and become intolerance."

Bryan, as usual, was all confidence. "Well, Mama," he said, "I have not made that mistake yet, have I?" Mary replied, "You are all right so far, but will you be able to keep to this narrow path?" A happy smile crossed his face as he said, "I think I can." Mary persisted, "But can you control your followers?" Confidently he said, "I think I can."

Winchester, with its comfortable homes, neat lawns, and treelined streets, was utterly delightful. Judge and Mrs. Raulston entertained at a luncheon in the Bryans' honor, with a hundred and more guests. After the meal, Mary, with the car and chauffeur, returned to Dayton before Bryan made his inevitable speech. He subsequently entrained for Dayton but en route made stops and rear platform addresses that reminded reporters of 1896. As wonderfully successful as ever, he electrified his listeners, and their extravagant cheering completely delighted him. Scopes' conviction, he cried, was a great victory for Christianity and a staggering blow "to the forces of darkness." His rear platform speaking on Saturday was estimated by reporters to have covered in excess of 200 miles, reaching at least 50,000 people. Any wounds the trial may have inflicted were for Bryan already well healed.[22]

The next morning, Sunday, July 26, he returned to Dayton and attended the Southern Methodist Church, which he led in an eloquent prayer calling for God's blessing upon the little Tennessee community, upon his country, and upon all humanity. From every corner of the church, he evoked a chorus of fervent Amens. After the service, practically every member of the congregation present pressed around to shake hands and exchange a word. Already all was forgiven Bryan for his strayings at the trial from the Fundamentalist faith. When he finally broke away, he arranged with the choir director the hymns for a sermon, "What Shall I Do With Jesus?," to be delivered on the following night.

Bryan returned to the Rogers cottage for his noonday Sunday dinner, which Mary had ordered within the guidelines of his diet. Buoyant from his successful speaking tour, he told Mary cheerily of a medical examination he had recently taken "just to ease your mind." His blood pressure, he exulted, was suitable for his age; his heart action was normal, and the other tests were entirely satisfactory. "According to that, Mama," he laughed, "I have several more years to live."

After dinner he made a few telephone calls to arrange for a vacation in the Smoky Mountains for himself and Mary and to his friend Milton concerning his soon-to-be-published speech. He then called to Mary who was on the side porch that he would take a nap and write a letter when he got up.

Bryan slept soundly. As shadows fell over the still house, Mary said to McCartney, "Go in and awaken Mr. Bryan. Such a long nap will break his rest tonight." McCartney returned and said that Bryan was sleeping so peacefully it seemed a pity to wake him. A chill foreboding raced over Mary. "Go back, raise the window curtains," she said, "and see if he is only sleeping." McCartney did so and called out, "Something is wrong. I cannot waken him." For Mary, crippled prisoner of her wheelchair, the world suddenly exploded into a frenzy of telephone calls for doctors, while upon her consciousness blazed the words "He was not, for God took him." [23]

The precise cause of Bryan's death remains somewhat obscure. No doctor was in attendance at the time, and no autopsy was performed. Newspapers reported that he died of apoplexy. His detractors continued to fight him even in death by suggesting that overeating brought him to his end. Clarence Darrow, after offering polite regrets, was told that Bryan had died of a broken heart. "Broken heart, nothing," Darrow is supposed to have responded, "he died of a busted belly." In 1931, Grace, still uncertain of the cause of her father's death, wrote to Dr. J. Thomas Kelly of Baltimore. Dr. Kelly, of course, had not been present when Bryan died, nor had he examined his body. He recalled to Grace that after examining Bryan in 1914, at Mary's request, he was satisfied from a urine test that Bryan had diabetes. "He was immediately put on an anti-diabetic diet," Dr. Kelly added, "*and continued on the diet up to the time of his death.*" After 1914, Dr. Kelly examined Bryan "at frequent intervals." During the Dayton trial, Kelly wrote, he studied many newspaper pictures of Bryan "and felt very apprehensive for him. You will remember it was very warm *and he was looking very thin*. Mr. Bryan died of diabetes mellitis, the immediate cause being the fatigue incident to the heat and his extraordinary exertions due to the Scopes Trial."

For the first twenty-four hours, Mary and the faithful McCartney faced their odeal alone. Early the following day Ruth and her husband arrived. Actually, she was never alone, for word of Bryan's death passed like a shock wave through the countryside. Mourners by the hundreds came to the little white cottage by auto, horse, mule, and foot. There were no celebrities among the endless human influx. They were tillers of the soil, mill hands, small shopkeepers, farmers' wives, children, and Negroes. The women mostly wore gingham, some linen, and a few silk. Some men wore black string ties, some blue shirts, and some overalls. Most had bronzed faces and the demeanor that tells of a life of hard work. There was much soft weeping. A man who had brought Bryan a basket of peaches a week before cried openly. On Tuesday afternoon a brief service was held on the lawn by local clergy, who used the veranda as a pulpit. The crowd filled the lawn, and prayers and hymns displaced the summer's quiet. Afterward, Mary, conversing with the Reverend Charles R. Jones, pastor of the Dayton Methodist Church, posed a question which showed that Bryan's loss had not overwhelmed her, that she, like he, looked always to the future and envisioned it in terms of unfinished work. After speaking with Jones of Bryan's career, she asked, "But I wonder who will take his place? Where is the man?"

Early the next morning, before the streaks of night had left the sky, Bryan's body, attended by Mary and her family, was placed aboard a special train destined for Washington, the chosen place of burial. Dayton was already stirring, and an immense crowd was at the station to watch sorrowfully as the train pulled away. Within minutes it was moving through the Tennessee Valley, with its lush fields of corn and sweet potatoes and peach orchards. Farther off, life stirred in little farmhouses nestled against the hills which rose to a cloudless sky. Increasingly, as the train moved on, country folk gathered at the stations or stood by the roadside to gaze, always bareheaded, at the train.

As the day and the train proceeded, the common people whom Bryan loved poured out in proof of their devotion. "This last journey," Mary reflected, "was like the early campaigns, except that now there was sorrow on the faces that pressed around the windows. The great crowds of people were silent and no one came to the back platform to greet them."

The mounds of flowers around the casket grew larger at every stop. At Jefferson City, Tennessee, a quartet of young men stood on a pile of railroad ties, hymnbooks in hand, singing as the train drew in a favorite Bryan anthem, "One Sweetly Solemn Thought." Nearby, an old man supported a large American flag. As the train pulled away, the hymn rose again from the crowd in a great chorus. In a small town where the train did not stop, a church service had been arranged so that it closed as the funeral train approached, and the congregation came in a body from its nearby chapel to the railroad embankment, where they stood with bowed heads as the train passed. At the Virginia cities of Bristol, Roanoke, and Lynchburg, thousands gathered. At Lynchburg, where the train arrived at 2:15 A.M., the huge crowd was so deeply reverent toward her father that Ruth ordered the doors of the funeral car opened to allow the crowd to pass through.[24]

In Washington, Bryan lay in state in the New York Avenue Presbyterian Church, "the church of Presidents." The city was in official mourning, and before the day was done, an estimated 20,000 persons moved past his bier, guarded by two Spanish-American War veterans. By now eulogies had been widely spoken. President Coolidge expressed "profound regret" and subsequently wrote to Mary of Bryan that "The sincerity of his motives was beyond dispute." Darrow, now less severe, acknowledged that he had voted for Bryan for President twice and respected his "sincerity and devotion." Political figures around the country swelled the eulogistic chorus.

The church services on the day of Bryan's burial, July 31, were simple. The Reverend Dr. Joseph R. Sizoo officiated, and to the family's surprise and delight they learned that Dr. Sizoo had been brought into the ministry through the influence of one of Bryan's addresses. Sizoo's eulogy of Bryan as "a rebuilder of God's altar" was carried by radio as far west as Minneapolis and into Canada.

The burial was at Arlington Cemetery, by Bryan's own request, thus affording the arresting final paradox of an ardent near pacifist choosing a soldier's grave. When the procession commenced from the church at about 4 P.M., fog and rain were so heavy that the streetlamps were turned on. At Arlington, Bryan was honored with a military burial. As throngs stood by in the rain, taps sounded over the flag-draped coffin, and Cabinet Secretaries, Senators and Representatives, politicians past and present, watched the lowering of the casket into a grave on a steep hillside which commanded a clear view of the White House. The Reverend George R. Stuart of Birmingham, Alabama, in a final prayer, broke in voice when he said, "We thank Thee for this great hero of the common people."

Mary returned to her Florida home and took up the task that Bryan had begun but could not finish. Despite illness and confinement, she completed the writing of her husband's memoirs, with the sense that her task was not a lonely one, that her working partnership with Bryan still endured. Bryan's soul, she always contended, is still marching on "just beyond our mortal vision." [25]

NOTES AND SOURCES

Notes

In order to avoid overwhelming numbers of notes, the references necessary for a particular passage are collected in a single note.
The following abbreviations have been used:

Manuscript Sources

BP	Bryan Papers, Library of Congress
BPNA	Bryan Papers, National Archives
OP	Bryan Papers, Occidental College Library
SDF	State Department File, National Archives
WP	Woodrow Wilson Papers, Library of Congress
WPNA	Woodrow Wilson Papers, National Archives

Newspapers

NSJ	*Nebraska State Journal*
NYT	New York *Times*
OWH	Omaha *World-Herald*
TC	*The Commoner*

Memoirs
William Jennings Bryan, *The Memoirs of William Jennings Bryan* (Philadelphia, 1925).

Chapter 1. A Rare Politician

1. *Memoirs*, 249–50.
2. *Ibid.*, 203–4.
3. Claude Bowers, *My Life* (New York, 1962), 122.
4. Charles McDaniel Rosser, *The Crusading Commoner* (Dallas, 1937), 264.
5. For discussions of ideology and pragmatism, see Giovanni Sartori, "Politics, Ideology and Belief Systems," *American Political Science Review* (June, 1969), 398. Daniels is quoted in Rosser, X.
6. Hewitt's statement is in Mark D. Hirsch, *William C. Whitney, Modern Maverick* (New York, 1948), 509.

Chapter 2. Illinois Beginnings

1. In Paxton Hibben, *The Peerless Leader: William Jennings Bryan* (New York, 1929), 21.
2. BP, Box 64, "William Jennings Bryan: Biographical Notes"; *Memoirs*, 22–24.
3. *Ibid.*, 34–35.
4. Paolo E. Coletta, "The Youth of William Jennings Bryan," *Nebraska History* (March, 1950), 5. *Memoirs*, 35–36, 29. On child-parent relations, see Harry Stack Sullivan, *The Interpersonal Theory of Psychiatry* (New York, 1953), 206–27.
5. *Memoirs*, 44.
6. Coletta, 2–3.
7. Implications are explored in Sullivan, 161, 165.

8. August 5, 1912, BP, Box 28.
9. WJB statement is in *Memoirs*, 40; and Silas' in Mrs. Mary E. Nickell to Mrs. W. J. Bryan, October 15, 1912, BP, Box 28.
10. *Memoirs*, 45.
11. William Jennings Bryan, *The Second Battle* (Chicago, 1900), 47–48; Coletta, 1; "Correspondence of Grace Bryan Hargraves," BP, Box 64.
12. *Memoirs*, 42; Coletta, 10; WJB statement in Mrs. Mary E. Nickell, *op. cit.*, BP, Box 28.

Chapter 3. Education of an Idealist

1. Quotations are from *Memoirs*, 52; William Jennings Bryan, *The Second Battle* (Chicago, 1900), 55.
2. *Memoirs*, 52–53; *Second Battle*, 53.
3. J. C. Long, *Bryan, the Great Commoner* (New York, 1928), 32.
4. Robert W. White, ed., *The Study of Lives* (New York, 1963), 417.
5. George R. Poage, "College Career of William Jennings Bryan," *Mississippi Valley Historical Review* (September, 1928), 166–68.
6. Poage, 169–70, 166. J. M. Sturtevant, Jr., *Julian M. Sturtevant, an Autobiography* (New York, 1896), *passim.*
7. *Memoirs*, 58–60. Storrs' statement in Poage, 171.
8. Poage, 176. On "Master Motives," see Illinois College *Rambler*, (April, 1880), 33; and Bryan's comments and reports on his college career in Jacksonville, Illinois, *Journal* (April 18, May 7 and 9, 1880).
9. Bryan on Virgil in "William Jennings Bryan: Biographical Notes, His Speeches, Letters and other Writings," typescript p. 16, BP, Box 64. Bryan on Cicero and "Perfection" in notebook, "William Jennings Bryan, Jacksonville, Illinois, Illinois College, Oct. 23, 1880," BP, Box 49.
10. Bryan discusses his college oratorical experiences in Bryan to F. C. Lockwood, February 23, 1920, BP, Box 33. Concerning the contests at Monmouth and Galesburg, extracts from the Monmouth *Courier* and the Galesburg *Plain Dealer* are in BP, Box 41.
11. *Memoirs*, 55–57.
12. For the St. Louis Convention, *Memoirs*, 97–98. Bryan's first political speech: *Second Battle*, 56. His experiences as college politician: Poage, 180–81.
13. Silas' statement is in *Second Battle*, 53. College references appear in Paolo E. Coletta, "The Youth of William Jennings Bryan—Beginnings of a Christian Statesman," 25, *Nebraska History* (March, 1960), 23–25; and Illinois College *Rambler*, October 24, 1896.
14. Bryan's struggle with religious doubts is discussed in his lecture "The Prince of Peace," *The Speeches of William Jennings Bryan* (New York, 1909), II, 282; Coletta, 12–13; Poage, 172–73. The classmate's remark is from Poage, 173.

Chapter 4. Mary

1. On Mary and Bryan's courtship, see Paolo E. Coletta, "Won, 1880–One, 1884," Illinois State Historical Society *Journal* (Autumn, 1957), 231 *passim;* George R. Poage, "College Career of William Jennings Bryan," *Mississippi Valley Historical Review* (September, 1928), 174–75; and Mrs. Mary Turner Carriel's comments in Jacksonville, Illinois, *Journal* (July, 1925). Mary's letter is in Coletta, 234–35.
2. Coletta, 232–36; Bryan's encounter with Mary's father is in William Jennings Bryan, *The Second Battle* (Chicago, 1900), 61. Silas' death is recounted in Paolo E. Coletta, "The Youth of William Jennings Bryan—Beginnings of a Christian Statesman," *Nebraska History* (March, 1950), 17, and the *Marion County Herald,* March 31 and April 23, 1880.

3. On Silas' will, see Coletta, "The Youth of William Jennings Bryan," 17–18, and the plan for an Oxford education is in Grace Dexter Bryan to Dan Bride, undated, BP, Box 41.
4. Bryan discusses his ambition to become a lawyer in William Jennings Bryan, *The Value of an Ideal* (New York and London, 1914), 10–12. Excerpts from the address on "Character" are from *Second Battle*, 56–58.
5. Law school details from Adolphus R. Talbot, address commemorating "79th Anniversary of the Birthday of William Jennings Bryan," Lincoln, Nebraska, March 19, 1939, BP, Box 65.
6. See William Jennings Bryan, *The First Battle* (Chicago, 1897), 46; Paolo E. Coletta, *William Jennings Bryan,* Vol. I, *Political Evangelist* (Lincoln, Nebraska, 1964), 24–26. The law school is described in Arthur Herbert White, *Northwestern University A History, 1855–1905* (New York, 1905), Vol. IV, 29–71. Bryan discusses his law school experiences in Bryan to F. C. Lockwood, February 23, 1920, BP, Box 33. The "Vigilance" speech is excerpted in "William Jennings Bryan: Biographical Notes, His Speeches, Letters and Other Writings," enlarged and edited by Grace Dexter Bryan, December 10, 1941, 21–24, BP, Box 64.
7. The penny-pitching episode is in *The Value of an Ideal*, 28–29; and the observation on England in Coletta, *William Jennings Bryan*, 24–25.
8. Bryan's appreciation of Trumbull is expressed in Willis J. Abbot, "William Jennings Bryan: A Character Sketch," *Review of Reviews* (August, 1896), 164. See also *Second Battle*, 60–61.
9. *Memoirs*, 223–24.

Chapter 5. The Young Lawyer

1. William Jennings Bryan, *The Memoirs of William Jennings Bryan* (Philadelphia, 1925), 61–63. On young adult psychology, see Robert W. White, *Lives in Progress* (New York, 1952), 397.
2. Mary-Bryan letters and wedding details from Paolo E. Coletta, "Won, 1880–One, 1884," *Illinois State Historical Society Journal* (Autumn, 1957), 241–42, and *Memoirs*, 230–31.
3. *Memoirs*, 67; George G. Waite to Bryan, March 29, 1887, BP, Box 1.
4. *Memoirs*, 232; James C. Davies, *Human Nature in Politics* (New York, 1963), 177–78.
5. Benjamin Harrison to Bryan, May 14, 1887, BP, Box 1; *Memoirs*, 232. Bryan's experiences coincide with the analysis by Lester W. Milbrath, *Political Participation* (Chicago, 1965), 42.
6. The speech episode: William Jennings Bryan, *The First Battle* (Chicago, 1897), 302. Bryan's temperance speech is in BP, Box 1. On the young adult ideologue, see Robert W. White, ed., *The Study of Lives* (New York, 1963), 417–18.
7. *Memoirs*, 71–74; Adolphus R. Talbot, address commemorating "79th Anniversary of the Birthday of William Jennings Bryan," Lincoln, Nebraska, March 19, 1939, BP, Box 65.
8. *Memoirs*, 74.
9. *Ibid.*, 76–77, 75; Paolo E. Coletta, "William Jennings Bryan's First Nebraska Years," *Nebraska History* (April–June 1947), 72–73. The contract with Harrison is in OP.

Chapter 6. O Pioneers!

1. Description of Lincoln: A. B. Hayes and Samuel D. Cox, *History of the City of Lincoln* (Lincoln, 1889), *passim.*
2. Talbot and Bryan advertisement: February 1, 1888, BP, Box 1. Data on the firm: Paolo E. Coletta, "William Jennings Bryan's First Nebraska Years," *Nebraska History* (June, 1952), 72–73.

3. Adolphus R. Talbot, address commemorating "79th Anniversary of the Birthday of William Jennings Bryan," Lincoln Nebraska, March 19, 1939, BP, Box 65.

4. Bryan's clubs and activities: M. R. Werner, *Bryan* (New York, 1929), 22; Paolo E. Coletta, "The Morning Star of the Reformation: William Jennings Bryan's First Congressional Campaign," *Nebraska History* (June, 1953), 113–14. Mary: Coletta, "William Jennings Bryan's First Nebraska Years," 88–89.

5. The tariff: Coletta, "William Jennings Bryan's First Nebraska Years," 77. Morton's letter is in BP, Box 1, and his reaction to Bryan is in James C. Olsen, *J. Sterling Morton* (Lincoln, 1942), 331.

6. Nebraska politics: Coletta, "William Jennings Bryan's First Nebraska Years," 77–78; J. Sterling Morton and Albert Watkins, *History of Nebraska* (Lincoln, 1913), III, 42–43, Nebraska's terrain and agriculture: Hayes and Cox, 57–58; Arthur F. Mullen, *Western Democrat* (New York, 1940), 4–10; *OWH*, November 11, 1894.

7. Nebraska farm life: Charles S. Reed, "Life in a Nebraska Soddy, A Reminiscence," *Nebraska History* (March, 1958), 63–69.

8. The farmer's plight: Paolo E. Coletta, "The Morning Star of the Reformation: William Jennings Bryan's First Congressional Campaign," *Nebraska History* (June, 1956), 103. J. R. Johnson, "Nebraska in the Seventies," *Nebraska History* (June, 1956), 81–100. Quotation, "Week after week . . ." is from John D. Barnhart, "Rainfall and the Populist Party in Nebraska," *American Political Science Review* (August, 1925), 534.

9. Bryan's first speeches: Coletta, "William Jennings Bryan's First Nebraska Years," 78–82. Wayne C. Williams, *William Jennings Bryan* (New York, 1923), 62. "William Jennings Bryan's Biographical Notes, His Speeches, Letters and Other Writings," enlarged and edited by Grace Dexter Bryan, December 10, 1941, 5, BP, Box 64. State leaders are impressed: Mullen, 95. Bryan's own evaluation: Bryan to L. C. Lockwood, February 23, 1920, BP, Box 33.

10. "A cradle made of hickory:" Coletta, "William Jennings Bryan's First Nebraska Years," 78–79. State convention: *OWH*, May 3, 1888. Democratic National Convention and Nebraska campaigning: Coletta, 80–83.

11. Fred Carey, *Mayor Jim* (Omaha, 1930), 63–65.

12. *Memoirs*, 248.

13. Bryan's speech with Morton: *OWH*, August 6, 1888. Morton asks Bryan to speak: Morton to Bryan, August 30, 1888, BP, Box 1.

14. Allan Nevins, *Grover Cleveland, A Study in Courage* (New York, 1932), 439–40.

15. Olson, 331.

16. Mary and family: *Memoirs*, 233–34, 193. A book on the tariff: G. P. competed and to Bryan, September 13, 1889; Democratic state convention: Morton to Bryan, October 10 and 11, 1889, BP, Box 1.

Chapter 7. A Victory

1. Mary: Paolo E. Coletta, *William Jennings Bryan*, Vol. I, *Political Evangelist* (Lincoln, 1964), 48. Newspaper interviews: *OWH*, April 15, 1890. R. W. Story to Bryan, June 24, 1890, BP, Box 1.

2. Bryan to Charles Brown, June 30, 1890, BP, Box 1. Lincoln *Call* clipping in BP, Box 1.

3. C. J. Smyth to Bryan, July 8, 1890, BP, Box 1.

4. Harold U. Faulkner, *Politics, Reform and Expansion, 1890–1900* (New York, 1959), 54.Verse from Arthur F. Mullen, *Western Democrat,* (New York, 1940).

5. John D. Hicks, *The Populist Revolt* (Minneapolis, 1931), 61–70.

6. *Ibid.*, 80–81; Faulkner, 58–59.

7. Richard Hofstadter, *The Age of Reform* (New York, 1956), 28–29; Faulkner, 55.

8. Hicks, 157–59.

9. J. W. Barnhart, to Bryan, July 22, 1890, BP, Box 1. C. J. Smyth to Bryan, July 25, 1890, BP, Box 1. Charles Brown to J. Sterling Morton, July 28, 1890, Morton Papers, Roll 15. Bryan to Morton, March 17, 1890, *ibid.*
10. *OWH,* July 31 and August 13, 1890, Bryan to Morton, March 17, 1890, Morton Papers, Roll 15.
11. *OWH,* July 31, 1890, BP, Box 1. On political ambition, see Joseph A. Schlesinger, *Ambition and Politics* (Chicago, 1966), 1–11. Miller: James C. Olson, *J. Sterling Morton* (Lincoln, 1942), 332. Bryan to Morton, August 20, 1890, Morton Papers, Roll 15.
12. John Sherman to Bryan, August 24, 1890, BP, Box 2. Bryan quoted: *OWH,* August 15, 1890.
13. "A child can understand . . ." *OWH,* September 17, 1890. Bryan on prohibition: *ibid.,* September 24, 1890. On the trust and tariff and Omaha Negroes: *ibid.,* October 9, 1890. The Bryan-Connell debates: William Jennings Bryan, *The Second Battle* (Chicago, 1900), 66–68.
14. *OWH,* October 30, 1890.
15. Ridicule of Bryan: Coletta, *William Jennings Bryan,* 45; Paolo E. Coletta, "The Morning Star of the Reformation: William Jennings Bryan's First Congressional Campaign," *Nebraska History* (June, 1956), 113. W. E. Johnson to Bryan, October 16, 1890, BP, Box 2.
16. Ballot-box stuffing: Coletta, *William Jennings Bryan,* 47; Bryan to Morton, November 10, 1890, OP, and Morton Papers, Roll 15. Bryan on his victory: *OWH,* November 6, 1890. Eli Doud: quoted in Coletta, "The Morning Star," 109.

Chapter 8. Congressman

1. Bryan's readings: William Jennings Bryan, *The First Battle* (Chicago, 1897), 71. Monetary theory: Davis R. Dewey, *Financial History of the United States,* 11th ed. (New York, 1931); John D. Hicks, *The Populist Revolt* (Minneapolis, 1931), *passim.*
2. "The Crime of 1873": Hicks, 301–5. Moreton Frewen: Stanley L. Jones, *The Presidential Election of 1896* (Madison, Wisconsin, 1964), 10–11.
3. The quantity of money: *OWH,* April 14, 1891; Jones, 7–8.
4. A. J. Warner to Bryan, May 10, 1891, BP, Box 2. J. Sterling Morton to Bryan, May 21, June 7, 1891, Morton Papers. Hitchcock: *OWH,* April 23, 1891, Roll 16. Ohio and other campaigning: Bryan to James A. Campbell, July 27, 1891, Bryan to J. E. Neal, September 11, 1891, Bryan to John Tomlinson, October 21, 1891, BP Box 2. Bryan to William Springer, June 26, 1891, BP, Box 42.
5. Political friend: Bryan to A. B. Farquar, October 3, 1891, BP, Box 2. State convention: *NSJ* and *OWH,* September 18, 1891. Morton's warning: Morton to Bryan, September 28, 1891, BP, Box 2. Bryan's reply: Bryan to Morton, October 3, 1891, Morton Papers, Roll 16.
6. *NSJ* and *OWH,* October 6, 1891.
7. Bryan to Mary, December 2, and December 6, 1891, BP, Box 2.
8. House hunting: William Jennings Bryan, *Memoirs of William Jennings Bryan* (Philadelphia, 1925), 237–38. Family living: Typescript by Dan Bride, November 15, 1920, BP, Box 33.
9. Bryan concerning House colleagues: Bryan to Mary, December 6, 1891, BP, Box 2. Mary's social genius: Bryan to Mary, December 2, 1891, BP, Box 2.
10. Springer's Speakership ambitions: William Springer to Bryan, November 8, 1890, BP, Box 2. Bryan on the Speakership fight: Bryan to Mary, December 6, 1891, BP, Box 2. Donald Dickinson's efforts: *OWH,* December 7, 1891. The "deal": *ibid.,* December 8, 1891. Champ Clark, *My Quarter Century of American Politics* (New York and London, 1920), I, 273. Attention centers on Bryan: *OWH, op. cit.* Bryan and Mills: *ibid.,* December 26, 1891.
11. Sarah Beck: *Congressional Record,* January 3, 1894, 487; May 4, 1894, 4, 430. Civil

war corn: Quartermaster General Office to Bryan, December 17, 1892, BP, Box 2. Buffalo Bill: *OWH*, March 7, 1891. Solomon Gerber: Bryan to Secretary of State J. G. Blaine, August 6, 1891, BP, Box 42. Postmasters: Bryan to Fred W. Bostrom, July 2, 1891, BP, Box 42. Bryan and the rivers study: *Congressional Record*, May 7, 1892, 4065.

12. Missouri bridge: *Congressional Record*, June 30, 1892, 5665. Loan sharks: Paolo E. Coletta, *William Jennings Bryan*, Vol. I, *Political Evangelist* (Lincoln, 1964), 50. Reed Rules: *OWH*, May 13, 1892. Contested election: *ibid.*, December 24, 1891. GAR: *Congressional Record*, June 30, 1892, 5961. Sugar beet industry: Omaha *Bee*, December 19, 1891; *OWH*, December 24, 1891; Lincoln *Daily Call*, December 27, 1891. Regulatory proposals: *OWH*, May 16, 1892; *NSJ*, May 17, 1892. Popular election of Senators: *OWH*, January 23, 1892.

13. Bryan on the tariff: William Jennings Bryan, *Speeches of William Jennings Bryan* (New York, 1911), 33–40, 60–72; *OWH*, March 17, 1892.

14. *OWH*, March 17, 1892.

15. Mary: *ibid.* The Washington scene: *ibid.*, March 2, 1891. The Bryan Sundays: typescript by Dan Bride, undated, BP, Box 41. Silver: *Congressional Record*, March 24, 1892, 656 ff.

16. *Congressional Record*, June 6, 1892, 5084.

Chapter 9. An Uncertain Election

1. *OWH*, April 12 and 13, 1892.

2. *Ibid.*, April 15, 1892.

3. *Ibid.*

4. Paolo E. Coletta, "William Jennings Bryan's Second Congressional Campaign," *Nebraska History* (December, 1959), 277.

5. *OWH*, July 14, 1892.

6. Coletta, 278. *OWH*, September 29, 1892; Jesse F. Boell, "The Career of William Jennings Bryan to 1896," unpublished MA thesis (University of Nebraska, 1919), 104.

7. The Albion *Argus* is quoted in *TC*, March 12, 1916; Bryan's campaign: Coletta, 280.

8. Democratic state convention: *OWH*, August 30 and 31, 1892; James C. Olson, *J. Sterling Morton* (Lincoln, 1942), 339. Jefferson Broady's collections: Lon V. Stephens to Jesse F. Boell, Jan. 25, 1925, BP, Box 64; Charles S. Thomas to Paxton Hibben, July 16, 1928; Paxton Hibben, *The Peerless Leader: William Jennings Bryan* (New York, 1929), 146. Rumors of a deal: Robert Clegg to J. B. Shrean, October 7, 1892, Morton Papers, Roll 17: Olson, 344; J. S. Morton to Emma Morton, October 6, 1892, Morton Papers, Roll 17.

9. Omaha *Bee*, November 4, 1892.

10. County fairs: *OWH*, September 23, October 6, 1892. Debate with Field: *ibid.*, September 23, 1892. Bryan on silver: *ibid.*, September 21, 1892. Bryan on his vote: *ibid.*, October 23, November 4, 1892; Omaha *Bee*, November 2, 1892.

11. Attacks on Bryan: Coletta, 286. Assessment of saloons: *OWH*, October 23 and November 4, 1892; Omaha *Bee*, October 25, November 7, 1892.

12. McKinley and Foraker: William Jennings Bryan, *The Second Battle* (Chicago, 1900), 69; *OWH*, September 22, 1892.

13. Shamp and railroads: A. J. Sawyer to J. Sterling Morton, August 22, 1893, Morton Papers, Roll 24; *OWH*, September 27, 1892. McKeighan: *ibid.*, October 27, 1892. "No chance to elect" Morton: H. J. Whitmore to Morton, October 9, 1892, Morton Papers, Roll 18.

14. Bryan on silver: *OWH*, September 23, 1892. Morton on Bryan: Morton to Michael D. Harter, January 9, 1893, in Olson, 344.

15. Coletta, 290; Omaha *Bee*, October 19, 1892; *OWH*, October 25, 1892.

16. Olson, 343.

17. "I never touch the stuff": *NYT,* August 2, 1925. Sec. Viii, 3. The floral piece episode, Mary's role, Bryan's friendships, and Willa Cather's comment concerning Bryan are in her "The Personal Side of William Jennings Bryan," *The Prairie Schooner* (Winter, 1949), 331 ff.

Chapter 10. The Silver Craze

1. Kansas City *Times* in Paolo E. Coletta, "William Jennings Bryan and the Nebraska Senatorial Election of 1893," *Nebraska History* (September, 1950), 191. John D. Calhoun to Bryan, January 23, 1893, BP, Box 2. Bryan to C. D. Casper, undated, BP, Box 41.
2. C. D. Casper to Bryan, February 8, 1893, BP, Box 2. T. S. Allen to Bryan, February 4, 1893, BP, Box 2. William V. Allen: Mittie Young Scott, "Life and Political Career of William V. Allen," MS Thesis, 1927, University of Nebraska; *OWH,* February 4 and 5, 1893; Omaha *Bee,* February 14, 1893; Coletta, 198. Allen—"shrewd politician": E. P. Weatherby to J. Sterling Morton, May 4, 1893, Morton Papers, Roll 26; C. D. Casper to Bryan, February 8, 1893, BP, Box 2.
3. Bryan's thank-you note: *Memoirs,* 239.
4. Grover Cleveland to John G. Carlisle is in Allan Nevins, *Letters of Grover Cleveland, 1850–1908* (Boston, 1933), 314–15. Bryan's "violent free silver tendencies": Omaha *Bee,* December 29, 1892. Cleveland and a special legislative session: James A. Barnes, *John G. Carlisle, Financial Statesman* (New York, 1931), 252–53; Horace S. Merrill, *Bourbon Leader: Grover Cleveland and the Democratic Party* (Boston, 1957), 172–76; Allan Nevins, *Grover Cleveland: A Study in Courage* (New York, 1932), 523–24.
5. Bryan on greenback cancellation: *Congressional Record,* February 27, 1893, 2237. Cleveland on yielding: Cleveland to L. Clarke Davis, January 25, 1893, in Nevins, Letters, 315.
6. Bryan's reading: Robert Beall to Bryan, May 3, 1893, BP, Box 3. J. Whitney, Bureau of Statistics, Treasury Department, to Bryan, May 11, 1893, BP, Box 3; Secretary of the Treasury, J. G. Carlisle to Bryan, August 23, 1893, BP, Box 3. Mary: "William Jennings Bryan: Biographical Notes, His Speeches, Letters and Other Writings," enlarged and edited by his daughter, Grace Dexter Bryan, typescript, 32, BP, Box 64.
7. W. H. Harvey to Bryan, March 28, 1893, BP, Box 3. University of Michigan: H. M. Jarrett to Bryan, April 13, 1893, BP, Box 3. Atlanta: W. Y. Atkinson to Bryan, April 18, 1893, BP, Box 3. Atlanta: W. Y. Atkinson to Bryan, April 18, 1893, BP, Box 3. Correspondent on Bryan's Southern tour: *OWH,* June 24, 1893.
8. Panic of 1893: Davis Rich Dewey, *Financial History of the United States,* 6th ed. (New York, 1918), 44, 445–47. Topeka: *OWH,* July 21, 1893. Lincoln, Nebraska, speech: *ibid.*
9. *OWH,* July 26, 1893.
10. Bryan to Mary, August 16, 1893, BP, Box 64. Bryan's speech: Nevins, *Grover Cleveland,* 539.
11. Much of the speech is in William Jennings Bryan, *The First Battle* (Chicago, 1897), 81 ff.
12. "No longer a British colony": *ibid.,* 93. Press coverage: *OWH,* August 17 and 23, 1893; Omaha *Bee,* August 17, 21, and 23, 1893. William Springer: *OWH,* August 17, 1893. William M. Stewart: *ibid.,* August 28, 1893.
13. Springer on Cleveland: Springer to Mrs. Springer, August 21, 1893, William Springer Papers. Patronage: James C. Olson, Jr., *J. Sterling Morton* (Lincoln, Nebraska, 1942), 379.
14. Cleveland's fight: Nevins, *Grover Cleveland,* 548. Castor and Martin: Olson, 380–81.
15. State convention: *OWH,* October 5, 1893. Morton on Bryan, in Olson, 381. Watson: C. Vann Woodward, *Tom Watson, Agrarian Rebel* (New York, 1938), 196.

16. The convention's aftermath: *OWH,* October 7 and 8, 1893. Irvine's abilities and help to Bryan: John Schomp to J. Sterling Morton, October 24, 1893, Morton Papers, Roll 24. Bryan on Irvine: Bryan to Gilbert Hitchcock, October 12, 1893, BP, Box 3. Morton and Irvine: Tobias Castor to J. Sterling Morton, October 22, 1893, Morton Papers, Roll 19; Olson, 382.
17. Bland's and Bryan's silver proposals: *OWH,* October 6 and 30, 1893. Tax on state bank notes: *Congressional Record,* June 5, 1894, 5814.
18. Bank reserves proposal: *Congressional Record,* June 5, 1894, 5808–15. Data on federal indirect taxes: Thomas G. Shearman, "The Owners of the United States," *Forum* (November, 1889), 262–73. C. H. Jones to Bryan, May 8, 1893, BP, Box 3.
19. Josephus Daniels, *Editor in Politics* (Chapel Hill, 1941), 75. *Congressional Record,* February 6 and 15, 1894, 1730, 1739, 1795–97; Appendix I, 203–5; 601–14; March 1, 1894, 1655–58.
20. *Congressional Record, ibid.*
21. *Ibid.,* June 18, 1894, Appendix I, 1074–75.
22. Bryan to Grover Cleveland, February 7, 1894, BP, Box 3. Daniels and Bryan: Daniels, 52. On Bryan's patronage fortunes: *OWH,* January 18, 1894; *NSJ* and Omaha *Bee,* May 24, 1894. Bryan to Tobias Castor, February 7, 1894, BP, Box 3; Paolo E. Coletta, "Bryan, Cleveland, and the Disrupted Democracy," *Nebraska History* (March, 1960), 12–13.
23. "Cross of Gold": *Congressional Record,* December 22, 1894, 785–789; *OWH,* January 7 and 10, 1895. Bryan on Morgan: *OWH,* February 12 and 13, 1895. Foreign syndicate's bribe: *The First Battle,* 137. Eastern creditors: *ibid.,* 146. Chastening the President: *ibid.,* 136. Bryan's speech is also in *Congressional Record,* February 14, 1894, 2182–83.
24. Populism: Arthur D. Mullen, *Western Democrat* (New York, 1940), 66; John D. Hicks, *The Populist Revolt* (Minneapolis, 1931), 159–63, 283, 316–20; C. Vann Woodward, *Tom Watson, Agrarian Rebel* (New York, 1938). Watson is quoted in Woodward, 195, 209, and 293. "The Call to Silver Men": *OWH,* March 2, 1895; *The First Battle,* 155–58.
25. Paxton Hotel meeting: *The First Battle,* 149. Nebraska silver conference: *ibid.,* 149–50; *OWH,* June 22, 1894.
26. *OWH, ibid.*
27. Consequences of the silver conference: *The First Battle,* 150. Bryan's speeches: *OWH,* February 23, 1894. Gresham to Cleveland: Wayne C. Williams, *William Jennings Bryan, a Study in Political Vindication* (New York, 1923), 118.

Chapter 11. The Almost Senator

1. Bryan to Broady: *NSJ,* May 18, 1894. Bryan to Hitchcock: April 14, 1894, BP, Box 3. Bryan to Abbot: Willis J. Abbot, "William Jennings Bryan: A Character Sketch," *The Review of Reviews* (August, 1896), 169.
2. Bryan's platform: *OWH,* August 5, 1894. Tobias Castor's statement concerning silver is in his letter to J. Sterling Morton, July 16, 1894, Morton Papers, Roll 27; concerning Bryan's strategy, *ibid.,* June 26, 1894; and concerning Tom Allen, *ibid.,* August 6, 1894. John Thomsen to Bryan, August 22, 1894, BP, Box 3. Winning county delegations: *OWH,* August 18 and September 16, 20 and 22, 1894. Omaha success: OWH, September 21, 1894.
3. Bryan becomes editor: *OWH,* August 28, 1894.
4. Bryan promotes fusion: J. C. Ecker to Bryan, September 5, 1894; S. B. Thompson to Bryan, September 5, 1894; E. B. Spackman to Bryan, September 7, 1894, BP, Box 3. Populist state convention: *OWH,* September 27, 1894. Nebraska gold Democrats: James C. Olson, *J. Sterling Morton* (Lincoln, 1942), 385–86.
5. Bryan's Senatorial campaign: *OWH,* October 6, 7, 9, 19, 20, 25, 26, and November 6, 1894.

6. Tom Reed's prophecy: William A. Robinson, *Thomas B. Reed, Parliamentarian* (New York, 1930), 321. Populist successes: John D. Hicks, *The Populist Revolt* (Minneapolis, 1931), 238 ff. James C. Dahlman to Bryan, November 15, 1894, BP, Box 3.

Chapter 12. Laying a Foundation

1. Statement by Dan Bride: November 15, 1920, BP, Box 33.
2. J. E. Brockway to Bryan, April 15, 1895; Bryan to Jefferson Myers, May 6, 1895, BP, Box 3.
3. Norbert R. Mahnken, "William Jennings Bryan in Oklahoma," *Nebraska History* (December, 1950), 250–54.
4. William Jennings Bryan, *The Memoirs of William Jennings Bryan* (Philadelphia, 1925), 101.
5. *U. S. E. C. Knight*, 156 U.S. 1 (1895). *Pollock v. Farmers' Loan and Trust Company*, 158, U.S. 60(1895). *In re Debs*, 158 U.S. 564 (1895). William H. "Coin" Harvey: William Jennings Bryan, *The First Battle* (Chicago, 1897), 153; Jeannette P. Nichols, "Bryan's Benefactor: Coin Harvey and His World," *The Ohio Historical Quarterly* October 1958, 299–325.
6. *OWH*, May 25, 1895.
7. William H. Hinrichsen to Bryan, April 15, 1895, BP, Box 3. Altgeld and Cleveland: Harvey Wish, "John Peter Altgeld and the Background of the Election of 1896," *Mississippi Valley Historical Review* (March, 1938), 504–5; Horace S. Merrill, *Bourbon Leader: Grover Cleveland and the Democratic Party* (Boston, 1957), 168. Altgeld at Chickamauga: Wish, 504. The Springfield convention: Chicago *Tribune*, June 2–7, 1895; *OWH*, June 6, 1895.
8. *The First Battle*, 155.
9. Bryan and Sibley: *OWH*, June 14, 1895. Democratic silver conference in Washington: *ibid.*, June 26, 1895.
10. *Ibid.*, August 16, 1895.
11. C. J. Smyth to Bryan, May 2, 1895, BP, Box 3; *OWH*, August 23, 1895.
12. James C. Olson, *J. Sterling Morton* (Lincoln, 1942), 387–88.
13. J. Sterling Morton to D. P. Rolfe, November 16, 1895, in Olson, 388.
14. Stanley L. Jones, *The Presidential Election of 1896* (Madison, Wisconsin, 1964), 72.
15. Bryan and Populist leaders: Jones, 75; Bryan to Ignatius Donnelly, January 1, 1896, Donnelly Papers: Western Populism and silver: John D. Hicks, *The Populist Revolt* (Minneapolis, 1931), 327–28.
16. Hicks, 353.
17. *OWH*, May 29, 1895.
18. Hicks, 313, 349; Jones, 31.
19. *OWH*, May 16, 1895; *The First Battle*, 155; H. F. Bartine to Bryan, December 18, 1895, BP, Box 3.
20. *OWH*, December 21–24, 1895; Robert C. Cotner, *James Stephen Hogg* (Austin, 1959), 464. Sidney Brooks is cited in Paolo E. Coletta, *William Jennings Bryan*, Vol. I, *Political Evangelist* (Lincoln, 1964), 110.
21. Charles McDaniel Rosser, *The Crusading Commoner* (Dallas, 1939), 19–20.
22. Marion Butler to Bryan, January 8, 1896; Benjamin Tillman to Bryan, December 7, 1895; James Weaver to Bryan, December 31, 1895, BP, Box 3. Illustrative of "Principles first" is Bryan's approach to James Hogg in Cotner, 465. Hogg's reply: Hogg to Bryan, May 2, 1896, BP, Box 3.
23. Bryan and Hogg: Cotner, *ibid.* C. S. Thomas in *Harper's Weekly*, October 11, 1913. Bryan's letter to Thomas of April 16, 1896, is in BP, Box 3.
24. *NSJ*, April 19, 1896.
25. *Ibid.*, April 23, 1896. The sound money Democratic convention: *ibid.*, April 30, 1896.
26. Illinois convention: *NYT*, June 24, 1896. Theodore Roosevelt: Elmer Ellis, *Henry Moore Teller* (Caldwell, Idaho, 1941), 288.

27. Wish, 513–15; Harry Barnard, *Eagle Forgotten, The Life of John Peter Altgeld* (Indianapolis, 1938), 368.

28. Bland's political standing: J. Rogers Hollingsworth, *The Whirligig of Politics* (Chicago, 1963), 47–48. Shelby Cullom is quoted in *NYT,* June 30, 1896.

29. Bland's limitations: Hollingsworth, 47. Populists oppose Bland: *NYT,* July 7, 1896. Bland's boom is launched: *OWH,* July 4, 1895. Boies described: Merrill, 150; Boies and Altgeld: Hollingsworth, 48.

30. Quotations are from *NYT,* June 4, 1896. The Bimetallic Democratic National Committee: *OWH,* August 15 and 16, 1895. Bryan to T. O. Towles, April 9, 1896, BP, Box 3.

31. Bryan to James K. Jones, June 23, 1896, BP, Box 3.

32. Henry Cabot Lodge to Moreton Frewen, February 17, 1896, Moreton Frewen Papers, Box 16. Cleveland's rallying cry: *NYT,* June 17, 1896.

33. Charles S. Hamlin is quoted by Merrill, 200.

34. William Whitney and his allies: Merrill, 73. Whitney on the convention's prospects: *NYT,* June 18, 1896. Perry Belmont and others come to Chicago: *ibid.,* June 21 and June 23, 1896. Whitney's strategy: Merrill, 205; *NYT,* July 2, 1896. Whitney is quoted in *NYT,* June 28, 1896.

35. Charles A. Towne to Moreton Frewen, March 16, 1896, Moreton Frewen Papers, Box 17. McKinley's letter to the Farmers' Alliance: *NYT,* June 5, 1896. McKinley's currency plank: Margaret Leech, *In the Days of McKinley* (New York, 1959), 79. Teller bolts: *NYT,* June 18, 1896.

36. Reactions to Teller's bolting: Leech, 80; *NYT,* June 19, 1896. A. J. Warner to Moreton Frewen, June 28, 1896, Moreton Frewen Papers, Box 17.

37. See Hadley Cantril, *The Psychology of Social Movements* (New York, 1941), 59–63, 185, and James C. Davies, *Human Nature in Politics* (New York, 1963), 40–41.

38. *Memoirs,* 31.

39. Chicago *Times-Herald* and Raleigh *News and Observer,* July 4, 1896. Bryan and J. W. Tomlinson: *Memoirs,* 102–3.

40. Charles G. Dawes, *A Journal of the McKinley Years* (Chicago, 1950), 88–89; Bascom Timmons, *Portrait of an American: Charles G. Dawes* (New York, 1953), 48.

Chapter 13. Cross of Gold

1. "The millionaire contingent": Mark D. Hirsch, *William C. Whitney, Modern Maverick* (New York, 1948), 497. Boies at the convention: *NYT,* July 5, 1896. Altgeld: Harvey Wish, "John Peter Altgeld and the Election of 1896," *Journal of Illinois Historical Society* (October, 1937), 357–58.

2. The Bland men at work: *NYT,* July 3, 1896: Stanley L. Jones, *The Presidential Election of 1896* (Madison, Wisconsin, 1964), 387. James K. Jones is quoted in *NYT,* June 30, 1896. Ben Tillman's conduct: *ibid.,* July 4, 1896. John Atwood to Bryan, June 8, 1896, BP, Box 4. Bryan departs for Chicago: Chicago *Record,* July 6, 1896.

3. The silver caucus: *NYT,* July 4, 1896. The convention hall: *ibid.*

4. James K. Jones is quoted on D. B. Hill in *NYT,* July 3, 1896. The convention begins: *ibid.,* July 8, 1896.

5. The strategy to contest delegations: D. C. Lewis to Bryan, May 8, 1896, and Thomas Maloney to Bryan, May 22, 1896, BP, Box 4. Nebraska's silver delegation is seated: Paolo E. Coletta, "Bryan, Cleveland and the Disrupted Democracy, 1890–1896," *Nebraska History* (March, 1960), 33; Charles M. Rosser, *The Crusading Commoner* (Dallas, 1937), 33; *OWH,* July 7, 1896.

6. Bryan and the permanent chairmanship: *NYT,* July 9, 1896. Bryan on the convention floor: *ibid.* Bryan's friends work for him: Willis J. Abbot, *Watching the World Go By* (Boston, 1933), 159. Bryan headquarters: *NSJ,* July 6, 1896. Bryan predicts his nomination: Abbot, 157. Abbot's interview with Altgeld: *ibid.,* 158.

7. Bryan and the Resolutions Committee chairmanship: *Memoirs,* 107. The money plank: Bryan statement concerning Senator James K. Jones, undated, BP, Box 41. The text of the plank is in Paolo E. Coletta, *William Jennings Bryan,* Vol. I, *Political Evangelist* (Lincoln, 1964), 129, and *NYT,* July 9, 1896, which also has texts of other planks. Tom Johnson concerning the platform: Abbot, 161. The platform and Grover Cleveland: Henry James, *Richard Olney and His Public Service* (Boston and New York, 1923), 175; Robert A. McElroy, *Grover Cleveland: The Man and Statesman* (New York, 1923), II, 237. Bryan on the Platform Committee's conflict: William Jennings Bryan, *The First Battle* (Chicago, 1897), 197. Texts of the majority and minority reports on the platform are in William Jennings Bryan, *The Second Battle* (Chicago, 1900) 312–17.

8. Selection of speakers to debate the platform: *Memoirs,* 109; Bryan statement concerning Senator James K. Jones, undated, BP, Box 41; Bryan, *The First Battle,* 615; Rosser, 35–37; Mark Sullivan, *Our Times: The United States 1900–1925* (New York, 1926), I, 123. Smyth's and Hitchcock's optimism: *NSJ,* July 6, 1896.

9. Delegations which first supported Bryan for President: "William Jennings Bryan: Biographical Notes, His Speeches, Letters and Other Writings," enlarged and edited by Grace Dexter Bryan, typescript, 62–63, BP, Box 64. Benton McMillin is quoted in Harold C. Syrett, ed., *The Gentleman and the Tiger: The Autobiography of George B. McClellan, Jr.* (Philadelphia and New York, 1956), 111–12. Legislators seek Bryan's support of Teller: *Memoirs,* 105–6. Bryan is optimistic about his speech and nomination: Rosser, 37–38.

10. The setting of Bryan's speech: Josephus Daniels, *Editor in Politics* (Chapel Hill, 1941), 163; *NYT,* July 9 and 10, 1896. A. B. Macdonald and Bryan: Rosser, 40. Tillman's speech: Francis Butler Simkins, *Pitchfork Ben Tillman, South Carolinian* (Baton Rouge, 1944), 334; Atlanta *Constitution* and *NYT,* July 10, 1896. Clark Howell and Bryan: Atlanta *Constitution,* July 11, 1896. Hill's speech: *Second Battle,* 322–25; Simkins, 337; *Memoirs* 112. Villas and Russell: *Memoirs,* 112–13; *NYT,* New York *Tribune, OWH,* July 10, 1896.

11. Bryan's speech: Chicago *Record, NYT, OWH,* New York *Tribune,* July 10, 1896; Daniels, 163–64; *Memoirs,* 114–15.

12. The convention's reaction to Bryan's speech: Daniels, 164; Chicago *Record, NYT, OWH,* New York *Tribune, ibid.* Altgeld's comment to Darrow is from Ray Ginger, *The Bending Cross: A Biography of Eugene Victor Debs* (New Brunswick, 1949), 188. Daniels' evaluation is in Daniels, 165. Instances of Bryan's previous use of the "Cross of Gold" theme are collected in *The Nation,* July 2, 1896, 40.

13. Delegates query Bryan: *Memoirs,* 115. Bryan delays his nomination: Abbot, 166–67. Bland forces look to Senator Vest: Chicago *Record,* July 10, 1896. Erstwhile detractors now support Bryan: Abbot, 166. McKinley's reaction: Chicago *Record* and Chicago *Times-Herald,* July 10, 1896.

14. Vest's speech: *NYT,* New York *World,* July 10, 1896. Judge Henry T. Lewis, *ibid.* John R. McLean's proposed deal: Rosser, 54. The balloting: *NYT, OWH,* Chicago *Record,* July 11, 1896. Altgeld and the Illinois delegation: Barnard, 371–73; Bryan, *Second Battle,* 329. Pre-fifth-ballot demonstration for Bryan: Syrett, 113–14. Delegations switch to Bryan: Abbot, 168; Barnard, 372; Bryan, *Second Battle,* 329–31.

15. Mary: *NYT,* July 11, 1896. Bryan in the barbershop: *Memoirs,* 116. Bryan rejects reelection: *NYT, ibid.* Bryan's interview with Abbot: Abbot, 168. Gifts for Bryan: Arthur W. Dunn, *From Harrison to Harding* (New York and London, 1922), 187. Bryan at his hotel rooms: Rosser, 56. Letters and telegrams of July 10–11, 1896, BP, Box 4. *The Nation* on Bryan: *The Nation,* July 16, 1896, 4. Henry Cabot Lodge to Moreton Frewen, July 14, 1896, Moreton Frewen Papers, Box 17.

16. Bryan caucuses on the Vice Presidential nomination: Daniels, 166–68. Sewall is nominated: *NYT, OWH,* New York *Tribune,* July 11, 1896. Hinckley is quoted in *NYT, ibid.*

Chapter 14. The Popocrat Candidate

1. The Bryans after the convention: William Jennings Bryan, *The First Battle* (Chicago, 1897), 219.
2. Speech at Salem: *The First Battle*, 233–34. Meeting with Bland: *ibid.*, 235.
3. Journey to Lincoln: *NYT, OWH*, July 17, 1896.
4. H. D. Lloyd is quoted in Caro Lloyd, *Henry Demarest Lloyd* (New York, 1912), I, 259. Taubeneck's and Weaver's maneuvers: Chester McArthur Destler, *Henry Demarest Lloyd and the Empire of Reform* (Philadelphia, 1963), 285; G. L. McKeon to Marion Butler, September 8, 1896, Marion Butler Papers, Box 3.
5. Butler's hopes: Marion Butler to R. K. Bryan, Jr., April 14, 1896, Marion Butler Papers, Box 3.
6. Convention scene: Martin Ridge, *Ignatius Donnelly* (Chicago, 1962), 352–53; Lloyd, 261. Populist delegates: *NYT,* New York *World,* July 23, 1896; Josephus Daniels, *Editor in Politics* (Chapel Hill, 1941), 173. Bryan's managers: Daniels, 171. J. H. Turner's prediction: *NYT,* July 15, 1896. Darrow supports Bryan and Sewall: Stanley L. Jones, *The Presidential Election of 1896* (Madison, 1964), 253. "Sockless" Jerry Simpson: *Rocky Mountain News,* July 11, 1896.
7. Debs declines to run: Eugene Debs to Bryan, July 27, 1896, BP Box 4. Convention scene: C. Vann Woodward, *Tom Watson, Agrarian Rebel* (New York, 1938) 296–97; Henry D. Lloyd, "The Populists at St. Louis," *American Review of Reviews* (September, 1896), 298–303; Robert W. Smith, "Comedy at St. Louis: A Footnote to Nineteenth Century Political Oratory," *Southern Speech Journal* (Winter, 1957), 122–23.
8. W. V. Allen becomes permanent chairman: Woodward, 297. Bryan men press Sewall for Vice President: *ibid.*
9. Tom Watson: *ibid,* 298. Theodore Roosevelt on Watson: *ibid.* 306.
10. Watson accepts the Vice Presidential nomination: *ibid.,* 298. Allen-Bryan communications: St. Louis *Republic,* July 25, 1896; John D. Hicks, *The Populist Revolt* (Minneapolis, 1931), 366.
11. The Populist financial plank is in *The First Battle,* 275–76. H. D. Lloyd on silver: Lloyd, 264. Allen's steamroller tactics: *ibid.,* 261.
12. Bryan's press interview on the Populist convention: *NYT,* July 26, 1896. James K. Jones: *ibid.,* July 28, 1896.
13. Press comment on Bryan as the Populist nominee: *NYT,* New York *Sun,* New York *World,* July 26, 1896. Watson opposes Sewall: T. E. Watson to Marion Butler, July 28, 1896, Marion Butler Papers, Box 3.
14. National Silver Party prepares for convention: Jones, 86–88. Warner's optimism for Bryan: A. J. Warner to Moreton Frewen, July 28, 1896, Moreton Frewen Papers, Box 17.
15. Bryan's dependence on the East for victory: E. E. Perry to Moreton Frewen, August 3, 1896, Moreton Frewen Papers, Box 17. Cleveland's silence: *NYT,* July 10, 1896. Morton urges Bryan's defeat: J. Sterling Morton to Albert Watkins, Roll 38, and James C. Olson, Jr., *J. Sterling Morton* (Lincoln, 1942), 394.
16. Louisville *Courier-Journal,* July 10, is quoted in *NYT,* July 11, 1896. Sound Money Democratic national convention: *NYT,* September 4, 1896; *The First Battle,* 386. Bryan on the National Democratic Party: *The First Battle,* 361.

Chapter 15. The First Battle

1. James S. Hogg to Bryan, July 28, 1896. James K. Jones to Bryan July 21, 1896; William J. Stone to Bryan, July 14, 1896, BP, Box 4.
2. McKinley's nomination: Margaret Leech, *In the Days of McKinley* (New York, 1959), 85–89. Farewell remarks at Lincoln: William Jennings Bryan, *The First Battle*

(Chicago, 1897), 300. Journey to the Atlantic: *ibid.*, 301; *NYT*, July 14, 1896; *OWH* and *NYT*, August 6–9, 1896. William V. Byars, *An American Commoner: The Life and Times of Richard Parks Bland* (Columbia, Missouri, 1900), 298. Bryan's failing voice and hand: *NYT*, August 12, 1896.

3. Madison Square Garden speech: *The First Battle*, 299, 307–37; *NYT*, August 13, 1896.

4. Press comments on Bryan's speech are collected in Bryan Scrapbook No. 2, Nebraska State Historical Society; *The First Battle*, 315. Foraker's comment is in Joseph B. Foraker, *Notes of a Busy Life* (Cincinnati, 1917), I, 494.

5. *NYT*, August 14, 1896.

6. Chicago as national campaign headquarters: *NYT*, August 14, 1896. Retreat to Upper Red Hook: *NYT*, August 16, 1896.

7. W. A. Swanberg, *Citizen Hearst* (Bantam ed., New York, 1963), 103.

8. In Upper Red Hook: *NYT*, August 18, 1896. Bourke Cockran's speech: *ibid.*, August 19, 1896.

9. Answering Cockran: *The First Battle*, 342–48. Visit to James Hinckley: *ibid.*, 349–50; *NYT*, August 21, 1896. Albany and D. B. Hill: *ibid.*, August 26, 1896.

10. Bryan's campaigning from New York to Chicago: *NYT* and *OWH*, August 27–September 7, 1896. Labor Day speech: *NYT* and *OWH*, September 8, 1896. Labor and Bryan's views: John R. Commons and Associates, *History of Labour in the United States* (New York, 1918), 509–14; Selig Perlman, *A History of Trade Unionism in the United States* (New York, 1950), 139–41; Philip Taft, *The A.F.L. in the Time of Gompers* (New York, 1957), 130.

11. Choosing a campaign strategy: *The Nation*, July 16, 1896, 43; A. H. Lewis to Bryan, July 29, 1896, and Joseph Sibley to Bryan, July 30, 1896, BP, Box 4; Willis J. Abbot, "James K. Jones," *American Review of Reviews* (October, 1896), 427.

12. Party realignment in the West: Arthur F. Mullen, *Western Democrat* (New York, 1940), 100. Silver as an issue: J. Rogers Hollingsworth, *The Whirligig of Politics* (Chicago, 1963), 90–94. Harvey Wish, "John Peter Altgeld and The Background of the Campaign of 1896," *Mississippi Valley Historical Review* (March, 1938), 505. Counsels of caution: William J. Stone to Bryan, July 14, 1896, BP, Box 4.

13. Roosevelt on Bryan and his associates is in Willis J. Abbot, *Watching the World Go By* (Boston, 1933), 178.

14. Indiana Bicycle Works: *NYT*, August 16, 1896. Railway Men's Sound Money Club: *The First Battle*, 362–63. Andrew Carnegie's views are in Andrew Carnegie, "The Ship of State Adrift," *North American Review* (October, 1896), 496. McKinley is quoted in Bascom Timmons, *Portrait of An American: Charles G. Dawes* (New York, 1953), 56.

15. Bryan on "mills" and "mints": *The First Battle*, 442. St. Louis: *ibid.*, 443. Louisville: *NYT*, September 16, 1896. Knoxville: *ibid.*, September 17, 1896.

16. Asheville and Raleigh: *The First Battle*, 451. New York State Democratic convention: *ibid.*, 455. The Rappahannock: *ibid.*, 457–58.

17. Bryan's collapse: Josephus Daniels, *Editor in Politics* (Chapel Hill, 1941), 193–94. New York State Democratic convention: *NYT*, September 17 and 18, 1896.

18. Blackburn in Brooklyn: *NYT*, September 24, 1896. New Haven: New York *Sun*, September 27, 1896; *OWH*, September 25–29, 1896, *The First Battle* 484–88. New England's hostility: Daniels, 196.

19. Daniels, 197.

20. Bryan and reporters: *The First Battle*, 441. Mary: *ibid.* Sam Weller: Abbot, 177. Marion Butler's paper on J. K. Jones: Jones, 298; reprinted in Chicago *Tribune*, August 7, 1896.

21. Hearst helps the campaign: Abbot, 181. "Coin" Harvey: Jeannette P. Nichols, "Bryan's Benefactor: Coin Harvey and His World," *Ohio Historical Quarterly* (October, 1958), 299. Homer Davenport: Abbot, 182. Silver campaign songs: "Silver Campaign Songs for 1896," BP, Box 52.

22. St. John's views are expressed in William P. St. John, "Free Silver and National Prosperity," *Arena* (September, 1896), 581. Further argument for free silver is made in Frank Parsons, "Free Silver vs. Free Gold," *ibid.*, 782 and in Parsons, "The Issue of 1896," *Arena* (November, 1896), 881. Argument against silver: Louis Windmuller and Walter Clark, "If Silver Wins," *North American Review* (October 1896), 459; J. Laurence Laughlin, "Would Free Coinage Double the Price of Silver—the Negative View," *American Review of Reviews* (September, 1896), 308. F. W. Taussig's views are presented in his *Silver Situation in the United States* (New York, 1893), 123.

23. Butler on Bryan's campaigning: Marion Butler to B. N. Richardson, September 18, 1896, Letterbook, Marion Butler Papers. Butler to J. K. Jones, September 21, 1896, *ibid.* Life aboard the Idler: "E.W.M." Jr. to "Joe," November 1, 1896, Ewing Young Mitchell Papers.

24. Bryan's warning to Palmer Democrats: *The First Battle*, 537. Democratic sabotage of Bryan: Arthur W. Dunn, *From Harrison to Harding* (New York and London, 1922), 198. Mary Lease is quoted in *NYT*, September 5, 1896.

25. Censures of Bryan are collected in *The First Battle*, 492–93.

26. Clergy hostile to Bryan: *ibid.*, 473–74; *NYT*, October 5, 1896.

27. Social clubs oppose Bryan: Abbot, 184. "Buffalo Bill" image: "William Jennings Bryan Biographical Notes, His Speeches, Letters and Other Writings," enlarged and edited by his daughter, Grace Dexter Bryan, typescript, 106, BP, Box 64.

28. Sewall and Maine: Marion Butler to L. C. Bateman, August 29, 1896, Marion Butler Papers. Howell and Watson: Woodward, 325.

29. Electoral vote division: William J. Stone to Bryan, July 31, 1896, BP, Box 4. Butler's electoral votes tactics: Marion Butler to J. S. Bradley, August 26, 1896, Letterbook, Marion Butler Papers. "Mark Hanna's money": John W. Breidenthal to Butler, September 20, 1896, *ibid.*

30. Horace G. Clark to Marion Butler, September 6, 1896, Marion Butler Papers, Box 3.

31. Daniels on Watson: Daniels, 176. Watson's Dallas speech: Marion Butler to Watson, September 8, 1896, BP, Box 3. Watson's Western speech: Woodward, 320. Watson on Populism's contribution to reform: Watson to Marion Butler, October 28, 1896, Marion Butler Papers, Box 3. Butler concerning the men around Bryan: Butler to J. P. Buchanan, September 14, 1896, Letterbook, Marion Butler Papers.

32. Ignatius Donnelly is quoted in Hicks, 356. Jerry Simpson is quoted in Richard Hofstadter, *The Age of Reform* (New York, 1956), 64. Bryan disavows anti-Semitism: *The First Battle*, 581.

33. Bryan on farmer-labor interests: *The First Battle*, 360. The income tax issue: Wish, "John Peter Altgeld and the Background of the Campaign of 1896," 505. The eight-hour day for labor: Horace S. Merrill, *William Freeman Vilas, Doctrinaire Democrat* (Madison, Wisconsin, 1954), 227.

34. Eugene V. Debs to Bryan, July 27, 1896, BP, Box 4.

35. Gompers' position: Norman Pollack, *The Populist Response to Industrial America* (Cambridge, 1962), 64. Gompers declines to join Bryan's Cabinet: Irving Bernstein, ed., "Samuel Gompers and Free Silver," *Mississippi Valley Historical Review* (December, 1942), 398; Omaha *Bee*, September 10, 1896; Samuel Gompers, *Seventy Years of Life and Labor: An Autobiography* (New York, 1925), II, 76, 87–88. Gompers on free coinage: Bernstein, 398.

36. Hanna becomes concerned: *OWH*, October 7 and 9, 1896; Fred E. Haynes, *Third Party Movements Since the Civil War with Special Reference to Iowa* (Iowa City, 1916), 369–70. Bryan crosses the Alleghenies: clipping, Bryan Scrapbook No. 2, Nebraska State Historical Society. Bryan in West Virginia: *NYT* October 1 and 2, 1896; *The First Battle*, 512.

37. *NYT*, October 4, 1896.

38. Bryan in Tennessee: *The First Battle*, 525. Kentucky, Ohio, and Indiana: *NYT* and *OWH*, October 6–9, 1896. Bryan concerning the National Democratic Party: *NYT*, October 7, 1896. Bryan threats in Indiana: *ibid.*

39. "Which McKinley are you for?": *NYT,* October 9, 1896. The Dakotas and Minnesota: *NYT* and *OWH,* October 8–13, 1896; *The First Battle,* 536–54.
40. *NYT,* October 18, 1896.
41. Michigan: *NYT,* October 17, 1896. Illinois: *ibid.,* October 22, 1896.
42. Threats of wealthy New York men: *OWH,* October 20, 1896. John Hay to Henry Adams, October 20, 1896, is in James Ford Rhodes, *The McKinley and Roosevelt Administrations, 1897–1909* (New York, 1893–1920), 143.
43. Gold, wheat, and straw: *The First Battle,* 602. Bryan on the gold syndicate: *NYT,* November 2, 1896.
44. Bryan on election day: *OWH* and *NYT,* November 3, 1896. Bryan to Dan Bride, undated, BP, Box 41. Election night: *ibid.,* William Jennings Bryan, *The Second Battle* (Chicago, 1900), 334.
45. Edgar Eugene Robinson, *The Presidential Vote 1896–1932* (Stanford, 1934), 4. William Diamond, "Urban and Rural Voting in 1896," *American Historical Review* (1941), 281–305; Woodward, 329–30.
46. George Fred Williams to Moreton Frewen, December 5, 1896, Moreton Frewen Papers, Box 17. A. J. Warner to Frewen, November 24, 1896, *ibid.* Josephus Daniels is quoted in Daniels, 198–99, and Donnelly in Ridge, 365.
47. The wheat factor: Mirabeau L. Towns to Bryan, November 6, 1896, BP, Box 9; Abbot, 186. The Altgeld factor: Wish, 357–58.
48. J. B. Hotaling to Bryan, November 23, 1896, BP, Box 16.
49. Henry T. Rainey to Bryan, November 6, 1896, BP, Box 9. Henry George is quoted in Barnard, 393.
50. Mrs. Henry Cabot Lodge's statement is from Daniels, 201, and Stephen Gwynn, *The Letters and Friendships of Sir Cecil Spring-Rice* (Boston, 1929), II, 197–98.

Chapter 16. The Legacy

1. Verse: L. J. Lamson to Bryan, November 4, 1896, BP, Box 5. Texas and Kansas: C. W. Bradenberg to Bryan, November 3, 1896, and Bryan's Silver Club, Sherman, Texas, to Bryan, November 3, 1896, BP, Box 5. Presidential election: William D. Trautham to Bryan, November 4, 1896, BP, Box 6. Claude Matthews to Mrs. Bryan, December 19, 1896, BP, Box 17. Joseph W. Bailey's statement is in *OWH,* June 7, 1897.
2. Joseph Sibley to Bryan, November 23, BP, Box 16. M. F. Dunlap to Bryan, November 11, 1896, BP, Box 16.
3. The quotation from the Topeka *Daily Capital* is in *NYT,* April 7, 1897.
4. Bryan's informant: J. J. Bailey to Bryan, July 2, 1897, BP, Box 20.
5. First Denver Speech: *OWH,* November 16, 1896. Second Denver speech: *NYT, OWH,* November 26, 1896.
6. Lincoln speech: *OWH,* January 7, 1897. Jeff Davis' picture: *NYT,* March 7, 1897.
7. Comstock: V. E. McBee to Bryan, December 2, 1896, BP, Box 17. W. P. St. John to Bryan, December 8, 1896, BP, Box 17. Applications and invitations: V. E. McBee to Bryan, November 23, 1896, BP, Box 17. *NYT,* December 29, 1896.
8. Charges for Bryan's lectures: Charles McDaniel Rosser, *The Crusading Commoner* (Dallas, 1937), 76. Bryan's statement is in *NYT,* February 27, 1897. Beatrice, Nebraska: W. P. Norcross to Bryan, June 28, 1897, BP, Box 19.
9. Willis Abbot to Bryan, September 2, 1897, BP, Box 20; Bradford Merrill to Bryan, September 2, 1897, *ibid.*
10. Mark Sullivan, *Our Times, the United States, 1900–1925* (New York, 1926), 304–5. Conkey's labor troubles: T. G. With to Bryan, November 22, 1896, BP, Box 16; W. B. Conkey to Bryan, November 28, 1896, *ibid.* Distributing the proceeds: James K. Jones to Bryan, March 26, 1897, BP, Box 18.
11. Bryan in the U.S. Supreme Court: *OWH,* April 6, 1897; *NYT,* April 7, 1897. The case eventually became known as *Smyth v. Ames,* 169 U.S. 466 (1898).

12. Boyd Carter, "William Jennings Bryan in Mexico," *Nebraska History* (March, 1960), 54; *NYT,* December 17, 1897.
13. Urey Woodson to Bryan, December 19, 1896, BP, Box 17. Silver's political apparatus: *NYT,* December 10, 1896. Manhattan, Kansas: A. C. Haulerbeck to Bryan, December 19, 1896, BP, Box 17. Central head of the movement: Thomas B. Skidmore to Bryan, November 10, 1896, BP, Box 13. John P. Altgeld to Bryan, March 25, 1897, BP, Box 18.
14. *OWH,* September 1 and 2, 1897; *NYT,* September 2 and 27, 1897.
15. W. H. Harvey to Bryan, December 1, 1896, BP, Box 17. J. Q. Thompson to Bryan, December 30, 1896, *ibid.* German-Americans: Hugo S. Grosser to Bryan, May 28, 1897, BP, Box 19. A. G. Thurman to Bryan, November 23, 1896, BP, Box 16. Bryan attacks Hanna: *NYT,* October 29, 1897.
16. Avoiding political contests: John H. Atwood to Bryan, December 8, 1896, BP, Box 16. Fred Dubois to Bryan, December 18, 1896, BP, Box 17; James K. Jones to Bryan, January 6, 1897, BP, Box 18; *NYT,* January 29 1897.
17. Arthur Sewall to Bryan, December 3, 1896, BP, Box 17. James K. Jones to Bryan, January 6, 1897, BP, Box 18. Elwood S. Corser to Bryan, June 21, 1897, BP, Box 19. Altgeld to Bryan, September 20, 1897, BP, Box 20. Louis R. Ehrich to Bryan, November 6, 1896, PB, Box 7.
18. Jackson Day banquet: *NYT,* January 8, 1897. McKinley's moves: *NYT,* March 3, 1897. Altgeld: J. P. Altgeld to Moreton Frewen, February 18, 1897, Moreton Frewen Papers, Box 16. Bryan on the Wolcott commission: *NYT,* October 27, 1897.
19. Davis H. Waite to Bryan, November 10, 1896, BP, Box 13.
20. *NYT,* September 16, 1897.
21. Bryan concerning Croker: Bryan to Willis J. Abbot, March 16, 1897, BP, Box 18; Willis J. Abbot, *Watching the World Go By* (Boston, 1933), 204–5. Henry George: *NYT,* September 27 and October 19, 1897.
22. Gorman: *NYT,* July 29, 1897. Bryan on the gold Democrats: *ibid.,* November 17, 1896, February 18, 1897. Grover Cleveland: *NYT* and New York *World,* January 9, 1897. William Bynum: *NYT,* November 21, 1897.
23. Purging the party: *NYT,* February 28, 1897; *ibid.* and *OWH,* December 14, 1896. William F. Harrity: *NYT,* August 31, 1897, and June 8, 1898.
24. Marion Butler to Bryan, December 16, 1896, Letterbook, Marion Butler Papers. George F. Washburn to Bryan, January 8, 1897, BP, Box 6.
25. Tom Watson is quoted in Davis H. Waite to Bryan, November 10, 1896, BP, Box 13. L. C. Bateman: A. V. Hartle to Bryan, July 2, 1897, BP, Box 20; *NYT,* June 24, 1897. Tom Watson: *NYT* and New York *World,* July 2, 1897.
26. Charles A. Towne to Bryan, April 2, 1897, BP, Box 19.
27. Editorial, *NYT,* November 4, 1897. Bryan: *ibid.*

Chapter 17. Colonel Bryan

1. Roosevelt is quoted in Harold U. Faulkner, *Politics, Reform and Expansion, 1890–1900* (New York, 1959), 230. Hanna concerning Bryan is quoted in Thomas Beer, *Mauve Decade* (New York, 1937), 552.
2. Bryan is quoted in Paolo E. Coletta, *William Jennings Bryan,* Vol. I, *Political Evangelist* (Lincoln, 1964), 221. Western attitudes toward war: Faulkner, 224. Henry Teller: *NYT,* February 17, 1898. William Sulzer: *ibid.,* March 9, 1898. Richard Pettigrew: Arthur W. Dunn, *From Harrison to Harding* (New York, 1922), I, 231–32. "War is a terrible thing": William Jennings Bryan, *The Second Battle* (Chicago, 1900), 83. Elihu Root is quoted in Ernest R. May, *Imperial Democracy* (New York, 1961), 152. Bryan in Boston: *NYT,* April 17, 1898.
3. James K. Jones to Bryan, May 11, 1898, BP, Box 20. Bryan to McKinley, April 25, 1898, *ibid.* Joseph Sibley to Bryan, May 16, 1898, *ibid.*

4. Joseph Wheeler to James K. Jones, May 14 and 16, 1898, BP, Box 21. Governor Holcomb's statement: *OWH*, May 18, 1898.
5. Lon V. Stephens to Bryan, May 31, 1898, BP, Box 21. "Old veteran": Oscar T. Taylor to Bryan, June 6, 1898, *ibid.* Bryan's regiment: J. C. Coovert, *Historical Sketch and Scenes of Camp Life of the Third Regiment Nebraska Volunteer Infantry* (Vicksburg, Miss., 1898), not paged. J. R. Johnson, "William Jennings Bryan, The Soldier," *Nebraska History* (June, 1950), 98.
6. Bryan's speech on the war and imperialism: *OWH*, June 15, 1898. Need for a new issue: Hadley Cantril, *The Psychology of Social Movements* (New York, 1941), 47. Roosevelt to Lodge, May 24, 1898, is in Henry Cabot Lodge, *Selections from the Correspondence of Theodore Roosevelt and Henry Cabot Lodge* (New York, 1925), I, 313.
7. Victor Vifquain: Johnson, 96–97; *OWH*, September 29, 1899; *NSJ*, September 28, 1899. William Schwind: "Souvenier Bryan's Regiment," BP, Folder 9, Box 52.
8. Induction ceremonies: *Memoirs*, 273; *OWH*, July 15, 1898, Bryan to William V. Allen, June 6, 1898, BP, Box 20. Third Regiment is destined for Florida: *NYT*, June 12 and July 14, 1898. The send-off: *OWH*, July 17, 1898.
9. Journey to Florida: Johnson, 99–100; *OWH*, July 19, 22, and 23, 1898. "Out of politics": *ibid.*, July 23, 1898.
10. Bryan to William, Jr., undated, OP; Albert Watkins, Jr., "Bryan as a Soldier," *OWH*, January 21, 1905. The Silver Third: *ibid.* July 31, 1898. Bryan to Mary, August 7, 1898, BP, Box 22. Bryan and his men: Johnson, 101–2, 100.
11. Bryan to Mary, July 31, 1898, BP, Box 22. O. N. Humphrey to Bryan, August 1, 1898, *ibid.* Bryan to Humphrey, undated, *ibid.*
12. Bryan's telegram is in *OWH*, August 9, 1898.
13. Johnson, 100–1. Bryan to Mary, undated, BP, Box 22. "William Jennings Bryan: Biographical Notes, His Speeches, Letters and Other Writings," enlarged and edited by his daughter, Grace Dexter Bryan, 142, BP, Box 64.
14. Bryan to Mary, August 24, 1898, BP, Box 22.
15. Telegrams: Alger to Allen, September 12, 1898; Alger to McKinley, September 12, 1898, McKinley Papers. Bryan's friends' comments are in P. H. Barry to Bryan, September 13, 1898, BP, Box 22.
16. Camp illnesses: Bryan to Mary, September 12, 1898. Stark's report: W. L. Stark to Bryan, September 17, 1898, BP, Box 22. The Bryan-McKinley meeting is reported by Lyman Gage, who was present at the President's request, in "Lyman Gage Memorandum, September 26, 1898," McKinley Papers.
17. Bryan's letter of October 26 to Mary is in BP, Box 22.
18. Bryan's homecoming: *OWH* and *NSJ*, November 8, 1898. Mark Hanna's statement is from Herbert Croly, *Marcus Alonzo Hanna* (New York, 1912), 291. Imperialist and anti-imperialist comment is in May, 253.
19. Bryan's comments on the election: *NYT*, November 16, 1898. Silver ratio: Charles A. Towne to Moreton Frewen, August 3, 1898, Moreton Frewen Papers, Box 17.
20. Jones, *ibid.*
21. Bryan to the Adjutant General, December 10, 1898, BP, Box 22.
22. Bryan's statement on colonialism: *The Second Battle*, 87–89.
23. Bryan's statement on resigning is in Johnson, 144.
24. Bryan in Washington: *OWH*, December 16 and 17, 1898. Distress over Bryan-Carnegie meeting: Bryan to William M. Stewart, December 19, 1898; Bryan to Andrew Carnegie, December 24, 1898, BP, Box 22.
25. Lincoln speech: *OWH*, December 24, 1898. A clipping from the Omaha *World-Herald* is enclosed in Bryan's letter concerning the speech, to Andrew Carnegie, December 24, 1898, Andrew Carnegie Papers, Vol. 59. Tillman and sugar trust: *NYT*, July 1, 1898. Anti-Imperialist League: *ibid.*, December 13, 1898.
26. Bryan's peace treaty strategy: Bryan to Albert Shaw, December 17, 1898, Albert Shaw Papers, Box 2. Denver speech: *NYT* and *OWH*, January 18, 1899.

27. The treaty in the Senate: Paolo E. Coletta, "Bryan, McKinley, and the Treaty of Paris," *Pacific Historical Review* (May, 1957), 131–46. Bryan works for the treaty: Dunn, 282–83; George F. Hoar, *Autobiography of Seventy Years* (New York, 1903), II, 322, 323.
28. Bryan's views on the Filipino insurrection are stated in his letter to Andrew Carnegie, January 30, 1899, BP, Box 22.
29. Why the treaty passed: May, 261; Hoar, *op. cit.*
30. W. V. Allen statement concerning Gorman is in *NYT*, February 7, 1899. Bryan's Washington's Birthday speech, *ibid.*, February 23, 1899.

Chapter 18. New Issues

1. Louis H. Ehrich to Bryan, March 27, 1899, BP, Box 22.
2. Hot Springs conference: *OWH*, March 26, 1899.
3. Jefferson Day dinner speech at Milwaukee: *ibid.*, April 14, 1899; at New York City: *ibid.*, April 16, 1899.
4. Bryan and the Philippines: *NYT*, July 8, 1899.
5. John Sherman: Mark Sullivan, *Our Times* (New York, 1927), II, 311. Trust data and personalities: George E. Mowry, *The Era of Theodore Roosevelt* (New York, 1958), 10–12. Bryan on the antitrust issue: *ibid.*; *NYT*, March 23, 1899. Evils of the trust: *The Second Battle*, 205–14.
6. *Ibid.*, 227.
7. Croker and silver: Lothrop Stoddard, *Master of Manhattan, The Life of Richard Croker* (New York, 1931), 219. Croker's manner: Willis J. Abbot, *Watching the World Go By* (Boston, 1933), 204–5. James K. Jones: *NYT*, October 16, 1899.
8. W. R. Hearst to Bryan, May 20, 1900; James Creelman to Bryan, June 2, 1900, BP, Box 24.
9. D. S. Jordan to Bryan, February 7, 1900, BP, Box 24. Bryan to Jordan, February 19, 1900, David Starr Jordan Papers.
10. P. S. Bennett to Bryan, Feb. 20, 1899, BP, Box 24. Bryan's speeches: *OWH*, June 15, 1900.
11. Hazen Pingree: *NYT*, April 15, 1899. Ohio campaign: *ibid.*, March 22, 1899. Cockran concerning Bryan: *OWH*, September 16–17, 1899. Bryan to Bradford Merrill, April 26, 1900, BP, Box 24.
12. Bryan to Perry Belmont, March 16, 1899, BP, Box 24.
13. Jefferson Day dinners in New York: *NYT*, April 16, 1899. Jerry Simpson: *ibid.*, March 22, 1899.
14. Croker and Bryan: Abbot, 204. O. H. P. Belmont and Bryan: *NYT*, April 25, 1899.
15. Norman Mack and Croker: Buffalo *Commerical*, August 21, 1899; Scrapbooks, Norman Mack Papers. Croker on the issues: *NYT*, August 13, 1899.
16. Croker's confidence: John Girdner to Bryan, September 20, 1899, BP, Box 23. G. F. Williams to Bryan, October 5, 1899, BP, Box 23. John Sheehan's victory: *NYT*, September 20, 1899. O. H. P. Belmont's dinner: New York *Journal*, January 23, 1900.
17. Mack and Hill: *NYT*, November 28, 1899.
18. Kentucky convention: *OWH*, June 2, 1899. J. P. Altgeld to Bryan, August 7, 1899, BP, Box 23. Bryan supporter A. W. G. Thurman to Bryan, *ibid.*, September 9, 1899. Also on the McLean contest: James A. Rice to Bryan, *ibid.*, September 7, 1899; A. J. Warner to Bryan, *ibid.*, September 19, 1899.
19. Election results: *NYT*, November 8 and 12, 1899. The New York *Press* is quoted in Sullivan, I, 305–6.
20. Omaha convention: *OWH*, August 23, 1899. Bryan campaigning: *ibid.*, September 19, 22, 28, October 1, 1899. The campaign's importance to Bryan, *NYT*, September 29, 1899. Hanna's slush fund: *OWH*, November 2, 1899. Sterling Morton's moves: *NYT*, October 15, 1899.

21. Campaigning in Nebraska: *NYT,* October 15, 1899; *OWH,* October 15–November 8, 1899. Meiklejohn's assessment: *NYT,* September 29, 1899.
22. Appointing a Senator: Bryan to W. A. Poynter, December 11, 1899, BP, Box 23. National committee meeting at St. Louis: *NYT,* May 25, 1899. Bryan's statement: *ibid.,* May 26, 1899. Bryan to Urey Woodson, July 22, 1899, BP, Box 23. Issues for the national committee meeting: *NYT,* June 11 and July 21, 1899.
23. Bryan reported on the national committee meeting to W. R. Hearst, July 22, 1899, BP, Box 23.
24. The state of Populism: Thomas Patterson to Bryan, June 9, 1899. BP, Box 23. H. D. Lloyd is quoted in Chester M. Destler, *Henry Demarest Lloyd and the Empire of Reform* (Philadelphia, 1963), 458. Populist-Democratic leaders conference: *NYT,* May 7, 1900. Marion Butler and H. S. Taylor are quoted in *OWH,* May 11, 1900. R. F. Pettigrew to Bryan, June 9, 1900, BP, Box 24. C. A. Towne to Bryan, May 15, 1900, BP, Box 24. Consequences of Towne's Vice Presidential nomination: *NYT,* May 14, 1900.
25. The Gorman boom: J. Rogers Hollingsworth, *The Whirligig of Politics* (Chicago, 1963), 160–61; *NYT,* June 17, 1899.
26. Augustus Van Wyck boom: *NYT,* August 6, 1899. Admiral Dewey's boom: Washington *Post,* January 20, 1900; *NYT,* April 5, 1900. Watterson is quoted in the Louisville *Courier-Journal,* January 1, 1899, and *NYT,* January 2, 1899. C. S. Thomas to Bryan, April 2, 1899, BP, Box 23. The Cockrell boom: Kansas City *Times,* January 19 and 20, 1899. Sylvester Pennoyer to Bryan, April 5, 1899, BP, Box 23.
27. Bryan to David Starr Jordan, February 19, 1900, David Starr Jordan Papers.
28. Hill visits Bryan: *OWH,* July 2, 1900. Bryan's article on the platform is discussed in *The Nation,* June 7, 1900, 431. Bryan's optimism: *OWH,* May 4, 1900.
29. Willa Cather, "The Personal Side of William Jennings Bryan," *The Prairie Schooner* (Winter, 1949), 332–33. The common man and his moral code are quoted from W. Lloyd Warner, *American Life: Dream and Reality* (Chicago, 1962), 231. Concerning the leader and followership relation and pressures for simplification: Giovanni Sarton, "Politics, Ideology and Belief Systems," *American Political Science Review* (June, 1969), 410–11.

Chapter 19. The Second Battle

1. The scene in Kansas City: *NYT,* July 1–3, 1900; Kansas City *Star,* July 1–6, 1900; *The Nation,* July 12, 1900, 22. Daniels and Bryan on the money plank: Josephus Daniels, *Editor in Politics* (Chapel Hill, 1941), 356. Vice Presidential nomination: *OWH,* July 4, 1900.
2. Bryan stays home: *NYT,* March 29, 1900. Metcalfe as Bryan's spokesman: *OWH,* July 3, 1900; *Memoirs,* 123.
3. Bryan and the reporters: *OWH,* July 4 and 6, 1900; *NYT,* July 5, 1900.
4. Sculpture of Bryan: *Harper's Weekly,* July 28, 1900. Bryan and the Colorado and Illinois delegations: *NYT,* July 3, 1900. Hill goes to Lincoln: "William Jennings Bryan: Biographical Notes, His Speeches, Letters and Other Writings," enlarged and edited by his daughter, Grace Dexter Bryan, December 10, 1941, 186, BP, Box 64; Hill is quoted in Paolo E. Coletta, *William Jennings Bryan* Vol. I, *Political Evangelist* (Lincoln, 1964) 256; *OWH,* July 2, 1900; New York *World,* July 1 and 2, 1900.
5. Platform drafts and debate: *NYT,* July 5, 1900. Bryan's adamancy on silver: *Memoirs,* 123–25. Bryan agrees to making imperialism the paramount issue: *ibid.*
6. Why Bryan clings to the silver issue: *The Nation,* July 19, 1900. Thomas B. Reed is quoted in Thomas A. Bailey, "Was the Presidential Election of 1900 a Mandate on Imperialism?" *Mississippi Valley Historical Review* (June, 1937), 43.
7. Tillman reads the platform: New York *Tribune* and New York *World,* July 6, 1900. The demonstration for the platform: *NYT,* July 6, 1900.

8. Bryan is nominated: *ibid., OWH,* July 6, 1900.
9. The Vice Presidential nomination: *NYT,* July 1, 1900 (Buffalo Bill); July 7 (Stevenson). Bryan prefers Towne: Grace Dexter Bryan, *WJB Biographical Notes,* 210. Towne declines: William Jennings Bryan, *The Second Battle* (Chicago, 1900), 246.
10. Croker: John H. Girdner to Bryan, July 10, 1900, BP, Box 24. Bryan's statement: *NYT,* Aug. 11, 1900.
11. Notification: *NYT* and *OWH,* August 8 and 9, 1900. J. G. Johnson to Bryan, July 20, 1900, BP, Box 24. Hanna is quoted in *NYT,* August 10, 1900.
12. Roosevelt in the West: *NYT,* August 10, 1900. Bryan's Nebraska campaign: *OWH,* August 23–25, 1900. Bryan and Roosevelt: *NYT,* September 27, 1900.
13. J. P. Altgeld to Bryan, July 7, 1900, BP, Box 24. Edgar Howard is quoted in *OWH,* July 11, 1900, Charles H. Gere in *NSJ,* July 11, 1900, and Henry Teller in Elmer Ellis, *Henry Moore Teller* (Caldwell, Idaho, 1941), 333.
14. Moorfield Storey's attitudes are conveyed in *OWH,* August 17, 1900. Bourke Cockran's statement is in Cockran to Edwin Burritt Smith, August 14, 1900, Bourke Cockran Papers, Box 1.
15. *Ibid.*
16. Bryan's homecoming remarks: *NYT* and *OWH,* August 17, 1900. Topeka speech: *The Nation,* August 30, 1900, 164.
17. Bryan on the Filipino, Boxer, and Boer conflicts, *OWH,* July 9, 1900; *NYT,* September 9 and 29, 1900. Evaluation of the anti-imperialism issue: *The Nation,* August 30, 1900, 162. Josephus Daniels is quoted in Josephus Daniels, *Editor in Politics* (Chapel Hill, 1941), 357; Elwood S. Corser to William A. Croffut, November 7, 1900, Croffut Papers, Box 2.
18. Secretary Gage's campaign activities; *NYT,* September 2 and 30, 1900.
19. *OWH* and *NYT,* September 15 and October 6, 1900.
20. *OWH* and *NYT,* August 17, 1900.
21. *Ibid.,* August 25, 26, and September 16, 1900.
22. Charles Daniel to Bryan, July 22, 1900, BP, Box 24. Labor Day speech: *OWH* and *NYT,* September 4, 1900. Debs is quoted in H. Wayne Morgan, *Eugene V. Debs* (Syracuse, 1962), 55.
23. Bryan to Carter Harrison, July 12, 1900, Carter Harrison Papers. Norman Mack to Bryan, July 16, 1900, BP, Box 25.
24. Bryan is quoted in *NYT,* September 20, 1900.
25. The Tillman problem: J. K. Jones to Bryan, July 23, 1900, BP, Box 25. United Colored Democracy: clipping, *ibid.,* and *NYT,* July 12, 1900. Negro National Democratic League: George E. Taylor to Bryan, July 16, 1900, BP, Box 25. J. M. Turner: *NYT,* August 14, 1900. W. P. McAllister to Bryan, July 20, 1900, BP, Box 25. Joves to Cockran, September 5, 1900; Cockran to Ervin Winslow, September 10, 1900, Cockran Papers, Box 1.
26. Max F. Ihmsen to Bryan, July 24, 1900, BP, Box 25. Bryan's appeal for Democratic clubs: *NYT,* August 10, 1900.
27. *Talkative Facts:* William Weir to Bryan, July 12, 1900, BP, Box 24. *National Watchman:* J. M. Devine to Bryan, August 3, 1900, BP, Box 25.
28. *NYT,* August 14, 1900.
29. Croker vs. Hill: *NYT,* September 5, 1900.
30. James K. McGuire to Bryan, August 3, 1900, BP, Box 25.
31. Josephus Daniels to Bryan, August 1, 1900, BP, Box 25.
32. Senator Lee Mantle is quoted in *NYT,* August 10, 1900, and Senator W. M. Stewart in *ibid.,* August 21, 1900. Populist national committee meeting in Chicago, *NYT,* August 10 and 28, 1900.
33. Data on Bryan's campaign: *NYT,* November 5, 1900. The episode of Bryan's railroad car: *OWH,* September 7, 1900.
34. *NYT* and New York *World,* October 17, 1900.

35. New York *World, ibid., OWH,* October 17–19, 1900. J. G. Schurman is quoted in *NYT,* October 19, 1900, and Schurz in Carl Schurz, *The Reminiscences of Carl Schurz* (New York, 1907–9), III, 447.
36. Hanna is quoted in Thomas A. Bailey, "Was the Presidential Election of 1900 a Mandate on Imperialism?" *Mississippi Valley Historical Review* (June, 1937), 48.
37. Bryan is quoted in *NYT,* October 20, 1900; Archbishop Ireland in *ibid.,* October 21, 1900.
38. Bryan's comments on thieves and on trust magnates is in *OWH,* November 6, 1900.
39. Bryan to Hitchcock, June 7, 1900; Hitchcock to Bryan, June 16 and July 15, 1900, BP, Box 25. Bryan concludes the campaign: *OWH,* November 6, 1900. Elwood S. Corser to William A. Croffut, November 3, 1900, Croffut Papers, Box 2.
40. Bryan on election night: "William Jennings Bryan: Biographical Notes, His Speeches, Letters and Other Writings," enlarged and edited by his daughter, Grace Dexter Bryan, 224, BP, Box 64. Bryan's telegram to McKinley is in *NYT,* November 9, 1900.
41. Causes of the election results: William Jennings Bryan, "The Election of 1900," *North American Review* (December, 1900), 789. Champ Clark's experience is from Wayne C. Williams, *William Jennings Bryan* (New York, 1923), 236. H. K. Jones to Bryan, November 20, 1900, BP, Box 25.
42. Epithets against Bryan are collected in Paolo E. Coletta, *William Jennings Bryan,* Vol. I, *Political Evangelist* (Lincoln, 1964), 282–83. Bryan's comments on his wealth are in *NYT,* October 16, 1900.
43. Bryan to Albert Shaw, December 19, 1900, Shaw Papers, Box 2; Bailey, 50–51.

Chapter 20. A Divided Party

1. Bryan's offer of a magazine editorship: George S. Benson to Bryan, November 9, 1900, BP, Box 25. His statement declining offers: Charles M. Rosser, *The Crusading Commoner* (Dallas, 1937), 102–3. The nature of Bryan's following and influence is discussed in Frederick Shepherd to Bryan, November 7, 1900, BP, Box 25. ". . . the war is still going . . .": John Altgeld to Bryan, November 7, 1900, *ibid.* Bryan declines to run for the Senate: *OWH, NYT,* November 9, 1900. "Principles Live": *ibid.,* December 27, 1900.
2. Bryan's statement on McKinley's assassination: *TC,* September 13, 1901. The Kansas City *Journal*'s criticism of Bryan is in *ibid.,* September 20, 1901. Bryan's statement condemning anarchy is in *NYT,* September 10, 1901.
3. Labor Day speech: *OWH,* September 3, 1901.
4. The statements of Bryan and Hadley are in *NYT,* March 12, 1901. Bryan's and Theodore Roosevelt's comments on fighting: *NYT,* August 8, 1902, "If the press . . . would not mention . . . Bryan . . .": *ibid.,* July 19, 1901.
5. Bryan's lecturing: *The Lyceum Magazine* (August, 1925), 1, and William Jennings Bryan, *The Memoirs of William Jennings Bryan* (Philadelphia, 1925), 288. Lecture schedule for "A Conquering Nation" is in *TC,* January 31, 1902.
6. Bryan's appreciation of lecturing's contribution to his career: *Memoirs,* 288–89. Willa Cather's observation is in her "The Personal Side of William Jennings Bryan," *The Prairie Schooner* (Winter, 1949), 333. Bryan on the lecture circuit: *Memoirs,* 302; Rosser, 111–13; "Correspondence of Grace Bryan Hargraves," BP, Box 64.
7. *The Commoner*'s sales data: *Memoirs,* 283; *TC,* January 30, 1901. Bryan's definition of the common people and *The Commoner*'s purpose: *Memoirs,* 283.
8. C. W. Bryan: *TC,* September, 1922; W. J. Bryan, "My Brother Charles," *World's Work* (September, 1924), 553; Paul N. Anderson, "Brother Charley," *The Nation* (October 22, 1924), 442. R. L. Metcalfe: *TC,* May 5, 1905. H. W. McVey: *ibid.,* December 26, 1902. Will Maupin: *ibid.,* November 10, 1905. "Whip Behind": *ibid.,* "Protected": *ibid.,* January 3, 1902. "Modern Definitions": *ibid.,* January 23, 1901. "Boomerleigh": *ibid.,* January 30, 1901.

9. Advertising policy: *ibid.*, January 24, 1902. Postcard campaign: *ibid.*, February 28, 1902. C. W. Bryan's county agent plan: W. J. Bryan to Thomas D. Gold, November 21, 1901, Mary W. Gold Mss. Subscription data: *TC*, December 26, 1902.

10. Bryan as employer: *ibid.*, January 30, 1903.

11. W. R. Hearst's counsel is in his letter to Bryan, March 25, 1901, BP, Box 26. The American scene: George E. Mowry, *The Era of Theodore Roosevelt*, (New York, 1958), *passim*. Progressivism: Richard Hofstadter, *The Age of Reform* (New York, 1956); Eric Goldman, *Rendezvous with Destiny* (New York, 1952); Mowry, *op. cit.* Negro lynchings: *TC*, January 23, 1901. Virginia's Negro schools: *ibid.*, May 10, 1901. Bryan on North-South racial differences: *ibid.*, October 2, 1903. B. T. Washington's visit to the White House: *ibid.*, August 21, 1903.

12. "The new woman": *ibid.*, March 29, 1901. Thanksgiving address: *ibid.*, December 18, 1903.

13. Holland Society address: W. J. Bryan, *Under Other Flags* (Lincoln 1904), 291–99. The evil of moneymaking: *TC*, January 29, 1904.

14. Madison Square Garden speech: *ibid.*

15. George Bancroft on "great principles": *ibid.*, July 3, 1903. Bryan on why he was nominated: *ibid.*, April 26, 1901. Bad principles: *ibid.*, April 19, 1901.

16. Bryan's views concerning "good and bad principles" and "truth" are in *TC*, January 30, 1901.

17. Fairview is inspired by Bryan's father: *ibid.*, June, 1922, Bryan's early visits to Fairview's site: *ibid.*, October 11, 1901. Building Fairview: *ibid.*, June, 1922. Ruth's education and work at Hull House: *NYT*, August 24, 1903.

18. Criticisms of Bryan as a wealthy demagogue: *TC*, February 6, 1903. Bryan's refutation: *ibid.* P. S. Bennett's financial aid to Bryan: Bennett to Bryan, February 14, 1901, BP, Box 26.

19. The Bennett will case is discussed in Wayne C. Williams, *William Jennings Bryan: A Study in Political Vindication* (New York, 1923), 250, and Grace Bryan's "William Jennings Bryan," I, 114, BP, Box 64. Trial and court action: *NYT*, November 7, 1903.

20. Bryan's farewell to Mary is in his letter to her of November 26, 1903, BP, Box 27. Bryan and the Henry Whites concerning Tolstoy: Allan Nevins, *Henry White: Thirty Years of American Diplomacy* (New York, 1930), 228.

21. Visit with Tolstoy: Bryan, *Under Other Flags*, 88–104; *TC*, October 18, 1901, and February 13, 1902; *Memoirs* 460–61.

22. "I am fighting on": *NYT*, July 3, 1901. Disclaimer of Presidential candidacy: *ibid.*, April 26, 1901. Bryan declines candidacy for other offices: *ibid.*, April 28, 1901.

23. Moves against Bryan: *ibid.*, June 17, 1901. Bryan's attack on Cleveland is in *ibid.*, November 12, 1903.

24. Bryan warns against the "harmony" theme: *TC*, May 3, 1901.

25. Political issues as moral issues: Lester W. Milbrath, *Political Participation* (Chicago, 1965), 70; Alexis de Tocqueville, *Democracy in America* (New York, 1954) I, 43–44; Robert E. Lane, *Political Ideology* (New York, 1962), 129. D. B. Hill's activities and the Brooklyn *Eagle*'s reports are treated in *TC*, March 13, 1903. Bryan opposes Rolla Wells: W. J. Stone to Bryan, February 15, 1901, BP, Box 26. Norman Mack to Bryan, April 15, 1901, *ibid.*; Kansas City *Star*, June 18 and 19, 1901.

26. Criticism of Mayor Carter Harrison: Charles K. Ladem to Bryan, September 8, 1901, BP, Box 26. Harrison fights Altgeld; *NYT*, April 4, 1901. The Ohio Democratic convention of 1901: *NYT*, July 11, 1901. Pennsylvania and the Kansas City platform: William T. Creasy to Bryan, July 24, 1901, BP, Box 26.

27. Bryan attacks John P. Hopkins: *TC*, March 21 and June 26, 1902. Displaying Bryan's portrait at the New York State Democratic convention: *NYT*, September 30, 1902. His statement on Republican tariff reformers: *ibid.*, September 10, 1902.

28. Theodore Roosevelt: Mowry, 106–23; William H. Harbaugh, *Power and Responsibil-*

ity: The Life and Times of Theodore Roosevelt (New York, 1961), 149–234. Congressman Bromwell characterizes Bryan as "a millstone": *NYT,* July 30, 1902. Bryan's comments on the 1903 elections: *TC,* November 13, 1903.

29. Square Deal: Mowry, 123–43; Harbaugh, 235–53. Bryan's observations on the Presidential nomination, in the New York *Independent,* appear in *TC,* November 13, 1903.
30. Stirrings of a Cleveland Presidential candidacy: *NYT,* May 5, 1903. Theodore Roosevelt's reaction: Roosevelt to H. C. Lodge, March 4 and 23, 1903; Joseph B. Bishop, *Theodore Roosevelt and His Times, Shown in His Own Letters* (New York, 1920), I, 241. Bryan attacks the Cleveland element: *TC,* August 28, 1903. Bryan opposes Gorman: *NYT* and *OWH,* March 20, 1903. Hugh McLaughlin booms Hill: *NYT,* January 22, 1901. Hill and the tariff: *ibid.,* April 14, 1903.
31. Edgar Howard condemns "traitors": *OWH,* May 24, 1902. Parker's strategy of silence: *NYT* and New York *Tribune,* April 6, 1904. Bryan rejects Parker: *NYT,* January 16, 1904.
32. Bryan's praise of Hearst in 1903: *TC,* February 27, 1903. Bryan denies being a candidate: *NYT,* January 16, 1904. He declines to endorse Hearst: *ibid.* Watterson discounts Hearst's candidacy: *NYT,* April 6, 1904.
33. Bryan's comment on Tom Johnson: *TC,* February 27, 1903.
34. Bryan's unknown candidates: *NYT,* November 27, 1903; *TC,* August 14, 1903.

Chapter 21. From the Ashes of Weakness

1. "Our fight is not against Mr. Bryan": *NSJ,* March 18, 1904. Edgar Howard's resolution: *NYT,* June 2, 1904.
2. Bryan denounces Parker and the Parker forces reciprocate: *NYT,* and New York *World,* July 4, 1904. John P. Hopkins' statement is in *OWH,* July 7, 1904. Bryan's reply is in *NYT,* July 3 and 4, 1904.
3. R. L. Holt and Bryan's bolting: *NYT,* July 8, 1904.
4. Bryan challenges the Illinois delegation: William Jennings Bryan, *The Memoirs of William Jennings Bryan* (Philadelphia, 1925), 147–48. Bryan presents a minority report on the floor: *NYT* and St. Louis *Post-Dispatch,* July 8, 1904.
5. Hamlin's comments concerning Bryan's planks are in Charles S. Hamlin, "Diary," 340, Hamlin Papers. Bryan's encounter with Hill concerning Parker's views: *TC,* July 15, 1904.
6. Fight in the Resolutions Committee: *NYT* and *OWH* and St. Louis *Post-Dispatch,* July 9, 1904.
7. Hamlin's observations concerning Bryan's behavior are in his "Diary," 346. The St. Louis *Globe-Democrat*'s views are in its issue of July 9, 1904. Hill's comment concerning platforms is in *TC,* December 15, 1905. The "closed mind": Milton Rokeach, *The Open and Closed Mind, Investigations into the Nature of Belief Systems and Personality Systems* (New York, 1960), *passim.*
8. Bryan's statement regarding the opposition is in *NYT,* July 6, 1904. John Brisben Walker's speech: *ibid.,* June 24, 1904. Bryan's petition against Parker: *NYT,* July 6, 1904.
9. J. G. Johnson to Bryan, February 26, 1904, James K. Jones Papers. Max Ihmsen's interview is in *NYT,* July 3, 1904. Bryan declines to nominate Hearst: Josephus Daniels, *Editor in Politics* (Chapel Hill, 1941), 474. Hearst as Bryan's rival for leadership of the progressives: Richard C. Bain, *Convention Decisions and Voting Records* (Washington, 1960), 167.
10. Praise for Cockrell: *Memoirs,* 152. Bryan also supports Pattison and Folk: *Under Other Flags,* 349–52. Parker's suspicion that Bryan was seeking the nomination is stated in his letter to George Bixby, March 20, 1920, Bixby Papers.
11. Littleton's conversation with Bryan: Rosser, 108. Carmack's statement is in *Official Report of the Proceedings of the Democratic National Convention, 1904,* 211–12.

Bryan's speech: *NYT*, July 10, 1904. August Belmont's comment: Rosser, 108; A. J. Beveridge's: Charles W. Thompson, "How Bryan Picked His Issues," *NYT*, August 2, 1925.

12. *Memoirs*, 154–55; *NYT*, St. Louis *Post-Dispatch*, July 10, 1904.
13. Bryan's affinity to Henry Gassaway Davis: "Correspondence Grace Bryan Hargraves," I, 364, BP, Box 64. Senator C. A. Culberson and Parker's telegram: *NYT* and St. Louis *Post-Dispatch*, July 10, 1904.
14. Bryan's speech concerning Parker's telegram: *ibid.*
15. The convention finishes its business: *NYT*, St. Louis *Post-Dispatch* and *OWH*, July 10 and 11, 1904. Bryan's statement at Fairview: *ibid.*, July 13, 1904.
16. W. V. Allen criticizes Bryan: *NSJ*, July 22, 1904. Nebraska's Populist and Democratic conventions: *ibid.*, August 10 and 11, 1904. A. C. Shallenberger's statement is in *ibid.*, August 11, 1904.
17. Proceedings of the Nebraska Democratic convention: *OWH* and *NSJ*, August 11, 1904. Bryan and Hitchcock help each other in the campaign: *ibid.*, September 9, 1904.
18. Parker prepares his letter of acceptance: Parker to Bryan, August 12, 1904, BP, Box 27.
19. Louis Post to Tom Johnson, July 24, 1904, is quoted in Paolo E. Coletta, *William Jennings Bryan*, Vol. I, *Political Evangelist, 1860–1908* (Lincoln, 1964), 346. Bryan "plan for party reform": *NYT* and *OWH*, July 22, 1904. Bryan's part in the campaign: *NYT*, September 17, 21, 25, 30; October 4, 5, 11, 13, 1904. The Tibbles-Allen "agreement": *NSJ*, August 4, 1904. Chancellor Andrews' interview is reported in *NYT*, September 21, 1904.
20. H. C. Frick's statement is in Oswald Garrison Villard, *Fighting Years: Memoirs of a Liberal Editor* (New York, 1939), 178–83. Bryan's Moses and Aaron speech: *NYT*, October 11, 1904.
21. Election results: *NYT*, New York *World*, and *OWH*, November 10, 1904.
22. Bryan's postmortem on the election and his analysis of the future: *ibid.*
23. Reorganization: *ibid.* Bryan to Louis Post, November 12, 1904, Post Papers, Box 1.
24. Dinner for W. S. Rodie: *ibid.*, November 22, 1904. Tom Watson's observation is in *NSJ*, November 14, 1904.

Chapter 22. The Road Back

1. Bryan's diversions: *NYT*, January 2, 1905. Praise for Roosevelt: *NYT* and New York *World*, January 6, 1905. Bryan on Capitol Hill: Washington *Post* and *NYT*, January 21, 1905.
2. Bryan confers with Roosevelt: *ibid.*, January 22, 1905.
3. Speech on Jefferson's Birthday: *NYT*, April 14, 1905. Mayor Dunne's remarks: *ibid.*
4. Bryan's plan for restoring "progressive Democracy": *TC*, March 17, 1905. His possible Presidential candidacy: *ibid.*, June 23, 1905.
5. Norman Mack on Bryan as party leader: *ibid.*, May 5, 1905. Taft attacks Bryan: *ibid.*, November 10, 1905. The Fulton *Gazette* replies: *ibid.*
6. Comment on Roosevelt's inaugural address: *ibid.*, March 17, 1905. A plea for stricter game laws: *ibid.*, May 5, 1905. Prodding Roosevelt's peace endeavors: *NYT*, September 15, 1905.
7. Roosevelt uses Democratic ideas: *TC*, August 4, 1905. Roosevelt "steals" Bryan's clothes: *NYT*, July 11, 1906.
8. Roosevelt's achievements: George E. Mowry, *The Era of Theodore Roosevelt* (New York, 1958), 197–210. "Social sin": *TC*, February 3, 1905; Coletta, 356–57. Bryan's citation of examples: *TC*, May 26, 1905.
9. Combating social sin: *ibid.*, May 26 and June 10, 1905.
10. Bryan concerning the Rockefeller gift: *TC*, April 7, 1905. Bryan resigns from the Illi-

nois College Board of Trustees: *ibid.*, February 23, 1906; Bryan to M. F. Dunlap, January 5, 1905, in *Minutes of Board of Trustees:* Illinois College; "Minutes of the Board of Trustees," January 17, 31, April 1, May 9, 1905. Charles H. Rammelkamp, *Illinois College: A Centennial History, 1829–1929* (New Haven, 1928), 457–58.

11. The articles Bryan wrote concerning his world trip appear in Hearst's newspapers and *TC,* January 19 to November 23, 1906. His letter to Roosevelt is in *TC,* September 29, 1905.

12. The Bryans' Pacific voyage: *ibid.*, January 19, 1906. Encounter with Admiral Togo: Grace Bryan Hargraves, "William Jennings Bryan," I, 402–4, BP, Box 64. "Steam has narrowed the Pacific": *TC,* October 27, 1905.

13. Korea: William Jennings Bryan, *The Memoirs of William Jennings Bryan* (Philadelphia, 1925), 312. China: *ibid.,* 312–13; William Jennings Bryan, *The Old World and Its Ways* (St. Louis, 1907), 139–49. Philippines: Bryan to C. W. Bryan, undated, OP; Manila *American,* December 28, 1905; January 3, 1906. Leonard Wood's comments are in his "Diary," January 31, 1908, Leonard Wood Papers.

14. Bryan in India: Bryan, *Under Other Flags,* 295–303.

15. The Holy Land: *ibid.,* 345–48. Bryan seeks to regain lost weight: Grace Bryan Hargraves, "William Jennings Bryan," I, 479, BP, Box 64. Bryan visits the Duma: Bryan, *Under Other Flags,* 406–7.

16. Coronation of King Haakon: Bryan, *Memoirs,* 318. Bryan in London: speech to the American Society: *TC,* July 6 and 13, 1906; Alice Roosevelt Longworth, *Crowded Hours* (New York, 1933), 123; Whitelaw Reid to Theodore Roosevelt, July 17, 1906, Reid Papers. King Edward's and Grey's comments are in Reid's letter to Roosevelt. Bryan's evaluations of British personalities are in Bryan to C. W. Bryan, July, 1906, Silas Bryan Papers, quoted in Paolo E. Coletta, *William Jennings Bryan,* Vol. I, *Political Evangelist, 1860–1908* (Lincoln, 1964), 367.

17. Momentum for Bryan's Presidential nomination: *NYT,* July 8, 1906; Wisconsin's action: *ibid.,* June 29, 1906; North Carolina's: *ibid.,* July 4, 1906. David Francis is quoted in *ibid.,* June 6, 1906; J. S. Williams in *ibid.,* July 4, 1906.

18. Statements to the press: *TC,* June 22, 1906; *NYT,* May 11, 1906. Bryan suggests possible Presidential nominees: *TC,* July 13, 1906; *NYT,* July 4, 1906.

19. George Harvey's meeting with Bryan: Willis F. Johnson, *George Harvey: A Passionate Patriot* (New York, 1929), 120–22.

20. J. S. Williams' mission is treated in George C. Osborn, *John Sharp Williams: Planter-Statesman of the Deep South* (Baton Rouge, 1943), 148; G. B. McClellan's in Harold C. Syrett, ed., *The Gentleman and the Tiger: An Autobiography of George Brinton McClellan, Jr.* (New York, 1956), 280–81.

21. Address to the Peace Congress: Clippings of the *Standard* and the *Daily Mail,* July 25, 1906, are in OP. The armament resolution: *NYT,* July 26, 1906. Bryan's amendment is in *TC,* January, 1922. Letter from Damascus: Bryan to C. W. Bryan, May 3, 1906, OP. Bryan's second letter looking forward to his homecoming is also to C. W. Bryan, undated, OP. Henry White's impressions: Coletta, 371–72.

22. Homecoming reception in New York: *TC,* September 7, 1906; *NYT,* August 30, 1906.

23. Address at Madison Square Garden: *NYT* and New York *World,* August 31, 1906.

24. G. F. Williams' observations: Coletta, 378. Roosevelt's observations are contained in his letter to Lodge of September 24, 1906, Henry Cabot Lodge, *Selections from the Correspondence of Theodore Roosevelt and Henry Cabot Lodge, 1884–1918* (New York, 1925), II, 223–24.

25. Speeches at Louisville and Raleigh: *NYT,* September 13 and 18, 1906. Bryan's statement to Nebraska audiences is in *ibid.,* September 11, 1906. The leftward Roosevelt: Mowry, 210–12, 221–24.

26. The moral awakening: *TC,* January 25, 1907. Bryan advocates the direct primary: *ibid.,* February 22, 1907.

27. Bryan's program is set out in *TC*, July 26, 1906. Government ownership of railroads will not be an issue: *OWH*, July 23, 1907. Taft: Mowry, 231–33; William Henry Harbaugh, *Power and Responsibility* (New York, 1961), 352–53.

28. Dr. G. L. Miller's statement: *NYT*, May 1, 1907. Bryan's adventures on the lecture circuit: *ibid.*, April 26 and July 26, 1907; *OWH*, July 9, 1907. Unity speech in New York; *NYT*, June 7, 1907. Bryan's observations concerning Roosevelt: *TC*, December 6, 1907.

29. Taft, the "postponer": *OWH*, September 6, 1907. Bryan prefers La Follette to Taft: *TC*, April 19 and October 18, 1907.

30. Tom Johnson supports Bryan: *OWH*, November 16, 1907. Other endorsements: *ibid.*, August 2 and November 13, 1907. Dahlman's mission: *NYT*, June 30, 1907. "Fingy" Connors opposes Bryan: *OWH*, November 17, 1907.

31. Efforts for Hearst: *NYT* and New York *World*, August 6, 1907. Jacob Ruppert concerning Chanler: *NYT*, September 1, 1907. Governor J. A. Johnson declines to contest with Bryan: *ibid.*, September 13, 1907. George Harvey's criticizing of Bryan: *TC*, April 26, 1907; Wilson's: *NYT*, November 24, 1907. Wilson's letter to Joline is quoted in Bryan, *Memoirs*, 332.

Chapter 23. Let the People Rule

1. Bryan's appearance: William Bayard Hale, "The Bryan of Twelve Years Ago and of Today," *NYT*, February 9, 1908; interview with Arthur Krock, January 20, 1969; Buffalo *Times*, July 6, 1908; *The Nation*, May 21, 1908, 458; Albert Shaw, "William Jennings Bryan," *American Review of Reviews* (July, 1925), 263. James Creelman is quoted in *NYT*, February 9, 1908. Bryan's comment concerning his age is in BP, Box 28.

2. Ruth's marital difficulties are recounted in *NYT*, November 28, 1908. Concerning Grace: *Memoirs*, 197; Buffalo *Times*, July 9, 1908.

3. William, Jr.: *Memoirs*, 195–96. Mabel Potter Daggett, "At Home with the Bryans," Buffalo *Times*, October 1, 1908.

4. *The Nation*, January 3, 1908, 93. Bryan in Washington: Washington *Post* and *NYT*, January 29, 1908. Bryan on principles and victory: Arthur W. Dunn, *From Harrison to Harding* (New York, 1922), II, 47–49. Ohio and Illinois: *NYT*, May 6 and 7, 1908. Roger Sullivan: Charles Bryan to Bryan, January 22, 1908, OP. Raymond Robins is quoted in *TC*, March 13, 1908. Illinois convention: *ibid.*, May 1, 1908.

5. *NYT*, April 19, 1908.

6. "Notes," December 5, 1907, Pulitzer Papers, Box 6. John Johnson: *TC*, February 14, 1908. Minnesota convention: *ibid.*, March 13, 1908; *NYT*, March 7, 1908.

7. New York *World*, June 2, 1908; *NYT*, June 3 and 5, 1908; *TC*, June 12, 1908.

8. Populist national convention: *TC*, April 10, 1908. W. R. Hearst: *ibid.*, July 24, 1908. Bryan's statement is in *NYT*, February 1, 1908. Joseph Pulitzer: "Conversation with Cobb," December 5, 1908, and "Notes," December 5, 1908, Pulitzer Papers, Box 6. Panic of 1907: George E. Mowry, *The Era of Theodore Roosevelt* (New York, 1958), 216–20.

9 "Favor-seeking corporations:" Chicago *Tribune*, March 19, 1908. Carnegie Hall speech: *TC*, February 7, 1908. Bank guarantee system: *ibid.*, June 5, 1908. Cooper Union speech: text, April 21, 1908, OP. Campaign contributions: *NYT*, May 27, 1908; Taft to Bryan, May 26, 1908, Letterbook Series 8, Taft Papers, Vol. 18.

10. A sure nominee: *NYT*, April 19, 1908; *TC*, June 19, 1908. Convention organization: *NYT*, June 28, 1908. Resolutions Committee chairman: Bryan to C. N. Haskell, June 18, 1908, Haskell Papers. Use the Nebraska platform: Bryan to Haskell, June 23, 1908, *ibid.* Visitors to Lincoln: *ibid.*, June 30, 1908.

11. Richard F. Pettigrew, *Imperial Washington* (Chicago, 1922), 259–60; W. A. Swanberg, *Citizen Hearst* (New York, 1961), 257. C. W. Bryan to Bryan, January 25, 1908, OP.

12. Dahlman as Bryan's emissary: *NYT,* January 19, 1908. Bryan vs. New York *World*: *TC,* February 28 and May 1, 1908.

13. *TC,* June 19 and 26, 1908.

14. The Denver scene: Samuel E. Moffett, "Mr. Bryan's Convention," *American Review of Reviews* (July, 1908), 179. Willis J. Abbot, *Watching the World Go By* (Boston, 1933) 261; *TC,* July 10, 1908; *NYT,* July 6, 1908; *Rocky Mountain News,* July 1–10, 1908. Bryan's managers at Denver: Charles McDaniel Rosser, *The Crusading Commoner* (Dallas, 1937), 127–28.

15. *OWH* and *NYT,* July 3, 1908.

16. Bryan vs. Guffey in Pennsylvania: *NYT,* February 28, 1908; *TC,* May 20, 1908. Bryan's statement on Guffey is in Bryan to Henry Watterson, July 6, 1908, Watterson Papers, Vol. 7. Bryan's statement at Fairview: *TC,* July 10, 1908. Credentials Committee and convention floor: C. W. Bryan to Bryan, undated, BP, Box 48.

17. *OWH* and *NYT,* July 9, 1908; Abbot, 262; "William Jennings Bryan: Biographical Notes, His Speeches, Letters and Other Writings," edited by his daughter, Grace Dexter Bryan, 6, BP, Box 64.

18. *OWH* and *NYT,* July 11, 1908.

19. *Ibid.,* July 10, 1908. C. W. Bryan to Bryan, undated, BP, Box 48.

20. Ground rules: Bryan to C. W. Bryan, undated, BP, Box 48. Arthur Mullen, *Western Democrat* (New York, 1940), 161. Railroad ownership: Bryan to C. W. Bryan, *op. cit.* Labor plank: *OWH* and *NYT,* July 10, 1908; Samuel Gompers, *Seventy Years of Life and Labor* (New York, 1925), II, 255–65.

21. Trust plank: Bryan to C. W. Bryan, *op. cit.* Further Bryan-Charles W. Bryan correspondence, *ibid.*

22. *NYT,* July 1 and 3, 1908. John Mitchell: Bryan to C. W. Bryan, undated, BP, Box 48. J. W. Kern, *NYT,* July 11, 1908.

23. Fairview's visitors: *NYT* and *OWH,* July 12, 1908. Campaign contributions: *ibid.,* July 22, 1908. TC: *ibid.,* July 24, 1908; *TC,* July 24, 1908. Bible class: Rosser, 132.

24. Norman Mack: *NYT* and *OWH,* July 26, 1908; "The Moore-Montgomery Families, with Biographical Sketch of Norman Mack," Mack Papers; Buffalo *Express,* July 1, 1900, clipping in scrapbook, Mack Papers.

25. Bryan to Henry Watterson, August 4, 1908, Watterson Papers, Vol. 7. Acceptance speech: *OWH,* and *NYT,* August 13, 1908; Edgar A. Hornig, "The Indefatigable Mr. Bryan in 1908," *Nebraska History* (September, 1956), 184–85; *The Nation,* August 20, 1908, 151–52; *Outlook,* August 22, 1908, 867; Joseph Pulitzer, "Notes on Bryan's Speech of Acceptance," August 8, 1908, Pulitzer Papers, Box 7.

26. Bryan to Henry Watterson, August 4, 1908, Watterson Papers, Vol. 7. Campaign plan: Buffalo *Times,* July 29, 1908. Topeka speech: *ibid.,* August 28, 1908; *TC,* September 4, 1908.

27. *NYT,* August 26, 1908; *TC,* August 28, 1908.

28. *OWH* and *NYT,* September 8, 1908.

29. *NYT,* September 14 and 16, 1908. D. B. Hill to Alton Parker, September 18, 1908; Hill to Edward Murphy, September 18, 1908, Hill Letterbooks, Bixby Papers.

30. *NYT,* September 18 and 19, 1908.

31. Campaign contributions: Buffalo *Times,* October 28, 1908; *TC,* October 2, 1908; *NYT,* August 15 and 27, 1908.

32. Lack of funds: Buffalo *Times,* October 15, 1908; Josephus Daniels to Mrs. Daniels, August 18, 1908, Daniels Papers, Box 27.

33. Phonograph records: *NYT,* September 6, 1908. Movie: *ibid.,* September 8, 1908. Textbook: Buffalo *Times,* September 8, 1908. Precinct club letter: *ibid.,* August 31, 1908.

34. Samuel Gompers: *OWH* and Buffalo *Times,* October 11, 1908.

35. Criticism of Gompers: *NYT,* July 22 and October 26, 1908. St. Louis *Post-Dispatch* is quoted in *TC,* July 31, 1908. Gompers' efforts: *NYT,* August 25 and October 20,

1908. Daniels' request of Gompers: Daniels to Gompers, undated, Daniels Papers, Box 28.

36. National Anti-Asiatic League: *NYT,* August 9, 1908. Wage earner in the Cabinet: *ibid.,* October 24, 1908. Bryan and the National Association of Manufacturers: *TC,* August 7, 1908. Eugene V. Debs is quoted in Ray Ginger, *The Bending Cross* (New Brunswick, 1949), 275.

37. *NYT,* March 27 and February 6, 1908.

38. Bryan to Henry Watterson, August 17, 1908, Watterson Papers, Vol. 7. Bryan and Catholics: Josephus Daniels, *Editor in Politics* (Chapel Hill, 1941), 540; *NYT,* August 29, 1908. Norman Mack: E. L. Scharf to Arthur Mullen, October 7, 1908, BP, Box 27. Taft's religious problem: Norman Mack to Henry Watterson, August 14, 1908, Watterson Papers, Vol. 7. Taft's minister: Charles Hilles to A. I. Vorys, August 31, 1908, Hilles Papers, Box 129.

39. Negro editors visit Fairview: *Broad Ax,* July 18, 1908. W. E. B. Du Bois: Emma Lou Thornbrough, "The Brownsville Episode and the Negro Vote," *The Mississippi Valley Historical Review* (1956), 490.

40. Negro convention at Philadelphia: Thornbrough, 489–90. Statements at Cooper Union: April 21, 1908, text in OP. Negro leaders support Bryan: Thornbrough, 490. Views of Negro newspapers: *Broad Ax,* May 16, 1908. C. H. Williams to Josephus Daniels October 27, 1908, Daniels Papers, Box 28. Forecasts of Negro vote: Thornbrough, 492.

41. New York politics: *NYT,* September 2, 1908. Cleveland wing: *ibid.,* October 21 and 23, 1908. Hearst: Buffalo *Times,* July 29 and 31, 1908. Haskell episode: *NYT,* September 25, 1908.

42. Bryan on Roosevelt's charges: *Rocky Mountain News,* September 23, 1908. Roosevelt and Taft: Telegrams, Roosevelt to Taft and Taft to Roosevelt, September 19, 1908; letters, Roosevelt to Taft, September 21 and 26, 1908, Taft Papers. Roosevelt attacks Bryan: *NYT,* September 24, 1908. Daniels and Haskell: Daniels, 543–46. Bryan's counterattack on Roosevelt: Oscar Straus, *Under Four Administrations* (Boston, 1922), 253–54; Roosevelt to Bryan, September 27, 1908. Taft attacks Bryan: *OWH* and *Rocky Mountain News,* September 23, 1908; discredits bank deposits guarantees: *NYT,* August 27, 1908. Bryan concerning Taft's position on campaign contributions: *TC,* August 7, 1908. Coercion and intimidation: *NYT,* October 10 and 22, 1908. Fears of Taft men: Charles Hilles to J. E. Mullen, October 19, 1908, Hilles Papers, Box 129; Hilles to Taft, September 4, 1908, *ibid.*

43. Bryan's electoral vote strategy: Edgar A. Hornig, "The Indefatigable Mr. Bryan in 1908," *Nebraska History* (September, 1956), 196–97. Nebraska campaigning: *OWH* and *NYT,* October 14–16, 1908. Bank deposits guarantee: *NYT,* October 24, 1908.

44. New York campaigning: New York *American* and *NYT,* October 26–29, 1908. Middle West: *OWH* and *NYT,* November 1, 1908. Gompers: Washington *Post* and *NYT,* October 31, 1908.

45. Election night: *TC,* November 6, 1908; *OWH* and *NYT,* November 4, 1908; "William Jennings Bryan: Biographical Notes," "Third Call to Leadership," 54, BP, Box 64. Bryan's statement to Grace: *ibid.*

46. Bryan to Louis Post, November 6, 1908, Louis Post Papers, Box 1. Bryan to Josephus Daniels, November 4, 1908, Daniels Papers, Box 37. Louis Post to Bryan, November 12, 1908, Louis Post Papers, Box 1. Tammany: *TC,* November 13, 1908; Raymond Robins' comment is in Chicago *Record,* November 6, 1908. Charles Murphy's statement is in *NYT,* November 6, 1908. Labor: Louis Post to Bryan, November 12, 1908, Louis Post Papers, Box 1. Labor "refused to participate": C. T. Callahan, November 7, 1908, BP, Box 27. *The Commoner* concerning labor: *TC,* November 20, 1908. J. B. Weaver to Bryan, November 13, 1908, BP, Box 28.

47. The Catholic vote: George C. Osborn, *John Sharp Williams* (Baton Rouge, 1943), 154–74. Clarence Darrow is quoted in his *The Story of My Life* (New York, 1932), 94. Editorial: *NYT,* November 4, 1908.

48. Robert E. Lane, *Political Ideology* (New York, 1962), 14–16; Hadley Cantril, *The Psychology of Social Movements* (New York, 1941), 66.

Chapter 24. Keeping the Progressive Faith

1. W. J. Gaynor to Bryan, November 13, 1908, BP, Box 28. Norman Mack: *NYT*, November 5, 1908. Bryan's statement is in *TC*, November 27, 1908.
2. William, Jr.'s marriage: Lincoln *Daily Star*, June 25, 1909; *TC*, July 2, 1909. Ruth reweds: *NYT*, May 4, 1909. Silver wedding anniversary: *NSJ*, October 2, 1909; *TC*, October 8, 1909. Forgiveness: *NSJ*, April 25, 1909. Baseball: *ibid.*, May 11, 1909.
3. Bryan on the lecture trail: *TC*, January 12, 1912. Edinburgh speech: June 10, 1910, excerpts BP, Box 49. Bryan to W. H. Taft, June 29, 1910, *ibid.*, Box 28.
4. *TC*, July 16 and October 8, 1909, June 2, 1911, and January 12, 1912.
5. Direct election of Senators: *ibid.*, July 16, 1909. Cannonism: *ibid.*, January 21, 1910. Recall of judges: *ibid.*, March 10, 1911. E. D. White: *ibid.*, October 13, 1911. Bryan's court: New York *World*, October 8, 1911; *TC*, October 20, 1911.
6. New Testament: *TC*, November 19, 1909. Saving one boy: *ibid.*, May 19, 1911. Havana speech: *ibid.*, January 14, 1910. Lake Mohonk: *ibid.*, July 8, 1910.
7. Bryan to Henry Rainey, January 13, 1909, Rainey Papers, Box 1.
8. *NYT*, March 2, 1910.
9. *TC*, February 11, 1910.
10. *Ibid.*, October 14, 1910; *NYT*, November 9, 1910.
11. Champ Clark: *TC*, April 21, 1911. Bryan concerning the Senate: *ibid.*, March 31, 1911. Senate leadership fight: *ibid.*, April 21, 1911; *NYT*, April 8, 1911.
12. *TC*, March 17 and February 3, 1911.
13. *Ibid.*, September 15 and April 7, 1911.
14. Hitchcock: *NYT*, February 3, 1934. Dahlman: *ibid.*, January 22, 1930. His gubernatorial candidacy: *NSJ*, August 8, 1910. Hitchcock's statement is in *NSJ*, March 14, 1910. Bryan declines candidacy: *ibid.*, June 15, 1910; *OWH*, July 4 and 6, 1910. Bryan endorses Metcalfe: *ibid.*, July 20, 1910.
15. Bryan on county option: Reverend Tinder's statement, *NSJ*, March 1, 1909. A. Mullen's statement is in Arthur Mullen, *Western Democrat* (New York, 1940), 140. Bryan's letter to Nebraska's Democratic legislators: *NSJ*, April 29, 1910. Dahlman is nominated for governor: Mullen, 144; *OWH*, July 27, 1910. Bryan repudiates Dahlman: Mullen, 145. Hitchcock praises Bryan: *OWH*, September 8, 1910. Nebraska Democracy's 1911 convention: *OWH*, July 26, 1911.
16. The New York *World* is quoted in *TC*, December 30, 1910. Bryan's test for Presidential aspirants: *ibid.*, December 30, 1910. Judson Harmon to Henry Rainey, November 16, 1908, Henry Rainey Papers, Box 1. Harmon displeases Bryan: *TC*, July 8, 1910. Praise for Wilson: *ibid.*, December 23, 1910, and Clark: *ibid.*, June 17, 1910.
17. Charles Bryan to Louis Post, January 14, 1911, Louis Post Papers, Box 1. ". . . devote all my time" is in *OWH*, August 15, 1911. Bryan on Harmon and plutocracy: *TC*, August 25, 1911; *NYT*, August 15, 1911.
18. Clark: Arthur S. Link. *Woodrow Wilson and the Progressive Era* (New York, 1954), 11. The New York *Sun* is quoted in *TC*, April 14, 1911. Wool tariff: Champ Clark, *My Quarter Century of American Politics* (New York and London, 1920), II, 397. Bryan's counsel to Clark: Bryan to Champ Clark, May 30, 1911, BP, Box 28, Bryan's statement on Underwood is in *NYT*, August 3, 1911. House of Representatives: *ibid.*, August 4, 1911.
19. Clark, liquor interests and J. J. Hill: *NYT*, May 1, 1912. Bryan despairs: *Memoirs*, 335–36. Wilson's statements and acts are in Arthur Link, *Wilson: The Road to the White House* (Princeton, 1947), 116–20. Pulitzer's statement: Editorial proof, 1911, Joseph Pulitzer Papers, Box 10. Bryan forgives Wilson: *TC*, February 3, 1911. Wilson to R. S. Baker: Willis J. Abbot, *Watching the World Go By* (Boston, 1933), 292.

The Philippines: Wilson to Bryan, August 15, 1911, BP, Box 65. The Joline letter: Joseph P. Tumulty, *Woodrow Wilson as I Knew Him* (Garden City, 1921), 95–97.
20. The "reactionary plot": *TC*, April 19, 1912. Bryan on Harmon and Wall Street: *ibid.*, April 5, 1912. Folk and Clark: *ibid.*, June 9 and 16, 1912.
21. Bryan's approval of Wilson: *ibid.*, January 26, 1912. How Wilson voted: Wilson to Bryan, April 3, 1912, BP, Box 28. Wilson and publication of prenomination subscriptions: Wilson to Bryan, March 15 and April 3, 1912, BP, Box 28. The Washington *Star* is quoted in *TC*, February 2, 1912. Bryan's disavowal of candidacy is in *NYT*, October 16, 1911, and April 14, 1912.
22. Bryan's statement of how he would vote as a delegate is in *TC*, March 29, 1912. His denunciation of Hitchcock: *ibid.*
23. Hitchcock's statement concerning Bryan: *ibid.* Clark should withdraw in Nebraska: *ibid.*; Arthur W. Dunn, *From Harrison to Harding* (New York and London, 1922), II, 186. His victory: Mullen, 171.
24. Bryan at the Republican convention: "William Jennings Bryan: Biographical Notes," 16, BP, Box 65. Daniels-Bryan conversation: Josephus Daniels, *The Wilson Era* (Chapel Hill, 1946), 50. Bryan's telegram and Wilson's and Clark's reply: *Memoirs*, 164–65.
25. Bryan and family in Baltimore: *NYT*, June 25, 1912. Bryan is not a candidate: *ibid.* Representatives of big business: *ibid.*, June 24, 1912. Bryan on the division of progressive strength: *TC*, June 14, 1912. The convention begins: *OWH*, June 25, 1912; *TC*, July 5, 1912.
26. Bryan on Parker's adamancy: *Memoirs*, 166. Bryan seeks an opponent to Parker: *ibid.*, 166–68. Vardaman and Bryan: *NYT*, June 24, 1912. Clark men fear Bryan's oratory: Henry A. Ashurst, *A Many Colored Toga* (Tucson, 1962), 17. Temporary chairman floor fight: *NYT*, June 26, 1912, *Memoirs*, 168–69. "Baltimore Letter": *TC*, July 5, 1912. Wilson men fear Bryan: *NYT*, June 25, 1912.
27. Clark men offer Bryan the permanent chairmanship: *Memoirs*, 170. Bryan and the platform: *ibid.*, 170–72.
28. Clark's strength: Abbot, 282. Bryan's criticism of Clark: *Memoirs*, 335–37. Wilson concerning Clark: Ray Stannard Baker, *Woodrow Wilson* (Garden City, 1931), III, 196. Men of wealth at the convention: Boyce House, "Bryan and Baltimore: The Democratic National Convention of 1912," *Nebraska History* (March, 1960), 32. Charles, Bryan, and the anti-Wall Street resolution: *Memoirs*, 90, 174–75; House, 46–47.
29. Bryan presents his anti-Wall Street resolution: *OWH*, *NYT* and New York *World*, June 28, 1912; Abbot, 65; *Memoirs*, 176–79. Convention is in progressive hands: *NYT*, June 28, 1912. Bryan's position on Clark and Wilson: *ibid.*
30. Bryan supports Clark: *Memoirs*, 182. Hitchcock demands poll of Nebraska's delegation: *ibid.*, 183. Bryan abandons Clark: *NYT*, New York *World*, *OWH*, June 30, 1912; "William Jennings Bryan: Biographical Notes," 16, BP, Box 65. Wilson gains: *NYT*, June 30, 1912.
31. Clark's response: *ibid.*; Baltimore *Sun*, July 1, 1912.
32. Movement to Wilson: *OWH*, July 3, 1912; Dunn, II, 192. Clark on Bryan's plan: Champ Clark, *My Quarter Century of American Politics* (New York and London, 1920), II, 424. Mary supports Wilson to help Bryan's candidacy: "William Jennings Bryan: Biographical Notes," 16, BP, Box 64.
33. Norman Mack: Charles McDaniel Rosser, *The Crusading Commoner* (Dallas, 1937), 144; editorial, Raleigh, North Carolina, *News and Observer*, October 23, 1929. Bryan profits from lengthy convention: *NYT*, June 30, 1912.
34. Murphy votes for Wilson: *ibid.*, June 28, 1912. Bryan's statement opposing a conservative Democratic ticket: *ibid.*, July 3, 1912. Wilson rejects pledge not to make Bryan Secretary of State: Daniels, *The Wilson Era*, 62; Tumulty, 118. McCombs' statement: *NYT*, July 3, 1912.

35. Bryan will campaign for Wilson: *ibid.* Charles Bryan visits Wilson: *ibid.,* July 5, 1912. Chautauqua lectures: *OWH,* August 17, 1912. Bryan campaigns: *Memoirs,* 340–41; praises Wilson: *OWH,* September 21, 1912. Bryan attacks Perkins: *ibid.,* October 5, 1912; criticizes Taft: *ibid.,* November 4, 1912.

36. Wilson and Bryan meet: *OWH,* October 6, 1912; *NYT,* October 7, 1912; *TC,* October 11, 1912.

37. Mrs. Champ Clark concerning Bryan: *TC,* August 2, 1912. Bryan concerning Clark: *ibid.,* July 26, 1912. Lancaster County convention: *OWH,* July 21, 1912. Grand Island convention: *ibid.,* July 31, 1912. Gilbert Hitchcock: *ibid.,* July 22, 1912.

38. *OWH,* November 4, 1912.

39. Bryan's statement on Wilson's victory: *TC,* November 8, 1912. Mary: *Memoirs,* 340–41. Wilson to Bryan, November 9, 1912, BP, Box 28; *Memoirs,* 339. Bryan and Wilson compared as vote getters: Link, *Road to the White House,* 525; Edgar Eugene Robinson, *The Presidential Vote, 1896–1932* (Stanford, 1934), 15.

40. Burleson-Wilson conversation: Link, *op. cit.,* 7–8. Wilson on Bryan's friends: *NYT,* December 11, 1912. Mrs. Wilson opposes Bryan's appointment: James Kerney, *The Political Education of Woodrow Wilson* (New York, 1926), 287–88.

41. Wilson-Bryan meeting: Charles McDaniel Rosser, *The Crusading Commoner* (Dallas, 1937), 212–14; *Memoirs,* 187–88.

42. Arthur Mullen's warning: Mullen, 176. Colonel House visits Bryan: Charles Seymour, *The Intimate Papers of Colonel House* (Boston, 1926), I, 104–6. Wilson to Bryan, February 23, 1913, BP, Box 29.

Chapter 25. A Pacifist Secretary of State

1. Bryan's statement to Mary at the inauguration: William Jennings Bryan, *The Memoirs of William Jennings Bryan* (Philadelphia, 1925), 344. Bryan is in "hearty accord" with Wilson; the Indianapolis speech: *TC,* March 14, 1913.

2. Eddie Savoy: *NYT,* March 11, 1913. Bryan's statement on tenure: *ibid.,* March 6, 1913. Manton Wyvell: *TC,* April 25, 1913. John Osborne: *NYT,* March 23, 1913.

3. J. B. Moore: Katharine Crane, *Mr. Carr of State* (New York, 1960), 126 and 153. J. B. Moore to Bryan, March 13, 1913, WP, C.F. 212. Bryan to Wilson, March 15; Wilson to Moore, March 17, 1913, *ibid.* Wilbur Carr's statement is in Crane, 155.

4. Improving diplomatic administration: Bryan to Wilson, November 20, 1913, BPNA. Bryan and the press: Bryan to Wilson, July 30, 1913, WP. Arthur W. Dunn, *From Harrison to Harding* (New York and London, 1922), II, 226.

5. Grape juice incident: *Memoirs,* 350–51. *NYT,* April 25 and May 18, 1913. *TC,* May 9, 1913. Madame Pezet: *NYT,* December 22, 1913.

6. Bryan and *The Commoner:* Charles Bryan to Bryan, June 30, 1913; Bryan to Charles Bryan, July 5, 1913, BP, Box 29. Chautauqua lectures: Manton Wyvell to J. P. Tumulty, July 21, 1913, WP, C.F. 40. Congressional outcry: *NYT,* July 16 and 19, 1913. Bryan's defense: *TC,* August, 1913.

7. Treaty of Ghent anniversary speech: *NYT,* May 10, 1913.

8. Beginnings of Bryan's peace treaties: *TC,* February 17, 1905; "William Jennings Bryan: Biographical Notes, His Speeches, Letters and Other Writings," enlarged and edited by his daughter, Grace Dexter Bryan, 1941, 2, BP, Box 64. Bryan provides an extended explanation in his letter to Harry Walker, January 20, 1915, BP, Box 29. The essence of the treaties is explained in "Memorandum by Mr. Bryan," 1913, BP, Box 29. Bryan's presentation to the Washington diplomatic circle: "Statement by the Secretary of State, in presenting the President's Peace Plan," April, 1913, BP, Box 29. Bryan's progress: Bryan to Wilson, January 17, 1914, WP, C.F. 63; Wilson to Bryan, March 16, 1913, BPNA. Diplomats' reactions: *NYT,* August 24, 1913.

9. D. F. Houston concerning Bryan's mission: David F. Houston, *Eight Years with Wilson's Cabinet* (Garden City, 1926), I, 60. Illinois land law: Bryan to Wilson, April 26, 1913, WP, C.F. 272A. Bryan's remarks to the California legislature: Bryan to Wilson,

April 28 and 29, 1913, *ibid.* Passage of the Webb bill: *NYT,* May 5, 1913; Bryan to Governor Hiram Johnson, May 11, 1913, BPNA. Moving the naval vessels: Houston, I, 66–67.

10. "To work out their own destiny": Bryan to Wilson, October 28, 1913, BP, Box 29. Bryan's counsel on first State of the Union message: Bryan to Wilson, November 20, 1913, BPNA. Panama loan: Bryan to Wilson, April 7, 1913, BPNA. Indemnity for Colombia: Washington *Post* and *NYT,* June 18, 1914.

11. Charles A. Douglas to Bryan, June 11, 1913, SDF, enclosing draft of new Nicaraguan treaty. Canal option: Bryan to Wilson, May 24, 1913, BPNA; Bryan to Wilson, June 16, 1913, WP. European interest in a Nicaraguan canal: *NYT,* June 19, 1914. Bryan's estimate of bankers' profits: Bryan to Wilson, August 16, 1913, WP, C.F. 506. Bryan's "good Samaritan" plan: *ibid.*

12. J. M. Sullivan concerning the revolution in Santo Domingo against Bordas: Bryan to Sullivan, September 9, 1913, SDF, 839.00/912a; Sullivan to Secretary of State, October 10, 1913, *ibid.,* 839.00/919. Vick opens Bryan's eyes: Walker W. Vick to Bryan, April 14, 1913, BPNA.

13. Bryan urges "freedom" and "order" for Haiti: Bryan to American legation, Haiti, February 26, 1914, SDF, 838.00/855. Bryan opposes intervention: Bryan to Wilson, January 7, 1915, WP, C.F. 612. J. F. Fort mission: "Report of Commission," headed by Fort, March 13, 1915, *ibid.*

14. J. B. Moore is quoted in Arthur S. Link, *Wilson: The New Freedom* (Princeton, 1956), 349.

15. Bryan's "progressive policy" toward Mexico: Bryan to Wilson, May 27, 1913, BPNA. Test of "constitutional legitimacy": Howard F. Cline, *The United States and Mexico* (Cambridge, 1953), 142.

16. The text of Bryan's memorandum of July 19, 1913, to the President is in BP, Box 29. Huerta's reaction to the Lind mission: *NYT,* August 9, 1913. Lind's comments concerning Mexico's elections: Lind to Bryan, August 28, 1913, WP, C.F. 95. ". . . the end of our trouble": Bryan to Wilson, September 25, 1913, WP.

17. *NYT,* June 18, 1913.

18. O'Shaughnessy concerning Carden: Nelson O'Shaughnessy to Secretary of State, October 14, 1913, WP, C.F. 95. Safety of Mexican deputies: Nelson O'Shaughnessy to Secretary of State, October 10, 1913, *ibid.* Bryan urges extending the Monroe Doctrine to Mexico: Bryan to Wilson, October 28, 1913, BP, Box 29.

19. Villa rejoices: *NYT,* February 4, 1914. Representative Gillett: *ibid.* January 16, 1914.

20. The *Dolphin* episode: Bryan to Wilson, April 9, 1914, WP. Bryan softens Lansing's language: Draft in BPNA, April 20, 1914. Bryan vs. Garrison: Arthur S. Link, *Woodrow Wilson and the Progressive Era* (New York, 1963), 126.

21. Bryan's speech to the Brooklyn League: *NYT,* May 16, 1914. Mediation: Commissioners to Bryan, May 20, 1914. SDF; Bryan to Commissioners, May 21, 1914, *ibid.* Bryan prefers Villa to Carranza, Bryan to Wilson, August 2, 1914. Wilson rejects Bryan's plan for all-American republics' appeal: Bryan to Wilson, Wilson to Bryan, March 11, 1915, BPNA.

22. Bryan recommends no legislation: *TC,* May 9, 1913. His delight in Wilson's New Freedom program: *ibid.,* March 14, 1913. Income tax amendment: *NYT,* February 7, 1913. Seventeenth Amendment: *ibid.,* June 1, 1913; *TC,* June 6, 1913. Bryan's friends in the Senate: *NYT,* March 6, 1913. Champ Clark's statement against "self-styled" Democrats: *ibid.* Bryan-Clark luncheon: *ibid.,* April 19, 1913.

23. Bryan's conversation with Wilson on the Federal Reserve bill: summary "as dictated" by Bryan to Mrs. Bryan, July 6, 1913, BP, Box 29; *Memoirs,* 370–71. Wilson's view of the conversation is in Tumulty, 178. Tumulty visits Bryan: *ibid.,* 178–79. Bryan lobbies: C. W. Thompson, *Presidents I Have Known* (Indianapolis, 1929), 97. Bryan speaks for the Federal Reserve bill: *NYT,* October 18, 1913. Bryan's encounters with Houston: Houston, I, 84–86.

24. Mary's statement concerning Bryan's campaigning: *Memoirs,* 417. Those for whom Bryan campaigned: *TC,* September, 1914. J. E. Martine concerning Bryan: *NYT,* May 1, 1913. Wilson's opposition to the single-term plank: *ibid.,* October 13, 1914.
25. C. W. Bryan's estimate of the Hitchcock forces: C. W. Bryan to Bryan, April 4, 1914, BP, Box 29. J. T. Maher attacks the Bryans: *OWH,* May 29, 1914. Convention at Columbus: *ibid.,* July 29, 1914.
26. Bryan opposes Whedon: Bryan to Albert S. Burleson, January 24, 1914, Burleson Papers, Vol. 10. Wilson proposes Bryan-Hitchcock meeting: Wilson to Bryan, August 22, 1914, BP, Box 29. The Bryan-Hitchcock negotiation: summary of meeting, undated, Hitchcock Papers. Bryan urges Wilson to follow his own wishes: Bryan to Wilson, January 14, 1915, BP, State Department Letterbooks, II, Box 43.
27. Wilson deems Bryan loyal: Thompson, 97. Bryan rejoices that Wilson is President: *NYT,* May 9, 1913. Wilson's affection for Bryan: Wilson to Bryan, March 18, 1915, WP, Series II. Wilson revises Bryan's telegram: Wilson to Bryan, August 19, 1914, WP, C.F. 1645.
28. Bryan and Mary when war breaks out: *Memoirs,* 415. The State Department's immediate responses to war: Bryan to Wilson, undated; Wilson to Bryan, August 20, 1914, WP, C.F. 1645.
29. The Bolivian minister's proposal: Bryan to Wilson, August 17, 1914; Wilson to Bryan, August 18, 1914, BPNA. Prayer Day: Bryan to Wilson, September 4, 1914, *ibid.* Bryan's address: *TC,* October, 1914.
30. Bryan and the Speyer dinner: Washington *Post,* September 13, 1914; clipping in Lansing Papers, Vol. 4. Bryan to Oscar Straus, March 17, 1914. Sir Edward Grey to Sir Cecil Spring-Rice, September 9, 1914, Straus Papers, Box 13. The offer to mediate: Bryan to Wilson with the dispatch, August 4, 1914, WP; Grey's response: summary, September 8, 1914, Lansing Papers, Vol. 4. Ambassador Herrick concerning France: *ibid.,* September 10, 1914. Germany's reaction: Bryan to Wilson, September 16, 1914, WP. Bryan's sentiment toward the responses: Bryan to Wilson, August 28, 1914, BPNA.
31. Bernstorff's optimism: Link, *Woodrow Wilson and the Progressive Era,* (New York, 1954), 161. Bryan again urges mediation: Bryan to Wilson, December 1, 1914, BP, State Department Letterbooks, II, Box 43. House, Bryan and the peace mission to Europe: E. M. House, *Diary,* January 13, 1915; Arthur S. Link, *Wilson: The Struggle for Neutrality, 1914–1915* (Princeton, 1960), 201–16. Peace-minded ladies visit Bryan: Bryan to Wilson, December 22, 1914, WP, C.F. 1645XYZ.
32. Bryan and the Chinese loan: Bryan, *Memoirs,* 362. Wilson's announcement of withdrawal: Bryan to Wilson, June 4, 1913, WP. "Neighborly spirit for China and Japan": Bryan to Wilson, March 25, 1915, BPNA. Chinda's influence on Bryan: Reinsch to Secretary of State, April 14, 1915, SDF. Bryan and Wilson stiffen: Bryan to Chinda, April 27, 1915, BPNA. Bryan's personal message to Okuma: Bryan to Chinda, May 5, 1915, BPNA; Bryan to Chargé Wheeler, May 6, 1915. U.S.–Japan exchanges: U.S. State Department, *The Lansing Papers* (Washington, 1939), II, 422–23.
33. Wilson asks for neutrality: *NYT,* August 4 and 19, 1914. Bryan and Belgian relief: *ibid.,* December 24, 1914. Theodore Roosevelt's disgust: *ibid.,* January 1, 1915. Bryan and the Morgan loan to France: *Memoirs,* 375–76. Lansing: Robert Lansing to Senator James A. O'Gorman, March 8, 1913, Lansing Papers, Library of Congress. Bryan protests the loan to Wilson: Bryan to Wilson, August 10, 1914, BP, Box 29. Wilson's typewritten response is in BP, *ibid.* Bryan hails Wilson's stand: *TC,* September 1914.
34. Bryan on limiting purchases of arms: Bryan to Wilson, January 6, 1915, WP, Series II. Senator W. J. Stone's views: *NYT,* January 25, 1915.
35. "Disputes about merchandise": Bryan to Wilson, March 23, 1915, BPNA. The British blockade: Bryan to Wilson, February 15, 1915, BP, Box 29.

36. War zone and food blockade: *ibid.* Germany's willingness to compromise: *NYT,* March 1, 1915; British adamancy: *ibid.,* March 15, 1915.
37. W. H. Page and Grey: Edward Grey, *Twenty-Five Years* (New York, 1925), II, 107. Lansing's attitude: Robert Lansing, *War Memoirs of Robert Lansing* (Indianapolis, 1935), 112.
38. The administration was lacking in neutrality: *Memoirs,* 404.
39. The *Falaba: NYT,* March 31 and April 1, 1915. Bryan's counsel: Bryan to Wilson, April 2, 1915, BP, State Department Letterbooks, II, Box 43. Bryan to Wilson, April 6 and 7, 1915, *ibid.* Wilson's decision: Wilson to Bryan, April 22, 1915, BP, Box 29; *Papers Relating to the Foreign Relations of the United States, The Lansing Papers, 1914–1920* (Washington, 1939–1940), I, 378. Bryan's objection: Bryan to Wilson, April 23, 1915, BP, Box 29. Wilson is "not confident": Wilson to Bryan, April 28, 1915, *ibid.*
40. Bryan objects to Americans traveling in the war zone: Bryan to Wilson, May 1, 1915, BPNA. The *Lusitania* sinks: *NYT,* May 8, 1915. Remarks to Mary: Bryan, *Memoirs,* 421. Munitions on the *Lusitania;* Samuel F. Bemis, *A Diplomatic History of the United States* (3d ed., New York, 1950), 616. Bryan's and Wilson's silence and Wilson's Philadelphia speech: *NYT,* May 9 and 11, 1915. Bryan forwards editorial: Bryan to Wilson, May 9, 1915, BP, Box 29.
41. The first *Lusitania* note: Bryan to Wilson, May 12, 1915, BP.
42. Lansing concerning Bernstorff: "Private Memoranda," 17 and 19–20, Lansing Papers, Box II, 47–A–1. Lansing warns of Dumba: *ibid.,* 80. Bryan's encounter with Dumba: *NYT,* June 28, 1915.
43. Wilson at Arlington: *ibid.,* June 1, 1915. Bryan's address: *ibid.*
44. Wilson invites Bryan's counsel on the reply to the German note: Wilson to Bryan, June 2, 1915, BP, Box 29. Bryan proposes delay: Bryan to Wilson, June 2, 1915, BP, State Department Letterbooks, II, Box 43. Wilson rejects delay: Wilson to Bryan, June 2, 1915, *ibid.* Cabinet meeting: Houston, I, 132–39.
45. Bryan urges arbitration: Bryan to Wilson, June 3 and June 3 (evening), 1915, State Department Letterbooks, II, BP, Box 43. Cabinet meeting of June 4: Houston, I, 139. Lansing's view: Lansing to Bryan, June 7, 1915, SDF, 763.72/1863–1/2.
46. Bryan's agony: *Memoirs,* 420–21. Bryan tells the President he will resign: *ibid.,* 422–24. Weekend at Silver Spring: *ibid.,* 424. Wilson discloses Bryan's resignation: Houston, I, 140. McAdoo's interview with Bryan: William G. McAdoo, *Crowded Years* (Boston, 1931), 334–46. The second *Lusitania* note: *NYT,* June 11, 1915. Bryan again argues his views: Bryan to Wilson, June 7, 1915, BP, Box 29. Bryan's unavailing interview with Wilson: *Memoirs,* 424–25; House, *Diary,* June 24, 1915. Bryan's distress: "William Jennings Bryan: Biographical Notes," BP, Box 65. Bryan's letter of resignation: Bryan to Wilson, June 9, 1915, State Department Letterbooks, II, BP, Box 43. Bryan's last Cabinet meeting: Houston, I, 146–47.
47. Bryan's farewell to Wilson: Washington *Star,* June 9, 1915; *TC,* June, 1915; Henry Ashurst, *A Many Colored Toga* (Tucson, 1962), 39–40. Reactions to the resignation: *NYT,* June 9, 1915. Wilson's surprise: Wilson to Cleveland Dodge, June 14, 1915, WP, Series II. Chandler Anderson: "Diary," June 9, 1915, Chandler Anderson Papers, Box 21. Nebraska editorial: *OWH,* June 11, 1915.
48. Hadley Cantril, *The Psychology of Social Movements* (New York, 1941), 27, 47. Musafer Sherif and Hadley Cantril, *The Psychology of Ego Involvements* (New York, 1947; reprinted 1966), 5. Robert W. White, ed., *The Study of Lives* (New York, 1963), 252–53. Lester W. Milbrath, *Political Participation* (Chicago, 1965), 46.

Chapter 26. War and Peace

1. Houston's statement is in David F. Houston, *Eight Years with Wilson's Cabinet* (Garden City, 1926), I, 147. Frank P. Glass to Wilson, June 10, 1915, WP, Series II.

2. Bryan's statements: *NYT,* June 11, 12 and 13, 1915. Louis Post to Bryan, June 11, 1915, Louis Post Papers, Box 1. A summary of press comments is in *NYT,* June 12, 1915.

3. Bryan opposes preparedness: *NYT,* June 19, 1915. Carnegie Hall speech: *ibid.,* June 20, 1915.

4. *OWH,* June 30, 1915.

5. Homecoming in Lincoln: *ibid.; Memoirs,* 425. Fairview becomes only a political home: *NYT,* June 29, 1915.

6. Speeches and lectures: Charles McDaniel Rosser, *The Crusading Commoner* (Dallas, 1937), 245; *Memoirs,* 427.

7. Bryan's condemnations of war: *TC,* August, 1915; Los Angeles *Tribune,* July 16, 1915. How to keep peace: *TC, ibid.* Cardinal Gibbons: *NYT,* August 25, 1915.

8. Bryan opposes preparedness: *TC,* August, 1915. "The greed of the preparers:" Bryan to Claude Kitchin, October 14, 1915, Kitchin Papers. "The duelist standard": *ibid.; OWH,* October 16, 1915.

9. Kitchin is "sorely disappointed": Claude Kitchin to Bryan, October 20, 1915, Kitchin Papers. Bryan's statement opposing the President on preparedness: *NYT,* November 6, 1915.

10. Wilson as "peacemaker": "Private Memorandum," September, 1916, Robert Lansing Papers, Box III-47-A-1 Ac. 3518 Add 2. Bryan's plea to Lloyd George: *NYT,* December 16, 1916. Wilson requests a statement of peace terms: *ibid.,* December 21, 1916. Bryan hails the President's action: *ibid.,* December 22, 1916.

11. Bryan declines to join Ford's peace ship: Bryan to Henry Ford, November 30, 1915, Ford Peace Plan Collection. Bryan sees the ship off: *NYT,* December 6, 1915. Dissension afflicts the ship: *ibid.,* January 3, 1916.

12. Bryan and Billy Sunday as evangelists: *OWH,* September 17, 1915. Bryan's prohibition rally in Philadelphia: Philadelphia *Public Ledger,* March 17, 1915; *TC,* April, 1915.

13. Bryan and woman's suffrage: Wayne C. Williams, *William Jennings Bryan, A Study in Political Vindication* (New York, 1923), 99–100. His statements and attitudes: *TC,* December, 1915, and March, 1916.

14. Villa Serena: *Memoirs,* 434–35. Bryan's Bible class: *TC,* March, 1916.

15. Charles Bryan in Nebraska politics: *TC,* May, 1915; *OWH,* September 30, 1915. Bryan's candidacy for delegate at large: *TC,* April, 1916. Bryan's fight against Hitchcock: *NSJ,* April 11, 1916.

16. Bryan seeks to forestall Wilson's intervention: Bryan to Josephus Daniels, April 10, 1916, Daniels Papers. Wilson favors Bryan in patronage: *NSJ,* April 8, 1916. Bryan courts German-Americans: *ibid.,* April 12, 1916. Bryan's defeat: *OWH,* May 2, 1916; *TC,* May, 1916.

17. Bryan lacks "political expectations": *TC,* August, 1915. He discourages instructions for him: Bryan to Daniel O'Connell, March 17, 1916, BP, Box 31. Watching the suffragettes: *Memoirs,* 440. Bryan arrives at the St. Louis convention: *NYT,* June 12, 1916. From "scrapheap" to "riding pole": *ibid.,* June 16, 1916.

18. Bryan's activities: *Memoirs,* 440. He supports the President's planks: *NYT,* June 15, 1916. Glynn's address: *NYT,* June 15, 1916.

19. The Wilson managers seek to avoid a Bryan address: *Memoirs,* 440–41. The convention demands he speak: *NYT,* June 16, 1916. His address: *ibid.* His City Club speech: *ibid.*

20. Bryan campaigns for Wilson: *Memoirs,* 444. Interview with David Lawrence: New York *Evening Post,* October 17, 1916; *TC,* December, 1916. Bryan helps Congressmen and Senators: *Memoirs,* 444–45. Wilson's and Bryan's positions concerning Hitchcock: *OWH,* October 31, 1916.

21. Election night: *Memoirs,* 444. Bryan's telegram to Wilson and his response: *TC,* November, 1916. Bryan's analysis of the victory: *ibid.*

22. Other analyses of Wilson's victory: *NSJ*, November 13, 1916; *TC*, November, 1916. C. W. Bryan's statement: C. W. Bryan to Bryan, November 22, 1916, BP, Box 31.

23. Bryan praises Wilson's offer of mediation: *TC*, January, 1917. Bryan urges a House resolution: Bryan to Claude Kitchin, January 2, 1917. Senator Ashurst concerning Bryan: Ashurst, 54. La Follette and Bryan consult: Belle Case La Follette and Fola La Follette, *Robert M. La Follette* (New York, 1953), I, 594. Bryan's appeal for peace: *NYT*, February 4 and 7, 1917. He meets with Bernstorff: *ibid.*, February 6, 1917. Bryan is discouraged: La Follette, 594.

24. Wilson asks for national unity: *NYT*, March 6, 1917. Theodore Roosevelt rejects debate with Bryan: *ibid.*, March 5, 1917. Alton Parker's telegram is in *ibid.*, March 6, 1917. Bryan's appeal to Congress demand for a referendum: *ibid.*, March 30, 1917. Senator James Vardaman's statement is in his letter to Bryan, April 2, 1917, BP, Box 31.

25. Bryan urges support for the President: *NYT*, April 13, 1917; offers his services: Bryan to Josephus Daniels, April 10, 1917, Daniels Papers, Box 37. Wilson acknowledges the offer: Wilson to Bryan, April 9, 1917, BP, Box 31. "Assistant chaplain": Bryan to Secretary of War Newton Baker, April 28, 1917, *ibid.* Bryan's home-front activities: William G. McAdoo to Bryan, June 2, 1917, BP, Box 31; *TC*, April, 1917; *OWH*, October 8, 1917. Bryan supports Kitchin's tax proposals: *NYT*, July 30, 1917; *TC*, May, 1917.

26. Bryan urges action on the prohibition amendment: Bryan to Claude Kitchin, April 25, 1917, Kitchin Papers. Bryan attacks the brewers: *TC*, January, 1917.

27. Madison, Wisconsin, speech: *TC*, February, 1917. Tiff with Gompers: *NYT*, December 19, 1917. Congress approves prohibition: *ibid.*

28. President of the National Dry Federation: *ibid.*, March, 1918. Bryan's nonpartisanship on prohibition: *ibid.*, September, 1918. New York *Sun's* criticism: New York *Sun*, December 17, 1917; *TC*, January, 1918.

29. New York speech for woman's suffrage: New York *World*, October 17, 1917; *TC*, November, 1917. Democratic Party should lead: *NYT*, February 3, 1917.

30. *TC*, January, 1918.

31. Bryan lectures: *Lyceum Magazine* (July, 1916), 22; *TC*, October, 1916. The observer is quoted in *Memoirs*, 286–87. Mary concerning Bryan diet: Mary Bryan to Bryan, March 12, 1916, BP, Box 31. The audience waits for Bryan: *Memoirs*, 285.

32. Birthday celebration: *OWH*, March 20, 1918. Bryan's sudden interest in prohibition: *ibid.*, April 1, 1918. Bryan's address to the state Democratic convention: *TC*, August, 1918; *NSJ*, August 2, 1918.

33. Bryan approves Wilson's Fourteen Points: Bryan to Claude Kitchin, October 14, 1918, Kitchin Papers; aspires to join U.S. peace commission: Bryan to Jonathan Daniels, October 14, 1918, Daniels Papers, Box 37. Bryan's statement that he is preparing himself: Bryan to Daniels, January 11, 1918, *ibid.* Bryan's position on peace issues: *TC*, February and July, 1919.

34. Bryan's approval of the League to Charley: Bryan to C. W. Bryan, March 2, 1919, BP, Box 32. Bryan hails League in Washington and offers proposals: *NYT*, March 12, 1919; *TC*, March, 1919.

35. Bryan predicts Senate approval of the peace treaty: Detroit *Free Press*, April 7, 1919; *TC*, April, 1919. Senator Lodge's mind: Thomas A. Bailey, *The American Pageant* (3d ed., Boston, 1966), II, 750.

36. Bryan is to see Senator Kenyon: Bryan to C. W. Bryan, March 2, 1919, BP, Box 32. Bryan's Senatorial supporters defend the League: *NYT*, July 15 and August 31, 1919. Bryan's speeches in Washington: Washington *Herald*, September 25, 1919; *TC*, October and August, 1919. Senator Hiram Johnson attacks the League: Thomas A. Bailey, *A Diplomatic History of the United States* (4th ed., New York, 1950), 668. Senator Brandegee's observation after visiting the President: *ibid.*, 660.

37. Senator Hitchcock asks Bryan to interneve with Wilson: Gilbert Hitchcock to Bryan,

November 30, 1919, BP, Box 32. Bryan works through his old Senate allies: *NYT,* January 7, 1920.

38. Bryan's compromises of Lodge's reservations; hostility to Bryan's plan: *ibid.* Keep the League "out of the campaign": *ibid.,* May 11, 1920. A petition urges compromise: *OWH,* April 15, 1920. Lansing; Arthur Walworth, *Woodrow Wilson* (2d ed., Boston, 1965), Book II, 348.

39. Prohibition is adopted: *NYT,* January 17, 1919. Lansing: Walworth, 380. Bryan's speech: *TC,* March, 1919. Bryan's compensation for prohibition speeches: Will Atkinson to Bryan, March 3, 1919, BP, Box 32; Bryan to C. W. Bryan, March 17, 1919, OP; *Memoirs,* 294. Prohibition in Omaha: *OWH,* April 27, 1918. Bryan celebrates the advent of prohibition: Wayne C. Williams, *William Jennings Bryan: A Study in Political Vindication* (New York, 1923), 108–9; *Memoirs,* 472–73.

40. Woman suffrage amendment: Mary Gray Peck, *Carrie Chapman Catt* (New York, 1944), 338–39. Wilson is quoted in *NYT,* August 27, 1920; and Cardinal Gibbons, *ibid.,* August 25, 1920. Bryan attacks the profiteers: *TC,* January, 1919. His postwar proposals: *ibid.,* November, 1919. Labor-management disputes: *NYT,* June 2, 1920. National bulletin: *TC,* July, 1920.

41. Mary's illness: Bryan to James Brown Scott, January 23, 1919. Bryan's optimism: Bryan to Josephus Daniels, September 29, 1919, Daniels Papers, Box 37.

42. Sixtieth birthday party: *NSJ,* March 20, 1920. Bryan's appearance: J. C. Long, *The Great Commoner* (New York, 1928), 352. Bryan's optimism: *NSJ, op. cit.* March 20, 1920. His vision of Miami: *TC,* December, 1920; Bryan to Josephus Daniels, December 29, 1920, Daniels Papers, Box 37.

43. Jackson Day dinner: *NYT,* January 9, 1920. Lansing's observations are contained in "Private Memoranda," January 10, 1920, Vol. VI, Box III–47–A–1. Bryan denies being a Presidential candidate: *NYT, op. cit.* Bryan disapproves of Governor Edwards: interview, Asheville, North Carolina, *Citizen,* January 30, 1920. Bryan criticizes Herbert Hoover: *TC, op. cit.*

44. Bryan identifies James Cox as a "wet" candidate: *TC,* June, 1920. Bryan says he is not a candidate: *TC,* February, 1920.

45. Bryan criticizes Gilbert Hitchcock: *NSJ* and *NYT,* March 10, 1920.

46. Hitchcock counterattacks Bryan: *OWH,* April 13, 1920; *NSJ,* April 17, 1920.

47. The wets fear Bryan's presence at the national Democratic convention: *NSJ,* April 20, 1920. WCTU helps Bryan's campaign: *ibid.* Bryan invites bipartisan support: *NSJ,* March 27, 1920. He warns women of intimidation: *NSJ,* April 19, 1920.

48. *OWH,* April 22, 1920.

49. Bryan seeks a Presidential candidate: *OWH,* June 30, 1920. The Wilson forces control the convention: *NYT,* June 30, 1920. Homer Cummings' address: *ibid.,* June 19, 1920; Bryan's reaction: *TC,* July, 1920. Bryan plans to fight for a dry plank: *NYT,* July 1, 1920. A lonely Bryan quotes the Bible: *ibid.* No "enemy of Woodrow Wilson": *NYT,* July 2, 1920.

50. *NYT, ibid.*

51. *Ibid.*

52. Bryan declines to support McAdoo: *TC,* July 1920. "My heart is in the grave . . .": *NYT,* July 6 and 7, 1920.

53. Bryan declines nomination by the Prohibition Party: Bryan to C. W. Bryan, July 22, 1920, printed in *TC,* August, 1920. Bryan endorses Cox: *NYT,* August 14, 1920; but declines to campaign for him: Bryan to Pat Harrison, undated, BP, Box 33. Cox courts Bryan: *NYT,* September 28, 1920.

54. Bryan and the Congressional elections: *TC,* August, 1920. Bryan to Wayne B. Wheeler, undated, BP, Box 33. Bryan votes for Cox: *TC,* November, 1920; but sulks "in his tent": H. J. Bailey to Bryan, November 6, 1920, BP, Box 33.

55. Bryan reviews the election and the future: *NYT,* November 5, 1920. Hitchcock and Kitchin are quoted in *ibid.,* November 10, 1920. H. D. Flood belittles Bryan: *ibid.,*

November 12, 1920. Bryan visualizes the future Democratic Party as progressive: *ibid.*, November 5, 1920.

Chapter 27. Normalcy

1. Bryan's observations in his sixtieth year: *TC*, April, 1921. Election to the Optimists Club: *ibid.*, May, 1921. Bryan becomes a citizen of Florida: Press release, May 31, 1921, BP, Box 34. The Washington *Star* is quoted in *TC*, June, 1921. Bryan's Bible class: *ibid.*, March and May, 1921; Miami *Herald*, April 4, 1921. Newspaper syndication of the Bible class: *TC*, November, 1921; the Republic Syndicate to Bryan, October 9, 1922, BP, Box 36.
2. Bryan's health: Mary to Bryan, March 12 and October 1, 1916, BP, Box 31. His voice: *NYT*, November 19, 1969. Bryan to Alben Barkley, June 13, 1922, Barkley Papers. Bryan hails radio: *NYT*, September 3, 1922. Bryan as a Washington lawyer: *ibid.*, May 26, 1921; Charles O. Douglas to Bryan, April 19, 1921, BP, Box 34. Attentions to Mary: Bryan to Dan Bride, January 14, 1922, BP, Box 35; Bryan to Frank Harris, April 13, 1922, *ibid.* Ruth concerning Bryan's political durability: *TC*, August, 1921.
3. Bryan visits Harding at Marion: *NYT*, December 18, 1920. They exchange visits at Miami: *TC*, February, 1921. Bryan approves of Harding's inaugural address: *ibid.*, March, 1921. Bryan's bonds with Harding: *ibid.*, February, 1921. Senator W. E. Borah opposes the League: *NYT*, December 23, 1920; *TC*, January, 1921.
4. Bryan urges disarmament: *NYT*, May 20, 1921. Harding's address at Hoboken: *TC*, June, 1921. Bryan's New York speech: *NYT*, July 10, 1921. Florence King Harding to Mary Bryan, July 28, 1921, BP, Box 34. Bryan and the Washington Naval Conference: *NYT*, November 2 and 26, 1921.
5. Bryan asks favoritism for the farmer: *TC*, May, 1921. He assails "rule of the rich": *ibid.*, November, 1922 and September, 1921.
6. The nineties all over again: Mark Sullivan to Bryan, January 25, 1921, BP, Box 33. "The farmer's power": *NYT*, January 24, 1922.
7. "The greatest moral reform": *NYT*, March 21, 1922. Bryan predicts there will be no more saloons: *ibid.* His observations on enforcement: *ibid.*, April 20, 1921.
8. Bryan's ideas for reorganizing the Democratic Party: *NYT*, February 17, 1921. C. W. Bryan calls for "purge": *ibid.*, January 21 and February 17, 1921. Moves against J. M. Cox: *TC*, February, 1921. Bryan prefers policies to Presidential candidates: *NYT*, February 17, 1921. His neutrality between factions: Bryan to Louis Post, February 28, 1921, Post Papers, Box 1. The liquor question as the test of party membership: *TC*, February, 1921. Prohibition and progressivism: Lawrence Levine, *Defender of the Faith* (New York, 1965), 104. Curbing market gambling: Senator Arthur Capper to Bryan, November 30, 1920, BP, Box 33. Minimum wage law: *TC*, November, 1922. Department of education: Senator William Kenyon to Bryan, December 10, 1920, BP, Box 33. Parks: *TC*, January, 1921. Federal Reserve Board: *ibid.*, October, 1921. Profits and speculation: *NYT*, February 17, 1921.
9. A paramount issue: *TC*, March, 1921.
10. Stirrings of a Bryan candidacy: *TC*, May, 1921. May M. Jennings to Bryan, December 15, 1921, BP, Box 34. Charles E. Jones to Bryan, December 30, 1921, *ibid.* Florida newspapers are quoted in *TC*, February, 1922; an undated clipping of the Jacksonville *Observer* is in the Bryan Papers, Box 34. Senator Park Trammell attacks Bryan: New York *World*, February 5, 1922. Bryan's statement that he is weighing his candidacy: *TC*, February, 1922. Bryan decides not to be a candidate: *ibid.*, May, 1922. He explains why to friends: Bryan to Frank Harris, April 13, 1922, BP, Box 35.
11. C. W. Bryan's observation concerning Nebraska's Progressive Party appears in his letter to Bryan of January 21, 1922, BP, Box 35. Charley deals with the Hitchcock men: C. W. Bryan to Bryan, January 21, 1922, BP, Box 35. Bryan appeals for

women's votes: *TC,* November, 1922. Bryan extols Hitchcock: *ibid.,* October, 1922. Hitchcock thanks Bryan in his letter of August 21, 1922, BP, Box 35. Bryan laments Hitchcock's defeat: *TC,* December, 1922.
12. Automobile accident: *NYT,* October 18, 1922. national Democratic chairman thanks Bryan: Cordell Hull to Bryan, November 11, 1922, BP, Box 36. Bryan urges progressive measures: *TC,* December, 1922.
13. William Jennings Bryan, *The Prince of Peace* (New York, 1909), 5.
14. Fairview is given to the Presbyterian Church: Bryan to "My dear Brother Master," November 10, 1921, BP, Box 34. Committee on Christian Life and Work: H. C. Swearingen to Bryan, June 13, 1921, *ibid.* Efforts to elect Bryan moderator: *NYT,* April 24 and May 23, 1921. Observations on Darwinism: *The Prince of Peace,* 13–15; Edward A. Ross, *Seventy Years of It* (New York, 1936), 88. Bryan's address to the World Brotherhood Congress: *TC,* November, 1920.
15. Bryan's address to the Nebraska Constitutional Convention: *ibid.,* February, 1920. Reverend A. W. Stalker to Bryan, November 15, 1920, BP, Box 33. "The Menace of Darwinism": *TC,* June, 1921. "Back to God": *ibid.,* August, 1921.
16. Mary's statement concerning Bryan's interest in youth is in *Memoirs,* 294. Bryan's observations regarding his crisis with Darwinism in his college years: *The Prince of Peace,* 11–12. Leuba's findings are contained in James H. Leuba, *The Belief in God and Immortality* (Boston, 1916), Chapters VII–IX. Information coming to Bryan from the campuses: *TC,* June, 1921; *NYT,* July 10, 1921.
17. E. R. Seligman's criticism of Bryan is in *NYT,* March 2, 1922; and E. G. Conklin's in *ibid.,* April 5, 1922. Bryan addresses the Kentucky legislature: *TC,* February, 1922. He counsels against penalties: *ibid.,* May, 1922. Bryan distinguishes between education and religion: Bryan to Martha Hughes, February 7, 1923, BP, Box 36. "Love makes money-grabbing contemptible": William Jennings Bryan, *In His Image* (New York, 1922), 232–34.
18. Bryan's perception of the interlocking of politics and religion: *ibid.,* 30. United States' resources for world peace: *ibid.,* 237–38. Bryan scolds the United States "for the calamity that may befall the world": *TC,* February, 1923. Bryan supports Harding on the World Court: *NYT,* February 29, 1923. "Another Dred Scott decision": *TC,* April, 1923. War veterans' bonus: Bryan to Cordell Hull, December 18, 1923, BP, Box 38. Bryan attacks Andrew Mellon's tax policies: *NYT,* December 11, 1923.
19. Congressman Upshaw's abstinence pledge: *TC,* January, 1923. Bryan addresses state legislatures: *NYT,* July 11, 1923. He clashes with Alfred E. Smith: *ibid.,* June 10, 1923. Bryan mourns Harding: *ibid.,* August 4, 1923; "tribute to President Harding," 1923, BP, Box 38.
20. *The Commoner*'s rededication: *TC,* January, 1923. Its farewell: *ibid.,* April, 1923. Bryan is distressed and oversees *The Commoner*'s dismantling: Bryan to C. W. Bryan, April 19, 1923, OP.
21. Mary takes "more interest": Bryan to C. W. Bryan, December 18, 1923, OP. "I owe it to her . . .": Bryan to Reverend J. Frank Norris, May 1, 1923, BP, Box 37. Consulting a faith healer: New York *World,* April 28, 1924; Bryan to Reverend H. C. Swearington, March 22, 1923, BP, Box 37. Bryan's sorrow for Mary: Clipping, Sacramento *Bee,* undated, OP. Mary counsels Bryan on his health: Mary to Bryan, March 12 and October 1, 1916, BP, Box 31. Reverend Percival H. Barker to Bryan, March 5, 1923, BP, Box 37. Samuel Untermyer to Bryan, February 24, 1924, BP, Box 39.
22. Lawrence Levine, *Defender of the Faith* (New York, 1965), 275.
23. On his candidacy for Presbyterian moderator: *NYT,* May 17, 1923. Wishart is elected and declines to appoint Bryan as vice-moderator: *ibid.,* May 18, 1923. Debate on Bryan's resolution: *ibid.,* May 23, 1923. His statement concerning the New York press: *ibid.,* May 21,1923.
24. The Fosdick question: *ibid.,* May 24 and 28, 1923. Bryan's differences with Fosdick:

William Jennings Bryan, *Seven Questions in Dispute* (New York, 1924), *passim;* Harry Emerson Fosdick and Sherwood Eddy, *Science and Religion: Evolution and the Bible* (New York, 1924). Bryan's address to the West Virginia legislature: *NYT,* April 14, 1923.

25. "my power . . . has waned": Bryan to Reverend John A. Marquis, May 4, 1923, BP, Box 37. Bryan identifies prohibition's enforcement with progressivism: *NYT,* January 19, 1923. His observation concerning Coolidge: Bryan to C. W. Bryan, December 18, 1923, OP. Bryan's progressive platform: *NYT,* July 8, 1923. He attacks Andrew Mellon: *ibid.,* May 11, 1924. Underwood and Smith: Congressman George Huddleston to Bryan, March 23, 1923, BP, Box 37. The Charles M. Lewis debate: *NYT,* February 24, 1924. McAdoo and Neff: Rosser, 280–81; W. G. McAdoo to C. W. Bryan, January 18, 1924, BP, Box 39. Bryan's observations concerning John W. Davis, typescript, February 11, 1924, BP, Box 39.

26. Bryan supports Pat Neff's candidacy: Bryan to Mr. Cherrington, Anti-Saloon League, August 16, 1923, BP, Box 37. Bryan endorses A. A. Murphree, *NYT* and editorial, Miami *Herald,* January 14, 1924; Bryan's press statement: typescript, January 14, 1924; Bryan's further statement, February 11, 1924, BP, Box 39. Charles Bryan's observations on Bryan's strength as a candidate: C. W. Bryan to Bryan, May 1, 1924, BP, Box 39. Bryan declines candidacy: Bryan to John J. Lentz, March 15, 1924, BP, Box 39. Teapot Dome and a Bryan candidacy: James A. Edgerton to Bryan, February 26, 1924, *ibid.* Bryan prefers "younger man": Bryan to Arthur Brisbane, March 15, 1924, *ibid.* He is available in a "remote contingency": Bryan to C. W. Bryan, March 3, 1924, *ibid.*

27. A heavy speaking schedule: Bryan to C. W. Bryan, *ibid.* Mary expects Bryan's nomination: *NYT,* June 20, 1924. John Temple Graves' formula: Graves to Bryan, June 18, 1924, BP, Box 39. Candidacy for delegate at large: Bryan to Senator Duncan U. Fletcher, February 18, 1924; Bryan to Senator Park Trammell, February 23, 1924, BP, Box 39. Mary is delighted: *Memoirs,* 474. Bryan's victory: *NYT,* June 5, 1924.

28. Convention eve dinner: Hotel Commodore, New York: *ibid.,* June 24, 1924. Housing of the Nebraska and Florida delegations: Bryan to C. W. Bryan, May 10, 1924, OP. Bryan planks: *NYT,* June 26, 1924. Debate on prohibition: *ibid.,* June 29, 1924. Struggle on the Resolutions Committee over the Ku Klux Klan plank: *ibid.,* June 30, 1924: "The Democratic National Convention," typescript edited by Bryan regarding the 1924 convention, BP, Box 50. Arthur Mullen's comment appears in his *Western Democrat* (New York, 1940), 243–44. Bryan and the floor debate on the Klan plank: "The Democratic National Convention," *ibid.; NYT,* July 1, 1924.

29. A. W. Gilchrist believes Bryan seeks the nomination: *ibid.,* June 22, 1924. Bryan rejects J. W. Davis: New York *American* and *NYT,* July 2, 1924. Bryan's speech supporting McAdoo and other candidates: *NYT,* July 3, 1924; Henry Ashurst, *A Many Colored Toga* (Tucson, 1962), 219; Rosser, 297; Claude Bowers, *My Life* (New York, 1962), 121. Doheny: Francis Russell, *The Shadow of Blooming Grove: Warren G. Harding and His Times* (New York, 1968), 615–16.

30. Bryan returns to the convention floor: *NYT,* July 10, 1924. Manhattan Club meeting concerning the Vice Presidency: *ibid.* Bryan's disappointment that Charles was Davis' running mate: Handcraft concerning the 1924 campaign, by Grace Bryan, BP, Box 65. Bryan pledges support to the ticket: *NYT,* July 11, 1924.

31. Bryan's part in the 1924 campaign: *NYT,* October 6 and 26, 1924.

32. La Follette fails to take over Western progressivism: C. W. Bryan to Bryan, December 5, 1924, BP, Box 39. Bryan's observations on the defeat: Miami *Herald* and *NYT,* November 7, 1924; statement to the press, December 4, 1924, BP, Box 39.

Chapter 28. Ordeal at Dayton

1. Statement by Bryan concerning Woodlock's appointment: February 17, 1925, BP, Box 39. Watching the eclipse: Washington *Post* and *NYT,* January 25, 1925. Bryan

weighs a 1926 race for the U.S. Senate: Bryan to the editor, Sanford, Florida, *Herald,* March 11, 1925, BP, Box 39; Bryan to Frank Harris, March 23, 1925, *ibid.*

2. Bryan's diabetes and diet: John A. Wesener, MD, to Bryan, January 23, and February 17, 1925, BP, Box 39. Birthday celebration and Mary's and Bryan's exchange of sentiments: March 19, 1925, BP, Box 41. James G. Bailey, "Mr. Bryan's Last Birthday Party," *Presbyterian Magazine* (March, 1927), 160.

3. Bryan prepares his memoirs: Mary Bryan to Dr. A. W. Anthony, February 5, 1926, Anthony Collection; *NYT,* June 4, 1925. Vice-moderator: *NYT,* May 23, 1924. Bryan as future Presbyterian moderator: Clarence E. MaCartney to Bryan, April 1, 1925, BP, Box 39. Bryan is rebuffed: *NYT,* May 22, 1925.

4. The lack of spirituality in education; even Charles is culpable: *NYT,* May 24, 1925. Bryan at Brown and Harvard: Bryan to Mary, undated, BP, Box 41; Bryan to C. L. Ficklin, undated, *ibid.* Bryan's comments concerning collective right vs. individual right: Bryan to Ficklin, *ibid.* Majority rule should determine religious education: Ray Ginger, *Six Days or Forever* (Boston, 1958), 36.

5. John A. Shelton to Bryan, February 5, 1925, BP, Box 41. Bryan opposes a penalty in the Tennessee law: Bryan to Shelton, February 9, 1925, *ibid.* Bryan congratulates Peay: Bryan to Governor Austin Peay, undated, BP, Box 47.

6. The American Civil Liberties Union seeks a test case: Ginger, 19; Lawrence W. Levine, *Defender of the Faith* (New York, 1965), 328. Beginnings of the Scopes case: Ginger, 19–21; L. Sprague de Camp, *The Great Monkey Trial* (Garden City, 1968), 13–14.

7. Bryan is invited to join the case: Sue K. Hicks to Bryan, May 14 and 25, 1925, BP, Box 47. He agrees to serve: *NYT,* May 13, 1925. Fundamentalists rejoice: L. M. Aldridge to Bryan, May 13, 1925, BP, Box 39. Church resolutions: Reverend A. J. Meiklejohn to Bryan, May 24, 1925, BP, Box 39. The WCTU approves: Mary Balch to Bryan, May 26, 1925, BP, Box 39. Reverend J. Frank Norris to Bryan, June 3, 1925, BP, Box 47.

8. Clarence Darrow enters the case: *NYT* and New York *World,* May 17, 1925; De Camp, 75–78; Ginger, 45–46. Dudley Field Malone: Ginger, 46. Arthur Garfield Hayes: De Camp, 92. Fathers and sons: Robert E. Lane, "Fathers and Sons: Foundations of Political Belief," *American Sociological Review,* 25 (August, 1959), 502–11. Darrow's statements are from his *The Story of My Life,* 14.

9. Bryan's fellow counsel: De Camp, 124, 156. Bryan corrals witnesses: Louis T. More, author of *The Dogma of Evolution,* to Bryan, July 7, 1925; BP, Box 47; De Camp, 158. George McReady Price's views are from his *A History of Some Scientific Blunders* (New York, 1930), 88–90. C. S. Thomas to Bryan, July 1, 1925, BP, Box 47. Bryan to Thomas, July 1, 1925, *ibid.*

10. S. K. Hicks to Bryan, June 12, 1925, BP, Box 47. Samuel Untermyer to Bryan, June 25, 1925, *ibid.* Bryan is optimistic: Bryan to Ed Howe, June 30, 1925, *ibid.*

11. The Dayton scene: De Camp, 120, 146–47, 159, 162; *NYT,* July 10, 1925; New York *Post,* June 11, 1925.

12. Bryan comes to Dayton: Progressive Club speech: *NYT,* July 8, 1925. His speech at Morgan Springs: *ibid.,* July 10, 1925.

13. The trial begins (July 10): De Camp, 83–84, 122; "Bulletin No. 1," July 11, 1925, BP, Box 47; *NYT,* July 11, 1925. Bryan's "Sunday school" remarks (July 12): *NYT* and New York *Herald Tribune,* July 13, 1925. Putting "God into the Constitution": *ibid.* "Interview" with the press, July 12, 1925, BP, Box 47.

14. The trial, July 13: *NYT,* New York *Herald Tribune,* Chattanooga *Times,* July 14, 1925; De Camp, 249. July 14–15: *NYT,* New York *Herald Tribune,* Chattanooga *Times,* July 15–16, 1925; De Camp, 249–63. *Record of the Proceedings of the State of Tennessee v. John Thomas Scopes,* Circuit Court, Rhea County, beginning July 10, 1925, Dayton, Tennessee, 120–199.

15. July 16: *NYT,* New York *Herald Tribune,* Chattanooga *Times,* July 17, 1925; De

Camp, 317–43; Leslie H. Allen, *Byran and Darrow at Dayton* (New York, 1925), 63 ff. Mary's assessment of Bryan's performance is in her letter to Grace of July 20, 1925, BP, Box 47. *Record,* 267–359.

16. July 17: *NYT,* New York *Herald Tribune,* Chattanooga *Times,* July 18, 1925; De Camp, 353–65; *NYT,* New York *Herald Tribune,* July 19 and 20, 1925. *Record,* 360–547.

17. July 20: *NYT,* New York *Herald Tribune,* Chattanooga *Times,* July 21, 1925; Ginger, 149 ff.; De Camp, 381–414; *Record,* 548–777; H. L. Mencken, "The Theatrical Performance at Dayton," *Outlook* (July 22, 1925), 421.

18. *Ibid.* Levine, 349–50.

19. Fundamentalists' disappointment in Bryan: De Camp, 410. July 21: *NYT,* New York *Herald Tribune,* Chattanooga *Times,* July 22, 1925; De Camp, 415–44.

20. Darrow's plan: De Camp, 416–17. The court begins: Raulston's, Darrow's, Stewart's, and Bryan's statements: *Record,* 791–800. Sentence is passed, Bryan speaks, and the court adjourns: *ibid.,* 818, 821–30; *NYT,* New York *Herald Tribune,* Chattanooga *Times,* and Louisville *Herald,* July 22, 1925; Ginger, 178–79.

21. Bryan's statement to the press on the case and Darrow's reply: De Camp, 428–29; *NYT* and New York *Herald Tribune, ibid.* Raymond Fosdick's comment: Fosdick to Roger Baldwin, October 19, 1925, Vol. 274, ACLU archives, 331; De Camp, 445. For evaluations of the trial, see Henry Steele Commager, *The American Mind* (New Haven, 1950), 182–84; Levine, 352.

22. George F. Washburn to Bryan, July 13, 1925, BP, Box 47. Visit to the site of a Bryan university: De Camp, 438; *Memoirs,* 484. Mary warns of dangers to religious liberty: *ibid.,* 485–86. Journey to Winchester and speeches: *NYT* and New York *Herald Tribune,* July 27, 1925.

23. Bryan's activities on July 26; his favorable medical report: *Memoirs,* 487. Mary discovers his death: *ibid.,* 487–88.

24. Darrow's comment on the cause of Bryan's death: De Camp, 440. Dr. Kelly's explanation: Kelly to Grace Bryan Hargraves, June 25, 1931, BP, Box 65. Mourning and a memorial service at Dayton: *NYT,* July 29, 1925. Mary's remarks to the Reverend C. R. Jones: "Correspondence of Grace Bryan Hargraves," undated, BP, Box 64. Mary's observations concerning the journey to Washington: *Memoirs,* 488–89. The journey is described in *ibid.,* 488–90; *NYT,* July 30 and 31, 1925.

25. President Coolidge's tribute: Washington *Post* and *NYT,* July 27, 1925. Darrow's comment: *ibid.* Church service and burial: *Memoirs,* 490–92; Washington *Post* and *NYT,* August 1, 1925. Mary's comment concerning Bryan's soul is in Levine, 357.

Sources

I. *Studies of Bryan*

Bryan is best represented in works of the last decade. The most comprehensive study is the three-volume biography by Paolo E. Coletta: *William Jennings Bryan,* Vol. I: *Political Evangelist, 1860–1908;* Vol. II: *Progressive Politician and Moral Statesman, 1909–1915;* Vol. III: *Political Puritan, 1915–1925* (Lincoln, University of Nebraska Press, 1964–1970). Coletta has also written many useful articles, some of which are referred to in the Notes. Most effective treatments are provided in Paul W. Glad, *The Trumpet Soundeth*: *William Jennings Bryan and His Democracy, 1896–1912* (Lincoln, University of Nebraska Press, 1960), and Lawrence W. Levine, *Defender of the Faith*: *William Jennings Bryan*: *The Last Decade, 1915–1925* (New York, Oxford University Press, 1965).

Earlier studies are either adulatory or hostile. Paxton Hibben, *The Peerless Leader: William Jennings Bryan* (New York, Farrar and Rinehart, 1929), completed after Hibben's death by C. Hartley Grattan, is perceptive but severe. Even more harsh is M. R. Werner, *Bryan* (New York, Harcourt, Brace and Co., 1929). J. C. Long, *Bryan, the Great Commoner* (New York, D. Appleton & Co., 1928) is useful, although oversympathetic. Altogether uncritical are Genevieve F. and John D. Herrick, *The Life of William Jennings Bryan* (Chicago, Grover C. Buxton, 1925), and Wayne C. Williams, *William Jennings Bryan* (New York, G. P. Putnam's Sons, 1936). Valuable for its personal recollections, the uncritical work of a longtime friend, is Charles McDaniel Rosser, *The Crusading Commoner: A Close-up of William Jennings Bryan and His Times* (Dallas, Mathis, Van Nort & Co., 1937).

Insightful essays concerning Bryan are found in Walter Lippmann, *Men of Destiny* (New York, The Macmillan Co., 1927); Merle E. Curti, *Bryan and World Peace* (Northampton, Massachusetts, Smith College Studies in History, Vol. XVI, Nos. 3–4, April–July, 1931), 111–258; Charles E. Merriam, *Four American Party Leaders* (New York, The Macmillan Co., 1926); William Allen White, *Masks in a Pageant* (New York, The Macmillan Co., 1939); and Richard Hofstadter, *The American Political Tradition* (New York, Vintage Book Edition, 1954).

II. *Manuscript Sources*

Bryan papers are widely scattered. The following manuscript collections have been consulted:

Bryan Collections
William Jennings Bryan Papers, Illinois State Historical Society
————, Library of Congress
————, National Archives
————, Nebraska State Historical Society
————, Occidental College Library
Other Collections Containing Bryan Papers or Papers Relating to Bryan

A–F

John Peter Altgeld Collection, Illinois State Historical Society
American Civil Liberties Union, Scrapbooks, Princeton University Library
Chandler P. Anderson Papers, Library of Congress
A. W. Anthony Collection, New York Public Library
Alben Barkley Papers, University of Kentucky Library
Bierce Papers, Stanford University Libraries
George S. Bixby Papers, New York State Library, Albany
Reuben Bowen Papers, Duke University Library
Waldo R. Brown Collection, Illinois State Historical Society
Albert Sidney Burleson Papers, Library of Congress
Marion Butler Papers, University of North Carolina Library
William Dallas Bynum Papers, Library of Congress
Joseph G. Cannon Papers, Illinois State Historical Society
Andrew Carnegie Papers, Library of Congress
Isaac Carrington Papers, Duke University Library
Thomas H. Carter Papers, Library of Congress
Grover Cleveland Papers, Library of Congress
John Clopton Papers, Duke University Library
Bourke Cockran Papers, New York Public Library
William Croffut Papers, Library of Congress
A. B. Cummins Papers, Iowa State Department of History and Archives
John W. Daniel Papers, Duke University Library
Josephus Daniels Papers, Library of Congress
Henry Gassaway Davis Papers, West Virginia University Library
Don Dickinson Papers, Library of Congress
Frederick Dixon Papers, Library of Congress
Henry P. Fletcher Papers, Library of Congress
Ford Peace Plan Papers, Library of Congress
Moreton Frewen Papers, Library of Congress

G–K

Carter Glass Papers, University of Virginia Library
Arthur Pue Gorman Papers, Maryland Historical Society
Charles S. Hamlin Papers, Library of Congress
Carter H. Harrison Papers, Newberry Library, Chicago
Edwin Harrison Papers, Duke University Library
Charles N. Haskell Collection, University of Oklahoma Library
John Hay Papers, Library of Congress
Hemphill Papers, Duke University Library
Charles D. Hilles Papers, Yale University Library
Gilbert Hitchcock Papers, Library of Congress
Edward M. House Papers and Diary, Yale University Library
David F. Houston Papers, Harvard University Library
James K. Jones Papers, University of North Carolina Library
David Starr Jordan Papers, Stanford University Libraries
Claude Kitchin Papers, University of North Carolina Library
Knollenberg Papers, Yale University Library
Philander C. Knox Papers, Library of Congress

L–S

Daniel S. Lamont Papers, Library of Congress
Robert Lansing Papers, Library of Congress
Logan Papers, Yale University Library
John A. Logan Papers, Library of Congress
Maurice F. Lyons Papers, Library of Congress
Norman Mack Papers, Buffalo Historical Society
James Manahan Papers, Minnesota Historical Society
William G. McAdoo Papers, Library of Congress
William McKinley Papers, Library of Congress
L. T. Michener Papers, Library of Congress
Ewing Young Mitchell Papers, University of Missouri Library
John Bassett Moore Papers, Library of Congress
John T. Morgan Papers, Library of Congress
J. Sterling Morton Papers, Nebraska State Historical Society
Albert A. Murphree Papers, University of Florida Archives
Francis Newlands Papers, Yale University Library
George W. Norris Papers, Library of Congress
Charles W. Osenton Papers, University of Kentucky Library
Thomas Nelson Page Papers, Duke University Library
Walter Hines Page Papers, Harvard University Library
George Peabody Papers, Library of Congress
John J. Pershing Papers, Library of Congress
Frank L. Polk Papers, Yale University Library
Louis F. Post Papers, Library of Congress
Chester Pugsley Papers, Duke University Library
Joseph Pulitzer Papers, Library of Congress
Henry T. Rainey Papers, Library of Congress
Whitelaw Reid Papers, Library of Congress
Robinson Collection, Stanford University Libraries
Theodore Roosevelt Papers, Library of Congress
Elihu Root Papers, Library of Congress
Albert Shaw Papers, New York Public Library
John C. Spooner Papers, Library of Congress
William M. Springer Papers, Chicago Historical Society
Walter Stuart Papers, West Virginia University Library
Oscar S. Straus Papers, Library of Congress
State Department File, National Archives

T–Z

William Howard Taft Papers, Library of Congress
Charles Talbott Papers, Duke University Library
Henry Moore Teller Papers, Colorado State Historical Society
Tucker Family Papers, University of North Carolina Library
Joseph P. Tumulty Papers, Library of Congress
Thomas J. Walsh Papers, Library of Congress
Henry Watterson Papers, Library of Congress
Edwin Yates Webb Papers, University of North Carolina Library
Wetmore Papers, Yale University Library
Stephen M. White Papers, Stanford University Libraries
Woodrow Wilson Papers, Library of Congress

————, National Archives
Leonard Wood Papers, Library of Congress
Robert W. Wooley Papers, Library of Congress

III. *Newspapers*

Atlanta *Constitution*
　Journal
Buffalo (New York) *Times*
Chicago *Inter-Ocean*
　Record
　Tribune
Denver *Rocky Mountain News*
Jacksonville (Florida) *Times-Union*
Lincoln (Nebraska) *Daily Call*
　Nebraska State Journal
　Herald
Louisville (Kentucky) *Courier-Journal*
Memphis *Commercial Appeal*
New York *American*
　Broad Ax
　Herald (and *Herald Tribune*)
　Journal
　Sun
　Times
　World
Kansas City *Star*
Omaha *Bee*
　Daily Herald
　World-Herald
Raleigh (North Carolina) *News and Observer*
St. Louis *Globe-Democrat*
　Post-Dispatch
Springfield (Illinois) *Illinois State Register*
Washington (D.C.) *Evening Star*
　Post
　Times

IV: *Works by William Jennings Bryan*

The First Battle (Chicago, 1896).
Republic or Empire, the Philippine Question (Chicago, 1899).
The Second Battle (Chicago, 1900).
British Rule in India (Westminster, 1906).
Letters to a Chinese Official (New York, 1906).
The Old World and Its Ways (Lincoln, 1907).
Under Other Flags (Lincoln, 1907).
Guaranteed Banks (Chicago, 1908).
The Prince of Peace (Chicago, 1909).
The Speeches of William Jennings Bryan (2 vols., New York, 1909).
A Tale of Two Conventions (New York, 1912).
The Forces That Make for Peace: Addresses at the Mohonk Conferences on International Arbitration (Boston, 1912).
The Making of a Man (New York, 1914).

Man (New York, 1914).
The Value of an Ideal (New York and London, 1914).
The Royal Art (New York, 1914).
The People's Law (New York and London, 1914).
Christ and His Companions: Famous Figures of the New Testament (New York, 1915).
Two Addresses Delivered by William Jennings Bryan at Peace Meetings Held in New York June 19 and 24, 1915 (no date or place).
Prohibition: Address by Hon. William Jennings Bryan Presenting in Substance the Line of Argumentation by Him in the Sixty Speeches Made in Ohio During the Week of October 25 to 30, 1915 (Washington, D.C., 1916).
Temperance Lecture Delivered Before the 128th General Assembly of the Presbyterian Church at Atlantic City, New Jersey, Sunday, May 21, 1916 (J. J. Hamilton, 1916).
Heart to Heart Appeals (New York, 1917).
Address of Hon. William Jennings Bryan to the Forty-Ninth General Assembly of the State of Missouri, January 24, 1917 (Jefferson City, Mo., 1917).
America and the European War: Address by William Jennings Bryan at Madison Square Garden, New York City, February 2, 1917 (New York, 1917).
World Peace: A Written Debate Between William Howard Taft and William Jennings Bryan (New York, 1917).
The First Commandment (New York, 1917).
Heart to Heart Appeals (New York, 1917).
In His Image (New York, 1922).
Famous Figures of the Old Testament (New York, 1922).
Orthodox Christianity versus Modernism (New York, 1923).
Seven Questions in Dispute (New York, 1924).
The Last Message of William Jennings Bryan (New York, 1925).
"The Last Speech of William Jennings Bryan," recorded and edited by Frank A. Pattie, *Tennessee Historical Quarterly*, VI (September, 1947), 265–83.
(With Mary Baird Bryan), *The Memoirs of William Jennings Bryan* (Philadelphia, 1925).

V. *Journals and Periodicals*

Most valuable is Bryan's own periodical, *The Commoner,* published from 1901 to 1923, containing texts of his addresses, presentations of his views on all sorts of subjects, accounts of his travels and political activities, digests of newspaper comment, including comment from sources critical of Bryan.

Many details on local history were secured from the *Journal of the Illinois State Historical Society* and *Nebraska History.*

The *Congressional Record* is the chief source for Bryan's career in the House of Representatives.

In Bryan's first two Presidential races, the periodicals most friendly were *The Arena* and the *National Bimetallist.* Most periodicals on public affairs opposed him. *The Nation,* which opposed Bryan in 1896, relented to support his anti-imperialist position in 1900. Certain periodicals on public affairs are useful for most, if not all, of Bryan's career. These include *Harper's Weekly, The Independent, The Nation, The Outlook,* and *The Public.* His Presidential campaigns are best reported in *The American Review of Reviews, North American Review,* and *Public Opinion.* From the Wilson era onward, the following are especially useful for political reporting or discussion: *America, Atlantic Monthly, Collier's, Literary Digest, The New Republic, Saturday Evening Post,* and *World's Work.*

Professional journals with material relating to Bryan include the *American Bar Association Journal, American Economic Review, American Historical Review, American Political Science Review, American Scholar, Annals of the Academy of Political and Social Science, Journal of Economic History, Journal of Political Economy, Journal of Politics, Journal of*

Southern History, Mississippi Valley Historical Review, Pacific Historical Review, Political Science Quarterly, Proceedings of the American Philosophical Society, The Virginia Magazine of History and Biography. Particularly useful articles are cited in the notes.

VI. *Published Papers, Memoirs, Autobiographies, and Biographies*

ACHESON, SAM HANNA, *Joe Bailey: The Last Democrat* (New York, 1932).

ADDAMS, JANE, *Hull House* (New York, 1930).

ALEXANDER, D. A. S., *Four Famous New Yorkers: The Political Careers of Cleveland, Platt, Hill, and Roosevelt* (New York, 1923).

ASHURST, HENRY, *A Many Colored Toga: The Diary of Henry Fountain Ashurst* (Tucson, 1962).

BAKER, RAY STANNARD, *American Chronicle: The Autobiography of Ray Stannard Baker* (New York, 1945).

———, *Woodrow Wilson: Life and Letters* (Garden City, 1927–1939), 8 vols.

BARNARD, HARRY, *"Eagle Forgotten": The Life of John Peter Altgeld* (New York, 1938).

BARNES, JAMES A., *John G. Carlisle: Financial Statesman* (New York, 1931).

BARRETT, JAMES W., *Joseph Pulitzer and His "World"* (New York, 1941).

BASS, HERBERT J., *"I Am a Democrat": The Political Career of David Bennett Hill* (Syracuse, 1961).

BEER, THOMAS, *Hanna* (New York, 1929).

BELMONT, PERRY, *An American Democrat: The Recollections of Perry Belmont* (New York, 1941).

BERNSTORFF, JOHANN H. VON, *My Three Years in America* (London, 1920).

BILLINGTON, MONROE L., *Thomas P. Gore: The Blind Senator from Oklahoma* (Lawrence, Kans., 1967).

BISHOP, JOSEPH B., *Theodore Roosevelt and His Times, Shown in His Own Letters* (New York, 1920), 2 vols.

BLUM, JOHN M., *The Republican Roosevelt* (Cambridge, Mass., 1954).

BOWERS, CLAUDE, *The Life of John Worth Kern* (Indianapolis, 1918).

———, *Beveridge and the Progressive Era* (New York, 1932).

———, *My Life* (New York, 1962).

BURNS, EDWARD M., *David Starr Jordan: Prophet of Freedom* (Stanford, 1953).

BURTON, THEODORE E., *John Sherman* (Boston, 1906).

BUSBEY, L. WHITE, *Uncle Joe Cannon: The Story of a Pioneer American* (New York, 1927).

BUTLER, NICHOLAS MURRAY, *Across the Years, Recollections and Reflections* (New York, 1939), 2 vols.

BUTT, ARCHIE, *The Letters of Archie Butt* (Garden City, 1924).

BYARS, WILLIAM VINCENT, ed., *An American Commoner: The Life and Times of Richard Parks Bland* (Columbia, Mo., 1900).

CAREY, FRED, *Mayor Jim: The Life of James Dahlman* (Omaha, 1930).

CLARK, CHAMP, *My Quarter Century of American Politics* (New York, 1921), 2 vols.

COBLENZ, EDMOND D., ed., *William Randolph Hearst: A Portrait in His Own Words* (New York, 1952).

CORTISSOZ, ROYAL, *The Life of Whitelaw Reid* (New York, 1921), 2 vols.

COTNER, ROBERT C., *James Stephen Hogg* (Austin, 1959).

COX, JAMES B., *Journey Through My Years* (New York, 1940).

CROLY, HERBERT, *Marcus Alonzo Hanna: His Life and Work* (New York, 1912).

DANIELS, JOSEPHUS, *Tar Heel Editor* (Chapel Hill, 1939).

———, *Editor in Politics* (Chapel Hill, 1941).

———, *The Wilson Era: Years of Peace, 1910–1917* (Chapel Hill, 1944).

———, *The Wilson Era: Years of War and After, 1917–1923* (Chapel Hill, 1946).

DARROW, CLARENCE, *The Story of My Life* (New York, 1932).

DAWES, CHARLES GATES, *A Journal of the McKinley Years, 1893–1913* (Chicago, 1950).

DENNETT, TYLER, *John Hay: From Poetry to Politics* (New York, 1933).

DEPEW, CHAUNCEY M., *My Memories of Eighty Years* (New York, 1922).
DESTLER, CHESTER M., *Henry Demarest Lloyd and the Empire of Reform* (Philadelphia, 1963).
DEWEY, GEORGE, *Autobiography of George Dewey* (New York, 1913).
DUNN, ARTHUR W., *From Harrison to Harding* (New York and London, 1922).
————, *Gridiron Nights* (New York, 1915).
DUNNE, F. P., *Mr. Dooley Says* (New York, 1910).
ELLIS, ELMER, *Henry Moore Teller* (Caldwell, Idaho, 1941).
FORAKER, JOSEPH BENSON, *Notes of a Busy Life* (Cincinnati, 1917), 2 vols.
FUESS, CLAUDE M., *Carl Schurz, Reformer* (New York, 1932).
GAGE, LYMAN J., *Memoirs of Lyman J. Gage* New York, 1937).
GARRATY, JOHN A., *Henry Cabot Lodge* (New York, 1953).
GEIGER, LOUIS G., *Joseph W. Folk of Missouri* (Columbia, Mo., 1953).
GERARD, JAMES W., *My First Eighty Years* (Garden City, 1951).
GINGER, RAY, *Altgeld's America* (New York, 1958).
————, *The Bending Cross: A Biography of Eugene Victor Debs* (New Brunswick, 1949).
GOMPERS, SAMUEL, *Seventy Years of Life and Labor: An Autobiography* (New York, 1925), 2 vols.
GRANTHAM, DEWEY W., JR., *Hoke Smith and the Politics of the New South* (Baton Rouge, 1958).
GRAYSON, CARY T., *Woodrow Wilson: An Intimate Memoir* (New York, 1960).
GREY, EDWARD, *Twenty-Five Years, 1892–1916* (New York, 1925), 2 vols.
GRIFFIN, SOLOMON B., *People and Politics, Observed by a Massachusetts Editor* (Boston, 1923).
GWYNN, STEPHEN, *The Letters and Friendships of Sir Cecil Spring-Rice* (Boston, 1929), 2 vols.
HARBAUGH, WILLIAM HENRY, *Power and Responsibility: The Life and Times of Theodore Roosevelt* (New York, 1961).
HARRISON, CARTER H., *Stormy Years: The Autobiography of Carter H. Harrison* (Indianapolis, 1935).
HARVEY, ROLAND H., *Samuel Gompers* (Stanford, 1935).
HAYNES, FRED E., *James Baird Weaver* (Iowa City, 1919).
HAYS, ARTHUR GARFIELD, *Let Freedom Ring* (New York, 1937).
HELMES, WINIFRED G., *John A. Johnson: The People's Governor* (Minneapolis, 1949).
HIRSCH, MARK D., *William C. Whitney, Modern Warwick* (New York, 1948).
HOAR, GEORGE, *Autobiography of Seventy Years* (New York, 1903), 2 vols.
HOOVER, HERBERT, *The Memoirs of Herbert Hoover*, Vol. I, *Years of Adventure, 1874–1920* (New York, 1951).
HOUSTON, DAVID F., *Eight Years with Wilson's Cabinet, 1913 to 1920* (Garden City, 1926), 2 vols.
HOWE, FREDERIC, C., *The Confessions of a Reformer* (New York, 1925).
HOWE, MARK A. DeWOLFE, *Portrait of an Independent: Moorfield Storey 1845–1929* (Boston, 1932).
ICKES, HAROLD, *Autobiography of a Curmudgeon* (New York, 1943).
JAMES, HENRY, *Richard Olney and His Public Service* (Boston and New York, 1923).
JESSUP, PHILIP, *Elihu Root* (New York, 1938), 2 vols.
JOHNSON, TOM, *My Story* (New York, 1911).
JOHNSON, WALTER, *William Allen White's America* (New York, 1947).
————, *Selected Letters of William Allen White, 1899–1943* (New York, 1947).
JOHNSON, WILLIS F., *George Harvey: A Passionate Patriot* (New York, 1929).
KENWORTHY, LEONARD S., *The Tall Sycamore of the Wabash: Daniel Wolsey Voorhees* (Boston, 1936).
KERR, WINFIELD S., *John Sherman: His Life and Public Services* (Boston, 1908), 2 vols.
LA FOLLETTE, BELLE CASE, and LA FOLLETTE, FOLA, *Robert La Follette* (New York, 1953), 2 vols.

LA FOLLETTE, ROBERT, *La Follette's Autobiography: A Personal Narrative of Political Experience* (Madison, 1913).

LAMBERT, JOHN R., *Arthur Pue Gorman* (Baton Rouge, 1953).

LANG, LOUIS J., comp., *The Autobiography of Thomas Collier Platt* (New York, 1910).

LANSING, ROBERT, *War Memoirs of Robert Lansing* (Indianapolis, 1935).

LEECH, MARGARET, *In the Days of McKinley* (New York, 1959).

LEWIS, ALFRED HENRY, *Richard Croker* (New York, 1901).

LIEF, ALFRED, *Democracy's Norris: The Biography of a Lonely Crusader* (New York, 1939).

LINK, ARTHUR S., *Wilson: The Road to the White House* (Princeton, 1947).

———, *Woodrow Wilson and the Progressive Era* (New York, 1954).

———, *Wilson: The New Freedom* (Princeton, 1956).

———, *Wilson: The Struggle for Neutrality* (Princeton, 1960).

———, *Wilson: Confusions and Crises* (Princeton, 1964).

LLOYD, CARO, *Henry Demarest Lloyd* (New York, 1912), 2 vols.

LLOYD GEORGE, DAVID, *The War Memoirs of David Lloyd George* (London, 1933–1936).

LODGE, HENRY C., *Selections from the Correspondence of Theodore Roosevelt and Henry Cabot Lodge, 1884–1918* (New York, 1925), 2 vols.

LONGWORTH, ALICE ROOSEVELT, *Crowded Hours* (New York, 1933).

LOWITT, RICHARD, *George W. Norris: The Making of a Progressive* (Syracuse, 1963).

MCCALL, SAMUEL W., *Life of Thomas B. Reed* (New York, 1914).

MCELROY, ROBERT, *Grover Cleveland: The Man and Statesman* (New York, 1923), 2 vols.

MCGURRIN, JAMES, *Bourke Cockran: A Free Lance in American Politics* (New York, 1948).

MCKENNA, MARIAN C., *Borah* (Ann Arbor, 1961).

MANAHAN, JAMES, *Trials of a Lawyer* (St. Paul, 1933).

MANDELL, BERNARD, *Samuel Gompers* (Yellow Springs, Ohio, 1963).

MARSHALL, THOMAS R., *Recollections of Thomas R. Marshall: A Hoosier Salad* (Indianapolis, 1925).

MASON, ALPHEUS T., *Brandeis: A Free Man's Life* (New York, 1946).

MASTERS, EDGAR LEE, *Across Spoon River: An Autobiography* (New York, 1936).

MERRILL, HORACE S., *William Freeman Vilas, Doctrinaire Democrat* (Madison, 1954).

———, *Bourbon Leader: Grover Cleveland and the Democratic Party* (Boston, 1957).

MILNER, LUCILLE, *Education of an American Liberal* (New York, 1954).

MORGAN, H. WAYNE, *Eugene V. Debs: Socialist for President* (Syracuse, 1962).

———, *William McKinley and His America* (Syracuse, 1963).

MORISON, ELTING E., and BLUM, JOHN H., *The Letters of Theodore Roosevelt* (Cambridge, Mass., 1951–1954).

MULLEN, ARTHUR, *Western Democrat* (New York, 1940).

NEUBERGER, RICHARD L., and KAHN, STEPHEN B., *Integrity: The Life of George Norris* (New York, 1937).

NEVINS, ALLAN, *Henry White: Thirty Years of American Diplomacy* (New York, 1930).

———, *Grover Cleveland: A Study in Courage* (New York, 1932).

———, *Abram S. Hewitt: With Some Account of Peter Cooper* (New York, 1935).

———, *John D. Rockefeller: The Heroic Age in America* (New York, 1940), 2 vols.

———, ed., *The Letters and Journal of Brand Whitlock* (New York, 1936), 2 vols.

NORRIS, GEORGE W., *Fighting Liberal: The Autobiography of George W. Norris* (New York, 1945).

OLCOTT, CHARLES S., *The Life of William McKinley* (Boston, 1912), 2 vols.

OLSON, JAMES C., *J. Sterling Morton* (Lincoln, 1942).

ORCUTT, WILLIAM DANA, *Burrows of Michigan and the Republican Party* (New York, 1917), 2 vols.

OSBORN, GEORGE, *John Sharp Williams: Planter-Statesman of the Deep South* (Baton Rouge, 1943).

PALMER, GEORGE T., *A Conscientious Turncoat: The Story of John M. Palmer* (New Haven, 1941).

PALMER, JOHN M., *Personal Recollections: The Story of an Earnest Life* (Cincinnati, 1901).
PARKER, GEORGE F., *Recollections of Grover Cleveland* (New York, 1909).
PECK, MARY GRAY, *Carrie Chapman Catt* (New York, 1944).
PEPPER, CHARLES M., *The Life and Times of Henry Gassaway Davis* (New York, 1920).
PERKINS, DEXTER, *Charles Evans Hughes and American Democratic Statesmanship* (Boston, 1956).
PHILLIPS, WILLIAM, *Ventures in Diplomacy* (Boston, 1952).
PRINGLE, HENRY F., *Theodore Roosevelt: A Biography* (New York, 1931).
———, *The Life and Times of William Howard Taft* (New York, 1939).
PROCTER, BEN H., *Not Without Honor: The Life of John H. Reagan* (Austin, 1962).
PUSEY, MERLO J., *Charles Evans Hughes* (New York, 1951).
PYLE, JOSEPH G., *Life of James J. Hill* (New York, 1917), 2 vols.
REINSCH, PAUL S., *An American Diplomat in China* (Garden City, 1922).
RICHBERG, DONALD R., *My Hero: The Indiscreet Memoirs of an Eventful but Unheroic Life* (New York, 1954).
RIDGE, MARTIN, *Ignatius Donnelly: The Portrait of a Politician* (Chicago, 1962).
ROBINSON, WILLIAM A., *Thomas B. Reed, Parliamentarian* (New York, 1930).
ROOSEVELT, THEODORE, *Autobiography* (New York, 1913).
ROPER, DANIEL C., with FRANK H. LOVETTE, *Fifty Years of Public Life* (Durham, 1941).
ROSEWATER, VICTOR, *Life and Times of Edward Rosewater* (privately printed, n.d.).
ROSS, EDWARD A., *Seventy Years of It: An Autobiography* (New York, 1936).
ROSS, THOMAS RICHARD, *Jonathan Prentiss Dolliver: A Study in Political Integrity and Independence* (Iowa City, 1960).
RUSSELL, CHARLES EDWARD, *Bare Hands and Stone Walls: Some Recollections of a Side-Line Reformer* (New York, 1933).
SCHURZ, CARL, *The Reminiscences of Carl Schurz* (New York, 1909), 3 vols.
SHERMAN, JOHN, *Recollections of Forty Years in the House, Senate and Cabinet* (Chicago, 1895).
SIEVERS, HARRY J., *Benjamin Harrison: Hoosier Statesman* (New York, 1959), 2 vols.
SIMKINS, FRANCIS B., *Pitchfork Ben Tillman, South Carolinian* (Baton Rouge, 1944).
SMITH, RIXEY, and BEASLEY, NORMAN, *Carter Glass: A Biography* (New York, 1939).
STEPHENSON, NATHANIEL, *Nelson W. Aldrich* (New York, 1930).
STEVENSON, ADLAI E., *Something of the Men I Have Known* (Chicago, 1909).
STODDARD, HENRY L., *As I Knew Them: Presidents and Politics from Grant to Coolidge* (New York, 1927).
STONE, CANDACE, *Dana and "The Sun"* (New York, 1938).
STONE, IRVING, *Clarence Darrow for the Defense: A Biography* (Garden City, 1941).
———, *They Also Ran* (Garden City, 1943).
STONE, MELVILLE E., *Fifty Years a Journalist* (Garden City, 1921).
STRAUS, OSCAR S., *Under Four Administrations* (Boston, 1922).
STURTEVANT, JULIAN M., JR., ed., *Julian Monson Sturtevant: An Autobiography* (New York, 1896).
SULLIVAN, MARK, *The Education of an American* (New York, 1938).
SUMMERS, FESTUS P., *William L. Wilson and Tariff Reform* (New Brunswick, 1953).
———, ed., *The Cabinet Diary of William L. Wilson, 1896–1897* (Chapel Hill, 1957).
SWANBERG, W. A., *Citizen Hearst: A Biography of William Randolph Hearst* (New York, 1961).
SYRETT, HAROLD C., ed., *The Gentleman and the Tiger: The Autobiography of George Brinton McClellan, Jr.* (New York, 1956).
TARBELL, IDA M., *All in the Day's Work* (New York, 1939).
THAYER, WILLIAM ROSCOE, *The Life and Letters of John Hay* (Boston, 1915), 2 vols.
THOMPSON, CHARLES WILLIS, *Party Leaders of the Time* (New York, 1906).
———, *Presidents I've Known and Two Near-Presidents* (Indianapolis, 1929).
TIMMONS, BASCOM N., *Portrait of an American: Charles G. Dawes* (New York, 1953).

TUGWELL, REXFORD G., *Grover Cleveland* (New York, 1968).
TUMULTY, JOSEPH P., *Woodrow Wilson as I Knew Him* (Garden City and Toronto, 1921).
VILLARD, OSWALD GARRISON, *Fighting Years: Memoirs of a Liberal Editor* (New York, 1939).
WALL, JOSEPH FRAZIER, *Henry Watterson: Reconstructed Rebel* (New York, 1956).
WALTERS, EVERETT, *Joseph Benson Foraker: An Uncompromising Republican* (Columbus, 1948).
WATTERSON, HENRY, *"Marse Henry": An Autobiography* (New York, 1919), 2 vols.
WEISS, NANCY JOAN, *Charles Francis Murphy, 1858–1924: Respectability and Responsibility in Tammany Politics,* (Northampton, Mass., 1968).
WHEELER, EVERETT P., *Sixty Years of American Life: Taylor to Roosevelt* (New York, 1917).
WHITE, HORACE, *The Life of Lyman Trumbull* (New York, 1913).
WHITE, WILLIAM ALLEN, *Masks in a Pageant* (New York, 1928).
WHITE, W. L., *Bernard Baruch* (New York, 1950).
WHITLOCK, BRAND, *Forty Years of It* (New York, 1914).
WINKLER, JOHN K., *W. R. Hearst: An American Phenomenon* (New York, 1938).
WILSON, EDITH BOLLING, *My Memoir* (Indianapolis, 1939).
WOODWARD, C. VANN, *Tom Watson: Agrarian Rebel* (New York, 1938).
ZUCKER, NORMAN L., *George W. Norris: Gentle Knight of American Democracy* (Urbana, 1966).

VII. *Topical Bibliographies*

A. *Agrarian Politics*
ARNETT, ALEX M., *The Populist Movement in Georgia* (New York, 1922).
BUCK, SOLON J., *The Granger Movement, 1870–1880* (Cambridge, Mass., 1913).
———, *The Agrarian Crusade: A Chronicle of the Farmer in Politics* (New Haven, 1920).
CLARK, JOHN B., *Populist in Alabama* (Auburn, 1927).
DICK, EVERETT E., *The Sod-House Frontier, 1854–1890* (New York, 1937).
DURDEN, R. F., *The Climax of Populism: The Election of 1896* (Lexington, Ky., 1965).
GLAD, PAUL W., *McKinley, Bryan, and the People* (Philadelphia, 1964).
HICKS, JOHN D., *The Populist Revolt: A History of the Farmers' Alliance and the People's Party* (Minneapolis, 1931).
JONES, STANLEY L., *The Presidential Election of 1896* (Madison, 1964).
MERRILL, HORACE S., *Bourbon Democracy of the Middle West* (Baton Rouge, 1953).
MORGAN, H. W., *William McKinley and His America* (Syracuse, 1963).
PETERSON, MERRILL D., *The Jefferson Image in the American Mind* (New York, 1962).
POLLACK, NORMAN, *The Populist Response to Industrial America* (Cambridge, Mass., 1962).
SALOUTOS, THEODORE, *Farmer Movements in the South, 1875–1933* (Berkeley, 1960).
———, and HICKS, JOHN D., *Agricultural Discontent in the Middle West* (Madison, 1951).
SHANNON, FRED A., *The Farmer's Last Frontier, 1860–1897* (New York, 1945).
SMITH, HENRY NASH, *Virgin Land: The American West as Symbol and Myth* (Cambridge, Mass., 1950).
STEVENS, G. W., *Land of the Dollar* (New York, 1897).
TAYLOR, CARL CLEVELAND, *The Farmers' Movement, 1620–1920* (New York, 1953).
UNGER, IRWIN, *The Greenback Era* (Princeton, 1964).
WILTSIE, CHARLES M., *The Jeffersonian Tradition in American Democracy* (Chapel Hill, 1935).

B. *The Money Question*
ANDREWS, ELISHA BENJAMIN, *An Honest Dollar* (New York, 1889).

BOLLES, ALBERT S., *Financial History of the United States, 1861–1885* (New York, 1886).

BOOKWALTER, JOHN W., *If Not Silver, What?* (Springfield, Ohio, 1896).

BROUGH, WILLIAM, *The Natural Law of Money* (New York, 1896).

DAWES, CHARLES G., *Banking System of the United States and Its Relation to the Money and Business of the Country* (Chicago, 1894).

DONNELLY, IGNATIUS, *American People's Money* (Chicago, 1896).

ELVIS, R., *Uncle Sam's Dream* (Chicago, 1896).

EMERY, MRS. S. E. V., *Seven Financial Conspiracies Which Have Enslaved the American People* (Lansing, 1888).

FONDA, ARTHUR I., *Honest Money* (New York, 1895).

FOOTE, ALLEN R., *A Sound Currency and Banking System: How It May Be Secured* (New York, 1895).

HAMMOND, BRAY, *Banks and Politics in America from the Revolution to the Civil War* (Princeton, 1957).

HARVEY, WILLIAM H., *Coin's Financial School* (Chicago, 1894).

———, *Coin Up-to-Date* (Chicago, 1895).

———, *Coin on Money, Trusts, and Imperialism* (Chicago, 1899).

———, with W. J. BRYAN, ET AL., *The Money of the People* (Chicago, 1895).

KELLER, BRONSON C., *History of Demonetization* (St. Louis, 1896).

KITSON, ARTHUR, *A Scientific Solution of the Money Question* (Boston, 1895).

LAUGHLIN, J. LAURENCE, *Facts About Money* (Chicago, 1896).

———, *Gold and Prices Since 1873* (Chicago, 1895).

———, *The History of Bimetallism in the United States* (3d ed., New York, 1898).

———, *The Principles of Money* (New York, 1903).

———, *Money and Prices* (New York, 1919).

LOCKWOOD, GEORGE R., *Some Facts and Figures Against the Unlimited Coinage of Silver* (St. Louis, 1896).

MCPHERSON, LOGAN C., *The Monetary and Banking Problem* (New York, 1896).

MITCHELL, WESLEY C., *A History of the Greenbacks* (Chicago, 1903).

NOYES, ALEXANDER D., *Forty Years of American Finance, 1865–1907* (New York, 1909).

ROBERTS, GEORGE E., *Coin at School in Finance* (Chicago, 1895).

RUSSELL, H. B., *International Monetary Conferences* (New York, 1898).

TAUSSIG, FRANK W., *The Silver Situation in the United States* (New York, 1896).

WALKER, FRANCIS A., *Money* (New York, 1891).

———, *International Bimetallism* (New York, 1897).

WHITE, HORACE, *Money and Banking Illustrated by American History* (Boston, 1896).

C. *Progressivism*

BROWN, WILLIAM G., *The New Politics and Other Papers* (Boston, 1914).

CROLY, HERBERT, *The Promise of American Life* (New York, 1909).

DAVIS, ALLEN F., *Spearheads for Reform: The Social Settlements and the Progressive Movement, 1890–1914* (New York, 1967).

GOLDMAN, ERIC, *Rendezvous with Destiny* (New York, 1952).

GREER, THOMAS H., *American Social Reform Movements: Their Pattern Since 1865* (New York, 1949).

HOFSTADTER, RICHARD, *The Age of Reform* (New York, 1956).

———, *The Progressive Movement* (Englewood Cliffs, 1963).

KOLKO, GABRIEL, *The Triumph of Conservatism, 1900–1916* (New York, 1963).

LINK, ARTHUR S., *Woodrow Wilson and the Progressive Era: 1910–1917* (New York, 1954).

LIPPMANN, WALTER, *Drift and Mastery* (New York, 1914).

LUBOVE, ROY, *The Progressives and the Slums* (Pittsburgh, 1962).

MARGULIES, HERBERT F., *The Decline of the Progressive Movement in Wisconsin* (Madison, 1968).
MAXWELL, ROBERT S., *La Follette and the Rise of the Progressives in Wisconsin* (Madison, 1956).
MOWRY, GEORGE E., *The California Progressives* (Berkeley, 1951).
NOBLE, DAVID W., *The Paradox of Progressive Thought* (Minneapolis, 1958).
NYE, RUSSEL B., *Midwestern Progressive Politics* (East Lansing, Mich., 1951).
PATTEN, SIMON, *The New Basis of Civilization* (New York, 1907).
SCHLESINGER, ARTHUR M., *Paths to the Present* (New York, 1949).
———, *The American as Reformer* (Cambridge, Mass., 1950).
WEYL, WALTER, *The New Democracy* (New York, 1912).
WOODWARD, C. VANN, *Origins of the New South* (Baton Rouge, 1951).

D. *The Roosevelt Era*

BEALE, HOWARD K., *Theodore Roosevelt and the Rise of America to World Power* (Baltimore, 1956).
BERMAN, EDWARD, *Labor Disputes and the President of the United States* (New York, 1924).
CLARK, JAMES D., *The Federal Trust Policy* (Baltimore, 1931).
COMMONS, JOHN R., and ASSOCIATES, *History of Labour in the United States* (New York, 1918).
DULLES, FOSTER RHEA, *Labor in America: A History* (New York, 1949).
FAULKNER, HAROLD U., *The Quest for Social Justice: 1898–1914* (New York, 1931).
———, *The Decline of Laissez-Faire, 1897–1914* (New York, 1951).
FILLER, LOUIS, *Crusaders for Liberalism* (Yellow Springs, Ohio, 1950).
FINE, SIDNEY, *Laissez Faire and the General Welfare State* (Ann Arbor, 1956).
HAYS, SAMUEL P., *The Response to Industrialism* (Chicago, 1957).
HECHLER, KENNETH W., *Insurgency: Personalities and Politics of the Taft Era* (New York, 1940).
JOSEPHESON, MATTHEW, *The President Makers* (New York, 1940).
LORD, WALTER, *The Good Years* (New York, 1960).
LORWIN, LEWIS L. *The American Federation of Labor* (Washington, 1933).
MOWRY, GEORGE E., *Theodore Roosevelt and the Progressive Movement* (Madison, 1946).
———, *The Era of Theodore Roosevelt, 1900–1912* (New York, 1958).
NOYES, ALFRED D., *Forty Years of American Finance, 1865–1907* (New York, 1909).
REGIER, C. C., *The Era of the Muckrakers* (Chapel Hill, 1932).
RIPLEY, WILLIAM Z., *Railroads: Rates and Regulation* (New York, 1912).
SULLIVAN, MARK, *Our Times*, Vol. II, *America Finding Herself* (New York, 1927).
TAUSSIG, F. W., *The Tariff History of the United States* (New York, 1923).
THORELLI, HANS B., *Federal Anti-Trust Policy: Organization of an American Tradition* (Baltimore, 1955).
THORNBROUGH, EMMA LOU, "The Brownsville Episode and the Negro Vote," *The Mississippi Valley Historical Review,* XLI (December, 1957), 469–83.
TINSLEY, JAMES A.,"Roosevelt, Foraker, and the Brownsville Affray," *Journal of Negro History,* XLI (January, 1956), 43–65.
SCHLUTER, WILLIAM C., *The Pre-War Business Cycle, 1907–1914* (New York, 1923).
SEAGER, HENRY R., and GULICK, CHARLES A., JR., *Trust and Corporation Problems* (New York, 1929).

E. *The Wilson Era*

CHILD, CLIFTON J., *The German-Americans in Politics, 1914–1917* (Madison, Wis., 1939).
CLENDENEN, CLARENCE E., *The United States and Pancho Villa* (Ithaca, N.Y., 1961).
DEPARTMENT OF STATE, *Papers Relating to the Foreign Relations of the United States, 1913* (Washington, 1920).

———, *Papers Relating to the Foreign Relations of the United States, 1914* (Washington, 1922).

———, *Papers Relating to the Foreign Relations of the United States, 1915* (Washington, 1924).

———, *Papers Relating to the Foreign Relations of the United States, 1914, Supplement, the World War* (Washington, 1928).

GRISWOLD, A. WHITNEY, *The Far Eastern Policy of the United States* (New York, 1938).

LaFARGUE, THOMAS E., *China and the World War* (Stanford, 1937).

LAURIAT, CHARLES E., JR., *The Lusitania's Last Voyage* (Boston, 1915).

LEVIN, N. GORDON, JR., *Woodrow Wilson and World Politics: America's Response to War and Revolution* (New York, 1968).

LINK, ARTHUR S., *Wilson the Diplomatist* (Baltimore, 1957).

MAY, ERNEST R., *The War and American Isolation* (Cambridge, Mass., 1959).

MONTAGUE, LUDWELL L., *Haiti and the United States* (Durham, 1940).

MUNSTERBERG, HUGO, *The Peace and America* (New York, 1915).

———, *The War and America* (New York, 1914).

MURRAY, GILBERT. *The Foreign Policy of Sir Edward Grey, 1906–1915* (Oxford, 1915).

OSGOOD, ROBERT E., *Ideals and Self-Interest in America's Foreign Relations* (Chicago, 1953).

PRATT, JULIUS W., *America's Colonial Experiment* (New York, 1952).

REED, JOHN, *Insurgent Mexico* (New York, 1914).

SINEY, MARION C., *The Allied Blockade of Germany* (Ann Arbor, 1957).

SMITH, DANIEL M., *Robert Lansing and American Neutrality* (Berkeley, 1958).

TANSILL, C. C., *America Goes to War* (Boston, 1938 and 1942).

U.S. Senate, *Inquiry into the Occupation and Administration of Haiti and the Dominican Republic.* 67th Congress, 2d Sess., Senate Report 794 (Washington, 1922).

WELLES, SUMNER, *Naboth's Vineyard: The Dominican Republic* (New York, 1928).

WITTKE, CARL, *German-Americans and the World War* (Columbus, 1936).

F. *The Dayton Trial*

ALLEN, LESLIE H., *Bryan and Darrow at Dayton (The Record and Documents of the "Bible-Evolution Trial")*, (New York, 1925).

AMERICAN CIVIL LIBERTIES UNION, *Annual Reports, 1925–1927* (New York, 1925–1927).

BOORSTIN, DANIEL J., *The Genius of American Politics* (Chicago, 1950).

COLE, STEWART G., *The History of Fundamentalism* (New York, 1931).

CASH, W. J., *The Mind of the South* (New York, 1941).

COMMAGER, HENRY STEELE, *The American Mind* (New Haven, 1950).

DANIELS, JONATHAN, *The Time Between the Wars: Armistice to Pearl Harbor* (Garden City, 1966).

DARWIN, FRANCIS, ed., *The Autobiography of Charles Darwin & Selected Letters* (New York, 1957).

DE CAMP, L. SPRAGUE, *The Great Monkey Trial* (Garden City, 1968).

FOSDICK, HARRY EMERSON, and EDDY, SHERWOOD, *Science and Religion: Evolution and the Bible* (New York, 1924).

FURNISS, NORMAN F., *The Fundamentalist Controversy* (New Haven, 1954).

GINGER, RAY, *Six Days or Forever* (Boston, 1958).

GREBSTEIN, SHELDON, *Monkey Trial* (Boston, 1960).

HOFSTADTER, RICHARD, *Anti-Intellectualism in American Life* (New York, 1962).

———, *Social Darwinism in American Thought* (Boston, 1955).

HUNTER, GEORGE WILLIAM, *A Civic Biology* (New York, 1914).

KEMLER, EDGAR, *The Irreverent Mr. Mencken* (Boston, 1950).

LAWRENCE, JEROME, and LEE, ROBERT E., *Inherit the Wind* (New York, 1955).

LEUBA, JAMES H., *Belief in God and Immortality* (Boston, 1916).
LIPPMANN, WALTER, *American Inquisitors* (New York, 1928).
MENCKEN, H. L., *Heathen Days* (New York, 1943).
———, *Prejudices (Fifth Series)* (New York, 1926).
OSBORN, HENRY FAIRFIELD, *The Earth Speaks to Bryan* (New York, 1925).
———, *Evolution and Religion* (New York, 1923).
POTTER, CHARLES FRANCIS, *The Preacher and I: An Autobiography* (New York, 1951).
RICE, STUART A., and WILLEY, M. M., *Dartmouth Charts Mr. Bryan's Arguments* (New York, 1924).
SCOPES, JOHN T., and PRESLEY, JAMES, *Center of the Storm: Memoirs of John T. Scopes* (New York, 1967).
SHIPLEY, MAYNARD, *The War on Modern Science* (New York, 1927).
SMALLWOOD, WILLIAM MARTIN, *Natural History and the American Mind* (New York, 1941).
STONE, IRVING, *Clarence Darrow for the Defense* (Garden City, 1941).
STRATON, JOHN ROACH, *The Famous New York Fundamentalist-Modernist Debates* (New York, 1925).
TOMPKINS, JERRY R., *D-Days at Dayton: Reflections on the Scopes Trial* (Baton Rouge, 1965).
WOODWARD, C. VANN, *The Origins of the New South* (Baton Rouge, 1951).

G. *Politics and the Politician*

BAIN, RICHARD C., *Convention Decisions and Voting Records* (Washington, 1960).
BELL, DANIEL, *The End of Ideology* (Glencoe, Ill., 1960).
CAMPBELL, ANGUS, ET AL., *Elections and the Political Order* (New York, 1966).
DAVIES, JAMES C., *Human Nature in Politics* (New York, 1963).
DEXTER, LEWIS ANTHONY, "Candidates Must Make the Issues and Give Them Meaning," *Public Opinion Quarterly*, XIX (Winter, 1955–1956), 408–14.
EDELMAN, MURRAY, *The Symbolic Uses of Politics* (Urbana, Ill., 1964).
HYMAN, HERBERT J., *Political Socialization: A Study in the Psychology of Political Behavior* (Glencoe, Ill., 1959).
KEY, V. O., "A Theory of Critical Elections," *Journal of Politics*, 17 (February, 1955), 3–14.
KLUCKHOHN, CLYDE, and MURRAY, HENRY A., *Personality in Nature, Society and Culture* (New York, 1953).
KORNHAUSER, WILLIAM, *The Politics of Mass Society* (Glencoe, Ill., 1959).
LANE, ROBERT E., *Political Life* (New York, 1959).
———, "Fathers and Sons: Foundations of Political Belief," *American Sociological Review*, XXIV (August, 1959), 502–11.
———, *Political Ideology* (New York, 1962).
LARNED, JOSEPHUS N., "A Criticism of Two-Party Politics," *Atlantic Monthly*, 107 (March, 1911), 289–94.
LIPSET, SEYMOUR MARTIN, *Political Man: The Social Basis of Politics* (Garden City, 1960).
MCCLOSKY, HERBERT, "Consensus and Ideology in American Politics," *American Political Science Review*, LVIII (June, 1964), 361–82.
MERELMAN, RICHARD M., "The Development of Political Ideology: A Framework for the Analysis of Political Socialization," *American Political Science Review*, LXIII (September, 1969), 750–67.
MILBRATH, LESTER, *Political Participation* (Chicago, 1965).
MINAR, DAVID, "Ideology and Political Behavior," *Midwest Journal of Political Science*, 5 (November, 1961), 317–31.
PORTER, KIRK, *National Party Platforms, 1840–1960* (Urbana, Ill., 1961).
ROBINSON, EDGAR EUGENE, *The Presidential Vote, 1896–1932* (Stanford, 1934).
ROSENZWEIG, ROBERT M., "The Politician and the Career in Politics," *Midwest Journal of Political Science*, 1 (May, 1957), 163–74.

SARTORI, GIOVANNI, "Politics, Ideology, and Belief Systems," *American Political Science Review,* LXIII (June, 1969), 398–411.

SCHLESINGER, JOSEPH A., *Ambition and Politics: Political Careers* (Chicago, 1966).

SIGEL, ROBERTA, "Effect of Partisanship on the Perceptions of Political Candidates," *Public Opinion Quarterly,* 28 (Fall, 1964), 483–96.

H. *Personality and Behavior*

CANTRIL, HADLEY, *The Psychology of Social Movements* (New York, 1941).

DONOVAN, ELIZABETH, and WALKER, W. M., "The Sense of Effectiveness in Public Affairs," *Psychological Monographs,* 70, no. 22 (1956).

EDINGER, LEWIS, "Political Science and Political Biography," *Journal of Politics,* 26 (May and August, 1964), 423–39, 648–62.

GREENSTEIN, FRED I., "Impact of Personality on Politics," *American Political Science Review,* 61 (September, 1967), 629–42.

———, "Personality and Politics: Problems of Evidence, Inference, and Conceptualization," *American Behavioral Scientist,* 11 (November–December, 1967), 38–53.

HALL, CALVIN S., and LINDZEY, GARDNER, *Theories of Personality* (New York, 1957).

LASSWELL, HAROLD D., *Power and Personality* (New York, 1948).

———, *Psychopathology and Politics* (New York, 1960).

MURRAY, Henry A., ed., *Explorations in Personality* (New York, 1938).

NEWCOMB, THEODORE M., *Personality and Social Change* (New York, 1943).

PYE, LUCIAN W., "Administrators, Agitators and Brokers," *Public Opinion Quarterly,* 22 (Fall, 1958), 342–48.

ROKEACH, MILTON, *The Open and Closed Mind: Investigations into the Nature of Belief Systems and Personality* (New York, 1960).

ROSE, ARNOLD M., ed., *Human Behavior and Social Processes* (London, 1962).

ROSENBERG, MORRIS, "Self-Esteem and Concern with Public Affairs," *Public Opinion Quarterly,* 26 (Summer, 1962), 201–11.

SHERIF, MUSAFER AND HADLEY CANTRIL, *The Psychology of Ego Involvements* (New York, 1947).

SMITH, M. BREWSTER, "Personal Values as Determinants of a Political Attitude," *Journal of Psychology,* 27–28 (October, 1949), 477–486.

———, BRUNER, JEROME S., and WHITE, ROBERT M., *Opinion and Personality* (New York, 1956).

SULLIVAN, HARRY Stack, *The Interpersonal Theory of Psychiatry* (New York, 1953).

SWANSON, GUY E., "Agitation in Face-to-Face Contacts: A Study of Personalities of Orators," *Public Opinion Quarterly,* 21 (Summer, 1957), 288–94.

ACKNOWLEDGMENTS

Research for this book made demands upon many libraries, and I am especially indebted to the exceptional kindness of William Mobley of the Manuscripts Division of the Library of Congress and Joseph Mask of the New York Public Library, where my needs were most concentrated. Duane J. Reed, archivist of the Nebraska State Historical Society, was fertile with suggestions for my many queries. In Washington, my many stays were brightened by the gracious hospitality of Mr. and Mrs. James L. Stuart.

At New York University, Dr. Charles Gosnell, director of libraries, and Julius Marke, librarian of the Law School, were generous in helping the progress of my task. Dean George Winchester Stone, Jr., of the Graduate School of Arts and Science and Ralph A. Straetz and Richard N. Swift, heads of the Department of Politics, kindly provided assistance for this project. I am grateful to Joyce Klein Gelb, Shirley Jacobson, and Elaine Wolfson for expertly handling several precise requests for research details.

To Robert Lescher, I am indebted for encouraging me to undertake the book, and to Harvey Ginsberg of G. P. Putnam's Sons for his careful and most considerate interest in the manuscript.

Once again, I am indebted to my wife, Eleanor, and daughter, Juliana, for patience which passes all understanding.

Index